The Crusader World

The Crusader World is a multidisciplinary survey of the current state of research in the field of crusader studies, an area of study which has become increasingly popular in recent years. In this volume Adrian Boas draws together an impressive range of academics, including work from renowned scholars as well as a number of thought-provoking pieces from emerging researchers, in order to provide broad coverage of the major aspects of the period. This authoritative work will play an important role in the future direction of crusading studies.

This volume enriches present knowledge of the crusades, addressing such wide-ranging subjects as: intelligence and espionage, gender issues, religious celebrations in crusader Jerusalem, political struggles in crusader Antioch, the archaeological study of battle sites and fortifications, diseases suffered by the crusaders, crusading in northern Europe and Spain and the impact of crusader art. The relationship between crusaders and Muslims, two distinct and in many way opposing cultures, is also examined in depth, including a discussion of how the Franks perceived their enemies.

Arranged into eight thematic sections, *The Crusader World* considers many central issues as well as a large number of less familiar topics of the crusades, crusader society, history and culture. With over 100 photographs, line drawings and maps, this impressive collection of essays is a key resource for students and scholars alike.

Adrian J. Boas is Professor of Medieval Archaeology in the Departments of Archaeology and Land of Israel Studies at Haifa University, Israel.

THE ROUTLEDGE WORLDS

THE OTTOMAN WORLD
Edited by Christine Woodhead

THE VICTORIAN WORLD
Edited by Martin Hewitt

THE ORTHODOX CHRISTIAN WORLD
Edited by Augustine Casiday

THE SUMERIAN WORLD
Edited by Harriet Crawford

THE ETRUSCAN WORLD
Edited by Jean MacIntosh Turfa

THE GOTHIC WORLD
Edited by Glennis Byron and Dale Townshend

THE WORLD OF THE REVOLUTIONARY AMERICAN REPUBLIC
Edited by Andrew Shankman

THE WORLD OF INDIGENOUS NORTH AMERICA
Edited by Robert Warrior

THE FIN-DE-SIÈCLE WORLD
Edited by Michael Saler

THE OCCULT WORLD
Edited by Christopher Partridge

THE ATLANTIC WORLD
Edited by D'Maris Coffman, Adrian Leonard, William O'Reilly

THE BUDDHIST WORLD
Edited by John Powers

Forthcoming:

THE MODERNIST WORLD
Edited by Stephen Ross and Allana Lindgren

THE POSTCOLONIAL WORLD
Edited by Jyotsna Singh and David Kim

THE SHAKESPEAREAN WORLD
Edited by Jill L. Levenson and Robert Ormsby

THE WORLD OF IONIA
Edited by Alan M. Greaves

THE WORLD OF FORMATIVE EUROPE
Edited by Martin Carver and Madeleine Hummler

THE CRUSADER WORLD

Edited by
Adrian J. Boas

Routledge
Taylor & Francis Group

LONDON AND NEW YORK

First published 2016
by Routledge

2 Park Square, Milton Park, Abingdon, Oxfordshire OX14 4RN
52 Vanderbilt Avenue, New York, NY 10017

Routledge is an imprint of the Taylor & Francis Group, an informa business

First issued in paperback 2019

British Library Cataloguing-in-Publication Data
A catalogue record for this book is available from the British Library

Library of Congress Cataloging-in-Publication Data
The crusader world / edited by Adrian J. Boas.
pages cm. — (The Routledge worlds)
Includes bibliographical references and index.
1. Crusades. I. Boas, Adrian J., 1952- editor, author.
D157.C763 2015
909.07—dc23
2015011532

ISBN: 978-0-415-82494-1 (hbk)
ISBN: 978-0-367-86788-1 (pbk)

Typeset in Times New Roman
by Swales & Willis Ltd, Exeter, Devon, UK

CONTENTS

———•➤•———

— Contents —

PART II: THE CRUSADER WEST

PART III: THE LATIN EAST

PART IV: MEDIEVAL BYZANTIUM

— Contents —

PART V: MEETING ISLAM

PART VI: ARCHAEOLOGY OF THE CRUSADES

PART VII: ART AND LITERATURE

PART VIII: STUDYING THE CRUSADES

ILLUSTRATIONS

———•◆•———

CONTRIBUTORS

———•◆•———

Reuven Amitai is Eliyahu Elath Professor of Islamic History at the Hebrew University of Jerusalem. He has recently published *Holy War and Rapprochement: Studies in the Relations between the Mamluk Sultanate and the Mongol Ilkhanate (1260–1335)* (Brepols, 2013) and *Nomads as Agents of Cultural Change: The Mongols and Their Eurasian Predecessors*, co-edited with Michal Biran (University of Hawai'i, 2014).

Michael Angold is Professor Emeritus of Byzantine History at the University of Edinburgh. He is the author of several books on the history of the Byzantine Empire, most recently *The Fall of Constantinople to the Ottomans: Context and Consequences* (2012). He also edited *Cambridge History of Christianity V: Eastern Christianity* (2008). He is working on a translation of the works of Nicholas Mesarites, Bishop of Ephesos.

Adrian J. Boas is Professor of Medieval Archaeology in the Department of Archaeology and the Department of Land of Israel Studies at the University of Haifa. He has excavated urban and rural sites and castles and is currently director the Montfort Castle Project. He has published several books including *Crusader Archaeology* (1999), *Jerusalem in the Time of the Crusades* (2001), *Archaeology of the Military Orders* (2006) and *Domestic Settings* (2010).

Karl Borchardt teaches medieval history at the University of Würzburg and is working at the Monumenta Germaniae Historica in Munich, preparing an edition of the letter-collections named after Petrus de Vinea (d. 1249). His fields of interest include the military-religious orders, especially the Hospitallers. He has published a number of articles on their commanderies in Central Europe and among his publications has co-edited the Hospitaller documents from Rhodes concerning Cyprus 1409–59 (2011). Together with Damien Carraz and Alain Venturini he is publishing circa 350 weekly accounts of the important Hospitaller commandery at Manosque in Provence from the 1280s.

Marcus Bull is Andrew W. Mellon Distinguished Professor of Medieval and Early Modern Studies at the University of North Carolina, Chapel Hill. His publications include *Knightly*

Piety and the Lay Response to the First Crusade (Oxford, 1993), *The Miracles of Our Lady of Rocamadour* (Woodbridge, 1999), *Thinking Medieval* (Basingstoke, 2005), and, with Damien Kempf, *The Historia Iherosolimitana of Robert the Monk* (Woodbridge, 2013). His latest research includes a study of the Great Siege of Malta (1565), and an investigation of the nature of eyewitness testimony in medieval and early modern historiographical texts.

Jochen Burgtorf is Professor of Medieval History at California State University, Fullerton (USA). He is the author of *The Central Convent of Hospitallers and Templars: History, Organization, and Personnel (1099/1120–1310)* (2008), a co-editor (with Helen J. Nicholson and Paul F. Crawford) of *The Debate on the Trial of the Templars (1307–1314)* (2010), and a collaborator of the international 'Regesta Pontificum Romanorum' project on pre-1198 papal documents.

Paul E. Chevedden (1986, UCLA) is an independent scholar specializing in the crusades and has published numerous studies pertaining to crusading warfare, the origins of the crusades, and post-crusade Muslim society in Spain, among them, with Robert I. Burns, *Negotiating Cultures: Bilingual Surrender Treaties in Muslim-Crusader Spain under James the Conqueror* (1999).

Nikolaos G. Chrissis (PhD London) is a Postdoctoral Research Fellow at the University of Athens. He has taught history at the universities of London and Birmingham and at the Hellenic Open University. His main interests revolve around Byzantine-Western interaction, the crusades, the papacy, and Byzantine identity. His publications include the monograph *Crusading in Frankish Greece: A Study of Byzantine-Western Relations and Attitudes, 1204–1282* (2012), while he also co-edited the volume *Contact and Conflict in Frankish Greece and the Aegean, 1204–1453* (2014).

Niall Christie teaches the history of Europe and the Muslim world at Langara College in Vancouver, Canada. His research focuses on interactions between the Middle East and Europe in the Middle Ages. He is the author of a range of publications, including two books: *Muslims and Crusaders: Christianity's Wars in the Middle East, 1095–1382, from the Islamic Sources* (2014), and *The Book of the* Jihad *of 'Ali ibn Tahir al-Sulami (d. 1106): Text, Translation and Commentary* (in press).

Nicholas Coureas works as a Senior Researcher at the Cyprus Research Centre in Nicosia on the history of Lusignan Cyprus (1191–1473). He has published various articles and books on this subject, including the monograph *The Latin Church of Cyprus, 1195–1312* (1997) and its sequel *The Latin Church of Cyprus 1313–1378* (2010). Together with Peter Edbury he will publish a new translation of the fifteenth-century anonymous Cypriot chronicle of 'Amadi' for the Cyprus Research Centre early in 2015.

Gary Dickson has a BA from Stanford, MA from Yale and PhD from Edinburgh. He is a medievalist at the University of Edinburgh; formerly Reader in History, currently Honorary Fellow. His publications include *Religious Enthusiasm in the Medieval West: Revivals, Crusades, Saints* (2000) and *The Children's Crusade: Medieval History; Modern Mythistory* (2008). Work in progress includes *Medieval Pentecostalism: Charismatic Christianity in Western Europe, 1000–1500*.

Gil Fishhof teaches medieval and crusader art history in the Department of Art History at Tel Aviv University. He specializes in French Romanesque art, and devotes his research to questions of Romanesque architecture in Burgundy; patronage; art within the order of Cluny; and the meaning of models in Romanesque architecture. Dr Fishhof's second area of research is crusader art, and his studies are dedicated to the mural cycle of the church of Emmaus (Abu-Gosh) and its Hospitaller patrons, as well as to the church of the Annunciation in Nazareth. His publications appeared in *Mediaevistik*, *Arte Medievale*, *Annales de Bourgogne* and *Viator*, among others.

Jaroslav Folda is the N. Ferebee Taylor Professor of the History of Art, emeritus, at the University of North Carolina at Chapel Hill. His recent publications include: *The Art of the Crusaders in the Holy Land, 1098–1187* (1995; awarded the Haskins Medal by the Medieval Academy of America in 1999); *Crusader Art in the Holy Land, from the Third Crusade to the fall of Acre: 1187–1291* (2005); and *Crusader Art: The Art of the Crusaders in the Holy Land, 1099–1291* (2008).

Alan Forey, who is now retired, taught in the universities of Oxford, St Andrews and Durham. He recently published a study of Western converts to Islam in the Middle Ages, but his main field of research has been military orders and crusades. His publications include *The Military Orders from the Twelfth to the Early Fourteenth Centuries* (1992) and *The Fall of the Templars in the Crown of Aragon* (2001).

John France is Professor Emeritus in the History Department at Swansea University specialising in the history of warfare and of crusading. His *Victory in the East. A Military History of the First Crusade* (1994) combines the two. His most recent book is *Perilous Glory, The Rise of Western Military Power* (2011). He is presently writing a history of warfare during the crusades.

Daniel P. Franke was an Assistant Professor at the United States Military Academy at West Point for three years. His fields of study are high and late medieval warfare, with particular concentrations in the Staufen and late Plantagenet eras. Currently he is working on an analysis of the earls of Suffolk in fourteenth-century England, to be followed by a military biography of Frederick Barbarossa. He has published various articles on medieval warfare and the crusades.

Yehoshua Frenkel has a PhD in History of the Middle East (Hebrew University) and is a senior lecturer in the Faculty of Humanities, University of Haifa. His research interests and teaching include social and legal history of the pre-modern Arabo-Muslim lands. Among his recent publication are two books: *Ḍaw' al-sārī li-ma'rifat ḫabar Tamīm al-Dārī* (*On Tamīm al-Dārī and His Waqf in Hebron*) Critical Arabic Edition of al-Maqrizi, Ibn Hajar and al-Suyuti epistles, annotated and translated into English with an English introduction (2014); and *The Turkic Peoples in Medieval Arabic Writings* (2015).

Yvonne Friedman is Lazarus Phillips Professor of General History in the Department of History and the Land of Israel Studies and Archeology at Bar-Ilan University and Chair of the Board of Israel Antiquities Authority. She has published several books and many articles on inter-religious historical subjects. Her latest project is a book on peace-processes between the Muslims and the crusaders in the Middle East in the twelfth and thirteenth centuries. Her book *Encounter between Enemies: Captivity and Ransom in the Latin Kingdom of Jerusalem* (2002) dealt with ransom as an inter-cultural and inter-religious phenomenon in the medieval Middle East and as a first step of peace-making.

Luis García-Guijarro Ramos is Reader in Medieval History at the University of Zaragoza and Secretary of the *Society for the Study of the Crusades and the Latin East*. He has published books and articles dealing with the *Reconquista*, the crusades, the military orders and the Latin Church in the Central Middle Ages. An additional line of his research is centred on the birth and development of political units in Eastern Iberia between the ninth and eleventh centuries.

Lydia Perelis Grossowicz obtained her BSc and MSc degrees on Geology from the Hebrew University of Jerusalem (1969–74) where she also acted as an educational and research assistant for two years. Since 1975 she has worked at the Geological Survey of Israel as a Senior Researcher on the field of Foraminifera (microfossils). She collaborates with oil and gas companies, water drilling companies, field geologists and archaeologists. She is the author/co-author of more than sixty publications.

Darius von Güttner-Sporzyński is a Historian and Research Fellow at the University of Melbourne, Australia. His research and teaching concentrates on cultural aspects of religious warfare, crusading, military orders and identity. His recent publication *Poland, Holy War and the Piast Dynasty, 1100–1230* (2014) examines the transmission of the ideology of holy war in Central Europe and its adaptation by the Piast Dynasty of Poland. He is currently working on the first English edition of the *Chronica Polonorum* by Bishop Vincentius of Kraków.

Bernard Hamilton is Emeritus Professor of Crusading History in the University of Nottingham, and President of the Society for the Study of the Crusades and the Latin East. Among his publications is *The Leper King and his Heirs: Baldwin IV and the Crusader Kingdom of Jerusalem* (2000). He is at present working with Andrew Jotischky on *Latin and Orthodox Monasteries in the Crusader States*, which will be published by Cambridge University Press.

David Jacoby is Professor Emeritus of Medieval History at the Hebrew University, Jerusalem. He has published extensively on intercultural exchange and maritime trade between the West and Byzantium, the Crusader states and Egypt in the eleventh to fifteenth centuries, medieval silk production and trade, and the Jews in the Eastern Mediterranean in the Middle Ages. His latest collection of studies is titled *Travellers, Merchants and Settlers across the Mediterranean, Eleventh–Fourteenth Centuries* (2014). He is currently working on a book on *Crusader Acre* and another on *Silk and Silk Textiles in Byzantium and the Medieval Mediterranean*.

Andrew Jotischky is Professor of Medieval History at Lancaster University, where he has taught since 1995. His main areas of research interest are crusading and the crusader states, and more widely the religious culture of the eastern Mediterranean, and monasticism in both the East and West. He has published articles and essays on Eastern/Western religious and cultural interactions, Orthodox influences on Western reform monasticism, pilgrimage and crusading origins. He is the author of *The Perfection of Solitude. Hermits and Monks in the Crusader States* (1995), *The Carmelites and Antiquity* (2002), *Crusading and the Crusader States* (2004) and *A Hermit's Cookbook. Monks, Food and Fasting in the Middle Ages* (2011).

Nurith Kenaan-Kedar is Professor of Medieval Art History in the Department of Art History, the Faculty of the Arts at Tel Aviv University. She has published widely on crusader art, monumental sculpture and architecture in the Holy Land, Eleanor of Aquitaine as patron of the Visual Arts, and Romanesque and Gothic Marginal sculpture in medieval France.

Rabei G. Khamisy has a PhD from the University of Haifa. His dissertation dealt with the history and archaeology of the region of Acre during the Crusader period. He was awarded the Rothschild post-doctoral Fellowship and has carried out a post-doctorate at Cardiff University during which he wrote a book titled *Fiefs, Fortresses, Villages and Farms in Western Galilee and Southern Lebanon in the Frankish period (1104–1291): Political, Social and Economic Activities* (in press). He has published articles in *Crusades, Ordenis Militares, Israel Exploration Journal, al-Masaq* and *Journal of Medieval Military History*. He has been involved in the University of Haifa's Montfort Castle Project since its foundation in 2006.

Raphael Y. Lewis is an archaeologist specialising in landscape archaeology and archaeology of conflicts. He received his PhD in Archaeology at the University of Haifa. He did a post-doctoral research at Harvard University and another at Tel Aviv University. Currently he works as a post-doctoral researcher at the University of Haifa as a member of the Montfort Castle Project. He is also a lecturer of archaeology in the Department of Political Science of Bar-Ilan University. He directed, co-directed and conducted a number of archaeological projects among these sites: Hattin, Arsuf and Mount Zion (Jerusalem).

Michael Lower teaches history at the University of Minnesota. He is the author of *The Barons' Crusade: A Call to Arms and Its Consequences* (2005). He is currently working on two book projects: a history of the Tunis Crusade of 1270, the last major expedition led by a European monarch in aid of the Holy Land; and a history of medieval mercenaries who crossed the religious divide in North Africa and the Iberian Peninsula.

Svetlana Luchitskaya is affiliated with the Russian Academy of Sciences, the Institute of Universal History as a Senior Researcher of the Department of Historical Anthropology. Her research interests include the history of the crusades and medieval Christian views of Islam. Among her publications are *Image of the Other: Muslims in the Crusader Chronicles* (2001, in Russian); 'Pictorial Sources, Coronation Ritual and Daily Life in the Latin Kingdom of Jerusalem' in *Ritual, Images and Daily Life* (ed. G. Jaritz, 2012); 'Veoir et oïr, legere et audire: réflexions sur les interactions entre tradition orale et écrite dans les sources relatives à la Première croisade' in *Homo legens. Styles et patiques de lecture, Analyses comparées des traditions orales et écrites au Moyen âge* (2010); and 'Wie starben die Jerusalemer Könige' in *Mediävistik. Internationale Zeitschrift für interdisziplinäre Mittelaltersforschung* (2009, 2010).

Sophia Menasche has a PhD from the Hebrew University of Jerusalem (1980) and is Professor of Medieval History at the Department of History, University of Haifa. She is a visiting fellow at Clare Hall, Cambridge. Her main areas of research are Church history, the papacy, the crusades, medieval communication (propaganda, stereotypes, etc.), the expulsions of Jews (France, England), the reign of Philip the Fair, and the approach to dogs in the Abrahamic religions. Her main books are: *The Vox Dei: Communication in the Middle Ages* (1990), *L'humour en chaire* (1996), *Clement V* (1998), and *The Catholic Church in the Middle Ages: Ideology and Politics* (2004).

Piers D. Mitchell is a biological anthropologist, medical historian and physician who teaches at the University of Cambridge. His research interests focus on disease in the past, and he is the leading authority on health, disease and medicine in the crusades. Piers is President of the Paleopathology Association, the worldwide organisation for the study of ancient diseases. His publications include *Medicine in the Crusades: Warfare, Wounds and the Medieval Surgeon* (2004), *Anatomical Dissection in Enlightenment England and Beyond: Autopsy, Pathology and Display* (2012), and *Sanitation, Latrines and Intestinal Parasites in Past Populations* (2015).

Helen J. Nicholson is Professor of Medieval History at Cardiff University in Wales, and has published extensively on the military orders, crusades, medieval warfare and various related subjects, including articles on 'Women on the Third Crusade' (1997) and 'Queen Sybil of Jerusalem (1186–1190) in History and Legend, 1186–1300' (2004). In 1997 she published a translation of the *Itinerarium peregrinorum et gesta regis Ricardi*, an important source for the Third Crusade. She has a particular interest in the role of women in warfare and in religious orders.

Aphrodite Papayianni teaches at the universities of London and Oxford. She has a particular interest in the Byzantine-Latin political and ecclesiastical relations, and has published articles on various topics of Byzantine history. Her publications include: 'The Reaction of the Greek-Orthodox Monastic Community to the Talks about the Reunification of the Two Churches, 1204–1261' in *Church, Society and Monasticism* (ed. A. Lopez-Tello Garcia and B. S. Zorzi, 2009); 'He Polis healo: The Fall of Constantinople in 1453 in Post-Byzantine Popular Literature' (2010); and 'The Papacy and the Fourth Crusade in the Correspondence of the Nicaean Emperors with the Popes' in *La Papauté et les Croisades/The Papacy and the Crusades* (ed. M. Balard, 2011).

Mathias Piana is an independent scholar and member of the scientific board of the Deutsche Burgenvereinigung e.V. His research topics include medieval fortified architecture of the Eastern Mediterranean and transfer processes in medieval architecture. His main publications include: 'The Crusader Castle of Toron: First Results of its Investigation' (2006); *Burgen und Städte der Kreuzzugszeit* (2008); 'From Montpèlerin to Óarābulus al-Mustajadda: The Frankish-Mamluk Succession in Old Tripoli' in *Egypt and Syria in the Fatimid, Ayyubid and Mamluk Eras VI* (ed. U. Vermeulen, K. D'hulster, 2010); (co-ed. with Christer Carlsson) *Archaeology and Architecture of the Military Orders: New Studies* (2014); and 'A Bulwark Never Conquered: The Fortifications of the Templar Citadel of Tortosa on the Syrian Coast' in *Archaeology and Architecture of the Military Orders*, 2014.

Aleksander Pluskowski is Lecturer in Medieval Archaeology at the University of Reading and Director of the Ecology of Crusading Project. His research interests include the relationship between ecological and cultural change in medieval Europe, especially in frontier regions. His publications include: *The Archaeology of the Prussian Crusade: Holy War and Colonisation* (2012), *The Ritual Killing and Burial of Animals: European Perspectives* (2012), *Breaking and Shaping Beastly Bodies: Animals as Material Culture in the Middle Ages* (2007) and *Wolves and the Wilderness in the Middle Ages* (2006).

Eytan Sass is Professor Emeritus of Geology at the Institute of Earth Sciences, the Hebrew University of Jerusalem. His interests and academic activity include: sedimentology of carbonate rocks, with emphasis on limestones and dolomites; carbonate platforms of Israel; carbonate geochemistry of major and trace elements, including stable isotopes; and brines, geochemical characterisation and evolution.

Vardit Shotten-Hallel is a PhD candidate at the Hebrew University of Jerusalem, European Forum. Her thesis focuses on building technologies and materials in churches of the Latin Kingdom of Jerusalem. She holds an MA in Archaeology (University of Haifa) and Diploma in Architecture (University of Cambridge). Since 2003 she has been working at the Israel Antiquities Authority, in the conservation and research of the Hospitaller Compound in Acre, where she recently curated the history and content for the newly opened museum.

Edna Stern is a Senior Archaeologist and a Medieval Ceramic Specialist in the Israel Antiquities Authority. She excavates at various sites in northern Israel and studies pottery from the crusader, Mamluk and Ottoman periods. Publications include: (with M. Avissar) *Pottery of the Crusader, Ayyubid, and Mamluk Periods in Israel* (2005) and *'Akko I: The 1991–1998 Excavations, The Crusader Period Pottery* (2012).

Daniella Talmon-Heller is a Senior Lecturer at the Department of Middle East Studies of Ben-Gurion University of the Negev. She is the author of *Islamic Piety in Medieval Syria* (2007); co-author (with Nehemia Levtzion and Daphna Ephrat) of *Islam – A History* (1999–2003) and (co-editor, with Katia Cytryn-Silverman) of *Material Evidence and Narrative Sources: Interdisciplinary Studies of the History of the Muslim Middle East* (2014). She is interested in social history, religious thought and practice, comparative religion and medieval historiography.

Heiki Valk is Senior Research Fellow at the University of Tartu (Estonia) at the Institute of History and Archaeology, specialising in the archaeology of Late Iron Age and Medieval Estonia. His research interests also include the transition to the Middle Ages, hill forts, and the relations between archaeology and folkloric/ethnographic traditions. His publications include: (with Silvia Laul) *Siksälä: A Community at the Frontiers. Iron Age and Medieval* (2007); *Rural Cemeteries of Southern Estonia 1225–1800 AD* (2001); and 'Strongholds and Power Centres East of the Baltic Sea in the 11th–13th Centuries' (2014).

CHAPTER ONE

INTRODUCTION

———•◆•———

Adrian J. Boas

Some of the most profound historical developments, when we look back on them, seem to have emerged without due warning out of a series of apparently minor, almost unnoticeable events which evolved and took on pace, eventually swelling out of all imaginable proportions, so that from our distant perspective it is almost impossible to understand how they even began. Such is the period discussed in this volume. It is in no small part the seemingly spontaneous nature of its origins that makes the crusades a field that has attracted the attention of modern scholars and has turned crusader studies into an increasingly popular academic field. Our fascination in the geneses of the crusades relates perhaps to a desire to comprehend the rapidly developing movements that have similarly impacted the modern world. But the mystery of its origins is only one aspect of the allure of crusader history. The enormous impact that the crusades and the Frankish East had on the Western world and on the Near East at the time, and on Western culture in later periods, is another. The crusades have been and remain a goldmine for story-tellers, from the romantic novelists of the nineteenth century to film producers of the twentieth. The role of the Latin East as meeting place between Occident and Orient has become of growing consequence in a time of cultural confrontation when the terms 'Crusade' and 'Holy War' or *jihad* are increasingly heard in reference to a whole range of ethnic and religious encounters. The clash in the Middle Ages of two distinct and, in many senses, opposing cultures (on the battlefield, in religion, in learning, in diplomacy, in commerce and in daily life) is perhaps more relevant today than it ever was in the past.

Over the past decades large numbers of scholars and students have become involved in crusader studies. Crusader sessions and papers are increasingly represented in international medieval conferences. A growing number of crusader courses appear in university curricula and numerous crusader-related websites have made their appearance. The Society for the Study of the Crusades and the Latin East (SSCLE) now numbers around 500 members, its quadrennial conferences are well attended and its journal, *Crusades*, has become a prestigious tool with a broad readership.

This volume does not attempt to cover every aspect of crusading. There are many excellent comprehensive histories of the crusades and the Latin East as well as major studies devoted to crusader warfare, art, architecture and archaeology. Rather, the aim of this collection has been to present the reader with a broad vista of the crusader world observed through a combination of chapters dealing with central issues together with studies on specific topics and with many examples of new and ongoing research and new approaches. The picture that emerges demonstrates the range and quality of modern scholarship which has advanced greatly over recent decades.

The five papers in Part I examine facets of the activity most prominent in crusader studies. The military aspects of crusading have always been a "hot topic" but recent studies have expanded our horizons, to look more deeply into not only the conflicts themselves but also motivation, participation and the interrelations between participants. Paul Chevedden takes a look at the manner in which Pope Urban II viewed crusading. Helen Nicholson examines the involvement of women in the crusading movement as supporters, victims and participants. John France discusses the contrasting styles of twelfth-century warfare, comparing the methods and leadership of the Western crusaders, Latin settlers and the Muslims. Alan Forey discusses the engagement of paid troops in the service of the military orders, and following these discussions on military activities, a chapter by Yvonne Friedman considers how peacemaking efforts and cross-religious alliances were regarded at the time.

Part II examines some aspects of crusading in the West. Karl Borchardt takes a look at the supportive role played by the principal military orders, in particular by expanding their assets and enabling the supplying of financial support to their houses in the East. Daniel Franke looks at German crusading in the late twelfth century and at recent German historiography. Darius von Güttner-Sporzyński looks at the expansion of Christendom in East Central and Eastern Europe, surveying the various crusades and missionary activities and the broad involvement of the various factions in subjugating and Christianising the pagans and Luis García-Guijarro Ramos presents an insightful examination of the *Reconquista* in medieval Iberia.

The outcome of the main endeavours of twelfth and thirteenth-century crusading was the occupation and settlement of the Syrian-Palestinian mainland states and the island of Cyprus. Various activities of Latins in the medieval Levant are the topic of five papers in Part III. The role of Italian merchant communes in the Latin East was a paramount one. David Jacoby takes a look at the vicissitudes of Venetian involvement in the Lordship of Tyre. Jochen Burgtorf writes about the complex struggles of succession of the principality of Antioch that evolved in the early thirteenth century. Rabei Khamisy observes settlement and land ownership in the western Galilee. A neglected example of Frankish monarchy is examined in Bernard Hamilton's study of Queen Alice of Cyprus. In the final chapter in this section, Andrew Jotischky takes a look at the Franciscan Order, the establishment of the custody of the Holy Land in the fourteenth century, and Mt Sion; its holy loci and role in pilgrimage.

In Part IV three papers take a look at different aspects of Byzantium in its relationship with crusading. Nikolaos Chrissis considers how the Byzantine Empire saw and represented itself with regard to the crusades. The manner in which Byzantine historians in the eleventh to thirteenth centuries regarded the crusades is the topic of Aphrodite Papayianni's chapter, followed by Michael Angold's examination of how the loss of Jerusalem to Saladin in 1187 was viewed in Byzantium.

The meeting between East and West, between Islam and Christianity, so quintessential a part of the crusader experience, is examined in Part V. Niall Christie argues that the Muslims were better acquainted with the Franks prior to the First Crusade than was sometimes represented by medieval Muslim historians and suggests why this 'illusion of ignorance' exists. At the other end of the period, Reuven Amitai takes a look at the early Mamluks from their first encounter with the Franks in 1250 through their defeat of the Mongols at Ayn Jālūt in 1260 until their final defeat of the crusader mainland states in 1291. Svetlana Luchitskaya discusses the manner in which chronicles of the First Crusade represent the Muslim political figures. Yehoshua Frenkel examines the manner in which medieval Muslim sources identified Saladin as a latter-day Joseph by making analogies between events in his life and those of the biblical figure. This theme continues in the chapter by Daniella Talmon-Heller, where medieval Muslim leaders are compared by Muslim authors to notables of the formative period of Islam, their victories to victories of the early Islamic leaders and traitors to former traitors of Islam. Nicholas Coureas examines the complex relationship between Latin Cyprus and the Mamluks. In his broad survey he covers the topics of warfare, diplomacy, cultural and religious exchanges, commerce and settlement, from the time of the establishment of the Mamluk sultanate in 1250 until its demise in 1517 at the hands of the Ottomans. In the final chapter of this section, Michael Lower looks at the legal status of Christian mercenaries in Muslim lands.

In Part VI the discussions are devoted to archaeological research. Mathias Piana expands on the topic of fortifications. Castles are the architectural form most identified with the crusades and Piana examines the history of crusader fortification research, and the development and form of castle building and urban fortifications in the Levant. Raphael Lewis studies two major battle sites: the region between Saforie and the Horns of Hattin in the eastern Galilee, site of perhaps the most significant battle in the history of the crusader states; and Arsur (modern Herzliya) on the central coast of Israel, the location in which the Battle of Arsuf, a significant encounter between the army of the Third Crusade under Richard I and the Ayyubid forces under Saladin, took place in 1191. Lewis exames how the environment of the battle site influenced the outcome of events. In this regard he takes a look at topography, geology, forests, fortifications, climate, water sources, road systems, and hours of sun and moonlight. Vardit Shotten-Hallel, Eytan Sass and Lydia Perelis Grossowicz present some architectural aspects from a new and ongoing study of what was certainly a landmark in castle design at the time of its construction shortly after 1168 – the Hospitaller castle of Belvoir in eastern Israel. In this chapter, emphasis is placed on the castle chapel, and topics discussed include layout, the types of building materials used and their possible source, and proposed dating of the chapel's construction. Edna Stern looks at how the examination of imported ceramic finds enlightens us on international commercial connections of the Latin East, most particularly evident in finds from the maritime cities of Acre and Jaffa. Adrian Boas examines different aspects of day-to-day life and the domestic surroundings in Frankish towns and villages. Aleksander Pluskowski and Heiki Valk survey archaeological evidence for conquest, colonisation and Europeanisation of the eastern Baltic. Piers Mitchell's chapter ends this section with a discussion of archaeological evidence for disease, diet and migration. He examines the eggs of intestinal parasites found in latrine waste in the castle of Saranda Kolones in western Cyprus and in the Hospitaller compound and private houses in Acre and shows how these finds reflect on sanitation, diet, cooking, migration of crusaders and pilgrims and general issues of health of the Frankish population.

The three papers in Part VII examine aspects of crusader art and literature. In many, perhaps most, of their endeavours, Frankish artist and artisans were influenced in varying degrees by the art they came into contact with. Nurith Kenaan-Kedar examines Eastern, Western and Armenian sources for the decorative sculpture found in crusader Jerusalem, concentrating on a specific feature – the goudron frieze, a decorative motif found in several Frankish churches in Jerusalem which she proposes to be an Armenian or north Syrian form adopted in buildings constructed under the patronage of Queen Melisende. Jaroslav Folda assesses the impact of the art of the crusader states on the medieval art of Western Europe. In the third chapter in this section, Marcus Bull takes a look at narratology in crusader texts through the examination of three crusader narratives: the anonymous *Gesta Francorum*, the *De expugnatione Lyxbonensi* and *La conquête de Constantinople.*

Remaining in the sphere of crusader art, the first chapter of the final section, Part VIII, which is devoted to the study of the crusades and the Latin East, is Gil Fishhof's examination of the scholarship of crusader art and his own observations on the sculptural programmes of the Church of the Annunciation in Nazareth. Sophia Menasche follows with an examination of the role of Joshua Prawer, one of the foremost historians of the crusader period in the twentieth century and founding father of Israeli crusader studies. In the concluding chapter, Gary Dickson asks the seemingly simple but in fact very complex question – What are the crusades?

These thirty-eight papers represent a small but notable portion of the vibrant scholarship that has evolved over recent decades and give an insight into not only the more studied aspects of crusader history but also many less familiar topics that form windows through which we can gain an enhanced view of the crusader world.

PART I

IDEOLOGY, CRUSADE, WARFARE AND PEACE-MAKING

———•◆•———

CHAPTER TWO

POPE URBAN II AND THE IDEOLOGY
OF THE CRUSADES

——•◆•——

Paul E. Chevedden

There's a battle outside and it is ragin' …
For the times they are a-changin'

—Bob Dylan[1]

God transfers rule when He wishes and changes the times

—Pope Urban II

A LOVELY ILLUSION

Historians of the crusades embark upon their task in the confident belief that the Jerusalem Crusade of 1095–99 provides a self-evident starting point. Yet this belief arises from an illusion. The illusion is created by the mass of chroniclers' accounts of this crusade (*Gesta francorum*; Fulcher of Chartres, *Historia*; Raymond of Aguilers, *Liber*; Robert the Monk, *Historia*; Guibert of Nogent, *Dei gesta*; Baldric of Bourgueil, *Historia*; Peter Tudebode, *Historia*; Ekkehard of Aura, "Chronica"; Ralph of Caen, "Gesta Tancredi"; William of Malmesbury, *Gesta*; Orderic, *Ecclesiastical History*; Albert of Aachen, *Historia*; William of Tyre, *Chronique*). The spotlight they direct on this single expedition so brilliantly illuminates it as to cause all that has gone before it to be thrust into the shadows. One sees only the Jerusalem Crusade and assumes that it is the only form that crusading took during the eleventh century. From this angle of vision, numerous histories of the crusades have been written (Grousset, 1934–36; Runciman, 1951–54; Waas, 1956; Rousset, 1957; Oldenbourg, 1965/1966; Cognasso, 1967; Setton, 1969–89; Balard, 1988; Zöllner, 1990; Platelle, 1994; Richard, 1996/1999; Mayer, 2005; Tyerman, 2006; Phillips, 2009, 2014; Asbridge, 2010; Jaspert, 2013/2006; Morrisson, 2012; Madden, 2013; Riley-Smith, 2014). What is lacking is an awareness of the wider world of crusading of which "the march to Jerusalem" (*iter Hierosolymitanum*) formed a part. The traditional paradigm of the crusades is not giving way easily to this wider world. It rejects the idea that a series of crusades constituted the point of departure for the earliest thinking about the crusades and instead contends that an individual crusade constitutes a self-evident "point from which" (*terminus a quo*) knowledge about the crusades can proceed forward. It rejects a Mediterranean-wide perspective in which to analyze the crusades in their initial form and comprehends them from a highly localized perspective—a Jerusalem-centered point of view—and projects this highly localized perspective onto all crusades, such that all crusades bear the stamp of the Jerusalem Crusade (Chevedden, 2013, 36–37). It also rejects a pluralistic conception of the crusades that recognizes crusade plurality as the general condition for understanding the crusades and instead adheres to a strict monism, according to which a single crusade—the Jerusalem Crusade—serves as the "standard" (Riley-Smith, 1987, xxix; 2005b, xxxi; Hehl, 1994, 318; 2004, 214), the "scale" (Riley-Smith, 1995a, 9; Tyerman, 2004, 228), the "touchstone" (Riley-Smith and Riley-Smith, 1981, 2; Schein, 2005, 117; Paul and Yeager, 2012, 3), the "template" (Housley, 2006, 19; Whalen, 2009, 70), the "model" (Blake, 1970, 12; Hehl, 1994, 318; Lloyd, 1995, 44; Starnawska, 2001, 418; Mitterauer, 2003, 208; Tyerman, 2004, 47; France, 2005, 97; Jensen, 2007, 17; Flori, 2010, 51; Price, 2011, 77, 78), the "blueprint" (Jotischky, 2004, 7), the "benchmark" (Frankopan, 2012, 5), and the "reference point" (Tyerman, 2011, 2) for all other crusades.

Such a Jerusalem-centric vision of the crusades leaves the false impression that these wars emerged *cum grano salis* fully developed, arising simultaneously as a political force and as an institutionalized tradition, which already consisted of a wide range of formalizing acts: authorization by a pope, the granting of an indulgence and privileges of protection, the taking of a vow, and the wearing of a cross. By elevating a single crusade into a general kind, as if its accidental and transitory features were necessary and permanent, the usual sequence by which political practice is connected to suitable instruments is reversed. Instead of seeing the institutional structures of crusading developing "by degrees and successively" (*gradatim et successive*), we see them emerging "altogether and at once" (*simul et semel*). And, instead of reasoning that these structures might spring from the fact that crusades have come into existence and that institutional mechanisms have been created to support and sustain them, we reason that there were crusades because institutional structures were combined in such and such a way, or because one or more institutional structures were persistently and recurrently attached to crusades (e.g., papal authorization, indulgence, vow, cross, and privileges) (Brundage, 1969, 25–26 n91, 30–190; Riley-Smith, 1977, 15; 2009b, 5; Bysted, 2014, 3–6, 276; Chevedden, 2013, 4–6, 10–11). Yet the crusades had a specific reality in deeds and events before they acquired institutional arrangements, conceptual formulations, theoretical understandings, and extrinsic rewards to affirm, validate, and reinforce this reality. Carl Erdmann (1935, 133/1977, 147) asserted as much in his statement that "the crusading idea became articulate only after it had developed in real life," but he found it impossible to develop a thesis based on this insight. To an extraordinary degree, the history of the crusades remains stuck on the examination of the Jerusalem Crusade. "All round and round in one vortex" (Melville, (1851) 2001, 623), the Jerusalem Crusade carries those that study the crusades. So unremitting is the flow from this single vortex that the modern observer cannot detect how the crusades were first apprehended—not in the form of an isolated vortex but in the form of separate vortices, whose parts were linked to a common movement.

MONISM *VERSUS* PERSPECTIVALISM

A focus on a single, self-existent, isolated crusade will not sharpen our understanding of the crusades; it will only dull it. What is needed is a de-emphasis on the usual theoretical framework into which the crusades have been cast and an emphasis on what contemporaries understood by crusading. Norman Housley (2006, 166) has observed that "the issue of what contemporaries understood by crusading, and above all the sense they made of their crusading past, has as yet received little attention." Housley seems to be suggesting that our understanding of the crusades be rebuilt on a completely new basis by taking into consideration the changing viewpoints and perspectives of contemporaries, who, admittedly, knew the crusades incompletely and restrictedly. Yet in the same breath that he proposes a perspectivalist approach[2] to the crusades, he also finds fault with this mode of analysis, because, as a way of "achieving an objective perspective on past events," it is clearly unsuccessful at "building up a historically accurate and nuanced picture of past crusading" (17). What Housley ignores in attempting to apply a perspectivalist methodology to the crusades is that this investigative method "seeks out the *entirety* of perspectival views in which reality is disclosed," without "prejudice about the character of [such] reality," and tries "to understand *every view* according to its own norms," knowing that "each form or 'view' carries in itself the measure of its reality," and that "true reality is the subject which is capable of all these 'views'" (Cassirer, 1953–96, 4:211–12). Rather than making some other perspective a standard by which to evaluate various perspectival views of the crusades, as Housley does, those adopting a perspectivalist approach should attempt to reconcile partial standpoints to one another in an effort to make them coherent.

Too often modern investigators judge historical sources for the crusades in the light of their own conceptions of crusading, as if their own ideas are universal and timeless, and fail to judge these sources in their own terms, according to the values and ideals implicit in them. Another pitfall for modern investigators has been anachronism—interpreting earlier periods of the crusades in the light of what crusading later became.[3] A perspectivalist approach to the crusades would recognize, for example, that all interpretations of crusading found in twelfth-century narrative accounts of the Jerusalem Crusade are interesting, valid, and important, but these interpretations should not submerge or supplant eleventh-century interpretations, nor should twelfth-century interpretations be read into the interpretations of the previous century. The so-called founding father of the crusades, Pope Urban II (r. 1088–99), saw crusading far differently from chroniclers writing after the events of the Jerusalem Crusade. According to Urban, crusading was not held in check until 1095, when "God," as claimed by Guibert of Nogent (*c.* 1055–1124), "ordained holy wars ... so that the knightly order and the erring mob ... might find a new way of earning salvation" (*Dei gesta*, 87; trans. Levine, *Deeds of God*, 28). Nor did crusading remain inert until 1147, when an account of the capture of Santarém (Shantarīn), north-east of Lisbon, in March of that year, speaks of God having "chosen new wars in our days" (*De Expugnatione Scalabis*, 94; Constable, 1953, 235). Still less did the crusades lie dormant until 1189–92, when Caesarius of Heisterbach (*c.* 1180–*c.* 1240) reports that "the first expedition to Jerusalem" (*prima exeditione Jerusolymitana*) took place (*Dialogus*, 1:300, 4:1986, 4:2014; Purkis, 2013, 113–14, 118).

None of these differing explanations of the start of the crusades offered by contemporaries can be considered incorrect. Each is correct in its own frame of reference, offering a valid account of events as seen from a particular angle of vision. From Guibert of Nogent's angle of vision, the history of the crusades has been particularly well researched and documented. What is lacking is a history of the crusades told from Pope Urban's angle of vision. Historians have studied this pope and developed a more complex image of the man and the times in which he lived without questioning the assumption that his 1095 summons to crusade must be seen as the key to the emergence of the crusading movement (Becker, 1964–2012). Urban, however, did not view crusading as his "creation," nor did he regard

9

the Jerusalem Crusade as the start of something new (Chevedden, 2013). Rather, he saw the Jerusalem Crusade as a part of a movement already underway. From his point of view, an individual crusade does not constitute a self-evident starting point for theorizing about the crusades; rather, a series of crusades constitutes the point of departure for thinking about the crusades. In his letters, he ponders the events "in [his] day" (*nostris diebus*)[4] and uncovers something new and original in them—a transition from Islamic to Christian rule taking place in large parts of the central, western, and eastern Mediterranean.

A MEDITERRANEAN POWER SHIFT IN THE MAKING

The shift from Islamic to Christian rule in which Pope Urban discovers the real essence of crusading was made possible by the strategic priorities and ambitions of a major Islamic state. In 358/969, the great power of the central Mediterranean, the Fatimid caliphate, turned its face eastward and conquered Egypt. This was the first step in its campaign to fulfill its historic mission of redeeming Islam by making a Shī'ī caliph, regarded as the infallible imam (*imām ma'ṣūm*) and the sole authority for the Law of God on earth, sovereign over the *ummah Muḥammadīyah*. As the Fatimids made their bid for political supremacy over Muḥammad's community and moved to dominate the central regions of the Middle East, they turned their backs on strategic possibilities in the central and western Mediterranean. Once this happened, other events followed as inevitable consequences. The central and western Mediterranean was left for others to exploit. Meanwhile, the Fatimid "march on Baghdad" directed toward the destruction of the Abbasid caliphate floundered. A Byzantine military resurgence (*c.* 940–*c.* 1030), which reduced northern Syria to tributary status, preoccupied Fatimid caliphs, as did uprisings against Fatimid rule in Syria and internal conflict within the Fatimid regime (Gil, 1992, 335–408; Whittow, 1996, 367–69, 371, 377, 379–82, 390; El-Cheikh, 2004, 162–87). As a result, the Fatimids were prevented from using Syria as a springboard for a drive on Baghdad. This setback turned the Fatimid thrust eastward into a strategic dead-end. Before long, the Fatimid attempt to achieve supremacy over the *ummah Muḥammadīyah* became the crucible for the Sunnī revival of the eleventh and twelfth centuries made possible by the Saljuq conquest of the Mashriq. As the great dialectic between Sunnī and Shī'ī Islam played itself out in the East, the strategic situation in the central and western Mediterranean changed dramatically.

Islam at first held the advantage. The Aghlabid conquest of Byzantine Sicily, between the years 212/827 and 289/902, signaled a new wave of Islamic aggression in the central Mediterranean. Muslim pressure against the Italian mainland remained constant throughout the ninth and tenth centuries in the form of raids and incursions, and even resulted in the establishment of coastal lodgments and pocket emirates (e.g., the lodgment on the Garigliano River and the emirates of Bari and Taranto). As the Fatimids replaced the Aghlabids as the premier power of the central Mediterranean in the early tenth century, the first faint stirrings of a Christian reaction began. In May 915, a coalition of papal, Byzantine, Campanian, and Spoletan forces attacked and destroyed the Muslim enclave at the mouth of the Garigliano River, thereby freeing central Italy from the Islamic threat. But Muslim raids and incursions intensified in southern Italy, culminating in the conquest of Reggio in 950. More Muslim raids during the 970s and 980s provoked Emperor Otto II (r. 973–83) to intervene with a large German army, but he was soundly defeated by a Muslim force in southern Calabria, near modern Villa San Giovanni, in July 982 (Vehse, 1927; Engreen, 1945; Cilento, 1959,

1971; Citarella, 1967, 1987; Bertolini, 1970; Krueger, 1969–89; Partner, 1972, 50–82; Kreutz, 1991, 18–62, 75–79; Marazzi, 1994, 251–78; Alvermann, 1995; von Falkenhausen, 2003; Hamilton, 2007).

Following Otto's debacle and retreat northward, the Byzantine Empire, in general recovery under emperor Basil II (976–1025), was able to stabilize its rule in southern Italy. This was greatly facilitated by the transfer of the Fatimid seat of power to the newly founded city of Cairo in 362/973. With the strategic deployment of the Fatimids now directed eastward, North Africa and Sicily gradually severed their links to the Ismāʿīlī Shīʿī caliphate and became independent. As power diffused into the hands of the Kalbids in Sicily, the Zirids in Ifrīqiyah, the Hammadids in Algeria, and the Banū Khazrūn in Tripoli, serious weaknesses developed for Islam in the central Mediterranean. After a brief heyday, Kalbid rule in Sicily collapsed, and power devolved into the hands of local *qāʾid*s, as the land fractured into a collection of petty states (*ṭawāʾif*; sing. *ṭāʾifah*). This situation was the "sign" that the Norman duke of Apulia, Robert Guiscard, was looking for to launch his invasion of Sicily, which he undertook with papal authorization that granted him rights of jurisdiction over the island as a "vassal" of the Holy See.[5]

Other "signs" could be seen in other parts of the Mediterranean, as the tide began to turn against Islam along the outer margins and hinterland of the Middle Sea. For more than eighty years (*c.* 889–*c.* 973) the Muslim lodgment at Fraxinetum (Jabal al-Qilāl in Arabic sources; modern La Garde-Freinet), on the French mainland east of Marseilles, was the epicenter for Muslim pillaging expeditions up the Rhône Valley and into the heart of the Alps and Piedmont. By the third decade of the tenth century, "while the bulk of the Muslim forces was entrenched in the mountainous canton of Fraxinetum, in the immediate vicinity of the sea," advance parties occupied and controlled the Alpine passes as far as Pontresina (Pons Saracenorum or "Bridge of the Muslims") in eastern Switzerland and "held—at least during the summer—all the country [from southern France to northern Italy and Switzerland] under a reign of terror" (Lévi-Provençal, 1950, 2:160; see also Dufourcq, 1978, 15–34; Wenner, 1980). In 954, the great Benedictine monastery of St. Gall, one of the main centers of Western culture from the ninth to the twelfth centuries, was sacked, and in the same year Grenoble fell to the Muslims. Cities as widespread as Embrun, Maurienne (Saint-Jean-de-Maurienne), Vienne, Marseille, Aix-en-Provence, Nice, Geneva, Lausanne, Chur, St. Maurice, Asti, Acqui, and Turin all suffered major attacks. The event that precipitated the overthrow of the Muslim enclave at Fraxinetum and forced the Muslims out of the Alps occurred on the night of 21/22 July 972. As Abbot Maiolus of Cluny and his entourage were crossing the Great Saint Bernard Pass (Mons Iovis) in the western Alps, they were taken captive and held for ransom by Muslim forces from Fraxinetum. This event shocked Western Christendom and spawned an immediate reaction. The considerable ransom of 1,000 pounds of silver was promptly paid to secure the abbot's release and shortly thereafter a coalition of local forces ousted the Muslims from Fraxinetum, thus ending Muslim plundering and captive-taking in Provence, Piedmont, and the Alpine region (Bruce, 2007).

By the turn of the eleventh century, Muslim attacks could now expect to be followed by Christian counterattacks. We see this pattern played out along the shores of the Ligurian Sea. In 934, the Fatimids launched an amphibious assault on Genoa and thoroughly sacked the city. Pisa suffered Muslim attacks in 1004 and 1011. In 1015, Mujāhid ibn ʿAbd Allāh al-ʿĀmirī, ruler of Denia (Dāniyah) and the Balearics (al-Jazāʾir al-Sharqīyah) from 1014 to 1045, launched his campaign to conquer Sardinia. This offensive posed an immediate threat to Pisa and Genoa, since Muslim ships operating out of Sardinia could take control of the sea-lanes essential to the economic survival of these two maritime cities. The Pisans and the Genoese immediately joined forces, and, with the support of Pope Benedict VIII (r. 1012–24), launched a coordinated attack on the Muslims on Sardinia. In 1034, the Pisans carried the war into the enemy's camp and captured Būnah (ancient Hippo Regius, colonial Bône, present-day ʿAnnābah) in North Africa. In 1050, the Genoese and Pisans turned their attention again to Sardinia and, at the behest of Pope Leo IX (r. 1049–54), ousted the Muslims from the island (Lewis, 1951, 184, 194, 198–99, 201, 204–05, 220–22, 224, 226, 232–33; Becker, 1964–2012, 2:284, 300–04; Citarella, 1967; Epstein, 1996, 14–23; Bruce, 2006).

In Iberia, a wave of Muslim attacks against the Christian states in the north of the peninsula from the late tenth to the early eleventh centuries eventually radicalized the Christian population into a Holy War reaction of its own. The architect of this onslaught was Muḥammad ibn Abī ʿĀmir (326–92/938–1002), the Umayyad *ḥājib*, or chief minister, who became the de facto ruler of al-Andalus from 368/978 to 392/1002. Taking the title al-Manṣūr billāh ("the one rendered victorious by God"; Almanzor in the Christian sources), Ibn Abī ʿĀmir made aggressive militarism the hallmark of his rule. He launched more than fifty campaigns of *jihād* against his northern Christian neighbors, sacking numerous cities, towns, and monasteries, among them Zamora (981), Simancas (983), Sepúlveda (984), Barcelona (985), the monastery of Sant Cugat del Vallès (San Cugat del Vallés) (985), Coimbra (987), León (988), Clunia (994), Santa María de Carrión (995), Astorga (995), Santiago de Compostella (997), Pamplona (999), Burgos (1000), Cervera (1000), and San Millan de la Cogolla (1002) (ʿUdhrī, *Nuṣūṣ*, 1:185–95, 2:196–205; *Dhikr bilād al-Andalus*, 1:185–95, 2:196–205; Ruiz Asensio, 1968; Lévi-Provençal, 1950, 2:233–59; Kennedy, 1996, 109–29; Chalmeta Gendrón, 1991, 430). Unfortunately for al-Andalus, he failed to translate his virtuoso operational performance into any strategic gain. In fact, Ibn Abī ʿĀmir's military successes worked to the advantage of the Christian kingdoms. The devastation wrought by the Muslim incursions became the cauldron of a Christian resurgence. Soon after the death of Ibn Abī ʿĀmir's son and successor, ʿAbd al-Malik al-Muẓaffar, in 399/1008, the ʿĀmirid dictatorship collapsed, and al-Andalus fragmented into a jumble of *ṭawāʾif* that soon fell easy prey to the rising Christian powers of the north. Financial exploitation, in the form of tribute or *parias*, soon transitioned into a movement of reconquest, followed by crusades from 1064 onward.[6]

As Christian powers in the Latin West gained the strategic momentum in the war with Islam and shifted to the offensive, the Islamic world found itself unable to offer effective resistance. Having created the conditions for a Christian Holy War reaction, Islam in the eleventh century was remarkably unprepared to deal with it. From the western Mediterranean to eastern Iran, the major Islamic powers that exercised dominance in the tenth century had either collapsed or fallen into a downward spiral by the eleventh century. Although momentum in the Mediterranean shifted in favor of the Latin West during the eleventh century, there was at first no dramatic turn of events. Even by mid-century, the most significant development in relations between the Latin West and the Islamic world lay not in any general European movement against Islamic powers in the Mediterranean but in unstable local situations along the Islamic frontier that invited a Christian reaction. The injection of the Latin West into Islamic political struggles in the central and western Mediterranean soon led to something much larger. Islamic weaknesses came to be exploited in ways that had not been anticipated. As certain Christian communities stirred themselves energetically for the fight with Islam, the Church was quick to follow.

TRANSLATIO REGNI

The idea of crusading in the eleventh century, as it emerged under the reform popes (Nicholas II, Alexander II, Gregory VII, Victor III, and Urban II), was an attempt by the papacy to get a handle on a highly fluid situation—the rise of the Latin West to political dominance and its changed relationship with Islam—and to provide western Christendom with a rationale for a transformation already underway in the Mediterranean world. In his attempt to do full justice to the novelty and uniqueness of what was happening "in [his] time" (*nostris temporibus*),[7] Pope Urban did not invent a new term or concept to account for what was occurring, but instead adopted and adapted a pre-existing conceptual framework taken from the Old Testament to explain the "world-historical" events of his day. These events, Urban found, were best understood through the prism of God's chosen people, in the redemptive cycle of sin, punishment, repentance, and restoration manifested in the history of ancient Israel, and through the idea that God directs the transfer of worldly power from one kingdom to another (*translatio regni*) and is doing so at present to restore the lost lands of Christendom.

In 1088, during the first year of his pontificate, Urban laid out the essential features of his crusading vision. He did so on the occasion of restoring the archbishopric of Toledo to primatial rank, which had been made possible by the capture of Toledo three years earlier by Alfonso VI of Léon-Castile (1072–1109).[8] Although the features of his crusading vision are specifically related to Toledo, they will be applied subsequently by the pope to other parts of Iberia,[9] to Sicily,[10] as well as to the eastern Mediterranean,[11] so that, "in the last three or four years of [Urban's] pontificate," these regions will be considered by the pope as "simply three different fronts … in which the same fight between Christianity and Islam was being played out, and in which everyone … took his assigned place and fulfilled a task of exactly equal value" (Becker, 1964–2012, 1:229–30; see also 3:675).

In his bull restoring Toledo as Iberia's primatial see, the pope begins by dividing the Christian history of the city into four major periods, the last two of which partly overlap and relate to the crusades. In the first period, Toledo enjoys an exulted status:

> It is apparent to all who know the holy decrees what a great position the Church of Toledo held from ancient times and what great authority it exercised in the regions of Iberia and Gaul, so much so that its authority in ecclesiastical matters increased.

In the second period, "the many sins of its people" bring about the conquest of Toledo by the Muslims and the destruction of "the liberty of the Christian religion":

> But due to the many sins of its people, this city was conquered by the Muslims, and the liberty of the Christian religion was destroyed completely there, so much so that over the course of nearly 370 years no Christian bishop could hold office there.

In the third period, "divine mercy" and human action combine to produce a movement of reconquest that returns Toledo to its Christian roots:

> In our time (*nostris temporibus*), however, with divine mercy pouring forth upon His people and through the efforts of the most glorious King Alfonso and with the hard work of the Christian people, after the Muslims were expelled, the city of Toledo was restored to the rite of the Christians.

In the fourth period, "the original authority of the Church of Toledo" is restored, making it possible "to consolidate and further enhance … the condition of the city":

> And, therefore, in response to God's grace and mercy, we have not refused to restore the original authority of the Church of Toledo, since you, through such hazards on land and sea, have humbly yearned for the authority of the Roman Church. Indeed, we rejoice, and, with a very joyful heart, offer great thanks to God, as is fitting, for the fact that He granted to the Christian people in our time (*nostris temporibus*) so magnificent a victory, as we ardently desire, with His help, to consolidate and further enhance, as far as it is possible for us, the condition of the city.[12]

In the lands lost to Islam by Christendom, Urban sees the same historical pattern repeating itself: (1) a period of greatness for the Church, followed by (2) a period of collective sin and punishment that takes the form of conquest and domination by the forces of Islam, followed by (3) a period of reconquest, that ultimately brings with it (4) a "[restoration of] the former position of the Holy Church" (*antiquum ecclesie sancte statum … reparavit*).[13] For Urban, these events give significance to the passage from the Book of Daniel telling of God's power to change the times and the seasons, and to depose kings and set up kings (Dan 2:20–21).[14] What the prophet Daniel said in the Old Testament, according to Urban, is once again being fulfilled *nostris temporibus* in an astounding *translatio regni* by which the Church of God (*ecclesiam Dei*) is being expanded into Muslim territory.[15] This *translatio regni* was no invention of Urban's, but the central fact of his age. By linking the *translatio* of his day with the *translatio* of scripture, Urban attempts to convey not merely a "change in rule" (*Herrschaftsübertragung*), but also a "change in era" (*Zeitenwende* or *Zeitenwandel*) (Becker, 1964–2012, 2:342, 344, 349, 352–54, 356, 361–63, 369, 372–75, 384, 398, 404, 3:356, 587, 675–76; Ringel, 1987, 139; Hehl, 1994, 303, 304, 319, 328, 335). The old era of Islamic ascendancy has ended and is being replaced by a new era of Christian reconquest and restoration. What caught Urban's imagination was not a *translatio regni* in the narrow sense—a localized effort to "rescue Jerusalem and the other Churches of Asia from the power of the Muslims" (Somerville, 1972, 124)—but a *translatio regni* in the broadest sense, a Mediterranean-wide movement to free the Christian world from Islamic rule and to rebuild the Church.

The separate events and actions that make up this sweeping *translatio regni*—in the central, western, and eastern Mediterranean—are in themselves dissimilar from one another in many ways. Urban overrides all dissimilarities and focuses on the one element that unites them: *translatio regni*. In doing so, he gives to these disparate events a conceptual identity by bringing them into a network of interrelations with other events. Urban's interpretation of the crusades as a *translatio regni* does not come from a centuries-old exegetical tradition (Gabriele, 2012),[16] but from an actual *translatio regni* already advancing across the Mediterranean, and it is this reality that gives the Book of Daniel contemporary importance because it is now seen to have a deeper meaning than previously thought.[17]

THE EXEGETE OF HISTORY

In providing a deeper meaning to the Book of Daniel by relating it to the events happening *nostris temporibus*, Urban becomes an "exegete of history" (Herder, (1803) 1985–2000, 930; Hamilton, 2003, 235). He is not only an interpreter of the events of his day but also a self-proclaimed "cooperator"[18] in the actualization of these events. In addition, he uses his exegetical powers to reconnect the past with the present, the Old Testament with events *nostris temporibus*, so that the past is no longer seen as alienated from the present. There is now nothing blocking access to the past because its meaning is now being fulfilled in the present. Urban contends that the past is not in fact detached from the present, but is intimately joined to it, and that the truth of the past is to be found in the present. To know the past, it is necessary to understand the present. The *translatio regni* spoken of in the Book of Daniel now takes on significance because Urban has placed it in relationship to the *translatio regni* occurring in the eleventh century.

As the "exegete of history," Urban, in Herder's words, "looks out at what is behind and what is before him ... and becomes an interpreter, indeed a creator of the times" (*rückwärts und vor sich hinausblickt ... und wird ein Ausleger, ja ein Schöpfer der Zeiten*) (Herder, (1803) 1985–2000, 930; Hamilton, 2003, 235). He not only looks for the present in the past, but he also searches for the future in the present. "What is" is connected to "what was," so that the present can inform the past. In addition, "what is" is also linked to "what ought to be," so that the developing Mediterranean *translatio regni* is projected onto a future in which the Church is to be regenerated through the recovery of ancient episcopal sees and ecclesiastical provinces that have fallen under Muslim domination. Urban feels certain that present efforts that have seen "the Church ... enlarged, the domination of the Muslims ... reduced" and "the ancient honor of episcopal sees ... restored"[19] contain the seeds of the future. These events signal a fundamental and radical change in the relations between Islam and Christendom. They mark the close of an old epoch in which Christendom had been under the heel of Islam and the beginning of a new epoch in which Christendom will be reborn. Out of these events Urban maps the course of Christianity's recovery and infuses the crusades with an underlying worldview and an ideology that is both powerfully attractive and inspirational.

POPE URBAN'S ESCHATOLOGICAL VISION AND HIS MANY "CRUSADES"

In Herder's words, Urban "shoots far out a prophetically strong shot into the heart of the future" (Herder, (1769) 1985–2000, 794; Hamilton, 2003, 234). Yet accounts of the crusades rarely do justice to Urban's eschatological vision and his commitment to epochal change, primarily because Urban does not fit the mold of a medieval apocalyptic thinker, such as Gerhoh of Reichersberg (1093–1169) or Joachim of Fiore (1135–1202). He was not at all like "those who dream by night," who, on waking in the day, find no change in their surroundings. Rather, he can be classified among "the dreamers of the day," to use T. E. Lawrence's expression (1935, 23), who are distinguished by the fact that "they may act their dream with open eyes, to make it possible." Urban did not consider the *Crusade of reconquest* (*reconquista*) and the *Crusade of rebuilding the Church* (*restauratio*) as ends in themselves. They were linked to the Church's mission to "proclaim the Gospel to all creation" (Mk 16:15). The *Crusade of reconquest* was to lead to the *Crusade of regenerating the Church*; and the *Crusade of rebuilding the Church* was to lead to the *Crusade of missionary evangelization* (*dilatatio fidei*). As a "dreamer of the day," Urban was faced with coming up with a way of achieving his many "crusades," or interlinked movements of the crusading enterprise. He realized that these "crusades" could not be achieved simultaneously; they could only be achieved in succession: achieving the first "crusade" was a condition for achieving the second "crusade," and achieving the first and second "crusades" was a condition for achieving the third "crusade."

Early in his pontificate, Urban clearly set the pattern for his many "crusades," when he promoted a policy of Muslim conversion upon the recovery of an ancient see. In 1088, Urban took action both "to restore the original authority of the Church of Toledo" and to fulfill the mission of the Church to "make disciples of all nations" (Mt 28:19). He restored the archiepiscopal see of newly reconquered Toledo to ecclesiastical primacy within Iberia and directed its incumbent Archbishop Bernard of Sédirac, himself a former Cluniac monk, to undertake a program of conversion: "With warm affection we exhort you, reverend brother, that you live worthy of so high and honored a pontificate, taking care always not to give offense to Christians or to Muslims; strive by word and example, God helping, to convert the infidels [i.e., the Muslims] to the faith."[20] Urban was following in the footsteps of his predecessor Pope Gregory VII (r. 1073–85), who had previously promoted conversionary activities in Sicily, Iberia, and North Africa (Kedar, 1988, 44–57), and had directly linked the crusade indulgence to the apostolic mission of the Church when he commanded Archbishop Arnald of Acerenza to grant Count Roger d'Hauteville (1031–1101) remission of his sins and to do the same for "his knights, who [were] about to fight with him against the pagans (i.e., the Muslims) [in Sicily]," which required that Roger and his knights receive the Sacrament of Penance and that Roger "keep himself from capital offences and … seek to spread the worship of the Christian name among the pagans (i.e., the Muslims)" (Chevedden, 2005b, 292; 2010, 216; see also Kedar, 1988, 49–50).[21]

One of the principal concerns of Pope Urban was to demonstrate the continuity of crusading with the history of the Church and God's plan for salvation. This meant above all seeing the crusades as playing a part in fulfilling the ultimate mission of the Church of making disciples through the preaching of the Gospel.[22] Why Urban's concern for the apostolic mission of the Church should not figure prominently in his extant letters dealing with the Jerusalem Crusade is perhaps best explained by his tripartite division of crusading activity. If conversion was to be achieved in an effective and enduring manner, it had to be pursued as part of a coherent overall crusading program. The stages that make up crusade—*reconquest*, *restoration*, and *evangelization*—could not all be achieved at once, but only in some sequential progression over time. So it is not surprising that Urban paid no heed to conversion in his appeals "to liberate the Churches of the East" (*ad liberationem Orientalium ecclesiarum*).[23] Only after Jerusalem was recovered and restored did evangelization enter the picture. Archbishop Anselm of Canterbury (*c.* 1033–1109) is the first to speak of evangelization as a crusading goal of the Jerusalem enterprise. In his letter to Baldwin I, following his coronation as the first king of Jerusalem (r. 1100–18), Anselm uses language that strongly echoes Urban's own view of crusading. He praises God for having raised Baldwin

> to the dignity of king in that country in which our Lord Jesus Christ Himself, having initiated the beginnings of Christianity, has reestablished (*novam plantavit*) His Church, which, because of the sins of men, had been, by the judgment of God, long oppressed by the infidels (i.e., the Muslims) there; but which, by His mercy, has in our time been so wonderfully raised to life again (*resuscitavit*), so that it might be spread from there throughout the whole world.[24]

The history of Jerusalem is laid out according to the same historical pattern that Urban first identified at Toledo, except for the fact that *reconquest* and *restoration* are combined under a single rubric: reestablishment of the Church. Yoked to the recovery of the Church is a final stage that has not been identified thus far as part of Urban's historical schema: the resumption of the mission of the Church. Anselm's version of Urban's schema may be summarized as follows: (1) "the beginnings of Christianity" in Palestine initiated by "our Lord Jesus Christ Himself," then (2) "oppress[ion] by the infidels there" of the Church "because of the sins of men," then (3) reestablishment of the Church there, and finally (4) the "spread [of the Church] from there throughout the whole world."

For Urban, as for Anselm, the *Crusade of battle*, the *Crusade of rebuilding the Church*, and the *Crusade of evangelization* were all conjoined activities. As these churchmen saw it, *reconquest* and *restoration* were means towards the ultimate goal of evangelizing the world. Another Church leader with whom Urban had strong ties and who shared Anselm's excitement about the new opportunities presented by the crusades for the evangelization of the world was Hugh of Semur, abbot of the great monastery of Cluny in Burgundy from 1049 until his death in 1109 (Hunt, 1967; Cowdrey, 1970b, 183–85; 1973; Kohnle, 1993; Constable, 2008). Hugh was at the forefront of the "evangelical awakening" (Chenu, 1979, 202–69; Constable, 1982, 53–56; 1996, 156–59)[25] at its birth during the second half of the eleventh century and promoted the new missionary enterprise to the Islamic world (Dunlop, 1952; Cutler, 1963, 1968; Turki, 1966; Hunt, 1967, 149; Cowdrey, 1978, 146–47; 1970a, 240–45; Kedar, 1988, 44–47, 55, 84; Kohnle, 1993, 38–39, 94–95, 227–29, 275; Constable, 2008, 191; Sarrió Cucarella, 2012). Hugh's interest in converting Muslims was doubtless known to, and most certainly shared by, the future Pope Urban II, who was prior of Cluny under Hugh from about 1070 to 1080 and who maintained his ties to Cluny after becoming a cardinal and, later, pope.

Hugh presided over the building of the largest church in Europe at the time, the great third church at Cluny, and served as a leading participant in the Council of Clermont (1095), which called for a crusading "march" (*iter*) to Jerusalem "to liberate the Church of God" in the East.[26] He, just like Urban and Anselm, placed the *Crusade of evangelization* in the context of the broader parameters of the crusading movement, and viewed the *Crusade of reconquest*, the *Crusade of rebuilding the Church*, and the *Crusade of evangelization* not only as interrelated phenomena but also as interpenetrating phenomena. Hugh incorporated these ideas into the decorative program of the Cluniac chapel of Berzé-la-Ville, located in Burgundy mid-way between Cluny and Mâcon (Chevedden, 2011, 281–88, 320–29). While a discussion still rages regarding who oversaw the actual execution of all the interior paintings of the chapel—Hugh or his successor, Pons de Melgueil (1109–22)—there is little doubt that the choice of the decorative program was made by Hugh (Wettstein, 1971–78, 1:77; Lapina, 2005, 311–12). Its overall purpose is to show the *Crusade of reconquest*, the *Crusade of rebuilding the Church*, and the *Crusade of evangelization* in mutual dependence and correlation (Figure 2.1).[27]

Benjamin Kedar (1988) posits a sharp distinction between crusading as "Europe's counteroffensive against the realm of Islam" (41) and "crusading for the advancement of missions" (159), the immediate consequence of which is that crusade and mission are each assigned their separate domain, so that they cannot interact. To forge a bridge between the two, Kedar constructs a scenario whereby crusading needed some development outside itself to bring it into harmony with the apostolic mission of the Church. The "mechanism" of change that brought about the union of crusade and mission, according to Kedar, was a growing emphasis within the Latin West on preaching to fellow Christians, which, eventually, by the middle of the twelfth century, turned outward and found a new destiny in

Figure 2.1 The priory chapel of Berzé-la-Ville (Saône-et-Loire), France: general view
of the mural paintings decorating the apse (early twelfth century). These paintings, which
give visual expression to crusading as a series of interlinked movements of *reconquest, restoration,*
and *evangelization,* represent the earliest artistic effort to articulate the ideology of the crusades
(Chevedden, 2011, 281–88, 320–29). With permission of the Académie de Mâcon.
Photograph © Scala / Art Resource, NY.

"preaching to the Muslims" (134). This reconstruction is a masterpiece of ingenuity and invention, but it fails to account for how contemporaries of the crusades understood the relationship between crusade and mission. As the crusades gathered momentum in the latter half of the eleventh century, hope for Islam's conversion was at the same moment being strongly asserted. The popular religious thought of the day was passionately concerned with converting Muslims. This finds its literary expression in the first heroic epic poetry of Europe, the *chansons de geste*, which speak of Muslims converting both collectively and individually (Burns, (1971), 1386; 1984, 81; Kedar, 1988, 68–70). Pope Urban, Anselm of Canterbury, and Hugh of Cluny were no bystanders to these currents of thought but active promoters of conversionist efforts. To them, crusade and mission were natural companions. No mysterious harmony needed to be created between crusade and mission. The concept of mission was not external to the concept of crusade, imposed upon it from outside, but was integral to crusade, part of its fundamental nature.

CRUSADING IDEOLOGY: A GUIDE, NOT A STRAITJACKET, FOR ACTION

Although Urban may not have been the originator of the crusades, he certainly must be credited with having systematized and refined a theory and an ideology of the crusades. As a theory, *translatio regni* explains the crusades; as an ideology, it provides a guide for action. It is both a theoretical and a practical principle, offering an explanation of the experience of crusading and a stimulus and a framework for guiding crusading action. Pope Gregory VII planted the seeds for this theory and ideology,[28] and Urban extended this theory and ideology and gave it a Mediterranean-wide scope. Yet for all of its power to inspire and galvanize political action, crusading theory and ideology never functioned as a straitjacket that bound the Latin West to "an aggressive war of religion for the expansion of Christendom" in which "religion itself provided the specific cause of war, unencumbered by the considerations of public welfare, territorial defense, national honor, or interests of sate" (Erdmann, 1935, 1, 7–8/1977, 3, 10). Crusading did not operate autonomously, unrelated to political, social, economic, and military circumstances. Crusading theory and ideology certainly gave to the immemorial struggle with Islam a new sense of purpose and design, but the rulers of Western Christendom that undertook to undo the Muslim occupation of former Christian territories and rebuild a subjugated Church performed their task, not only to serve the interests of wider Christendom but also to serve their own interests. These rulers contributed to the common war with Islam in unequal measure, depending on their own relations with the Islamic world and their own political ambitions. Whenever they did engage in crusading, they did so on their own terms. When their interests conflicted with the papacy, they could hold out with remarkable stubbornness, by passive, as well as by blatant, opposition.

By ceding no role whatsoever to the papacy or the hierarchical Church in establishing the crusades, other than as a "*cooperator* in the works of God and the proclaimer of God's will regarding the *translatio regni* and the *restauratio* of religion and the Church" (Becker, 1964–2012, 2:357), Pope Urban accentuates with the greatest emphasis the part played by Christian rulers of the Latin West in initiating the crusades. This is not an eccentric view but the shared sentiment of many contemporaries of Urban, which finds its literary manifestation in the most famous medieval crusading epic, *The Song of Roland*. In this greatest of all medieval epic poems, crusading is presented as a royal, not a papal, enterprise (*La Chanson de Roland*).[29] What this indicates is that the crusades arose and took root because these wars pertained to important interests of newly emerging European polities, whether in the form of Italian maritime city-states, such as Genoa, Pisa, and Venice, or in the form of larger territorial entities, such as Norman South Italy, or various Catalan counties that would gradually be brought under the rule of the count of Barcelona, or the recently minted kingdoms of Aragon and León-Castile, or the Cid's principality of Valencia (1094–1102). Much of the impetus for the crusades can be traced to the realm of politics in terms of the rise of Christian polities and the expansion of Christendom, rather than to the realm of religion, as the word "religion" is understood nowadays, in a privatized and individualized way (Riley-Smith, 1997, 75; 2000, 20; 2001, 135; 2005a, 555; 2005b, xxx–xxxi; 2008, 33;

2009b, 58; 2014, 19), not a public way (Burns, 1989a, 127; 1989b, 100). Over the course of the eleventh century, Christian powers seized the opportunity both to deliver a counterattack against Islam and to create, or further expand, independent political realms in regions that had been lost to Christendom. In such circumstances, it is easy to see why these powers promoted crusading and the concept that sustained it: *translatio regni*. The crusades were driven by political realities rather than by ideology. Yet ideology played a key role in giving political coherence to the crusading movement, and Pope Urban was instrumental in making the crusading enterprise an ideologically and politically coherent movement.

Following his celebrated call for a crusade in 1095 "to liberate the Churches of the East," Urban soon feared that this expedition would "[pull] the whole [crusading] enterprise in this one direction" (Mayer, 2005, 20; see also O'Callaghan, 2003, 33), that is, toward Jerusalem, to the detriment of crusading fronts elsewhere. Urban foresaw the disastrous consequences of Iberia becoming the "forgotten front," the Burma of the crusading enterprise. If the Jerusalem Crusade were considered to be the one and only expression of crusading, such a narrow and myopic vision of the crusading enterprise would endanger Christendom by putting at risk the "Churches [in Iberia] suffering from the incursions of the Muslims."[30] If the Jerusalem campaign became the sole supreme model for crusading, then crusading would have value only insofar as it was pursued to liberate the Eastern Churches. And if crusading consisted solely of acting to aid Eastern Christendom, then the Islamic threat in the broader Mediterranean region would not be addressed.

Urban believed that he could avoid these undesirable consequences by considering the war with Islam in its full range, across the entire Mediterranean, rather than viewing it as a series of discrete campaigns unrelated to one another. Accordingly, he promoted a comprehensive approach to the crusades that recognized the need to maintain pressure against Islam in both the western and the eastern Mediterranean. When a number of Catalan counts and their knights were contemplating joining the expedition "to aid the Churches of Asia and to liberate their brothers from the tyranny of the Muslims," Urban admonished them in a letter (*c.* July 1096), saying, "if anyone of you plans to go to Asia, let him try to fulfill the desire of his devotion here [in Iberia]." The pope begged and commanded them, "for the sake of the city and Church of Tarragona ... to carry out its restoration in every way," and he affirmed the Mediterranean-wide focus of crusading in the bluntest of terms: "it is no feat of valor to liberate Christians from Muslims in one place [i.e., in Asia] only to deliver Christians to Muslim tyranny and oppression in another place [i.e., in Iberia]."[31] Urban's broader vision of crusading is also on display in the spring of 1099, when, as Erdmann recounts, "Archbishop Bernard of Toledo appeared in Rome ... wishing to proceed from there to Syria to join the crusading army." Instead of being commended for his action, the pope absolved the prelate of his crusading vow and sent him home, because, as Erdmann explains, "the pope did not wish the Spaniards to take less heed for the church of their own land than for that of the East" (Erdmann, 1935, 295/1977, 318; see also Becker, 1964–2012, 1:230, 2:381; O'Callaghan, 2003, 34).

PAPAL PARTICIPATION IN THE CRUSADES: A STEP-BY-STEP DEVELOPMENT

Urban's prominent role in the Jerusalem Crusade was not at all indicative of the papacy's participation in the crusades from the beginning. For example, the Norman assault on Islamic Sicily, starting in the late fall of 1060 with a reconnaissance operation in the north-eastern corner of the island, gives no sign of papal direction or leadership in the enterprise. To the contrary, the direct evidence seems to suggest that the initiative behind the Norman undertaking came from Robert Guiscard. The title that he gives to himself in his oath to Pope Nicholas II at Melfi in August 1059, "future Duke of Sicily" (*dux ... futurus Sicilie*), indicates, according to Graham Loud (2007, 138), that "the invasion of Sicily was already contemplated [by Guiscard], and hence the return of the island to Christian rule."[32] Regardless of the limited role that the papacy exercised in Guiscard's venture at its outset, beyond papal authorization of the project, this role soon grew.

In 1063, following the Norman victory at the critical Battle of Cerami in the Sicilian interior fifteen miles north-west of Troina, Pope Alexander II (r. 1061–73) granted a crusade indulgence to the participants in the Sicilian enterprise (Geoffrey Malaterra, *De rebus gestis*, 44–45 [II.33]; trans. Wolf, *Deeds*, 111; Erdmann, 1935, 125/1977, 138–39; Chevedden, 2010, 214–16). In the same year, Pope Alexander also granted a crusade indulgence to Christian warriors setting off for Iberia on a campaign against the Muslim frontier town of Barbastro (Loewenfeld, (1885) 1959, 43 (no. 82); Chevedden, 2005b, 277–86; 2006, 134–35; 2010, 193, 214–16). The most detailed account of the Barbastro Crusade (1064–65), written by Ibn Ḥayyān (377–469/987 or 988–1076), identifies its senior leader as "the commander of the papal mounted army" (*qāʾid khayl rūmah*),[33] and Amatus of Montecassino identifies this individual as the Norman adventurer Robert Crispin (*Storia*, 13–14 (I.5); trans. Dunbar, *History*, 46–47).[34] Whether the term *qāʾid khayl rūmah* can be equated with the Latin title *romani exercitus princeps militiae* ("the commander of the papal army"), as Dozy (1881, 2:351) believed, it is Ibn Ḥayyān's thoroughgoing contention that the papacy, spearheaded by its Norman allies, played the dominant role in the Barbastro Crusade. This crusade was followed up "in the next decades by a series of similar undertakings," that included, according to Erdmann, the "bands of crusaders, especially from France," that rushed to aid Alfonso VI in the fight against the North African Almoravids (al-Murābiṭūn), who intervened in al-Andalus to bolster Islam's rapidly deteriorating position, due to Castile's conquest of Toledo. "The severe defeat suffered by the Christians," at the battle of Sagrajas (Zallāqah), near Badajoz (Baṭalyūs), in 479/1086, Erdmann contends, provided "new stimulus to the idea of a Spanish crusade" (*Spanienkreuzzuges*). In the following year, "substantial contingents of knights reached Spain from various parts of France under high-placed leadership," and "these knights continued to attribute to the Moorish war the crusading character it had had in the Barbastro campaign" (Erdmann, 1935, 267–68/1977, 288).

The papacy played a crucial part in providing new stimulus to crusading in Iberia. To shore up Christian defenses in the peninsula, Pope Urban issued a crusade bull on 1 July 1089 to Catalan nobles and bishops and urged them to rebuild Tarragona (Ṭarrakūnah) so that it might "be celebrated as a concentric system of defense (*in murum et antemurale*) against the Muslims for the Christian people," offering to all those who heeded his call "the same indulgence that they would gain if they had undertaken the long journey [to Jerusalem or to some other (pilgrimage) site]."[35] In the early 1090s, the crusading vow was first made compulsory upon those taking part in the Tarragona Crusade (Villanueva and Lorenzo Villanueva, 1821, 326–29, Appendix 39, nos. 1–2; McCrank, 1974, 255–56, 280–81 nn30–34; 1978, 162). As the Tarragona enterprise was slowly evolving, the Almoravids were busy methodically obliterating one Muslim *ṭāʾifah* state after another in al-Andalus. This development prompted the Castilian nobleman and military leader Rodrigo Díaz de Vivar to capture Valencia in Jumādá I 487/June 1094.

RODRIGO DÍAZ DE VIVAR (EL CID): CRUSADER PRINCE AND "PROPAGATOR OF THE FAITH"

Known to history and legend by the honorific title El Cid, Rodrigo Díaz de Vivar (*c.* 1043–99) continues to be an enigmatic figure (Figure 2.2). History seems to cast him in the role of a freebooter and a soldier of fortune, while legend has made him the quintessential Christian hero and crusading warrior. Historians mostly prefer an either/or choice between these two contrasting images, but it is obvious that both characterizations of Rodrigo are equally valid. The continuing debate over which image is the correct one—Christian hero (Menéndez Pidal, 1969) or military adventurer (Dozy, 1881, 2:1–233; Wasserstein, 1985, 148, 262–64; Linehan, 1987; Fletcher, 1987, 36; 1989; 2004, 72–73, 86, 89, 92; Catlos, 2004, 76–78; 2014a, 10, 69–123, 148, 319–20; Purkis, 2010, 445; Hitchcock, 2014, 130–33)—and recent efforts to judiciously strike a balance between the two (Martin, 2007; Barton, 2011) overlook a very important part of Rodrigo's diverse and complex career: his role as a crusading ruler, during the years 1094 to 1099, when he exercised sovereign power over the principality of Valencia. Like Robert Guiscard d'Hauteville (*c.* 1015–85), who legitimized control over lands to which he had no rightful claim by gaining papal recognition in 1059 of his sovereignty over Apulia, Calabria, and Islamic Sicily,[36] Rodrigo also consolidated his hold on the greater part of the former *ṭā'ifah* of Valencia by obtaining papal recognition of his sovereignty over this territory. The document that confirms this is the endowment charter that Rodrigo granted in 1098 to the newly restored cathedral of Valencia and its newly installed bishop, Jerome of Périgord. Although it is the only document that the Cid put in writing that has survived, and contains his own autograph subscription (lines 34–35), it has received surprisingly little attention (Figure 2.3).[37]

Figure 2.2   Charlton Heston in a publicity still for the 1961 Anthony Mann film *El Cid,* in which he played the title role. By permission of the Heston Family Trust. © AF archive / Alamy

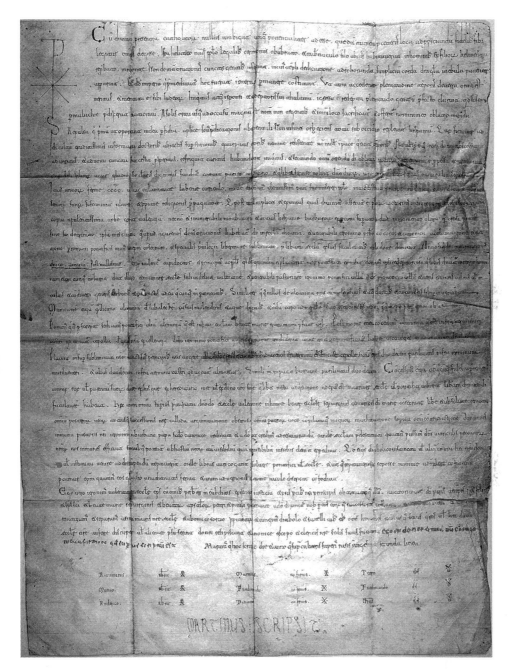

Figure 2.3   The endowment charter issued by Rodrigo Díaz de Vivar in 1098 to the cathedral of
Valencia and its bishop, Jerome of Périgord. It presents Rodrigo as the independent ruler
of the Christian principality of Valencia, and it applies Pope Urban II's fourfold schema of
Christian history to Valencia. Salamanca, Archivo Diocesano, caja 43, legajo 2, no. 72. See:
http://commons.wikimedia.org/wiki/File:Dotación_del_Cid_a_la_catedral_de_Valencia_1098.jpg
http://es-la.dbpedia.org/page/resource/Jerónimo_de_Perigord

There is no trace in this document of Rodrigo Díaz as the unscrupulous adventurer, who is willing to offer his services to Muslim and Christian alike. Instead, what we find are the basic elements of Pope Urban's crusading vision and the part played by Rodrigo in this vision. Rodrigo is presented as an independent ruler, with the titles *princeps* (prince) and *campidoctor* (Sp. Campeador = victor), whose authority is underwritten by God Himself. The preamble, or introduction, of the document establishes Rodrigo's right to rule by invoking the principle of God's sovereignty over the kingdoms of the world, the primary principle that is the source and origin of the idea of *translatio regni*, as well as other *translatio*-based concepts, such as *translatio imperii* (transfer of empire), *translatio legis* (transfer of the Law (from Moses to Christ, and from Christ to his two chief apostles, Peter and Paul)), *translatio religionis* (transfer of religion (from Judaism to Christianity)), and *translatio studii* (transfer of knowledge and learning). The preamble begins with a general statement:

> Although no one among the Catholic people doubts that the divine presence is powerfully manifested everywhere, it is read nonetheless that the Almighty has chosen certain places over others to show mercy to those who are faithful to Him.[38]

This declaration is then set within the larger framework of the history of salvation, beginning with "the transformation of priesthood and kingship" (*sacerdotium regnumque mutatum est*), described in Augustine's *The City of God*, and continuing through to the contemporary deeds of the Cid. God's shift of the priestly lineage of ancient Israel from Eli to Samuel, and God's changes in rulership from priestly judges to kings, and in kings, from Saul to David, coupled with the change in the center of cultic worship from Shiloh to Jerusalem, all have a function within the divine purpose of establishing the eternal priesthood and kingship of Christ (*De civitate Dei*, 17.4–8; trans. Dyson, *City of God*, 770–93) by which God's universal plan of salvation is fulfilled. These changes would eventually lead to the Old Testament hope that the temple of Jerusalem would one day become the center of worship for all the nations (Ps 77 (78):68–69; Isa 2:2–3; 56:6–7; Zech 8:20–23) and the Christian understanding that Christ's "own body, first destroyed and then raised from the dead is to be the true Temple, the house of prayer for all the nations" (Barrett 1978, 195; see also Mk 11:17, 14:58; Jn 2:19, 21; Mt 26:61). The Old Testament hope and the New Testament realization of that hope are founded upon God's preconceived plan of redemption for all people made possible by the primordial sovereignty of God:

> When the Israelite people had become dominated by the rites of their law, and the tabernacle of Shiloh, where God had dwelt among men, had been rejected [by God] (Ps 77 (78):60; Jer 7:12–14) on account of the wickedness of the sons of Eli (1 Sam 2:12–26), He founded on Mount Zion (Ps 77 (78):68–69) *a house of prayer for all the nations* (Isa 56:7; Mk 11:17). At the consecration of this temple, in order to strengthen the hearts of the simple, the glory of the Lord plainly appeared in a cloud (3 Kings (1 Kings) 8:10–12), and He who had conceived of this beforehand assigned sovereignty to God (Ps 21:29 (22:28), 61:12 (62:11); Zech 14:9; Rom 9:5; 1 Tim 6:14–15) to endure forever (2 Sam 7:16; Ps 44:7 (45:6); Isa 9:7; Dan 2:44; 3:100 (4:3); 4:31 (34); 6:26; 7:14; Lk 1:32–33; Heb 1:8; *De civitate Dei*, 17.6, 8, 12, 16; trans. Dyson, *City of God*, 785–86, 790–93, 800, 804–07).[39]

God's sovereignty extends over all the nations on earth, and these nations, the preamble emphasizes, will ultimately join in the worship of God, because the coming of Christ into the world has inaugurated "the fullness of time" (Gal 4:4; Eph 1:7–10), the eschatological age in which the Old Testament prophecies are fulfilled in the person and work of Christ and "the full number of the Gentiles" (Rom 11:25) are brought to the worship of God by being united in "spiritual marriage" (*De civitate Dei*, 17.16; trans. Dyson, *City of God*, 805; Jensen 2012, 197, 199, 200) in baptism to Jesus Christ, "their Bridegroom and Redeemer":

> But with *the fullness of time* (Gal 4:4; Eph 1:10; cf. Mk 1:15) coming, *truth has sprung up from the earth* (Ps 84:12 (85:11); Augustine, *En. Ps.* 84:13), the *iniquity* of the Jews *has deceived itself* (Ps 26 (27):12), and *the full number of the Gentiles* (Rom 11:25), entering into the bridal chamber of their Bridegroom (Ps 18:6 (19:5); Mt 25:1–13; Mk 2:19–20; Jn 3:28–29) and Redeemer (Job 19:25; Ps 18:15 (19:14); 77 (78):35; Is 41:14; 43:14; 44:6, 24; 47:4; 48:17; 49:7, 26; 54:5, 8; 59:20; 60:16; 63:16; Jer 50:34; Lam 3:58; Rom 3:24; 1 Cor 1:30; Gal 3:13; Titus 2:14; Apc 5:9), are redeemed. That doubtless the Holy Spirit has foretold [and] was made manifest in the prophecy of Malachi: *From the rising of the sun to its setting My name is great among the nations, and in every place incense is offered to My name, and a pure offering* (Mal 1:11).[40]

Having established that all the nations will one day be united under the worship of one God, as the Psalmist and the Prophets predicted (Ps 21:28 (22:27); 85 (86):9; Isa 45:22–23; 66:18–23; Jer 3:17; Zech 2:11; 8:20–23), the preamble describes how the followers of Christ brought the message of the Gospel to the Gentile world:

> Once Jewish faithlessness (Rom 3:1–3) was rejected, as it ought to have been, the sound of apostolic preaching went forth from Zion in the east to the ends of the earth, and filled the whole of Iberia in the west. Iberia, soundly instructed in the worship of God by most learned teachers, with superstitions cast aside and errors rooted out, meeting no resistance, remained at peace for a long time.[41]

At this point, the preamble jumps ahead to the Islamic overthrow of Visigothic rule in Iberia, and, in the same way that Augustine had argued that the rise of "great evils" in Rome was due to "the prosperous condition of things" (*De civitate Dei*, 1.30; trans. Dyson, *City of God*, 45), the preamble assumes an inverse relationship between prosperity and virtue and blames the triumph of Islam over the Visigoths on the "wickedness" and "idleness" that emerged out of the prosperity that God had lavished upon Iberian Christians:

> But as soon as adversity departed altogether, as a gift from God, and was followed by as much prosperity as could be desired, charity grew cold [and] wickedness abounded (Mt 24:12); and, by pursuing idleness (Ezek 16:49), oblivious of the terrible judgment of God, Iberia suffered sudden destruction (1 Thess 5:3), and the splendor of worldly rule together with that of the Church was completely overthrown by the cruel sword of the sons of Hagar (i.e., the Muslims); and, he, who had been as a free man unwilling to serve the *Lord of lords* (1 Tim 6:14–15; Apc 17:14; 19:16), was compelled by authority to become a slave of those who are slaves by nature.[42]

Islamic subjugation lasted for a considerable time, but God interceded in the end and gave to Iberia a deliverer:

> After nearly four hundred years following this calamity, the most merciful Father deigned to take pity on His people, and He raised up the most invincible prince Rodrigo the Campeador to be the avenger of the disgrace of His servants and the propagator of the Christian faith (*christiane religionis propagatorem*).[43] And he, after many famous

victories in battle, accomplished through divine assistance, captured the very wealthy city of Valencia, with its vast riches and abundance of inhabitants. Furthermore, after defeating a large army made up of Almoravids and barbarians from all of Iberia in an incredibly short space of time and without harm to himself, he dedicated to God as a church the [main] mosque [of Valencia city] that the Hagarenes (i.e., the Muslims) had used as a house of prayer, and he granted the abovementioned church, with the following endowment from his own assets, to the venerable priest Jerome, who was consecrated bishop by the hands of the Roman Pope, [upon being] unanimously and canonically acclaimed and elected, and who was elevated [to this position] by an exemption under a special privilege (*specialis privilegii libertate*).[44]

It is only after this lengthy preamble that the endowment clause of the charter begins, giving the particulars of the properties assigned to the cathedral, but even here we are reminded that temporal authority derives from God, and, by implication, that Rodrigo's authority too comes from God and is sanctioned by God. Particularly noteworthy is a direct appeal to the Book of Daniel to indicate that rulers are beholden to God for their sovereignty:

In the year 1098 of the Incarnation of the Lord, I, Rodrigo the Campeador, and my commanders, as well as the people whom God has entrusted to my power for as long as it pleases Him, give to our Redeemer—who alone *has sovereignty over the kingdom of mortals and gives it to whom He will* (Dan 4:14, 22, 29 (17, 25, 32); cf. 5:21)—and to our Mother Church of Valencia and our venerable pastor, Bishop Jerome, the village of Picassent, with its farms, lands, and vineyards, cultivated and uncultivated, together with its trees of various sorts and all that belongs to it in any way.[45]

The charter, at this point, records other properties included in the endowment, followed by threats of anathema for non-compliance with the charter, Rodrigo's autograph subscription ("I, Rodrigo, together with my wife, confirm what is written above"),[46] the names of a number of witnesses, and, finally, the scribe's name.

The endowment charter of 1098 does, of course, serve the obvious purpose of providing the Cathedral of Valencia with properties for its material upkeep, but it also serves to establish and underwrite the Cid's legitimacy as an independent ruler of the principality of Valencia. In fact, the charter is a bold attempt to create a political foundation for the Cid's rulership based completely upon the principle of God's sovereignty over earthly powers and authorities. That is why Pope Urban's fourfold schema of Christian history is presented in the most explicit and complete form found in any eleventh-century document, with the Cid incorporated into this schema. In addition, this schema is itself embedded in the wider framework of "the transformation of priesthood and kingship brought about by the new and everlasting priest-king Who is Christ Jesus" (*De civitate Dei*, 17.4; trans. Dyson, *City of God*, 770), which directly relates the Cid's exploits to the propagation of the Christian faith through the reestablishment of the Valencian Church. The basic tenet undergirding both *translatio sacerdotii* (change of the priesthood) and *translatio regni* is the same: "the Almighty has chosen certain places over others to show mercy to those who are faithful to Him."

After linking *translatio sacerdotii* and *translatio regni* in the priesthood and kingship of Christ, the charter shows the working of God's purpose of salvation in the history of the Christian people, with particular reference to Iberia and Valencia. In the first stage of history, Iberia is Christianized and enjoys peace and prosperity. In the second stage, a "calamity" befalls Iberia and "the splendor of worldly rule together with that of the Church

[is] completely overthrown by the cruel sword of the sons of Hagar." In the third stage, God raises up "the most invincible prince Rodrigo the Campeador to be the avenger of the disgrace of His servants and the propagator of the Christian faith," who succeeds in winning "many famous victories in battle, accomplished through divine assistance," and "captur[ing] the . . . city of Valencia." And in the fourth stage, Rodrigo consecrates for Christian use the main mosque (*jāmiʿ*) of Valencia city and reestablishes the Church of Valencia by restoring the cathedral and creating a new ecclesiastical apparatus for his realms.

THE VALENCIA–ROME CRUSADING AXIS

What is significant in the endowment charter of 1098 is that Pope Urban is associated directly with it. In the long preamble, he is designated as "the Roman Pope" (*romani pontificis*); in the endowment part of the document, he is mentioned under his name, Pope Urban II (*Urbano papa secundo*).[47] In both instances, the pope is linked to an act which of itself appears of trivial importance: Bishop Jerome's direct papal consecration by reason of an exemption privilege. The exemption privilege is not spelled out in so many words, but it can be inferred from the reference to Jerome's consecration by the pope. Personal consecration by the pope was one of the key mechanisms by which a bishopric was made directly subject to the Holy See and outside the administrative structure of a metropolitan province (Loud, 2007, 201–2).[48] The significance of Pope Urban personally consecrating Jerome can now be understood. In 1088, the pope had confirmed that the see of Valencia, then in Muslim hands, was under the jurisdiction of the archbishop of Toledo. Valencia, however, had been conquered by the Cid, who "[had] prayed to God, Our Lord, to give it to me," and, as "a man who has never possessed a kingdom," he now wanted to be "master" over that which "God gave me the grace to conquer."[49] Not only that, the Cid had political ambitions that stretched far beyond *Sharq al-Andalus* (eastern Islamic Iberia), and included all al-Andalus.

Contemporary Andalusī historians Ibn ʿAlqamah (428–509/1037–1116) and Ibn Bassām (d. 543/1147) both remark on the scope of the Cid's territorial desiderata. Ibn ʿAlqamah says that the Cid declared that he would force the other rulers of al-Andalus to submit to his authority, and that "just as King Rodrigo [i.e., Roderic, the last Visigothic king of Hispania] (r. 710–711), who was lord of al-Andalus without being of royal lineage, yet was king and reigned, so he too would reign and be the second King Rodrigo."[50] Ibn Bassām records that "someone told me that he heard [the Cid] say, when his ambition was at its height and his greed was relentless: 'On account of a Rudharīq [Roderic, i.e., the last Visigothic king of Hispania], this Peninsula was laid open to invasion, and a Rudharīq [Rodrigo, i.e., El Cid] will take it back.'"[51] Before such dreams could begin to take shape, the Cid had first to gain sovereignty over the principality of Valencia and that required freeing the Valencian Church from foreign manipulation. Although Toledo had a better claim to the see of Valencia than did the Cid, the Cid could not maintain his independence in Valencia if he were to allow so important a vassal as the Valencian bishop to fall under the control of Castile. He therefore requested that Pope Urban make the Valencian see directly subject to the Holy See, so that Valencia would have its own separate ecclesiastical organization, independent of the archbishopric of Toledo. Bishop Jerome's personal consecration by the pope indicates that the pope granted this request, which put Valencia's ecclesiastical establishment under the Cid's vassal, Bishop Jerome, and placed the Valencian Church under the watchful eye of Valencia's new master, who functioned now both as an autonomous temporal ruler and as an independent religious sovereign endowed directly by God with transcendent obligations for his interwoven political and religious realms.

This concession by the pope not only reveals the means by which the Cid consolidated his position as the independent ruler of the principality of Valencia, but also establishes the pope as a "cooperator" in the Cid's drive for independence. The Cid had taken the most active role in refounding and redeveloping the Church of Valencia, and Pope Urban amply rewarded him by granting Valencia ecclesiastical independence from Castile, which served to secure the sovereignty of the new ruler.[52] For the Cid, the papal grant of exemption from the ecclesiastical jurisdiction of Toledo was a means of converting the practical sovereignty of the new Christian principality of Valencia into a genuine sovereignty. For the pope, it signaled a new way of thinking about the crusades. In 1088, it seemed possible for the pope to envision a unified crusade against the Muslims in Iberia under the leadership of Castile.[53] Even Castile's disastrous defeat at the battle of Zallāqah in 479/1086 by the Almoravids was not sufficient reason to lay aside such a strategy, since the North African state did not initially intend to establish a permanent presence in Iberia. Its interventions in 479/1086 and 481/1088 were followed by withdrawal, which afforded Castile the chance to recover, "as if the victory at Zallāqa had never been won" (Kennedy, 1996, 164). It is only when the Almoravids, beginning in 483/1090, substituted their strategy of periodic engagement in Iberia with one of territorial expansion in the peninsula, sending Castilian forces in retreat, that Pope Urban abandoned his strategic assumptions of 1088 and did his utmost to aid other Christian powers in Iberia in conflicts against the Muslims. His constant urging in the 1090s of Catalan counts to reconquer and repopulate Tarragona,[54] his jubilation at the recovery of Huesca by King Peter I of Aragon (1094–1104) in 1096,[55] and his support of the Cid's independent Valencian principality are all part of a concerted effort to champion rulers whose deeds indicate that they have been raised up by God as liberators of the Christian people and as propagators of the Christian faith, understood broadly to mean Christian princes engaged in the recovery of ancient sees and ecclesiastical provinces.

The endowment charter of 1098 gives us insight into Urban's understanding of the crusades. The document presupposes a connection between the Valencian *translatio* from Islamic to Christian rule and a network of interrelations with other events of the same kind, such that the *translatio* achieved by the Cid can take on a conceptual identity only in so far as it is brought into this network of interrelations to other similar events. Neither the Cid's crusading deeds nor the crusading nature of his principality of Valencia can be determined in isolation of other crusading deeds and events. And the specific content of the Cid's crusading acts is not the starting point but the end point of the conceptual process by which one can postulate the existence of crusading phenomena. The starting point is a unifying principle by which certain events are connected and held together, so that the specific character of crusading, whether in Valencia or elsewhere, becomes known only when it is understood in relationship to this unifying principle and to other events whose identity is determined by this principle. For Urban, the unifying principle of the crusades, which governs and connects all crusades together, is *translatio regni*, the transfer of power from Islam to Christianity, expressing the sovereignty of God. As Urban looks upon the Cid's actions in taking Valencia and in reestablishing Christian dominion there, he recognizes a *translatio* from Islamic to Christian rule and, in response, becomes actively involved as a "cooperator" in this endeavor. The key players in the crusading enterprise were the "princes chosen by God" (Becker, 1964–2012, 2:354), such as the Cid, who acted as agents of God's sovereignty on earth and exercised dominion in His name.

CRUSADER SOVEREIGN OR *ṬĀʾIFAH* KING?

The Cid was not "a sort of *taifa* ruler of Valencia" (Smith, 1983, 50) or a founder of "a personal taifa kingdom" (Cobb, 2014, 64). Nor was he "a Muslim hero" who, "once in the possession of Valencia," acted "in the capacity of a Taifa [ruler]" (Hitchcock, 2014, 130, 132). Nor was he a "Christian *taifa* king" (Catlos, 2014a, 71, 74, 2014b, 26), who "ruled Islamic Valencia as sultan" (2014a, 70), or who reigned as "the sultan of Islamic Valencia" (10), and to whom "thanks" should be directed for "Muslim Valencia [being] saved" (114). Modern scholars have found it difficult to accept the fact that the Cid was a Christian crusading ruler of an independent Christian crusader principality, either because they are looking for more worthy standard-bearers for the crusading cause, or because they find Dozy's (1881, 2:233) verdict that the Cid was "more Muslim than Catholic" not far from the truth. Barton (2011) places the Valencian phase of the Cid's career in the context of the Spanish *reconquista*, not the crusading movement, and regards the 1098 endowment charter "as a manifesto for [it]." Yet the Cid and his charter have emphatically nothing to do with the Spanish *reconquista*, which is not a historical fact, but a completely discredited historical theory. This anachronistic theory treats medieval Iberia as if it were simply an earlier or primitive version of the modern nation-state of Spain, and reads modern nationalist and secularist ideals into the Iberian past, as if it were always the mission of Iberian Christian rulers to wrest control of the Iberian peninsula from the Muslims (Ríos Saloma, 2011).[56] If one departs from the "narcissistic framework" of nineteenth-century historiography that isolates medieval Iberia from the rest of the Latin West as "a quirky appendage to Christendom ... and bloody semi-Africa" (Burns, 1979, 238; 1984, 1), the crusades will emerge in quite a new and revealing light. The static model of the crusades will be replaced by a dynamic model, and even the checkered and conflict-ridden life of the Cid will be seen as intersecting with the crusades.

When the Cid took up position at Jubaylah (Cat. Puig; present-day El Puig de Santa Maria) to besiege Valencia in Jumādá II 486/July 1093, no St. Ferdinand III of Castile (r. 1217–52) or St. Louis IX of France (r. 1226–70) came to direct the operation, and the troops assembled there were not observed to be wearing devotional and penitential crusading ideals on their sleeves. Today, it is possible to envisage better standard-bearers for the Valencian Crusade than the Cid and his followers, but in the eleventh century in the east of Iberia there were none. As bent upon the "ruthless pursuit of plunder" (Catlos, 2014a, 108) as the Cid and his forces may have been before the walls of Valencia, lack of crusading religious purity never stood as a barrier to the development of the crusades. The Cid certainly was no saint, but in terms of the religious sensibilities, pieties, and beliefs of his era, he was every bit a crusading hero and champion of the faith for his conquest of Valencia. Muslim sources attest to this. Ibn ʿAlqamah presents the Cid's self-understanding of his winning of Valencia as the work of God. He "prayed to God" that it might happen, and, when it did, he credited God with giving him the grace to make it happen. We have no reason to doubt that his gratitude to God was genuine.

The Cid's subsequent construction and defense of his independent Christian principality, not "a Christian *taifa* kingdom" (Catlos, 2014b, 25), upon the ruins of a Muslim *ṭāʾifah* state, was the fulfillment of a long-held desire for "a man who [had] never possessed a kingdom." In his capacity as organizer of newly won Valencia, the Cid set about Christianizing his realms by rebuilding the physical, institutional, and social structure of the Valencian Church. Ibn al-Kardabūs (fl. twelfth–thirteenth centuries) comments on the Cid's Christianizing mission in his history of Islamic Iberia, *Taʾrīkh al-Andalus* (103), when

29

he speaks out against the "contemptible, shameless, and depraved Muslims" who joined the Cid after the conquest of Valencia in 487/1094, "most" of whom, he says, converted to Christianity. This assessment of the number of converts to Christianity in conquered Valencia may be wildly exaggerated, inspired by a desire to pour scorn on the inhabitants for having lost the city to the Christians, but it conveys an underlying reality: Christian reconquest did not stop at a change in government, as if the process merely amounted to "a Christian *taifa* kingdom" replacing a Muslim *ṭā'ifah* kingdom. It entailed the restoration of the land to its former state as a part of Christendom, which involved the reestablishment of the Church and the Church community.

In this respect, the Cid's objective was no different from that of another conqueror of Valencia, King James I of Aragon-Catalonia (r. 1213–76), who secured the city permanently for Christendom in 1238. The great Catalan conqueror regarded his task as multifaceted: to reconquer former Christian lands and "to restore and assimilate [the conquered areas] to Christian worship" (Burns, 1989b, 102–3; see also 1967, 1:15, 2:376 n56). In these varied pursuits, the "founding [of] even the clerical institutions of the Church of Valencia was neither a decorous work of piety nor a routine accompaniment of [a] secular conquest," but rather an act aiming to express, transmit, and diffuse a religious culture that served as the foundation of societal existence, so that "the Church, even in its purely clerical functions, was to be King Jaume's major transforming agency in [an] alien and dangerous land" (1989b, 110; see also 1989a, 137). What was true for King James in the thirteenth century was equally true for the Cid in the eleventh century, and just as King James's "greatest renown was to come from his conquest of Valencia and from his energetic reorganization of that area as a Christian kingdom" (Burns, 1967, 1:3), so too the Cid would win his greatest fame for his conquest of Valencia and for his valiant but ultimately doomed effort to reorganize that area as a Christian realm. Without understanding this, one cannot grasp why the exploits of the Cid should appeal to wider Christendom (Chevedden, 2011, 284–86) and inspire one of the world's greatest epic poems, the *Poema de mio Cid* (Smith, 1972).

Scholars have questioned the Cid's religious piety. "Of any sign of special Christian devotion in the Cid," asserts Smith (1983, 50), "we know nothing." Yet the Cid did not need to display "any sign of special Christian devotion" in order to win over the hearts and minds of his followers and instill fear and dread into his adversaries; the normal kind for a Christian warrior was quite sufficient. Like King James, the Cid's faith was grounded in a "theology of military 'deeds'" (Burns, 1976, 10) that gave evidence of God's mighty power working through him. His battles and his victories were in partnership with God. As the great king of Aragon would later say, "God gives [victories in battle] to those to whom He wants to give them" (James I, *Llibre dels fets*, 430.14–15; Burns, 1967, 2:375 n43). The Cid's generation lived in this view of the military arena and could only conclude from the Cid's long run of successes on the battlefield that God had made this possible. In the eyes of his contemporaries, divine assistance had rendered the Cid unconquerable, earning him the epithets of "the most invincible prince" and "the Campeador." The Cid need not have embodied the purest piety in order to be seen, as Ibn Bassām (*Dhakhīrah*, 3/1:100 and n1) did, as "a gift from his [divine] Lord" (*āyah min āyāt rabbih*), even though one might feel obliged, as the Andalusī historian did, to invite God's curse upon him: *la'anahu Allāh* ("May God curse him!").

Catlos (2014a) contends that the Cid "captured the imagination of the inhabitants of the [Iberian] peninsula and beyond in the 1100s," not because he was "the most successful soldier of fortune in pre-Crusade Spain," but because "he was one of the first" (111). For him, it was the Cid's "ruthless pursuit of plunder and his steady distribution of the spoils of war that made him a popular Christian hero in his own time" (108), and "although even during his own life he was beginning to be portrayed as a dedicated holy warrior, he was, in fact, an indirect champion of Christianity" (108–09). It matters little what indirect, circuitous, roundabout, meandering, crooked, oblique, twisting, and torturous path the Cid took to becoming a champion of Christianity, or that non-religious motives may have been to the fore, rather than religious ones, when the Cid entered into his fame as a champion of the faith. What matters is that he did become a champion of faith, and that is what "captured the imagination of the inhabitants of the [Iberian] peninsula and beyond in the 1100s," not the fact that he was a successful soldier of fortune.

Catlos's sharp dualism between the epoch of the Cid, featuring "struggles between Christian and Muslim warlords who had little regard for the religious identity of their enemies or allies, and who pursued political, personal, and often short-term goals" (87–88), and "the era of the Crusades" (5, 10, 267), featuring "a war of religion" (225) "launched" (223) by Pope Urban II that "constituted an anomaly, having no precedent in the history of either Europe or the Middle East" (242), is premised on the notion that Iberian history, as well as the history of the Mediterranean world, is wholly discontinuous, one period with the next. "The era of the Crusades" does not grow organically from the preceding period, with the result that one can see clearly the connection between El Cid the warlord and El Cid the crusader. Rather, these two periods are discrete and exist in some "pure" state, so that any change that occurs is not developmental, but *sprunghaft*, and signifies a new start. For that reason, Catlos places the Cid at "the end of an era" (120–23) and not at the beginning of a new era that he helped to create. In addition, he sees the new era, "the era of the Crusades," as "a by-product of aggression among Christians" (316) that was "not a reaction on the part of the Christian West to Muslim attacks, but rather the consequence of transformations and tensions within Christian society" (7). Out of these inter-Christian "transformations and tensions" emerged a struggle between "Latin and Byzantine Christendom" that had been brewing "since the fifth century" (323), and that ultimately culminated in "the conquest by Christians of the greatest Christian empire in history" (316), the Byzantine Empire. The crusades provided "the framework for this clash, and the threat of Islam, its pretext" (323), so that the crusades were a product, not of a real struggle between Islam and Christendom, but of an earlier clash between Eastern and Western Christendom, and the crusades were simply a cloak by which the Latin Church covered up the real nature of an internal Christian conflict.[57]

Whatever the imaginings of modern historians, it is absurd to think that the crusades were the outcome of an internal Christian dispute, and not the result of a real struggle between two opposing Mediterranean societies, Islam and Western Christendom, both defined by a deeply rooted religio-cultural identity. Catlos tries to downplay the importance of religion in these two religious societies, reducing warfare between the Dār al-Islām and the Latin West to a purely political or power-related phenomenon, presented occasionally in religious guise: "The struggles and conflicts of the golden age of Crusade and *jihad*, the period from the mid-eleventh to the twelfth centuries, were first and foremost struggles between individuals and between clans that did not act as representatives of theological principles, but rather pursued personal and earthly agendas," to which "at times religious ideology may have provided a firm and convincing basis for their actions," in order to give "a sense of higher purpose for their ambitions, or a moral justification for their violence, but it was neither a prerequisite nor a cause [of struggles and conflicts]" (324). For Catlos, the history of medieval Mediterranean societies can be explained by the doings of minority political elites in their quests to accumulate and retain power. Ideas, especially religious ideas, were mere devices used by those wielding power in the Middle Ages to advance their "worldly agendas" (145), because "as integrated and cosmopolitan as [medieval] societies may have appeared, they were built on relationships of power" (321) and were controlled by "opportunists who cloaked their avarice and ambition in piety" (324).

Catlos portrays the politics of "the Middle Ages, and the era of Crusade and *jihad*" (318), as essentially an affair of the elites, with a corresponding neglect of the non-elites, the *populus christianus*, the society of Christian peoples, and the *ummah Muḥammadīyah*, the society of Muslim peoples founded by the Prophet Muḥammad. The process by which the non-elites were brought into the activities of crusading and *jihād* was by manipulation. The consciousness of a people as a *res publica Christiana* and an *ummah* as "a body politic as well as the body of true believers" (von Grunebaum, 1962, 48) that is important to maintain, develop, and protect is denied. The very possibility of a civilization being conceived in terms of the values of a given religion and being threatened by an alien society similarly organized is also denied. And the actual historical experience of a prolonged struggle between Islam and Christendom is denied, replaced by power politics and self-interest of minority ruling elites, so that "as a rule, the various campaigns of conquest that took place across the Mediterranean in the eleventh and twelfth centuries were clearly prosaic in nature: their goals were territory, resources, and the expansion of trade," with "religious difference [providing] a justification for a war, endowing it with greater meaning for its participants and bolstering their morale, but it was rarely, if ever, a *cause* of war" (Catlos, 2014a, 322).

Catlos defends his position by arguing that "for many among the warrior elites of the Middle Ages, religion was for Sundays (or Fridays or Saturdays, depending on one's faith), at most." As "professional killers," Muslim and Christian warriors enjoyed a "vocational solidarity" that transcended political and confessional boundaries, represented by a shared "ethos of honor, a hunger for power and wealth, a sense of entitlement, and an appreciation of prestige, all of which often took precedence over religious differences." Because these warriors had much in common, "a sense of mutual respect" developed among them "that easily transcended the dictates of faith." Catlos writes that "Muslim warriors and Christian knights swore oaths to each other, exchanged weapons, falcons, and tack, sang each other's praises, and bore each other gifts. They competed in tournaments, hunted together, feasted with each other, attended religious services together, and gave each other the 'kiss of peace'—knowing full well that on another day they might be fighting each other to the death" (109–10). In addition, "the peoples of the Mediterranean adopted elements of one another's style of dress, cuisine, art, and architecture more than ever before. They shared and borrowed ideas, technologies, and techniques, fueling a tremendous wave of innovation—agricultural, medical, navigational, mathematical, philosophical, theological, literary, and technological." At the same time, "the collaborations and disputes among theologians, philosophers, and mystics of the three faiths transformed each, and laid the intellectual foundation for the European Renaissance, European Judaism, and Islamic modernity" (323–24).

Yet it matters little that in the realms of Islam and Christendom the common run of humanity (not to mention the rulers and the military elite) turned deeply and intensely to religion only spasmodically and infrequently, or that cultural interchange occurred between the Islamic and Christian worlds. No vast interpenetration of cultures, no "history of encounters among Christianity, Islam, and Judaism" (8), no "[engagement] in relationships of mutual benefit and support with those [deemed] 'infidels'" (7), and no amount of "collaborative relations between kingdoms that should have been, according to the principles of their religions, deeply opposed [to one another]" (320–21) was able to reduce or mitigate what Goitein (1967–93, 4:xii, 5:502) calls the "all-embracing religiosity" of, not only "the Geniza society," which he studied so thoroughly, but also of all the otherwise very worldly societies of the medieval Mediterranean. That is because religion was the permanent feature of medieval man's identity, the enduring substratum that gave the fundamental shape for all other determinations of human identity. "Religion formed the frame [of the social body]" around which the entire societal edifice was constructed, and "that 'frame,'" Goitein reminds us, "was fairly substantial." Regardless of the quality of the religious behavior, or the degree of belief or lack of belief, of "an ordinary person in the Middle Ages" (Catlos, 2014a, 319), the identity and self-image of a denizen of the medieval Mediterranean world was unreservedly religious. This identity was seen as vital to the individual and to the society to which he or she belonged, important and even critical to the survival of one's social group, defined in a religious sense by membership in "a people ... the Lord your God has chosen" ('*am ... bāḥar YHWH 'ĕlōhêḳā*) (Deut 7:6), "a Christian people" (*populus christianus*), or "a community submitting to [God]" (*ummatan muslimatan laka*) (Qur'ān 2:128).

The crusades cannot be properly comprehended without an understanding of two pre-existing communities, the *populus christianus* and the *ummah Muḥammadīyah*, or without an understanding of a pre-existing conflict between these two societies. Seen from the standpoint of Pope Urban, this conflict had entered a new phase during the second half of the eleventh century, the phase of Christian reconquest, restoration, and evangelization, and he saw in the Cid a champion of the faith for the recovery of the Church, which is seen not only in terms of brick and mortar and of "prelates and clergy" but also, and more fundamentally, in terms of "the entire body of true Christians who are to be found in the whole world" (Alfonso X, *Siete partidas*, 1:156 (1.10.1)). With an ever-growing sense that the Cid's taking of Valencia formed part and parcel of this new phase of history, the pope took steps to inspire and sustain the Valencian crusading project. He put Valencia on a truly independent footing by siding with the Cid in the struggle for control of the Valencian Church. He conferred upon the Cid an exemption privilege in order to protect the interests of this crusading ruler in governing his domain, just as he had done for Roger I of Sicily (Loud 2007, 200, 213), because he regarded both men as "princes chosen by God" (Becker, 1964–2012, 2:354) for "the great task of the reconquest of the Mediterranean from the power of Islam" (Dawson, 1932, 285). The pope took an active role in the creation of the Cid's crusader principality, and the Cid's endowment charter of the cathedral of Valencia incorporates the fullest expression of the pope's ideas about the crusades.

What counted in the process of aiding and orchestrating crusading activity in the Mediterranean and giving to the crusades a degree of ideological and political coherence was weakness, not strength, and a type of authority that could be asserted and acted upon internationally. It was the very weakness of the papacy vis-à-vis the secular realm that allowed the papacy to rise to a position of leadership in the crusading movement. At a time when the German Empire was a spent force as a pan-European polity, unable to command the internationalist convictions of the peoples of the Latin West in either the political realm or the spiritual realm, and unable to respond adequately to the new political challenges of the day, particularly to the kaleidoscopic changes in the Mediterranean world, the papacy asserted its "supremacy over the entire Western Church" and "the independence of the Church from secular control" (Berman, 1983, 50). To achieve independence for the Church and make it a truly self-governing body, the papacy had to secure new protectors other than the German Empire, which viewed the papacy as an integral part of its own governmental apparatus. The papacy found such protectors in the newly emerging polities of Western Christendom, which made common cause with Rome in its struggle with the Empire because they needed a higher power than themselves to legitimize their own claims to sovereignty. The papacy not only conferred legitimacy upon individual rulers and polities in the Latin West, but also assisted rulers in maintaining their independence by giving them their own separate ecclesiastical organization. In addition, the papacy recognized the territorial claims of Christian rulers to lands that had "originally belonged to the Christians" but had been conquered by Islam and subjected to Islamic rule ('Abd Allāh ibn Buluggīn, *Tibyān*, 100; trans. Tibi, *Tibyān*, 90), and supported rulers that took up the struggle with Islam. In this effort, the papacy was able to draw upon the internationalist convictions of Christianity that stretched back to the early Church and to forge effective coalitions to undo the Islamic occupation of Christian territories and to restore, reorganize, and assimilate these territories back into Christendom. It was able to do this quite effectively because of its ability to appeal to the conscience of the wider Christian community in a way that the secular powers could not, and because of its capacity to rise above national and territorial rivalries. Secular polities, for their part, were ready to accept papal direction in situations where the interests of wider Christendom were at stake and where their own self-interest and Church interests were widely aligned.

THE 1095 PARADIGM *VERSUS* POPE URBAN'S UNDERSTANDING OF THE CRUSADES

Scholars have long sought to determine the ideational content of the crusades. Yet when it comes to considering Pope Urban's ideas about the crusades, his views cannot be examined or explained without seeing them within the framework of the 1095 crusade paradigm. Another approach is available to us. Instead of imposing ideas upon Urban by forcing his ideas into a preconceived mold, we should try to interpret Urban in his own terms. We should take into account the distinctions he made, the concepts he used, and the terminology he employed. Above all, this means that we should consider his own depiction of crusading as a true *translatio regni* and how he differentiates the crusading period from the period before it. Once we formulate the crusades in Urban's terms, by using the concept of *translatio regni*, we will begin to see some of the advantages of his conceptualization.

Crusading began when Western Christian powers initiated a counteroffensive against Islam (Kedar, 1988, 41, 43, 56, 57, 83, 134) and undertook to restore the lost lands of Christendom. The term "crusade" can therefore be applied to this counteroffensive and restoration program that became a Mediterranean-wide phenomenon during the course of the eleventh century, evident in the central, western, and eastern regions of the Middle Sea. Pope Urban properly describes and designates crusading phenomena as *translatio regni*, in the sense of a dramatic shift in the power relationship between Islam and Latin Christendom in the Mediterranean world. This power shift was discernible by the 1060s, when the Latin West gained the strategic and operational initiative in the war with Islam and shifted to the offensive. Despite tactical setbacks, the West was never to lose the strategic momentum in this war. Islamic sources fully corroborate Urban's vision of the crusades by depicting the early crusades as a three-pronged assault on the power of Islam by the Christian West directed at Sicily, al-Andalus, and the eastern Mediterranean (Chevedden, 2006, 2008, 2010, 2011). Urban's conception of crusading was not a narrow and myopic one, limited to a single event, the Jerusalem Crusade, or to a single aspect of that event, namely the "objective ... to acquire or to preserve Christian dominion over the Sepulcher of Our Lord in Jerusalem" (Mayer, 1965, 263; Chevedden, 2013, 17–18). Rather, his vision was as expansive as it was ambitious.

Urban's great insight was that the nature of crusading could best be determined by looking at how it was that crusades were actually undertaken. He therefore focused attention on the activities of Christian rulers who were engaged in exploits of *translatio regni*, the actual process of crusading, rather than on speculative theories about crusading. He found that contemporary history—the events taking place "in [his] time" (*nostris temporibus*)— could be an indispensable guide to a theoretical understanding of crusading. Urban had a willingness to allow the facts of history to set the terms of his conceptualization of the crusades. He refused to impose an *a priori* notion of what the crusades were, but instead sought to respond to what actually appeared to be happening "in [his] time" (*nostris temporibus*) in the struggle "to liberate the Church of God" (*ad liberandam ecclesiam Dei*) (Somerville 1972, 74) and to "restore the Christian [Churches] to their former freedom."[58] In other words, he finds crusading in history.

History has not been where scholars have been looking for the crusades. When Erdmann (1935/1977) reduced the crusades to an idea, he eliminated any relation of this idea to history. While his study maintains the pretense of a historical reconstruction, its actual underpinning is Herder's famous "genetic method," which looks to the origin of a phenomenon in order to learn "the entire nature of its product" (Herder, (1764) 1984–2002, 1:10; trans. Forster, 2011, 233), and discovers "in the origin of a phenomenon the whole treasure of elucidation through which the explanation of the phenomenon becomes *genetic*" (Herder, (1767–68) 1985–2000, 1:602/2002, 53). Building upon Erdmann's "genetic" doctrine of "crusade," Hans Eberhard Mayer (1965, 263–65) reified crusading activity into a definable and defined entity and invited other scholars to do likewise. Many responded to his invitation (Riley-Smith, 1977, 1986, 1997, 2008, 2009b, 2014; Flori, 1992, 1999, 2001, 2004, 2010; Bull 1993, 2009; Hehl, 1994; Richard, 1996/1999; Tyerman, 1998, 2004, 2005, 2006, 2011; Asbridge, 2004, 2010; Demurger 2006; Housley, 2006, 2008; Jaspert, 2013/2006; Purkis, 2008; Phillips, 2009, 2014; Madden, 2013), so that today it has become common practice to cull and classify the crusading enterprise into a discrete, knowable, and essentialized object for study. Yet crusading was not a discrete, static, and pedestalled object standing in one place. Rather, it was a historical entity that was exceedingly dynamic and heterogeneous, and that stood to be discovered and rediscovered, imagined and reimagined, made and remade and remade again, and repeatedly renewed, revitalized, and transformed.

During the eleventh century, the crusades took on as many shapes as Proteus. This fact alone is sufficient, in the eyes of many, to disqualify all but one crusade in this century as being truly legitimate. Yet one of the defining characteristics of the early crusades was their protean character, encompassing a wide range of activities. A single large enterprise, such as the Jerusalem Crusade, would have been considered a crusade, but so too would have been a small-scale enterprise, such as the restoration of the monastery of Sant Cugat del Vallès, near Barcelona, destroyed by Ibn Abī ʿĀmir in 985.[59] The crusades not only involved many crusades, varying from small to very large, but they also involved a number of interlinked movements, or "crusades," mutually related to each other and mutually reinforcing one another: a *Crusade of reconquest*, a *Crusade of rebuilding the Church*, and a *Crusade of evangelization*. In time, the Church would add to these another "crusade": the *Crusade of settlement and colonial control* (Burns, 1989b, 101; 1962, 245–46).[60] Many varieties of "crusades" took place at any given time during the crusades, and still more "crusades" may be waiting to be discovered. Each of these "crusades" gathered strength from the idea that an old era had ended and an entirely new era had begun. Pope Urban looks into the face of Proteus and sees both a changeability of character and a unity of being. By recovering something of what Urban understood by crusading, we might come to a better understanding of the crusades.

ACKNOWLEDGMENT

My warm thanks to Donald J. Kagay for his assistance and guidance with many of the letters of Pope Urban II discussed in this chapter.

NOTES

1 Lyrics reproduced by kind permission of Special Rider © 1963, 1964 by Warner Bros. Inc.; renewed 1991, 1992 by Special Rider Music.

2 On "perspectivalism" in the study of history, see Chladenius, (1742) 1969, 181–370; 1752, 91–155; Beiser, 2011, 40–62.

3 Riley-Smith (2007, 29) has described his own consciously anachronistic understanding of the crusades. Lambert (2007, 93) criticizes this approach.

4 Urban II to Bishop Peter of Huesca, 11 May 1098, in Durán Gudiol, 1962, 193 (no. 20). Becker, 1964–2012, 1:228, 2:334, 348–49, 351, 383, 400, 425, 3:77; 1989, 15–16.

5 For the "sign" that signaled to Robert Guiscard that it was God's will that he take Sicily, see Amatus of Montecassino, *Storia*, 229–31 (V.7–9); trans. Dunbar, *History*, 136. The oath that Robert Guiscard swore at Melfi in August 1059 to Pope Nicholas II (r. 1058–61) acknowledged Robert's supreme authority over all of Apulia and Calabria, even though Bari, the Byzantine capital of Apulia and the seat of the Byzantine governor (*catepano*) of Italy, did not fall until April 1071, and recognized Robert as the rightful ruler of Islamic Sicily (*dux ... futurus Sicilie*), thereby endorsing the Norman conquest of the island and its return to Christian rule. For the text of this oath, see *Liber censuum*, 1:422. Translations of this oath are found in Tierney, 1988, 44; Norwich, 1992, 128–29; Loud, 2000, 188–89.

6 On the Iberian Crusades, see now O'Callaghan, 2003, 2011, 2014.

7 Urban II to Bernard of Sédirac, archbishop of Toledo, Anagni, 15 October 1088, in Mansilla Reoyo, 1955, 43–45 (no. 27), at 43; Urban II to Daibert, bishop of Pisa, Anagni, 21 April 1092, in Urban II, "Epistolae et privilegia," letter 63, in Migne, 1841–64, 151:345A; Urban II to Bishop Peter of Huesca, 11 May 1098, in Durán Gudiol, 1962, 193 (no. 20); Urban II to Bishop Gerland of Agrigento (d. 1101), 10 October 1098, in Collura, 1961, 22 (no. 5); Urban II to Bishop Pons of Barbastro, 1099, in Kehr, 1926, 298 (no. 31); Becker, 1964–2012, 2:342, 351, 353, 357.

8 Becker (1989, 10) claims that "one can observe the evolution of [Pope Urban II's] idea of Crusade" by studying his bulls and letters, and that the "essential and characteristic elements" of his concept of crusade "appear already from the very start of his pontificate, in 1088." Others disagree and argue that the essential and characteristic elements that make up the idea and ideology of crusade emerged as a result of the Jerusalem Crusade, and that Urban served as a catalyst, but not a guiding

force, in the creation of the ideational and ideological content of crusading; cf. Mayer, 2005, 18–52; Riley-Smith, 1986, 1–2, 30, 99, 135–55; 1987, 10; 1993, 10; 2005b, 112; 2009a, 3; 2014, 69–70.

9 Urban II to Berenguer Sunifred de Lluçà (d. 1099), bishop of Ausona-Vic, 1 July 1091, in Mansilla Reoyo, 1955, 50–51 (no. 32); Urban II to Count Ermengol IV of Urgell, 1 July 1091, in Kehr, 1926, 286 (no. 22); Urban II to Bishop Gomez of Burgos, Piacenza, 14 March 1095, in Urban II, "Epistolae et privilegia," in Migne, 1841–64, 151:407B–D; Urban II to Bishop Peter of Huesca, 11 May 1098, in Durán Gudiol, 1962, 193 (no. 20); Urban II to Bishop Pons of Barbastro, 1099, in Kehr, 1926, 298 (no. 31); Becker, 1964–2012, 1:228, 2:334, 341–42, 346–49, 351, 359, 383, 398, 400, 3:65, 77, 91, 586–88, 600, 712–13; 1989, 15–16.

10 Urban II to Ambrose, first abbot of the monastery of St. Bartholomew on Lipari, just off the north-east tip of Sicily, 3 June 1091, in Urban II, "Epistolae et privilegia," in Migne, 1841–64, 151:329C–D; Urban II to Abbot-Bishop Ansgar of Catania, 9 March 1092, in Scalia, 1961, 48 (no. 1); Urban II to Bishop Roger of Syracuse, 23 November 1093, in Urban II, "Epistolae et privilegia," in Migne, 1841–64, 151:370C–371A (under the date 17 November 1093); Urban II to Bishop Gerland of Agrigento (d. 1101), 10 October 1098, in Collura, 1961, 22 (no. 5); Becker, 1964–2012, 2:340, 342–46, 349–50, 359–60, 383, 3:146–47, 355–56.

11 In two letters, Pope Urban links the campaign "to aid the Churches in Asia and to liberate their brothers from the tyranny of the Muslims" with the movement of Christian liberation in Iberia: Urban II to the counts Bernat of Besalú, Hugo of Ampurias, Guislabert of Roussilon, and Guillem of Cerdanya and their knights, *c.* July 1096, in Kehr, 1926, 287–88 (no. 23); Urban II to Bishop Peter of Huesca, 11 May 1098, in Durán Gudiol, 1962, 193 (no. 20). In a third letter, Urban declares "that in our time (*nostris temporibus*) the Church has been enlarged, the domination of the Muslims has been reduced, the ancient honor of episcopal sees has been, by the gift of God, restored (*restauratur*)," thereby connecting the movement of *translatio regni* to the central, western, and eastern Mediterranean. Urban II to Bishop Pons of Barbastro, 1099, in Kehr, 1926, 298 (no. 31); Becker, 1964–2012, 1:227–30, 2:334, 347–49, 351, 383, 400, 425, 3:77, 600, 713.

12 Urban II to Bernard of Sédirac, archbishop of Toledo, Anagni, 15 October 1088, in Mansilla Reoyo, 1955, 43 (no. 27): "Cunctis sanctorum decretales scientibus institutiones liquet, quante Toletana ecclesia dignitatis fuerit ex antiquo, quante in Hispaniis et Gallicis regionibus auctoritatis extiterit, quanteque per eam in ecclesiasticis negotiis utilitates accreverint; sed peccatorum populi multitudine promerente a saracenis eadem civitas capta et ad nihilum christiane religionis illic libertas redacta est, adeo, ut per annos CCC° pene LXXᵃ nulla illic viguerit christiani pontificii dignitas. Nostris autem temporibus, divina populum suum respiciente misericordia, studio Aldefonsi gloriosissimi regis et labore christiani populi, sarracenis expulsis, christianorum iuri Toletana est civitas restituta. ... Et nos ergo miserationi superne gratie respondentes, quia per tanta terrarum mariumque discrimina Romane auctoritatem ecclesie suppliciter expetisti, auctoritatem pristinam Toletane ecclesie restituere non negamus. Gaudemus enim et corde letissimo magnas, ut decet, Deo gratias agimus, quod tantam nostris temporibus, dignatus est christiano populo prestare victoriam statumque eiusdem urbis, quoad nostra est facultas, stabilire atque augere, ipso adiuvante, peroptamus." Becker, 1964–2012, 2:337, 342, 359, 3:384–86; 1989, 14. I thank Prof. Donald J. Kagay for translating this text.

13 Urban II to Bishop Gerland of Agrigento (d. 1101), 10 October 1098, in Collura, 1961, 22 (no. 5). For Urban's fourfold schema of Christian history, reduced to its simplest expression, see Becker, 1964–2012, 2:352–53; Cowdrey, 1995, 723; Flori, 1998, 73–74; Chevedden, 2005b, 274 n48; 2011, 271–72; 2013, 19.

14 Dan 2:20–21: "Deus ... mutat tempora, et aetates; transfert regna, atque constituit" ("God ... changes times and seasons, deposes kings and sets up kings"). For Urban's letters that give expression to the biblical foundation upon which his conception of the crusades is based, see Becker, 1964–2012, 2:235 n179, 3:356 and 356 n284. For a discussion of these letters, see Becker, 1964–2012, 1:227–30, 2:342, 344, 349, 352–54, 356, 361–63, 369, 372–75, 384, 398, 404,

3:356–57, 587–88, 675–76; Chevedden, 2013, 32–46. According to Becker (1964–2012, 3:675), Dan 2:20–21, which Urban explicitly references in three of his extant letters (1964–2012, 2:353 n180; Ringel 1987, 137–39), forms the basis for his theology of history (*Geschichtstheologie*), and this theology of history, I would add, offers not only a theoretical understanding of the crusades but also an ideological framework for carrying out the crusades.

15 See below n43.

16 Gabriele (2012) examines an exegetical tradition that supposedly "gave weight to some of the biblical citations in Urban II's letters" (799), which refer to the movement of "reconquest and restoration" (812) taking place across the Mediterranean *nostris temporibus*, instead of examining the historical context that gave substance and meaning to the biblical passages. He describes the movement of "reconquest and restoration" as "a ninth-century promise come true" (812), because Urban, "steeped in ninth-century exegesis" (814), continued "the work of his ninth-century predecessors, [in] calling the Christian people (*populus christianus*) to mend their ways and strike back against the pagans" (796), with the result that "at the end of the eleventh century, the work that had begun centuries before could be completed" (814). Yet it is far-fetched to think that the eleventh-century movement of "reconquest and restoration" began with the bookish pursuits of ninth-century exegetes. Instead of asking, "What religio-intellectual current caused the emergence of a political movement built on religious foundations?" Gabriele should be asking, "What type of activity or movement intensified to the point where it provoked a validating intellectual rationalization?" In referring to Pope Urban as "the last Carolingian exegete," Gabriele misunderstands the type of exegesis that Urban was engaged in. Urban does not see his function as shedding more light on various biblical texts after the fashion of a textual exegete. Rather, he attempts to shed light on events *nostris temporibus*, and, in this pursuit, he is interested in biblical texts only to the extent that they support his analysis of events. *Contra* Gabriele, Urban maintains that a purely exegetical understanding of the present is insufficient precisely because it ignores the present—or, more specifically, a present that is capable of informing scripture.

17 According to Goez (1958, 8), "the idea of transfer of power (*Translation der Macht*) arose, not from speculation, but from the fact that it was so experienced." Quoted, with approval, in Becker, 1964–2012, 2:353 n180.

18 Urban II to Berenguer Sunifred de Lluçà (1076–99), bishop of Ausona-Vic, 1 July 1091, bestowing on him the title *archiepiscopus Tarraconensis*, in Mansilla Reoyo, 1955, 49–52 (no. 32), at 51; Becker, 1964–2012, 2:341–42.

19 Urban II to Bishop Pons of Barbastro, 1099, in Kehr, 1926, 298 (no. 31): "quod nostris temporibus ecclesia propagatur, Sarracenorum dominatio diminuitur, antiquus episcopalium sedium honor prestante Domino restaurateur." Becker, 1964–2012, 2:351, 3:600, 713.

20 Urban II to Bernard of Sédirac, archbishop of Toledo, Anagni, 15 October 1088, in Mansilla Reoyo, 1955, 44 (no. 27): "Te, reverentissime frater, affectione intima exortamus, quatenus dignum te tanti honore pontificii semper exhibeas christianis ac sarracenis sine offensione semper esse procurans et ad fidem infideles convertere, Deo largiente, verbis studeas et exemplis"; trans. in Burns, 1971, 1389; 1984, 82–83.

21 Gregory VII to Archbishop Arnald of Acerenza, 14 March 1076, in Caspar, 1920–23, 1:271–72 (no. 3.11): "Quapropter pastorali cura hoc laboris onus tibi imponimus, immo ex parte beati Petri imperamus, ut postposita omni torporis desidia illum [Rogerum] adeas eumque huius nostri precepti auctoritate fultus, si nobis parere sicut pollicitus est voluerit et poenitentiam, ut oportet christianum, egerit, ab omni peccatorum vinculo tam illum quam etiam suos milites, qui cum eo contra paganos, ita tamen ut agant poenitentiam, pugnaturi sunt, peccatis maxime absolvas. Addimus praeterea, ut eum pia admonitione admoneas, ut se a capitalibus criminibus custodiat et christiani nominis culturam inter paganos amplificare studeat, ut de eisdem hostibus victoriam consequi mereatur."

22 Others disagree. Reflecting the views of Riley-Smith (2001, 135), who considers crusading as being "primarily about benefiting the crusaders themselves, through the imposition of condign

self-punishment, and as such ... an act of self-sanctification," MacEvitt (2008, 18) contends that the Jerusalem Crusade was "not ... concerned with the salvation of others, but only about the salvation of the warrior himself. The infidel represented a path to salvation, not a focus of concern for the crusader." Whalen (2009, 58) also sees no connection between the Jerusalem Crusade and conversion, but he considers only forcible conversion: "Medieval contemporaries did not initially link crusading with an effort to convert Muslims 'by the sword' or by the threat of violence." In the main, Whalen follows in the footsteps of Kedar on this topic: "According to the crusade chronicles, individual acts of conversion did happen, but the effort to expand Christendom by 'recovering' lands from the infidels did not entail any systematic effort to convert the non-Christian inhabitants of those regions. There was, in fact, little discussion in the Roman Church during the period leading up to the crusade about the necessity or desire for converting infidel societies en masse. ... A full-fledged theory of mission to the Muslim world would not develop until the thirteenth century, when ideas of crusading and conversion would begin to compete and mutually reinforce each other, both contributing to Christian visions of world order." Cutler (1968), Flori (2002), Loutchitskaja (2002), and Birk (2011) challenge the notion that the Jerusalem Crusade was entirely devoid of any idea of conversion or missionary focus.

23 Urban II to all the faithful in Flanders, *c.* December 1095, in Hagenmeyer, 1901, 136 (ep. II.3).

24 Saint Anselm (archbishop of Canterbury), Epistle 235, "Ad Baldewinum regem Hierosolymorum" (to Baldwin king of Jerusalem), *c.* spring 1102, in Schmitt, 1946–61, 4:142: "Benedictus deus in donis suis et *sanctus in omnibus operibus suis* [Ps. 144:13, 17], qui vos ad regis dignitatem sua gratia in illa terra exaltavit, in qua ipse dominus noster Iesus Christus, per se ipsum principium Christianitatis seminans, ecclesiam suam, ut inde per totum orbem propagaretur, novam plantavit, quam propter peccata hominum iudicio dei ab infidelibus diu ibidem opressam, sua misericordia nostris temporibus mirabiliter resuscitavit." See Chevedden, 2011, 280–81.

25 Chenu (1979), who coined the term "evangelical awakening," gives Pope Gregory VII credit for providing the Awakening with its original impetus, but he studies this movement, not in its early stages, but in its twelfth-century context.

26 Somerville, 1972, 74: "Quicumque pro sola devotione, non pro honoris vel pecunie adeptione, ad liberandam ecclesiam Dei Hierusalem profectus fuerit, iter illud pro omni penitentia ei reputetur"; Chevedden, 2005a. On Hugh's participation in the Council of Clermont, see Somerville, 1974, 75. Iogna-Prat (1998, 330/2002, 329) accepts Erdmann's finding (1935, 304 n73/1977, 329 n73) that there is no evidence that Cluny actually played a role in the propaganda or execution of the "First" Crusade and states that "as far as we know, Hugh of Semur and his Cluniac brethren did not work directly to launch the [Jerusalem] expedition." Although the surviving direct evidence linking Cluny with the Jerusalem Crusade is meager—a handful of charters attesting to the financing of a few individual crusaders—many other monasteries, especially in the Mâconnais region where crusade recruitment was heavy, also have an imperfect record of their participation in the Jerusalem Crusade. Such an imperfect record, however, does not permit us to conclude that Cluny did not work directly to launch the Jerusalem Crusade, let alone argue that there is no evidence that Cluny had any real role in the propaganda or implementation processes for this expedition. The surviving evidence from Cluny and its dependencies indicates that this stronghold of Christendom did work directly with crusaders to launch them on their great march to Jerusalem by contributing its vast organizational and financial resources to this enterprise.

27 Precisely the same purpose is accomplished by the scheme of the tympanum above the central entrance of the Benedictine abbey church of Sainte-Marie-Madeleine at Vézelay in Burgundy (*c.* 1120–32). See Katzenellenbogen, 1944.

28 In 1083, when Pope Gregory confirmed the restoration of Palermo to its ancient metropolitan status in Sicily and allowed the first Norman archbishop of the city to wear the *pallium*, he spoke of the Church of Palermo as having once been "distinguished and famous." Due to sin, however, it "was delivered over to the faithless power of the Muslims, but, with God's help, it is now restored to the Christian faith through the vigorous action or unremitting efforts of the glorious

Duke Robert." Pope Gregory VII to Archbishop Alcherius, 16 April 1083, in Santifaller, 1957, 253 (no. 212); Becker, 1964–2012, 2:305; Cowdrey, 1998, 436–37. All the stages of Pope Urban's *translatio regni* find expression in Gregory's schema: (1) important achievement of a Christian community, then (2) dreadful calamity caused by sin, then (3) "the vigorous action or unremitting efforts" of reconquest, then (4) restoration. Pope Gregory's bull of 18 January 1074 confirming the rights and privileges of the monastery of Saint Mary on the island of Gorgona, located in the Ligurian Sea between Corsica and Livorno, also adheres to this schema when it speaks of a monastery, once "under the special right and dominion of St. Peter," which suffered calamity when Gorgona was subjected to "the cruelty of the Muslims" and Christian worship was banned on the island, but then, "by Divine piety," was restored. Santifaller, 1957, 40 (no. 61); Whalen, 2009, 36. It seems very likely therefore that Urban's own theoretical views of the crusades took shape under the influence of Pope Gregory and were already fully mature by the time he became pope in 1088. Others disagree; cf. Gabriele, 2012, 812–13, who argues that "Gregory VII and Urban II belonged to similar, yet distinct, textual communities" and held differing views on Christian reconquest and restoration.

29 Others disagree; cf. Ashe, 1999, who fragments medieval religious experience and medieval crusading experience by suggesting that the Church expounded one model of crusading, reflecting papal resolve to assert control over secular rulers, while the *Song of Roland* expounded "a subversive antimodel of reality," reflecting "its own, distinctive, form of secularized Christianity ... opposed not only to Church theology, but to Church power."

30 Urban II to the counts Bernat of Besalú, Hugo of Ampurias, Guislabert of Roussilon, and Guillem of Cerdanya and their knights, *c.* July 1096, in Kehr, 1926, 287–88 (no. 23); trans. based on O'Callaghan, 2003, 33, with additions and amendments made by the author.

31 Ibid. See also Erdmann, 1935, 294–95/1977, 317; Riley-Smith and Riley-Smith, 1981, 40; Goñi Gaztambide, 1958, 60–61; Becker, 1964–2012, 2:347–48; Housley, 1992, 32–33; McCrank, 1974, 264, 284–85 n51; Chevedden, 2005b, 299–302. Pope Urban's coordinated strategy of engaging the enemy on two fronts simultaneously finds a parallel in the Islamic world. When Aḥmad ibn Ḥanbal (d. 241/855) was asked about a man who wished to journey to Tarsus to fight the Byzantines while his own region of Islamic Central Asia was contending with the Turks, Ibn Ḥanbal responded by quoting the Qur'ānic *Sūrat al-tawbah*, āyah 123: "'O believers, fight the unbelievers around you.' It is not for anyone that he go from his own land while the enemy is in it, and fight someone other than them. Let him fight in defense of his lands, and drive away the enemies of God" (quoted in Sizgorich, 2009, 211).

32 For the Oath of Melfi, see above n5.

33 Ibn Ḥayyān's account of the siege of Barbastro in his lost *Kitāb al-Matīn* is preserved in Ibn Bassām, *Dhakhīrah*, 1/3:179–90. See 1/3:182, for his reference to *qā'id khayl rūmah*. According to Dozy (1881, 2:350), this designation can only mean "the commander of the cavalry of Rome": "The Arabic words *qā'id khayl Rūmiyah* [according to the Gotha manuscript of Ibn Bassām's *Dhakhīrah*], or *Rūmah* according to manuscript B [of the *Dhakhīrah* in the collection of Pascual de Gayangos], cannot have any other meaning." Ibn Ḥayyān's phrase consists of three terms. The first term, *qā'id* (pl. *quwwād*), means "leader." In a military setting it denotes a "commander" and may even be translated as "general," depending on the context. When Ibn Ḥayyān uses the term in his account of Roman Iberia (Ibn Ḥayyān, *Muqtabis*, 273; trans. Jesús Viguera and Corriente, *Muqtabis V*, 207), as in *qā'id ahl rūmah*, he is referring to "the Roman general" (lit., "the general of the people of Rome"). The second term, *khayl*, is a collective noun signifying "horses." By extension, *khayl* can be applied to a "mounted troop," a "cavalry force," or a "mounted army" (Viré, 1978, 1143). The third term, *rūmah*, or *rūmiyah*, is the Arabic word for the city of Rome. By extension, *rūmah/rūmiyah* can be applied to the papacy. Dozy notes that medieval authors used either *rūmah* or *rūmiyah*. Al-Idrīsī and Abū Ḥamīd al-Gharnāṭī employed *rūmah*, while Ibn Khurradādhbih, Yāqūt, and al-Dimashqī employed *rūmiyah*. Other authors, such as Ibn al-Athīr, employed both terms (Dozy, 1881, 2:350). Ibn Ḥayyān clearly favors *rūmah*: *Muqtabis*, 272, 273,

274, 482 (*rūmah* = Rome); trans. Jesús Viguera and Corriente, *Muqtabis V*, 206, 207, 208, 362 (Roma); Ibn Ḥayyān, as quoted in Maqqarī, *Nafḥ al-ṭīb*, 1:203 (*madīnat rūmiyah* = city of Rome); 1:566 (*madīnat rūmah* = city of Rome); 1:134, 138, 139, 147, 150, 354, 366, 414; 4:449, 525, 526; 5:34; 6:462 (*rūmah* = Rome). Corriente (1997, s.v. "RWM") lists only *rūmah* as the Arabic term for Rome.

34 Amatus doubtless derived his account of the Barbastro Crusade directly from Robert Crispin, who was at Montecassino in June 1066 where he witnessed a charter of Richard I of Capua (Loud, 1981, 121–22 (no. 13)).

35 Urban II to Catalan counts Berenguer Ramon II, Armengol VI of Urgel, and Bernard II of Besalú, and "omnibus Tarrraconensis et Barchinonensis provincie episcopis vicecomitibus et ceteris nobilis et potentibus sive clericis sive laicis," Rome, 1 July 1089, in Mansilla Reoyo, 1955, 46–47 (no. 29).

36 See above n5.

37 Salamanca, Archivo Diocesano, caja 43, legajo 2, no. 72; Menéndez Pidal, 1918, 11–13; 1969, 2:868–71; Martín Martín, 1977, 79–81 (no. 1); Lacombe, 1999, 119–121 (no. 1), fig. 12; Martin, 2007, 133–35. An abridged edition of the charter, with an English translation, is available in Smith, Melville, and 'Ubaydlī, 1988–92, 1:130–133. All references will be made to the edition of this document in Martín Martín, 1977.

38 Martín Martín et al., 1977, 79: "Christus [MS: XPS]. Cum divinam presentiam catholicorum nullus ambigat ubique potencialiter adesse, quedam tamen pre ceteris loca ad propiciandum fidelibus sibi legitur Omnipotens elegisse."

39 Martín Martín, 1977, 79: "Israhelico [MS: Israhelitico] namque populo legalibus cerimoniis obumbrato, et tabernaculo Silo, ubi Deus habitaverat in hominibus, ex filiorum Heli nequitia reprobato, in monte Syon domum orationis cunctis gentibus instituit, in cuius templi dedicatione, ad roboranda simplicium corda, Domini gloria in nebula patenter apparuit, et Deo imperium qui premeditatus hoc fuerat in eternum permanere constituit."

40 Martín Martín, 1977, 79: "Ut autem accedente plenitudine temporis, de terra orta est veritas et mentita est sibi iudeorum iniquitas, atque in Sponsi et Redemptoris sui thalamum ingressa est redempta plenitudo gentium, profecto claruit quod Sanctus Spiritus per Malachie predixerat vaticinium; a solis ortu usque ad occasum magnum est nomen meum in gentibus, et in omni loco sacrificatur et offertur nomini meo oblatio munda."

41 Martín Martín, 1977, 79: "Repulsa igitur primum ut oportuit iudea perfidia, apostolice sonus predicationis ab orientali Syon in fines orbis exiens, totam sub occiduo replevit Hispaniam; que firmiter ad Dei cultum eruditissimis informata doctoribus, abiectis supersticionibus, extirpatis erroribus, nemine resistente, nonnullis in pace quievit temporibus."

42 Martín Martín, 1977, 79: "At ubi prorsus ex Dei dono abscessit adversitas et ad votum cuncta successit prosperitas, refriguit caritas, habundavit iniquitas, et sectando ocium orrendum Dei oblita iudicium, repentinum est perpessa exterminium, et crudeli filiorum Agar gladio secularis dignitas funditus corruit pariter cum sanctuario: et qui liber servise [MS: servire] noluit Domino dominorum, iure cogitur fieri servus naturalium servorum."

43 In the same year that the Cid is praised as *christiane religionis propagator*, Pope Urban pays tribute to Count Roger of Sicily for having "greatly expanded the Church of God into Muslim territories" (*in Saracenorum finibus Ecclesiam Dei plurimum dilatavit*). Urban II to Count Roger, 5 July 1098, Urban II, "Epistolae et privilegia," in Migne, 1841–64, 151:506C; Geoffrey Malaterra, *De rebus gestis*, 108 (IV.29); trans. Wolf, *Deeds*, 213; Becker, 1964–1012, 2:350–51, 3:38, 66–69. This title is reminiscent of the title that Paul the Deacon gave to Charlemagne ("Letter to Charlemagne," 230–31): "propagator and defender of the Christian faith" (*propagatori ac defensori christianiae religionis*).

44 Martín Martín, 1977, 79–80: "Itaque annorum ferme CCCC^{orum} in hac calamitate labente curriculo, tandem dignatus clementissimus Pater suo misereri populo, invictissimum principem Rudericum Campidoctorem obprobrii servorum suorum suscitavit ultorem et christiane religionis propagatorem; qui post multiplices et eximias quas divinitus assecutus est preliorum victorias,

diviciarum gloria et hominum copia opulentissimam urbem cepit Valentiam; necnon et innumera-
bili moabitarum et tocius Hispanie barbarorum exercitu superato, velut in momento ultra quam
credi potest sine sui detrimento, ipsam meschitam, que apud agarenos domus oracionis habebatur,
Deo in ecclesiam dicavit, et venerabili Ieronimo presbitero, concordi et canonica acclamatione
et electione per romani pontificis manus in episcopum consecrato et specialis privilegii libertate
sublimato, prelibatam ecclesiam ex suis facultatibus tali dote ditavit."

45 Martín Martín, 1977, 80: "Anno siquidem incarnationis Dominice LXXXX° VIII° post millesi-
mum, ego Ruderius Campidoctor et principes, ac populos quos Deus quandiu ei placuerit mee
potestati comisit, donamus ipsi Redemptori nostro, qui solus dominatur in regno hominum et
cuicunque voluerit dat illud, et matri nostre ecclesie sedi videlicet Valentine, et venerabili pas-
tori nostro Ieronimo pontifici, villam que dicitur Pigacen, cum villis et terris et vineis cultis vel
incultis, et cum diversi generis arboribus, et cum cunctis ad eam quocunque modo pertinentibus."

46 Martín Martín, 1977, 81: "Ego Ruderico, simul cum coniuge mea, afirmo oc quod superius scrip-
tum est."

47 Martín Martín, 1977, 80: "Ego Rudericus ... donamus in manu pastoris nostri Ieronimi ab Urbano
papa secundo canonice ordinati et a Deo."

48 On exceptions from episcopal jurisdiction, see Loud, 2007, 89, 197–213, 243, 260–61, 329, 382.

49 Muḥammad ibn Khalaf Ibn ʿAlqamah, *al-Bayān al-wāḍiḥ fī al-mulimm al-fāḍiḥ* [The clear exposition of the shameful calamity], as reproduced in Old Castilian in Alfonso X, *Primera crónica
general*, 2:588b–589a: "Yo soy omne que nunca oue regnado, nin omne de mi linage non lo ouo;
et del dia que vin a esta villa, pagueme della mucho et cobdiçiela, et rogue a Nuestro Sennor Dios
que me la diesse; et veet qual es el poder de Dios que el dia que yo pose sobre Juballa [Arabic:
Jubaylah] non auia mas de quatro panes, et fizome Dios merçed que gane Valençia et so apoderado
della." Barton, 2011, 534.

50 Ibn ʿAlqamah, *al-Bayān al-wāḍiḥ*, in Alfonso X, *Primera crónica general*, 2:564b: "Et dixo que
ell apremiarie a quantos sennores en ell Andaluzia eran, de guisa que todos serien suyos; et que el
rey Rodrigo que fuera sennor dell Andaluzia que non fuera de linnage de reys, et pero que rey fue
et regno, et que assi regnarie ell et que serie el segundo rey Rodrigo." Barton, 2011, 533.

51 Ibn Bassām, *Dhakhīrah*, 3/1:99: "Ḥaddathanī man samiʿahu yaqūlu wa-qad qawiya ṭamaʿuhu wa-
lajja bihi jashaʿuhu: ʿalá Rudharīq futiḥat hādhihi al-jazīratu wa-Rudharīqu yastanqidhuhā."

52 Both Fletcher (1989, 183) and Martin (2007, 126–27) understand the exemption privilege in the
1098 endowment charter as a likely tool for making the Valencian bishopric directly subject to the
Apostolic See and outside of the control of Toledo, and they both argue that this privilege is a clear
sign of the Cid's ambition to be independent. Barton (2011, 529), on the other hand, understands
the exemption privilege as a vehicle for achieving "Bishop Jerome's independence from secular
power," making "it all the more likely that the prelate had earlier served as a Cluniac [monk], for
which Order the defence of independence against secular encroachment was a perennial concern."

53 Urban II to Bernard of Sédirac, archbishop of Toledo, Anagni, 15 October 1088, in Mansilla
Reoyo, 1955, 44 (no. 27); Burns, 1967, 1:257–58.

54 Urban II to Bishop Berenguer of Vic, 1 July 1091, in Mansilla Reoyo, 1955, 49–52 (no. 32); Urban
II to Count Ermengol IV of Urgell, 1 July 1091, in Kehr, 1926, 286 (no. 22); Urban II to the counts
Bernat of Besalú, Hugo of Ampurias, Guislabert of Roussilon, and Guillem of Cerdanya and their
knights, c. July 1096, in Kehr, 1926, 287–88 (no. 23).

55 Urban II to Bishop Peter of Huesca, 11 May 1098, in Durán Gudiol, 1962, 193 (no. 20).

56 For attempts to abolish the concept of the Spanish *reconquista* as a framework for viewing Iberia's
medieval past, see Burns, 1979, 242; 1998; Chevedden, 2013, 41–42. The monumental study of
crusade bulls in Iberia by Goñi Gaztambide (1958) should have been sufficient to bury the idea
of the Spanish *reconquista*, as well as the 1095 start date for the crusades, but his findings were
ignored by scholars.

57 Just as Catlos argues that the Latin West placed no intrinsic value in crusading as an activity
that should be pursued for its own sake, as an end in itself, but rather made use of it as a mere

tool to serve the needs of an internal Christian conflict, Hirschler (2014) argues that the Islamic world, when faced with the crusader advance in the eastern Mediterranean, was drawn to *jihād*, not because it held any intrinsic value for Muslims, but because *jihād* was called upon to serve as a tool in "the rivalry between the Abbasid Caliphate and the Saljuq Sultanate." For Catlos and Hirschler, it is not necessary to postulate an external cause for either the crusades or the *jihād* response to them, since internal struggles within Christendom and the Dār al-Islām have the power to produce both crusade and *jihād*. The overall intention of both scholars is to remove the ongoing conflict between Islam and Western Christendom in the medieval Mediterranean world from the causes of hostility between these two civilizations, and to demonstrate that either inter-Christian disputes (Catlos) or inter-Muslim disputes (Hirschler) were to blame for whatever strife arose between Cross and Crescent. A thesis such as Catlos's and Hirschler's that maintains that actions were determined by causes internal to a society must show an absence of external causes, that external causes could not be a factor in their determination.

58 Urban II's letter to the monks of Vallombrosa, 7 October 1096, in Hiestand, 1985, 88–89 (no. 2); trans. in Jensen, 2003, 121.

59 Urban II to Bishop Bertrand of Barcelona and the counts of the city, Berenguer Ramon and Ramon, 9 December 1093, in Kehr, 1926, 290–92 (no. 27); Becker, 1964–2012, 2:346; Chevedden, 2005b, 299 n112.

60 The *Crusade of settlement and colonial control* is explored at length in its Valencian context in Burns, 1973 and 1975.

REFERENCES

Narrative primary sources

ʿAbd Allāh ibn Buluggīn al-Zīrī, *Kitāb al-Tibyān lil-amīr ʿAbd Allāh ibn Buluqqīn, ākhir umarāʾ Banī Zīrī bi-Gharnāṭah*. Edited by A. T. al-Ṭayyibī [al-Ṭībī]. Rabat: Manshūrāt ʿUkāẓ, 1995; translated by A. T. Tibi as *The Tibyān: Memoirs of ʿAbd Allāh ibn Buluggīn, Last Zīrid Amīr of Granada*. Leiden: Brill, 1986.

Albert of Aachen. *Historia Ierosolimitana: History of the Journey to Jerusalem*. Edited by S. B. Edgington. Oxford: Clarendon Press, 2007; translated by S. B. Edgington as *Albert of Aachen's History of the Journey to Jerusalem*. 2 vols. Farnham: Ashgate, 2013.

Alfonso X, King of Castile and Leon. *Primera crónica general de España que mandó componer Alfonso el Sabio y se continuaba bajo Sancho IV en 1289*. Edited by R. Menéndez Pidal. 2 vols. Madrid: Editorial Gredos, 1955.

———. *Las Siete partidas*. Edited by R. I. Burns; translated by S. P. Scott. 5 vols. Philadelphia: University of Pennsylvania Press, 2001.

Amatus of Montecassino. *Storia de' Normanni di Amato di Montecassino volgarizzata in antico francese*. Edited by V. de Bartholomaeis. Rome: Tipografia del Senato, 1935; translated by P. N. Dunbar as *The History of the Normans*, revised with introduction and notes by G. A. Loud. Woodbridge, UK: Boydell Press, 2004.

Augustine. *Sancti Aurelii Augustini De civitate Dei libri I–XXII*. Edited by B. Dombart and A. Kalb. 2 vols. Turnholt: Brepols, 1955; translated by R. W. Dyson as *The City of God against the Pagans*. Cambridge: Cambridge University Press, 1998.

———. *Sancti Aurelii Augustini Enarrationes in Psalmos*. Edited by Eligius Dekkers and Johannes Fraipont. 3 vols. Turnhout: Brepols, 1956; translated by M. Boulding as *Expositions of the Psalms*. 6 vols. Hyde Park, NY: New City Press, 2000–04.

Baldric of Bourgueil. *The Historia Ierosolimitana of Baldric of Bourgueil*. Edited by S. Biddlecombe. Woodbridge, UK: Boydell Press, 2014.

Caesarius of Heisterbach. *Dialogus miraculorum = Dialog über die Wunder*. Edited and translated by H. Schneider and N. Nösges. 5 vols. Turnhout: Brepols, 2009.

La Chanson de Roland = The Song of Roland: The French Corpus. Edited by J. J. Duggan. 3 vols. Turnhout: Brepols, 2005.

De Expugnatione Scalabis. In *Portugaliae monumenta historica: a saeculo octavo post Christum usque ad quintumdecimum, Scriptores*, edited by A. Herculano de Carvalho e Araújo and J. José da Silva Mendes Leal. 1 vol. in 3 pts. Lisbon: Academia das Ciências de Lisboa, 1856–61, 1:93–95.

Dhikr bilād al-Andalus li-muʾallif majhūl (*Una descripción anónima de al-Andalus*). Edited by L. Molina. 2 vols. Madrid: Consejo Superior de Investigaciones Científicas, 1983.

Ekkehard of Aura. "Ekkehardi chronica." In *Frutolfs und Ekkehards Chroniken und die Anonyme Kaiserchronik* [*Frutolfi et Ekkehardi Chronica necnon Anonymi Chronica Imperatorum*], edited by F.-J. Schmale and I. Schmale-Ott, 123–209. Darmstadt: Wissenschaftliche Buchgesellschaft, 1972.

Fulcher of Chartres. *Historia Hierosolymitana (1095–1127)*. Edited by H. Hagenmeyer. Heidelberg: C. Winter Universitatsbuchhandlung, 1913; translated by M. E. McGinty as *Chronicle of the First Crusade (Fulcheri Carnotensis Historia Hierosolymitana)*. Philadelphia: University of Pennsylvania Press, 1941; translated by F. R. Ryan as *A History of the Expedition to Jerusalem, 1095–1127*. New York: W. W. Norton, 1969.

Geoffrey Malaterra. *De rebus gestis Rogerii Calabriae et Siciliae comitis et Roberti Guiscardi Ducis fratris eius*. Edited by E. Pontieri. Bologna: Zanichelli, 1927–28; translated by K. B. Wolf as *The Deeds of Count Roger of Calabria and Sicily and of his Brother Duke Robert Guiscard*. Ann Arbor, MI: University of Michigan Press, 2005.

Gesta francorum et aliorum Hierosolymitanorum: The Deeds of the Franks and other Pilgrims to Jerusalem. Edited and translated by R. Hill. London: T. Nelson, 1962.

Guibert of Nogent. *Dei gesta per Francos et cinq autres textes*. Edited by R. B. C. Huygens. Turnhout: Brepols, 1996; translated by R. Levine as *The Deeds of God through the Franks: A Translation of Guibert de Nogent's Gesta Dei per Francos*. Woodbridge, UK: Boydell Press, 1997.

Ibn Bassām, Abū al-Ḥasan ʿAlī al-Shantarīnī. *al-Dhakhīrah fī maḥāsin ahl al-jazīrah*. Edited by I. ʿAbbās. 4 vols. in 8. Beirut: Dār al-Thaqāfah, 1975–79.

Ibn Ḥayyān, Abū Marwān Ḥayyān ibn Khalaf al-Qurṭubī. *al-Muqtabis fī taʾrīkh al-Andalus: al-juzʾ al-khāmis*. Edited by P. Chalmeta Gendrón and F. Corriente. Madrid: al-Maʿhad al-Isbānī al-ʿArabī lil-Thaqāfah; al-Ribāṭ Kulliyat al-Ādāb, 1979; translated by M. Jesús Viguera and F. Corriente as *Crónica del califa ʿAbdarrahman III An-Nasir entre los años 912 y 942 (al-Muqtabis V)*. Zaragoza, Anubar: Instituto Hispano-Arabe de Cultura, 1981.

Ibn al-Kardabūs, ʿAbd al-Malik. *Taʾrīkh al-Andalus li-Ibn al-Kardabūs wa-waṣfuhu li-Ibn al-Shabbāṭ*. Edited by A. M. al-ʿAbbādī. Madrid: Instituto de Estudios Islámicos, 1971.

James I, King of Aragon-Catalonia. *Llibre dels fets del rei En Jaume*. Edited by J. Bruguera. 2 vols. Barcelona: Barcino, 1991.

Le liber censuum de l'église romaine. Edited by P. Fabre and L. Duchesne. 3 vols. Paris: Fontemoing, Thorin, 1889–1952.

al-Maqqarī, Shihāb al-Din Abū al-ʿAbbās Aḥmad ibn Muḥammad al-Tilimsānī. *Nafḥ al-ṭīb min ghuṣn al-Andalus al-raṭīb*. Edited by I. ʿAbbās. 8 vols. Beirut: Dār Ṣādir, 1968.

Orderic Vitalis. *The Ecclesiastical History of Orderic Vitalis*. Edited and translated by M. Chibnall. 6 vols. Oxford: Clarendon Press, 1969–80, 5:8–191.

Paul the Deacon. "Letter to Charlemagne." In Saint Benedict, *The Rule of Saint Benedict*, edited and translated by B. L. Venarde, 230–42. Cambridge, MA: Harvard University Press.

Peter Tudebode. *Historia de Hierosolymitano itinere*. Edited by J. H. Hill and L. L. Hill. Paris: Librairie Orientaliste Paul Geuthner, 1977; translated by J. H. Hill and L. L. Hill as *Historia de Hierosolymitano Itinere*. Philadelphia: American Philosophical Society, 1974.

Ralph of Caen. "Gesta Tancredi in expeditione Hierosolymitana." In *Recueil des historiens des Croisades: Historiens occidentaux*, edited by Académie royale des inscriptions et belles-lettres. 5 vols. Paris: Imprimerie royale, 1844–95, 3:587–716; translated by B. S. Bachrach and D. S. Bachrach as *The* Gesta Tancredi *of Ralph of Caen: A History of the Normans on the First Crusade*. Farnham, UK: Ashgate, 2005.

Raymond of Aguilers. *Le "Liber" de Raymond d'Aguilers*. Edited by J. H. Hill and L. L. Hill. Paris: Librairie Orientaliste Paul Geuthner, 1969; translated by J. H. Hill and L. L. Hill as *Historia Francorum qui ceperunt Iherusalem*. Philadelphia: American Philosophical Society, 1968.
Robert the Monk. *The Historia Iherosolimitana of Robert the Monk*. Edited by D. Kempf and M. G. Bull. Woodbridge, UK: Boydell Press, 2013; translated by C. Sweetenham as *Robert the Monk's History of the First Crusade* = Historia Iherosolimitana. Aldershot, UK: Ashgate, 2005.
al-ʿUdhrī, Abū al-ʿAbbās Aḥmad ibn ʿUmar ibn Anas al-maʿrūf bi-Ibn al-Dalāʾī. *Nuṣūṣ ʿan al-Andalus min Kitāb tarṣīʿ al-akhbār wa-tanwīʿ al-āthār, wa-al-bustān fī gharāʾib al-buldān wa-al-masālik ilá jamīʿ al-mamālik*. Edited by ʿA. ʿA. al-Ahwānī. Madrid: Maṭbaʿat Maʿhad al-Dirāsāt al-Islāmīyah, 1965.
William of Malmesbury. *Gesta regum Anglorum: The History of the English Kings*. Edited and translated by R. A. B. Mynors; completed by R. M. Thomson and M. Winterbottom. 2 vols. Oxford: Clarendon Press, 1998–99.
William of Tyre. *Chronique* [= *Historia rerum in partibus transmarinis gestarum*]. Edited by R. B. C. Huygens. 2 vols. Turnholt: Brepols, 1986; translated by E. A. Babcock and A. C. Krey as *A History of Deeds Done Beyond the Sea*. 2 vols. New York: Columbia University Press, 1943.

Documentary primary sources

Caspar, E., ed. 1920–23. *Das Register Gregors VII (Gregorii VII registrum lib. I-IX)*. 2 vols. Berlin: Weidmann.
Collura P., ed. 1961. *Le più antiche carte dell'Archivio capitolare di Agrigento (1092–1282)*. Palermo: Manfredi.
Hagenmeyer, H., ed. 1901. *Epistulae et chartae ad historiam primi belli sacri spectantes: Die Kreuzzugsbriefe aus den Jahren 1088–1100*. Innsbruck: Verlag der Wagner'schen Universitäts-Buchhandlung.
Hiestand, R., ed. 1985. *Vorarbeiten zum Oriens Pontificius, III, Papsturkunden für Kirchen im Heiligen Lande*. Göttingen: Vandenhoeck & Ruprecht.
Kehr, P., ed. 1926. *Papsturkunden in Spanien: Vorarbeiten zur Hispania Pontificia*, vol. 1, *Katalanien*, pt. 2, *Urkunden und Regesten*. Berlin: Weidmann.
Loewenfeld, S., ed. (1885) 1959. *Epistolae pontificum Romanorum ineditae*. Leipzig: Veit; Graz: Akademische Druck- u. Verlagsanstalt. Reprint, Graz: Akademische Druck- u. Verlagsanstalt.
Mansilla Reoyo, D., ed. 1955. *La documentación pontificia hasta Inocencio III (965–1216)*. Rome: Instituto Español de Estudios Eclesiásticos.
Martín Martín, J. L., et al., eds. 1977. *Documentos de los Archivos Catedralicio y Diocesano de Salamanca (siglos XII-XIII)*. Salamanca: Universidad de Salamanca.
Migne, J.-P., ed. 1841–64. *Patrologiae cursus completes: Series latina*. 221 vols. Paris: J.-P. Migne.
Santifaller L., ed. 1957. *Quellen und Forschungen zum Urkunden- und Kanzleiwesen Papst Gregors VII*, pt. 1, *Quellen: Urkunden, Regesten, Facsimilia*. Vatican City: Biblioteca apostolica vaticana.
Schmitt, F. S., ed. 1946–61. *S. Anselmi cantuariensis archiepiscopi opera omnia*. 6 vols. Edinburgh: Thomas Nelson and Sons.
Somerville, R., ed. 1972. *The Councils of Urban II*, vol. 1, *Decreta claromontensia*. Amsterdam: Adolf M. Hakkert.
Villanueva, J., and J. Lorenzo Villanueva, eds. 1821. *Viage literario à las iglesias de España*, vol. 6, *Viage a la iglesia de Vique: año 1806*. Valencia: Imprenta de Oliveres, antes de Estévan.

Secondary literature

Alvermann, D. 1995. "La battaglia di Ottone II contro i Saraceni nel 982." *Archivio storico per la Calabria e la Lucania* 62: 115–30.

Asbridge, T. 2004. *The First Crusade: A New History*. Oxford: Oxford University Press.

———. 2010. *The Crusades: The War for the Holy Land*. London: Simon & Schuster.

Ashe, L. 1999. "'A Prayer and a Warcry': The Creation of a Secular Religion in the *Song of Roland*." *Cambridge Quarterly* 28 (4): 349–67.

Balard, M. 1988. *Les croisades*. Paris: MA editions.

Barrett, C. K. 1978. *The Gospel According to St John: An Introduction with Commentary and Notes on the Greek Text*, 2nd ed. Philadelphia: Westminster Press.

Barton, S. 2011. "El Cid, Cluny and the Medieval Spanish *Reconquista*." *English Historical Review* 126: 517–43.

Becker, A. 1964–2012. *Papst Urban II (1088–1099)*. 3 vols. Stuttgart: Hiersemann; Hannover: Hahn.

———. 1989. "Urbain II, pape de la croisade." In *Les champenois et la croisade: actes des quatrièmes Journées rémoises, 27–28 novembre 1987*, edited by Y. Bellenger and D. Quéruel, 9–17. Paris: Aux Amateurs de livres.

Beiser, F. C. 2011. *The German Historicist Tradition*. Oxford: Oxford University Press.

Berman, H. J. 1983. *Law and Revolution: The Formation of the Western Legal Tradition*. Cambridge, MA: Harvard University Press.

Bertolini, P. 1970. "La serie episcopale napoletana nei secoli VIII e IX: Ricerche sulle fonti per la storia dell'Italia meridionale nell'alto medioevo." *Rivista di storia della Chiesa in Italia* 24: 349–440.

Birk, J. C. 2011. "The Betrayal of Antioch: Narratives of Conversion and Conquest during the First Crusade." *Journal of Medieval and Early Modern Studies* 41 (3): 463–85.

Blake, E. O. 1970. "The Formation of the 'Crusade Idea.'" *Journal of Ecclesiastical History* 21: 11–31.

Bruce, S. G. 2007. "An Abbot between Two Cultures: Maiolus of Cluny considers the Muslims of La Garde-Freinet." *Early Medieval Europe* 15 (4): 426–40.

Bruce, T. 2006. "The Politics of Violence and Trade: Denia and Pisa in the Eleventh Century." *Journal of Medieval History* 32 (2): 127–42.

Brundage, J. A. 1969. *Medieval Canon Law and the Crusader*. Madison: University of Wisconsin Press.

Bull, M. 1993. *Knightly Piety and the Lay Response to the First Crusade: The Limousin and Gascony, c. 970–c. 1130*. Oxford: Clarendon Press.

———. 2009. "Crusade and Conquest." In *The Cambridge History of Christianity*, vol. 4, *Christianity in Western Europe, c. 1100–c. 1500*, edited by M. Rubin and W. Simons, 340–52. Cambridge: Cambridge University Press.

Burns, R. I. 1962. "The Parish as a Frontier Institution in Thirteenth-Century Valencia." *Speculum* 37 (2): 244–51.

———. 1967. *The Crusader Kingdom of Valencia: Reconstruction on a Thirteenth-Century Frontier*. 2 vols. Cambridge, MA: Harvard University Press.

———. (1971) 1984. "Christian-Islamic Confrontation in the West: The Thirteenth-Century Dream of Conversion." *American Historical Review* 76 (5): 1386–434. Reprint (with modifications) in Burns, 1984, 80–108.

———. 1973. *Islam under the Crusaders: Colonial Survival in the Thirteenth-century Kingdom of Valencia*. Princeton, NJ: Princeton University Press.

———. 1975. *Medieval Colonialism: Postcrusade Exploitation of Islamic Valencia*. Princeton, NJ: Princeton University Press.

———. 1976. "The Spiritual Life of James the Conqueror, King of Arago-Catalonia (1208–1276): Portrait and Self-Portrait." *Catholic Historical Review* 62 (1): 1–35.

———. 1979. "Muslim-Christian Conflict and Contact in Medieval Spain: Context and Methodology." *Thought* 54: 238–52.

———. 1984. *Muslims, Christians, and Jews in the Crusader Kingdom of Valencia: Societies in Symbiosis*. Cambridge: Cambridge University Press.

———. 1989a. "L'Església com a institució fronterera." In *Història del País Valencià: obra en cinc volums*, vol. 2, *De la conquesta a la federació hispànica*, edited by E. Belenguer Cebrià, 125–37. Barcelona: Edicions 62.

———. 1989b. "Igelesia y sociedad de Valencia, durante la generacion de la conquista." In *En torno al 750 aniversario: antecedentes y consecuencias de la conquista de Valencia*. 2 vols., 2:97–114. Valencia: Generalitat Valenciana, Consell Valencià de Cultura.

———. 1998. "The Many Crusades of Valencia's Conquest (1225–1280): An Historiographical Labyrinth." In *On the Social Origins of Medieval Institutions: Essays in Honor of Joseph F. O'Callaghan*, edited by D. J. Kagay and T. M. Vann, 167–77. Leiden: Brill.

Bysted, A. L. 2014. *The Crusade Indulgence: Spiritual Rewards and the Theology of the Crusades, c. 1095–1216*. Leiden: Brill.

Cassirer, E. 1953–96. *The Philosophy of Symbolic Forms*. Translated by R. Manheim and J. M. Krois. 4 vols. New Haven: Yale University Press.

Catlos, B. A. 2004. *The Victors and the Vanquished: Christians and Muslims of Catalonia and Aragon, 1050–1300*. New York: Cambridge University Press.

———. 2014a. *Infidel Kings and Unholy Warriors: Faith, Power, and Violence in the Age of Crusade and Jihad*. New York: Farrar, Straus and Giroux.

———. 2014b. *Muslims of Medieval Latin Christendom, c. 1050–1614*. Cambridge: Cambridge University Press.

Chalmeta Gendrón, P. 1991. "al-Manṣūr." In *The Encyclopaedia of Islam*, 2nd ed., vol. 6, edited by C. E. Bosworth, E. van Donzel, and C. Pellat, 430–32. Leiden: Brill.

Chenu, M.-D. 1979. *Nature, Man, and Society in the Twelfth Century: Essays on New Theological Perspectives in the Latin West*. Translated by J. Taylor and L. K. Little. Chicago: University of Chicago Press. Originally published as *La théologie au douzième siècle*. Paris: J. Vrin, 1957.

Chevedden, P. E. 2005a. "Canon 2 of the Council of Clermont (1095) and the Goal of the Eastern Crusade: 'To liberate Jerusalem' or 'To liberate the Church of God'?" *Annuarium Historiae Conciliorum* 37 (1): 57–108.

———. 2005b. "Canon 2 of the Council of Clermont (1095) and the Crusade Indulgence." *Annuarium Historiae Conciliorum* 37 (2): 253–322.

———. 2006. "The Islamic Interpretation of the Crusade: A New (Old) Paradigm for Understanding the Crusades." *Der Islam* 83 (1): 90–136.

———. 2008. "The Islamic View and the Christian View of the Crusades: A New Synthesis." *History* 93: 181–200.

———. 2010. "'A Crusade from the First': The Norman Conquest of Islamic Sicily, 1060–1091." *al-Masāq: Islam and the Medieval Mediterranean* 22 (2): 191–225.

———. 2011. "The View of the Crusades from Rome and Damascus: The Geo-Strategic and Historical Perspectives of Pope Urban II and ʿAlī ibn Ṭāhir al-Sulamī." *Oriens* 39 (2): 257–329.

———. 2013. "Crusade Creationism *versus* Pope Urban II's Conceptualization of the Crusades." *Historian* 75 (1): 1–46.

Chladenius, J. M. (1742) 1969. *Einleitung zur richtigen Auslegung vernünftiger Reden und Schriften*. Introduction by Lutz Geldsetzer, photomechanical reprint of the 1742 Leipzig edition. Düsseldorf: Stern-Verlag Janssen.

———. 1752. *Allgemeine Geschichtswissenschaft: worinnen der Grund zu einer neuen Einsicht in allen Arten der Gelahrtheit gelegt wird*. Leipzig: Friedrich Lanckischens Erben.

Cilento, N. 1959. "I Saraceni nell'Italia meridionale nei secoli IX e X." *Archivo storico per le provincie napoletani* 77: 109–22.

———. 1971. "Le incursioni saraceniche nell'Italia meridionale." In N. Cilento, *Italia meridionale longobarda*, 2nd ed., 175–89. Milan: R. Ricciardi.

Citarella, A. O. 1967. "The Relations of Amalfi with the Arab World before the Crusades." *Speculum* 42 (2): 299–312.

———. 1987. "The Political Chaos in Southern Italy and the Arab Destruction of Monte Cassino in 883." In *Montecassino dalla prima alla seconda distruzione: Momenti e aspetti di storia cassinese (secc. VI-IX): Atti del II Convegno di studi sul Medioevo meridionale (Cassino-Montecassino, 27–31 maggio 1984)*, edited by F. Avagliano, 163–80. Cassino: Montecassino.

Cobb, P. M. 2014. *The Race for Paradise: An Islamic History of the Crusades*. Oxford: Oxford University Press.

Cognasso, F. 1967. *Storia delle cruciate*. Milan: Dall'Oglio.

Constable, G. 1953. "The Second Crusade as Seen by Contemporaries." *Traditio* 9: 213–79.

———. 1982. "Renewal and Reform in Religious Life: Concepts and Realities." In *Renaissance and Renewal in the Twelfth Century*, edited by R. L. Benson and G. Constable, 37–67. Cambridge, MA: Harvard University Press.

———. 1996. *The Reformation of the Twelfth Century*. Cambridge: Cambridge University Press.

———. 2008. "Cluny and the First Crusade." In G. Constable, *Crusaders and Crusading in the Twelfth Century*, 183–96. Farnham, UK: Ashgate.

Corriente, F. 1997. *A Dictionary of Andalusi Arabic*. Leiden: Brill.

Cowdrey, H. E. J. 1970a. *The Cluniacs and the Gregorian Reform*. Oxford: Clarendon Press.

———. 1970b. "Pope Urban II's Preaching of the First Crusade." *History* 55: 177–88.

———. 1973. "Cluny and the First Crusade." *Revue Bénédictine* 83: 285–311.

———. 1978. "Two Studies in Cluniac History, 1049–1126." *Studi Gregoriani per la storia della "libertas ecclesiae"* 11: 1–298.

———. 1995. "Pope Urban II and the Idea of the Crusade." *Studi medievali* 36: 721–42.

———. 1998. *Pope Gregory VII, 1073–1085*. Oxford: Clarendon Press.

Cutler, A. 1963. "Who Was the 'Monk of France' and When Did He Write? A Note on D. M. Dunlop's 'A Christian Mission to Muslim Spain in the 11th Century.'" *Al-Andalus, Revista de las Escuelas de Estudios Árabes de Madrid y Granada* 28: 249–69.

———. 1968. "The First Crusade and the Idea of 'Conversion.'" *Muslim World* 58 (1): 57–71; 58 (2): 155–64.

Dale, A., ed. 2007. *Crusades: Authors and Audiences*. Sydney: History Teachers' Association of NSW.

Dawson, C. 1932. *The Making of Europe: An Introduction to the History of European Unity*. New York: Sheed & Ward.

Demurger, A. 2006. *Croisades et croisés au Moyen Âge*. Paris: Flammarion.

Dozy, R. 1881. *Recherches sur l'histoire et la littérature de l'Espagne pendant le moyen âge*. 3rd ed. 2 vols. Leiden: Brill.

Dufourcq, C.-E. 1978. *La vie quotidienne dans l'Europe médiévale sous domination arabe*. Paris: Hachette.

Dunlop, D. M. 1952. "A Christian Mission to Muslim Spain in the Eleventh Century." *Al-Andalus, Revista de las Escuelas de Estudios Árabes de Madrid y Granada* 17: 259–310.

Durán Gudiol, A. 1962. *La Iglesia de Aragón durante los reinados de Sancho Ramírez y Pedro I (1062?–1104)*. Rome: Iglesia Nacional Española.

El-Cheikh, N. M. 2004. *Byzantium Viewed by the Arabs*. Cambridge, MA: Distributed for the Center for Middle Eastern Studies of Harvard University by Harvard University Press.

Engreen, F. E. 1945. "Pope John the Eighth and the Arabs." *Speculum* 20 (3): 318–30.

Epstein, S. 1996. *Genoa and the Genoese, 958–1528*. Chapel Hill, NC: University of North Carolina Press.

Erdmann, C. 1935/1977. *Die Entstehung des Kreuzzugsgedankens*. Stuttgart: W. Kohlhammer, 1935; translated by M. W. Baldwin and W. Goffart as *The Origin of the Idea of Crusade*, foreword and additional notes by M. W. Baldwin. Princeton, NJ: Princeton University Press.

Fletcher, R. A. 1987. "Reconquest and Crusade in Spain, *c.* 1050–1150." *Transactions of the Royal Historical Society*, 5th Ser., 37: 31–47.

———. 1989. *The Quest for El Cid*. New York: Oxford University Press.

————. 2004. *The Cross and the Crescent: Christianity and Islam from Muhammad to the Reformation*. New York: Viking.

Flori, J. 1992. *La première croisade, 1095–1099: L'Occident chrétien contre l'Islam (aux origines des idéologies occidentals)*. Brussels: Éditions Complexe.

————. 1998. "Réforme, *reconquista*, croisade: l'idée de reconquête dans la correspondance pontificale d'Alexandre II à Urbain II." In J. Flori, *Croisade et chevalerie: XIᵉ-XIIᵉ siècles*, 51–80. Brussels: De Boeck Université.

————. 1999. *Pierre l'Ermite et la première croisade*. Paris: Fayard.

————. 2001. *La Guerre sainte: La formation de l'idée de croisade dans l'Occident chrétien*. Paris: Aubier.

————. 2002. "Première croisade et conversion des 'païens.'" In *Migrations et diasporas méditerranéennes: Xᵉ–XVIᵉ siècles: actes du colloque de Conques, octobre 1999*, edited by M. Balard and A. Ducellier, 449–57. Paris: Publications de la Sorbonne.

————. 2004. "Pour une redéfinition de la croisade." *Cahiers de civilisation medievale* 47: 329–49.

————. 2010. *La croix, la tiare et l'épée: la croisade confisquée*. Paris: Payot.

Forster, M. 2011. "Genealogy." *American Dialectic* 1: 230–50.

France, J. 2005. *Crusades and the Expansion of Catholic Christendom, 1000–1714*. London: Routledge.

Frankopan, P. 2012. *The First Crusade: The Call from the East*. London: Bodley Head.

Gabriele, M. 2012. "The Last Carolingian Exegete: Pope Urban II, the Weight of Tradition, and Christian Reconquest." *Church History* 81 (4): 796–814.

Gil, M. 1992. *A History of Palestine, 634–1099*. Translated by E. Broido. Cambridge: Cambridge University Press.

Goez, W. 1958. *Translatio imperii: ein Beitrag zur Geschichte des Geschichtsdenkens und der politischen Theorien im Mittelalter und in der frühen Neuzeit*. Tübingen: Mohr.

Goitein, S. D. 1967–93. *A Mediterranean Society: The Jewish Communities of the Arab World as Portrayed in the Documents of the Cairo Geniza*. 6 vols. Berkeley: University of California Press.

Goñi Gaztambide, J. 1958. *Historia de la bula de la cruzada en España*. Vitoria: Editorial del Seminario.

Grousset, R. 1934–36. *Histoire des Croisades et du Royaume Franc de Jérusalem*. 3 vols. Paris: Plon.

Hamilton, B. 2007. "Pope John X (914–928) and the Antecedents of the First Crusade." In *In Laudem Hierosolymitani: Studies in Crusades and Medieval Culture in Honour of Benjamin Z. Kedar*, edited by I. Shagrir, R. Ellenblum, and J. S. C. Riley-Smith, 309–18. Aldershot, UK: Ashgate.

Hamilton, J. T. 2003. *Soliciting Darkness: Pindar, Obscurity, and the Classical Tradition*. Cambridge, MA: Harvard University Department of Comparative Literature.

Hehl, E.-D. 1994. "Was ist eigentlich ein Kreuzzug?" *Historische Zeitschrift* 259 (2): 297–336.

————. 2004. "War, Peace and the Christian Order." In *The New Cambridge Medieval History*, vol. 4, *c. 1024–c. 1198*, edited by D. Luscombe and J. Riley-Smith. 2 vols., 1:185–228. Cambridge: Cambridge University Press.

Herder, J. G. (1764) 1984–2002. "Versuch einer Geschichte der lyrischen Dichtkunst (1764)." In J. G. Herder, *Werke*, edited by W. Pross. 3 vols. in 4, 1:7–62. München: Carl Hanser.

————. (1767–68) 1985–2000/2002. *Über die neuere deutsche Literatur; Fragmente; Erste Sammlung; Zweite völlig umgearbeitete Ausgabe; 1768*. In Herder 1985–2000, 1:541–649; translated by M. N. Forster as "Fragments on Recent German Literature (1767–8)," in J. G. Herder, *Philosophical Writings*, edited by M. N. Forster, 33–64. Cambridge: Cambridge University Press.

————. (1769) 1985–2000. "Der Genius der Zukunft." In Herder, 1985–2000, 3:793–95.

————. (1803) 1985–2000. "Pindar, ein bote der Götter, Ausleger alter Geschichten." In Herder, 1985–2000, 10:927–30.

————. 1985–2000. *Werke in zehn Bänden*. Edited by M. Bollacher et al. 10 vols. in 11. Frankfurt am Main: Deutscher Klassiker Verlag.

Hirschler, K. 2014. "The Jerusalem Conquest of 492/1099 in the Medieval Arabic Historiography of the Crusades: From Regional Plurality to Islamic Narrative." *Crusades* 13: 37–76.

Hitchcock, R. 2014. *Muslim Spain Reconsidered: From 711 to 1502*. Edinburgh: Edinburgh University Press.

Housley, N. 1992. "Jerusalem and the Development of the Crusade Idea, 1099–1128." In *The Horns of Hattīn*, edited by B. Z. Kedar, 27–40. Jerusalem: Yad Izhak Ben-Zvi and Israel Exploration Society; London: Variorum.

———. 2006. *Contesting the Crusades*. Oxford: Blackwell Publishers.

———. 2008. *Fighting for the Cross: Crusading to the Holy Land*. New Haven: Yale University Press.

Hunt, N. 1967. *Cluny under Saint Hugh, 1049–1109*. London: E. Arnold.

Iogna-Prat, D. 1998/2002. *Ordonner et Exclure: Cluny et la société chretiènne face à hérésie, au judaisme, et à l'islam, 1000–1150*. Paris: Aubier; translated by G. R. Edwards as *Order and Exclusion: Cluny and Christendom Face Heresy, Judaism, and Islam, 1000–1150*. Ithaca, NY: Cornell University Press.

Jaspert, N. 2013/2006. *Die Kreuzzüge*, 6th ed. Darmstadt: WBG (Wissenschaftliche Buchgesellschaft); translated by P. G. Jestice as *The Crusades*. London: Routledge.

Jensen, J. M. 2003. "*Peregrinatio sive expeditio*: Why the First Crusade was not a Pilgrimage." *al-Masāq: Islam and the Medieval Mediterranean* 15 (2): 119–37.

———. 2007. *Denmark and the Crusades: 1400–1650*. Leiden: Brill.

Jensen, R. M. 2012. *Baptismal Imagery in Early Christianity: Ritual, Visual, and Theological Dimensions*. Grand Rapids, MI: Baker Academic.

Jotischky, A. 2004. *Crusading and the Crusader States*. Harlow, UK: Pearson/Longman.

Katzenellenbogen, A. 1944. "The Central Tympanum at Vézelay: Its Encyclopedic Meaning and Its Relation to the First Crusade." *Art Bulletin* 26 (3): 141–51.

Kedar, B. Z. 1988. *Crusade and Mission: European Approaches toward the Muslims*. Princeton, NJ: Princeton University Press.

Kennedy, H. 1996. *Muslim Spain and Portugal: A Political History of al-Andalus*. Harlow, UK: Longman.

Kohnle, A. 1993. *Abt Hugo von Cluny (1049–1109)*. Sigmaringen: Jan Thorbecke Verlag.

Kreutz, B. M. 1991. *Before the Normans: Southern Italy in the Ninth and Tenth Centuries*. Philadelphia: University of Pennsylvania Press.

Krueger, H. C. 1969–89. "The Italian Cities and the Arabs before 1095." In Setton, 1969–89, 1:40–53.

Lacombe, C. 1999. *Jérôme de Périgueux, 1060–1120, chapelain du Cid: évêque de Valence et de Salamanque: un moine-chevalier dans la Reconquista*. Périgueux: Fanlac.

Lambert, S. 2007. "Interview with Sarah Lambert." In Dale, 2007, 85–97.

Lapina, E. 2005. "The Mural Paintings of Berzé-la-Ville in the Context of the First Crusade and the Reconquista." *Journal of Medieval History* 31 (4): 309–26.

Lawrence, T. E. 1935. *Seven Pillars of Wisdom: A Triumph*. London: Jonathan Cape.

Lévi-Provençal, É. 1950. *Histoire de l'Espagne musulmane*, nouv. éd. rev. et augm. 3 vols. Paris: G. P. Maisonneuve.

Lewis, A. R. 1951. *Naval Power and Trade in the Mediterranean, A.D. 500–1100*. Princeton, NJ: Princeton University Press.

Linehan, P. 1987. "The Cid of History and the History of the Cid." *History Today* 37 (9): 26–32.

Lloyd, S. 1995. "The Crusading Movement, 1096–1274." In Riley-Smith 1995b, 34–65.

Loud, G. A. 1981. "A Calendar of the Diplomas of the Norman Princes of Capua." *Papers of the British School at Rome* 49: 99–143.

———. 2000. *The Age of Robert Guiscard: Southern Italy and the Norman Conquest*. Harlow, UK: Longman.

———. 2007. *The Latin Church in Norman Italy*. Cambridge: Cambridge University Press.

Loutchitskaja, S. 2002. "L'idée de conversion dans les chroniques de la première croisade." *Cahiers de civilisation médiévale* 45: 39–53.

MacEvitt, C. 2008. *The Crusades and the Christian World of the East: Rough Tolerance*. Philadelphia: University of Pennsylvania Press.

Madden, T. F. 2013. *The Concise History of the Crusades*, 3rd ed. Lanham, MD: Rowman & Little-field.

Marazzi, F. 1994. "Le 'città nuove' pontificie e l'insediamento laziale nel IX secolo." In *La storia dell'alto Medioevo italiano (VI-X secolo) alla luce dell'archeologia: convegno internazionale (Siena, 2–6 dicembre 1992)*, edited by R. Francovich and G. Noyé, 251–78. Florence: All'insegna del giglio.

Martin, G. 2007. "Le premier témoignage chrétien sur la prise de Valence (1098)." In *Balaguer, 1105: Cruïlla de civilizations: Reunió científica: X Curs d'Estiu Comtat d'Urgell celebrat a Balaguer els dies 13, 14 i 15 de juliol de 2005*, edited by F. Sabaté Curull, 121–35. Lleida: Pagès.

Mayer, H. E. 1965. *Geschichte der Kreuzzüge*, 1st ed. Stuttgart: Kohlhammer.

———. 2005. *Geschichte der Kreuzzüge*, 10th ed. Stuttgart: Kohlhammer.

McCrank, L. J. 1974. "Restoration and Reconquest in Medieval Catalonia: The Church and Principality of Tarragona, 971–1177." PhD diss., University of Virginia.

———. 1978. "The Foundation of the Confraternity of Tarragona by Archbishop Oleguer." *Viator* 9: 157–78.

Melville, H. (1851) 2001. *Moby-Dick, or, The Whale*. New York: Penguin Books.

Menéndez Pidal, R. 1918. "Autógrafos inéditos del Cid y de Jimena, en dos diplomas de 1098 y 1101." *Revista de filología española* 5: 1–20.

———. 1969. *La España del Cid*, 7th ed. 2 vols. Madrid: Espasa-Calpe.

Mitterauer, M. 2003. *Warum Europa? Mittelalterliche Grundlagen eines Sonderwegs*. Munich: C. H. Beck.

Morrisson, C. 2012. *Les Croisades*, 11th ed. Paris: Presses universitaires de France.

Norwich, J. J. 1992. *The Normans in Sicily: The Normans in the South, 1016–1130, and, the Kingdom in the Sun, 1130–1194*. London: Penguin.

O'Callaghan, J. F. 2003. *Reconquest and Crusade in Medieval Spain*. Philadelphia: University of Pennsylvania Press.

———. 2011. *The Gibraltar Crusade: Castile and the Battle for the Strait*. Philadelphia: University of Pennsylvania Press.

———. 2014. *The Last Crusade in the West: Castile and the Conquest of Granada*. Philadelphia: University of Pennsylvania Press.

Oldenbourg, Z. 1965/1966. *Les croisades*. Paris: Gallimard; translated by A. Carter as *The Crusades*. New York: Pantheon Books.

Partner, P. 1972. *The Lands of St. Peter: The Papal State in the Middle Ages and the Early Renaissance*. Berkeley: University of California Press.

Paul, N. and S. Yeager. 2012. "Introduction." In *Remembering the Crusades: Myth, Image, and Identity*, edited by N. Paul and S. Yeager, 1–25. Baltimore: Johns Hopkins University Press.

Phillips, J. 2009. *Holy Warriors: A Modern History of the Crusades*. London: Bodley Head.

———. 2014. *The Crusades, 1095–1204*, 2nd ed. London: Routledge.

Platelle, H. 1994. *Les croisades*. Paris: Desclée.

Price, J. 2011. "Alfonso I and the Memory of the First Crusade: Conquest and Crusade in the Kingdom of Aragón-Navarre." In *Crusades: Medieval Worlds in Conflict*, edited by T. F. Madden, J. L. Naus, and V. T. Ryan, 75–94. Aldershot, UK: Ashgate.

Purkis, W. J. 2008. *Crusading Spirituality in the Holy Land and Iberia, c. 1095–c. 1187*. Woodbridge, UK: Boydell Press.

———. 2010. "The Past as a Precedent: Crusade, Reconquest and Twelfth-Century Memories of a Christian Iberia." In *The Making of Memory in the Middle Ages*, edited by L. Doležalová, 441–61. Leiden: Brill.

———. 2013. "Crusading and Crusade Memory in Caesarius of Heisterbach's *Dialogus Miraculorum*." *Journal of Medieval History* 39: 100–27.

Richard, J. 1996/1999. *Histoire des croisades*. Paris: Fayard; translated by J. Birrell as *The Crusades, c. 1071–c. 1291*. Cambridge: Cambridge University Press.

Riley-Smith, J. 1977. *What Were the Crusades?* 1st ed. London: Macmillan.

———. 1986. *The First Crusade and the Idea of Crusading*. Philadelphia: University of Pennsylvania Press.

———. 1987. *The Crusades: A Short History*. New Haven, CT: Yale University Press.

———. 1993. "History, the Crusades and the Latin East, 1095–1204." In *Crusaders and Muslims in Twelfth-Century Syria*, edited by M. Shatzmiller, 1–17. Leiden: Brill.

———. 1995a. "The Crusading Movement and Historians." In Riley-Smith 1995b, 1–12.

———, ed. 1995b. *The Oxford Illustrated History of the Crusades*. Oxford: Oxford University Press.

———. 1997. *The First Crusaders, 1095–1131*. Cambridge: Cambridge University Press.

———. 2000. "Rethinking the Crusades." *First Things: A Journal of Religion and Public Life* 101: 20–23.

———. 2001. "The Crusading Movement." In *War, Peace, and World Orders in European History*, edited by A. Hartmann and B. Heuser, 127–40. London: Routledge.

———. 2005a. "Christians of the Middle East under the Franks: I. Motives for the Crusades: A European Perspective." In *Christianity: A History in the Middle East*, edited by H. Badr, S. Abou el Rouss Slim, and J. Abou Nohra, 548–58. Beirut: Middle East Council of Churches, Studies & Research Program.

———. 2005b. *The Crusades: A History*, 2nd ed. New Haven, CT: Yale University Press.

———. 2007. "Pluralism and Sentient Empathy." In Dale, 2007, 26–31.

———. 2008. *The Crusades, Christianity, and Islam*. New York: Columbia University Press.

———. 2009a. *The First Crusade and the Idea of Crusading*, 2nd ed. Philadelphia: University of Pennsylvania Press.

———. 2009b. *What were the Crusades?* 4th ed. San Francisco: Ignatius Press.

———. 2014. *The Crusades: A History*, 3rd ed. London: Bloomsbury Academic.

Riley-Smith, L. and J. Riley-Smith. 1981. *The Crusades: Idea and Reality, 1095–1274*. London: E. Arnold.

Ringel, I. H. 1987. "*Ipse transfert regna et mutat tempora*: Bemerkungen zur Herkunft von Dan. 2,21 bei Urban II." In *Deus qui mutat tempora: Menschen und Institutionen im Wandel des Mittelalters; Festschrift für Alfons Becker zu seinem fünfundsechzigsten Geburtstag*, edited by E.-D. Hehl, H. Seibert, and F. Staab, 137–56. Sigmaringen: J. Thorbecke.

Ríos Saloma, M. F. 2011. *La Reconquista: una construcción historiográfica (siglos XVI-XIX)*. Madrid: Marcial Pons Ediciones de Historia.

Rousset, P. 1957. *Histoire des croisades*. Paris: Payot.

Ruiz Asensio, J. M. 1968. "Campañas de Almanzor contra el reino de León (981–986)." *Anuario de Estudios Medievales* 5: 31–64.

Runciman, S. 1951–54. *A History of the Crusades*. 3 vols. Cambridge: Cambridge University Press.

Sarrió Cucarella, D. 2012. "Corresponding across Religious Borders: Al-Bājī's Response to a Missionary Letter from France." *Medieval Encounters: Jewish, Christian, and Muslim Culture in Confluence and Dialogue* 18 (1): 1–35.

Scalia, G. 1961. "Nuove considerazioni storiche e paleografiche sui documenti dell'Archivio Capitolare di Catania per il ristabilimento della sede vescovile nel 1091." *Archivio storico per la Sicilia orientale*, 57 (4th ser., 14): 5–53.

Schein, S. 2005. *Gateway to the Heavenly City: Crusader Jerusalem and the Catholic West (1099–1187)*. Aldershot, UK: Ashgate.

Setton, K. M., ed. 1969–89. *A History of the Crusades*, 2nd ed. 6 vols. Madison, WI: University of Wisconsin Press.

Sizgorich, T. 2009. *Violence and Belief in Late Antiquity: Militant Devotion in Christianity and Islam.* Philadelphia: University of Pennsylvania Press.

Smith, C., ed. 1972. *Poema de mio Cid.* Oxford: Clarendon Press.

———. 1983. *The Making of the* Poema de mio Cid. Cambridge: Cambridge University Press.

Smith, C., C. Melville, and A. ʿUbaydlī. 1988–92. *Christians and Moors in Spain.* 3 vols. Warminster, UK: Aris & Phillips.

Somerville, R. 1974. "The Council of Clermont (1095), and Latin Christian Society." *Archivum Historiae Pontificiae* 12: 55–90.

Starnawska, M. 2001. "Military Orders and the Beginning of Crusade in Prussia." In *The Crusades and the Military Orders: Expanding the Frontiers of Medieval Latin Christianity; In Memoriam Sir Steven Runciman (1903–2000)*, edited by Z. Hunyadi and J. Laszlovszky, 417–28. Budapest: Department of Medieval Studies, Central European University.

Tierney, B. 1988. *The Crisis of Church and State, 1050–1300: With Selected Documents.* Toronto: Published by University of Toronto Press in association with the Medieval Academy of America.

Turki, A. 1966. "La lettre du 'Moine de France' à al-Muqtadir Billāh, roi de Saragosse et la réponse d'al-Bāŷī, le faqīh andalou." *Al-Andalus, Revista de las Escuelas de Estudios Árabes de Madrid y Granada* 31: 73–153.

Tyerman, C. 1998. *The Invention of the Crusades.* Toronto: University of Toronto Press.

———. 2004. *Fighting for Christendom: Holy War and the Crusades.* Oxford: Oxford University Press.

———. 2005. *The Crusades: A Very Short Introduction.* Oxford: Oxford University Press.

———. 2006. *God's War: A New History of the Crusades.* London: Allen Lane.

———. 2011. *The Debate on the Crusades.* Manchester: Manchester University Press.

Vehse, O. 1927. "Das Bündnis gegen die Sarazenen vom Jahre 915." *Quellen und Forschungen aus italienischen Archiven und Bibliotheken* 19: 181–204.

Viré, F. 1978. "Khayl." In *The Encyclopaedia of Islam*, 2nd ed., vol. 4, edited by E. van Donzel, B. Lewis, C. Pellat, and C. E. Bosworth, 1143–46. Leiden: Brill.

von Falkenhausen, V. 2003. "Between Two Empires: Byzantine Italy in the Reign of Basil II." In *Byzantium in the Year 1000*, edited by P. Magdalino, 135–59. Leiden: Brill.

von Grunebaum, G. E. 1962. "An Analysis of Islamic Civilization and Cultural Anthropology." In von Grunebaum, *Modern Islam: The Search for Cultural Identity*, 30–72. Berkeley: University of California Press.

Waas, A. 1956. *Geschichte der Kreuzzüge.* 2 vols. Freiburg: Herder.

Wasserstein, D. 1985. *The Rise and Fall of the Party-Kings: Politics and Society in Islamic Spain 1002–1086.* Princeton, NJ: Princeton University Press.

Wenner, M. W. 1980. "The Arab/Muslim Presence in Medieval Central Europe." *International Journal of Middle East Studies* 12 (1): 59–79.

Wettstein, J. 1971–78. *La fresque romane: études comparatives*, 2 vols. Geneva: Droz.

Whalen, B. E. 2009. *Dominion of God: Christendom and Apocalypse in the Middle Ages.* Cambridge, MA: Harvard University Press.

Whittow, M. 1996. *The Making of Byzantium, 600–1025.* Berkeley: University of California Press.

Zöllner, W. 1990. *Geschichte der Kreuzzüge*, 6th ed. Berlin: Dt. Verl. d. Wiss.

CHAPTER THREE

WOMEN'S INVOLVEMENT IN THE CRUSADES

———·◆·———

Helen J. Nicholson

Modern readers could be forgiven for assuming that women could have no role in the crusades. Canonists and preachers alike discouraged women's active involvement. The reforming Church wished to enforce chastity on anyone involved in spiritual undertaking, and so crusaders must avoid all contact with women (Holt 2008). Failures on crusade could be blamed on women's sexual temptation. Maureen Purcell went so far as to claim (1979) that women could not be true crusaders: *crucesignatae*, literally 'cross-signed', bearing the sign of the cross.

Against this view, we have the leadership of noblewomen in holy wars and the Holy Land. From 1131 to 1152 the Kingdom of Jerusalem was ruled by a queen, Melisende, who ruled jointly with her husband, Fulk of Anjou, until 1143, and then as queen in her own right with her underage son Baldwin III, until 1152. Melisende was praised by her contemporary Abbot Bernard of Clairvaux and many of the nobles of the kingdom supported her against her eldest son (Hamilton 1978: 152–5; Newman 2014: 215–16). In the Iberian Peninsula, Queen Teresa of Portugal (1112–28) and Queen Urraca of León and Castile (1109–26) continued their father King Alfonso VI of Castile's wars of expansion against the Moors, wars which Pope Paschal II declared to be the equivalent of crusades. In Italy, Countess Matilda of Tuscany ruled her county in her own right from 1076 to 1115, and gave military support to the reforming papacy (Hay 2008). She also sponsored an attack on the North African coastal city of al-Mahdiyyah in 1087, in which the Pisan participants wore a pilgrim's badge and the warriors claimed to be fighting a holy war against godless Muslims (Cowdrey 1977).

It is clear that women were involved in crusades. Sabine Geldsetzer (2003) traced ninety-one clear *crucesignatae* from the period 1096–1291, in addition to another seven possible *crucesignatae* and a further fifty-nine whose status is unclear but who were present or involved in some way. It is evident that women's involvement was limited by cultural and religious expectations, and also that contemporary sources do not give us a full picture of their activity. All narrative sources from the medieval period had a didactic and moralising as well as an informative role, but those composed by clerical writers especially so. The imperative to produce a moralising discourse distorted the depiction of women, recreating them as pious virgins, faithful wives, carers or impious whores, but with little acknowledgement of their fulfilling wider roles (Hodgson 2005, 2007). The writings of the crusaders' opponents were little better in this respect, offering a different but equally distorted image. Modern scholars attempt to read between the lines and against the grain, but all too often the narrative sources have not given sufficient information to allow effective analysis (Gerish 2005; Nicholson 2004: 124). In the case of noblewomen, we may be able to refer to the evidence of charters, wills or material culture to counter the distorted view of the narrative sources, but there is little evidence for non-noblewomen's involvement beyond the narrative sources.

Beyond the question of whether women could legally be *crucesignatae* lie other debates. Did women fight on crusade? Was their role in supporting crusaders their main contribution to the crusading movement? Were women, as some contemporary clergy claimed, an impediment to a successful crusade?

We must remember that although the first crusades were depicted by contemporaries as mass-movements, by the beginning of the thirteenth century the papacy discouraged the involvement of all but warriors. Non-warriors – such as all male clergy, merchants, peasant farmers and women of all classes – were encouraged to redeem their vows through a money payment unless they were wealthy enough to lead soldiers to the crusade. If women played only a minor role in crusading from the early thirteenth century, they were in the same position as most men. However, in fact women did continue to be involved in crusading in various ways, but – as for men – the most important contributions were made by wealthy women.

RECRUITMENT

Women's sufferings in the Holy Land at the hands of Islam were used by crusade propagandists to urge support for the crusade (Lambert 2001: 9). Yet accounts of Pope Urban II's preaching of the First Crusade suggest that the pope did not expect women to take part (Rousseau 2001: 32–4). Fewer women joined crusading expeditions from the early thirteenth century: the crusade was preached to everyone, but increasingly women were encouraged to commute their crusading vows and pay a sum of money in support of the expedition instead (Powell 1992: 295; Rousseau 2001: 37–39). Nevertheless, women continued to join expeditions during the thirteenth century (Kedar 1972). Even after the final loss of Acre to the Mamluks in 1291, women continued to promote crusading.

Pope Urban II promised that those who took part in the First Crusade would be relieved of all penance due for their confessed sins (Riley-Smith 1997: 68). This guarantee would have made the expedition equally attractive to all Catholic Christians of Europe. So far as motivations can be established, the same incentives drew women as men: remission of confessed sins, the desire to visit the holy places, to imitate Christ and support the Christians of the East, in addition to a host of other less spiritual motives such as dynastic connections (Geldsetzer 2003: 45–67).

Pope Urban II advised that men should have their wives' consent before undertaking the crusade, but crusade preachers quickly saw the danger that men would allow their wives to hold them back from taking the cross. Gerald of Wales, recording Archbishop Baldwin of Canterbury's preaching mission in Wales before the Third Crusade, recalled that one man had refused to ask for his wife's consent because the crusade was men's business. Yet he also recorded cases of men who had been dissuaded from taking the cross by their wives – or at least claimed that their wives had dissuaded them as an excuse for not fulfilling their vow – and a woman who accidently smothered her baby in her sleep after preventing her husband from taking the cross (Edbury 1996a).

Despite such claims by contemporary preachers that women held back their husbands and sons from joining the crusade, much of the historical evidence is the other way. Jonathan Riley-Smith (1991) demonstrated that involvement of noble French families in the Second Crusade was connected through the female line, while James Powell (1992) showed how the women of Genoa promoted the Fifth Crusade. When a prominent woman took the cross, as did Queen Isabella of England in 1313, it would encourage wide recruitment and donation of resources, even if (as in Isabella's case) she never set out on crusade (Guard 2013: 139). A near-contemporary narrative of the Third Crusade, the *Itinerarium peregrinorum*, records women encouraging their menfolk to participate and regretting that they could not join the crusade themselves 'because of the weakness of their sex' (p. 48). The contemporary Muslim historian Ibn al-Athīr recorded a conversation he had with a Christian prisoner who told him that although he was his mother's only son, she had sold the family home in order to equip him for the Third Crusade, and had sent him to recover Jerusalem (Nicholson 1997: 339).

Women played a role in organising crusades as well as encouraging recruitment. In 1301 Pope Boniface VIII endorsed a project by a group of Genoese noblewomen to sponsor a crusading expedition. They selected a leader, the famous Genoese admiral Benedetto Zaccaria, and planned to join the crusade. The pope noted 'that the women were venturing where the men had refused to go', but like many crusade plans of this time it came to nothing (Luttrell 1990: 187).

Later in the fourteenth century, Catherine of Siena, mystic and writer, promoted the concept of a crusade against the infidel, to be made up of both men and women. In 1372 a Tuscan hermit wrote that he had heard that a group of pious young men and women wished to go overseas – a euphemism for going on crusade; by 1374 Catherine of Siena had asked the pope for permission to go on pilgrimage to Jerusalem with a group of holy women, and wrote of her intended journey as if she envisaged it as a crusade; in 1375 she wrote about a crusade against the Turks. But her plans came to nothing (Luttrell 1990: 187; Maier 2004: 78–81).

WOMEN IN CRUSADE CAMPAIGNS

As Christoph Maier has pointed out, although most women who were involved in crusade campaigns were not formally called *crucesignatae*, the same is true for most men in crusade armies, especially before the start of the thirteenth century (2004: 69–70). James Brundage (1969) has shown that, despite Purcell's arguments to the contrary, medieval canon lawyers did acknowledge that women's crusading vows were valid. Having said this, women who took part in crusades did not normally fight.

Noblewomen who accompanied the First Crusade travelled with their husbands, brothers and other male relatives. Conor Kostick points out that they 'were brought to generate families should the conquest be successful' (2008: 278). That said, only one of the leaders of the crusade, Raymond of St Gilles, was accompanied by wife, Elvira of Castile. Alan V. Murray (2012: 256) suggests that as Raymond had passed his estates to his son Bertrand, he intended to 'found a new principality for himself in the East'.

Noblewomen and queens also accompanied their husbands on later crusades: Eleanor of Aquitaine accompanied King Louis VII of France on the Second Crusade, while Richard I of England was accompanied from Sicily by his widowed sister Joanna and his wife-to-be Berengaria of Navarre. In 1248–54, Margaret of Provence accompanied her husband, King Louis IX of France, on crusade to Egypt; in 1271 Eleanor of Castile accompanied her husband the Lord Edward, soon to be King Edward I of England, on his crusade to the Holy Land. For the majority of these cases, men and women travelled together to seek the blessing of the pilgrimage, but Richard I also needed his sister's dowry to finance his campaign. Queens also had a role in diplomacy: Eleanor of Aquitaine and the German-born Empress Bertha communicated by letter, and Emperor Manuel I Komnenos tried to arrange a Greek marriage through her for one of the ladies accompanying the French army (Martindale 2004). According to Muslim accounts, Richard I used the possibility of marriage between Saladin's brother al-Adil and his sister Joanna as a bargaining tool with Saladin (Luttrell 1990: 185–6). When King Louis IX was captured during his campaign in Egypt, his wife Margaret directed the defence of Damietta from her childbed (Joinville 1963: 262–3).

Presumably many women of lesser status also took part in these crusades with their families, for the crusade was a pilgrimage as well as a holy war and therefore participation was open to all. Yet Catholic clerical writers depicted women participants in crusades as a source of sexual pollution and an encouragement to sin – as the crusade was a spiritual undertaking, it was essential that participants avoid sex during the campaign (Brundage 1985; Holt 2008). Women should therefore not take part in crusades, should be strictly segregated from men during the expedition, or at least should be respectably married and under male control. Alan V. Murray has pointed out that in fact most of the single women on crusade were not prostitutes but women whose male protectors, whether husbands, fathers or employers, had died during the campaign: many would have been domestic servants, members of crusaders' households. The common crusaders were concerned to support these women when they were left without protection or employment (Murray 2012).

Western contemporary writers recording crusades also depicted the non-noblewomen in crusading armies providing a military support role during the expedition, supplying food, bringing water to the warriors during battles, helping with manual labour such as filling in ditches, and giving encouragement and advice (Powell 1992: 300; Lambert 2001: 8; Maier 2004: 67). They also killed Muslim prisoners (*Itinerarium peregrinorum* nd: 89). The popular story that Eleanor Castile sucked poison from her husband Edward I's wound following an assassination attempt during his crusade is no more than a story, but reflects the traditional caring role of women, and Eleanor's reputation as a devoted wife (Parsons 2004).

Even non-combatant women were in conditions of considerable danger during a crusade campaign. Albert of Aachen's First Crusade story of the beautiful woman captured at the siege of Antioch while playing dice in an orchard outside the city has a moralising function but expresses the constant danger of war: the woman and her companion the archdeacon were captured and killed because they failed to keep a good look-out or set an effective armed guard (Kostick 2008: 277). Ambroise and the *Itinerarium peregrinorum* recount the death of a woman engaged in filling in the ditch defences of the city of Acre (Ambroise 2011: 2:83; *Itinerarium peregrinorum* nd: 106). An account of the Fifth Crusade mentions women present during one battle outside the city of Damietta, on the banks of the river Nile, 19 August 1219: 'By the waterside were the Romans and women who carried fresh water for the infantry to drink. The Bedouins, who were above the river, charged them and killed them' (*Fragmentum de captione Damiatæ* nd: 187).

Western crusade chroniclers depicted Muslim women in various roles during these campaigns. Like Christian women, they could give sound advice to their menfolk (Hodgson 2001).

Abbot Guibert of Nogent, who was not an eye-witness of the First Crusade, imagined exotically dressed Saracen women in the Muslim camp, carrying quivers full of arrows, who he wrote seemed to have come 'not to fight but to reproduce' but who later ran away, abandoning their children (Lambert 2001: 8–9). Christian writers in Western Europe imagined Muslim women to be beautiful and well-educated, ready to be impressed by and to marry doughty Christian warriors. The reality was rather different, as Usama ibn Munqidh describes the suicide of a young Muslim woman who was captured by a Frankish knight (Nicholson 2013: 109–10). The continuator of William of Tyre recounted that the sergeants in the King Guy of Jerusalem's army, on their way to relieve the fortress at Tiberias in early July 1187, captured a Saracen sorceress who said she had been employed by Saladin to curse the Christian army. The Christians killed her and then burned her body, but the continuator comments 'it was indeed true that few knights escaped [from the battle of Hattin] and avoided being killed or taken', suggesting that Muslim magic could not be easily nullified (Edbury 1996b: 40). This story reflects the Western European belief that the Muslims, as 'other', had magical knowledge; but also reflects the actual Arab knowledge of science that had become known to the Catholic West since the capture of the city of Toledo in 1085, with its extensive collection of Greek and Arabic scientific texts. In contrast to these highly imaginative Western depictions, contemporary Islamic sources indicate that Muslim women were prepared to fight Christians or assist Muslim warriors in defence of home and family, but they did not become involved in military campaigns (Nicholson 1997: 341).

COMBATANTS

Saladin's secretary 'Imād al-Dīn al-Isfahani echoed the Christian clerical image of crusading women as a source of sexual pollution, writing of Christian prostitutes taking the cross and coming to the siege of Acre in 1189 to provide sexual services for the crusaders. But he also described women bringing supplies and merchandise to the siege, and depicted old women stirring up the crusaders to fight. He and the *qadi* Bahā al-Dīn ibn Shaddad gave the Christian women active military roles too, depicting a Christian woman using a bow against Muslim soldiers and Christian women fighting in the field against Muslims (Nicholson 1997: 337–9). The Catholic Christians writers make no mention of women fighting. If women on this crusade were stepping out of their normal sphere, it is strange that Christian writers did not blame the failure of the Third Crusade on female misbehaviour: one of the contemporary reasons given for the failure of the Second Crusade was the presence of Eleanor of Aquitaine, wife of King Louis VII of France, who was accused of sexual misbehaviour with her cousin Prince Raymond of Antioch (Holt 2008: 454, 465–6; Geldsetzer 2003: 107–12). The Muslim commentators, however, set out to depict their Christian enemies as morally corrupt barbarians who were incapable of fulfilling proper manly functions (such as defending their women folk) and whose society was cursed by God. Their depiction of Christian women fighting on the battlefield would have formed part of this image of the morally corrupt enemy heading for destruction (Nicholson 1997: 340–2, 348).

In contrast, the women in power in the crusader states would have acted as military leaders, even though they did not fight in the field in person. As fief holders, military service was their duty, although their feudal lord would normally expect an heiress to marry and for her husband to perform the military service due (Edbury 2004: 286). However, if circumstances demanded, a woman holding a lordship could take part in military action herself. Queen

Melisende defended her kingdom against her son Baldwin III when he rebelled against her (Newman 2014: 211–12). Queens Sybil and Isabel of Jerusalem, cousins of King Richard I of England, commanded the fortified cities of Jerusalem and Tyre respectively against Sultan Saladin's forces; in July 1187 Lady Eschiva of Tiberias commanded the defence of her castle of Tiberias against Saladin's siege (*Itinerarium peregrinorum* nd: 38, 312–13; Edbury 1996b: 37, 38, 48). But even these high-status women never fought on the battlefield; they commanded, but the contemporary sources do not record that they bore arms.

One Muslim noblewoman directed military forces against crusaders, although she did not fight herself. Shajar or Shajarat al-Durr (d. 1257) (Duncan 2000). Originally a Turkish slave, from 1240 she was concubine of al-Ṣāliḥ Ayyūb, Ayyūbid sultan of Egypt and was promoted to being his wife. In November 1249, while King Louis IX of France's first crusade was attacking Egypt, the sultan fell ill and died. According to the Arab historian al-Maqrīzī, writing nearly two centuries later, Shajar al-Durr called together the emir Fakhr al-Dīn ibn Shaykh al Shuyūkh, commander of her late husband's armies, and Djamāl al-Dīn Moḥzsin, explained that her husband was dead and asked them to keep the death a secret, for fear of demoralising the Muslims and encouraging the invaders. The three worked together to maintain government until the heir, al-Malik al-Muʿaẓẓam Tūrān-Shāh Ghiyath al-Dīn, could arrive from Ḥiṣn Kaīfā (now Hasankeyf in south-eastern Turkey). Shajar persuaded the emirs and government officials to swear to acknowledge Tūrān-Shāh as heir.

The crusaders, who had already captured the important port of Damietta, heard rumours of the sultan's death and advanced towards Cairo. Fakhr al-Dīn led the Muslim defence. After a series of battles, on 8 February 1250 the crusaders were defeated at Manṣūra and forced to withdraw, but Fakhr al-Dīn himself was killed. Shajar al-Durr continued to conduct affairs of state in the name of her dead husband until Tūrān-Shāh arrived at Cairo and was proclaimed sultan. The crusaders, meanwhile, began to retreat, but were surrounded by Muslim troops and forced to surrender. Many were executed, but the leaders, including King Louis himself, were held for ransom. Having dealt with this danger, Tūrān-Shāh demanded that Shajar al-Durr hand over the dead sultan's treasure to him. Shajar al-Durr denied having the treasure and appealed to her late husband's mamluks for aid. They murdered Tūrān-Shāh, and made Shajar al-Durr sultana.

However, the Syrian emirs would not acknowledge Shajar al-Durr as ruler of Egypt and threatened to invade Egypt, so the Mamluks appointed a military commander to rule jointly with Shajar; she then abdicated. Shajar came into the public sphere only because she was acting on behalf of a man, her late husband, and her authority lasted only until a male replacement was found.

PILGRIMS AND CRUSADERS

During the crusades, women continued to visit the Holy Land as pilgrims and might take the cross as a symbol of their intention to travel to Jerusalem. The English royal clerk Roger of Howden, an eyewitness of the Third Crusade, noted in his 'Chronicle' that when King Béla III of Hungary died (1196) his wife Margaret, sister of King Philip of France and former queen of England as wife of Henry the young king, took the cross for the journey to Jerusalem, *accepit crucem Jerosolimitanae profectionis*, and remained in the land of Jerusalem at Acre in the Lord's service until the end of her life. So she was a *crucesignata*, a crusader; but there is no evidence that she took part in warfare when she reached the Holy Land (Nicholson 1997: 337).

Yet women who were in the Holy Land as pilgrims during crusades did become involved in the military action. Perhaps the best-known example is that of Margaret of Beverley, whose life was recorded by her younger brother Thomas of Froidmont. Margaret was in Jerusalem at the time of Saladin's siege of 1187, and assisted in the defence of the city by bringing water to the warriors. She was made a prisoner after the fall of the city and went through many sufferings before she was able to return to Europe, where she became a nun. Thomas's spiritual biography of his sister remains within the traditional narrative of women's involvement in warfare; she acts in a supportive role and suffers a living martyrdom through imprisonment and slavery (Luttrell 1990: 185; Maier 2004: 64–7).

Another pilgrim saint depicted being caught up in events in the Holy Land just before the Third Crusade is St Hildegund, who joined the Cistercian abbey of Schönau as a monk, died during her first year there on 20 April 1188, and was discovered after her death to have been a woman. Her biographers recorded that following her mother's death her father took her on pilgrimage to Jerusalem but died *en route*. According to an account written by one of her fellow novices, Hildegund's father had dressed her as a boy in order to travel more safely, *ut sic securior iens*, and given her the name of Joseph. 'Joseph' arrived in Jerusalem and visited Jerusalem and the Holy Sepulchre. Destitute and without support, she did not know where to turn, but a pious man helped her and gave her food. She stayed in Jerusalem for a year in the Templars' house, visiting the Holy Places, before returning to Europe with an old friend and relative of her father. Her male biographers praised her virtue, seeing her male disguise as a sign of spiritual strength (Hotchkiss 2012: 36, 39; *Acta Sanctorum April II* 1865: 781). However, they do not state that Hildegund ever fought with arms while she was staying with the Templars.

For both of these women, their suffering in the Holy Land allowed them to share in Christ's sufferings even though contemporary culture did not permit them to take part in military combat to defend Christians; but sometimes female pilgrims were depicted as taking part in combat. Anthony Luttrell has noted that 'in 1350 an English woman pilgrim was reputed, presumably with considerable exaggeration, single-handedly to have killed more than a thousand Turkish captives at Rhodes'. The event was recorded by the traveller Ludolph von Sudheim, who admitted that that story was only rumour (Luttrell 1990: 187). Over a hundred years later, Lucy, an English sister of the Trinitarian Order, was reported to have fought in the 1480 defence of Rhodes against the Ottoman Turks (Guard 2013: 140). Such accounts demonstrated the power of even weak Christian women over their Muslim enemies.

WOMEN LIVING IN CRUSADING REGIONS

According to both Catholic Christian and Islamic cultural ideals, women should have been excluded from fighting in crusades, and should have been regarded as inviolate non-combatants. Heath Dillard has noted an account in the anonymous *Chronica Adefonsi Imperatoris* which was predicated on this assumption:

> One reliable anonymous narrative describes the shrewd command of the Empress Berengaria at Toledo in 1139 when the garrison was caught unawares and ill-defended in the absence of Alfonso VII. She successfully averted a Muslim attack by concealing her few soldiers and shaming the besiegers' vanity, asking them what honour they could hope to win by taking the city from a woman. To make her point, she retired with her

ladies to the summit of the castle, and the Muslims, beholding these non-combatants deliberately arrayed in finery and playing musical instruments, withdrew from the field.

(Dillard 1984: 15)

But in practice, women were not normally spared the violence of holy war. Margaret of Beverley has already been mentioned as a female pilgrim who was captured and enslaved during Saladin's campaigns which resulted in the Third Crusade. Almost two centuries later in January 1366 the Englishwoman Isolda Parewastrell informed Pope Urban V that she had been imprisoned and tortured while she was on pilgrimage to the Holy Land: perhaps she was caught up in the reprisals against Christians following King Peter I of Cyprus's attack on Alexandria in October 1365 (Luttrell 1990: 189). In the first decades of the thirteenth century, the crusaders taking part in the Albigensian Crusade dealt with women just as they dealt with men, hacking them to pieces. Most notorious was the killing of the noblewoman Girauda of Lavaur, who was thrown into a well and then covered in stones (Barber 2001: 48; Shirley 1996: 41). Women and young girls on both sides were captured in the course of crusades; sometimes they were killed, but often they were enslaved, and contemporary writers assumed that they would be sexually abused (Friedman 2001).

It is therefore no surprise that women living in crusading regions expected and were expected to take part in military activity. According to the author of the *Chanson de la croisade albigeois*, women brought about the death of the leader of the crusade, Simon de Montfort, on 25 June 1218. He was besieging the city of Toulouse when he was killed by a stone hurled by a catapult operated by ladies, girls and married women (Shirley 1996: 172). According to this writer, Montfort's actions were so abhorrent to God that He permitted weak and feeble women to kill him – a shameful death for such a renowned warrior.

The Catalan writer Ramon Muntaner, writing in the early fourteenth century, recorded an incident during the French crusade against Aragon in 1285. Na Mercadera, a woman of Peralada in Aragon, went out of her house armed with a lance and shield so that she could defend herself if necessary against the French crusaders, who were besieging the town. She encountered a French knight, whom she captured (Nicholson 1997: 343–4). Muntaner used this story to demonstrate God's support for the Catalans, for even their weak women could defeat the supposedly superior French knights.

Moving forward to the early fifteenth century: on 14 June 1419 the people of Prague, including many women, held off a fierce attack by the army of King Sigismund, king of Hungary and heir to Bohemia, during the first crusade against the Hussites. Prague had declared for the Hussite heresy; Sigismund and his army were determined to enforce orthodox Roman Catholicism. A Czech contemporary, Lawrence of Březová, described the crusaders' attack:

They strongly attacked the … wooden bulwark. They succeeded in crossing the moat, and they took the old watchtower on top of the vineyards. And when they tried to scale the wall erected from earth and stone, two women and one girl together with about twenty-six men who still held the bulwark defended themselves manfully, hurling stones and lances, for they had neither arrows nor guns. And one of the two women, though she was without armour, surpassed in spirit all men, as she did not want to yield one step. Before Antichrist, so she said, no faithful Christian must ever retreat! And thus, fighting with supreme courage, she was killed and gave up her spirit.

(Heymann 1955: 138)

A letter from the margrave of Meissen claimed that 156 Hussite women had been captured during this encounter, wearing men's clothes and armed (Heymann 1955: 138). This was a crucial day in the formation of the Czech nation: it was the battle which saved Prague and the Hussite faith from German and Catholic invasion. For the Czech writer, the presence of courageous women among the fighters underlined the rightness of the Czech cause. For the Germans, the presence of women dressed and armed as men among the enemy's forces demonstrated their otherness.

The above instances all occurred in crusades in which Christians fought Christians, but Rasa Mazeika has shown that the same situation pertained in the regions where the Teutonic Order was militarily active against non-Christians from the 1230s onwards, in Prussia, Livonia and Lithuania. The chronicler Peter von Dusburg and others described women fighting alongside men against the pagans, and the pagan women encouraging their menfolk to fight against the Christians. A Christian woman attacked by a pagan man and chased into a swamp turned on him and drowned him in the mud; captive Christian women also turned on their Lithuanian captors and killed them, through the power of God. Like the Muslim women who fall in love with Christian heroes in the Old French epics of the crusade, an Estonian woman was depicted helping two brothers of the Teutonic Order who had been taken captive by her fellow pagans (Mazeika 1998). The situation was the same in the eastern Mediterranean, where a Greek woman was recorded to have died as a martyr fighting at Rhodes against the Turks in the siege of 1522: she was apparently the partner of a Hospitaller officer (Vertot 1726: 3:342–3).

As Mazeika explains apropos of the crusades in the Baltic region, 'Women in heaven and on earth were not excused from participation in battle … there could be … no bystanders in a war seen as an elemental struggle between war and demons', and in such circumstances God would give even weak women strength to fight like men (Mazeika, 1998: 247). These heroic tales, however, must conceal many instances where women suffered death, torture and enslavement, the invariable fate of non-combatants in wartime.

SUPPORTING THE CRUSADE

Although women did not normally fight on crusade campaigns, noblewomen could use their wealth to support the defence of Christendom. Pietro Collivaccino, a notary of the Roman curia under Pope Innocent III who finished his work on canon law in 1209, wrote that a woman should normally redeem her crusading vow by paying a sum of money so that a man could go in her place, unless she was wealthy and would be accompanied by a retinue of soldiers (Brundage 1969: 77). Pope Innocent III himself also stated that a wealthy woman could lead warriors to the East at her own expense (Rousseau 2001: 39). Women certainly did finance campaigns. For example, in 1288 Countess Alice of Blois travelled to the city of Acre in Palestine with a large military force and financed the construction of a tower to defend against Muslim attack (*Annales de Terre Sainte* nd: 459–60).

Obviously, women were better able to give such support to crusades if they had control of resources of their own. At Genoa in the second decade of the thirteenth century, the crusade preacher Jacques de Vitry found that the wealthy and noble women were eager to take the cross. James Powell has pointed out that Genoese women 'wielded considerable economic power', making commercial contracts, investing in trade, 'active in real estate and in the borrowing and lending of money' (1992: 296–7). Of the surviving wills from

Genoa from the period of the Fifth Crusade, fifteen contain legacies for the crusade; ten of these were the wills of women (1992: 296).

In effect, every wife who remained at home running the family estates or business while her husband was on crusade was supporting the crusade effort (Maier 2004: 75–6). In theory, the crusaders' wives, children and possessions were under the protection of the Church during their absence (Muldoon 2005: 46). But in practice this did not always come about. During a crusader's absence, his wife and daughters were vulnerable to force from those with land claims against them: both physical force and legal attack through the courts. It was not always clear whether a crusader who had not returned was dead or captured, and hence the status of his wife and heirs remained uncertain. The widow of a crusader might have to resort to the law courts to obtain her dower lands. Women could be pressured to sell their own dowry and dower lands to support their husband's crusade, which would leave them in financial difficulties in the future, unable to pay their absent husband's debts or support themselves and their children (Brundage 1967a, 1967b; Tyerman 1988: 208–211).

In addition to financial aid, women gave prayer support to this spiritual undertaking. In 1212, in preparation for King Alfonso of Castile's expedition against the Muslims in Spain, Pope Innocent III commanded that there should be a liturgical procession in which men and women formed separate contingents and prayed to God for his support for the campaign. His encyclical for the Fifth Crusade, *Quia Maior* (1213), ordered monthly liturgical processions on the same lines, in which men and women were to pray for God to liberate the Holy Land from the Muslims (Rousseau 2001: 36). Men and women would take part in daily prayers at mass and almsgiving for the crusade (Rousseau 2001: 37).

Another means of supporting the Catholic Christian cause was to support the military religious orders which developed in the Holy Land and the West, dedicated to the care of Christian pilgrims and defence of Christendom. Women gave valuable donations and patronage to these institutions. They could also become members or associates. Although they did not fight, they provided a support role of prayer and sometimes nursing care (Luttrell and Nicholson, 2006; Born, 2012).

As those who were left behind, women were also involved in the commemoration of crusaders. Idonea de Camville and Countess Ela of Salisbury, respectively wife and mother of William Longespee, English hero of King Louis IX's first crusade who perished at the Battle of Manṣūra in February 1250, may have instigated the references to William's deeds in historical records created at the abbeys of Barlings and Lacock (Lloyd 1992: 86–87).

Natasha Hodgson has noted that in the early fourteenth century the crusade propagandist Pierre Dubois proposed a new role for women in the effort against Islam. His suggestion was that women should be trained in theology and logic and then married to Eastern Christians and Muslims, so that they could convert their husbands through reasoned argument. Alternatively, they could be educated in the medical care of women's ailments and thereby they would influence non-Christians to convert (Hodgson 2006: 1290). Such suggestions reflected the fictional narratives of Muslim heroes converting to Christianity for love of Christian women (Kangas 2013: 125–6). Like King Richard I's sister Joanna who was reported to have refused to marry Saladin's brother al-Adil, it is unlikely that any western European Christian noblewoman would have been willing to give up her culture and society in this way, even for the good of Christendom; or that their menfolk would have been willing to allow them to do so. That said, Catholics did intermarry with Armenian

Christians, both parties hoping to secure alliances, gain territory and extend power and influence. This was not always successful: despite these alliances, neither side wished to be ruled by the other (Hodgson 2011).

Certain female Christian saints, including Christ's mother the Blessed Virgin Mary, were the focus of crusaders' special religious devotion. Eric Christiansen has described Mary as a 'warrior goddess' in her role as the patron of the Teutonic Order in its military campaigns in the Baltic, and Rasa Mazeika has pointed out that the priest Henry of Livonia described her as 'a cruel wreaker of vengeance on her enemies' (Christiansen 1997: 222; Mazeika 1998: 244–7). Although elsewhere she was not usually depicted in such a martial setting, nevertheless she was the outstanding female supporter of the crusades. The military religious orders claimed a number of female saints as patrons, probably because they presented valuable spiritual examples of long suffering and martyrdom (Nicholson 2005).

CONCLUSION

It is clear that women were deeply involved in the crusades, as participants and supporters. As James Powell noted, 'The enthusiastic response with which Genoese women greeted Jacques de Vitry's preaching of the crusade demonstrates the degree to which they felt involved in one of the major enterprises of the Latin West' (1992: 296). Women in Catholic Christendom could not fail to be involved in a movement that was so central to their society and culture, but both the form that involvement took and its depiction by contemporary commentators were circumscribed by social convention and expectations. For contemporaries, prayer, finance and commemoration were as valuable in support for the crusade as actual fighting. In contrast, women who lived in the warzone or who were travelling there as pilgrims could not avoid being drawn into the conflict, either as victims or active participants in war. Even female saints were co-opted as supporters of the crusade; a few women tried to initiate crusade expeditions. For most women, however, as for most men, the crusade was an expression of faith which they supported but in which they were not personally involved.

REFERENCES

Acta Sanctorum April II. 1865, Paris and Rome: Victor Palme.
Ambroise. 2011. *A History of the Holy War: Ambroise's* Estoire de la Guerre Sainte, translated from the Old French by Marianne Ailes with Malcolm Barber. Woodbridge: Boydell.
Annales de Terre Sainte. [no date]. In: *Archives de l'Orient Latin,* 2. 1884, repr. 1978.
Barber, Malcolm. 2001. The Albigensian Crusades: Wars Like any Other? In: Balard, Michel, Kedar, Benjamin Z. and Riley-Smith, Jonathan, eds, *Dei Gesta per Francos:* Études *sur les croisades dédiées à Jean Richard; Crusade Studies in Honour of Jean Richard.* Aldershot: Ashgate, 45–5.
Born, Myra. 2012. *Women in the Military Orders of the Crusades.* New York: Palgrave.
Brundage, James A. 1967a. The Crusader's Wife: A Canonistic Quandary. *Studia Gratiana* 12, 425–41.
———. 1967b. The Crusader's Wife Revisited. *Studia Gratiana* 14, 243–51.
———. 1969. *Medieval Canon Law and the Crusader.* Madison: University of Wisconsin Press.
Brundage, James A. 1985. Prostitution, Miscegenation and Sexual Purity in the First Crusade. In: Edbury, Peter, ed., *Crusade and Settlement.* Cardiff, UK: University College Cardiff Press, 57–65.
Christiansen, Eric. 1997. *The Northern Crusades: The Baltic and the Catholic Frontier 1100–1525.* New edition. London: Penguin.

Cowdrey, H. E. J. 1977. The Mahdia Campaign of 1087. *English Historical Review* 92 (1), 1–29.

Dillard, Heath. 1984. *Daughters of the Reconquest*. Cambridge: Cambridge University Press.

Duncan, David J. 2000. Scholarly Views of Shajarat al-Durr: A Need for Consensus. *Arab Studies Quarterly* 22 (1), 51–69.

Edbury, Peter W. 1996a. Preaching the Crusade in Wales. In: Haverkamp, Alfred and Vollrath, Hanna, eds, *England and Germany in the Middle Ages*. The German Historical Institute. London: Oxford University Press, 221–33.

———. 1996b. *The Conquest of Jerusalem and the Third Crusade: Sources in Translation*. Aldershot: Ashgate.

———. 2004. Women and the Customs of the High Court of Jerusalem according to John of Ibelin. In: Coulon, Damien, Otten-Froux, Catherine, Pagès, Paul and Valérian, Dominque, eds, *Chemins d'outre mer*. Études *d'histoire sur la Méditerranée medieval offertes à Michel Balard*. Paris: Publications de la Sorbonne, 285–92.

Fragmentum de captione Damiatæ [no date]. In: Röhricht, Reinhold, ed., *Quinti Belli Sacri Scriptores Minores*. Geneva: J.-G. Fick.

Friedman, Yvonne. 2001. Captivity and Ransom: The Experience of Women. In: Edgington Susan B. and Lambert, Sarah, eds, *Gendering the Crusades*. Cardiff, UK: University of Wales Press, 121–39.

Geldsetzer, Sabine. 2003. *Frauen auf Kreuzzügen*. Darmstadt: Wissenschaftliche Buchgesellschaft.

Gerish, Deborah. 2005. Gender Theory. In: Nicholson, Helen J., ed, *Palgrave Advances in the Crusades*. Basingstoke: Palgrave Macmillan, 130–47.

Guard, Timothy. 2013. *Chivalry, Kingship and Crusade: The English Experience in the Fourteenth Century*. Woodbridge: Boydell Press.

Hamilton, Bernard. 1978. Women in the Crusader States: The Queens of Jerusalem (1100–1190. In: Baker, Derek, ed., *Medieval Women*. Oxford: Blackwell, 143–74.

Hay, David J. 2008. *The Military Leadership of Matilda of Canossa, 1046–1115*. Manchester: Manchester University Press.

Heymann, Frederick G. 1955. *John Žižka and the Hussite Revolution*. Princeton, NJ: Princeton University Press.

Hodgson, Natasha. 2001. The Role of Kerbogha's Mother in the *Gesta Francorum* and Select Chronicles of the First Crusade. In: Edgington, Susan and Lambert, Sarah, eds, *Gendering the Crusades*. Cardiff, UK: University of Wales Press, 162–76.

———. 2005. Women and Nobility in the Narrative Sources for the Crusades and the Latin East. *Al-Masaq; Islam and the Medieval Mediterranean* 17 (1), 61–85.

———. 2006. Women and Crusade. In: Murray, A.V., ed., *The Encyclopaedia of the Crusades*. Santa Barbara: ABC-Clio, 1285–91.

———. 2007. *Women, Crusading and the Holy Land in Historical Narrative*. Woodbridge: Boydell Press.

———. 2011. Conflict and Cohabitation: Marriage and Diplomacy between Latins and Cilician Armenians, c. 1097–1253. In: Kostick, Conor, ed., *The Crusades and the Near East: Cultural Histories*. Abingdon: Routledge, 83–106.

Holt, Andrew. 2008. Feminine Sexuality and the Crusades: Clerical Opposition to Women as a Strategy for Crusading Success. In: Classen, Albrecht, ed., *Sexuality in the Middle Ages and Early Modern Times: New Approaches to a Fundamental Cultural-Historical and Literary-Anthropological Theme*. Berlin: De Gruyter, 449–69.

Hotchkiss, Valerie R. 2012. *Clothes make the Man: Female Cross Dressing in Medieval Europe*. New York: Routledge.

Itinerarium peregrinorum et gesta regis Ricardi. [no date]. Translated by Helen Nicholson, 1997, as *Chronicle of the Third Crusade*. Aldershot: Ashgate.

Joinville, Jean de. 1963. *The Life of Saint Louis*. In: Joinville, J. de and Villehardouin, G. de, *Chronicles of the Crusades*. Translated from the French by M. R. B. Shaw. Harmondsworth: Penguin.

Kangas, Sini. 2013. First in Prowess and Faith. The Great Encounter in Twelfth-Century Crusader Narratives. In: Jensen, Kurt Villads, Salonen, Kirsi and Vogt, Helle, eds, *Cultural Encounters during the Crusades*. Odense: University Press of Southern Denmark, 119–34.

Kedar, Benjamin Z. 1972. The Passenger List of a Crusader Ship, 1250: Towards the Popular Element on the Seventh Crusade. *Studi Medievali* ser. 3 (13), 269–79.

Kostick, Conor. 2008. *The Social Structure of the First Crusade*. Leiden: Brill.

Lambert, Sarah. 2001. Crusading or Spinning. In: Edgington, Susan and Lambert, Sarah, eds, *Gendering the Crusades*. Cardiff: University of Wales Press, 1–15.

Lloyd, Simon. 1992. William Longespee II: The Making of an English Crusading Hero. Part II. *Nottingham Medieval Studies* 36, 79–125.

Luttrell, Anthony. 1990. Englishwomen as Pilgrims to Jerusalem: Isolda Parewastrell, 1365. In: Holloway, Julia Bolton, Bechtold, Joan and Wright, Constance S., ed., *Equally in God's Image: Women in the Middle Ages*. New York: Peter Lang, 184–97.

Luttrell, Anthony and Nicholson, Helen J., eds. 2006. *Hospitaller Women in the Middle Ages*. Aldershot, Hants and Burlington, VT: Ashgate.

Maier, Christoph T. 2004. The Roles of Women in the Crusade Movement: A Survey. *Journal of Medieval History* 30, 61–82.

Martindale, Jane. 2004. Eleanor, *suo jure* duchess of Aquitaine (*c*.1122–1204). In: Matthew, H. C. G. and Harrison, Brian, eds, *Oxford Dictionary of National Biography*. Oxford: Oxford University Press. Online edn. ed. Lawrence Goldman.

Mazeika, Rasa. 1998. 'Nowhere was the Fragility of Their Sex Apparent': Women Warriors in the Baltic Crusade Chronicles. In: Murray, Alan V., ed., *From Clermont to Jerusalem: The Crusades and Crusader Societies*. Turnhout: Brepols, 229–48.

Muldoon, James. 2005. Crusading and Canon Law. In: Nicholson, Helen J., ed., *Palgrave Advances in the Crusades*. Basingstoke: Palgrave Macmillan, 37–57.

Murray, Alan V. 2012. Sex, Death and the Problem of Single Women in the Armies of the First Crusade. In: Gertwagen, Ruthy and Jeffreys, Elizabeth, eds, *Shipping, Trade and Crusade in the Medieval Mediterranean: Studies in Honour of John Pryor*. Farnham: Ashgate, 255–70.

Newman, Sharan. 2014. *Defending the City of God: A Medieval Queen, the First Crusade, and the Quest for Peace in Jerusalem*. New York: Palgrave Macmillan.

Nicholson, Helen. 1997. Women on the Third Crusade. *Journal of Medieval History* 23, 335–49.

———. 2004. 'La roine preude femme et bonne dame': Queen Sybil of Jerusalem (1186–1190) in History and Legend, 1186–1300. *The Haskins Society Journal* 15, 110–24.

———. 2005. Saints Venerated in the Military Orders. In: Sarnowsky, Jürgen and Czaja, Roman, eds, *Selbstbild und Selbstverständnis der geistlichen Ritterorden*, Ordines Militares: Colloquia Torunensia Historica XII. Toruń: Uniwersytetu Mikołaja Kopernika, 91–113.

———. 2013. The Hero Meets his Match. Cultural Encounters in Narratives of Wars against Muslims. In: Jensen, Kurt Villads, Salonen, Kirsi and Vogt, Helle, eds, *Cultural Encounters during the Crusades*. Odense: University Press of Southern Denmark, 105–18.

Parsons, John Carmi. 2004. Eleanor [Eleanor of Castile] (1241–1290). In: Matthew, H. C. G. and Harrison, Brian, eds, *Oxford Dictionary of National Biography*. Oxford: Oxford University Press. Online edn. ed. Lawrence Goldman.

Powell, James M. 1992. The Role of Women on the Fifth Crusade. In: Kedar, Benjamin Z., ed., *The Horns of Hattin*. Jerusalem: Yad Izhak Ben-Zvi Institute, 294–301.

Purcell, Maureen. 1979. Women Crusaders, a Temporary Canonical Aberration? In: Frappell, L. O., ed., *Principalities, Power and Estates: Studies in Medieval and Early Modern Government and Society*. Adelaide: University Union Press, 57–67.

Riley-Smith, Jonathan. 1991. Family Tradition and Participation in the Second Crusade. In: Gervers, Michael, ed., *The Second Crusade and the Cistercians*. New York: Palgrave Macmillan, 101–08.

Riley-Smith, Jonathan. 1997. *The First Crusaders (1095–1131)*. Cambridge: Cambridge University Press.

Rousseau, Constance M. 2001. Home Front and Battlefield: The Gendering of Papal Crusading Policy (1095–1221). In: Edgington Susan B. and Lambert, Sarah, eds, *Gendering the Crusades*. Cardiff, UK: University of Wales Press, 31–44.

Shirley, Janet. 1996. *The Song of the Cathar Wars: A History of the Albigensian Crusade*. Aldershot: Ashgate.

Tyerman, Christopher. 1988. *England and the Crusades, 1095–1588*. Chicago: University of Chicago Press.

Vertot, L'Abbé René Aubert de. 1726. *Histoire des Chevaliers Hospitaliers de S. Jean de Jerusalem, appellez depuis Chevaliers de Rhodes, et aujourd'hui Chevaliers de Malthe*. Paris: Rollin, Quillau and Desaint.

CHAPTER FOUR

'CRUSADING' WARFARE IN THE TWELFTH CENTURY

——•◆•——

John France

Since the crusades were wars in God's name, pious acts for which salvation could be obtained not by the traditional good deeds but by slaughter, the warfare of the era has exercised enormous interest. It has also produced a great deal of confusion because all Western warfare in the Eastern Mediterranean in the twelfth and thirteenth centuries has been characterised as crusading. Since crusades faced a Muslim reaction in the form of *jihad*, these have been seen as wars of religious fanaticism, and indeed an observation by William of Tyre has often been taken as proof of that:

> War is waged differently and less vigorously between men who hold the same law and faith. For even if no other cause for hatred exists, the fact that the combatants do not share the same articles of faith is sufficient reason for constant quarrelling and enmity.[1]

It is not hard to find examples of fanaticism in the course of the crusades. Antioch was besieged by the First Crusade for eight months, and when they finally broke in on the night of 2 June 1098, according to Albert of Aachen they massacred as many as 10,000, including local Christians, which Albert of Aachen justified rather casually as the consequence of fighting in the dark.[2] When they broke into Jerusalem in July 1099, there was an orgy of killing and an eyewitness testified that:

> In the Temple and porch of Solomon, men rode in blood up to their knees and bridle reins.[3]

After the capture of Acre, Saladin delayed in paying the ransom for the garrison who had surrendered on terms and Richard the Lionheart (1189–99) ordered that all 2700 of them should be massacred.[4] In the ensuing fighting, Saladin in turn ordered that all prisoners should be killed.[5] These are famous and notable occasions, but it should be noted that brutality and massacre were far more pronounced than in the West. In the fighting between Antioch and Aleppo in the first third of the twelfth century, prisoners were routinely killed, as Kemal ad-Din makes clear.[6]

68

But such brutality was actually only episodic, even when Western crusades were present in the East. Saladin's forces were defeated by Richard's crusaders at the Battle of Arsuf, after which it became obvious that the war would be protracted, and exchange of prisoners was once more resumed. In fact in a very rough and ready way both sides respected the laws of war as practised in the Islamic and Christian worlds, though it has to be said that this was very rough and ready and exceptions were very numerous.[7] This convergence was due to a number of factors. On the face of it, Islamic and European societies were very different. European rulers depended on lords who exercised power in their names, but often very independently. Literacy was confined largely to the clergy and it was only slowly that government was systematised, and even then it remained very decentralised. The East had great cities, on a scale unknown to Europeans. Their rulers enjoyed the support of quite complex and literate bureaucracies which collected and accounted for taxes. However, since 1055 the Middle East had been dominated by a steppe people, the Seljuk Turks, whose concept of power was deeply personal. Cities such as Mosul, Damascus, Diyarbakir and Aleppo were ruled by Turkish grandees presiding over the bureaucrats and nominally responsible to the sultan at Baghdad. Both European lords and Turkish magnates attached great importance to redeeming family members and their more notable followers when they were captured in war, it being the case that only people of wealth and importance could escape death or enslavement as a result of captivity.[8]

But there was a more fundamental reason why war to the knife, whether in battle or siege, occurred less often than might be expected. While the rulers of the Islamic cities would impose tax on trade, both societies fundamentally depended on agriculture, which produced only relatively limited surpluses that had to support the magnificence of courts and religious institutions as well as warfare. This had a profound influence on the recruitment of armies. Turkish grandees could usually support a small standing force, the *askar*, but for anything bigger they needed to accumulate wealth. Western lords relied very heavily on agriculture, keeping about them only a limited number of soldiers in their military households; the raising of major forces depended on negotiation with their subordinates and potential allies. For both sides, therefore, warfare had to be episodic. And since an army represented a huge political and financial investment, leaders tended to be risk averse. As a result, truces were a commonplace and warfare was discontinuous, except in relatively rare cases such as the Third Crusade (1189–92). It was simply not possible to maintain the kind of constant murderous warfare seen on the Eastern Front in the Second World War. Of course, the greater a ruler's dominions, the bigger the army he could raise. It has been calculated that by the 1180s Saladin's huge empire had the potential to raise 34,000 mounted men. But such a force could only be concentrated by a great effort and in particular political circumstances. That is, when the magnates of a ruler agreed and there was no other external threat – the greater the empire, the more enemies it had. In 1187 Saladin created an enormous army because political circumstances were favourable, but without the success of Hattin it is doubtful whether he could have done it again, and his resources were soon after deeply stretched by the Third Crusade.

The warfare between Westerners and Turks was in part a clash of contrasting styles, and all the more fascinating because of that. The Turks brought with them into the Middle East a form of warfare developed on the open steppe of Asia. They were primarily horse-archers whose way of life made them highly disciplined warriors. The possession of strings of horses enabled them to move long distances over the steppe lands and to manoeuvre at high speed over periods of time when in contact with their enemies. Such light cavalry could move around clumsier enemies, surrounding them or tempting them to lose formation by feigned retreats. Their strength lay in manoeuvre and sapping the power of their enemies. This style fitted well into the open plains of the Middle East and could be sustained by the easy raising of small horses possible in such areas. It is worth noting that the Middle East to this day is regarded as excellent tank country. The anonymous author of the *Gesta Francorum*, who may himself have been a knight, remarked on the sudden appearance of the enemy which so surprised the army:

> Our men wondered exceedingly whence had arisen so great a multitude of Turks, Arabs, Saracens and others, for almost all the mountains and hills and valleys and all the level places, within and without, were on all sides covered with that excommunicate race.[9]

And Fulcher of Chartres, a priest trapped in the crusader camp, observed acutely the novelty of the enemy's methods:

> Altogether they numbered 360000 fighters all on horses and armed with bows as was their custom. We, on the other hand, had both foot-soldiers and knights. ... The Turks crept up, howling loudly and shooting a shower of arrows. Stunned, and almost dead, and with many wounded, we immediately fled. And it was no wonder, for such warfare was new to us all.[10]

But this form of warfare had a fatal flaw which was picked out by the anonymous author of the *Gesta Francorum* as he later reflected on the course of the battle of Dorylaeum, 1 July 1097:

> Turks, who thought that they would strike terror into the Franks as they had done into the Arabs and Saracens, Armenians, Syrians and Greeks, by the menace of their arrows?
>
> (GF, 21)

At Dorylaeum the crusaders, though surprised, held their formation and crushed the Turks. In the circumstances of the Middle Ages, battle usually had to be settled by close-quarter combat, in which the heavily armoured crusaders had an advantage. This was why Turkish armies tried to have a leavening of more heavily armoured men, and indeed the same author recognised that they did when he later noticed:

> The Agulani numbered 3000; they fear neither spears nor arrows nor any other weapon, for they and their horses are covered all over with plates of iron.
>
> (GF, 49)

The priest Raymond of Aguilers remarked on the same thing when he discussed the make-up of the garrison of Antioch:

> There were, furthermore, in the city two thousand of the best knights, and four or five thousand common knights.
>
> (RA, 41, trans. 127)

It was relatively easy for Islamic armies to recruit horse-archers, either from their native steppe-lands or from the Turcomen tribes who roamed the Middle East, often displacing the Bedouin and semi-nomadic Arab tribes. Such men were brave and able fighters, and they could sometimes prevail against the crusaders either by sheer weight of numbers or by luring them into breaking formation, as they seem to have done in the battle of Harran in 1104.[11] It was perhaps no coincidence that it was the failure of the Latin's light cavalry, their Turcopoles, which played a part in the catastrophic defeat of the army of Antioch at the Field of Blood in 1119.[12]

But light horsemen found it difficult to break down close formations of heavily armoured knights whose horses were protected from arrow fire by surrounding foot soldiers. Thus on occasion the armies of the settlers opted for what Smail called the 'fighting march'.[13] In 1147 the Latins, under Baldwin III of Jerusalem, had marched on Bosra but found Nur ed-Din in great strength, so they formed a column to retreat. In consequence:

> General orders had been given that the bodies of all the dead in the Christian ranks were to be placed upon camels and other pack animals, that the knowledge of the massacre of our forces might not tend to strengthen the enemy. The weak and wounded were also to be placed on beasts of burden so as to give the impression that not a single Christian had been killed or wounded. It was a source of amazement, therefore, to the wiser heads among the enemy that, after such a volley of arrows, such repeated conflicts, such torture of thirst, dust and unbearable heat, not a single dead Christian could be found. This people must indeed, be made of iron, they thought.
>
> (WT, Bk 16: ch. 11)

Such a tactic was only possible against masses of light cavalry who did not close to kill – the reference here to 'such a volley of arrows' is highly significant. The problem for Muslim armies was to amass sufficiently large numbers of the heavily armed and armoured horse-men who could challenge the Latin knights at close quarters. William of Tyre noted the large number of such elite troops in the army of Shirkuh at the battle of Babayn in 1167:

> Shirkuh had twelve thousand Turks, of whom nine thousand wore the breastplate and the other three thousand used only bows and arrows.
>
> (WT, Bk 19: ch. 25)

Again at the battle of Montgisard in 1177, William distinguished 8000 'splendid soldiers', including Saladin's personal bodyguard of 1000, from the remainder of the 26,000 cav-alry.[14] The proportion of this elite, the *tawashi*, seems to have increased, and this marched with an increasing emphasis on heavy equipment for the army in the 1170s and 1180s.[15] They continued to use the bow and were never as heavily armed as the Christian knights who they outnumbered. As Saladin's empire grew, so the numbers of such troops at his disposal grew, enabling him to concentrate large numbers of them in the forces gathered for the great confrontation at Hattin in 1187. Overall, by the time of Saladin, the capacity of Islamic armies for the close-quarter battle had increased enormously, while their capacity for manoeuvre remained very substantial.[16]

When we come to analyse the military methods of the Westerners who invaded the Middle East, we have to distinguish two distinct forms of warfare:

1   The warfare of crusaders from the West in or moving towards the East.
2   The warfare of those who had settled in the East.

It is the case of the present article that in the twelfth century the Latin settlers adapted the Western style of war to the different circumstances of the Middle East. However, in the thirteenth century their armies were usually only a part of Western forces, so that the distinction between them and crusaders proper disappeared. This process was the more rapid because the armies coming from the West became increasingly sophisticated.

In Western Europe the predominant style of war was what I have called 'agro-urban'.[17] Concentrations of power, usually castles in Europe, were supported by arable and pastoral farming. Extensive agriculture left little ground for horse-rearing compared with the steppe and the open plains of the Middle East. As a result armies were composed of masses of foot soldiers and rather small numbers of cavalry. The horsemen were members of the elite. They could afford to raise big horses capable of bearing their owners' equipped with strong heavy armour and fine weapons, and even to equip small numbers of followers. Since political structures were weak and kings had only very limited administrations, much power rested with the most powerful magnates of the realm. So armies came to war in their retinues, and while infantry and cavalry might be separated for the purposes of the campaign, the soldiers would have known only those from their own locality. Such armies were, therefore, incoherent, rather clumsy and slow-moving. Their focus was siege because castles and cities were the lynchpins of their political structure. And because this was complex, the simple business of ravaging, destroying the land to feed yourself and deny the enemy, was the staple of war:

> Destroy your foes and lay waste their country
> By Fire and burning let all be set alight
> That nothing be left for them, either in wood or meadows
> Of which in the morning they could have a meal.[18]

Because of the limits of the economy, armies could not be maintained for long and even most members of the elite were soldiers only part of the time – for the rest they needed to supervise the activities of the agricultural year. So armies were rather incoherent because they were usually kept together only for short periods. Further, since communications were poor, political structures were relatively weak and all armies were in the nature of alliances, raised for a purpose and then dispersed. In this they were not unlike the armies of Islam, though Western rulers could not draw on Turcomen and steppe peoples with their military expertise. Western armies were thus major economic and political investments which rulers were cautious about exposing to the chance hazards of battle.

The result was armies of retinues whose connection to an overall commander was generally weak. For the most part they were engaged in ravaging or defending against it, which meant many small-scale engagements. This fostered amongst the elite an individualistic ethos which valued bravery and comradeship within the group, rather than discipline, an attitude essentially unhelpful to overall command. Because of this and their lumbering style, manoeuvre was not a strong point, and when battle was desired, Western armies sought to go straight to the close-quarter battle. Any major Western army was essentially a collection of retinues, and crusading armies were collections of armies made up of retinues.

The First Crusade, therefore, ushered in a fascinating clash of contrasting military styles. When it came to sieges, the army was competent and able, but the lack of a real command structure put it at risk in field operations. Its people were deeply disconcerted by Turkish tactics at their first contact at the battle of Dorylaeum, but their army was so numerous that, with some good luck, they overcame the Turks of Anatolia. And the crusade leaders were good soldiers who adapted quickly to the challenges of their new situation. At the very end of 1097, a large foraging expedition ran into the army of Duqaq of Damascus who was attempting to raise the siege of Antioch. The presence of a rearguard protected the crusaders from encirclement. At the Lake Battle of 9 February 1098 they appointed Bohemond of Otranto as sole commander and ambushed the army of Ridwan of Aleppo, while by the time of the Battle of Ascalon it was their habit to throw infantry forward to protect their horses from the arrows of their enemies.[19] Above all they learned solidity of formation, which could hold off their more numerous enemies. These adaptations reflected well on the crusader leaders, but there was no means by which such lessons could be passed on to later expeditions. The 'Crusade of 1101' came to grief in Anatolia as did the Second Crusade (1145–49).[20]

But the Latin settlers in the East had to adapt to their new circumstances. Lordship was the basic Western social, political and economic institution which they brought with them. It was natural, therefore, for castles which were estate centres to be built in large numbers, especially as in the early years almost all of the states were open to enemy raiding. In a country lacking in wood, they built in stone, much of it taken from the ancient ruins which studded the Holy Lands. Many of these were not especially strong, but they proved able to innovate when necessary. Belvoir, built 1168–70, was a superb concentric castle in which the outer wall could be supported by the inner, while the defences of both were multi-tiered with ample fully enclosed shooting-galleries.[21] Even weaker castles had their uses. In 1182 Saladin invaded the Kingdom of Jerusalem with a huge army against which only 700 knights could be deployed. But they attacked aggressively and when driven back anchored themselves on Baisan and Forbelet and so repelled the enemy.[22]

But their greatest innovations occurred in field warfare. Because they were so heavily outnumbered, the Latins had to be prepared to launch their entire strike-force, the cavalry, in one stroke if they were to achieve a decisive success. The mass charge was possible because the settlers fought time after time and were used to working together. Timing, of course, was vital, for if it did not strike the heart of the enemy force, the horses would be blown and vulnerable and the enemy did their best to provoke them into unconsidered action. This was the importance of the fighting march which did not serve a merely defensive purpose. Protected, at least to a degree by a screen of foot soldiers, the knights could at a moment of their choosing be launched at the enemy. Turcopoles were light cavalry, usually horse-archers, and the crusaders recruited them from their own people in the native Christian population.[23] However, numbers were limited because the local population was relatively small and had undergone long centuries of demilitarisation under Islam.

But perhaps the greatest military innovations of the Latins were the monastic Military Orders of the Temple and the Hospital. An enormous amount has been written about these two organisations which were so immensely popular in medieval Europe and powerful in the Latin states.[24] What is important in this context about the Orders is that they established standing armies. This was a startling innovation in the context of the twelfth century. They each seem to have been able to field some 300 knights.[25] In addition the *Templar Rule* makes it clear that the Order had Turcopoles and sergeants, some of whom were mounted; there is no indication of their numbers, but they were presumably proportionate to the knights.[26] This means that the Orders could field 600 knights, approximately the same as the mounted strength of the entire Kingdom of Jerusalem.[27] At the end of the twelfth century, Richard I of England (1189–99) conceived of the idea of raising a permanent body of 300 knights, apparently to be paid for by remitting 'feudal' service for taxes. Magnate resistance scuppered the force, and Richard could not pay for it out of his own resources because it would have cost over half the normal annual income of the crown.[28] It is interesting that each of the Military Orders, in terms of a field-force alone, could raise a standing cavalry force beyond that which could be managed by the English Crown. By contemporary standards the forces of the Orders were well disciplined, and given their motivation they seem to have been formidable fighters. This was an important innovation in military affairs. Moreover the wealth of the Orders enabled them to build great castles: Belvoir, already noted above, was built by the Hospital.

The full military capacity of the Islamic powers and the Latin settlers was rarely mobilised. The stuff of war was mainly raiding across the frontiers, although this was backed up by the existence of strong regular forces. In 1184 Saladin besieged Kerak, tying down the army of Jerusalem and permitting his forces to enjoy a highly destructive raid on Galilee.[29] Once Saladin had created his great empire, after 1174 the balance of advantage between him and the settlers had changed, clearly in his favour. However, he faced a formidable enemy. The strength of the Kingdom of Jerusalem lay in the walled cities, any one of which could only be taken by a major siege. There was nothing in siege technique between the Muslims and their settler enemies. By 1154 all the great cities of the Palestinian coast had succumbed to Latin attack.[30] The Muslims were no less adept at this form of warfare, as Saladin showed by his capture of Jacob's Ford.[31] But an invading army which stopped to besiege a city would be subject to attack by the field army of the kingdom, which could count on close knowledge of the area and active support from the numerous castles which studded the countryside and served as centres of supply and support. The strength of the kingdom was made very evident in 1177 when Saladin entered the kingdom from Egypt. So formidable was his army that Baldwin IV's much smaller force retreated into Ascalon. However, Saladin permitted his forces to disperse to ravage the countryside, so that when Baldwin's men approached, he had to call them together in haste. He then allowed himself to be lured into an area unfavourable for manoeuvre, and suffered a heavy defeat at Montgisard.[32]

Montgisard was a heavy blow to Saladin's prestige as the self-appointed champion of Islam, especially as he was much concerned with fighting Islamic enemies such as the Zengid clan. In October 1178 Baldwin IV of Jerusalem tried to follow up his victory by building a new castle at Jacob's Ford to threaten Damascus, but his army suffered heavy losses in a raid into the Beqaa valley. Saladin then attacked Jacob's Ford unsuccessfully and as he withdrew Baldwin pursued him only to be defeated at Marj Ayun, opening the way for Saladin's successful attack on Jacob's Ford in 1179. In 1180 drought in Syria and Egypt brought both sides to a truce which lasted until 1182 when Saladin first attacked Kerak, then led a major army across the Jordan into Galilee from whence it was ejected by an aggressive defence. When Saladin then attacked Beirut, Baldwin raised the siege. By 1183 Saladin had gained control of Aleppo and once more attacked the Galilee. On this occasion the defenders were poorly led by Guy of Lusignan and enormous damage was done. In November 1183 and August 1184 Saladin again attacked Kerak. By 1185 Zengid hostility in Mosul forced him to a truce with the Latins. Jacob's Ford marked a turning point in the military balance because from then on the fighting took place within Christian territory.

The only exception was the raid Reynald of Chatîllon led which disrupted pilgrimage to Mecca in 1184, causing great scandal in the Muslim world and increasing pressure on Saladin.[33]

These campaigns must have been difficult and expensive for Saladin, but they placed enormous pressure on Jerusalem, whose leaders in 1184 sent an embassy to Europe asking for help. They returned with money but no major commitment of military aid. The sheer variety of Muslim assaults, raids, sieges and battles all caused substantial physical damage which sharpened disagreements in the Latin leadership over how to proceed. There were no typical battles. In fact the confrontations at Marj Ayun and elsewhere were battles of encounter in which luck and opportunism were more important than any kind of planning. By the mid-1180s Saladin clearly recognised that he needed to destroy the field-army of his enemies if he was to damage them seriously, and in the end this could only be done by battle. He could take comfort in the thought that if he was defeated, he could absorb the punishment because the Latins were unlikely to be able to do anything far-reaching. But defeat, or even failure to do much, could erode his aura as the champion of Islam. He needed success. However, Guy, the new king of Jerusalem, was deeply unpopular and needed a success. And many of his leading subjects, exasperated by a long period on the defensive, were eager to fight. In short, both sides were prepared for battle, and this was why Hattin happened. And there followed its consequence, the Third Crusade and the Battle of Arsuf in 1191. These two major confrontations were not typical, but they illustrate the nature of warfare in the Middle East at this time.

In late 1186 or early 1187 Reynald of Chatîllon lord of Kerak, in open breach of the truce with Saladin, attacked a caravan travelling between Egypt and Syria. This set the scene for a great confrontation, for Saladin seized the opportunity to end the truce negotiated in 1185. The newly crowned king of Jerusalem, Guy of Lusignan, was a bitter enemy of his greatest lord, Raymond of Tripoli lord of Tiberias, who concluded a treaty with Saladin who agreed to aid him against Guy and in return was given the right to pass Raymond's lands to raid the kingdom. On 1 May 1187 the Muslims took advantage of this and launched 7000 troops on a major raid into the Galilee. They massacred a force of 140 knights, mostly Templars, who tried to take them on. This was a disastrous loss at a time when it was known that Saladin was gathering a huge army of between 30,000 and 40,000 near Damascus. At its heart were 12,000 regular cavalry augmented by huge numbers of Turkish and Arab horse-archers and substantial infantry forces. On 30 June Saladin crossed the Jordan at Sinnabra and entered the Kingdom of Jerusalem. His army ascended the mighty slope of the western side of the Jordan valley and established its main camp at Kafr Sabt, and laid siege to Tiberias. According to Ibn al-Athir, Saladin was using the siege of Tiberias as a lure:

> His purpose in besieging Tiberias had only been that the Franks should leave their position so that he could engage them.[34]

Saladin was seeking such a battle, and so was King Guy who needed a success to win over his sullen and hostile barons.[35] As Saladin had prepared his army, so too had the kingdom, and some 18,000 troops, with 1200 knights at its heart gathered at Saforie, some 26 km due east of Tiberias. The crusader leaders were divided about the response to Saladin's onslaught, with some urging an immediate attack and others preferring Fabian tactics, certain that the huge enemy army would in the end melt away. The mass of the knights, however, were eager for a fight. Perhaps because of the damage they had suffered in recent raids they wanted vengeance:

All advised that at dawn they should march out, accompanied by the Lord's cross, ready to fight the enemy, with all the men armed and arrayed in battle formation.[36]

Because of the disaster which ensued, King Guy has been much blamed for joining battle but there was a case for attacking because it offered the opportunity to inflict a terrible defeat on a dangerous enemy. The problem is that we have no idea how Guy intended to use his army. The debate over how to counter Saladin had been fractious and lasted into the night of 2 July, concluding with the decision to continue to avoid battle. However, overnight Guy changed his mind and ordered an immediate advance on the morning of 3 July. In such circumstances, if he had a plan there was hardly any opportunity to communicate it to his soldiers who were astonished by the change of plan. Saforie was on the south side of a west–east valley through which a Roman road passed via Turan then up a long slope to the plateau of Hattin. It seems unlikely that Guy intended to march to Tiberias 26 km to the east. In 1182 a Latin army marched 8 km against major opposition, and in 1183 Guy himself had made only 6 km.[37] It seems likely, therefore, that he was bent on forcing a battle but we have no idea how and no knowledge of his instructions to the army.

On the morning of 3 July, Guy and his army set off eastwards, probably via Mashhad.[38] They turned north down onto the road to Tiberias, and advanced towards Turan. They were organised in three boxes. The vanguard was commanded by Raymond of Tripoli, for it was the custom that the army should be led by the lord across whose lands they were fighting. The king, accompanied by the Holy Cross, commanded the central box, while Balian of Ibelin was in charge of the rearguard which was largely manned by the Templars and Hospitallers. Within each box were the mounted knights, the strike force of the army, and they were surrounded by infantry and archers whose task was to hold off the enemy horse-archers who would try to wound the all-important horses. As they debouched onto the Roman road to Tiberias, this formation would have extended over a considerable distance. The road was about 10 metres wide, which means that the knights could have advanced along it in a column six wide.[39] It seems likely that each block of knights numbered about 400, so that allowing 3 metres for each horse, the heavy cavalry in any one box would have occupied about 200 metres of road. In addition the army also had a large number of light horse, Turcopoles, who probably kept close to the knights. We know that the army had a substantial amount of baggage because towards the end of the battle they tried to set up tents to block enemy charges. We are not told if this paraphernalia was carried on wagons or pack-animals, but we can assume they covered at least an additional 60 metres of road. In addition a contemporary Muslim letter reports that after the battle many women and children were captured, so presumably there were non-combatants as well. Around this core were the infantry and archers, forming a perimeter at least 10 metres outside and all around the knights and the baggage. Thus any one of these boxes would have extended over some 400 metres or more of road. Since the boxes would have been somewhat separated, the army would have been spread out over more than 1 km of road, rolling like a battering-ram towards the enemy. In the heat and dust of this movement, communication between the three commanders would have been enormously difficult.

The departure of this huge force seems to have surprised Saladin, who may well have had some knowledge of the decision taken the night before to stay at Saforie. He was supervising the siege of Tiberias and arrived at the top of the slope overlooking Turan only at midday, by which time the Jerusalemite army had arrived at Turan where there was a spring.[40] This movement significantly changed the balance of advantage between the two armies because Guy was now only about 14–15 km from Tiberias and just 10 km from Saladin's main camp at Kafr Sabt.

As Saladin looked down on the enemy, he must have been deeply worried lest they establish themselves at Turan. Certainly, if there was enough water, at Turan Guy would have been in an unassailable position very like that at Saforie, and from there he could threaten to advance and oblige Saladin to keep his forces on the edge of the plateau in readiness. This was a game which Saladin's army could not play indefinitely because it was profitless in every sense. It has been suggested that Guy was trying to tempt Saladin's army down the slope where it would be away from its own water supplies.[41] But after a short pause, Guy led his army up the slope towards Saladin's forces ensconced on the plateau in great strength. Saladin's relief was palpable in a letter he wrote shortly after to Baghdad speaking of 'the hawks of the Frankish infantry and the eagles of their cavalry hovering around the water'. But, he went on, 'Satan incited Guy to do what ran counter to his purpose', that is to say, Guy left Turan and mounted the slope up to the plateau.[42] This was, indeed, the crucial decision which led to defeat because they were marching through great heat into an almost waterless area. It is possible that Guy was encouraged by the relatively easy progress to Turan, and he may have thought that as in 1183 Saladin would harass but not directly challenge his march.[43] As the army climbed up the northern edge of the valley towards the plateau, Saladin sent substantial sections of his army to cut them off from Turan and to harass them, concentrating especially on the rearguard. This could easily have been disastrous if the Latins had charged them, but they could not do that because the central mass of the Muslim army remained to the east at the top of the slope, standing off but threatening.

After 4–5 km the army had reached the edge of the plateau, but it was demoralised and Guy called a halt at Maskana where there was a small and wholly inadequate pool. In the words of one account:

At this place they were so constrained by enemy attacks and by thirst that they wished to go no further.[44]

The pause was hardly beneficial because night was spent tightly surrounded by the huge enemy army whose infantry swarmed into the rocky land to the north and set fire to the grass increasing the horrors of thirst. During the night there were desertions and it was a thoroughly demoralised army which resumed formation in the morning of 4 July, totally surrounded. Saladin once more held his forces back, allowing the heat of the day to further weaken the enemy army. When fighting resumed, Guy seems to have had no plan. His infantry fled up onto the slopes of the ancient volcano called the Horns of Hattin, uncovering the cavalry who were overwhelmed.

The collapse of what was normally a strong and disciplined Latin army was probably down to poor leadership. Guy was deeply unpopular and he had hesitated many times about how to tackle Saladin. By contrast Saladin was in command and worked through trusted and experienced lieutenants. Then there was the sheer size of the Muslim army. It was so numerous that powerful elements engaged the Christians on 3 July and did great damage, yet its main force under Saladin himself never engaged, though its menace protected those who did. There was nothing inevitable about victory at Hattin. The Muslims were very numerous, but Saladin knew how deadly the charge of the knights could be and his entire strategy was to weaken them to the utmost before closing. Even at the last such a charge almost broke through the Muslim army. According to Saladin's son, al-Afdal:

I was alongside my father during this battle. When the king of the Franks was on the hill with that band, they made a formidable charge against the Muslims facing them, so that they drove them back to my father ... I looked towards him and he was overcome with grief and his complexion pale. He took hold of his beard and advanced, crying out 'Give the lie to the Devil'. The Muslims rallied, returned to the fight and climbed the hill. ... But the Franks rallied and charged again like the first time and drove the Muslims back to my father. He acted as he had on the first occasion and the Muslims turned upon the Franks and drove them back to the hill.[45]

It is one of the curiosities of history that only about four years later, on 7 September 1191, there was a rematch, but fought on very different terms: the Battle of Arsuf. The disaster of Hattin and the consequent capture of almost all the land of the Kingdom of Jerusalem inspired Europe to launch the Third Crusade. Between 1189 and 1191 the focus of the crusaders was the siege of Acre which capitulated to the crusaders on 11 July 1191. On 22 August, Richard the Lionheart, now the undisputed leader of the crusader forces, marched south determined to seize Jaffa, which would be the base for any assault on Jerusalem. The core of his army were his own troops, mostly tough professional mercenaries and knights long in his service.[46] There were plenty of other crusaders of many nationalities, all well seasoned after the long siege at Acre. Numerous amongst them were the French who had no love for Richard. But his military reputation was high and since he was the sole king left on the expedition, his leadership was inevitable. And they had been fighting together for some time, and this gave them much greater coherence than was common in crusader armies. The numbers in Richard's army are uncertain. A recent writer has suggested about 20,000 in all, but his calculations are based on the original numbers of those coming to the East with Philip and Richard, and this makes no allowance for deaths and defections. But certainly he had no less than 10,000 and perhaps many more. Saladin seems to have had about 25,000, all cavalry.[47]

Richard arranged his men in three blocks with the infantry surrounding the cavalry as at Hattin.[48] But unlike at Hattin, Richard's fleet hovered offshore providing food and water. Moreover, although his infantry on the landward (left) side of the army were exposed to enemy assaults, Richard could rotate them to the shore-side, where they were virtually immune from attack, to give them rest. Richard was always careful about logistics and these dispositions were vital to his aim of seizing Jaffa.[49] As at Hattin, on 3 July, Saladin, with a larger army, savagely harassed his enemy and both sides suffered heavy casualties. Saladin's biographer described with admirable clarity the military situation as Richard moved south:

The Muslims were shooting arrows on their flanks, trying to incite them to break ranks, while they controlled themselves severely and covered the route in this way, travelling very steadily as their ships moved along at sea opposite them, until they completed each stage and camped.[50]

The discipline which Richard imposed was remarkable and even his enemies admired it:

The enemy army was already in formation with the infantry surrounding it like a wall, wearing solid iron corselets and full-length well-made chain-mail, so that arrows were falling on them with no effect ... I saw various individuals amongst the Franks with ten arrows fixed in their backs, pressing on in this fashion quite unconcerned.[51]

On 7 September, Saladin deployed for battle in the narrow plain, 1.5–3 km deep between the wooded hills and the sea. In the classic pattern, massive harassing attacks were sent against the crusader column, and increasingly they focused on the rearguard where the Hospitallers took terrible punishment. It has been suggested that Richard did not want to fight and that he kept his army in column striving to shake off Saladin and so reach Jaffa.[52] However, it seems unlikely he could have avoided battle entirely and he certainly could not move towards Jerusalem with Saladin's army intact and close. In addition he would have recognised that a decisive victory would open the way to both Jaffa and Jerusalem. That morning he reorganised his cavalry from three groups into five and issued orders that all were to keep formation until he ordered otherwise. In the event, Saladin attacked the Hospitaller rear savagely, presumably hoping to bring them to a halt which would separate them from the rest of the army. The Hospitallers, provoked beyond endurance, launched a charge of their own and Richard recognised that they must be supported. The massive charge which followed did enormous damage to the Muslim army:

> The enemy's situation worsened still more and the Muslims thought they had them in their power. Eventually the first detachments of their infantry reached the plantations of Arsuf. Then their cavalry massed together and agreed on a charge, as they feared for their people and thought that only a charge would save them. I saw them grouped together in the middle of the foot-soldiers. They took their lances and gave a shout as one man. The infantry opened gaps for them and they charged in unison. One group charged our right wing, another our left, and the third our centre. It happened that I was in the centre which took to wholesale flight. My intention was to join the left wing, since it was nearer to me. I reached it after it had been broken utterly, so I thought to join the right wing, but then I saw that it had fled more calamitously than all the rest.[53]

Though their losses were heavy, many of the light Turkish horse got away and rallied, so that Saladin's army remained in being. Richard achieved what Guy had sought to do at Hattin.

The tactics in both battles were remarkably similar, and they were alike in another respect. Both battles, though climactic, were indecisive. After Hattin, most of the cities of the Latin Kingdom surrendered, but Tyre held out and Saladin never launched an all-out attack. Later he moved to Tripoli and Antioch, but although he made important gains, achieved nothing decisive. It is worth considering why this was. Saladin relied on an army grouped around a core of his own followers, but even amongst his own men – predominantly like himself, Kurds – most fought for gain and like their Western counterparts needed to keep an eye on the agricultural year. Siege was bloody and difficult. Moreover, great though the victory at Hattin was, Saladin could not strike at Europe despite his incautious boasting:

> As soon as Allah the most high enables me to wrest the rest of the maritime plain, I plan to divide my realm among my aides, give them instructions, bid them farewell and cross the seas, pursuing the enemy to their island. There I shall destroy the last on the surface of the earth of those who do not believe in Allah.[54]

The prospect of relief forces arriving was therefore ever present, and indeed the prompt arrival of a Sicilian fleet saved Tripoli in 1188.[55]

Saladin lacked the power, not the will, to destroy the European settlements in Palestine. Richard, by contrast, knew from the first that he could not conquer what had been lost. He hoped to use military pressure to persuade Saladin to leave the kingdom and Jerusalem. From the moment of his landing he opened negotiations which would go on until his departure.

For he knew that even if he won Jerusalem, the armies would melt away and the land could not be held. This was the significance of his unceasing negotiations with Saladin. As it was, the military advantage which he gained at Arsuf was too marginal and too transient to be of much use. He subsequently showed remarkable reluctance to attack Jerusalem, and quite sensibly suggested that if anything was going to be conquered, it should be Egypt, Saladin's financial powerbase. Subsequent crusades in the thirteenth century saw the sense of this, but at the time the army as a whole was focused on Jerusalem. Subsequently, the quarrels between its individual components and leaders brought to an end the remarkable discipline demonstrated in the march to Jaffa and the Battle of Arsuf.

For all his military ability, Richard was unable to manage the crusader army, which was quickly crippled by its inner tensions, though it is doubtful whether it ever had enough strength to reconquer the Holy Lands. It is remarkable that Richard, whose entire experience before 1191 was European, should have been able to adapt to the fighting march and to have conducted it so skilfully in an alien environment. He enjoyed the advantage of leading a very seasoned army, but it was no less divided at heart than that which Guy had led. Subsequently the tensions between the various elements in the army were to come to the fore. But when it came to battle the personality and capacity of a leader could make all the difference. Guy never seems to have had a plan and to have ignored the demands of logistics, quite unlike Richard.

Conquest in medieval circumstances was always difficult, largely because armies were so episodic and great powers had so many distractions. It is sobering to reflect that it took two and a half centuries for England to conquer its tiny neighbour, Wales. The events of the First Crusade were altogether so remarkable and so exceptional that it is no wonder that contemporaries regarded them as truly the work of God. At first sight the Latin colonies which it established appeared weak, especially in comparison to the vast empire which Saladin created. But large empires have many enemies, and the Latin kingdom, based upon well-fortified cities supported by a formidable field army, was a tough nut to crack. In its own way Hattin was as wonderful as the outcome of the First Crusade, and like it partly the result of chance events. But Saladin's armies were too episodic to destroy all vestiges of the European settlement and much too weak to triumph once the Third Crusade arrived. Correspondingly, Richard never had enough support from a divided and quarrelsome Europe to reverse the decision of 1187. The triumph of Islam came with the creation of a new army, that of Mamluks, whose hard core was a very substantial number of highly trained professional soldiers gathered in a standing army.[56] The Mamluks defeated not only the Latin settlers but also the Mongols, and their triumph is witness to what a real standing army could do.

NOTES

1 William of Tyre, *Historia Rerum in partibus transmarinis gestarum*, ed. R.B.C. Huygens, Corpus Christianorum, Continuatio Medievalis 63A, 2 vols (Tournhoult: Brepols, 1986) 13:16, also as *A History of Deeds done beyond the Sea by William of Tyre*, trans. E.A. Babcock and A.C. Krey, 2 vols (New York: Columbia University Press, 1943) 2:25. Subsequently cited as WT.

2 Albert of Aachen, *Historia Hierosolymitana* ed. S.B. Edgington (Oxford: Clarendon Press, 2007), 4:22.

3 Raymond of Aguilers, *Liber*, ed. J.H. and L.L. Hill (Paris: Geuthner, 1969), 150, trans. A. C. Krey, *The First Crusade* (Gloucester MA: Smith, 1958), 261. Subsequently cited as RA. There is some disagreement about the scale of the massacre. J. France, *Victory in the East: A Military History of*

the First Crusade (Cambridge: Cambridge University Press, 1994), 355–6 suggests that this was a fairly normal result of a city holding out until stormed, and that many survived. The case for the massacre being quite exceptional is persuasively stated by B.Z. Kedar, 'The Jerusalem Massacre of 1099 in Western Historiography of the Crusades', *Crusades* 3 (2004), 15–76.

4   *L'Estoire de la Guerre Sainte par Ambroise* ed. and trans. G. Paris (Paris, 1897), ll. 5506–59 trans. M. Ailes and M. Barber, *History of the Holy War* (Woodbridge: Boydell, 2003), 108.

5   Ibn al-Athir, *Chronicle of Ibn al-Athir for the Crusading Period from al-Kamil fi'l-Ta'rikh,* trans. D.S. Richards, 3 vols (Aldershot: Ashgate, 2006–08), Part 2, 390.

6   Kemal ad-Din, *The Chronicle of Aleppo,* in *Recueil Des Historiens des Croisades, Historiens Orientaux,* 3:577–665.

7   See Y. Friedman, *Encounter Between Enemies: Captivity and Ransom in the Latin Kingdom of Jerusalem* (Leiden: Brill, 2002); J. France, 'Siege conventions in Western Europe and the Latin East', in P. de Souza and J. France (eds), *War and Peace in Ancient and Medieval History* (Cambridge: Cambridge University Press, 2008), 158–72 and 'Surrender and capitulation in the Middle East in the Age of the Crusades', in H. Afflerbach and H. Strachan (eds), *How Fighting Ends – A History of Surrender* (Oxford: Oxford University Press, 2012), 73–84.

8   For the East, see Friedman, *Encounter,* 35–54, and for the West, M. Strickland, *The Conduct and Perception of War under the Anglo-Norman and Angevin Kings* 1075–1217 (Cambridge: Cambridge University Press, 1996).

9   Anonymous, *Gesta Francorum et aliorum Hierosolimitanorum,* ed. R. Hill (Edinburgh: Nelson, 1962), 19. Subsequently cited as GF.

10 Fulcher of Chartres, *Historia Hierosolymitana,* ed. H. Hagenemyer (Heidelberg: Winter, 1913), 85, trans. F.R. Ryan and H.S. Fink, *A History of the Expedition to Jerusalem 1095–1127* (Knoxville: University of Tennessee Press, 1969), 64. Subsequently cited as FC.

11 Ibn al-Qalanisi, *Damascus Chronicle of the Crusades,* ed. H.A.R. Gibb (London: Luzon, 1932), 60–1, and Ralph of Caen, *Life of Tancred,* trans. B.S. and D.S. Bachrach (Woodbridge: Boydell, 2005), 164–7.

12 Walter the Chancellor, *The Antiochene Wars,* trans. T.S. Asbridge and S.B. Edgington (Aldershot: Ashgate, 1999), 127.

13 R.C. Smail, *Crusading Warfare 1097–1193* (Cambridge: Cambridge University Press, 1956, 2nd edn 1995), 156–64.

14 WT 21:23.

15 C. Cahen, 'Les changements techniques militaires dans la Proche Orient médiévale et leur importance historique', in V.J. Parry and M.E. Yapp (eds), *War, Technology and Society in the Middle East* (London: Oxford University Press, 1975), 113–24.

16 For a fine analysis of the Egyptian element of Saladin's army, see Y. Lev, *Saladin in Egypt* (Leiden: Brill 1999), 141–60.

17 J. France, *Perilous Glory. The Rise of Western Military Power* (London: Yale, 2011), 4–6.

18 Jordan Fantosme, *Chronicle,* ed. R.C. Johnston (Oxford: Clarendon, 1981), 41:33–4.

19 France, *Victory,* 173–85, 237–41, 360–1.

20 J.L. Cate, 'The Crusade of 1101', in K. Setton and M.W. Baldwin (eds), *History of the Crusades* 6 vols (Philadelphia and Madison: University Presses of Pennsylvania and Wisconsin, 1955–86), 1:343–67; J. Phillips, *The Second Crusade: Extending the Frontiers of Christendom* (London: Yale, 2007), 168–206.

21 H. Kennedy, *Crusader Castles* (Cambridge: Cambridge University Press, 1994), 58–61.

22 M. Ehrlich, 'The Battle of Hattin: A chronicle of a defeat foretold?' *Journal of Medieval Military History* 5 (2007), 16–32.

23 Y. Harari, 'The military role of the Frankish Turcopoles: A reassessment', *Mediterranean Historical Review* 12 (1997), 75–116.

24 The standard works on the Orders are J. Riley-Smith, *The Knights of St. John in Jerusalem and Cyprus, c.1050–1310* (London: Macmillan, 1967) and his *The Knights Hospitaller in the Levant,*

c.1070–1309 (Basingstoke: Palgrave, 2012); M. Barber, *The New Knighthood. A History of the Order of the Temple* (Cambridge: Cambridge University Press, 1994).

25 For the figure of 300, see S. Schein, 'The Templars: The regular army of the Holy Land and the spearhead of the army of its reconquest', in G. Minicci and F. Sardi (eds), *I Templari: mito e storia* (Sienna: A.G. Viti-Riccucci, 1989), 15–28.

26 H. de Curzon, *La Règle du Temple: French Text of the Rule of the Order of the Knights Templar* (Paris: Nogent-le-Rotrou, 1886), English trans. J.M. Upton-Ward, *The Rule of the Templars* (Woodbridge: Boydell, 1992), especially 39–66.

27 At Hattin in 1187 a maximum effort by the kingdom mustered some 1200 knights, on which see the finest scholarly study of Hattin by B.Z. Kedar, 'The Battle of Hattin revisited', in B.Z. Kedar (ed.) *The Horns of Hattin* (London: Variorum, 1992), 190–207.

28 J. France, *Western Warfare in the Age of the Crusades* (London: UCL Press, 1999), 58.

29 Abu Shama, *The Book of the Two Gardens*, trans. M.C. Lyons and D.E.P. Jackson, *Saladin. The Politics of Holy War* (Cambridge: Cambridge University Press, 1982), 217.

30 R. Rogers, *Latin Siege Warfare in the Twelfth Century* (Oxford: Clarendon, 1997) charts this process and explains its mechanisms well.

31 M. Barber, 'Frontier warfare in the Latin Kingdom of Jerusalem: The Campaign of Jacob's Ford, 1178–79', in J. France and W.G. Zajac (eds), *The Crusades and Their Sources. Essays Presented to Bernard Hamilton* (Aldershot: Ashgate, 1998), 9–22.

32 M. Ehrlich, 'Saint Catherine's Day Miracle – the Battle of Montgisard', *Journal of Medieval Military History* 11 (2013), 95–106.

33 B. Hamilton, 'The Elephant of Christ: Reynald of Châtillon', in D. Baker (ed.), *Religious Motivation: Biographical and Sociological Problems for the Church Historians* (Oxford: Oxford University Press, 1978), 97–108.

34 Ibn al-Athir, *Chronicle*, Part 2 (1146–93), 321.

35 R.C. Smail, 'The predicaments of Guy of Lusignan,' in B.Z. Kedar et al. (eds), *Outremer* (London: Variorum, 1982), 168–9.

36 Anonymous, *De Expugnatione Terrae Sanctae libellus*, ed. J. Stevenson (London, RS 66, 1875), 221–2, trans. in J.A. Brundage (ed.), *The Crusades: A Documentary Survey* (Milwaukee: Marquette University Press, 1962), 155.

37 M.C. Lyons and D.E.P. Jackson, *Saladin* (Cambridge: Cambridge University Press, 1984), 259.

38 In this article I am not seeking to discuss the course of the battle, but merely to pick out elements which bear on my subject. I would like, however, to acknowledge my debt to some distinguished writing on the subject: J. Prawer, 'La bataille de Hattin', *Israel Exploration Journal* 14 (1964), 160–79, English trans. in his *Crusader Institutions* (Oxford: Oxford University Press, 1980); P. Herde, 'Die Kämpfe bei den Hörnern von Hittin und der Untergang des Kreuzritterheeres', *Römische Quarttalschrift für christliche Altertumskunde und Kirchengeschichte* 61 (1966), 1–50; Lyons and Jackson, *Saladin*, 255–66; Kedar, 'The Battle of Hattin revisited'. My own study of Hattin is presently in press.

39 Kedar, 'The Battle of Hattin revisited', 195.

40 Kedar, 'Battle of Hattin revisited', 197 thinks its flow would not have watered the whole army, but we cannot know this definitely.

41 Lyons and Jackson, *Saladin*, 260.

42 C.P. Melville and M.C. Lyons, 'Saladin's Hattin letter', in Kedar, *The Horns of Hattin*, 216–20.

43 M. Ehrlich, 'The Battle of Hattin: A chronicle of a defeat foretold?' *Journal of Medieval Military History* 5 (2007), 16–32, at 20–3.

44 Anonymous, *De expugnatione*, 156.

45 Ibn al-Athir, *Chronicle*, Part 2 (1146–93), 327.

46 P. Edbury, 'Preaching the crusade in Wales', in A. Haverkamp, H. Vollrath, K. Leyser (eds), *England and Germany in the High Middle Ages* (London: German Historical Institute, 1996),

221–33 has suggested that Richard never had the crusade preached in England, which means that it is likely that his troops were paid men.

47 F. McLynn, *Lionheart and Lackland* (London: Cape, 2006), 182.

48 Good accounts of the course of the march to Jaffa and the battle are those of: S. Painter, 'The Third Crusade: Richard the Lionhearted and Philip Augustus', in Setton and Baldwin, *History of the Crusades*, 2:45–86; J. Gillingham, *Richard I* (Yale: Yale University Press, 1999), 173–8; McLynn, *Lionheart and Lackland*, 182–94.

49 McLynn, *Lionheart and Lackland*, 184 comments on Richard's logistical provisions.

50 Baha al-Din Ibn Shaddad, *The Rare and Excellent History of Saladin*, ed. D.S. Richards (Aldershot: Ashgate, 2002), 74.

51 Baha ad-Din, *The Rare and Excellent History of Saladin*, 170.

52 T. Asbridge, *The Crusades. The War for the Holy Land* (London: Simon and Schuster, 2010), 466, contested convincingly by M. Ehrlich, 'The Battle of Arsur: A short-lived victory', *Journal of Medieval Military History* 12 (2013), 109–18.

53 Baha ad-Din, *The Rare and Excellent History of Saladin*, 175.

54 P.K. Hitti, *Makers of Arab History* (London: Macmillan, 1968), 116.

55 M.W. Baldwin, 'The decline and fall of Jerusalem 1174–89', in Setton and Baldwin, *History of the Crusades*, 1:618.

56 On the Mamluks, see especially R. Amitai-Preiss, *Mongols and Mamluks: The Mamluk-Ilkhanid War, 1260–1281* (Cambridge: Cambridge University Press, 1995) and 'Ayn Jalut revisited', *Tarih* 2 (1992), 119–50, reprinted in J. France (ed.), *Medieval Warfare 1000–1300* (Aldershot: Ashgate, 2006).

CHAPTER FIVE

PAID TROOPS IN THE SERVICE OF MILITARY ORDERS DURING THE TWELFTH AND THIRTEENTH CENTURIES[1]

———•◆•———

Alan Forey

Many who participated in crusades during the twelfth and thirteenth centuries received payment. From the time of the First Crusade, those going to the aid of the Holy Land included men who were paid, either from the start of an expedition or at a later stage (Tyerman 2013: 1–40; Murray 2006: 246–8). The practice is also encountered in the Iberian peninsula and the Baltic region: in the thirteenth century, for example, indulgences were offered both to individuals who provided money for others to serve in these areas and to those whom they sent (Fonnesberg-Schmidt 2007: 139, 143, 185, 194–5; Mansilla 1955: 161–2, 274–5); and thirteenth-century Spanish chronicles mention payments made by the Castilian King Alfonso VIII during the Las Navas campaign in 1212 (Charlo Brea 1997: 57; Fernández Valverde 1987: 263).[2] The use of *stipendiarii* is reflected in several crusader treatises written in the late thirteenth and early fourteenth centuries, which advocated the recruitment of paid soldiers for crusading expeditions (Leopold 2000: 63–5). The forces which local secular rulers mobilised in the crusader states against Muslims also included paid troops: in the Kingdom of Jerusalem, for example, money-fiefs were common (Murray 2008: 275–86), and in the later thirteenth century hired troops in the Holy Land included a contingent which was maintained at the expense of the French king, while some other Western rulers also offered to pay for troops there (Marshall 1992: 77–83; Tyerman 2006: 815–16). Sancho IV of Castile was similarly using paid troops to defend frontier castles in Castile in the later thirteenth century (García Fitz 1988: 275–323). Detailed information has survived of paid troops in the service of military orders on various fronts during the later Middle Ages (Biskup 1991: 49–74; Luttrell 1991: 133–53; Ekdahl 2008: 345–61; Kreem 2001: 26–42), but precise evidence about fighting men in the pay of these orders in the twelfth and thirteenth centuries is more elusive; it has in fact sometimes been claimed that in the Baltic region the Teutonic order did not need to hire troops until the fourteenth century (Tumler 1955: 495; Ekdahl 2008: 345).

It is certainly clear that those fighting under the command of military orders in the twelfth and thirteenth centuries often included many who were not brothers. On numerous occasions auxiliary troops far outnumbered brethren in an order's contingent. This is apparent from information about garrisons of castles, forces in the field and losses sustained in warfare. In the Kingdom of Jerusalem, the Templar garrison at Safed after the castle had been restored in the thirteenth century comprised fifty brother knights, thirty brother sergeants, fifty *turcoples* (these usually constituted a light cavalry) and 300 crossbowmen (*ballistarii*), and a Limoges chronicle asserts that when the stronghold fell in 1266 some 150 Templars and a further 767 fighting men were killed (Huygens 1965: 384; 'Majus Chronicon Lemovicense' 1855: 773–4). Wilbrand of Oldenburg reported that when he visited the Holy Land in 1211–12 the night watch at the castle of Margat, in the principality of Antioch, consisted of four Hospitaller knights and twenty-eight other guards (Pringle 2012: 121). A similar impression is conveyed by sources for other regions, such as eastern and north-eastern Europe. In 1236 the master of the Temple in France wrote that six brothers, three knights, two sergeants and 500 other men under Templar command had been killed in Hungary by the Mongols (Holder-Egger 1882: 604–5). Peter of Dusburg, a fourteenth-century chronicler of the Teutonic order, stated that in 1242 a contingent of five brothers of the Teutonic order and twenty-four men-at-arms (*armigeri*) attacked Sartowitz, and that in 1289 Ragnit, on the river Memel farther north, was garrisoned by forty-one brothers and a hundred *armigeri*; he also mentioned a force of thirteen brothers and 250 mounted troops on campaign in Prussia in 1281 (1984: 138–40, 320, 350). Nine years later, according to the *Livonian Rhymed Chronicle*, a force of twelve brothers and 350 Kurs and *armigeri* undertook an expedition against the Lithuanians (Smith and Urban 1977: 139).

Yet paid troops were just one of several types of outsider who fought under the command of military orders. Others included unpaid vassals, who provided both cavalry and infantry forces. There were also fighting men, such as 'knights at term' (*milites ad terminum*) who voluntarily entered the service of a military order for a period on an unpaid basis (Forey 2008a: 5–11). Further service was provided by offenders who had a penance imposed upon them of serving for a period with a military order: among these were the murderers of Becket, as well as Bertrand of Cares, who in 1224 was ordered to serve with the Temple after killing the bishop of Le Puy (Vincent 2003: 248–62; Forey 2008b: 164 n. 66; Claverie 2005: 98). There was even the expectation on the part of the papacy, though not always fulfilled, that all crusaders in Prussia would accept the leadership of the Teutonic order (Philippi and Seraphim 1882–1909: 1.1:218; 1.2:47–8, 84–5). Such troops might provide not only service in the field but also castleguard. Crusaders might help in the task of defending strongholds,[3] especially as some stayed for a year: in 1239–40 Otto of Brunswick and his following resided at the Teutonic order's stronghold of Balga in Prussia for this period of time (Peter of Dusburg 1984: 126–8; Rüdebusch 1972: 192–3). *Milites ad terminum* could also help to provide garrisons, and in some instances vassals had an obligation of castleguard, as at the Hospitaller stronghold of Margat (Delaville Le Roulx 1894–1906: 1:491–6), although there are few references to this duty and it may not have been common.

Unpaid troops were, however, not necessarily available when they were needed. Vassals' obligations for unpaid service were often restricted in time, distance or numbers; and in some cases service was commuted into a money payment to an order (e.g. Ayala Martínez 2003: 544–5). The loyalty of subject populations was also sometimes in doubt. Although in the Baltic region converted native inhabitants as well as settlers were expected to fight (Philippi and Seraphim 1882–1909: 1.1:77–81, 131–3, 158–65; Murray 2013: 33–7), there were in the thirteenth century several periods of widespread revolt by the native population against the Teutonic order in Prussia. In the Holy Land and the Iberian peninsula, subject Muslims could not be relied to fight against fellow Muslims.

The Muslims of the Templar lordship of Chivert in northern Valencia, for example, were obliged to give military service only of a defensive kind when Chivert itself came under attack (Febrer Romaguera 1991: 10–16; Guinot Rodríguez 1991: 100–5), and in the crusader states Muslim subjects were not summoned for military service (Kedar 1990: 158–9). Although western settlements in the Kingdom of Jerusalem were often established in places where there was a considerable population of oriental Christians and not where Muslims predominated (Ellenblum: 1998: *passim*), and although these Christians at times fought alongside Westerners, doubts have been expressed about their reliability and in some instances their competence (Smail 1956: 46–53). It has also been suggested that the numbers of *milites ad terminum* in the service of military orders in the Holy Land declined in the thirteenth century (Forey 2008a: 9–11), while there were apparently no 'guest knights' (*Gastritter*) with the Teutonic order in Prussia in the last quarter of the thirteenth century (Paravicini 1989: 23; Ehlers 2001: 25).

It is not, however, always easy to identify those who fought for pay in the service of military orders. Obviously, not all who were in the paid employment of these orders were fighting men: outsiders were commonly engaged to undertake domestic or agricultural work. Unfortunately, many sources which refer to paid employees do not specify the nature of the tasks undertaken. A reference to *mercennarii* in early regulations of the order of Calatrava has been taken to indicate the use of paid troops, but the word could apply to any who were in the order's paid employment (Lomax 1961: 490, 493).[4] Gregory IX's comment in 1237 in a privilege to the Templars that 'in a number of houses directly subject to them, some men served for pay, and others freely' has been considered to refer to warriors (Auvray: 1907: 567; Marshall 1992: 58), but this is not a necessary conclusion; and the paid sergeants mentioned in Hospitaller statutes in 1262 may similarly not have been fighting men; while a Templar inventory of the Aragonese commandery of Castellote in southern Aragon in 1289 which states that 'the company (*companyes*) has been paid up to the last Sunday of May' was probably not alluding to troops (Delaville Le Roulx 1894–1906: 3:43–54; Miret y Sans 1911: 67).

Sources which clearly refer to military personnel often fail to differentiate between paid and unpaid service. In some instances those for whom an order is known to have been providing may have been receiving merely maintenance and not cash. This is true, for example, of the crusaders to whom in 1158 Adrian IV promised spiritual rewards if they served with the Templars in Spain at their own expense for a year or 'at the expense of the brothers ... for two years' (Kehr 1926: 363–4). In many sources troops serving with an order are described merely by type, such as knights (*milites*), sergeants (*servientes*), *turcoples* and foot soldiers (*pedites*), with no indication of the terms on which they were engaged. It has admittedly sometimes been assumed that *turcoples* were all paid troops, but some in fact were recruited on a different basis. Although Hospitaller statutes of 1303 refer to the engaging and dismissing of *turcoples* (Delaville Le Roulx 1894–1906: 4:57–8) – these were obviously paid men – in Templar ordinances and in those of the Teutonic order a distinction was made between *turcoples* who served 'for charity' (*à charité*) and those who were paid: the former would be maintained by the order, just as the *milites ad terminum* were, but did not receive a salary, although those in the Temple were given three besants at the end of a year's service (Upton-Ward 2003: 74–6; Perlbach 1890: 141–2). *Turcoples* might also receive fiefs (Richard 1986: 264–5; Mayer 2010: 375–7, 455–7; Mas Latrie 1861: 606–7). The Templar Customs imply that a *turcople* might even be a brother; although, as *turcoples* are often distinguished from brothers in many of the surviving sources, it would seem that they were only rarely members of an order (Curzon 1886: 273: Amatuccio 2009: 268).

Nor did *turcoples* always fulfil a military function: leading officials of military orders in the East commonly had one or more *turcoples* in their entourage, and in the regulations of the Teutonic order it was ruled that of the three assigned to the master, one was to carry his shield and lance, the second was to act as a messenger and the third was to be a chamberlain (Perlbach 1890: 98–9, 103, 106; Curzon 1886: 75, 86, 89, 94, 100, 102: Amatuccio 2009: 46, 58, 62, 72, 75; Delaville Le Roulx 1894–1906: 2:31–40). Yet relatively few *turcoples* would have been occupied in such tasks: the vast majority had a military role, and probably most were paid.

Apart from references to *turcoples* serving for pay, there are comparatively few direct statements about paid service. Some of these relate to men who served a military order but were financed by others. The indulgence granted to those who went on crusade at another's expense was given to some who in these circumstances fought under the banner of a military order: thus in 1250 Innocent IV promised an indulgence to those who, at the expense of others, assisted the order of Santiago in its campaigns in the Iberian peninsula for a year (Quintana Prieto 1987: 602–3; Aguado de Córdoba et al. 1719: 181–2). Evidence also survives of particular arrangements by which men were to serve an order at the expense of others. The penance imposed on the English King Henry II in 1172 for the murder of Becket included the requirement that he should provide enough money to maintain 200 knights for a year in the defence of the Holy Land 'according to the judgement of the brothers of the Temple' (Duggan 2000: 657–8; Robertson and Sheppard 1885: 516–18), and in a letter to the archbishop of Sens, the cardinals who imposed the penance wrote that Henry had promised to give the money to the Templars (Robertson and Sheppard 1885: 520–2). It would seem therefore that the Templars were to engage 200 knights at the expense of the English king, although it is doubtful whether the money was in fact made available (Mayer 1982: 722–3; Tyerman 1988: 54). In his will, the French king Philip Augustus left money to the king of Jerusalem, the Temple and the Hospital on the condition that they would maintain 300 knights, 'apart from the convents of the said houses', for three years (Delaville Le Roulx 1894–1906: 2:305). In 1217 Philip of Dreux, bishop of Beauvais, similarly left 100 marks in aid of the Holy Land 'so that they are sent there for hiring paid troops by the Templars' (Guyotjeannin 2004: 151); and Peter of Dusburg reported that in 1244 the duke of Austria sent thirty mounted archers at his own expense to Prussia, where they were presumably under the command of the Teutonic order (1984: 156). A few years later, when the French king Louis IX was in the East, he was maintaining a force of paid troops at the Templar castle of Atlit, on the coast of the Holy Land, where his wife Marguerite was then staying: they were apparently subject to the Templar commander there (Claverie 2001: 627, 635). In the thirteenth century the English kings Henry III and Edward I also granted fifty marks annually to the Templars for the maintenance of a knight in the Holy Land, although it is not known exactly how the order utilised the money (*Calendar of Liberate Rolls, 1251–1260* 1959: 53–4, 482; *Calendar of Close Rolls, 1279–1288* 1902: 70; *Calendar of Charter Rolls, 1257–1300* 1906: 237–8).

It may not only have been rulers, nobles, prelates and others seeking indulgences who paid for men to serve with military orders. Some communities which owed military service to an order probably hired men to fulfil their obligations, and in 1233 Hermann of Salza, Master of the Teutonic order, ruled that if any resident of the towns of Culm or Torun in Prussia defaulted in giving service, the town judge was to find a substitute to be maintained from the goods of the defaulter (Philippi and Seraphim 1882–1909: 1.1:77–81).

Of paid troops who were financed by military orders themselves, some held money fiefs and received cash payments: in the early 1260s, when the Hospitallers in the Holy Land rented Arsur from Balian of Ibelin, a list was drawn up of the sums of money which were to be paid by the Hospitallers to knights and sergeants who held fees there (Delaville Le Roulx 1894–1906: 3:6–7). Other paid troops were engaged as the need arose. William of Tyre reported that in 1168, when an attack on Egypt was being planned, the master of the Hospital had brought his order into serious debt because he had used the Hospital's own resources and also loans to pay all the knights that he could recruit (1986: 917). Several manuscripts of Templar regulations refer to 'secular knights who are in Jerusalem and are attached to the house for pay' (Curzon 1886: 102; Amatuccio 2009: 74).[5] It was further reported by Matthew Paris that in 1237 the prior of the English Hospitallers went out to the East 'with a paid militia and household' (1876: 406), and a letter written by Thomas Berard, master of the Temple, in 1260 to the English provincial master referred to the hiring of *stipendiarii* by his order for the defence of castles in the Holy Land ('Annales de Burton' 1864: 494). The employment of *stipendiarii* by the next Templar master, William of Beaujeu, was mentioned by a Templar in his testimony during the Templar trial, and a notary, who also then gave evidence and who at one time had been in Templar service, said that he had witnessed an altercation in Italy between the same Templar master and a body of sergeants who had been engaged at pay to help defend Templar castles (Michelet 1841–51: 1:646). Lastly, a letter written by the master of the Hospital to the prior of St Gilles after the loss of Acre in 1291 mentions paid troops employed by his order during the siege of the city (Delaville Le Roulx 1894–1906: 3:592–3).

The relative paucity of direct references to the hiring of troops by the orders themselves does not, of course, imply that this was merely an occasional practice. There was never any attempt systematically to record the employment of men on a paid basis. That the hiring troops by military orders was a regular custom which was widely known is implied by the comment attributed to a Templar in Jacquemart Giélée's *Renart le Nouvel*, written in the late thirteenth century:

> Mout nous couvient de saudoiers
> Et mout or et argent despendre
> Tout pour sainte Eglize desfendre
> (1961: 306)[6]

There are in fact a number of other sources which, while not alluding directly to the hiring of men to fight, strongly suggest the employment of paid troops. Clause thirty-three of the rule of the Teutonic order refers to outsiders serving freely or for pay, and as the clause mentions the prayers to be said for a dead knight who had been serving freely, it was clearly including military personnel (Perlbach 1890: 53). In 1218, during the fifth crusade, Honorius III mentioned the sums of money which the Temple and Hospital were daily expending at Damietta 'on knights, sergeants, crossbowmen and others capable of fighting and on the poor': he stated that they were each providing for some 2000 persons, while Oliver of Paderborn, who participated in that crusade, claimed that the Temple was daily feeding 4000 troops (Rodenburg 1883: 57–8; Oliver of Paderborn 1894: 255). The size of the numbers suggests that many of those mentioned were paid men, as the orders could put only a limited number of brothers in the field: a recent estimate places the total number of Hospitaller warrior brethren in the East at never more than 200 (Riley-Smith 2012: 82), and many of these were needed for garrisoning castles, while masters of the orders could not rely on being able to assemble a considerable number of unpaid volunteers. Even without William of Tyre's comment, it could be assumed that the 500 knights promised by the Hospitaller master in 1168 for an invasion of Egypt would have included some engaged for pay (Delaville Le Roulx 1894–1906: 1:275–6). In 1246 the master of Santiago undertook to take to the Latin Empire of Constantinople a force of 300 knights, made up of brothers and laymen (the *infante* Alfonso sought to ensure that the order's contingent included no more than fifty brother knights), together with 200 crossbowmen, of whom a hundred should be mounted, and a thousand foot. As it was said that all crusaders accompanying the order should be included in these totals, it was obviously not expected that these would comprise all those who were not brothers, and – given that the contingent was to be stationed in the East for two years – it would seem that a very considerable part of the force would have consisted of paid troops (Benito Ruano 1952: 30–4). The wording of Peter of Dusburg's *Chronica* further implies that some of the *armigeri* who formed part of the garrisons of the Teutonic order's castles in Prussia and Livonia were paid: he stated that the *armigeri* defending the newly built stronghold of Georgenburg in 1259 were drawn from Prussia and Livonia, and an *armiger* who deserted from Ragnit in 1293 was said by the chronicler to be a native of Bartenland, farther south (1984: 202, 368). These were not local inhabitants who owed service to the Teutonic order. It may also be assumed that the reference to *stipendiarii* in the account of the rebuilding of the Templar castle of Safet referred at least in part to some of the non-Templars who helped to form the garrison of the castle (Huygens 1965: 384); and the Syrian archers who later participated in the defence of the small island of Ruad, off the Syrian coast, which the Templars had occupied in 1300, could hardly have been other than paid troops (Raynaud 1887: 310). No doubt some of the other troops listed in the surviving sources merely by type, with no further explanation, were also paid.

Yet, although the military orders appear to have made widespread use of paid troops in the twelfth and thirteenth centuries, their ability to recruit such men must in some instances have been affected by declining financial resources. In the later thirteenth century the Templars and Hospitallers were no longer making large-scale acquisitions of property through donation or purchase in most parts of western Europe; they were losing revenues derived from estates in the Holy Land as these fell into Muslim hands; and in some parts of the West financial privileges and exemptions were being reduced, while the orders were expected to contribute to new forms of royal and papal taxation. Letters from Templar and Hospitaller officials in the East bewailing the plight of the two orders are common: on several occasions the fear was even expressed that they might have to abandon the Holy Land to its fate because of lack of resources ('Annales de Burton' 1864: 494; Kohler and Langlois 1891: 55–6).[7] In the Holy Land there was the further problem of the availability not only of Westerners, as fewer journeyed to the East, but possibly also of others who could be hired. This is suggested by a letter of the Templar master Thomas Berard, who wrote in 1260 that in defending his order's castles in the East 'we have to sustain four times the normal level of expenses, as paid troops cannot be had unless they are provided with food and the risk of death is reflected in their pay' ('Annales de Burton' 1864: 494). Shortage allowed potential hired troops to make large demands.

Troops recruited for pay by military orders were drawn from various backgrounds. Western Christians were no doubt engaged for warfare in the Iberian peninsula and the

Baltic region, and paid troops serving in the Holy Land included some from western Europe.[8] These either went to the East in search of employment or were hired in the West. Gerard of Ridefort, who became Templar master in 1185, was said to have been employed at pay by Raymond III of Tripoli after travelling out to the Holy Land (France 1999: 61). The sergeants recruited by William of Beaujeu mentioned by the notary during the Templar trial were drawn from France and other Western countries, and it has already been mentioned that paid troops were sent out to the East from England by the Hospital (Michelet 1841–51: 1:646). Those who served with the orders at the expense of Westerners were presumably also themselves Westerners. That *turcoples*, whether paid or not, included some Westerners is suggested not only by a reference to a brother *turcople* in Templar regulations, but also by the appearance as a witness of Frevol '*turcople* of the house of the militia' at the Catalan convent of the Temple at Tortosa in 1211 and by references to Berenguer *Turcople* in Templar documents drawn up there in 1229 and 1234 (Curzon 1886: 273; Amatuccio 2009: 268; Pagarolas i Sabaté 1999: 44–6, 53–4; 'Cartulario de Tortosa' 23–23v); and it would seem that *turcoples* giving unpaid service were normally Western Christians, possibly including some who had converted from Islam. But evidence about the origins of *turcoples* is slight and differing opinions have been expressed about their provenance (Richard 1986: 262–4, 269–70; Saavides 1993: 122–3; Harari 1997: 100–14). Probably most in the Holy Land were of Eastern origin and were Christians of various sects or Muslim converts. Paid *turcoples* could, however, also have included some Muslims, for it was at times claimed that military orders had Muslim troops in their employ, presumably usually for pay. The chronicler Ibn al-Athir mentions a Muslim at Crac des Chevaliers who raided with the Franks: he was referring here to the Hospitallers, who held that stronghold (Richards 2007: 364). In 1242 the Spanish bishops of Cuenca and Sigüenza asserted that the order of Santiago had used Muslim archers against them, and during the Templar trial brother Hugh of Narsac stated that the master William of Beaujeu 'had some Saracens in his pay when he wanted them' (Lomax 1959: 360–5; Rivera Garretas 1985: 387–90; Michelet 1841–51: 2:209). Christian rulers were certainly prepared not only to ally with Muslim states but also to employ paid Muslim troops in their armies, just as Christians entered the paid service of Muslim rulers: in the later thirteenth century, for example, the Aragonese kings were employing Muslim *jenetes*, mainly against Christian enemies but at times also against Muslim powers (Gazulla 1927: 174–96: Catlos 2004: 257–302; Fancy 2013: 39–73). Muslim troops were occasionally even employed by Western rulers in more northerly parts of Europe (Powicke 1910: 104–5). Although James of Vitry warned the military orders not to put their trust in Muslims (Pitra 1888: 421), these orders often negotiated and made treaties with Muslim powers in the East in the thirteenth century (Holt 1995: 33–41, 49–57, 66–8), to the consternation of some recently recruited brothers (Michelet 1841–51: 1:44–5), and in 1304 Aragonese Templars were raiding into Granada alongside the Muslim mercenary leader Alabes Abenraho, who was in the employ of the Aragonese king James II ('Templarios' 101; Finke 1922: 122–4; Giménez Soler 1905: 365–9). During the Templar trial, brother Bernard of Fuentes escaped and fled to Tunis, where he became head of the Christian militia there (Forey 2001: 17, 28, 216). It would not therefore be very surprising if some of the paid troops employed by military orders in the Mediterranean region were Muslims.

It may, of course, be asked why military orders engaged paid troops instead of relying on their own members, especially as hired men were more expensive to maintain than brothers.

Turcoples admittedly received smaller rations than fighting brothers (Curzon 1886: 119, 208, 210–11; Amatuccio 2009: 92, 190, 192; Perlbach 1890: 116), but the overall cost of a paid warrior was greater than that of a brother. A notary who gave evidence during the Templar trial asserted that the rank of sergeant brother had in fact been introduced into the Temple because there had been insufficient funds to pay all the sergeants who had earlier been in the order's employ (Michelet 1841–51: 1:643).

In obtaining service through money fiefs, the orders were merely continuing an existing practice, encouraged by the nature of the local economy, and they had little control over the employment of troops financed by others. Yet the majority of Templars and Hospitallers resided in Western Europe, remote from the frontiers of Christendom, and in 1291 the French clergy argued that most of the brothers of these orders should serve in the East, with only a few remaining in the West, and a similar idea was considered by Gregory XI with regard to the Hospital in the later fourteenth century, while about the year 1340 it had been proposed that the paid troops on the Hospitaller island of Rhodes should be replaced by a hundred brother sergeants (Bartholomew Cotton 1859: 213; Legras 1987: 37–8, 40; Luttrell 1991: 144). But brothers were needed in the various regions of Western Europe away from frontier districts in order to encourage recruitment and donations; many were not skilled warriors; and some were too old to fight (Forey 1980: 330). For orders to maintain a larger fighting establishment of brothers, further recruitment would often have been necessary.

Some military orders – especially minor ones – appear, however, to have experienced difficulties in recruiting brothers. In 1180 the order of Mountjoy petitioned Alexander III to allow it to accept Brabanzon, Aragonese and Basque mercenaries, who had been condemned at the Lateran Council in the preceding year: this recently founded order, which acquired considerable estates in Aragon, was apparently having difficulty in attracting recruits, and was seeking to convert mercenaries into brothers (Delaville Le Roulx 1893: 54; Hiestand 1972: 319–21; Forey 1971: 254–5). The Swordbrethren in Livonia were amalgamated with the Teutonic order after losing fifty brothers in the battle of the Saule in 1236. The dispatch of brothers of the order of Santiago to Germany in 1250 with powers to admit recruits suggests that it had then become necessary to seek new members outside the Iberian peninsula, where most of its brothers originated, and when fifty-five brothers of Santiago were killed in the defeat at Moclín in 1280, the order merged with the small military order of Santa María de España (Aguado de Cordóba et al. 1719: 178; Forey 1986: 160). Yet not all institutions encountered recruiting difficulties. In the twelfth and thirteenth centuries the leading orders appear to have been able to replace losses of manpower. According to the *Flores historiarum*, after the defeat at La Forbie in 1244 'to make good the loss of brothers, the Templars and Hospitallers admitted to their orders many selected laymen, and sent assistance to the Holy Land' (Luard 1890: 287); and in 1289, following the fall of Tripoli, where the Hospital lost forty brothers, the master of that order wrote that 'we have ordered that some of our brethren should be summoned to these parts from each province, so that the convent may be brought up to strength' (Delaville Le Roulx 1894–1906: 3:541).[9] Yet it is not known, of course, whether these orders' losses could easily have been made good if much larger contingents of brothers had been maintained in the Holy Land and casualties among brethren had therefore been greater.

In some instances additional troops were, however, needed for only a limited period. Although the Temple and Hospital were able to replace losses, the slowness of communications – caused partly by the restricted periods of sailing across the

Mediterranean – inevitably delayed the transfer of brothers from Western Europe to the Holy Land: in the meantime paid troops might be hired. It has been suggested that some knights in the Templar and Hospitaller contingents at Hattin in July 1187 were paid, as these orders had suffered heavy losses at Cresson two months earlier (France 2000: 2:59). Other heavy losses in the East included those sustained at Hattin itself and in 1244. On some occasions paid troops may also have been hired temporarily to replace vassals whose term of service had expired, and on occasion it may also have been necessary to pay vassals to keep them in the field for a period beyond their normal term of service.

But clearly paid troops were not engaged merely on a very short-term basis: as has been seen, garrisons of castles were composed partly of men recruited for pay. The reasons for the long-term hiring of troops by orders such as the Temple and the Hospital need therefore to be considered.

In the twelfth and thirteenth centuries the recruitment of certain types of soldier was not usually prevented by social exclusiveness within military orders: the only limitation was that, as in other religious orders, recruits should not be serfs. Many brothers of military orders resident in Western Europe in fact spent their lives engaged in menial domestic or agricultural tasks (Forey 1973: 280–1). Yet brothers of an order may not at times have been able to provide the kind of military service which was needed. Before it became militarised, the Hospital may have hired men to protect pilgrims along the roads of the Holy Land: this is suggested by a letter of Innocent II, sent between 1139 and 1143, which refers to 'sergeants, whom the brothers of that house retain at their own expense especially for this task' (Delaville Le Roulx 1894–1906: 1:107–8). The Temple at first consisted only of a group of *milites* – a term which at that time referred to a type of soldier rather than to a social rank – and during the Templar trial it was said that in the order's early days 'they rated each of their esquires and sergeants at a certain amount of money, which they used to pay them for their salaries as paid employees' (Forey 1998: 294–5; Michelet 1841–51: 1:643): but it is not clear whether any of these paid sergeants had military functions comparable with those of later brother sergeants-at-arms, who were more lightly armoured than *milites*. It was, however, probably necessary to resort to payment in order to obtain the service of *turcoples*, as there would not have been enough Westerners who were skilled in the *turcoples'* manner of fighting. Some other specialised troops, such as crossbowmen, could probably also only be obtained through hiring. Admittedly, when writing of campaigns in Prussia, Peter of Dusburg mentioned Henry Tupadel, 'fully skilled in the crossbowmen's art', who later became a brother of the Teutonic order (1984: 240); and certainly in the later thirteenth century some brothers of the leading military orders did possess bows, including crossbows; but they were not primarily archers (Forey forthcoming). The use of bows and crossbows within Western Christendom was in fact condemned by the Church (Alberigo et al. 1962: 179; Friedberg 1881: 805), and although this did not prevent the employment of archers in wars in Western Europe, crossbowmen were apparently used to only a limited extent in the West during the twelfth century and were often mercenaries (Bradbury 1985: 8, 171). It may therefore not have been easy for orders to attract large numbers of recruits who could serve as *ballistarii*. For some military orders, the hiring of troops may therefore have been necessitated at least in part by an inability to recruit certain types of fighting men as brothers. And already in the first half of the twelfth century, of course, the engaging of troops for pay was a well-established practice in the secular world.

NOTES

1 I have avoided the use of the term 'mercenary' when discussing troops paid by military orders as this word has been defined in more than one way: the question is examined in several essays published in France (2008). 'Paid' is used in this chapter in the sense of remuneration in cash.

2 On the hiring of troops during the Albigensian crusade, see Horoy (1880: 143, 154).

3 Several papal bulls refer to crusaders who assisted orders in the defence of the latter's castles in various frontier regions (Ortega y Cotes et al. 1761: 57; Mansilla 1955: 251; Bunge 1853: 109).

4 The same comment can be made about a reference in 1238 to *mercenarii* of the order of Alcántara (Palacios Martín 2000: 92).

5 Other manuscripts omit the words 'for pay' (*aus solz*).

6 The sixteenth-century historian Rades y Andrada (1572: Santiago 23v, 30v) states that the order of Santiago had paid troops (*gente de sueldo*) on its campaigns, but provides no reference.

7 The fear that the Holy Land might have to be abandoned was expressed not only by the military orders (Weiland 1874: 547–9).

8 Differing views have been expressed about the numbers of Westerners available for hire (France 2004: 1:353; Murray 2008: 279).

9 On the supply of recruits generally, see Forey (1986: 157–62).

REFERENCES

Manuscript sources

'Cartulario de Tortosa', in Barcelona, Archivo de la Corona de Aragón, Ordenes Religiosas y Militares, San Juan de Jerusalén.

'Templarios', in Archivo de la Corona de Aragón, Cancillería Real, Cartas Reales Diplomáticas, Jaime II.

Printed works

Alberigo, J., Joannou, P., Leonardi, C. and Prodi, P. (eds) (1962) *Conciliorum oecumenicorum decreta*. Basel: Herder.

Aguado de Córdoba, A. F., Alemán y Rosales, A. A. and López Agurleta, J. (eds) (1719) *Bullarium equestris ordinis S. Iacobi de Spatha*. Madrid: Aritzia.

Amatuccio, G. (ed.) (2009) *Il Corpus normativo templare. Edizione dei testi romanzi con traduzione e commento in italiano*. Galatina: Congedo.

'Annales de Burton' (1864) in H. R. Luard (ed.) *Annales monastici*, vol. 1, Rolls Series 36. London: Longman.

Auvray, L. (ed.) (1907) *Les registres de Grégoire IX*, vol. 2. Paris: Fontemoing.

Ayala Martínez, C. de (2003) *Las órdenes militares hispánicas en la edad media (siglos XII-XV)*. Madrid: Marcial Pons.

Bartholomew Cotton (1859) *Historia Anglicana*, ed. H. R. Luard, Rolls Series 16. London: Longman.

Benito Ruano, E. (1952) 'Balduino II de Constantinopla y la orden de Santiago. Un proyecto de defensa del Imperio Latino de Oriente', *Hispania*, 12: 3–36.

Biskup, M. (1991) 'Das Problem der Söldner in den Streitkräften des Deutschordensstaates Preussen vom Ende des 14. Jahrhunderts bis 1525', in Z. H. Nowak (ed.), *Das Kriegswesen der Ritterorden im Mittelalter*. Torun: Uniwersytet Mikołaja Kopernika, 49–74.

Bradbury, M. (1985) *The Medieval Archer*. Woodbridge: Boydell.

Bunge, F. G. von (ed.) (1853) *Liv-, Esth-, und Curländisches Urkundenbuch nebst Regesten*, vol. 1. Reval: Laakmann.

Calendar of Charter Rolls, 1257–1300 (1906) London: HMSO.

Calendar of Close Rolls, 1279–1288 (1902) London: HMSO.

Calendar of Liberate Rolls, 1251–1260 (1959) London: HMSO.

Catlos, B. A. (2004) '"Mahomet Abenadalill": A Muslim Mercenary in the Service of the Kings of Aragon (1290–1291)', in H. J. Hames (ed.), *Jews, Muslims and Christians in and around the Crown of Aragon. Essays in Honour of Professor Elena Lourie*. Leiden: Brill, 257–302.

Charlo Brea, L. (ed.) (1997) *Chronica Latina regum Castellae*, CCM 73. Turnhout: Brepols.

Claverie, P.-V. (2001) 'Un nouvel éclairage sur le financement de la première croisade de Saint Louis', *Mélanges de l'Ecole Française de Rome. Moyen Age*, 113: 621–35.

———. (2005) *L'ordre du Temple en Terre Sainte et à Chypre au XIIIe siècle*, vol. 3. Nicosia: Recherche Scientifique de Chypre.

Curzon, H. de (ed.) (1886) *La règle du Temple*. Paris: Renouard.

Delaville Le Roulx, J. (1893) 'L'ordre de Montjoye', *Revue de l'orient latin*, 1: 42–57.

———. (1894–1906) *Cartulaire général de l'ordre des Hospitaliers de Saint-Jean de Jérusalem*, 4 vols. Paris: Leroux.

Duggan, A. J. (2000) '*Ne in dubium*: The Official Record of Henry II's Reconciliation at Avranches, 21 May 1172', *English Historical Review*, 115: 643–58.

Ehlers, A. (2001) 'The Crusade of the Teutonic Knights against Lithuania reconsidered', in A. V. Murray (ed.), *Crusade and Conversion on the Baltic Frontier, 1150–1500*. Aldershot: Ashgate, 21–44.

Ekdahl, S. (2008) 'The Teutonic Order's Mercenaries during the "Great War" with Poland-Lithuania (1409–11)', in J. France (ed.) *Mercenaries and Paid Men. The Mercenary Identity in the Middle Ages*. Leiden: Brill, 345–61.

Ellenblum, R. (1998) *Frankish Rural Settlement in the Latin Kingdom of Jerusalem*. Cambridge: Cambridge University Press.

Fancy, H. (2013) 'Theologies of Violence: The Recruitment of Muslim Soldiers by the Crown of Aragon', *Past and Present*, 221: 39–73.

Febrer Romaguera, M. V. (ed.) (1991) *Cartas pueblas de las morerías valencianas y documentación complementaria*. Zaragoza: Anubar.

Finke, H. (1922) *Acta Aragonensia*, vol. 3. Berlin: Rothschild.

Fonnesberg-Schmidt, I. (2007) *The Popes and the Baltic Crusades, 1147–1254*. Leiden: Brill.

Forey, A. J. (1971) 'The Order of Mountjoy', *Speculum*, 46: 250–66.

———. (1973) *The Templars in the Corona de Aragón*. London: Oxford University Press.

———. (1980) 'The Military Orders in the Crusading Proposals of the Late-Thirteenth and Early-Fourteenth Centuries', *Traditio*, 36: 317–45.

———. (1986) 'Recruitment to the Military Orders (Twelfth to Mid-Fourteenth Centuries)', *Viator*, 17: 139–71.

———. (1998) 'Rank and Authority in the Military Orders during the Twelfth and Thirteenth Centuries', *Studia monastica*, 40: 291–327.

———. (2001) *The Fall of the Templars in the Crown of Aragon*. Aldershot: Ashgate.

———. (2008a) '*Milites ad terminum* in the Military Orders during the Twelfth and Thirteenth Centuries', in J. Upton-Ward (ed.) *The Military Orders. Volume 4. On Land and by Sea*. Aldershot: Ashgate, 5–11.

———. (2008b) 'Henry II's Crusading Penances for Becket's Murder', *Crusades*, 7: 153–64.

———. (forthcoming) 'Were Brothers of Military Orders equipped with Bows in the Twelfth and Thirteenth Centuries?'

France, J. (1999) *Western Warfare in the Age of the Crusades, 1000–1300*. London: UCL.

———. (2000) 'Crusading Warfare and its Adaptation to Eastern Conditions in the Twelfth Century', *Mediterranean Historical Review*, 15, 2: 49–66.

———. (2004) 'The Crusades and Military History', in *Chemins d'outre-mer. Etudes d'histoire sur la Méditerranée médiévale offertes à Michel Balard*, vol. 1. Paris: Publications de la Sorbonne, 345–52.

————. (ed.) (2008) *Mercenaries and Paid Men. The Mercenary Identity in the Middle Ages*. Leiden: Brill.

Friedberg, E. (ed.) (1881) *Corpus iuris canonici*, vol. 2. Leipzig: Tauchnitz.

García Fitz, F. (1988) 'La defensa de la frontera del bajo Guadalquivir ante las invasiones benimerines del siglo XIII', in M. García-Arenal and M. J. Viguera (eds), *Relaciones de la Península Ibérica con el Magreb (siglos XIII-XVI)*. Madrid: CSIC.

Gazulla, F. D. (1927) 'Las compañías de zenetes en el reino de Aragón (1284–1291)', *Boletín de la Real Academia de la Historia*, 90: 174–96.

Giménez Soler, A. (1905) 'Caballeros españoles en Africa y africanos en España', *Revue hispanique*, 12: 299–372.

Guinot Rodríguez, E. (ed.) (1991) *Cartes de poblament medievals valencianes*. Valencia: Generalitat Valenciana.

Guyotjeannin, O. (2004) 'Le testament de l'évêque de Beauvais Philippe de Dreux (2 novembre 1217)', in *Retour aux sources. Textes, études et documents d'histoire médiévale offerts à Michel Parisse*. Paris: Picard, 143–54.

Harari, Y. (1997) 'The Military Role of the Frankish Turcoples: a Reassessment', *Mediterranean Historical Review*, 12, 1: 75–116.

Hernández Valverde, J. (ed.) (1987) *Roderici Ximenii de Rada Historia de rebus Hispanie*. Turnhout: Brepols.

Hiestand, R. (1972) *Papsturkunden für Templer und Johanniter*. Göttingen: Vandenhoeck and Ruprecht.

Holder-Egger, O. (ed.) (1882) 'Ex historiae regum Franciae continuatione Parisiensi', in *MGH, Scriptores*, vol. 26. Hannover: Hahnsche Buchhandlung, 603–10.

Holt, P. M. (1995) *Early Mamluk Diplomacy (1260–1290). Treaties of Baybars and Qalawun with Christian Rulers*. Leiden: Brill.

Horoy, C. A. (1880) *Medii aevi bibliotheca patristica*, vol. 4. Paris: Imprimerie de la Bibliothèque Ecclésiastique.

Huygens, R. B. C. (1965) 'Un nouveau texte du traité "De constructione castri Saphet"', *Studi medievali*, 3rd series, 6: 355–87.

Jacquemart Giélée (1961) *Renart le Nouvel*, ed. H. Roussel. Paris: Picard.

Kedar, B. Z. (1990) 'The Subjected Muslims of the Frankish Levant', in J. M. Powell (ed.) *Muslims under Latin Rule, 1100–1300*. Princeton: Princeton University Press, 135–74.

Kehr, P. (1926) *Papsturkunden in Spanien. I. Katalanien*. Berlin: Weidmann.

Kohler, C. and Langlois, C. V. (1891) 'Lettres inédites concernant les croisades (1275–1307', *Bibliothèque de l'Ecole des Chartes*, 52: 46–63.

Kreem, J. (2001) 'The Business of War. Mercenary Market and Organization in Reval in the Fifteenth and Early Sixteenth Centuries', *Scandinavian Economic History Review*, 49, 2: 26–42.

Legras, A.-M. (ed.) (1987) *L'enquête pontificale de 1373 sur l'ordre des Hospitaliers de Saint-Jean de Jérusalem*. Paris: Centre National de la Recherche Scientifique.

Leopold, A. (2000) *How to Recover the Holy Land: The Crusade Proposals of the Late Thirteenth and Early Fourteenth Centuries*. Aldershot: Ashgate.

Lomax, D. W. (1959) 'El arzobispo don Rodrigo Jiménez de Rada y la orden de Santiago', *Hispania*, 19: 323–65.

————. (1961) 'Algunos estatutos primitivos de la orden de Calatrava', *Hispania*, 21: 483–94.

Luard, H. R. (ed.) (1890) *Flores historiarum*, vol. 2, Rolls Series 95. London: Longman.

Luttrell, A. T. (1991) 'The Military and Naval Organization of the Hospitallers at Rhodes, 1310–1444', in Z. H. Nowak (ed.), *Das Kriegswesen der Ritterorden im Mittelalter*. Torun: Uniwersytet Mikołaja Kopernika, 133–53.

'Majus Chronicon Lemovicense' (1855) in M. Bouquet (ed.), *Recueil des historiens des Gaules et de la France,* vol. 21. Paris: Palmé, 761–802.

Mansilla, D. (ed.) (1955) *La documentación pontificia de Honorio III (1216–1227)*. Rome: Instituto Español de Historia Eclesiástica.

Marshall, C. (1992) *Warfare in the Latin East, 1192–1291*. Cambridge: Cambridge University Press.

Mas Latrie, L. de (1861) *Histoire de l' île de Chypre sous le règne des princes de la maison de Lusignan*, vol. 3. Paris: Imprimerie impériale.

Matthew Paris (1876) *Chronica majora*, ed. H. R. Luard, vol. 3, Rolls Series 57. London: Longman.

Mayer, H. E. (1982) 'Henry II of England and the Holy Land', *English Historical Review*, 97: 721–39.

———. (2010) *Die Urkunden der Lateinischen Könige von Jerusalem*, vol. 1. Hannover: Hahnsche Buchhandlung.

Michelet, J. (1841–51) *Procès des Templiers*, 2 vols. Paris: Imprimerie Royale.

Miret y Sans, J. (1911) 'Inventaris de les cases del Temple de la Corona d'Aragó en 1289', *Boletín de la Real Academia de Buenas Letras de Barcelona*, 6: 61–75.

Murray, A. V. (2006) 'Money and Logistics in the Forces of the First Crusade: Coinage, Bullion, Service and Supply, 1096–99', in J. H. Pryor (ed.) *Logistics of Warfare in the Age of the Crusades*. Aldershot: Ashgate, 229–49.

———. (2008) 'The Origin of Money-Fiefs in the Latin Kingdom of Jerusalem', in J. France (ed.), *Mercenaries and Paid Men. The Mercenary Identity in the Middle Ages*. Leiden: Brill, 275–86.

———. (2013) 'The Sword Brothers at War: Observations on the Military Activity of the Knighthood of Christ in the Conquest of Livonia and Estonia (1203–1227)', *Ordines militares. Colloquia Torunensia historica*, 18: 27–37.

Oliver of Paderborn (1894) 'Historia Damiatina', in O. Hoogeweg (ed.), *Die Schriften des Kölner Domscholasters späteren Bischofs von Paderborn und Kardinal-Bischofs von S. Sabina Oliverus*. Tübingen: Litterarischer Verein in Stuttgart.

Ortega y Cotes, I. J., Alvarez de Baquedano, J. F. and Ortega Zúñiga y Aranda, P. de (eds) (1761) *Bullarium ordinis militiae de Calatrava*. Madrid: Antonio Marin.

Pagarolas i Sabaté, L. (1999) *Els Templers de les terres de l'Ebre. De Jaume I fins a l'abolició de l'orde (1213–1312)*, vol. 2. Tarragona: Diputació de Tarragona.

Palacios Martín, B. (ed.) (2000) *Colección diplomática medieval de la orden de Alcántara (1157?–1494). I. De los orígenes a 1454*. Madrid: Editorial Complutense.

Paravicini, W. (1989) *Die Preussenreisen des Europäischen Adels*, vol. 1. Sigmaringen: Jan Thorbecke.

Perlbach, M. (1890) *Die Statuten des Deutschen Ordens nach den* ältesten *Handschriften*. Halle: Max Niemeyer.

Peter of Dusburg (1984) *Chronica terre Prussie*, ed. and trans. K. Scholz, D. Wojtecki and M. Toeppen. Darmstadt: Wissenschaftliche Buchgesellschaft.

Philippi, R. and Seraphim, A. (eds) (1882–1909) *Preussisches Urkundenbuch*. vol. 1. Königsberg: Hartung.

Pitra, J. B. (1888) *Analecta novissima spicilegii Solesmensis: altera continuatio*, vol. 2. Paris: Typis Tusculanis.

Powicke, F. M. (1910) 'The Saracen Mercenaries of Richard I', *Scottish Historical Review*, 8: 104–5.

Pringle, D. (2012) 'Wilbrand of Oldenburg's Journey to Syria, Lesser Armenia, Cyprus and the Holy Land (1211–1212): A New Edition', *Crusades*, 11: 109–37.

Quintana Prieto, A. (ed.) (1987) *La documentación pontificia de Inocencio IV (1243–54)*, vol. 2. Rome: Instituto Español de Historia Eclesiástica.

Rades y Andrada, F. de (1572) *Chronica de las tres ordenes y cavallerias de Sanctiago, Calatrava y Alcantara*. Toledo: Juan de Ayala.

Raynaud, G. (ed.) (1887) *Les Gestes des Chiprois*. Geneva: Fick.

Richard, J. (1986) 'Les turcoples au service des royaumes de Jérusalem et de Chypre: musulmans convertis ou chrétiens orientaux?', *Revue des études islamiques*, 54: 259–70.

Richards, D. S. (trans.) (2007) *The Chronicle of Ibn al-Athir for the Crusading Period from al-Kamil fi'ta'ikh*, vol. 2. Aldershot: Ashgate.

Riley-Smith, J. (2012) *The Knights Hospitallers in the Levant, c. 1070–1309*. Basingstoke: Macmillan.

Rivera Garretas, M. (1985) *La encomienda, el priorato y la villa de Uclés en la edad media (1174–1310)*. Madrid-Barcelona: CSIC.

Robertson, J. C. and Sheppard, J. B. (eds) (1885) *Materials for the History of Thomas Becket, Archbishop of Canterbury*, vol. 7, Rolls Series 67. London: Longman.

Rodenburg, C. (ed.) (1883) *Epistolae saeculi XIII e regestis pontificum Romanorum selectae*, vol. 1. Berlin: Weidmann.

Rüdebusch, D. (1972) *Der Anteil Niedersachsens an den Kreuzzügen und Heidenfahrten*. Hildesheim: A. Lax.

Saavides, G. C. (1993) 'Late Byzantine and Western Historiographers on Turkish Mercenaries in Greek and Latin Armies: the Turcoples/Tourkopouloi', in R. Beaton and C. Roueché (eds), *The Making of Byzantine History. Studies dedicated to Donald M. Nicol*. Aldershot: Brookfield, 122–36.

Smail, R. C. (1956) *Crusading Warfare (1097–1193)*. Cambridge: Cambridge University Press.

Smith, J. C. and Urban W. L. (trans.) (1977) *The Livonian Rhymed Chronicle*. Bloomington: Indiana University.

Tumler, M. (1955) *Der Deutsche Orden im Werden, Wachsen und Wirken*. Vienna: Panorama.

Tyerman, C. (1988) *England and the Crusades, 1095–1588*. Chicago: University of Chicago.

———. (2006) *God's War. A New History of the Crusades*. London: Penguin.

———. (2013) 'Paid Crusaders. "*Pro honoris vel pecunie*"; "*stipendiarii contra paganos*"; Money and Incentives on Crusade', in Tyerman, *The Practices of Crusading*. Farnham: Ashgate, Essay 14.

Upton-Ward, J. (ed. and trans.) (2003) *The Catalan Rule of the Templars. A Critical Edition and English Translation from Barcelona, Archivo de la Corona de Aragón, Cartes Reales, MS 3344*. Woodbridge: Boydell.

Vincent, N. (2003) 'The Murderers of Thomas Becket', in N. Fryde and D. Reitz (eds) *Bischofsmord im Mittelalter. Murder of Bishops*. Göttingen: Vandenhoeck and Ruprecht, 211–72.

Weiland, L. (ed.) (1874) 'Menkonis chronicon', in *MGH, Scriptores*, vol. 23. Hannover: Hahnsche Buchhandlung, 523–61.

William of Tyre (1986) *Chronicon*, ed. R. B. C. Huygens, CCM 63. Turnhout: Brepols.

CHAPTER SIX

PEACEMAKING IN AN AGE OF WAR: WHEN WERE CROSS-RELIGIOUS ALLIANCES IN THE LATIN EAST CONSIDERED TREASON?

———•◆•———

Yvonne Friedman

The history of the crusades and the Latin Kingdom of Jerusalem is fundamentally one of war, conquest, and ultimately defeat. From the romantic histories of Christian heroism to the modern historiography of warfare, much emphasis has been placed on the ideologies of holy war and *jihad*. As the almost yearly publication of new histories of the crusades proves, this topic continues to exercise its fascination in both scholarly and lay circles. Most histories of the crusades focus on war and heroic battles, with the second stage—that of coexistence between clashing cultures and religions—a more recent newcomer on the scholarly scene.

Even if the prevailing perception of the 1096 to 1291 era is one of perennial holy war, this epoch of holy war was in fact punctuated by interludes of peace. These treaties were accepted by both sides as legally binding and, although in principle a temporary remedy for inability to continue to fight a holy war, in fact both the Muslim and the Christian political entities could legitimately enjoy periods of peace (Friedman, 2011: 229–32; Forey, 2012: 41, 42). These treaties were not only between religious adversaries and, from the very first encounters, included cross-religious alliances as Christians leaders tried to play off rival Muslim powers by siding with one against another and sometimes gaining tribute; similarly, Muslims made alliances against a too formidable Muslim neighbor or used internal divisions in the Christian camp to gain power (Köhler, 2013: 37–40). Such alliances were criticized as opposing the ideology of holy war and sometimes the initiator was seen as a traitor to the cause, as in the case of Shams al-Khilafa, emir of Ascalon, who was described as "more desirous of trading than of fighting and inclined to peaceful and friendly relations and the securing of the safety of travelers" (Ibn al-Qalanisi, 1932: 109–10; Hillenbrand, 2000: 396).[1] After he made an alliance with King Baldwin I in 1111 he was assassinated by his local coreligionists who objected to his pro-Frankish policy (Ibn al-Qalanisi, 1932: 108–9; Albert of Aachen, 2007: 11:35–37). Ibn al-Athir claimed that Shams al Khilafa wanted to assert his independence from Egypt and that was the reason for the truce with Baldwin (2007: 1:52). When were such alliances perceived as pragmatic policy and when were they seen as treason?

In modern history, based on a reality of nation-states, private negotiations with an enemy delegate are clearly designated treason and harshly punished, sometimes even by capital punishment.[2] In the medieval Middle East, however, in the absence of nation-states, the lines between individual and societal prerogatives were often more blurred. This chapter examines the question of treason in the context of the Christian–Muslim contacts in the Latin East, asking when the Christian side viewed a Christian–Muslim alliance as an example of prudent pragmatic policymaking and when similar overtures ranked as high treason.

The search for a Frankish definition of treason brings us to the *Livre au roi* (*c.* 1200). Chapter 16 stipulates various acts of treason against his seignor and his land as grounds for confiscation of a vassal's fief *sans esgart de cort*: "*La segonde raison si est, c'il avient que aucun home lige fait traïson contre son seignor ou contre sa terre, si juge la raison qu'il det estre deserités a tous jors mais*" (Greilsammer, 1995: 179). Treason, under the rubric of apostasy in Roman law, was considered in our *assise* in the special case of surrendering a town or manor to the Saracens:

> 7: La septime raison est se aucun home lige entre par force de Sarasins contre la volonté de son seignor et sans esgart de cort en saisine et de casaus et de sa terre don il det servise et homage au roi, si juge la raison qu'il det estre desiretés a tous jors mais.

> [If a vassal seized against the will of his lord and without judgement of court with the help of Saracens such villages and such lands for which he owes service and homage to the king.]

> (Greilsammer, 1995: 182)

Betrayal was a crime of treason against a sovereign who personified the state and not the betrayal of the lord by his vassal (La Monte, 1932: 276–80). Prawer (1980: 435) defined such acts as "cases of treason against the state or against Christendom." Such a definition assumed that there existed at the time a concept of state or Christendom against which one might perform an act of treason, a kind of identity that was defined not by personal ties of fidelity to a person but to a higher concept. Acts defined as treasonous included: armed rebellion; taking legal action against the king; plotting to poison him and his family; deserting him in battle; converting to Islam; and, what is most germane to this consideration, entering into possession of a fief with the help of Muslim forces against the will of the king (Riley-Smith, 1973: 146). Similarly, Jean d'Ibelin's *Livre de Assises* (Edbury, 2003: 86–87) also notes asking for assistance from Muslim forces in order to keep a fief as an act of treason, citing the Roman law that saw this as a capital offense (Edbury, 2003: 230–35, 433–38). Accordingly, an alliance between a private Christian power and a Muslim ruler in a period of crusade and holy war was defined as treason by both law and custom.

In and of itself, a Muslim–Christian peace treaty was not necessarily negative or exceptional. Notwithstanding the propaganda on both sides that depicted the enemy as an infidel, pragmatic alliances were alien neither to the crusaders nor to the Muslims. Agreements were made when deemed expedient, as Köhler has shown (2013: 165–69; 230–35). Although both the Muslim concept of *jihad* and the Christian ideal of holy war legitimated peacemaking only in cases of dire need, there were in fact many treaties from the beginning of the encounter between the enemies. These treaties not only included agreements between the two former religious enemies, but also Christian–Muslim alliances against their own coreligionists. Thus political considerations could override inter-religious enmity. We find Muslims joining with Christians to oppose a Muslim ruler, or Christians inviting Muslims to oppose a Christian rival. This, however, was the prerogative of the king or military leader.

But when was negotiating with the enemy considered treason? In order to answer that question I investigate some test cases in chronological order to see what notions governed the contemporary Christian attitude toward private alliances with the Muslims.

Two early twelfth-century cases serve as examples of the different perspectives on whether making an alliance with a Muslim ruler was considered a pragmatic step or treason. William of Tyre describes the princess Alice of Antioch as a "*mulier callida supra modum et maliciosa nimis*" (WT bk 14, ch. 4, p. 635, ll. 9–10): a woman of "wicked malice" (WT 13, 27, 265, 70). In 1130–31, after her husband's death and before she was aware that her father Baldwin II intended to come to Antioch, "*nequam agitate spiritu rem concepit nefariam*" ("an evil spirit led her to conceive a wicked plan") (13, 27, 623, 254). In order to strengthen her rule and maintain her independence, she sent messengers to the ruler of Mosul, Imad ad-Din Zengi, the arch-enemy of the northern principalities. Her envoy to Zengi was one of her *familiares* and with him she sent a snow-white palfrey decorated with silver trappings. Intercepted by Baldwin's men, the messenger was tortured and put to death, a fate that William of Tyre seemed to think was appropriate. Thomas Asbridge, who analyzed the event as an example of female power in the Latin East, tends to view the story as a tale that was perhaps invented by those opposed to Alice's rule (Asbridge, 2003: 34, 36). However, if true, approaching the enemy would be enough to discredit Alice as ruler of Antioch. It should, however, be noted that sending a costly horse as a gift was normal negotiating procedure in the East and not necessarily a romantic tale (Friedman, 2007: 31–48). If Alice wanted to forge an alliance with Zengi there was nothing unusual in her behavior. As the legitimate ruler of Antioch, she was simply using her prerogative as princess to deal with questions of war and peace, seeking an ally against those who opposed her rule. Although William of Tyre does not use the word "treason" to describe her deeds, he probably viewed her "wicked" behavior as such. Accordingly, William states that the unfortunate messenger paid the just price for her deeds, whereas she was spared by Baldwin's paternal love. Although he ousted her from Antioch, Baldwin allowed her to keep Latakia and Jabala, her dowry, as a power base. Thus, her, to us, treasonous actions were punished by exile and loss of power, but not by a capital sentence.

Taking place almost contemporaneously, the revolt of Hugh of Puiset against Fulk, the king of Jerusalem ("For certain reasons some of the highest nobles of the realm: namely Hugh, count of Jaffa, and Romain de Puy, lord of the region beyond the Jordan, are said to have conspired against the lord king" [WT 14, 15, 651, 3–4]), seems like double treason—that of a vassal against his king by having an affair with the queen, and of a vassal who asks for Muslim aid when summoned to court. If William of Tyre's insinuations are true, an affair with the queen would amount to a classical *crimen laesae maiestatis*. William claims that, in the middle of this revolt, Hugh approached the Fatimid enemy and enlisted their help. When the Fatimids attacked Arsur, Hugh's behavior was seen as clear treason and he was deserted by his former supporters. In this case too, Asbridge doubts that Hugh could have made such a move:

> Hugh was not so politically naïve as to make a choice that would automatically turn all his supporters against him. Instead, I would suggest that, once Hugh had been accused of this treasonous act, whether on the basis of fact or not, his supporters deserted him, not because they were disgusted by his act, but because they judged his political position to be untenable.
>
> (2003: 36 n31)

If Hugh was indeed guilty of high treason, King Fulk's reaction seems surprisingly lenient. Hugh did not show up for the duel to which his stepson had challenged him—accusing him of high treason—("*more accusatoris obicit comiti quod maiestatis crimine reus erat et quod contra domini regis salutem cum quibusdam factionis eiusdem complicibus, contra bonos mores et contra nostrorum disciplinam temporum, conspirasset*" [WT 14, 16, 652, 5–8]); "he publicly accused Hugh in the royal presence of high treason and of having conspired with certain accomplices of the same faction against the life of the king, contrary to good morals and the laws of the times" (WT trans., II, 72)—and fled to Egyptian shelter instead. When finally tried, the king and his court decided on a three-year exile as the appropriate punishment. This seems a very light sentence for what appears to be high treason and, at the very least, a feudal revolt ("*Contra dominum regem ab hostibus opem postulaturus ingressus est*" [WT 14, 16, 653, 23–24]). Apparently, if the king was unable to execute him lawfully, Hugh had strong forces backing him (Mayer, 1972: 102–12). An assassination attempt was made which ended in the execution of the assassin. Surprisingly, William of Tyre's final assessment of Hugh states: "Roger of Apulia thought that Hugh was a noble and valiant man (*virum strenum et nobilem*) who had been driven from the kingdom through the jealousy of his rivals" (WT 14, 18, 655, 43–44).

The punishment of exile in both of these cases shows that allying oneself with the Muslim enemy in an internal Christian power dispute apparently did not merit capital punishment. It seems that the definition of this act was more one of infringing on the king's prerogatives, not necessarily treason against kingdom and Christendom.

My next example comes from the fateful days before the battle of Hattin. This battle was preceded by a period of court intrigue and shifts in regency. According to one contemporary description, the ultimate villain of the day was Raymond III of Tripoli. Head of one of the political factions in the kingdom in this decisive period, he endorsed a policy of making treaties with the Muslims. However, Raynaud de Chatillon and Guy de Lusignan, the so-called court party, have been described as more hawkish. In 1185, while serving as regent for the infant king, Baldwin V, Raymond signed a treaty with Saladin. This took place after a year of drought, considered by both sides as a good pretext or reason for peacemaking. After Baldwin V's death a year later, the court faction staged a coup d'état, crowning Sybilla queen and accepting her unpopular husband Guy de Lusignan as king. Raymond, who refused to accept Guy as ruler, went from being the lawful regent of the kingdom to rebellious prince of Galilee. His standing treaty with Saladin was transformed from a truce between rulers to a private alliance between a rebel and an alien enemy against the crowned king of Jerusalem. At the same time, Saladin was pressured into making *jihad* after a long period of empire-consolidating battles against other Muslims (Köhler, 2013: 250–51).

What made Raymond a traitor in the eyes of some of his contemporaries? It was that, at Saladin's request, he allowed Saladin's son al-Afdal to invade his territory for one day, on 1 May 1187. The battle of Cresson, with its dreadful carnage of the Templars and Hospitallers, transformed Raymond's treaty with Saladin into an act of treason. Or as the Lyon Eracles defined it: if he agreed (to al-Afdal's raid) he would "bear great shame and reproach in Christendom" ("*grant honte et grante blasme en avroit de la crestienté*" [Morgan, 1982: 38; Edbury, 1996: 31]). The modern historian Bernard Hamilton summarizes: "The plain name for Raymond's action is treason" (2005: 224). In fact, similar political motivations drove Raymond's act and Reynaud's attack on Saladin's sister's caravan during a period of truce. Raymond's famous reply to the king when asked to make reparations for breaking the truce was "that he was lord of his land, just as Guy was lord of his and he had no truces with the Saracens" (Morgan, 1982: 36; Edbury, 1996: 29). Both princes infringed on Guy's regal rights but in opposite directions: one honored a truce with the Muslims; the other broke a truce with the Muslims. In both cases their behavior had dire consequences for the kingdom.

If a traitor, what was Raymond's punishment? Following the battle of Cresson, Raymond paid homage and fealty to Guy and they were reconciled, even though he could have been regarded as a traitor and punished accordingly. Raymond then joined the fight against Saladin. An anonymous chronicle still pegged him as the main villain in the great disaster at Hattin from the Frankish viewpoint. According to the chronicle, Raymond dispensed bad military advice, and his charge against Saladin's troops that enabled him to escape to Tyre and save his life was suspicious, but the chronicle did not name him a traitor (Colbert-Fontainebleau Eracles, 1859: 62–64; Edbury, 1996: 159). According to another version of the continuation of William of Tyre, the chronicle does report that before the battle Gerard de Ridefort told the king not to trust Raymond as he was a traitor (Morgan, 1982: 34). Ernoul rather placed the blame for the defeat at Hattin on Guy and his lack of leadership (Mas Latrie, 1871: 162–63). Depending on the writer and his political views at the time, Raymond could be seen either as a valiant leader worthy of the crown or a traitor.

In 1192, at the end of the Third Crusade, when Conrad of Montferrat tried to negotiate a private peace with Saladin, Richard the Lionheart's propagandist saw it, not unreasonably, as treason (Ambroise, 1897, ll. 8665–700). It certainly weakened Richard's position in his negotiations with Saladin. Beha a Din ibn Shadad explains how Saladin used the duplicity of peace offers as a card in the diplomatic play (Richards, 2001: 195–99). But as neither Richard nor Conrad were kings of Jerusalem at the time, this act could be harshly criticized, but not as treason, which is, by definition, against the king. When Richard signed a truce with Saladin in 1192, Ambroise explained that Richard had no choice, and that he promised to return and fight a holy war in three years' time (Ambroise, 1897, ll. 11761–800, 11805–15). Thus, making peace during the crusades was part of the lawful ruler's prerogative; nevertheless, an explanation was required.

To this point, the examples of "treason" have been related to political factors: what was acceptable for a ruler (namely to make an alliance with the enemy) was not acceptable for a private individual, who thereby manifested opposition to the legitimate regime. How then are we to regard the strange case of St. Francis, whom modern historians describe as a paradigm of private peacemaking? (Powell, 1986: 158–59; 2007: 271–80; Runciman, 1954: 159–60; Queffélec, 1982: 228; Tolan, 2009: 305). Leaving the crusader camp near Damietta in September 1219, Francis crossed the lines accompanied only by another friar and was either received by the sultan al-Kamil or captured and brought before him. Although Francis tried to preach Christianity to him, al-Kamil did not kill Francis, returning him some days later to the camp at Damietta. I suggest that perhaps the sultan regarded Francis as an envoy sent to negotiate a ceasefire and therefore granted him an audience and safe-conduct. This took place shortly before al-Kamil offered a truce to the crusaders, whose terms included the return of all the territories west of the Jordan to the Kingdom of Jerusalem if the Fifth Crusade would leave Egypt:

> Therefore the Sultan, fearing dearth and famine, and also because of his desire to keep Damietta, offered the Christians a peace with Coradin his brother on these terms: That he would give back the Holy Cross, which had formerly been captured in the victory of Saladin, along with the Holy City and all the captives who could be found alive

throughout the kingdom of Babylon and Damascus and also funds to repair the walls of Jerusalem, in addition he would restore the kingdom of Jerusalem entirely, except Krak and Monreal.

(Hoogeweg, 1894: 222–24; Gavigan, 1948: 48)

This offer was refused by the papal legate Pelagius, the military orders and Italian communes. The king of Jerusalem and some of the local nobility, however, were in favor of accepting the truce. Francis's endeavor has been seen by modern historians as an implicit criticism of the crusade and perhaps even as his working against crusader interests. But the contemporary sources do not support the modern image of Francis as an individual peacemaker. Jacques de Vitry portrayed St. Francis as an ardent preacher of Christianity who tried to convince the sultan to convert; thus he exemplified mission rather than crusade:

Lord Rayner, Prior of St. Michael, has entered the Order of the Lesser Brothers. The Order is multiplying rapidly throughout the world, because it expressly imitates the pattern of the primitive church and the life of the apostles in everything. Nevertheless, this Order seems dangerous to us, because it sends out two by two throughout the world, not only formed religious, but also immature young men who should first be tested and subjected to conventual discipline for a time.

The head of these brothers, who also founded the Order, came into our camp. He was so inflamed with zeal for the faith that he did not fear to cross the lines to the army of our enemy. For several days he preached the Word of God to the Saracens and made little progress. The Sultan, king of Egypt, privately asked him to pray to the lord for him, so that he might be inspired by God to adhere to that religion which most pleased God ... I am having a difficult time holding on to the cantor and Henry and several others.

(Huygens, 1960, letter 6; trans. from Tolan, 2009: 19)

Although his mission was not effective, Francis could still be admired for his piety. The chronicle of Ernoul emphasizes that the friars asked for permission to cross the lines in order to preach Christianity to the sultan and that this was reluctantly granted by Pelagius (Mas Latrie, 1871: 431; Tolan, 2009: 42). Whether the motivation was missionary zeal or seeking the glory of martyrdom, Francis's initiative was not a private negotiation for peace. St. Francis may have become a symbol of the individual fighting for peace and love in a society organized for war, but the contemporary sources do not support such a view. Ernoul does, however, elaborate on the friar's pure intentions, noting that, although the sultan offered them great riches, "They said they would take nothing, since they could not have his soul for God for it was in their eyes more valuable to them than all that he possessed" (Mas Latrie, 1871: 435; Tolan, 2009: 42). Unlike the examples discussed earlier, where the peace initiative was motivated by personal or political gain, it was clear to all sides that Francis sought no personal gain. His very presence in the crusader camp suggests that he did not perceive missionizing and crusading as opposing tasks and did not criticize crusader policy (Kedar, 1984: 129–31). Indeed, the sultan may have thought him insane and therefore spared his life or he may have been impressed by his personality and sanctity, as the hagiographic Franciscan stories have it. It is doubtful that al-Kamil used Francis as a tool for promoting his offer of a truce. In any event, in the hagiographic descriptions Francis does not undermine the military aim of conquering Egypt once and for all.

Another saintly crusader, Louis IX, returned to Damietta in 1249 and made almost exactly the same political and military mistakes as his predecessors, the leaders of the Fifth Crusade. He too declined an Egyptian offer of a treaty in hopes of crushing Egypt completely, only to end up in captivity along with his entire army. Nonetheless, in 1250, on his return to Acre, he was received with royal magnificence as the leader of the crusade (Gaposchkin, 2013: 85–60). On hearing that the Templars had conducted private negotiations for a truce with the Damascus Muslims in 1252, the saintly king reacted with fury. He did not, however, term the deed treason, but an infringement of the king's sole authority to decide on matters of peace. The Templars' marshal, Hugues de Jouy, had encroached on these rights and therefore had to be punished publicly: the king insisted on his expulsion from the kingdom (Joinville, 1888, chs. 511–14). Thus in the mid-thirteenth century such initiatives had to be nipped in the bud to elucidate that the king, and only he, possessed the right to enter into peace negotiations with the enemy. Whereas in Spain the kings were able to enforce the principle that the military orders could not make peace privately and had to honor truces that the king made, it was apparently less clear in the Latin East (Forey, 2012: 42–44). In 1168 Bohemond III of Antioch conceded that the Hospitallers could make war or peace from the places he gave them (Delaville le Roulx 1894, doc. 391: 266–68; Forey, 2012: 45) and the Templars received tribute from the Assasins in the 1170s (WT 20, 29–30; Forey, 2012: 45) and in 2012 the pilgrim Wilbrand of Oldenburg reported that the Hospitallers received tribute from Aleppo (Wilbrand, 1873: 170) and in the Kingdom of Jerusalem there were many cases of private negotiations without asking the king's permission (Forey, 2012: 47–49). When Louis IX was in Cyprus before his crusade to Damietta, he ordered the Templar master not to negotiate with the Muslims without his permission (Guillaume de Nangis, 1840: 366–69; Forey, 2012: 49). The king's reaction did therefore fit his concepts of kingship and the king's prerogative to have the sole authority to decide on matters of war and peace. The punishment of expulsion fitted that of a treasonous infringement of royal rights.

This show of central power was not lasting. Although Louis was not king of Jerusalem, his personal authority as king of France and prestige as holy warrior, in spite of his failure, were enough to restrain other factions. However, with Mamluk ascendance and the fact that the kings of Jerusalem were absentee kings, the dwindling kingdom made desperate efforts to be saved by making truces with the Mamluk sultan Baybars and his heirs. In the 1280s Baybars and Qalawun made numerous peace treaties with separate entities in the Latin Kingdom: the Hospitallers (1271), the Templars (1281), certain cities as in the case of Tripoli (1281), the lady Margaret of Tyre (1285), and also entered into short-term private peace treaties where each entity did its best to save its own skin without much thought for the good of the kingdom. These treaties illustrate the disintegration of the kingdom into petty political and geographical entities, which enabled the Mamluks to dictate ever more humiliating terms (Holt, 1995). Given the absence of a central authority to prevent them from seeking their own interest, the Genoese, the Hospitallers, and the lady of Tyre could not be viewed as treasonous.

The last "treasonous" accord discussed here comes from the story of the Templar of Tyre concerning the final years of the Kingdom of Acre. This involved the Templar master William of Beaujeu, who engaged in private contacts with the sultan of Egypt, including financial dealings and safe conducts. Although not defined as a traitor, his coreligionists distrusted him. Time and again he warned the rulers of Tripoli and Acre of the Mamluk sultan's imminent plans to conquer the kingdom. But, because of the suspicion aroused by his lucrative contacts with the sultan, his warnings and mediation endeavors went unheeded.

> They did not want to believe this ... Others said ugly things about the master, to the effect that he wanted to alarm them so that they would need him as an intermediary between them and the sultan, so that it would seem as though the master had induced the Saracens to go back, but that in fact they were not coming at all.
>
> (Crawford, 2003: 99)

When the sultan prepared the final attack on Acre, William again tried to warn the Franks, in vain (Crawford, 2003: 102, 104). On the one hand, the king was unable to curb the Templar master as Louis IX had, but, on the other, he also did not use the intelligence to be gained from the master's peaceful relations with the sultan. In a way, the master was regarded as a traitor. This was in fact proven incorrect when the Templars fought courageously in the final battles for Acre and went to their deaths as martyrs.

To return to the question with which I opened this chapter: the classic definition of treason, with its sentences of long imprisonment or capital punishment, belongs more to the notion of the nation-state than to the medieval landscape with its petty, warring principalities. Pursuit of personal political or financial gain through alliances with the enemy placed the individual in question under suspicion of lack of loyalty to the "central" government of the day. However, when kings engaged in peacemaking initiatives or alliances, they were seen as exercising their royal prerogative. As always, treason is in the eye of the beholder.

NOTES

1 For the economic background to treaties, see, for example, the treaties between Baldwin I and Tughtigin of Damascus in 1108–09, 1111, and 1113 sharing the income from territories held as condominiums, in Ibn al-Qalanisi, 1932, 92, 113, 147.

2 See, e.g., the British code of 1351 which is still in force: Declaration what Offences shall be adjudged Treason. Compassing the Death of the King, Queen, or their eldest Son; violating the Queen, or the King's eldest Daughter unmarried, or his eldest Son's Wife; levying War; *adhering to the King's Enemies*; killing the Chancellor, Treasurer, or Judges in Execution of their Duty. Similar definitions of treason as helping enemies of one's country are found in US Code, Title 18, Part I, Chapter 115, § 2381 (the punishment being death or not less than five years' prison) and Israeli penal law 1977, 93–103.

REFERENCES

AA=Albert of Aachen, 2007. *Historia Ierosolimitana: History of the Journey to Jerusalem*, ed. S. Edgington. Oxford: Clarendon.

Ambroise, 1897. *L'Estoire de la Guerre Sainte par Ambroise: Histoire en vers de la troisième croisade*, ed. G. Paris. Paris: Imprimerie nationale.

Asbridge, T., 2003. Alice of Antioch: A Case Study of Female Power in the Twelfth Century. In P. Edbury and J. Phillips, eds. *The Experience of Crusading II: Defining the Crusader Kingdom*. Cambridge: Cambridge University Press, 29–47.

Colbert-Fontainebleau Eracles 1859. *L'Estoire de Eracles Empereur et la conqueste de la terre d'Outremer c'est la continuation de l'estoire de Guillaume arcevesque de Sur, RHC, Historiens Occidentaux* vol II. Paris: Imprimerie Impériale.

Crawford, P., trans., 2003. *The "Templar of Tyre". Part III of the "Deeds of the Cypriots."* Aldershot: Ashgate.

Delaville Le Roulx, J., ed., 1894. *Cartulaire général de l'ordre des Hospitaliers de Saint-Jean de Jérusalem.* Paris: Leroux.

Edbury, P.W., trans., 1996. *The Conquest of Jerusalem and the Third Crusade.* Aldershot: Ashgate.

Edbury, P.W. ed., 2003. *John of Ibelin: Le Livre des Assises.* Leiden: Brill.

Forey, A., 2012. The Participation of the Military Orders in Truces with Muslims in the Holy Land and Spain during the Twelfth and Thirteenth Centuries. *Ordines Militares: Yearbook for the Study of the Military Orders*, 17.

Friedman, Y., 2007. Gestures of Conciliation: Peacemaking Endeavors in the Latin East. In I. Shagrir, R. Ellenblum, and J. Riley-Smith, eds. *In laudem Hierosolymitani. Studies in Crusades and Medieval Culture in Honour of Benjamin Z. Kedar.* Aldershot: Ashgate.

————, 2011. Peacemaking: Perceptions and Practices in the Medieval Latin East. In C. Kostick, ed. *The Crusade and the Near East.* London: Routledge.

Gaposchkin, C., 2013. The Captivity of Louis the IX. *Quaestiones Medii Aevi Novae*, 18.

Gavigan, John J., trans. 1948. *The Capture of Damietta by Oliver Paderborn.* Philadelphia: University of Pennsylvania Press.

Greilsammer, M., ed., 1995. *Le Livre au roi.* Paris: L'Académie des inscriptions et belles-lettres.

Guillaume de Nangis, 1840, repr. 1968. *Vita Sancti Ludovici.* In M. Bouquet, *Recueil des historiens des Gaule et de la France* vol. 20. Paris: Académie des inscriptions et belles-lettres, Victor Palmé; reprint, Gregg International Publishers.

Hamilton, B., 2005. *The Leper King and His Heirs: Baldwin IV and the Crusader Kingdom of Jerusalem.* Cambridge: Cambridge University Press.

Hillenbrand, C., 2000. *The Crusades: Islamic Perspectives.* New York: Routledge.

Holt, P.M., 1995. *Early Mamluk Diplomacy (1260–1290).* Leiden: Brill.

Hoogeweg, H., 1894. *Die Schriften des Kölner Domscholasters, späteren Bischofs von Paderborn und Kardinal-bischofs con S.Sabina Oliverus.* Tübingen: Litterarischer Verein in Stuttgart.

Huygens, R.H.C., ed., 1960. *Lettres de Jacques de Vitry 1160/70–1240 éveque de Saint Jean d'Acre.* Leiden: Brill.

Ibn al-Athir, 2007. *The Chronicle of Ibn al-Athir for the Crusading Period from al-Kamil fi'l-ta'rikh.* Aldershot: Ashgate.

Ibn al-Qalanisi, 1932. *The Damascus Chronicle of the Crusades.* London: Luzac.

Joinville, J. sire de, 1888. *Histoire de Saint Louis: Credo et Lettre a Louis IX*, ed. N. de Wailly. Paris: Hachette.

Kedar, B.Z., 1984. *Crusade and Mission: European Approaches to the Muslims.* Princeton, NJ: Princeton University Press.

Köhler, M.A., 2013. *Alliances and Treaties between Frankish and Muslim Rulers in the Middle East: Cross-Cultural Diplomacy in the Period of the Crusades.* Leiden: Brill.

Mas Latrie, L. de, ed., 1871. *Chronique d'Ernoul et de Bernard le Trésorier.* Paris: J. Renouard.

Mayer, H.E., 1972. Studies in the History of Queen Melisende of Jerusalem. *Dumbarton Oaks Papers,* 26.

La Monte, J., 1932. *Feudal Monarchy in the Latin Kingdom of Jerusalem, 1100 to 1291.* Cambridge, MA: Medieval Academy of America.

Morgan, M.R., ed., 1982. *La continuation de Guillaume de Tyr (1184–1197).* Paris: Paul Geuthner.

Powell, J., 1986. *Anatomy of a Crusade, 1213–1221.* Philadelphia: University of Pennsylvania Press.

————, 2007. St. Francis of Assisi's Way of Peace. *Medieval Encounters*, 13.

Prawer, J., 1980. *Crusader Instititutions.* Oxford: Clarendon.

Queffélec, H., 1982. *François d'Asisse, le Jongleur de Dieu.* Paris: Calmann-Lévi.

Richards, D.S., trans., 2001. *The Rare and Excellent History of Saladin by Baha al-Din Ibn Shadad.* Aldershot: Ashgate.

Riley-Smith, J., 1973. *The Feudal Nobility and the Kingdom of Jerusalem.* London: Macmillan.

Runciman, S., 1954. *History of the Crusades,* vol. III: *The Kingdom of Acre and the Later Crusades.* Cambridge: Cambridge University Press.

Tolan, J., 2009. *Saint Francis and the Sultan: The Curious History of a Christian-Muslim Encounter.* Oxford: Oxford University Press.

Willbrand of Oldenburg, 1873. *Peregrinatio* 1,11. In J.C.M Laurent, ed. *Peregrinatores medii aevi quatuor.* Leipzig.

WT=William of Tyre, 1986. *Chronicon,* ed. R.B.C. Huygens, Corpus Christianorum continuatio medievalis 63, 63A. Turnhout: Brepols.

WT trans.=William of Tyre, 1943. *A History of Deeds Done beyond the Sea,* trans. E.A. Babcock and A.C. Krey. New York: Columbia University Press.

PART II

THE CRUSADER WEST

———•◆•———

CHAPTER SEVEN

THE MILITARY-RELIGIOUS ORDERS IN THE CRUSADER WEST

———•◆•———

Karl Borchardt

Templars, Hospitallers and the Teutonic Order were founded in the East to support the Latin Christians there with supplies from the West. Their role in the West was twofold: spiritual and practical. Setbacks in the East were usually explained as happening *peccatis nostris exigentibus*, and so life in the West had to be reformed to regain God's favour in the East. On the practical side, the West provided men, armour and money for fighting in the East. The concept of an order itself was new. Its evolution was not complete before the thirteenth century when general councils forbade the creation of new orders. Before the twelfth century, mother houses might found *filie* and try to maintain there some kind of uniformity regarding the rule, the statutes and the *consuetudines*. The military-religious orders primarily tried to organise an efficient exploitation of Western resources. During the twelfth and thirteenth centuries, they acquired rich possessions in the West which were administered by brethren known as preceptors or commanders. For administrative purposes the commanderies formed various geographical entities usually called provinces, priories or bailiwicks. Such geographical divisions were a twelfth-century innovation made popular by Templars, Hospitallers and Premonstratensians, whereas so far Cluniacs, Cistercians and other religious communities had controlled their new houses through the immediate mother house, that is, by the principle of filiation. This, however, soon proved to be awkward for long distances. In the context of reforms after the failure to regain Jerusalem, the Lateran Council of 1215 c. 12 prescribed triennial chapters according to ecclesiastical dioceses, *in singulis regnis sive provinciis*, for all Benedictine and Cistercian abbots and priors (Tanner and Alberigo 1990: 240–1). In the thirteenth century, the Dominicans, the Franciscans and other mendicants followed the example of the military-religious orders and established provinces (see Schmidt 2013 with further references). Neither the history of the administrative divisions of the three great military-religious orders in the West nor the development of their Western possessions in general have been studied thoroughly so far. The major reason for this is not the lack of documentation but, on the contrary, the huge number of relevant charters in archives throughout Latin Europe. Especially the prosopography of the leading brethren and the regional officers has so far not been established on a critical and reliable basis, and therefore the history of their offices cannot be described here with confidence as such offices were formed and reshaped not only due to changing political situations but also for individual brethren. The purpose of the present chapter is merely to highlight some of the open questions in this context.

All three great military-religious orders had their headquarters in Jerusalem or elsewhere in the East, at least until Acre was lost in 1291. Their central convents were in the Levant, their chapters general usually assembled there, and their masters were as a rule elected in the East and lived there, although they sometimes travelled to the West trying to organise support (Burgtorf 2008: 115). From the twelfth century onwards both the Hospitallers and the Templars empowered envoys to represent the respective order in the West, at first probably for special missions and later on a permanent basis. In Western documents and sources such an officer might be called *maitre deça mer* or *magister citra mare*. And there might be several of them at the same time for different Western regions. In due course, possessions and administrative tasks multiplied. Regional officers had to be established in the West, and for controlling them, visitations were introduced during the thirteenth century. There could be different *visitatores* for different Western regions at the same time, and sometimes a *maitre deça mer* or *magister citra mare* could himself serve as a *visitator*. After the 1250s the Templars tended to have one such officer for Spain and another for France, England and Germany, whereas their Italian possessions were apparently surveyed by the Eastern headquarters directly (Forey 1973: 328–9; Barber 1994: 245; Vogel 2007: 283–5). Similarly, the thirteenth-century Hospitallers empowered grand commanders for the West in general, for specific regions, or for special purposes. They must not be confused with the regional priors who held a permanent office (Riley-Smith 1967: 366–71).

ADMINISTRATION IN THE WEST

The brethren in charge of Western affairs and possessions were at first usually called *magistri*, following the example of the supreme *magister* in the Eastern headquarters, *preceptores*, referring to their special authority, or *procuratores*, as one of their tasks was to represent their order at negotiations and law-courts; the Hospitallers also used the monastic term *priores*. Later on, especially in the thirteenth century, the terms *baiulus* and *commendator* came to be more frequently used, the former from the Anglo-Norman and French royal and princely administrations, the latter probably from the merchants' *commenda*, a well-known commercial institution in the Mediterranean. These officers could be special *missi*, envoys with specific tasks. Yet the increasing number of donations soon made it necessary to appoint permanent officers for specific geographical regions. In the thirteenth century such permanent officers even began not only to use their personal seal but also to have a seal for their office. The size of the geographical entities was never stable and would be changed according to political or personal conditions. Nor was there always a clear-cut hierarchy of such regional officers. In remote regions, subordinate officers might be de facto independent. The local administrative unit was supposedly the commandery, a house where a group of brethren, *milites*, priests and *servientes* formed a convent. The officers in charge of such a house used the same titles as the regional officers: *magister, preceptor, procurator, baiulus* or *commendator*. This makes it difficult to distinguish whether such an officer was in charge of only a single house or of his order's possessions in a whole region. Furthermore, houses came into existence only when there were enough brethren available in the region. Sources may mention the acquisition of a certain property. Yet such an acquisition did not necessarily mean that a house or a commandery was established at this particular place immediately. Finally, the series of office-holders is difficult to establish, because they are mentioned only occasionally in charters, and because such sources are not always accessible in reliable editions. Furthermore, until the end of the thirteenth century many officers were mentioned only with their first or Christian name, and family names would often vary. Therefore it is almost impossible to establish the prosopographies of the Western office-holders of the military-religious orders for the twelfth and thirteenth centuries. It is clear, however, that the Eastern headquarters usually appointed only the higher Western officers who in turn had their own chapters where they dealt with the local commanders. Conflicts might arise of course when the headquarters wanted to reward brethren who had served in the East with particular Western commanderies, and when kings, princes or other influential people in the West wanted to secure the appointment of their favourites as officers among the military-religious orders.

The starting-point for any discussion of the regional divisions of the three military-religious orders in the West has to be the situation at the beginning of the fourteenth century. For the Hospitallers, there is a list from the year 1317 when Pope John XXII appointed priors and *preceptores* for ten years who had to repay debts of the order to the societies of the Bardi and the Peruzzi (Mollat 1904: nos. 4450–72). At this stage, the Hospital had seven priors – Venice, Pisa, Lombardy, Rome, Barletta, Capua and Messina – and three preceptors – (1) Santissima Trinità in Venosa and San Giovanni de Pizonibus in Naples, (2) Sant'Euphemia in Calabria and (3) Santo Stefano in Monopoli – in Italy, seven priors – Provence, Saint-Gilles, Toulouse (separated from Saint-Gilles in 1315), Auvergne, Francia, Aquitaine, Champagne (the latter two separated from *Francia* in 1317, Legras 1987: 73–74) – in France, three priors – England, Ireland, Scotland – on the British Isles, four priors – (1) Castile and León, (2) Portugal, (3) Navarre and (4) the Castellany of Amposta for Aragón – on the Iberian Peninsula, where in 1319 Catalonia was formed as another separate priory, and finally four priories – (1) *Alamania superior* and *inferior*, (2) Bohemia, Moravia, Poland and Austria, (3) *Dacia*, Sweden and Norway, (4) Hungary – for central, eastern and northern Europe. This amounted to a total of twenty-six priories and, in Italy, three preceptories. When brethren, supplies and moneys were sent to the conventual headquarters in the East, they were grouped there according to seven *langues*: (1) Provence, (2) Auvergne, (3) France, (4) Italy, (5) Spain, (6) England and (7) Germany (Riley-Smith 1967: 353–9).

For the Templars, who were dissolved between 1307 and 1312, the documentation concerning their trial permits a reconstruction of their regional divisions in the West. They had about a dozen provincial *preceptores* for Francia – Poitou and Aquitaine, Provence, Auvergne – for England and other parts of the British isles, for Aragón and for Portugal, for Lombardy and other parts of Italy, for Sicily and for Apulia, for Alamania and the Slavic lands east of Alamania, and finally for Hungary including Slavonia (Vogel 2007: 285–90). It is difficult to establish a precise figure, because some of these regional entities had subdivisions which might have separate *preceptores*, among them Normandy and Ireland. When the Hospitallers were awarded the Templar possessions in 1312, they had to retrocede to the papacy certain commanderies in the Comtat Venaissin by 1317, among them the Hospitaller houses of Avignon, Châteauneuf, Orange and Pernes, Beaulieu, Thoronne and Saint-Paul-Trois-Châteaux, plus the former Templar houses at Cavaillon, Roaix and Richerenches (Carraz 2005: 536–7 with n. 98 and fig. 29).

The Teutonic Order was formed only between 1190 and 1197, and its possessions centred on Germany, the Mediterranean and the Baltic. At the beginning of the fourteenth century its regional administrative structures included three provincial masters (*Landmeister*) for Germany, Prussia and Livonia. Outside Prussia and Livonia the Teutonic Order had also *Landkomture, provinciales*, for certain groups of commanderies called bailiwicks, an innovation copied from Templars and Hospitallers in Western Europe. There were some twelve bailiwicks in the Empire north of the Alps: (1) Franconia, (2) Alsace and Burgundy, (3) Lorraine, (4) Koblenz, (5) the *partes inferiores* or Netherlands, (6) Westphalia, (7) Marburg, (8) Thuringia, (9) Saxony, (10) Bohemia and Moravia, (11) Austria and (12) Bozen on the Etsch. The possessions around the Mediterranean were grouped into more than half a dozen bailiwicks – Sicily, Apulia, (Central) Italy, Lombardy, Spain, Romania (Greece), Cyprus, and Armenia – the latter two being more or less titular by 1300 (Forstreuter 1967: 56–7, 65–6).

The Western officers had to report to the Eastern headquarters from time to time. For their chapters general and for the magistral elections, all three military-religious orders tried to ensure that Western officers went to the Eastern headquarters. For the Templars, a section of the French rule datable probably to the mid-1160s mentions eight regional *preceptores*, two in the East – Tripoli and Antioch – and seven in the West – France, England, Poitiers, Aragón, Portugal, Apulia and Hungary. By the late thirteenth century there were also important *preceptores* for Aquitaine, Normandy and Auvergne (Barber 1994: 244–5). The Hospitaller chapter general of 1182 mentioned the priories of France, Saint-Gilles, Italy, Pisa and Venice: later on, a number of Western officers were regarded as capitular bailiffs and participated in chapters general alongside with the conventual officers (Riley-Smith 1967: 287–8). According to the mid-thirteenth-century statutes, the Teutonic Order summoned seven regional *preceptores* to its annual chapters in the Eastern headquarters, from Livonia, Germany, Prussia, Austria, Apulia, Romania and Armenia. In a fourteenth-century French translation, Armenia was replaced in this list by Spain (Perlbach 1890: 59, 97). The reason was probably that the Armenian possessions had been lost meanwhile.

WESTERN POSSESSIONS
Hospitallers and Templars

The lesser nobility of Western Europe being the primary supporters of the military-religious orders in the twelfth century, both Hospitallers and Templars had their major possessions in Capetian and Angevin realms. French or Occitan were the dominant languages in both orders. For Western Europe, Provence was the major centre of communication with the Levant, and the port of Saint-Gilles became a major administrative centre for both Hospitallers and Templars. The first Templar master, Hugues de Paiens, however, originated from near Troyes, and therefore many early donations to the new militia came from Champagne. Nobles in other French and in Plantagenet lands soon followed suit. So from their beginnings the Templars tended to have three regional *magistri*: the first for Provence, the second for *Francia* including Champagne and the third for Angevin Poitou. As donations multiplied, subregions were created which sometimes received separate officers. The following survey is primarily based on Léonard (1930), who merits ample revisions but may serve as a starting-point for future research. In the twelfth century there were two clear-cut divisions: one between the Capetian and the Angevin spheres of influence, and one between the northern regions and Provence. Already in the 1140s the Templars had a *magister* for Provence (Forey 1973: 420–1), responsible especially for Saint-Gilles, Arles,

Avignon, Orange, Roaix, Richerenches, Valence, Jalez and Montpellier. His province being large and having numerous possessions, there came to be masters for smaller regions such as Carcassonne and Redez (including Douzens), Rodez (including Sainte-Eulalie-du-Larzac), Albi (including La Selve), the Rouergue (mentioned in 1233 and 1256; Selwood 1999: 150 n. 60), the region of Cahors, Toulouse with the house of Villedieu and the diocese of Comminges, Gascony with the Agenais including the houses between the Garonne and the Dordogne, finally the Roussillon with Mas-Déu and Perpignan. From the 1240s onwards the preceptor of Provence lost his Spanish responsibilities (Selwood 1999: 148). Poitou or, as the regional master styled himself from the 1190s, Aquitaine included Bordeaux, La Rochelle and the Saintonge, Anjou, Touraine and Brittany with Nantes. Since the 1180s the Limousin and Auvergne had a separate officer, with unclear competences for the region of Bourges. *Francia* included Paris with the Île-de-France, Orléans, and separate bailiwicks for Brie (with Provins and Moisy), for Picardy, for Beauvais, for Vermandois, for Artois, for Laon (with Reims), for the duchy of Burgundy (with Bure) and for Chalons-sur-Saône. In the early thirteenth century Capetian expansion created many problems, not only in the south with the Albigensian war. Conquered by Philip Augustus in 1204, Normandy (with Bretteville, Renneville, Sainte-Vaubourg) had a separate officer dependent upon *Francia*, whereas Brittany agreed to stay with the province of Aquitaine in 1225 (Josserand 2012: 22). The borders between France and the Empire were of no importance for the socio-political networks and the administrative divisions, neither in the south for Provence nor in the north for Francia, which included separate bailiwicks for Flanders, Hainault and Brabant, for Lorraine, and for the Franche-Comté or county of Burgundy. For some houses the territorial divisions are so far unclear, among them for the Lyonnais and the Dauphiné.

For the Hospitallers, the situation was more or less similar, with the exception that they lacked any founder such as Hugues de Paiens in Western Europe. Their possessions centred only on Saint-Gilles at first. The Hospitaller officer there originally held some sort of responsibility also for the Iberian peninsula until the 1150s and the British Isles until around 1150. The Hospitaller priory of *Francia* is mentioned from 1179 onwards, first at Paris, then at Corbeil, a donation from Ingeborg, widow of King Philip Augustus, in 1223, and after the suppression of the Templars again at Paris (Mannier 1872). The Hospitaller priory of Auvergne came into being some time between 1229 and 1245 (Riley-Smith 1967: 353–4; Legras 1987: 73).

In England the troublesome times of King Stephen (1135–54) saw many donations to both Templars and Hospitallers, whom nobles trusted to pray for them regardless of changing political alliances. A Templar master for England is known since the 1140s, a Hospitaller prior since about 1180. London, the capital and the most important economic centre, had their most important houses, the Old Temple, sold between 1155 and 1162 to Robert de Chesney, bishop of London, and the New Temple on the north banks of the Thames, for the Hospitallers Clerkenwell just outside the northern walls of London. The Templars used the big city to sell agricultural surpluses from their estates in Essex, especially at Temple Cressing, donated in 1137 by Queen Matilda, Stephen's wife, and at Witham. In the north, Yorkshire had ten, Lincolnshire five commanderies. According to the 1185 inquest, some Templar possessions in the south were administered by the master for England directly, whereas elsewhere tasks were so numerous or estates so remote that the Templars had special bailiffs for London, Kent, Warwick, Weston, Lincolnshire, Ogerston and Yorkshire. The Hospitallers may have imitated this, as in 1189, at a prioral chapter in London, there was regional *preceptor* for Kent (Delaville 1894: no. 869). By the thirteenth century both the Templars and the Hospitallers had separate masters for the commanderies in Ireland and for Scotland. Both of them were usually appointed by and responsible to the master or prior of England and his chapter, a fact that caused political tension primarily in Scotland, for example, when in 1291 both the Templar and the Hospitaller master of Scotland swore fealty to King Edward I of England (Parker 1963; Lord 2002; Nicholson 2011: xv–xvi).

On the Iberian peninsula both the Hospitallers and the Templars participated in the *reconquista*, and both had to compete with regional military-religious orders such as Santiago or Calatrava. Already in 1113 a certain *Palaicus a Ierosolimitani xenodochii preposito Geraldo missus* was empowered to collect alms for the Hospital *per Yspaniam* (Delaville 1894: no. 31). A plan by King Alfonso I of Aragón to bequeath his whole realm to the Templars, the Hospitallers and the Holy Sepulchre failed in 1134. But both the Templars and the Hospitallers held important castles, churches and estates in all Iberian kingdoms, not only on the frontiers with the Muslims but also in the hinterland. These included for the Templars six castles awarded in 1143 when the order renounced its claims to the kingdom, among them Monzón and Belchite (at first the seat of an independent militia founded by Alfonso I of Aragón; Lourie 1982), and the city of Tortosa in the Crown of Aragón, the latter being exchanged for the castle of Peñiscola in 1294, the castles of Soure and Almourol plus the house of Tomar in Portugal; for the Hospitallers the castle of Caspe, the castellany of Amposta and the female convent of Sigena in the Crown of Aragón, the castles of Consuegra and Alcázar de San Juan in Castile, the castle of Belver and the convent of Crato in Portugal. The Templars at first administered their possessions in Catalonia, Aragón and Navarre together with those in Provence, all belonging to Occitan political and cultural networks. Only Portugal had at least five separate masters from the 1140s onwards, followed by probably four separate masters for Castile and León from the late 1170s onwards. From 1210 to 1288, seventeen officers administered both provinces, Portugal and Castile-León, but already in 1286 Castile-León had its own subordinate administrator. Then the two realms were separated again, Portugal under at least three, Castile-León under at least four successive officers. It was only after the Albigensian crusades that the Templars separated their Spanish lands from Provence. In 1240 an independent Templar master for Aragón and Catalonia was mentioned. He and his successors were in charge of more than thirty commanderies, among them two in kingdom of Navarre. Among the Hospitallers, Saint-Gilles was apparently never in charge of Iberian possessions. They had separate priories for all Iberian kingdoms, including not only Portugal but also small Navarre. The majority of their Iberian possessions was administered by the prior of Castile-León and the castellan of Amposta, who acted as the regional prior for the Crown of Aragón (Forey 1973; Martinez Diez 1993; Josserand 2004; Miret i Sans 2006). When in 1312 the papacy planned to give the Templar possessions to the Hospital, the kings of Aragón and Portugal protested as this would have tilted the balance of power in their realms. Finally, in 1319 the Templar possessions in Portugal were awarded to a new military-religious order, the Order of Christ, and in the Crown of Aragón the Hospitallers got only the Templar estates in Catalonia, which formed a separate priory, but had to relinquish their own estates in Valencia, which together with the Templar estates in Valencia were transferred to another new military-religious order, the Order of Montesa (Forey 2001).

The Italian peninsula was important to all military-religious orders because of its maritime connections with the Levant. Many early possessions were to be found in ports or along pilgrim routes. For the Templars such early possessions included houses and churches in the Ligurian ports of Genoa and Albenga and in communes such as Milan, Vercelli and

Bergamo. Until around 1200 seven further convents were established, followed by no fewer than twenty-seven new houses in the thirteenth century (Bellomo 2008: 13–14, 23, 26). On the Italian peninsula the Templars had a provincial preceptor for Lombardy or *tota Italia* who is attested since the 1160s. His exact title varied. He was in charge of the whole peninsula north of the kingdom of Sicily. This included Rome and the papal dominions, that is, the *patrimonium Petri in Tuscia, Campania, Maritima*, the duchy of Spoleto, the march of Ancona, and Sardinia. Occasionally, there were regional bailiffs, the first in the East for the march of Verona or the march of Treviso, the second in the south for Rome, Tuscia and Sardinia and the third for Lucca, that is, Tuscany north of the papal dominions (Bellomo 2008: 363–6). The southern part of the Italian peninsula formed the kingdom of Sicily ruled by the Normans and from 1197 by the Hohenstaufen, followed by the Anjou in 1266, who from 1282 onwards quarrelled with Aragón (Bramato 1991; Houben 2002; Guzzo 2003; Petracca 2006; Ricci 2009).

In central Europe two Hospitaller priories were known from the 1180s onwards: one in the West for *Alamania* and one in the East for Bohemia, which included Austria, Moravia and Poland (Silesia). The first acquisitions occurred at the times of the Second Crusade. In the thirteenth century, competition with the Teutonic Order was fierce. The Hospitallers, however, received enough donations to consider regional subdivisions for Upper und Lower Germany, *superior* and *inferior Alamania*. Quarrels between empire and papacy under Frederick Barbarossa (d. 1190) and especially under Frederick II (d. 1250) fostered this regionalism. Some princely families such as Wittelsbach or Wettin were loath to support centralised orders who might not be willing to continue masses and prayers during papal excommunication, and as a consequence there were no Hospitaller possessions in Bavaria or Meißen. In about 1250 Poland and Lower Germany with its centre at Cologne sided with the papacy, whereas Upper Germany and Austria supported the Hohenstaufen. Early in the fourteenth century the priory of *Alamania* included even a third geographical entity, *media Alamania* for the Wetterau near Frankfurt, Franconia and Thuringia, but this was not continued when by 1318 the north-eastern houses became a separate bailiwick centred on the March of Brandenburg and by 1319 the houses in Frisia were made dependent upon (Burg)Steinfurt, the centre of the bailiwick of Westphalia. Other bailiwicks included Utrecht and Cologne for Lower and Oberland for the Upper Germany, the regions along the Rhine from Swabia to Mainz where Heimbach near Speyer and Heitersheim near Freiburg im Breisgau were frequently meeting-places for prioral chapters. The priory of Bohemia with its major house at Prague suffered from tensions between the Přemyslid kings of Bohemia and the dukes of Austria as well as from ethno-linguistic diversity between German and Slavic *fratres*. Its unity was nevertheless preserved. Only Pomerania was transferred to the priory of *Alamania* in the 1230s, in view of the German colonisation (Borchardt 1998, 2011). A Templar *magister* for *Alamania* is known from only the 1230s. The acquisition of many properties in the lands east of the Elbe and Saale meant that he was sometimes called master for the German and Slavic lands. By the end of the thirteenth century, political tensions between the four Rhenish electors and the kings of Bohemia may have sparked off attempts to form a separate Templar province for the eastern parts of central Europe including Bohemia, Austria, Poland and Pomerania (Labonde 2010; Jan 2011a, 2011b; Vogel 2011).

Scandinavia and Hungary were closely related to central Europe. Hungary's importance rested on the overland routes to the Levant, which ceased to be used after the Third Crusade. Both Hospitallers and Templars had a regional officer and some possessions for Hungary, though only south and west of the Danube, the Templars also in Croatia and Dalmatia, including Zengg and the castle of Vrana on the shores of the Adriatic (Hunyadi 2010, 2011). In Scandinavia only the Hospitallers had a priory of *Dacia* for Denmark with just one house in Norway, at Varna, and in Sweden, at Eskilstuna. Apparently, there were no Templars, although in 1308 Clement V's nine commissioners for the trial of the Templars on the British Isles were also licensed to act in Scandinavia (Nicholson 2011: xii), probably only an addition by the papal chancery for the sake of completeness. Until the fourteenth century there were no, or only very few, Teutonic Knights in Scandinavia either.

The Teutonic Order

The Teutonic Order was different from both the Hospitallers and the Templars. Founded about hundred years later and based on the Hohenstaufen Empire, its Western possessions were located primarily in Germany and in Italy. As late-comers the Teutonic Knights faced many difficulties in the Holy Land. So from 1212 to 1225 they accepted an invitation by King Andrew II of Hungary to settle in Transylvania. Between the 1230s and the 1280s they fought heathen natives on the eastern shores of the Baltic. They conquered Prussia and, merged with the Sword-Brethren in 1237, they subdued Livonia. In the 1230s Hermann Balk acted as *magister per Sclavoniam et Prusciam* and administered also the order's possessions in Bohemia, Silesia and Cujavia; in the newly conquered territories he had two *provisores* at his side – one for the Kulmerland and one for Prussia proper. These two *provisores* existed still in the 1250s. In Livonia a *Landmeister* of the Teutonic Order succeeded the master of the Sword-Brethren, and soon Prussia also became only one *Landmeister*. Neither Prussia nor Livonia had bailiwicks between the *Landmeister* and the single commanderies; Prussia and Kulmerland at first had twelve commanderies, later twenty-six, and in Livonia about twelve. There were also a few *Vögte* for regions where the order maintained no convent but just an officer; for example, at Tapiau/Gwaresk, Goldingen/Kuldīga and Rositten/Rēczekne (Militzer 1999: 334–87). In Germany and around the Mediterranean, however, the Teutonic Order developed bailiwicks – an institution which the Hospitallers imitated for central Europe. The quarrels between the Hohenstaufen and the papacy posed a problem, especially for the Teutonic Order. Master Hermann von Salza (1209–39) tried to mediate on behalf of Emperor Frederick II but failed (Cohn 1930/78; Kluger 1987). When Master Gerhard von Malberg sided with the pope, he was forced to resign in 1244. This produced a schism as Prussia, Livonia, Venice and some Italian houses favoured Innocent IV. From 1250 to 1252 there were apparently two competing masters: Günther von Wüllersleben for the Hohenstaufen and Wilhelm von Urenbach for the pope. Gradually the supporters of the papacy gained ground. Master Poppo von Osternohe, elected in 1252, had to resign in 1256, and from then on his successors were papal partisans. Templars and Hospitallers were more affected by quarrels between France and England, Venice and Genoa, but in the early 1250s, the Hospitaller Raimbaud de Voczon, prior for Hungary and Slavonia, clearly supported Conrad IV, Frederick II's son and successor and for this reason he became responsible also for Austria, Styria and, partially, Italy (Hunyadi 2010: 71–2).

The major supplies for the Teutonic Order were of course produced by Germany. Donations and purchases came from the Hohenstaufen, many ecclesiastical and some lay princes, but mostly from nobles and lesser knightly families, the so-called *ministeriales* whose sons dominated the order as *milites*. The properties in Germany were administered by a *magister*, *preceptor* or *procurator* for *Alemania* or *Teutonia* from the 1210s onwards. Quite often the master from the East came to Germany himself in the thirteenth century, and evidence is too scarce to decide whether Koblenz and adjacent houses which produced valuable quantities of good wine were already exploited by the supreme master himself at this time, as was certainly the case in the fourteenth century (Militzer 1970: 90–4, 143–9; 1999: 285–90). Bohemia and Moravia were administered by the Prussian *Landmeister* in 1233, and were taken over by the supreme master from Marienburg in the fourteenth century (Militzer 1967: 57–63, 149–51; 1999: 239–50). For Austria and Styria a separate commander was instituted by Emperor Frederick II and Master Hermann von Salza in 1236, when the emperor had just deposed the Babenberg duke of Austria. From that time onwards the *Landkomtur* for Austria, Styria, Carinthia and Crain continued to be directly subordinate to the central master (Militzer 1967: 63–9, 152–5; 1999: 261–7). The same may be true for the rich hospital at Bozen, two lesser hospices at Lengmoos and Sterzing and several parishes around the River Etsch/Adige, which formed a separate bailiwick (Militzer 1967: 100–6, 155–7; 1999: 299–302). For possessions in the kingdom of France, most of them donated by participants of the Damietta crusade, there was a separate *preceptor in regno Francie* already in 1225 (Militzer 1999: 191–3). The Low Countries had their own Landkomtur in 1228 but later on were subordinate to the *Deutschmeister*; the most important houses were (Alten)Biesen and Utrecht (Militzer 1967: 55–6; 1999: 223–39), contrary to France which remained under the central master. Primarily possessions in Franconia and on the Upper Rhine were administered by the *Deutschmeister* himself. More remote possessions he ceded to bailiffs: in 1236 at Thuringia-Saxony, centred around Altenburg and Zwätzen; in 1243 at Alsace-Burgundy, centred first at Rufach; from the 1250s at Beuggen and later sometimes also at Altshausen; in 1245 at Lorraine centred at Trier. There were *Landkomture* for Marburg in 1258, where since 1235 saint Elizabeth was venerated, and for Franconia in 1268, where the major houses were at Würzburg and Nuremberg. Finally, a bailiwick of Westphalia was created in 1285, centred at Münster and including the house at Bremen, and in 1287 Thuringia-Saxony was split into two separate bailiwicks – the new *Landkomtur* for Saxony usually living at Lucklum. Possessions such as Horneck, Speyer and Sachsenhausen near Frankfurt, however, remained directly under the *Deutschmeister*. So for most parts of the empire north of the Alps, the Teutonic Order had finally a four-layered administrative structure – *Hochmeister, Deutschmeister, Landkomtur, Komtur* – contrary to the three-layered structure everywhere else (Militzer 1967: 70–137; 1999: 193–332). This four-layered structure was imitated by the German Hospitallers whose leading members usually originated from the same social strata of *ministeriales*.

Until early in the fourteenth century, however, the Teutonic Order did not relinquish its Levantine aspirations, and this ensured the importance of the Italian peninsula. When Acre was lost in 1291, the order's headquarters was moved to Venice, and only in 1309 Master Siegfried von Feuchtwangen (1303–11) moved on to Marienburg/Malbork on the Vistula in Prussia. How controversial this decision was in the early fourteenth century can be inferred from the fate of Master Karl von Trier (1311–24), who was forced to leave Prussia (Nieß 1992). Only his successors finally took up their residence at Marienburg. Around the Mediterranean, the Teutonic Order acquired possessions and shaped their administration with the help of the Hohenstaufen and their partisans, including the Venetians, but against the Genoese and the Guelph supporters of the papacy. The Hohenstaufen kingdom of Sicily figured prominently in this context. On the island of Sicily the Teutonic Order held possessions in the important harbour of Messina, from an unknown but probably very early date, and in 1197 was given the monastery of Santissima Trinità at Palermo by King Henry VI, because the Cistercians there had supported Henry's enemies. From the 1210s onwards several *preceptores* of Sicily are known, and from the 1260s onwards also for Calabria, which in the royal administration formed part of Sicily; at the turn of the century this officer began to be called *generalis* or *magnus preceptor* of Sicily. More important than Sicily was Apulia where the Teutonic Orders held an important hospital, St Thomas, at Barletta (confirmed by Henry VI in 1197), a German hospice at Brindisi mentioned already in 1191, furthermore the castle of Mesagne near Otranto (a donation by Henry VI), and finally in Siponto the monastery of San Leonardo, incorporated by Pope Alexander IV in 1260. From the 1220s several *preceptores* of Apulia are known; from the 1280s onwards they also began to be called *generales* or *magni preceptores* of Apulia (Forstreuter 1967: 110–11, 120–1, 124–7, 132–3; Militzer 1999: 172–7; Houben 2002; 2004; Toomaspoeg 2003). Possessions on the Peloponnese, since 1209 in the principality of Achaia, centred around Mosteniza, a remote place on the borders of Elis and Arcadia, plus the Venetian harbours of Modon and Coron, and had their separate *preceptor* of *Romania* from the 1230s onwards at the latest. Plans for expansion failed: first, because Innocent IV gave the hospital of St James at Andravida, the then capital of Achaia, to the Templars in 1246; second, after 1259, because of the Greek reconquests (Forstreuter 1967: 72–5, 86; Militzer 1999: 177–8; Kiesewetter 2004). After the fall of Acre in 1291, the Teutonic Order united Apulia, *Romania* and Cyprus under the *(magnus) preceptor* Guido of Amigdala, mentioned from 1293 to 1311 (Houben 2008). His title sometimes included Sicily, referring to the kingdom, not to the island, as from 1282 onwards the conflict between Anjou and Aragón rendered it inadvisable if not impossible to have one and the same officer for the two regions.

In central and northern Italy the Teutonic Order strove to acquire possessions to ensure communication over the Alps to its German centres. These included Brixeney/Precenicco (confirmed in 1232), in Venice the monastery Santissima Trinità (founded by the Doge Reniero Zeno in 1258), houses in Padua, Bologna and Parma (here only until 1247 when the city sided with the papacy against the Hohenstaufen), and finally the castle and town of Stigliano between Padua and Treviso (donated in 1282). In Rome in 1220, Honorius III bestowed the church Santa Maria in Domnica on the order to house its procurator at the curia, but in 1312, when both the curia and the procurator were in Avignon, Clement V transferred this church to his nephew. The Teutonic Order kept, however, possessions in Viterbo, Montefiascone and Orvieto, favourite papal residences in the thirteenth century, plus a hospital at Castiglione near Arezzo acquired in 1229. From the 1240s there was a preceptor of Lombardy and the March of Treviso. The possessions in the papal dominions were probably administered by the procurator at the curia; only after 1312 a Landkomtur for *Tuscia* was mentioned (Forstreuter 1967: 136–8, 140–2, 146–52, 155, 158–67; Militzer 1999: 178–80, 183–9).

At Montpellier the town council gave the suburban hospital of St Martin to the Teutonic Order in 1228. At Arles the Teutonic Order had possessions near the suburban hospital of St Thomas. In the fourteenth century these revenues were supervised by the order's procurator at the Roman curia, then in Avignon (Militzer 1999: 189–91). In Spain the Teutonic Order received a few noble and royal donations between the 1230s and 1250s, as the Castilian court had dynastic ties with the Hohenstaufen. The donations included Figares (Higares) on the Tajo north-east of Toledo, La Mota (del Marquez) north of the Duero between Valladolid and Zamora, and Carmona east of Seville. Two *commendatores* or *provinciales* of Spain are known, in the 1250s Fr. Eberhard von Mörsberg, formerly preceptor of Lorraine and probably French-speaking, in the 1280s Fr. Volmar von Bernhausen, who in 1287 was killed fighting against the Lithuanians in Livonia (Forstreuter 1967: 89–5; Militzer 1999: 180–3).

WESTERN RESOURCES

The primary aim of the military-religious orders was certainly to collect alms for the Latin East. To avoid conflicts, alms-collecting, the *questia*, was organised according to dioceses by the Latin church. As a consequence, alms-collectors were licensed for a particular diocese or group of dioceses. For practical purposes they would stay in a house at the episcopal see or in another important town of the diocese. Such houses might be rented, and only at a later stage they might be bought. This is perhaps one of the reasons why the military-religious orders were often recorded at episcopal sees only at a very late date, although their regular presence in such cities may be much older. It may also be a reason why both Hospitallers and Templars quite frequently used to have houses in the same cities, from Arles, Avignon, Orange to Milan or London. In the countryside or in lesser towns, the military-religious orders owed their presence to particular founders, patrons or purchases, and only rarely two or more orders would have a house in the same town; for example, Rothenburg or Mergentheim in Franconia.

Alms would include cash money, weapons, horses, cloth or other valuable commodities which were taken to the Holy Land or sold on behalf of the Holy Land. Ports on the Mediterranean and hospices on roads leading towards the Mediterranean were therefore essential for the military-religious orders, and it is not by chance that already in 1113 the Hospitallers coveted *xenodochia sive ptochia in occidentis partibus* near Saint-Gilles, Asti, Pisa, Bari, Otranto, Taranto and Messina (Delaville 1894: no. 30). In north-western Europe they may have started to collaborate with a fraternity of *Ierosolimitani* at Utrecht at about the same time (van Winter 1996). Although regular shipping through the Straits of Gibraltar did not begin before the end of the thirteenth century, people from north-western Europe did participate with ships in crusading expeditions throughout the twelfth century. Overland-routes to the Holy Land through Hungary, the Balkans, Constantinople and Asia Minor ceased to the useful after the Third Crusade. So Hungary lost some of its importance for the military-religious orders in favour of Venice and the Adriatic. Eastern central Europe would use roads from Moravia through Austria to Venice. From the Rhineland others would cross the Alps to reach ports in Italy, Genoa, Venice, Ancona, Brindisi or Messina. People from Western Europe would follow the Rhône valley to reach places such as Marseille or Aigues-Mortes, the latter a newly established port by Louis IX of France in the 1240s. Between 1216 and 1233 both the Hospitallers and the Templars increased their regular shipping from Marseilles to the Levant (Barber 1994: 237–41).

The acquisition of landed estates required local administration for their exploitation. The military-religious orders must have tried to avoid this, and so they tried to sell such estates. The Italian Templars, for example, sold a remote donation in Bavaria in 1167 to the Wittelsbach family (Labonde 2010: 223–5). Of course they could not avoid accepting donations in regions such as Eastern Europe where money was not as commonly used as in Italy or in Western Europe. The lack of permanent administration is highlighted by special *missi* acting for a military-religious order; for example, a certain Oberto, *missus de Templo de Ierusalhem*, at the Ligurian port of Albenga in 1143 and 1145 (Bellomo 2008: 229–33), or by laymen, local nobles, receiving donations on behalf of a military-religious order, such as Count Poppo of Wertheim in 1192 on behalf of the Hospitallers near Würzburg in Franconia (Delaville 1894: no. 924).

Donations were frequently made in the context of crusades proclaimed by the papacy, especially after the fall of Edessa in 1144 and the fall of Jerusalem in 1187. Before leaving for the East, crusaders might try to secure the services of a military-religious order, or after returning from the East they might show their gratitude by making donations. For the Hospital, the immense acts of charity in their conventual hospital in the East became a standard phrase for justifying the donation of privileges and estates. Threatened by Nur ad-Din and by Saladin, the East needed a more continuous support than merely alms and donations. So from the second half of the twelfth century both Hospitallers and Templars accepted permanent revenues from estates and other possessions in the West, despite the fact that this required the costly maintenance of an administration. Moreover, the failure of the Third Crusade in 1191 and the defeat at La Forbie in 1244 made it clear to everyone that the Latin East would be dependent upon continuous support from the West. So all three military-religious orders began to invest money in the West, to build castles or to keep fighters, but also to produce enough surpluses that could be sent to the East as *responsiones* on a regular basis (Bronstein 2005). These *responsiones* were fairly high – in the second half of the twelfth century one-third of the incomes. In the thirteenth century the amount of money was fixed for each officer. Soon complaints started that because of wars or similar disasters the money could not be paid (Riley-Smith 1967: 344–6; Forey 1973: 319–27). By the end of the thirteenth century, as fighting both in the East and on other frontiers of Latin Christendom ceased, the military-religious orders became integrated into ordinary religious networks, becoming local houses to prayer and prestige.

The sources for the military-religious orders in the West are mostly charters referring to particular legal acts, donations, purchases, exchanges of properties, and economically profitable privileges. There must have also been inventories of estates and accounts, but such sources are rarely extant. There is an inventory for the Templars in England started by 1185 and completed probably around 1190 (Lees 1935). Most such inventories only date from the fourteenth century for confiscated Templar possessions after 1307 or for the Hospitallers in Provence (Beaucage 1982) and England (Larking and Kemble 1856), both of them made following a commission by Benedict XII in 1338. There are a few accounts written on paper from thirteenth-century Manosque (Carraz and Borchardt 2015). Furthermore, there are a few obituaries with the names of patrons to be commemorated by houses of the military-religious orders; for example, by the Templar commandery in Reims (Barthélemy 1882). Sometimes it is possible to use later evidence, even early modern surveys, to reconstruct the size and the components of estates. Yet more than a fairly general enumeration of agricultural and other revenues is not possible for the period prior to the early fourteenth century.

The bulk of the Western revenues was certainly due from agricultural production, both grain and livestock. The orders had estates which they managed themselves with servants, corvees and hired workers, and they had peasants who paid rents, either commodities or cash. The arable land would produce wheat, oats, rye and barley. Mills were frequently mentioned, usually for grain, in a few cases perhaps for fulling purposes; participation in the production of cloth warrants further investigation. Cattle, sheep and swine would graze on pastures or in woods, which also produced timber. In some places salt and iron were important. To earn money, grain and wine, meat, hides, dairy products such as cheese and wool might be sold on the markets, sometimes also fish, salt and metals. The Templars had ships to transport wine from Bordeaux to England. Usually, however, there is only indirect evidence for such commercial activities through royal and other privileges which provided access to markets for free or at reduced fees. The market-orientation may have been especially important for large population centres such as Milan, Paris, Cologne or London, for commercial regions such as Tuscany, Flanders or Champagne; it may not be by chance that the Templars held two houses at Provins (Barber 1994: 262–4). The Templars and Hospitallers in Paris and London were involved in accepting valuables and giving loans to crusaders and others. From Haimard in 1202 to Jean de la Tour in 1307, many Paris Templars served not only their order but also the king of France to administer his revenues. Both the Templars and the Hospitallers accepted valuables and cash for deposit and disbursement, lent money, transferred funds over long distances, sometimes using letters of exchange, issued and used credit instruments, and guaranteed future interests. Apparently, however, the orders were less frequently involved in such business in southern France, Provence and Italy where both the papacy and the military-religious orders usually worked with merchants and lay bankers (Barber 1994: 266–79). Only the Aragonese Templars were active money lenders and bankers (Forey 1973: 346–52). A typical administrative centre would include the residence of the personnel, a chapel, stables and barns, mills, ovens, forges and an enceinte. Not all such manors or houses would necessarily have a convent of *fratres*, but if so, there would have to be a refectory and a dormitory; later on, *fratres* would have separate chambers. In the second half of the twelfth century, Richerenches, north-east of Avignon, had between ten and twenty Templars resident, and eight dependent houses with perhaps two or three Templars each. In the late thirteenth century, Mas-Déu in Roussillon had a preceptor, some twenty-five Templars plus seven dependent houses with one or two Templars each; all these establishments closely worked together with the urban house of Perpignan where six or seven Templars lived (Barber 1994: 254). From these examples one can easily understand how misleading and futile is would be just to count houses, convents or commanderies. Some of these military-religious order centres could include castles, parishes, hospitals and temporal jurisdiction.

Generally, the military-religious orders were not supposed to fight in the West against Christians. Whenever they were given possessions on the frontiers of territories, this was mainly done because any raiders would incur excommunication for plundering *bona ecclesiastica*. Warfare being costly, the orders would not usually undertake this in the West, except for the defence of their local princes and rulers against enemies of the faith such as the Mongols in 1241, or if the orders themselves were local lords, such as at Manosque. Parish churches were also costly, as they required the maintaining of priests. However, parish churches permitted the continuous collection of alms, tithes and other dues from a steadily growing population, especially in newly founded towns. The founders of such new towns might wish to give the parish church to a military-religious order, especially as this meant ensuring prestigious support for the new foundation against possible envy and as the orders would be able to increase and decrease the number of priests serving in such a parish without the costly and legally cumbersome procedure of founding permanent benefices.

Hospitals were quite often entrusted to both the Hospitallers and the Teutonic Knights, because both orders were renowned for keeping a prestigious hospital at the convent in the East. The Templars in the East did not have a conventual hospital, but nevertheless they received a few hospices in the West, either because Western patrons did not know enough about the differences of the military-religious orders or because they were supposed to keep stations for pilgrims on their way to the East. Eagle in Lincolnshire may have been used to house Templar *fratres* who were sick or too old and infirm to fulfil their duties (Parker 1963: 41). Most military-order establishments in the West were subject to temporal lords, yet in a few cases they were also donated secular jurisdiction, lesser or even higher. Manosque is an example in the county of Forcalquier. In a similar way the military-religious orders were sometimes awarded older monastic houses with rich possessions, such as the Hospitallers by Boniface VIII in 1297 at Venosa in Apulia, the Teutonic Knights' two Augustinian houses at Zschillen, diocese of Meißen, in 1278 and at Trient/Trento in 1283, from the local bishops respectively (Militzer 1967: 75, 102; 1999: 273, 301).

Compared with Cistercians and Premonstratensians in the twelfth century and Dominicans and Franciscans in the thirteenth century, the military-religious orders were unique because their primary aim was not spiritual reform or economic innovation in the West. However, they did try to improve their possessions by founding new villages, castles and towns, such as in Gascony (Higounet 1986), and especially on the Iberian peninsula and east of Germany (Smoliński 2011; Wihoda 2011; Borchardt 2013). And as a rule, the military-religious orders did not produce learned preachers, although a few of their brethren did study at schools or became prelates. Their Western officers were *milites*, sometimes *servientes* and, except for the Templars, also priests. Some of them also served popes and prelates, kings and princes or communes in the West, a fact that could produce conflicts of loyalty with the order. A lot of future research has to be done, yet in sum the importance of the Western possessions can hardly be underestimated, for both religious and economic reasons. Although until the fourteenth century evidence is scarce and casual, the military-religious orders established important networks within Latin Christendom to support defence against the enemies of the faith. This was certainly helped by the existence of *(con)fratres*, *-sorores* and donats, noble and non-noble affiliates and members of the orders' confraternities who made regular donations, shared the prayers of the order and choose to be buried in the orders' churches. The knights of the orders also had squires, each Templar knight one squire, each Hospitaller knight two squires. Such squires could be paid commoners or young aspirant knights who took up service as a *donzel* or attendant (Selwood 1999: 159–60). It should be noted, however, that such networks could easily be converted to other uses, supporting younger sons of the nobility who could not inherit family possessions but still aimed at noble careers and at supporting temporal lords, kings or princes in the West. The prestigious goal of fighting for Jerusalem, the Holy Land or the faith rendered administrative innovations acceptable among the nobility (Borchardt 2012). Yet one should not over-emphasise this. The good documentation for the higher social strata may produce a somewhat distorted view of the Western social networks on which the military-religious orders relied. The orders also had many not fully professed affiliates who joined the prayers, paid dues, sometimes were paid stipends, although all this would not be kept in long-term archival records. All this has to be taken into consideration when we focus on the role of the military-religious orders in the West during the times of the crusades in the twelfth and thirteenth centuries. Afterwards things changed. From the second half of the thirteenth century onwards, and especially after the fall of Acre in 1291, the demise of the Levantine crusades profoundly affected the role of the military-religious orders in the West. The Templars whose sole raison d'être had been fighting the enemies of Christ were suppressed, whilst both the Hospitallers on Rhodes and the Teutonic Knights on the Baltic desperately tried to keep up some semblance of performing pious acts of charity by defending Christians and by running their hospitals. The military-religious orders kept their organisation and their administrative structures. Nevertheless, they lost many of the special features which had made them unique earlier on.

BIBLIOGRAPHY

d'Albon, A. (1913) *Cartulaire général de l'ordre du Temple, 1119?–1150*. Paris: Champion.

Barber, M. (1994) *The New Knighthood: A History of the Order of the Temple*. Cambridge: Cambridge University Press.

Barthélemy, E. (1882) 'Obituaire de la Commanderie du Temple de Reims', in *Mélanges historiques: Choix de documents*, 4. Paris: Imprimerie nationale, 301–41.

Baudin, A., Brunel, G. and Dohrmann, N., eds. (2013) *L'économie templière en Occident. Patrimoines, commerce, finances. Actes du colloque international (Troyes, abbaye de Clairvaux, 24–26 octobre 2012)*. Langres: Guéniot.

Beaucage, B., ed. (1982) *Visites générales des commandéries de l'ordre des hospitaliers dépendantes du Grand Prieuré de Saint-Gilles (1338)*. Aix-en-Provence: Université de Provence.

Bellomo, E. (2008) *The Templar Order in North-west Italy (1142–c.1330)*. Leiden: Brill.

Borchardt, K. (1998) 'The Hospitallers in Pomerania: Between the Priories of Bohemia and Alamania.', in Nicholson, 295–306.

———. (2011) 'Verwaltungsstrukturen bei den deutschen Johannitern (12. bis 14. Jahrhundert)', in Borchardt and Jan, 51–77.

———. (2012) 'The Military-Religious Orders: A Medieval "School for Administrators"?', in Edbury, 3–20.

———. (2013) 'The Templars and Thirteenth-Century Colonisation in Eastern Central Europe', in Baudin, Brunel and Dohrmann, 419–56.

———. (2014) 'Die Johanniter und ihre Balleien in Deutschland während des Mittelalters', in Gahlbeck, Heimann and Schumann, 63–76.

Borchardt, K. and Jan, L., eds. (2011) *Die geistlichen Ritterorden in Mitteleuropa: Mittelalter*. Brno: Matice moravská.

Bramato, F. (1991) *Storia dell'Ordine dei Templari in Italia*, vol. 1. Roma: Anatór.

Bronstein, J. (2005) *The Hospitallers and the Holy Land: Financing the Latin East 1187–1274*. Woodbridge: Boydell.

Bulst-Thiele, M. L. (1974) *Sacrae domus militiae Templi Hierosolymitani magistrii*. Göttingen: Vandenhoeck & Ruprecht.

Burgtorf, J. (2008) *The Central Convent of Hospitallers and Templars: History, Organization, and Personnel (1099/1120–1310)*. Leiden: Brill.

Carraz, D. (2005) *L'Ordre du Temple dans la basse vallée du Rhône (1124–1312): Ordres militaires, croisades et sociétés méridionales*. Lyon: Presses Universitaires de Lyon.

———, ed. (2013) *Les Ordres militaires dans la ville médiévale (1100–1350)*. Clermont-Ferrand: Presses Universitaires Blaise-Pascal.

Carraz, D. and Borchardt, K. (2015) 'Les pratiques comptables de l'ordre de l'Hôpital en Provence: Le cas de la commanderie de Manosque (années 1260–1350)', in Th. Pécout, *De l'autel à l'ecriture. Aux origines des comptabilités en Occident (XIIe–XIVe siècles), Actes du colloque international d'Aix-en-Provence, 13–14 juin 2013*. Paris: De Boccard, in print.

Cohn, W. (1930/78) *Hermann von Salza*. Breslau: M. & H. Marcus; reprint with an annex *Hat Hermann von Salza das Deutschordensland betreten? Hermann von Salza im Urteil der Nachwelt*. Aalen: Scientia-Verlag.

Delaville le Roulx, J. (1894/1906) *Cartulaire général de l'ordre des Hospitaliers de S. Jean de Jérusalem*, 4 vols. Paris: Leroux.

Edbury, P., ed. (2012) *The Military Orders*, vol. 5: *Politics and Power*. Farnham: Ashgate.

Fleckenstein, J. and Hellmann, M., ed. (1980) *Die geistlichen Ritterorden Europas.* Sigmaringen: Thorbecke.

Forey, A. (1973) *The Templars in the* Corona de Aragón. London: Oxford University Press.

———. (2001) *The Fall of the Templars in the Crown of Aragon.* Aldershot: Ashgate.

Forstreuter, K. (1967) *Der Deutsche Orden am Mittelmeer.* Bonn: Verlag Wissenschaftliches Archiv.

Gahlbeck, C., Heimann, H.-D. and Schumann, D., eds. (2014) *Regionalität und Transfergeschichte: Ritterordenskommenden der Templer und Johaniter im nordöstlichen Deutschland und in Polen.* Berlin: Lukas Verlag.

Guzzo, C. (2003) *Templari in Sicilia: la storia e le sue fonti tra Federico II e Roberto d'Angiò.* Genoa: Name.

Higounet, Ch. (1986) 'Hospitaliers et Templiers: Peuplement et exploitation rurale dans le sud-ouest de la France,' in *Les ordres militaires, la vie rurale et le peuplement en Europe occidentale (XIIe-XVIIIe siècles),* Auch, 61–78.

Houben, H. (2002) 'Templari e Teutonici nel Mezzogiorno normanno-svevo', in *Il Mezzogiorno normanno-svevo e le crociate. Atti delle quattordicesimo giornate normanno-sveve, Bari, 17–20 ottobre 2000,* ed. G. Musca. Bari: Dedalo, 251–88.

———, ed. (2004) *L'Ordine Teutonico nel Mediterraneo: Atti del convegno internazionale di studio, Torre Alemanna (Cerignola), Mesagne, Lecce, 16–18 ottobre 2003.* Galatina: Congedo.

———. (2008) 'Guido von Amigdala/Amendolea. Ein Italo-Palestinenser als Landkomtur des Deutschen Ordens im Mittelmeerraum (1289–1311)', *Quellen und Forschungen aus italienischen Archiven und Bibliotheken* 88, 48–60.

Hunyadi, Z. (2010) *The Hospitallers in the Medieval Kingdom of Hungary, c. 1150–1387.* Budapest: METEM.

———. (2011) 'The Formation of the Territorial Structures of the Templars and Hospitallers in the Medieval Kingdom of Hungary', in Borchardt and Jan, 183–97.

Jan, L. (2011a) 'Die Entwicklung des böhmischen Priorats der Johanniter', in Borchardt and Jan, 79–98.

———. (2011b) 'Die Templer in Böhmen und Mähren', in Borchardt and Jan, 171–82.

Josserand, P. (2004) *Église et pouvoir dans la péninsule Ibérique: Les ordres militaires dans le royaume de Castille (1252–1369).* Madrid: Casa de Velázquez.

———. (2012) 'Les Templiers en Bretagne au Moyen Âge', *Annales de Bretagne et des Pays de l'Ouest* 119–14, 7–33.

Kiesewetter, A. (2004) 'L'Ordine Teutonico in Grecia e in Armenia', in Houben, 73–107.

Kluger, H. (1987) *Hochmeister Hermann von Salza und Kaiser Friedrich II. Ein Beitrag zur Frühgeschichte des Deutschen Ordens.* Marburg: Elwert.

Labonde, J. (2010) *Die Templer in Deutschland.* Heimbach: Bernardus.

Larking, L. B. and Kemble, J. M. (1857) *The Knights Hospitallers in England.* London: Camden Society.

Lees, B. A., ed. (1935) *The Records of the Templars in England in the Twelfth Century. The Inquest of 1185.* London: Milford; reprint (1981) München: Kraus.

Legras, A.-M. (1987) *L'enquête pontificale de 1373 sur l'ordre des Hospitaliers de Saint-Jean de Jérusalem.* Paris: Éditions du Centre national de la recherche scientifique.

Léonard, É.-G. (1930) *Introduction au Cartulaire manuscrit du Temple (1150–1317).* Paris: Champion.

Lord, E. (2002) *The Knights Templar in Britain.* Harlow: Pearson Education.

Lourie, E. (1982) 'The Confraternity of Belchite, the Ribat, and the Temple', *Viator* 13, 159–76.

Mannier, E. (1872) *Les commanderies du Grand-Prieuré de France d'après les documents inédits conservés aux Archives nationales.* Paris: Aubry; reprint (1987) Brionne: Saint-Pierre-de-Salerne.

Martinez Diez, G. (1993) *Los Templarios en la Corona de Castilla.* Burgos: Olmeda.

Miguet, M. (1995) *Templiers et Hospitaliers en Normandie.* Paris: Comité des Travaux Historiques et Scientifiques.

————. (2009) *Les Templiers en Bourgogne*. Précy-sous-Thil: Éd. de l'Armançon.

————. (2012) *Templiers et Hospitaliers de Bure: Histoire et rayonnement d'une commanderie bourguignonne*. Langres: Guéniot.

Militzer, K. (1970) *Die Entstehung der Deutschordensballeien im Deutschen Reich*. Bonn and Bad Godesberg: Verlag Wissenschaftliches Archiv.

————. (1999) *Von Akkon zur Marienburg. Verfassung, Verwaltung und Sozialstruktur des Deutschen Ordens 1190–1309*. Marburg: Elwert.

Miret i Sans, J. (2006) *Les cases de Templers i Hospitalers a Catalunya*, reprint of the 1910 edition with introduction by Sans i Travé, J. M. Lleida: Pagés.

Mollat, G. (1904) *Jean XXII, Lettres communes*, Paris: A. Fonternoing.

Nicholson, H., ed. (1998) *The Military Orders*, vol. 2: *Welfare and Warfare*. Aldershot: Ashgate.

————, ed. (2011) *The Proceedings Against the Templars in the British Isles*, 2 vols. Farnham: Ashgate.

Nieß, U. (1992) *Hochmeister Karl von Trier (1311–1324). Stationen einer Karriere im Deutschen Orden*. Marburg: Elwert.

Parker, Th. W. (1963) *The Knights Templars in England*. Tucson: University of Arizona Press.

Perlbach, M. (1890) *Die Statuten des Deutschen Ordens*. Halle: Viemeyer.

Petracca, L. (2006) *Giovanniti e templari in Sicilia*. Galatina: Congedo.

Ricci, V. (2009) *I templari nella Puglia medievale*. Bari: Edizioni del Sud.

Richard, J. (1980) 'Les Templiers et les Hospitaliers en Bourgogne et en Champagne du Sud (Xiie-XIIIe siècles)', in Fleckenstein and Hellmann, 231–242; reprint (1983) *Croisés, missionaires et voyageurs: Les perspectives orientales du monde latin médiéval*. London: Variorum, item III.

Riley-Smith, J. (1967) *The Knights of St. John in Jerusalem and Cyprus c. 1050–1310*. London: Macmillan.

Schenk, J. G. (2012) *Templar Families. Landowning Families and the Order of the Temple in France, c. 1120–1307*. Cambridge: Cambridge University Press.

Schmidt, H.-J. (2013) 'Contested Frontiers: Mendicant Provinces Between Germany and Poland During the Late Middle Ages', in Jamroziak, E. and Stöber, K. (eds.), *Monasteries on the Borders of Medieval Europe: Conflict and Cultural Interaction*. Turnhout: Brepols, 129–45.

Selwood, D. (1999) *Knights of the Cloister: Templars and Hospitallers in Central-Southern Occitania, 1100–1300*. Woodbridge: Boydell.

Smoliński, M. (2011) 'Der Johanniterorden in Pommern und Pommerellen im Mittelalter – Politik, Wirtschaft, Menshcen', in Borchardt and Jan, 139–55.

Starnawska, M. (1999) *Między Jerozolimą a Łukowem: Zakony krzyżowe na ziemiach polskich w średniowieczu*. Warszawa: Wydawn. DiG.

Tanner, N. and Alberigo, G. (1990) *Decrees of the Ecumenical Councils, vol. 1: Nicaea I to Lateran V*. London and Washington/DC: Sheed & Ward and Georgetown University Press.

Toomaspoeg, K. (2003) *Les Teutoniques en Sicile, 1191–1492*. Rome: École Française de Rome.

Vogel, C. (2007) *Das Recht der Templer*. Berlin: LIT Verlag.

————. (2011) 'Die Templer in Mitteleuropa und ihre Organisationsstrukturen', in Borchardt and Lan, 157–170.

van Winter, J. (1996) 'Les seigneurs de Sainte-Catherine à Utrecht, les premiers Hospitaliers au nord des Alpes', in Balard, M., ed., *Autour de la première croisade*. Paris: Publications de la Sorbonne, 239–46.

Wihoda, M. (2011) 'Die geistlichen Ritterorden und ihre Haltung zum Landesausbau im böhmischen Mittelalter', in Borchardt and Jan, 245–63.

CHAPTER EIGHT

CRUSADE, EMPIRE AND THE PROCESS OF WAR IN STAUFEN GERMANY, 1180–1220

———•◆•———

Daniel P. Franke

The crusade in the kingdom of Germany enjoyed a long, vigorous, and bloody life from 1096 to well beyond the fall of Acre in 1291.[1] Nevertheless, German crusading is frequently under-covered in English-language scholarship, being most often presented either as a narrative or a series of examples that support general conclusions about crusading.[2] This is due partly to the fact that most scholarship on the medieval German kingdom remains in German, and in part because this German scholarship is both dense and situated against a complex historiography that only specialists have the time or inclination to master.[3] It also, until recently, tends to exhibit particularly "German" traits, such as a dubious preoccupation with demonstrating that Germany had as good a claim as France to the crusades.[4] Furthermore, the previous English-language survey of German crusading, Rudolf Hiestand's "Kingship and Crusade," is twenty years old, and while some of its questions have proved to be of abiding interest, others reflect approaches to medieval German politics that have been heavily modified or superseded in the last two decades. At the same time, however, there are a number of instances where we are really no further along in 2015 than in Hiestand's analysis from 1996.[5]

This chapter, therefore, has two aims: first, to acquaint otherwise unfamiliar readers with the themes and sources of German crusading in the late twelfth century; second, to indicate the state of German crusades historiography in the twenty years after Hiestand's "Kingship and Crusade." In particular, it focuses on the "initial conditions" of the Third Crusade as the essential foundation for understanding the subsequent political-religious situations that confronted German monarchs from Henry VI's coronation in 1191 to Frederick II's coronation in 1220. It gives a sense of the available sources and the state of the scholarship, and indicates some avenues of research that are still in need of exploration. Since space is limited, many of the references given in the footnotes will guide the interested reader to scholarship with extensive citations and bibliographies. What follows shifts among three different aspects of the German crusade experience: the crusade itself, the empire, and the process by which a medieval kingdom went to war, since, as Hiestand remarked, "the crusade itself was a sort of mobilization."[6]

CRUSADE AND EMPIRE: FREDERICK I[7]

Except for the reign of his grandson Frederick II, the reign of Frederick I (known as "Barbarossa" on account of his red beard) receives more attention than nearly any other period of medieval German history. There have been two enduring insights into Barbarossa's involvement in crusading, and into German crusading in general. The first is Hiestand's insistence on the political potential of crusade, specifically that "[i]t was the crusade that gave [Barbarossa] the opportunity to arrive at peace with the Church and force the princes and nobles to peace, and not a standing peace prior to 1187 that allowed the possibility of the crusade."[8] The second insight, developed in several publications by Knut Görich, is the way that Barbarossa's actions as emperor were guided by the concept of *honor imperii*, the honor of the empire. In particular, Görich draws attention to precisely those aspects of medieval German political culture that are largely absent from Hiestand's analysis, but which are crucially important when attempting to understand how crusade impacted the empire—history and literature, chivalry, aristocratic memory, consensual lordship, the court, etc.[9]

Görich's approach allows for a more nuanced interpretation of Barbarossa's crusade, as it asks us to think of the context of 1187 before considering the crusade's events. To start, imperial concerns rested on a popular enthusiasm for pilgrimage whose influence on crusade still needs investigation. Despite the defeat of Conrad III's army in the Second Crusade, German interest in the Levant remained strong throughout the twelfth century, even before news of the Battle of Hattin reached Europe in October 1187.[10] The most prominent examples of this interest are John of Würzburg's famous guidebook to the Latin Kingdom and the pilgrimage of Henry the Lion, duke of Bavaria and Saxony, in 1172. Henry's diplomatic visits to both the Seljuk and Byzantine capitals signaled a new interest in and commitment to the eastern Mediterranean by Germany's ruling elite.[11] At roughly the same time, Raymond of Tripoli had begun negotiations with Frederick Barbarossa for the marriage of Raymond's niece Sibylla to one of Frederick's cousins, William of Montferrat. By the time the marriage took place in November 1176, however, the entire diplomatic landscape had changed: Barbarossa had been defeated at Legnano by the Lombard League and was seeking a negotiated peace with the papacy and the Lombard cities.[12] Meanwhile, Henry the Lion had refused to support the campaign of 1176, and Frederick's rapprochement with the papacy meant that many of Henry's clerical henchmen would likely have to vacate their positions. By 1181, the Lion had been stripped of his titles and exiled to England, while Frederick and Lucius III continued to negotiate the administrative and legal mess that sixteen years of war had created in Italy and, to a lesser extent, Germany. While a crusade was a standing long-term goal of their negotiations, much had to be done at home first. Thus domestic and papal political issues exerted a decisive influence on the empire's geopolitical involvement with the crusader states, whatever the popularity of Jerusalem as a pilgrimage destination.

These internal political issues had reached crisis proportions by autumn 1187, and it is this crisis, often overlooked or downplayed by historians, that is the essential context for understanding whether Frederick "used" the crusade, and how successfully he did so. No matter how foregone a conclusion Barbarossa's participation may have been, the Crisis of 1187 had to be *at least temporarily* solved before he could formally commit to the Jerusalem crusade.[13] It consisted of two separate but interrelated problems: a conflict with Urban III over the disputed election to the archbishopric of Trier, and a rebellion of Archbishop Philipp of Cologne, who fancied himself the papacy's champion in Germany against Barbarossa's tendency to use church property as a petty-cash box.

In 1184, Pope Lucius III, frustrated at Barbarossa's obstinacy over ecclesiastical property negotiations, signaled his intent to resist imperial demands by refusing to crown young King Henry VI.[14] Meanwhile, the disputed archiepiscopal election in Trier, ongoing since late 1183, underwent an unexpected escalation. According to the *Gesta Treverorum*, what might have been a minor dispute between papal and imperial factions became much larger when Werner von Bolanden, imperial legate in Burgundy, arrived and proceeded to drive the pro-papal candidate, Folmar, from the city. It seems that Folmar enjoyed widespread sympathy, since shortly afterward Barbarossa's son Henry arrived in Trier at the head of a large retinue, revoking all tolls, rights, and privileges held by the metropolis. Folmar appealed directly to Lucius III to intervene.[15] Although Lucius died in November 1185, his successor, Urban III, actually proved a far more vigorous supporter of Folmar.[16] As a native of Milan and a supporter of Thomas Becket, Urban was one of Frederick's most inveterate enemies, and the papal registers testify to the energy with which he defended the Church's interests.[17] Upon his accession, he retained the archbishopric of Milan, so that the emperor would not be able to collect its revenue,[18] and he refused to crown Henry emperor unless Barbarossa first renounced his crown, as Lucius III had insisted previously.[19] The emperor's response was to have his son's marriage to Constance of Sicily celebrated in Urban's native Milan on January 27, 1186. Henry VI occupied the papal lands in Italy: Urban responded by personally consecrating Folmar as archbishop in May. Meanwhile, Folmar had crossed the frontier to take refuge with the archbishop of Rheims; by May 1187 the bishop of Metz had also fled to Cologne, his estates being occupied by Werner's imperial troops; and the bishop of Verdun had lost his temporalities.[20]

With several of the major Western sees under imperial occupation, attention shifted at this point to the ambitious Philipp of Heinsberg, archbishop of Cologne. Philipp's reasons for opposing Barbarossa were complex, but in broad terms consisted of his confidence in his power as duke of Westphalia and archbishop, his ongoing conflicts with the ambitious Count of Hainault (who had secured the Staufen's favor), pressure from the citizens of Cologne, and a genuine concern for the freedom of the Church.[21] Caesarius of Heisterbach, not a friend to the Staufen, wrote in his addendum to the Cologne annals that "Frederick, as was supposed by many, secretly envied the glory of the archbishop, and feared his power."[22] But this is mere partisanship: Frederick had no reason to fear Cologne. To the contrary, imperial economic initiatives in the lower Rhineland gave the citizens of Cologne cause to resent the emperor.[23] At the Diet of Gelnhausen in November 1186, Philipp alone refused to subscribe to the German prelates' collective rejection of Urban III's appeals for support. Archbishop Wichmann of Magdeburg, however, endorsed Barbarossa's measures as supporting "justice and the empire's honor."[24] Philipp officially withdrew from the imperial court, and by 1187 both sides were cautiously preparing for open war.[25] When Philipp began to negotiate with the king of France for aid, Barbarossa opened his own negotiations with the French king, and concluded a treaty in July 1187 whereby the Staufen promised Philip II Augustus support against Henry II of England in return for the Capetians withdrawing all support from Cologne.[26] Although both Eickhoff and Huffman have stressed Cologne's increasing isolation, neither the papacy nor the emperor shared this point of view: Urban escaped from Verona and was about to pronounce Friedrich's excommunication, when he died on October 24, supposedly after learning of the Battle of Hattin.[27]

Such was the general situation when Gregory VIII ascended the papal throne in October 1187 with the overriding objective of organizing a new crusade.[28] Our narrative at this point is well known: Gregory, who had opposed Urban's confrontational attitude, imme-diately indicated that he would align his views on both Trier and the imperial succession with those of the emperor, and the emperor lifted the siege of Verona and gave the pope an imperial escort.[29] At Strasbourg in December 1187, the imperial court listened to Henry, bishop of Strasbourg, exhort the assembled nobles and knights to take the cross. Many knights came forward, but Barbarossa said little; the *Historia Peregrinorum* claims that he hid his true intentions until he knew that enough nobles had committed themselves.[30] At the Pentecost diet of March 1188, the "curia Jhesu Christi" as the chroniclers reverently called it, Philipp of Cologne finally submitted to Barbarossa, throwing himself unconditionally on the emperor's mercy, formally abjuring his defiance and agreeing to pay a fine. In addition, Cologne's fortifications were to be degraded (though the outraged citizens quickly rebuilt them). Meanwhile, Gottfried of Würzburg, Barbarossa's chancellor and a diplomat of some acumen, preached a rousing sermon, Barbarossa and hundreds of knights and nobles took the cross, and several popular riots against the Jews were crushed by Henry of Kalden, the imperial marshal.[31] The imperial army departed Regensburg on May 11, 1189; the survivors reached Acre toward the end of 1190, but without the emperor, who had drowned in Asia Minor on June 10, 1190.

The above is an all-too-brief exposition of the conditions in which the call for crusade was issued in 1187. The reliability of our sources continues to stir a great deal of debate, in particular the collection of letters from the Abbey of Hildesheim.[32] More fundamental to our understanding of Barbarossa's crusade is the dating of the *Landfriede* (the general peace) against "incendiaries," which for years had been dated to 1186, although Burchard of Ursberg's chronicle places it in early 1188. Currently, while a date of 1188 is preferred, the full implications of locating a key piece of imperial legislation within the crusade are still largely unexplored.[33] But even more significantly, our usual focus on *Audita tremendi* and the Diet of Mainz have obscured the actual limitations of crusade as a vehicle for political peace. We will never know how Urban, a true enemy of the Staufen, would have planned the new campaign, and far more importantly, it would be a serious mistake to imagine the princes of the empire standing united behind Barbarossa at Mainz in 1188 for longer than the duration of the diet.[34] The conflicts in the empire were far greater in extent than can be conveyed here, and they were not extinguished simply because the emperor took the cross. Even as late as March 1189, the bishop of Metz's holdings were still in Barbarossa's possession, while Philipp of Cologne held a great sale of his properties in Cologne and Westphalia, raising nearly forty-seven thousand marks thereby, which the chronicler says he used "to guard against the future."[35] Although Philipp went on to serve Henry VI faith-fully, after Henry's death in 1197 Cologne rather naturally sided with the Welf Otto IV, and suffered siege, economic loss, and military defeat at the hands of the Staufer Philip of Swabia from 1205 to 1207.[36] The Count of Hainault's intrigues continued unabated in 1189, as did the Italian cities' feuds.[37] Simply put, Hiestand's recognition of the political aspects of crusading did not go far enough.

EMPIRE AND CRUSADE: HENRY VI AND FREDERICK II[38]

The initial conditions of Barbarossa's crusade discussed above serve as a template for understanding the issues in subsequent crusades. Upon learning of his father's unex-pected death in Lesser Armenia, Henry VI assumed the reins of imperial government.

His crusade, launched just before his death in 1197, has generally been the preserve of specialists, and is usually subsumed within discussions of his hopes to make the empire an hereditary monarchy rather than an elective one. Van Cleve's 1937 discussion of Henry's dreams of world empire expressed a general fascination with a larger-than-life character, and it has proved impossible for historians, as it proved for Henry's contemporaries, to separate crusade and the imperial succession. Csendes has emphasized just how serious are the gaps in the surviving evidence of Henry's negotiations with Celestine III concerning crusade and empire—unknown locations, unknown correspondence, unknown contents of known correspondence. Despite these limitations, Naumann has argued persuasively that in Henry's case the crusade likely preceded a serious effort to secure the throne for his infant son Frederick, and that the succession issue was likely a byproduct of Henry's crusade plans, brought up by those of his loyal followers who planned on participating. Loud has recently argued that Henry's insistence on the succession provoked a groundswell of discontent, even from nobles who had supported the dynasty and the crusade to that point.[39]

However, the precise political context of Henry's crusade is also difficult to ascertain, for reasons largely the opposite of his father's crusade. Where we know much about Barbarossa's court and itinerary, we know comparatively less about Henry's. The sources for his crusade are also fewer and less detailed. As king of Germany, he inherited a fairly sophisticated administrative establishment of *ministeriales* (unfree knights) in Germany, followed itineraries separate from those of his father, and secured the cooperation of many of his father's former supporters such as Berthold of Künigsberg, and even Philipp of Cologne.[40] With Henry VI, identification with knightly culture seems to have been accentuated, both because Henry had been "knighted" at Mainz in 1184 and because his inner circle seems to have been largely composed of *ministeriales*: of his top nine advisors, six were from ministerial families.[41] There was also a corresponding decrease of princely involvement with the imperial court, and an increased location of the court away from centers of princely or ecclesiastical power, though as Theo Kölzer has remarked, "we have yet to determine whether these tendencies had already begun under Barbarossa."[42] These circumstances doubtless affected the way he recruited and organized his crusade.

While it is hard to shake the impression that Henry prioritized war and empire over crusade, and there can be no doubt that most of his surplus cash was spent on military affairs, "the sheer size of the expedition suggests that he genuinely wanted to win back Jerusalem."[43] After spending most of Richard the Lionheart's ransom on the conquest of the Norman kingdom of Sicily, the emperor appeared ready to devote even more resources to the crusade. Henry planned to expend sixty thousand ounces of gold for his three thousand knights and sergeants when his revenues, even after the conquest of Sicily and the extortion of Byzantium, likely amounted to less than that.[44] Arnold of Lübeck writes of the seemingly endless numbers of knights pouring into Apulia in 1197 to take the emperor's wages for the upcoming expedition.[45]

Yet this image of the German emperor, pouring resources into his crusade and precipitating a constitutional crisis in the process, is not how his partisans wished to present him—and this contrast, curious in itself, has by and large escaped historians' notice. There is undoubtedly a strong connection, even subordination, of crusade to empire in surviving artifacts such as the perennially popular *Liber ad honorem Augusti*, produced by Peter of Eboli around 1196, and replete with symbolism that continues to prompt new analyses.[46] Crusade and empire are given a very prominent place throughout the manuscript, particularly Frederick I's crusade. Particularly noteworthy is the famous scene on folio 107r depicting his death (which in later versions of the manuscript was painted over) and the composition of images depicting the capture of Richard I of England on folio 129v, in which Richard's crusader cross is explicitly subordinated to Henry's imperial authority. It was also no accident that eulogists such as Gottfried of Viterbo appropriated Maccabean imagery to describe Henry's secular wars, despite his well-documented failures in Sicily. The appellation was used of his father and was specifically associated with crusade: its use in this non-crusade context should be considered in conjunction with Henry's treatment of Jews and heretics.[47]

As events unfolded, the expedition proved to be of short duration and lacking in firm direction: the first fleet set sail on September 22, 1197, and most crusaders had returned home by the summer of 1198 after learning of Henry's death. Konrad of Hildesheim, Henry VI's chancellor and previously court chaplain to Barbarossa, was the chief executor of Henry's plans for crusade in 1198, but did not command the army. However, the operational commander Heinrich of Kalden, the imperial marshal who had served first Barbarossa and then Henry with spectacular success, was resented by the nobles who looked to Henry duke of Brabant as their natural leader.[48] The Germans did not make a good impression on the Franks of the Levant, with the *Estoire d'Eracles* complaining of the arrogance they displayed at the siege of Toron, where they rejected several offers to surrender in favor of attempting to storm the place.[49]

After the death of Henry VI in 1197 and the election of Innocent III in 1198, many aspects of Western Christian experience changed, crusading perhaps most of all. Innocent's election coincided with a double royal election in Germany, in which the Staufen candidate Philip of Swabia struggled to maintain the family's position against the Welf candidate Otto IV. In the aftermath of Philip's murder in 1208 and then Otto's defeat at Bouvines in 1215, young Frederick II emerged as the sole claimant to the royal and imperial throne, and from the very start of his reign the crusade hung over his head. Frederick's world seemed "wider, more varied, and livelier" than that of his grandfather Barbarossa, and those political aspects of crusade that we examined under Barbarossa were magnified tenfold due to Frederick's path to power and the complexity of his social and political networks.[50] Both at his royal coronation in 1215 and at his imperial coronation in 1220, he made a crusade vow, but, as is well known, did not fulfill it before the Fifth Crusade unraveled at Egypt. Not until 1228 would the emperor fulfill his vow, and then while excommunicated.[51] In the meantime, in 1213 the papal bull *Quia maior* had foregrounded many of the political aspects of crusade, so that taking the cross was "not only a vassal's duty, but also a demonstratively symbol-laden affirmation of loyalty."[52] The near-constant presence of crusade preaching in Frederick's court and the papacy's more systematic approach to preaching could only result in an increased awareness of the potential and pitfalls of a deceptively spontaneous commitment to Jerusalem.[53]

THE PROCESS OF WAR

The final aspect of crusade discussed here is one that is only gradually being incorporated into studies of German crusading: crusade as war and the process of going to war. The emperor's personal devotion aside, his participation in crusade was not just a matter of pilgrimage, but a state affair of the first order. Although this fact has long been acknowledged, a systematic study has yet to be completed of how the empire's resources were mobilized for these multiple crusades. There are two major aspects to this mobilization: diplomatic and socio-military.

The diets held by emperors in preparation for crusade still contain unmined data, in part because there have been no major follow-ups to Plassmann's and Seltmann's work on court networks. There are also two very important caveats that researchers must make to any conclusions from the records, namely that much documentary evidence is lost or fragmentary, and that, as Kölzer has remarked, what survives often does not tell us what we want to know. For example, to return to Barbarossa and the Third Crusade: between December 1187 and May 1189, Barbarossa held nine diets of significance, as well as various smaller gatherings as he prepared the empire and himself for the army's embarkation from Regensburg. These diets were held in Strasbourg (December 1187), Nuremberg (February 1188), Mainz (March 1188), Seligenstadt (April–May 1188), Goslar (July–August, 1188), Nuremberg (December 1188), Strasbourg (April 1189), Hagenau (mid-April 1189), and Regensburg (May 1189). For most we lack much more than a few surviving documents. In particular the great diet of Mainz in March 1188, the great crusading affair of state, has left us very little material. With a couple of exceptions such as the treaties with Clement III and Alfonso of Castile, few diplomatic initiatives are well documented, in particular the embassies to Constantinople or Iconium.[54] So, although we can easily deduce imperial agendas (Goslar and Nuremberg focused on the northern nobles and diplomatic affairs, Hagenau and Donauworth largely on Staufen family affairs), details that would complicate or nuance our understanding of the crusade preparations are largely missing.[55]

For strictly military resources, in particular manpower, we continue to await new, comprehensive studies that analyze the troops, supplies, bases, and extensive planning necessary to carry out this kind of venture.[56] However, there are several points worth pondering in looking at the military resources of the German crusades.

For Barbarossa's crusade, the mobilization of troops was not so much controlled as guided and influenced by the emperor; the limits of technology and communication did not allow for much more than that. Some participants who joined the imperial army were not known as Staufen supporters. Others, who were known to be sympathetic to the Staufen, took the sea route instead, and there is no transparent logic behind who went by land and who by sea. This includes Barbarossa's nephew Ludwig "the Pious," Landgrave of Thuringia, who traveled by sea with various Dutch and Hessian nobles, and the famous expedition of the north German sea-faring peoples, who stopped to assist the king of Portugal on their way to the Levant.[57] Why certain groups chose the sea route over the emperor's land route was a matter of individual circumstance, and the *Historia de Expeditione* can safely be ignored when attributing sea-route decisions to the devil. After all, even Gottfried of Würzburg's first impulse, so the author says, had been to go by sea.[58] If the Brussels chronicle fragment is anything to go by, the sea-route had been considered and rejected due to concern over lack of shipping, and Henry VI's sea-borne crusade was made with naval resources not quite available to his father.[59]

There was expectation that any campaign led by the emperor would de facto consist largely of troops from his own estates and vassals. This, after all, is the thrust of Walther von der Vogelweide's poem "You princes—all who'd gladly be king-free," and is supported by many of the known allegiances of the nobles in the imperial army in 1189.[60] Yet recent studies have moved away from the connected suppositions that only Staufen supporters joined the emperor's army, and that this expenditure of manpower put the dynasty at a disadvantage in the wars of Henry VI and Philip of Swabia. Tabulated, if incomplete, data of imperial land holdings indicate that they grew substantially during the reign of Barbarossa, and Henry VI's ability to sustain extended wars in Germany and Italy (albeit with difficulty) also suggests that, whatever reserves of manpower had been expended by his father's *passagium*, they did not seriously impact the dynasty's ability to project power against potential rivals.[61] It is often argued that manpower and force-projection issues were eased by the militarization of the German Hospital at Acre, transforming it into a fully-fledged military order dominated by Staufen political interests.[62] However, as Nicholas Morton has shown, while the order certainly benefitted from imperial patronage, other patrons' "donations generally seem to have been made in the wake of a pilgrimage or a crusade, not in reaction to an act of imperial benevolence."[63] The Order's reaction to the split royal election in 1198 and the subsequent war between Otto IV Welf and Philip of Swabia indicates that, rather than being a Staufen auxiliary, it was "an institution which represented the combined commitment of the German people to the recovery of the Holy Land."[64] It was only at the end of the period considered here, during the Fifth Crusade, that the order appears as an agency equal to the Hospitallers or the Templars.[65]

Lastly, the backbone of any German crusading army from our time period was knights. The character, motivations, and political aspirations of the knightly class have been studied in exhaustive detail by German scholars, and *Rittertum* forms the keystone of many interpretations of crusade and empire in the twelfth century.[66] Barbarossa, as discussed below, seems to have encouraged and specifically identified with the *ritter* as a means of promoting a unifying martial culture in his empire. The number of designated *ministeriales* appearing in the charter witness lists actually declined over the course of Frederick I's reign, while the presence of major *ministerial* families increased in the charters of Henry VI, indicating, according to Thomas Zotz, the general tendency of the *ministeriales* to integrate into the lower rungs of nobility.[67] Yet non-knightly participants counted not only for a far greater percentage of a crusade army, but also, as *De Itinere Navali* suggests, for a great deal of its combat power and technical expertise. David Bachrach has already examined the military capabilities of German cities in the mid-thirteenth century, and a similar study of urban crusade contributions would be welcome.[68]

BEYOND THE STATE

This chapter has focused primarily on what could be called a state-centric view of crusading. Yet in the end, while the imperial perspective will likely continue to dominate most discussions, more profitable may be those avenues of investigation that leave imperial politics behind altogether and approach the subject from the point of view of local crusading spirituality. After all, medieval resources for war were decentralized to the point that crusade to the Levant or against the Slavs on the eastern frontier did not absolutely require an imperial presence—the Fifth Crusade is an excellent example of this. The notorious "Children's" Crusade of 1212 is another. Both Peter Raedts' classic 1977 article as well as more recent work by Gary Dickson encourage us to think of German crusading outside the imperial box in which Henry VI and his supporters tried to place it.[69] Similarly, questions of German regionalism, identity, and religious belief are thrown into sharper relief when we look to the crusades across the Elbe and Oder than when we examine Germans on the Jerusalem pilgrimage.[70] As Tyerman has indicated, the crusade idea in the Baltic inhabited a world very different from that of the Jerusalem crusade—conversion of non-Christian peoples was a key difference, for one thing, and the re-purposing of crusade to a different geography was another.[71]

Also absent from this chapter, but essential to bring into the conversation, is the rich crusading material in medieval German literature, on which there have been consider-able recent advances. In particular, the cultural functions of medieval German romance are extremely important to the current discussion, since, as Will Hasty has remarked, they "seem to reflect or continue preceding cultural developments (such as the crusades), [and] they provide ... a new method for archiving, remembering, and processing" the displace-ment of aggression to the peripheries of society.[72] The work of Wolfram von Eschenbach, in particular his *Willehalm*, has proved fertile ground for literary analyses of crusade and empire, as has the lyric poetry of Walther von der Vogelweide.[73] Reception of French *chan-son de geste* has received new treatment, and will add to the already-plentiful scholarship on German poets and crusade-lyricists such as Hartmann von Aue who either apostrophize the emotions of crusading or else extol the character of their Muslim opponents. At the same time, Jarold Frakes has cautioned us not to over-apply modern discourses of "tolerance" to a medieval German literature that lacked the concept as we would understand it.[74]

Integral to both crusade and empire, according to Josef Fleckenstein, was the monarch's identity as a warrior. Barbarossa in particular seems to have recognized the benefits of fostering a *ritterlich* identity among his unfree knights, his *ministeriales*.[75] This achieved its highest form with the crusade, and the concept of the *milites Christi*, such as Barbarossa enacted when he took the cross at Mainz in 1188. With this, "the ideal superorder became reality, a reality in which the emperor took the protection of all Christendom as his high-est duty."[76] While Fleckenstein has argued that the dynamics of *rittertum* were at once "national" and universal, it has also been argued that knighthood was gaining social promi-nence in part because of the growing economic challenges to fielding good cavalry, much as Jean Scammell has argued happened in Henry II's England. It is thus reasonable to consider whether the "chivalric" ceremonies at Mainz in 1184 and 1188 represent the conscious fulfillment of the emperor's goals, or perhaps instead the shrewd appropriation of a larger historical social transformation.[77] In any case, much of the rhetoric about chivalry, crusade, and empire has focused on Barbarossa, and overlooks the changing and often unstable rela-tionship of subsequent emperors to these items. Frederick II is a case in point.[78]

CONCLUSION

On May 18, 1190, Frederick Barbarossa had led his followers against the Seljuk army shouting "Christus regnat, Christus vincit, Christus imperat," the *laudes regiae* used at his imperial coronation in 1155.[79] Such an explicit identification of crusade with empire was the hallmark of the later twelfth century, and of the dynasty that gave the era its moniker. Yet it was hardly confined to the Staufen: the *Rolandslied*, after all, was composed under the patronage of Barbarossa's cousin, Henry the Lion, and completely imbued with the spirit of imperial crusade.[80] Both examples are instances of the appropriation of a concept much larger than a particular ruling house, and Hiestand's "Kingship and Crusade," by implicitly separating concept from appropriation, has held up quite well after twenty years. At the same time, a continued fascination with the narrative sweep of Staufen Germany has not prevented increasingly complex approaches to the crusade, frequently embedding the cru-sade within social analysis and imperial ideologies. Unfortunately for English audiences, much of this new work is in German and we are in sore need of more translations in order to make this field accessible to a wider audience. Frederick I's crusade remains the most approachable of the German crusades, and analyzing his preparations remains an excellent case study of how the religious imperatives of "crusade" were negotiated in a world shaped by faction, interest, and personality. Even if we accept that there was a general expectation in the empire that the emperor would lead the *passagium* to Jerusalem, his path to doing so was not straightforward. The same goes for every subsequent German crusade to the Latin East.

At the same time, there are several areas of research that are not much further advanced than they were twenty years ago. The impact of heavy crusading mortality on the political landscape remains imperfectly understood, not least because our understanding of German government and administration, on which Hiestand based his conclusions, has changed. As an event, mortality could be decisive enough: Frederick of Swabia's death at Acre basically ensured a contested royal election in 1198. Of the sixty-seven nobles serving in the imperial army in 1189, at least a third died on the expedition.[81] However, by itself that statistic means little. To date, there have also been few follow-ups to Plassmann's and Seltmann's work on power networks, or applications of network analysis to power and crusade in the German realms. The relationship of crusade as political act to crusade as act of personal devotion is also still in need of development. We also have much to learn about the connections between crusading ideas in literary and historical writing. A full analysis of crusading must also examine persecution, and we are in need of a more comprehensive revision of the Jewish experience in the German crusades.[82] Finally, while the ultimate success of the effort might be limited, more attention should be given to attempts, like Andrew Latham's, to bring the crusades into dialog with the social sciences; this may have potential for uniting the disparate strands of crusade activity in the German realm.[83]

It could also be said that the way we assess medieval actors has changed significantly since the 1990s. "The crusades," remarked Hiestand, "were wasteful of both men and money."[84] That judgment remains by and large an accurate one; after all, war tends to be a wasteful activity, no matter how skillfully handled or adroitly planned. Neither Frederick Barbarossa nor his uncle Conrad III, or even, in the final analysis, his son Henry VI, were especially remarkable for the efficiency of their operations. Yet the "waste" of which Hiestand speaks was regarded as acceptable loss in pursuit of a goal that superseded the normal calculations of statecraft, or rather directed diplomatic, military, and economic resources to an end that, to the German realm at least, was considered an obligation as well as a privilege. Both Barbarossa and his son found the intersection of crusade, empire, and the process of war a messy and costly one. But, had they lived long enough, they likely would have agreed with Wolfram von Eschenbach that "whoever desires the Grail has to approach that prize with the sword. So should a prize be striven for."[85] As subsequent centuries demonstrated, it was not a mentality that would soon fade.

NOTES

1 The "Roman Empire" technically consisted of three kingdoms: Germany, Italy, and Burgundy. Nevertheless, following medieval German practice, the "Kingdom of Germany" and the "Empire" are often used synonymously, and, for ease of reference, that is how they are used in this chapter. Non-German parts of the empire are indicated by name.

2 Recent English-language works that have helped to redress this imbalance include Graham Loud's excellent article "The German Crusade of 1197–98," in *Crusades* 13 (2014), 143–170, Loud's

translation of the Ansbertus Chronicle, *The Crusade of Frederick Barbarossa: The History of the Expedition of the Emperor Frederick and Related Texts* (Farnham: Ashgate, 2010), Nicholas Morton's *The Teutonic Knights in the Holy Land 1190–1291* (Woodbridge: Boydell, 2009), Jonathan Lyon's *Princely Brothers and Sisters: The Sibling Bond in German Politics, 1100–1250* (Ithaca: Cornell University Press, 2013), and John Freed's much-anticipated study of Frederick Barbarossa (New Haven: Yale University Press, 2015).

3 For German medieval scholarship through 2010, see Jonathan Lyon, "The Medieval German State in Recent Historiography," *German History* 28 (2010), 85–94; Hans-Werner Goetz, "Historical Studies on the Middle Ages in Germany: Tradition, Current Trends, and Perspectives," *The Journal of English and Germanic Philology* (Special issue: *The State of Medieval Studies*), 105 (2006), 207–230; and Joachim Ehlers, "Das Kaisertum Barbarossas und seine Folgen für das Reich," in *Staufisches Kaisertum im 12. Jahrhundert*, ed. Stefan Burkhardt et al. (Regensburg: Schnell & Steiner, 2010), 295–319.

4 Rudolf Hiestand, "Kingship and Crusade in Twelfth-Century Germany," in *England and Germany in the High Middle Ages*, ed. Alfred Haverkamp and Hannah Vollrath (Oxford: Oxford University Press, 1996), 235–240. This topic was recently discussed in Susan B. Edginton's presentation "Did the Franks suppress the German Contribution to the First Crusade?", which addressed John of Würzburg's claim in the 1160s that the Franks had done just that. For more details, see abstract at the 34th Annual Conference of the Center for Medieval Studies at Fordham University, 29 March 2014, http://legacy.fordham.edu/mvst/conference14/program.html (accessed January 14, 2015).

5 Rudolf Hiestand, "Kingship and Crusade," 235–265; "Precipua tocius christianismi columpna: Barbarossa und der Kreuzzug," in *Friedrich Barbarossa: Handlungsspielräume und Wirkungsweisen des staufischens Kaisers*, ed. Alfred Haverkamp (Sigmaringen: Jan Thorbecke, 1992), 51–108.

6 Hiestand, "Kingship and Crusade," 258. Hiestand understates the matter: the military aspects of crusading are often overlooked, but were essential to the enterprise.

7 The key studies on Frederick I's crusade, aside from those already mentioned, are mostly in German, and are dominated by Ekkehard Eickhoff's work. See Eickhoff, *Friedrich Barbarossa im Orient: Kreuzzug und Tod Friedrichs I* (Tübingen: Ernst Wasmuth, 1977); "Die Bedeutung de Kreuzzüge für den deutschen Raum," in *Die Zeit der Staufer*, vol. 3 (Stuttgart: Württembergisches Landesmuseum, 1977), 239–248; and "Friedrich Barbarossa in Anatolien," in *Stauferzeit–Zeit der Kreuzzüge*, ed. Karl-Heinz Rueß (Göppingen: Gesellschaft für staufische Geschichte, 2011), 58–85. See also Alan V. Murray, "Finance and Logistics of the Crusade of Frederick Barbarossa," in *In Laudem Hierosolymitani*, ed. Iris Shagrir et al. (Aldershot: Ashgate, 2007), 357–368. For a detailed analysis of how chroniclers reported Frederick's death on crusade, see Leila Bargmann, "Der Tod Friedrichs I. im Spiegel der Quellenüberlieferung," *Concilium medii aevi* 13 (2010), 223–249.

8 Rudolf Hiestand, "Precipua tocius," 57. See also Marcel Pacaut, *Frederick Barbarossa*, trans. A. J. Pomerans (New York: Charles Scribner's Sons, 1970), 193–201; and for Conrad III's crusade, see Conor Kostick, "Social Unrest and the Failure of Conrad III's March Through Anatolia, 1147," *German History* 28 (2010), 125–142; and Knut Görich, "Schmach und Ehre: Konrad III. auf dem Zweiten Kreuzzug," in *Stauferzeit–Zeit der Kreuzzüge*, ed. Karl-Heinz Ruess (Göppingen: Gesellschaft für staufische Geschichte e. V., 2011), 42–57.

9 See Knut Görich, "Die 'Ehre des Reichs' (*honor imperii*): Überlegungen zu einem Forschungsproblem," in *Rittertum und höfische Kultur der Stauferzeit*, ed. Johannes Laudage and Yvonne Leiverkus (Cologne: Böhlau Verlag, 2006), 36–74; *Die Ehre Friedrich Barbarossas: Kommunikation, Konflikt und Politisches Handeln im 12. Jahrhundert* (Darmstadt: Wissenschaftliche Buchgesellschaft, 2001); and *Friedrich Barbarossa: Eine Biographie* (Munich: C. H. Beck, 2011).

10 See Reinhold Röhricht's dated but still useful *Die Deutschen im Heiligen Lande* (Innsbruck, 1894).

11 See John Wilkinson, *Jerusalem Pilgrimage 1099–1185* (London: Hakluyt Society, 1988) for John of Wurzburg's account. For Henry the Lion's pilgrimage to Jerusalem, see Joachim Ehlers, *Heinrich der Löwe: eine biographie* (Munich: Siedler Verlag, 2008), 197–211. For the most recent overview of scholarship on Henry, see Wilhelm Störmer, "Heinrich der Löwe–ein europäischer Fürst des Hochmittelalters," *Zeitschrift für bayerische Landesgeschichte* 73 (2010), 779–789.

12 See Malcolm Barber, *The Crusader States* (New Haven: Yale University Press, 2012), 266. See also Jonathan Phillips' *Defenders of the Holy Land: Relations between the Latin East and West, 1119–1187* (Oxford: Oxford University Press, 1996).

13 Joseph P. Huffman, *The Social Politics of Medieval Diplomacy* (Ann Arbor: University of Michigan Press, 2000), 103–132, and esp. 120–123 and 128–132, insists that Philip of Cologne's policy was territorial, and not part of a larger anti-Staufen coalition. Görich, while downplaying the chances of the dispute becoming an empire-wide conflict, does recognize the gravity of the situation, as well as the crucial way in which the Capetian-Angevin wars affected it. See Görich, *Friedrich Barbarossa*, 527–530.

14 Görich, *Friedrich Barbarossa*, 520–525; Pacaut, *Friedrich Barbarossa*, 183–185. The points at issue are too complex for analysis here: they revolved around Barbarossa's use of church incomes in Italy, his refusal to remove bishops unacceptable to Rome, his occupation of the Matildine estates, which had been bequeathed to the papacy, and above all his negotiations with William II of Sicily for a marriage alliance.

15 *Gesta Treverorum Continuata*, ed. G. Waitz, MGH SS 24, 383–5.

16 Arnold of Lübeck describes Urban as a "zealot for justice, who constantly worked for the defense of the holy Roman church, not fearing the imperial earthly principality." *Chronica Slavorum*, ed. G. Pertz, SRGS 14 (reprinted Hannover: Hahnsche Buchhandlung, 1978), 102.

17 See I. S. Robinson, *The Papacy 1073–1198: Continuity and Innovation* (Cambridge: Cambridge University Press, 1990), 499. Robinson's remains the most concise account of the papacies of Lucius III, Urban III, Gregory VIII, and Celestine III, 497–507. For Urban's energy, see letters to Wichmann of Magdeburg, protesting imperial use of church property (*Regesta Pontificum Romanorum*, vol. 1, ed. Jaffe [RPR] 15534), and to Barbarossa himself, protesting Henry VI's behavior in central Italy (RPR 15634, June 18, 1185).

18 Robinson, 503.

19 Ibid., 502, 503.

20 *Gesta Trev.*, 387; Folmar resided at the archbishop of Rheims' castle at Mouzon. *Chronica Regia Coloniensis*, ed. G. Waitz, MGH SRG 18, 135, for the bishop of Metz; Görich, *Friedrich Barbarossa*, 526–527, for Henry VI and Folmar's consecration.

21 For Philipp's earlier career and central role in the fall of Henry the Lion, duke of Saxony and Bavaria, see Görich, *Friedrich Barbarossa*, 466–475.

22 *Catalogi Archiepiscoporum Coloniensium: Continuatio II*, ed. Hermann Cardauns, MGH Scriptores 24, 345.

23 See Manfred Groten, "Köln und das Reich: Zum Verhältnis von Kirche und Stadt zu den staufischen Herrschern 1151–1198," in *Stauferreich im Wandel*, ed. Stefan Weinfurter (Stuttgart: Jan Thorbecke, 2002), 237–252, for an overview of this larger (but often overlooked) debate over Barbarossa's relationship with Cologne.

24 The position of the German prelates and papal legates to the German church are both subjects in need of more study. For an overview, see Bernhard Töpfer, "Kaiser Friedrich Barbarossa und der deutsche Reichsepiskopat," in *Friedrich Barbarossa: Handlungsspielräume und Wirkungsweisen des Staufischen Kaisers*, ed. Alfred Haverkamp (Sigmaringen: Jan Thorbecke, 1992), 394–402. For the political influence of the bishops after the Peace of Venice in 1177, see Wolfgang Georgi, "Wichmann, Christian, Philipp und Konrad: Die 'Friedensmacher' von Venedig?", in *Stauferreich im Wandel: Ordnungsvorstellungen und Politik in der Zeit Friedrich Barbarossas*, ed. Stefan Weinfurter (Stuttgart: Jan Thorbecke, 2002), 41–84. For Wichmann of Magdeburg, see *Erzbischof Wichmann (1152–1192) und Magdeburg im hohen Mittelalter: Stadt – Erzbistum – Reich*, ed. Matthias Puhle

(Magdeburg: Magdeburg Museum, 1992). For Cologne, see Wilhelm Weise, *Der Hof der Kölner Erzbischöfe in der Zeit Kaiser Friedrich Barbarossas* (Düsseldorf: Droste, 2004).

25 Görich, *Friedrich Barbarossa*, 527–528. *Constitutiones* 1, 441–448, Controversio cum Urbano III. Philipp's diet of March 1187 supposedly had upwards of four thousand knights present; see *Die Regesten der Erzbischöfe von Köln im Mittelalter*, vol. 2 1100–1205, ed. Richard Knipping (Bonn: Hanstein, 1901), nos. 1280, 1281, 1282.

26 Ferdinand Opll, *Das Itinerar Friedrich Barbarossas (1152-1190)* (Vienna: Hermann Böhlaus, 1978), 92; Görich, *Friedrich Barbarossa*, 529–530.

27 Eickhoff, *Friedrich Barbarossa im Orient*, 33–34.

28 See Gregory's first bull, "Nuntio cladis Hierosolimitanae," RPR 16013, October 24, 1187. The founding document of the Third Crusade, *Audita tremendi*, has been translated in Loud, *The Crusade of Frederick Barbarossa*, 37–41, and in *Crusade and Christendom: Annotated Documents in Translation from Innocent III to the Fall of Acre, 1187–1291*, ed. Jessalynn Bird et al. (Philadelphia: University of Pennsylvania Press, 2014), 4–9.

29 Robinson, *The Papacy 1073–1198*, 505–506.

30 Loud, *The Crusade of Frederick Barbarossa*, 143.

31 For Mainz, see Fleckenstein, "Friedrich Barbarossa und das Rittertum: Zur bedeutung der großen Mainzer Hoftage von 1184 und 1188," in *Festschrift für Hermann Heimpel*, vol. 2, ed. Fellows of the Max Planck Institute for History (Göttingen: Vandenhoeck & Ruprecht, 1972), 1023–1141. For Würzburg, see Hiestand, *Die päpstlichen Legaten*, 286; Hiestand compares Gottfried to Adhemar le Puy, papal legate during the First Crusade. For the Jews, see Robert Chazan, "Emperor Frederick I, the Third Crusade, and the Jews," *Viator* 8 (1977), 83–93.

32 Rolf de Kegel, ed., *Die Jüngere Hildesheimer Briefsammlung* (Munich: Monumenta Germaniae Historica, 1995). For the most part, these letters seem to belong to a genre called *Stilübungen*, that is, stylistic exercises produced by clerks to gain practice in scribal duties. However, there has long been an argument that the content of the exercises is historically valuable, and if this is true there is much to be learned about the Crisis.

33 MGH Diplomata vol 10, part 4, *Urkunden Friedrichs I 1181-1190*, ed. Heinrich Appelt (Hannover: Hahnsche, 1990), no. 987, 273–277; Burchard von Ursberg, *Chronicon*, MGH SRG 16, 2nd ed., ed. Oswald Holder-Egger and Bernhard von Simson (Hannover: Hahnsche, 1916), 65–69; Loud, *The Crusade of Frederick Barbarossa*, 209–212.

34 Cf. Eickhoff, *Friedrich Barbarossa im Orient*, 35, who argues with comparative accuracy that "nobles and church in Germany, Burgundy, and Italy at no point and for no other undertaking stood so closely behind an emperor in the Middle Ages."

35 DFI 991, 280–281, Frederick giving salt flats to the Monastery of Trois-Fontaines while the temporalities of the bishop of Metz were in imperial hands. For Philipp, see Chron. Reg. Col., 140.

36 *Catalogi Archaepiscoporum Coloniensium*, 352.

37 See Gilbert of Mons, *Chronicle of Hainault*, trans. Laura Napran (Woodbridge: Boydell, 2005), 122–134; *Annales Placentini Guelfi*, MGH SS 188, 417.

38 The key studies on Henry VI are almost entirely in German: Claudia Naumann, *Der Kreuzzug Kaiser Heinrich VI* (Frankfurt am Main: Peter Lang, 1994); Peter Csendes, *Heinrich VI* (Darmstadt: Wissenschaftliche Buchgesellschaft, 1993); Ingeborg Seltmann, *Heinrich VI: Herrschaftsprxis und Umgebung* (Erlangen: Palm & Enke, 1983). At St. Louis University, Daniel Webb is currently conducting major new research on Henry's crusade, which will be a very welcome addition to the literature.

39 Thomas Curtis Van Cleve, *Markward of Anweiler and the Sicilian Regency* (Princeton: Princeton University Press, 1937), chapter 1; Csendes, *Heinrich VI*, 184–188; Naumann, *Der Kreuzzug Kaiser Heinrichs VI*, 108–110; Loud, "The German Crusade," 143–147.

40 For Henry's itinerary, see *Regesta Imperii* vol. 4, part 3 *Heinrich VI 1165 (1190)–1197*, ed. J. Böhmer, revised Gerhard Baaken (Cologne: Böhlau, 1972), at http://daten.digitale-sammlungen.de/~db/bsb00009243/images/ (accessed June 25, 2015). For Berthold of Künigsberg, castellan of modern

Haute Kounigsberg, crusader with Barbarossa, and commander of the imperial army in 1192, see Loud, *Crusade*, 54. For Philipp of Cologne, see Hubert Houben, "Philipp von Heinsberg, Heinrich VI. und Montecassino," *Quellen und Forschungen aus Italienischen Archiven und Bibliotheken* 68 (1988), 52–73.

41 This was one of the conclusions of Ingeborg Seltmann's study of Henry's court, *Heinrich VI: Herrschaftspraxis und Umgebung* (Erlangen: Palm & Enke, 1983).

42 Theo Kölzer, "Der Hof Friedrich Barbarossa und die Reichsfürsten," in *Stauferreich im Wandel: Ordnungsvorstellungen und Politik in der Zeit Friedrich Barbarossas*, ed. Stephan Weinfurter (Stuttgart: Jan Thorbecke, 2002), 224.

43 Peter W. Edbury, "Celestine, the Crusade and the Latin East," in *Pope Celestine III (1191–1198): Diplomat and Pastor*, ed. John Doran and Damian J. Smith (Farnham, Surrey: Ashgate, 2008), 129–143, 134.

44 MGH *Constitutiones*, vol. 1, #365, Encyclical on the Expedition to Jerusalem, 12 April, 1195.

45 Arnold of Lübeck, *Chronica Slavorum*, 197.

46 The two best versions of the manuscript are *Petrus de Ebulo: Liber ad honorem Augusti sive de rebus Siculis*, ed. Theo Kölzer, Marlis Stähli, and Gereon Becht-Jördens (Sigmaringen: Jan Thorbecke, 1994), and Gwenyth Hood, *Book in Honor of Augustus (Liber ad Honorem Augusti)* (Tempe, AZ: Arizona Center for Medieval and Renaissance Studies, 2012).

47 Gottfried von Viterbo, *Gesta Friderici I. et Heinrici VI.*, MGH SRG 30, ed. G. H. Pertz (Hannover: Hahnsche, 1870), 48, line 70; Nicholas Morton, "The Defence of the Holy Land and the Memory of the Maccabees," *Journal of Medieval History* 36 (2010), 275–293. For Henry's policy toward heretics in Italy, see Peter D. Diehl, "Henry VI, Heresy and the Extension of Imperial Power in Italy," in *Plentitude of Power: The Doctrines and Exercise of Authority in the Middle Ages. Essays in Memory of Robert Louis Benson*, ed. Robert C. Figueira (Aldershot: Ashgate, 2006), 37–46.

48 Csendes, *Heinrich VI*, 197–202; Loud, "The German Crusade," 143–147. For Hildesheim, see Gerhard Bach, *Konrad von Querfurt, Kanzler Heinrichs VI., Bischof von Hildesheim und Würzburg* (Hildesheim: Bernward, 1988), 33–45. For Henry of Kalden, see Loud, *The Crusade of Frederick Barbarossa*, 74.

49 Peter W. Edbury, *The Conquest of Jerusalem and the Third Crusade* (Aldershot: Ashgate, 1998), 144–145.

50 See the discussion in Bodo Hechelhammer, *Kreuzzug und Herrschaft unter Friedrich II: Handlungsspielräume von Kreuzzugspolitik (1215–1230)* (Stuttgart: Jan Thorbecke, 2004), 41.

51 The most recent overview of Frederick II's crusade is by Wolfgang Stürner, "Der Kreuzzug Kaiser Friedrichs II," in *Stauferzeit-Zeit der Kreuzzüge*, 144–157.

52 Heckelhammer, *Kreuzzug und Herrschaft*, 50.

53 Ibid., 50–55.

54 See *Constitutiones* I, 461–463 for the treaty with Clement, *Constitutiones* I, 452–457, and DFI 4:247–251 for the treaty with Alfonso of Castile.

55 See Opll, *Das Itinerar*, 92–97 and the maps in Karl Bosl's two-volume study, *Die Reichsministerialität der Salier und Staufer* (Stuttgart: Hiersemann, 1950).

56 For the Third Crusade, Dana Cushing and Stephen Bennett are working on separate projects that explore recruitment for the Third Crusade. For Cushing's new, expandable inventory of German crusaders which substantially corrects and expands Röhricht's list; see her "ICHS-CrusaderDatabase," www.academia.edu/4204567/ICHS-CrusaderDatabases (accessed January 15, 2015). Interested readers should peruse Loud's translation of the *Historia de Expeditione*, cited above; also Sylvain Gouguenheim's "Die Perspktive der Erforschung der Ritterorden im Lichte der 'neuen Militärgeschichte': einige Bemerkungen aus der Geschichte des Deutschen Ordens," *Ordines Militares: Colloquia Torunensia Historia* 18 (2013), 7–25. For Henry VI's crusade, see Loud, "The German Crusade," 155–158.

57 See Dana Cushing's exhaustive new analysis of the northern group's chronicle, *De Itinere Navali* (Antimony Media, 2013).

58 Loud, *The Crusade of Frederick Barbarossa*, 44.

59 Freiherrn von Reiffenberg, ed., *Bruckstück über den Kreuzzug Friderich's I* (Stuttgart, 1844), 24. For an excellent survey of twelfth-century shipping and extensive bibliography, see Dana Cushing, "New Information about Cogs and Medieval Naval Logistics from an Eyewitness Crusade Chronicle, *De itinere navali*," AVISTA Forum Journal 20 (Fall, 2010), 24–34, available at www. academia.edu/671249/New_Information_about_Cogs_and_Esneccar_from_an_Eyewitness_ Account_of_the_Third_Crusade_De_Itinere_Navali (accessed January 28, 2015).

60 Walther von der Vogelweide, Poem no. 52 "Ir fürsten die des küniges gerne waeren âne," in *Walter von der Vogelweide: The Single-Stanza Lyrics*, ed. and trans. Frederick Goldin (New York: Routledge, 2003).

61 Hiestand, in particular "Kingship and Crusade," 258–259, has argued that crusade inadvertently weakened, or at least complicated, Staufen internal power. However, see Loud's analysis of the imperial army in 1189, *The Crusade of Frederick Barbarossa*, 20–25, and Murray, "Finance and Logistics." See also Loud, "The German Crusade," 158–167, for an in-depth analysis of the political sympathies of Henry's crusaders in 1197. For royal and imperial holdings, see Andreas Schlunk's controversial *Königsmacht und Krongut: Die Machtgrundlage des deutschen Königtums im 13. Jahrhundert–und eine neue historische Methode* (Stuttgart: Franz Steiner, 1988). While the mechanics and assumptions behind his argument have not found acceptance with most scholars, the carefully tabulated spreadsheets of royal and imperial holdings remain extremely valuable.

62 Udo Arnold, "Die Staufer und der Deutschen Orden," in *Medieval Spirituality in Scandinavia and Europe: A Collection of Essays in Honor of Tore Nyberg*, ed. Lars Bisgaard et al. (Odense: Odense University Press, 2001), 145–155.

63 Morton, *Teutonic Knights in the Holy Land*, 25.

64 Ibid., 30. See also Bodo Hechelhammer, "Mittler zwischen Kreuz und Krone: Hermann von Salza und der Kreuzzug Friedrichs II," *Zeitschrift des Vereins für Thüringische Geschichte* 61 (2007), 31–58.

65 See James Powell's *Anatomy of a Crusade, 1213–1221* (Syracuse: Syracuse University Press, 1990); Morton, *Teutonic Knights in the Holy Land*, chapter 2, and especially Oliver of Paderborn's chronicle *Historia Damiatina*, in *Die Schriften des Kölner Domscholasters*, ed. Dr. Hoogeweg (Tübingen: Litterarischen Verein in Stuttgart, 1894), 253–255.

66 The classic study, though now obsolete, is Karl Bosl's two-volume *Die Reichsministerialität der Salier und Staufer: Ein Beitrag zur Geschichte des hochmittelalterlichen deutschen Volkes, Staates und Reiches*, MGH Schriften 10 (Stuttgart: Hiersemann, 1950/1951). Another important study is Josef Fleckenstein's edited collection *Herrschaft und Stand: Untersuchungen zur Sozialgeschichte im 13. Jahrhundert* (Göttingen: Vandenhoeck & Ruprecht, 1977).

67 See Thomas Kotz, "Die Ministerialen und der Hof Friedrich Barbarossas," in *Friedrich Barbarossa und sein Hof*, ed. Caspar Ehlers and Karl Heinz Rueß (Göppingen, 2009), 59–77.

68 David Bachrach, "Making Peace and War in the 'City State' of Worms, 1235–1273," *German History* 24 (2006), 505–525.

69 Peter Raedts, "The Children's Crusade of 1212," *Journal of Medieval History* 3 (1977), 279–323. Reprinted in *The Crusades: Critical Concepts in Historical Studies*, vol. 4, ed. Andrew Jotischky (London: Routledge, 2008), 264–317. See the most recent work by Gary Dickson, *The Children's Crusade: Medieval History, Modern Mythistory* (London: Palgrave Macmillan, 2010). However, see Loud, "The German Crusade," 170, who argues that historians have read "imperial ambitions" into Henry's crusade preparations where a "crusading ethic" may be the more convincing explanation.

70 The two most important works on the Baltic crusade for this period are the 2003 edition of *The Chronicle of Henry of Livonia*, trans. James Brundage (New York: Columbia University Press, 2003) and Marek Tamm et al., eds., *Crusading and Chronicle Writing on the Medieval Baltic Frontier: A Companion to the Chronicle of Henry of Livonia* (Farnham: Ashgate, 2011). See also Alan Murray, ed., *Crusade and Conversion on the Baltic Frontier 1150–1500* (Aldershot:

Ashgate, 2001); and Rasa Mažeika, "Granting Power to Enemy Gods in the Chronicles of the Baltic Crusades," in *Medieval Frontiers: Concepts and Practices*, ed. David Abulafia and Nora Berend (Aldershot: Ashgate, 2002), 153–171. Friedrich Lotter's older "The Crusading Idea and the Conquest of the Region East of the Elbe" remains an excellent survey of the topic, in *Medieval Frontier Societies*, ed. Robert Bartlett and Angus MacKay (Oxford: Clarendon Press, 1989), 267–306.

71 Christopher Tyerman, "Henry of Livonia and the Ideology of Crusading," in *Crusade and Chronicle Writing*, 26.

72 Will Hasty, "Bounds of Imagination: Grail Questing and Chivalric Colonizing in Wolfram von Eschenbach's *Parzival*," in Hasty, ed. *The Grail, the Quest, and the World of Arthur* (Woodbridge: Boydell and Brewer, 2008), 48–61.

73 See in particular *Wolfram's Willehalm: Fifteen Essays*, ed. Martin H. Jones and Timothy McFarland (Woodbridge: Boydell and Brewer, 2002), and Frederick Goldin, ed. and trans., *Walther von der Vogelweide: The Single-Stanza Lyrics* (New York: Routledge, 2003).

74 See Bernd Bastert, *Helden als Heilige: Chanson de geste-Rezeption im deutschsprachigen Raum* (Tübingen: A. Francke, 2010), and Jerold C. Frakes, *Vernacular and Latin Literary Discourse of the Muslim Other in Medieval Germany* (London: Palgrave Macmillan, 2011).

75 Josef Fleckenstein, "Friedrich Barbarossa und das Rittertum." The best introduction to the issues of knighthood in later twelfth-century Germany remains chapter 2 of William Henry Jackson's *Chivalry in Twelfth-Century Germany: The Works of Hartmann von Aue* (Cambridge: D. S. Brewer, 1994).

76 Fleckenstein, "Kaisertum und Rittertum in der Stauferzeit," *Ordines Militares–Colloquia Torunensia Historica* 5 (1990), 18.

77 See William Henry Jackson, "Aspects of Knighthood in Hartmann's Adaptations of Chrétien's Romances and in the Social Context," in *Chrétien de Troyes and the German Middle Ages*, ed. Martin H. Jones and Roy Wisbey (Cambridge: D. S. Brewer, 1993), 49. Jean Scammell, "The Formation of English Social Structure: Freedom, Knights, and Gentry, 1066–1300," *Speculum* 68 (1993), 591–618.

78 Josef Fleckenstein, "Friedrich II und das Rittertum," in *Federico II e le nouve culture* (Spoleto, 1995), 27–44.

79 Loud, *The Crusade of Frederick Barbarossa*, 111.

80 Jeffrey Ashcroft, "*Honor imperii—des riches ere*: the Idea of Empire in Konrad's *Rolandslied*," in *German Narrative Literature of the Twelfth and Thirteenth Centuries*, ed. Volker Honemann et al. (Tübingen: Niemeyer, 1994), 139–156.

81 Hiestand, "Kingship and Crusade," 248; Loud, *The Crusade of Frederick Barbarossa*, 47–55.

82 Resources for further reading on this complicated topic can be found in Daniel Franke, "The Crusades and Medieval Anti-Judaism: Cause or Consequence?" in *Seven Myths of the Crusades*, ed. Alfred J. Andrea and Andrew Holt (Cambridge: Hackett, 2015).

83 Andrew A. Latham, *Theorizing Medieval Geopolitics: War and World Order in the Age of the Crusades* (New York: Routledge, 2012). Latham's "corporate-sovereign Church" thesis and "conditions-of-possibility" thesis for crusade are not completely satisfying, but his book represents a serious attempt to rethink medieval politics, and deserves wider consideration.

84 Hiestand, "Kingship and Crusade," 261.

85 Wolfram von Eschenbach, *Parzival*, X:503, trans. Helen Mustard and Charles Passage (Vintage Books, 1962); "wan swer sgrâles gerte/ dô muoste mit dem swerte / sich dem prîse nâhen. / sus sol man prîses gâhen." See the TITUS database, University of Frankfurt, http://titus.fkidg1.uni-frankfurt.de/texte/etcs/germ/mhd/parzival/parzi.htm (accessed January 2, 2015).

CHAPTER NINE

NORTHERN CRUSADES: BETWEEN HOLY WAR AND MISSION

———•◆•———

Darius von Güttner-Sporzyński

The impact of the holy wars and crusades in East Central and Eastern Europe was transformative and enduring, expanding the frontier of Christendom spiritually, culturally and geographically. The precursor to these military expeditions was pacifist missionary activity, which in many areas preceded the holy wars by up to a century. In the historiography of the crusades, the Northern Crusades are rarely considered on the same footing as crusades directed at the Holy Land. This is because, among other reasons, the Northern Crusades were characterised by a combination of forced conversion and conquest to a degree not found in the Levantine crusades. The issue of papal authorisation of the Northern Crusades is also questioned as many of the campaigns did not receive explicit sanction. Notwithstanding that the Northern Crusades were, like the 'true crusades', 'fought against those perceived to be the external or internal foes of Christendom', the association of the crusades to the Holy Land with 'the recovery of Christian property' and the 'defence of the Church or Christian people' accorded them primacy. Whilst this latter objective was often also claimed by the participants of the Northern Crusades, concrete evidence that Christian property or peoples were directly threatened by the pagan targets of a specific military action is often difficult to substantiate.[1]

The traditional view that the Northern Crusades were a uniquely German endeavour is no longer accepted as an increasing body of research testifies to active involvement by Danes, Poles, Swedes and Russians.[2] This former view was influenced by the arrival of the Teutonic Order in Prussia in 1226 at the invitation of the Poles and its subsequent establishment of theocratic lordship in the lands the order conquered from the Prussians. What has become increasingly clear in the growing scholarship is that from the early days of Christian–pagan interaction, the relationship was characterised by the heavy-handed involvement of secular rulers from the newly converted monarchies of the region. The Danes were involved in Christianising the Wends, Prussians and Estonians; the Swedes acted in Finland; the Poles with the Wends, Pomeranians and Prussians and there was Russian involvement in Estonia and Finland. The Teutonic Order, a military religious order established in the Holy Land took up the challenge of converting the pagans and declared a perpetual crusade against the Prussians and other Balts, the last pagan communities in Europe. The Prussians were annihilated; their culture and language vanished and their name was appropriated by a German dynasty. Among the Balts, the Lithuanians survived by forming an alliance when its ruler accepted Christianity, delivered his people and territories into a union with Poland and in exchange was crowned the king of Poland.

INTO THE NEW LANDS

In the middle of the tenth century, German colonisation began encroaching on the lands of the pagan Slavs between the Elbe and Oder rivers. In these colonised marches new bishoprics were founded and the mission to Christianise the local Slav tribes began. The pagan Slavs, collectively referred to as Wends, did not form a unified polity. Across the Oder River a pagan warlord Mieszko accepted baptism in 966 and was recognised as the duke of the Poles by the empire and the papacy. A missionary bishopric for Mieszko's subjects was established in Poznań in 968. Similar processes were underway in Bohemia, whose rulers were influenced by the Christianisation of Moravia attributed to the earlier mission of Cyril and Methodius in 863. The first bishopric was established in Prague in 973. Within a century of Mieszko's baptism other regional pagan elites had followed suit and the dynasties of Denmark, the Rus, the Hungarians, Norway and Sweden converted to Christianity.

Yet, while the Wendish elites were receptive to a degree to Christian preaching they demonstrated a selective and calculated approach to the new religion espoused by their neighbours. Significantly, the Wends were not unified under a single dynasty who could enforce the adoption of Christianity and they rejected German missionary efforts. With the military conquest of Pomerania (*c.* 1102–28) by the Poles and a campaign of Christianisation conducted by Otto of Bamberg (*c.* 1060–1139) in 1124 and 1128 under the auspices of Bolesław III Krzywousty of Poland (1086–1138), the Wends were increasingly seen as a target for missionary bishops.[3] The involvement of devout and energetic bishops such as Norbert of Xanten (†1134), archbishop of Magdeburg, Otto Bamberg's acolyte Adalbert of Pomerania (†1160/1164) and Alexander of Malonne (†1156), bishop of Płock ensured that the early Northern Crusades acquired a distinctive missionary character.

THE MAGDEBURG CHARTER OF 1108

The success of the First Crusade, increasing missionary activity among the Wends and the political situation in the Holy Roman Empire, provided fertile ground for the evolution of the idea of crusade into legitimacy for wars of defence against a perceived pagan threat. The lands of the Wends (fertile, resource rich and strategically located), where missionary work often led to the martyrdom of Christians, provided contemporaries with vivid examples of the newly converted being oppressed by pagans. In 1108 an appeal was drafted advocating a war in defence of the Christian communities and for the conversion of the pagans of the region.[4] The appeal or the *Magdeburg Charter* is the first extant document to advocate a Christian war of conversion in North Central Europe.[5] It was most likely written by a cleric and claims to represent the ideas of Archbishop Adelgot of Magdeburg.[6] Its author calls for action against the pagans in language reminiscent of the chronicles of the First Crusade; addressing Christian warriors as 'lovers of Christ'[7] and urging them to follow in the foot-steps of the Franks and liberate 'our Jerusalem'.[8] The Wends are described as the 'most cruel heathens', attacking Christians and profaning churches.[9] The imagery used in the charter sought to provoke the intended audience to act against the inhumanity and cruelty of the Wends presenting such a war as an opportunity to both secure salvation and acquire land.[10] Whilst there is no evidence of a military or political response to the appeal in 1108, the charter is evidence of the spread of the idea of crusade to North Central Europe within a decade of the First Crusade and is an example of the adaptation of the idea of crusade in the form of missionary war to suit a local environment.[11]

THE CONQUEST OF POMERANIA

The conquest of Pomerania by Bolesław III of Poland is an early example of the adoption of the ideas expressed in the *Magdeburg Charter*. Pomerania's Latin Slavic-derived name referred to its location 'along a sea' and in the Middle Ages it encompassed almost the whole southern shore of the Baltic Sea, from the Recknitz River near Stralsund in the west to the delta of the Vistula River near Gdańsk in the east and to Chełmno Land in the south. The Pomeranians were a group of West Slavic tribes who spoke a Lechitic language akin to Polish. Archaeological evidence suggests a long history of skirmishes between the southern 'Polish' and northern 'Pomeranian' tribes long before the arrival of Christianity. From the tenth century, Pomeranian communities faced continuous attempts by the Piast dynasty from neighbouring Poland to incorporate Pomerania into the Piasts' expanding realm and Polish communities were subject to violent pillaging raids in return.[12] The Piast military expeditions accompanied by forced Christianisation resulted in the short-lived subjugation of Pomerania. Taking advantage of the eleventh-century pagan reaction in Poland (when all church structures were destroyed and Piast authority collapsed), the Pomeranians reasserted their independence, which earned them the appellation of 'viper race'.[13] By the twelfth century, the Piasts and the Church had regained control and the dynasty undertook a concentrated and sustained military effort to bring the Pomeranians under Piast political control and conducted a systematic Christianisation of the population in a series of wars which contemporary apologists glorified in their chronicles as holy wars.

The oldest extant Polish narrative source, the *Cronicae et Gesta ducum sive principum Polonorum*, written between 1112 and 1118 by an anonymous monk,[14] describes the early efforts by Bolesław to convert 'the most savage nations of pagan barbarians' listing amongst these the Pomeranians and Prussians.[15] According to the *Gesta*, the leading motivation for the conquest of Pomerania was its conversion but its author also wrote that the wars gave the Poles opportunity for enrichment and land, and the defeat of the Pomeranians would put an end to their devastating pillaging raids.[16] Another dynastic consideration was that the incorporation of Pomerania into the Piast realm would place its population within the administrative structures of the Church and specifically, within a Church hierarchy subordinated to Poland and not to the encroaching Empire.

The *Cronicae et Gesta ducum sive principum Polonorum* presents the conquest of Pomerania and fighting the pagans as a transcendent holy act directly commanded by God. In practical terms, however, the Christian religion was used to bond the newly acquired territory to the Piast monarchy.[17] After the successful military conquest of Pomerania, Bolesław III initiated a mission led by Bishop Otto of Bamberg to Christianise its population. Bolesław provided the mission with armed guards and threatened the return of his armies should the population not convert and keep the Christian observances. Bolesław sought to make the conquest permanent and in the process created a new model of forcible conversion.[18] Under the new approach, the military and political subjugation of the pagans by a Christian ruler was followed by intense missionary activity which through baptism of the population and the destruction of the symbols of paganism 'welcomed' them as a new Christian community into Christendom. Otto undertook two missions, the first in 1124 and the second in 1128, and their success earned him the appellation 'Apostle of Pomerania'.[19] Otto's methods stood in contrast to the approach of his predecessor, the pacifist Spanish missionary Bernard the Eremite, who ventured to the Pomeranians in ascetic garb and without shoes. Contemporary accounts relate that Bernard's appearance failed to impress the pagans, who surmised he was lacking in divine favour.[20] According to the chronicles, Bernard advised Otto that in order to 'win over the brute hearts of these barbarians he must go there with a splendid retinue of companions and servants and a plentiful supply of foodstuffs and garments'. Only then 'those who, with unbridled neck, despised the burden of humility will bend their necks in worship'.[21] Otto heeded this advice and utilised local superstitions. He presented himself to the Pomeranians as the messenger of a potent deity, wearing rich pontifical vestments suggesting he was a person of great importance, influence and power, and was supported by an almighty god.[22] Otto's mission, although described as a peaceful conversion, was underlined by military threat. It involved a powerful combination of traditional warfare with the ideals of Christian holy war aimed at the evangelisation of the pagans.[23] The threat of force was an overriding consideration and where previous attempts had failed, achieved the submission of the Pomeranians to the Christian faith. Later, this strong missionary element remained a crucial part of crusading in Northern Europe and was sanctioned by the papacy.

THE WENDISH CRUSADE

In 1146 Pope Eugenius III (1145–53) enlisted Bernard of Clairvaux to preach the Second Crusade.[24] Bernard persuaded some reluctant European monarchs, including Conrad III of Germany, to take the Cross.[25] Saxo Grammaticus, the author of the first history of Denmark, wrote about fifty year later that the reception of the summons to this crusade was received as the call 'upon the faithful to fight against all enemies of the faith', requiring each province of the Church 'to fight the pagans living closest to them'.[26] On 13 March 1147 in Frankfurt, Henry the Lion and Albert the Bear approached Bernard of Clairvaux to gain his support to obtain papal approval for a crusade against the Wends instead of joining the crusade to the Holy Land. Bernard's response was enthusiastic, he immediately approved and endorsed the launch of a Wendish Crusade. Within a month the papal bull *Divini dispensatione* extended crusading privileges to those who fought against the Wends. In addition to announcing papal authorisation of the crusade, Bernard of Clairvaux proclaimed that the crusaders were forbidden to make any truce with the pagans 'until such a time as, with God's help, they shall be either converted or wiped out'.[27] There has been much debate over interpretation of this startling declaration. The prevailing view is that Bernard's statement was intended as a declaration of missionary war and that it's not clear whether Bernard actually meant the physical annihilation of the pagans.[28] The experience of the Northern Crusades and in particular the conquest and conversion of Prussia demonstrates that the crusaders interpreted this statement literally.

The forces of the Wendish Crusade gathered in two separate groups after the departure of the crusaders for the Holy Land and, like the departed crusaders, were marked as *cruces-ignati* with a cross which resembled *globus cruciger*.[29] In early July 1147, the first Wendish crusading army besieged Dobin under the command of Henry the Lion and with the support of the Danish fleet.[30] After early losses to the Danes, a truce was concluded with the terms providing for the release of Danish prisoners, the nominal conversion of the Wendish ruler to Christianity and the resumption of an earlier, lapsed tribute payment.[31] The second Wendish crusader army, which included a contingent commanded by the younger brother of the duke of Poland, Mieszko III (c. 1126–1202), gathered in Magdeburg before the end of July 1147.[32] Its command was assumed by Albert the Bear together with the papal legate Bishop Anselm of Havelberg (*c.* 1100–58). They marched north towards the Wendish stronghold of Dymin, which did not surrender, and later towards Szczecin in Pomerania.[33] The siege of Szczecin was a fiasco. It was already a predominantly Christian town and the seat of Bishop Adalbert of Pomerania. The siege was lifted as a result of negotiations by Bishop Henry of Olomouc and the Pomeranian duke's public affirmation of his adherence to the Christian faith.[34] Similarly after the siege of Malachow, the Wendish ruler Niklot acknowledged Saxon overlordship. Before the end of September the crusaders dispersed. The Wendish Crusade was considered a failure and attracted criticism: it failed to deliver new land to the Christians and it failed to achieve new converts. In the long term, however, the crusade which was in essence a significant frontier raid, enabled further missionary activity and ultimately facilitated the conversion of the last Slavic bastion of paganism and with it the incorporation of Wendish territory into Latin Christendom.[35]

THE POLISH EXPEDITIONS TO PRUSSIA IN 1147, 1166, 1192

Prussia remained a target of expansionary policy for the Piast dynasty of Poland, which officially drew inspiration from the martyrdom of Saint Adalbert of Prague, slain by pagans in 997. In 1147, shortly after the conclusion of the Wendish Crusade, an army led by Bolesław IV of Poland (c. 1125–1173) successfully subjugated some of the Prussian tribes.[36] This expedition is referred to by the Polish historian Stanisław Smolka as 'the truly Polish crusade' but its extant descriptions suggest a missionary war which bore similarities to the Wendish Crusade.[37] The two sources which provide evidence for this expedition are the *Annales Magdeburgenses* and the twelfth-century narrative source the *Chronica Polonorum* written by Bishop Vincentius of Kraków.[38] The *Annales Magdeburgenses* also contained reports on the crusader armies of the Wendish Crusade, including the size of the Polish contingent, and gives information on the duke of Poland's expedition against the Prussians. According to the *Annales Magdeburgenses*, Bolesław IV with 'a boundless army went against the cruellest barbarian Prussians and remained there a long time'.[39] The placement of information about the Prussian campaign immediately following a narrative of the events of the Wendish Crusade suggests that Bolesław's expedition against the Prussians was equated with, or was at least as significant as, the Wendish Crusade. In the *Chronica Polonorum*, Bolesław's expedition is presented as a holy war to eradicate the pagan's threat to salvation: Prussians are 'dangerous not so much to the body as to the "soul"'.[40] The Prussians need to be compelled by Bolesław and his army to undergo baptism and should be presented with a choice – baptism or death.[41] Such a declaration could be understood as a repeat of Bernard of Clairvaix's instructions to the crusaders against the Wends. The outcomes of Bolesław's expedition did not, however, result in the lasting subjugation of the Prussian tribes and the Piast dynasts of Poland organised at least another two punitive strikes against the Prussians, now considered as apostates, in 1166 and 1192.[42] Neither expedition was proclaimed a crusade. The 1166 expedition against the Prussian apostates claimed the life of the only twelfth-century Piast prince who is known to have travelled to the Holy Land, Bolesław's second youngest brother, Henry.[43] Only the *Chronica Polonorum,* whose author Bishop Vincentius of Kraków was a member of the Piast court and would have had access to living witnesses, offers information on the 1166 expedition. The account in the *Chronica Polonorum* reflects on the deep loss the dynasty suffered with the death of Henry; its author remarking on the surprising defeat of Polish troops and pleading that 'oratory of the most eloquent kind would not suffice to relate' the details of the tragic event. He then declines to give the 'names, personages, noble lineage, ancestry, dignities, valour, diligence [and] standing of those who were killed'.[44] Such a deliberate omission perhaps reflects the Chronicle's author's own view of the expedition against the Prussians as God's judgement on the Poles as they had not been zealous enough in ensuring adherence to the Faith, a view consistent with contemporary understanding of the outcomes of holy wars related in the Old Testament.[45] The 1192 expedition is also mentioned by the *Chronica Polonorum.* Vincentius compares the pagan Prussians as 'enemies of the Holy Faith' to the 'Saladinistas', kinsmen of the Muslim leader Saladin (*c.* 1138–93) and the 'most obstinate enemy of the Holy Sepulchre'.[46] Such a direct link could be only a literary device used by the erudite Bishop Vincentius of Kraków, but it can also be interpreted as a comparison used to demonstrate the merit of the Prussian campaign as a holy war and a just war. Could it also indicate that the Piast dynasts and the participants of these expeditions have assumed that the provisions of *Divini dispensatione* authorising crusade 'against the Slavs and other pagans inhabiting the north'[47] extended to them in the absence of papal action to the contrary? The 1147 expedition against the Prussians and the expeditions of 1166 and 1192 certainly matched other examples of Northern Crusades.[48]

THE BALTIC CRUSADES

In the second half of the twelfth century attempts to Christianise the pagans who lived in the east Baltic region coincided with or were a by-product of warfare conducted to eliminate the pagan threat to the dominions of Christian rulers.[49] Denmark fought in the Baltic against the pagan Wendish and Estonian pirates through strategic raids using the Danish fleet. The first target of the Danes were the islands of Rugen, whose pagan population continued to raid and devastate the Danish coast. In 1168 Valdemar I (1157–82) destroyed the pagan temple at Arkona, forced the Wends to accept Christianity and initiated the Christianisation of the population with the foundation of a network of Cistercian houses. The Danish conquest of the southern shores of the Baltic followed with victories over the Pomeranians, who were already nominally Christian following the missions of Otto of Bamberg.

In the 1170s, missionary activity began amongst the Estonians and Livonians who lived in the lands between the Dvina River and the Gulf of Finland. Missions were often assisted by military protection from Denmark, Sweden and Germany. The missionaries, who aimed at 'helping to propagate the Catholic faith' and assuring that 'the infidel people gain salvation',[50] gained some measures of success in the short term, however, they were met with fierce and sustained resistance from local communities. Defence of the new Christian outposts in the Baltic became a new, if reluctant, concern of the papacy still preoccupied with the Levantine crusades.[51] The bull *Non parum animus,* issued in September 1171 or 1172, offered an indulgence to all those in Denmark, Sweden and Norway who supported military missions in Estonia against the brutal reprisals of the pagans.[52]

In Livonia, the mission started by Meinhard around 1180 established its base at Üxküll on the Duna River. Support for this Christian outpost came from Archbishop of Hamburg-Bremen, resulting in Meinhard becoming the Bishop of Üxküll.[53] In 1200 Albert of Buxhövden, who was consecrated a missionary bishop in 1199, organised an expedition of crusaders and clerics, colonists and traders to secure the survival of the Livonian mission. Albert established his seat as the Bishop of Livonia in a new town of Riga and successfully repelled numerous attacks by the pagan Livonians. The new frontier crusading outpost was supported by a militia established before 1202. The Order of the Sword Brothers, also known as the *Fratres Militiae Christi*, was a military religious order which provided armed support to the missionary work of the bishop and played a key role in all crusading campaigns organised in Livonia and Estonia. Albert worked energetically to secure the stability in the lands under his control and the security of his community.[54] The establishment of Livonia as an imperial fief was announced in 1207, followed in 1215 by subordination of the diocese of Riga directly to the pope. The extension of the jurisdiction of the bishop of Riga over the whole of Livonia and Estonia was approved by the pope in 1219. The measure of independence won by Albert led Valdemar II of Denmark to reassert his rights in respect of Estonia by forcing Albert in 1221 to acknowledge the authority of the archbishop of Lund over Riga.[55] Denmark was victorious in its conquest of Estonia and by the end of Valdemar's reign in 1241 its population was subject to Danish rule. Within decades, however, there were significant changes to the method and purpose of the Northern Crusades as a result of the bishops' disagreements with the Order of the Sword Brothers and the arrival of the Teutonic Order in Prussia in 1226. Denmark sold Estonia to the ascendant Teutonic Order in 1346 as the knights consolidated their south and east Baltic dominion.

THE CHRISTIANISATION OF PRUSSIA

At the same time as the missionary activity was in progress in the eastern Baltic, Cistercians from Poland and Pomerelia were undertaking the evangelisation of the pagan Prussians. Within a decade after the establishment of the mission among the pagan Livonians, the Cistercian community of Oliwa in Pomerelia and its sister house in Łekno in Greater Poland sent their monks on a mission to the Prussians. For the Cistercians from Łekno, the mission was the continuation of the tradition of Saint Adalbert of Prague who was martyred in Prussia in 997.[56] In 1206, Innocent III recognised the efforts of the abbot of Łekno, authorised the mission[57] and in 1210 he placed it under the protection of the archbishop of Gniezno.[58] The mission's success was marked by the establishment of the Cistercian convent in the Prussian town of Zantyr with the monk Christian as its superior.[59]

The mission attracted a measure of interest from the papacy. In 1212 Pope Innocent III forbade the dukes of Poland and Pomerania to impose higher taxes dues on the converts, perhaps in an enlightened policy aimed at reducing apostasy among the new Christian communities in Prussia, a lesson learned from the outcomes of the 1147 Polish expedition against the Prussians.[60] The progress of the mission was communicated to Innocent III in person in 1216 by its leader, Abbot Christian, who travelled with a number of neophytes to Rome. Innocent recognised the enthusiasm and the ability of Christian and ordained him bishop with jurisdiction over Prussia.[61] Christian's energy for the establishment of the support for his mission matched that of Albert of Buxhövden in Livonia and his efforts were recognised accordingly. In 1217 Honorius III empowered Christian to form a militia for the defence of the Christian neophytes and in 1218 authorised the bishop to erect new dioceses in Prussia as and when it was warranted for the evangelisation of the local population.[62] During 1218, the pope also made an appeal to the faithful of Poland and Pomerania and the dioceses of Cologne, Salzburg and Mogunz and called on them to support the crusade against the Prussians. Honorius singled out those who were unable to support Christian efforts in the Holy Land by agreeing to the commutation of crusading vows from the Levant to Prussia.[63] Those who were unable to participate in person were able to receive a full crusading indulgence if they were able to equip and financially support others who went on crusade in their stead.[64] On 6 May 1218, Honorius III authorised the crusade in Prussia to defend the newly converted Christian communities against the pagans.[65] Within a year the pope placed sole authority over the newly baptised Prussians in the hands of Bishop Christian.[66] However, some uncertainty on jurisdiction over the mission must have remained, because in 1221 Pope Honorius III again decreed his control of the course of the mission and military activities in Prussia, requesting that Prussian prisoners be handed over to the bishop.[67]

In 1222, the Piast dynasts Conrad I of Mazovia, Leszek the White of Lesser Poland and *crucesignatus* Henry I of Silesia organised a joint expedition for the recovery of Chełmno from the Prussians.[68] Involvement by Bishop Christian of Prussia and other Polish bishops suggests a coordinated effort against the Prussians, although there is no other evidence of the 1222 Polish crusade, and the borderland region of Chełmno was recovered from the Prussians. Subsequently, Conrad I of Mazovia granted the bishop of Prussia fiefdom over the land of Chełmno, further expanding the economic base for the mission to the Prussians.[69]

The increasing resources of the mission and presumably the complexity of the task attracted armed men and knights to the mission's cause. These men became the core of Bishop Christian's local militia. It is not unreasonable to assume that a local military force existed from the very early days of the Cistercian mission in Prussia. There is no evidence of its formal structures until 1217 and only in 1228 was the militia recognised as a military religious order called the Knights of Christ, *Fratres Milites Christi de Prussia*.[70] In the same year, Conrad I, granted the Knights of Christ the town of Dobrzyń. The town and the surrounding land were territorially located in Mazovia, south of and adjacent to Prussia. Conrad aimed for the Knights of Christ to provide assistance to the Cistercian missionaries in Prussia and protect Christian communities in Mazovia from raids by pagan Prussians. The military religious order of the Knights of Christ received the rule modelled on the Knights Templar. The knights wore white cloaks with the symbols of a raised red sword and a red star over their armour.[71] As a fighting force, the Knights of Christ reached perhaps no more than 150 knights.[72]

A significant change in papal policy towards the Cistercian mission in Prussia occurred under Honorius's successor, Gregory IX (1227–41). Gregory formulated a new strategy combining missionary activity with pastoral care of the new Christian communities. In the pope's view, the Cistercians would no longer hold a monopoly over the mission in Prussia and he considered the Dominican Order and other mendicant orders such as the Franciscans ideally suited, given the evangelising character of their vocation and focus on pastoral care. This shift in papal policy coincided with the arrival in Prussia of the Teutonic Knights, which heralded fundamental changes to the quest for Prussian souls and the overlordship of their lands.

In 1226 the Teutonic Order responded, at first reluctantly, to the repeated requests of Conrad I of Mazovia for the leadership of the order to consider establishing an outpost in the borderlands of Poland and Prussia.[73] The order was to settle in lands donated for this purpose by Conrad and to pursue the crusade against the pagans. The Teutonic Knights' zeal in pursuing the conquest of Prussia surprised all contenders in the region and their arrival marked the rapid decline in influence and control by Bishop Christian.

Papal documents revoked its blanket support for the Cistercian mission[74] and in 1231 the pope authorised the Dominicans to preach and organise crusades against the remaining pagan Prussians, further limiting the scope of Bishop Christian's authority.[75] Between September 1230 and January 1232, Pope Gregory IX issued a number of documents which subordinated the crusading effort in Prussia to the Teutonic Order. In October 1233 and again in September 1234, Gregory IX repeated his directive that all crusaders in Prussia (and this time also the converts) support and follow the command of the Teutonic Knights.[76]

The position of the Dominicans and the Teutonic Order towards Bishop Christian was made clear in 1233 when the bishop was unexpectedly taken hostage by the Prussian pagan tribe of Sambs. Neither the Dominicans nor the Teutonic Order attempted to secure his release.[77] Instead, the Teutonic Order began to take control of the estates and the property of the Cistercian mission which hindered the missionaries' work.[78] Over the course of Bishop Christian's five-year imprisonment, the Teutonic Order systematically undermined and destroyed the structures established in support of the bishop's mission and effectively removed Cistercian influence from Prussia. The Teutonic Knights' actions provoked the disapproval of the Piast dynasts for whom Prussia had a natural sphere of influence.

The papal legate William of Modena received explicit instructions from Gregory to endorse the role of the Teutonic Order and to assist its work in Prussia. However, the legate was not to take over administration of the crusade.[79] It could be argued that when William arrived in Prussia in 1234, he attempted to deal with the power vacuum left by Christian's absence. In 1235 the Teutonic Order also secured the takeover of the military order of the Knights of Christ.[80] In 1236, without any reference to the bishop of Prussia, Pope Gregory IX decided to divide Prussia into three dioceses to be ruled by Dominican bishops. Before Bishop Christian's release from captivity in 1239 (secured after his own family paid the ransom), the Teutonic Order, with the agreement of the curia, had Christian removed from all positions of authority in Prussia.[81] The removal of Bishop Christian and the Cistercians achieved domination and control of the Prussian crusade for the Teutonic Order.

The Teutonic Knights established a tightly controlled, territorial lordship which became the base for a permanent crusade against the pagans. By the end of the thirteenth century the Teutonic Order had successfully, if nominally, Christianised the Prussians and the order directed its activities against the pagan Lithuanians through brutal annual seasons of *Reisen*.[82] The last pagan tribe in Europe, the Lithuanians, outmanoeuvred the Teutonic Knights when the queen of Poland, Jadwiga (1373/4–99) accepted in marriage Lithuania's Grand Duke Jogaila on the condition that he and his people convert to Christianity.[83] At a stroke, Jogaila removed the pretext for Teutonic raids and became king of Poland as Władysław II Jagiełło (c. 1351/1362–1434) and Jadwiga secured vast new territories making the Polish-Lithuanian Commonwealth the largest political unit in Europe. By the fifteenth century there were no pagan strongholds left within the Teutonic Order's Baltic territories or within its reach, yet despite the entreaties of its neighbours and the obvious completion of its mission, the Teutonic Knights did not leave. The crusading state of the order in Prussia existed until 1525 when the order's grand master staged a coup, and in defiance of the rule, converted to Protestantism, accepted Polish sovereignty and secured for his family hereditary rule over Prussia.

CONCLUSION

The Northern Crusades resulted in the incorporation of large and significant territories into Latin Christendom subordinated to the adherence to one God. The roots of the Northern Crusades lay in pacifist missionary activity and wars of expansion which facilitated the 'making of Europe'. The work of the missions among the pagan communities, the conversion of some of its members, and the often violent reaction actions taken by Christian missionaries, later provided a justification for holy war, missionary war and crusades. These episodes of violence against those who were seen as the enemies Christendom were thus justified on the basis of 'the recovery of Christian property' and the 'defence of the Church or Christian people'. The experience of the Northern Crusades shaped the region. In the absence of the conveniently distant authority of the papacy, the Northern Crusades often began as local initiatives, most often dominated by secular rulers motivated by religious fervour and who adopted and actively adapted the ideology of Christian holy war to satisfy their need for salvation, their ambition and their dynastic needs.

NOTES

1 See the definition of the crusades suggested in Jonathan Riley-Smith, *The Crusades: A Short History* (London: Athlone, 1987), xxviii.

2 For example: Eric Christiansen, *The Northern Crusades: The Baltic and the Catholic Frontier, 1100–1525* (Minneapolis: University of Minnesota Press, 1980); William L. Urban, *The Baltic Crusade*, 2nd edn (Chicago, IL: Lithuanian Research and Studies Center, 1994); William Urban, *The Prussian Crusade* (Chicago, IL: Lithuanian Research and Studies Center, 2000); Alan V. Murray, ed., *Crusade and Conversion on the Baltic Frontier: 1150–1500* (Aldershot: Ashgate, 2001); Carsten Selch Jensen, Kurt Villads Jensen, and John H. Lind, 'Communicating Crusades and Crusading Communications in the Baltic Region', *Scandinavian Economic History Review* 49, 2 (2001): 5–25; Jerzy Gąssowski, ed., *Christianization of the Baltic Region*, Castri Dominae Nostrae Litterae Annales vol. 1 (Frombork, Pułtusk: Bałtycki Ośrodek Badawczy, Wyższa Szkoła Humanistyczna, 2004); Sven Ekdahl, 'Crusades and Colonization in the Baltic', in *Palgrave Advances in the Crusades*, ed. Helen J. Nicholson (Basingstoke: Palgrave Macmillan, 2005), 172–203; Iben Fonnesberg-Schmidt, *The Popes and the Baltic Crusades: 1147–1254* (The Northern World. North Europe and the Baltic c. 400–1700 AD: Peoples Economies and Cultures) (Leiden: Brill, 2007); Alan V. Murray, ed., *The Clash of Cultures on the Medieval Baltic Frontier* (Farnham: Ashgate, 2009); Marek Tamm, Linda Kaljundi, and Carsten Selch Jensen, eds., *Crusading and Chronicle Writing on the Medieval Baltic Frontier: A Companion to the Chronicle of Henry of Livonia* (Farnham: Ashgate, 2011); William L. Urban, *The Teutonic Knights: A Military History* (Barnsley, South Yorkshire: Frontline Books, 2011); Darius von Güttner-Sporzyński, 'Constructing Memory: Holy War in the Chronicle of the Poles by Bishop Vincentius of Cracow', *Journal of Medieval History* 40, 3 (2014): 276–91; Darius von Güttner-Sporzyński, *Poland, Holy War, and the Piast Monarchy, 1100–1230*, Europa Sacra (Turnhout: Brepols, 2014).

3 von Güttner-Sporzyński, *Poland, Holy War*, 77–106.

4 Gerard Labuda, 'Wezwanie wschodnioniemieckich feudałów do walki ze Słowianami roku 1108', in *Fragmenty dziejów Słowiańszczyzny Zachodniej*, ed. Gerard Labuda (Poznań: Poznańskie Towarzystwo Przyjaciół Nauk, 1975), 233–69; Marian Dygo, 'Crusade and Colonization: Yet

Another Response to the Magdeburg Charter of 1108', *Quaestiones Medii Aevi Novae* 6 (2001): 319–25.

5 Wilhelm Wattenbach, 'Handschriftliches', *Neues Archiv der Gesellschaft für Ältere Deutsche Geschichtskunde* 7 (1882): 624–6. English translation in Louise Riley-Smith and Jonathan Riley-Smith, *The Crusades, Idea and Reality: 1095–1274*, Documents of Medieval History (London: Edward Arnold, 1981), 74–7.

6 Friedrich Lotter, 'The Crusading Idea and the Conquest of the Region East of the Elbe', in *Medieval Frontier Societies*, ed. Robert Bartlett and Angus MacKay (Oxford: Clarendon Press, 1989), 267–306, here 275–8; Giles Constable, 'The Place of the Magdeburg Charter of 1107/08 in the History of Eastern Germany and of the Crusades', in *Vita religiosa im Mittelalter: Festschrift fur Kaspar Elm zum 70. Geburtstag*, ed. Franz J. Felten and Nikolas Jaspert (Berlin: Duncker und Humblot, 1999), 283–99, here 290.

7 'Amatores Christi'. Wattenbach, 'Handschriftliches', 626.

8 'Hierusalem nostra'. Wattenbach, 'Handschriftliches', 626. Christopher Tyerman highlights the incoherence of crusader ideology developing as 'a thing of shreds and patches in the regions remote to the influence of the papacy and learned elites, ill-formed'. Christopher Tyerman, 'Henry of Livonia and the Ideology of Crusading', in *Crusading and Chronicle Writing on the Medieval Baltic Frontier: A Companion to the Chronicle of Henry of Livonia*, ed. Marek Tamm, Linda Kaljundi and Carsten Selch Jensen (Farnham: Ashgate, 2011), 23–44, here 24.

9 'Insurrexerunt in nos et prevaluerunt crudelissimi gentiles, viri absque misericordia et de inhumanitatis sue gloriantes malicia.' Wattenbach, 'Handschriftliches', 626.

10 von Güttner-Sporzyński, *Poland, Holy War*, 130–1.

11 Constable, 'The Place of the Magdeburg Charter', 286–7; Mikołaj Gładysz, *The Forgotten Crusaders. Poland and the Crusader Movement in the Twelfth and Thirteenth Centuries* (The Northern World. North Europe and the Baltic c. 400–1700 AD: Peoples Economies and Cultures) (Leiden: Brill, 2012), 31; von Güttner-Sporzyński, *Poland, Holy War*, 131. Cf. Tyerman, 'Henry of Livonia and the Ideology of Crusading', 23–44, here 44.

12 Stanisław Rosik, *Conversio gentis Pomeranorum. Studium świadectwa o wydarzeniu (XII wiek)* (Wrocław: Chronicon, 2010).

13 'Viperalis progenies'. *Gesta Principum Polonorum*, ed. Frank Schaer, trans. Paul W. Knoll and Frank Schaer, Central European Medieval Texts 3 (Budapest and New York: Central European University Press, 2003), I:Prohem, p. 12. [=Gesta].

14 Darius von Güttner-Sporzyński, 'Gallus Anonymus', in *Encyclopedia of the Medieval Chronicle*, ed. Graeme Dunphy (Leiden: Brill, 2009), 659–60.

15 'Ad mare autem septemtrionale vel amphitrionale tres habet affines barbarorum gentilium ferocissimas naciones, Selenciam, Pomoraniam et Pruziam, contra quas regiones Polonorum dux assidue pugnat, ut eas ad fidem convertat. Sed nec gladio predicacionis cor eorum a perfidia potuit revocari, nec gladio iugulationis eorum penitus vipperalis progenies aboleri. Sepe tamen principes eorum a duce Poloniensi prelio superati ad baptismum confugerunt, itemque collectis viribus fidem christianam abnegantes contra christianos bellum denuo paraverunt.' *Gesta*, I:Prohem, p. 12.

16 *Gesta*, II:14, p. 141; II:44, p. 201; II:47–8, pp. 204–7; III:1, pp. 220–7. A wider context is provided in Jerzy Strzelczyk, 'Bolesław Krzywousty i Otton z Bambergu', in *Pomorze Zachodnie w tysiącleciu*, ed. Paweł Bartnik and Kazimierz Kozłowski (Szczecin: Archiwum Państwowe w Szczecinie, 2000), 47–67, here 51.

17 Józef Umiński, 'Rola Bolesława Krzywoustego w uchrześcijanieniu Zachodniego Pomorza', *Collectanea Theologica* 21 (1950): 384–417.

18 Cf. Lech Leciejewicz, 'Społeczne i polityczne warunki chrystianizacji Pomorza', *Pomorania Antiqua* 16 (1995): 51–74; Benedykt Zientara, 'Stosunki polityczne Pomorza Zachodniego z Polską w drugiej połowie XII wieku', *Przegląd Historyczny* 61, 4 (1970): 546–76.

19 *Herbordi dialogus de vita s. Ottonis episcopi Babenbergensis*. Monumenta Poloniae Historica. Nova Series 7 (Warszawa: Państwowe Wydawnictwo Naukowe,1974), II:16, p. 90. Maleczyński outlines the itinerary and progress of the mission. Karol Maleczyński, *Bolesław III Krzywousty* (Kraków: Universitas, 1975; reprint, 2010), 189–236. See also Jürgen Petersohn, 'Apostolus Pomeranorum', *Historisches Jahrbuch* 86 (1966): 257–94, here 262.

20 'Quomodo [...] credere possumus te nuntium summi Dei esse, cum ille glorious sit et omnibus divitiis plenus, tu vero despicabilis at tante pauperitatis, ut nec calciamenta habere possis?' *Ebonis vita sancti Ottonis, episcopi Babenbergensis*. Monumenta Poloniae Historica. Nova Series 7 (Warszawa: Państwowe Wydawnictwo Naukowe,1969), III:1, p. 51; Robert Bartlett, 'Conversion of a Pagan Society in the Middle Ages', *History* 70, 229 (1985): 185–201, here 198.

21 'Lucrum aliquod in brutis barbarorum pectoribus agere volueris, assumpta cooperatorum et obsequentium nobili frequentia, sed et victus ac vestitus copioso apparatu, illuc tendas; et qui humilitatis iugum effrenata cervice spreverunt, diviciarum gloriam reveriti, colla submittent.' *Ebonis vita sancti Ottonis, episcopi Babenbergensis*. II:1, p. 55.

22 *Herbordi dialogus de vita s. Ottonis episcopi Babenbergensis*. III:19, pp. 181–2.

23 Cf. Bartlett, 'Conversion of a Pagan Society in the Middle Ages', 194–7. I don't agree with the assertion made by James Westfall Thompson that Pomerania's 'transition from paganism to Christianity and from barbarism to civilization' was achieved 'by transformation and not by force'. James Westfall Thompson, *Feudal Germany* (New York: Frederick Ungar, 1928; reprint, 1962), 430.

24 Eugenius III reissued *Quantum praedecessores* on 1 March 1146 with minor changes.

25 Jonathan Phillips, 'Papacy, Empire and the Second Crusade', in *The Second Crusade: Scope and Consequences*, ed. Jonathan Phillips and Martin Hoch (Manchester: Manchester University Press, 2001), 20–2. Cf. Harold Cosack, 'Konrads III. Entschluss zum Kreuzzug', *Mitteilungen des Instituts für Österreichische Geschichtsforschung* 35 (1914): 278–96.

26 *Gesta Danorum*, ed. Jørgen Olrik and Hans Ræder (København: Levin & Munkesgaard, 1931), XIV: 3.5, p. 376. Cf. Fonnesberg-Schmidt, *The Popes and the Baltic Crusades*, 46.

27 'Donec, auxiliante Deo, aut ritus ipse, aut nation delegatur.' Jean Leclercq, Charles H. Talbot, and Henri-Marie Rochais, eds., *Sancti Bernardi Opera*, 8 vols (Rome: Cistercienses, 1957–77), 8: 433 (doc. 457), dated after 13 March 1147; Bruno Scott James, trans., *The Letters of Saint Bernard of Clairvaux*, 2nd edn (Stroud: Sutton, 1998), 467. See also discussion of a range of propositions in John R. Sommerfeldt, 'The Bernardine Reform and the Crusading Spirit', *The Catholic Historical Review* 86, 4 (2000): 567–78.

28 Fonnesberg-Schmidt, *The Popes and the Baltic Crusades*, 32–3.

29 *Annales Magdeburgenses*. Monumenta Germaniae Historica. Scriptores (Hannover: Hahn, 1859), 188. 'Eramus in obsidione castri Dimin sub vexillo Crucifixi.' 'Wibaldi epistolae', in *Monumenta Corbeiensia*, ed. Philip Jaffé, *Bibliotheca Rerum Germanicarum* (Berlin: Berolini, 1864), I, doc. 150, p. 244. 'Saxones [...] cruces [...] assumpserunt, a nostris in hoc distantes, quod non simpliciter vestibus assutae, sed a rota subterposita in altum protendebatur.' *Ottonis et Rahewini Gesta Friderici I. imperatoris*, ed. Georg Waitz, 3rd edn, Monumenta Germaniae Historica. Scriptores rerum Germanicarum in usum scholarum separatim editi (Hannover: Hahn, 1912), I:42, p. 61. 'Magna christiane militiae multitudo contra paganos, assumpto signo vivifice crucis exiverat.' *Annales Magdeburgenses*. 188.

30 *Ex Saxonis Gestis Danorum*. Monumenta Germaniae Historica. Scriptores (Hannover: Hahn, 1892), XIV: 87. *Vincentii Pragensis Annales*. Monumenta Germaniae Historica. Scriptores (Hannover: Hahn, 1861), 663.

31 *Auctarium Gemblacense*. Monumenta Germaniae Historica. Scriptores (Hannover: Hahn, 1874), 392; *Ex Saxonis Gestis Danorum*. XIV: 87.

32 von Güttner-Sporzyński, *Poland, Holy War*, 123–5.

33 Johannes Schultze, 'Der Wendenkreuzzug 1147 und die Adelsherrschaften in Prignitz und Rhingebiet', *Jahrbuch für Geschichte des deutschen Ostens* 2 (1953): 114–15. Cf. Jay T. Lees,

Anselm of Havelberg: Deeds into Words in the Twelfth Century, Studies in the History of Christian Thought (Leiden: Brill, 1998), 75–82.

34 *Vincentii Pragensis Annales*, 663.

35 The criticism can be found in *Vincentii Pragensis Annales*, 663; *Annales Palidenses*. Monumenta Germaniae Historica. Scriptores (Stuttgart: Hahn, 1859), 87; *Helmoldi presbyteri Bozoviensis cronica Slavorum*. Scriptores rerum Germanicarum in usum scholarum separatim editi (Hannover: Hahn, 1937), 129. Cf. varied interpretation in Otto von Heinemann, *Albrecht der Bär: Eine quellenmässige Darstellung seines Lebens* (Darmstadt: G. G. Lange, 1864; reprint, 2001), 171; Margret Bünding-Naujoks, 'Das Imperium Christianum und die deutschen Ostkriege vom zehnten bis zum zwölften Jahrhundert', in *Heidenmission und Kreuzzugsgedanke in der Deutschen Ostpolitik des Mittelalters*, ed. Helmut Beumann, *Wege der Forschung* (Darmstadt: Wissenschaftliche Buchgesellschaft, 1963), 107; Friedrich Lotter, *Die Konzeption des Wendenkreuzzugs: ideengeschichtliche, kirchenrechtliche und historisch-politische Voraussetzungen der Missionierung von Elb- und Ostseeslawen um die Mitte des 12. Jahrhunderts* (Sigmaringen: Thorbecke, 1977), 70–2.

36 Magdalena Biniaś-Szkopek, *Bolesław IV Kędzierzawy – książę Mazowsza i princeps* (Poznań: Wydawnictwo Poznańskie, 2009), 277–92.

37 Stanisław Smolka, *Mieszko Stary i jego wiek*, ed. Aleksander Gieysztor, 2nd edn (Warszawa: Państwowe Wydawnictwo Naukowe, 1881; reprint, 1959), 255.

38 *Annales Magdeburgenses*, 188; *Chronica Polonorum*, 15 vols, Monumenta Poloniae Historica. Nova Series (Kraków: Polska Akademia Umiejętności, 1994), III: 30.

39 'Cuius etiam frater maior [Bolesław IV] cum infinito exercitu adversus Pruscos crudelissimos barbaros venit, et diutius ibi moratus est.' *Annales Magdeburgenses*, 188.

40 'Quos non tam personis quam animabus constat esse infestos.' *Chronica Polonorum*, III: 30.

41 'Quorum quibusdam uix tandem post multa bellorum discrimina subactis, hoc edictum iussit promulgari, ut qui Christiane caracterem religionis elegisset, absolutissima donatus libertate, nullum in personis, nullum in fortuna pateretur dispendium; qui autem sacrilegum gentilitatis ritum deserere neglexisset, ultimo capitis infortunio indilate plecteretur.' *Chronica Polonorum*, III: 30.

42 The expeditions are discussed in detail in von Güttner-Sporzyński, 'Constructing Memory', 276–91.

43 Henry died on 18 October 1166. He travelled to the Holy Land perhaps even twice, first during the Second Crusade in 1147, and again in 1154. Henry has been tentatively identified as the 'king of the Poles' who, according to John Kinnamos, led a Polish contingent in 1147 and who also founded the Hospitaller commandery in Zagość, Poland before 1166. 'Dux Hinricus interfectus est cum exercitu suo in bello in Prussica': *Annales Cracovienses priores cum kalendario*, ed. Zofia Kozłowska-Budkowa, in *Monumenta Poloniae Historica*, n.s., 13 vols (Warszawa: Państwowe Wydawnictwo Naukowe; Kraków, Polska Akademia Umiejętności, 1946–2007), V (Warszawa: PWN, 1978), 62; 'Dux Henricus cum exercitu suo interficitur in bello in Prussia': *Annales Poloniae Maioris*, ed. Brygida Kürbis, in *Monumenta Poloniae Historica*, n.s., 13 vols (Warszawa: Państwowe Wydawnictwo Naukowe; Kraków, Polska Akademia Umiejętności, 1946–2007), VI (Warszawa: PWN, 1962), 114.

44 'Quorum nomina, personas, generositatem, prosapiam, dignitates, strennuitatem, industriam, fortunas nec superficietenus quidem cursu attingere, nedum disserendo exequi omnis dissertissimorum sufficeret facundia, quos lamentationum varietates, a diversis diverso modo deplorate, usque hodie lugubriter deplangunt.' *Chronica Polonorum*, IV: 30.

45 Writing some three hundred years later Jan Długosz (1415–80) summed the reasons for the 1166 Polish defeat: 'just God has rightly punished the Poles for their transgressions and thus in a short time [the Prussians] achieved their cunning aims'. 'Neque illos spes opinioque fefellit, sed callido vafroque eorum ingenio, Polonos pro suis transgressionibus iusto puniente Deo, effectus brevi respondit.' *Joannis Dlugossii Annales seu Cronicae incliti Regni Poloniae. Lib. 5–6*, ed. Krystyna Pieradzka, Zofia Kozłowska-Budkowa and Danuta Turkowska (Warszawa: Państwowe Wydawnictwo Naukowe, 1973), 83.

46 'Atrocissimum Dominici sepulcri hostem Saladinum.' *Chronica Polonorum*, IV: 16.

47 'Contra Sclavos ceterosque paganos, habitantes versus aquilones.' *Patrologiae Cursus Completus.* Series Latina, ed. Jacques P. Migne (Paris: Garnier, 1844–55), vol 180, cols 1203–4.

48 von Güttner-Sporzyński, *Poland, Holy War*, 165–86. See also von Güttner-Sporzyński, 'Constructing Memory', 276–91.

49 See, for example, Edgar Andreson, 'Early Danish Missionaries in the Baltic Countries', in *Gli inizi del Cristianesimo in Livonia-Lettonia: Colloquio internazionale di storia ecclesiastica*, ed. Michele Maccarrone (Città del Vaticano: Libreria Editrice Vaticana, 1989), 245–75.

50 Adam Afzelius et al., *Diplomatarium Danicum* (København: C.A. Reitzel, 1938), 1:3, doc. 22. Cf. Fonnesberg-Schmidt, *The Popes and the Baltic Crusades*, 56. *PL* 200, cols 852–3.

51 Fonnesberg-Schmidt, *The Popes and the Baltic Crusades*, 64–5.

52 Fonnesberg-Schmidt, *The Popes and the Baltic Crusades*, 59.

53 Fonnesberg-Schmidt, *The Popes and the Baltic Crusades*, 65–7.

54 Fonnesberg-Schmidt, *The Popes and the Baltic Crusades*, 79–116.

55 Fonnesberg-Schmidt, *The Popes and the Baltic Crusades*, 81–3.

56 Tadeusz Manteuffel, 'Próba stworzenia cysterskiego państwa biskupiego w Prusach', *Zapiski Historyczne* 18 (1953): 165–6. Mikołaj Gładysz offers a concise summary of the early mission originating in Łękno, Gładysz, *The Forgotten Crusaders*, 177–80.

57 *Preussisches Urkundenbuch*, ed. Rudolf Philippi, vol. 1 (Königsberg: Hartungsche Verlagsdruckerei, 1882), doc. 4, pp. 2–4. [dated 26 October 1206]. [=PrUB]

58 *PrUB* 1, doc. 5, p. 4 [dated 4 September 1210].

59 *PrUB* 1, doc. 6, p. 5 [dated 10 August 1212]. Cf. Emilia Jamroziak, 'Centres and Peripheries', in *The Cambridge Companion to the Cistercian Order*, ed. Mette Birkedal Bruun (Cambridge: Cambridge University Press, 2013), 68.

60 *PrUB* 1, doc. 7, p. 6 [dated 13 August 1212].

61 *PrUB* 1, doc. 9–10, p. 7 [dated 18 February 1216].

62 *PrUB* 1, doc. 7, p. 6 [dated 13 August 1212]. *PrUB* 1, doc. 19, p. 14 [dated 5 May 1218].

63 *PrUB* 1, doc. 21, pp. 15–16 [dated 6 May 1218]

64 Johannes Voigt, ed., *Codex diplomaticus Prussicus*, 6 vols, vol. 1 (Königsberg: Gebrüdern Borntränger, 1836), doc. 2 [dated 5 May 1218]. [=CDPr]

65 'Ad defendum fideles predictos contra barbaras nations.' *CDPr* 1, doc. 3 [dated 6 May 1218].

66 *PrUB* 1, docs 30–1, pp. 21–2 [dated 11 and 12 May 1219].

67 *PrUB* 1, doc. 38, p. 25 [dated 17 January 1221]. Tadeusz Manteuffel argued that Bishop Christian was effectively working towards the establishment of a monastic Cistercian lordship in Prussia. Whilst Christian was unsuccessful, the leadership of the Teutonic Order made these ideas reality. Manteuffel, 'Próba stworzenia cysterskiego państwa biskupiego w Prusach', 157–73. Cf. László Pósán, 'Prussian Missions and the Invitation of the Teutonic Order into Kulmerland', in *The Crusades and the Military Orders: Expanding the Frontiers of Medieval Latin Christianity*, ed. Zsolt Hunyadi and József Laszlovszky, *CEU Medievalia* (Budapest: Central European University, 2001), 429–48.

68 Cf. Gładysz, *The Forgotten Crusaders*, 197–8.

69 'Ego Conradus, dei gratia dux Mazovie et Cuiavie, notum facio omnibus fidelibus tam futuris quam presentibus, quod venerabili domino Christiano Episcopo Prutscie primo et suis succesoribus pro eo, quod H. ducem Slesie, L. Wratzlauiensem, L. Lubusensem episcopos cruce signatos et eorum barones, ceterosque cruce signatos versus Prusciam, ad peticionem meam baronumque meorum, castrum Colmen, per multos annos a Prutenis destructum et totaliter desolatum, reedificare cum eius bona voluntate permisit, partem predicti Culmensis territorii, [...] in remissionem peccatorum meorum liberi me donavi.' *PrUB* 1, doc. 41, pp. 27–31 [dated 5 August 1222]. The grant was confirmed in 1223 by Pope Honorius III, *PrUB* 1, doc. 44, p. 33 [dated 18 April 1223]. Tadeusz Manteuffel, *Papiestwo i cystersi: ze szczególnym uwzględnieniem ich roli w Polsce na przełomie XII i XIII wieku* (Warszawa: Państwowe Wydawnictwo Naukowe, 1955), 99–105; Paul

Milliman, *'The Slippery Memory of Men': The Place of Pomerania in the Medieval Kingdom of Poland* (Leiden: Brill, 2013), 38–40.

70 Zenon Hubert Nowak, 'Milites Christi de Prussia. Der Orden zu Dobrin und seine Stellung in der preußischen Mission', in *Die geistlichen Ritterorden Europas*, ed. Josef Fleckenstein and Manfred Hellmann, *Vorträge und Forschungen* (Sigmaringen: Thorbecke, 1980), 339–52. Cf. Wanda Polkowska-Markowska, 'Dzieje Zakonu Dobrzyńskiego', *Roczniki Historyczne* 2 (1926): 145–210; Friedrich Benninghoven, *Der Orden der Schwertbrüder. Fratres Milicie Christi de Livonia*, Ostmitteleuropa in Vergangenheit und Gegenwart (Köln, Graz: Böhlau, 1965), 265–6. In the older historiography the order is referred to as the Knights of Dobrzyń because of the order's association with Dobrzyń (located in Mazovia and not in Prussia). Dobrzyń, however, is related to the order's final years of existence of the Order. It is more accurate to refer to it as the Knights of Christ of Prussia. Jan Karol Kochanowski, ed. *Codex diplomaticus et commemorationum Masoviae generalis*, vol. 1 (Warszawa: z zasiłku Kasy im. J. Mianowskiego, 1919), docs 258–9, pp. 276–7. Maria Starnawska argues for the earlier foundation of the order. Maria Starnawska, *Między Jerozolimą a Łukowem: zakony krzyżowe na ziemiach polskich w średniowieczu* (Warszawa: DiG, 1999), 109; Maria Starnawska, 'Military Orders and the Beginning of Crusades in Prussia', in *The Crusades and the Military Orders: Expanding the Frontiers of Medieval Latin Christianity*, ed. Zsolt Hunyadi and József Laszlovszky (Budapest: Central European University, 2001), 417–28, here 420.

71 Petrus de Dusburg, 'Chronica terrae Prussiae', in *Pomniki Dziejowe Polski. Seria 2 = Monumenta Poloniae Historica. Series 2* (Kraków: Polska Akademia Umiejętności, 2007), II:4, pp. 25–6.

72 Nowak, 'Milites Christi de Prussia', 339–52, here 348.

73 For example, Tomasz Jasiński, 'The Golden Bull Allegedly Issued in 1226 by Friedrich II for the Teutonic Order', *Quaestiones Medii Aevi Novae* 3 (1998): 221–44. Cf. *PrUB* 1, doc. 58, p. 44 [dated 5 May 1227].

74 *PrUB* 1, doc. 85, pp. 65–6 [dated 18 July 1231].

75 Cf. Dariusz Aleksander Dekański, 'Cystersi i Dominikanie w Prusach – działania misyjne zakonów w latach trzydziestych XIII wieku. Rywalizacja czy współpraca?', in *Cystersi w społeczeństwie Europy Środkowej: materiały z konferencji naukowej odbytej w klasztorze oo. Cystersów w Krakowie Mogile z okazji 900 rocznicy powstania Zakonu Ojców Cystersów, Poznań-Kraków-Mogiła 5-10 października 1998*, ed. Józef Dobosz and Andrzej Marek Wyrwa (Poznań: Wydawnictwo Poznańskie, 2000), 227–50.

76 *PrUB* 1, doc. 102, p. 76 [dated 7 October 1233]; docs 115–16, pp. 88–9 [dated 9 September 1234].

77 *PrUB* 1, doc. 133, p. 100 [dated 23 March 1240]; doc. 135, p. 102 [dated 28 April 1240]. The pope referred to the imprisonment of Christian in a letter addressed to the Dominicans in Prussia. *PrUB* 1, doc. 100, pp. 74–5 [dated 7 October 1233]. After his release, Christian complained to the pope that the Teutonic Order did nothing to secure his release from imprisonment in Sambia. He also gave examples of the exchange of ransoms, hostages and prisoners by the Order for other Christian prisoners. *PrUB* 1, doc. 134, pp. 100–2 [dated 11 April 1240].

78 *PrUB* 1, doc. 134, pp. 100–2 [dated 11 April 1240].

79 *PrUB* 1, doc. 111, p. 86 [dated 9 September 1234].

80 *PrUB* 1, doc. 119, p. 90 [dated 19 October 1235]. William of Modena adjudicated in the dispute between Conrad I of Mazovia and the Teutonic Knights. Conrad objected to the transfer of the property of the Knights of Christ to the Teutonic Order arguing that Dobrzyń should be restored to him.

81 The investigation into Bishop Christian's complaints against the order did not change Gregory's policy favouring the Teutonic knights. *PrUB* 1, doc. 134, p. 100 [dated 11 April 1240]. Cf. Fonnesberg-Schmidt, *The Popes and the Baltic Crusades*, 200–2.

82 Aleksander Pluskowski, *The Archaeology of the Prussian Crusade: Holy War and Colonisation* (London: Routledge, 2012), 18–20.

83 Jadwiga was the queen regnant of Poland from 1384 until her death. On her coronation she was actually crowned 'king' (*rex*) to highlight her position as queen in her own right. Her role in the Christianisation of Lithuania contributed to her canonisation in 1997 by a Polish pope.

REFERENCES

Afzelius, Adam, Aage Andersen, Franz Blatt, C. A. Christensen, Russell Friedman, Gustav Hermansen, Herluf Nielsen, Kåre Olsen, Thomas Riis, Niels Skyum-Nielsen, and Lauritz Weibull. 'Diplomatarium Danicum.' København: C. A. Reitzel, 1938.

Andreson, Edgar. 'Early Danish Missionaries in the Baltic Countries.' In *Gli inizi del Cristianesimo in Livonia-Lettonia: Colloquio internazionale di storia ecclesiastica*, ed. Michele Maccarrone, 245–75, 1989.

Annales Magdeburgenses. Ed. Georg H. Pertz, Monumenta Germaniae Historica. Scriptores. Hannover: Hahn, 1859.

Annales Palidenses. Ed. Georgius H. Pertz, Monumenta Germaniae Historica. Scriptores. Stuttgart: Hahn, 1859.

Auctarium Gemblacense. Ed. Ludowicus C. Bethmann, Monumenta Germaniae Historica. Scriptores. Hannover: Hahn, 1874.

Bartlett, Robert. 'Conversion of a Pagan Society in the Middle Ages'. *History* 70, 229 (1985): 185–201.

Benninghoven, Friedrich. *Der Orden der Schwertbrüder. Fratres Milicie Christi de Livonia*, Ostmitteleuropa in Vergangenheit und Gegenwart. Köln, Graz: Böhlau, 1965.

Biniaś-Szkopek, Magdalena. *Bolesław IV Kędzierzawy – książę Mazowsza i princeps*. Poznań: Wydawnictwo Poznańskie, 2009.

Bünding-Naujoks, Margret. 'Das Imperium Christianum und die deutschen Ostkriege vom zehnten bis zum zwölften Jahrhundert.' In *Heidenmission und Kreuzzugsgedanke in der Deutschen Ostpolitik des Mittelalters*, ed. Helmut Beumann, 65–120. Darmstadt: Wissenschaftliche Buchgesellschaft, 1963.

Christiansen, Eric. *The Northern Crusades: The Baltic and the Catholic Frontier, 1100–1525*. Minneapolis: University of Minnesota Press, 1980.

Chronica Polonorum. Ed. Marian Plezia. 15 vols, Monumenta Poloniae Historica. Nova Series. Kraków: Polska Akademia Umiejętności, 1994.

Constable, Giles. 'The Place of the Magdeburg Charter of 1107/08 in the History of Eastern Germany and of the Crusades.' In *Vita religiosa im Mittelalter: Festschrift fur Kaspar Elm zum 70. Geburtstag*, ed. Franz J. Felten and Nikolas Jaspert, 283–99. Berlin: Duncker und Humblot, 1999.

Cosack, Harold. 'Konrads III. Entschluss zum Kreuzzug.' *Mitteilungen des Instituts für Österreichische Geschichtsforschung* 35 (1914): 278–96.

Dekański, Dariusz Aleksander. 'Cystersi i Dominikanie w Prusach – działania misyjne zakonów w latach trzydziestych XIII wieku. Rywalizacja czy współpraca?' In *Cystersi w społeczeństwie Europy Środkowej: materiały z konferencji naukowej odbytej w klasztorze oo. Cystersów w Krakowie Mogile z okazji 900 rocznicy powstania Zakonu Ojców Cystersów, Poznań-Kraków-Mogiła 5-10 października 1998*, ed. Józef Dobosz and Andrzej Marek Wyrwa, 227–50. Poznań: Wydawnictwo Poznańskie, 2000.

Dusburg, Petrus de. 'Chronica terrae Prussiae.' In *Pomniki Dziejowe Polski. Seria 2 = Monumenta Poloniae Historica. Series 2*. Kraków: Polska Akademia Umiejętności, 2007.

Dygo, Marian. 'Crusade and Colonization: Yet Another Response to the Magdeburg Charter of 1108.' *Quaestiones Medii Aevi Novae* 6 (2001): 319–25.

Ebonis vita sancti Ottonis, episcopi Babenbergensis. Ed. Jan Wikarjak and Kazimierz Liman, Monumenta Poloniae Historica. Nova Series 7. Warszawa: Państwowe Wydawnictwo Naukowe, 1969.

Ekdahl, Sven. 'Crusades and Colonization in the Baltic.' In *Palgrave Advances in the Crusades*, ed. Helen J. Nicholson, 172–203. Basingstoke: Palgrave Macmillan, 2005.

Ex Saxonis Gestis Danorum. Ed. Georg Waitz, Monumenta Germaniae Historica. Scriptores. Hannover: Hahn, 1892.

Fonnesberg-Schmidt, Iben. *The Popes and the Baltic Crusades: 1147–1254*, The Northern World. North Europe and the Baltic c. 400–1700 AD: Peoples Economies and Cultures. Leiden: Brill, 2007.

Gąssowski, Jerzy, ed. *Christianization of the Baltic region*, Castri Dominae Nostrae Litterae Annales vol. 1. Frombork, Pułtusk: Bałtycki Ośrodek Badawczy, Wyższa Szkoła Humanistyczna, 2004.

Gesta Danorum. Ed. Jørgen Olrik and Hans Ræder. København: Levin & Munkesgaard, 1931.

Gesta Principum Polonorum. Trans. Paul W. Knoll and Frank Schaer. Ed. Frank Schaer, Central European Medieval Texts 3. Budapest and New York: Central European University Press, 2003.

Gładysz, Mikołaj. *The Forgotten Crusaders. Poland and the Crusader Movement in the Twelfth and Thirteenth Centuries*, The Northern World. North Europe and the Baltic c. 400–1700 AD: Peoples Economies and Cultures. Leiden: Brill, 2012.

von Güttner-Sporzyński, Darius. 'Gallus Anonymus.' In *Encyclopedia of the Medieval Chronicle*, ed. Graeme Dunphy, 659–60. Leiden: Brill, 2009.

———. 'Constructing Memory: Holy War in the Chronicle of the Poles by Bishop Vincentius of Cracow'. *Journal of Medieval History* 40, 3 (2014): 276–91.

———. *Poland, Holy War, and the Piast Monarchy, 1100–1230*, Europa Sacra. Turnhout: Brepols, 2014.

Heinemann, Otto von. *Albrecht der Bär: Eine quellenmässige Darstellung seines Lebens*. Darmstadt: G. G. Lange, 1864. Reprint, 2001.

Helmoldi presbyteri Bozoviensis cronica Slavorum. Ed. Bernhard Schmeidler, Scriptores rerum Germanicarum in usum scholarum separatim editi. Hannover: Hahn, 1937.

Herbordi dialogus de vita s. Ottonis episcopi Babenbergensis. Ed. Jan Wikarjak and Kazimierz Liman, Monumenta Poloniae Historica. Nova Series 7. Warszawa: Państwowe Wydawnictwo Naukowe, 1974.

Jamroziak, Emilia. 'Centres and peripheries'. In *The Cambridge Companion to the Cistercian order*, ed. Mette Birkedal Bruun, 65–79. Cambridge: Cambridge University Press, 2013.

Jasiński, Tomasz. 'The Golden Bull Allegedly Issued in 1226 by Friedrich II for the Teutonic Order'. *Quaestiones Medii Aevi Novae* 3 (1998): 221–44.

Jensen, Carsten Selch, Kurt Villads Jensen, and John H. Lind. 'Communicating Crusades and Crusading Communications in the Baltic Region'. *Scandinavian Economic History Review* 49, 2 (2001): 5–25.

Joannis Długossii Annales seu Cronicae incliti Regni Poloniae. Lib. 5–6. Ed. Krystyna Pieradzka, Zofia Kozłowska-Budkowa and Danuta Turkowska. Warszawa: Państwowe Wydawnictwo Naukowe, 1973.

Kochanowski, Jan Karol, ed. *Codex diplomaticus et commemorationum Masoviae generalis*. Vol. 1. Warszawa: z zasiłku Kasy im. J. Mianowskiego, 1919.

Labuda, Gerard. 'Wezwanie wschodnioniemieckich feudałów do walki ze Słowianami roku 1108.' In *Fragmenty dziejów Słowiańszczyzny Zachodniej*, ed. Gerard Labuda, 233–69. Poznań: Poznańskie Towarzystwo Przyjaciół Nauk, 1975.

Leciejewicz, Lech. 'Społeczne i polityczne warunki chrystianizacji Pomorza.' *Pomorania Antiqua* 16 (1995): 51–74.

Lees, Jay T. *Anselm of Havelberg: Deeds into Words in the Twelfth Century*, Studies in the History of Christian Thought. Leiden: Brill, 1998.

Lotter, Friedrich. *Die Konzeption des Wendenkreuzzugs: ideengeschichtliche, kirchenrechtliche und historisch-politische Voraussetzungen der Missionierung von Elb- und Ostseeslawen um die Mitte des 12. Jahrhunderts*. Sigmaringen: Thorbecke, 1977.

———. 'The Crusading Idea and the Conquest of the Region East of the Elbe.' In *Medieval Frontier Societies*, ed. Robert Bartlett and Angus MacKay, 267–306. Oxford: Clarendon Press, 1989.

Maleczyński, Karol. *Bolesław III Krzywousty*. Kraków: Universitas, 1975. Reprint, 2010.

Manteuffel, Tadeusz. 'Próba stworzenia cysterskiego państwa biskupiego w Prusach'. *Zapiski Historyczne* 18 (1953): 157–73.

———. *Papiestwo i cystersi: ze szczególnym uwzględnieniem ich roli w Polsce na przełomie XII i XIII wieku*. Warszawa: Państwowe Wydawnictwo Naukowe, 1955.

Milliman, Paul. *'The Slippery Memory of Men': The Place of Pomerania in the Medieval Kingdom of Poland.* Leiden: Brill, 2013.

Murray, Alan V., ed. *Crusade and Conversion on the Baltic Frontier: 1150–1500.* Aldershot: Ashgate, 2001.

———, ed. *The Clash of Cultures on the Medieval Baltic Frontier.* Farnham: Ashgate, 2009.

Nowak, Zenon Hubert. 'Milites Christi de Prussia. Der Orden zu Dobrin und seine Stellung in der preußischen Mission'. In *Die geistlichen Ritterorden Europas*, ed. Josef Fleckenstein and Manfred Hellmann, 339–52. Sigmaringen: Thorbecke, 1980.

Ottonis et Rahewini Gesta Friderici I. imperatoris. Ed. Georg Waitz. 3rd edn, Monumenta Germaniae Historica. Scriptores rerum Germanicarum in usum scholarum separatim editi. Hannover: Hahn, 1912.

Petersohn, Jürgen. 'Apostolus Pomeranorum.' *Historisches Jahrbuch* 86 (1966): 257–94.

Phillips, Jonathan. 'Papacy, Empire and the Second Crusade.' In *The Second Crusade: Scope and Consequences*, ed. Jonathan Phillips and Martin Hoch, 15–31. Manchester: Manchester University Press, 2001.

Polkowska-Markowska, Wanda. 'Dzieje Zakonu Dobrzyńskiego.' *Roczniki Historyczne* 2 (1926): 145–210.

Pósán, László. 'Prussian Missions and the Invitation of the Teutonic Order into Kulmerland'. In *The Crusades and the Military Orders: Expanding the Frontiers of Medieval Latin Christianity*, ed. Zsolt Hunyadi and József Laszlovszky, 429–48. Budapest: Central European University, 2001.

Preussisches Urkundenbuch. Ed. Rudolf Philippi. Vol. 1. Königsberg: Hartungsche Verlagsdruckerei, 1882.

Riley-Smith, Jonathan. *The Crusades: A Short History.* London: Athlone, 1987.

Riley-Smith, Louise and Jonathan Riley-Smith. *The Crusades, Idea and Reality: 1095–1274*, Documents of Medieval History. London: Edward Arnold, 1981.

Rosik, Stanisław. *Conversio gentis Pomeranorum. Studium świadectwa o wydarzeniu (XII wiek).* Wrocław: Chronicon, 2010.

Schultze, Johannes. 'Der Wendenkreuzzug 1147 und die Adelsherrschaften in Prignitz und Rhingebiet.' *Jahrbuch für Geschichte des deutschen Ostens* 2 (1953): 95–125.

Smolka, Stanisław. *Mieszko Stary i jego wiek.* Ed. Aleksander Gieysztor. 2nd edn. Warszawa: Państwowe Wydawnictwo Naukowe, 1881. Reprint, 1959.

Sommerfeldt, John R. 'The Bernardine Reform and the Crusading Spirit.' *The Catholic Historical Review* 86, 4 (2000): 567–78.

Starnawska, Maria. *Między Jerozolimą a Łukowem: zakony krzyżowe na ziemiach polskich w średniowieczu.* Warszawa: DiG, 1999.

———. 'Military Orders and the Beginning of Crusades in Prussia.' In *The Crusades and the Military Orders: Expanding the Frontiers of Medieval Latin Christianity*, ed. Zsolt Hunyadi and József Laszlovszky, 417–28. Budapest: Central European University, 2001.

Strzelczyk, Jerzy. 'Bolesław Krzywousty i Otton z Bambergu.' In *Pomorze Zachodnie w tysiącleciu*, ed. Paweł Bartnik and Kazimierz Kozłowski, 47–67. Szczecin: Archiwum Państwowe w Szczecinie, 2000.

Tamm, Marek, Linda Kaljundi and Carsten Selch Jensen, eds. *Crusading and Chronicle Writing on the Medieval Baltic Frontier: A Companion to the Chronicle of Henry of Livonia.* Farnham: Ashgate, 2011.

Thompson, James Westfall. *Feudal Germany.* New York: Frederick Ungar, 1928. Reprint, 1962.

Tyerman, Christopher. 'Henry of Livonia and the Ideology of Crusading.' In *Crusading and Chronicle Writing on the Medieval Baltic Frontier: A Companion to the Chronicle of Henry of Livonia*, ed. Marek Tamm, Linda Kaljundi and Carsten Selch Jensen, 23–44. Farnham: Ashgate, 2011.

Umiński, Józef. 'Rola Bolesława Krzywoustego w uchrześcijanieniu Zachodniego Pomorza.' *Collectanea Theologica* 21 (1950): 384–417.

Urban, William. *The Prussian Crusade*. Chicago, IL: Lithuanian Research and Studies Center, 2000.

Urban, William L. *The Baltic Crusade*. 2nd edn. Chicago, IL: Lithuanian Research and Studies Center, 1994.

———. *The Teutonic Knights: A Military History*. Barnsley, South Yorkshire: Frontline Books, 2011.

Vincentii Pragensis Annales. Ed. Wilhelm Wattenbach, Monumenta Germaniae Historica. Scriptores. Hannover: Hahn, 1861.

Voigt, Johannes, ed. *Codex diplomaticus Prussicus*. 6 vols. Vol. 1. Königsberg: Gebrüdern Bornträger, 1836.

Wattenbach, Wilhelm. 'Handschriftliches'. *Neues Archiv der Gesellschaft für Ältere Deutsche Geschichtskunde* 7 (1882): 621–6.

'Wibaldi epistolae.' In *Monumenta Corbeiensia*, ed. Philip Jaffé. Berlin: Berolini, 1864.

Zientara, Benedykt. 'Stosunki polityczne Pomorza Zachodniego z Polską w drugiej połowie XII wieku'. *Przegląd Historyczny* 61, 4 (1970): 546–76.

CHAPTER TEN

CHRISTIAN EXPANSION IN MEDIEVAL IBERIA: *RECONQUISTA* OR CRUSADE?

———•◆•———

Luis García-Guijarro Ramos

In the spring of 711, Mūsā ibn Nuṣayr, the Arab governor of the recently conquered territories of western North Africa, sent an expedition to southern Iberia under the command of his Berber subordinate Ṭārīq Ibn Ziyād. Previous raids had taken place in 709 and 710, but this new operation seems to have originated as support to one of the aristocratic parties coveting royal power in the complex and unstable panorama of Visigothic high politics. The turn of events quickly transformed assistance into conquest of territories as the political structures of the kingdom collapsed among continuous quarrels between its ruling classes. King Roderic was engaged at the time in one of the usual campaigns against the unrestful Basque peoples in northern Iberia. He became alarmed at the news of the Muslim landing and depredations and decided to rush to the theatre of events, although he and his army were at a considerable distance from the most southern tip of Iberia. In July that year he met the invaders in the mountains west of Tarifa – *Transductini promonturii* – not far from the rock of Gibraltar, which was later named after Ṭārīq who was supposed to have landed there with his forces. The Visigothic army was put to rout. The utter defeat may have been favoured by the lack of unity on the Christian side caused by deep rivalries within the higher nobility after the election of Roderic as king in 710, which was contested by the late King Wittiza's sons and their followers, who may have sought help from the Arabs in North Africa.[1]

The disastrous defeat and the disappearance of Roderic, who probably perished in combat, was a turning point in the history of Iberia. The Muslims soon turned from assistants to one of the Visigothic aristocratic factions to invaders who found no effective military resistance. They soon reached the Guadalquivir valley and headed for Cordoba which fell. Late in 711 or early in the following year, Mūsā set foot on the Iberian peninsula with an Arab contingent which controlled Seville and Merida before joining Ṭārīq and the Berbers in Toledo, the former centre of the Visigothic royalty, which had been taken by Ṭārīq. The occupation of most of the regions of southern, central and eastern Iberia was completed very soon with little fighting through pacts with the regional and local Visigothic aristocracy. The best known of such accords was the one signed by Duke Theodemir, lord of the region of Murcia, on 5 April 713.[2] The Christians of these territories retained their socio-economic status and the religious cult on condition of total loyalty and payments to the Muslim authorities. Pacts became the usual way of transferring political power to the Arab invaders because their reduced numbers made it difficult to control wide territories in another way. That policy had been used before in the first wave of conquests that had extended Arab rule to Syria, Palestine and Egypt in the late 630s and early 640s. This sort of agreement was also favoured by the vanquished side. The break up of any sign of overall Visigothic political power forced aristocracies to come to terms with the newcomers to keep as much economic and social control of men and lands as possible.

North-eastern Iberia, especially the coastal regions of the old Tarraconensis Roman province, and Septimania were the last Iberian or Trans-Iberian territories to be occupied by the Muslims. Some form of aristocratic power and apparently even an elected king delayed Arab conquest for a few years and forced the Muslims to stronger action than in other parts of Iberia, although pacts continued to be common. In the end they managed to extend control beyond the Pyrenees to the most important cities of Septimania: Narbonne was taken in 721 and Carcassonne and Nimes in 724. They became the most northerly outposts of a series of conquests which soon began to be known as al-Andalus. In little over a decade, all the former lands which formed the Visigothic kingdom had passed to the Arabs, who had quickly developed in less than a century since the times of Muhammad a radically different culture, although such a clear divide from Christianity was neither perceived by Iberian Christians at that moment nor in the immediate times to come.

The second decade of the eighth century left a distinctive mark on the Iberian Middle Ages. Muslims were politically dominant in the peninsula for three hundred years, had territorial control over half of Iberia for another two hundred and kept an emirate in Granada and its wide region until 1492. No other part of Latin Christendom consistently and predominantly based external expansion on snatching lands from the Muslims since the late eighth down to the late fifteenth centuries. Although it was by no means an even process in its rhythm, intensity and quality, it is no wonder that medieval Iberia is generally related to that very long struggle. Spanish nationalism found in it the signs of identity of Spain as a modern nation since the mid-1800s and developed sophisticated and sometimes conflicting intellectual views to support that view in the following century.[3] Although essentialist proposals either of conflict or *convivencia* with the Moors such as those put forward by Claudio Sánchez Albornoz and Américo Castro in the 1950s cannot be subscribed nowadays,[4] there is little doubt that Muslims played a substantial role in the Iberian Middle Ages and that Christian kingdoms and counties basically expanded by way of conquests in al-Andalus. Social formations made that territorial enlargement possible, but the ideology which mixed with and gave meaning to social impulses was also of paramount importance. Controversies about the conception of such ideological background, either as *Reconquista* or crusade, has generated nowadays a historiographical debate which shows different ways of structuring contemporary ideas on the character of Christian conquests in al-Andalus all through the Middle Ages.

The *Reconquista*, or continuous struggle against and submission of Muslims in al-Andalus, was considered the specific trait which differentiated Spaniards from other Europeans and which provided modern Spain with a character of its own at the time when nations were being built. This nineteenth-century intellectual view which offered Spanish nationalism a solid historical background had liberal origins but was soon appropriated by conservative thinking and by Francisco Franco's regime well into the twentieth century; the post-1939 authorities found in the medieval protracted conflict with Muslims arguments for the historical peculiarity of Spain of which the authoritarian regime was a continuation. Such a dichotomous look at the Iberian Middle Ages which demonised the Moors served the black and white ideology of the nationalists in the Spanish Civil War (1936–39). No wonder that they strengthened their approach by considering the conflict a crusade.[5] This labelling had a wider international echo than the ambiguous concept of *Reconquista* and it served to mix, in the practice of an internal modern military conflict which had a wide appeal abroad, terms which were coeval and somewhat related, but mutually independent in the Middle Ages.

In the first third of the twentieth century, *Reconquista* and crusade had been loosely related by both liberal and conservative historians, but there was no study specifically devoted to that relationship.[6] In 1958, José Goñi Gaztambide, canon archivist of the cathedral of Pamplona, produced a seminal work of conceptualisation of the *Reconquista* from the perspective of the crusade once this movement emerged in the late eleventh century.[7] Goñi Gaztambide thought that both shared an ultimate religious goal and that the more universal scope of the crusade absorbed the ideological and doctrinal expression of war with Islam in the Iberian Peninsula. The Reconquest, originally a 'sacred war', switched to 'proper crusade' in that century.[8] This intellectual approach was influenced by the ideological climate of post-civil war Spain. Goñi Gaztambide was a rigorous historian of conservative leanings. He offered a thorough institutionalist account of the fusion of *Reconquista* and crusade which had been vaguely referred to by historians before the 1930s and had been used as a potent ideological weapon by the nationalist side during and after the Spanish Civil War.

Goñi Gaztambide's book is an insufficient formal approach to the complexities of ideology, or ideologies to be more precise, of Christian expansion in medieval Iberia, but it was and still is a reservoir of details and sources, especially of papal bulls. He was highly praised by historians on that account, but not fully used to view the *Reconquista* as crusade until pluralism became dominant in crusading studies in the last decades of the twentieth century. His book was an isolated brilliant study until Joseph O'Callaghan turned to this question in 2003 and reaffirmed Goñi's views for a period which covered the great Christian expansion, from the campaign of Barbastro (1064) to the conquest of Seville (1248).[9] O'Callaghan's line of reasoning is crystal clear from the preface of the book: 'The clash of arms between Christians and Muslims in the Iberian peninsula from the early eighth century onward, commonly labelled the Reconquest, was transformed into a crusade by the papacy during the twelfth and thirteenth centuries.'[10] The chosen period is well suited to the purpose of twisting Christian Iberian campaigns into a crusading pattern, but the character of the *Reconquista* before the crusade appeared receives no treatment. Thus there is no link between both ages and the deep change is attributed to the external agency of popes following Goñi's trail. O'Callaghan has later focused on the Battle for the Strait and on the War of Granada as crusading campaigns, thus encompassing the whole medieval time and reinforcing Goñi's arguments which extended well into the early modern period.[11]

The most influential contribution, at least in the anglophone world, of the vanishing of the *Reconquista* into the crusade has been, however, a momentous article published by Richard Fletcher in 1987.[12] The main difference with Goñi's and O'Callaghan's views lies in the consideration that the background of Iberian Christian fighting against the Muslims down to the mid-eleventh century had no religious undertones and that conflicts lacked the uncompromising virulence fuelled by religion on both sides: 'There is a degree of mutual restraint in the political dealings of Christian and Muslim with one another.'[13] According to Fletcher, this situation changed around the 1060s due to external influences and not internal developments either in Christian Iberia or in al-.Andalus so that 'the restraint which had marked them [the relations] was gradually replaced by more aggressive attitudes'.[14] French adventurers, ecclesiastic and lay – Cluniacs most notably among them all – were the agents of hard-line policies towards the Muslims in the Christian kingdoms and counties, while North African newcomers, namely the Almoravids, produced similar effects in al-Andalus. This new climate introduced religion as the main element of sharper attitudes on both sides and eased the way for crusade monopoly of Christian expansion in Iberia via military actions.

Richard Fletcher's reasoning is debatable on two points. Religion was at the core of western or eastern Iberian Christian campaigns since at least the ninth century. The Asturian-Leonese monarchy and the Carolingian or post-Carolingian Pyrenean or Pre-Pyrenean counties were nascent polities with a firm religious ideological grip when shaping the new political entities or when waging war against the Muslims, who were beginning to be considered pagans. The Trinitarian controversy of Adoptianism in the late eighth century showed the will of the Western Christian kingdom to build up a religious foundation of its own that would cement a new polity away from Mozarabic compromises with Islam. Eastern counties under Carolingian rule stuck to imperial orthodoxy which repeatedly condemned Bishop Felix of Urgel for his defence of what were considered heretical views. Two centuries later, Almanzor's seizure as a trophy of the bells of the main church at Santiago of Compostela in 997 was a symbol of the intense religious character of the conflict between Christians and Muslims. Two instances picked at random at different periods prior to the eleventh century show that religion was instrumental in building up Christian kingdoms and counties and in protecting or enlarging them. Islam had obviously the same function in al-Andalus. Joseph O'Callaghan is then right in asserting that 'discord was obviously based on religious antagonism'.[15]

The second questionable point relates to the external impulses which transformed *Reconquista* into crusade. No basic structural traits are imported and made to work in societies throughout history. There may be important influences from outside, but the main developments tend to be always internal. That general historical evidence must affect any consideration of the ideological elements which gave consistence to Christian expansion in Iberia through war against the Moors leading to conquest or political submission. It is not conceivable that peninsular kingdoms and counties had to wait for agents coming from abroad, be they French or papal, to develop a religiously coherent mental structure to support and motivate fighting against Islam. It is far more logical to assume that native ideological constructions, which had a distinct religious flavour and shared common traits between eastern and western Iberia, appeared and developed according to specific socio-economic basis while impelling political strategies of expansion. They received external influences and above all used the crusade on special occasions as a prestigious religious addition. Their signs of identity were, however, distinguishably native and geared towards restoration of political unity and Christianity as they were at the time of the Visigoths. *Restauratio* was the term widely used in medieval chronicles. *Reconquista* was coined much later, at the end of the eighteenth century.[16]

The relation of the great Christian Iberian expansion in the Central Middle Ages with a pan-crusading ideological deployment seems to dismiss the factors which made possible conquests and extension of territories in the peninsula. They were specific to Iberia, although the nature of many of its elements is recognisable elsewhere in Latin Christendom. Sedentary societies begin to expand when the social relations that structure them reach a considerable degree of permanence and stability. The great leap forward is the outcome of maturity. That means the full development of the qualitative potential of cohesive principles and their extension to all levels of society. The beginning of this process favoured piecemeal expansion east and west in Iberia in the second half of the ninth century. The maturity of social relations of dependence began to unleash great potential for expansion since the second third of the eleventh century. From the very start expansion was not only rationalized but also made possible by ideological structures which grew especially in the Kingdom of Asturias-Leon. The interrelationship of social aspects and ideology is the key to understanding Christian expansion in medieval Iberia.

A second factor conditioned the possibility of still embryonic or mature Christian societies to gain territories beyond the frontier with al-Andalus: the political cohesion and strength of Muslim power or powers in Iberia. It is well known that the emirate, the caliphate of Cordoba or the North African empires which intermittently crossed the Strait and swept Iberian lands from the late eleventh century onwards had difficulties in keeping control over different parts of al-Andalus. The weaker the Muslim opponents, the greater the possibilities to Christian expansion according to the social and political strength of their polities. It is not a mere coincidence that disruption or *fitna* in the emirate favoured Christian occupation down to the rivers Duero, Gállego and Llobregat in the second half of the ninth century. Neither it is questionable that the great expansion of the period 1145–1248, dates of the conquests of Calahorra on the Ebro and Seville on the Guadalquivir, was made possible by the collapse of the caliphate of Córdoba and the fragmentation of Muslim political power into petty kingdoms at odds with each other, nor that the temporary control of al-Andalus by North African empires put a momentary brake to territorial enlargement at certain times in the twelfth, thirteenth and fourteenth centuries.

The interaction of Christian and Muslim powers at different degrees of social cohesion and strength over a long period of time is the basic factor to understand Christian expansion in Iberia and its process which extended over seven centuries. The crusade, once it emerged in the late 1000s, contributed to Christian military conquests only in a subsidiary way. It certainly appeared as reinforcement, but papal bulls or passing references in chronicles should not lead historians to think that it became the main element which made possible the great conquests of the twelfth and thirteenth centuries or the occupation of the emirate of Granada at the close of the Middle Ages. The *Reconquista*, or *restauratio* (the medieval term), was a native ideological construction which expressed and promoted expansion in different ways and with varied rhythms and intensities from the ninth to the fifteenth centuries. Kings and counts lived in that ideological Iberian humus and only occasionally resorted to crusading apparatus as additional support to domestic impulses.

The *Reconquista*, as ideology both of expansion and of the political powers related to it, was present throughout the entire Middle Ages. It did not stick to a stereotyped form and meaning, but changed according to the times, although it kept a common perception of the character of confrontation with the Muslims and of the will to subdue them which was adapted to the peculiarities of each epoch in both cultures. Permanence and adjustment to different times are basic characteristics of a wide time spectrum in historical concepts. The territorial expansion of Christian polities in Iberia and consequently the ideology which explained and propelled it had three distinctive periods: resistance to Islam, formation of Christian polities and first territorial acquisitions, eighth to early eleventh century; the great expansion, mid-eleventh to mid-thirteenth century; the emirate of Granada, last Muslim enclave, from vassalage to conquest, second half of the thirteenth century to late fifteenth century. The main aspects of each period shall be dealt below in a summary way to reveal how the *Reconquista*, and not the crusade, was the ideology of war against the Moors and of feudal submission of them in medieval Iberia with nuances and different characteristics at each epoch. Special attention shall be given to the origins. Post-1030s developments are difficult to understand, ignoring their roots which lay in earlier centuries.

RESISTANCE, SOCIAL CHANGES AND EMERGENGE AND GROWTH OF NEW IBERIAN CHRISTIAN POLITIES, EIGHTH TO EARLY ELEVENTH CENTURIES

Traditional Spanish nationalism converted a skirmish, the Battle of Covadonga (718/722), and the figure of Pelayo, reckoned as first king of Asturias (718–737), into symbols of the will to recover the Visigothic unity and reinstate Christianity only a few years after the rout of Guadalete. According to this view, there was no break between the collapse of the Kingdom of Toledo and the early conscious efforts to recover it. But the idea of an early purpose to restore the immediate Gothic past shattered to pieces in 711 is anachronistic; it only served later medieval purposes of a clear-cut beginning of the *restauratio* or modern images of the *Reconquista* based on essentialist views of a medieval neo-gothic past as origin of the Spanish nation. Muslims did not control, or did it superficially and briefly, those northern territories of Iberia which first the Romans and then the Visigoths had not fully held sway over. Regions north of the Cantabrian Mountains and some places in the Pyrenees soon reacted against Muslim dominion, as they had done in previous centuries, especially the Basques, against the unifying policies of Rome or of the kings of Toledo. By the early 720s, Muslims ruled the Iberian regions which had been socially and culturally integrated in the Visigothic kingdom from Septimania to Baetica, from the Mediterranean to the Atlantic seas. Northern peripheries of the peninsula resisted integration into al-Andalus more as a result of backward disunited social structures which rejected control of more developed societies than of deliberate impulses to recover what had been lost in the summer of 711. Visigothic immigrants arrived at these lands and had a considerable impact in speeding up developments towards more complex societies, but they did not head any movement which aimed at reinstating the Gothic world soon after its collapse. The social and political character of the Asturian-Cantabrian world could not have backed it. Resistance to a much more powerful culture, Islam, was the only alternative for more than a century, especially when the Umayyad emirate tried after 756 to put some order into fractioned Muslim policies in al-Andalus. Pressure on the Asturian kingdom grew when Cordoban emirs managed to curtail autonomous powers and achieved some degree of overall control, albeit only temporarily.

The situation in north-eastern Iberia was somewhat different and much related to the birth of the Carolingian world. Pepin the Short's coup d'état of 751 reinforced kingship and allowed an expansionist policy which soon put an end to Muslim power north of the Pyrenees. In 759 Narbonne was rendered to the Frankish king by the Visigothic notables; by the end of the 750s the Muslims had lost control of Septimania. Charlemagne's interest in the Upper March of al-Andalus, which had its centre at Zaragoza, was prompted by the need to protect Aquitania and conquered Septimania from possible attacks. The unstable situation in the mid-Ebro valley led the Frankish king into an Iberian expedition in 778 which became widely known thereafter by the Carolingian defeat at Roncesvalles significantly caused by local peoples, Basques or converts to Islam (*muladíes*), and not by Muslims of

Arab stock. The reverse at Roncesvalles did not weaken Charlemagne's aggressive policies in the region. The lands of Gerona, Urgel and Cerdaña were occupied in 785–789. The control of the coastal area was more difficult. Barcelona was taken in 801 but attempts further south at Tarragona (809) and Tortosa (811) were unsuccessful.

At the turn of the ninth century, conquered territories in north-eastern Iberia were politically structured as counties heavily dependent on the Carolingian administration. These were highly Romanised and Visigothised territories. Perception of and relations to the neighbouring Muslims were those decreed by Charlemagne and his entourage. There had been conquests south of the Pyrenees, but they did not come out of any restoration ideology. The situation was socially and politically different at that time in the Asturian kingdom. Social structures were far more backward than in the newly born Carolingian counties and political power shakier than that of Charlemagne. There was no strong European power at hand to check Muslim inroads and thus resistance had been the main political aim of Asturian kings until the end of the eighth century. Neither in eastern nor western Iberia were there at that time signs of a restoration ideology.

A specific Christian ideological approach to fighting with Muslims was made possible in the ninth century when social developments and political stability consolidated the Asturian monarchy which became ready for territorial expansion at any sign of weakness in al-Andalus. The political autonomy of the most eastern counties and of Aragon, which also had a similar Frankish origin, was a natural outcome of the crisis of Carolingian power in the second half of that century. Break-up of imperial rule allowed native outlooks and policies towards neighbouring Moors that were no longer dependent on the overall schemes of the Frankish kings and emperors. Greater strength and cohesion in the west and autonomy in the east of Iberia favoured the development of ideologies of war with the Muslims regardless of the fact that these mental perspectives were overtly expressed in chronicles in the western kingdom and not in the eastern counties or in the embryonic kingdom of Navarre.

The long reign of Alfonso II of Asturias (791–842) was a turning point for the history of Christian enclaves in north-western Iberia. Submission to Cordoba was abandoned and an autonomous policy adopted based on the development of more solid and complex social relations and on an autochthonous ideology which severed links with southern Mozarabism. Matriarchal royal lines of succession which had probably helped Alfonso I (739–757) and Silo (774–783) to become kings of Asturias in the previous century vanished. They were signs of archaic social practices in which women transmitted rights. Patrilineal practices existed but were not absolutely dominant. The fact that they became so in the ninth century implied deep social changes which favoured a stronger and more cohesive society. This situation made it possible to abandon passive resistance to the Muslims, to develop a political entity of its own and to confront the Moors at a time when the emirate had managed to impose power from Cordoba to the regions but was periodically affected by local rebellions (Toledo, Cordoba, Mérida) which weakened its external power. The new position versus Cordoba, which had internal social roots and was facilitated by problems in al-Andalus, was also expressed in the efforts to separate northern Christians from al-Andalus Mozarabs. A new programme of religious autonomy, that is to say, of explicit distinctiveness of the Asturian polity, was developed. A brand new royal centre, Oviedo, in which churches had as much importance as royal buildings, expressed the new significance and purpose of the monarchy. New bishoprics and the reshuffle of the diocesan map, as well as the foundation of monasteries, showed regional vitality and desire for autonomy from the metropolitan see of Toledo, which the anti-adoptianist standing of northern clerics had already made clear at the end of the eighth century. The beginnings of the cult of St James, through whom a much coveted apostolic link was found, added prestige to the Asturian Church that was increasingly becoming unrelated to Christian Mozarabism in the south. All aspects of the rich reign of Alfonso II pointed towards building up a new polity with no formal connections with the al-Andalus Christians, who inevitably had to come to terms with the Muslims. An organic dependence of the Asturian Church to the metropolitan of Toledo would have meant a de facto Muslim protectorate of the new kingdom, as religion was obviously the main ideological asset to the nascent monarchy.

This background has to be taken into account when dealing with the great territorial advance in the second half of the ninth century which transferred the frontier of the Kingdom of Asturias from the Cantabrian Mountains to the valley of the River Duero and tripled the extension of lands controlled by the monarchs of a kingdom which soon was centred on the city of León. Kings Ordoño I (850–866) and Alfonso III (866–910) relied on the sound social and political foundations established at the time of their predecessor Alfonso II to occupy the west (Oporto, 868), the centre (León, 856; Zamora, 893) and the east (Burgos, 884) of the river valley. Two circumstances favoured this momentous expansion: the region down to the Duero and immediately beyond was not uninhabited, as Claudio Sánchez Albornoz once presumed,[17] but had no consistent Muslim effectives since the Berbers abandoned the region in the 740s; besides, Cordoba could not send armies to check the Christian advance because it was in the midst of the worst disruptive internal crisis that it experienced before the ruin of the Caliphate in the first third of the eleventh century. Internal strength could lead to territorial enlargement due to temporary weakness in al-Andalus.

The control of the Duero valley from the Atlantic sea to the eastern frontiers of the nascent county of Castile was a half-century process (Tuy, Astorga, 854; Osma, 912) which was also made possible by an ideological construction that was rooted in conceptions that emerged at Alfonso II's time and were refined in chronicles composed by court clerics since the 880s. In that decade a series of texts began to offer a general view of the place in history of the Kingdom of Asturias and of contemporary events.[18] They gave form to the idea that Christians on both sides of the Cantabrian Mountains were directly connected with the Visigoths and were also entrusted by God to recover and restore what their Gothic predecessors had lost through sinful behaviours. It is obvious that the *restauratio* ideology – what in modern times has been labelled *Reconquista* – is a high cultural product structured in the midst of a great process of territorial expansion and that it was designed to give sense not only to the occupation of the Duero valley but also to the Kingdom of Asturias itself. But this in no way means that this construct was invented by learned men, some probably of Mozarabic origins, and that it was imposed from above to a passive aristocracy or to other social layers.[19] It is a historical truism to view ideology as a long process that stretches from bottom to top of society and which exists and has an informal coherence long before it is given its final form, by clerics in this case. It is not conceivable that the first phases of the Duero expansion were deprived of any ideological meaning and support until some court intellectuals illuminated the scene *post eventum* or in the middle of events. This ideology was religious throughout before and after it was given literary form. Religion was thus at the centre of relationships with Islam whether there were military actions or not. It is not acceptable to detach Christian ideals from the *Reconquista* and defend that only Cluny and the crusade introduced them aggressively in the late eleventh century in the war against the Muslims in Iberia, as Richard Fletcher and many historians thereafter have proposed.

One of the main arguments of nationalist Catalan historiography in favour of a distinctiveness of Catalonia from Castile and other parts of present-day Spain since the early post-Visigothic period touches on the Carolingian origins of the north-eastern Iberian counties and on developments which made them different from the Kingdom of Asturias – they do not take into account that early Aragon was also a county of Carolingian stock which followed ways different in many respects to other eastern counties. This historiographical approach assumes that no explicit ideological construct was developed in them to make sense of their new polities and of war to the Muslims, and that the set of ideas which coalesced in *restauratio* or *Reconquista* was alien to the autonomous counties. As they did not share common ideological origins, they were utterly different from other Christian Iberian polities from the start, so it is argued. Their identity was related to the wide autonomy from Carolingian rulers that the counties enjoyed from the second half of the ninth century. Guifre the Hairy (870/878–897), the head of various comital dynasties which controlled the region when Frankish power ceased to be effective, was the founder of Catalonia according to this essentialist vision, no less so than that centred on Pelayo and Covadonga.

There were social and geopolitical differences between the Kingdom of Asturias and the north-eastern counties. The latter had a far more developed social structure – mainly in the coastal areas – had experienced Carolingian administration of which they may have felt followers at the beginning, and had faced thriving Muslim communities which repeatedly struggled for autonomy from Cordoba and put a brake on significant Christian expansion. When the counts ceased to be accountable to Carolingian kings and emperors, they became de facto solely responsible for the welfare of their polities that was based on harnessing aristocracies and on confronting nearby Muslims who were a barrier but not a too aggressive obstacle. The *fitna* or great rebellion in al-Andalus during the late ninth century increased the autonomy of Muslim powers of the Superior March but prevented joint action of Iberian Moors against the new comital powers and so the need of help from their still Frankish overlords. Differences between eastern and western Iberia existed but were confined to social developments – the gap was nonetheless narrowing – and to the potential pressure across the frontier. It is not easy to perceive the ideology towards Muslims in eastern Iberia, basically because there were no parallel chronicles to the ones written at the time of Alfonso III of Asturias and after, nor were there for a long time. However, the absence of such evidence is not a concluding proof of lack of *restauratio* concepts or of basic aspects of them. The more the counties became part of an Iberian setting as consequence of their autonomy, the more their rulers probably took an ideological standing similar to other peninsular counts and political leaders. The confinement to Asturias-Leon and later to a mythicised Castile of the origins of the idea of Reconquista and of its development in following centuries is a presentist approach which serves all kind of modern Spanish or regional nationalisms. When chronicles widely appeared in the Crown of Aragon in the thirteenth century – James I of Aragon's 'Book of Deeds' is perhaps the best example[20] – they depicted similar attitudes of kings and nobles to the Muslims that were and had been common in León-Castile.

The great territorial advances which had extended Christian occupation to the Duero valley, or more modestly to the lines of the rivers Aragon, Llobregat and Cardoner in the central Pyrenees and in eastern Iberia, came to a stop after 'Abd al-Raḥmān III succeeded his grandfather as Cordoban emir in 912. His control of revolts which had put the emirate on the brink of collapse and the establishment of a caliphate in al-Andalus in 929 altered the relations of power between Christians and Muslims in Iberia clearly in favour of the latter. The tenth century was the golden age of al-Andalus. Northern kingdoms and counties, some of them weakened by serious internal political succession crisis, were on the defensive for decades. *Reconquista* principles had to wait for more propitious times to be again active elements of expansion. The caliphate was not particularly aggressive. It did in fact opt for a conservative strategy of fortifying the extensive frontier. The situation changed when Almanzor (c. 980–1002), a distinguished courtier, rose to prominence over the feeble caliph Hishām II (976–1009). Harsh punitive expeditions were repeatedly sent deep into Christian territory to boost morale and the *ḥājib*'s power in Cordoba. The raids afflicted many regions in the north, but they did not disrupt polities nor add significant number of lands to the Muslims. However, these activities artificially kept the power of Almanzor and his son Abd al Malik (1002–08) but did not solve the basic problem of legitimacy and consequent lack of authority which the Amirid regime could never come to terms with. When these two powerful personalities vanished, the system that they had tried to impose fell and dragged with it a caliphate which had been eroded without repair into oblivion after three decades of systematic snub.

The caliphate of Cordoba broke up into pieces in 1031 and al-Andalus was split in a number of petty kingdoms (*taifas*) which were relevant culturally but not politically. Their Christian counterparts were at that time developing greater social and political cohesion and were prepared to take advantage of the situation not only by waging expansive wars along *Reconquista* ideas, but also by adapting their socio-political feudal principles to relations with the Muslims through the submission of *taifas* by vassalage and tributes. This policy was not contrary to *restauratio* aims, but an alternative expression of them because it implied supreme overlordship over the Moors, a different option to outright conquest when conditions so demanded.

AL-ANDALUS DWINDLES TO MINIMA: THE GREAT CHRISTIAN EXPANSION, MID-ELEVENTH TO MID-THIRTEENTH CENTURIES

Most works which associate *Reconquista* at its prime with crusade begin the story of this connection with the expedition to Barbastro in 1064. There has been copious literature discussing if this event may be considered a pre- or protocrusade, or no crusade at all. But the debate has missed the essential question. Regardless of Pope Alexander II's impulse, if he ever gave it, the campaign was a strictly Iberian issue. It was involved in the strategies of the eastward expansion of the kingdom of Aragon – King Ramiro I was killed in the attempt to take Graus, north-east of Brabastro, in 1063 – and of the westward expansion of the county of Urgel beyond both Noguera rivers and eventually even beyond the Cinca river where Barbastro lay. This expansive policy had been already at work in the 1050s and it was continued after Barbastro was lost back to the Muslims in 1065 while significantly being defended by Count Armengol III of Urgel, who died in the attempt to keep it in Christian hands. One of the main agents of this policy had been Arnau Mir de Tost, an Urgellian noble who based expansion and control of new areas on the building of castles much in the same way as Fulk Nerra had done in Anjou shortly before.

The Barbastro campaign shows quite clearly that this and other much more important expeditions in the late eleventh and in the twelfth and thirteenth centuries were conceived as part of the expansion strategies of the different Christian kingdoms and counties and not primarily as crusades. The *restauratio* ideology, which had been present openly or silently in Christian Iberia since at least the late ninth century, was an inextricable part of those schemes which were put to work in military actions long before the crusade was added only on very specific occasions from the short-lived capture of Tarragona in the 1090s to the War of Granada at the end of the fifteenth century.

Focusing on Barbastro, many historians tend to disregard previous campaigns in Iberia since the 1030s, when Muslim unitary power collapsed and the Christian political map, which was a reflection of a dynamic and increasingly cohesive social world in most areas, became established for the rest of the Middle Ages at the death of Sancho III the Great of Navarre in 1035: Kingdoms of León-Castile – united or separated at different times until their final union in 1230 – Navarre and Aragon; the eastern counties, which came to be known collectively as Catalonia in the early twelfth century; and Portugal, separated from León in 1139, completed the Iberian Christian territories in the Central Middle Ages. Each of them tended to expand according to well-established strategic lines. Navarra was focused on the Upper Ebro valley: Calahorra was taken in 1145. León-Castile tried to consolidate its hold over the entire Duero valley and go beyond it at the mouth of the river: conquests of Lamego, 1157, Viseu, 1158, and Coimbra, 1164. In the year when a pre- or protocrusade was apparently at work in Barbastro, Fernando I of León-Castile succeeded in snatching from much weakened Muslims Coimbra, an important position south of the Duero; both campaigns had the same intrinsically Iberian nature, although the former has fallen under the spell of crusading interpretations. The next step for Leonese-Castilian kings was to consolidate positions between the Duero and the Cordillera Central, and thus make settlements safe in the northern Castilian plateau, by winning a strategic city south of the range of mountains. Toledo was taken in 1085. The control of the royal centre in Visigothic times made kings Alfonso VI (1065–1109) and Alfonso VII (1126–57) feel superior to other Christian Iberian rulers. They began to use the title of emperor to mark the difference in status. *Restauratio* principles were clearly at work.

Attention to campaigns between the 1040s and 1080s should not obscure the fact that Christian polities had at the time an alternative way of dealing with the Muslim petty kingdoms, weak and in conflict with each other, which combined pressure, protection and extortion that produced substantial tributes (*parias*). Traditional views stress the point that northern kingdoms and counties had yet no military or demographic strength to undertake overall conquests and resettlement of new territories and were driven to a policy of beneficial accords with the *taifas*. This may have been true at that time, the mid-eleventh century, but not at other periods of the Central and Late Middle Ages in which submission was preferred to conquest in specific situations – the survival of the emirate of Granada until 1492 is the most obvious example. Armed interventions and vassalage of Muslim petty kingdoms were not conflicting options, but different possibilities to expand in polities which regarded feudal submission as effective in terms of authority and power as direct control of territories. The *restauratio* was also achieved through pacts with the Muslims. These treaties determined the terms of subjection of the latter which may have been at times more profitable to Christians than outright conquest. Medieval societies at their prime were based on a growing number of dependants. The control of territories was only relevant when they offered native or most commonly new settlers means to pay rents or tributes.

Reconquista ideals aimed at restoring jurisdiction over entire Iberia. This was done through war and occupation of lands or through the forced subordination of tributaries whose overlord was a Christian king who thought he was enlarging his dominion that way, as in fact he was according to the socio-political structure of that age. The double option of conquest or submission of Muslims which the social and ideological Christian Iberian background offered is beautifully attested by the way Ferdinand III of Leon-Castile

(1217/1230–52) addressed his son Alfonso on the point of death: 'My Lord, I leave you the whole realm from the sea hither that the Moors won from Rodrigo, king of Spain. *All of it is in your dominion, part of it conquered, the other part tributary*' (italics are mine).[21] There was thus no black and white distinction or preference in military actions between direct conquest and imposing vassalage. Both were expression of the *Reconquista*, namely of feudal social relations and of the ideology that pervaded them.

There were short- or long-term conditions which determined either policy. Among the latter, unity or fragmentation of al-Andalus was the basic factor. Only when the several post-Caliphate attempts to control Muslim Iberia by North African empires failed one after the other (Almoravids, Almohads, Marīnids) and second or third *taifas* rose, there was the possibility to impose subjection on the weakened parts of al-Andalus. This was also the setting which favoured the conquest of much coveted positions which had been strategic targets for decades. The surrender of Tortosa on 30 December 1148 is a good example. Ramón Berenguer IV, prince of Aragon and count of Barcelona, who had been able to unite the conflicting expansive strategies of both territories after marrying Petronila of Aragon in 1137, forced the capitulation of the city at the mouth of the Ebro valley when no relieving Muslim force helped the besieged within the established truce of forty days. Al-Andalus was then experiencing a re-emergence of the petty kingdoms (the so-called second *taifas*) after the Almoravid power had cracked and the Almohads had only just disembarked in the Iberian Peninsula. Ramon Berenguer IV blocked any help from the south by winning the allegiance of the *taifa* king who controlled the area north and south of Valencia. Submission elsewhere made the conquest of Tortosa possible or at least easier than it might have been if any Muslim expedition had been sent to rescue the besieged.

The specific example of Tortosa shows how little impact the crusade had in the character of this and other campaigns in the crowns of Aragon and Castile in the Central Middle Ages. The key to their understanding lies on the long-term strategies of Christian kings and on the strength or weakness of al-Andalus at specific moments. Only at the level of specific military operations did the crusading call have any relevance through warriors who may have taken the cross. Some kings also used the crusade to enhance their positions in Latin Christendom. James I of Aragon (1213–76) resorted to the crusade in late 1236 to achieve the conquest of the city of Valencia, but the Christian campaign against the *taifa* kingdom had started successfully in 1233 with no crusading undertones. Once he had completed that aim, he tried to compete with Louis IX of France for pre-eminence among Christian monarchs by devising an expedition to Outremer which did not take place. All these aspects are obviously not enough to unify *Reconquista* campaigns under the umbrella of the crusade. Views which do so are much influenced by papal sources that show opinions, intentions and desiderata of popes and their entourage. This type of information cannot be taken for granted because it did very seldom correspond exactly to what was happening in situ. Papal bulls, for example, are as ideological as any chronicle and can be considered tools in the struggle between popes and kings, between overarching ecclesiastic ambitions and secular restrictions to them. They phrased struggle against Islam in Iberia in the way most favourable to the power of popes in the peninsula, thus enhancing the crusading perspective, and they devalued the ideological and military autonomy of the policies of kings.

Traditional periodisation of medieval Christian expansion in Iberia emphasised the access to successive great river valleys. This approach is still very useful because it stresses the geopolitical lines of expansion which each kingdom or county consistently followed over a long time. The Duero, Ebro, Tagus, Jucar and Guadalquivir were fluvial frontiers which Iberian Christians aimed at reaching to consolidate previous conquests and look forward to new ones. Al-Andalus was a culture of cities and river valleys teemed with urban centres. Their capture by Christian kings has been a symbol of expansion: Toledo (1085) on the Tagus; Zaragoza (1118) and Tortosa (1148) on the Ebro; Valencia (1238), Alcira (1242) and Jativa (1244) on the Jucar; Cordoba (1236), Jaén (1246) and Seville (1248) on the Guadalquivir. Toledo apart, many modern historians consider that the other conquests were products of crusading campaigns. I have already dealt briefly with the nature of the expeditions which brought the mouth of the Ebro river or the Muslim Kingdom of Valencia into Christian hands. Similar arguments may be put forward when touching on the above mentioned or on many other conquests in the great expansive thrust of the twelfth and thirteenth centuries. The traditional ideals of *Reconquista* welded dynamic social forces to achieve goals which were easier to attain when the Muslims were disunited. The crusading framework did not substitute the *Reconquista* as the main ideological ethos. It only supplemented Iberian principles which were tightly linked to social aspirations to expand when the additional energy of non-Iberian warriors was needed, when an extra ideological impulse was added to face the conquests of important cities or to check the advance of potent North African armies, as it happened at the battle of Las Navas de Tolosa (1212), or finally when kings thought that a crusading appendage increased their prestige.

RECONQUISTA AFTER THE END OF THE *RECONQUISTA*? CHRISTIAN KINGDOMS AND THE EMIRATE OF GRANADA, MID-THIRTEENTH TO LATE FIFTEENTH CENTURIES

The greatest Christian territorial advances in Iberia took place in the 1230s and 1240s led by Kings James I of Aragon and Ferdinand III of Castile-León. The Balearic Islands, the region of Valencia and a considerable part of Andalusia fell to them after the Almohads failed to consolidate unity in al-Andalus and new *taifas* began to emerge as a result of the Muslim defeat at Las Navas (1212) and the retreat of the Almohad contingent to North Africa. Historians who identify *Reconquista* with seizure of Moorish territories assume that the long process of expansion had finished by the middle of the thirteenth century. Once Jaén, south of the Guadalquivir river, was captured in 1246 the emir of Granada decided to cut his prospective losses and became a vassal of the Leonese-Castilian king. Seville opted for confrontation, but it became clear not long after that it stood little chances of success. The city capitulated in 1248. By that time the most substantial part of the Guadalquivir valley was in Christian hands.

Reconquista was, however, mainly concerned with restoring Christian rule, which was done not only through conquests and land acquisition, but also through submission leading to vassal emirates. Ferdinand III chose that alternative in 1246 in relation to Granada and the region kept that status for nearly two hundred and fifty years. Few Moorish districts were fully integrated into the Crown of Castile since the 1250s, but *Reconquista* principles still shaped relationships with the remaining autonomous Muslims in south-eastern Iberia in the following centuries. Two were the major questions under consideration in Castilian policy towards Granada: the control of the Strait of Gibraltar and the nature of the contacts with the Naṣrid emirate.

From North Africa came the only possibility of help to the Muslims of Granada, although relationships between al-Andalus and the African empires had always been shifty: the need of military assistance was counterbalanced by utter reluctance to the unitary purposes of either Almoravids, Almohads or Marīnids. The Strait was the sea route to keep assistance to Granada active. It was centred on the key posts of Algeciras and Gibraltar, once the Atlantic side came under the control of the Castilians after the seizure of Niebla (1262) and Cadiz (early 1260s), and the most southern point of the Iberian Peninsula, Tarifa, was taken in 1292. The main strategic objective of Castilian kings was for decades to check an easy connection between the Iberian and African shores. The battle of El Salado (1340) was decisive in this regard. Once again and following the trail of crusading views on so many conquests and battles, it has been considered primarily a crusade. The much repeated argument is valid here: Iberian Christian strategies structured and fuelled by *Reconquista* principles were at the heart of that conflict on the Christian side. Crusade was the usual resort to boost native ideology and military efficiency. No more than that.

Victory at El Salado was followed by the capture of Algeciras in 1344, but these campaigns abruptly ended with Alfonso XI of Castile's death caused by the bubonic plague in 1350 while laying siege to Gibraltar. The Crown of Castile soon entered years of inner turmoil which concluded with the killing of Alfonso's successor Peter I (1350–69) and with a new dynasty, the Trastamaras, reaching power. Then came a long period of social and political readjustment at times of severe structural crisis that was common to most European regions. The emirate of Granada was not the first priority either to kings who were reasserting their rule or to a new nobility, formed by upstarts who benefitted from the dynastic change and who were finding their way to and through power. Only at the beginning of the fifteenth century did the regent Fernando, soon to become king of Aragon, resume campaigns against Granada and seize the important post of Antequera (1410). The Naṣrid emirate was again on the agenda of Castilian kings and nobles, and some positions on the frontier were taken, but no fully fledged effort for an outright conquest of the whole territory was made until the Catholic kings started operations in the early 1480s, which concluded with their entry into the city of Granada on 2 January 1492.

The key aspect related to the long campaign of Granada is not the deconstruction of its crusading nature (it may be done following the arguments put forward above), but the understanding of what *Reconquista* principles meant to Isabella of Castile (1474–1504) and Ferdinand of Aragon (1479–1516) who married in 1469. Ideas about *restauratio* were central to Iberian political ideology all along the Middle Ages, but they were interpreted by monarchs, ruling elites and societies in general in very different ways depending on the times. They were expression of specific periods and were coloured by them, as happened to any other contemporary aspect. *Restauratio/Reconquista* was certainly not an immutable message that had run through without alterations since its inception in ninth-century Asturias. Kings and nobilities had perspectives in the later Middle Ages which were dissimilar from those of the thirteenth or earlier centuries. The previous precarious balance between monarchs and nobles had given way to the construction of states around kings with the help of the new ruling classes. The aim of reinforcing royal power to levels unknown in previous centuries and of converting it into a potent political and administrative machinery tainted *Reconquista* ideals. These began to be not only focused on reinstating Christian religious and territorial domination as in times past. Ferdinand and Isabella abandoned practices of vassalage, related in this case to the Muslims, in favour of religious and political unity, and this implied a certain degree of uniformity in rulership and beliefs. The Castilian-Aragonese monarchy began to change the focus from vassals and vassalage to subjects fully integrated in the project of a new political structure: a state of which kings were the axis.

Granada, as a vassal emirate that was integrated into a feudal political structure, had its place and meaning at the time of its establishment in the thirteenth century. It had to be conquered when it ceased to be operative to Castile in the late fifteenth century. Then the *Reconquista* finished. The nature of the War of Granada was strictly no longer related to a question of 'restoring' what had been lost in 711, but of building up a new political frame, post-medieval in many aspects though it may keep the neo-Visigothic rhetoric (King Ferdinand as a new Pelayo) and the use of crusading apparatus. Resorting to the crusade in the way of papal bulls rather than in the contribution of non-peninsular warriors served the Catholic kings as a financial bonus and as a speedy way of building up a positive image of the Castilian-Aragonese monarchy in the papal court. Ferdinand II was especially interested in this last point due to the Italian commitments of the Crown of Aragon. Soon after Granada fell, war broke out between France and Castile-Aragon on account of the Kingdom of Naples. The pope's support to Ferdinand II's anti-French policies was a quick response to favour whom the papacy regarded as a crusading king. High Roman ecclesiastical circles conceived the crusade in the most traditional papally centred way. But it was only instrumental for the Catholic kings who wrapped the last *Reconquista* campaign in such bright institutional colours with purposes which mostly were related to it only in an indirect way; one of the most relevant was to benefit the Mediterranean policy of the Crown of Aragon. The usual Iberian policy of 'crusadising' the most important military operations of the *Reconquista* was this time highly successful in terms of propaganda: on 19 December 1496 Pope Alexander VII conferred upon Isabella and Ferdinand the title of 'Catholic kings'.

NOTES

1 A recent approach to this complex series of events is in Luis A. García Moreno, *España, 702–719: La conquista musulmana* (Seville, 2013).

2 An English translation from Arabic by Olivia R. Constable in *Medieval Iberia: Readings from Christian, Muslim and Jewish Sources*, ed. Olivia Remie Constable (Philadelphia, 1997), 37–8.

3 Martín F. Rios Saloma, *La Reconquista. Una construcción historiográfica (siglos XVI-XIX)* (Madrid, 2011).

4 Both authors produced abundant literature to support their arguments. The basic texts which had many updated re-editions to fuel the controversy are: Claudio Sánchez Albornoz, *España, un enigma histórico*, 2 vols (Buenos Aires, 1956), English translation by Colette Joly Dees and David Sven Reher (Madrid, 1975); Americo Castro, *La realidad histórica de España* (México, 1954), English translation by Williard F. King and Selma Margaretten as *The Spaniards. An Introduction to their History* (Berkeley and Los Angeles, 1971).

5 Stanley G. Payne, *Spanish Catholicism: An Historical Overview* (Madison, WI, 1984), 171–9. The first Francoist official history of the war unambiguously referred to it as a crusade: Joaquín Arrarás Iribarren, *Historia de la cruzada española*, 8 vols (Madrid, 1939–43).

6 One among many possible examples is included in one of Rafael Altamira's contributions to the *Cambridge Medieval History*: 'Spain, 1031–1248', *CMH*, vol. 6: *Victory of the Papacy*, ed. J. R. Tanner, C. W. Previté-Orton and Z. N. Brooke (Cambridge, 1929), 420–1: 'Meanwhile, the Spain of the reconquest, by continual crusades against the Muslims, was the strongest rampart for the rest of Europe, and saved the Christian world from an invasion which would otherwise had been easier on the Western side.'

7 José Goñi Gaztambide, *Historia de la Bula de la Cruzada en España* (Vitoria, 1958).

8 Goñi Gaztambide, *Historia de la Bula de la Cruzada en España*, ch. 2 '*La Reconquista, guerra santa*', 14–42, and ch. 3 '*La Reconquista, verdadera cruzada*', 43–62.

9 Joseph F. O'Callaghan, *Reconquest and Crusade in Medieval Spain* (Philadelphia, 2003).

10 O'Callaghan, *Reconquest and Crusade in Medieval Spain*, xi.

11 Joseph F. O'Callaghan, *The Gibraltar Crusade: Castile and the Battle for the Strait* (Philadelphia, 2011); Joseph F. O'Callaghan, *The Last Crusade in the West: Castile and the Conquest of Granada* (Philadelphia, 2014). For the fifteenth century, see also John Edwards, 'Reconquista and Crusade in Fifteenth-Century Spain' in *Crusading in the Fifteenth Century: Message and Impact*, ed. Norman Housley (Basingstoke, 2004), 163–81.

12 Richard A. Fletcher, 'Reconquest and Crusade in Spain, c.1050–1150', *Transactions of the Royal Historical Society*, 5th series, 37 (1987), 31–47.

13 Fletcher, 'Reconquest and Crusade in Spain, c.1050–1150', 36.

14 Fletcher, 'Reconquest and Crusade in Spain, c.1050–1150', 38.

15 O'Callaghan, *Reconquest and Crusade in Medieval Spain*, p. 11.

16 Martín F. Ríos Saloma, 'De la Restauración a la Reconquista: la construcción de un mito nacional (Una revisión historiográfica. Siglos XVI–XIX)', *En la España Medieval* 28 (2005), 379–414, here 398–402; also in Ríos Saloma, *La Reconquista. Una construcción historiográfica (siglos XVI–XIX)*, 147–52.

17 Claudio Sánchez Albornoz, *Despoblación y repoblación del valle del Duero* (Buenos Aires, 1966).

18 The 'cycle of Asturian chronicles', as historians label this remarkable production, comprises the *Chronica Albeldensia*, 881–3, the 'Prophetic Chronicle', 883, and the two 'Chronicles of Alfonso III', which mention the latter and so are post-883: *Crónicas asturianas*, ed. Juan Gil Fernández and Juan Ignacio Ruiz de la Peña, Spanish trans. José Luis Moralejo (Oviedo, 1985); also *Chroniques asturiennes (fin du IXe siècle)*, ed. Yves Bonnaz (Paris, 1987).

19 Derek Lomak assumed that the *Reconquista* 'was an ideal invented by Spanish Christians soon after 711': *The Reconquest of Spain* (London, 1978), 1. Peter Linehan placed the invention in the 880s: *History and the Historians of Medieval Spain* (Oxford, 1993), 103 and in general ch. 4 'The Invention of the Reconquest', 95–127. He came to the conclusion that it was a myth which was not shaped as such in the medieval centuries. It was rather moulded in modern times as the central part of the ideological historical basis of Spanish nationalism.

20 *Crònica o Llibre del feits*, in *Les quatre grans cròniques*, ed. Ferran Soldevila, 2nd edn (Barcelona, 1983). English translation: *The Book of Deeds of James I of Aragon: A Translation of the Medieval Catalan Llibre dels Fets*, trans. Damian Smith and Helena Buffery (Aldershot, 2003).

21 'Sennor te dexo de toda la tierra de mar aca, que los moros del rey Rodrigo de Espanna ganado ovieron; *et en tu sennorio finca toda: la una conquerida, la otra tributada*' (italics are mine), *Primera Crónica General de España*, ed. Ramón Menéndez Pidal, 2nd edn, 2 vols (Madrid, 1955), II:1132, p. 772. English translation from J. F. O'Callaghan, *Reconquest and Crusade*, 8.

PART III

THE LATIN EAST

———•◆•———

CHAPTER ELEVEN

THE VENETIAN PRESENCE IN THE CRUSADER LORDSHIP OF TYRE: A TALE OF DECLINE

———— •◆• ————

David Jacoby

Tyre was among the last Fatimid strongholds along the Levantine coast resisting Christian conquest after the First Crusade. It was eventually captured in 1124 by the forces of the Latin kingdom, supported by a contingent from the County of Tripoli and a Venetian fleet. The lordship of Tyre, which consisted of the city and its countryside, was included in the royal domain until 1187, except for the years 1129–31 when Fulk of Anjou held it as fief before ascending the throne of Jerusalem. Following the Frankish defeat at the battle of Hattin in 1187, Tyre remained for some four years the only city of the Latin kingdom under Frankish rule, while its countryside was occupied by Sultan Saladin of Egypt. The lordship of Tyre was once more included in the royal domain after the conclusion of the Third Crusade in 1191. The forces of Emperor Frederick II of Hohenstaufen occupied the city from autumn 1231 until June 1242. They were defeated then by the baronial party, backed by Marsilio Zorzi who had arrived at Acre in the spring of that year to serve as Venetian bailo or state representative in the Levant. Following Tyre's conquest, Balian of Ibelin, lord of Beirut, was appointed royal custodian of the lordship of Tyre on behalf of Queen Alice of Cyprus, regent of the Kingdom of Jerusalem (Jacoby, 1986a; Jackson, 1986). In 1246 King Henry I of Cyprus, regent of the kingdom, assigned the lordship's custody to Philip of Montfort, who proclaimed himself lord of Tyre. King Hugh III recognized his possession of the lordship around 1269. Philip was succeeded in 1270 by his son John, who was compelled in the same year to enter a treaty with Sultan Baybars I of Egypt. John maintained his rule over the city of Tyre and its immediate surroundings, he retained ten villages, yet five others were transferred to the sultan and the revenue from the remaining rural territory was divided between them. John of Montfort died in 1283, and his widow Margaret agreed in 1285 to a ten-year truce with Sultan Qalawun of Egypt, which confirmed the treaty of 1270 (Holt, 1995: 106–117). Frankish rule over the lordship of Tyre came to an end with the Mamluk occupation of the city in 1291.

Venice's presence and Venetian activity in the lordship of Tyre until 1291 are documented by royal and seigniorial charters, chronicles, notary records, resolutions adopted by Venetian state institutions, and above all by a report compiled by Marsilio Zorzi between 1242 and 1244. He collected extensive oral evidence, some from old people

(Berggötz, 1991: 29, 101: "per anticos nostros qui in Syria demorantur"), as well as from documents regarding Venetian privileges, assets, and losses incurred in the lordship of Tyre, Acre, and Cyprus. Zorzi completed his report by August 1244 at the latest, and after returning to Venice in the autumn of that year submitted it to the Venetian doge (Berggötz, 1991: 1–42; Jacoby, 1986a: 85–87, 93). Once the scattered evidence is collected and assembled in proper chronological order, it may be possible to determine to what extent Venice managed to uphold its interests in the city and countryside of Tyre.

The foundation of Venice's standing, property and privileges in the lordship was established in 1123 by its treaty with Gormond of Picquigny, Patriarch of Jerusalem, acting in the name of Baldwin II who was in Muslim captivity. The so-called *Pactum Warmundi* assigned one-third of the city and its countryside to Venice as a reward for its expected naval assistance in the city's conquest. Venice was to hold its section of the lordship as a collective *allodium* in which it would exercise the same rights as the king in his own domain (Mayer, 2010: III, 1333–1337, no. 764; Jacoby, 1997a: 157–163, especially 157–158). The inclusion of an extensive section of the countryside was clearly made at Venice's insistence. This was a striking departure from the Venetian policy regarding the acquisition of property in a foreign land, which in Byzantium had been limited to an urban center, namely Constantinople (Jacoby, 2001: 154–156).

The treaty of 1123 was apparently implemented shortly after Tyre's conquest in the following year. Marsilio Zorzi does not always accurately date past events, yet his statement that Venice held its portion of the countryside "since the conquest of the city of Tyre" may be taken at face value. By 1123 that rural area had already been occupied for several years by Christian forces and the Venetians were thus fully acquainted with its resources, which included extensive sugar-cane plantations (Berggötz, 1991: 149–150). Since there is some confusion in Marsilio Zorzi's report, it is impossible to arrive at the exact number of villages included in Venice's section of the countryside, yet it appears to have consisted of some twenty whole villages and one-third of some fifty villages, in fact, one-third of their revenue. The treaty of 1285 between Sultan Qalawun of Egypt and Margaret, John of Montfort's widow, describes how shared revenue from villages in the Levant was assembled and divided (Holt, 1995: 111–114, pars. 4–8).

Venice also obtained a section of the city of Tyre and a yearly lump sum of 300 bezants from the revenue of the royal *funda*, the toll station at the city's land gate. In addition, the parties determined the sources of royal revenue from which one-third would be allocated to Venice. These included the remaining revenue from the *funda*, the revenue from the *chaine* or toll office in the harbor, as well as sales and other taxes, listed later by Marsilio Zorzi (Berggötz, 1991: 166–167, and see below). The Venetian church of San Marco in Tyre was built shortly after the conquest with revenue from the Venetian quarter (Berggötz, 1991: 143, ll. 1–2; Tafel and Thomas, 1856–1857: I, 140 = Pozza, 1994, 70–71). It is first attested in 1137 (Morozzo della Rocca and Lombardo, 1940: I, 126–127, no. 126).

After returning from captivity, King Baldwin II concluded a new treaty with Venice in 1125, by which he reasserted royal authority over the Venetian share of the lordship. Its section of the city and the countryside lost its allodial status and became a fief held from the king. This change was closely linked to a new clause in the treaty. It defined Venice's obligation to participate in the defense of the Kingdom of Jerusalem "to the extent that the revenue of the third portion [of the lordship of Tyre granted to Venice] can suitably bear" (Mayer, 2010: I, 245). This rather vague formula implies some kind of relation between revenue and military service, yet it obviously also concealed a more precise understanding between Venice and the king. In order to fulfill its obligation Venice established several fiefs within its portion of the lordship soon after the latter's conquest (Berggötz, 1991: 156, 169). The fiefs consisted of land in the countryside, a house in town (Berggötz, 1991: 159, ll. 1–2; 161, ll. 14–15; 169, ll. 14–19), and in some cases also revenue in cash (see below). The fiefholders owed military service as horsemen (Jacoby, 1997a: 163–164). Marsilio Zorzi mentioned two of the original fiefholders, both members of prominent families in Venice, namely Vitale Pantaleo and Rolando Contarini *maior*.

The fief of Vitale Pantaleo, surnamed *Malvisino*, consisted of two entire villages, Dairrham and Gaifiha, a third of the villages of Maharona and Cafardani, both shared with the king; some other landed property; a house in Tyre, inhabited in Marsilio Zorzi's time by Guglielmo Zorzani and his wife of the Pantaleo family, which incidentally reveals that the fief was hereditary; finally, sixty bezants from Venice's portion of the revenue yielded by a royal market of musical instruments (Berggötz, 1991: 156–159, 167). Precious information regarding Vitale Pantaleo and his fief appears in a notary charter, the full implications of which have been overlooked so far (Morozzo della Rocca and Lombardo, 1940: I, 126–127, no. 126). Around 1137 he asked Pietro Morosini, the parish priest of the Venetian church of San Marco in Tyre, to draft his will, since he feared "sudden death when going to the army and [in] battle." In 1137, the reference is either to the expedition of King Fulk of Anjou to counter in the county of Tripoli the offensive of Zengi, the atabeg of Mosul, or to the forces gathered somewhat later by William of Messines, Patriarch of Jerusalem, to assist the king (Runciman 1952–54: II, 203–204).

In his will, Vitale Pantaleo bequeathed his fief to his own brother Pietro, who had visited him two or three times since 1124, obviously in the course of commercial operations. Vitale entrusted a pouch containing the document and additional charters bearing on his fief and other land to the priest, who was to deliver them after his death to Pietro. Vitale Pantaleo died without offspring in Tyre in the first months of 1157. Shortly afterwards his nephew Giovanni, Pietro's son, was informed of this event while trading in the Byzantine Empire and hastened to Tyre. He settled in Vitale's house and requested the latter's pouch of charters from the priest in his own father's name. It was his intention to keep the house until his father's arrival and thereby uphold the latter's claim to the fief. When the priest Pietro Morosini refused to comply with his request, Giovanni Pantaleo assembled in April 1157 in the local church of San Marco all the Venetians he could find in Tyre, who unanimously supported him. After a lively and noisy debate, the priest finally gave in, but duly stated that he had done so under duress, "because of the calls and shouting at me" ("propter voces et vociferaciones que fuerunt facte supra me"). The notary charter recording the episode of 1157 was drafted at the request of two residents of Tyre. One of them was Ambrogio Bon, *milex* (*sic*), whose surname appears among those of Venetian prominent families and whose title suggests that he too was a Venetian fiefholder, probably one of the original ones settled in the city. We have no other information about him.

The episode of 1157 reveals three important facts. First, prior to 1137 Vitale Pantaleo had apparently participated in military operations and in any event had been called up for another one in or around that year. Venice had thus duly implemented its military obligation to contribute to the defense of the kingdom. It had established a clear link between the holding of fiefs granted by the doge to its citizens (Berggötz, 1991: 156, ll. 12–13) and military service, in accordance with the custom prevailing in the Kingdom of Jerusalem. Venice had also borrowed the term *miles* for fiefholder from 'feudal' terminology. Second, there was no permanent or even temporary Venetian state representative or administration in Tyre in 1137, nor in 1157. Instead, the parish priest of San Marco, settled in the city for more than twenty years, acted as substitute for the state, fulfilling administrative functions such as drafting the will of Vitale Pantaleo and safeguarding documents at his church, like contemporary Venetian clerics and their establishments in Byzantium (Jacoby, 2015: 77–78). In addition, in the absence of a state representative or state institution, the Venetian citizens who happened to be in Tyre, both settlers and visiting merchants, acted collectively as a decision-making body in a specific case. Third, since Vitale Pantaleo was childless in 1137, he willed his fief to his brother, considering that it was hereditary or transmissible within the family, which indeed it was, and as noted above further evidence in that respect will be adduced below.

The earliest datable loss incurred by Venice is related to the annual allocation of 300 bezants from the royal *funda* of Tyre, which in 1243 yielded 1,900 bezants (Berggötz, 1991: 167). We may safely assume that Baldwin II was the king who transferred that royal obligation to the *catena* or harbor customs of Acre, after granting the lordship of Tyre to Fulk of Anjou in 1129. The latter unilaterally suspended the yearly payment, clearly during his rule as king of Jerusalem from 1131 to 1143. Venice attempted yet failed to recover it in 1164 (Tafel and Thomas, 1856–57: I, 141 = Pozza, 1994, 71).

A few years later Venice suffered a far more serious blow by losing a large portion of its property in the lordship of Tyre, namely almost the entire fief of Rolando Contarini *maior*, who lived during the reign of King Fulk of Anjou which extended from 1131 to 1143. The formula "since the time of Rolando Contarini," used by Doge Vitale Michiel in 1164 (Tafel and Thomas, 1856–57: I, 140–144, especially 141 = Pozza, 1994, 70–73, especially 71), points to the standing of this Venetian citizen as the most prominent Venetian fiefholder with the largest holdings in the lordship of Tyre soon after 1124. The whole issue of his fief has been obscured by the fact that two additional members of the same family bearing an identical name later appeared in the lordship. His fief included twelve whole villages, most of which formed a compact territory south of Tyre, a third of four additional villages, and a house in the Venetian section of Tyre. The fief owed the service of three horsemen (Berggötz, 1991: 72–73, 169). Rolando Contarini's widow, Guida, a member of the Venetian Gradenigo family, held in fief from Venice the village of Mahallia, one-third of four other villages, and a house in the city of Tyre, none of which is included in the inventory of her husband's fief (Berggötz, 1991: 157, 161, 169).[1] These assets presumably belonged to Guida's inheritance, which suggests the presence of her father among the original Venetian fiefholders. According to Marsilio Zorzi, when Rolando Contarini died childless, sometime between 1131 and 1157,[2] the Venetian *baiulus* or state representative requested his widow to return his fief to the state, or Commune as it was called. In fact, there was no Venetian state officer in Tyre at that time, as noted above, which explains why the Commune failed to take hold of the fief. Guida placed herself under royal protection and, moreover, bequeathed the fief of her deceased husband to the king in order to keep it during her lifetime. The king seized the rural assets of the fief after her death, which occurred before 1187 (Berggötz, 1991: 31). Most usurped property was never recovered by Venice (Berggötz, 1991: 169–170). Still, Venice managed to retain Guida's village of Mahallia (Berggötz, 1991: 156–157).

Around the time at which Rolando Contarini's fief was lost or somewhat later another development affected Venice's rights and assets, this time in the city of Tyre. Pisa's property in the city was at first limited to five houses in the vicinity of the harbor, conferred by King Baldwin II within the years 1124–29. The grant was confirmed and additions were made in 1156 and 1165 (Mayer, 2010: I, 263–265, no. 106; 446–449, no. 242; II, 541–544). Pisa also bought a *fondaco* or caravanserai from one of the kings of Jerusalem, possibly in 1168 when King Amalric granted the Pisans a quarter in Acre (Mayer, 2010: II, 564–568, no. 327), or somewhat later.[3] The *fondaco* was situated east of the Venetian quarter, faced the harbor, and extended along a street shared by the king and Venice leading to the harbor customs (*catena*), along which there was a shop and a city gate. After obtaining the *fondaco*, the Pisans built their church of San Pietro above the shop and the city gate in such a way that it encroached upon Venetian territory and left a passageway in the street only some five Venetian feet or 1.74 meters wide. Zorzi states that this had happened so long ago that he could not find anyone remembering it (Berggötz, 1991: 167–168; Pringle, 1993–2009: IV, 220, and map on 212).[4] Only the absence of Venetian reaction and possible royal connivance while construction was underway may explain this violation of Venetian territorial rights.

Originally Venice must have owed the service of five horsemen, if not more: the fief of Rolando Contarini *maior* providing three, as noted above, Vitale Pantaleo's one, Ambrogio Bon's one, and the fief of Guida Contarini's father possibly one. Yet according to a list dated to 1185 or 1186, included in the *Livre des Assises* compiled by John of Ibelin, Venice's obligation of military service to the king was limited to three out of a total of twenty-eight "chevaliers," or horsemen, owed by the lordship of Tyre (John of Ibelin, 2003: 613; Edbury, 1997: 122, 129–131). Clearly, Venice had obtained a reduction of its military burden, undoubtedly following the loss of the fief of Rolando *maior* and most of Guida's fief. These losses had seriously curtailed Venice's holdings in the lordship of Tyre.[5]

The service of three Venetian fiefholders was renewed after the recovery of Tyre's countryside from Saladin in 1191. Vitale Falier was then reinstated in the fief he had obtained in 1171. In 1206 he returned it to the doge, most likely because he was unable to further perform his military service (Tafel and Thomas, 1856–57: II, 11–13). The fief of Vitale Pantaleo, acquired by his brother Pietro in 1157 or shortly afterwards, was in the hands of an unknown descendant or relative of his after 1191. Some fifty years later, in Marsilio Zorzi's time, it was held by Guglielmo Zorzani (Berggötz, 1991: 150, l. 7: Guillielmus Iordanis) in the name of his wife, who was a Pantaleo (Berggötz, 1991: 153, ll. 17–18; 155, ll. 2–3; 158, l. 23–159, l. 2). The third fiefholder was Rolando Contarini (here Rolando II), a relative yet not a direct descendant of the one surnamed *maior*, who had died without issue and whose fief had been lost, as noted above. Rolando II arrived in Tyre at an unknown date and held a Venetian fief while Pantaleo Barbo served as Venetian state representative in the Kingdom of Jerusalem during the rule of Count Henry of Champagne, which extended from May 1192 to September 1197 (Berggötz, 1991: 155, 159–161, 171).[6] This was a new fief, especially established for Rolando II. Significantly, none of its components had ever belonged to the fiefs of either Rolando Contarini *maior* or his wife Guida. This also applies to a house in town, distinct from the one held by Rolando *maior*, although the two were contiguous (Berggötz, 1991: 169). Pantaleo Barbo authorized Rolando II to sell a piece of land called Fossa, a move that in fact reduced the fief's revenue. Vitale Galafarius, tutor of the grandson of Rolando II called Rolando *minor*, who had inherited his fief, recovered Fossa and thus restored the territorial integrity of the fief while Stefano Giustinian served as Venetian state representative in the kingdom (Berggötz, 1991: 161), presumably in the early 1230s.[7]

Marsilio Zorzi may have obtained a confirmation of the reduced load of military service in 1242. Significantly, he tacitly recognized the seemingly irreversible royal annexation of Rolando's fief. While he minutely describes its content and relates the circumstances of its loss (Berggötz, 1991: 169–170), he fails to insist upon Venice's legal rights to the property, as he systematically does with expressions such as "in eo habemus ius" or "in quo dicimus habere terciam [partem]" when mentioning other lost Venetian assets (Berggötz, 1991: 159–160).

Venice's position in the lordship of Tyre was considerably weakened in the years following the Frankish defeat at Hattin in 1187. Conrad of Montferrat arrived at Tyre shortly afterwards. From the summer of 1189 until the fall of Acre in 1191 the two commanders of the Venetian fleet operating in Levantine waters, who served as official state representatives in Tyre, refrained from supporting him in his dispute with King Guy of Lusignan over the royal crown (Jacoby, 1993: 190, 193–194, 213–223). In that period, Conrad confiscated a large house in which he established a royal mint, yet later granted the house to the Genoese Ansaldo Bonvicini, whose son held it when Zorzi compiled his report (Berggötz, 1991: 159, 168).[8] In May 1188 Conrad also granted to the Pisan *Societas Vermiliorum*, a military association created in Tyre during the city's siege by Saladin, several villages of which Venice was entitled to one-third of the revenue (Mayer, 2010: II, 882–885, no. 524). It is unclear whether Venice had already lost its portion of these villages, or whether Conrad disregarded Venice's rights because it failed to support him. In any event, the grant remained meaningless, since the villages were situated in the countryside occupied by Saladin at that time, and the *Societas Vermiliorum* is not attested after the Christian forces recovered that territory, presumably because it dissolved once Tyre's siege ended.

In 1191 Venice submitted a copy of the *Pactum Warmundi* to Conrad of Montferrat, although the charter issued by King Baldwin II to Venice in 1125 had superseded it and was the authoritative document defining Venice's assets and privileges (Jacoby, 1997a: 165–166). Uncertainty about the recovery of Venice's property in Tyre's countryside may have prompted the choice of the *Pactum Warmundi*, since it lacked the military obligations based on that property included in the charter of 1125 issued By Baldwin II. Conrad's confirmation of the *Pactum Warmundi* in 1191 or 1192 (Mayer, 2010: II, 900–904) did not prevent further Venetian losses.

Indeed, the recovery of the rural hinterland of Tyre in 1191, after almost four years of Muslim occupation, signaled the beginning of an accelerated and continuous erosion of Venetian property and rights in that area. It was far more extensive than in the city. Several lords previously sharing villages with Venice usurped the latter's portion or curtailed its revenue, as illustrated by numerous entries in Marsilio Zorzi's report. He recorded that in the village of Betheron, jointly held by Venice and the archbishops of Tyre, three pieces of land belonging to Venice had been held by the archbishops for fifty years, "since the time of Sultan Saladin," a reference to 1191. Other Venetian pieces of land had been entirely taken over by successive archbishops during the previous forty, twenty, fifteen, ten or five years respectively (Berggötz, 1991: 161–162). Vitale Galafarius, an old man by the 1240s, testified how the Venetian section of Sedim, a village shared with the king, had been lost. He was in charge of its cultivation at the time of Pantaleo Barbo, thus between 1192 and 1197. Barbo requested the implementation of the customary division of the total revenue from the village, presumably because it was not implemented or had been curtailed. Henry of Champagne, who ruled over the kingdom, flatly refused and seized the Venetian section, which since then had remained in royal hands (Berggötz, 1991: 170, ll. 4–6; 171).

Tommaso Dulce, Vitale Galafarius and others reported that because of neglect the Venetian state representative Domenico Acotanto had lost the Venetian section of the village of Teyrfebne, presumably in 1198 or 1199. When royal officers realized that it was abandoned and not effectively supervised by Venice, they seized it for the king (Berggötz, 1991: 170; Favreau-Lilie, 1999: 228, n. 49, for the dating of his office). A vineyard planted "at the time of the capture of Damietta" in Egypt during the Fifth Crusade, thus in 1219, had also been lost (Berggötz, 1991: 161–165, especially 163). In the village of Hanoe shared with the Templar Order, Venice had enjoyed for a long time no more than one-eighth of the revenue, instead of the third it was entitled to (Berggötz, 1991: 154).

Venice was also deprived of property confiscated by the royal administration on judicial grounds. At an unspecified date, yet many years before 1231 when Riccardo Filangieri occupied Tyre on behalf of Frederick II, a Venetian mill in the vicinity of Tyre had been leased out for five years at the annual rate of 100 bezants. After the miller committed a murder, he was arrested and the mill confiscated by royal officers as if it were the king's property. Marsilio Zorzi failed to recover it and it remained in royal hands (Berggötz, 1991: 151, 171). Criminal justice, a royal prerogative (see below), thus provided the king's officers with opportunities to encroach upon Venetian property.

Venice also suffered losses in jurisdiction and taxation inside its own quarter of Tyre. According to Zorzi, Jews living in the quarter had been subjected to royal jurisdiction and taxation for some fifty years, thus from the 1190s either under the rule of Conrad of Montferrat or of Henry of Champagne. The royal treasury collected the annual tax of one bezant levied from all Jewish males in the city having reached the age of fifteen. Royal jurisdiction had also been imposed upon the Syrian or Oriental Christian weavers residing in the Venetian quarter, who were required to pay to the king what appears to be a monthly license fee imposed upon their workshops (Berggötz, 1991: 139–140).[9]

The infringements of Venetian privileges markedly increased during the reign of John of Brienne, whose rule extended from 1210 to 1225. King John exempted the Syrians living in the royal section of the city from dues at the *catena* or harbor customs, in order to lure their brethren residing in the Venetian quarter, who did not enjoy such an exemption, to move to his own section of the city (Berggötz, 1991: 166–167). Apparently the measure was only partly successful and, therefore, the king extended royal jurisdiction over all the Syrians remaining in the Venetian quarter, while previously only Syrian weavers had been submitted to it (Berggötz, 1991: 139). He also extended royal taxation to the Venetian quarter and unified tax collection under the royal *muhtasib* or *iusticiarius* in the entire city of Tyre, regardless of Venice's rights in its own quarter. Without referring to John, Zorzi mentions in his report a specific case which illustrates this step, namely the royal tax of 4 denarii on the slaughtering of pigs called *tuazo*, a survival from Fatimid times (Berggötz, 1991: 140–141, 167; Riley-Smith, 1973: 84). In view of the various measures introduced by John of Brienne, we may safely ascribe to him the usurpation of Venice's portion of the revenues from customs dues at the *catena* and at the city's land gate, as well as from sales taxes on musical instruments, grain, wine, beer, olive and sesame oil, milk, fish, spices, glass and candles, the collection of which the royal treasury granted to individuals under lease (Berggötz, 1991: 140, 166–167). The extension of royal jurisdiction and taxation over the Venetian quarter of Tyre, as if it were part of the royal domain, amounted to the collapse of the quarter's de facto exterritorial status, and the loss of revenue previously shared with the king outside the quarter abolished the remnants of Venetian rights and privileges obtained in 1123 and 1125. John of Brienne's harsh measures against Venice were most likely prompted by the dire state of the royal treasury, attested by various sources, following his participation in the military campaign in Egypt from 1218 to 1220, in the framework of the Fifth Crusade (Favreau-Lilie, 1986: 437, n. 13, on his indebtedness).

Venice must have recovered some assets and revenues after the reign of John of Brienne, at the latest in the first years following Riccardo Filangieri's occupation of Tyre in 1231 on behalf of Emperor Frederick II. The emperor was attempting then to ensure Venice's support in Italy. A renewed loss occurred after Venice turned against the emperor from 1237 onward, in any event following its treaty of September 1239 with Genoa and Pope Gregory IX, followed by attacks of the Venetian navy against imperial ships and cities in Apulia (Kretschmayr, 1905–1934: II, 42–45). Zorzi accused Filangieri of having stripped Venice of its revenue in the entire lordship of Tyre and requested its restoration, but to no avail (Berggötz, 1991: 135). He therefore supported the baronial forces in their attack on Tyre (Jacoby, 1986a: 87, 93–94). Yet even after the city's conquest in June 1242, to which he had contributed, Marsilio had to wait several months before achieving some measure of success.

The developments affecting Venice's assets and privileges from 1187 to 1242 did not prevent Venetian individuals from remaining in Tyre and retaining their private property in the city, even under the rule of Riccardo Filangieri. Such was the case with members of the Dulce (Dulsi, Dous) family. Giacomo was *habitator* of Tyre in 1189 (Morozzo della Rocca and Lombardo, 1940: I, 366–367, no. 373). Tommaso, *burgensis Tyri*, is mentioned in 1200 and 1221. At an unspecified date before 1242 he served as *procurator* of the local church of San Marco and as such bought some property on its behalf. He leased various pieces of property from the Commune. In 1243 he owned a plot of land and several houses. Tommaso provided Marsilio Zorzi with invaluable information regarding the loss of Venetian state property in the countryside due to Pantaleo Barbo and Domenico Acotanto, respectively between 1192 and 1197 and presumably in 1198–99 (Berggötz, 1991: 143, 145, 146, 148, 170–171; Favreau-Lilie, 1999: 228, n. 49, for the second dating). Manasse Dulce, another member of the family, appears in 1221 and was appointed Venetian *vicecomes* in Tyre by Marsilio Zorzi (Favreau-Lilie, 1987: 94, no. 6; Berggötz, 1991: 147, 159). Pietro is recorded in a document of 1209 dealing with Tyre, yet drafted in Acre, and in 1221 in Tyre (Morozzo della Rocca and Lombardo, 1940: II, 52–53, no. 513; Favreau-Lilie, 1987: 94, no. 6). Domenico served as witness in Tyre in 1211 (Morozzo della Rocca and Lombardo, 1940: II, 69–70, no. 529). Vitale Galafarius had been in charge of the cultivation of the Venetian section of Sedim at the time of Pantaleo Barbo, thus between 1192 and 1197, and as tutor of Rolando Contarini *minor* he bought a piece of land at the time of Stefano Giustiniani, presumably in the early 1230s (see above). He further served as witness in Tyre in 1218 and 1221 (Favreau-Lilie, 1987: 92, no. 5, Vitale Calefai; 94, no. 6, Vitale Callafatus).

Some other Venetian citizens had also remained in Tyre by 1242 (Berggötz, 1991: 146). According to Marsilio Zorzi, the city's Venetian *burgenses* or residents decisively contributed to its conquest by the baronial party, presumably by offering information regarding Riccardo Filangieri's forces. Some of these Venetians also provided Zorzi with precious data regarding Venice's rights, interests and losses in the lordship of Tyre (Berggötz, 1991: 137; see also above). However, Venetian merchants based in other ports most likely refrained from trading or limited their activity in Tyre, once they were denied the exemptions and special judicial status previously enjoyed by Venetian citizens and subjects.

Following the ouster of the imperial forces from Tyre in June 1242, Balian of Ibelin, lord of Beirut, one of the two leaders of the baronial party, became royal custodian of the lordship, and it is with him that Marsilio had henceforth to deal. Balian restored to Venice its urban quarter and the Commune's property within its ancient boundaries, except for a few houses. Marsilio Zorzi mentions one that had belonged to the dowry of a widow, without referring to the date at which its loss had occurred. The house should have reverted to the Commune after the widow's death, since she was not entitled to alienate it (Berggötz, 1991: 168). Balian of Ibelin held the house that had once belonged to the fief of Guida, the wife of Rolando Contarini *maior*. He also held the house that had originally belonged to the fief of Rolando himself (Berggötz, 1991: 161, 169). Zorzi claims that Pantaleo Barbo had resided in it when he visited Tyre while serving as Venice's representative between 1192 and 1197. This would imply that Venice had recovered the house sometime after the death of Rolando Contarini *maior*, which is unlikely. It would seem that Zorzi confused this house with another one that had belonged to the Commune and had occasionally served as residence of the Venetian representatives based in Acre, when they temporarily stayed in Tyre. Hugh l'Amiral, a supporter of the baronial party opposing Frederick II, lived in that house and claimed that it belonged to the dowry of his wife, a daughter of Zunzulino Gazel (Berggötz, 1991: 168). He had seized it, as well as the Venetian third of the village of Joie situated in the countryside of Tyre, presumably after his appointment as royal castellan of Tyre, a function he still held by April 1243 (Berggötz, 1991: 139, 160, 168; Kohler, 1899: 179–180, no. 71).

Following Tyre's conquest in June 1242, Marsilio Zorzi recovered Venice's share of the taxes collected in the royal section of the city and cites the sums obtained (Berggötz, 1991: 166–167). He also regained Venice's fiscal and judicial authority over its own quarter and all the latter's residents, whether Latins, Syrians or Jews (Berggötz, 1991: 139–141). However, when he asserted that Venice's jurisdiction over Venetian nationals also extended to High Justice, he encountered strong opposition, since it was viewed as one of the foremost expressions of royal and baronial authority. Zorzi and the royal party eventually worked out a compromise. The royal officers refused to recognize Zorzi's contention, while transferring to him Venetian criminals and enabling him to exercise High Justice openly. Zorzi boasts that he retained this jurisdiction for the rest of his term of office in the Levant. "And these things we did," he wrote, "so that our court should be seen doing them." He was obviously eager to establish precedents, because he knew that his claim to High Justice was groundless (Berggötz, 1991: 139; Jacoby, 1997a: 159, 169–171). In order to ensure his enlarged judicial prerogatives, which he considered crucial for Venice's position in Tyre, he had to forgo the recovery of the houses of the Venetian quarter that had been lost. As noted earlier, two of these were held by Balian of Ibelin and another by Hugh l'Amiral, the royal castellan of Tyre, precisely the two officials who tacitly agreed to Zorzi's exercise of High Justice with regard to Venetian nationals.

Zorzi also recovered some of the Commune's assets in the countryside of Tyre, as illustrated by references to *angaria* or labor services and payments in kind by peasants to the Commune and to the bailo (Berggötz, 1991: 45–46; 153, ll. 5–7, 11–12, 24–26; 154, ll. 10–13; 155, ll. 13–16; 156, ll. 2–4, 10–11). Payments in kind are also mentioned in 1256 (Cessi, 1931–50: II, 357, par. I). However, most Venetian rural assets usurped by royal officers or by other lords were lost (Berggötz, 1991: 170–171). The policy adopted by Balian of Ibelin after the conquest of Tyre in 1242 toward Venice was entirely consistent with royal interests. The renewal of Venice's territorial, fiscal and judicial privileges in the city of Tyre was bound to encourage private Venetian trade and shipping and thereby enhance the income of the royal treasury. This goal could be achieved without restoring the Commune's share of the countryside.

Marsilio Zorzi's achievements in Tyre were lost during the so-called War of St. Sabas, which from 1256 to 1258 opposed Venice to Genoa in Acre. Philip of Montfort, lord of Tyre, who sided with Genoa, expelled the Venetians from his city shortly before the resumption of the war in autumn 1257 (Jacoby, 2003: 243–246). As a result, Venice and its citizens incurred heavy losses of income in the following twenty years. Philip of Montfort confiscated the assets of individual Venetians, as implied by the charter of March 1264 confirming his treaty with Genoa, which refers to the former shops of Vitale Galefarius (Calefat) and Pietro Dulce (Dous) and the former two houses of Tommaso Dulce (Dous) (Madia, 1999: 7–12, especially 9). The church, campanile and *loggia* of San Marco in the Venetian quarter suffered damage, whether purposely inflicted or as a result of neglect, which implies that these buildings had not been used for a long time (Tafel and Thomas, 1856–57: III, 153). Not surprisingly, Tyre does not appear in the anonymous Venetian trading manual compiled in Acre around 1270 (Jacoby, 1986b).

Fearing a joint attack by Ruggero di San Severino, the representative of Charles of Anjou, king of Sicily, in the Kingdom of Jerusalem and by Venetian forces, Philip's successor, John of Montfort, reached an agreement in July 1277 with Venice's bailo in Acre, Albertino Morosini. In principle it provided for a return to the situation existing during Marsilio Zorzi's tenure of office. The Commune recovered its privileges in the lordship of Tyre, both in the city and in its rural hinterland, and individual Venetians regained possession of their assets (Tafel and Thomas, 1856–57: III, 150–159; Jacoby, 2003: 172–174). However, the territorial clause regarding the countryside was clearly unrealistic, following the agreement concluded by John of Montfort with Sultan Baybars in 1270. The revenue from villages previously shared by Venice with the kings of Jerusalem and from 1246 with the lords of Tyre was now divided between John of Montfort and the sultan (Holt, 1995: 111–114, pars. 4–8). The whole of Batiole, which had belonged to Venice according to Marsilio Zorzi (Berggötz, 1991: 152), was among the villages retained by the lord of Tyre, and a section of its territory had been seized by the Mamluk governor of Safed (Tafel and Thomas, 1856–57: III, 398–400).

In the field of jurisdiction, the whole formulation of the agreement of 1277 was supposedly in accordance with the terms of the charter issued by Baldwin II in 1125 and represented a return to the situation existing during Zorzi's tenure of office. In fact, John of Montfort acknowledged the Venetian doge and Commune as the "true lords" of their possessions (Tafel and Thomas, 1856–57: III, 152); in other words, the latter's exterritorial status. He also recognized Venice's right to exercise criminal, in addition to civil justice over Venetians, as well as over the permanent and temporary residents of its portion of Tyre, except for his own liegemen and burgesses. This amounted to a shift from tolerated exercise of High Justice, as in Marsilio Zorzi's days, to full authority in that field. John of Montfort also granted full exemption from taxation on both seaborne and land trade, an improvement on the privilege of 1125. He further promised to transfer to Venice's representatives the revenue yielded by the property belonging to the Commune and to Venetian individuals that he and his father had collected in the city and its rural hinterland from 1257 to 1277.

The implementation of the agreement of 1277 was far from smooth. John of Montfort's numerous infringements prompted Venice to conduct new negotiations with him in 1283. All the major issues supposedly settled in 1277 were raised again. Venice instructed its bailo in Tyre to demand full implementation of the charters of 1125 and 1277 with respect to fiscal matters and the exercise of justice. The Commune should enjoy its share of the land and the fiscal revenues of the city and countryside of Tyre, in conformity with their original partition, once more a completely unrealistic demand (Cessi, 1931–50: III, 43–44, par. 129; Jacoby, 2003: 174). There is no evidence regarding the outcome of the negotiations between Venice and John of Montfort. Despite the territorial losses suffered by the lordship of Tyre, it is noteworthy that Venice still retained some sugar-cane plantations in the city's rural hinterland at the time of Marco Zen, who must have served as bailo of Tyre shortly before 1286 (Cessi, 1931–50: 149–150, par. 75). He may have been identical to the one serving as podestà of Chioggia in that year (Rösch, 1989: 23).

The absence of a permanent Venetian state administration in the Kingdom of Jerusalem was undoubtedly the most important factor responsible for the ongoing erosion of Venice's position in the lordship of Tyre from the 1140s to the 1220s. This absence is rather puzzling, yet once we consider it within the context of Venetian expansion in the eastern Mediterranean, it is clear that this was a matter of general policy. Venice appears to have avoided whenever possible direct administration in its outposts and colonies in that region (Jacoby, 2015: 101–102). Tyre's rulers and their officers, as well as landlords sharing villages with Venice in the countryside, took advantage of these conditions to usurp Venetian property, rights and revenue, whether temporarily or definitively. After 1187 the aggressive royal policy in that respect was also prompted by the constant need to compensate for the severe curtailment of royal territory and revenue following the Frankish defeat of Hattin. Venice's losses were further compounded by adverse political circumstances, such as its conflict with Frederick II and the War of St. Sabas in Acre.

Venice resorted to various devices to solve the problems arising from the absence of a state presence in the lordship of Tyre, namely the grant of fiefs, the lease of property instead of direct exploitation, and delegation of authority to ecclesiastical institutions. The fiefs must have represented about half the total number of Venice's villages in the countryside. By granting them, Venice also transferred the administration and revenue of a large section of its territory to the beneficiaries. The remaining rural territory and property in the city were leased to Venetian citizens in return for payments, as Venice's sugar-cane plantations in 1204 (Lombardo and Morozzo della Rocca, 1953: 103, no. 90). The collection of the yearly rent from leased property did not require the permanent presence of a Venetian state official in Tyre. It could be performed by Venetian settlers or visiting merchants, as in Constantinople (Jacoby, 2015: 79–80). We have no information regarding the exercise of Venetian judicial and fiscal authority affecting the indigenous population.

As noted above, in the city of Tyre the priest of San Marco and his church replaced the state in certain administrative functions as late as 1157. However, somewhat later Venice entrusted San Marco with more extensive functions, in view of the state's losses of property from the 1140s. It transferred to the church a section of its urban quarter, at first temporarily some time before August 1164, and definitively in that month. In January 1165 Venice granted to San Marco its entire quarter in Tyre and the remainder of its rural possessions for five years, except for sugar-cane plantations in the countryside of Tyre, and extended that transfer two more times, until 1180. Still, Venice considered that state supervision over these assets was required, and by 1171 Leo Falier, as *prelatus tercie divisionis Tyri*, was in charge of the entire Venetian section of the lordship, a function that apparently continued to exist until 1187. There is good reason to believe that Leo Falier and his successors leased the function of *prelatus*, were not paid a salary, and recouped themselves with the revenue from the assets they supervised on behalf of the state.

The heavy losses Venice suffered soon after 1191 prompted it to exercise firmer authority over its share of the lordship of Tyre under a *vicecomes in terra Tyri*, yet this function too was leased from the state. Domenico Acotanto's appointment to that office in 1198 yielded some positive results. He reached an agreement with the local church of

San Marco regarding the division of revenue accruing from the lease of two ovens, one of which was adjacent to a *fondaco* of the church (Berggötz, 1991: 143, ll. 12–16). He also took a strong stand with respect to the royal administration. Venice was entitled to four yearly installments from the revenue yielded by the royal *fondaco*, according to an agreement by which it had relinquished its share of the revenue deriving from a soap factory and a dyeing installation. Acotanto enforced the closure of the dyeing plant when the payments were withheld, and maintained it until they were renewed (Berggötz, 1991: 149, ll. 1–8). It would seem that Acotanto paid less attention to the Commune's assets in the rural hinterland of Tyre, since he was responsible for the loss of the Venetian section of a village (see above).

By August 1204, Venice's interests in Acre and the lordship of Tyre were under the control of a single individual. Giovanni Dandolo had been appointed for five years *vicecomes et prelatus* of Venice's quarter in Acre and of its share in the lordship of Tyre. He resided in Acre, yet his title *miles* suggests that he was one of Venice's fiefholders in the lordship of Tyre at that time (Lombardo and Morozzo della Rocca, 1953: 103, no. 90, insert of 1204 in a document of 1240). In 1214 Andrea Vitale appears as the first bailo *in partibus Syrie*, thus in the entire Kingdom of Jerusalem. A further upgrading of Venice's presence took place after Vitale left the office, when a full permanent state administration was established under salaried officials sent from Venice. In 1217 Teofilo Zeno is the first securely attested salaried bailo in charge of that administration. A separate apparatus for Tyre headed by a *vicecomes*, yet under the authority of the bailo in Acre, was created in 1221. This step was presumably prompted by the severe royal encroachments upon Venetian property, rights and jurisdiction in the lordship of Tyre under John of Brienne (see above). All these developments did not halt Venetian losses (Jacoby, 2015: 88–94, for the last three paragraphs).

Marsilio Zorzi was the first Venetian official who managed to recover a significant portion of Venice's state authority and revenue. He was less successful with respect to property. It is possible that he was the one who suggested a further upgrading of the office of state representative in Tyre. Between his return to Venice in the autumn of 1244 and January 1249 Venice appointed a bailo for the lordship, distinct from the one serving in Acre. Political circumstances brought about a total loss of Venetian interests in Tyre in 1257, which lasted twenty years. The achievements and precedents established by Zorzi determined Venice's position in its negotiations with John of Montfort in 1277. As noted above, the implementation of their agreement proved to be arduous.

Venice was one of the three powerful maritime powers active in the Kingdom of Jerusalem throughout the latter's existence. Surprisingly, though, for about a whole century it displayed considerable weakness in the lordship of Tyre. It appears to have been unconcerned about its property and rights there and inefficient in their management and preservation, especially in the countryside. When it finally adopted a firm policy to recover lost assets and privileges, it was too late. It achieved only partial success in the city of Tyre, and failed in the rural area. The developments in the lordship of Tyre sharply contrast with those affecting Venice's quarter in Acre. To be sure, in Acre individual Venetians suffered from increased royal taxation, which they considered illegal and a breach of their privileges (Berggötz, 1991: 179–180: Jacoby, 1997a: 168–169). However, there was no loss of state assets or revenue (Berggötz, 1991: 172–179). At first state rents and taxes must have been handled by local clerics or merchants, as presumably done in the city of Tyre. The regular arrival and especially the continuous presence of Venetian settlers in Acre, the precise boundaries of the quarter, and the absence of property-sharing with other lords, as in Tyre's rural hinterland, were decisive factors in the preservation of Venice's interests. Once Venice established direct state control over its property in the Kingdom of Jerusalem, Venice's quarter in Acre became its main base and was administered separately from its assets in the lordship of Tyre, also more efficiently. Venice's focus upon Acre is not surprising: it was the major port and market of the Kingdom of Jerusalem.

NOTES

1 Strangely, Marsilio Zorzi ascribes four villages to Guida's fief (Berggötz, 1991: 156–157), yet elsewhere mentions them as belonging to Rolando's fief (169). Berggötz (1991: 246) wrongly ascribes Mahallia to that fief.

2 The first date is implied by the correspondence between "the time of Rolando Contarini" and the reign of Fulk of Anjou (Tafel and Thomas 1856–57: I, 141). Since Rolando does not appear among the Venetian witnesses in the document of 1157 mentioned above, he must have been dead by that time.

3 In 1187 Conrad of Montferrat confirmed the grant of assets close to the Pisan *fondaco* in Tyre made by Raymond III of Tripoli when acting as regent of the kingdom in 1185–86 (Mayer, 2010: II, 863, no. 519). The phrasing implies that Pisa was already in possession of the *fondaco*.

4 Pringle's translation of the relevant passage fails to reflect Zorzi's implicit complaint. The use and meaning of the feminine *trivia* in that context (instead of neuter *trivium*) is unusual. *Trivium* generally refers to a T crossroads with three branches.

5 Berggötz (1991: 73–74) argues that the service of three knights only was justified, since it corresponds proportionally to the number of villages included in the Venetian fiefs out of the total number in the lordship of Tyre at the time of Marsilio Zorzi's tenure. However, revenue, rather than territorial extension, determined the amount of service required, as implied by the cash allocated to Vitale Pantaleo in addition to territory, noted above. This was in line with the extensive use of money fiefs by other lords in the Kingdom of Jerusalem (Prawer, 1980: 153–155).

6 Pantaleo Barbo was back in Venice by April 1198 (Lombardo and Morozzo della Rocca, 1953: 51–52, no. 45). Marsilio Zorzi wrongly ascribes to all Venetian state representatives who preceded him in the kingdom the title "bailo," which is not attested by other sources before 1214 (see below). He also uses an anachronistic vocabulary in other instances.

7 He is attested in Tyre in 1211, yet without a title (Morozzo della Rocca and Lombardo 1940: II, 69–70, no. 529). He served in high offices in Venice in the years 1227–29 and 1232–33, and as duke of Crete in 1236–38 (Berggöz, 1991: 62). Rolando *minor* was already an adult in 1221 (Favreau-Lilie, 1987: 94, no. 6). Marsilio Zorzi notes that he "nunc est," thus in the early 1240s (Berggötz, 1991: 169 line 17).

8 A proper reading of the second entry points to Conrad's time, "in tempore marchionis Montisferati, qui fuit dominus rengni (*sic*)," for the expropriation of the house, the existence of the mint, and the grant to the Genoese Ansaldo Bonvicini, who arrived with Conrad in Tyre and who in October 1187, September 1189 and April 1190 appears among the witnesses to charters issued by Conrad, in the last case as castellan of Tyre (Mayer, 2010, II, 865, no. 519, 888, no. 525, 894, no. 526; Jacoby, 1993: 189, 204–205, 216, 222, 228, 233). There is no evidence for the existence of a Venetian mint in Tyre, as claimed by several modern authors: see the generally overlooked note by Heyd (1879).

9 Zorzi's reference to the weavers is rather perplexing, since they paid a tax on a *fovea*, pit and by extension vats as in dyeworks "where they wove." The tax amounted to two *cartata*, an unexplained term. Still, Riley-Smith (1973: 84) considers this a tax on vats and Berggötz (1991: 45) a tax paid by dyers.

REFERENCES

Airaldi G e Kedar BZ (ed) (1986) *I Comuni italiani nel Regno crociato di Gerusalemme* (Collana storica di fonti e studi, diretta da Geo Pistarino, 48). Genova: Università di Genova, Istituto di medievistica.

Berggötz O (1991) *Der Bericht des Marsilio Zorzi. Codex Querini-Stampalia IV3 (1064)* (Kieler Werkstücke, Reihe C: Beiträge zur europäischen Geschichte des frühen und hohen Mittelalters, herausgegeben von Hans Eberhard Mayer, 2). Frankfurt am Main: Peter Lang.

Cessi R (ed) (1931–50) *Deliberazioni del Maggior Consiglio di Venezia*. Bologna: Nicola Zanichelli.

Edbury PW (1997) *John of Ibelin and the Kingdom of Jerusalem*. Woodbridge: Boydell Press.

Favreau-Lilie M-L (1986) Friedensversicherung und Konfliktbegrenzung: Genua, Pisa und Venedig in Akkon, ca. 1200–1224. In: Airaldi e Kedar, 429–447.

——— (1987) Die italienischen Kirchen im Heiligen Land (1098–1291). *Studi Veneziani*, N. S., 13: 15–101.

——— (1999) Der Fernhandel und die Auswanderung der Italiener ins Heilige Land. In: Stromer W (ed) *Von Venedig und die Weltwirtschaft um 1200*. Sigmaringen: Jan Thorbecke Verlag, 203–234.

Heyd W (1879) Über die angeblichen Münzprägungen der Venetianer in Accon, Tyrus und Tripolis. *Numismatische Zeitschrift* 11: 237–242.

Holt PM (1995) *Early Mamluk Diplomacy (1260–1290). Treaties of Baybars and Qalawun with Christian Rulers*. Leiden: Brill.

Imperiale di Sant'Angelo C (ed) (1936–42) *Codice diplomatico della Repubblica di Genova*. Rome: Tipografia del Senato.

Jackson P (1986) The End of Hohenstaufen Rule in Syria. *Bulletin of the Institute of Historical Research* 59: 20–36.

Jacoby D (1986a) The Kingdom of Jerusalem and the Collapse of Hohenstaufen Power in the Levant. *Dumbarton Oaks Papers*, 40: 83–94, reproduced in Jacoby (1989), no. III.

——— (1986b) A Venetian Manual of Commercial Practice from Crusader Acre. In: Airaldi e Kedar, 403–428, reproduced in Jacoby (1989), no. VII.

——— (1989) *Studies on the Crusader States and on Venetian Expansion*. Northampton: Variorum Reprints.

——— (1993) Conrad, Marquis of Montferrat, and the Kingdom of Jerusalem (1187–1192). In: Balletto L (ed) *Atti del Congresso Internazionale Dai feudi monferrini e dal Piemonte ai nuovi mondi oltre gli Oceani, Alessandria, 2–6 Aprile 1990* (Biblioteca della Società di Storia, Arte e Archeologia per le province di Alessandria e Asti, N. 27). Alessandria: Società di Storia, Arte e Archeologia, Accademia degli Immobili, 187–238, reproduced in Jacoby (1997b), no. IV.

——— (1997a) The Venetian Privileges in the Latin Kingdom of Jerusalem: Twelfth and Thirteenth-Century Interpretations and Implementation. In: Kedar BZ, Riley-Smith J, and Hiestand R (ed) *Montjoie. Studies in Crusade History in Honour of Hans Eberhard Mayer*. Aldershot: Ashgate, 155–166, reproduced in Jacoby (2005), no. V.

——— (1997b) *Trade, Commodities and Shipping in the Medieval Mediterranean*. Aldershot: Ashgate Variorum.

——— (2001) The Venetian Quarter of Constantinople from 1082 to 1261: Topographical Considerations. In: Sode C and Takács S (ed) *Novum Millennium. Studies on Byzantine History and Culture dedicated to Paul Speck*. Aldershot: Ashgate, 153–170, reproduced in Jacoby (2005), no. III.

——— (2003) New Venetian Evidence on Crusader Acre. In: Edbury P and Phillips J (ed), *The Experience of Crusading, II: Defining the Crusader Kingdom*. Cambridge: Cambridge University Press, 240–256, reproduced in Jacoby (2014), no. IV.

——— (2005) *Commercial Exchange Across the Mediterranean: Byzantium, the Crusader Levant, Egypt and Italy*. Aldershot: Ashgate Variorum.

———— (2014) *Travellers, Merchants and Settlers across the Mediterranean, Eleventh-Fourteenth Centuries*. Farnham: Ashgate Variorum.

———— (2015) The Expansion of Venetian Government in the Eastern Mediterranean until the Late Thirteenth Century. In: Ortalli G, Schmitt OJ, Orlando E (ed) *Il* Commonwealth *veneziano tra 1204 e la fine della Repubblica. Identità e peculiarità*. Venezia: Istituto Veneto di Scienze, Lettere ed Arti, 73–106.

John of Ibelin (2003) *Le Livre des Assises*, ed. Edbury PW. Leiden-Boston: Brill.

Kohler Ch (ed) (1899) Chartes de l'abbaye den Notre-Dame de la vallée de Josaphat en Terre-Sainte, 1108–1291. *Revue de l'Orient Latin* 7: 108–222.

Kretschmayr H (1905–34) *Geschichte von Venedig*. Gotha-Stuttgart: FA Perthes.

Lombardo A and Morozzo della Rocca R (ed) (1953) *Nuovi documenti del commercio veneto dei sec. XI-XIII*. Venezia: Deputazione di Storia Patria per le Venezie.

Madia E (ed) (1999) *I Libri Iurium della Repubblica di Genova, I/5* (Fonti per la storia della Liguria, XII; Pubblicazioni degli Archivi di Stato, Fonti XXIX). Genova: Società Ligure di Storia Patria.

Mayer HE (ed) (2010) *Die Urkunden der lateinischen Könige von Jerusalem* (Monumenta Germaniae Historica, Diplomata regum latinorum hierosolymitanorum). Hannover: Hahnnsche Buchhandlung.

Morozzo della Rocca R and Lombardo A (ed) (1940) *Documenti del commercio veneziano nei secoli XI-XIII*. Torino: Editrice Libraria Italiana.

Pozza M (ed) (1994) *Gli atti originali della cancelleria veneziana, I, (1090–1198)*. Venice: Il Cardo.

Prawer J (1980) *Crusader Institutions*. Oxford: Clarendon Press.

Pringle D (1993–2009) *The Churches of the Crusader Kingdom of Jerusalem. A Corpus*. Cambridge: Cambridge University Press.

Riley-Smith J (1973) *The Feudal Nobility and the Kingdom of Jerusalem, 1174–1277*. London: Archon Books.

Rösch G. (1989) *Der venezianische Adel bis zur Schliessung des Grossen Rats. Zur Genese einer Führungsschicht* (Kieler Historischen Studien, Band 33). Sigmaringen: Jan Thorbecke Verlag.

Runciman S (1952–54) *A History of the Crusades*. Cambridge: Cambridge University Press.

Tafel GLF and Thomas GM (ed) (1856–57) *Urkunden zur älteren Handels- und Staatsgeschichte der Republik Venedig*. Vienna: Kaiserliche Akademie der Wissenschaften.

CHAPTER TWELVE

THE ANTIOCHENE WAR OF SUCCESSION

———•◆•———

Jochen Burgtorf

Domestic abuse, torture-induced suicide, death by poison, murder in the cathedral, and excommunication: the Antiochene war of succession features many of the ingredients popularly associated with the Middle Ages, as well as some of the staples of warfare, such as sieges, campaigns of devastation, and even a few minor battles. Fought between 1201 and 1219 to determine the succession to the throne of the principality of Antioch, the northernmost Syrian crusader state, after the death of its ruler, Prince Bohemond III, this conflict pitched Antioch's northern neighbor, King Leo of Cilician Armenia, against Antioch's southern neighbor, Count Bohemond IV of Tripoli. For the first decade of the war, Leo represented the rights of a minor, his great-nephew Raymond-Roupen, who was also the late prince's grandson from the marriage of his oldest, but also deceased son Raymond to Leo's niece Alice, thereby stressing the Antiochene custom of primogeniture and an existing agreement between Leo and Bohemond III. Meanwhile, emphasizing the latter's final wishes and the alleged will of the people, Bohemond of Tripoli, Bohemond III's younger son, sought the succession for himself. The war lasted until 1219, the year Bohemond of Tripoli managed to seize Antioch permanently for himself, Leo died, and Raymond-Roupen lost the support of both Antiochenes and Armenians. The war's repercussions, however, were felt well into the second half of the thirteenth century.

What makes the Antiochene war relevant to the history of the "Crusader World" is the range and diversity of its direct and indirect participants. At one time or another, and to varying degrees of intensity, this conflict involved the Seljuks of Anatolia to the north and west of the main theaters of war; the Ayyubids of Aleppo, Hamah, Homs, and Damascus to the east; the Assassins (Ismailis) to the south-east; the pope and the papal legates of the Fourth and Fifth Crusades; the Latin empire of Constantinople and the Byzantine empire of Nicaea; the Latin kingdoms of Jerusalem and Cyprus; the military religious orders of the Templars, Hospitallers, and Teutonic Knights; the Italian cities of Genoa, Pisa, and Venice; and the members and clergy of the various Christian denominations of Antioch and Armenia, particularly the Greek Orthodox, the Armenians, and the Latins (Roman Catholics).

The primary sources available for the study of this war include a number of charters, and while the archives of the rulers of Antioch, Tripoli, and Armenia have not survived, the documents preserved by Hospitallers and Teutonic Knights shed some light on the events. It is here, however, that the loss of the Templars' Eastern archives is most acutely felt, because the conflict repeatedly focused on Baghras (Gaston), a castle situated north-east of Antioch and claimed by the order but held by the Armenians for much of the war. There are also letters, especially the correspondence between Leo and Pope Innocent III, as well as the 1204 report of the papal legates; travel accounts, for example, that of Wilbrand of Oldenburg, a canon of Hildesheim; the Old French continuations of the chronicle of William of Tyre; the "chronography" of the Syriac Orthodox (Jacobite) Gregory Bar Hebraeus; several Armenian texts, including the "history" of Sempad the Constable, the brother of King Hethoum; the Arabic chronicle of Ibn al-Athir; and some archaeological evidence, for example, at Antioch and Baghras. In scholarly treatments of the crusades, the Antiochene war usually features as a side show of the Fourth and Fifth Crusades, while historians of the crusader states have tended to focus more on the twelfth rather than the thirteenth century. Researchers can, however, gather much from the analysis of the pre-war Antiochene affairs by Hans Eberhard Mayer (1993), the still invaluable reconstruction of the war by Claude Cahen (1940), and the recent study of the Armenian side of the story by Claude Mutafian (2012). This chapter first outlines the history of the region prior to the death of Prince Bohemond III. It then discusses the military history of the war itself, addresses the key legal debates, and lastly turns to the question of real and imagined alliances.

ROADS TO WAR

In the second half of the eleventh century, Antioch was one of the Byzantine Empire's most important frontier duchies. Its existence, however, was challenged by several demographic and military developments. Due to the Seljuks' incursions from the east, groups of Armenians, particularly the rival Roupenid and Hethoumid clans, moved into Cilicia just north of Antioch, where they established an Armenian principality with the capital in Sis, and a Byzantine general of Armenian background even briefly became duke of Antioch (1078). Traveling on the Armenians' heels, the Seljuks migrated into Anatolia, founded the sultanate of Rum, and captured Antioch (1084). When the First Crusade arrived in the region, the Byzantine emperor expected that Antioch, once retaken from the Seljuks, would revert to his control. Thus, the formation of the crusader principality of Antioch (1098) was countered by several successful imperial campaigns to assert Byzantine overlordship. However, the Byzantines' loss to the Seljuks at the battle of Myriocephalum in Anatolia (1176) effectively ended their sway over Cilicia and northern Syria. Consequently, Antioch found itself surrounded by the increasingly independent principality of Armenia to the north; Ayyubid-controlled Aleppo, Hamah, and Homs to the east; the territory of the Assassins to the south-east; and the crusader county of Tripoli, closely allied with the Latin kingdom of Jerusalem, to the south. At Antioch's northern border, the Templars held a number of castles, most notably Baghras, and at the principality's southern border the Hospitallers were building a strong presence around the castle of Margat (Nersessian 1969; Boase 1978; Riley-Smith 1978).

The dominant figure in Antioch at this time was Prince Bohemond III. Born around 1148, he had succeeded to the throne upon reaching legal age around 1163, and it appears that Prince Thoros of Armenia assisted with his succession, which had been blocked by Bohemond's own mother Constance. From his first marriage to Orgueilleuse of Harem, an Antiochene noblewoman, Bohemond III had two sons, Raymond (born 1169) and Bohemond IV (born 1171). Around 1177, he married Theodora Comnena, the niece of the Byzantine emperor Manuel Comnenus who had already wed Bohemond III's sister Mary. While this Antiochene–Byzantine rapprochement caused considerable discomfort in Armenia and the kingdom of Jerusalem, it was not to last: following Manuel's death in 1180, Bohemond separated from his Byzantine wife, which may have hastened the downfall of his own sister in Constantinople, to marry Sibyl, an Antiochene noblewoman, whose reputation ranged from spying for Saladin to being a whore and sorceress. Those Antiochene nobles who opposed the match found refuge at the court of Prince Roupen III of Armenia, which soured the relationship between Bohemond and Roupen. Thus, in 1185, when Roupen's Armenian rivals, the Hethoumids, turned to Bohemond for help, the latter assisted them by detaining Roupen during a visit to Antioch, demanding and receiving an oath of fealty from him, which made Armenia a vassal of Antioch, and collecting a ransom, including territorial concessions, for his release (Hiestand 1993; Mayer 1993: 45–65; Mutafian 2012, 1: 89; but see also Rüdt de Collenberg 1983; Hodgson 2011). It must be noted that the Normans had considerable experience with forcing their "guests" to swear oaths of this kind: William of Normandy had required Harold Godwinson to do so, an event famously recorded on the Bayeux Tapestry; however, the shame associated with Roupen's kidnapping of 1185 would long be remembered by the Armenians.

After the battle of Hattin (1187), Count Raymond III of Tripoli, who did not have any children of his own, named his godson Raymond of Antioch, Bohemond III's oldest son, as his successor in Tripoli. However, Raymond's father had other plans and sent his younger son Bohemond IV instead, so that, prior to his death that same year, the ailing count of Tripoli made his nobles swear fealty to Bohemond IV. Yet, the charter evidence suggests that, at least for a few years, Raymond of Antioch was considered a titular count of Tripoli (Mayer 1993: 133–134, 184–202). To secure his legacy in Tripoli, Bohemond IV, within a few years, married Plaisance Embriaco, a Tripolitan noblewoman from the Genoese family of the lords of Jubayl (Gibelet), who bore him several children, among them Raymond, a future bailli of Antioch, Bohemond V, and Philip. Meanwhile, Roupen III had retired to a monastery and subsequently died (1187), whereupon his brother Leo (born around 1150) assumed the regency for his brother's daughters, Alice and Philippa, but eventually sidelined them. He married Alice to an Armenian noble, Hethoum of Sason, and pursued a foreign connection for himself by wedding Isabel, the niece of Bohemond III's third wife Sibyl. In 1188, Leo achieved military successes against the Seljuks, and Bohemond III obtained a truce agreement from Saladin, making Armenia and Antioch the beacons of Christendom in southern Asia Minor and northern Syria. (Hardwicke 1969; Nersessian 1969; Mutafian 2012, 1: 96).

At this time, with both reaching their early forties, Leo and Bohemond III appear to have developed royal ambitions, perhaps because of their position of relative strength, the dynastic weakness of the kingdom of Jerusalem, and the soon-to-arrive Third Crusade's cast of crowned rulers. As early as 1187, Bohemond had offered to submit Antioch to the overlordship of his Italo-Norman relative, King William II of Sicily, in exchange for Sicilian troops to be sent to the aid of the crusader states. This was likely an attempt to extricate Antioch from subordination to any other political entity in the eastern Mediterranean, and it may not be a coincidence that Bohemond's son from his third marriage was also named "William." A few years later, in 1190, Bohemond rendered hommage for his principality to Duke Frederick VI of Swabia, the son of the late Western Emperor Frederick Barbarossa. This, too, was not a random act: on his way to the East, Duke Frederick had become engaged to Constance of Hungary, the daughter of Bohemond III's step-sister Agnes, and he was the younger brother of the future emperor Henry VI who, in turn, had married into the royal house of Sicily (Hiestand 1993; Mayer 1993: 135). Bohemond's overtures toward these western rulers came to naught, but they must have made Leo nervous. In 1191, Leo seized the Templar castle of Baghras, the northern gateway to the Antiochene plain, which had been abandoned by Saladin's troops after a three-year occupation. Bohemond responded by entering into a new truce agreement with Saladin (1192) that did not include his Armenian vassal. By 1193, a conspiracy was underway that involved Leo, as well as Bohemond's third wife Sibyl, ostensibly concerned about the rights of her son William. Thus, when Bohemond followed Leo's invitation to come to Baghras to discuss the terms for the return of the castle to Antioch or the Templars, he was seized and deported to Sis (1194), an unmistakable retaliation for Bohemond's previous kidnapping of Leo's brother Roupen III (Mutafian 2012, 1: 96).

In exchange for Bohemond's release, Leo initially demanded Antioch, and he sent Hethoum of Sason, the husband of his niece Alice, to effect the surrender. However, the Greek Orthodox population of Antioch opposed the idea of an Armenian ruler, as did the principality's Italian communities, who may have feared for their existing privileges (Röhricht 1893: 113, 124, 192). To ensure that their government would continue to operate, the Antiochenes formed a commune and installed Bohemond's oldest son Raymond as ruler. Eventually, to obtain his freedom, Bohemond had to accept Armenia's independence from Antioch, forfeit Baghras, and agree to the wedding of his son Raymond to Leo's recently widowed niece Alice (1195) with the understanding that a male heir from this union would rule over both Armenia and Antioch. Alice's late husband, Hethoum of Sason, had died shortly after his failed attempt to take possession of Antioch, and it takes little imagination to think that Leo must have played a part in his convenient demise. Nothing further was heard of Sibyl, Bohemond III's third wife, or her son William; given her role in the conspiracy to kidnap her own husband, one may assume that she stayed in Armenia; after all, her niece Isabel was still married to Leo (Mayer 1993: 183; Mutafian 2012, 1: 96).

Having dealt with Antioch, Leo turned his attention to obtaining a royal crown, which had to come either from the pope or from an emperor. The pope's condition, namely the union between the Armenian Church and the Roman Church, required the Armenian clergy's consent, which was slow in coming. Not surprisingly, the Byzantine emperor was not approached in the matter due to his historical claim to the region. Only the Western emperor's respective expectations, namely to be recognized as the overlord of the king of Armenia, seemed instantly acceptable. In 1197, Aimery of Lusignan had been crowned king of Cyprus by representatives of the Western emperor, and Leo's coronation as king of Cilician Armenia with insignia sent by the Western emperor followed in 1198. Now only Antioch remained without a royal crown, but Antioch had other problems. In 1197, Bohemond III's oldest son Raymond had died while his wife, Leo's niece Alice, was pregnant. Their child, Raymond-Roupen, born shortly after his father's death, was the heir apparent to the principality of Antioch, yet Bohemond sent the newborn and his mother to Armenia, perhaps to ensure their safety, but more likely to suggest that Raymond-Roupen's claim to Antioch would not be honored. As if to emphasize this, Bohemond III's younger son, Bohemond IV of Tripoli, came to Antioch to stage what looked like a coup, but may have had his father's tacit approval (1198/1199). As Bohemond III's surviving, albeit younger son, Bohemond IV asked for and received the Antiochene commune's acknowledgment of his claim to the principality, thereby countering Raymond-Roupen's right of primogeniture with the commune's popular mandate bestowed on him. By the time Leo arrived in Antioch to restore Bohemond III's rule, Bohemond IV had returned to Tripoli, and it is noteworthy that the latter, in charters issued in 1199, referred to himself as the 'son of Prince Bohemond of Antioch and by the grace of God count of Tripoli', thereby stressing his Antiochene lineage. Leo, meanwhile, set up a military presence at Baghras and reported the recent developments to the new pope, Innocent III, who responded by inquiring about the status of the anticipated Church union, promising an investigation led by papal legates, and encouraging a focus on fighting the Muslims (Maleczek 1988: 160–163; Mayer 1993: 201; Mutafian 2012, 1: 97–99).

MILITARY CAMPAIGNS

Bohemond III died in April 1201. Bohemond IV had been alerted of his father's imminent passing and managed to arrive in Antioch just in time for the funeral. Presenting himself as the heir in accordance with his father's final wishes, he obtained the commune's renewed oath of allegiance; however, a considerable number of Antiochene nobles, claiming to be bound by feudal law to uphold the rights of Raymond-Roupen, chose exile in Armenia (Cahen 1940: 594–595; Richard 1985: 202). The Antiochene war was about to begin, and it is to its military history that we now turn. In hindsight, it is clear that neither side had the resources to field an army that was substantial enought to annihilate the enemy, permanently garrison Antioch, secure its surrounding plain, and simultaneously keep that army's own homeland, namely Armenia or Tripoli, safe from internal and external dangers. To start with this last point, Armenia was permanently threatened by the Seljuks of Anatolia in the north and the Ayyubids of Aleppo in the east, and its Roupenid king also had to stay alert with regard to his inner-Armenian rivals, the Hethoumids. Tripoli, meanwhile, had its own share of rebellious nobles, and one of its count's priorities, if he ever wanted to rule over both Tripoli and Antioch, had to be the restoration of the mainland connection between the two crusader states, which had been severed by Saladin's conquests and was currently controlled by the Ayyubids of Hamah and Homs. Thus, one of the reasons why the Antiochene war lasted as long as it did was because both sides were fighting several wars at the same time. That Leo was twenty years older than Bohemond IV also appears to have had an interesting effect: while Leo launched military campaigns on an almost annual basis, Bohemond stalled whenever possible, perhaps figuring that time was on his side.

Shortly after Bohemond IV's Antiochene takeover in the spring of 1201, Leo invaded the principality to press the claim of his great-nephew Raymond-Roupen, and laid siege to the capital. Thereupon Bohemond called on Az-Zahir Ghazi, the Ayyubid ruler of Aleppo, as well as Rukn ad-Din Suleiman, the Seljuk sultan of Anatolia, who responded with invasions of Armenia from the east and the north, thereby forcing Leo to abandon the siege of Antioch and return to the defense of his homeland. In the process, Leo was able to intercept some of Bohemond's envoys to the Seljuks and promptly informed the pope of his opponent's collusion with the Muslims. In 1202, some participants of the Fourth Crusade traveled directly to the East, rather than assembling at Venice. Since they were comparatively few, King Aimery of Cyprus and (by now also) Jerusalem refused to break the existing truce with the Muslims, which is why these crusaders temporarily involved themselves in the Antiochene war: some joined Leo in his next campaign against Antioch, while others rode with Bohemond in an attack against his Ayyubid neighbors. After a campaign of devastation through the Antiochene plain in the spring of 1203, Leo almost prevailed in the fall of that same year. In November, a small Armenian contingent managed to enter Antioch by night, while Bohemond was absent, and, to avoid an all-out battle, asked the city's Latin Patriarch Peter of Angoulême to help them negotiate with the commune. However, the Antiochene Templar garrison drove the Armenians out of the city, and the commune sent carrier pigeons with calls for help to Aleppo, whose ruler Az-Zahir Ghazi immediately dispatched troops to invade Armenia; once again, Leo had to lift the siege (Cahen 1940: 600–605; Lock 2006: 83–85).

Bohemond had been away from Antioch because trouble had been brewing in Tripoli. One of his vassals, Lord Renard of Nephin, had married Isabel, the daughter and heiress of Akkar (Gibelacar), without Bohemond's consent. The Tripolitan court of barons sided with Bohemond, but Renard refused to comply, wherefore the court authorized Bohemond to seize Renard's possessions. Renard proceeded to ravage the countryside around Tripoli, and in 1204 Bohemond even lost an eye in a battle against this rebellious baron, earning him the nickname 'the one-eyed'. Renard was enjoying the support of King Aimery and some barons in the kingdom of Jerusalem who were troubled by Bohemond's 'pretensions to autonomy' (Hardwicke 1969: 534), but King Aimery's death in 1205 changed things, because the new regent, John of Ibelin, sided with Bohemond against Renard: the latter was forced to surrender his fiefs and retire to Cyprus, allowing Bohemond to refocus on Antioch. In the background of all this, the Hospitallers of Margat were fighting to gain control over Latakia, part of the mainland connection between Tripoli and Antioch, but this was based on their right to wage their own wars rather than a desire to function as Bohemond's agents (Richard 1985: 216; Lock 2006: 85–87; Burgtorf 2013: 229).

That Bohemond did not lose Antioch to Leo while dealing with Renard of Nephin was due to the simultaneous altercations between Leo and Az-Zahir Ghazi. In addition to Baghras, Leo had occupied several other fortresses in the Amanus mountains, thus not only blocking the northern access to the plain of Antioch, but also threatening Aleppo's western border. In 1205/1206, the two sides came to blows, with Az-Zahir Ghazi receiving Antiochene support and, in turn, supporting Antioch whenever Leo was turning against the city. On Christmas Day of 1205, Leo attacked Darbsak (Trapessac), a castle just north of Baghras and held by the Ayyubids of Aleppo, but was defeated in the ensuing battle and had to escape through a snowstorm that made pursuit impossible. By the summer of 1206, Leo was suing for peace and eventually gained an eight-year truce according to which he was expected to refrain from attacks against Antioch. It appears that Leo followed the letter, but not the spirit of this agreement, as it was probably no coincidence that opposition against Bohemond now arose inside Antioch, thus expanding the "foreign" war by adding a "civil" war. In 1207/1208, Leo's main ally in Antioch, the Latin Patriarch Peter of Angoulême, brought some of the exiled nobles back from Armenia, staged an uprising, replaced the existing communal authorities with new ones, and forced Bohemond to seek refuge in the citadel. However, Bohemond managed to gather his troops, returned into the city, defeated the rebels, and incarcerated the patriarch. When the latter refused to declare Bohemond the legitimate ruler of Antioch, he was tortured by drink deprivation, whereupon he consumed the oil of his lamp and died (Cahen 1940: 609–613; Nersessian 1969: 649).

Since it was clear that Leo was not letting up on his efforts to gain Antioch, despite his existing truce with Aleppo, and, in 1208, even led a new campaign of devastation through the Antiochene plain, Bohemond called on Kaykhusraw, the Seljuk sultan of Rum, who, in 1208/1209, attacked Armenia from the north. Leo had to seek terms, which included the restoration of Baghras to the Templars and the ceasing of hostilities toward Antioch, neither of which the Armenian king intended to do. While Leo was dealing with the Seljuks, Bohemond had to face his Ayyubid neighbors yet again: the Hospitallers' various campaigns, launched from their castles at Margat and Krak des Chevaliers against Hamah, Homs, and Latakia, had enraged Al-Adil, the sultan of Damascus, who held Bohemond responsible for the order's actions, led a campaign against Tripoli in 1208/1209, and forced Bohemond to ransom himself and his city (Cahen 1940: 614–615; Mutafian 2012, 1: 105–109). Leo's refusal to surrender Baghras to the Templars reached all new heights in 1211, when he attacked one of the order's convoys that was transporting provisions to northern Syria. The Templar master William of Chartres, who happened to be traveling with the convoy, was injured, which seriously upset Pope Innocent III and caused him to call on John of Brienne, the king of Jerusalem, to support a retaliatory expedition against Leo. Leo does not seem to have been too impressed with this and, in 1212, sent his great-nephew Raymond-Roupen, who was just about to reach legal age and had been crowned Leo's heir the previous year, on yet another campaign of devastation through the Antiochene plain (Cahen 1940: 616–619; Bulst-Thiele 1974: 164). Meanwhile, Bohemond remained busy in his county of Tripoli, where, in 1213, his eighteen-year-old firstborn son Raymond, bailli of Antioch, had been murdered by Assassins while visiting the cathedral of Tartus (Tortosa). The following year, to avenge his son's death, Bohemond launched a campaign against the Assassins who, in turn, called on Az-Zahir Ghazi of Aleppo for help. By that time, the Ayyubids of Aleppo had set aside their long-standing differences with the Ayyubids of Damascus and therefore summoned the latter to their aid, whereupon Bohemond abandoned his campaign, sent an apology to his old ally in Aleppo, and focused his attention on keeping Tripoli safe (Riley-Smith 1967: 158; Hardwicke 1969: 537–538; Major 2001: 65).

Exhausted from almost annual campaigns of devastation against the surrounding countryside and feeling abandoned by Bohemond, the Antiochene may have been ready to give Armenian rule a try. In early 1216, Armenian troops swarmed into the city by night and occupied all strategic points, so that Antioch changed hands without bloodshed. In February 1216, Leo and Raymond-Roupen entered the city. The latter was ordained as prince of Antioch by the Latin Patriarch Peter II of Ivrea, and he received oaths of allegiance from the nobles and the leaders of the commune. Concluding that no assistance would be forthcoming, Bohemond's Antiochene garrison surrendered the citadel, which prompted Bohemond to abandon his intended relief expedition. Now that the Armenians were in control of Antioch, Leo returned Baghras to the Templars and dispatched embassies of goodwill to Aleppo and Damascus. The Anatolian Seljuks, however, took Leo's triumph in Antioch as a sign that it was time for an all-out war against Armenia. This must have shifted Leo's attention immediately back to Armenia, and perhaps he called on Raymond-Roupen, the new prince of Antioch, to assist him against the Seljuks. By 1217, the relationship between Leo and Raymond-Roupen had deteriorated to the point that the latter intended to detain his great-uncle. Leo, however, was warned by the Templars who, now that Baghras had been returned to them, no longer held a grudge against the Armenian king, and Leo was able to escape to Armenia to deal with the Seljuk invasion (Cahen 1940: 621–623; Hardwicke 1969: 538; Mutafian 2012, 1: 108–109).

Without his great-uncle's backing, Raymond-Roupen's days in Antioch were numbered. While he was able, in 1218, to make good on a promise to help the Hospitallers occupy Jableh (Gabula), situated just south of Latakia, but not with lasting success, the

Antiochene war had left the principality impoverished, and no medieval prince without resources was ever able to remain in power for long. Bohemond had initially lacked the troops to fight back and therefore participated in the Fifth Crusade, but by 1219 his supporters in Antioch were ready to orchestrate his comeback. As Bohemond entered the city, it was Raymond-Roupen's turn to flee to the citadel, which he entrusted to the Hospitallers, before escaping to Armenia to call on his great-uncle for help. Leo, however, was dying and, in the interim, had made plans for his legacy that no longer involved his great-nephew. Thus, with Raymond-Roupen's ouster from Antioch, Bohemond's restoration to power, and Leo's death in May 1219, the Antiochene war came to a rather unspectacular end. Few may have noticed this, though, because it was immediately followed by an Armenian postlude. At first, Raymond-Roupen's prospects to gain the Armenian throne appeared promising: he had the support of his mother Alice, the daughter of the late Roupen III, of some Armenian nobles, of the pope and his Fifth Crusade legate Pelagius, and, within their territorial spheres of interest, of the Hospitallers who helped him with the occupation of Tarsus. However, Constantine of Barberon, a member of the Armenian Hethoumid clan and regent for the late Leo's infant daughter and heiress Isabel (Zabel), took swift action: he captured Tarsus after a three-month siege, and by 1221/1222 Raymond-Roupen was spending the final days of his life in an Armenian prison; he was in his mid-twenties. In an ironic twist of fate, the Armenians now turned to Bohemond to secure a husband for young Isabel. He offered his younger son Philip, the two were married in 1222, and Philip initially even made a good impression by repelling a Seljuk attack. However, Philip's contempt for the Armenians soon got the better of him, which is why, in 1224, a group of Armenian nobles kidnapped and poisoned him. Bohemond planned to avenge his son; however, in another ironic twist of fate, the Armenians were able to forestall his military intervention by forging an alliance with his own former allies, the Ayyubids of Aleppo, who, now that Bohemond was established in both Tripoli and Antioch, were no longer interested in supporting him and even joined the Armenians in an unsuccessful attack against Baghras (1226). Relations between Antioch–Tripoli and Armenia remained frosty well beyond Bohemond IV's death (1233), and the Antiochene (and Armenian) war of succession left northern Syria substantially weakened (Riley-Smith 1967: 159; Hardwicke 1969: 540–541; Mutafian 2012, 1: 115–117).

LEGAL DEBATES

Military force was not the only means employed to determine the Antiochene succession. Therefore, as we leave the battlefield, we enter the courtroom and, thus, the legal debates pertaining to this war. While the Armenians emphasized the Antiochene custom of primogeniture and the 1195 agreement between Leo and Bohemond III, the Tripolitans argued that all this was overruled by the Antiochene commune's acknowledgment of Bohemond IV's claim, represented by the more recent oaths of allegiance sworn to him in 1198 and 1201, which amounted to a popular mandate based on Bohemond III's final wishes. However, could new realities really invalidate existing practices and arrangements? Who was to judge, and what if the opposing parties could not agree on a judge?

It is this last question that set Leo and Bohemond IV on a collision course right from the start. Initially, Leo appeared confident that the vision of a union between the Armenian Church and the Roman Church, as well as the prospect of the Armenian king championing a crusade, would secure the pontiff's support; and, after all, the pope had the power to send legates, excommunicate evildoers, and place entire territories under the interdict. Yet, Leo seems to have overlooked several critical points. His opponent Bohemond regarded the whole succession affair as a dispute under feudal law, was prepared to revive Antioch's status as a territory under imperial suzerainty, and did not recognize the pope and his legates as appropriate arbiters. Second, Leo's use of Baghras as a pawn eventually had to antagonize the pope, because the Templars claimed that they owned Baghras, apparently based on an Antiochene donation, and that their right to defend it had been confirmed by Pope Alexander III (reigned 1159–81); they were an exempt order of the Church under the pope's protection; and therefore any attack on their property was an attack on the Church. Third, Leo's argument that he was holding Baghras by right of recent conquest, which, to him, set aside the Templars' older claim, since they had failed to protect the castle against the Muslims, amounted to an admission that new realities could indeed invalidate existing practices and arrangements. Fourth, the Greek Orthodox commune of Antioch was suspicious of any outsider, especially a Roman Catholic legate, to intervene in their affairs; likewise, Antioch's patriarch, be he Latin or Greek, was historically averse to papal or legatine claims of jurisdiction. Lastly, excommunication as a means of coercion had become so overused that those hit by it often felt at liberty to ignore it for years, which is exactly what Bohemond IV, much like the Hohenstaufen Frederick II a few years later, was prepared to do (Lawrence 1978: 42; Maleczek 1988: 160–163; Mutafian 2012, 1: 103–104).

In 1198/1199, when Leo alerted Pope Innocent III of the impending Antiochene succession crisis, the pontiff assured him that he would be sending legates. The first legate to arrive, in the fall of 1202, was Soffred Gaetani of Pisa, cardinal priest of St. Praxedis; he was followed by his colleague, Peter Capuano of Amalfi, cardinal priest of St. Marcellus, who made the trip to the East in the late spring of 1203. Soffred's attempt to schedule negotiations hit its first roadblock when Bohemond stated that he was not allowed to meet with the papal legate, because he had been excommunicated by the patriarchs of Jerusalem and Antioch for his disagreement with the Hospitallers over certain incomes in the region of Krak des Chevaliers. When Soffred traveled to Tripoli to broker a settlement between Bohemond and the Hospitallers, the count insisted that the legate's name not be mentioned in the respective agreement, thus indicating that he was not willing to recognize the papal legate as an arbiter. Upon Soffred's arrival in Antioch in 1203, Leo's envoys told him that both the Church union and the Armenian support for the crusade would only be forthcoming once the Antiochene succession would be resolved in Leo's favor. However, Antioch's predominantly Greek Orthodox commune was not interested in a Church union that would give the Armenians any additional legal standing; the city's Latin patriarch Peter of Angoulême categorically opposed Bohemond with whom he had had a contentious relationship ever since his tenure as bishop of Tripoli; and Bohemond's representatives insisted that the Antiochene succession was entirely a matter of feudal law and not under papal or legatine jurisdiction. Where Soffred had not been able to make any headway, his colleague Peter Capuano was hoping to succeed, and things even seemed to be off to a good start when he and representatives of the Armenian clergy were finally able to celebrate the Church union. Yet, during his stay in Antioch in 1203/1204, Peter quickly found that neither side was willing to budge: Leo was unwilling to surrender the Templar castle of Baghras from where he was terrorizing the Antiochene plain, and Bohemond was unwilling to remove his troops from Antioch and, thus, allow the Armenians to move in. Peter now focused on Baghras, perhaps speculating that returning the castle to the Templars would create a much-needed buffer between Antioch and Armenia.

He summoned Leo three times, and when the latter declined to appear, excommunicated him and placed Armenia under the interdict, sentences that the Armenian clergy refused to publicize. Frustrated with this whole new level of legal deadlock, Leo and the legates sent separate reports to Rome, where the pope must have realized that Leo was going to be no help with the crusade for the time being (Hiestand 1972: 323–354; Maleczek 1988: 164–167; Jamil and Johns 2003: 167).

In the spring of 1204, as a consequence of the crusade, Baldwin of Flanders had become the Latin emperor of Constantinople. When his wife, Mary of Champagne, stopped in Acre that same year on her way from Europe to Constantinople, Bohemond IV seized the opportunity to pay hommage to her for Antioch, thus reviving the principality's status as a territory under imperial suzerainty and sending a clear message to Leo, the pope, and the legates that any legal proceedings between Tripoli and Armenia pertaining to Antioch would have to involve the Latin emperor as Antioch's overlord and, by implication, the Western emperor as Armenia's overlord. With this, the case was placed well outside of the current legates' legal reach (Cahen 1940: 606; Hardwicke 1969: 535). Nonetheless, in 1205/1206, Innocent III asked Peter Capuano to return to the East, where the latter quickly became embroiled in the internal affairs of the Antiochene clergy. He and the Latin patriarch Peter of Angoulême sparred over who had the right to appoint the successor to the Antiochene archdeaconate which had recently become vacant, and when the city's cathedral chapter appealed to Rome, the legate responded with suspension and excommunication. While Peter of Angoulême was still appealing the legate's sentence, Bohemond seized the opportunity to elevate a Greek Orthodox, Symeon, to Antioch's patriarchal throne. Soon thereafter, however, the pope reversed the legate's sentence, and Peter of Angoulême used his restored patriarchal powers to excommunicate Symeon, Bohemond, and their supporters, and placed Antioch under the interdict, which was not really effective because the Antiochene commune allowed all excommunicated Latin Christians to attend Greek Orthodox services. The breaking point was reached in 1207/1208, when the Latin patriarch conspired with Leo to overthrow Bohemond. As we have already seen, the coup failed and led to Peter of Angoulême's incarceration and death. Thus, Bohemond had demonstrated that, while he was willing to drag legal proceedings out for years, he would act swiftly, should his legal opponents decide to resort to arms (Hardwicke 1969: 535; Richard 1985: 230, 234; Jamil and Johns 2003: 167).

Innocent III now asked Patriarch Albert of Jerusalem to publicize Bohemond's excommunication and oversee the election of a new Latin patriarch in Antioch, which led to the elevation of Peter II of Ivrea in 1208/1209, but it was not until 1212/1213 that the latter was able to push Symeon out of the city (Jamil and Johns 2003: 168). As it turns out, Peter of Angoulême was not to remain the only one whose patience had run short with regard to drawn-out legal debates. In the dispute over the ownership of Baghras, the pope and his legates had consistently refused to back Leo, leading the Armenian king to his above-mentioned 1211 attack on the Templar convoy in northern Syria. If he had hoped, though, that the use of arms would improve his legal standing, Leo did not know Innocent III very well. The pope responded by calling on all the clergy in Syria and Cyprus to publish the sentence of excommunication that had been hanging over Leo's head ever since Peter Capuano had first uttered it in 1204. However, Leo had yet another legal card to play: he now called into question the Church union, expelled the Latin clergy from his kingdom, installed Armenians and in some cases even Greeks in their places, and received Symeon, the Greek Orthodox patriarch of Antioch, who had been driven into exile by Peter II, at his court. In February 1213, Innocent III finally found Leo's (then) soft spot, when he threatened to extend the apostolic sentences, so far only leveled against Leo himself, to his grand-nephew Raymond-Roupen. Leo now quickly signaled his willingness to negotiate, and the pope, for his part, instructed the patriarch of Jerusalem to lift Leo's excommunication. This latest development has to be seen in the context of Innocent III's plans for the immediate future, which required peace among the Christians of the East, for, in April 1213, the pontiff issued the bull 'Quia maior,' thereby calling for a new crusade (Cahen 1940: 616–619; Claverie 2005, 1: 43).

Unlike his predecessors, Pelagius Galvani, cardinal bishop of Albano and legate of the Fifth Crusade, largely stayed out of the legal debates pertaining to the Antiochene succession, perhaps because he had himself been a contender for Antioch's patriarchal throne after the death of Peter II in 1217. In 1219, when Raymond-Roupen was ousted from Antioch and not welcomed as his great-uncle's successor in Armenia, he turned to Pelagius for help. However, the contingent that the legate sent to his aid from Damietta via Cyprus was not able to reach him in time. Raymond-Roupen was captured and incarcerated by his Hethoumid opponents, and died shortly thereafter. Meanwhile, Pelagius did have to deal with some of the legal complications caused by the Antiochene war. In 1221, he divided Jableh, part of the mainland connection between Tripoli and Antioch, between Templars and Hospitallers; the former argued that it had been given to them by Bohemond IV, while the latter stated that it had been donated to them by Raymond-Roupen. It was, however, actually held by the Muslims, so the whole affair was a case of 'shadow boxing' (Mayer 1993: 203). Pelagius's Solomonic judgment created a 'terra partitioni' in the region that kept both orders in arbitration well into the 1260s. As for the legal status of the two main antagonists, Leo's excommunication, as we have seen, had been lifted in 1213; Bohemond IV, however, would be excommunicated several more times, but, perhaps the ultimate evidence that he was indeed 'one of the great Syrian jurists' (Hardwicke 1969: 549), he did manage to have the sentence lifted just before his death in 1233 (Riley-Smith 1967: 161; Burgtorf 2008: 489–490; Mutafian 2012, 1: 109).

REAL AND IMAGINED ALLIANCES

At first glance, the Antiochene war was a conflict between Armenians and Tripolitans, and it involved Antiochenes on both sides: the city's Latin patriarch and the majority of the principality's nobility held with the Armenians, while the Greek Orthodox commune, generally speaking, supported the count of Tripoli. Leo benefitted from the papal hope that the Armenians would agree to a Church union and play a significant part in a future crusade, while Bohemond IV was able to use his diplomatic relations with the Seljuks of Anatolia and the Ayyubids of Aleppo to considerable advantage. This brings us to the war's real and imagined alliances, particularly those with the Muslims, military religious orders, and various ruling families (Hitti 1985).

According to Claude Cahen, the history of northern Syria in the first half of the thirteenth century was characterized by 'a lack of conflicts with the Muslims, [but] constant conflicts with the Armenians' (Cahen 1940: 579). As we have seen, the Muslim neighbors of Armenia, Antioch, and Tripoli did nonetheless factor into the Antiochene war. They did not unite against the Christians, and they even entered into alliances with them, because they were fighting their own wars of succession, as well as wars with their "other" neighbors, the governing principle being: "my enemy's enemy is my friend." Thus, following the death of

Kilij Arslan II in 1192, the Seljuks of Anatolia went through succession struggles involving his sons and grandsons that lasted well into the second decade of the thirteenth century, and while Leo tried to take sides in these struggles, this did not really benefit him. After 1204, the new Byzantine empire of Nicaea developed into a formidable foe to the north, which distracted the Seljuks at least temporarily. Consequently, the Seljuk invasions of Armenia during the Antiochene war were primarily intended to protect the sultanate from Leo's ambitions of expansion, but they were frequently timed to occur whenever Leo was already occupied with Bohemond IV, making them look like invasions on Bohemond's behalf. That Leo was able to simultaneously defend Armenia against the Seljuks (and Ayyubids) and wage a war over the Antiochene succession is a testament to his military and diplomatic abilities (Cahen 1940: 600–623; Mutafian 2012, 1: 105–111).

The Ayyubids, too, experienced succession disputes after Saladin's death in 1193 that involved the latter's son Az-Zahir Ghazi of Aleppo, his great-nephew Al-Mansur Muhammad of Hamah, his second cousin Al-Mujahid of Homs, and his brother Al-Adil of Damascus and Egypt. Aleppo, a direct neighbor of both Armenia and Antioch, initially supported Bohemond IV as the lesser of two evils, and because Aleppo and Tripoli had a joint rival, namely Damascus. Usually, this took the form of Aleppine invasions into Armenia whenever Armenia was moving against Antioch. That these invasions were actions on Bohemond's behalf can be seen from the conditions imposed on Leo, whenever he lost against the Ayyubids, because these conditions usually included the surrender of Baghras to Antioch, rather than Aleppo, whose ruler certainly had an interest in this castle on his western border as well. However, the alliance between Aleppo and Tripoli slowly cooled over the years. Bohemond's 1202 attack on his Ayyubid neighbors, primarily intended to occupy some participants of the Fourth Crusade, left a bad aftertaste. Second, his Ayyubid neighbors held Bohemond, despite his protestations that he was not involved, increasingly responsible for the regular attacks against their territories by the Hospitallers of Margat and Krak des Chevaliers. Third, the 1212 marriage between Az-Zahir Ghazi and Dayfa Khatun, Al-Adil's daughter, ended the rivalry between Aleppo and Damascus, and therefore neutralized Aleppo with regard to any future altercations between Tripoli and Damascus. Fourth, Bohemond's 1214 campaign against the Assassins, intended to avenge his son who had been murdered by them, prompted the Assassins to seek the protection of Aleppo, which forced Bohemond to abandon his plans. Fifth, Aleppo's neutrality during the 1216 Armenian takeover of Antioch must have disappointed Bohemond. Sixth, Az-Zahir Ghazi's death in 1216 left Aleppo and Damascus under the regency of Dayfa Khatun, which, in effect, terminated Bohemond's alliance with the Ayyubids. Lastly, Bohemond's triumph in Antioch in 1219 made him too powerful in the eyes of his Ayyubid neighbors who, henceforth, occasionally sided with the Armenians (Cahen 1940: 600–630; Hardwicke 1969: 536–540; Mutafian 2012, 1: 108–109).

The military religious orders have been credited with key roles in the Antiochene war, namely the Templars as Bohemond IV's allies, the Hospitallers first as Bohemond's and later as Leo's allies, and the Teutonic Knights as Leo's allies (Riley-Smith 1978: 99–101; see also Morton 2009: 56). Yet, quite like the Seljuks and Ayyubids, the orders acted primarily out of self-interest, and the term "alliance" is probably too strong to characterize their involvement. Since it included repeated campaigns of devastation, the Antiochene war went against the orders' economic interests. Moreover, the fact that members of the Armenian, Antiochene, and Tripolitan ruling houses occasionally joined the confraternity of these orders should not be overstated: one had to pay to be a "confrater," and one received prayers and basic goodwill, but no unwavering military alliance, in return. Lastly, the loss of the Templars' Eastern archives, compared to the surviving documentation for both Hospitallers and Teutonic Knights, leaves us with a distorted image. For the Templars it was apparently all about Baghras. As long as Leo was using this castle as a pawn, they stood against him, as evidenced by their swift intervention when he tried to seize Antioch in November 1203. However, after Baghras had been returned to them (1216), they even alerted Leo to his great-nephew's conspiracy against him, not because they had suddenly developed an affection for him but, rather, because his detention would have destabilized Armenia, where the Templars were just reestablishing themselves. The Hospitallers were particularly keen on expanding their interests around Margat and Krak des Chevaliers against the neighboring Ayyubids and Assassins. When Leo established them in western Anatolia to create a buffer against the Seljuks by entrusting Silifke (Seleucia) to them (1210), the Hospitallers did not disappoint and, in 1216, repelled a Seljuk attack (Bronstein 2005: 18, 49–50). However, in 1224, when Silifke briefly became the focus of an extradition demand involving Isabel, the late Leo's daughter and heiress, the order sold it rather than getting involved in inner-Armenian disputes. The Teutonic Knights were especially courted by Leo who owed his crown to the Western (German) emperor and, in 1212, gave them the castle of Amuda (Hemite). It was at Amuda that Bohemond IV's son Philip was allegedly poisoned (1224), for which, however, the order should not be held responsible, or, if so, then only to the extent that the Hospitallers should be blamed for the incarceration of Isaac Comnenus at Margat during the Third Crusade; in both cases, the orders merely permitted someone else to use their castles (Cahen 1940: 590–634; Favreau 1974: 73–79; Arnold 1980; Edwards 1983; Chevalier 2006; Molin 2008; Burgtorf 2013).

It has been said that 'dynastic alliances' are 'the linchpin of political stability' (Hodgson 2011: 86; see also Ryan 2001: 57). They certainly can be, as long as they hold. The 1195 marriage between Bohemond III's oldest son Raymond and Leo's niece Alice had been intended, at least by Leo, to forge such a dynastic alliance, but when, with Raymond's death in 1197, the Antiochenes and Tripolitans viewed this alliance as "over," while the Armenians did not, the stage was set for the Antiochene war, which was fought by way of matrimony just as much as it was fought with arms and legal arguments. In 1210, Leo, who had meanwhile separated from his first wife, married Sibyl of Lusignan, a daughter of the late King Aimery and his second wife Isabel of Jerusalem, while his great-nephew Raymond-Roupen married Helvis of Lusignan, a daughter of the same King Aimery and his first wife Eschiva of Ibelin. However, Bohemond IV was not to be sidelined by this dynastic alliance between Armenia and Cyprus/Jerusalem: in 1218, shortly after the death of his first wife, he married Melisende of Lusignan, a younger sister of Leo's new wife, thereby establishing the curious scenario that, one year before the end of the Antiochene war, all its major players were married to daughters of King Aimery, raising the inevitable question: At what point do dynastic alliances cancel each other out?

Since he was aware of his inner-Armenian Hethoumid rivals, Leo was determined to diversify his family's dynastic portfolio; however, to rather dubious effect: the 1188 marriage of his niece Alice to Hethoum of Sason ended with the husband's mysterious death; Leo's own 1188 marriage to Isabel, the niece of Bohemond III's third wife Sibyl, ended in separation; the 1195 (second) marriage of Leo's niece Alice to Raymond of Antioch led to the Antiochene war; the 1210 marriage of Leo's great-nephew Raymond-Roupen to Helvis of Lusignan ended with the husband's death in prison; the 1214 marriage of Leo's other niece Philippa to Theodore I Laskaris, the Byzantine emperor of Nicaea, ended in an annulment; the 1214 marriage of Rita (Stephanie), the daughter from Leo's first marriage to the Antiochene Isabel, to John of Brienne, the royal widower of Jerusalem, brought domestic abuse and ultimately death to the wife and their child; the 1218 engagement of Isabel, the daughter from Leo's second marriage to Sibyl of Lusignan, to Prince Andrew of Hungary was dissolved when the Hungarians learned of Leo's death; the 1219 (third) marriage of Leo's niece Alice to Vahram of Korykos ended with the husband's murder; the 1222 marriage of Leo's daughter Isabel to Bohemond IV's son Philip found a premature end when the husband was kidnapped and poisoned; only the 1226 (second) marriage of this same Isabel to Hethoum, the son of Constantine of Barberon, eventually brought about the successful union of these two as king and queen of Armenia, and reconciled the Hethoumid and Roupenid clans. From the perspective of dynastic alliances, it was not until 1254, when Prince Bohemond VI of Antioch-Tripoli married Sibyl of Armenia, one of the daughters of King Hethoum and Queen Isabel, that the Antiochene war of succession truly came to an end (Cahen 1940: 619–635; Mutafian 2012, 1: 102–116).

CONCLUSION

The Antiochene war of succession was, first and foremost, a "game of thrones," born from royal and territorial ambitions. It was a struggle between two strong individuals, Leo and Bohemond IV, both diplomats, the former a strategist, the latter a jurist. It was a conflict between denominations, namely Latins, Armenians, and Greek Orthodox. It was a war that ultimately engulfed Christian and Muslim neighbors. It was a war of succession surrounded by other wars of succession, a side show of two crusades, and a distraction to the activities of the military religious orders. It was fought by means of arms, legal debates, and alliances. It cited imperial overlords in both West and East, and it involved the first and the second seat of St. Peter, namely Antioch and Rome. It resulted in the personal union of Tripoli and Antioch under one ruler, a wedding that brought together two rival clans, and, albeit years later, another wedding that reconciled the former enemies. Above all, while its economic damage outweighed its actual loss of lives, it left northern Syria impoverished and vulnerable: Antioch fell to the Mamluks in 1268, Tripoli followed in 1289, and only Cilician Armenia survived until 1375 (Cahen 1940: 644; Claverie 2009: 410). However, the war did not interrupt the cross-cultural exchange in this "Crusader World": the "Assises of Antioch," a significant law code, were translated into Armenian; the Jacobite Theodore of Antioch undertook a veritable academic 'peregrinatio' that took him to Mosul, Baghdad, Cilician Armenia, and eventually the court of the Emperor Frederick II (Kedar and Kohlberg 1996); and, in 1227, King Hethoum donated a beautifully carved wooden door to the Church of the Nativity in Bethlehem with both an Armenian and an Arabic inscription, perhaps out of gratitude that the Antiochene war of succession, and its Armenian postlude, had finally come to an end (Boas 1999: 166–168; Mutafian 2012, 2: plate 213).

REFERENCES

Arnold, U. (1980). "Entstehung und Frühzeit des Deutschen Ordens," in *Die geistlichen Ritterorden Europas*, ed. J. Fleckenstein and M. Hellmann, Sigmaringen, 81–107.

Boas, A. J. (1999). *Crusader Archaeology: The Material Culture of the Latin East*, London.

Boase, T. S. R. (1978). "The History of the Kingdom," in *The Cilician Kingdom of Armenia*, ed. T. S. R. Boase, Edinburgh, 1–33.

Bronstein, J. (2005). *The Hospitallers and the Holy Land: Financing the Latin East, 1187–1274*, Woodbridge.

Bulst-Thiele, M. L. (1974). *Sacrae domus Templi Hierosolymitani magistri: Untersuchungen zur Geschichte des Templerordens 1118/19–1314*, Göttingen.

Burgtorf, J. (2008). *The Central Convent of Hospitallers and Templars: History, Organization, and Personnel (1099/1120–1310)*. Leiden.

———. (2013). "Der antiochenische Erbfolgekrieg," *Ordines Militares Colloquia Torunensia Historica: Yearbook for the Study of the Military Orders*, 18: 219–239.

Cahen, C. (1940). *La Syrie du nord à l'époque des croisades*, Paris.

Chevalier, M. A. (2006). "La vision des ordres religieux-militaires par les chrétiens orientaux (Arméniens et Syriaques) au Moyen Age (du début du XIIe siècle au début du XIV siècle)," *Crusades*, 5: 55–84.

Claverie, P. V. (2005). *L'ordre du Temple en Terre sainte et à Chypre au XIIIe siècle*, Nicosia.

———. (2009). "Guerre de succession d'Antioche," in *Prier et combattre: Dictionnaire européen des ordres militaires au moyen âge*, ed. N. Bériou and P. Josserand, Paris, 409–410.

Edwards, R. W. (1983). "Bagras and Armenian Cilicia: A Reassessment," *Revue des études arméniennes*, 17: 415–455.

Favreau, M. L. (1974). *Studien zur Frühgeschichte des Deutschen Ordens*, Stuttgart.

Hardwicke, M. N. (1969). "The Crusader States, 1192–1243," in *A History of the Crusades II*, ed. R. L. Wolff and H. W. Hazard, Madison, 522–554.

Hiestand, R. (1972). *Die päpstlichen Legaten auf den Kreuzzügen und in den Kreuzfahrerstaaten*, Kiel.

———. (1993). "Antiochia, Sizilien und das Reich am Ende des 12. Jahrhunderts," *Quellen und Forschungen aus italienischen Archiven und Bibliotheken*, 73: 70–121.

Hitti, P. K. (1985). "The Impact of the Crusades on Moslem Lands," in *A History of the Crusades V*, ed. N. P. Zacour and H. W. Hazard, Madison, 33–58.

Hodgson, N. (2011). "Conflict and Cohabitation: Marriage and Diplomacy between Latins and Cilician Armenians, c.1097–1253," in *The Crusades and the Near East: Cultural Histories*, ed. C. Kostick, London, 83–106.

Jamil, N. and Johns, J. (2003). "An Original Arabic Document from Crusader Antioch (1213 AD)," in *Texts, Documents, and Artefacts: Islamic Studies in Honour of D. S. Richards*, ed. C. F. Robinson, Leiden, 157–191.

Kedar, B. Z. and Kohlberg, E. (1996). "The Intercultural Career of Theodore of Antioch," in *Intercultural Contacts in the Medieval Mediterranean*, ed. B. Arbel, London, 164–176.

Lawrence, A. W. (1978). "The Castle of Baghras," in *The Cilician Kingdom of Armenia*, ed. T. S. R. Boase, Edinburgh, 34–84.

Lock, P. (2006). *The Routledge Companion to the Crusades*, London.

Major, B. (2001). "Al-Malik Al-Mujahid, Ruler of Homs, and the Hospitallers: The Evidence in the Chronicle of Ibn Wasil," in *The Crusades and the Military Orders: Expanding the Frontiers of Medieval Latin Christianity*, ed. Z. Hunyadi and J. Laszlovszky, Budapest, 61–75.

Maleczek, W. (1988). *Petrus Capuanus: Kardinal, Legat am Vierten Kreuzzug, Theologe (+1214)*. Vienna.

Mayer, H. E. (1993). *Varia Antiochena: Studien zum Kreuzfahrerfürstentum Antiochia im 12. und frühen 13. Jahrhundert*, Hanover.

Molin, K. (2008). "Teutonic Castles in Cilician Armenia: A Reappraisal," in *The Military Orders, 3: History and Heritage*, ed. V. Mallia-Milanes, Aldershot, 131–137.

Morton, N. E. (2009). *The Teutonic Knights in the Holy Land, 1190–1291*, Woodbridge.

Mutafian, C. (2012). *L'Arménie du Levant*, Paris.

Nersessian, S. D. (1969). "The Kingdom of Cilician Armenia," in *A History of the Crusades II*, ed. R. L. Wolff and H. W. Hazard, Madison, 630–659.

210

Richard, J. (1985). "The Political and Ecclesiastical Organization of the Crusader States," in *A History of the Crusades V*, ed. N. P. Zacour and H. W. Hazard, Madison, 193–250.

Riley-Smith, J. (1967). *The Knights of St. John in Jerusalem and Cyprus c.1050–1310*, London.

———. (1978). "The Templars and the Teutonic Knights in Cilician Armenia," in *The Cilician Kingdom of Armenia*, ed. T. S. R. Boase, Edinburgh, 92–117.

Röhricht, R. (1893). *Regesta Regni Hierosolymitani (MXCVII-MCCXCI)*, Innsbruck.

Rüdt de Collenberg, W. H. (1983). "A Fragmentary Copy of an Unknown Recension of the "Lignages d'Outre-Mer" in the Vatican Library," *The English Historical Review*, 98: 311–327.

Ryan, J. D. (2001). "Toleration Denied: Armenia between East and West in the Era of the Crusades," in *Tolerance and Intolerance: Social Conflict in the Age of the Crusades*, ed. M. Gervers and J. M. Powell, Syracuse, 55–64.

CHAPTER THIRTEEN

WESTERN UPPER GALILEE UNDER CRUSADER RULE

——— •◆• ———

Rabei G. Khamisy

Western Upper Galilee can be divided into a few small areas in its different parts. The term refers to the area which is located west of the highest summits of Upper Galilee (the watershed between the Mediterranean and the Jordan Valley), east of the Mediterranean, south of the Ladder of Tyre and the mountain range that continued farther east of the Ladder and north of Sahl al-Biʿna (the plain of al-Biʿna) – which is called after the Frankish village of St George de Labeyne (see below).

The natural division between Upper and Lower Galilee is very clear owing to the great difference in elevation between them. While Lower Galilee reaches the 602m above sea level, Upper Galilee is twice as high, with the Shāghūr mountains rising very steeply northwards above the plain of al-Biʿna to form the border between the two Galilees. This mountain range rises up in some points for 700m above the plain, and more than 1000m above sea level.

In general, Lower Galilee is consists of long Horsts oriented east–west and separated by quite wide plains (Grabens), while Upper Galilee consists of two different areas: the eastern one is the Mount Meron range comprising high hills reaching 1,208m above sea level and is very rocky, steep and difficult for cultivation, and the western part comprising long spurs oriented east–west with comparatively flat summits but, unlike Lower Galilee, here very deep and wild valleys separate the spurs. West of these, a thin and fertile coastal plain is located.[1] Thus, on the one hand, Lower Galilee was much more suitable to serve as a passage connecting the Mediterranean and the Jordan valley through its plains, and, on the other hand, Upper Galilee is much more suitable for refugees, especially for small ethnic groups and entities that needed a kind of separation from their surroundings. However, this does not mean that the inhabitants of Upper Galilee were refugees. In fact, this area had been extensively settled and developed during several periods, especially in the Byzantine period.[2] The current chapter aims, *inter alia*, to examine the reasons that stand behind the Frankish settlement there.

In addition to the differences mentioned above between the two Galilees, other important differences can be distinguished in terms of the rainfall and the availability of water sources. In both aspects, Upper Galilee is richer.

Western Galilee had been regarded as part of Acre region during the crusader period, a fact that naturally had contributed in developing the region and expanding its importance. Many landowners, including the kings, the military orders, noble families, ecclesiastical bodies and private persons were active there during the crusader period, and landownership changed for different reasons such as political and economic factors. Thus, this chapter will try also to examine the Franks' use of the northern part of this region and will try to identify the relationship between the development of the region and the natural resources available there. To do so, I will refer to historical documents, archaeological remains and topographical situations as well.

PREVIOUS RESEARCH

Many scholars since the second half of the nineteenth century tried to discuss the Frankish documents dealing with the area under study and succeeded to identify many of the places that were mentioned as part of it. For example, Emmanuel Rey tried to identify these places in his *colonies franques* which, although published in 1883, is still regarded alongside the most important studies in the field (Rey, 1883: 471–509). Three years earlier, in 1880, Victor Guérin published his journey through Galilee in which he tried to give some identifications, dealing with just few documents, such as those regarding Kuwaykāt (Guérin, 1969). One year later, in 1881, Claude Conder and Horatio Kitchener published their survey in Galilee, but without referring to many documents or trying to identify the majority of the crusader places (Conder and Kitchener, 1881). However, in his later studies, Conder dealt, *inter alia*, with identifications (Conder, 1889a, 1889b, 1890). In the 1880s and 1890s, Reinhold Röhricht also published a few studies with many suggestions of identifications (see, for example, Röhricht, 1887). Although few of the abovementioned studies have also discussed the fiefs which contained these villages and tried to locate them and give their borders, the most important studies in the nineteenth century about fiefs were carried out by Louis De Mas-Latrie (Mas-Latrie, 1965: 107–20; 1882). Later, in 1945, Gustav Beyer published one of the most important and extensive studies about the region of Acre in the crusader period in which he tried to identify all the places that were mentioned in the Frankish documents and to locate the Galilean fiefs (Beyer, 1945). Joshua Prawer and Meron Benvenisti published a map containing many crusader places in the crusader Kingdom of Jerusalem, and some work had also been done by Jonathan Riley-Smith and in the Tübinger Atlas (Prawer and Benvenisti, 1970; Riley-Smith, 1991; Tübinger Atlas). Hans Mayer also took part in this research and published some of the most important studies about the region, giving detailed discussions about the *seigneurie* of Joscelin III and the Teutonic Order, and also about the fief of ʿArrāba which is situated in Lower Galilee. In his recent publication, he dealt with these issues in each document that included information about these places (Mayer, 1977, 1980, 2010). Rafael Frankel, in 1988, published the first and only study that includes an accurate division between many Galilean fiefs and properties. He also presented several new identifications of places that were not identified in the earlier studies. Later on, few researchers from the Israel Antiquities Authority, led by Frankel, published three important studies which include information about the crusader period in Galilee (Frankel, 1988; Frankel and Getzov, 1997, 2013). Throughout his *Churches* and *Secular Buildings*, Denys Pringle mentioned all the names that he found of each place included in his studies, and added several new identifications (Pringle, 1993–2009, 1997). In my PhD thesis I discussed the crusader villages and properties in Galilee, presenting new identifications, a few corrections of previously error identifications and chronological mapping of all the Galilean fiefs (Khamisy, 2012, forthcoming(a)).[3]

GENERAL HISTORY OF THE REGION DURING THE CRUSADER PERIOD

The nearest two main urban settlements to the area, Tiberias and Acre, were occupied by the crusaders in 1099 and 1104 respectively (Pringle, 1997: 101 no. 222; 1993–2009: II, 351; IV, 5; Prawer, 2001: I, 270). Therefore, it is reasonable to assume that all Western Galilee fell to them around this time, most probably in 1104, shortly after the occupation of Acre. Since that time, the Frankish entities, led by the kings of Jerusalem, started to carry out activities in the region. However, in 1187, following the crusader defeat by the Ayyūbid forces in the Battle of Ḥaṭṭīn, the whole area, as well as most of the crusader Kingdom of Jerusalem, fell to Ṣalāḥ al-Dīn who probably damaged most of the Frankish places. It seems likely that Western Galilee was recovered by the Franks with the recovery of Acre by the Third Crusade. In fact, scholars have suggested that Miʿilyā and al-Biʿna, which are located in the middle of Western Galilee, had been recovered by the Franks in 1192 (Mayer, 2010: III, 1047; Pringle, 1993–2009: II, 30). According to Mayer's map, Miʿilyā seems to belong to the Franks in 1192 (Mayer, 1982: 324). However, it seems likely that the Franks had recovered all the Acre region until the watershed. This can be understood from the terms of the truce which were given in some details by Bahāʾ al-Dīn Ibn Shaddād, a biographer of Ṣalāḥ al-Dīn (Bahāʾ al-Dīn Ibn Shaddād, 1994: 344–5; 1872–1906: III, 343; Richards, 2001: 229) (this truce will be published by me in detail in Khamisy forthcoming(a)), who clearly stated that the Franks should keep the region of Acre. The terms of the treaty did not exclude any of Acre's parts, as was clarified while mentioning other places that were included in the truce. This might mean that the entire region of Acre (the coastal plain and Western Galilee) had been recovered by the Franks.[4]

The situation in the region had not been changed following the Crusade of Frederick II in the late 1220s,[5] but did change in 1241 when the Franks doubled their area in Galilee following their agreement with the Muslims (Mayer, 1982: 257, 324 map 2; Prawer, 2001: II, 285–7, 284 map 8).[6] Things had not changed in Galilee until 1266 when half of the area was lost to the Mamluks following their occupation of the major castle of Safed. The biographer of Baybars, Muḥyī al-Dīn Ibn ʿAbd al-Ẓāhir, described the occupation in detail, but neither he nor his successors dealt with the conquest of Western Galilee (for the fall of Safed, see Ibn ʿAbd al-Ẓāhir, 1976: 250–63; for some studies, see Thorau, 1992: 166–71). Five years later, on June 1271, Montfort Castle fell to Baybars (Ibn ʿAbd al-Ẓāhir, 1976: 385–7; for a detailed discussion, see Khamisy, forthcoming(c)), leading few scholars to suggest that large areas in the region, including Castellum Regis, fell to the Mamluks sometime between 1266 and 1271 (see, for example, Pringle, 1993–2009: II, 31). However, based on both Latin and Arabic sources, it is reasonable to assume that during Baybars's first campaign in 1266, he captured all the Frankish areas between Castellum Regis and Safed including Castellum Regis itself (see Khamisy, 2014b: 156–9). This new political situation affected the Frankish activities and their day-to-day life in the region; Montfort's close vicinity became a real frontier for the first time since establishing the crusader kingdom; this in turn reduced the number of the Frankish inhabitants in the area whose settlements were either dismantled or re-inhabited by Muslims. In fact, after 1266 the Franks seem likely to control only a very small area surrounding Montfort (Khamisy, 2014b: 155, fig. 1). Yet, in

June 1271 Montfort fell to Baybars who put an end to the Frankish existence in Western Galilee except for a very thin strip of land, no more than 11km wide including the coastal plain running north–south and forming the Acre region in the last two decades, and more precisely, since 1272. In my recent studies, I raise the possibility that some of the locales inside this strip of land, which contained the first hills east of the coastal plain, had been previously taken by the Mamluks (between 1266 and 1271) and later granted to the Franks in the truce that was concluded between the two parties in 1272 (Khamisy, 2014a, 2014b). Finally, on May 1291 Acre fell to the Mamluk forces led by sultan al-Ashraf Khalīl (Mayer, 1982: 286), and the Franks lost the entire region.

FRANKISH OWNERSHIP AND ACTIVITIES IN THE REGION OF ACRE

As noted above, Frankish entities started to carry out activities in Western Galilee from 1104. I will start with the kings who formally owned the land, but granted part of it as fiefs to different entities. However, not every single activity by the kings of Jerusalem will be discussed in this chapter, but rather, a few of their most important and interesting acts will be presented.

A charter dated 1153 proves that King Baldwin III was planning to establish Frankish settlement in Casal Imbert (al-Zīb, Akhziv, map ref. 1598.2728) which was earlier granted to a knight called Hubert de Paci, probably by King Baldwin I in the very beginning of the Frankish control in the region, that is, directly after 1104 (Mayer, 2010: I, 419–22, no. 228. For discussion, see Ellenblum, 1998: 65–8; Prawer, 1980: 140–1; Pringle, 1997: 110; 1993–2009: II, 384; Boas, 2010: 328. For the first mention which relates the village with Hubert, see Delaborde, 1880: 37–8, no. 12). The document of 1153 stated that the king owned a bakery and bath-house in Casal Imbert and a mill in the village of Ferge (al-Faraj, map ref. 1617.2678), *c.* 6km south-south-east of Casal Imbert. A document from 1197 mentions sugar production under the control of the king in the same village of Ferge (Mayar, 2010: II, 983–6, no. 609). Later documents, from 1253, 1256 and 1261, prove that Casal Imbert was the centre of a region which included the majority of the coastal plain between the Ga'ton stream (Wādī Ja'thūn) and the Ladder of Tyre (for the documents see Mayer, 2010: III, 1396–400, no. 802, 1403–4, no. 805; Strehlke, 1975: 106–9, no. 119. For the region and its borders, see Frankel, 1988: 251 fig. 1; Khamisy, 2012: 303–31). In addition, other documents from 1160, 1182, 1220 and 1226 prove that the area under discussion had been expanded during the years, presumably after 1220, by attaching some villages that previously belonged to the area of Castellum Regis (for the documents, see Mayer, 2010: I, 460–2, no. 253; II, 730–3, no. 430; III, 1041–52, 1071–75, nos 639, 652. For discussions, see ibid; Frankel, 1988: 259–60; Khamisy, 2012: 303–31). In fact, the Casal Imbert area had been granted as a fief to Balian of Ibilin, possibly sometime after 1232 and held by the family until 1261. The history of the area will not be examined in detail, but I will assume that its location and its natural resources, especially the existence of the only three perennial streams to the north of Acre, played an important role in its history. That was the only area in the region of Acre to be controlled by the throne for such a long time. This in turn sheds light on the kings' participation in the activities in the region. It seems likely that they encourage Franks to settle in the villages in the vicinity and also encourage the development of the agriculture and industry (milling and sugar producing). Casal Imbert had been mentioned by Fulcher of Chartres (d. *c.* 1127) as being a castle ('*Castellum*') which they passed by on their way between Tyre and Acre in 1099 (Fulcher of Chartres, nd: 354). In 1183 it was described by Ibn Jubayr as a big fortress (Ibn Jubayr, 1952: 319; Ibn Jobair, 1956: 356), and in 1187 it appeared alongside the stronghold mentioned by al-Iṣfahānī ('Imād al-Dīn, 1995: XIII, 5914). It is not known whether this stronghold was built by one of the kings or by Hubert, the knight who owned the village in the early dates of Frankish control. However, although Fulcher of Chartres mentioned it as '*Castellum*' which already existed there before the Franks arrived, it is logical to assume that the 'castle' or perhaps 'the settlement fortifications' had been later expanded or strengthened by King Baldwin III who wanted to carry out the project of developing the village and settling it with Franks. If judging the existence of a castle according to Fulcher's use of the term '*Castellum*', we should assume that a pre-Frankish castle really existed there.[7]

Although the situation of the Castellum Regis area is quite different, its documentation sheds light on the kings' activities there. In 1160 the administration of the area was granted to John of Haifa with a hope that new villages would be inhabited (Mayer, 2010: I, 460–2, no. 253). Ellenblum assumes that the purpose was to settle Franks (Ellenblum, 1996: 105; 1998: 41–2), and I agree with him. This political action, which seems to be carried out, *inter alia*, in order to change the demographical situation in the region, had been achieved sometime before 1220, but surely not before 1182 when the area was granted as a fief to Joscelin III of Courtenay (for the document, see Mayer, 2010: II, 730–3, no. 430). Whether it was the case or not, it is the second time that we are informed about the desire of King Baldwin III to settle new villages, especially by Christians, and most probably by Franks. In addition, King Baldwin III seems to build Castellum Regis not only as an administrative centre in the middle of Western Upper Galilee but also in order to strengthen the region against the Muslim threat from the north, or maybe against his mother Queen Milesende, with whom he had great conflict which ended with a civil war in 1152 (for the historical events in the late 1140s and the early 1150, see Mayer, 1982: 107–15; 1972a; Holt, 2004: 61–4). It is worth noting that the 1160 charter mentioned only nine villages by name in the Castellum Regis area, and it recorded that the king hoped to settle others. The Franks did not receive a completely empty area, and certainly part of the inhabited villages continued to be settled from earlier period.[8] Thus, it seems that minimal activities had been carried out by the kings in this area before 1160.

These facts show that the kings, especially King Baldwin III, should be regarded with the most active entities in the region in all political, social and economic fields; settling the area with new inhabitants in newly established villages would affect all aspects. In addition to the demographical change, it will develop the agriculture by cultivating additional lands, which certainly will greatly increase the amount of crops. This in turn will need more agricultural installations such as mills, wine presses, olive presses and so forth. Such activities have certainly increased the incomes of the inhabitants but mainly those of the lords – the kings in this specific case.

The same document from 1153 mentioned above refers to the abbey of St Mary of the valley of Jehoshaphat as being the owner of properties in Casal Imbert. In fact, the abbey's properties in the settlement had been mentioned several times between 1120 and 1255 (for the documents, see Delaborde, 1880: 37–8, 45–7, 60–1, 63–70, 100–5, nos 12, 18, 26, 28, 29, 49). However, the first of the abbey's properties in the region of Acre appeared in a document dated 1115 when two *carruca* of land were granted to it by King Baldwin I (for the document, see Mayer, 2010: I, 195–8, no. 640). Our study of the abbey's documents revealed that this property should be identified with the place in which the village of Kisrā is situated (map ref. 1787.2630), on one of the highest hills of the southernmost spur of Upper Galilee.

It is worth noting that the abbey did not expand his properties in the Acre region after the first half of the twelfth century. Moreover, the documentation of Kisrā threw light on its history during the crusader period, and might be summarised as follows: it is possible that the village had been established by the abbey between 1115 and 1120 and most probably settled by Christians (see discussion, Khamisy, 2012: 23–30). It was captured in 1187 and for unknown reasons, probably economic, and in unknown time, probably after 1192, a knight called John of Cannay had rented properties in the village and tried to carry out activities there; however, in 1230, both John and the abbey passed the rights to the Teutonic Order who, at the time, tried to control as much property as it could in Western Galilee (see below). It should be noted, however, that the Teutonic Order seems to have been interested in this area more for political reasons than for economic ones (Khamisy, 2012: 23–30). Owing to the documentation of the adjacent territories, it is possible to locate the areas which had been controlled by the abbey and centred by Kisrā, with high degree of accuracy (Khamisy, 2012: 23–30).

This 8km square area lacks perennial streams and springs, but its average rainfall is almost 900mm a year. The topographical and hydrological situations were not suitable, thus, for the developing of irrigated agriculture and building agricultural installations that used water power. Presumably that is why no major development of this territory had been traced yet through its documentation and archaeological remains.[9] We might conclude that the abbey of St Mary of the valley of Jehoshaphat was not notably active in the region but it was one which had long existed there. It controlled Kisrā between 1115 and 1266 when it was lost to Baybars,[10] and the properties in Casal Imbert were owned between 1120 and the fall of Acre in 1291.

The abbey of St Mary of the valley of Jehoshaphat was not the only ecclesiastical entity to take part in the activities in Galilee. For example, the church of the Holy Sepulchre owned lands in Mīmās (map ref. 1643.2633) which is located in the plain north-east of Acre. The documents prove that the church received the lands there from Lambert Hals in the 1130s and continued to own them during the 1250s (for the documents mentioning this property, see references by Pringle, 1993–2009: II, 32; VI, 52; Röhricht, 1893: I, 313, no. 1187). If that were the case, it might be assumed that they kept the lands until the fall of the region in 1291. However, except for building a church in the late 1130s, which is also not certain (Pringle, 1993–2009: II, 32; for the site in the crusader period, see Khamisy, 2012: 39–45), no archaeological remains or historical accounts prove that the area or the village had been developed under the church's control. The church of the Holy Sepulchre owned also a parcel of land near Castellum Regis (Mayer, 2010: III, 1030–2, no. 632).[11]

The third group to be discussed is the knights and other leading figures in the kingdom who received fiefs from the kings, perhaps for their help during the crusades or for their social and administrative positions. This is why we are informed that Hubert de Paci owned Casal Imbert, which was named after him, and that Lambert Hals owned extensive lands in Mīmās. We are also told that Barda Armenus and his wife granted the village of Kuwaykāt (map ref. 1642.2639) to the Hospitaller Order in 1129 (Mayer, 2010: II, 270–3, no. 111). This man seems to have been a knight in order to have been granted such an important village in the plain of Acre (for the village, see Khamisy, 2012: 31–5). In the year 1179, Petronalla, the viscount of Acre and her sons, sold properties in Galilee to Joscelin III. These included two separated villages – Suḥmātā (map ref. 1787.2679) and Shufayya (map ref. 1715.2685) (Mayer, 2010: II, 706–7, no. 413. Petronella seems to have been the widow of Clarembald, the viscount of Acre, who was mentioned for the first time in 1149 and the last time on 13 August 1169 (Mayer, 2010: I, 354, no. 175; II, 590, no. 340. For suggestions by Mayer, see Mayer, 2010: II, 706, no. 413). Nevertheless, the most important of this group were the chamberlains of Acre who owned a fief containing some of the most important lands and villages in the region of Acre. This fief had passed from one chamberlain to another and finally was sold to Joscelin III in 1179 (Mayer, 2010: II, 700–3, no. 410. For research see Mas Latrie, 1882; Frankel, 1988: 251, fig, 1, 258–9; Khamisy, 2012: 36–53). A document dated one month after the sale, confirms that the chamberlain who sold the fief had previously granted the Hospitallers one *quintar* of sugar from a village in his area (Mayer, 2010: II, 704–5, no. 412). This is the only hint we have for a serious activity taking place in the fief under the leadership of the chamberlain. It is interesting to note, however, that both the chamberlain and Petronella sold their fiefs to Joscelin III in 1179, and this put an end to a stage in which this group of owners held large areas in Western Upper Galilee. From now onwards, most of the lands were divided between the king and the noble families. It might thus be asked, what were the real reasons for the sales in 1179? In fact, many suggestions might arise and many answers can be given, but I would like to argue that between the many reasons, two are more probable. The first is that the region had been harmed by a natural or political catastrophe and the owners could not renovate their properties. This might find support by the fact that a severe earthquake hit the region in 1170 and caused huge damage in both Frankish and Muslim areas, probably also in Acre and its vicinity (Ibn al-Athīr, 1987: 24; Amiran et al., 1994: 270; Mayer, 1972b: 296–7). The second reason, which for me looks more reliable, is that Joscelin III was a very promising figure who had a familial relationship with the throne and was part of a very influential family in the Latin East.[12] This made things easier for him, and probably there was a programme to create his lordship instead of the much greater one that the Courtenay family lost in Edessa (Hamilton, 1985: esp. 200–1). Here I will start with the fourth group and one of the most important, which is the noble families who controlled extensive areas throughout long periods.

Joscelin III had consolidated his lordship in a very extensive area in Galilee, with its majority in Western Upper Galilee. He combined the two villages of Petronella, the fief of the chamberlain, the area of Castellum Regis (in 1182) and the fief of Gofri le Tor (in 1183), which also belonged to a noble family who controlled a wide area in the eastern part of Western Upper Galilee. In addition, Joscelin owned a third of the fief of Henri de Milly (see below), by marrying his daughter, Agnes, in the second half of the 1170s (for this marriage, see Hamilton, 1985: 200). Joscelin and his family seem to have been very active in the region in all aspects: political, social and economic. They established a series of new villages and settled them with Franks, they developed their own sugar production and certainly built mills and other installations to produce products from their lands.[13] However, Gofri le Tor does not seem to have been particularly active in his eastern area, probably because of the lack of perennial streams there, but he was in Manueth (al-Manawāt, map ref. 1645.2717), the western fief that he owned in the plain of Acre, where he produced sugar and probably developed the village. This part of Gofri's fief continued to be held by him for later periods, and in 1212 the Courtenays appeared as the owners of some rights there, probably acquired from Gofri between 1183 and 1187. In later charters from 1217 and 1231, the king and a person called Nicholas of Manueth appeared as owning rights there (for the relation between Nicholas's father and Gofri le Tor, see Ellenblum, 1998: 201, 202). However, all three owners sold their rights to the Hospitaller Order between 1212 and 1231.[14]

Here again, we witness the influence of the natural resources on the activity of the land lords and the development of their properties. When water sources are available more activities can be done.

The greater fief of St George de Labeyne surrounds the Kisrā area from its eastern, western and southern sides. It was controlled by the Milly family, most probably since the first half of the twelfth century. However, our knowledge about the fief comes from documents dealing especially with the properties of Joscelin III and the Teutonic Order. Until the late 1160s, the fief was controlled by Henri de Milly (Le Bufle), and in 1171, probably one year after his death, the fief was divided between his three daughters (for the dates of Henri's death and the division, see Edbury, 2009: 330). The first third belonged to Joscelin, who seems to own some rights in the whole fief in 1182 (for the document and discussion about the rights of 1182, see Mayer, 2010: II, 730–3, no. 430. For other discussions on the fief, see for example Mayer, 1980, esp. 181–9; Frankel, 1988: 251–5, 256–7; Mas-Latrie, 1878; Khamisy, 2012: 252–87). The second third was sold to the Teutonic Order in 1249 by John l'Aleman of Casarea, who was a descendant of one of Henri's daughters (Strehlke, 1975: 78–80, no. 100; see Frankel, 1988: 251–5, 256–7; Khamisy, 2012: 252–87), and the last third had not been mentioned in the contemporary documents but seems to have been located in the north-eastern side of Western Upper Galilee, and remained with the descendants of Henri until its fall to Baybars in 1266 (Khamisy, 2012: 282–4). The archaeological survey in the area belonging to Hinri's fief had greatly contributed to the identification of the fief's boundaries and some of the important activities there. However, the lack of documentation and archaeological excavations prevents us from knowing precisely when and why each activity had been carried out and who is responsible for them.

However, in the centre of this fief stands the village of al-Biʿna which contains remains of a Frankish building, probably a small stronghold, and a fortified ecclesiastical building (monastery) dedicated to St George, which is the source of the name 'St George de Labeyne' (in Dayr al-Asad at present) (for the abbey, see Pringle, 1993-2009: I, 80–92. For the stronghold in al-Biʿna, see Boas, 2006: 91; 2010: 234–6; Ellenblum, 1998: 166–71). These religious and administrative buildings shed some light on the activity carried out by the owners. In addition, Gothic art was found during my survey in Bayt Jann – one of the mountainous villages there (map ref. 1860.2634). Gothic art might point to the existence of a thirteenth-century church in a Frankish settlement (see, for example, Khamisy, 2012: 275–7). In fact, the archaeological remains and the historical accounts throughout the crusader, Mamluk and Ottoman periods suggest that part of the villages in the Mount Meron range were settled by Christians, part of them were certainly Franks (Khamisy, 2012). It would not be strange, thus, if future research proves that Frankish inhabitants settled in some villages further east and as far as the major castle of Safed.

Thus, the owners, whether the noble families or the Teutonic Order, seem to have carried out extensive activities including settling the mountainous villages with Christians, and certainly with Frankish inhabitants in some of them. This contradicts Ellenblum's assumption that the Franks inhabited villages eastwards from the Mediterranean until the middle of Western Galilee, reaching the area between Fassūta (map ref. 1768.2710) and al-Bi'na (Ellenblum, 1998: 213, 215).

Unlike the area of Kisrā, Hinri's fief contained extensive agricultural lands in both the mountains and the plains, and also contained many springs and small perennial streams which helped in developing the agriculture and the industry as well. Moreover, its lands contained low plains, small hills and part of the highest mountains of Galilee. This combination had certainly increased the number of different plants that could have been cultivated there.

The fifth and most important entities to take part in the activities were the military orders. As noted above, the Hospitaller Order received its first property in the plain of Western

Upper Galilee in 1129, and continued to expand its properties throughout the twelfth and thirteenth centuries by owning extensive lands in the plain north-east of Acre, but mainly in Manueth (for these properties and their location see Khamisy, 2013a). The Templar Order was also very active in the region, but, unfortunately, the loss of its archive prevents us from knowing any precise details. However, the documentation of the other entities greatly helps in locating its properties and studying its activities (Khamisy, 2013a). Both military orders seem to have been very active, especially in the agricultural fields, but most interesting is their absence from the hilly areas of Western Upper Galilee. This leads us to believe that they mainly dealt with agriculture, but the Templars probably also tried to defend the highway which connected Haifa with Tyre (Khamisy, 2013a). This was not the situation with the Teutonic Order, which tried to control the mountainous region and wide areas of the plain, as mentioned above. Its activity seems to be mainly political, but did also involve many economic activities. The construction of its main castle in the kingdom, Montfort Castle, began in 1226/27, when Western Upper Galilee was in Frankish hands. However, Montfort seems to be located in an area very close to the frontier with the Muslims in the east and north. Once Montfort fell to Baybars in 1271, no strong fortress remained in Frankish hands in the Acre region. The historical accounts as well as the archaeological remains suggest that the Teutonic Order, in addition to building the castles of Montfort and Jiddīn (for Jiddīn, see Pringle et al., 1994: 135–66) and controlling Castellum Regis, it also established new villages (see, for example, Khamisy, 2014b: 159, n. 65), strengthened and fortified few others (see Khamisy, forthcoming(a)) and built mills and sugar refineries.[15]

CONCLUSIONS

In 1104 the Franks started to control the Acre region including Western Upper Galilee. Activities started to be carried out by the Frankish kings and also by few entities such as ecclesiastical bodies, knights and officers who were close to the throne and received properties from the kings. At the same time, especially in the St George fief, noble families started to own lands and to take part in activities. In a slightly later stage, some properties were transferred by the knights to the Hospitallers and a few ecclesiastical bodies. However, by the 1170s, when Joscelin III appeared again in the Kingdom of Jerusalem, the majority of the land in the region was being controlled by the noble families with some areas remaining with the throne and others with the military orders. In a later stage, the Teutonic Order became the most dominant in the mountainous area and in the northern part of the coastal plain, while the Templars and Hospitallers owned the majority of the lands in the southern section of the plain, north of Acre. However, a few properties remained under the control of other entities such as the Church of the Holy Sepulchre and the Genoese community (for the Genoese's property, see Frankel, 1980; Khamisy, 2013a).

Three stages of major developments seem to take place in the region: the first under the leadership of King Baldwin III; the second was under Joscelin III's leadership between 1179 and 1187; and the third and most impressive under the leadership of the Teutonic Order, especially between 1220 and 1271. However, before, during and after these stages, the same three entities and many others carried out different activities in all political, social and economic fields, reflected in building small strongholds, establishing new settlements, constructing industrial and agricultural installations, erecting churches and, above all, cultivating wide areas of lands to support the day-to-day life in the region. In fact, throughout the period of Frankish rule, private individuals owned properties in the region and took their part and contributed to the development of the region. Evidence to such owners can be found in one document dealing, *inter alia*, with properties that had been acquired by the Teutonic Order from many inhabitants from Castellum Regis (Strehlke, 1975: 120–1, no. 128. For discussion in the document, see Ellenblum, 1996; 1998: 41–53; Khamisy, 2013b). Unfortunately we have no information about the inhabitants of the other villages, their properties and activities, and thus, it is impossible to know the value of their influence on the above mentioned activities.

It is also worth noting that there was a direct relationship between the development of each area and the availability of the natural recourses, especially the perennial streams. In addition, there was a direct relationship in the different periods between the kind of activity done to develop each area and the owners of these areas.

NOTES

1 The topographical information is based on my personal observations and the 1:20,000 Mandatory maps of Upper and Lower Galilee (Mandatory map of El-Baṣṣa, 1940, 1:20,000 (sheet 16–27), the Survey of Palestine; Mandatory map of Tarbīkhā, 1941, 1:20,000 (sheet 17–27), the Survey of Palestine; Mandatory map of Sasa, 1940, 1:20,000 (sheet 18–27), the Survey of Palestine; Mandatory map of Nahariya, 1941, 1:20,000 (sheet 16/25, 16/26), the Survey of Palestine; Mandatory map of Tarshīḥā, 1940, 1:20,000 (sheet 17/26), the Survey of Palestine; Mandatory map of Beit Jann, 1940, 1:20,000 (sheet 16/25, 18/26), the Survey of Palestine; Mandatory map of Acre, 1946, 1:20,000 (sheet 15/25, 16/25), the Survey of Palestine; Mandatory map of Majd El Kurūm, 1944, 1:20,000 (sheet 17/25), the Survey of Palestine; Mandatory map of Maghār, 1944, 1:20,000 (sheet 18/25), the Survey of Palestine; Mandatory map of Haifa, 1942, 1:20,000 (sheet 14/24, 15/24), the Survey of Palestine; Mandatory map of Shafā ʿAmr, 1940, 1:20,000 (sheet 16/24), the Survey of Palestine; (sheet 17/24); Mandatory map of Turʿān, 1940, 1:20,000 (sheet 18/24), the Survey of Palestine; Mandatory map of Nahalal, 1940, 1:20,000 (sheet 16/23), the Survey of Palestine; Mandatory map of Nazareth, 1942, 1:20,000 (sheet 17/23), the Survey of Palestine).

2 For the settlements throughout the different periods, see Frankel et al. 2001.

3 Other works with additional information including new identifications have already been published by the author (all the following articles contains information about few Galilean villages and fiefs: Khamisy, 2013a, 2014a, 2014b).

4 Based on the descriptions given by contemporary Arabic sources, one could understand that the Ayyūbids were well informed about the Frankish regions and their inner divisions including the small districts and their centres. Thus, I believe that when talking about the region of Acre in the truce, the two parties, as well as Ibn Shaddād, knew exactly what they were talking about. Detailed discussion will be published later in Khamisy, forthcoming(a).

5 The additional areas were the city of Jerusalem, ten estates on the road between Acre and Jerusalem and according to Christian sources also Nazareth, as well as the lordship of Toron and Sidon (Mayer, 1982: 236, 324 map 2; Prawer, 2001, 2: 201, 207 map 7).

6 As these issues are not essential to the current chapter, I have not discussed them in detail here or referred to other research that deals with them.

7 Fulcher came from Chartres which is located some 90km south-west of Paris. That means that he was influenced by the north-western European terminology which used the word ‘*Castellum*’ to describe strongholds at the time, unlike the use of the term ‘*castella*’ in early medieval Italy to describe a simple village, not necessarily fortified (Pringle, 2010: 223).

8 This point is being discussed in Khamisy forthcoming(a).

9 This information will published in detail in Khamisy forthcoming(a).

10 It is true that the abbey moved many of the village’s rights to the Teutonic Order in 1230, but it continued to be the official owner.

11 Collecting tithes by churches and bishops is not regarded as an activity for developing the area, and thus will not be discussed here.

12 The Courtenay family, and especially Joscelin III, have been discussed in many studies such as in Nicholson, 1973 and Hamilton, 1985. The current chapter will not discuss it.

13 I will not discuss these issues in detail here, but they will be published in Khamisy forthcoming(a). See Khamisy, 2012, 371–8.

14 This was one of the most important villages and sugar producers in the crusader period. It drew the attention of many scholars how had dealt with it, sometimes in detail. For researches, see, for example, Boas, 2006: 246; Ellenblum, 1998: 200–2, n. 13; Frankel and Getzov, 1997: 106–7; Frankel and Stern, 1996; Stern, 1998, 2001; Khamisy, 2012: 228–31. For the documents and other historical accounts, see Khamisy, 2014a: 88, n. 41; Mayer, 2010, vol. 3: 1019–20, 1033–4, 1034–6, 1359–61, nos. 627, 634, 635, 783.

15 Many studies had been carried out regarding the Teutonic Order and its activities, and many others studied the three castles controlled by it, especially Montfort (for Montfort, see for example Pringle, 1986; Piana, 2008; Khamisy, 2004; but mainly see the publications by Adrian Boas who is leading a major project in the castle including survey and excavations: Boas, 2012a, 2012b, 2013a, 2013b. For Jiddīn, see for example Pringle et al., 1994; Khamisy, 2004. For Castellum Regis, see Ellenblum, 1996; Pringle, 1997: 71–2; 1993–2009: II, 30–2; Khamisy, 2013b. However, none of these had precisely examined the Teutons' political, social and economic activities through the archaeological remains they left in their rural settlements in Galilee. For these points see Khamisy, 2012, through the whole thesis. For a brief discussion on the landownership in Montfort region see Khamisy, forthcoming(b).

ACKNOWLEDGEMENT

I would like to thank Yad Hanadiv for the Rothschild Fellowship, the Council for Higher Education for the VATAT Fellowship, Haifa University for its generous grants, and Cardiff University for its hospitality during my post-doctorate.

REFERENCES

Amiran D., E. Arieh and T. Turcotte, 1994, 'Earthquakes in Israel and Adjacent Areas: Macroseismic Observations since 100 B.C.E.', *IEJ* 44: 260–305.

Bahā' al-Dīn Ibn Shaddād, 1994, *al-Nawādir al-sulṭāniyya wa'l maḥāsin al-yūsufiyya: sīrat Ṣalāḥ al-Dīn*, ed. Jamāl al-Dīn al-Shayyāl, Cairo.

——, 1872–1906, *Anecdotes et beaux traits de la vie du sultan Youssof (Salah ed-Din)*, in *Recueil des historiens des croisades: historiens orientaux (RHC Or)*, 5 vols, Paris.

Beyer, G., 1945, 'Die Kreuzfahrergebiete Akko und Galilaea', *ZDPV* 67 (1944–45): 183–260.

Boas, A.J., 2006, *Archaeology of the Military Orders: A Survey of the Urban Centres, Rural Settlement and Castles of the Military Orders in the Latin East (c. 1120–1291)*, London and New York.

——, 2010, *Domestic Settings: Sources on Domestic Architecture and Day-to-Day Activities in the Crusader State*, Leiden.

——, 2012a, 'The Montfort Castle Project: A Programme of Research, Conservation and Development at the Teutonic Castle in the Western Galilee', in *Mons Fortis alias Mons Feret. Il castello dei Teutonici in Terrasanta*, ed. C.M.R. Luschi and L. Aiello, Florence, 87–91.

——, 2012b, 'Some Preliminary Findings at the Teutonic Castle of Montfort', in *Christ is Here! Studies in Biblical and Christian Archaeology in Memory of Michele Piccirrillo ofm*, ed. L. Daniel Chrupcala, Milano, 11–27.

——, 2013a, 'Archaeological Evidence for the Two Sieges of Montfort Castle', *Castelos das Ordens Militares*, vol. 1, Lisbon, 73–85.

———, 2013b, 'Renewed Research at Montfort Castle', *Archaeology and Architecture of the Military Orders*, ed Mathias Piana, Ashgate, 175–92.

Conder, C.R., 1889a, 'Norman Palestine', *PEFQSt*: 195–201.

———, 1889b, 'The Norman Fiefs in Palestine', *PEFQSt*: 201–2.

———, 1890, 'Norman Palestine', *PEFQSt*: 29–37.

Conder, C.R. and H.H. Kitchener, 1881, *The Survey of Western Palestine: Memoirs of the Topography, Orography, Hydrography and Archaeology,* vol 1: Galilee, London.

Delaborde, H.F., (ed.), 1880, *Chartes de la Terre Sainte provenant de l'abbaye de Notre-Dame de Josaphat*, Bibliothèque des Écoles françaises d'Athènes et de Rome, vol. XIX, Paris.

Edbury, P. (ed. and trans.), 2009, *Philip of Novara: Le Livre de Forme de Plait*, Nicosia.

Ellenblum, R., 1996, 'Colonization Activities in the Frankish East: The Example of Castellum Regis (Mi'ilya)', *The English Historical Review* 111: 104–22.

———, 1998, *Frankish Rural Settlement in the Latin Kingdom of Jerusalem*, Cambridge.

Frankel, R., 1980, 'Three Crusader Boundary Stones from Kibbutz Shomrat', *Israel Exploration Journal* 30: 199–201.

———, 1988, 'Topographical Notes on the Territory of Acre in the Crusader Period', *IEJ* 38: 249–72.

Frankel, R. and N. Getzov, 1997, *Archaeological Survey of Israel: Map of Akhziv, Map of Hanita (2)*, Jerusalem.

———, 2013, *Archaeological Survey of Israel: Map of 'Amqa (5)*, Jerusalem.

Frankel, R. and E. Stern, 1996, 'A Crusader Screw Press from Western Galilee – The Manot Press', *Techniques and Culture* 27: 89–123.

Frankel, R., Getzov, N., Aviam, M. and A. Dagani, 2001, *Settlement Dynamics and Regional Diversity in Ancient Upper Galilee: Archaeological Survey of Upper Galilee*, IAA, Report 14, Jerusalem.

Fulcher of Chartres, nd, *Gesta peregrinantium francorum cum Armis Hierusalem pergentium*, in *RHC Occ*. III.

Guérin, V., 1969; orig. edn 1868–80, *Description géographique, historique et archéologique de la Palestine*, 7 vols., Galilée, vol. VII, Amsterdam.

Hamilton, B., 1985, 'The Titular Nobility of the Latin East: The Case of Agnes of Courtenay', in ed. P. Edbury, *Crusade and Settlement*, Cardiff, 197–203.

Holt, P.M., 2004, *The Crusader States and their Neighbors 1098–1291*, London.

Ibn 'Abd al-Ẓāhir, 1976, *al-Rawḍ al-zāhir fī sīrat al-malik al-ẓāhir*, ed. Abdulaziz al-Khuwaitir, al-Riyad, 250–63.

Ibn al-Athīr, 1987, *al-Kāmil fī al-ta'rīkh*, vol. 10: *Dār al-Kutub al-'Ilmiyya*, ed. Muḥammad al-Daqqāq, Beirut.

Ibn Jubayr, 1952, *The Travels of Ibn Jubayr*, trans. R.J.C. Broadhurst, London.

Ibn Jobair, 1956, *Voyages*, vol. 3, trans. M. Gaudefroy-Demombynes, Paris.

'Imād al-Dīn al-Iṣfahānī, *al-Fath al-qussī fī al-fath al-qudsī*, in Suhayl Zakkār, ed., *al-Mawsū'a al-shāmiyya fī ta'rīkh al-ḥurūb al-ṣalībiyya*, 40 vols, Damascus, 1995, 13.

Khamisy, R.G., 2004, The Influence of German Military Architecture in the Medieval Period on the Teutonic Castles in the Western Galilee (Montfort Castle and Jiddin Castle), unpublished MA thesis, University of Haifa (Hebrew).

———. 2012, Political, Social and Economic Activities of the Franks in the Western Galilee, 1104–1291, unpublished PhD diss., University of Haifa (Hebrew).

———, 2013a, 'The Templar Estates in the Territory of Acre', *Ordines Militares* 18: 267–85.

———, 2013b, 'The History and Architectural Design of Castellum Regis and Some Other Finds in the Village of Mi'ilya', *Crusades* 12: 13–51.

———, 2014a, 'The Treaty of 1283 between Sultan Qalāwūn and the Frankish Authorities of Acre: A New Topographical Discussion', *Israel Exploration Journal* 64(1): 72–102.

———, 2014b, 'The Un-ratified Treaty between the Mamlūks and the Franks of Acre in 1268', *al-Masaq* 26(2): 147–67.

————, forthcoming(a), *Fiefs, Fortresses, Villages and Farms in Western Galilee and Southern Lebanon in the Frankish period (1104–1291): Political, Social and Economic Activities.*

————, forthcoming(b), 'The Region of Montfort and Land Ownership in the Frankish Period', in *Montfort: History, Early Research and Recent Studies*, ed. A. J. Boas, assist. ed. R. G. Khamisy, Leiden and Boston.

————, forthcoming(c), 'Montfort Castle (Qal'at al-Qurayn) in Mamluk Sources', in *Montfort: History, Early Research and Recent Studies*, ed. A. J. Boas, assist. ed. R. G. Khamisy, Leiden and Boston.

Mas-Latrie, L., 1965; orig. edn 1878, 'Mélanges et Documents de Quelques Seigneurs de Terre Sainte Oubliés dans les Familles d'Outremer et du Cango. Les Seigneurs de St. George, du Bouquiqu et de Saor', *Revue Historique*, 8: 107–20.

————, 1882, 'Le Fief de Chamberlaine et les Chambellans de Jérusalem', *BEC* 43: 647–52.

Mayer, H.E., 1972a, 'Studies in the History of Queen Melisende of Jerusalem', *Dumbarton Oaks Papers* 26: 93–182.

————, 1972b, 'Two Unpublished Letters on the Syrian Earthquake of 1202', in *Medieval and Middle Eastern Studies in Honor of A. S. Atiya*, ed. Sami A. Hanna, Leiden.

————, 1977, 'Die Kreuzfahrerherrschaft *'Arrābe*', *ZDPV* 93: 198–212.

————, 1980, 'Die Seigneurie de Joscelin und der Deutsche Orden', in *Die geistlichen Ritterorden Europas (Vorträge und Forschungen, 26)*, ed. J. Fleckenstein and M. Hellman, Sigmaringen, 171–216.

————, 1982, *The Crusades*, trans. John Gillingham, New York.

————, 2010, *Die Urkunden der Lateinischen Könige von Jerusalem*, 4 vols, Hannover.

Nicholson, R.L., 1973, *Joscelyn III and the Fall of the Crusader State*, Leiden.

Piana, M., 2008, 'Die Deutschordenburg Montfort (Qal'at al-Qur'ain) in Galiläa', in *Burgen und Städte der Kreuzzugszeit*, ed. M. Piana, Petersberg.

Prawer, J., 1980, *Crusader Intitution*, Oxford.

————, 2001; orig. edn 1969–70, *Histoire du royaume latin de Jérusalem*, 2 vols, 2nd edn, Paris.

Prawer, J. and M. Benvenisti, 1970, 'Palestine under the Crusades', in *Atlas of Israel*, sheet IX/10, Jerusalem and Amsterdam.

Pringle, R.D., 1986, 'A Thirteenth Century Hall at Montfort Castle in Western Galilee', *The Antiquaries Journal* 66: 52–81.

————, 1997, *Secular Buildings in the Crusader Kingdom of Jerusalem*, Cambridge.

————, 1993–2009, *The Churches of the Crusader Kingdom of Jerusalem*, 4 vols, Cambridge.

————, 2010, 'Perceptions of the Castle in the Latin East', *Château Gaillard* 24: 223–29.

Pringle, R.D., A. Petersen, M. Dow and C. Singer, 1994, 'Qal'at Jiddin: A Castle of the Crusader and Ottoman Periods in Galilee', *Levant* 26: 135–66.

Rey, G.E., 1883, *Les colonies franques de Syrie aux XII et XIII siècles*, Paris.

Richards, D.S., trans., 2001, *The Rare and Excellent History of Saladin or al-Nawādir al-sulṭāniyya wa'l maḥāsin al-yūsufiyya by Bhā' al-Dīn Ibn Shaddād*, Crusader Texts in Translation, vol. 7, Aldershot and Burlington.

Riley-Smith, J., ed., 1991, *The Atlas of the Crusades*, London.

Röhricht, R., 1887, 'Studien zur mittelalterlichen Geographie und Topographie Syriens', *ZDPV* 10: 195–345.

————, (ed.), 1893, *Regesta Regni Hierosolymitani*, 2 vols., Innsbruck.

Strehlke, E. (ed.), 1975; orig. edn 1869, *Tabulae Ordinis Theutonici*, ed. H.E. Mayer, Berlin.

Stern, E.J., 1998, 'Horbat Manot (Lower)', *Excavations and Surveys in Israel* 18: 10–11.

————, 2001, 'The Excavations at Lower Horbat Manot: A Medieval Sugar -Production Site', *Atiqot* 42: 277–308.

Thorau, P., 1992, *The Lion of Egypt: Sultan Baybars I and the Near East in the Thirteenth Century*, trans. P.M. Holt, London and New York.

Tübinger Atlas, *Syria and Palestine, The Religious Military Orders*, 1:1,000,000 MAP 56-V3–1,000-BVIII12–1982 Tübinger Atlas des Vorderen Orients.

CHAPTER FOURTEEN

QUEEN ALICE OF CYPRUS

———•◆•———

Bernard Hamilton

Alice of Cyprus was interested in exercising political power. In this she resembled Melisende of Jerusalem and Eleanor of Aquitaine, from both of whom she was descended. Although some reference is made to her in most works dealing with the Latin East in the first half of the thirteenth century, she has not hitherto been the subject of any single study, and consequently her influence has often been underestimated.

She was the daughter of Isabel I of Jerusalem (1190–1205) by her third marriage. Isabel's first marriage to Humphrey IV of Toron, which had been childless, had been annulled in 1190 and she had then married Conrad of Montferrat to whom she bore a daughter, Maria. After his assassination in 1192, she married Count Henry II of Champagne, a nephew of both Richard I of England and Philip Augustus of France. Isabel and Henry had three daughters: Alice, born in *c.* 1193, Philippa and Margaret who almost certainly died in childhood (*Lignages*, 2003: 164).

Henry and Isabel's right to rule was contested by Guy of Lusignan who had become Lord of Cyprus in 1192. He had been married to Isabel's elder sister Sibyl and had been king of Jerusalem from 1186 until her death in 1190, but he continued to claim the throne for the rest of his life. When Henry married Isabel, Guy's brother Aimery was constable of the Kingdom of Jerusalem and lord of Jaffa. Henry stripped him of both dignities and exiled him to Cyprus, of which he became lord when Guy died childless in 1194. It was not until 1197 that Henry and Aimery made peace in preparation for the arrival of a new crusade led by the Western emperor Henry VI. One of the provisions of their agreement was that when their children came of age, Aimery's eldest surviving son should marry Henry's eldest surviving daughter who should receive the county of Jaffa as her dowry (*L'Estoire d'Eracles* (henceforth *Eracles*), 1859, XXVI, xxi, *RHC Occ.* II, p. 209; the Florence manuscript (Bibl. Laurentiana, Pluteus 61, 10) gives details of the dowry, 1982: 177). A few months later, in September 1197, the imperial chancellor, Conrad of Hildesheim, who came to the Levant with the vanguard of the crusade, crowned Aimery king of Cyprus while in return Aimery acknowledged that his kingdom was an imperial fief.

On 10 September 1197, Henry of Champagne fell to his death from the first-floor gallery of the palace of Acre, and after a short interval Queen Isabel married Aimery of

Cyprus who had recently become a widower (*Eracles*, XXVII, iii–v, pp. 219–23). The projected imperial crusade was abandoned because Emperor Henry VI died in December 1197, and the defence of the Latin East undoubtedly benefited from the union of Cyprus and Jerusalem, but no attempt was made to perpetuate it. When Aimery died on 1 April 1205, he was succeeded as king of Cyprus by Hugh I, the son of his first marriage. Isabel had borne him three children, a son who died in infancy, and two daughters, Sibyl and Melisende (*Lignages*, 2003: 81).

Isabel resumed sole rule of Jerusalem and, with the assent of the High Court, appointed John of Ibelin as her *bailli*, or executive regent. John and his brother Philip were her half-brothers. Isabel was the only child of King Amalric (1163–74) and Maria Comnena, while John and Philip were the sons of Maria's second marriage in 1177 to Balian of Ibelin (*Eracles*, XXX, xi, p. 305).

Isabel died a few months after her husband, leaving five daughters. A clear precedent existed for the succession when there were only female heirs: that of Baldwin II, who in 1131 had been succeeded by his eldest daughter, Melisende. So Isabel was succeeded by her eldest daughter, Maria, the child of Conrad of Montferrat. She was about fourteen years old, and it was thought necessary to appoint a regent until she married. The custom of the kingdom, recorded for Aimery of Lusignan in the *Livre au Roi*, stated that: 'The regency of the kingdom should be entrusted to the nearest relation, male or female, on the mother's side, if the claim to the throne comes through the mother' (*Le Livre au roi* c.5, 1995: 146). Since Maria's sisters were all still minors, her closest maternal kin was her uncle, John of Ibelin, who was already *bailli*, and who was now appointed as her regent (*Eracles, * XXX, xi, p. 305). Alice, who was the next oldest of Queen Isabel's daughters, became Queen Maria's heir-presumptive.

Under the terms of the agreement made between her father and Aimery of Lusignan in 1197, Alice, the eldest surviving daughter of Henry, should have been betrothed to Hugh I of Cyprus, Aimery's eldest surviving son. Hugh was still a minor and the regency was held by Walter of Montbéliard, husband of his sister Burgundia (*Eracles, * XXX, xii, p. 305). A papal dispensation was needed to allow Alice and Hugh to marry, because as a result of Aimery's marriage to Isabella they had become stepbrother and stepsister although no blood relationship existed between them. Innocent III delegated the inquiry to Albert, Patriarch of Jerusalem, and if either of the regents had been opposed to the marriage, they could have raised objections at that point, but neither of them did so (*Bullarium Cyprium* I, doc. b.-27, pp. 145–6). Walter of Montbéliard no doubt welcomed a marriage which, if Queen Maria should die childless, would bring the Kingdom of Jerusalem under the rule of King Hugh. John of Ibelin, it may be conjectured, hoped that the marriage would strengthen the interests of his family, for Hugh's mother had been Eschiva of Ibelin, and his marriage to John's niece Alice might restore Ibelin influence at the court of Cyprus.

The marriage was in Alice's own best interests, because there was no more eligible bachelor in the Latin East than Hugh of Cyprus. A papal dispensation was granted, and Alice received the county of Jaffa as her dowry, as had been specified in the 1197 agreement. Her marriage contract was supervised by her grandmother, Maria Comnena, who may have been her guardian (*Thesaurus Novus Anecdotorum*, 1717: I, 806–7). The marriage probably took place in 1210, the year in which Hugh was fifteen and came of age. Alice, who was about seventeen, was escorted to Cyprus by her uncles John and Philip of Ibelin (*Eracles*, XXX, xv, p. 309). The marriage preceded the end of the truce with al-Adil and the arrival of John of Brienne at Acre in September 1210. Peter Edbury argues that the first half of 1210 was the most likely date for the marriage (Edbury, 1991: 43, n. 18).

The High Court of Jerusalem had asked Philip Augustus to choose a husband for Queen Maria, and he nominated John of Brienne, a first cousin of Walter of Montbéliard, the regent of Cyprus. John of Brienne reached Acre in September 1210 and his marriage to Maria marked the end of John of Ibelin's regency (*Eracles* XXX, xiii–xiv, XXXI, i, pp. 306–8, 311–12). The regency of Walter of Montbéliard also came to an end at about the same time, when Hugh I attained his majority. When the young king demanded that Walter should account for the revenues which he had received while regent and hand over the treasures which he had amassed, Walter fled to the court of John of Brienne, where he died in 1212 (*Eracles* XXXI, v, pp. 315–16; Rudt de Collenberg, 1977–1979: 131, n. 45).

John was not popular with some of the nobility of Jerusalem: this was particularly true of his relations with the Ibelins and their supporters.[1] There was no open breach while Queen Maria was alive (Mayer, no. 626, 2010: III, 1017–19), but after her death in 1212 neither John nor Philip of Ibelin appeared at John of Brienne's court again. As they were kinsmen of King Hugh, it seems likely that they went to live in Cyprus, and it would appear that they were not alone in this, for in 1213 Innocent III reprimanded Hugh for supporting John of Brienne's rebellious vassals, although he did not name them (*Bullarium Cyprium* I, doc. b.-36, pp. 162–4). The first secure evidence for the presence of the Ibelin brothers in Cyprus comes from 1217, when they headed the list of witnesses in a diploma of King Hugh for the Teutonic Order (Röhricht, 1893–4: no. 900, I, 241).

The constitutional position of John of Brienne after the death of Queen Maria was uncertain. The heir to the throne was their only child, Isabel II, sometimes called Yolande, who was at most about a year old when her mother died. Her father, as her nearest kinsman, was undoubtedly the lawful regent during her minority, but there was some uncertainty about whether he should continue to be king after his wife's death. Had John's daughter Isabel died, the throne would certainly have passed to the heir-presumptive, Alice of Cyprus and her husband King Hugh, and it was an awareness of this, no doubt, which led John of Brienne's disaffected vassals to seek refuge at the Lusignan court.

Alice's younger sister, Philippa, remained in Acre as a ward of John of Brienne. In c. 1213, as *L'Estoire d'Eracles* reports: 'While King John was visiting Tyre, Philippa, the daughter of Count Henry, left the castle of Acre secretly by night and went to the lodgings of Erard of Brienne, who married her at dawn on the next day, which was a Friday' (*Eracles*, XXXI, viii, p. 319). Erard was King John's cousin, and he and Philippa went to France, where they advanced Philippa's claim to the County of Champagne.

When Alice and Philippa's father, Henry of Troyes, count of Champagne, took the cross, he designated his younger brother, Theobald, as his heir should he die on crusade without issue. When Henry died in 1197, Theobald III was invested with Champagne by Philip Augustus without reference to the rights of Henry's daughters, living in Acre. Theobald III died in 1201, leaving his wife, Blanche of Navarre, pregnant with the future Theobald IV. During his minority, she acted as regent of the county and vigorously defended his rights against Erard and Philippa's claims. First she disputed the validity of their marriage. Innocent III ruled that they were related within the prohibited degrees because one each of their great-grandfathers had been brothers.[2] Despite this ruling, the marriage was not annulled, perhaps because in 1215, before the case had been resolved, the Fourth Lateran Council reduced the number of the prohibited degrees of kinship, so that Erard and Philippa's marriage no longer contravened canon law (*De restricta prohibitione matrimonii*, 1973: Canon 50, pp. 257–8). Philip Augustus made a pragmatic ruling that the dispute about the succession to Champagne should not be judged until 1222

227

when Theobald IV would come of age at twenty-one (Dossier, documents IV, V, VI, PL 216, cols 975–77).

Countess Blanche realised that the question of the validity of Erard and Philippa's marriage was at best a delaying tactic rather than a secure defence of Theobald IV's rights, because even if Philippa's marriage was annulled, her claims to the county would be unaffected. The regent therefore raised a different objection: that Philippa's father's marriage to Isabel of Jerusalem had been invalid because the annulment of her first marriage to Humphrey IV of Toron had been uncanonical. From this it followed that she had not been free to marry either Conrad of Montferrat or Henry of Champagne, and that the daughters she had borne to Henry were illegitimate and had no claim to their father's inheritance. Isabel's marriage to Humphrey had been dissolved by the papal legates on the Third Crusade, but all the sources agree that the proceedings had been brief and arbitrary, and that although Humphrey had been opposed to the divorce, the court had given him no opportunity to present his case (Hamilton, 1978: 172–3). Cardinal Robert of S. Stefano, to whom Innocent III entrusted this inquiry, took statements from a group of knights who had served on the Third Crusade and witnessed the annulment proceedings. They were unanimous in declaring that the marriage had been dissolved against the wishes of the young couple (Dossier, document XI, PL 216, cols 980–1). Nevertheless, Pope Innocent, like many of his contemporaries, was struck by the way in which Isabel's second and third husbands had met with violent deaths: Conrad at the hands of the Assassins and Henry by falling headlong from a balcony, and supposed that this indicated divine displeasure. He therefore ordered that the annulment should be reviewed by a tribunal of the Roman curia (Champagne Dossier, documents VII, VIII, PL 216, cols 978–9).

This challenge to the validity of Queen Isabel's second and third marriages had implications for the succession to the throne of Jerusalem as well as to that of the county of Champagne. Odoard, the marshal of Champagne, swore on oath to the papal legate that Isabel's three daughters (Maria, Alice and Philippa) were born while Humphrey IV of Toron was still alive (Champagne Dossier, document XII, PL 216, col. 980; Migne incorrectly dates this document 1200, but the text itself gives the correct date of 1213). None of the witnesses who gave evidence made any reference to Isabel's fourth marriage to Aimery of Lusignan, perhaps because Humphrey of Toron died in 1198 soon after it was solemnised (Mayer, 1990: 241). If Innocent III had upheld the objections to the annulment of Isabel's marriage to Humphrey of Toron, not merely would Alice and Philippa have had no claim to the county of Champagne, but they and their elder half-sister Queen Maria would have had no claim to the throne of Jerusalem either. In that case the rightful heir to the crusader kingdom would have been Sibyl, the elder daughter of Isabel and Aimery of Lusignan. Hugh of Cyprus, who was her half-brother and guardian, had arranged her marriage to Leo II of Armenian Cilicia in *c.* 1210 (*Eracles*, XXX, xi, p. 305; *Lignages*, 2003: 81–2; Rudt de Collenberg, 1979–80: 99–100), but it is doubtful how far an Armenian king-consort would have been acceptable to the baronage of Jerusalem. This may explain why, although the question of Isabel I's divorce from Humphrey was not forgotten by the Holy See, it was never pursued with any degree of rigour, because the political implications for the Latin East would have been very difficult to handle. Consequently Maria's daughter, Isabel II, remained queen of Jerusalem, while her aunt, Queen Alice of Cyprus, remained the heir-presumptive.

Alice and Hugh had two daughters, Maria and Isabel, and a son Henry, born on 3 March 1217 (*Lignages*, 2003: 90; Rudt de Collenberg, 1979–80: 100–3). In September of that year, the first contingent of the Fifth Crusade, led by King Andrew II of Hungary, reached the Levant. King Hugh took a force of Cypriot crusaders to the mainland and joined with Andrew's army and that of the Kingdom of Jerusalem in raids on Muslim-held Galilee and the lands to the east of the Jordan. Andrew II, having fulfilled his crusading vow, set out for home with his army in January 1218 and Hugh accompanied him as far as Tripoli, where he attended the marriage of his half-sister Melisende, the younger daughter of King Aimery and Queen Isabel I, to the recently widowered Bohemond IV of Antioch. During the celebrations, Hugh was taken ill, and died at Tripoli on 10 January 1218 (*Eracles*, XXXI, xiii, p. 325; Powell, 1986: 123–36.

Henry I of Cyprus was eight months old when he succeeded to the throne, and there are two contemporary accounts of the provision made for the government of the kingdom during his long minority. One is in the *Mémoires* of Philip of Novara, who at the end of his life was described as 'the best legal counsel this side of the sea' ('Sire Phelipe de Nevaire, qui lon tient au meillour plaideour de sa mer', Edbury, 1979: 25). In his youth he had entered the service of John of Ibelin, Lord of Beirut, with whom he remained until John's death in 1236, and his account of events in Cyprus after Hugh's death is heavily weighted in favour of his patron's family (Philippe de Novare, 1913, pp. iii–vi):

> All the liegemen of the king did homage to Queen [Alice] as regent, and they all begged my lord Philip of Ibelin to be *bailli* of Cyprus, to rule the land, preside over justice and command the army. King Hugh himself as he was dying had asked that this should be done. Lord Philip received the office of *bailli*, which caused him a great deal of work and harm, and the queen received the revenues and spent the money lavishly.
>
> (Philippe de Novare, 1913, c. iii, p. 6)

The account given by *L'Estoire d'Eracles*, the Old French continuation of William of Tyre's *Chronicle*, is rather different:

> Queen [Alice] required the people of the land to do homage to her, and they did so immediately and without reservation, because she was the regent. After she had received homage, she handed over the government of the kingdom on her behalf to her uncle, Philip of Ibelin, and required her vassals to swear to obey him until her son Henry came of age. This was a stupid thing to do, because when she wished to change her mind she was unable to do so.
>
> (*Eracles*, XXXII, xxi, pp. 360–1)

Alice's appointment as regent set a constitutional precedent in the kingdoms of Jerusalem and Cyprus because the mother of a sovereign had not previously held power there during a minority.[3] This may account for the degree of hostility which Alice initially faced, which led Honorius III to instruct Cardinal Pelagius of Albano, his legate on the Fifth Crusade, together with the Masters of the Temple and the Hospital, to defend the queen from 'certain men inspired with wicked fervour, who rashly presume to do injury to her, her children and her kingdom' (*Bullarium Cyprium*, I, docs. c.-17, c.-19, pp. 199–202). It was presumably in response to this opposition that Alice appointed an executive regent, or *bailli*, to govern on her behalf. Philip of Ibelin was an obvious choice. He was her uncle, but he had no claim to the throne and therefore had a vested interest in insuring the safety of the child king.

After the death of King Hugh, the Cypriot crown took no further official part in the Fifth Crusade, although individual barons from Cyprus played a distinguished role in it. In May 1218 the crusade was directed against Egypt, and Alice maintained regular contact with its leaders to whom she relayed information about Muslim troop movements in Syria (Oliver of Paderborn, 1894: 268). As regent she also had dealings with the legate, Cardinal Pelagius, who was charged with negotiating a religious settlement in Cyprus. Virtually the entire indigenous population belonged to the Orthodox Church of Cyprus, a venerable and self-governing institution, which had been granted autocephalous status by the Council of Ephesus in 431 (Janin, 1955: cols 791–820). A Latin hierarchy had been established in the island by Pope Celestine III (1191–98), consisting of an archbishop at Nicosia, with suffragans at Famagusta, Limassol and Paphos, but when Alice became regent, relations between the two hierarchies had not been resolved.

Alice was sympathetic to the Orthodox of Cyprus. This may reflect the influence of her grandmother, Maria Comnena, or it may simply indicate that she had sound political sense and did not wish to offend Greek Christians, who formed the majority of her subjects. In the Agreement drawn up in October 1220 between the queen, the Frankish nobility and the Latin hierarchy of Cyprus, in the presence of Cardinal Pelagius, Alice specified that the Orthodox clergy should be freed from the payment of taxes and from *corvées* of labour. Her intervention was important, since, as Nicholas Coureas has pointed out, the Orthodox hierarchy was not represented at the discussions. The queen also wanted the Greek bishops to remain in office and this matter was referred to the pope, who was adamant that the Orthodox hierarchy should be suppressed (Coureas, 1997: 12; *Bullarium Cyprium*, I, docs c.-35, c.-37, pp. 223–5, 227–8). In the end, as a result of Alice's persistence, a compromise was reached whereby an Orthodox bishop was allowed to live as a suffragan of his Catholic colleague in each of the four Latin sees, although many other Orthodox bishoprics were suppressed (*The Cartulary of the Cathedral of the Holy Wisdom of Nicosia* (henceforth, *Holy Wisdom*), 1997: no. 95, p. 251).

The Frankish nobility did not object to these provisions, but opposed very strongly the concession made by the queen in the 1220 Agreement that all Frankish landowners should pay tithe to support the Latin hierarchy. Honorius III was not satisfied with the terms of the Agreement either, because no decision had been reached about Orthodox church property sequestered by the Franks, which the pope proposed should be given to the Latin Church. A fresh Agreement was therefore drawn up in 1222 despite the protests of the Frankish nobility. The provisions about payment of tithe were allowed to stand, but the Crown and its Frankish vassals declined to restore any of the former property of the Orthodox Church to the Latin bishops. The papal legate, and in due course the pope himself, had no alternative but to accept this decision (the First Agreement, *Holy Wisdom*, 1997: no. 84, pp. 220–2; confirmation by Pelagius, no. 82, pp. 213–16; the papal requirement to reconsider the Agreement, no. 80, pp. 208–9; the Second Agreement, no. 95, pp. 249–52; confirmation by Pelagius, no. 83, pp. 216–219; confirmation by Honorius III on 16 May 1224, no. 98, pp. 255–6; Coureas, 1997, pp. 11–31). As these negotiations show, Queen Alice was not simply a nominal head of state but took an active part in shaping policy which affected her vassals. This may have contributed to the tension which developed between her and her *bailli*, Philip of Ibelin.

Alice was also anxious to pursue her claim to her father's inheritance in Champagne. She may have been encouraged in this by the judgment of Innocent III that Erard of Brienne had been blinded by ambition and avarice in claiming Champagne on behalf of his wife

Philippa, 'because she is not the firstborn daughter, who ought to succeed if it were right that either of them should succeed' (Dossier, no. VI, PL 216, cols 976–7). Alice does not seem to have raised the issue in her husband's lifetime, but on 23 June 1219 Honorius III reported that the Countess Blanche of Champagne had complained to him that Alice had sent a representative to advance her claim to the county. The pope later informed Philip Augustus, as overlord of Champagne, that no action should be taken until the curia had determined whether Alice was of legitimate birth (*Bullarium Cyprium*, I, docs c.-23, c.-24, pp. 209–11). Erard of Brienne was no longer in contention: he had renounced his claims to Champagne in return for a monetary indemnity and a substantial land grant, and had even undertaken to support Blanche against Alice (Dossier, nos XIII, XVII, PL 216, cols 982–4, 986–7). Alice did not attempt to use force to make good her claim, which would have been both expensive and impractical, but more subtly sought to arrange a marriage for herself with William II of Dampierre who, as constable of Champagne, would have been a powerful advocate of her rights. Theobald IV, who had come of age in 1222, presumably alerted Honorius III to this proposal, and in August 1223 the pope declared that Alice and William were related within the prohibited degrees and refused to grant them a dispensation (*Bullarium Cyprium*, I, doc. c.-49, pp. 250–1; Evergates, 1975: 177).

Alice made no further attempt to assert her claim to Champagne for some years because a crisis had arisen in her government of Cyprus. Philip of Ibelin resented the fact that the queen did not delegate the financial administration to him as *bailli*. The *Chronique de Terre Sainte* relates: 'Queen Alice was very generous and spent the revenues of the kingdom liberally, and disposed of them entirely as seemed good to her' (*Chronique de Terre* Sainte, c. 96, 1869: II, 669). Unfortunately there is no way of testing the truth of this assertion because the only surviving financial document issued by Alice as regent is a modest grant of alms for the repose of the soul of King Hugh (*Holy Wisdom*, 1997: no. 62, pp. 167–8). *L'Estoire d'Eracles* reports that Philip of Ibelin made the queen's position so untenable that 'she was not able to endure any longer the injuries and lack of respect to which she was subjected' and went into voluntary exile, initially in the Kingdom of Jerusalem, where her dowry, the county of Jaffa, was situated. Subsequently she married Prince Bohemond of Antioch-Tripoli, the son of Bohemond IV. The date given by *L'Estoire d'Eracles* for this, the late summer of 1225, is unlikely to be correct, 'ele ne pot soffrir moult de leidenges et de despis que l'en li faisoit' (*Eracles* XXXII, xxi, *RHC Occ.* II, p. 361), because on 11 August 1225 Honorius III ordered Archbishop Eustorgius of Nicosia to hold an inquiry to determine whether Alice and Bohemond were related within the prohibited degrees. Since a request about this matter must have had time to reach the curia from the Latin East, it seems likely that the marriage had taken place earlier, perhaps in the winter of 1224–25 (*Bullarium Cyprium*, I, doc. c.-63, pp. 271–2).

According to Philip of Novara, the members of the High Court of Cyprus feared that Alice would try to make Bohemond *bailli* in place of Philip of Ibelin, a contingency to which they were unanimously opposed (Philip of Novara, 1913: c. viii, p. 8). This was almost certainly the reason why the pope had been alerted to the possibility that Alice's marriage to Bohemond was uncanonical. In fact the barons of Cyprus were not so solidly behind Philip of Ibelin as Philip of Novara claimed. A group led by Aimery Barlais, Amaury of Bethsan, Hugh of Jubail, William Rivet and Gawain of Chenéché were members of families which had settled in Cyprus under Guy and Aimery of Lusignan (Edbury, 1991: 51–2; Hamilton, 1997: 16). When Aimery Barlais quarrelled with Philip of Ibelin and sought refuge with Alice and Bohemond in Tripoli, Alice appointed him her *bailli* in Cyprus. The High Court refused to accept him, claiming that Philip of Ibelin had been appointed *bailli* until the king reached his majority and that Alice did not have the power to change the terms of his appointment which the High Court had ratified. Aimery Barlais therefore returned to Tripoli for, as Philip of Novara comments, 'his expectation was that with imperial help he would be able to subdue the house of Ibelin' (Philip of Novara, 1913: c. x, p. 9). Other opponents of the Ibelins joined him at Tripoli, among them William de Rivet, whom Alice and Bohemond chose, together with the master of the cathedral school of Antioch, to defend the validity of their marriage before the Roman curia (*Bullarium Cyprium*, I, doc. c.-76, pp. 285–6).

Philip of Novara's mention of 'the expectation of imperial help' related to the forthcoming crusade of the Emperor Frederick II. In 1223 he had betrothed Isabel II of Jerusalem and had given a solemn undertaking to Honorius III that he would lead a crusade to the East in 1225. Although the crusade was deferred until 1227, Isabel was married to the emperor by proxy in 1225 and crowned queen of Jerusalem at Tyre. Alice, the queen's aunt and heir-presumptive, attended the coronation and led the official delegation which bade her farewell when she left for the Sicilian Kingdom, where her marriage to Frederick was solemnised on 9 November (*Eracles*, XXXII, xxi, *RHC Occ.* II, p. 361; *Chronique de Terre Sainte*, 1869: II, 668).

Alice and all Philip of Ibelin's opponents looked to Frederick II for help. As emperor he had an interest in the Kingdom of Cyprus because Aimery of Lusignan had received it as a fief from Frederick's father, Henry VI. After his imperial coronation in 1220, Frederick considered himself overlord of Cyprus, and Philip of Novara reports that he had several times asked Alice to recognise him as the true regent. These claims were at first theoretical, but after he had married Isabel II and announced his intention of coming on crusade, it was necessary to take them seriously. In 1225 the High Court of Cyprus arranged for Archbishop Eustorgius to crown the eight-year-old king Henry. This was done without reference to Alice. What they hoped to achieve by it is not clear: perhaps the barons believed that the king, once he had been crowned, would be able to validate the acts carried out by Philip of Ibelin in his name. The coronation angered Frederick, since it was performed without reference to him as overlord: the rite should have taken place in presence of his representative, and Henry should have done homage for his kingdom ('Et aucune fois manda l'empereor a la reyne Alis de Chypre qu'ele li laissast tenir le baillage de grace, tant com il li plairoit', Philip de Novara, 1913: c. iv, p. 6).

In 1226, in preparation for his coming, the emperor appointed the Sicilian Count Thomas of Acera as his *bailli* in the Kingdom of Jerusalem in place of John of Brienne's nephew, Odo of Montbéliard. This showed that Frederick intended to control the government of his wife's kingdom (on Odo of Montbéliard, see Hamilton, 1997: 'Entourages', p. 21, n. 57; on Frederick II's appointment of *baillis* see Riley-Smith, 1973: 166–7, 319). At that time he was well disposed towards Alice and Bohemond. He persuaded Honorius III, shortly before his death in March 1227, that Archbishop Eustorgius, to whom the pope had delegated the inquiry into the validity of their marriage, was not an impartial judge, and Honorius appointed two new judges to investigate the case, an arrangement which was ratified by the new pope, Gregory IX (Honorius III appointed the patriarch of Jerusalem and the bishop of Acre as judges delegate, and Gregory IX confirmed this, *Bullarium Cyprium*, I, docs. c.-75, c.-76, d.-1, pp. 284–8). In the summer of 1227 the Frankish leaders from Cyprus and the mainland, including Queen Alice and her husband, gathered at Limassol to greet the emperor. Alice and Bohemond no doubt hoped that he would recognise them as regents for King Henry, but Frederick did not arrive. He had fallen ill when about to leave Sicily and was forced to postpone his departure until late June 1228 (*Eracles*, XXXII, xxiii, *RHC Occ.* II, p. 364).

Before he set out for the East, his constitutional position in the Kingdom of Jerusalem changed. In the first place he had been excommunicated by Gregory IX in 1227 for failing to leave the West on the scheduled date, and the pope renewed this censure in 1228 because the emperor left on crusade before making his peace with the Church. The problems which this caused him as a crusade commander were fairly minimal, although the repercussions in the Sicilian Kingdom were more serious (Pacifico, 2012: 155–86). A change in his position in the Kingdom of Jerusalem had come when Isabel II of Jerusalem died on 4 May 1228, having given birth on 25 April to a son named Conrad (Mayer, 2010: III, 1070). According to the law of the kingdom, Frederick then, like John of Brienne in 1212, ceased to hold the crown matrimonial and became regent for his daughter.

The emperor's constitutional position in Cyprus remained unchanged. Philip of Ibelin had died in 1227 and had been succeeded as *bailli* by his brother John, Lord of Beirut. John was appointed without reference to Queen Alice and presumably owed his position entirely to the High Court, but it is doubtful whether that body had the right to appoint a *bailli* without the consent of the regent (the exact date of Philip of Ibelin's death is unknown; Edbury, 1997: 38, n. 50).

Frederick learned about this development from a group of dissident Cypriot noblemen who joined his fleet off the coast of Frankish Greece as he brought his crusading force to the Levant in the summer of 1228 (Philip of Novara, 1913: c. xviii, p. 12). When he reached Limassol he found a delegation from the Kingdom of Jerusalem waiting for him, together with the barons of Cyprus (*Eracles,* XXXII, i, *RHC Occ.* II, p. 367).

Soon after this he was joined by Prince Bohemond IV of Antioch at the head of a crusading force of sixty knights and an unspecified number of mounted sergeants and infantrymen (*Eracles,* XXXII, iii, *RHC Occ.* II, p. 368). It is not known whether his son and daughter-in-law, Bohemond and Queen Alice, accompanied him, but, as Philip of Novara relates, cordial relations between Bohemond IV and the emperor soon broke down because Fredrick ordered the prince and his vassals to take an oath of fealty to him. The prince, '*se tint a mort et dezerité*', fled secretly by night, together with his army, to the castle of Nefin in the county of Tripoli (Philip of Novara, 1913: c. xxxix, pp. 22–3). Although Frederick might have argued that the counts of Tripoli had traditionally been vassals of the kings of Jerusalem (John of Jaffa, *Le Livre des Assises*, c. x; Edbury, 1997: 113–14), the princes of Antioch had never been. Prince Bohemond had no intention of accepting the suzerainty of the Western emperor and took no further part in Frederick's crusade. One consequence of this was that Alice and the young prince Bohemond lost the emperor's goodwill and received no help from him in being restored to power as regents of Cyprus.

This did not mean that the emperor had any sympathy with the Ibelins. He asked John of Ibelin to account for his administration of the finances of the kingdom. John's defence was a technical one: as *bailli* he did not receive the revenues, which were paid to Queen Alice as regent, but Fredrick was not impressed by this claim, not least perhaps because there is no evidence that any revenues had been paid to Queen Alice since she had left Cyprus in 1224 (Edbury,1991: 56–8). Frederick removed John from power and required the little King Henry to do homage to him, but Henry's vassals refused to do homage directly to Frederick, claiming that they owed homage only to Queen Alice as regent, though they were prepared to do homage to the emperor as King Henry's overlord, and Frederick was content with that (Philip of Novara, 1913: cc. xxvii, xxxvii, pp. 16–17, 21–2). When he left for Italy in 1229 he appointed the five chief opponents of the Ibelins as joint *baillis* of Cyprus (Philip of Novara, 1913: c. xlv, p. 25). Frederick did not question Alice's right to be regent, but he did nothing to restore her powers. He did not seek her confirmation of the *baillis* whom he appointed, nor was she consulted about the marriage which Frederick arranged for her twelve-year-old son Henry with Alice of Montferrat, which took place on 15 May 1229. That marriage was in Frederick's interest, since the bride was a cousin of his son Conrad (Alice of Montferrat was a granddaughter of Boniface of Montferrat; Conrad of Jerusalem was a great-grandson of Boniface's brother, Conrad (Hamilton, 1997: 'Entourages', p. 22, n. 65)). Alice officially remained regent until Henry came of age on 3 May 1232 when he was fifteen, but her title conferred no power and during those years she did not return to Cyprus (see the 'Table chronologique' appended by Kohler to his edition of Philip of Novara's *Mémoires* (1913: 137)).

Queen Alice was a woman of combative temperament. Although Frederick had ignored her during his time in the East, she remained heir-presumptive to the crown of Jerusalem and countess of Jaffa, The High Court had recognised Conrad as king, and did not dispute that Frederick, as his closest kinsman, had the right to be his regent, or that as regent he had the right to appoint *baillis* to rule the kingdom during his son's minority. Before he left Acre on 1 May 1229, Frederick appointed Balian Lord of Sidon and Garnier l'Aleman as *baillis* in Acre, and Rainald of Haifa as *bailli* in the city of Jerusalem, recently restored to Frankish rule (Riley-Smith, 1973: 319).

A few weeks later Alice appeared before the High Court to point out that the laws of the kingdom required an heir to a fief living in the West to come in person and claim his inheritance within a year and a day of his succession. Isabel II had died on 5 May 1228, and the time of grace for Conrad to make his claim had expired on 6 May 1229. He had therefore forfeited the throne, and Alice demanded that she should be recognised as queen because she was the legitimate heir of her grandfather King Amalric I (1163–74). The members of the Court were clearly flustered and pointed out that they had just done homage to the emperor as regent for King Conrad. Nevertheless, they accepted the force of Alice's argument and adopted a compromise solution. Geoffrey le Tor and John of Bailleul were sent to Italy to require the emperor to send his son to receive seisin of the kingdom within a year and a day. If he did so they would receive him as their lord, and the emperor is said to have agreed to those terms (*Eracles*, XXXIII, xiii, *RHC Occ.* II, 380).

Frederick, of course, never complied with this unrealistic undertaking. There was considerable opposition to him in the Latin East, but initially on quite different grounds. John of Ibelin, Lord of Beirut, led a revolt against the imperial *baillis* in Cyprus which spread to the mainland (Edbury, 1991: 60–5).

The Ibelins and their supporters recognised the absent Conrad of Hohenstaufen as lawful king, while disputing the emperor's right to appoint *baillis* for him *in absentia*. That function, they claimed, devolved on the High Court in the emperor's absence. John of Ibelin, it may be inferred, had no interest in supporting Alice's claim to the throne, even though she was his niece, because she had opposed the rule of his brother Philip and of himself in Cyprus. Yet without the support of her Ibelin kinsmen Alice had no hope of success, and she was aware of this.

No mention is made of Alice's husband Bohemond in the accounts of her suit before the High Court of Jerusalem, because their marriage had been dissolved before then. This is known from the fact that Pierre Mauclerc, Count of Brittany, had made public his intention of marrying Queen Alice. This alliance did not take place because on 21 July 1229 Pope Gregory IX refused to grant the couple a dispensation from consanguinity (*Bullarium Cyprium*, I, doc. d.-2, pp. 288–9).

Queen Alice did not perceive her exclusion from the Kingdom of Cyprus, the rejection by the High Court of her claims to the throne of Jerusalem, or the annulment of her marriage to the heir to the principality of Antioch/Tripoli, as reasons why she should retire from public life. Instead, she decided to pursue her claim to the county of Champagne. Her cousin Theobald IV was by this time well established, but had made many enemies among the high nobility of France and, indeed, among some of his own vassals, all of whom were inclined to support Alice's claims. She went to France in person in 1233, and Theobald alerted Gregory IX to this and reminded him that the question of Alice's legitimacy had never been resolved. The pope ordered Alice to come to Rome, so that the matter might be examined by a papal tribunal and wrote to her supporters in Champagne forbidding them to withdraw their allegiance from Theobald until the Church had given judgment about Alice's legitimacy. The sheer volume of this correspondence is an index of the support which Alice enjoyed (*Bullarium Cyprium*, docs. d.-11, d.-12, d.-13, d.-14, pp. 301–7). Louis IX helped to formulate a peaceful settlement in September 1234, by which Alice renounced her claim to Champagne and Brie and in return received from Theobald IV an outright payment of 40,000 livres of Tours, together with estates in freehold tenure which would yield a further 2,000 livres annually (Dossier, nos 20, 21, PL 216, cols 988–92). Jean Richard observed: 'Quelle que fût la richesse de Thibaud … l'énormité de cette somme le contraignit à aliéner une partie de ses terres' (1983: 95). Although Gregory IX complained in August 1234 that Alice had refused to appear before the papal tribunal, her agreement with Theobald obviated any need for her to do so, and the question of whether Isabel I had been lawfully married to Conrad of Montferrat and Henry of Champagne remained permanently unresolved (*Bullarium Cyprium*, I, doc. d.-19, pp. 311–12).

When Alice left Cyprus in 1224, her daughters Maria and Isabel had stayed behind with the young King Henry (in 1232 they were living in the castle of Dieudamour/St Hilarion; *Eracles*, XXXIII, xxxiii, *RHC Occ.* II, p. 399). When Henry came of age in 1232, John of Ibelin, who hoped to enlist the support of Bohemond IV of Antioch in his war against Frederick II's supporters in the Latin Kingdom, persuaded King Henry to arrange a marriage between his younger sister Isabel and Bohemond's younger son, Henry (Philip of Novara, 1913: c. xcv, p. 61). There is no evidence that King Henry consulted his mother about this marriage, but he certainly seems to have enlisted her help in arranging the marriage of his elder sister, Maria.

Maria married Walter IV of Brienne, one of the chief vassals of Theobald IV of Champagne, and the nephew of King John of Brienne (*Lignages,* 2003: 90). He was also the only credible alternative to Frederick II as King of Sicily, because his mother, Alberia, was the daughter of King Tancred (1189–94) (van Cleve, 1972: 43; Longnon, 1978: 15–18). He married Maria in 1235, the year in which Queen Alice returned to the Latin Kingdom and a confederate Frankish army besieged Montferrand (*Annales de Terre Sainte,* 1884: II, part ii, p. 439). *L'Estoire d'Eracles* records among the Frankish participants in that campaign, 'Gautier li cuens de Briene, qui avoit esposée en cele année Marie la suer dou roi Henri' (*Eracles,* XXXIII, xxxviii, *RHC Occ.* II, p. 403; the editor has wrongly dated this siege to 1233). Walter became count of Jaffa, but that county was Alice's dowry.

Mayer has rightly pointed out that the use of this title by Walter during Alice's lifetime implies that the county had been transferred to Maria when she married Walter, and that Walter held it in his wife's right (Mayer, 1984: 143–44 acknowledges that he is indebted to a suggestion made earlier by Jean Richard about Maria's marriage settlement). Peter Edbury is reluctant to accept this solution, observing that it was the normal custom for a woman to keep her dowry for life and for it to pass to her heir at her death, and suggesting that Walter was merely administering the fief on Alice's behalf (Edbury, 1997: 81). This, however, fails to explain why Walter of Brienne was called Count of Jaffa by all his contemporaries. I can see no reason why Alice should not have transferred the dower-fief to her elder daughter Maria on her marriage. She would have needed the assent of her natural heir, King Henry of Cyprus, but he would no doubt have welcomed the suggestion, since it would have provided his sister with a dowry at no cost to himself (*Eracles* states that Henry had given land to Walter, but does not specify where it was situated, XXXIII, xxxviii, *RHC Occ.* II, p. 403). In the light of this evidence, it seems probable that Alice had consulted with Henry about the marriage of Maria before she went to Champagne in 1233 and that they had agreed on Count Walter of Brienne as a suitable husband. Not merely was he rich, well connected and single, but also, because of his descent from the twelfth-century Norman Kings of Sicily, he would be acceptable to the Ibelins who by that time controlled much of the Kingdom of Jerusalem. Having received a generous settlement in Champagne, Alice was no longer solely dependent on the income of her dower lands and might well have been prepared to surrender the county in order to secure a good marriage for her daughter. It is possible that she returned to Palestine in Walter's company; certainly they arrived there in the same year.

By 1235 a virtual stalemate had occurred in the struggle between the supporters of Frederick II and the native baronage led by John of Ibelin, lord of Beirut. The cities of Tyre and Jerusalem obeyed the imperial *bailli*, Richard Filangieri, while the rest of the kingdom was ruled by the *baillis* Odo of Montbéliard and Balian of Sidon, recognised by the baronial party.[4] When John of Beirut died in 1236, the leadership of the baronial party passed to his son, Balian of Ibelin, and Balian's cousin, Philip of Montfort, lord of Toron (Edbury, 1997: 74–6).

In September 1239 Theobald IV of Champagne, who had also become king of Navarre, led a crusade to the East. Among his followers was Ralph, brother of the count of Soissons, and he and Alice married, probably in the winter of 1239–40 (*Continuation de Guillaume de Tyr de 1229 à 1261, RHC Occ.* II, p. 527; Toury, 1989). Alice was about forty-seven years old, but remained an attractive marriage prospect because she was a very rich woman who was also queen-mother of Cyprus and heir-presumptive to the throne of Jerusalem.

Peter Jackson and David Jacoby independently proved that Hohenstaufen rule in the Kingdom of Jerusalem was successfully challenged in 1242, not 1243 as had been generally assumed before they published their articles (Jackson, 1986; Jacoby, 1986). Philip of Novara reports that in 1242 a group of citizens of Tyre, discontented with imperial rule, approached Balian of Ibelin and Philip of Montfort offering to admit baronial forces to the city, while the new Venetian *bailli* in Syria, Marsilio Zorzi, was prepared to give the barons naval help because Venetian privileges in Tyre had been eroded under imperial rule (Philip of Novara, 1913: c. clxviii, p. 93; *Marsilii Georgii, Venetum in Syria Bajuli, ad Ducem Relatio* (henceforth *Relatio*), 1856–57: 354–5). The baronial party, while wishing to avail themselves of this opportunity of regaining control over Tyre, were concerned about the legality of such a plan. Philip of Novara, who was a distinguished lawyer, masterminded a constitutional *coup d'état*. His case rested on a false premise, that the absent King Conrad had come of age in April 1242, whereas he was not fifteen until 26 April 1243. Philip argued that because Conrad had come of age Frederick II's regency was at an end, and that his right to appoint *baillis* in the kingdom on his son's behalf was also at an end.[5] He further maintained that it was the custom of the kingdom that if an absentee ruler did not present himself to be invested, power should be held by his nearest kin living in the kingdom until he did so. Conrad's nearest kin in the Latin East were Queen Alice and her husband Ralph of Soissons (Philip of Novara, 1913: c. clxx, p. 94). Philip claimed that a written agreement was drawn up at this stage and endorsed by Alice and Ralph, which stated that if they became regents, custody of the royal castles would be vested in Balian of Ibelin and Philip of Toron (Philip of Novara, 1913: c. clxxiii, p. 95). It was ironic that the Ibelin cousins, whose elder kinsmen had driven Alice from power in Cyprus, and excluded her from the throne of Jerusalem in 1229, should have needed her help in 1242 to forward their ambitions, but there was no constitutional alternative. They were not members of the blood royal, and Alice was the heir-presumptive: should Conrad die without legitimate heirs, the throne would automatically pass to her. Yet they clearly intended to reserve all-important powers to themselves. On 5 June 1242, a meeting of the *curia generalis* took place in Acre: this consisted of the members of the High Court, with representatives of the Church, the military orders and the Italian communes in attendance (*Relatio*, 1856–57: 355).

Those present agreed to Philip of Novara's proposal and, as he relates: 'Queen Alice was then given seisin of the Kingdom of Jerusalem, Then the lord of Beirut and the lord of Toron did homage to her, followed by the other knights present in Acre' (Philip of Novara, 1913: c. clxxvi, p. 96).

The attack on Tyre took place exactly a week later on 12 June. Ralph of Soissons accompanied the baronial forces, and they were admitted to the city by a group of dissidents who opened a postern to them. There was, nonetheless, fierce fighting on the walls between the garrison and the invading force in which Ralph took a leading part. When the city capitulated, he expected to receive it on his wife's behalf because it was part of the royal domain, but Balian of Ibelin and Philip of Montfort took charge instead (Philip of Novara, 1913: cc. clxxix, clxxx, pp. 97–8; *Eracles*, XXXIII, cc. lii, liii, *RHC Occ.* II, pp. 422–3). When they also refused to hand over the other important part of the royal domain, the city of Acre, Ralph was disgusted. *L'Estoire d'Eracles* relates: 'it seemed to him that he was just a shadow [ruler]. So because of the resentment he felt and the double-dealing to which he had been subjected, he abandoned everything and, leaving his wife behind, returned to his own country' (*Eracles*, XXXIII, c. l, *RHC Occ.* II, p. 420). Ralph returned to the Holy Land with the crusade of Louis IX in 1248, bur Alice was dead by then, and he no longer had any claim to office in the Latin Kingdom (John of Joinville, 1868: c. 92, p. 167).

Alice recognised Conrad as king, but Frederick II did not recognise her as regent. In 1244 he sent Thomas of Acera to the kingdom as his son's *bailli*, but he was not received there and made his headquarters at Tripoli, where he acted as Conrad's representative, under the protection of Alice's former husband, Bohemond V (Riley-Smith, 1973: 210, 302, n. 109, 321, n. 2). Frederick was unable to react more vigorously on his son's behalf, because he was locked in a bitter struggle with the Holy See and the Lombard communes which only ended with his death in 1250 (Pacifico, 2012: 399–481).

It is difficult to be certain how much power Alice had as regent of Jerusalem. Nominally she ruled the kingdom. Philip of Novara records that that she gave him a money-fief of 1,000 Saracen bezants as well as paying off his debts of 1,000 silver marks (Philip of Novara, 1913:

c. clxxvii, p. 96), but this might be regarded simply as the payment of generous legal fees to him for securing her appointment as regent. Marsilio Zorzi, the Venetian *bailli*, reports that when he claimed the restoration of the rights which Venice had formerly enjoyed at Tyre and which the imperial representatives had diminished, the queen took a firm line: 'She replied that if any of our rights in the kingdom had been diminished by any *bailli* they would freely be restored to us, but if any of our rights had been diminished by the lord king they would not be restored, because the queen was not the lawful ruler of the kingdom, King Conrad was' (*Relatio*, 1856–57: 357). The queen had clearly taken legal advice and a way had been found to deny the Venetians the full restitution of their rights despite the support they had provided in the attack on Tyre. Alice also revoked all the appointments and grants made by Frederick II since the death of Isabel II in 1228 (*Documents relatifs à la succes-sibilité au trône et à la régence*, 1841–3: II, 401). It is not clear how far any of these acts represented Alice's own wishes and how far she was implementing policies decided by her Ibelin cousins. There are no acts which may unequivocally be construed as the outcome of decisions taken by her alone.

The office of regent conferred status on Alice. She already had a large fortune and per-haps she was resigned to allowing her kinsmen to decide policy in her name. Certainly she made no attempt to follow her husband's example by retiring from office because it conferred no real power. She presided over the kingdom for four years, and died in 1246 when she was about fifty-three years old. Her heir was her son, King Henry of Cyprus, who succeeded her as regent of the Kingdom of Jerusalem (*Annales de Terre Sainte*, text B, *AOL* II, part ii, pp. 441–2).

A NOTE ON THE COUNTY OF JAFFA AFTER ALICE'S DEATH

Alice's son-in-law, Walter IV of Brienne, was captured by the Ayyubids at the battle of Gaza in 1244 and died a prisoner in Egypt (John of Joinville, 1868: 188–92). In 1252 the Sultan of Egypt returned Walter's remains to Louis IX who was in the Holy Land, and the arrangements for their re-burial were made by Walter's cousin, the lady of Sidon, which indicates that his wife, Alice's daughter Maria, was already dead at that time (John of Joinville, 1868: c. 91, p. 166). Mayer considers it probable that her death had occurred in or before 1247 (H.-E. Mayer, 1984: 145–7). John of Brienne, the son of Walter IV and Maria, cannot have been older in 1252 than ten or eleven and King Henry of Cyprus, his uncle and closest kinsman, must have been his legal guardian. John would have inherited the county of Jaffa from his mother, but in 1247, Henry, in his capacity as regent of the Kingdom of Jerusalem, granted the fief to John, the son of Philip of Ibelin. In the same year, Henry granted his nephew, John of Brienne, 'all the rights he possessed in the counties of Champagne and Brie' that is, the estates granted to Alice by the settlement of 1234, which had passed to King Henry at her death in 1246. It would appear that Henry intended this to be compensation to his young nephew for the sequestration of the county of Jaffa, which was rightfully his. This is only an inference: there is no written evidence to substantiate this view ('La terre que li cuens Tybaus donna a la royne de Cypre, tiennent il cuens de Brienne qui ore est [presumably Walter V (1297–1311)], et le cuens de Joigny por ce que l'aiole li conte de Brienne fu fille a la royne de Cypre et femme li grant conte Gautier de Brienne', John of Joinville, 1868: c. 19, p. 32).

NOTES

1 The problems faced by John of Brienne are not central to this chapter. The interested reader should consult the excellent study by Guy Perry, *John of Brienne, King of Jerusalem, Emperor of Constantinople, c. 1175–1237* (2013).

2 J. Richard, 'Les affaires de Champagne, 1227–1236', in his *Saint Louis* (1983: 88–96); J.P. Migne printed a dossier of the documents relating to the inheritance of Champagne as an Appendix to the Registers of Innocent III (henceforth this collection is referred to as Dossier) documents I, II, III, IX, X, XII relate to Erard and Philippa's marriage, Patrologia Latina (henceforth PL), 216, cols 973 5, 979 82.

3 In Jerusalem, Melisende, who was queen in her own right, ruled jointly with the young Baldwin III after the death of King Fulk in 1143, not as his regent; Agnes of Courtenay could not act as regent during Baldwin IV's minority (1174–76) because her marriage to King Amalric had been annulled; Sibyl was barred from being regent for her infant son Baldwin V (1185–86) by Baldwin IV's arrangements for the succession; Maria and Isabel II, who both became queens while minors, did so on the deaths of their mothers.

4 After the death of Balian of Sidon in 1239, Odo alone was recognised as *bailli* by the baronial party (Riley-Smith, 1973: 319).

5 Philip told Balian of Ibelin: 'Je vos fais assaver que le roy Conrat est d'aage, et par raison estes vous mais quite a l'empereor', 1913: c. clxix, 93.

REFERENCES

Annales de Terre Sainte, R. Röhricht (ed.), *Archives de l'Orient Latin*, 2 vols, Paris, 1884.

Bullarium Cyprium, I, *Papal Letters Concerning Cyprus, 1196–1261*, C. Schabel (ed.), Cyprus Research Centre, Texts and Studies in the History of Cyprus LXIV, Nicosia, 2010.

The Cartulary of the Cathedral of the Holy Wisdom of Nicosia, N. Coureas and C. Schabel (eds), Cyprus Research Centre, Texts and Studies in the History of Cyprus XXV, Nicosia, 1997.

Chronique de Terre Sainte (1132–1224), RHC Documents Arméniens, 2 vols, Paris, 1869.

van Cleve, T.C., *The Emperor Frederick II of Hohenstaufen. Immutator Mundi*, Oxford, 1972.

Continuation de Guillaume de Tyr de 1229 à 1261, dite du manuscrit de Rothelin, RHC Occ. Recueil des Historiens des Croisades. Historiens Occidentaux II, Paris, 1859.

Coureas, N., *The Latin Church in Cyprus, 1195–1312*, Aldershot, 1997.

De restricta prohibitione matrimonii, in *Conciliorum Oecumenicorum Decreta*, Istituto per le scienze religiose, 3rd edn, Bologna, 1973.

Documents relatifs à la successibilité au trône et à la régence, Comte Beugnot (ed.), *RHC Lois*, 2 vols, Paris, 1841–43.

Edbury P.W., *John of Ibelin and the Kingdom of Jerusalem*, Woodbridge, 1997.

———, *The Kingdom of Cyprus and the Crusades 1191–1374*, Cambridge, 1991.

——— (ed.), 'The Disputed Regency of the Kingdom of Jerusalem, 1264/6 and 1268', Camden Miscellany XXVII, Royal Historical Society, London, 1979.

Evergates, T., *Feudal Society in the Bailliage of Troyes under the Counts of Champagne, 1152–1284*, Baltimore, 1975.

Florence manuscript (Bibl. Laurentiana, Pluteus 61, 10), M.R. Morgan (ed.), *La Continuation de Guillaume de Tyr (1184–1197)*, DRHC XIV, Paris, 1982.

Hamilton, B. 'Women in the Crusader States: the Queens of Jerusalem (1100–1190)', in D. Baker (ed.), *Medieval Women*, Studies in Church History, Subsidia Oxford, 1978.

———, 'King Consorts of Jerusalem and their Entourages from the West, from 1186–1250', in H-E. Mayer and E. Müller-Luckner (eds), *Die Kreuzfahrerstaaten als multikulturelle Gesellschaft*, Munich, 1997.

Jackson, P. 'The End of Hohenstaufen Rule in Syria', *Bulletin of the Institute of Historical Research* LIX, no. 139, 1986, 20–36.

Jacoby, D., 'The Kingdom of Jerusalem and the Collapse of Hohenstaufen Power in the Levant', *Dumbarton Oaks Papers* 40, 1986, 83–101.

Janin, R. 'Chypre', *Dictionnaire d'histoire et de géographie ecclésiastique* XII, 1955.

John of Joinville, *Histoire de Saint Louis*, N. de Wailly (ed.), Paris, 1868.

Longnon, J., *Les compagnons de Villehardouin*, Geneva, 1978.

L'Estoire d'Eracles, empereur et la conqueste de la terre d'Outremer, Recueil des Historiens des Croisades. Historiens Occidentaux II, Paris, 1859.

Le Livre au roi, ed. M. Greilsammer, *DRHC* 17, Paris 1995.

Lignages d'Outremer, M-A. Nielen (ed.), Documents relatifs à l'histoire des Croisades, publiés par l'Académie des Inscriptions et Belles Lettres XVIII, Paris, 2003.

Marsilii Georgii, Venetum in Syria Bajuli, ad Ducem Relatio, G.L.F. Tafel and G.M. Thomas (eds.), *Urkunden zur älteren Handels- und Staatsgeschichte der Republik Venedig mit besonderer Beziehung auf Byzanz und die Levante*, Fontes Rerum Austriacarum, section III, vols 12–14, Vienna, 1856–57, II, no. CCXCIX.

Mayer, H-E. *Die Kreuzfahrerherrschaft Montréal*, Wiesbaden, 1990.

———, 'John of Jaffa, his Opponents and his Fiefs', *Proceedings of the American Philosophical Society* 128, Philadelphia, 1984.

——— (ed.), *Diplomata Regum Latinorum Hierosolymitanorum*, Monumenta Germaniae Historica, 4 vols, Hanover, 2010.

Oliver of Paderborn, *Historia Damiatina*, H. Hoogeweg (ed.), *Die Schriften des Kölner Domscholasters ... Oliverus*, Bibliothek des Literarischen Vereins in Stuttgart, 202, Tübingen 1894.

Pacifico, M., *Federico II e Gerusalemme al tempo delle crociate*, Rome, 2012.

Philippe de Novare, *Mémoires, 1218–1243*, Ch. Kohler (ed.), Paris, 1913.

Powell, J.M., *Anatomy of a Crusade 1213–1221*, Philadelphia, 1986.

Richard, J. *Saint Louis, roi d'une France féodale, soutien de la Terre Sainte*, Paris, 1983.

Riley-Smith, J., *The Feudal Nobility and the Kingdom of Jerusalem, 1174–1277*, London, 1973.

Röhricht, R., *Regesta Regni Hierosolymitani*, 2 vols. Innsbruck, 1893–1904.

Rudt de Collenberg, W-H., 'Les Ibelins aux XIIIe et XIV siècles', *Epeteris* IX, 1977–79.

———, 'Les Lusignans de Chypre', *Epeteris* 10, 1979–80.

Thesaurus Novus Anecdotorum, E. Martène and U. Durand (eds), 5 vols, Paris, 1717.

Toury, M.N., 'Raoul de Soissons', in Y. Bellenger and D. Quéruel (eds), *Les Champenois et la Croisade*, Paris, 1989, 97–107.

CHAPTER FIFTEEN

THE FRANCISCAN RETURN TO THE HOLY LAND (1333) AND MT SION: PILGRIMAGE AND THE APOSTOLIC MISSION

——— • ◆ • ———

Andrew Jotischky

The association between the Franciscan Order and the Holy Land is almost eight centuries old, and for several of those after the 1330s, the Franciscans represented the major Latin religious presence there. The custody of the holy places, established in 1333, permitted the Franciscans to establish a convent at Mt Sion, just outside the south-west corner of the current walls of the Old City of Jerusalem, and to celebrate Latin rites there. Soon afterwards these rights were extended by the Mamluk Sultan of Egypt an-Nasir to other holy places, including the Holy Sepulchre. The return of the Franciscans to the Holy Land as the sole representatives of the Latin Church, only forty years after the fall of Acre had signalled the end of the Latin presence on the mainland, was a remarkable turn of events, both for the Franciscan Order itself and for Christianity in the Holy Land. Equally surprising is the manner of the Franciscan establishment of the custody in 1333, following as it did a series of negotiations that had taken several years between an-Nasir and two separate Christian kingdoms: Aragon and Naples. No less remarkable is the preparedness of the Franciscans to undertake such an ambitious venture at a time when the Order was still undergoing the traumas of serious internal conflict and division resulting from the split between conventuals and Spirituals.[1]

The circumstances of the Franciscan return are well known from the surviving sources, but they have rarely been commented on in the context of Franciscan internal affairs, nor indeed of Franciscan spirituality. This chapter will examine in some detail the initiation and significance of the custody in the light of Franciscan perceptions of the Order's mission, the place of Mt Sion in the pilgrimage tradition, and the connections between the principal sponsors of the custody and the Spiritual movement within the Order.

I

A group of Franciscans arrived in the Holy Land to establish the custody in 1333, but final settlements regarding its nature, legal status and physical parameters were not made until 1336. In 1335 the Franciscans Roger Guérin and John, together with Margaret of Sicily, the director of a pilgrims' hospice in Jerusalem, acquired by purchase from the qadi Sharaf

241

ad-Din Muhammad, the administrator of the public treasury in Jerusalem, four properties and some ruins on Mt Sion, which probably formed the basis for a convent on the site.[2] More land was purchased in 1337 and 1345, and a cistern in 1357.[3] In 1361 permission was granted by Pope Innocent VI to build a convent next to the tomb of the Blessed Virgin in the Kidron Valley just beyond the eastern wall of Jerusalem; in 1391 the Franciscans bought a garden on Mt Sion from its Armenian owners, and four years later another house was purchased on Mt Sion.[4]

Only one of the Franciscans involved is known by name, and that is from a later source. The Franciscan *Chronicon XXIV Generalium*, written in *c.* 1375, records the dispatch by the Minister-General Gerald Odonis of Roger Guérin, a friar from Provence, with an unspecified number of companions, in 1333.[5] According to the *Chronicon*, Roger and his companions were part of a larger group en route for the Franciscan mission in Armenia. The legal basis for the Franciscan authority to represent the Catholic Church at the holy places is outlined in two bulls of Pope Clermont VI from 1342.[6] Up to twelve friars and their households are permitted to serve the shrines in perpetuity, maintained through an annuity paid by the crown of Naples, which also purchased a plot of land on Mt Sion for the construction of a convent for the friars. The custody thus secured rights to maintain religious provision in specific named churches, but no rights of residence in those churches or buildings associated with them. By the time the bull was granted, the custody had been extended to include rights in the tomb of the Blessed Virgin, in the Church of the Nativity in Bethlehem, and in the Cenacle on Mt Sion. Only on this last site did the Franciscans also exercise rights of ownership of land, but this ownership was negotiated through local authorities by purchase from the previous owner. The precise dates at which the later custody rights were granted remains unclear, but the Franciscans seem to have been present in Bethlehem and at the Tomb of the Virgin from 1334, and to have secured rights over the Cenacle and over various parts of the Holy Sepulchre in 1335. The drawn-out nature of these concessions suggests that the initial agreement must have secured permission for Roger Guérin to enter the Holy Land, after which he then had to negotiate the further concessions piecemeal. As regards Mt Sion, the bull confirms the concession of the Cenacle (the room where the Last Supper supposedly took place), of the chapel of the Holy Spirit (the room where the Holy Spirit descended in the form of fire on the Apostles), and the chapel of St Thomas, the 'lower room' where the disciples met secretly after the crucifixion.[7]

The custody entrusted the provision of religious offices to the Franciscans, but – with the exception of the Cenacle, where property was purchased – no proprietary rights of ownership over the shrines. The Lanercost Chronicle, a Franciscan source deriving from the bishopric of Carlisle, implies that the settlement permitted the return of Latin clergy to Outremer in order to re-open churches, but that no sovereignty was ceded over territory occupied by any shrines.[8] Although allowed permanent rights within the Holy Sepulchre, the Franciscans did not gain entitlement to the church. The sultan's officials even controlled access to the church, and the keys were retained by Mamluk officials.[9] Thus the Franciscan pilgrim Niccolo da Poggibonsi, who wanted to spend a night in prayer at the Sepulchre, had to resort to the stratagem of changing places with one of the resident Franciscans so that he could enjoy the illicit privilege.[10]

So much for the immediate circumstances of the establishment of the custody. In order to understand the significance of this series of events, however, it will first be necessary to go back to the first arrival of the Francsicans in the Holy Land, and to examine how the friars' presence there embodied aspects of Franciscan spirituality.

Franciscan interest in the Holy Land dates from 1217, when the province was established at the Order's first chapter-general.[11] One of Francis's followers, Giles, made a pilgrimage to Jerusalem in 1215 that may have provided the impetus for this,[12] but the first evidence for the activities of the Franciscans in the Holy Land dates from 1220. In a letter, Jacques de Vitry, bishop of Acre, complains that three of his clergy, including a canon of Acre, had joined the Order and that he had had to dissuade others from doing the same.[13] In 1230 Pope Gregory IX instructed the Latin ecclesiastical authorities throughout the crusader states to ensure that laypeople who wished to build chapels for Franciscan use should not be impeded.[14] A Franciscan convent was established in Jerusalem, probably after 1229 when most of the city was restored to the kingdom, and in 1252–53 King Louis IX built a convent for the Order in Jaffa.[15] Subsequently convents were built at Sidon in 1253 and Tyre before 1255, by which time there was also one at Acre.[16] In general, however, evidence for Franciscan activities in the province of the Holy Land is limited, certainly when compared to the rest of Christendom.[17]

For Franciscans themselves, however, their presence in the land of Christ's birth was only natural. Biblical prophecy seemed to legitimise it: the Franciscans saw themselves as the 'gens iusta' of Isaiah 26.2, who were entrusted with the 'custodia veritatis', and as the 'populus egenus et pauper' of Wisdom 3.11.[18] Parallels were made in Franciscan literature of the thirteenth and fourteenth centuries between Francis himself and Christ. The Holy Land, moreover, features strongly in the Franciscan literary tradition of the fourteenth century. The Spiritual Franciscan Angelo da Clareno, retelling the story of St Francis' preaching to Sultan al-Kamil on the Fifth Crusade in 1219, asserts that Francis went on to pray at the Holy Sepulchre afterwards, a detail repeated by the *Chronicon XXIV Generalium*.[19] Another Spiritual work, the *Actus beati Francisci* (in which Francis secretly converts the sultan to Christianity), places part of Francis' preaching in the Holy Land.[20] The Franciscans had a history of martyrdom in the Holy Land, and the custody was to provide further such opportunities. According to his biographer, Francis specifically desired martyrdom as the outcome of preaching to the Muslims, and his *Regula non bullata* specified martyrdom as a possible outcome of the mission.[21] In 1266 the Templar grand master asked the Franciscan provincial of the Holy Land to send friars to give spiritual aid to the Templars besieged in Safed. James of Podio and his three Franciscan companions who undertook the mission persuaded the Templars to accept martyrdom rather than conversion to Islam, a fate in which the friars also shared.[22] Seven Franciscans were killed in the sack of Tripoli in 1289, while the fall of Acre in 1291 resulted in the deaths of fourteen Franciscans and some Claresses.[23] In 1391 four of the friars of the custody were martyred when they tried to preach to a crowd of Muslims at the Dome of the Rock.[24]

The Franciscan presence after 1333 was determined by the relationship to specified shrines. Naturally, the sites of the birth, death and resurrection of Christ – the Churches of the Nativity and the Holy Sepulchre – were universally recognisable as the most important of all holy places. Latin worship in the Holy Sepulchre was emblematic of the rightful possession of the site by Western Christendom. Mt Sion, however, was particularly important to the custody, for it marked the only place over which the Franciscans enjoyed rights of ownership. Moreover, Mt Sion offered to the Franciscans a set of symbols that conformed in very particular ways to the Order's perception of itself and its mission. This meaning can only be understood if we first consider briefly its previous history as a pilgrimage site.

II

Mt Sion's history as a holy site is complex. The site included the Cenacle – the room where the Last Supper had been held – and the house where Jesus first appeared to the Apostles after the Resurrection, and where at Pentecost the Holy Spirit descended in the form of flames on the Apostles. It was also celebrated in Christian tradition as the place where the Blessed Virgin had died, and as the burial place of the first martyr, Stephen.[25] Not all these topographical identifications were made at the same time, however. Even before the Constantinian foundation of the Anastasis Church in the 320s, Mt Sion may have provided a topographical focus for Christians in Jerusalem.[26] During the growth of pilgrimage to Jerusalem in the fourth century, Mt Sion retained a special place in a complex and physically demanding liturgical drama. Cyril of Jerusalem (*c.* 348) mentions Mt Sion as the place where the Apostles gathered in the upper room after the death of Jesus, and it is clear that there was already a church on the site by this date.[27] Egeria, in the 380s, reported that the Easter and Pentecost celebrations included processions of the faithful with the bishop of Jerusalem to Mt Sion on Easter Sunday and a week later. Having just celebrated the Passion and Resurrection, Christians now looked forward to the return of Jesus to his disciples as they gathered in the Upper Room with locked doors.[28] At Pentecost, the Church's oldest feast, the role of Mt Sion was even more central. After the Sunday service, the congregation processed with the bishop to the Upper Room, where the relevant passage from the *Acts of the Apostles* was read aloud. The whole congregation then crossed the city to ascend the Mount of Olives, where the Ascension was commemorated, returned to Calvary for another service, and finally – late at night, by this time – processed once again to Mt Sion for further readings.[29]

Mt Sion's physical presence in the observance of ritual in Jerusalem confirmed its place as 'the mother of all the churches', as it was called in the Jerusalem liturgy itself, and as it became known in the Palestinian monastic tradition.[30] As the location where the Holy Spirit had descended on the Apostles at the first Pentecost, it was, in effect, the site of the origin of the Church itself. Hence the importance of the translation of the relics of St Stephen, the first martyr, to Mt Sion, the place where he had been chosen as one of the first deacons of the Church by the disciples, even though the relics themselves were discovered several miles away from Jerusalem.[31] Stephen himself enjoyed a particular importance in the Jerusalem liturgy, and among the relics associated with him and preserved at the church of Sion were some of the stones used at his martyrdom.[32] Another of the relics at Mt Sion important to early Christians was the throne of St James, the first bishop of the Church. This, and the liturgical presence of the bishop in the early Christian celebrations of Easter and Pentecost, reinforced the identity of Mt Sion as the original site of authority in the Church.

Pilgrimage accounts consistently identify Mt Sion with Pentecost, but added importance was bestowed by the identification of the Upper Room, from the fifth century onward, as the site of the Last Supper.[33] Saewulf, the Anglo-Saxon pilgrim who visited Jerusalem in 1101–03, believed he had seen the very table at which the Last Supper took place. He also knew Mt Sion as the place of the burial of St Stephen, and as the 'Galilee' – the place where the Apostles had taken refuge after the crucifixion.[34] In most Western pilgrimage accounts of the twelfth and early thirteenth centuries, the biblical events of the Last Supper and the descent of the Holy Spirit at Pentecost provide a constant thread in the descriptions of Mt Sion.[35] A service book made for the canons of the Holy Sepulchre gives details of the Maundy Thursday procession to Mt Sion for the service of the blessing of the holy oil, led by the patriarch, in which the diocesan bishops and heads of religious houses in Jerusalem also participated.[36] Slight variations occur in Orthodox pilgrimage; for example, the Cretan monk John Phokas (1185) knows Sion by the early Christian formulation 'mother of all the churches', and both he and Abbot Daniel (1106–07) followed a tradition that the house where the Last Supper took place and where the Virgin died belonged to John the Evangelist.[37]

Another such variation, which places the house of Caiaphas the High Priest on Mt Sion, is found both in Orthodox pilgrimage accounts and in a Latin account, the *Work on Geography* (1128–37), which is itself derived from Jerome's *De Interpretatione Nominum* and another topographical work of the same period attributed to Jerome.[38] There thus appears to have been an early Christian tradition that the judgement of Christ at the *lithistratos*, or stone pavement, took place on Mt Sion. From *c*. 1170 some Western pilgrims also observed this tradition, including some or all of the elements of the Passion such as the scourging of Jesus and the wearing of the crown of thorns.[39] This extension of the role of Mt Sion in the Passion beyond the Last Supper drew pilgrims physically back to the site during the liturgical re-enactment of the Passion in Holy Week.

The tradition associating the judgement of Jesus with Mt Sion was not uncontested, however. In the Gospel narratives, Jesus underwent two separate trials: one at the hands of the Jewish Temple authorities, Caiaphas and his father-in-law Annas, and the other presided over by the Roman governor Pontius Pilate. Early Christian tradition located the house of Caiaphas on Mt Sion, and assumed therefore that the first trial had taken place there. However, the pilgrim Theoderic (1169–74), while affirming the identification of both trials on Mt Sion, also hinted that the Praetorium, the official seat of Pilate's government, lay instead to the north of the Temple enclosure. It is also clear from Theoderic's account that by *c*. 1170 the Templars were promoting the Praetorium as the place of the second trial, on the grounds that it was near here, in the Sheep Pool, that the wood that formed Jesus's cross was taken.[40] The Gospel narrative of the trial made better sense if Jesus went straight from the second trial to Golgotha; therefore, if the source of the cross were securely identified, the site of the trial by Pilate must be nearby. It was, of course, no coincidence that both sites lay just to the north of the wall of the Templars' own precinct. This meant that pilgrims re-enacting the drama of the Passion were drawn back from Mt Sion to the Temple precinct for the last stage of the procession to the Holy Sepulchre, and from the orbit of the Augustinian canons to that of the Templars themselves.

The Cenacle itself seems to have undergone extensive rebuilding in the 1180s, and possibly minor renovations when Jerusalem once again came under Frankish control between 1229 and 1244.[41] This building campaign comprised the ribbed vaulting of the Upper Room and the renovation of Galilee below, providing a model of a second-floor refectory that may have been imported to Augustinian houses in England in the late twelfth and thirteenth centuries.[42] As Folda has observed, the Cenacle was in terms of its architectural sculpture the most advanced church building in the Crusader kingdom in the 1180s, and may represent the transmission of architectural ideas between Angevin England and Jerusalem.[43] If so, it surely also suggests a huge investment by the canons of Mt Sion to wrest back from the Templars the initiative in the identification and control of Passion sites that played an important role in pilgrimage.

After 1187, the use of the Templars' Sheep Pool site, and the route from it to Golgotha, was in any case no longer available. Even in 1229, the treaty through which Frederick II negotiated the return of Jerusalem specifically excluded the Temple area. But from 1192, pilgrims had been permitted controlled access once again to the Holy Sepulchre and certain other sites, among them Mt Sion.[44] Thirteenth-century pilgrims identified the Cenacle as the place of both the house of Caiaphas and the judgement and the trial at Pilate's hands and the punishment that followed it.[45] Even the report of conditions in the Holy Land sent to Rome by Patriarch Aimery the Monk at the pope's request made this identification.[46] Confirmation of the importance of Mt Sion as a holy site in the thirteenth century is given in Jacques de Vitry's *Historia Orientalis*. Although he says nothing about the Praetorium or the second trial, Jacques brackets Mt Sion alone of all other pilgrimage sites with the Holy Sepulchre: 'Among other holy places, this enjoys the greatest honour.'[47] Jacques reinvigorates the early Christian tradition associating Mt Sion directly with the origins of the Church itself: here, in the place where Jesus dined with the Apostles and established the commemoration of the event through the breaking of bread, where later he was to appear to them after the resurrection, and where they received the gift of the Holy Spirit, 'the new Testament was instituted'.

In the thirteenth century, especially after the loss of the rival sites at the Temple Mount promoted by the Templars, the importance of Mt Sion was given a further boost. The Franciscan Albertus Stadensis reports that it was by way of Mt Sion that Jesus entered Jerusalem on Palm Sunday. This was probably a rationalisation of the loss of the traditional route for the Palm Sunday procession from Bethany to Golgotha via the 'Golden Gate' in the eastern wall of the Temple precinct.[48] Since the topographically correct route was no longer available, attention shifted back to Mt Sion, which had since the fourth century been identified with some elements of the Passion narrative. Similar emphasis on the role of Mt Sion in pilgrimage processions and re-enactments is noticeable in other Franciscan accounts, such as the anonymous *De via eundi de Iope ad Jerusalem*.[49] Although the existence of a Franciscan house in Jerusalem is uncertain, Mt Sion may have been served by Franciscans between 1229 and 1244, during the period when Jerusalem was once again in Frankish hands but when the Augustinian canons of Mt Sion remained in Acre.

The early Christian traditions surrounding Mt Sion explain why the Cenacle was so important to the Franciscans, possibly as early as 1229–44 but certainly from 1333 onward. The crusader rebuilding of the Cenacle housed sites that had an iconic quality for an Order whose profession – like that of the Augustinian canons whose tenure of the site preceded the Franciscans' – was centred on the *vita apostolica*.[50] Mt Sion, as Fergusson has noted, was the site of the 'principal sacramental, missionary and miraculous acts of Christian history'.[51] Since the mid-fourth century it had been recognised as the birthplace of the Church itself through its identification as the place of the Upper Room where the disciples had received the gift of the Holy Spirit and the commission to preach the Gospel – a commission consciously imitated by Francis in his injunctions to the friars minor. The connection with the Last Supper reinforced this association through the institution of the Eucharist, which by the 1330s had been established through the feast of Corpus Christi as the regular salvific act mediated by the Church. The doctrine of transubstantiation, which placed the physical presence of Christ at the centre of late medieval spirituality, also served to focus attention on the site where the Eucharist had been born.[52] That this Eucharist-centred spirituality was critical to Franciscan self-perception in a general sense is demonstrated by the cycle of Passion scenes, including the Last Supper, which are interspersed with scenes from the life of St Francis in the Lower Church at Assisi.

The Franciscans also had the opportunity, through the identification of the house of Caiaphas on Mt Sion, to commemorate the part of the Passion narrative centred on the trial of Jesus. This was surely of particular significance at a time when the iconography of the Passion in Western art had undergone a shift towards more representational depictions of the suffering of Jesus, including concentration on the episodes of the Flagellation and Mocking.[53] Moreover, the burial of Stephen the proto-martyr on Mt Sion centred at the same site an association with the early Church's priestly ministry through the institution of the diaconate – the office held by Francis himself.[54] Likewise, the institution of episcopal authority could be identified with Sion through the throne of the first bishop of Jerusalem, the Apostle James. It is significant in this regard that the Franciscan custody, according to Clement VI's bull of 1342, acted as a surrogate for patriarchal authority.[55] Mt Sion thus offered a unique combination of physical sites that reinforced its place at the heart of the Church's mission: the Eucharist, the evangelical commission, the priestly and episcopal offices. In short, the Cenacle provided the Franciscans with the opportunity to embody their mission as restorers of the early Church with public reference to the places in which the Church had been founded.

III

From the last quarter of the thirteenth century, the legacy of Francis came to be contested within his Order between those who wished to observe his rule in its strictest form, including absolute poverty, and the mainstream who saw the need to modify it in order to establish the internal efficacy of the Order. By the 1280s the conflict had centred on the question of whether the Franciscans could legitimately own property. The Sprituals argued that since the Apsotles had not practised ownership, they too were prohibited from doing so.

Thus far, there is nothing to suggest that the Franciscan custody was accented with any specifically Spiritual overtones. Given that Pope John XXII had condemned the Spirituals in 1317 and actively persecuted them from 1322 onward, it is inconceivable that Clement VI would in 1342 have sanctioned the custody if it were seen to promote 'Spiritual' ideals. Indeed, the Spiritual movement is generally reckoned to have had its day by this time. Nevertheless, there was much in the symbolism of the custody to attract Spirituals. The apocalypticism of Angelo da Clareno's *Historia de septem tribulationum* drew on perceived links between the Spirituals and the suffering and martyrdom of the Apostles.[56] For those who clung to the ideal of apostolic poverty, the Holy Land was a homeland. Here as nowhere else on earth, friars could follow to the letter biblical injunctions and examples by walking in the very footprints of Christ and the Apostles.[57]

The terms of the custody may also be significant here. As we have seen, the Franciscans were granted rights of dwelling in the Holy Sepulchre, Church of the Nativity and Tomb of the Virgin, but no rights of ownership. In this respect the unwillingness of Sultan an-Nasir to cede any territory in the Holy Land may have coincided with the principles of apostolic poverty to which some Franciscans still clung even after the papal condemnation of the doctrine. Francis himself had insisted that the Minors should not own property, but simply make use of what was given to them for the purpose. The arrangements made by Roger Guérin for the custody in the 1330s resemble, coincidentally perhaps, the conditions of the *usus pauper* theory developed by Peter John Olivi to clarify Francis' teaching on apostolic poverty. Even the undoubted ownership exercised over the property on Mt Sion could be seen as a purchase by Queen Sancia for the use of the Franciscans.

When we turn to examine the source of the Franciscans' patronage in the Holy Land, an undercurrent of Spiritual interest becomes visible. Clement VI's bulls cannot mask the fact that the papacy's involvement in the establishment of the custody was from the beginning minimal. All that Clement did in 1342 was to recognise the fait accompli of the custody established by Sancia and Robert of Naples. Both Robert and Sancia, however, had family connections with the Franciscans. The Angevin royal house had been linked with the Franciscans through the patronage given the Order by Sancia's great-aunt Elizabeth of Hungary (1207–31) and Louis IX of France (1226–70), Robert's grand-uncle. Robert's own brother, Louis of Toulouse (1274–97), who renounced his throne for the Franciscan habit, was canonised in 1317. Sancia's own upbringing in the court of Majorca was imbued with Franciscan-inspired spirituality. Her mother, Sclaramanda of Foix, was a patron of the Franciscans; one of her brothers, James, renounced his claim to the throne for the religious life; another, Fernando, abdicated as prince of Achaia and the Morea to become a friar.[58] Sancia herself, who already enjoyed the concession of having two Claresses in her personal retinue, petitioned the pope in 1317 to divorce Robert in order to enter a convent. Although Pope John XXII refused, from *c.* 1328 onward Robert and Sancia entertained a mutual regard for the Franciscans. Robert was buried in the Franciscan habit (in which he had been painted by Benozzo Gozzoli) while after his death in 1343 Sancia herself entered the Clares' convent of Santa Croce in Naples.[59]

So far, so orthodox. But her youngest brother, Philip, who had become a disciple of Olivi and Angelo Clareno, renounced the regency of Majorca in 1328–29 to enter a community in Naples that was dominated by Franciscan Spirituals. Sancia's predilection for the Spiritual Franciscans became sufficiently marked for John XXII to write to her complaining about the preaching of evangelical poverty in her kingdom, and warning her not to continue to harbour heretics and schismatics. In 1334 she wrote to the chapter-general of the Franciscans outlining her involvement with the Order and the direction of her sympathies.[60] The letter, which survives in the *Chronicon XXIV Generalium*, includes the texts of previous letters to the Order: one written to Michael of Cesena during his minister-generalship in 1316, another to the chapter-general after Michael's deposition in 1329, and a third to the chapter meeting held under Gerald Odonis in 1331.[61]

It is clear from the letters not only that Sancia had a profound knowledge of the Franciscan literary tradition, but also that she regarded the Spirituals much as they saw themselves, as the true followers of St Francis. She calls on Franciscans to defy the pope, to remain faithful to Francis' teaching on apostolic poverty, and to adhere to the literal prescriptions in the Rule. Sancia's involvement with the Spiritual tendency, however, is marked by her actions as well as her words. She deliberately snubbed the Conventual mainstream of the Order by opening the kingdom of Naples to dissenting Spirituals and fraticelli.[62] At the very time that the Franciscan custody in the Holy Land was beginning, in 1332–33, a group of about fifty Spirituals from Ancona settled in Castel Lettere, in the Bay of Naples.[63] Among Sancia's advisors was a man who was later to be tried for being one of the fraticelli, Adhemar de Mosset, a friend of her brother Philip of Majorca.[64] Philip himself had been a protégé of one of the leaders of the Anconan Spirituals, Angelo da Clareno, since 1311. Nine of Angelo's letters between 1316 and 1334 were addressed to Philip, and another of Philip's friends, Robert of Mileto, asked to borrow Angelo's translation of the Rule of St Basil.[65] Philip benefited from his sister's protection to found an openly extreme Spiritual community at Santa Chiara in Naples. His preaching against the pope's condemnation of the Spirituals provoked a letter from John XXII objecting to his activities, and in 1331 the pope tried to compel him to join an 'approved' order.[66] In 1336 Sancia and Robert banished the Franciscan minister-general, Gerald Odonis, from Naples, in retaliation for the Order's attack on another of Philip's friends, the Spiritual Andreas da Gagliano, on the grounds of disobedience both to the pope and the Franciscan Order.[67] As Musto has suggested, the inquisitorial process directed against Andreas was a means of attacking a queen who was 'a major protagonist in the later history of the Spirituals'.[68] Robert, whose sympathies probably lay with the mainstream of the Order, nevertheless had to defend Sancia against such interference.[69]

The provocative favour shown by Sancia to Spiritual Franciscans, and her willingness to snub the Order itself, naturally raise questions about her sponsorship of the Franciscan custody in the Holy Land in the 1330s. It is true that at the time when the Franciscans arrived in the Holy Land, in 1333, Sancia and Robert had not yet taken formal action against the Conventuals in the kingdom of Naples. Nevertheless, Sancia's insistence on adherence to apostolic poverty, as attested in her letters to the Order, dates from well before this, and she can hardly have been well disposed to Odonis after 1331, when he had tried to get John XXII to abrogate the Franciscan Rule's prohibition on receiving money.[70] Her letter of 1329 had begged the Franciscans assembled in chapter to elect a new minister of the same high qualities as Michael of Cesena; when she heard about Odonis' attempt to have the Rule changed, she wrote again, in 1331, to recommend disobedience to the minister-general if he succeeded in his objective.[71] In the very year that Odonis sent Roger Guérin to the Holy Land, Robert and Sancia were intervening with John XXII on behalf of Andreas da Galgliano and another Spiritual, Peter of Cadeneto.

None of this evidence for Sancia's defence of Spirituals, *fraticelli* or other Franciscan rebels and their principles necessarily means that in the 1330s she *only* supported the remnants of the extreme wing of the Order. For one thing, it is difficult to be precise about the nomenclature of 'Spirituals' and 'fraticelli' in this period.[72] The kingdom of Naples under Robert and Sancia was a haven for a wide variety of disaffected mendicants; it was, as one historian has put it, a 'great melting-pot of Franciscan dissidence'.[73] Robert's most recent biographer has challenged the assumption that he shared his wife's sympathies for the Spirituals and their ideals.[74] Dissident Franciscans from different provinces had suffered varied experiences and had absorbed different traditions; those who took refuge in Sicily cannot necessarily be classed with the Anconans or Provencals. The sheer variety of dissident Franciscans to be found in Robert and Sancia's Naples, however, may have made it more representative of the Spiritual movement as a whole.[75] Her letters to the Franciscans indicate that she saw herself not so much as a partisan of one particular side over another in the Spiritual debate, but as a mother-figure to the whole Order.[76] Sancia's letter of 1334, written to remind the Franciscans of the care with which she had always nurtured the Order, coincides with the beginning of the Franciscan custody in the Holy Land for which she was paying out of her own purse.

The only contemporary narrative of the establishment of the custody, the *Chronicon XXIV Generalium*, places these events in the context of Franciscan missionary activity that the chronicler sees as part of a Spiritual agenda. Roger Guérin is named as the friar who negotiated the return of the Cenacle on Mt Sion from the Sultan.[77] The whole passage, however, makes it appear that this was simply a side-show in the larger Franciscan mission to the Armenians. Roger was apparently one of the Aquitainian friars sent by Gerald Odonis in 1332–33 to reconvert those Armenians who had slipped away from Roman obedience. After a short aside explaining the significance of the Cenacle as the place where the Last Supper had been held, and furthermore as the site of the descent of the Holy Spirit on the Apostles, the chronicler returns to the main story of the Armenian mission and the martyrdoms that resulted from it; following this, he inserts the letters of Queen Sancia to the Franciscan chapter-general.

The Franciscan mission to Armenia had become in the 1280s a predominantly Spiritual affair, and one moreover dominated by dissenting friars from Ancona. The Armenian king Hethoum II, anxious to maintain diplomatic channels to Rome after the fall of Tripoli in 1289, asked for Franciscan preachers to be sent to his country to re-invigorate the union of the Armenian Church with Rome. This request must be seen in the context of a long-standing Franciscan involvement in Armenia, which by mid-century had resulted in the foundation of convents in Sis and Siwas. The minister-general used the request as an opportunity to defuse a potential revolt from the province of Ancona, by sending a group that included friars who had been imprisoned for their extreme views – Peter da Macerata, Thomas of Tolentino, Marco da Montelupone, Fraymundo and Angelo da Clareno.[78] The Spirituals enjoyed a cordial reception from Hethoum, who was personally sympathetic to the Order, but in 1290 they were forced out of Armenia as a result of rumours spread by the conventual establishment in the province of the Holy Land, and withdrew to Cyprus.[79] In 1292 Marco and Thomas pleaded unsuccessfully at Rome for military help for Armenia; in the face of the Mamluk invasion of Armenia in that year, Hethoum II himself became a Franciscan at Sis. The Order's chapter-general, held in the same year, placed the Franciscan convents in Armenia under the obedience of the province of the Holy Land, which was firmly in the hands of conventuals.[80]

After they were withdrawn from Armenia in 1290, they found that the province of the Holy Land was being contested between conventuals and Spirituals. Cyprus, for example, was divided in its opinion: at the convent in Nicosia, Peter of Macerata was welcomed, but in Paphos he encountered hostility.[81] John of Parma, a 'protospiritual' who had resigned as minister-general in 1257,[82] was from 1270 to 1279 custodian of the Franciscan province of the Holy Land. The chapter-general of 1287, however – the same that found against the teachings of Peter John Olivi on the 'usus pauper' – decreed that no more 'insolent' friars (the term used to describe those with extreme sympathies) were to be sent to the Holy Land.[83] Eastern mission fields were used by the Order as a means of getting rid of troublesome Spirituals: Thomas of Tolentino, one of the Anconans sent to Armenia in 1289–90, was eventually martyred in India in 1321.[84] If this was the case with Armenia in the 1280s, why not also in the 1330s, when the need to be rid of Spirituals and *fraticelli* after the papal condemnation was more pressing still? Spiritual sympathisers, indeed, seem to have been alive to this strategy: a bull of John XXII from 1325, censures Spirituals who undertook missionary work in the East in order to evade the authority of their Order, and without proper licence.[85] If the friars sent by Gerald Odonis to Armenia in 1333 were in fact going into a missionary exile, and if Roger Guérin and his diversion to the Holy Land was part of this mission, then it follows that the friars of the custody may also have been suspected of Spiritual sympathies.

There is no 'silver bullet' that links the surviving Spirituals in the 1330s definitively to the Franciscan custody of the Holy Land. Yet hints have been dropped by historians before now suggesting that such a connection may have been real.[86] In any event, the custody of the Holy Land offered the opportunity for the Franciscans to revive a reputation that had suffered through internal dissent by taking on the responsibility of representing Christendom in the holy places. In providing spiritual ministry and practical help for pilgrims to the Holy Land under Mamluk rule, the custody enabled the Order to rediscover and reinvigorate pilgrimage to Jerusalem, but at the same time also to re-define their own spiritual direction. In due course, over centuries of exercising their ministry to Catholic Christians in the Jerusalem, the Franciscans would become synonymous with the Holy Land in ways that belied their quiet beginnings there in the 1220s but that reconnected them with the spirituality of the first Church.

NOTES

1 David Burr, *The Spiritual Franciscans. From Protest to Persecution in the Century after Saint Francis* (University Park, PA, 2001) provides the most recent survey of these events.

2 Girolamo Golubovich (ed.), *Serie cronologica dei superiori di Terra Santa* (Jerusalem, 1898), 131–3; Margaret is mentioned by the pilgrim Ludolf von Sudheim, 'Liber terrae sanctae Jerusalem', ed. G.A. Neumann, *Archives de l'Orient latin*, ii (1884), 352.

3 Golubovich, *Serie cronologica*, 143–4, 153–4, 160.

4 Sabino de Sandoli, *The Peaceful Liberation of the Holy Places in the Fourteenth Century*, Studia Orientalia Christiana Monographia 3 (Cairo: Franciscan Center of Oriental Studies, 1990), 26–9, for summary of these acquisitions.

5 *Chronicon XXIV Generalium ordinis Minorum*, in *Analecta Francescana*, iii, (Quaracchi, 1897), 510. The anonymous author is mistaken in thinking that permission to occupy Mt Sion was given at this stage. For introduction to the chronicle, Bert Roest, *Reading the Book of History. Intellectual Contexts and Educational Functions of Franciscan Historiography 1226–ca.1350*, (Groningen, 1996), 37–8.

6 L. Wadding (ed.) *Annales* III (Rome, 1635), an. 1342, n. 17, also Girolamo Golubovich, *Biblioteca bio-bibliografia della Terra Santa e dell'Oriente francescano*, 5 vols (Quaracchi 1906–27), iv, 52–6.

7 Wadding, *Annales*, III, an. 1342, n. 17.

8 *Chronicon de Lanercost 1201–1346*, ed. Joseph Stevenson (Edinburgh, 1839), 289–90; however, the author seems to have confused the 1333–36 proceedings with negotiations resulting from an earlier embassy by Peter de la Palud in 1329–30. On the authorship of the chronicle, see A.G. Little, 'The Authorship of the Lanercost Chronicle', in *Franciscan Papers, Lists and Documents* (Manchester, 1943), 42–54, and H.S. Offler, 'A Note on the Northern Franciscan Chronicle', *Nottingham Medieval Studies*, xxviii, (1984), 45–59. In general, see the remarks of Antonia Gransden, *Historical Writing in England, I, c.550 to c.1307* (London, 1974), 494, and idem, *Historical Writing in England, II, c.1307 to the Early Sixteenth Century* (London, 1982), 115–17.

9 An anonymous Franciscan pilgrim of 1345 reports that the door to the church was opened by a Mamluk gatekeeper, 'Itinerarium cuiusdam Anglici', in Golubovich, *Biblioteca*, IV, 453. Another Franciscan pilgrim, Niccolo da Poggibonsi (1346), says that eight Muslims held the keys to the church, *Libro d'Oltramare (1346–50)*, ed. B. Bagatti (Jerusalem 1945), XXXII, 25–6. Even after the Franciscan custody had been granted, however, there is some doubt as to who kept the key to the edicule of the Holy Sepulchre itself. Ludolf of Sudheim, who visited Jerusalem at Christmas 1336, thought that the key was kept by Georgian monks, G.A. Neumann, 349–52.

10 Niccolo da Poggibonsi, *Libro d'Oltramare*, XXXIII, 26.

11 J. Moorman, *A History of the Franciscan Order from its Origins to the Year 1517* (Oxford, 1968), 62, for a full account of these events.

12 Moorman, *History*, 227.

13 Jacqes de Vitry, *Lettres*, VI, ed. R.B.C. Huygens, Corpus Christianorum Continuatio Medievalis (Turnhout, 2000), 620–3.

14 Golubovich, *Biblioteca*, I, 160.

15 Denys Pringle, *The Churches of the Crusader Kingdom of Jerusalem. A Corpus*, 4 vols (Cambridge, 1993–2009), IV, no. 381, 48–50; William of St Pathus, *Vie de Saint Louis*, ed. H-F. Delaborde (Paris, 1899), 46–7.

16 Pringle, *Churches,* II, no. 243, 328; Golubovich, *Biblioteca,* I, 234.

17 M. Roncaglia, *I francescani in Oriente durante le Crociate* (Cairo, 1954), 33.

18 Salimbene de Adam, *Cronica,* CCCLXXIII-IV, ed. G. Scalia, Corpus Christianum Continuatio Medievalis 125 and 125A (Turnhout, 1998, 1999), 393–4; Marjorie Reeves, *The Influence of Prophecy in the Later Middle Ages: A Study in Joachimism* (Oxford, 1969), 179–81.

19 Angelo Clareno, *Chronicon seu Historia septem tribulationum,* ed. Alberto Ghiniato, (Rome, 1958–9), 35–6; Golubovich, *Biblioteca,* I, 56; *Chronicon XXIV Generalium,* 331. Angelo may be following the sense of Thomas of Celano, *Vita prima sancti Francisci,* XX, ed. E. Alençon, *S. Francisci vita et miracula* (Rome, 1906), 57–60, who includes 'Syria' within the geographical orbit of Egypt. The Old French continuation of William of Tyre, *Eracles,* RHC Occ ii, 348, also has Francis going on to Syria from Egypt. See now John V. Tolan, *Saint Francis and the Sultan* (Oxford, 2009).

20 *Actus beati Francisci et sociorum eius,* XXVII, ed. P. Sabatier (Paris 1902), 90–1.

21 Thomas of Celano, *Vita Prima,* XX, ed. E. Alençon, *S. Francisci vita et miracula* (Rome, 1906), 57–60. For general discussion, see Christopher MacEvitt, 'Martyrdom and the Muslim World through Franciscan Eyes', *Catholic Historical Review* 97 (2011), 1–23.

22 *Les gestes des Chiprois,* Receuil des Historiens des Croisades, Documents Arméniens, 2 vols (Paris 1869–1906), II, 765.

23 Golubovich, *Biblioteca,* I, 351–2.

24 P. Durnieu, 'Procès-verbal du martyre de quatre frères mineurs, 1391', *Archives de l'Orient Latin,* i, (1881), 539–46.

25 Pringle, *Churches,* III, 261–87.

26 Thus E.D. Hunt, *Holy Land Pilgrimage in the Later Roman Empire, AD 312–460,* (Oxford, 1982), 19, but see Joan Taylor, *Christians and the Holy Places. The Myth of Jewish-Christian Origins,* (Oxford, 1993), 208–9, for the view that Mt Sion was too up-market an area for the earliest Christians to have resided there; on these grounds she dismisses the idea of a Jewish-Christian house church on the site. On the early Church in Jerusalem, see Jerome Murphy-O'Connor, 'Pre-Constantinian Christian Jerusalem', in A. O'Mahony (ed.) *The Christian Heritage in the Holy Land* (London, 1995), 13–21.

27 Cyril of Jerusalem, *Catecheses* XVI, 4, PG 33: 924; Taylor, *Christians and the Holy Places,* 211, for dating the church to *c.* 336.

28 *Itinerarium Egeriae,* XXXIX, 5, ed. A. Franceschini and R. Weber, *Itineraria et alia Geographica,* [C]orpus [C]hristianorum [S]eries [L]atina 175 (Turnhout, 1965), 83. A twelfth-century liturgical synaxarion from the Greek Orthodox community in Jerusalem records the procession to Mt Sion and the services of Vespers and the blessing of the holy oil in the Upper Room on Maundy Thursday, A. Papadopoulos-Kerameos (ed.), *Analekta Ierosolymitikes Stachyologias,* ii (Athens 1894, repr. Brussels 1963), 83–108, from Jerusalem Holy Sepulchre MS 43.

29 *Itinerarium Egeriae,* XLIII, 8, 86.

30 *Liturgy of St James* ed. G. Mercier, *Patrologia Orientalis* 26 (Paris, 1946), 206; Cyril of Scythopolis, *Vita Sabae,* LVII. ed. E. Schwartz, *Kyrillos von Skythopolis* (Leipzig, 1939), 176.

31 Hunt, *Holy Land Pilgrimage,* 212–20.

32 *Antoninus Placentinus Itinerarium* XXII, ed. P. Geyer, *Itineraria et alia Geographica* CCSL 175, 140.

33 The first mention is in Ps-Hesychius, *Commentarium in Psalmos,* I, 17, LIV, 14, CIX, 2; see Taylor, *Christians and the Holy Places,* 207.

34 *Saewulf,* ed. R.B.C. Huygens, *Peregrinatores Tres,* CCCM 139 (Turnhout, 1994), 71.

35 The architectural layout of the church and shrines is difficult to reconstruct exactly from pilgrims' accounts, Jaroslav Folda, *The Art of the Crusaders in the Holy Land, 1099–1187* (Cambridge, 1995), 282.

36 Ch. Kohler (ed.) 'Un ritual et un bréviaire du Sait-Sépulcre', *Revue de l'Orient latin,* viii (1900–1), 414–15.

37 John Phokas, *Descriptio Terrae Sanctae*, PG 133: 942; *The Life and Journey of Daniel, Abbot of the Russian Land*, trans. W.F. Ryan, in J. Wilkinson (ed. and trans.) *Jerusalem Pilgrimage 1099–1185* (London, 1988), 142.

38 P.C. Boeren (ed.) *Rorgo Fretellus de Nazareth et sa Description de la Terre Sainte: histoire et Edition du Texte* (Amsterdam, 1980), 127, *Daniel*, 142.

39 *John of Würzburg*, ed. R.B.C. Huygens, *Pergrinatores Tres*, CCCM 139, 115: 'Traditus est, ut diximus, dominus noster a discipulo suo, captus et ligatus a milite romano reductus ad Montem Syon, ubi tunc est pretorium Pilati nuncupatum lithistrotos, hebraice autem Gabatha.' *Innominati VII Descriptio Terrae Sanctae*, ed. S. de Sandoli, *Itinera Hierosolymitana Crucesignatorum*, iii (Jerusalem, 1983), 80; Thietmar, *Iter ad Terram Sanctam*, VIII, 264.

40 *Theoderic*, ed. R.B.C. Huygens, *Peregrinatores Tres*, CCCM 139, 195, and see Wilkinson, *Jerusalem Pilgrimage*, fig. 19. The tradition is first recorded, however, in the *Itinerarium Burdigalense (333)*, ed. P. Geyer and O. Cuntz, *Itineraria et alia Geographica*, CCSL 175, 16–17.

41 Folda, *Art of the Crusaders*, 601.

42 Peter Fergusson, 'The Refectory at Easby Abbey: Form and Iconography', *Art Bulletin*, lxxi (1989), 334–51. Arguments for a late twelfth-century date for the rebuilding of the Cenacle are provided by Hugh Plommer, 'The Cenacle on Mount Sion', in Jaroslav Folda (ed.) *Crusader Art in the Twelfth Century* (London, 1982), 139–66, correcting Camille Enlart, *Les Monuments des Croisés dans le royaume de Jérusalem*, 2 vols (Paris, 1925–8), ii, 249–62, and H. Vincent and F-M. Abel, *Jérusalem: Recherches de topographie, d'archéologie et d'histoire*, 2 vols (Paris, 1914–26), ii, 421–40.

43 Folda, *Art of the Crusaders*, 471.

44 Between 1187 and 1229 the Cenacle seems to have been in the control of the Greek Orthodox, who maintained a monastery on Mt Sion, Wilbrand of Oldenburg, *Itinerarium Terrae Sanctae* II, 9, in De Sandoli, *Itinera*, iii, 242.

45 For example, Thietmar, *Iter*, VIII, 264; *Les pelerinages por alher in Jerusalem*, IX, in De Sandoli, *Itinera*, iii, 456; *De via eundi de Iope in Ierusalem*, ed. Golubovich, *Biblioteca*, i, 406.

46 B.Z. Kedar, 'The *Tractatus de locis et statu sancte terre Ierosolimitane*', in J. France and W.G. Zajac (eds) *The Crusades and their Sources. Essays Presented to Bernard Hamilton* (Aldershot, 1998), 127.

47 Jacques de Vitry, *Historia Orientalis*, LXI, ed. F. Moschus (Douai, 1597), 103–4.

48 Albertus Stadensis, *Itinerarium Terrae Sanctae*, ed. Golubovich, *Biblioteca*, i, 182. For discussion of the Palm Sunday procession, see Molly Lindner, 'Topography and Iconography in Twelfth-Century Jerusalem', in B.Z. Kedar (ed.) *The Horns of Hattin* (Jerusalem, 1992), 81–98.

49 Golubovich, I, 406.

50 On the Augustinians and the *vita apostolia*, see *inter alia* C.N.L. Brooke, 'Monk and Canon: Some Patterns in the Religious life of the Twelfth Century', in W.J. Shiels (ed.) *Monks, Hermits and the Ascetic Tradition*, Studies in Church History, xxii (Oxford, 1985), 109–29, Caroline W. Bynum, 'Did the Twelfth Century Discover the Individual?' *Journal of Ecclesiastical History*, xxxi (1980), 1–17.

51 Fergusson, 'The Refectory at Easby Abbey', 341.

52 See in this context, Francis' instructions to clergy and to the *custodes* of the Order on the handling and positioning of the Eucharistic host, Kajetan Esser (ed.) *Die opuskula des hl. Franziskus von Assisi. Neue textkritische Edition* (Grottaferrata, 1976), 192–4, 207–9.

53 Anne Derbes, *Picturing the Passion in Late Medieval Italy. Narrative Painting, Franciscan Ideologies and the Levant* (Cambridge, 1996), 7–8.

54 The only contemporary evidence for Francis as a deacon comes from Thomas of Celano, *Vita Prima* LXXXVI, *Analecta Franciscana*, x, 64, and idem, *Vita Secunda* CCXIX, 257. For discussion of Francis' deaconate in the context of contemporary views of the office, see C.N.L. Brooke, 'Priest, Deacon and Layman, from St. Peter Damian to St. Francis', in Diana Wood and W.J. Sheils (eds) *The Ministry, Clerical and Lay*, Studies in Church History, xxvi (1989) 65–85.

55 Wadding, *Annales*, II, an. 1342, n. 17.

56 Gian Luca Potestà, *Angelo Clareno: dai poveri eremiti ai fraticelli* (Rome, 1990), 199–200; but see also Stephen Wessley, 'The Role of the Holy Land for the Early Followers of Joachim of Fiore', in R.N. Swanson (ed.) *The Holy Land, Holy Lands and Christian History*, Studies in Church History, xxxvi (Woodbridge, 2000), 181–91, for the argument that Joachists were indifferent to the Holy Land.

57 Consider the importance attached to the literal following of apostolic conduct in the debate between English Franciscans and Dominicans in the 1290s, Thomas Sutton, *Contra aemulos fratrum Praedicatorum*, ed. F. Pelster, 'Eine Kontroverse zwischen englischen Dominikanern und Minoriten über einige Punkte der Ordensregel', *Archivum Fratrum Praedicatorum*, iii (1933), 74–80.

58 Welbore St Clair Baddeley, *Robert the Wise and His Heirs 1278–1352* (London, 1897), 154, 232.

59 Ronald G. Musto, 'Queen Sancia of Naples (1286–1345) and the Spiritual Franciscans', in Julius Kirshner and Suzanne Wemple (eds) *Women of the Medieval World* (Oxford, 1985), 185–7, 189–90. On the piety of Sancia and Robert, see Domenico Ambrasi, *Storia di Napoli* (Naples, 1969), iii, 502–12.

60 Musto, 'Queen Sancia', 207–14, for a translation of the letter.

61 *Chronicon XXIV Generalium ordinis Minorum*, 508–14.

62 Ambrasi, *Storia di Napoli*, iii, 487–522; Francesco Russo, 'I Fraticelli in Calabria nel secolo XIV. Fatti e personaggi', *Miscellanea Francescana*, lxv (1965), 349–68.

63 *Bullarium Franciscanum*, ed. J. Sbaralea, vi, 601, 607, 611.

64 Musto, 'Queen Sancia', 195.

65 Musto, 'Queen Sancia', 196. The letters are discussed in Ronald G. Musto, 'The Letters of Angelo Clareno (*c.*1250–1337)', unpub. PhD dissertation, Columbia University, 1977, 307–43, 367–98; for the loan of St Basil's Rule to Robert, see Lydia von Auw (ed.) *Angeli Clareni Opera. I. Epistolae* (Rome, 1980), 203–7.

66 Musto, 'Queen Sancia', 196–7.

67 Baddeley, *Robert the Wise*, 233; Edith Pásztor, 'Il processo di Andreas da Galgiano (1337–8)', *Archivum Franciscanum Historicum*, xlviii (1955), 252–97.

68 Musto, 'Queen Sancia', 200–1.

69 Samantha Kelly, *The New Solomon. Robert of Naples (1309–1343) and Fourteenth-Century Kinghip* (Leiden, 2003), 83–6.

70 Alvanus de Pelayo, *De planctu ecclesiae* (Lyons, 1517), ii, 219.

71 Musto, 'Queen Sancia', 210–11, 212–13.

72 David Burr, *The Spiritual Franciscans* (Philadelphia, 2001), 11–12.

73 Duncan Nimmo, *Reform and Division in the Franciscan Order 1226–1538* (Rome, 1987), 265.

74 Samantha Kelly, 'Robert the Wise (1309–1343) and the Spiritual Franciscans', *Cristianesimo nella storia*, xx (1999), 41–80.

75 Nimmo, *Reform and Division*, 260.

76 Musto, 'Queen Sancia', 206–14; Wadding, *Annales*, vii, 1334, 172.

77 *Chronicon XXIV Generalium*, 506.

78 Angelo Clareno, *Historia septem tribulationum ordinis minorum*, ed. Franz Ehrle, *Archiv für Literatur und Kirchengeschichte*, ii (Berlin 1886), 305–6.

79 Angelo Clareno, *Historia septem tribulationum*, 306–8.

80 F. Ehrle (ed.) 'Die ältesten Redaktionen der Generalconstitutionen des Franziskanordens', *Archiv für Literatur und Kirchengeschichte*, vi (1892), 64. For a summary of the mission to Armenia, see Lydia von Auw, *Angelo Clareno et les spirituals italiens* (Rome, 1979), 31–3. On the Franciscan province of the Holy Land in the thirteenth century, see Marshall W. Baldwin, 'Franciscan Missions to the East in the Thirteenth and Fourteenth Centuries', in Kenneth Setton (gen ed.) *History of the Crusades*, 5, *The Impact of the Crusades on the Near East*, ed. Norman P. Zacour

and Harry W. Hazard (Madison, 1985), 452–89; Martiniano Roncaglia, *Storia della Provincia di Terra Santa. Vol 1. I Francescani in Oriente durante le Crociate (sec. XIII)* (Cairo, 1954).

81 Angelo Clareno, *Historia septem tribulationum*, 307–8. See also G. Golubovich, 'Cipro francescana', *Archivum Franciscanum Historicum*, x (1917), 357–66.

82 Burr, *Spiritual Franciscans*, 29–32.

83 M. Bihl (ed.), 'Statuta generalia ordinis edita in capitulis generalibus celebratis Narbonae an.1260, Assisii an.1270 atque Parisiis an.1292', *Archivum Franciscanum Historicum*, xxxiv (1941), 69.

84 *Chronicon XXIV Generalium*, 609–10.

85 Golubovich, *Biblioteca*, iii, 291

86 Kaspar Elm, 'La custodia di Terra Santa. Franziskanisches Ordensleben in der Tradition der lateinischen kirche Palästinas', in *I Francescani nel Trecento. Atti del XIV Convegno Internazionale Assisi 16–18 Ottobre 1986* (Assisi, 1988), 129–66.

PART IV

MEDIEVAL BYZANTIUM

———•◆•———

CHAPTER SIXTEEN

BYZANTINE CRUSADERS: HOLY WAR AND CRUSADE RHETORIC IN BYZANTINE CONTACTS WITH THE WEST (1095–1341)[1]

———•◆•———

Nikolaos G. Chrissis

Seeing the Holy Land, where our Saviour suffered for the salvation of the world [...], occupied by the infidels and the impious, and [seeing] the innumerable army of the Latin peoples who rushed to assist its deliverance [...] turn back having achieved nothing and profited in no way [...] deeply touches the heart of our Highness, afflicting us with constant sadness, making us wander around sullenly and mournfully each day, washing with tears not only our bed but even the streets and roads. My Highness urges your Holiness: [...] sounding your trumpet and wielding your pastoral staff, muster all the Christians in one flock, and instruct them all to be enemies only to the Serpent. Not only the spiritual Serpent, Satan [...], but also the impious who ally with him and at his instigation hasten to trample upon the Holy Land; their head will not be crushed, unless the common bond of love to Christ unites all the Christians in one and makes them a single mouth, a single tongue, a single hand against the perpetrators of impieties.

These words, so full of pathos for the fate of the Holy Land, are not the words of a Western king or a crusading lord. They rather come from a letter of the Byzantine emperor Isaac II to Pope Celestine III, composed around 1193 (Darrouzès, 1970: 336–45). That is, the same emperor who had tried to hinder the passage of Frederick Barbarossa during the Third Crusade, and whose negotiations with Saladin had given rise to scandalous (if exaggerated) rumours in the West that an alliance had been forged between the two rulers (Brand, 1962; Neocleous, 2010, 2013). Why did Isaac declare his commitment to the cause of the Holy Land and the crusade despite the rather different choices of his foreign policy at the time?

It will be argued here that Byzantine policymakers realised early on that they could not afford to ignore the crusade and the Western sensitivities on the affair of the Holy Land. Consequently, it became established practice for Byzantine emperors when dealing with the West to express their concern for the Holy Sepulchre and profess their support for 'the common cause of Christendom'. It was this established practice of Byzantine diplomacy that Isaac was following. We will examine the characteristics of this policy and the way it developed over the following two centuries. The focus will be mostly on Byzantine propaganda towards the West, that is, the self-representation of the empire, rather than its actual policy towards the crusade.

BYZANTIUM AND HOLY WAR

The examination touches upon a wider and controversial issue: namely, the Byzantine attitudes towards the notion of Holy War, and particularly its Western variety, the crusade. There is no doubt that the crusades greatly affected Byzantium. The armies of the First and Second Crusade, as well as the host of Frederick Barbarossa during the Third Crusade, made their way to the East through Byzantine territory, with alternating phases of cooperation and growing tension with the Byzantine authorities. Furthermore, the creation of the crusader states within the sphere of Byzantine interests reconfigured the balance of power and the political landscape in the area (Lilie, 1993; Harris, 2003). It was only reasonable that imperial diplomacy would have to readjust and take the new circumstances into consideration. Its reaction would necessarily depend on Byzantine understanding of the motives and incentives behind crusading.

The subject is a complex one and we will not presume to solve it here. However, it will be useful to summarise the main directions of the debate so far and the basic underlying issues, as they are pertinent to our topic.[2] George Dennis has put it like this:

> For the Byzantines [...] both ideas and forms of holy war – jihad and crusade – were abhorrent. They absolutely rejected both. [...] They never seemed to understand why all those Western knights and their followers were marching through their land. [...] The Byzantines did not have any concept of a true holy war.
>
> (2001: 32–3)

This view reflects the opinion of a sizeable proportion of the scholars who have dealt with the issue of Byzantine attitudes to Holy War and the crusade. It harks back to a seminal contribution by Vitalien Laurent (1946), while similar views have been expressed by major scholars, such as Paul Lemerle (1955), Angeliki Laiou (1993, 2006) and Nicholas Oikonomides (1995). The argument against Byzantine understanding of Holy War is twofold: first, no wars fought by Byzantium qualify as Holy Wars; and second, the very notion of a Holy War was alien and repugnant to Byzantine thought.

The question largely depends on definitions. In general, Dennis, Laiou and Oikonomides accept three criteria as essential for defining a Holy War. First, promulgation: the war should be declared by a religious authority (and not a secular one), theoretically at the instigation of the Divine. Second, it should be in pursuit of a religious objective. This can have a 'defensive', re-active character, namely the protection of the faith, of sacred places and of co-religionists – including the effort to avenge past injuries in such matters. Alternatively, it can have an 'offensive', pro-active character, namely the conversion, elimination or subjection of the 'infidels'. Finally, it should entail the promise of a spiritual reward for the participants, such as the remissions of sins, the crown of martyrdom, and the promise of heaven.

Byzantine wars are seen by these scholars as not fulfilling any of the three criteria. The authority responsible for declaring and waging war in Byzantium was indisputably the emperor and never the Church. The aim of fighting, for all its possible religious overtones, was generally to defend or reclaim imperial territory. Finally, Byzantine soldiers were not granted any spiritual rewards for their service as the Byzantine Church never sanctioned such a development.

This latter point and the view that Byzantines rejected the notion of Holy War in general rest primarily on the Byzantine Church's adherence to the thirteenth canon of St Basil, which states: 'Our Fathers did not consider killings in war to be murders, but, in my opinion, pardoned those who fight in defence of virtue and piety. Still, it is perhaps well to advise them to abstain only from communion for three years, since their hands are not clean' (Courtonne, 1957–66: II, 130, no. 188). An event from the tenth century is usually cited to illustrate the point: Emperor Nikephoros Phokas (963–9), famous for his military exploits against the Arabs, requested for the Byzantine soldiers who fell in the fighting to be awarded the status of martyrs by the Church. Patriarch Polyeuktos and the synod rejected the petition, citing the canon of St Basil as justification (Thurn, 1973: 273–5). The incident was also reported and commented upon by later canonists from the twelfth to the fourteenth century: John Zonaras, Theodore Balsamon and Matthew Blastares all seemed to approve of the patriarchal decision – although, it should be noted, they were less clear-cut about the possibility or even the desirability of enforcing St Basil's 'suggestion' of exclusion from the sacraments (Beck, 1981: 20–39; Viscuso, 1995; Stouraitis, 2011: 52–8). Therefore, though fighting can be unavoidable or indeed desirable when it is for a just cause, it can by no means be a 'holy' activity bestowing spiritual benefits to the participants. Rather, it is necessary for soldiers to do penance and be purified from the shedding of blood.

A parallel point often made is that in Byzantine thought there was an emphasis on peace, while war was not seen as meritorious or glorious in itself but rather as a necessary evil, a last resort if all efforts at peace had failed. This was stressed even in the preface of a military treatise, the *Taktika*, attributed to Emperor Leo VI (886–912), which stated:

> all men ought to embrace peace and foster love for one another instead of taking up murderous weapons in their hands to use against their own people. But since the devil […] has made use of sin to bring men to the point of waging war against their own kind, it becomes entirely necessary for men to wage war […] and, without flinching, to take their stand against those nations that want war.
>
> (Dennis, 2010: 2–5)

Following this line of argument, the combination of the abovementioned elements could only mean that the Byzantines faced the crusade with shock and incomprehension as to the motives of the participants. It was something outside their experience and opposite to their values and worldview.

However, this is not the only way to interpret Byzantine attitudes to Holy War, and this view has not gone unchallenged. Some scholars have taken a different approach to the subject. Athina Kolia-Dermitzaki (1991a, 2012) has argued for the existence of a particular variety of Byzantine Holy War distinct from both the crusade and the jihad, whereas Tia Kolbaba (1998) has similarly taken a more nuanced view to the question, re-examining the defining elements of a Holy War. These scholars pointed out that criteria and definitions have often been based upon the model of the crusade and the jihad, and therefore they lack the flexibility to allow for different forms of Holy War originating from different societies, such as the Byzantine one. Even allowing for the three aforementioned criteria to stand, it is argued that some Byzantine wars fulfilled them in their own particular way. Indeed, Byzantine political ideology viewed the emperor as God's regent on earth and his office was by no means a solely secular one. The emperor was 'sacred' and his position as the only competent authority to declare war was never challenged, rendering the direct involvement of the Byzantine Church in this matter unnecessary, unlike what had been the case with the papacy in the West. Similarly, the objective was to protect the emperor's subjects, identified as the 'Christians' and the 'chosen people', and to defend the 'sacred empire', which was seen as a part of God's plan for the salvation of humanity – in other words, aims that transcended the temporal plane.

The most important issue for our examination, however, is that of spiritual rewards, as it is connected with the Byzantines' own understanding and attitude towards holy or sanctified war, rather than our definitions of it. We have already seen how the official Church rejected the request by Nikephoros Phokas for fallen soldiers to be recognised as martyrs. Another relevant incident comes from the early thirteenth century. Patriarch Michael IV Autoreianos (1207–13), resident with the exiled Byzantine government at Nicaea, in one of his acts granted remission of sins to the Byzantine soldiers who fell in battle against the Latins who held Constantinople (Oikonomides, 1967: 117–19). This is dismissed by those who reject the existence of Byzantine Holy War as a unique exception and a temporary aberration from the practice of the Byzantine Church under the pressure of Emperor Theodore I Lakaris.

However, the most important counter-argument is exactly the point that the idea of a sanctified war, whereby the warriors would be proclaimed martyrs or given remission of sins, obviously held *some* allure for both emperors, Nikephoros II and Theodore I. They evidently also thought that it would be good for the soldiers' motivation; therefore it is to be expected that the idea would be far from incomprehensible or repugnant *to them*. Furthermore, there is evidence that Byzantine commanders actually went 'further than what was admissible for the Byzantine church' in telling their soldiers of the holy nature of the war and divine rewards to be had (Oikonomides, 1995: 66–7). A military treatise from the tenth century speaks of the soldiers as protectors and liberators of the Christian people (Dagron and Mihaescu, 1986: 284–6). It is important that in the same source which was mentioned earlier as evidence for the negative Byzantine attitude towards war in general, the *Taktika* of Leo VI, Byzantine soldiers who die in battle are presented as martyrs for the faith, fighting 'for the salvation of [their] souls and for God' (Dennis, 2010: par. XIV.31, XVIII.16, 19, 127). The author also advises that:

> [the soldiers should be reminded] of the divine reward and the imperial generosity [...] and that the fight is for God and for love of God and for the brothers and co-religionists and for the women and children and the homeland [...] and that such a fight is against the enemies of God, and that we have God as a friend [...] whereas they have Him as an adversary, because they are infidels.
>
> (Dennis, 2010, par. XII.57)

This was not the earliest reference to divine rewards. Back in the seventh century, in a climate of heightened religious antagonism during the great Byzantine-Persian war, Herakleios reportedly encouraged his soldiers by telling them that they were fighting to avenge the insult against God and their fellow Christians, in return for eternal life and the crown of martyrdom (de Boor, 1883–85: I, 307, 310–11; Mango and Scott, 1997: 439, 442–3; Stoyanov, 2011; Kaegi, 2012).

The difference of opinion between secular and ecclesiastic leadership on the matter should not be exaggerated either. Around 915, the patriarch of Constantinople, Nicholas I

Mystikos, wrote a letter to congratulate the Byzantine general of the theme of Longobardia in southern Italy for the great victory against the Arabs at Garigliano. In this letter, the patriarch stated that he hoped for even greater victories for 'the race of coreligionists' to honour the name of God, and expressed the wish that the general might enjoy 'both in the present life the greatest honours, as the fruits of your own labours [...] and in the afterlife the common reward for those who fight for Christ our God and for His glory' (Jenkins and Westerink, 1973: no. 44, 262–3; Kolia-Dermitzaki, 1997: 226). In this case, therefore, the view that the fight against infidels can bring rewards after death was expressed by no less an authority than the head of the Orthodox Church. Further evidence that ecclesiastical authorities occasionally recognised in practice fallen soldiers as martyrs and saw fighting as connected to the salvation of the soul is provided, for example, by some surviving liturgies (Kolia-Dermitzaki, 1991a: 252–60; Stephenson, 2012).

Finally, a more general critique regarding the notion of a Byzantine Holy War is that there should be a meaningful way of distinguishing between a 'holy' war and any other war waged by the empire, particularly any other 'just' war. Ioannis Stouraitis (2012) proposes that the distinction is essentially between a war fought for 'rational' state reasons and one waged on the basis of an 'irrational' divine command. Consequently, only when religious incentives were the basic motive for the fighting (or at least for the soldiers' participation in it), can we speak of Holy War. Since Byzantium's wars were mostly motivated by 'political' (or natural-law) reasons – that is, the defence or the expansion of the state – they cannot be rightly called Holy Wars. For all the merits of this argument, however, its main flaw is the overly theoretical rigidity of the proposed model. On real, historical grounds it is unlikely that any war – not only Byzantine ones, but also most crusading and jihadist campaigns – would meet the criteria imposed by such a strict dichotomy. Virtually none of them was 'untainted' by practical considerations and circumstances other than a perceived divine mandate. Jihad was connected intimately to the ambitions and needs of the Muslim regimes that had recourse to it, while crusading activity followed closely the political circumstances in both the West and the crusader states in the Levant. This is obviously too prescriptive an approach and does not allow for gradations of real-life religious devotion and for the dynamic relationship between the holy and the temporal. A more balanced analysis of the interplay between political exigencies, imperial ideology and the attitudes towards warfare inherited by the Christian and Roman traditions is offered by Yuri Stoyanov (2011: 25–75).

In any case, most recent discussions of the topic confirm that an often intense sacralisation of warfare was present in Byzantium (see Stephenson, 2007). Ideas of Holy War, therefore, were not necessarily alien and automatically repudiated by the Byzantines.[3] This is the most pertinent point here – and not whether Byzantium had its own variety of Holy War – as we turn to consider the Byzantine attitudes and reactions towards Western crusading.

BYZANTIUM AND THE CRUSADE[4]

The source most frequently cited to highlight the allegedly uncomprehending Byzantine attitude towards crusading is the Byzantine princess Anna Komnene who, in her account of the First Crusade, stated that the real aim of the leaders of the expedition, and particularly of the Norman prince Bohemond, was to seize Constantinople (Reinsch and Kambylis, 2001: Bk 10, pars. V.10, VI.7, IX.1, and XI.7). A similar view was held by John Kinnamos who, recounting the Second Crusade, stated that Jerusalem was merely a pretext, whereas the crusaders' real aim was the conquest of the Byzantine capital (Meineke, 1836: Bk II, par. 12, 67). Byzantine fears seemed to be confirmed, when the Fourth Crusade, instead of going to the Holy Land, captured Constantinople in 1204. Nicholas Mesarites, describing the looting of the churches of Constantinople by the crusaders, commented: 'Such was the reverence for holy things of those who bore the Lord's cross on their shoulders; thus their own bishops taught them to act' (Heisenberg, 1973: no. II.i, 47; Brand, 1968: 269).

But this criticism, it should be stressed, was levelled against the eventual actions of the crusaders and not their initial or professed aim. Anna Komnene's attitude was not much different in that respect: she explicitly contrasted the leaders' designs on Constantinople with the genuine desire of the 'simpler folk' to go to the Sepulchre of the Lord. It was not the notion of the crusade as a Holy War that was criticised by these Byzantine authors but rather the discrepancy between the professed ideal and the crusaders' actions and designs (real or imaginary) against the empire. The criticism presupposes an awareness of the underlying principles of crusading. What is more, Niketas Choniates, himself an eyewitness of the conquest of Constantinople by the Latins in 1204, accepted the motives of the participants in the Second and Third Crusade as sincere, that is, aiming to bring assistance to the Kingdom of Jerusalem and the Christians of the Holy Land. Furthermore, he displayed a clear understanding – and essentially an appreciation – of crusading ideology in his History, in the speech he put in the mouth of King Louis VII of France and in his portrayal of Emperor Frederick Barbarossa. In the speech purportedly given by the French king there is even a reference to gaining heaven through the crusade (van Dieten, 1975: I, 60–71, 401–17; Harris, 2003: 138–9; Kolia-Dermitzaki, 1991b: 177–9). The notion of spiritual rewards for crusaders was not only known but also accepted by at least one high-ranking member of the Byzantine clergy. Patriarch Symeon II of Jerusalem (resident in Cyprus after fleeing his see) issued joint admonitions with the papal legate in the early stages of the First Crusade, calling those who had taken crusade vows to fulfil them or face excommunication. In a letter of October 1097 it was even stated that the patriarch had a vision in which Christ told him that those who participated in the expedition would wear crowns at the Last Judgement, an allusion to martyrdom (Hamilton, 1980: 5–7). Regardless of Symeon's actual role in composing these letters, the Orthodox prelate was evidently content to add his name to them and was not appalled by the Holy War waged by the crusaders.

Thus, the Byzantines were far from oblivious of the ideology and practice of crusading. This is confirmed also by the way Byzantine imperial diplomacy towards Latin powers incorporated language and imagery revolving around the Holy Land and the affair of the cross. Indeed, Byzantine emperors in the twelfth century took care to project an image of their actions that was acceptable to the Latin West.

The Byzantine emperor's status as a Christian ruler and the empire's proximity to the Holy Land raised expectations in the West for Byzantine participation in the common enterprise – even more so, as one of Urban II's stated objectives for launching the First Crusade was to assist the Eastern Christians against the Muslims, following Alexios Komnenos's appeal to the West (Charanis, 1949; Riley-Smith, 1993: 13–30). During a large part of the First Crusade, it was hoped or even assumed that the emperor would accept the honourable obligation to lead the expedition. For example, according to Raymond of Aguilers and Peter Tudebode, the envoys sent by Raymond of St Gilles to Constantinople reported back that the count should hurry to meet Alexios and come to an agreement with him: 'since the Emperor had taken the cross, he said he would take the Jerusalem journey as their commander-in-chief and head' (Hill and Hill, 1974: 29; 1968: 22). Even at the meeting of the crusade leaders with Byzantine ambassadors at 'Arqah, after relations had seriously deteriorated between the two sides, Raymond advocated that the host should wait for Alexios, since they would benefit from his help and they would 'be united under his leadership' (Hill and Hill, 1968: 105–6).

Alexios foresaw the potential benefits and took advantage of the passage of the First Crusade to effect the re-stabilization of Byzantine authority in Asia Minor. The above testimonies indicate that the emperor, already at the time of the crusaders' arrival at Constantinople, invoked arguments that were in tune with their sensitivities and aims, cultivating the expectation that he would join the campaign. The flip side of crusading for Byzantium was made evident in 1107–08, when Bohemond launched a propaganda campaign depicting the emperor as behaving treacherously against the pilgrims and hindering the way to the Holy Land, in an effort to stir Western emotion against Constantinople. He eventually diverted the crusade under his command to an invasion of the empire (Rowe, 1966–67; Whalen, 2010). Alexios managed to defeat Bohemond at Dyrrachium but the implications of this attack were clear: the emperor needed to project a positive image to the West and counter the impression that he was hostile to the crusaders. These considerations set the tone for Byzantine diplomacy for decades to come. The Byzantine leadership was acutely aware of the danger, because Latin recriminations against Byzantine unhelpfulness and unwillingness to contribute to the 'war of the faith' became commonplace over the following years and the argument was often used to justify aggression against the empire (Harris, 2012).

Though Alexios' heir, John Komnenos (1118–43), followed a more aggressive policy towards the Latin principality of Antioch, he did not lose sight of the importance of invoking a crusade-related rationale to legitimise his actions. In his first expedition against Antioch in 1137–38, the emperor opted not to persist with direct aggression, which could provoke Western opinion. Instead, he concluded a treaty with Prince Raymond for common action against Aleppo, Shaizar and Homs, as the capture of these cities would not only be exchanged with the cession of Antioch but it would also, in Lilie's words, 'invest the Byzantine Emperor with the glory of a successful crusader and raise the dignity of the Empire in the West' (Lilie, 1993: 120–123, 140). Imperial propaganda evidently projected John as a defender of the faith, both internally and towards the Latins, as has been argued by Augé (2000: 228–49, 336–7; 2001) and Papageorgiou (2007: 225–45, 308–59; forthcoming).[5]

But the Byzantine ruler whose policy most persistently made use of the crusade was Manuel Komnenos (1143–80). Magdalino (1993) and Lilie (1993: 142–221) have extensively and convincingly demonstrated how Manuel fashioned and projected his image towards the West as a protector of the Christian peoples and the Holy Land, with a view to strengthening his influence in both the Latin States in the Levant and in western Europe. This propaganda climaxed in his expedition against the Seljuk Sultan Kiliç Arslan which ended with the defeat of Myriokephalon (1176) – 'the Byzantine Crusade' as has been termed by both scholars (Magdalino, 1993: 95–8; Lilie, 1993: 211–14). Reasonable objections have been raised regarding this term (Stouraitis, 2011: 42–9; Chrysos, 2012); however, as we will see, it is beyond doubt that Manuel presented it as such to the Latin world.

This brief outline of Komnenian policies corroborates our basic premise that Byzantine emperors took crusade ideology under consideration in their diplomacy towards the West. This will be demonstrated even more clearly through a thematic examination of: a) the means used by imperial propaganda, and b) the major developments over time.

MEANS AND METHODS OF BYZANTINE PROPAGANDA

Byzantine diplomacy resorted to three general methods in order to portray imperial policy in a favourable light regarding Western sensitivities for the Holy Land: the use of relevant crusading rhetoric; symbolic gestures; and actual (and widely advertised) cooperation with the Latins against the Muslims.

Starting with rhetoric: virtually all twelfth-century emperors took care to explicitly state their interest for the Holy Land in their correspondence with Latin powers. In this context, the evocative power of Jerusalem and the Holy Sepulchre was repeatedly exploited. John Komnenos wrote to King Fulk and expressed his wish to visit and assist the Holy City, at the time of his second campaign against Antioch in 1142–43 (Huygens, 1986: par. 15.21). The court orator Nikephoros Basilakes rejoiced that 'the Christ-loving emperor [John] had made the way safe for pilgrims to Jerusalem', which indicates that the theme was a current one in the Byzantine court (Garzya, 1984: 56; Magdalino, 1993: 41, 420; Kolia-Dermitzaki, 1991a: 332–7). Manuel Komnenos consistently presented himself in this light, particularly from the 1160s onwards, when he stepped up his policy of actively interfering in the affairs of Outremer. An example that stands out is the lavish reception of King Amalric in Constantinople, in 1171, when Manuel promised assistance to the Kingdom of Jerusalem (Huygens, 1986: par. 20.22–4; Runciman, 1982). When preparing his major campaign against the Seljuks in 1176, the emperor wrote to Pope Alexander III presenting the re-fortification of Dorylaion in the Anatolian plateau as an important contribution to opening up the road to the Holy Sepulchre. Consequently, he asked the pope to incite Western (crusading) support, for his forthcoming expedition. The pope, indeed, called the French king and nobles to take up this task which would be 'for the exaltation of the name of the Christian Faith' (Bouquet et al., 1738–1904: XV, 952–3, no. 385; Stone, 2003). Manuel described his campaign in similar terms also to King Henry II of England (Vasiliev, 1929–30; Harris, 2003: 103). Later in the twelfth century, Isaac II, as we saw in our opening quotation, did not spare rhetorical exaggerations to depict his anguish for the tribulations of the Holy Land. His successor, Alexios III, affirmed his fiery zeal to assist the Sepulchre for which, he claimed when writing to Innocent III, he would not only devote the riches and manpower of the empire but would in fact 'gladly lay down [his] own life' (Hageneder et al., 1964–: II, 391, no. 201; Powell, 2003).

Furthermore, in communications with the West, crusading was routinely depicted as a worthy enterprise which the Byzantine emperors approved of. For example, Manuel applauded the prospect of the Second Crusade in his letters to King Louis VII of France and to Pope Eugenius III:

> [we were informed that] the aforementioned most noble king of France set out, along with numerous other glorious men, on God's journey, in order to avenge the holy churches and on account of the capture of Edessa by the godless enemies of God. Our Imperial Majesty received the news of this great mobilisation most gladly. For it will be for the benefit of the Christians and for the fall and eradication of the godless enemies of God.
>
> (Lampros, 1914: 112–13)

As we will see below, even in the thirteenth century, when crusading was actually turned against the Byzantines, Theodore Laskaris and John Vatatzes expressed their indignation at this perversion of the crusade, thereby implying that the original aim was praiseworthy.

Another instrument in the hands of Byzantine diplomacy was the invocation of the common bond of Christianity coupled with calls for unity among the Christian peoples. Isaac II urged Celestine III to bring all Christians together, as this was the only way to crush the impious who trampled upon the Holy Land (Darrouzès, 1970: 345). The theme of unity was further elaborated when the emperors stressed their unwillingness to shed Christian blood and affirmed their preference to fight against the infidels. Any conflict among Christians, it was pointed out, would be to the detriment of the affair of the cross. Alexios III warned Pope Innocent III that he had prepared a fleet to reclaim Cyprus from the Latins but he delayed the expedition 'lest [he] shed the blood of Christians and prevented the aid to the Holy Land' (Powell, 2003: 94–5; 2004, par. 64).

Except for rhetoric, Byzantine diplomacy also resorted to symbolic gestures, aimed at confirming the emperors' commitment to the common cause and advertising their role as protectors of the Christians and of the Holy Land. Ransoming Christians from Muslim captivity was an effective gesture, as the emperor's generosity was also publicised by the gratitude of the released prisoners who were bound to disseminate his charitable act throughout Europe. Alexios I was the first to employ this measure to counter accusations against him when he ransomed the Latins that had been captured by the Egyptians at the battle of Ramla (Lilie, 1993: 71–2). Manuel, likewise, ensured the release of Christian captives as part of his truce with Nur-ad-Din in 1158–59 and, later on, ransomed Bohemond III of Antioch and Raynald of Châtillon (Magdalino, 1993: 71–3, 97; Hamilton, 1988: 360–1). Another symbolic gesture meant to highlight the emperor's protectorate over the Holy Land was the restoration of the Churches of Nativity in Bethlehem and of the Holy Sepulchre in Jerusalem which was carried out at Manuel's orders and expenditure in 1169 (Carr, 1982; Hunt, 1991; Folda, 1995: 347–78). Alexios Komnenos had evidently made a similar point in the 1100s, when he founded a hospice for Latin pilgrims at Civetot and entrusted it to the care of Cluniac monks (Gay, 1931). Under 'gestures' one could also include Manuel's arrangement of diplomatic marriages: one of his nieces was married to King Amalric of Jerusalem, his daughter Maria married Renier of Montferrat, and his son and heir, Alexios [II], was betrothed to Agnes, the daughter of Louis VII of France. Besides the obvious case of Jerusalem, the marriage of Manuel's children into the royal family of France and the house of Montferrat, both with notable connections to crusading and to Outremer, enhanced the reputation of Byzantium regarding its solicitude for the Holy Land (Hamilton, 1988: 370; Madgalino, 1993: 100–4).

Finally, a number of joint Byzantine-Frankish expeditions were undertaken against Muslims, usually at Byzantine initiative. No doubt, other practical aims were usually more important for the empire to take such action but the allusions to the cause of the Holy Land were not lost from sight. Such were, for example, the expeditions of John and the principality of Antioch against Aleppo and Shaizar in 1138, and the ones by Manuel and the Kingdom of Jerusalem against Nur ad-Din in 1158–59 and against Egypt in 1167–68 and 1177 (Lilie, 1993: 120–8, 198–202, 215–20, 309–20; Madgalino, 1993: 70–5; Hamilton, 1988: 357–66). Even though none of these campaigns achieved much in practical terms, they were evidently successful in raising the empire's prestige and improving Byzantium's reputation among the Latins – at least, if the opinions expressed by William of Tyre are any guide, when he praised the bravery and the commitment of the emperors and their soldiers while criticizing the passive and unenthusiastic role played by the Latin lords of the Levant (Huygens, 1986: par. 15.1–2, 20.16). Similarly, Byzantine emperors repeatedly held out the prospect of their participation in a crusade for the Holy Land. As we will see below, this was done in various times and circumstances; for example, by Alexios III on the eve of the Fourth Crusade, by Theodore Laskaris when dealing with its aftermath, and by Michael VIII after the recovery of Constantinople.

DEVELOPMENT OF BYZANTINE 'CRUSADING' DIPLOMACY (TWELFTH TO FOURTEENTH CENTURY)

This brings us to the examination of how the abovementioned characteristics of Byzantine diplomacy evolved over time. There were three critical turning points in Byzantine–Western interaction from the twelfth to the fourteenth century: first, after the death of Manuel Komnenos; second, after the conquest of Constantinople by the Fourth Crusade; and third after the growth of the Turkish threat in the Aegean. What was the impact of those developments on Byzantine crusade-related rhetoric?

After Manuel's death in 1180, Byzantium's policy drifted away from cooperation with the Latins, and its influence in the affairs of Outremer gradually diminished (Lilie, 1993: 222–45). But that change of policy hardly affected the pronouncements of Byzantine diplomacy towards the West – with the exception of Andronikos I, for whom little relevant evidence survives. As we saw, both Isaac II and Alexios III kept on asserting their commitment to the struggle against the infidels. But the fact that they did not support their proclamations with actions gave rise to widespread criticism in the West (for Western attitudes towards Byzantium in this period, see Lilie, 1993: 232–40, 252–8; Harris, 2003: 127–43, 146–51; Neocleous, 2009: 174–271). The Byzantine leadership was aware of that and tried to counter the accusations with the argument that it was Western aggression that hindered Byzantine participation in the crusade and consequently harmed the cause of Christendom and the Holy Land. Isaac, in his letter to Celestine III, explained the setbacks of crusading efforts as the outcome of internal strife between the Christian leaders, and pointed specifically to the hostility of the Hungarian king, Béla III, against Byzantium (Darrouzès, 1970: 343–5). Alexios III, responding to Innocent's reproof that Byzantium was unhelpful to the Holy Land, spoke of the danger that Frederick Barbarossa had presented for Constantinople, and asserted that such aggression was a hindrance to Byzantine cooperation (Hageneder et al., 1964–: II, 389–94, no. 201). The emperor used similar crusade-related rhetoric in response to the threat presented by his nephew (the future Alexios IV) who had fled to the West and had appealed, among others, to the leaders of the Fourth Crusade. Alexios III tried to convince Innocent III not to support the claims of the young prince to the Byzantine throne, urging the pope not to use the crusade against Christians, something which would 'offend God and weaken the attack against the enemies of Christ' (Hageneder et al., 1964–: V, 239–43, no. 121). Alexios III brought up the same arguments in his attempt to convince the leaders of the Fourth Crusade to desist from any aggression against Constantinople in 1203, while the fist skirmishes between Latins and Byzantines were taking place. According to Geoffrey of Villehardouin, the emperor's envoy addressed the following words to the heads of the crusading army:

> [Emperor Alexios] seriously wonders why, and for what purpose, you have entered this land over which he rules. For you are Christians just as he is, and he knows very well that you have left your own country to deliver the Holy Land oversea and the Holy Cross and Sepulchre. If you are in want of supplies, he will give you a share of his provisions

and his money, provided you withdraw from his land. If you refuse to leave, he would be reluctant to do you harm, yet it is in his power to do so.

(Faral, 1961: par. 143; Shaw, 1963: 63)

The chronicler's report has the ring of authenticity, for we can see here the emperor taking up most of the themes mentioned earlier: the common bond of Christianity between the Greeks and the crusaders; the positive reference to the latter's crusading mission; the prospect of Byzantine assistance to the expedition; and Alexios' unwillingness to use force against fellow Christians.

However, the conquest of Constantinople brought an end to such discussions. Byzantine failure to contribute to the war against the 'infidels' had, in fact, been one of the main arguments of justification for the attack by the army of the Fourth Crusade, while providing assistance to the Holy Land was perceived as the *raison d'être* of the Latin Empire, which was set up at Constantinople (Chrissis, 2012a: 22–5). What's more, the rump Byzantine states of Nicaea and Epiros became the target of a series of crusading expeditions in the thirteenth century, aimed at buttressing the Latin possessions in Romania (Chrissis, 2012b). The two main arguments used by the papacy when proclaiming these crusades were the schism between the Greek and the Latin Church, and – crucially – the fact that Byzantium had been unhelpful or even a hindrance to the Holy Land. This illustrates vividly the significance of Byzantium's diplomacy which aimed at projecting itself favourably regarding the latter affair, despite its eventual failure to avert the events of 1204.

Nevertheless, it is striking that Byzantine rulers continued to invoke the crusade in their correspondence with the West during the period of exile, although there were two significant changes. First, there were now Byzantine protests and criticism for the use of crusading against them as a betrayal of Christendom. Theodore I Laskaris, in a letter to Innocent III, accused the soldiers of the Fourth Crusade of perverting the expedition by turning against Constantinople and raising their weapons against Christians, whereas they had assumed the cross of the Lord and vowed to go to the help of the Holy Land; they, therefore, were guilty of apostasy, treason and sacrilege (Hageneder et al., 1964–: XI, no. 44). Then, in 1237, in a vehement letter to Gregory IX, John Vatatzes expressed his scorn at the use of the crusade by the pope to support the Latin Empire against the Greeks of Nicaea. The emperor dismissed such plans as 'mockery against the Holy Land and games at the expense of the cross'. The implication is that the emperor appeared to approve of the theoretical objective of crusading for the Holy Land. His bitter criticism made exactly the point that the use of the crusade against the Christian Greeks was a perversion of an otherwise worthy cause. In response to Pope Gregory's threat that a crusading army was making its way to Romania, Vatatzes ironically remarked that he was overjoyed since he hoped that 'the avengers of the Holy Land would start their revenge in our homeland, inflicting just punishment on the conquerors [of Constantinople] as desecrators of churches, defilers of holy vessels, and perpetrators of all kinds of impious crimes against Christians' (Sakellion, 1872: 376; Grumel, 1930).

The other notable development in this context is that the statements of commitment to the crusade receded from the Byzantine rulers' policy towards the West. The only time Byzantine promises for cooperation against the Muslims appear during the period of exile is early on: around 1208 Theodore Laskaris asked the pope to intervene so that peace could be established between Nicaea and Constantinople. In return, Laskaris promised that he would cooperate with the Latins against the 'Ismaelites' (Hageneder et al., 1964–: XI, no. 44).

However, after that point, promises of participation to a crusade or help to the Holy Land no longer feature in the contacts of Nicaea or Epiros with the West.[6] There were basically two reasons for this: first, the deployment of the crusade against the Byzantines after 1204 obviously created an ideological (not to mention emotional) complication to the invocation of crusading by the Byzantine rulers; second, and most importantly, the successor states lacked the international standing and resources of the empire for such promises to carry any weight.

Once the empire was reinstated at Constantinople in 1261, however, Michael Palaiologos resumed vigorously the policy of professing his commitment to the Holy Land and promising Byzantine help for forthcoming crusades (see Chrissis, 2012b: 227–9). This came along with the revival of a number of the rhetorical themes which were associated with Byzantine diplomacy towards the West in the past. Already in his contacts with Pope Urban IV (1261–64), Michael returned to the argument of Christian unity, expressing his surprise that the Holy See 'preferred war to peace among Christians', while at the same time alluding to Byzantine assistance to the crusading effort for the Holy Land (Guiraud, 1892–1958: no. 748). In 1266–68, Michael VIII offered Pope Clement IV not only Byzantine but also Armenian participation in a crusade (Jordan, 1893: no. 1201). The emperor similarly invoked the crusade in his contacts with James I of Aragon and Louis IX of France, in 1269 and 1270 respectively (Geanakoplos, 1959: 220, 223–8). But by far the most extensive and successful of Michael's efforts in that field were the negotiations with Gregory X, which culminated in the Union of the Churches at Lyons in 1274. Crucially, the Union was accompanied by the agreement for a common Byzantine–Latin crusade in Asia Minor. The plan for this expedition, which aimed to wrest the formerly Christian lands of Anatolia from Turkish hands so that they could be returned to the empire, was discussed at some length between the pope and the imperial envoy, George Metochites (Giannelli, 1947; Geanakoplos, 1959: 285–94). This remarkable proposal actually meant that Michael could now put the crusading powers of Western Christendom at his service rather than trying to dodge their blows. The project did not proceed, as Pope Gregory died shortly afterwards and papal policy towards Byzantium was soon reversed. The fact remains, however, that by this point Michael had astutely manipulated Western crusading sensitivities to his advantage – and, apparently, not only through his rhetoric but also through some more tangible gestures. If we are to believe Marino Sanudo's report a few decades later, Michael had built a tower in Acre at his own expense (Papadopoulou, 2000: 157), something we can compare with Manuel's acts of patronage in the twelfth century.

We will conclude our examination with a quick look at the developments after 1282, under Michael's successors, Andronikos II (1282–1328) and Andronikos III (1328–41): a significant part of Andronikos II's reign was dedicated to reversing his father's policies, particularly regarding contacts with the West. Bowing to internal pressures, Andronikos followed an isolationist policy, repudiating the Church Union with Rome. As a result, the opportunities for (or the usefulness of) crusade-related rhetoric were limited. However, the emperor had to change his approach later in his reign, on account of the threat posed by Western claimants to Byzantine lands and, even more, by the Turkish encroachment in Asia Minor (Laiou, 1972).

The first of those problems was similar to the situation in the previous century – and so was the response. Marino Sanudo, writing to Andronikos in 1324 and 1326, advised the emperor that in order to stop Western aggression he should promise Byzantine participation in a crusade and restart negotiations for Church Union (Bongars, 1661: II, 299, 301; Lock, 2014). Indeed, when the Dominican Benedict of Como visited Constantinople in 1326 as an envoy of the French king Charles IV, Andronikos responded not only by professing his inclination for the Union but also by indicating his wish to take part in the Franco-papal expedition for the Holy Land which was under preparation at the time (Bosch, 1965: 108). Given the state of the empire, which was unable to protect its territories from Turkish invasions and Catalan looting, there could be no realistic hope for such a far-fetched and distant involvement. Yet, it was still important for Byzantine diplomacy to assert its commitment to the cause of the Holy Land.

The effort to stem the Turkish advance was taken up more actively by Andronikos III, who also turned more decisively to the West. It is striking that he took an active role in promoting and even proposing crusade plans to Latin powers. In 1332 he was one of the initial signatories of the first anti-Turkish naval League, along with Venice and Hospitaller Rhodes (Thomas, 1880–99: II, 224–30, nos. 114–17; Zachariadou, 1983: 21–40; Ivanov, 2012). The agreement of 6 September set out the League's mission statement in clear terms of religious warfare. It denounced the violence of the Turks, 'the enemies of the cross', against Latins *and* Greeks in Romania. The signatories (the Byzantine emperor, the doge and the Hospitaller grand master) agreed to act in common, out of reverence to God, for the exaltation of the orthodox faith and for the consolation of the aforementioned Christians. Such language – which referred jointly to both Greeks and Latins as the faithful who were to be delivered from the attacks of the 'infidels' – is even more striking if one considers that up to a few years earlier Holy War was proclaimed against the Byzantines by John XXII, the same pope who would now agree to join this alliance (Mollat, 1904–47: nos. 2128, 8241, 16672).

Andronikos actually went one step further. In 1339, he dispatched Barlaam of Calabria to the papal court for negotiations. The imperial envoy argued that some common action should come before Church Union. In a move reminiscent of George Metochites' mission to the papacy at the time of Michael VIII, Barlaam proposed a plan by which a Greco-Latin crusade would first reclaim Asia Minor, before moving on to Jerusalem. Among Barlaam's proposals was the suggestion that the crusade indulgence should be given to anyone who came to the help of the Greeks against the Turks (Tautu, 1958: nos. 42–43; Gill, 1979: 196–9). So, Byzantine diplomacy now not only took the lead in suggesting crusade action to the curia but also advocated for the indulgence to be offered for services rendered to the empire.

Barlaam's plan and proposal eventually came to nothing as the empire descended into chaos after the emperor's death in 1341. Nevertheless, Andronikos III's crusade rhetoric came closer to matching his actions than that of any of his predecessors since the time of Manuel Komnenos. Two factors had made this possible: first, a revival of Byzantine fortunes under the leadership of the determined emperor; and second, the fact that the main theatre of crusading in the Eastern Mediterranean was shifting from the Holy Land to the Aegean, and from reclaiming Jerusalem to stopping Turkish expansion. Even if the empire no longer had the status to make a difference in the affair of Outremer, its role on the Turkish front was crucial and immediate. However, as Byzantium was embroiled once again in devastating civil wars in the 1340s and 1350s, the inability to contribute significantly to the crusades against the Turks came as a corollary of its once again diminishing importance in international and regional affairs.

CONCLUSION

The Byzantine leadership familiarised itself early on with the crusade. Relevant language and imagery were incorporated in diplomatic contacts with the West, while declarations of interest for the Holy Land and commitment to the service of the cross became a pattern of Byzantine propaganda. This approach persisted to the end of the twelfth century, hardly altered by the death of Manuel Komnenos. Even after the radical change of circumstances in 1204, the policy of exploiting Western sensitivities on the issue of the Holy Land persisted, as it could still serve Byzantine objectives.

The impact of such proclamations varied. It is difficult to distinguish it from the effect of actual Byzantine policy towards the West and the crusader states. Not only was the development of this propaganda closely tied to the current political situation in the Levant, but also its success depended on whether the emperors could couple words with actions. This is mostly evident in the case of Manuel Komnenos. His policy of active interference in the Latin East and dynamic interaction with the West, along with his consistent self-representation as a pious ruler interested in the fate of the Holy Land, resulted in the creation of a Byzantine protectorate over Outremer. At the height of this influence, factions within the crusader states advocated a pro-Byzantine policy, and notable figures turned to Byzantium for support and help. Doubtless, these actions were mostly motivated by the dire need of the Latins in Syria and Palestine, but Byzantine propaganda helped legitimise intervention that could otherwise be denounced as external interference. An indication of the potential effectiveness of this propaganda was Manuel's reputation in later times. In the West, he was often regarded as a model for his successors on account of his services to the Holy Land (Neocleous, 2009: 167–73; Carrier, 2006: 312–52). However, Byzantine failure to provide help to the crusade meant that proclamations to that end could be – and indeed were – criticised as mere lip-service and Byzantine policy dismissed as duplicity and treason against the common cause. That negative impression was further aggravated when set against the background of Manuel's 'legacy'. For example, Innocent III, writing in 1202 to Alexios III, stated that after the time of 'Manuel of blessed memory' the Byzantine emperors had been serving the cause of the Holy Land with words rather than actions, and warned Alexios to redress his and his predecessors' omissions so as to avert 'the fire burning in far-away parts from coming to [his] lands' (Hageneder et al., 1964–: V, 239–43, no. 121).

Diplomacy did not save the empire from the disaster of 1204. But the arguments used to justify the conquest and, subsequently, the crusades against the Byzantines highlight how important it was for Byzantium to have at least attempted to negotiate with the Latins in such terms. The successes of Michael VIII and of Andronikos III are proof that this diplomacy could be efficiently used to neutralise threats and even turn the crusade to Byzantium's advantage when favourable circumstances were coupled with a strong political will on the Byzantine side and when the empire appeared to regain its influence in the area.

To return to our initial discussion, the agents of imperial diplomacy were well aware of Western crusading sensitivities. They had a more than passing understanding of the motivations and ideology behind the crusade, even if they did not entirely share these views. The explanation for the failure of Byzantium to avoid the disastrous clash with Latin powers in the late twelfth and early thirteenth century should be sought elsewhere rather than in a supposed Byzantine incomprehension and ignorance of Western mentality. The ease with which the Byzantine imperial diplomacy took up Western crusading themes and language is another argument against blanket statements that the Byzantine mind found ideas of Holy War repelling. Without overlooking the substantial differences between the two societies, the answer to this question needs to be rephrased in more nuanced terms.

NOTES

1 Part of the research for this chapter was carried out in the context of the project "Worlds Apart? Identity and Otherness in Late Byzantine Perceptions of the West" (SH6–1345). The research project was implemented within the framework of the Action "Supporting Postdoctoral Researchers" of the Operational Program "Education and Lifelong Learning" (Action's Beneficiary: General Secretariat for Research and Technology), and was co-financed by the European Social Fund (ESF) and the Greek State. The chapter is based on papers I presented at Leeds (IMC, 2007), London (Royal Holloway, 2009; Crusades Seminar, IHR, 2012) and Athens (Oikonomides Seminar, 2013).

2 A great number of studies touching upon the subject have appeared in recent years. See, for example, the works cited by Koder and Stouraitis (2012: 133–4), and Stoyanov (2011: 25–36).

3 I have also made this point more extensively, from a rather different angle, in a recent paper on 'Byzantine Criticisms of the Crusade' at the International Medieval Congress (Leeds, 9 July 2014).

4 On Byzantine views of crusaders and crusading, see in general the works by Charanis (1952), Kolia-Dermitzaki (1991b), Gounaridis (2006), Stouraitis (2011) and Dagron (2012).

5 I would like to thank Dr Papageorgiou for providing a copy of her article prior to publication.

6 Without being possible to positively exclude the presence of such elements in other sources now lost, there are no surviving references to Byzantine participation in a crusade in: the correspondence of Honorius III with Theodore Doukas of Epiros; in the correspondence of John Vatatzes with either Gregory IX or Frederick II (even during the extensive unionist negotiations between Rome and Nicaea in 1232–34 and 1249–54); in the submission of Manuel of Thessalonica to the Roman Church; in the unionist negotiations between Theodore II Laskaris with Alexander IV in 1256; or even in the contacts between Vatatzes and Henry I Lusignan of Cyprus.

REFERENCES

Augé, I. (2001) 'La reconquête des Comnènes en Orient vue par les panégyristes byzantins', *Bizantinistica* 3, 313–28

———. (2000) *Politique religieuse et reconquête en Orient sous les Comnènes (1081–1185)*, doctoral thesis, Montpellier: Université Montpellier III

Beck, H.-G. (1981) *Nomos, Kanon und Staatsraison in Byzanz*, Vienna: Verlag der Österreichischen Akademie der Wissenschaften

Bongars, J. (ed.) (1661) *Gesta Dei per Francos*, 2 vols, Hanover: Typis Wechelianis

Bosch, U. (1965) *Kaiser Andronikos III. Palaiologos: Versuch einer Darstellung der byzantinischen Geschichte in den Jahren 1321–1341*, Amsterdam: A. M. Hakkert

Bouquet, M. et al. (eds) (1738–1904) *Recueil des historiens des Gaules et de la France*, 24 vols, Paris: Palmé

Brand, C. M. (1962) 'The Byzantines and Saladin, 1185–1192: Opponents of the Third Crusade', *Speculum* 37, 167–81

———. (1968) *Byzantium Confronts the West, 1180–1204*, Cambridge, MA: Harvard University Press

Carr, A. W. (1982) 'The Mural Paintings of Abu Ghosh and the Patronage of Manuel Comnenus in the Holy Land', in Folda, J. (ed.) *Crusader Art in the Twelfth Century*, Oxford: British School of Archaeology in Jerusalem, 215–34

Carrier, M. (2006) *L'Image des byzantins et les systèmes de représentation selon les chroniqueurs occidentaux des croisades, 1096–1261*, doctoral thesis, Paris: Université Paris I

Charanis, P. (1952) 'Aims of the Medieval Crusades and How They Were Viewed by Byzantium', *Church History* 21, 123–34

———. (1949) 'Byzantium, the West and the Origin of the First Crusade', *Byzantion* 19, 17–36

Chrissis, N. (2012a) 'The City and the Cross: The Image of Constantinople and the Latin Empire in Thirteenth-Century Papal Crusading Policy', *Byzantine and Modern Greek Studies* 36, 20–37

———. (2012b) *Crusading in Frankish Greece: A Study of Byzantine-Western Relations and Attitudes, 1204–1282*, Turnhout: Brepols

Chrysos, E. (2012) '1176 – A Byzantine Crusade?', in Koder and Stouraitis, 81–6

Courtonne, Y. (ed.) (1957–66) *Saint Basile: Lettres*, 3 vols, Paris: Belles Lettres

Dagron, G. (2012) 'Byzance entre le djihad et la croisade: quelques remarques', in idem, *Idées byzantines*, 2 vols, Paris: Association des amis du Centre d'histoire et civilisation de Byzance, II, 376–86

Dagron, G. and Mihaescu, H. (eds) (1986) *Le traité sur la guérilla (De velitatione) de l'empereur Nicéphore Phocas (963–969)*, Paris: Editions du centre national de la recherche scientifique

Darrouzès, J. (ed.) (1970) *Georges et Dèmètrios Tornikès: Lettres et discours*, Paris: Éditions du Centre national de la Recherche scientifique

de Boor, C. (ed.) (1883–85) *Theophanis Chronographia*, 2 vols, Leipzig: Teubner

Dennis, G. T. (2001) 'Defenders of the Christian People: Holy War in Byzantium', in Laiou, A. E. and Mottahedeh, R. P. (eds) *The Crusades from the Perspective of Byzantium and the Muslim World*, Washington, DC: Dumbarton Oaks, 31–9

———. (2010) *The Taktika of Leo VI: Text, Translation and Commentary*, Washington DC: Dumbarton Oaks Research Library and Collection

Faral, E. (ed.) (1961) *Geoffroi de Villehardouin: La Conquête de Constantinople*, 2nd edn, 2 vols, Paris: Belles Lettres

Folda, J. (1995) *The Art of the Crusaders in the Holy Land, 1098–1187*, Cambridge: Cambridge University Press

Garzya, A. (ed.) (1984) *Nicephori Basilacae orationes et epistolae*, Leipzig: Teubner

Gay, J. (1931) 'L'abbaye de Cluny et Byzance au début du XIIe siècle', *Echos d'Orient* 30, 84–90

Geanakoplos, D. J. (1959), *Emperor Michael Palaeologus and the West, 1258–1282: A Study in Late Byzantine-Western Relations*, Cambridge, MA: Harvard University Press

Giannelli, C. (ed.) (1947) 'Le Recit d'une mission diplomatique de Georges le Metochite (1275–1276) et le Vat. Gr. 1716', in Laurent, M.-H. (ed.) *Le Bienheureux Innocent V (Pierre de Tarentaise) et son temps*, Studi e Testi 129, Vatican City: Biblioteca apostolica vaticana, 419–43

Gill, J. (1979) *Byzantium and the Papacy, 1198–1400*, New Brunswick: Rutgers University Press

Gounaridis, P. (2006), 'L'Image de l'autre: les croisés vus par les Byzantins', in Ortalli, G., Ravegnani, G. and Schreiner, P. (eds) *Quarta crociata: Venezia, Bisanzio, impero latino*, 2 vols, Venezia: Istituto veneto di scienze, lettere ed arti, 1: 81–95

Grumel, V. (1930) '*L'Authenticité de la lettre de Jean Vatatzès, empereur de Nicée, au pape Grégoire IX*', *Echos d'Orient* 29, 450–8

Guiraud, J. (ed.) (1892–1958) *Les Registres d'Urbain IV*, 4 vols, Paris: Fontemoing

Hageneder, O. et al. (eds) (1964–) *Die Register Innocenz' III*, 10 vols to date, Graz, Rome and Vienna: Verlag der Österreichischen Akademie der Wissenschaften

Hamilton, B. (1980) *The Latin Church in the Crusader States*, London: Variorum

——— (1988) 'Manuel I Comnenus and Baldwin IV of Jerusalem', in Chrysostomides, J. (ed.) ΚΑΘΗΓΗΤΡΙΑ: *Essays Presented to Joan Hussey for her 80th Birthday*, Camberley: Porphyrogenitus, 353–75

Harris, J. (2003) *Byzantium and the Crusades*, London: Hambledon and London

———. (2012) 'Collusion with the Infidel as a Pretext for Western Military Action against Byzantium (1180–1204)', in Lambert, S. and Nicholson, H. (eds) *Languages of Love and Hate: Conflict, Communication, and Identity in the Medieval Mediterranean*, Turnhout: Brepols, 99–117

Heisenberg, A. (ed.) (1973) 'Neue Quellen zur Geschichte des lateinischen Kaisertums und der Kirchenunion, I. Der Epitaphios des Nikolaos Mesarites auf seinen Bruder Johannes', in idem, *Quellen und Studien zur spätbyzantinischen Geschichte*, London: Variorum, no. II.i, 3–75

Hill, J. H. and Hill, L. (trans.) (1968) *Raymond d' Aguilers: Historia Francorum qui ceperunt Iherusalem*, Philadelphia: American Philosophical Society

———. (trans.) (1974) *Peter Tudebode: Historia de Hierosolymitano itinere*, Philadelphia: American Philosophical Society

Hunt, L.-A. (1991) 'Art and Colonialism: The Mosaics of the Church of the Nativity at Bethlehem (1169) and the Problem of "Crusader" Art', *Dumbarton Oaks Papers* 45, 69–85

Huygens, R. B. C. (ed.) (1986) *Willelmi Tyrensis Archiepiscopi chronicon*, Turnhout: Brepols

Ivanov, V. (2012) '*Sancta Unio* or the Holy League 1332–36/37 as a Political Factor in the Eastern Mediterranean and the Aegean', *Études Balkaniques* 48, 142–76

Jenkins, R. J. H. and Westernik, L. G. (eds and trans.) (1973) *Nicholas I Patriarch of Constantinople: Letters*, Washington DC: Dumbarton Oaks Center for Byzantine Studies

Jordan, E. (ed.) (1893) *Les Registres de Clement IV*, Paris: Thorin

Kaegi, W. E. (2012) 'The Heraclians and Holy War', in Koder and Stouraitis, 17–26

Koder, J. and Stouraitis, I. (eds) (2012) *Byzantine War Ideology between Roman Imperial Concept and Christian Religion*, Vienna: Verlag der Österreichischen Akademie der Wissenschaften

Kolbaba, T. M. (1998) 'Fighting for Christianity: Holy War in the Byzantine Empire', *Byzantion* 68, 194–221

Kolia-Dermitzaki, A. (1991a) *Ο βυζαντινός «ιερός πόλεμος». Η έννοια και η προβολή του θρησκευτικού πολέμου στο Βυζάντιο* [The Byzantine 'Holy War': The Idea and Propagation of Religious War in Byzantium], Athens: St. D. Basilopoulos

———. (1991b) 'Die Kreuzfahrer und die Kreuzzüge im Sprachgebrauch der Byzantiner', *Jahrbuch der Osterreichischen Byzantinistik* 41, 163–188

———. (1997), 'Το εμπόλεμο Βυζάντιο στις ομιλίες και τις επιστολές του 10ου και 11ου αι.: Μια ιδεολογική προσέγγιση', [Byzantium at War in 10th- and 11th-century Orations and Letters: An Ideological Approach], in *Byzantium at War (9th-12th c.)*, Athens: Goulandri-Horn Foundation, 213–38

———. (2012) '"Holy War" in Byzantium Twenty Years Later: A Question of Term Definition and Interpretation', in Koder and Stouraitis, 121–32

Laiou, A. E. (1972) *Constantinople and the Latins: The Foreign Policy of Andronicus II, 1282–1328*, Cambridge, MA: Harvard University Press

———. (1993) 'On Just War in Byzantium', in Langdon, J. et al. (eds) *To Hellenikon: Studies in Honor of Speros Vryonis Jr*, vol. 1: *Antiquity and Byzantium*, New Rochelle, NY: Aristide D. Caratzas, 153–77

———. (2006) 'The Just War of Eastern Christians and the "Holy War" of the Crusade', in Sorabji, R. and Rodin, D. (eds) *The Ethics of War: Shared Problems in Different Traditions*, Aldershot: Ashgate, 30–43

Lampros, S. (1914) 'Αυτοκρατόρων του Βυζαντίου χρυσόβουλλα και χρυσά γράμματα αναφερόμενα εις την ένωσιν των εκκλησιών' [Byzantine Imperial Chrysobulls Relating to the Union of the Churches], *Νέος Ελληνομνήμων* 11, 99–128 and 241–54

Laurent, V. (1946) 'L'idée de guerre sainte et la tradition byzantine', *Revue historique du sud-est européen* 23, 71–98

Lemerle, P. (1955) 'Byzance et la croisade', in *Relazioni del X Congresso internazionale di scienze storiche*, 7 vols, Florence: Sansoni, III: 595–620 [repr. in Lemerle, P. (1978) *Le Monde de Byzance: histoire et institutions*, London: Variorum, no. VIII]

Lilie, R.-J. (1993) *Byzantium and the Crusader States, 1095–1204*, trans. Morris, J. C. and Ridings J. E., Oxford: Clarendon Press

Lock, P. (2014) 'Sanudo, Turks, Greeks and Latins in the Early Fourteenth Century', in Chrissis, N. G. and Carr, M. (eds) *Contact and Conflict in Frankish Greece and the Aegean, 1204–1453*, Farnham: Ashgate, 135–49

Magdalino, P. (1993) *The Empire of Manuel I Komnenos, 1143–1180*, Cambridge: Cambridge University Press

Mango, C. and Scott, R. (trans.) (1997) *The Chronicle of Theophanes Confessor*, Oxford: Clarendon Press

Meineke, A. (ed.) (1836) *Ioannis Cinnami Epitome rerum ab Ioanne et Alexio Comnenis gestarum*, Corpus Scriptorum Historiae Byzantinae, Bonn: Impensis Ed. Weberi

Mollat, G. (ed.) (1904–47) *Jean XXII: Lettres communes analysées d'après les registres dits d'Avignon et du Vatican*, 16 vols, Paris: Fontemoing

Neocleous, S. (2009) *Imaging the Byzantines: Latin Perceptions, Representations and Memory, c. 1095–c. 1230*, doctoral thesis, Dublin: Trinity College Dublin

———. (2010) 'The Byzantines and Saladin: Opponents of the Third Crusade?', *Crusades* 9, 87–106

———. (2013) 'The Byzantines and Saladin: Some Further Arguments', *Al-Masaq* 25, 204–21

Oikonomides, N. (1967) 'Cinq actes inédits du Patriarche Michel Autôreianos', *Revue des études byzantines* 25, 113–45

———. (1995) 'The Concept of "Holy War" and Two Tenth-Century Byzantine Ivories', in Miller, T. S. and Nesbit, J. (eds) *Peace and War in Byzantium: Essays in Honor of George T. Dennis*, Washington DC: The Catholic University of America Press, 62–87

Papadopoulou, E. (ed.) (2000), *Marin Sanudo Torsello: Istoria di Romania*, Athens: National Hellenic Research Foundation, Institute for Byzantine Research

Papageorgiou, A. (2007) Ο *Ιωάννης Β΄ Κομνηνός και η εποχή του (1118–1143)* [John II Komnenos and his era (1118–1143)], doctoral thesis, Athens: National and Kapodistrian University of Athens

———. (forthcoming) 'The Political Ideology of John II Komnenos' Foreign Policy', in Bucossi, A. and Suarez, A. R. (eds) *John II Komnenos, Emperor of Byzantium*, Farnham: Ashgate

Powell, J. M. (2003) 'Alexius III and Innocent III: A Crusade Plan that Failed', in Bull, M. and Housley, N. (eds) *The Experience of Crusading*, 2 vols, Cambridge: Cambridge University Press, I: 96–102

———. (trans.) (2004) *The Deeds of Pope Innocent III*, Washington, DC: Catholic University of America Press

Reinsch, D. R. and Kambylis, A. (eds) (2001) *Annae Comnenae Alexias*, Corpus Fontium Historiae Byzantinae 40, 2 vols, Berlin: De Gruyter

Riley-Smith, J. (1993) *The First Crusade and the Idea of Crusading*, London: Athlone Press

Rowe, J. G. (1966–67) 'Paschal II, Bohemund of Antioch and the Byzantine Empire', *Bulletin of the John Rylands Library* 49, 165–202

Runciman, S. (1982) 'The Visit of King Amalric I to Constantinople in 1171', in Kedar, B. Z., Mayer, H.-E. and Smail, R. C. (eds) *Outremer: Studies in the History of the Crusading Kingdom of Jerusalem Presented to Joshua Prawer*, Jerusalem: Yad Izhak Ben-zvi Institute, 153–8

Sakellion, I. (ed.) (1872) 'Ανέκδοτος επιστολή του Αυτοκράτορος Ιωάννου Δούκα Βατάτση προς τον Πάπαν Γρηγόριον, ανευρεθείσα εν Πάτμω' [Unpublished Letter of the Emperor John Ducas Vatatzes to Pope Gregory, Discovered in Patmos], *Athinaion* 1, 369–78

Shaw, M. R. B. (trans.) (1963) *Chronicles of the Crusades: Joinville and Villehardouin*, Harmondsworth: Penguin

Stephenson, P. (2007) 'Imperial Christianity and Sacred Warfare in Byzantium', in Wellman Jr., J. K. (ed.), *Belief and Bloodshed: Religion and Violence across Time and Tradition*, Lanham MD: Rowman and Littlefield Publishers, 81–93

———. (2012) 'Religious Services for Byzantine Soldiers and the Possibility of Martyrdom: c.400–c.1000', in Hashmi, S. H. (ed.), *Just Wars, Holy Wars and Jihads*, Oxford: Oxford University Press, 25–46

Stone, A. E. (2003) 'Dorylaion Revisited: Manuel I Komnenos and the Refortification of Dorylaion and Soublaion', *Byzantion* 61, 183–99

Stouraitis, I. (2011) 'Jihād and Crusade: Byzantine Positions towards the Notions of "Holy War"', *Byzantina Symmeikta* 21, 11–63

———. (2012) '"Just War" and "Holy War" in the Middle Ages: Rethinking Theory through the Byzantine Case-Study', *Jahrbuch der Österreichischen Byzantinistik* 62, 227–64

Stoyanov, Y. (2011) *Defenders and Enemies of the True Cross: The Sasanian Conquest of Jerusalem in 614 and Byzantine Ideology of Anti-Persian Warfare*, Vienna: Verlag der Österreichischen Akademie der Wissenschaften

Tautu, A. L. (ed.) (1958) *Acta Benedicti XII (1334–1342)*, 2 vols, Vatican City: Typis Polyglottis Vaticanis

Thomas, G. M. (ed.) (1880–99) *Diplomatarium Veneto-Levantinum: sive acta et diplomata res Venetas Graecas atque Levantis illustrantia*, 2 vols, Venice: Deputazione veneta di storia patria

Thurn, J. (ed.) (1973) *Ioannis Scylitzae Synopsis historiarum*, Corpus Fontium Historiae Byzantinae 5, Berlin: De Gruyter

van Dieten, J. L. (ed.) (1975) *Nicetae Choniatae Historia*, 2 vols, Corpus Fontium Historiae Byzantinae 11, Berlin: De Gruyter

Vasiliev, A. A. (1929–30) 'Manuel Comnenus and Henry Plantagenet', *Byzantinische Zeitschrift* 29, 233–44

Viscuso, P. (1995) 'Christian Participation in Warfare: A Byzantine View', in Miller, T. S. and Nesbit, J. (eds), *Peace and War in Byzantium: Essays in Honor of George T. Dennis*, Washington DC: Catholic University of America Press, 33–40

Whalen, B. E. (2010) 'God's Will or Not? Bohemond's Campaign against the Byzantine Empire (1105–1108)', in Madden, T. F. et al. (eds) *Crusades: Medieval Worlds in Conflict*, Farnham: Ashgate, 111–25

Zachariadou, E. (1983) *Trade and Crusade: Venetian Crete and the Emirates of Menteshe and Aydin: 1300–1415*, Venice: Hellenic Institute of Byzantine and Post-Byzantine Studies

CHAPTER SEVENTEEN

MEMORY AND IDEOLOGY: THE IMAGE OF THE CRUSADES IN BYZANTINE HISTORIOGRAPHY, ELEVENTH–THIRTEENTH CENTURIES

———— •◆• ————

Aphrodite Papayianni

In March 1095, the ambassadors of the Byzantine emperor Alexios I Comnenos addressed the council Pope Urban II had summoned in Piacenza, requesting the pope's help to muster an army of Western mercenaries to come to Byzantium's aid against the Turks in Asia Minor. Responding to the appeal, the pope did indeed encourage 'many to promise, by taking an oath, to aid the [Byzantine] emperor most faithfully in so far as they were able against the pagans' (Bernold of St Blasien 1844: 462; Riley-Smith 1986: 13). What Alexios had petitioned for was a Western army a few hundred strong to be sent to fight under his command. What he received the following year were numerous Western armies made up of allies, together with their women and children, over whom he had no control. Until 1204, the presence of crusaders in the lands of the Byzantine Empire caused nothing but friction and frustration between them and both the local population and the authorities, culminating in the conquest of Constantinople in April 1204 and the atrocities that ensued.

The aims of this chapter are to examine the terminology employed by contemporary (i.e., eleventh to thirteenth century) Byzantine historians to describe the crusade movement and its participants, to analyse their choice of terminology and to explore the ideology behind them.

The notion of the First Crusade as a divinely ordained war against the Muslims who had conquered the lands of the Byzantine Empire and now had Jerusalem under their control, with the aim to liberate those lands and reclaim Jerusalem, is articulated unequivocally in Urban II's sermon delivered in Clermont in March 1095 and is clearly reflected in the terminology used in the Latin West to describe the movement and its participants (*Robert of Monk*, 2005: 80–2; Fulcher of Chartres 2005: 513–17; Baldric of Bourgueil 2014: 6–10). For the Latins, a crusade was '*via*', '*iter*', '*itenirarium*', '*iter hierosolymitanum*', '*profectio*', '*passagium*', '*Hierosolymitana expeditio*', '*expeditio Dei*' or simply '*expeditio*', '*expugnatio Dei*', '*agmen*', '*causa*', '*bellum*', '*negotium*', '*peregrinatio*', '*peregrinatio Iherosolimitana*', '*via Dei*' or '*via Jesu Christi*', '*sancta via*', '*opus Dei*', and, later, '*crux*'. The crusaders were '*milites Dei*' or '*milites Christi*', '*athletae Christi*', '*athletae Dei*', '*christocoli*', '*fideles*

Christi', '*bellatores Dei*' or '*bellatores Christi*', '*paupers*', '*Hierosolymitani*', '*peregrini Dei*' or just '*peregrini*', and collectively they were an '*exercitus christianus*', '*exercitus Dei*' or '*exercitus Domini*', '*militia Christi*' or '*militia Dei*', '*agmen Dei*', '*populus Dei*' or simply '*populus*', '*plebs*', '*gens Dei*' or '*gens Christi*', who participated in the operation '*peregrinationis gratia*'.[1] At the end of the twelfth century, the term '*crusesignatus*' or '*cruciferus*' also started to be used to refer to a crusader (Markowski 1984).

Contemporary Byzantine historians, however, very rarely used the terminology of pilgrimage, journey or crucifix to describe the crusades and their participants, but almost exclusively employed the vocabulary of war or military expedition. In the twelfth century, Anna Comnena, daughter of Emperor Alexios I, characterised the First Crusade as an 'ἐπέλευσιν' ('attack'), 'ἔφοδον' ('journey through' but also an 'assault') and 'συγκίνησιν' ('concerted movement', 'assault') and the crusaders as 'ἐπερχομένους' ('[those] coming in order to attack') (Comnena, 2001: 297–9; Leib, 1943: II, 206–9). Writing in the same century, the imperial secretary Ioannes Kinnamos, called the Second Crusade 'πορείαν ἐπὶ Παλαιστίνην' ('a march on Palestine') (Kinnamos, 1836: 73; Brand, 1976: 63) and 'ἐμβολὴν' ('an incursion') (Kinnamos, 1836: 88, 92; Brand, 1976: 72, 76), whilst the thirteenth-century statesman, theologian and orator Nicetas Choniates called the crusades 'κίνησιν' (lit. 'a movement') (Choniates, 1975: 61; Magoulias, 1984: 35), and in reference to the Third Crusade 'ἐπιδρομὴ ἐθνῶν' ('invasion of nations') (Choniates, 1975: 403; Magoulias, 1984: 222), and 'ἔξοδον' ('expedition') (Choniates, 1975: 61; Magoulias, 1984: 35). The statesman George Acropolites, also writing in the thirteenth century, claimed similarly that 'those from Italy *campaigned* against Constantinople' (Acropolites, 1978: 5; Makrides, 2007: 106). The terminology used is martial and clearly speaks of an aggressive approach on the part of the crusaders towards the Byzantines.

Nor are the crusaders themselves described in terms used in the Latin West. Instead, they are designated by ethnic terms, though these do not necessarily represent their true origin: Gauls, British (Kinnamos, 1836: 67; Brand, 1976: 58), *Alamanoi* (Kinnamos, 1836: 68, 69, 77, 80, 81, 84, 85, 88, 188, 228; Brand, 1976: 59, 60, 65, 67, 68, 70, 72, 73, 143, 172), *Germanoi* (Kinnamos, 1836: 67, 69, 82, 84, 86, 87, 188; Brand, 1976: 58, 60, 68, 70, 71, 72, 143),[2] Celts (Comnena, 2001: 297 and *passim*; Leib, 1943: II, 207 and *passim*; Kinnamos, 1836: 67; Brand, 1976: 58),[3] or Franks (Comnena, 2001: 321 and *passim*; Leib, 1943: II, 235 and *passim*; Choniates, 1975: 553, 588, 647; Magoulias, 1984: 303, 323, 357);[4] or by generic terms: 'Λατινικὰ γένη' ('Latin races') (Kinnamos, 1836: 199; Brand, 1976: 151), Latins (Comnena, 2001: 301 and *passim*; Leib, 1943: II, 212; Choniates, 1975: 551 and *passim*; Magoulias, 1984: 302 and *passim*)[5] or 'Λατινικὰ στρατεύματα' ('Latin troops') (Choniates, 1975: 67; Magoulias, 1984: 39), 'Φραγκικὰ στρατεύματα' ('Frankish troops') (Comnena, 2001: 297, 302; Leib, 1943: II 1: 206, 214), 'Φραγκικὰ τάγματα' ('Frankish regiments'), 'Κελτικὸ στράτευμα' ('Celtic troops') (Comnena, 2001: 298, 331; Leib, 1943: II, 208–9; 1945: III, 18) or simply 'στρατεύματα' ('troops') (Comnena, 2001: 315; Leib, 1943: II, 228; Acropolites, 1978: 5; Makrides, 2007: 107), as 'πανστρατιὰ' ('[the result of] a general military mobilisation') (Comnena, 2001: 298; Leib, 1943: II, 208), 'κατάφρακτοι Λατινικαὶ ... φάλαγγαι' ('Latin battalions in full armour') (Choniates, 1975: 572; Magoulias, 1984: 314), 'ἐξ ἑσπέρας στρατοὶ' ('armies from the Occident') (Choniates, 1975: 61; Magoulias, 1984: 36), or 'army' (Kinnamos, 1836: 67, 76; Brand, 1937–45: 58, 64; Choniates, 1975: 65, 402; Magoulias, 1984: 38, 221), as 'a cloud of enemies ... a dreadful and death-dealing pestilence' (Choniates, 1975: 60; Magoulias, 1984: 35), as 'Κελτικὰ πλήθη' ('Celtic hordes') (Comnena, 2001: 303; Leib, 1943: II, 215), as 'δυσμικὰ ἔθνη' ('Western nations') (Kinnamos, 1836: 88, 92; Brand, 1976: 72, 76), as 'ἅπαν … τὸ ἑσπέριον … κράτος' ('the whole Western array') (Kinnamos, 1836: 67; Brand, 1976: 58), as 'ἑσπέρια γένη' ('peoples from the West') (Choniates, 1975: 648; Magoulias, 1984: 357) or as the 'scattered nations of the West' (Choniates, 1975: 585; Magoulias, 1984: 322). Anna Comnena and Choniates also at times call them 'barbarians', mainly when commenting on the crusaders' undisciplined conduct in the Byzantine Empire (Comnena, 2001: 297, 298, 307, 315, 357; 358, 428, 429, 433, 440; Leib, 1943: II, 207, 208, 218, 228; 1945: III, 51, 52, 146, 147, 153, 161; Choniates, 1975: 68, 560, 574, 590, 591, 594, 648, 649, 653; Magoulias, 1984: 39, 306, 315, 324, 325, 327, 357, 358, 360), whilst John Kinnamos uses the appellation when referring to the crusade army of the Second Crusade collectively (Kinnamos, 1836: 67, 69, 70, 72, 73; Brand, 1976: 59, 60, 61, 63). The only time that Western terms are found in contemporary Byzantine historiography to describe the crusaders are when Anna Comnena cites the treaty of Devol (1108), where Prince Bohemud of Otranto (and later of Antioch) describes the crusaders as 'περεγρῖνοι' (the Greek transliteration of the term *peregrini*) (Comnena, 2001: 421; Leib, 1945: III, 135); when Nicetas Choniates notes that King Conrad of Germany 'had taken up the cross at home' ('σταυροφορήσας') long before he arrived in the Byzantine Empire (Choniates, 1975: 395; Magoulias, 1984: 217); and when the same historian records that one of the leaders of the Third Crusade, the German king Frederick I Barbarossa, referred to his army as 'soldiers of Christ' (Choniates, 1975: 412; Magoulias, 1984: 227).

The choice of vocabulary raises questions about the extent to which the Byzantines were aware of the crusade ideology. What considerations informed their choice of terms? Was it a matter of ignorance, of empathy or of experience? What fashioned their views? Byzantine historians appear to have had limited knowledge of the idea of the crusade as a divine enterprise organised through the agency of the pope. They were aware of the aim of the crusades, however, that is to say, the liberation of Jerusalem from Muslim rule (the other purpose, at least of the First Crusade, namely the freeing of the Eastern Churches from Muslim oppression, is not mentioned at all), although at times they express doubts about the sincerity of some of the participants. As for the absolution of sins offered to crusaders who died on crusade, that seems to have been known only to Nicetas Choniates (Choniates, 1975: 69; Magoulias, 1984: 40).[6]

In regard to the crusaders' motives, the Byzantine historians' views do not differ significantly. Remarkably, Anna Comnena fails to mention her father's appeal to Pope Urban for military aid in the fight against the Turks. Nevertheless, she seems to have been aware that Peter the Hermit claimed that a divine plan had been revealed to him to exhort Frankish noblemen to accompany him to the Holy Land to liberate Jerusalem from the Muslims and characterised it as a 'wise' one (Comnena, 2001: 297; Leib, 1943: II, 207). Although Anna does not distinguish between a crusader and an unarmed pilgrim, she does make a distinction between the pure religious motives of the 'more simple-minded' participants of the First Crusade, who certainly did wish to visit Christ's tomb, and the 'more devious ones', whose unspoken motivation might have been to capture Constantinople on their way to the Holy Land. She includes Peter the Hermit in the first category and Prince Bohemud and other noblemen in the second. Furthermore, she states unequivocally that certain crusaders, like Bohemud, used Peter the Hermit's proclamation as a pretext to deceive the 'most honourable' crusaders by claiming that they were going to the Holy Land, when in reality their aim was to conquer the Byzantine Empire. The reason for that, Anna claims, was Alexios' victory over Bohemud near Larisa a few years earlier. To support her argument that some of the noblemen crusaders had a hidden agenda, she states that they had sold their lands in the West before they set out for the East (Comnena, 2001: 299, 301, 309, 319–20; Leib, 1943: II, 209, 212, 220–1, 233–4). Similarly, Kinnamos states baldly that the Western nations that participated in the Second Crusade used the liberation of the Holy Sepulchre as a pretext for attacking Byzantine lands; their real aim was to gain possession of them (Kinnamos, 1836: 67, 73; Brand, 1976: 58, 63). The violence perpetrated against local merchants in the empire during the Second Crusade exposed the 'hostile intent' of the crusaders, in Kinnamos' view (Kinnamos, 1836: 70; Brand, 1976: 61). The same historian also questions the motives of Frederick I stating that 'Frederick ... had set his sights on the office of [the Roman] emperor' (Kinnamos, 1836: 229; Brand, 1976: 173), and that he 'intended to invade the Romans' land' (Kinnamos, 1836: 262; Brand, 1976: 197).

Of all contemporary Byzantine historians, Choniates, an eyewitness to the Third and Fourth Crusades, seems to have had the most complete insight into the ideology of crusading. He appears to have been aware that the crusaders of the Second Crusade 'declared and affirmed by oath that Jerusalem was the motive for their expedition' and admits that 'later events proved their declarations were not false' (Choniates, 1975: 61; Magoulias, 1984: 36). He also notes Frederick I's request, and the consequent accord between him and the Byzantine Emperor Isaac II, in the course of the Third Crusade, for German crusaders who 'were heading towards Palestine' to be allowed to pass unhindered through Byzantine territory (Choniates, 1975: 401–2; Magoulias, 1984: 221). In the fictitious speech of exhortation (Simpson, 2013: 316) that he attributes to Conrad, Choniates includes all key elements of the crusade ideology: that the crusaders' expedition was taken on behalf of Christ, that they were seeking the glory of God, that it was their duty to bear suffering, that the crusader army was 'a sacred host and God-chosen army', that those who fell in battle would be rewarded with access to heaven, that the enemy would be crushed by the power of Christ, that the liberation of the Holy Sepulchre was the ultimate goal of their expedition and that they would take vengeance on the infidels who had defiled Christ's tomb (Choniates, 1975: 68–70; Magoulias, 1984: 39–41). In his epitaph to Frederick I, he confirms his knowledge of crusade ideology by stating that Frederick 'died *for the name of Christ*' (Choniates, 1975: 416; Magoulias, 1984: 229). However, his judgement of crusaders is not blunted by this knowledge, for he also claims that the Lord's empty tomb was a pretext for the Second Crusade (Choniates, 1975: 61; Magoulias, 1984: 35), and records that the patriarch of Jerusalem, Dositheos (1189–91), 'prophesied' that Frederick intended to march on Constantinople, not to take possession of Palestine, during the course of the Third Crusade (Choniates, 1975: 405; Magoulias, 1984: 222). Moreover, he describes Frederick as 'the evil beyond our borders ... [who] burst upon us' (Choniates, 1975: 401; Magoulias, 1984: 221) and characterises the Fourth Crusade as a 'voyage of piracy', stating that its participants used the restoration of Isaac II as their pretext, 'like a painted mask concealing their true motives' (Choniates, 1975: 585–6; Magoulias, 1984: 322), and pointing out that they were exposed as 'λογοποιοί' ('people who make up excuses', 'liars') who, seeking to avenge the Holy Sepulchre, raged against Christ and sinned by overturning the Cross with the cross they wore on their backs for the sake of a little gold and silver (Choniates, 1975: 576; Magoulias, 1984: 316). George Acropolites makes similar assertions in regard to the Fourth Crusade (Acropolites, 1978: 5; Makrides, 2007: 107).

Riley-Smith has remarked in regard to the First Crusade that 'even the propagandists agree that the crusading armies had adventurers and charlatans among their number, although most of these were not knights' (Riley-Smith, 1986: 40). The odd composition of the participants in the crusades did indeed surprise the Byzantines, while their unruly behaviour and vast numbers dismayed them. Although one cannot be certain about the objectivity of contemporary Byzantine historians' accounts of the activities of the crusaders whilst in the Byzantine Empire, besides the attribution of stereotypical Latin characteristics to them,[7] it should be noted that these historians do not hesitate to acknowledge the virtues of some groups of them or of individuals, and also to record and comment on incidents when the crusaders were treated unjustly by the local population. For instance, Kinnamos comments that the mounted Frankish knights excelled in the use of the spear and surpassed the German cavalry in speed, whilst the Germans were outstanding in the use of the sword and better than the French in combat on foot (Kinnamos, 1836: 84–5; Brand, 1976: 70). In regard to the French crusaders, participants in the Fourth Crusade, Choniates comments that they 'were unlike the others in temperament or physique and boasted that the only thing they feared was heaven' (Choniates, 1975: 588; Magoulias, 1984: 323). Anna Comnena, Kinnamos and Choniates often describe individual crusaders in positive terms too: Anna characterises Bohemud, a long-standing enemy of the empire, as a 'most able individual in adjusting to the circumstances' and 'braver than all other crusaders' (Comnena, 2001: 319; Leib 1943: II, 233) and Raymond of Saint Gilles, one of the leaders of the First Crusade, as a man of 'superior spirit, rightness in his judgement, purity in life and sincerity' (Comnena, 2001: 320; Leib, 1943: II, 235). Kinnamos likens Prince Raymond of Antioch to the 'legendary Herculeis' (Kinnamos, 1836: 125; Brand, 1976: 99) and remarks that he was 'most active in martial affairs' (Kinnamos, 1836: 122; Brand, 1976: 97), whilst in regard to Conrad he notes that 'he was courageous in warfare' (Kinnamos, 1836: 82; Brand, 1976: 68). Choniates comments favourably on Marquis William of Montferrat and especially his son Conrad, later king of Jerusalem, whom he calls 'brave and prudent beyond measure, and full of rigour and bodily strength' (Choniates, 1975: 201; Magoulias, 1984: 114), a man who 'was so excelled in bravery and sagacity that his fame was widespread, not only among the Romans [Byzantines] but also among his countrymen ... graced with acute intelligence and strength of arm' (Choniates, 1975: 382; Magoulias 1984: 210). The French Baron Peter of Bracieux, according to the same historian, was a man of 'heroic strength' (Choniates, 1975: 601; Magoulias, 1984: 330), whilst Baldwin I, the first Latin emperor of Constantinople and one of the leaders of the Fourth Crusade, 'was devout in his duties to God and ... temperate in his personal conduct' (Choniates, 1975: 597; Magoulias, 1984: 328). Choniates is also full of praise for Frederick I, who caused so many problems in the empire during the course of the Third Crusade: '[he was] endlessly acquiring recognition for his sagacity', he writes, and, after mentioning his drowning in the River Salef, states:

> He was a man who deserved a blessed and never to be forgotten memory ... also, because his burning passion for Christ was greater than that of any other Christian monarch of his age ... he chose ... to suffer with the Christians of Palestine for the name of Christ and due regard to the life-saving tomb ... following the example of the Apostle Paul, he did not count his life dear unto himself but pressed forward ... Thus the man's zeal was apostolic, his purpose dear to God, and his achievements beyond perfection.
> (Choniates, 1975: 416–17; Magoulias, 1984: 228–9)

Nevertheless, Byzantine historians also highlight the negative traits of individual crusaders. Anna Comnena considers Bohemud a cunning man who for a long time harboured a desire to conquer the Byzantine Empire (Comnena, 2001: 299, 301; Leib, 1943: II, 209,

212). Kinnamos attributes to Conrad 'haughtiness' and 'arrogance' (Kinnamos, 1836: 78, 79, 80; Brand, 1976: 65, 66, 67), to Baldwin III of Jerusalem 'innate arrogance' (Kinnamos, 1836: 185; Brand, 1976: 141), to Frederick I 'immoderate wilfulness' (Kinnamos, 1836: 71; Brand, 1976: 61) and calls Frederick's intention to divide the Byzantine lands, that he intended to attack in the course of the Second Crusade, among his followers 'some kind of barbaric folly' (Kinnamos, 1836: 262; Brand, 1976: 197).

In an apparent expression of impartiality, one that can be explained if one considers his criticism of Byzantine society and also his *Kaiserkritik*,[8] Choniates is scathing about local Byzantines who, either following the Byzantine Emperor Manuel I's orders or on their own initiative, violated agreements with the German army of the Second Crusade regarding supplying them with provisions. Some Byzantines were 'ruthless' (Choniates, 1975: 63; Magoulias, 1984: 37), their acts were 'knowingly unlawful' and their deeds 'iniquitous and unholy' (Choniates, 1975: 66; Magoulias 1984: 39). In a similar vein, he calls senseless the indiscriminate animosity Byzantines expressed towards Latin inhabitants of Constantinople during the course of the Fourth Crusade (Choniates, 1975: 552; Magoulias, 1984: 302) and openly accuses Emperor Manuel of minting debased silver coins for trading with the crusaders and for inciting the Turks, through an exchange of letters, to take action against the crusaders (Choniates, 1975: 66–7; Magoulias, 1984: 39). He also blames Isaac II's representatives, who did not fulfil their duty to facilitate Frederick I's passage through Byzantine lands, for the strained relations between the Byzantines and the crusaders of the Third Crusade because 'through ignorance of their obligations and their cowardliness ... they provoked the king's [Frederick] anger against the Romans and induced the emperor [Isaac II] to think of the king as an enemy' (Choniates, 1975: 402–3; Magoulias, 1984: 221; also see Choniates, 1975: 411; Magoulias, 1984: 226). Interestingly, he also records Frederick's message to the Byzantine emperor's representative, the *protostrator* Manuel Kamytzes, that he had never plotted anything 'detrimental or offensive to the Romans' and that 'he had observed the terms of the agreement unviolated' (Choniates, 1975: 403–4; Magoulias, 1984: 222).[9] Similarly, Kinnamos notes King Conrad's and the French King Louis' messages to the Byzantine emperor's envoys during the course of the Second Crusade in which they affirmed that they had not entered the Byzantine empire in order to inflict harm on the Byzantines (Kinnamos, 1836: 68, 82; Brand, 1976: 59, 68).[10]

Apart from the crusaders' behaviour, what also surprised the Byzantines was the heterogeneity of crusade participants, as well as their sheer numbers. Ekkehard of Aura notes that some of the participants of the First Crusade had taken their crusade vows under 'all kinds of personal disadvantages. In fact many of them were burdened on the journey with wives and children and all their domestic goods' (Ekkehard of Aura, 1895: 17; Riley-Smith, 1986: 39). Anna Comnena records similarly that 'women and children' (Comnena, 2001: 297–8; Leib, 1943: II, 207–8), 'a crowd of all kinds [of people]', followed the First Crusade (Comnena, 2001: 315; Leib, 1943: II, 227). Other contemporary Byzantine historians too commented on the mixed composition of the crusader groups. What, however, surprised them most was their numbers. Anna describes the First Crusade as made up of 'countless Frankish armies' (Comnena, 2001: 297; Leib, 1943: II, 206; also see Comnena, 2001: 304, 315; Leib, 1943: II, 215, 227), 'a crowd as innumerable as grains of sand and the stars' (Comnena, 2001: 297, 440; Leib, 1943: II, 207–8; 1945: III, 160), 'a countless multitude of people' (Comnena, 2001: 315, 321, 322, 330, 439; Leib, 1943: II, 235, 227; 1945: III, 7, 18, 160), 'setting out from everywhere, they burst upon us' (Comnena, 2001: 439; Leib, 1945: III, 160), 'like rivers which, flowing from all directions, were converging and ... came against our [lands]' (Comnena, 2001: 298; Leib, 1943: II, 208). 'Neither man nor woman could remember anything like it', she remarks in regard to the Western mobilisation. Before the crusaders' arrival, Peter the Hermit had arrived in the empire with 80,000 foot soldiers and 100,000 cavalry, she claims (Comnena, 2001: 299; Leib, 1943: II, 209–10). Writing about the Second Crusade, Kinnamos states that 'the whole of the western army had been mobilised' and that the number of participants in the crusade was 'beyond count' (Kinnamos, 1836: 67; Brand, 1976: 58). They were 'innumerable and greater than the grains of sand on the shore' so that the Byzantine emperor's officials, who had been appointed to count each crusade ship's cargo that was crossing the Danube, gave up when they had reached 900,000, he notes (Kinnamos, 1836: 69; Brand, 1976: 60). Choniates claims similarly that the crusader army of the Second Crusade was so large that the Byzantine officials who were supposed to register every man ferried across to the Asiatic side, facing Constantinople, abandoned the task (Choniates, 1975: 66; Magoulias, 1984: 38). That is certainly an exaggeration but it is indicative of the impression made on the Byzantines by the numbers of crusaders arriving in the empire. Anna Comnena states that 'the whole of the West and all barbarian races who inhabited the land beyond the Adriatic [Sea] and up to the Herculean Columns [that is, Gibraltar], all of them travelled together ... and were making their way to Asia through Europe' (Comnena, 2001: 297; Leib, 1943: II, 207). Elsewhere, she reports that 'these people did not all arrive together nor did they come at the same time ... some came first, some second, others [followed] them' (Comnena, 2001: 298; Leib, 1943: II, 208; also see Comnena, 2001: 303–4, 308, 314, 315; Leib, 1943: II, 215, 220, 226, 227–8). Indeed, the crusaders of the First Crusade did arrive in waves: in July and August 1096 Walter's and Peter the Hermit's contingents came, while between December 1096 and May 1097 four more, under the command of Western noblemen, arrived. In regard to the Fourth Crusade, Acropolites reports that 'large crowds' ('πλήθη πολλὰ') from the realms of the Franks, Italy, Venice and elsewhere had assembled in Italy to join the crusade (Acropolites, 1978: 5; Makrides, 2007: 107). Not surprisingly, the Byzantines gained the impression that the West had been mobilised to invade the East and, given the behaviour of the crusaders and their leaders, they were fearful of their presence in the empire.

Interestingly, on occasion, the Byzantine historians hint poignantly at the common religion of the Byzantines and the crusaders. Alexios I was reluctant to attack the crusaders massed outside the walls of Constantinople because he wanted to 'avoid the brotherly killing ('ἐμφύλιον [πόλεμον]')', Anna reports. When the crusaders persisted in storming the walls of the city, however, he commanded his men to fire on them, but ordered them to aim wide because it was 'most important that Christians not to be killed' (Comnena, 2001: 310–12; Leib, 1943: II, 222–3, 225).[11] George Dennis has pointed out that the Byzantines were not belligerent people and, in fact, this led the crusaders to accuse them of cowardice. For the Byzantines, killing, even when deemed justifiable, was considered evil (Dennis, 2001: 37–8). Choniates also refers to the two sides' common religion when he castigates the way some locals treated the crusaders who wanted to buy provisions from them, because they did not take into consideration the fact that they were 'co-religionists' (Choniates, 1975: 66; Magoulias, 1984: 39). Anna is surprised by the active involvement of a Latin clergyman in a naval battle and explicitly denounces it (Comnena, 2001: 306–8; Leib, 1943: II, 218–20),[12] whilst Choniates denounces the atrocities of the 'forerunners of Antichrist', as he calls them (i.e., the Latin Christians), committed against the local population who, in vain, tried to propitiate them by greeting them holding up crosses and icons when they entered Constantinople in April 1204. The rape of women of all ages, including nuns, the destruction and looting of churches and the desecration of holy relics, among other atrocities, clearly left Choniates feeling revulsion for the Western Christians (Choniates, 1975: 572–4, 595; Magoulias, 1984: 314–15, 327).

Nevertheless, beside the crusaders' attacks on the local population, plunder, theft of food, the destruction of sacred, private and public property, assaults on the walls of Constantinople and of other cities, and the slaughter of the local population in conquered Byzantine cities and towns, attacks on the crusaders by local populations are also documented in Byzantine accounts. Kinnamos records that the 'braggart' crusaders of the Second Crusade 'slew many Romans who resisted them', whilst the Byzantines made 'a great slaughter of barbarians [crusaders]' in retaliation for Frederick's torching of a monastery in Adrianople, an act the German prince inflicted in revenge for the killing of a distinguished German, who was treated in that monastery, by Byzantine soldiers (Kinnamos, 1836: 71–2; Brand, 1976: 61–2). Later, another 'great slaughter of Germans' occurred during a battle waged against the Byzantines, he notes (Kinnamos, 1836: 77; Brand, 1976: 65). Choniates states that, in the course of the Second Crusade, the Byzantines 'slew no small number' of crusaders, a deed which, in combination with other misdemeanours perpetrated against the crusaders, aimed to incite fear in the latter and deter them from attacking the Byzantines in the future (Choniates, 1975: 66–7; Magoulias, 1984: 38–9).

Even before the First Crusaders arrived, the Byzantines were weary of them, mainly because of the disastrous financial and territorial impact and human losses that had resulted from the Norman attacks on Byzantine territories in the eleventh century, and also because of the commercial privileges accruing to Venice and the consequent financial implications that had had for Byzantium. These factors had given rise to tension and distrust between the Greek East and the Latin West. According to Anna, when Alexios heard that the crusaders were advancing, he was fearful because 'he had got to know their [the Latins'] unstoppable rush, their unpredictable and changeable views ... that they adore money, that whenever they have the chance they readily dishonour their own agreements ...' (Comnena, 2001: 297; Leib, 1943: II, 206–7; also see Comnena, 2001: 319, 325, 327; Leib, 1943: II, 233; 1945: III, 11, 13; Choniates, 1975: 551; Magoulias, 1984: 302). Moreover, he was aware, even before the crusaders arrived, that the Latins 'were dreaming of the throne of the Roman empire' (Comnena, 2001: 439–40; Leib, 1945: III, 160). Nevertheless, he treated them with courtesy and provided them with military assistance in their passage through Asia Minor. Emperor Manuel too had little trust in the crusaders, according to Choniates: '*with little sincerity* [Manuel] lavished high praise on their [crusaders'] action and *pretended* to admire them for their pious intention' (Choniates, 1975: 61; Magoulias, 1984: 36). Summing up his personal views on the 'western nations', Choniates states: 'these men were braggarts, undaunted in spirit, lacking all humility and trained to be ever bloodthirsty ... they also nurtured an unsleeping hostility towards the Romans [Byzantines], a restless, raving hatred as they viewed them with suspicion' (Choniates, 1975: 199; Magoulias, 1984: 113). To that one could add Anna's claim that the Latins' treachery, among other negative attributes, had been 'πάνυ ἐπαληθεῦον' ('many times verified') (Comnena, 2001: 297; Leib, 1943: II, 206–7). The events of 1204 proved that the Byzantines who, in the eleventh and twelfth centuries, suspected or feared that the religious warriors from the West had nothing less in mind than the conquest of the empire were right.

In conclusion, and based on the crusaders' activities whilst in the Byzantine Empire, can one accuse contemporary Byzantine historians of prejudice? It has been argued that the

Byzantines perceived the crusades as a military expedition, one that was no different from others (Kolia-Dermitzaki, 1991). This is partly right. Indeed, in the eyes of contemporary Byzantines the crusaders were unwelcome invaders. However, some Byzantines seem to have had a little insight into the fundamental elements of the ideology that inspired these invaders and understood its main principles. Interestingly, they did not seem to object to those core ideological elements. What they objected to was the political implication of the crusaders' enterprise – that is, their behaviour and demands while they were in the empire. We should not forget that all the Byzantine narratives were written after the crusades they describe. Therefore the contemporary Byzantine historians judged the crusade movement by the outcome of each crusade. With the benefit of hindsight, the Byzantine historians had no interest in dwelling on the ideological background of the crusades because of the overwhelmingly negative consequences of the crusaders' actions in the empire, men who, in their eyes, constituted nothing less than a numberless, demanding and unruly mob. Georgina Buckler points out that 'on the whole it is remarkable that Anna should have been so little prejudiced [against the crusaders] rather than so much' (Buckler, 1929: 459). George Dennis has argued that in general the Byzantines never seemed to understand why all those Western knights and their followers were marching through their land; pilgrimage they understood, warfare they understood, but the conjoining of the two the Byzantines did not understand (Dennis, 2001: 33). Steven Runciman writes of a 'most complete misunderstanding' in regard to the crusade movement and Byzantium (Runciman, 1986: 22). It might have started like that, but later the actions of the crusaders taken against the Byzantine Empire and its interests fell short of being considered by the Byzantines as a barbarian invasion. Nicetas Choniates, referring to the sack of Thessalonika by the Normans in 1185, had remarked that 'χάσμα διαφορᾶς ... μέγιστον' ('an enormous chasm') separated the two worlds of Greeks and Latins (Choniates, 1975: 301; Magoulias, 1984: 167; Luke 16:26). By their conduct in the empire, the crusaders contributed nothing to alter that opinion. On the contrary, they created an even wider chasm, one that was not bridged throughout the Middle Ages.

NOTES

1 For an overview of the terminology of crusading in the West, see Constable, 2008: 349–52; Kolia-Dermitzaki, 1994: 24–5.
2 Kinnamos calls the French 'Germans'.
3 Kinnamos calls the Normans 'Celts'.
4 On the use of the term 'Franks' in Byzantium in the eleventh century, see Shepard, 1993.
5 Anna uses the terms 'Latins', 'Celts' and 'Franks' interchangeably when referring to the crusaders. On the use of the terms 'Latins' and 'Franks' in Byzantium, see Kazhdan, 2001.
6 On the absolution of sins to the crusaders who died in battle, see various Western contemporary views in Riley-Smith, 1986: 19–20, 28, 36.
7 The unruly behaviour of the crusaders of the first four crusades, whilst in the Byzantine empire, has been described extensively in modern works, therefore I will not refer to them in detail in this chapter. For bibliography about the image of the Latins in Byzantine sources during the period of the Crusades see Stouraitis, 2011: 17, note 17.
8 On Choniates *Kaiserkritik*, see Magdalino, 1993: 3–26 and *passim*; Angold, 1997: 173–80; Simpson and Efthymiadis, 2009: 17–22, 24; Simpson, 2013: 3–6, 295, 319 and *passim*.
9 One ought to take into consideration Nicetas Choniates's rather biased views on emperors Isaac and Manuel.

10 Kinnamos' account of the relationship between Emperor Manuel and King Louis seems to be partial; Brand, 1976: 4, 7.

11 Another reason for his reluctance to attack the crusaders was because it was Maundy Thursday. Anna points out that the crusaders were not deterred by that. Cf. the behaviour of the Latins against the Byzantine Christian population of an unnamed town in Asia Minor in 1101: Comnena, 2001: 346; Leib, 1945: III, 37. Note that on Easter Sunday 1069, the Byzantine forces of Emperor Romanos IV attacked the forces of the Norman mercenary leader Robert Crispin: *Michaelis Attaliotae*, 1853: 123–4.

12 The Byzantines were aware of the existence of this practice by Latin bishops before the start of the crusades: Stouraitis, 2011: 31.

REFERENCES

Acropolites, G., 'Historia', ed. A. Heisenberg and P. Writh, in *Georgii Acropolitae Opera*, Stuttgart 1978, vol. 1.

Angold, M., *The Byzantine Empire, 1025–1204*, London 1997.

Anne Comnène Alexiade, trans. B. Leib, 3 vols, Paris 1937–45 (cited in the text as Leib).

Bardric of Bourgueil, *The Historia Ierosolimitana of Bardric of Bourgueil*, ed. S. Biddlecombe, Boydell 2014.

Bernold of St Blasien, 'Chronicon', *Monumenta Germaniae Historica Scriptorum* 5, Hanover 1844.

Buckler, G., *Anna Comnena: A Study*, London 1929.

Choniates, N., *O City of Byzantium: Annals of Niketas Choniatēs*, trans. H. Magoulias, Detroit 1984 (cited in the text as Magoulias).

Comnena, A., *Alexias*, ed. D. R. Reinsch and A. Kambylis, *Corpus Fontium Historiae Byzantinae* 40/1, Berlin 2001.

Constable, G., *Crusaders and Crusading in the Twelfth Century*, Ashgate 2008.

Deeds of John and Manuel Comnenus by John Kinnamos, trans. Charles Brand, New York 1976 (cited in the text as Brand).

Dennis, G. T., 'Defenders of the Christian People: Holy War in Byzantium', in *The Crusades from the Perspective of Byzantium and the Muslim World*, ed. Angeliki E. Laiou and Roy Parviz Mottahedeh, Dumbarton Oaks 2001, 31–9.

Ekkehard of Aura, 'Hierosolymita', *Recueil des Historiens des Croisades, Historiens Occidentaux* 5, Paris 1895.

Fulcher of Chartres, in *A Source Book for Medieval History*, ed. Oliver J. Thatcher and Edgar Holmes McNeal, New York 1905.

Ioannis Cinnami epitome rerum ab Ioanne et Alexio Comnenis gestarum, ed. A. Meineke, *Corpus Scriptorum Historiae Byzantinae*, Bonn 1836 (cited in the text as Kinnamos).

Kazhdan, A., 'Latins and Franks in Byzantium: Perception and Reality from the Eleventh to the Twelfth Century', in *The Crusades from the Perspective of Byzantium and the Muslim World*, ed. Angeliki E. Laiou and Roy Parviz Mottahedeh, Dumbarton Oaks 2001, 83–100.

Kolia-Dermitzaki, A., Συνάντηση Ανατολής και Δύσης στα εδάφη της Αυτοκρατορίας, Athens 1994.

———, Die Kreuzfahrer und die Kreuzzüge im Sprachgebrauch der Byzantiner', *Jahrbuch der Österreichischen Byzantinistik* 41, 1991, 163–88.

Magdalino, P., *The Empire of Manuel I Comnenos, 1143–1180*, Cambridge 1993.

Makrides, R., *George Akropolites. The History*, Intro., trans. and commentary Ruth Makrides, Oxford 2007.

Markowski, M., '*Crusesignatus*: Its Origins and Early Usage', *Journal of Medieval History* 10, 1984, 157–65.

Michaelis Attaliotae Historia, ed. I. Bekker, Bonn *Corpus Fontium Historiae Byzantinae* 11/1 1853.

Nicetae Choniatae Historia, ed. I. A. van Dieten, Berlin and New York 1975 (cited in the text as Choniates).

Riley-Smith, J., *The First Crusade and the Idea of Crusading*, London 1986.

Robert of Monk's History of the First Crusade. Historia Iherosolimitana, trans. C. Sweetenham, Ashgate 2005.

Runciman, S., 'Byzantium and the Crusades', in *The Meeting of Two Worlds. Cultural Exchange between East and West during the Period of the Crusades*, ed. V. Goss, Michigan 1986.

Shepard, Jonathan, 'The Uses of the Franks in Eleventh-Century Byzantium', *Anglo-Norman Studies* 16, 1993, 275–305.

Simpson, A., *Niketas Choniates. A Historiographical Study*, Oxford 2013.

Simpson, A. and S. Efthymiadis, eds., *Nicetas Choniates. A Historian and a Writer*, La Pomme d'Or 2009.

Stouraitis, I., 'Jihād and Crusade: Byzantine Positions towards the Motions of "Holy War"', *Vyzantina Symmeikta* [Βυζαντινὰ Σύμμεικτα] 21, 2011, 11–63.

CHAPTER EIGHTEEN

THE FALL OF JERUSALEM (1187) AS VIEWED FROM BYZANTIUM

————•◆•————

Michael Angold

An important development in the historiography of the crusades in recent years has been a reassessment of Byzantine attitudes to war. It is now becoming clear that far from condemning the notion of Holy War as unchristian, the Byzantines accepted that in practice war might be divinely sanctioned. It could hardly be otherwise with the example of the Emperor Constantine held up before them. Not only was campaigning in Byzantium accompanied by a special liturgy, but also in some cases cults of martyrdom developed around soldiers, such as the forty martyrs of Amorion, who had perished at enemy hands.[1] The high moral standing of soldiers at Byzantium in the tenth century is a theme of a military handbook of the time, which underlines their willingness to lay down their lives in the service of the emperor and in defence of Christianity.[2] Authorship of this military handbook has been ascribed to the Emperor Nikephoros Phokas (965–69), who unsuccessfully sought patriarchal approval of the popular notion that a soldier dying in battle against the infidel acquired the status of martyr. Once military retrenchment became the order of the day in the course of the eleventh century, ideas about war having spiritual rewards and goals began to have less resonance at Byzantium, while at the same time the notion of the emperor as peacemaker rather than warrior took hold.[3] However, the traditions of Holy War, which had sustained Byzantine expansionism in the tenth century were not forgotten among the military families, who came to form the core of the Comnenian regime at the end of the eleventh century, and allowed some measure of understanding of – and even sympathy for – the aims of the crusading armies.

The letters despatched by Alexius I Comnenus to Oderisius, abbot of Monte Cassino, at the time of their passage through Byzantine territory in 1097 and 1098 suggest not only good relations with the crusading armies, but also approval of the ideal of crusade. The emperor regretted that so many of the crusaders had gone 'to the eternal tabernacles', but adds 'They are blessed, since they met death with the right intention, wherefore we should scarcely consider them dead, but rather living, having departed to the eternal and incorruptible life'.[4] The stress not only on right intention, but also on spiritual rewards for death in battle reveals the awareness there was at Alexius Comnenus's court of the crusading ideal in its earliest stages. The fullest account of the First Crusade comes from the pen of the emperor's daughter Anna Comnena. Completed nearly half a century after the passage of the First Crucsade, it represents studied reflection rather than immediate reaction. If there is an underlying anxiety about the way the undoubted piety of the crusaders might be exploited by unscrupulous leaders, the undertaking itself is not called into question. On the contrary, it is presented as a noble enterprise, which had the full support of her father. He even ransomed crusade leaders, who had been captured by the Fatimids of Egypt. His daughter claims that this was because he found it intolerable for men, who 'seemed to rival the heroes of old', to be held in captivity.[5] Anna Comnena was writing as the Second Crusade was making its way eastwards.[6] She was therefore aware that the crusade was not an exceptional incident, but a recurrent movement, which harnessed the spiritual and military energies of Latin Christendom. This might hold dangers for the Byzantine Empire, but it did not prevent her from approving its underlying motivation. This applied with equal force to Niketas Choniates, who was writing on the eve of the Fourth Crusade. Even in such a climate of uncertainty his sympathies still lay with the crusade and its leaders. In his account of the passage of the Second Crusade through the Byzantine Empire he went out of his way to criticise the Emperor Manuel I Comnenus for his hostile handling of the crusade. He puts into the mouth of the German Emperor Conrad II (in mistake for the French king Louis VII) a speech, which reveals a sensitive understanding of the spiritual ideals underlying the crusade.[7] Only in the sections of his *History* written after 1204 do we find outright condemnation of the crusade. Only then did Byzantine writers subject the crusade to a rigorous analysis and reject it as a perversion of Christian ideals. There can be no doubt that it was the crusader conquest of Constantinople which was the critical event in turning Byzantine opinion against the crusade. However, playing a subsidiary – but not unimportant – part in this was the fall of Jerusalem to Saladin some twenty years earlier in 1187.

As always, Jerusalem was contested by the different faiths. If the crusade itself was an enterprise that the Byzantines had little difficulty in countenancing, the Frankish occupation of Jerusalem and the holy places together with the appropriation of the patriarchate of Jerusalem produced a different set of problems. It challenged the Byzantine claim to the protection of the Holy places. Long before the crusades the Byzantine emperor John Tzimiskes (969–76) had for propaganda purposes proclaimed his intention of liberating the Holy Sepulchre.[8] Though not seriously meant, it directed attention to the Holy Sepulchre, which became the focus of the campaign directed by the Fatimid caliph al-Hakim (996–1021) against the Christians in his territories. In 1009 he ordered the destruction of the Holy Sepulchre, which resulted in razing the Constantinian basilica to the ground and serious damage to the Anastasis rotunda.[9] In 1027 his successor made formal approaches to Constantinople for help in making good the damage. Furthermore, he restored the rights – long in abeyance – of the Byzantine emperor in the appointment of the patriarch of Jerusalem, thus formalising the Byzantine claims to the protection of Jerusalem and the Holy places.[10] The crusader conquest of Jerusalem in July 1099 called these into question. It so happened that the patriarchal throne was vacant; the last incumbent Symeon II having died a year earlier. The crusaders therefore elected one of their own as patriarch without reference to the papacy; still less to Byzantium. An Orthodox successor to Symeon II was forced to seek refuge at Constantinople.[11]

If Antioch was the main focus of Byzantine policy in the aftermath of the creation of the crusader states, it did not mean that Jerusalem and the holy places were forgotten. Their appropriation by Latin Christians in the wake of the First Crusade forced a reappraisal of a string of Byzantine attitudes. It brought clarification and intensification of existing views rather than any radical change. Before the crusades it would have been difficult to say how important Jerusalem and the holy places were in practice to the Byzantines. There was never a tradition at Byzantium of popular pilgrimage to Jerusalem, of the kind, which burgeoned in the West over the eleventh century.[12] Instead, pilgrimage to Jerusalem was to a large extent the preserve of ascetics, for many of whom it was part of a spiritual education and might be combined with retreat – sometimes for a number of years – at one of the famous Palestinian monasteries, such as the Lavra of St Saba and the monastery of Choziba,[13] which were noted for their ascetic expertise.

Counterbalancing Jerusalem in the popular imagination was the New Jerusalem of Constantinople. The idea of Constantinople as the new Sion had ancient roots, going back to the fifth century. Scholars have recently argued that from the mid-tenth century this idea was given clearer focus with the transfer of the imperial collection of relics of the passion to the chapel of the Pharos within the precinct of the imperial palace.[14] It is further maintained that the chapel thus became another Holy Sepulchre: a line of thought which receives some support from the Emperor Manuel Comnenus' decision in 1169 not merely to transfer Christ's burial slab from Ephesus to the Pharos chapel, but to carry it in person into the chapel; in the words of Niketas Choniates, 'as if it were the body of God Himself'.[15] This and the other relics of the passion were put on display.[16] But the question is not so much who had access to them, but who controlled access? If ultimately it was the emperor, more immediately it was the sacristan or *skeuophylax* of the holy churches within the imperial palace. In other words, entry into the chapel was carefully supervised. However, it was not the exclusive preserve of the imperial court. This is borne out not only by its inclusion in guide books of the eleventh and twelfth century,[17] but also by the story of a Canterbury monk, who was able to gain access through the good offices of a fellow countryman in the Varangian guard.[18] But equally such information cannot be taken to mean that the Pharos chapel was a site of popular pilgrimage. There is a story of its icon of the Mother of God *Oikokyra* acting as a godmother to children brought by their mothers, but this practice is unlikely to have had any wide application.[19] The main importance of the chapel continued to be the role it played in imperial ceremonial. Its collection of relics contributed to imperial prestige and was regularly shown off to visiting rulers.[20] The parallel drawn by contemporaries was not with the Church of the Holy Sepulchre, but with Shiloh, the original resting place of the Ark of the Covenant, the equivalent of which in the new dispensation were the relics of the passion.[21]

The parallel with the Church of the Holy Sepulchre can be misleading, particularly when it is suggested that Manuel Comnenus deliberately promoted the chapel of the Pharos to compensate for the Church of the Holy Sepulchre falling under Latin control. In the context of his policy of entente towards the crusader states, the two were seen as complementary rather than in competition, even if by the end of his reign it was becoming difficult to disguise the limitations of this formula. But it was never a matter of disengaging from Jerusalem and the holy places now that they came under Latin auspices. Manuel Comnenus was building on the intense interest in Jerusalem shown by his father John II at the very end of his reign. It was John's brother Isaac who is the first member of the Comnenian dynasty known to have gone on pilgrimage to Jerusalem.[22] After the discovery of his conspiracy against his brother John, he sought refuge among the Turkish emirs of eastern Anatolia. When they failed to back his bid for the Byzantine throne, he went on pilgrimage to Jerusalem. While in the Holy Land he paid for the construction of an aqueduct to bring water from the spring of Elisha ('Ain as-Sultan) to the Orthodox monastery of St John by the River Jordan.[23] It is perhaps best to see Isaac's sojourn in the Holy Land as an act of atonement, which prepared the way for his reconciliation for his brother and his return to Constantinople in 1136. It certainly made an impact at court. A court orator credited the emperor with smoothing the path for pilgrims to Jerusalem.[24] In 1137 his cousin, the monk Adrian/John Comnenus, 'took that blessed route and tasted the joys of the holy city'. He 'steeped himself in our Saviour's birthplace and everywhere connected to Him, including Golgotha, the burial place of our Saviour'.[25] Though the orator, who celebrated his visit to the Holy Land, cloaks it in the usual pieties, he reveals that it was also combined with a diplomatic mission to the king of Jerusalem, which discussed among other things an exchange of prisoners. Circumstantial evidence suggests that another topic will have been the emperor's fervent wish to make the pilgrimage to Jerusalem himself. The deathbed speech that Niketas Choniates put into his mouth came close to turning him into an apologist for the crusade. The emperor talked of his desire to visit Palestine 'to ascend the mountain of the Lord, as the Psalmist puts it, and to stand in His holy place; justified by the law of war to drive away the encircling enemy, who have often seized the Sepulchre of our Lord, just as in former times the gentiles took the ark by force of arms'.[26] As a token of his sincerity, he had already had a large golden lamp made, which he hoped to present in person to the Church of the Holy Sepulchre.[27] His death following a hunting accident prevented the wish being fulfilled.

Manuel I Comnenus was not immediately able to build on his father's achievements. The passage of the Second Crusade and the Norman incursions into Greece left him with little time to devote to the crusader states. It was not until 1159, when he made a ceremonial entrance into the city of Antioch, that he recovered the ground lost since his father's death sixteen years before. Thereafter there was a period of entente with the crusader states lasting until almost the end of his reign.[28] It was characterised by an increase in pilgrimage traffic overland. Eustathios of Thessaloniki applauded the way that Emperor Manuel had made the routes across Anatolia safe for pilgrims. You no longer had to be armed to make the crossing. Even 'women brought up to a life of luxury … were venturing along these roads, prompted by a holy desire to frequent the holy places of that land'.[29] At a diplomatic level there were exchanges of embassies and a series of marriage alliances linking the great families of crusader Outremer to the Comnenian dynasty. Manuel chose as his second wife a princess from Antioch, while King Baldwin III of Jerusalem (1143–63) married one of Manuel's nieces and his brother and successor Amalric I (1163–74) another Comnenian princess. In 1171 Amalric made a state visit to Constantinople, when he grudgingly recognised Manuel as in some sense overlord of the Kingdom of Jerusalem. In practice, it was unlikely to have been much more than acceptance of his role as protector of the holy places. Later events suggest parallels with the principality of Antioch, where in 1159 the ruler Reynald of Châtillon not only did homage to Manuel, but also promised to restore the cathedral of Antioch to the Orthodox patriarch, though it took several years of Byzantine pressure before this happened. Later events suggest that at Jerusalem Manuel was equally determined to secure agreement on the part of the Latin authorities to Orthodox claims on the Church of the Holy Sepulchre. He contributed to the decoration of the church, as he did to the refurbishment of the church of the Nativity at Bethlehem, where a bilingual inscription of 1169 celebrates his work. The first part of the inscription is in Latin and pride of place is given to King Amalric, while Emperor Manuel is remembered as a generous donor. It dutifully recalls that the bishop of Bethlehem at that time was called Ralph and that the artist in charge of the decoration of the church was one Ephraim. By way of contrast, the Greek inscription gives pride of place to the monk Ephraim, described as designer and mosaicist, who completed the work under the imperial auspices of the Great Emperor Manuel in the days of the Great King of Jerusalem Amalric and of Bishop Ralph. The prominence given to the mosaicist is best explained by the importance of the iconography of the church's decoration.[30] That it reflected Manuel's ideas is suggested by the way that Manuel's portrait was set up at various points in the church, including the sanctuary. The emperor was without any doubt the moving spirit behind the refurbishment of the church. A Greek pilgrim can be forgiven for suggesting erroneously that the emperor was responsible for the construction of the whole church, but his insistence that he decorated the whole church with gold mosaic is much closer to the truth, because the mosaic decoration is substantially new. There is no way of telling how much of the original mosaic decoration was included, but for our purposes it is not important, because the iconography of the church was a way of proclaiming Manuel Comnenus's commitment to the union of churches. The devices of ecumenical and local councils, which decorate the walls of the nave to the north and to the south, were an effective declaration of adherence to a common set of beliefs. Lucy-Anne Hunt has argued that 'taken as a whole, the mosaic program proclaimed the reconciliation of the divine and human natures of Christ'.[31] This was the theme of the *Ekthesis* issued by Manuel I Comnenus in 1166 pronouncing on the controversy over the verse 'My Father is greater than I' (John 14:28), which had divided the church of Constantinople. The emperor had relied heavily for his formulation on the Pisan theologian Hugo Eteriano and was deliberately making concessions to Western opinion at a time, when he was actively seeking an understanding with the papacy.[32] Manuel's patronage of the church of the Holy Nativity at Bethlehem was well designed to emphasise the sincerity of his overtures. But it was something more than this. It reflected the place that Jerusalem and the Holy Land held in Manuel's thinking. It was a symbol of the integrity of Christianity, for which the Byzantine emperor as the heir of the emperor Constantine bore a direct responsibility. In lavishing care on the shrines of the Holy Land, Manuel Comnenus had Constantine's example before him. In the preamble to the *Ekthesis*, he claimed to be 'the heir of the crown of Constantine the Great and in his spirit holding sway over all his rightful possessions'.[33] But there was another way in which Manuel Comnenus could carry out his responsibilities. Palestine was a Holy Land not only because it witnessed the life and death of Christ, but also because it had been a cradle of monasticism. At the church of the Nativity at Bethlehem, the columns of the nave bore the images of St Euthymios, St Theodosios and St Sabas, who were the founders of noted Palestinian monasteries, all of which were still functioning in the twelfth century.[34] While the crusader conquest had relegated the hierarchy of the Orthodox Church to a position of inferiority, Orthodox monasteries continued to flourish. They benefited immensely from the patronage of the Emperor Manuel Comnenus.[35]

This was a theme of the description of the holy places written by *Sevastos* John Doukas,[36] who is to be identified with Grand Hetaireiarch John Doukas, one of the leaders of an embassy despatched to Jerusalem in 1177.[37] His description of the holy places was the fruit of this mission. It was written either in the course of his stay in the Kingdom of Jerusalem or immediately after his return to Constantinople; certainly before the death of Manuel I Comnenus, who was still alive at the time of writing. In dating this text, scholars have been mislead by two things: the date 1185 (Latin style), which is ascribed to the text in one of the manuscripts (Bibl. Vall. Rome Ms. 153) and a reference to the late emperor Comnenus Porphyrogenitus, which must not be to Manuel Comnenus, but to his father John II, because Manuel is always referred to as either 'my' or 'our' emperor, indicating that he was still alive. The 1185 date (Latin style – MCLXXXV) has no direct relationship with the original Greek text. It has been suggested that it may be a misreading for 1485 (Latin style – MCDLXXXV) – a possible date for the copying of the manuscript. It has, in any case, no bearing on the dating of the text. After John Doukas returned from the Holy Land his life was far too crowded for him to have had time for literary composition. In 1179 he was sent by Manuel Comnenus to Thessalonica to rescue its archbishop, Eustathios, who in gratitude produced a eulogy in his honour, where his journey to the Holy Land is admiringly commented on.[38]

His *ekphrasis* of the holy places must be the most elegant of Palestinian pilgrimage accounts and might even have satisfied Eustathios of Thessalonica. Not only did he manage a reference – which may be more pointed than it seems – to the romance of *Leukippe and Kleitophon* by Achilles Tatios,[39] but he was also able to weave into his narrative some verses of Chorikios celebrating paintings of the Mother of God.[40] These would be nods in the direction of a Constantinopolitan audience, but the author's piety quite patently informed his literary endeavours. With the naivety of a pilgrim he recounted what purported to be recent miracles at two different shrines, but these turned out to be just the recycling of old stories.[41] His underlying purpose was to emphasise the immediate importance to Byzantium of the holy places and the spiritual value of pilgrimage. It was also to celebrate all that Emperor Manuel I Comnenus had done to put a Byzantine stamp on the Holy Land by his donations to major pilgrimage shrines, such as the Church of the Holy Sepulchre at Jerusalem[42] and of the Holy Nativity at Bethlehem,[43] and by his rebuilding of Orthodox monasteries.[44]

It is more than possible that it was intended to counter an earlier account of a visit to the Kingdom of Jerusalem made by Constantine Manasses in 1160,[45] who was also on a diplomatic mission. John Doukas's invocation of Achilles Tatios looks like a veiled reference to Constantine Manasses's literary pretensions evident in his romance of *The Loves of Aristander and Kallithea*.[46] John Doukas and Constantine Manasses undoubtedly had rather different views about the importance of the Holy Land from the Byzantines.[47] Constantine Manasses dutifully visited the holy sites of Jerusalem and then took the pilgrim trail to Jericho and the Jordan, where he became increasingly disillusioned.[48] He had no wish to see Jericho ever again; even in his sleep. He had bathed in the waters of the Jordan, but they were murky and unfit to drink.[49] Capernaum was an abomination and Nazareth a hellhole. Manasses could not understand why Christ should have chosen to live there.[50] He invokes the city of Byzantium, which had nurtured him, as his only hope. O to be under its sheltering wing![51]

Given the comparative lack of Constantinopolitan interest in Jerusalem and Palestine before the twelfth century, to have two detailed accounts of journeys to the holy places written within twenty years of each other is quite unprecedented and underlines their importance to the Byzantines in the mid-twelfth century. Admittedly, Constantine Manasses's poem was a very different work from John Doukas's *Ekphrasis* of the holy places. Manasses was dealing in personal experience – the more miserable the better, largely for comic effect. But his underlying theme was the superiority of Constantinople over the outside world as the proper setting for civilised society. There is no hint of any religious dimension. Constantinople is not held up as a New Sion. John Doukas might well have agreed with Manasses about the benefits of civilised life in Constantinople, but he was urging the importance of a spiritual life, as exemplified by pilgrimage to Jerusalem and by Palestinian monasticism.

On occasion, Constantinople and Jerusalem might come into conflict, as happened in the case of a young Constantinopolitan patrician, John Mesarites. Towards the end of Manuel

Comnenus's reign, when Mesarites was in his teens, he formed a plan to run away and become a hermit in the Palestinian desert, to which end he took a ship for the Holy Land. His father was distraught and begged the emperor to get him back, which at no small cost he did. The young man was hauled before the emperor, who rebuked him in the following terms:

> What turned you, who are short in stature and lacking discernment, into such a daredevil? Despite your youth you intended to cross the open sea in order to live in foreign parts and to choose to stay among Barbarian peoples, whose way of life is entirely incompatible with our own. Their gaze is scarcely human, while ours is full of humanity; our speech is agreeable, while theirs is harsh and garbled. They are all armed and ready to set out along any route; they are bloodthirsty as just a look will tell, while we are peaceful and compassionate and refuse to carry weapons needlessly, not being in thrall to Ares.[52]

This comes from the *Epitaphios*, composed for John by his brother Nicholas Mesarites in 1207. Whether after a lapse of thirty years the words attributed to Emperor Manuel were completely accurate is one thing, but the incident itself is more than believable. Manuel took great pains to keep control of his aristocracy, as his supervision of aristocratic marriages shows.[53] It was certainly not in the state's interest to have talented youngsters shutting themselves away in Palestinian monasteries rather than becoming high-powered administrators. It posed in very clear terms a dilemma, which runs through Byzantine life: how to balance the *vita activa* and the *vita contemplativa*. The emperor ignored the spiritual dimension and simply emphasised the superiority of the Byzantine way of life over the Latin. John Mesarites had no compunction in demonstrating the weaknesses of the emperor's position. His father, by way of contrast, treated his son more sympathetically and more astutely. He pointed out the advantages of life in Constantinople, but emphasised that it was not lacking spiritual benefits.

> There is no need for you to settle in a foreign land or to live among strangers, whose way of life is at variance with your own, still less among aliens. Christ may have made himself known in Judaea, but he has not forsaken us. The tomb of our Lord may be there, but we have the veils and shrouds; the place of the skull may be there, but we are privileged by the possession of the Holy Cross and its base, the Crown of Thorns, the sponge, the lance and the reed, which are here. What more should I add? The Uncircumscribed, who appeared among us in human form, thus received definite shape. The form he then had has been preserved impressed on the Holy Towel and applied to the fragile Holy Tile by some superhuman artistic skill (*acheiropoieta*). This land of ours, my child, is Jerusalem, Tiberias, Nazareth, Mount Thabor, Bethany and Bethlehem [all rolled into one] and partakes of salvation because our Lord watches over us and fulfils the wishes of those that fear him throughout the whole world.[54]

If these words were intended in the first instance to assuage a young man's spiritual longings, they pointed to a discrepancy between Manuel Comnenus's promotion of Palestine, as the holy land, and his celebration of the relics of the passion, which turned Constantinople into a holy city. If the former had as one of its goals a justification for a Byzantine protectorate over the crusader states, the latter was a way not only of enhancing imperial prestige, but also of placating Constantinopolitan *amour-propre*. They were predicated on the assumption of a broad community of interest between Byzantium and the West, the limits of which became increasingly clear after Manuel Comnenus's death. These created serious divisions within Byzantine society that only the crusader conquest of 1204 finally resolved. But even before Manuel's death, cracks were beginning to appear; never so obviously as on the occasion, when Leontios, the Orthodox patriarch of Jerusalem, attempted to take up residence in his see.[55] He was a famous ascetic, who became abbot of the monastery of St John the Theologian on the island of Patmos.[56] He was an appropriate choice as patriarch of Jerusalem, because his way of life was likely to meet with approval from the heads of the Orthodox monasteries in Palestine. He set out from Patmos in the winter of 1176, spending time on the islands of Rhodes and Cyprus. He reached Acre in 1177 almost certainly in tandem with the Byzantine embassy, of which John Doukas was one of the leaders. The patriarch negotiated with the Latin authorities over the possibility of performing the Orthodox liturgy in the Church of the Holy Sepulchre, but they were adamant that any visit had to be made as a private individual.[57] It put an end to any hopes of a triumphant recovery of the Church of the Holy Sepulchre. He made his way to Jerusalem and visited the church as unobtrusively as possible. He went as a pilgrim rather than as a patriarch.[58] But his presence soon became known. It happened to coincide with a storm, which ended a drought at Jerusalem. The patriarch's supporters immediately claimed it as a miracle, which increased Latin hostility.[59] There was an assassination attempt or more probably the threat of one, as a way of persuading the patriarch to leave Jerusalem.[60] Rather than jeopardise relations with the Kingdom of Jerusalem, Emperor Manuel summoned him back to Constantinople,[61] but not before Saladin had got wind of what was happening and invited him to take up residence at Damascus. The patriarch politely declined the offer on the grounds that he was returning on imperial orders to Constantinople. Saladin replied post haste offering him every support for his journey home. On his return to Constantinople, the patriarch presented Saladin's letter to the emperor as reproof to the Latins.[62] It was an episode from which Saladin emerged in Byzantine eyes with credit. It allowed him not only to open up diplomatic channels to the Byzantine court, but also to put out feelers to the Orthodox community in the Kingdom of Jerusalem.

Saladin's victory over the armies of the Kingdom of Jerusalem at the battle of the Horns of Hattin in July 1187 left the city of Jerusalem depleted of defenders and it was only a matter of time before it surrendered on terms to Saladin. The official Byzantine reaction was muted. It was left to the Cypriot hermit St Neophytos the Recluse to express his regrets: 'Who would not lament from the depths of his heart and soul such a disaster, upon seeing and hearing of such a turn of events – how the holy flock in that Holy Land was ousted, and the holy of holies was delivered to the dogs?'[63] This was very much a personal reaction. As a young man he had visited the holy places and stayed in the monasteries of Palestine. This was an experience, which will have left him with a strong emotional attachment to Jerusalem. Given the isolation of Cyprus from Constantinople at this juncture Neophytos's thoughts can hardly be taken as a reflection of Constantinopolitan attitudes, but he remained in close touch with monastic circles in Palestine. Andrew Jotischky is therefore almost certainly correct, when he dismisses as erroneous the information contained in the *History of the Patriarchs of Alexandria* to the effect that the Orthodox community of Jerusalem was instrumental in handing over Jerusalem to Saladin.[64] If there had been any collusion with local Christians, Saladin might have been expected to hand over the Church of the Holy Sepulchre to the Orthodox clergy on his victorious entry into Jerusalem on 2 October 1187, which did not happen. Instead Saladin's initial action was to close the church down, as he debated with his advisers whether or not to raze it to the ground. It was only after being struck by the futility of any such action that he turned the church over to the Orthodox clergy.[65]

The lack of any clear response to the fall of Jerusalem to Saladin on the part of the Byzantine government needs little explanation. It was in a state of disarray following the troubles – coups, counter-coups, rebellions and foreign invasions – which the Byzantine Empire experienced in the aftermath of the death of Manuel Comnenus in September 1180. The reigning Byzantine emperor, Isaac II Angelos, had come to the throne in 1185 by sheer luck, when a popular uprising unseated the usurper Andronikos I Comnenus. His hold on power was uncertain. In 1187 he faced a rebellion by his most successful general Alexios Branas. He survived thanks to the martial skills of his brother-in-law Conrad of Montferrat, whose marriage to the emperor's sister was negotiated in the course of the previous year. It was one of Isaac Angelos's earliest forays into the field of foreign policy. It revived Manuel I Comnenus's alliance with the house of Montferrat, which among other things was a way of procuring specialised military assistance. Everything suggests that at the outset of his reign Isaac Angelos intended to continue lines of policy followed by Manuel Comnenus. Surviving stalwarts of the old regime rallied round Isaac Angelos. It would follow from this that Isaac would have wished to re-establish Manuel's alliance with the crusader states, but events conspired to push Isaac into seeking an alliance with Saladin. For example, no sooner had Conrad of Montferrat defeated the rebel commander than he abandoned his new bride, Isaac's sister, and took ship with his retinue to the crusader states; arriving off Acre on 13 July 1187 a few days after the defeat suffered by the Franks of Jerusalem at the battle of Hattin. There was very little that Isaac Angelos could do to influence events because Cyprus had passed under the control of a member of the Comnenus family in 1184. Isaac Angelos despatched an expedition to recover the island in 1186, but it was a total failure.[66] Without Cyprus it was difficult, if not impossible, to revive Emperor Manuel Comnenus's *entente* with the crusader states. We can surely discount stories of an alliance between Saladin and the previous Byzantine emperor, Andronikos I Comnenus, as Western propaganda, but it may well be that even before the fall of Jerusalem Isaac Angelos was exploring the possibility of a deal with Saladin, because Isaac's elder brother Alexios was a presence at Saladin's court. He had fled there to escape the vengeance of Andronikos I Comnenus, but mysteriously he stayed on for two years or more after his brother Isaac had secured the Byzantine throne.[67] He could have acted as an intermediary with Saladin. Even so, meaningful negotiations only began after the fall of Jerusalem and had as their background the gathering of the Third Crusade, the passage of which through Byzantine territories presented Isaac II Angelos with immense difficulties.[68]

It was these that at some point after the fall of Jerusalem decided Isaac Angelos that there was more to be gained from an alliance with Saladin than from co-operation with Emperor Frederick I Barbarossa, who proposed to follow the overland route to the Holy Land. It had as its corollary a preference for Muslim rather than Latin control of the holy places. This represented a clear break with Comnenian policies. There were many in the Byzantine administration, such as the historian Niketas Choniates, who were critical and ascribed the reversal of policy to the emperor's spiritual father Dositheos, a Studite monk of Venetian extraction.[69] The attractions, which an alliance with Saladin held for Isaac Angelos, were largely pragmatic. Once it became clear that reviving Manuel Comnenus's policy of *entente* with the crusader states was impractical – largely because of the loss of the island of Cyprus – an understanding with Saladin was the most effective way of protecting Byzantine interests in Anatolia, where Saladin could bring his influence to bear on the Seljuqs of Rum. If Byzantine foreign policy was almost always pragmatic, short term – and usually reactive – it had to be dressed in religious and even eschatological terms for respectability's sake. Dositheos was used as a propagandist, but with a twist: Isaac Angelos appointed him patriarch of Jerusalem in succession to Leontios, who had died on 14 May 1185. Such an appointment reflected the continuing importance of the Church of Jerusalem in Byzantine thinking. It was designed to press Orthodox claims over the Church of the Holy Sepulchre, which became even more necessary once the city had fallen to Saladin. If Jerusalem as a symbol of Christendom united in the common enterprise of the crusade had little appeal for Isaac Angelos and his spiritual mentor, more attractive was the use increasingly made of it by Byzantine apologists as a symbol of Orthodox ecumenicism as opposed to Roman exceptionalism.[70] In order to secure control over the Church of the Holy Sepulchre, Isaac offered to place the mosque in Constantinople under Saladin's auspices by transferring the *khutba* from the Fatimid to the Abbasid caliph. Saladin willingly accepted and despatched a new *mihrab* (or pulpit) to be installed in the mosque at Constantinople.[71] Saladin and his advisers were convinced that Isaac's overtures were merely a reaction to the dangers presented by Frederick I Barbarossa and should be treated accordingly, which meant that Isaac obtained no worthwhile help from Saladin. He even failed to obtain any concessions over the Church of the Holy Sepulchre.[72] Saladin was willing to place it in the care of the local Orthodox clergy. He was not willing, however, to countenance the return of an Orthodox patriarch, even during the vacancy that occurred after 1190/91 with the death of the Latin Patriarch Heraclius. Isaac was compre-hensively outplayed.[73]

Isaac Angelos's opposition to the passage of Frederick I Barbarossa's armies produced deep dissatisfaction at the heart of government. It was, in any case, self-defeating because he was quickly brought to terms by the German emperor. The historian Niketas Choniates had first-hand experience of the events. He was governor of Thrace and had a part to play in organising opposition to the Germans – ineffective as it was. He wrote up this section of his history before the coming of the Fourth Crusade. In his hands, Frederick I Barbarossa becomes a hero figure designed to underline the inadequacies of the Byzantine emperor. The historian's sympathy for the crusade ideal, which Barbarossa exemplifies, seems gen-uine.[74] It reveals a split in Byzantine opinion: there were those opposed to the crusade, who were happy to accept a reversion to an older state of affairs, when the holy places came under the control of a Muslim ruler. Against them were those at Byzantium, such as Niketas Choniates, who still clung to a belief in the moral value of holy war as waged by the crusaders. This might appear to be at odds with his famous denunciation of the Latins for their arrogance and their pomposity and their double-dealing and their contempt for the Byzantines.[75] This was not a passage, as it would be easy to imagine, that Choniates added to his *History* after 1204, but one written before the arrival of the Fourth Crusade, when he was generally speaking well disposed to the Latins. It forms part of his description of the sack of Thessaloniki in 1185 by the Normans of Sicily. The outrages they committed were in contrast to the comparatively orderly progress of crusader armies through the Byzantine Empire. Niketas Choniates was still under the illusion that the crusade was a force for moral good and acted as a restraint on the unbridled instincts of Westerners.

That the fall of Jerusalem to Saladin should have had such a muted reception in con-temporary Byzantine sources is a reflection of the failure of Isaac Angelos's attempted alliance with Saladin. It deprived the Byzantine emperor of his moral standing and prepared the way for the coup, which brought his brother Alexios to power in 1195. The weakness of his position is evident from the fate of his spiritual adviser Dositheos. With the threat of the German crusade hanging over Byzantium, he imposed Dositheos on the patriarchal throne of Constantinople in February 1189 – though strictly speaking such a transfer was uncanonical. Niketas Choniates has great fun describing how the emperor tricked the great canonist Theodore Balsamon into giving a favourable opinion, which allowed Isaac to place his mentor on the patriarchal throne. But the patriarchal synod was not so easily fooled and almost immediately forced Dositheos to resign. Isaac understood that his authority was being called into account and in June 1189 once again imposed Dositheos on the patriarchal throne of Constantinople. The patriarch was at the very centre of resistance to the Germans. He is alleged by the chronicler of the German crusade to have preached in the church of St Sophia that convicted murderers could atone for their sins by killing crusaders, which is perhaps a garbled version of something less sensational. In any event, when peace was made between Frederick I Barbarossa and Isaac Angelos in February 1190, the former insisted the patriarch append his signature to the peace treaty.[76] The latter's stance at the time of the passage of the German crusade did not endear him to the Episcopal bench. In September 1191 he was once again examined before synod. Despite his best efforts, the emperor could no longer protect him and Dositheos was forced to resign. The patriarch was at the heart of one of the bitterest disputes to divide the Church of Constantinople in the twelfth century.[77] It was superficially about infringements of canon law, but beneath the surface were far larger questions about the place of the Church of Jerusalem in the Byzantine scheme of things: was it a symbol of the co-operation of Byzantium and the West within the framework of the crusade or was it a symbol of Byzantium's emancipation from Western interference?

It was a question, which Isaac Angelos did his best to avoid in the letter he sent in *c.* 1193 to Pope Celestine III. He was trying to mend fences after the failure of his opposition to the passage of the Third Crusade. He claimed to be sorrowed by the spectacle of the holy places in the possession of the infidel; but still more dismayed by the fiasco of the Third Crusade. He attributed this to the divisions between the leaders of the crusade. His argument is interesting. His premiss is as follows: a simple gift to a shrine only becomes acceptable to God, when the donor has made his peace with his enemy. 'How then,' he asks, 'is it admissible for those who have vowed their bodies and souls to God to behave in a way that offends against Christ's love, when at the moment of making their offering they quarrel bitterly with one another?'[78] To an extent it was a matter of shifting the blame, but it also pointed to a practical failing of the crusade ideal. Isaac Angelos refrained from pointing out that the fall of Jerusalem might equally be ascribed to divisions among the Franks.

It was only after the crusader conquest of Constantinople in 1204 that Byzantine views about the fall of Jerusalem received any definitive expression. That they had failed to materialise earlier is best explained by the overlay of the traumatic events connected with the passage of the Third Crusade. Our best witness is Niketas Choniates. Following Alicia Simpson we can compare the version of his *History*, which was completed on the eve of the arrival of the Fourth Crusade in August 1203, with that written in exile at Nicaea. In the earlier version the fall of Jerusalem to Saladin is treated in passing and dismissed as of little importance.[79] It was only after the fall of Constantinople that its relevance became apparent. He now compares the treatment of Constantinople by the crusaders with that of Jerusalem by Saladin. He notes that the latter

> allowed one and all to depart having set the ransom money at a few gold coins for each man and permitted them to keep the rest, even though they were like grains of sand. It was in this fashion that the enemies of Christ behaved towards the Latin

infidels; magnanimously they inflicted upon them neither sword, nor fire, nor hunger, nor persecution, nor nakedness, nor bruises, nor tortures. Quite differently, as we have superficially recounted, were we treated by those, who [were supposed] to love Christ and be our fellow believers, guiltless, as we were, of any wrong.[80]

This was not an isolated reaction: while Niketas Choniates was revising his *History* at Nicaea, Theodosios Goudeles was on the island of Patmos writing his *Life of St Leontios of Jerusalem*. His account of Leontios's time in Jerusalem reflected grudging admiration for Saladin, which could now be openly expressed. As Theodosios Goudeles put it, even if '[Saladin] did not seek after the good in an appropriate fashion, he was in many things good and kind and honourable';[81] far more so than the Franks, who refused Leontios access to the Church of the Holy Sepulchre. Their intrinsic evil was amply displayed in the sack of Constantinople. It was left to the exiled patriarch of Constantinople John Kamateros to make this connection in a tract entitled 'On the Harm done to us by the Latins' written shortly before he died in 1206.[82] He dismisses them as tomb robbers for their depredations in Constantinople and contrasts this with their claim to be venerators of the Lord's sepulchre, who have devoted themselves to its rescue from the Muslims. 'It is your desire to wrest Ailia [Jerusalem] from the Arabs. Wherefore Christ allowed your "carcasses to be scattered in the wilderness" (Hebrews 3.17), knowing that [His] Sepulchre would be a cause of trouble and that possession of Constantinople would become an issue'.[83] He makes clear what he means by this a little further on: 'Not so long ago you were driven from Jerusalem by the Arab. Does that mean that the Arabs are stronger in their faith than your church and its leader? But the Scythian and the Bulgarian also overcame you and slaughtered you. Does that mean that they are holier than you?'[84] This is the clearest expression of an idea, which began to emerge after the fall of Jerusalem to Saladin. It revealed that the crusade was an enterprise, which was not pleasing to God; which in Sir Steven Runciman's words was 'nothing more than a long act of intolerance in the name of God, which is the sin against the Holy Ghost'.[85] All this was to be confirmed by the sack of Constantinople in 1204.

It was accompanied by a deep contempt for the wearing of the cross, which is denounced in the following terms by Niketas Choniates:

Still more [to blame] were those who bore the cross on their shoulders, who had oft-times sworn by it and by holy scripture to pass through Christian lands without spilling blood, neither nodding to the left nor inclining to the right, and to take up arms against the Saracens and to stain their swords purple in their blood; those [they were] who were going to take Jerusalem by storm, [having sworn an oath] not to marry or to have sex with women, while they bore the cross on their shoulders, because they were consecrated to God and were ready to follow in his footsteps. They were exposed as frauds. Seeking to avenge the Holy Sepulchre they raged openly against Christ and criminally encompassed the destruction of the Cross with the cross they bore on their backs![86]

These were the bitter words of a man who had once admired the crusade ideal, but which to his dismay proved to be entirely false. Choniates's words were echoed by Nicholas Mesarites, who concluded his account of the sack of Constantinople as follows: 'Such was the reverence displayed towards the things of God by those, who bore the cross of our Lord on their shoulder!'[87] He also took to task those 'who bear our Lord's cross on their shoulders' for a completely different reason. He accused them of persevering with Jewish customs, despite their claim to have abolished them. In justification they could only offer their oath 'by the holy sepulchre', which to Mesarites's way of thinking was tantamount to death to the Jews.[88] 'By the holy sepulchre' was the battle cry of the armies of the Latin Empire of Constantinople.[89] Mesarites was therefore employing sarcasm as a way of underlying how nonsensical the ideal of the crusade had become in Byzantine eyes.

Admittedly, it took the sack of Constantinople to bring out the significance of the fall of Jerusalem to Saladin. It was only after 1204 that the Byzantines became critical of the ideas and practices, which sustained the crusade. In his 'Griefs against the Latins', Constantine Stilbes, the bishop of Kyzikos, presented Latin Christianity in a new light.[90] It had been perverted by its espousal and promotion of war, at the heart of which was the crusade.[91] He pointed to the use of indulgences, which made possible the forgiveness of not only past sins and crimes, but also those still to be committed.[92] He pointed to the way those dying in battle were supposed to go directly to paradise, which may have had no canonical foundation, but was widely believed by those participating in the crusades.[93] He also claimed that bishops sprinkled holy water over naked youths, which turned them into invincible warriors. This sounds like a garbled version of the making of a knight.[94] Constantine Stilbes devoted a section of his treatise to the excesses of the crusaders during the sack of Constantinople. He paid special attention to one bishop carrying the sign of the cross, who had a prominent part to play in the storming of the city.[95] This was proof, if proof was needed, of the perversion of Latin Christianity. It was something picked up by Nicholas Mesarites, when he observed: 'Thus did their own bishops teach them to behave! What name could you give them? Bishop-soldiers or warrior-bishops?'[96]

To the fall of Jerusalem to Saladin, the ideal of the crusade not only had the general approval of Byzantine opinion, but also provided a framework for the co-operation of Byzantium and the crusader states. Though it took time to articulate the precise meaning of the fall of Jerusalem in 1187, the difficulties encountered by Isaac II Angelos in his handling of the Third Crusade revealed in a practical way the loss of understanding and trust between crusader and Byzantine now that Jerusalem was gone. However, it was only with the crusader conquest of Constantinople that the true importance of the fall of Jerusalem for Byzantium's relations with the West became apparent. Without Jerusalem, the Byzantines were unwilling to credit the crusade with any moral force. In retrospect, the loss of Jerusalem magnified the enormity of what had been perpetrated in 1204 and convinced Byzantine opinion that the crusade was a work of evil. It explains why the Byzantines were loath to accept Latin rule. It explains too why, much later, Michael VIII Palaiologos found it more or less impossible to persuade Byzantine opinion of the legitimacy of co-operation with the papacy within the framework of the crusade.

NOTES

1 See A. Kolia-Dermitzaki, *Ο βυζαντινός <ιερός πόλεμος>. Η έννοια και η προβολή του θρησκευτικού πολέμου στο Βυζάντιο* (Athens: S.D. Vasilopoulos, 1991); T.M. Kolbaba, 'Fighting for Christianity: Holy War in the Byzantine Empire', *Byzantion*, 68 (1998), 194–221; P. Stephenson, '"About the Emperor Nikephoros and How He Leaves his Bones in Bulgaria". A context for the controversial *Chronicle of 811*', *Dumbarton Oaks Papers*, 60 (2006), 87–109; P. Stephenson, 'Religious Services for Byzantine Soldiers and the Possibility of Martyrdom ca. 400-ca.1000', in *Just Wars, Holy Wars and Jihad*, ed. S.H. Hashmi (Oxford: Oxford University Press, 2012), 25–46; esp. I. Stouraitis, 'Jihad and Crusade: Byzantine Positions Towards the Notions of Holy War', *Byzantina Symmeikta*, 21 (2011), 11–63, for a survey of earlier literature.

2 *Le traité sur la guerrilla de l'empereur Nicéphore Phocas*, ed. G. Dagron and H. Mihăescu (Paris, 1986), 110.35–38.

3 A.P. Kazhdan, 'The Aristocracy and the Imperial Ideal', in *The Byzantine Aristocracy IX to XIII centuries*, ed. M.J. Angold [BAR International Series 221] (Oxford: BAR, 1984), 43–57.

4 H. Hagenmayer, *Die Kreuzzugsbrief aus den Jahren 1088–1100* (Innsbruck: Wagner'sche Universitäts-Buchhandlung, 1901), no. XI.

5 Anna Comnena, *Alexiad*, ed. D.R. Reinsch and A. Kambylis [CFHB, ser. Berol. 40] (Berlin and New York: De Gruyter, 2001), XI, vii, 4: 343.72.

6 P. Magdalino, 'The Pen of the Aunt: Echoes of the Mid-twelfth Century in the *Alexiad*', in *Anna Komnene and her Times*, ed. T. Gouma-Peterson (New York and London: Garland, 2000), 24–9.

7 Alicia J. Simpson, *Niketas Choniates: A Historiographical Study* [Oxford Studies in Byzantium] (Oxford: Oxford University Press, 2013), 316–18.

8 P.E. Walker, 'The "Crusade" of John Tzimiskes', *Byzantion*, 47 (1977), 301–27.

9 M. Canard, 'La destruction de l'église de la Résurrection par le Calife Hākim et l'histoire de la descente du feu sacré', *Byzantion*, 35 (1965), 16–43.

10 M. Biddle, *The Tomb of Christ* (Stroud: Sutton, 1999), 74–88; D. Pringle, *The Churches of the Crusader Kingdom of Jerusalem*: III – *The City of Jerusalem* (Cambridge: Cambridge University Press, 2007), 10–12.

11 J. Pahlitzsch, 'The Greek Orthodox Church in the First Kingdom of Jerusalem (1099–1187)', in *Patterns of the Past; Prospects for the Future: The Christian Heritage in the Holy Land*, ed. Th. Hummel et al. (London: Melisende, 1999), 195–207.

12 A.-M. Talbot, 'Byzantine Pilgrimage to the Holy Land from the Eighth to the Fifteenth Century', in *The Sabaite Heritage in the Orthodox Church from the Fifth Century to the Present*, ed. J. Patrich [Orientalia Lovaniensia Analecta, 98] (Louvain: Peeters, 2001), 96–110.

13 Pringle, *Crusader Churches*, I, nos 77–9; A. Jotischky, 'Greek Orthodox and Latin Monasticism around Mar Saba under Crusader Rule', in Patrich, *Sabaite Heritage*, 85–96.

14 P. Magdalino, 'L'église du Phare et les reliques de la Passion à Constantinople (viie/viiie–xiiie siècles)', in *Byzance et les reliques de Christ*, ed. J. Durand and B. Flusin [Monographies, 17] (Paris: Association des amis du centre de recherché et d'histoire et civilisation de Byzance, 2004), 15–30; A. Lidov, 'The Imperial Pharos Chapel as the Holy Sepulchre', in *Jerusalem as Narrative Space*, ed. A. Hoffmann and G. Wolf (Leiden and Boston: Brill, 2012), 63–103. Cf. E. Patlagean, 'La double terre sainte de Byzance. Autour du XIIe siècle', *Annales HSS*, 49/2 (1994), 459–69.

15 Niketas Choniates, Χρονικὴ Διήγησις, ed. J.L. van Dieten 222 [CFHB, ser. Berol., 11] (Berlin and New York: De Gruyter, 1975), 222.80.

16 K.N. Ciggaar, 'Une description de Constantinople dans le Tarragonensis 55', *Revue des études byzantines*, 53 (1995), 123.62–3.

17 K.N. Ciggaar, 'Une description anonyme de Constantinople du XIIe siècle', *Revue des études byzantines*, 31 (1973), 340–1; K.N. Ciggaar, 'Une description de Constantinople traduite par un pelerin anglais', *Revue des études byzantines*, 34 (1976), 245–6; M. Bacci, 'Relics of the Pharos Chapel: A View from the Latin West', in *Eastern Christian Relics*, ed. A. Lidov (Moscow: Progress-traditsija, 2003), 234–48.

18 C.H. Haskins, 'A Canterbury Monk at Constantinople, c. 1090', *English Historical Review*, 25 (1910), 293–5.

19 J.P. Migne, *Patrologia graeca* (Paris: J.P. Migne, 1865), 145, 548C.

20 P. Magdalino, *The Empire of Manuel I Komnenos, 1143–1180* (Cambridge: Cambridge University Press, 1993), 242–3.

21 A. Heisenberg, *Nikolaos Mesarites: Die Palastrevolution des Johannes Komnenos* (Würzburg: H. Stürtz, 1907), 29.25, 34.29.

22 K. Varzos, Ἡ Γενεαλογία τῶν Κομνηνῶν [Βυζαντινὰ κείμενα καὶ μελέται, 20α](Thessaloniki: Centre of Byzantine Studies, 1984), I, no. 36, 238–54.

23 E. Kurtz, 'Unedierte Text aus der Zeit des Kaisers Johannes Komnenos', *Byzantinische Zeitschrift*, 16 (1907), no.4, 107–8; W. Horänder, *Theodoros Prodromos: historische Gedichte* [Wiener byzantinische Studien, 11] (Vienna: Österreichische Akadamie der Wissenschaften, 1974), no. xl, 391–3.

24 *Nicephori Basilacae orationes et epistolai*, ed. A. Garzya (Leipzig: Teubner, 1984), no. 3, 567 12–17.

25 Ibid., no. 2, 46–7.

26 Choniates, 42.26–31.

27 *Ioannes Cinnami epitome: rerum ab Ioanne et Alexio Comnenis Gestarum*, ed. A. Meineke (Bonn: E. Weber, 1836), 25; *Deeds of John and Manuel Comnenus*, tr. C.M. Brand (New York: Columbia University Press, 1976), 28–9. Cf. *Michel Italikos: Lettres et Discours*, ed. P. Gautier [Archives de l'Orient Chrétien, 14] (Paris: Institut français d'études byzantines, 1972), no. 44, 290.1–6.

28 See R.-J. Lilie, *Byzantium and the Crusader States 1096–1204* (Oxford: Clarendon Press, 1993), 142–221.

29 *Fontes rerum Byzantinarum*: fasc.1–2 – *rhetorum saeculi XII orationes politicae*, ed. W. Regel (Petrograd: Eggers and I. Glasunof, 1892 [repr. Leipzig, 1982]), 30.6–13.

30 See L.-A. Hunt, 'Art and Colonialism: The Mosaics of the Church of the Nativity in Bethlehem (1169) and the Problem of "Crusader Art"', *Dumbarton Oaks Papers*, 45(1991), 69–85; Pringle, *Crusader Churches*, I, 137–56; A. Jotischky, 'Manuel Comnenus and the Reunion of the Churches: The Evidence of the Conciliar Mosiacs in the Church of the Nativity in Bethlehem', *Levant*, 26 (1994), 207–24.

31 L.-A. Hunt, 'Art and Colonialism', 81.

32 P. Classen, 'Das Konzil von Konstantinopel und die Lateiner', *Byzantinische Zeitschrift*, 48(1955), 339–68; M.J. Angold, *Church and Society in Byzantium under the Comneni 1081–1261* (Cambridge: Cambridge University Press, 1995), 83–6.

33 C. Mango, 'The Conciliar Edict of 1166', *Dumbarton Oaks Papers*, 17 (1963), 324.5–8.

34 Pringle, *Crusader Churches*, I, 146.

35 A. Jotischky, *The Perfection of Solitude: Hermits and Monks in the Crusader States* (University Park PA: Pennsylvania State University Press, 1995), 65–100; A. Weyl Carr, 'The Mural Paintings of Abu Ghosh and the Patronage of Manuel Comnenus in the Holy Land', in *Crusader Art in the Twelfth Century*, ed. J. Folda [BAR Int. Ser. 152] (Oxford: BAR, 1982), 215–43.

36 J.P. Migne, *Patrologia graeca* (Paris: J.P. Migne, 1864), 133, 928–61; ed. I. Troitskii in *Pravoslavnii Palestinskii Sbornik*, 8 (1889), 1–28; trans. J. Wilkinson, *Jerusalem Pilgrimage 1099–1185* [Hakluyt Society, ser.ii, 167] (London: Hakluyt Society, 1988), 315–36.

37 For the important identification of the author of this text, traditionally named John Phokas, with John Doukas, see Ch. Messis, 'Littérature, voyage et politique au XIIe siècle: *L'ekphrasis des lieux saints* de Jean Phokas', *Byzantinoslavica*, 69 (2011), Suppl., 146–66. Cf. A.F. Stone, 'The *Grand Hetaireiarch* John Doukas: The Career of a Twelfth-century Soldier and Diplomat', *Byzantion*, 69 (1999), 146–64.

38 *Eustathii Thessalonicensis Opera Minora: magnam partem inedita*, ed P. Wirth [CFHB, ser. Berol., xxxii] (Berlin and New York: De Gruyter, 2000), 198.15–19.

39 Migne, *PG* 133, 932D (§6.1–2); ed. Troitskii, 5.7–8; trans. Wilkinson, 318.

40 Migne, *PG* 133, 936B (§10.7), 957D (§27.14); ed. Troitskii, 7.23–31, 25–6; trans. Wilkinson, 320, 333–4.

41 Migne, *PG* 133, 952D–953B (§23.4–13), 960D–961A (§29.4–6); ed. Troitskii, 21–2, 27.15–23; trans. Wilkinson, 330–1, 335.

42 Migne, *PG* 133, 944B (§14.18); ed. Troitskii, 13.21–23; trans. Wilkinson, 324.

43 Migne, *PG* 133, 957A–B (§27.6); ed. Troitskii, 24.18–24; trans. Wilkinson, 333.

44 Migne, *PG* 133, 952B (§22.1), 956D (§27.3); ed. Troitskii, 20.9–14, 24.1–5; trans. Wilkinson, 329, 332.

45 K. Horna, 'Das Hodoiporikon des Konstantin Manasses', *Byzantinische Zeitschrift*, 13(1904), 313–55 (Text: 325–47); W.J. Aerts, 'A Byzantine Traveller to One of the Crusader States', in *East*

and West in the Crusader States. Context–Contacts–Confrontations, ed. K. Ciggaar and H.G.B. Teule [Orientalia Lovaniensia Analecta, 125] (Louvain: Peeters, 2003), 165–221 (Text: 172–219). Cf. M. Marcovich, 'The *Itinerary* of Constantine Manasses', *Illinois Classical Studies*, 12 (1987), 277–91; É. Malamut, 'Le récit de voyage (*Hodoiporikon*) de Constantin Manassès (1160–1162)', in *Géographes et voyageurs au Moyen Âge* ed. H. Bresc and E. Tixier du Mesnil (Paris: Presses universitaires de Paris Ouest, 2010), 253–73.

46 P. Magdalino, 'In Search of the Byzantine Courtier: Leo Choiosphaktes and Constantine Manasses', in *Byzantine Court Culture from 829 to 1204*, ed. H. Maguire (Washington DC: Dumbarton Oaks, 1997), 161–4. Cf. I. Nilsson, 'Constantine Manasses, Odysseus, and the Cyclops: On Byzantine Appreciation of Pagan Art in the Twelfth Century', *Byzantinoslavica*, 69 (2011), Suppl. 123–36.

47 Cf. A. Külzer, 'Konstantinos Manasses und Johannes Phokas – zwei byzantinische Orientsreisende des 12. Jahrhunderts', in *Erkundung und Beschreibung der Welt. Zur Poetik der Reise- und Länderberichte*, ed. X. von Ertzdorff and G. Gieseman [Chloe (Beihefte zum Daphnis), 34] (Amsterdam and New York: Rodopi, 2003), 185–209.

48 Constantine Manasses, *Hodoiporikon*, §I, vv.218–93: ed. Horna, 331–3; ed. Aerts, 186–90.

49 Ibid., §I, vv.286–91; ed. Horna, 333; ed. Aerts, 190.

50 Ibid., §I, vv.294–330; ed. Horna, 333–4; ed. Aerts, 190–2.

51 Ibid., §I, vv.331–6; ed. Horna, 334–5; ed. Aerts, 192.

52 Nicholas Mesarites, *Epitaphios*, ed. A. Heisenberg, 'Neue Quellen zur Geschichte des lateinischen Kaisertums und der Kirchenunion I', *Sitzungsberichte der bayerischen Akademie der Wissenschaften,* philos.-philol und hist. Klasse, 1922, Abh.5 (= A. Heisenberg, *Quellen und Studien zur spätbyzantinischen Geschichte* (London: Variorum, 1973), no. II), §12, 25–6.

53 Angold, *Church and Society*, 413.

54 Mesarites, *Epitaphios*, I, §13, 27–8.

55 R.B. Rose, 'The *Vita* of St Leontius and its account of his visit to Palestine during the Crusader period', *Proche Orient Chrétien*, 35 (1985), 238–57; M. Kaplan, 'Un patriarche byzantin dans le royaume latin de Jérusalem: Léontios', in *Chemins d'Outremer. Études d'histoire sur la Méditerranée médievale offerts `a Michel Balard* [Byzantina Sorbonensia, 20], ed. D. Coulon et al. (Paris: Publications de la Sorbonne, 2004), II, 475–88.

56 D. Tsougarakis, *The Life of Leontios, Patriarch of Jerusalem* (Leiden, New York and Cologne: Brill, 1993), 1–11.

57 *Life of Leontios*, §88, 138.1–4.

58 Ibid., §84, 1–5.

59 Ibid., §85, 132–34.1–23.

60 Ibid., §85, 134.23–36.

61 Ibid., §87,134–36.6–11.

62 Ibid., §87, 136.11–43.

63 C. Galatariotou, *The Making of a Saint: The Life, Times and Sanctification of Neophytos the Recluse* (Cambridge: Cambridge University Press, 1991), 206–7.

64 Cf. A. Jotischsky, 'The Fate of the Orthodox Church in Jerusalem at the End of the Twelfth Century', in Hummel et al., *Patterns of the Past*, 179–94.

65 'Imâd ad-Dîn al-Isfahânî, *Conquête de la Syrie et de la Palestine par Saladin*, trans. H. Massé (Paris: Paul Geuthner, 1972), 59.

66 C.M. Brand, *Byzantium Confronts the West 1180–1204* (Cambridge, MA: Harvard University Press, 1968), 114–16.

67 Choniates, 531.71–74; M.C. Lyons and D.E.P. Jackson, *Saladin: The Politics of the Holy War* [University of Cambridge Oriental Publications, 30] (Cambridge: Cambridge University Press, 1982), 251–2.

68 C.M. Brand, 'The Byzantines and Saladin, 1185–1192: Opponents of the Third Crusade', *Speculum*, 37 (1962), 176–81, but for a more nuanced reading of the situation, see S. Neocleous, 'The Byzantines and Saladin: Opponents of the Third Crusade?', *Crusades*, 9 (2010), 87–106;

S. Neocleous, 'The Byzantines and Saladin: Some Further Arguments', *Al-Masaq*, 25 (2013), 204–21.

69 Choniates, 404–7. Cf. D.G. Angelov, 'Domestic Opposition to Byzantium's Alliance with Saladin: Niketas Choniates and his Epiphany Oration of 1190', *Byzantine and Modern Greek Studies*, 30 (2006), 44–68.

70 J. Darrouzès, 'Documents byzantins sur la primauté romaine', *Revue des études Byzantines*, 23 (1965), 51–59. The first instance of this usage seems to have been by Niketas Seides in 1112.

71 Bahâ' al-Din Ibn Shaddad, *The Rare and Excellent History of Saladin*, trans. D.S. Richards [Crusader Text in Translation] (Aldershot and Burlington VT: Ashgate, 2001), 121–2,

72 Ibid., 201–2.

73 'Imâd ad-Dîn, 244–5.

74 Choniates, 416–17.

75 Ibid., 301–2.

76 Brand, *Byzantium Confronts the West*, 176–88.

77 Angold, *Church and Society*, 122–4.

78 J. Darrouzès, *Georges et Dèmètrios Tornikès Lettres et discours* (Paris, 1970), 341.20–26.

79 Choniates, 417.66.

80 Ibid., 576.89–95.

81 *Life of Leontios*, §87, 136.14–15.

82 Archimandrit Arsenij, *Tri stat'i neizvestnago grechescago pisatelia nachala XIII veka* (Moscow: A.P. Spegirevoj, 1892), 84–115.

83 Ibid., 85.20–28.

84 Ibid., 90.10–20.

85 S. Runciman, *A History of the Crusades*: III – *The Kingdom of Acre* (Cambridge: Cambridge University Press, 1954), 480.

86 Choniates, 575–6.

87 Nicholas Mesarites, *Epitaphios*, I, 47.1–2.

88 Nicholas Mesarites, *Katechetikos Logos*, III, 27.22–29.

89 Henri de Valenciennes, *Histoire de l'empereur Henri de Constantinople*, ed. J. Longnon (Paris: Paul Geuthner, 1948), §539.

90 J. Darrouzès, 'La mémoire de Constantin Stilbès contre les Latins', *Revue des études Byzantines*, 21 (1963), 50–100. See T.M. Kolbaba, *The Byzantine Lists: Errors of the Latins* (Urbana and Chicago: University of Illinois Press, 2000), 32–87.

91 Angold, *Church and Society*, 516–17.

92 Stilbes, 69.133–42.

93 Ibid., 77.273–75.

94 Ibid., 67.106–109.

95 Ibid., 84.400–403.

96 Nicholas Mesarites, *Epitaphios*, I, 47.2–4.

REFERENCES

Sources

Anna Comnena (2001) *Alexiad*, ed. D.R. Reinsch and A. Kambylis [CFHB, ser. Berol. 40] Berlin and New York

Archimandrit Arsenij (1892) *Tri stat'i neizvestnago grechescago pisatelia nachala XIII veka*, Moscow

Ciggaar, K.N. (1973) 'Une description anonyme de Constantinople du XIIe siècle', *Revue des etudes byzantines* 31: 335–54

——— (1976) 'Une description de Constantinople traduite par un pelerin anglais', *Revue des* études *byzantines* 34: 211–67

———— (1995) 'Une description de Constantinople dans le Tarragonensis 55', *Revue des* études *byzantines* 53: 117–40

Cinnamus (1836) *Ioannes Cinnami epitome: rerum ab Ioanne et Alexio Comnenis Gestarum*, ed. A. Meineke, Bonn

———— (1976) *Deeds of John and Manuel Comnenus*, trans. C.M. Brand, New York

Dagron, G. and Mihaescu, H. (1986) *Le traité sur la guerrilla de l'empereur Nicéphore Phocas*, ed. G. Paris

Darrouzès, J. (1963) 'La mémoire de Constantin Stilbès contre les Latins', *Revue des etudes byzantines*, 21: 50–100

———— (1970) *Georges et Dèmètrios Tornikès Lettres et discours*, Paris

Garzya, A. (1984) *Nicephori Basilacae orationes et epistolai*, Leipzig: Teubner

Gautier, P. (1972) *Michel Italikos: Lettres et Discours* [Archives de l'Orient Chrétien, 14] Paris

Hagenmayer, H. (1901) *Die Kreuzzugsbrief aus den Jahren 1088–1100*, Innsbruck

Haskins, C.H. (1910) 'A Canterbury Monk at Constantinople, c. 1090', *English Historical Review* 25: 293–5

Henri de Valenciennes (1948) *Histoire de l'empereur Henri de Constantinople*, ed. J. Longnon, Paris

Horänder, W. (1974) *Theodoros Prodromos: historische Gedichte* [Wiener byzantinische Studien, 11] Vienna

Kurtz, E. (1907) 'Unedierte Text aus der Zeit des Kaisers Johannes Komnenos', *Byzantinische Zeitschrift* 16: 69–119

Manasses, Constantine (1904) 'Das Hodoiporikon des Konstantin Manasses', ed. K. Horna, *Byzantinische Zeitschrift*, 13: 313–55

———— (2003) 'A Byzantine Traveller to One of the Crusader States', ed. W.J. Aerts, in *East and West in the Crusader States. Context – Contacts-Confrontations*, ed. K. Ciggaar and H.G.B. Teule [Orientalia Lovaniensia Analecta, 125] Louvain, 165–221

Mango, C. (1963) 'The Conciliar Edict of 1166', *Dumbarton Oaks Papers* 17: 317–30

Massé H. (1972) *'Imâd ad-Dîn al-Isfahânî, Conquête de la Syrie et de la Palestine par Saladin*, Paris

Niketas Choniates (1975) Χρονικὴ Διήγησις, ed. J.L. van Dieten 222 [CFHB, ser. Berol., 11] Berlin and New York

Nicholas Mesarites (1907) *Die Palastrevolution des Johannes Komnenos*, ed. A. Heisenberg, Würzburg

———— (1922) *Epitaphios*, ed. A. Heisenberg, 'Neue Quellen zur Geschichte des lateinischen *Akademie* Kaisertums und der Kirchenunion I', *Sitzungsberichte der bayerischen der Wissenschaften*, philos.-philol und hist. Klasse, 1922, Abh.5 (= A. Heisenberg, *Quellen und Studien zur spätbyzantinischen Geschichte*, London, 1973)

———— (1923) *Katechetikos Logos*, ed. A. Heisenberg, 'Neue Quellen zur Geschichte des lateinischen Kaisertums und der Kirchenunion III', *Sitzungsberichte der bayerischen der Wissenschaften*, philos.-philol und hist. Klasse, 1923, Abh.3 (= A. Heisenberg, *Quellen und Studien zur spätbyzantinischen Geschichte*, London, 1973)

Phokas (Doukas), John (1864) *Ekphrasis*, in J.P. Migne (ed.), *Patrologia graeca* 133, Paris, 928–61

———— (1889) *Ekphrasis*, ed. I. Troitskii, *Pravoslavnii Palestinskii Sbornik*, 8: 1–28

———— (1998) *A General Description*, trans. J. Wilkinson, *Jerusalem Pilgrimage 1099–1185* [Hakluyt Society, ser.ii, 167], London, 315–36

Regel, W. (1892) *Fontes rerum Byzantinarum*: fasc.1–2 – *rhetorum saeculi XII orationes politicae*, Petrograd

Richards, D.S. (2001) *Bahâ' al-Din Ibn Shaddad, The Rare and Excellent History of Saladin* [Crusader Text in Translation], Aldershot and Burlington VT

Tsougarakis, D. (1993) *The Life of Leontios, Patriarch of Jerusalem*, Leiden, New York and Cologne

Wirth, P. (2000) *Eustathii Thessalonicensis Opera Minora: magnam partem inedita* [CFHB, ser. Berol., xxxii], Berlin and New York

Secondary literature

Angelov, D.G. (2006) 'Domestic Opposition to Byzantium's alliance with Saladin: Niketas Choniates and his Epiphany oration of 1190', *Byzantine and Modern Greek Studies* 30: 44–68.

Angold, M.J. (1995) *Church and Society in Byzantium under the Comneni 1081–1261*, Cambridge.

Bacci, M. (2003) 'Relics of the Pharos Chapel: A View from the Latin West', in *Eastern Christian Relics*, ed. A. Lidov, Moscow, 234–48.

Biddle, M. (1999) *The Tomb of Christ*, Stroud.

Brand, C.M. (1962) 'The Byzantines and Saladin, 1185–1192: Opponents of the Third Crusade', *Speculum* 37: 167–81.

———— (1968) *Byzantium Confronts the West 1180–1204*, Cambridge MA.

Canard, M. (1965) 'La destruction de l'église de la Résurrection par le Calife Hākim et l'histoire de la descente du feu sacré', *Byzantion* 35: 16–43.

Classen, P. (1955) 'Das Konzil von Konstantinopel und die Lateiner', *Byzantinische Zeitschrift* 48: 339–68.

Darrouzès, J. (1965) 'Documents byzantins sur la primauté romaine', *Revue des* études *Byzantines* 23: 42–88.

Galatariotou, C. (1991) *The Making of a Saint: The Life, Times and Sanctification of Neophytos the Recluse*, Cambridge.

Hunt, L.A. (1991) 'Art and Colonialism: The Mosaics of the Church of the Nativity in Bethlehem (1169) and the Problem of "Crusader Art"', *Dumbarton Oaks Papers* 45: 69–85.

Jotischky, A. (1994) 'Manuel Comnenus and the Reunion of the Churches: The Evidence of the Conciliar Mosiacs in the Church of the Nativity in Bethlehem', *Levant*, 26: 207–24.

Jotischky, A. (1995) *The Perfection of Solitude: Hermits and Monks in the Crusader States*, University Park PA.

———— (1999) 'The Fate of the Orthodox Church in Jerusalem at the End of the Twelfth Century', in *Patterns of the Past; Prospects for the Future: The Christian Heritage in the Holy Land*, ed. Th. Hummel et al., London, 179–94.

———— (2001) 'Greek Orthodox and Latin Monasticism around Mar Saba under crusader rule', in *The Sabaite Heritage in the Orthodox Church from the Fifth Century to the Present*, ed. J. Patrich [Orientalia Lovaniensia Analecta, 98], Louvain, 85–96.

Kaplan, M. (2004) 'Un patriarche byzantin dans le royaume latin de Jérusalem: Léontios', in *Chemins d'Outremer. Études d'histoire sur la Méditerranée médievale offerts `a Michel Balard* [Byzantina Sorbonensia, 20], ed. D. Coulon et al., Paris, II, 475–88.

Kazhdan, A.P. (1984) 'The Aristocracy and the Imperial Ideal', in *The Byzantine Aristocracy IX to XIII centuries*, ed. M.J. Angold [BAR International Series 221] Oxford, 43–57.

Kolbaba, T.M. (1998) 'Fighting for Christianity: Holy War in the Byzantine Empire', *Byzantion* 68: 194–221.

———— (2000) *The Byzantine Lists: Errors of the Latins*, Urbana/Chicago.

Kolia-Dermitzaki, A. (1991) Ο βυζαντινός <ιερός πόλεμος>.Η έννοια και η προβολή του θρησκευτικού πολέμου στο Βυζάντιο, Athens.

Külzer, A. (2003) 'Konstantinos Manasses und Johannes Phokas – zwei byzantinische Orientsreisende des 12. Jahrhunderts', in *Erkundung und Beschreibung der Welt. Zur Poetik der Reise- und Länderberichte*, ed. X. von Ertzdorff and G.Gieseman [Chloe (Beihefte zum Daphnis), 34], Amsterdam and New York, 185–209.

Lidov, A. (2012) 'The Imperial Pharos Chapel as the Holy Sepulchre', in *Jerusalem as Narrative Space*, ed. A. Hoffmann and G. Wolf, Leiden and Boston, 63–103.

Lilie, R.J. (1993) *Byzantium and the Crusader States 1096–1204*, Oxford.

Lyons M.C. and Jackson, D.E.P. (1982) *Saladin: The Politics of the Holy War* [University of Cambridge Oriental Publications, 30], Cambridge.

Magdalino, P. (1993) *The Empire of Manuel I Komnenos, 1143–1180*, Cambridge.

—— (1997) 'In Search of the Byzantine Courtier: Leo Choiosphaktes and Constantine Manasses', in *Byzantine Court Culture from 829 to 1204*, ed. H. Maguire, Washington DC, 141–6.

—— (2000) 'The Pen of the Aunt: Echoes of the Mid-twelfth Century in the *Alexiad*', in *Anna Komnene and her Times*, ed. T. Gouma-Peterson, New York and London, 15–43.

—— (2004) 'L'église du Phare et les reliques de la Passion à Constantinople (viie/viiie-xiiie siè-cles', in *Byzance et les reliques de Christ*, ed. J. Durand and B. Flusin, Paris, 15–30.

Malamut, É. (2010) 'Le récit de voyage (*Hodoiporikon*) de Constantin Manassès (1160–1162)', in *Géographes et voyageurs au Moyen Âge* ed. H. Bresc and E. Tixier du Mesnil, Paris, 253–73.

Marcovich, M. (1987) 'The *Itinerary* of Constantine Manasses', *Illinois Classical Studies*, 12: 277–91.

Messis, Ch. (2011) 'Littérature, voyage et politique au XIIe siècle: *L'ekphrasis des lieux saints* de Jean Phokas', *Byzantinoslavica*, 69, Suppl.: 146–66.

Neocleous, S. (2010) 'The Byzantines and Saladin: Opponents of the Third Crusade?', *Crusades*, 9: 87–106.

—— (2013) 'The Byzantines and Saladin: Some Further Arguments', *Al-Masaq*, 25: 204–21.

Nilsson, I. (2011) 'Constantine Manasses, Odysseus, and the Cyclops: On Byzantine Appreciation of Pagan Art in the Twelfth Century', *Byzantinoslavica*, 69 Suppl.: 123–36.

Pahlitzsch, J. (1999) 'The Greek Orthodox Church in the First Kingdom of Jerusalem (1099–1187)', in *Patterns of the Past; Prospects for the Future: The Christian Heritage in the Holy Land*, ed. Th. Hummel et al., London, 195–207.

Patlagean, E. (1994) 'La double terre sainte de Byzance. Autour du XIIe siècle', *Annales HSS*, 49: 459–69.

Pringle, D. (1993–2009) *The Churches of the Crusader Kingdom of Jerusalem*, 4 vols, Cambridge.

Rose, R.B. (1985) 'The *Vita* of St Leontius and Its Account of his Visit to Palestine During the Crusader Period', *Proche Orient Chrétien*, 35: 238–57.

Runciman, S. (1952–54) *A History of the Crusades*, 3 vols, Cambridge.

Simpson, A.J. (2013) *Niketas Choniates: A Historiographical Study* [Oxford Studies in Byzantium], Oxford.

Stephenson, P. (2006) '"About the Emperor Nikephoros and How He Leaves his Bones in Bulgaria". A Context for the Controversial *Chronicle of 811*', *Dumbarton Oaks Papers* 60, 87–109.

—— (2012) 'Religious Services for Byzantine Soldiers and the Possibility of Martyrdom ca. 400–ca.1000', in *Just Wars, Holy Wars and Jihad*, ed. S.H. Hashmi, Oxford, 25–46.

Stone, A.F. (1999) 'The *Grand Hetaireiarch* John Doukas: The Career of a Twelfth-Century Soldier and Diplomat', *Byzantion*, 69: 146–64.

Stouraitis, I. (2011) 'Jihad and Crusade: Byzantine Positions Towards the Notions of Holy War', *Byzantina Symmeikta* 21: 11–63.

Talbot, A.-M. (2001) 'Byzantine Pilgrimage to the Holy Land from the Eighth to the Fifteenth Century', in *The Sabaite Heritage in the Orthodox Church from the Fifth Century to the Present*, ed. J. Patrich [Orientalia Lovaniensia Analecta, 98], Louvain, 96–110.

Varzos, K. (1984) Ἡ Γενεαλογία τῶν Κομνηνῶν [Βυζαντινὰ κείμενα καὶ μελέται, 20], Thessaloniki, 2 vols.

Walker, P.E. (1977) 'The "Crusade" of John Tzimiskes', *Byzantion* 47: 301–27.

Weyl Carr, A. (1982) 'The Mural Paintings of Abu Ghosh and the Patronage of Manuel Comnenus in the Holy Land', in *Crusader Art in the Twelfth Century*, ed. J. Folda [BAR Int. Ser. 152], Oxford, 215–43.

PART V

MEETING ISLAM

———•◆•———

CHAPTER NINETEEN

AN ILLUSION OF IGNORANCE? THE MUSLIMS OF THE MIDDLE EAST AND THE FRANKS BEFORE THE CRUSADES

———•◆•———

Niall Christie

INTRODUCTION

A reader of the contemporary Muslim sources for the First Crusade and its aftermath (1095–1146) would likely conclude that one of the major reasons that the Muslim writers found the crusaders to be such intimidating foes was the fact that they knew almost nothing about them before their arrival in the Levant. It seems that the crusaders exploded onto the scene, sweeping the shocked Muslims before them, while the Muslims were themselves mystified and confused about why the Franks had seen fit to invade their territories. Some authors attributed the crusaders' activities to greed for plunder or territory, while others linked them in a basic way to the Franks' Christian faith, with their campaigns being undertaken either as a form of revenge for the abuse of Christian pilgrims to the East or an attempt to spread Christianity by force. Only one author of the time, a Damascene jurisprudent named 'Alī ibn Ṭāhir al-Sulamī (d. 1106), seems to have been aware that the Franks were fighting a *jihād*, here understood in its aspect as a formal military campaign for their religion, seen by al-Sulamī as being analogous to the Muslim military *jihād* doctrine (Christie, 2006). Al-Sulamī's description of the motives of the Franks, which is found in his *Kitāb al-Jihād* (the Book of the *Jihād*), a treatise on the *jihād* in all its aspects that he composed in public over the course of the year 1105, has been described as 'remarkable', and indicative of 'an understanding, probably unique at this early stage of the Crusades, of what the Franks were planning to do' (Christie, 2006: 71; Hillenbrand, 1999: 71).

Yet how far was al-Sulamī's recognition of the impetus behind the First Crusade really indicative of an unusual level of insight, and how far is it actually the case that the Muslim authors contemporary with the first decades of the crusading period knew more in general about the Franks than they reveal in their works? In this chapter we will contend that while the Muslim writers of the Middle East, and by extension the Muslims of the region as a whole, seem to have known very little about the Franks before their arrival in the Levant, there are elements in the sources that suggest that this apparent ignorance is in fact an illusion, and that other factors led the Muslim authors of the crusading period to avoid providing full descriptions of their enemies. We will then provide some suggestions regarding what these other factors may have been.

311

MUSLIM GEOGRAPHERS' IMAGES
OF THE FRANKS

The principal genre of sources that we have for Muslim knowledge of the Franks from before the crusading period is the Muslim geographical literature, the earliest known examples of which date from the ninth century. It is worth noting from the outset that the Muslim authors who wrote about the Franks before the crusades had a different understanding of the term 'Frank' itself. The Arabic term *ifranj*, along with other variations on the root consonants *f-r-n-j* such as *firanj* or *faranj*, was originally used by the Muslim writers to refer to the inhabitants of, roughly, the area corresponding to the Frankish empire of the Carolingians. As John Tolan has recently observed, it is not clear how the term came to be transformed into one that, by the time of the First Crusade, referred to Europeans in general. Latin sources for the crusade refer to the Christian forces using the overall term *Franci*, even though a limited number of the first crusaders were French; was this a term picked up from the Muslims, or was it one that they already used for themselves, which led the Muslims to adjust the way in which they understood the similar Arabic word *ifranj* (Tolan, 2013: 311)? The scarcity of sources from the time makes it unlikely that this question will ever be fully answered.

In structuring their works, the Muslim geographers followed the model of the second-century Greco-Alexandrian author Ptolemy (*c.* 100–*c.* 170), who divided the world up into seven climes, essentially horizontal bands that enjoyed different climates; the most temperate zones were the third and fourth climes, in which Greek civilisation consequently flourished. The Muslim geographers divided the world similarly, placing their own lands in the temperate third and fourth climes (Hillenbrand, 1999: 268–70). The Franks, however, lived in the frigid sixth clime, the effects of which are illustrated in the following famous passage from *Kitāb al-Tanbīh wa'l-Ishrāf* (The Book of Instruction and Supervision), by the Muslim traveller and geographer 'Alī ibn al-Ḥusayn al-Mas'ūdī (d. 956):

> As for the peoples of the northern region, who of those who reach the north are the ones for whom the sun is far from the zenith, like the Slavs, the Franks and those nations next to them, the sun shines weakly upon them because of their distance from it, cold and damp have overcome their region, and snow and ice come upon them in uninterrupted succession. They have little warm temperament in them; their bodies have become enormous, their humour dry, their morals crude, their intellect stupid and their tongues sluggish. Their colour has become excessively white, to the point of becoming blue, their skins thin, their flesh coarse, their eyes blue in accordance with their colouring, and their hair lank and reddish-brown because of the excess of steam and damp. Their beliefs have no solidity, and this is because of the nature of the cold and the lack of warmth. The ones who are from further north have become overcome with ignorance, dryness of humour and brutishness. This increases in them the further north that they go.
>
> (Al-Mas'ūdī, 1894: 23–4)

Thus the Muslim geographers, like their Greek predecessors, attributed a direct impact on the physical and mental characteristics of the peoples whom they described to the climes in which they lived.

Al-Mas'ūdī's commentary on the Franks, above, is actually relatively copious in comparison to the rather briefer references to them that we see in the works of other Muslim geographers. These writers also show confusion regarding the location of the capital of the

Franks (Paris or Rome), their religion (possibly Christian, possibly the same as that of the Byzantines) and their relationship to the Byzantines (possibly allies, or possibly subjects) (Christie, 1999: 10–27). Examples of knowledge of the Franks' internal affairs are few and far between, though in his other great geographical work, *Murūj al-Dhahab wa Ma'ādin al-Jawhar* (Meadows of Gold and Mines of Gemstone), al-Mas'ūdī presents us with an important exception to the rule:

> The Franks are the strongest of [the] races, the most fearsome and the most numerous. They have the most widespread power and the most numerous cities. They are the best organised, the most obedient to their kings and the most compliant, except that the Galicians [whom al-Mas'ūdī regards as a subspecies of the Franks] are stronger and more harmful than the [other] Franks. One Galician is a match for several Franks.

> All of *Ifranja* is unified in one kingdom. There is no competition between them about that, nor is there any factionalism. The name of the capital of their kingdom at this time is Paris. It is a great city.

Al-Mas'ūdī then provides a partial list of the Frankish kings, which he has apparently drawn from a book that he read in Cairo that had originally been given to the future Umayyad ruler of Spain, al-Ḥakam II (r. 961–76) in 939 or 940 by the bishop of Girona in Catalonia:

> The first of the kings of *Ifranja* was Clovis [r. 481–511]. He was a Zoroastrian, but his wife converted him to Christianity. Her name was Clotild. Then his son Theuderic [r. 511–24] ruled after him. Then Theuderic's son Dagobert ruled after him. Then Dagobert's son Theuderic ruled after him, then after him ruled his brother Carloman. Then his son Charles [probably Charles Martel, *major domo* of the Merovingian kings, 714–41] ruled after him. Then his son Pippin [III, *major domo*, 741–51, king of the Franks, 751–68] ruled after him. Then after him ruled his son Charles [Charlemagne, r. 768–814], who ruled for 26 years, and he was in the days of al-Ḥakam, the ruler of *al-Andalus* [Muslim Iberia, r. 796–822]. After him his children fought each other and fell into disputes until *Ifranja* was ruined because of them. Then Louis, the son of Charles [Louis the Pious, r. 814–40] became the ruler of their kingdom, and he ruled for 28 years and six months, and he was the one who advanced on Tortosa and besieged it.
>
> (Al-Mas'ūdī, 1965–79: II, 145–8)

Al-Mas'ūdī continues to list the Carolingian kings up to the time that he read the book in 947 or 948.

Confused and incomplete as the details of his list may be, al-Mas'ūdī's insight into the affairs of the Franks is strikingly detailed in comparison to the works of his contemporaries. This apparent lack of attention to the Franks in particular, and to Europeans in general, in the Muslim geographical literature led Bernard Lewis, in his seminal work, *The Muslim Discovery of Europe* (first published in 1982), to conclude that despite the conflicts between Muslims and Europeans that took place in various parts of the Mediterranean region in the eighth to tenth centuries, there was 'a complete lack of interest and curiosity among Muslim scholars about what went on beyond the Muslim frontiers in Europe' (Lewis, 2001: 142). Lewis' view has enjoyed considerable influence in the decades since its publication, as is apparent in the publications of a number of scholars, including the early work of the author of this chapter (Christie, 1999: 23–30; Hillenbrand, 1999: 267–74). However, it has been convincingly challenged by a number of scholars, who have re-examined and re-interpreted the source material to demonstrate that Muslim scholars were in fact at times greatly interested in the world outside the *dār al-islām* (Tolan et al., 2013: 17). One work particularly pertinent to the topic of this chapter is Nizar F. Hermes' *The [European] Other in Medieval Arabic Literature and Culture* (2012), in which the author demonstrates, through the use of a wide range of sources, that 'generally speaking there was no shortage of Muslims who cast curious eyes and minds toward Europe and the Europeans' (Hermes, 2012: 174). We will be drawing on a number of the same sources as we seek to uncover the 'hidden' knowledge of the Muslims.

PROBLEMS WITH THE ACCEPTED IMAGE

The two images that al-Mas'ūdī gives us of the Franks are of course markedly different. In the *Tanbīh* he depicts the Franks as brutish, stupid and sluggish of speech, while in the *Murūj* he presents them as fierce fighters who have established a well-organised state with many cities and a powerful capital. While the two passages that we have cited do not *explicitly* contradict each other, they are hard to reconcile with each other. How can we understand this disparity? We are fortunate to have information on the history of these two texts. Al-Mas'ūdī wrote the first draft of his *Murūj* in 943, then revised it twice, in 947 and 956; however, the only version of the text that we have is the version from 947. Meanwhile, al-Mas'ūdī wrote the *Tanbīh* in 955 and revised it in 956 (Pellat, 1991: VI, 785–6; Shboul, 1979: 68–72). What is of note here is that the description of the Franks that seems to be less well informed and more driven by imagination is the one that appears in the *later* text. It would of course be nonsensical to suggest that al-Mas'ūdī's knowledge of the Franks deteriorated over time, so we must seek out other explanations, the most likely of which is that with his account in the *Tanbīh* al-Mas'ūdī intended not to provide an accurate depiction, but rather to contrast the heathen barbarity of the northern peoples with the enlightened civilisation of the Muslims, in a way that echoes the stereotypes of the northern peoples found in the Classical sources upon which the Muslim geographical works were modelled (Hermes, 2012: 49–50). Thus we see polemic trumping any attempt to preserve accuracy. This is of course an important sign that we must be cautious in assuming that the limited depictions of the Franks that we see in the works of the Muslim geographers represent an honest indication of the true extent of their knowledge of them.

Another Muslim geographer makes us similarly suspicious. In his *Mukhtaṣar Kitāb al-Buldān* (Abridgement of the Book of Countries), written in about 903, the Persian scholar Ibn al-Faqīh states, 'The sixth climate consists of *Firanja* and other countries. In it are women whose custom it is to cut off their breasts and cauterise them while they are small, so that they will not grow large' (1967: 6). The influence of the Greek tradition is apparent here, since the women whom the author describes are clearly based on the Amazons of Greek myth, who were said to engage in similar practices so that their breasts would not interfere with their use of bows and arrows. While it is not clear whether or not Ibn al-Faqīh believes what he has written, this account certainly makes us, again, wary of taking the words of the Muslim geographers at face value, given the fact that the tradition in which they were writing clearly had an overwhelming influence on the subject matter at times.

Turning away from the geographical tradition, another important clue appears in a text by the Christian physician al-Mukhtār ibn al-Ḥasan ibn Buṭlān (d. 1066), who was originally from Baghdad but travelled widely in the Levantine region. In his *Risāla Jāmi'a li-Funūn Nāfi'a fī Sharī al-Raqīq wa Taqlīb al-'Abid* (Comprehensive Epistle on Useful Techniques in Trading Slaves and Inspecting Bondservants), Ibn Buṭlān notes the following:

> It is said: Whoever wants a slave girl for pleasure should take on a Berber; whoever wants her to look after treasure and keep things safe [should take on] a Byzantine; whoever wants her to bear children [should take on] a Persian; whoever wants her for nursing [should take on] a Frank; and whoever wants her to earn wealth [should take on] a Meccan. [...] This is a saying of which we have gathered the scattered parts and put the fragments in order from the epistles of the teacher of Alexander [Aristotle] and others of the *'ulama'* and philosophers.
>
> (Hārūn 2001: I, 383)

Ibn Buṭlān is of course perpetuating stereotypes here, but what is interesting is that in his almost casual mention of the activity to which Frankish slave girls are best suited, he does not suggest that Franks are a particularly exotic or unknown element among the slave population of the Muslim world, nor does he seem to feel the need to describe them in any more detail for an unfamiliar audience. The Franks seem instead to be as well known as Berbers, Byzantines, Persians and even Meccans, at least in Ibn Buṭlān's eyes. This again makes us question the traditional view that the Muslims were particularly unaware of the Franks and their characteristics before the crusades.

SOURCES OF INFORMATION

Having established that the Muslims of the Levant may well have known more about the Franks than they let on, we will now explore the means through which they are likely to have gained that information. A number of Muslim sources written both before the First Crusade and during the first decades of the crusading period provide us with important clues in this regard.

Muslims and Franks at war

The Muslims, of course, came into conflict with the Franks on a number of occasions before the crusading period. Al-Mas'ūdī refers to some of these, though he mixes up the Franks and the Byzantines in the process. Thus he refers to Rhodes, Crete, Sicily and North Africa as territories that the Muslims took from the Franks, rather than the Byzantines (al-Mas'ūdī, 1965–79: II, 145–6). Al-Mas'ūdī is not alone in confusing the Franks and Byzantines in this way, and this is a tendency that continues to appear during the first half of the twelfth century (Christie, 1999: 17–20, 64).

Other writers present more accurate accounts; for example, the tenth-century geographer Ibn Ḥawqal, in his *Kitāb Ṣūrat al-'Arḍ* (the Book of the Shape of the Earth) describes the Muslim presence in Fraxinetum, near Saint-Tropez in Provence, which he notes was once in Frankish hands and has become a well-supplied stronghold 'in the faces of the Franks', from which its Muslim occupiers cannot be dislodged (Ibn Hawqal, 1967: 204). The Muslims held this site from about 890 to 973. This was just one of a number of sites in modern-day France and Switzerland that the Muslims occupied in the tenth century (Versteegh, 1990).

It is perhaps surprising, then, that the Battle of Poitiers (Tours) in 732 receives so little mention in the Muslim sources. The account of the Egyptian historian Ibn ʿAbd al-Ḥakam (d. 871) is a typical example:

> ʿAbd al-Raḥmān [al-Ghāfiqī, the governor of *al-Andalus*,] raided the *Ifranja*, who are the most distant enemies of *al-Andalus*, and gained great booty and conquered them [...] then he also went out to raid them and was martyred along with all his companions. His death [...] was in the year 115 [733].
>
> (Ibn ʿAbd al-Ḥakam, 1922: 216–17)

This lack of detail in the Muslim sources has led modern historians to debate the significance of this event, such that their depictions range from the defeat of a small-scale Muslim raid that has been over-valued by other modern scholars to the breaking of a Muslim advance that would have seen European civilisation subordinated to that of Islam (Lewis, 2001: 18–20; Watson, 1993). Whatever the truth of this, for the purposes of this chapter the significance of the battle is that it represents another example of a direct military confrontation between Muslims and Franks that made enough of an impression to be recorded, albeit vaguely, in the chronicles of the writers of the Levant, despite time, distance and the arguably negligible impact that it made upon them personally. It may have been encounters like these that al-Masʿūdī had in mind when he referred to the strength and fearsomeness of the Franks.

When one looks at the earliest Muslim sources for the crusading period itself, one sees attention still being paid to the activities of the Franks in the west. Al-Sulamī refers to the *reconquista* in Iberia (as well as the Norman conquest of Sicily), in the process depicting the First Crusade as being part of a wider Frankish offensive that also includes these other military campaigns (Christie, 2006: 64). The chronicler Ibn al-Qalānisī (d. 1160) wrote a history of his hometown, *Dhayl Taʾrīkh Dimashq* (The Continuation of the History of Damascus), which focuses first and foremost on the history of the city; however, he likewise clearly still felt that he should mention Frankish military activities in Iberia and North Africa in his account of the Muslim years 478–79 (1085–87) (Ibn al-Qalānisī, 1983: 193–4). Thus it would seem that the Muslim writers were both aware of and feeling an obligation to report on Frankish activities at the other end of the Mediterranean.

Starting in the eleventh century, the Byzantines began employing significant contingents of Frankish (and especially Norman) mercenaries in their forces (Haldon, 1999: 85–94; Kazhdan, 2001: 89–93). For the Muslims of the Levant the Franks were now not only involved in military operations in the distant West, but also a more immediate and proximate threat as part of the armed forces of their traditional Christian enemies. This means that the Muslims of the Levant had direct experience of fighting the Franks even before the arrival of the First Crusade. The presence of Franks in the Byzantine forces was also likely a contributory factor to the confusion of the two that can be seen in the Muslim sources, as noted above. Of course, it is also worth noting that Frankish slaves were inducted into the armies of Muslim rulers, which would have provided another way for the Muslims to learn more about them (Tolan et al., 2013: 68).

Muslim contacts with the Franks were not only restricted to the battlefield. Some Muslim and Frankish rulers also engaged in diplomatic exchanges. The best known of these, of course, are the embassies exchanged between Charlemagne and the ʿAbbāsid caliph Hārūn al-Rashīd (r. 786–809), which are directly attested to only in the Frankish sources and have been the subject of much scholarly discussion (Sénac, 2002: 37–8, 46–51). These exchanges formed part of a wider exchange of intermittent embassies between the Carolingians and the 'Abbāsids that began with a diplomatic mission sent to the caliph al-Manṣūr (r. 754–75) by Pippin the Short in 765, continued with the embassies between Charlemagne and Hārūn al-Rashīd, and ended after ambassadors from the caliph al-Ma'mūn (r. 813–33) visited Louis the Pious in 831; again, none of these are mentioned in the Muslim chronicles of the time. Scholars have suggested a number of reasons for these diplomatic exchanges. Strategic concerns are likely to have played a major part. The Carolingians and the Abbāsids shared mutual enemies in both the Umayyads of Cordoba and the Byzantines, not to mention the possibility of these two powers providing assistance to other opponents of the Carolingians and 'Abbāsids, such as Byzantine support of the Lombards against the Carolingians. The second motivation for diplomatic contact relates to Carolingian interest in giving patronage to the sacred sites of the Holy Land. It is generally accepted that the authority that Hārūn al-Rashīd allegedly gave Charlemagne over the holy places of the region, described with such enthusiasm by Einhard (d. 840) and Notker the Stammerer (d. 912) (Thorpe, 1969: 70, 148–9), is a fabrication, but the diplomatic contacts between the two seem to have been intended to make it easier for Charlemagne to respond to calls for support that came from the Christians of Jerusalem in 799 and 810, and to make wider donations to the Christian communities of the Muslim world. Finally, the diplomatic exchanges between the caliphs and the Carolingian kings may have been intended to promote trade and safeguard trade routes between the two powers, which were threatened by the activities of the Umayyads and Byzantines (Sénac, 2002: 38–41, 46–51). The third proposed incentive for diplomatic contact in some senses reflects the first, reminding us that these motivations were, of course, not mutually exclusive.

As noted above, these exchanges between the 'Abbāsids and the Carolingians are not mentioned in the Muslim sources of the period, something that Runciman ascribes to a desire by the 'Abbāsids to avoid besmirching their pious reputation by leaving an official record of cordial relations with infidels (Runciman, 1935: 607). However, a reflection of them is found in the pages of the *Arabian Nights*, a collection that dates back at least as far as the eighth century and has been added to, expanded, and revised repeatedly since (Irwin, 1994: 48). The tale of *Nur al-Din and Miriam the Sash-Maker* tells of a Muslim merchant's son, Nūr al-Dīn, who buys a Frankish slave girl. She turns out to be the daughter of the king of *Ifranja*, who after being captured by Muslim pirates was enslaved and during her captivity converted to Islam. Nūr al-Dīn and Miriam fall in love and experience a series of adventures, including two forced sojourns in the land of the Franks, after the second of which they escape back to Muslim lands once more. However, the king of the Franks sends an ambassador to Hārūn al-Rashīd with a letter requesting that his daughter be returned to him and offering the caliph half of the city of Rome in exchange. The lovers are duly arrested and taken to the caliph's court in Baghdad, where they tell their story. Upon learning that Miriam has become a Muslim, the caliph refuses to return her to her father, and Miriam herself executes the Frankish king's ambassador. Miriam and Nūr al-Dīn are married and live the rest of their lives happily together (Lyons, 2008: III, 341–428).

What is noteworthy here, of course, is that the last challenge that Nūr al-Dīn and Miriam face stems from the fact that Hārūn al-Rashīd enjoys friendly relations with the king of the Franks, and the caliph fully intends to return Miriam to her father before he learns that she has become a Muslim, sending orders to his agents across the Muslim world that they should find her (Lyons, 2008: III, 424). While the king of the Franks is not identified by name in the tale, the co-operative diplomatic contact that the king and the caliph enjoy is strongly reminiscent of that between the 'Abbāsid and the Carolingian rulers recorded by the Frankish sources. We must also acknowledge that the difficulties involved in dating folk literature such as the *Arabian Nights*, along with its explicitly fictional nature, must make us wary of placing too much faith in its depictions of real historical figures, but the trans-Mediterranean echo remains, nevertheless, striking as a recollection of the 'Abbāsid-Carolingian relations that are not found in the Muslim chronicles.

We do have, however, other occasional historical records of Muslim-Frankish diplomacy written by Muslim authors. One intriguing example is the correspondence exchanged between Bertha, the daughter of Lothair II of Lotharingia and the self-styled 'queen' of Tuscany (d. 925), and the 'Abbāsid caliph al-Muktafī (r. 902–08). In 906 Bertha sent an embassy to the caliph that has been recorded in passing by the well-known Baghdadi bibliographer Ibn al-Nadīm (d. 995 or 998) and in considerably more detail by the rather less famous author al-Awḥadī. According to both authors, Bertha sent the embassy in order to create ties of friendship with the caliph and to ask his hand in marriage, even though she was married at the time (Ibn al-Nadīm, 1970: I, 38; Hamidullah, 1953: 273, 279)! Al-Awḥadī's version of events also includes a list of the presents that Bertha sent with her embassy, as well as describing the circumstances of its arrival and the caliph's response, though we do not learn exactly how the caliph reacted to Bertha's amorous advances (Hamidullah, 1953: 273–86). Needless to say, no wedding ensued, but Bertha's embassy provides further evidence of periodic diplomatic contact taking place between the Muslims and the Franks before the crusades. In addition, one interesting feature of al-Awḥadī's account is that we are told that upon receipt of Bertha's letter, the caliph or his vizier sought out someone who could read it, eventually finding a Frank in the caliphal wardrobe who translated it into Greek, after which someone else translated the Greek into Arabic (Hamidullah, 1953: 274, 280). If this is not a case of confusion of Franks and Byzantines, this suggests that Frankish slaves could be found, in the caliphal household at least, as early as the tenth century, further supporting the hypothesis that Franks were a known quantity in the Muslim world from an early stage.

It was not only through direct contact that diplomatic relations gave the Muslims opportunities to learn about the Franks. The Aleppine chronicler al-'Aẓīmī (d. after 1161) asserts that the Byzantine emperor Alexius Comnenus (r. 1081–1118) wrote to the Muslims in 1096, warning them that the Franks were on their way (1984: 358). It is not clear *which* Muslims the emperor wrote to; Carole Hillenbrand suggests that the most likely candidates were the Fāṭimids of Egypt, who had enjoyed diplomatic links with the Byzantines for a long time before the First Crusade (Hillenbrand, 1999: 45, 69). Whatever the truth of this, for the purposes of this discussion the important thing is that, if we can trust al-'Aẓīmī's claims, at least *some* of the Muslims of the Levantine region were receiving information about the Franks through indirect channels, complementing any direct contact that they may have had with them.

Travellers and trade

Ambassadors were not the only Westerners visiting the Muslim world before the First Crusade. European pilgrims, both Christian and Jewish, had been visiting the Holy Land long before both the crusading period and the first appearance of Islam in Arabia; with regard to Christian pilgrims in particular, Wilkinson notes that the earliest record we have of such a visitor dates back to 333 CE (2002: 1). The Muslim conquest of Jerusalem in 638 only caused a temporary hiatus in Western pilgrimages to the region, as the Muslim rulers themselves on the whole did not seek to prevent such visits (Wilkinson, 2002: 18). Indeed, they seem to have become used to seeing European pilgrims passing through the Levant en route to the holy places of the East. In her *Life of St Willibald*, the nun Hugeburc (fl. 780) records the words of one influential Muslim citizen at the Syrian city of Homs, apparently dictated to her by Willibald himself after his own pilgrimage to the area: 'Many times I have seen people coming here, fellow-tribesmen of theirs, from those parts of the world. They mean no harm. All they want to do is to fulfil their law' (Wilkinson, 2002: 236). A more direct attestation to the passing of European pilgrims through the Holy Land from the Muslim side is given by al-'Azīmī, who notes in his account of the year 486 AH (1093–94 CE), 'The people of the coastal ports prevented Frankish and Byzantine pilgrims from crossing to Jerusalem. News of what happened spread from those who escaped to their countries, and they prepared to invade [the Levant]. The news of that reached the coast and all the lands of the Muslims' (1984: 356). In this way al-'Azīmī indicates an awareness of the presence of European pilgrims in the Holy Land, depicting the First Crusade as having been undertaken in revenge for their mistreatment at the hands of the Muslims. It is also noteworthy, of course, that he claims that Muslims as a whole became aware of the impending European attack, years before the crusaders arrived, though he is probably exaggerating for effect here. However, this does not detract from the fact that European, including Frankish, pilgrims had been visiting the Levant for centuries, providing another way in which the Muslims may have learned about them.

Muslim travellers also came from West to East. For example, in 1092–95 the Sevillan pilgrim and scholar Ibn al-'Arabī (d. 1148) visited various places in the Holy Land, and has left his impressions of the region in various works (Drory, 2004). Ibn al-'Arabī spent significant portions of his visit studying and debating with Muslim and Jewish scholars. It is not unreasonable to assume that he might in the process have informed his listeners of developments in Iberia, including Frankish activities in the region. It is likely that he and other travellers like him were important sources for Levantine writers who recorded events in the Muslim west, like the examples of al-Sulamī and Ibn al-Qalānisī that we have noted above.

We should also not neglect the role that trade played in interactions between East and West. There had been trade taking place between Europe and the Muslim world from as early as the eighth century, and this expanded in the eleventh century as Egypt became the centre of commerce in the eastern Mediterranean (Tolan et al., 2013: 72–6). At the forefront of this trade were two major groups: the Jews and the Italians. The Jewish trade networks of the Mediterranean, which were studied so masterfully by Shlomo D. Goitein (Goitein and Sanders, 1967–99), enabled goods and information to pass between the Jewish communities as far apart as France, Egypt and India, though it is not clear how far information, at least, passed between these Jewish communities and their non-Jewish neighbours in Europe and the Muslim world (Christie, 1999: 39–43). The various Italian trading cities, especially Amalfi, Venice, Pisa and Genoa, also established themselves as major carriers of trade between Europe and the Levant in the eleventh century, and the Venetians, Pisans and Genoese in particular would go on to become prominent in the crusading movement as the twelfth and thirteenth centuries unfolded (Tolan et al., 2013: 74–8). The Franks, however, seem to have been far less significant participants in the commerce between Europe and the Middle East, receiving only occasional mentions in Muslim descriptions of East–West trade. For example, the Persian traveller and poet Nāṣir Khusraw (d. *c.* 1077) who visited Tripoli in February 1047, remarks that it is 'a trade centre frequented by ships coming from the Byzantines, the land of the Franks, al-Andalus and the Maghrib' (1970: 12 [Persian] and 41 [French translation]). It is possible that Nāṣir Khusraw is using the term 'Frank' in its later sense of 'western European' here, given that the Italians were the dominant European trading power in the Levant at the time, but it is also possible that he is referring to genuinely Frankish merchants who had found their way to the East. It is striking that they are in Tripoli, rather than Egypt, which was the primary destination of Italian merchants travelling to the region, which could represent an attempt by Frankish merchants to avoid coming into conflict with Italian commerce.

AN ILLUSION OF IGNORANCE?

It is clear from the above that there is simply too much evidence, even though much of it is circumstantial, to support the idea that the Muslims of the Middle East knew little about the Franks before the arrival of the First Crusade in the Levant. If we accept that the Muslim writers of the periods before and contemporary with the crusade and its aftermath both had greater access to information and knew more than has commonly been assumed, we must, then, consider why they reveal so little in their accounts of the events. Space will not permit a full consideration of Muslim attitudes towards the Franks during this period; such discussions are available elsewhere (Hillenbrand, 1999; Christie, 1999: 62–113). However, a review of some of the major characteristics of the Franks in the contemporary Muslim sources will help to provide some understanding of why this might be the case.

The Muslims knew that the crusaders were Christian, and very quickly they used the different religion of the Franks to depict them in their writings as a religious enemy that had to be opposed through military *jihād* for the sake of the Muslim faith. In doing so, they also sought as far as possible to emphasise the points of conflict between Christian and Muslim doctrine; thus the crusaders are described as *kuffār* (blasphemers or infidels), highlighting the fact that Christian claims that Jesus was the son of God are blasphemy from a Muslim point of view; and *mushrikūn* (polytheists), in that they worship three gods (the Holy Trinity) when God is in fact only one, with no partners or associates. In an evocative passage, an anonymous poet from the period provides a negative depiction of Christianity and the crusaders' observance thereof, stating, 'How many a mosque have they made into a church, a cross set up in its mihrab? Pig's blood in it is suitable for them, and the burning of *Qur'ans* in it as incense' (Ibn Taghrī Birdī, 1963: V, 152). In the process he not only accuses the Franks of committing sacrilege by burning copies of the *Qur'an*, but also accuses them of using the blood of pigs, an animal considered unclean in Islam, as part of their worship. Thus Christianity, sacrilege and pollution go hand in hand.

Another prominent feature of the Franks is their greed for wealth and power. A number of Muslim writers highlight this feature. Al-Sulamī depicts the crusaders as having found the conquest of the Levantine coast more successful than they had expected and states, 'Still now they are spreading further in their efforts, assiduous in seeking an increase in their achievements. Their desires are multiplying all the time [...] until they have become convinced that the whole country will become theirs and all its people will be prisoners in their hands' (Christie, 2014: 133). Thus he presents the ambitions of the Franks as being unbridled, with them always seeking to gain more territory and wealth. While material gain is not seen as inherently evil in Islam (the Prophet was, after all, a merchant), overweening desire for gains of the type demonstrated by the Franks is seen as unacceptable and flying in the face of pious contentment with what one has been given by God, so their behaviour thus makes them both evil and impious. Al-Sulamī's representation of the Franks as being greedy is echoed in the other Muslim sources from the period.

A third noted feature of the Franks is their tendency to be treacherous. As an example, Ibn al-Qalānisī gives the following description of the Franks' conquest of Jubayl in 1104:

> They took it with an assurance of safety, and when it passed under their control, they dealt treacherously with its people and did not stand by the assurance of safety that they had offered. They seized the people and took possession of their property and wealth using punishments and various tortures.
>
> (Ibn al-Qalanisi, 1983: 231)

It is of course noteworthy that by breaking the agreement, the Franks were taking the opportunity to gain the possessions and wealth of the people of the town. Thus their avarice and their treachery are combined in the Damascene chronicler's narrative.

The three features of the Franks highlighted here exemplify the fact that on the whole, Muslims depictions of them from the time tend to be negative. This is of course not surprising; they had, in the eyes of the Muslim writers, invaded, plundered, and occupied Muslim lands, and the writers were trying to motivate their listeners or readers to oppose the ongoing Frankish activities. We might suggest, therefore, that the rather limited portrayal of the Franks that we get in the Muslim sources stems not from ignorance but rather from a desire to focus only on their negative qualities, so that they will be seen clearly and unambiguously as an enemy. The lack of detail about the Franks may also in part owe its origin to a technique beloved of horror movie directors, in that the less that is revealed to the audience about the villain, the more dangerous and frightening they seem. Thus we see the Muslim sources being economical with the information that they have in order to present the Franks as a clear and present danger, against which the Muslims are obliged to take action. What was important for the Muslim writers was not what the Franks were like, but what was to be done about them.

CONCLUSION

In this chapter we have argued that there is too much evidence in the sources from before the period of the crusades to support the notion that the Muslims knew almost nothing about the Franks before their arrival in the Levant. As noted above, we must acknowledge that much of the evidence for this argument is circumstantial. In addition, the references that we have to the Franks in the Muslim sources before the crusades are still relatively few and scattered, and even the contemporary sources for the First Crusade are limited in number, so it is difficult to determine how far they speak for the Muslims of the Middle East in general, and the Levant in particular, as a whole. The question is also complicated by the lack of clarity that surrounds the changing use of the term 'Frank' in the Muslim sources. However, the evidence that does exist remains too significant to ignore, and must therefore be borne in mind as we refine our understanding of both the first encounters between the Muslims of the Levant and the crusaders, and the ways in which these encounters are depicted by the contemporary Muslim sources for the period.

REFERENCES

Al-'Azīmī, Muḥammad ibn 'Alī, 1984, *Ta'rīkh Ḥalab*, ed. I Za'rūr, n.p., Damascus.

Christie, N, 1999, *Levantine Attitudes towards the Franks during the Early Crusades (490/1096–564–1169)*, PhD diss., University of St Andrews, http://hdl.handle.net/10023/2741 (accessed 30 April 2014).

——— 2014, *Muslims and Crusaders: Christianity's Wars in the Middle East, 1095–1382, from the Islamic Sources*, Routledge, Abingdon.

——— 2006, 'Religious Campaign or War of Conquest? Muslim Views of the Motives of the First Crusade', in *Noble Ideals and Bloody Realities: Warfare in the Middle Ages*, eds N Christie and M Yazigi, E.J. Brill, Leiden, 57–72.

Drory, J, 2004, 'Some Observations during a Visit to Palestine by Ibn al-'Arabī of Seville in 1092–1095', *Crusades*, 3, 101–24.

Goitein, SD and Sanders, P, 1967–99, *A Mediterranean Society: The Jewish Communities of the Arab World as Portrayed in the Documents of the Cairo Geniza*, 6 vols, University of California Press, Berkeley.

Haldon, J, 1999, *Warfare, State and Society in the Byzantine World 565–1204*, UCL Press, London.

Hamidullah, M, 1953, 'Embassy of Queen Bertha of Rome to Caliph al-Muktafi Billah in Baghdad 293 H./906', *Journal of the Pakistan Historical Society*, 1, 273–300.

Hārūn, 'Abd al-Salām (ed.), 2001, *Nawādir al-Makhṭūṭāt*, vol. 1, al-Hay'a al-'Āmma li-Quṣūr al-Thaqāfa, Cairo.

Hermes, NF, 2012, *The [European] Other in Medieval Arabic Literature and Culture: Ninth-Twelfth Century AD*, Palgrave Macmillan, New York.

Hillenbrand, C, 1999, *The Crusades: Islamic Perspectives*, Edinburgh University Press, Edinburgh.

Ibn 'Abd al-Ḥakam, 'Abd al-Raḥmān ibn 'Abd Allāh, 1922, *Futūḥ Miṣr*, ed. CC Torrey, Yale University Press, New Haven.

Ibn al-Faqīh, Aḥmad ibn Muḥammad, 1967, *Kitâb al-Boldân*, ed. MJ de Goeje, E.J. Brill, Leiden.

Ibn Ḥawqal, Abu'l-Qāsim ibn 'Alī, 1967, *Opus Geographicum*, ed. MJ de Goeje, E.J. Brill, Leiden.

Ibn al-Nadīm, Muḥammad ibn Isḥāq, 1970, *The Fihrist of al-Nadīm*, ed. and trans. B Dodge, vol. 1, Columbia University Press, New York.

Ibn al-Qalānisī, Ḥamza ibn Asad, 1983, *Tarīkh Dimashq: 360–555*, ed. S Zakkār, Dār Ḥassān li'l-Ṭibā'a wa'l-Nashr, Damascus.

Ibn Taghrī Birdī, Jamāl al-Dīn Yūsuf, 1963, *Al-Nujūm al-Zāhira fī Mulūk Miṣr wa'l-Qāhira*, ed. M 'Abd al-Qādir Ḥātim, vol. 5, Dar al-Kutub al-Misriyya, Cairo.

Irwin, R, 1994, *The Arabian Nights: A Companion*, Allen Lane, London.

Kazhdan, A, 2001, 'Latins and Franks in Byzantium: Perception and Reality from the Eleventh to the Twelfth Century', in *The Crusades from the Perspective of Byzantium and the Muslim World*, eds AE Laiou and RP Mottahedeh, Dumbarton Oaks Research Library and Collection, Washington DC, 83–100.

Khusraw, Nāṣir, 1970, *Sefer Nameh*, ed. and trans. C. Schefer, Philo Press, Amsterdam.

Lewis, B, 2001, *The Muslim Discovery of Europe*, re-issued edn, W.W. Norton, New York.

Lyons, MC (trans.), 2008, *The Arabian Nights: Tales of the 1001 Nights*, vol. 3, Penguin Books, London.

Al-Mas'ūdī, 'Alī ibn al-Ḥusayn, 1894, *Kitâb at-Tanbîh wa'l-Ischrâf*, ed. MJ de Goeje, E.J. Brill, Leiden.

——— 1965–79, *Murūj al-Dhahab wa Ma'ādin al-Jawhar*, ed. Ch Pellat, Manshūrāt al-Jāmi'a al-Lubnāniyya, Beirut.

Pellat, Ch, 1991, 'Al-Mas'ūdī', in *The Encyclopaedia of Islam*, new (2nd) edn, eds CE Bosworth, E van Donzel, B Lewis and Ch Pellat, E.J. Brill, Leiden, VI: 784–9.

Runciman, S, 1935, 'Charlemagne and Palestine', *English Historical Review*, 50(200), 606–19.

Sénac, P, 2002, 'Les Carolingiens et la Califat Abbasside (VIIIᵉ-IXᵉ Siècles)', *Studia Islamica*, 95(1), 37–56.

Shboul, AMH, 1979, *Al-Masʿūdī and his World: A Muslim Humanist and his Interest in Non-Muslims*, Ithaca Press, London.

Thorpe, L (trans.), 1969, *Einhard and Notker the Stammerer: Two Lives of Charlemagne*, Penguin Books, London.

Tolan, J, 2013, Review of Nizar F. Hermes, *The [European] Other in Medieval Arabic Literature and Culture*, *Speculum: A Journal of Medieval Studies*, 88(1), 310–12.

Tolan, J, Veinstein, G and Laurens, H, 2013, *Europe and the Islamic World: A History*, trans. JM Todd, Princeton University Press, Princeton.

Versteegh, K, 1990, 'The Arab Presence in France and Switzerland in the 10th Century', *Arabica*, 37(3), 359–88.

Watson, WE, 1993, 'The Battle of Tours-Poitiers Revisited', *Providence: Studies in Western Civilization*, 2(1), 51–68.

Wilkinson, J, 2002, *Jerusalem Pilgrims before the Crusades*, Aris & Phillips, Ltd., Warminster.

CHAPTER TWENTY

THE EARLY MAMLŪKS AND THE END OF THE CRUSADER PRESENCE IN SYRIA (1250–1291)[1]

———•◆•———

Reuven Amitai

At the battle of Manṣūra in the Nile Delta on February 8, 1250, the Ayyūbid army was caught completely off guard by a surprise crusader attack under the general command of King Louis IX of France, coming after a standoff of several weeks across a large channel of water. The sultan, al-Malik al-Ṣāliḥ Ayyūb, had recently died (November 22, 1249), and the commander of his army, Fakhr al-Dīn ibn Shaykh al-Shuyūkh, was cut down before he could organize resistance. Frankish knights broke through the Muslim lines, reaching the city of Manṣūra itself. Things looked grim for the Muslims, but the tables were turned with the appearance of a large group of Mamlūks of the late sultan. This is what the contemporary Syrian chronicler Ibn Wāṣil (d. 1298) writes:

> [And then,] the Turkish band, Mamlūks of the Sultan—may God have mercy on him— from the Jāmadāriyya and the Baḥriyya[2]—lions of war, and horsemen [who were masters in the use of] lance and bow—appeared on the scene. They launched a concerted attack against the Franks, violently rocking their pillars, demolishing their building and overturning their crosses.[3] The Turkish swords and maces wreaked havoc with them, inflicting death and wounds, and threw them down on the ground in the alleys of Manṣūra.

A little later, when summing up the battle, the author writes:

> This was the first encounter in which the polytheist dogs were defeated by means of the Turkish lions (*wa-kānat hādhahi awwal waqʿa untuṣira fīhā bi-usūd al-turk ʿalā kilāb al-shirk*).[4]

In aftermath of this defeat, the Franks under Louis IX began withdrawing to the north, hoping to make it back to their base at Damietta on the Mediterranean coast. They were, however, unsuccessful, stymied by difficult conditions and incessant Muslim attacks. Many died, while Louis and most of his troops were taken captive in April.[5] The fate of the French king, however, is not our concern, at least not yet. Rather, we should look at what was going on in the Muslim camp, while the above described Mamlūks—and the Muslim army in general—were basking in their victory.

On February 23, al-Mu'aẓẓam Tūrānshāh, son of al-Ṣāliḥ Ayyūb and heir apparent, had arrived from his governorship north of the Euphrates. The new ruler soon managed to alienate the veteran leadership of the army (mainly Mamlūk officers from various units), not the least by advancing quickly his own men to top positions. The result, not for the first time in Muslim history, was that the son of the previous ruler was removed from power; as was often the case, he was killed in the process. Yet, unlike similar occurrences in the past, this time the military leadership did not seek another young member from the dynasty to serve as a malleable puppet, but decided to forgo this fiction. Instead, they officially placed on the throne the beloved wife of the late al-Ṣāliḥ Ayyūb, Shajar (or Shajarat) al-Durr ("Tree of Pearls"), who was also of Inner Asian Turkish origin like most of the Mamlūks. Soon afterward, aware of the unprecedented nature of naming a woman as ruler, they picked a non-descript Mamlūk officer by the name of Aybak al-Turkmānī, also a Mamlūk of al-Ṣāliḥ Ayyūb but not part of either of the two above-mentioned units, to serve as Aṭābak (commander of the army and also guardian or regent) and to wed her.[6]

This was a real revolution. For the first time in the Muslim Middle East, a legitimate ruling dynasty had been completely cast aside,[7] and replaced by nothing less than a former slave girl and an officer of slave provenance. This was not a planned revolution, as had been the case when the 'Abbāsids took power in 750, or as Shī'ī groups had been trying to do for centuries. As there was no ideological basis for this change in 1250, and no thinking about the day after, this was indeed a time of political and military confusion. However, before going on to examine how the leadership of the new political entity resolved some of the outstanding issues, and then strengthened its rule internally and externally, let us look at the conditions that led to this change in the nature of politics.

BACKGROUND TO POLITICAL CHANGE

Muslim armies had long a strong component of Mamlūks, or slave soldiers, who were usually Turks from the Eurasian Steppe. Certainly from the time of Saladin, Turkish Mamlūks had played an important role in Ayyūbid military (and sometimes political affairs). The number and role of such Mamlūks were strengthened through the ongoing efforts of Saladin's great nephew, al-Ṣāliḥ Najm al-Dīn Ayyūb (b. 1205). Already as a young prince in the 1220s, while left as regent in Egypt by his father al-Kāmil Muḥammad (r. 1218–38), al-Ṣāliḥ had obtained Mamlūks in large numbers to augment his position in the internal politics of the Ayyūbid federation.[8] His father put an end to such mischief, as he saw it, sending al-Ṣāliḥ off to serve as governor in some of the Ayyūbid possession east of the Euphrates. After his father's death, al-Ṣāliḥ was raised to the throne, but soon lost it, due to the disloyalty of the former's troops. Later, when al-Ṣāliḥ gained control over Syria for a second time, in 1240, he showed that he had learned his lesson.[9] Thus, the historian Ibn Wāṣil writes, while summing up al-Ṣāliḥ Ayyūb's life:

> He bought from among the Turkish Mamlūks what no one in his family had bought [before him], so that they became the main part of his army. [This happened] when he saw the perfidy of the Kurds and others on the day that Damascus was taken. He [also noted] the steadfastness of his Mamlūks with him, when his [other] people fled from him while he was Qaṣr bin Mu'īn in the Jordan Valley (al-Ghawr). He thus preferred his

Mamlūks, giving them precedence. When he took over in Egypt (in 1240), he discontinued the service of the officers who had been with his father (al-Kāmil) and brother (al-ʿĀdil Abū Bakr II), and imprisoned them. In Egypt, he bought a large group of Turks, and made them his inner entourage and those who surrounded him in his pavilion (*al-dihlīz*), calling them the Baḥriyya.[10]

This is, however, only part of the story. It was not enough only to have a heightened desire for more Turkish Mamlūks, one had to find a ready supply. Around 1240, this was exactly the situation, as the historian al-Nuwayrī (d. 1332) tells us:

> The [Mongols] fell upon [the Qipchaq Turks] and brought upon most of them death, slavery and captivity. At the same time, merchants bought [these captives] and brought them to the [various] countries and cities. The first who demanded many of them and made them lofty and advanced them in the army was al-Malik al-Ṣāliḥ Najm al-Dīn Ayyūb.[11]

Our source is tersely telling us that it was the Mongol campaigns of the late 1230s in the steppe region north of the Black Sea and the Caucasus (i.e. southern Russia and Ukraine of today), where the Qipchaq (also known as Cumans or Polovtsy) tribes lived, practicing a lifestyle of nomadic pastoralism, that led to the flooding of local slave markets with young Turks, both boys and girls. Most of these slaves were probably shipped through the Crimean Peninsula, brought through the Bosporus or over land via Anatolia by merchants of various origins. In Syria and Egypt, the boys were enrolled in the Mamlūk units of various princes or officers; the girls, at least in part, became household slaves and concubines, not the least in this or that princely court.[12] Al-Ṣāliḥ Ayyūb, then, had the means to build with relative ease his new Mamlūk formation, setting in motion events that helped to propel the Mamlūk takeover of 1250.

THE EARLY YEARS OF THE MAMLŪK RULE

The leadership of the fledgling Mamlūk state did not find Aybak's marriage to Shajar al-Durr provided enough legitimacy to rule, especially in the face of growing Ayyūbid opposition in Syria. Thus, after about three months they found a suitable Ayyūbid scion to fill void, al-Malik al-Ashraf Mūsā, the ten-year-old great-grandson of the above-mentioned al-Kāmil Muḥammad, with Aybak remaining Aṭābak (again, a combination of guardian and army chief). However, while they may have thought to have found a solution to the problem of legitimacy, the Ayyūbid princes in Syria thought otherwise. Led by al-Nāṣir Yūsuf b. al-ʿAzīz, the erstwhile ruler of Aleppo (from 1234), who also took over in Damascus soon after al-Ṣāliḥ Ayyūb's death, they launched an invasion of Egypt at the beginning of 1251 (following intermittent fighting in the previous months in the area of Gaza). It is not surprising that the Syrian Ayyūbids were unhappy with the effective end of Ayyūbid rule in that country, no matter who the ostensible ruler was. The armies met in Kurāʿ, to the east of Cairo at the beginning of February. While the Syrians were initially successful, Aybak was ultimately victorious, and al-Nāṣir Yūsuf and most of his troops fell back in disarray. Aybak made some moves to launch a campaign into Ayyūbid Syria to wrest it from the Ayyūbids, and thus initiated negotiations with King Louis IX, now in Acre after having ransomed himself out of captivity in Egypt. The Mamlūk leader, however, soon became aware that that even a partial conquest of Syria was beyond his powers; likewise, al-Nāṣir Yūsuf surely despaired of regaining Egypt for the Ayyūbids. There was thus likely relief on both sides at the offer by Caliph al-Mustʿaṣim in Baghdad to broker an agreement. In April 1253, a peace treaty was signed: Mamlūk sovereignty was recognized in Egypt, including the Sinai Peninsula, up to, but not including Nablus; soon Shawbak in Transjordan was also under their control. However, in 1255, in a second agreement facilitated by a caliphal envoy, Aybak gave up any claims to territory north and east of al-ʿArīsh in north-east Sinai.[13]

The resolution of the difficulties with the Syrian Ayyūbids opened up the possibility of infighting among the Mamlūks themselves. The Baḥriyya (along with their colleagues from the Jāmadāriyya) may have been the driving force behind the Mamlūk victory at Manṣūra, but they were far from controlling the government. Aybak was also a Mamlūk of al-Ṣāliḥ Ayyūb, but not one of them, and there were other factions represented in the ruling group. While Aybak may have been picked originally for his apparent lack of political strength, his position had become stronger during his time in office. He had begun assembling his own unit of Mamlūks, and he had the support of various military refugees from Syria, from many of the Turkish ʿAzīziyya regiment (the Mamlūks of al-Nāṣir Yūsuf's father) and from some members of the Kurdish Qaymariyya, a large group that until then had been stalwarts of the Syrian Ayyūbid regime. The Baḥriyya and their allies, however, had not been idle, and under the dynamic leadership of Fāris al-Dīn Aqṭāy were angling for taking real and formal control of the State. They certainly behaved as if they were already running things: Aqṭāy was already referred to with the royal title of al-Malik al-Jawād and was allocating *iqṭāʿāt* (revenue-generating land allocations).[14] A clash between Aqṭāy and Aybak was inevitable, and probably most observers of the political game in Cairo thought that the victory of the former was a foregone conclusion. However, Aybak moved first, and his trusted Mamlūk Quṭuz struck down Aqṭāy on January 1, 1254. Some of the Baḥrīs were arrested, other escaped to the north: a small group went on to Anatolia (gaining employment with the Seljuq ruler of Rūm, i.e. Anatolia), while the majority—some 700—stayed in Syria under the command of one Rukn al-Dīn Baybars al-Bunduqdārī. We will return to this Baybars and his comrades shortly, but first let us continue with developments in Egypt.[15]

Aybak had surely been frustrated by the problems he had hitherto encountered trying to rule, and thus took the opportunity to bolster his position. Almost immediately after disposing of the Baḥriyya, he got rid of the Ayyūbid puppet ruler, al-Ashraf Mūsā, and declared himself sultan, with the royal title of al-Malik al-Muʿizz ("the King who brings glory"); coins, however, were still struck in the name of al-Ṣāliḥ Ayyūb, with Aybak as his viceroy! Aybak also sought the hand of a "princess" from far away: the daughter of Badr al-Dīn Luʾluʾ, ruler of Mosul. This brought about a final rupture with his erstwhile wife, Shajar al-Durr (who had been an ally of the Baḥriyya). In a series of events worthy of *Games of Throne*, Shajar al-Durr murdered her husband (April 1257), and she was in turn killed by his concubines. Unable to decide on one of their own to rule, the military grandees (now bereft of most of the Baḥriyya) raised Aybak's son fifteen-year-old son, ʿAlī to the throne with the royal name of al-Malik al-Manṣūr. The regime's strongman was Quṭuz, Aybak's trusted Mamlūk. Here we see what will be a pattern throughout most of the Mamlūk period: a ruling sultan—himself a former Mamlūk officer—dies a natural death or otherwise; the powerful officers are unable to agree on a successor, or none of them is strong enough to force the issue, and so the late ruler's son is appointed. The latter invariably plays the role of a puppet ruler, with one or more of the senior officers acting as the power behind the throne. This present charade was put to an end in November 1259: with the approach of the Mongols, it was clear to the political and military elite that a strong leader was needed. The hapless boy sultan was replaced by Quṭuz, who took the royal title of al-Malik al-Muẓaffar ("The Victorious King").[16] In retrospect, this was surely a good thing for the Mamlūks military class, the Egyptian and Syrian populations and perhaps the Muslims in a more general sense.

In the meantime, things had been busy in Syria. The presence of Baybars and his comrades from the Baḥriyya was a catalyst for political and military troubles among the Ayyūbid princes. Originally, the Baḥriyya attached themselves to al-Nāṣir Yūsuf, ruler of Damascus and Aleppo, but eventually relations between him and Baybars soured, leading to fighting near Nablus in October 1257. The Baḥriyya, discomforted in this engagement, then joined up with al-Mughīth 'Umar, Ayyūbid prince of Karak in Transjordan. Here Baybars and company continued their encouragement of an attack on Egypt, and in at the end of November of that year, a small army under Baybars drew close to Cairo, but was repulsed. Still undeterred, Baybars and his supporters again tried their luck in March 1258 against the Mamlūk regime in Cairo, and were again defeated. Thereupon began a confused period in which part of the time Baybars and various groups of troopers were independently active in Palestine, mostly against the troops and interests of al-Nāṣir Yūsuf. Yet, by early 1259, Baybars was reconciled with the al-Nasir, and with some of his comrades was back in his service in Damascus.[17]

At this point, we might ask ourselves two questions: first, what about the Franks, local and from across the sea; and second, what about the ever-approaching Mongols? Regarding the former question it appears that ever since Louis IX had left the country in late April 1254,[18] the Frankish-Ayyūbid frontier had generally been quiet. Not only were the Muslim rulers preoccupied with their own affairs but also the local Franks had neither time nor energy for their traditional adversaries. The one significant exception to this relative quiet was a Frankish raid in January 1256 in the area between Ashkelon and Gaza, and the resulting Muslim attack on Jaffa. Besides booty and some destruction of the countryside, nothing was accomplished by this fighting, perhaps with the exception of keeping alive Christian–Muslim enmity.[19] It was not long after that the "War of Saint Sabas" commenced in Acre between the Genoese and the Venetians (and their respective allies), certainly reducing the ability of the Franks in Acre (and beyond) to launch campaigns against Muslim-controlled territory.[20]

THE COMING OF THE MONGOLS

The matter of the Mongols, who were very soon to change the whole nature of politics and warfare in the region, is a weighty one. This is not the place to discuss in any detail the rise of the Mongol empire under Chinggis Khan (d. 1227) and its expansion south into China, and westward across Asia, reaching eastern Europe by the late 1230s (as we have seen above), and we will limit ourselves to a few remarks.[21] The first Mongol invasion of the Islamic world began in 1219 under the direct command of the great conqueror. This campaign covered what is today known as Uzbekistan, Turkmenistan, northern Afghanistan and north-east Iran, although one column reached western Iran before turning north and advancing through Azerbaijan and the Caucasus. Chinggis Khan and most of his army returned to the eastern Steppe in 1223, but smaller Mongol forces remained in the area, and over the next three decades expanded the area under Mongol control, including all of Iran, the Caucasus, most of Anatolia, with occasional raids into Upper Mesopotamia and northern Syria.[22] In the mid-1250s, a new wave of Mongol campaigns in the whole region began with the arrival of a large army under Hülegü, grandson of Chinggis Khan and brother of the Great Khan Möngke (r. 1251–59). Hülegü's orders included re-organizing all territories that had hitherto been conquered by the Mongols, gaining the surrender of the Nizārī Ismāʿīlīs (known in the West as the Assassins) in their mountain fortresses, obtaining the submission of the ʿAbbāsid caliph in Baghdad, and pushing on to Egypt, enacting in all conquered territories the "law (*yasa*) of Chinggis Khan." By the end of 1259, Hülegü had taken almost all the Ismāʿīlī fortresses (killing also their leader), had conquered Baghdad (also executing the caliph and most of his family), had consolidated Mongol rule in the entire region, and was poised to enter north Syria.[23]

Al-Nāṣir Yūsuf, the Ayyūbid ruler of Syria, made some efforts to organize its forces to meet the Mongol invasion, while conducting desultory negotiations with Hülegü. The ability of the Ayyūbid regime to meet the upcoming Mongol challenge was surely compromised by activities of both high civilian officials and princes to strike deals with the enemy: at least one of the former, Zayn al-Dīn al-Ḥāfiẓī, was actively working on behalf of the Mongols, to weaken moral and to confuse planning. The lion's share of the Ayyūbid army was with al-Nāṣir outside of Damascus, but there were forces to the north, primarily as garrisons. Around the beginning of 1260, a large Mongol army under the Ilkhan[24] crossed the Euphrates, entering northern Syria. It soon invested Aleppo, taking it after one week (January 25), with much killing and looting (from which local Christians and Jews seemed to have at least been partially protected); the citadel held up for another month, eventually surrendering and its defenders spared. Meanwhile, Mongol forces began to spread throughout the country, and soon an advanced division under Kitbuga, Hülegü's most trusted general, moved south.[25]

At Damascus, matters soon came to ahead. Even before the Mongol takeover of north Syria, al-Nāṣir Yūsuf's position had become even weaker. Baybars—who had despaired of a concerted or effective resistance to the Mongols in Syria under this ruler—had joined a conspiracy to remove him. When this plan fell through, he left with his supporters and some allies for Gaza, and from there made his way back to Egypt, effecting a reconciliation with his old enemy Quṭuz (March 1260). When news arrived of Aleppo's fall, al-Nāṣir Yūsuf lost his nerve, and fled with part of his army to the south. Reaching Gaza, he soon made his way to Egypt, approaching Cairo, with the hope of a rapprochement with Quṭuz. However, al-Nāṣir's fears got the better of him, and he then turned around, heading east. Mongol scouts caught up with him in Transjordan. He was brought before Hülegü, and later—after ʿAyn Jālūt—executed. So ended Ayyūbid rule over the main parts of Syria. In Damascus, pro-Mongol elements asserted themselves, and Kitbuga soon arrived to take over. Mongol administrators and governors were appointed in Damascus and elsewhere, and Mongol raiders and scouts were soon spreading out over Palestine and Transjordan, reaching Jerusalem and as far south as Gaza.[26]

From the beginning of his reign, Quṭuz had adopted a resolute attitude toward the Mongols. This policy was surely reinforced when he learnt that toward the end of winter, Hülegü had withdrawn from north Syria with the bulk of his troops, leaving behind as governor Kitbuga with a division of about 10,000 men.[27] When in the late spring Mongol envoys arrived in Cairo carrying a bellicose letter from Hülegü, calling on the Mamlūks to unconditionally surrender, Quṭuz had them all cut in half, and their heads hung up around

Cairo. The die was now cast for a confrontation, to the chagrin of some of the Mamlūk officers, who were far from one mind regarding the wisdom of challenging the Mongols. In mid-July 1260, the Mamlūk army left Cairo for Syria. At Gaza, it ran into a Mongol forward force, repulsing it before continuing up the coast. At Acre, around the end of August, the Franks wisely decided to adopt a neutral attitude in the upcoming conflict, but passed on supplies to the nearby Mamlūks, who soon entered the Valley of Esdraelon, heading south-east looking for the Mongols; the vanguard was under the command of Baybars.[28] The Mongols had taken up position in the plain to the north of the Gilboa Mountains, near the Spring of Goliath ('Ayn Jālūt in Arabic, the bliblical 'Ein Ḥarōd). The two armies came into contact on Friday, September 3, 1260; after a long and difficult battle, the Mamlūks emerged victorious. Kitbuga was killed in the fighting and the Mongols abandoned Syria. The Mamlūks occupied the country up to the Euphrates, earning much prestige and exploding the myth of Mongol invincibility.[29]

In order to understand the background to this Mamlūk victory, and their continued success in the wars against the Mongols, lets look at what one of the Mamlūk historians themselves write. Aḥmad Ibn Faḍl Allāh al-'Umarī (d. 1349), a senior bureaucrat in Syria and author of a comprehensive encyclopedia, writes in the section on the Mongols:

> And the Turks of these lands [i.e., the Mongol state of the Golden Horde, in the southern Russian Steppe] are the best Turkish race, because of their faithfulness and bravery and their shunning treachery ... they constitute the overwhelming majority of the Egyptian army, for since the time that al-Malik al-Ṣāliḥ Najm al-Dīn Ayyūb had made his mind to buy Qipchaqi Mamlūks, the sultans and commanders of this country have been of these Turks. Then, when the rule [of Egypt] passed into their hands, their kings inclined toward the people of their own race, and they decided to increased their numbers, until Egypt had become populated and protected by means of them ... Islam had praised their stand in the protection of the Muslim religion as well as their waging the holy war in the name of God, against their own relatives and against the people of their own race. Their first victory over the Mongols in the battle of 'Ayn Jālūt is sufficient [to give them praise and glory]. The Egyptian army had succeeded where all the kings of the earth had failed.[30]

Here the point is made that the Mamlūks had fought well, in spite of their ethnic closeness to the Mongols. In fact, this ethnic affinity (and thus similar fighting methods) made possible for concerted and successful resistance to the Mongols. Another writer, the Damascene jurist and historian Abū Shāma (d. 1268), puts it in even more unequivocal terms:

> The amazing thing is that the Mongols were defeated and annihilated by people of their own race (*bi-anbā' jinsihim*) from among the Turks. I said about this:
>
> > The Mongols conquered the land and there came to them
> > From Egypt a Turk, who sacrificed his life.
> > In Syria he destroyed and scattered them.
> > To everything there is a pest of its own kind (*min jinsihi*).[31]

Thus, to the minds of learned Arabic-speaking Muslims, the combination of military abilities (similar to those of their Mongol "cousins") and commitment to *jihād* are the keys to understanding the ongoing Mamlūk successes to defeat the Mongols and to keep them at bay.[32] These two elements also played a major role in the ultimate Mamlūk victory over the Franks in the Levant.

Quṭuz, the victor at ʿAyn Jālūt, did not long enjoy the glory of his success. The Mongol danger had been removed, at least for now, and internal struggles within the Mamlūk leadership soon reappeared. Baybars, who had been reunited with the Sultan in the face of the Mongol danger, was now part of a conspiracy (and maybe its leader) that assassinated Quṭuz on October 23, 1260. After some discussion and political jostling, Baybars was elected sultan by the senior Mamlūk commanders, launching a seventeen-year reign that would be very formative for the Mamlūk state, have a decisive impact on the Franks in the Levant, and also be of significant consequence for the Mongols in both Iran (the Ilkhanate) and southern Russia (the Golden Horde).[33] After a two-year interregnum, when two of Baybars' sons were sultans (in name, if not always in fact), his comrade Qalāwūn al-Alfī took the throne, adopting the regal title of al-Malik al-Manṣūr ("The [Divinely Assisted] Victorious King"). Qalāwūn worked to consolidate Baybars' achievements, ruling until his death in 1290; he also made more significant inroads into Frankish territory.[34] He, in turn, was succeeded by his son, al-Malik al-Ashraf Khalīl ("The Most Noble King," r. 1290–93), whose great accomplishment was the conquest Acre in 1291, thus putting an effective end to the Frankish polity in the region.[35] We will examine the following themes over the reigns of all three sultans: the strengthening of military and state institutions; the war with the Mongols; and, the conflict with the Franks. We will conclude with some brief remarks about the culture and society under the early Mamlūks and the long-term history of the sultanate, which remained the leading power in the region until its demise in 1517 at the hands of the Ottomans.

THE MAMLŪK SULTANATE COMES INTO ITS OWN

After a somewhat chaotic first decade, the Mamlūk state was now set to become more organized and institutionalized. Led by a military elite, and born in war with serious and determined enemies, this polity was infused with a martial ethos and an ideology of holy war (*jihād*). Probably at no other time in Islamic history has the state and the army been so intertwined.[36] This was not a chance occurrence, resulting from the culmination of uncoordinated actions by a ruling group, but to a large degree, the result of the decisions and actions of one individual, Sultan Baybars al-Bunduqdārī, who took the royal title of al-Malik al-Ẓāhir ("The Triumphant King") upon his accession in the fall of 1260.

At the center of Baybars' activities was the expansion and strengthening of the army. Under his rule, both the Egyptian and the Syrian armies probably doubled in size, and they underwent frequent drilling in the hippodromes, along with inspections to check equipment and general readiness. The ongoing campaigns in Syria and beyond the frontier there (especially against the Armenian Kingdom in Cilicia) provided ample opportunity for ongoing "hands-on" practice of individual skills, small and large unit training, and the inculcation of esprit de corps. A logistic system to equip and feed such an army, which probably numbered some 40,000 troopers (not all of them, however, going on campaign at a given time), was set up, although we have little information about it. The vast majority of the soldiers were mounted archers, so much attention and many resources were devoted to procuring, training, and maintaining horses, not the least during campaigns in Syria, since most of the Mamlūk army was based in Egypt. The bulk of the cavalry were Mamlūks, organized in the corps of Royal Mamlūks (*al-mamālīk al-sulṭāniyya*), and in the units of the amirs (*umarāʾ*, plural of *amīr*), "officers," who generally commanded units of 100, 40, or 10 Mamlūks (this could be flexible, certainly in the early period). Baybars had some 4000 personal Mamlūks (the Ẓāhiriyya), while Qalāwūn purchased at least 6000 (the Manṣūriyya). Most of these were Turks, although other ethnic groups were represented, including some Mongols of various provenance. Qalāwūn also established a large sub-unit known as the Burjiyya ("[those living in] the towers [of the Cairo Citadel]"), composed of Circassians from the Caucasus. In addition, there were many battalions of *Ḥalqa* ("ring," as in the circle surrounding the ruler, or perhaps that encircling the enemy), composed mainly of non-Mamlūk troopers: sons of Mamluks, Kurds, Muslims military refugees from neighboring countries, not insignificant Mongol deserters, and even some declassé Mamlūks. These *Ḥalqa* soldiers were all cavalry, and in fact, in the early Mamlūk period, were of a fairly high quality; the abilities and readiness of *Ḥalqa* formation, however, declined over time. In addition, there were specialist units, such as sappers and engineers to build and operate trebuchets and other machines of war. In Syria, there were also units of foot archers (*uqciyya*) and other infantry, especially in the border fortresses. Civilians, on the whole, did not fight in the Mamlūks armies, but in frontier areas, some were used to combat, and could take part in defense or even offensive operations if necessary.[37]

In order to build and maintain such a large military force, two conditions had to be met: a continual and organized supply of young Mamlūks (as sons of Mamlūks—*awlād al-nās*—could not serve in elite Mamlūk units, but only in the secondary *Ḥalqa*); and, the commanders and their soldiers needed to be paid. Building on earlier traditions, the supply of young Mamlūks generally continued on an annual basis. Young candidates for "mamlūkhood," as well as young girls destined for concubinage or domestic slavery, were collected from the realm of the Golden Horde (with the agreement of the authorities there), and were brought to the trading cities of Crimea. There Muslim merchants were involved, as were ships from the sultanate. The Genoese, however, played a major role in transporting these young Qipchaq slaves (as well as the occasion Mongol and others who were swept up in this trade), and their importance increased with over time. From the Black Sea, the ships carrying the slaves passed the Bosporus with the agreement of the Byzantine ruler (Anatolia, under Mongol rule, was now impassable for this trade). Emperor Michael Palaeologus had expelled the Latin rulers and their Venetian allies in 1261, permitting the establishing of a Genoese colony, again to the advantage of the trade in young Mamlūks.[38] Once in Egypt or Syria, the young slaves were bought by agents of the sultan or officers, thus beginning their years of training.[39] For the economic support of the Mamlūk—the troops in the units and their commanders—the agricultural lands of Egypt and Syria were divided up into *iqṭāʿāt*, allocations that were awarded to officers, who continued to reside in the cities, but collected the taxes from the agricultural yields. The *iqṭāʿ* did not mean local administration, and generally were not passed on to heirs. Rather, the *iqṭāʿ* system represented a relatively efficient way to transfer the surplus from the countryside to the military-political elite, including the ruling sultan, who also enjoyed extensive revenues from this source. With these revenues, the *iqṭāʿ*-holders would support their households, train their personal Mamlūks and then support them in the long run.[40]

Baybars also established efficient communications systems to enable the rapid transference of urgent military and political information between Syria and Egypt. This included a network of postal horse relays connecting the important cities of Syria with Cairo, the capital, a pigeon post, and lines of bonfires from the Euphrates frontier to send word of an impending Mongol raid or invasion.[41] Once news reached the sultan (whether in Egypt or Syria), he could dispatch or lead the Egyptian troops, concentrated in Cairo.[42] Fighting with the Mongols tended to be in the winter months; the Mongols had even larger cavalry-based armies, and needed both the water then available in the riverbeds and the fresh grasslands to nourish their mounts.[43] For the Mamlūks, the movement of large numbers of troops (and animals) in winter meant crossing many full riverbeds in Syria. To meet this challenge, Baybars constructed or rebuilt a number of bridges in southern Syria to expedite the movement of his armies with relative ease.[44]

Fortifications also received the attention of the Mamlūk rulers. Overall, castles and fortified cities were destroyed on the coast as they were taken from the Franks (more about that below), while those further inland were rebuilt, well maintained and garrisoned.[45] Thus, Baybars states in the mid-1265, in an announcement issued after the conquest of Arsūf (Apollonia) and Caesarea in Palestine:

> One part [of the Muslim armies] uproots Frankish fortresses, and destroys [their] castles, while [another] part rebuilds what the Mongols destroyed in the east and increases the height of their ramparts.[46]

Special attention was devoted to keeping up the morale of the inhabitants of the frontier fortresses, especially Bīra and Raḥba along the Euphrates. We learn that:

> The people [in the frontier castles] were reassured that the Sultan [Baybars] did not neglect an act, [but rather] carried it out, and he did not abandon his servants. The hearts of the castle defenders were calmed at this, and they said: "The Sultan moves quickly to our aid and his armies reach the besieging enemy before news [of these approaching armies] comes.[47]

An important component of military preparedness is intelligence gathering, and starting with Baybars, a far-reaching and well-organized foreign espionage service was set up. This included a director in Cairo who was a trusted personal of the sultan; a special, secret government office (*dīwān*) for payments; covert operatives (*quṣṣād*, sing. *qāṣid*, literally "couriers") who deep went into enemy territory to make contacts with local informants. We find the Mamlūk espionage operators active among the Franks, the Mongols and the Armenians, bringing information about impending attacks, political changes and other important matters, along with regular scouts (usually called *kashshāfa*) active in the frontier area.[48]

Baybars' activities, however, were not limited only to the strictly military sphere. He reestablished the ʿAbbāsid caliphate in Cairo, after its extinction in Baghdad in 1258, having a scion of the ʿAbbāsid family acknowledged in 1261 and given the title of al-Mustanṣir. During this carefully orchestrated ceremony, this new caliph's first act was to transfer all executive power to Sultan Baybars, as well as authority over all territories that will be conquered by him. Henceforth, Baybars was also known as *qasīm amīr al-muʾminīn*, "the associate of the Commander of the Faithful." The importance of this epithet, which was surely to strengthen the sultan's legitimacy in the eyes of the Muslim subjects, can be seen in that it is found in the gold and silver coins issued by Baybars and his successors.[49]

The Mamlūk sultans also strove to integrate Syria into a centralized state controlled from the Egyptian capital. In this, they were following the precedent set by their patron al-Ṣāliḥ

Ayyūb, who would not abide the confusion and difficulties experiences of the earlier Ayyūbid rulers of Egypt with their recalcitrant and all-but-independent family members in Syria. Over major cities (Damascus, Aleppo, Hama, Homs and Karak, later Gaza, Safad and Tripoli, but note, usually not Jerusalem) were appointed governors (*nuwwāb*, plural of *nā'ib*) directly by the sultan. Each governor answered directly to the Sultan, and usually, the commander of the local urban citadels did likewise.[50] This process was intensified even further under Qalāwūn and his successors, and was to remain in place until the end of the Mamlūk rule in Syria in 1516.[51]

THE ONGOING STRUGGLE WITH THE MONGOLS

The Mongols were the most important foreign concern of the Mamlūks for sixty years starting from 1260, and they long remained a significant factor in their thinking. The Mongols in Iran and the surrounding countries, the so-called Ilkhanate, were the most serious enemies of the sultanate. For the Mamlūk leadership it was clear that they had defeated only a small Mongol force at ʿAyn Jālūt, and it was just a question of time before the Mongols would return in force to avenge their defeat. At the same time, the "Golden Horde," the Mongol state to the north of the Black Sea and the Caucasus, was the most important ally of the Mamlūk sultanate. As noted above, this was the main source for young Mamlūks, the lifeblood of the sultanate; in addition, from the winter of 1261–62, the *khan*s (rulers) of the Golden Horde were at war with their (literal) cousins, the Ilkhans. Although many of the rulers of the Golden Horde were Muslims (as compared to shamanist and Buddhist Ilkhans), the struggle was apparently not mainly a religious one, but rather for control of the Caucasus and Azerbaijan, as well as tax revenues and other concrete matters. This "civil war" in the Mongol ruling family was of course a great boon to the Mamlūks, since the Ilkhanid Mongols were frequently pre-occupied with these wars (and those with the Chaghatayid Mongols from Central Asia).

However, this recurrent fighting in the north did not free the Mamlūks from almost existential dread of the Mongols from over the Euphrates, and they reacted accordingly. Most of the military measures described above were directed first and foremost toward this danger. There was virtually no year in the first two decades after ʿAyn Jālūt where there was not some fighting on the frontier, and sometimes in the north of Syria. Already at the end of 1260, another Mongol force—of about 6000 horsemen—was back in the country, and was defeated by the combined forces from Aleppo, Hama and Homs, near the last mentioned location. In the aftermath of these two battles, it was clear to the Mamlūk leadership that it was only a matter of time until the Mongols would come back again, most probably in force. They could not know then, of course, that only in 1281 would conditions be such that a large Mongol army would be back. Meanwhile, over the years they tried to take the border fortress of Bīra, in a small Mamlūk-controlled enclave on the east of the Euphrates (today in Turkey): 1265, 1272, and 1275. Later, Raḥba further south was the focus of Mongol attacks: the Ilkhans Gazan and Öljeitü in 1303 and 1312 respectively put it under siege, but were unable to take it (although possibly, at least according to pro-Mongolian sources, the governors made symbolic submissions). Time and again, with news of impending Mongol invasions or even raids, there was massive mobilization of the Mamlūk armies in Egypt and Syria, and frenzied preparations were made to meet this possible challenge. Overall, the Mamlūk leadership was not ready to let the frontier be breached or northern Syria be taken by default. To keep the Mongols off their guard, Mamlūk forces (either regular troops from the center and from the fortresses or Bedouin irregulars) raided across the frontier and collected intelligence. Another tactic to make life difficult for the advancing Mongols was to set grasslands in the frontier area on fire, and thus to reduce available pastureland so necessary for the Mongol armies.[52]

In the framework of the present volume, I will note in a little more detail one Mongol raid. In 1271, a Mongol force of some 1500 horsemen raided in north Syria, with another 10,000 or so waiting along the Euphrates for further orders. This particular raid was in conjuncture with the Franks, particularly Prince Edward of England who had arrived in Acre with some troops earlier that year. This is how Abaga Ilkhan (1265–82) is reported to have responded to Edward's original letter:

After talking over the matter, we have on our account resolved to send to your aid Cemakar [Samagar, commander of Mongol forces in Upper Mesopotamia] of a mighty force; thus, when you discuss among yourselves the other plans involving the forementioned Cemakar be sure to make explicit arrangements as to the exact month and day on which you will engage the enemy.[53]

Yet, no meeting or practical coordination between the Franks and Mongols was effected at this time, Edward dissipating his strength on pointless raids in Palestine. The opportunity for a potentially effective coordinated campaign between the Franks and the Mongols was wasted, largely due to Edward's dithering. The Mongol force in north Syria eventually withdrew with the approach of a Mamlūk army, when it became clear that there would be no help from the Franks in Acre. The Mamlūks were aware of these contacts between the Mongols and Franks, a point to which I will return below.[54]

As mentioned above, the Mamlūks at times took the war across the frontier, again usually with success. The most serious of these campaigns was Baybars' 1276 invasion of Anatolia, then ruled by the Seljuqs of Rūm, vassals of the Mongols. The local Mongol garrison of the country was defeated at Abulstayn (today Elbistan in southeastern Turkey), and Baybars advanced as far as the Seljuq capital at Caesarea (Kaiseri) in the center of the country. It was, however, impossible to hold the country, and Baybars withdrew before a new advancing Mongol army; the sultan died soon afterwards in Damascus (1277).[55] The next stage of the Mongol–Mamlūk war was early in the reign of his comrade Qalāwūn: already in 1280 there were Mongol probes, and the following year, an enormous army (perhaps even 80,000 troops, mostly cavalry) invaded the country. Qalāwūn mobilized the Egyptian army, and moved into Syria. Joined by local Mamlūk forces, the two armies met north of Homs on October 29, 1281. After difficult fighting and much uncertainly, the Mamlūks emerged victorious; the long-term efforts to build the Mamlūk military machine by Baybars had proven itself.[56]

Over the next fifteen years, the Mamlūk-Ilkhanid struggle was somewhat muted, although there was occasional fighting along the border. Between 1282 and 1284, during the short reign of Tegüder Aḥmad Ilkhan, there were desultory peace negotiations. Some scholars have thought that Tegüder, a long-time convert to Islam, was sincere in his démarche, while others detect the traditional Mongol truculence (albeit more subtly expressed) and calls for Mamlūk surrender.[57] In any case, these discussions via missives and ambassadors came to naught, and ended with Tegüder's death after his removal from office by his nephew Argun (1284–91). This new Ilkhan, an unequivocal Buddhist, devoted much effort—like that of his father, Abaga, ultimately unsuccessful—to organizing a military alliance with the West.

The most famous of these Ilkhanid embassies was that of the important Nestorian cleric, Rabbān Ṣauma, who in 1287 met with the kings of France and England, and the following year with the new pope, Nicholas IV; luckily the story of this trip has been preserved in some detail by an anonymous account in Syriac.[58] Under Abaga's successor, Geikhatu (1291–95), there was virtually no anti-Mamlūk initiative on the diplomatic or military front, which did not prevent the Mamlūks themselves from taking the initiative. In 1292, fresh from his victory at Acre, Sultan al-Ashraf Khalīl, took the Armenian fortress Qalʿat al-Rūm (Hromgla), in Mongol controlled eastern Anatolia, and was threatening to invade Iraq to retake Baghdad when he was assassinated.[59] Matters began to heat up along the frontier in the second half of the 1290s, after the accession of Gazan Maḥmūd to the Ilkhanid throne in 1295. This ruler, son of Argun and thus the great-grandson of Hülegü, became a Muslim during the struggle for the throne with his cousin Baidu, and henceforth, the Ilkhanate can be called a Muslim state. The implications for the Mongol–Mamlūk war were great, but that goes beyond the framework of this chapter. We may note just that between 1299 and 1303, Gazan (who died in 1304) launched three large campaigns. In spite of a setback in December 1300, when the Mamlūks were defeated near Homs and the Mongols occupied Syria for some 100 days, in the long run the Mamlūks kept control of the country. By 1320, negotiations began between the two powers that resulted in a treaty in 1323, leading to a peace that remained in force until the dissolution of the Ilkhanate in 1335.[60]

To what might we attribute this ultimate success of the Mamlūks over the Mongols, who had a much larger army? Several reasons can be considered: the similarity of fighting techniques (disciplined masses of mounted archers) on both sides; the logistical problems faced by the Mongols (although the Mamlūks needed to deal with some of the same problems); the Mamlūks were fighting on home turf, enjoying civilian support (most of the time) and having supply bases and castles nearby. Of great significance was the ongoing conflict— alluded to above—between the Mongols of the Ilkhanate with those of the Golden Horde and the Chaghatayid Khanate of Central Asia (to a lesser degree). This often prevented the Ilkhanids from devoting all of their attention to the Mamlūks, in spite of unequivocal bellicose rhetoric toward them and clear aspirations to take Syria and then to eradicate this enemy. In fact, it was the inability (and perhaps unwillingness) to devote themselves to the Mamlūk enemy, due to external and internal matters, that surely stymied the Mongol effort on the Syrian front. The Mamlūk leadership, however, clearly recognized the Ilkhanid Mongols as an existential enemy, and prepared themselves accordingly. This single-minded devotion to the Mongol danger gave the Mamlūks the strategic edge in this struggle, along with other reasons adduced above.[61]

ACTIVITIES VIS-À-VIS THE FRANKS IN THE LEVANT

When not dealing with the Mongol peril, the Mamlūks frequently devoted themselves to reducing the Frankish presence in the Levant. This was not a forgone conclusion in the aftermath of ʿAyn Jālūt and the establishment of Mamlūk rule in Syria. There is not a priori reason to think that the Mamlūks would change the policies of the Ayyūbids, which generally meant a continuation of the status quo with the Franks. True, the Mamlūk sultanate was a military state, which earlier had adopted a public *jihādī* ethos that had been forged in encounters, such as against the Franks at Manṣūra in 1250 and the Mongols at ʿAyn Jālūt in 1260. This may have contributed to increased truculence against the Franks. I believe, however, that something more concrete was involved. This is the growing understanding by the Mamlūk leadership that the Franks of Syria, as well as those in Europe, were increasingly in contact with the Ilkhanid Mongols, in order to come to some type of agreement with regard to a joint campaign against the Mamlūks. For example, after the Mongols attacked the frontier fortress of Bīra in 1265 (withdrawing with the approach of a large Mamlūk army), Baybars wrote to the castellan of Jaffa to complain about the Frankish leaders in Syria: "This people have committed many offences against me, such as their writing to the Mongols to attack my territories."[62] The possibility of real Mongol-Frankish military cooperation was the Mamlūks' worst nightmare. They might be able to deal with each enemy individually, but the possibility of fighting simultaneously on two fronts, let alone a combined enemy on one battlefield, was more than the Mamlūks could abide. I can suggest that in order to pre-empt such a possibility, and to generally weaken the Frankish presence in Syria, the Mamlūks under Baybars initiated a systematic program of conquering Frankish castles and fortified cities, invariably when the war with the Mongols was in abeyance. In the case of coastal cities, generally the fortifications and harbors were at least partially dismantled (the statements of the written sources to the effect that these were totally destroyed is belied by the extant fortifications today). The aim was clearly to deny the Franks as much as possible potential facilities for bringing troops, horses and supplies, not the least so that they could not combine forces with the Mongols.[63] As we have seen above, this potential for Mongol–Frankish cooperation was never realized, even when a small crusading army—as under Edward of England in 1271—was present in the country.

There had been some somewhat inconsequential skirmishing with the Franks in the early 1260s, but fighting began in earnest in 1263, with the attacks against Nazareth, the taking of Mt. Tabor and the raids in the environs of Acre. In 1265, the first serious offensives were carried, resulting in the conquest of Arsūf (Apollonia) and Qaysariyya (Caesarea) after well-prepared sieges. The following year, Safad was taken, also a lengthy siege, and most of the Templar garrison was massacred. Unlike the first two cities, the fortifications and ports of which were at least partially destroyed, Safad was rebuilt, and became the capital of a new Mamlūk province (*niyāba*). In 1268, more locations were taken: Jaffa, Shaqīf Arnūn (Beaufort) and, most significantly, Antioch, again with much bloodshed. In the first half of 1271, with news that King Louis IX of France had taken his crusading army to Tunis, and would not be coming to Holy Land in the near future, Baybars launched a series of attacks on various fortresses, taking many in relatively short order: Safītha/Safīta (Chastel Blanc, of the Templars), Hisn al-Akrād (Crac des Chevaliers, of the Hospitallers), Hisn ʿAkkār (Gibelacar, also of the Hospitallers) and al-Qurayn (Montfort, headquarters of the Teutonic Knights). This is pretty much the end of Baybars' campaigns against the local Franks, although surely he and his governors were alert to renewed activity on their parts: the raids launched by Edward of England later in 1271 occasioned a vigorous Mamlūk response.[64]

Under Sultan Qalāwūn, further Frankish territory was taken, but at a less frenetic rate. Early in his reign, Qalāwūn was preoccupied with the Mongols, and in general he devoted more attention than his comrade and illustrious predecessor to consolidating power in Egypt. However, by 1285 he was ready to take another slice from the Frankish kingdom: Marqab (Margat), was soon conquered, and then rehabilitated and heavily garrisoned. Qalāwūn's big achievement vis-à-vis the Franks was the conquest of Tripoli in 1289; the town was destroyed, but rebuilt further inland, again becoming the center of another *niyāba*. Preparations were in full swing in 1290 for a siege of Acre, but were curtailed by Qalāwūn's death in November of that year. A few months later, his son and successor, al-Ashraf Khalīl, realized his father's plan, and took the city (end of May 1291). Soon afterwards, the few remaining Frankish strongholds were abandoned or surrendered and with this the political presence of the Franks came to an end (although individual Franks and small communities may have remained).[65]

Of course, relations with the Franks in these thirty-one years did not only involve fighting. There was also plenty of diplomatic activity, leading at times to long-term treaties with various entities (the Kingdom of Jerusalem centered at Acre, individual lords, the military orders and the Italian cities). These agreements were generally very much in the sultanate's favor; as the stronger side, the sultan got the better deal, and could break these agreements when necessary or convenient without too much ado. In the case of Genoa and Venice, however, these agreements were more even handed, as befitting partners who provided important services to the sultanate (not the least, with regard to Genoa, young Mamlūks). We cannot survey all of these treaties, but can note that those treaties were discussed in detail by the late Peter M. Holt, in his exemplary exposition (with full translations) in 1995: Baybars' treaty with the Hospitallers in 1267; his treaty with Lady Isabel of Beirut in 1269; yet another treaty with the Hospitallers in 1271, who now controlled much less territory; Qalāwūn's treaty with Bohemond VII of Tripoli (having lost Antioch in 1269); Qalāwūn's treaty with the Templars in 1282; Qalāwūn's treaty with the Latin kingdom in 1283; Qalāwūn's treaty with Lady Margeret of Tyre in 1285.[66] From these treaties (most of which were for either ten years, or for ten years, ten months, and ten days), we learn—sometimes *en passant*—of commercial relations between the Franks of the Levant and their Muslim neighbors, even while the Mamlūk armies were pursuing a clear policy of territorial aggrandizement at the expense of these same Franks. This is not the first or last time in the late medieval history of the region that political and military considerations would not get in the way of economic concerns, or rather, vibrant economic relations belied ongoing tension in other spheres.

With the complete elimination of the Frankish entities in the Levant, it is instructive to cite the words of the later Syrian bureaucrat and encyclopedist, Ibn Faḍl Allāh al-'Umarī:

> If [al-Ashraf Khalīl b. Qalāwūn] had not cleansed the country [of the Franks], and not [taken upon himsef] the duty during his reign to rid any remnant of them [there], then in the 699/1299–1300 when the sultan Mahmud Ghazan came to the country and withdrew, [the Franks] would have gained control of the country and annihilated the inhabitants, taking advantage of the absence of the [Mamlūk] army, the distance of the [Mamlūk] officers from Syria], and the disagreements [among the Muslims].[67]

This passage, written perhaps two generations after the disappearance of the Frankish entity, may attribute to them too much power in its waning days, but this does clearly show the perceived connection between the Franks and the Mongols, and the danger that this represented to Mamlūk rule, at least in Syria.

THE WIDER PICTURE

In this short survey of the early Mamlūk sultanate, no mention has been made of the vigorous intellectual and cultural life of both Syria and Egypt, at least partially facilitated by the patronage of the Mamlūk elite: this included a massive construction effort of religious and secular buildings, along with much infrastructure. The religious buildings were very often supported by the creation of endowments (*awqāf*, the plural of *waqf*), which directed the revenues from urban and rural properties toward such projects, among which were *madrasas* (Muslim religious colleges), *khānqāhs* and *zāwiyas* (ṣūfī centers), mosques, caravanserais (which, in spite of their clear economic value were considered pious projects), etc. One result was the strengthening the groups of 'ulamā' (religious scholars) and ṣūfīs (mystics); often the border between these two groups was unclear. Other areas of cultural and intellectual activity were in the natural sciences (medicine and astronomy stand out), historical writing and the "minor" arts (work in metal, glass and other media).[68] This sets the stage for further developments in these and related areas in the coming generations. The Mamlūks ruled over a varied and multi-confessional society, besides Sunni Muslims, there were Shī'īs in Syria (and several splinter groups, mainly Druze and Nuṣayrīs), large Christian communities in both Egypt and Syria, concentrations of Jews in both countries and a small Samarian community in Palestine. There is concrete evidence that in the Mamlūk period there were waves of conversion to Islam among the Christians of Syria and Egypt, setting the stage for the demographic situation that lasted up to the nineteenth century.[69]

The Mamlūk sultanate in the first decades of its existence played an essential role in stopping the Mongols in south-west Asia and bringing the Crusading presence in the Levant to an end. The success of the Mamluks was due to the creation of a relatively centralized state, the judicious use of available resources, the building of a large and powerful mobile field army, outstanding leadership and a sound ideological program. In the framework of the present volume we have concentrated on the achievements of this early period, yet we should not forget that the Mamlūk state continued for more than another two centuries as the leading regional power. As such, it dealt with powers big and small in all directions, and provided a reasonably stable framework for an overall robust cultural, intellectual, economic and social life. Thus, the period surveyed in this chapter is more than just the story of the end of the crusading presences in the Levant or even the war against the Mongols: it is the time in which the foundations were laid down for a quarter millennium of rule, with great influence on regional and even world history.

NOTES

1 The initial research for this chapter was conducted with the support of Israel Science Foundation grant no. 1676/2009, but it was written while I was a fellow at the Annemarie Schimmel Kolleg ("History and Society of the Mamlūk Sultanate 1250–1517") at the University of Bonn, Germany in the fall of 2014. I am grateful to the directors and staff of the Kolleg for their warm, hospitable support.

2 These were the two main components of the Ṣāliḥiyya, the Mamlūk regiment of al-Ṣāliḥ Ayyūb. The Jāmadāriyya (literally: "wardrobe attendants") were apparently a special bodyguard, while the Baḥriyya (from *baḥr*, "sea," but in this case, meaning a large river, referring to their camp on the island of Rawḍa in Baḥr al-Nīl, or the Nile River), were also an elite body of fighters. On these units, and al-Ṣāliḥ Ayyūb's Mamlūks in general, see Amalia Levanoni, "The Mamlūks' Ascent to Power in Egypt," *Studia Islamica*, 72 (1990), 124–125; idem, "The Consolidation of Aybak's Rule: An Example of Factionalism in the Mamlūk State," *Der Islam*, 71 (1994), 241, n. 2.

3 These are metaphors for the complete disarray that the Mamlūks caused among the Franks.

4 Ibn Wāṣil (Jamāl al-Dīn Muḥammad), *Mufarrij al-kurūb fī akhbār banī ayyūb*, in Mohamed Rahim, *Die Chronik des ibn Wāṣil: ... Untergang der Ayyūbiden und Beginn der Mamlūkenherrschaft* (Wiesbaden: Harrassowitz, 2010), 55, 57. This seems to be the ultimate source for the rousing passage in the chronicle by Nāṣir al-Dīn 'Abd al-Raḥmān b. Muḥammad Ibn al-Furāt (d. 1405):

Ursula and Malcolm C. Lyons (trans.) and Jonathan S.C. Riley-Smith (intro. and notes), *Ayyubids, Mamlukes and Crusaders. Selections from the Tārīkh [sic] al-Duwal wa'l-Mulūk of Ibn al-Furāt*, (Cambridge: Heffers, 1971), I, 27–28 (Arabic text); II, 22–23 (trans.). NB: The earlier work does not mention the role of Baybars in this episode.

5 For the fate of these Franks, see Joshua Prawer, *Histoire du royaume latin de Jérusalem*, trans. G. Nahon (Paris, 1970), II, 343–344.

6 These events are surveyed in some detail in the following: Robert Irwin, *The Middle East in the Middle Ages: The Early Mamluk Sultanate 1250–1382* (London: Croom Helm, 1986), 20–27; R.S. Humphreys, *From Saladin to the Mongols: The Ayyubids of Damascus, 1193–1260* (Albany: SUNY Press, 1977), 301–305; Julien Loiseau, *Les Mamelouks, XIIIe–XVIe siècle: une experience du pouvoir dans l'Islam médiéval* (Paris: Éditions du Seuil, 2014), 112–115.

7 We can note, however, that earlier in the thirteenth century, a parallel type of political entity was established by Muslim commanders of slave origin, again mostly Turkish, in northern India and centered at Dehli. See Peter Jackson, "The Mamlūk Institution in Early Muslim India," *Journal of the Royal Asiatic Society*, 2 (1990), 340–358.

8 Hans Gottschalk, *Al-Malik Al-Kāmil von Egypten und seine Zeit. Eine Studie zur Geschichte Vorderasiens und Egyptens in der ersten Hälfte des 7./13. Jahrhunderts* (Wiesbaden: Harrassowitz, 1958), 175.

9 For these events, see Humphreys, *From Saladin to the Mongols*, 250–265.

10 Ibn Wāṣil, ed. Rahim, 19. This is surely the origin of the oft-cited passage by al-Maqrīzī (Taqī al-Dīn Aḥmad b. ʿAlī, d. 1441), *al-Sulūk li-maʿrifat duwal al-mulūk*, ed. M.M. Ziyāda and S.ʿA. ʿĀshūr (Cairo, 1934–73), I, 339–340.

11 Al-Nuwayrī (Shihāb al-Dīn Aḥmad b. ʿAbd al-Wahhāb), *Nihāyat al-arab fī funūn al-adab* (Cairo, 1992), XXIX, 417. For other sources that relate similar sentiments, see Reuven Amitai-Preiss, *Mongols and Mamlūks: The Mamlūk-Ilkhanid War, 1260–1281* (Cambridge: Cambridge University Press, 1995), 18, n. 63.

12 See below for more on this trade in young Mamlūks. We should note that some of these young slaves, particularly the girls, also made their way to the western–and Christian–part of the Mediterranean, becoming there household slaves.

13 Humphreys, *From Saladin to the Mongols*, 314–323; Prawer, *Histoire du royaume latin*, II, 346–347; 14, *The Middle East*, 27–28; Peter Thorau, *The Lion of Egypt: Sultan Baybars I and the Near East in the Thirteenth Century*, trans. Peter M. Holt (London and New York: Longman, 1992), 46–47, 52.

14 For the growing tension between the Baḥriyya and other sections of the military-political elite, especially Aybak, see Levanoni, "The Mamlūks' Ascent to Power," 141–144.

15 Humphreys, *From Saladin to the Mongols*, 326; Irwin, *The Middle East*, 28. For the origins and very early career of Baybars, see Thorau, *The Lion of Egypt*, 27–32. The *nisba* (adjective denoting descent or origin ending in an –ī) of Bunduqdārī refers to Baybars' first Mamlūk patron, the amir (officer), ʿAlāʾ al-Dīn Aydakin al-Bunduqdar. Aydakin, also originally a Mamlūk of al-Ṣāliḥ Ayyūb, who had early in his career been the bearer (*dār* < Persian) of a pellet shooting arbalest (<*bunduq*, lit. "hazelnut") for his master; this weapon was used for hunting birds. Subsequently, Baybars became a personal and close Mamlūk of al-Ṣāliḥ.

16 Irwin, *The Middle East*, 29; Thorau, *Lion of Egypt*, 51–53, 64–65; Amitai-Preiss, *Mongols and Mamlūks*, 19.

17 Irwin, *The Middle East*, 30, succinctly summarizes these events, which are rendered in greater detail in Thorau, *The Lion of Egypt*, 51–58, and Humphreys, *From Saladin to the Mongols*, 326–333.

18 For Louis' activities in Palestine, see Humphreys, *From Saladin to the Mongols*, 321–326; Prawer, *Histoire du royaume latin*, II, 339–356. Irwin (*The Middle East*, 30) notes that Louis was "fairly successful" in playing off al-Nāṣir Yūsuf against the Mamlūks.

19 Prawer, *Histoire du royaume latin*, II, 357.

20 Linda Goldsmith, "St. Sabas, War of (1256–1258)," in Alan V. Murray (ed.), *The Crusades: An Encyclopedia* (Santa Barbara, Denver and Oxford: ABC-CLIO, 2006), III, 1059; Prawer, *Histoire du royaume latin*, II, 359–373.

21 For excellent introductions to the history of the Mongol empire, with extensive bibliographies, see: Michal Biran, *Chinggis Khan*, "Makers of the Muslim World" (Oxford: One World, 2007); David Morgan, *The Mongols*, 2nd ed. (Oxford, Malden MA and Carlton, Victoria: Blackwell Publishing, 2007). The forthcoming *Cambridge History of the Mongol Empire*, edited by Michal Biran and Hodong Kim, will surely be an extremely useful reference work on this particular chapter in Asian, Middle Eastern and world history.

22 The best survey of this interim period is still John A. Boyle, "Dynastic and Political History of the Īl-Khāns," in *The Cambridge History of Iran*, vol. 5, ed. J.A. Boyle (Cambridge: Cambridge University Press, 1968), 322–340.

23 Ibid., 340–350; Amitai-Preiss, *Mongols and Mamlūks*, 8–17. For the wider Mongol context, see: Thomas T. Allsen, *Mongol Imperialism: The Policies of Grand Qan Möngke in China, Russia and the Islamic Lands 1251–59* (Berkeley and Los Angeles: University of California Press, 1987).

24 Hülegü was now frequently referred to with this title, meaning probably "submissive ruler [to the Great Khan]." It was also often applied to his successors, and thus this Mongol state is conveniently referred to as the Ilkhanate.

25 Humphreys, *From Saladin to the Mongols*, 348–351; Amitai-Preiss, *Mongols and Mamlūks*, 26–27; Reuven Amitai, "Im Westen nichts Neues? Re-examining Hülegü's Offensive into the Jazīra and Northern Syria in Light of Recent Research," in Frank Krämer, Katharina Schmidt and Julika Sinder (eds.), *Historicizing the "Beyond". The Mongolian Invasion as a New Dimension of Violence?* (Heidelberg: UniversitätverlagWinter Heidelberg, 2011), 83–96.

26 Thorau, *The Lion of Egypt*, 64–69; Humphreys, *From Saladin to the Mongols*, 345–348, 351–355; Reuven Amitai, "Mongol Raids into Palestine (A.D. 1260 and 1300)," *Journal of the Royal Asiatic Society* (1987), 236–55; idem, "Mongol Provincial Administration: Syria in 1260 as a Case-Study," in Iris Shagrir, Ronnie Ellenblum and Jonathan Riley-Smith (eds.), *In Laudem Hierosolymitani: Studies in Crusades and Medieval Culture in Honour of Benjamin Z. Kedar* (Aldershot: Ashgate, 2007), 117–143.

27 For Hülegü's withdrawal, see Amitai-Preiss, *Mongols and Mamlūks*, 27–29; cf. David Morgan, "The Mongols in Syria, 1260–1300," in Peter Edbury (ed.), *Crusade and Settlement. Papers Read at the First Conference of the Society for the Study of the Crusades and the Latin East and Presented to R.C. Smail* (Cardiff: University College Cardiff Press, 1985), 231–235; John M. Smith, Jr., "'Ayn Jālūt: Mamlūk Success or Mongol Failure," *Harvard Journal of Asiatic Studies*, 44 (1984), 307–345, esp. 328–345.

28 For the relations between the Franks and the Mongols at this time, see: Peter Jackson, "The Crisis in the Holy Land in 1260,"*English Historical Review*, 95 (1980), 481–513, esp. 486–507; cf. Prawer, *Histoire du royaume latin*, II, 425–434.

29 The most detailed description of the battle remains Reuven Amitai, "'Ayn Jālūt Revisited," *Tārīḫ* (Philadelphia), 2 (1992), 119–150, reprinted in R. Amitai, *The Mongols in the Islamic Lands: Studies in the History of the Ilkhanate* (Aldershot and Burlington, VT: Ashgate, 2007); additional bibliography in R. Amitai, "'Ayn Jālūt," *Encyclopdaedia of Islam*, 3rd ed., online version.

30 Al-'Umarī (Shihāb al-Dīn Aḥmad b. Yaḥyā ibn Faḍlallāh), *Masālik al-abṣār fī 'l-mamālik al-amṣār*, partial ed. and trans. in Klaus Lech, *Das Mongolische Weltreich: al-'Umarīs Darstellung der mongolischen Reiche in seinem Werk Masālik al-abṣār fī 'l-mamālik al-amṣār* (Wiesbaden: Harrassowitz, 1968), 70–71 (Arabic text), 139–140 (German translation). This rendition in English is based on that given in David Ayalon, "The Great Yāsa of Chingiz Khān. A Reexamination," *Studia Islamica*, Part C1, 36 (1972), 122–123; reprinted in D. Ayalon, *Outsiders in the Lands of Islam: Mamlūks, Mongols, and Eunuchs* (London: Variorum, 1988).

31 Abū Shāma (Shihāb al-Dīn 'Abd al-Raḥmān b. Ismā'īl), *Tarājim rijāl al-qarnayn al-sādis wa 'l-sāb' al-ma'rūf bi 'l-dhayl 'alā al-rawḍatayn*, ed. Muḥammad al-Kawtharī (Cairo: Maktab Nashr

al-Thiqāfa al-Islāmiyya, 1947, 208, cited and trans. by David Ayalon, "The European-Asiatic Steppe: A Major Reservoir of Power for the Islamic World," *Proceedings of 25th Congress of Orientalists–Moscow, 1960* (Moscow: Izdatel'stvo vostochnoy literatury, 1963), II, 47–52 [reprinted in D. Ayalon, *The Mamlūk Military Society* (London: Variorum, 1979)].

32 For more citations to this effect, see: Ayalon, "The Great Yāsa of Chingiz Khān," 117–124; Amitai-Preiss, *Mongols and Mamlūks*, 45, n. 119.

33 Thorau, *The Lion of Egypt*, is the best available survey of this sultan's reign, with particular empha-sis on the relations with the Franks in the Levant and Europe. Also useful is Abdul-Aziz Khowaiter, *Baibars the First: His Endeavors and Achievements* (London: Green Mountain Press, 1979).

34 Linda Northrup, *From Slave to Sultan: The Career of al-Manṣūr Qalāwūn and the Consolidation of Mamlūk Rule in Egypt and Syria (678–689 A.H./1279–1290 A.D.)* (Stuttgart: Franz Steiner Verlag, 1998).

35 There is no biography of this sultan, nor a detailed review of his reign. However, this energetic ruler's deeds (ended abruptly when he was assassinated by a group of senior officers who were dismayed by some of his policies) are surveyed in the following general works on the Mamlūks, which are also very informative for the entire period discussed here: Irwin, *The Middle East*; Peter M. Holt, *The Age of the Crusades: The Near East from the Eleventh Century to 1517* (London and New York: Longman, 1986); Linda Northrup, "The Baḥrī Mamlūk Sultanate, 1250–1390," in Carl Petry (ed.), *The Cambridge History of Egypt*, vol. 1: Islamic Egypt, 540–1517 (Cambridge: Cambridge University Press, 1998), 242–289.

36 Reuven Amitai, "Dealing with Reality: Early Mamlūk Military Policy and the Allocation of Resources," in Stefan Leder (ed.), *Crossroads between Latin Europe and the Near East: Frankish Presence in the Eastern Mediterranean (12th to 14th Centuries)* (Würzburg: Ergon Verlag, 2011), 127; idem, "Mamlūks, Franks and Mongols: A Necessary but Impossible Triangle," in Robert Hillenbrand, Firuza Abdullaeva and Andrew Peacock (eds.), *Ferdowsi, the Mongols and the History of Iran: Art, Literature and Culture from Early Islam to Qajar Persia* (Charles Melville Festschrift) (London: I.B. Tauris, 2013), 140.

37 For Baybars' organization of the army, see Amitai-Preiss, *Mongols and Mamlūks*, 71–74; for Qalāwūn's purchase of Mamlūks and his military policy, see Northrup, *From Slave to Sultan*, 183–199; for the organization of the Mamlūk army, see David Ayalon, "Studies on the Structure of the Mamlūk Army," *Bulletin of the School of Asian and African Studies*, 15/2 (1953), 203–228; 15/3 (1953), 448–476; 16/1 (1954), 57–90 (reprinted in D. Ayalon, *Studies on the Mamlūks of Egypt (1250–1517)* [London: Variorum, 1977]; for the infantry in the Mamlūk army and the role of civilians, see Reuven Amitai, "Foot Soldiers, Militiamen and Volunteers in the Early Mamlūk Army," in Chase F. Robinson (ed.), *Texts, Documents and Artifacts: Islamic Studies in Honour of D.S. Richards* (Leiden: E.J. Brill, 2003), 232–249.

38 Andrew Ehrenkreutz, "Strategic Implications of the Slave Trade between Genoa and Mamluk Egypt in the Second Half of the Thirteenth Century," in Avram L. Udovitch (ed.), *The Islamic Middle East, 700–1900: Studies in Economic and Social History* (Princeton: Darwin Press, 1981), 335–345; Reuven Amitai, "Diplomacy and the Slave Trade in the Eastern Mediterranean: A Re-examination of the Mamlūk-Byzantine-Genoese Triangle in the Late Thirteenth Century in Light of the Existing Early Correspondence," *Oriente Moderno*, NS, 87/2 (2008), 349–368 [Special issue entitled: *Les relations diplomatiques entre le monde musulman et l'occident latin (XIIe-XVIe siècle)*, ed. Denise Aigle and Pascal Buresi].

39 David Ayalon, *L'esclavage du Mamelouk*, "Oriental Notes and Studies," No. 1 (Jerusalem: Israel Oriental Society, 1951) [reprinted in D. Ayalon, *The Mamlūk Military Society* (London: Variorum, 1979)]; see also the forthcoming two articles by Yehoshua Frenkel, "Some Notes Concerning the Trade and Education of Slave-Soldiers during the Mamlūk Era" and Amir Mazor, "The Early Experience of the Mamlūk in the First Period of the Mamlūk Sultanate (1250–1382 CE)," both to appear in Christoph Cluse and Reuven Amitai (eds.), *Slavery and the Slave Trade in the Eastern Mediterranean (c. 1000–1500 CE)*.

40 Robert Irwin, "*Iqṭā*' and the End of the Crusader States," in Peter M. Holt (ed.), *The Eastern Mediterranean Lands in the Period of the Crusades* (Warminster: Aris and Phillips, 1977), 62–77 [reprinted in R. Irwin, *Mamlūks and Crusaders: Men of the Sword and Men of the Pen* (Farnham, Surrey and Burlington: Ashgate, 2010)]; Hassanein Rabie, *The Financial System of Egypt, A.H. 564–741/A.D, 1169–1341* (London: Oxford University Press), 26–72.

41 Amitai-Preiss, *Mongols and Mamlūks*, 74–75; Adam J. Silverstein, *Postal Systems in the Pre-Modern Islamic World* (Cambridge: Cambridge University Press, 2007), 165–185.

42 On the movement of the Mamlūk army to Syria, see David Ayalon, "Ḥarb, iii. – The Mamlūk Sultanate," *The Encyclopedia of Islam*, III, 184–185

43 For the logistical challenges faced by the Mongols in their wars with the Mamlūks, see Morgan, "The Mongols in Syria"; Smith, "'Ayn Jālūt"; Reuven Amitai, "Some More Thoughts on the Logistics of the Mongol-Mamlūk War (with Special Reference to the Battle of Wādī al-Khaznadār)," in John Pryor (ed.), *Logistics of War in the Age of the Crusades* (Aldershot: Ashgate, 2006), 25–42.

44 Amitai-Preiss, *Mongols and Mamlūks*, 75.

45 Kate Raphael, *Muslim Fortresses in the Levant: Between Crusaders and Mongols* (Abington, Oxon and New York: Routledge, 2011); Amitai-Preiss, *Mongols and Mamlūks*, 76–77.

46 Ibn al-Dawādārī (Abū Bakr b. 'Abd Allāh), *Kanz al-durar wa-jāmi' al-ghurar*, vol. 8: al-durra al-zākiyya fī akhbār al-dawla al-turkiyya, ed. Ulrich Haarmann (Cairo: Deutsches Archäologisches Institut Kairo, 1391/1971), 109; trans. and analysis in David Ayalon, "The Mamlūks and Naval Power: A Phase of the Struggle between Islam and Christian Europe," *Proceedings of the Israel Academy of Sciences and Humanities*, 1, 8 (1967), 12 [reprinted in D. Ayalon, *Studies on the Mamlūks of Egypt (1250–1517)* (London: Variorum, 1977)].

47 Ibn 'Abd al-Ẓāhir (Muḥyī al-Dīn), *al-Rawḍ al-zāhir fī sīrat al-malik al-ẓāhir*. ed. 'Abd al-'Azīz al-Khuwayṭir (Riyad: n.pub., 1396/1976), 227.

48 Reuven Amitai, "Mamlūk Espionage among Mongols and Franks," *Asian and African Studies*, 22 (1988), 173–181; Amitai-Preiss, *Mongols and Mamlūks*, 139–156.

49 Peter M. Holt, "Some Observations of the 'Abbāsid Caliphate of Cairo," *Bulletin of the School of Oriental and African*, 47 (1984), 501–507; Reuven Amitai, *Holy War and Rapprochement: Studies in the Relations between the Mamlūk Sultanate and the Mongol Ilkhanate (1260–1335)* (Turnhout: Brepols, 2013), 56–57.

50 Peter M. Holt, *The Age of the Crusades: The Near East from the Eleventh Century to 1517* (London and New York: Longman, 1986), 149–150. Actually, in the aftermath of 'Ayn Jālūt, three of these localities remained under the direct rule of Ayyūbid princes who had submitted to the Mamlūk sultan: Karak (prince was removed and executed in 1263); Homs (with the death of the prince in 1263, replaced by Mamlūk governor); and Hama (generally remained under Ayyūbid princes until 1341); see Thorau, *The Lion of Egypt*, 134–141.

51 Irwin, *The Middle East*, 45, 65–67.

52 For the border war in general, see Amitai-Preiss, *Mongols and Mamlūks*, ch. 5.

53 Reinhold Röhricht, "La croisade du Prince Édouard d'Angleterre (1270–1274)," in *idem*, "Études sur les deerniers temps du royaume de Jérusalem," *Archives de l'orient latin*, 1 (1881), 623, n. 35, citing *Liber de Antiquis Legibus*, ed. T. Stapleton (London: Camden Society, 1846), 143; trans. from Denis Sinor, "On Mongol Strategy," in *Proceedings of the Fourth Altaistic Conference*, ed. Ch'en Ch'ieh-shien (Tainan, Taiwan: Dept. of History, Natinoal Ch'engkung University, 1975), 224 [reprinted in D. Sinor, *Inner Asia and Its Contacts with Medieval Europe* (London: Variorum, 1977)].

54 On this episode, see: Prawer, *Histoire Histoire du royaume latin*, II, 499–505; Reuven Amitai-Preiss, "Edward of England and Abagha Ilkhan: A Reexamination of a Failed Attempt at Mongol-Frankish Cooperation," in Michael Gervers and James M. Powell (eds.), *Tolerance and Intolerance: Social Conflict in the Age of the Crusades* (Syracuse, NY: Syracuse University Press, 2001), 75–82 (nn. 160–163).

55 Claude Cahen, *Pre-Ottoman Turkey: A General Survey of the Material and Spiritual Culture and History c. 1071–1330*, trans. J. Jones-Williams (London: Sidgwick and Jackson, 1968), 285–292; Amitai-Preiss, *Mongols and Mamlūks*, ch. 7.

56 Boyle, "Dynastic and Political History of the Īl-Khāns," 363–364; Amitai-Preiss, *Mongols and Mamlūks*, ch. 8.

57 Adel Allouche, "Tegüder's Ultimatum to Qalāwūn," *International Journal of Middle Eastern Studies*, 22 (1990), 437–446; Reuven Amitai, "The Conversion of Tegüder Ilkhan to Islam," *Jerusalem Studies in Arabic and Islamic Studies*, 25 (2001), 15–43; Judith Pfieffer, "Aḥmad Tegüder's Second Letter to Qalā'ūn (682/1283)," in Judith Pfeiffer and Shjoleh A. Quinn (eds.), in collaboration with Ernest Tucker, *History and Historiography of Post-Mongol Central Asia and the Middle East: Studies in Honor of John E. Woods* (Wiesbaden: Harrassowitz, 2006), 167–202.

58 John A. Boyle, "The Il-Khans of Persian and the Christian West'" *History Today*, 23/8 (1973), 554–563 [reprinted in J.A. Boyle, *The Mongol World Empire 1206–1370* (London: Variorum, 1977)]; Peter Jackson, *The Mongols and the West, 1221–1410* (Harrow: Pearson Longman, 2005), 169, 173, 179; Morris Rossabi, *Voyager from Xanadu: Rabban Sauma and the First Journey from China to the West* (rpt., Berkeley and Los Angeles: University of California Press, 2010).

59 Boyle, "Dynastic and Political History of the Īl-Khāns," 373; Irwin, *The Middle East*, 78–82; Angus Stewart, "Qal'at al-Rūm / Hromgla / Rumkale and the Mamlūk Siege of 691 AH/1292 CE," in Hugh Kennedy (ed.), *Muslim Military Architecture in Greater Syria: From the Coming of Islam to the Ottoman Period* (Leiden: Brill, 2006), 269–280.The role of the Armenia Kingdom of Cilicia in the Mongol–Mamlūk war is beyond the scope of this chapter; see Bayarsaikhan Dashdondog, *The Mongols and the Armenians (1220–1335)* (Leiden: Brill, 2010); Reuven Amitai, "Dangerous Liaisons: Armenian-Mongol-Mamlūk Relations (1260–1292)," in Gérard Dédéyan and Claude Mutafian (eds.), *La Méditerranée des Arméniens, XIIe-XVe siècle* (Paris: Geuthner, 2014), 191–206; Angus Stewart, *Armenian Kingdom and the Mamlūks: War and Diplomacy During the Reigns of Het'um II (1289–1307)* (Leiden: Brill, 2001).

60 Boyle, "Dynastic and Political History of the Īl-Khāns," 376–413; Charles Melville, "'Sometimes by the Sword, Sometimes by the Dagger': The Role of the Isma'ilis in Mamlūk-Mongol Relations in the 8th/14th Century," in Farhad Daftary (ed.), *Medieval Isma'ili History and Thought* (Cambridge: Cambridge University Press, 1996), 247–263; Reuven Amitai, "The Resolution of the Mongol-Mamlūk War," in Reuven Amitai and Michal Biran (eds.), *Mongols, Turks and Others: Eurasian Nomads and the Sedentary World* (Leiden: E.J. Brill, 2005), 359–390.

61 See the elaboration on this theme in Amitai, *Holy War and Rapprochement*, 35–36; idem, "Dealing with Reality," 131–132.

62 Shāfi' b. 'Alī al-Kātib (Nāṣir al-Dīn), *Ḥusn al-manāqib al-sirriyya al-muntaza'a min al-sīra al-ẓāhiriyya*, ed. 'Abd al-'Azīz al-Khuwayṭir (Riyad: Maṭābi' al-Quwāt al-Musallaḥa al-Su'ūdiyya, 1396/1976), 87–88; trans. in Peter M. Holt, "Some Observations on Shāfi' b. 'Alī's Biography of Baybars," *Journal of Semitic Studies*, 29 (1984), 127, who suggests that the Castellan was most probably John d'Ibelin.

63 For general Mamlūk policy regarding the Syrian coast, see: Albrecht Fuess, "Rotting Ships and Razed Harbours: The Naval Policy of the Mamlūks," *Mamlūk Studies Review*, 5 (2001), 45–71; David Ayalon, "The Mamlūks and Naval Power: A Phase of the Struggle between Islam and Christian Europe," *Proceedings of the Israel Academy of Sciences and Humanities*, 1/8 (1967), 1–12 [reprinted in David Ayalon, *Studies on the Mamlūks of Egypt (1250–1517)* (London: Variorum, 1977)]; Amitai, "Dealing with Reality," 136–137.

64 Irwin, *The Middle East*, 47–49; Thorau, *The Lion of Egypt*, 142–162, 166–171, 175–178, 187–192, 203–206; Prawer, *Histoire du royaume latin*, II, 436–505.

65 Irwin, *The Middle East*, 73–78; Prawer, *Histoire du royaume latin*, II, 519–557; Northrup, *From Slave to Sultan*, 130–132, 151–154; Donald P. Little, "The Fall of 'Akkā in 690/1291: The Muslim Version," in Moshe Sharon (ed.), *Studies in Islamic History and Civilization in Honour of Professor David Ayalon* (Leiden: Brill and Jerusalem: Cana, 1986), 159–181.

66 Peter M. Holt, *Early Mamlūk Diplomacy (1260–1290), Treaties of Baybars and Qalāwūn with Christian Rulers* (Leiden: Brill, 1995). See the short discussion in Northrup, "The Baḥrī Mamlūk Sultanate," 275–276, as well as Thorau, *Lion of Egypt, passim*; Northrup, *From Slave to Sultan*, 112–115. It is impossible here to review the important information regarding diplomatic relations with the Byzantine Empire, the Armenians, the Italian city-states and other European political entities, but see the comments in Holt's introduction to *Early Mamlūk Diplomacy*.

67 This section of the encyclopedia by Ibn Faḍl Allāh al-ʿUmarī, *Masalik al-absar wa'l-mamalik al-amsar*, has been edited by Michele Amari, "'Al ʿUmari. Condizioni degli stati cristiani dell'occidente." *Atti della Reale Accademia dei Lincei. Memorie della Classe di scienze morali, storiche e filologiche*, Ser. III, 11 (1882–83) (=Anno 280), 102–103; see also Arieh Gribetz, "Some Notes by al-ʿUmarī on the Franks," in Benjamin Z. Kedar, *The Crusaders in Their Kingdom 1099–1291* (Jerusalem: Yad Ben Zvi, 1987), 268–269 [Hebrew].

68 See the surveys in Northrup, "The Baḥrī Mamlūk Sultanate," 265–271; Jonathan Berkey, "Culture and Society during the Late Middle Ages," in Petry (ed.), *Cambridge History of Egypt*, I, 400–411; Donald P. Little, "Historiography of the Ayyūbid and Mamlūk Epochs," in Petry, *Cambridge History of Egypt*, I, 420–441.

69 Donald P. Little, "Coptic Conversion to Islam under the Baḥrī Mamlūks, 692–755/1293–1354," *Bulletin of the School of Oriental and African Studies*, 39 (1976), 552–569; Nimrod Luz, "Aspects of Islamization of Space and Society in Mamlūk Jerusalem and its Hinterland," *Mamlūk Studies Review*: 6 (2002), 133–154; Tamer El-Leithy, "Sufis, Copts and the Politics of Piety: Moral Regulation in Fourteenth-Century Upper Egypt," in Richard J.A. McGregor, and Adam A. Sabra (eds.), *Le développement du soufisme en Égypte à l'époque mamelouke* (Cairo: Institut français d'archéologie orientale, 2006), 75–119 [= *Cahier des Annales Islamologiques*, 27].

CHAPTER TWENTY-ONE

THE MUSLIM POLITICAL WORLD AS MIRRORED IN THE FIRST CRUSADE CHRONICLES

———•◆•———

Svetlana Luchitskaya

Both the chronicles of the First Crusade and the "Song of Antioch" contain this same fictive scene: Muslim warriors bring to their camp a rusty sword, a wooden bow and a completely useless spear supposedly seized from the crusaders.[1] At the sight of those primitive weapons, the Muslim leader Karbuqa depicted in the Crusade sources as a typical epic Saracen, the embodiment of pride and vainglory, bursts out with a long bombastic speech: "Are those the warlike and splendid weapons which the Christians have brought into Asia and by which they hope to drive us out of the limits of Khurāsān and to blot out our names beyond the river of Amazonia? Are those the people who drove our forefathers away from Romania and from the royal city of Antioch which is the honourable capital of the whole of Syria?" Thereafter Karbuqa calls his secretary and says: "Be quick as to write many letters which should be read in Khorasan by the Calip our bishop and the sultan, our king and lord, and the strongest knight as well by all the wisest knights of the kingdom Khorasan," and he dictates: "I have got all the Franks shut in Antioch. They are now in my hands, I shall either put them to death or lead them captured to Khorasan because they threaten to expel us by their weapons beyond Khorasan ... as they expelled our forefathers out of Rum and Syria."[2]

This passage from the crusade chronicle, albeit fictitious, gives a vivid image of the Muslim political world. In this chapter I will try to see this world through the eyes of the medieval writers. I will contrast the accounts of chronicles with what we know about the political structure of the Muslim East. Analyzing the relationship between fiction and reality in the texts, I will try to find out to what extent the medieval authors were able to grasp Islamic realities.

The scene mentioned above takes place in the land of Khurāsān, or the "kingdom of Khorasan." The province of Khurāsān, whose name referred the medieval readers to the eschatological connotations (Matthew 11:21; Luke 10:13), was identified in the medieval treatises with the birthplace of the Antichrist.[3] In the chronicles, Khurāsān is described as the remote land situated on the edge of the earth and surrounded by mountains and marshes.[4]

After the capture of Antioch by the crusaders, the twelve ambassadors of Yaghi-Syan, the emir of Antioch, set out for this land in quest for the help against the Christians.

Chems-ad-Daul (Sensadolus) is at the head of this embassy, one of the ambassadors is Kilj-Arslan, the sultan of Nicea, previously defeated by the crusaders.

Having passed through this territory, the ambassadors find themselves in the town of Sammarthan (may be Samarkand) where they meet the "king of Khorasan" and his "servant" (*familiaris*) Karbuqa. Both of them, especially Karbuqa, take the story of the Turkish defeats by Christians with a sneer and distrust.[5] But after a close look at the lists of the Christian kingdoms and chieftains fighting the Muslims, the "king of Khorasan" starts preparing for a war against the crusaders: he sends "throughout the kingdom of Khorasan" the order to assemble the best troops followed by the inquiries of magicians and fortune-tellers about the outcome of the forthcoming battle. In the chronicles, Khurāsān appears as a kind of the border area controlled by the Muslims – embassies are sent there for the reinforcement, Muslims fear to be driven outside its limits, Christians taken prisoner are led there.[6] This is evidently a political center of the Muslims for the chroniclers mention the capital of the "kingdom of Khorasan"; strange as it may seem, it is the city of Bagdad located in the Near East.[7]

According to the chroniclers, Khurāsān is the residence of the ruler to whom they give majestic titles: "king," "sultan,"[8] "the sultan, carrying the scepter," "the great ruler over all the kings and rulers of the Oriental land.[9] We can say with certainty that the chroniclers mean the sultan Berqyārūq, at that time the head of the Persian sultanate of Bagdad, the greatest of the Seljuk states that came into being after the death of Malik-shāh. The Seljuk Turks are the major branch of the Oghuz Turks named after the chief of their horde Seljuk converted to Islam around 985. The migration of these nomadic tribes in the western direction started at the beginning of the eleventh century. Their first greatest conquest was the province of the medieval Persia Khurāsān that takes up the most part of contemporary north-eastern Iran. In Khurāsān the Seljuk Turks adopted the tradition of the strong political power and created the powerful state while gradually subjugating Western Iran, Xorazm, and Azerbaijan. Finally their chief Toghrul-bek captured the city of Baghdad in 1055. From this time onward the Seljuks chose to move toward Western Asia where two mighty dynasties were struggling with each other—the one being the (Sunni) Abbasids based in Baghdad, the other being the (Shi'a) Fatimids based in Cairo. The Seljuk chieftain Toghrul-bek became the faithful vassal of the Abbasids and promised to fight against the Fatimids.[10] The Baghdad caliph delegated him the temporal power and conferred to him the title of the sultan of the West and the East. Under Toghrul-bek and his successors alp-Arslan (1063–72) and Malik-shāh (1063–95), the Turks at first subjugated Armenia, then occupied the whole of Minor Asia, where the Seljuk chief Suleiman ibn-Kutulmish (1077–86) created the Rūm sultanate with the capital in Nicea. Finally the Seljuk Turks established their control over Syria and Palestine and deprived the Fatimids of Jerusalem in 1071, Damascus in 1076 and Antioch in 1085. That is how the great Seljuk state has arisen.

Just like his predecessors, Berqyārūq mentioned in the First Crusade chronicles was recognized by the Baghdad caliph as the sultan of the Arab provinces of the Seljuk state. At that time Syria was divided between the sons of Tutush I (+1095): Dukak, the emir of Damascus, and Redwan, the emir of Aleppo, Malik-Shāh being their uncle. In Iran, Berqyārūq succeeded in taking control over the above mentioned Khurāsān and handed it over to his younger brother Sanjar.[11] In spite of the general negative attitude of the Western provinces toward the power of Berqyārūq, Khurāsān was still perceived in terms of central power.

On the eve of the First Crusade, the Seljuk states were absorbed in the dynastic wars between the successors of Malik-shāh.[12] However, these conflicts do not receive much attention of the chroniclers who rather focus on the fight in Western Asia between the Fatimids, on the one hand, and the Seljuk Turks supporting Abbasids, on the other. All the First Crusade chroniclers distinctly differentiate between the "Turks" and the "Arabs," calling the former "Turci" or "Turci, gens Persica" and the latter "Arabes" or "Saracens."[13] They also know about religious discords between the Shi'a Arabs and Sunnite Turks.[14]

On the whole, the chroniclers underline the hostility between the two great rivaling Oriental states—the "kingdom of Khorasan," on the one hand, and "the empire of Babylon" (or the kingdom of Babylon) on the other. The former in general stands for the Abbasid caliphate and the latter for the Fatimid Egypt. Just as there exists the "king" in the "kingdom of Khorasan," there is also the "king" or the "emperor" in Babylonia.[15] Babylon is known to be the name of the fortress near Cairo, the capital of the Fatimid Egypt. But it is also the city on the bank of the river Euphrates that is interpreted in the Prophetic books and in the "Apocalypse" as the symbol of evil and is associated with the Antichrist.

Just as in the case of the toponym of "Khurāsān," there might have been eschatological connotations associated with the name of Babylon. As said by medieval writers, there were "severe discord and hatred" between the "Babilonium regnum" and the "regnum Perisidis."[16] The chroniclers give a detailed account of the conquest of the Fatimid (Babylonian) territories by the Seljuk Turks who stand out for their "military talent and great courage."[17]

As stated by the chroniclers, the "Babylonian empire" used to be one of the most powerful states in the Orient and subjugated Syria, Palestine and other provinces but in the long run it gave up these lands to the Seljuk Turks known for their "ferocious spirit." As a result, the "Persian king" who ruled over the people who were more "dexterous in fighting" "seized the greatest part of the Babylonian empire."[18] One of the most important episodes in the history of the struggle between the two powers is the capture of Jerusalem by the Fatimids. Suqman ibn Ortoq (+1105), the Turkish ruler of the holy city, was expelled by the Egyptians in August 1098. This fact is mentioned in all the First Crusade chronicles.[19]

This is the general image of the Muslim political world which emerges from the First Crusade chronicles. How distinctly do they perceive its political structure and hierarchy? We have seen that according to the chronicles emperors and kings rule in "Babylonia" and the "Persian realms." Kilij-Arslan and Yaghi-Syan are also kings.[20] Besides, the sources familiarize readers with other "kings," "dukes," and even "majordomos."[21] Such a play of symmetry can be observed in the traditional *chansons de geste* representing the political hierarchy of the Saracenic world. In the epic literature, particularly in the "Song of Roland," we come across Saracenic kings, barons, and viscounts.[22] The medieval authors consider the political structure of the Orient analogous to that of Western Europe.[23] But the titles of the former are not fixed; on the contrary, they are instable, changeable. For instance, Redwan the ruler of Aleppo is sometimes called king by the chroniclers, sometimes emir.[24] His brother Duqaq, the ruler of Damascus, is referred to as either king or emir.[25] One can get a wrong impression that the medieval authors confuse some titles. But the rank of the emir is mentioned more frequently, so we may assume that the medieval writers were clear about it. Probably this title was a clue to convey the specific character of the Oriental hierarchy so the analysis of this term may help us to elucidate the crusade chroniclers' ideas concerning the political structure of the Muslim Orient.

The title of "emir" (derived from the Arabic word *amara* meaning "to order, to rule") is a very general designation of a Muslim ruler or a military leader. In the twelfth century the emirs were the deputies of the Seljuk sultans in the towns and fortresses of the Seljuk state.[26] Just like poets, the First Crusade chroniclers sometimes do not even translate the title and give only exotic names: am(d)miraldus, am(d)miratus, admiralis, admiralius, ad(m)miravisus, miraldus, am(d)mirabilis etc.[27] But in contrast to the poets, chroniclers are aware of the difference between the Christian and the Muslim hierarchies and they try to make sense of it. In particular, they look in their language for the equivalent of the term designating the rank of an emir and for this purpose they antiquate it by identifying "emir" with "prefect," "procurator" and other Roman title-holders.[28] For instance, bearing in mind the ruler of Jerusalem Soqman ibn-Ortoq, Guibert of Nogent refers to him as "the prefect of Jerusalem whom they call emir in their barbarian language."[29] Thus accepting the difference between the Muslim and Christian political hierarchies Guibert is reluctant to recognize the foreign language while calling it barbarian. Sometimes he goes even further by comparing the Seljuk emirs with the Ancient Persian rulers and speaking about the "twelve noblest who are called satraps in Chaldean language and emirs in their barbarian manner."[30]

From among the Egyptian and Seljuk rulers the chroniclers single out twelve of them— a kind of the *corps d'elite*. As the Christian writers state, "twelve noblest leaders of the Turkish army called emirs were killed" during the battle of Antioch in March 1098.[31] This figure is mentioned not by chance. The story about the twelve emirs is surely a literary topos of the *chansons de geste* where twelve most distinguished Saracens are usually opposed to the twelve peers of France.[32] This topos also goes back to the ancient tradition. Drawing upon this tradition, the chroniclers try to display the administrative structure of the Muslim world. They claim that "those they call emirs are in fact kings who rule the provinces out in the regions. The definition of a province is an area with a metropolitan, twelve consuls and a king."[33]

Shems-ad-Daul lists the names of the provinces (Syria, Romania, Khorasan, Jerusalem, and the kingdom of Damascus) in the presence of the kings who rule over them.[34] Karbuqa intends to send his boastful letter to these various provinces appealing not only to "the pope and the king" but also to "the prefects and their companions-in-arms in different regions."[35] It is clear that the knowledge of the chroniclers concerning the political structure of the Muslim world is rather vague but nevertheless they try to get an insight into the unfamiliar political realities. No doubt, they look at them through the prism of the ancient and literary traditions as well as of their concept about their own political hierarchy.

After all they characterize quite correctly the functions of the emirs, this title being applied to the rulers of large cities and the military leaders as well as commanders of towers and fortresses.[36] The emirs of fortresses who serve the higher rulers are depicted in the chronicles as their vassals.[37] The chroniclers clearly differentiate between these vassals and important hierarchy representatives called *maiores* or *potentes*.[38] Who are these great members of the Egyptian and Seljuk hierarchies?

The Egyptian political hierarchy is described poorly. Specific names are missing— "Babylonian emir" or "king of Babylon" and even "Babylonian emperor" being mentioned most often.[39] It seems reasonable to assume that chroniclers mean by these titles the vizier al-Afdal who was the actual ruler of Egypt under the reign of the weak caliph al-Mustali and his son. But such is not always the case. The example to prove is the "king of Babylon" giving orders to his commander Lavedalius who is easily recognizable as al-Afdal.[40] Do the medieval writers imply al-Mustali addressing him "king" in this case? We shall never know it. In other cases it is even more difficult to identify the holders of the titles[41].

The chroniclers let us know how Jerusalem was won over from the Turks and it is undoubtedly al-Afdal who is hidden under the title of the "king of Babylon." The news about the Christian victories over the Turks prompted the Egyptian vizier to besiege the city of Jerusalem ruled by the Turkish garrison led by Soqman ibn Ortoq and he took it.[42] After the reconquest of the holy city, "the king," "in accordance with the rituals of gentils," paid homage to the shrines of Jerusalem by visiting the Temple of the Lord and the Church of the Holy Sepulchre. He even permitted the Christians to observe their religious rites and finally he offered gifts (candles and incense) to the Holy Sepulchre and the mount Calvary.[43]

The Egyptian king demonstrated his skills as a ruler maneuvering between Turks and Christians.[44] The chroniclers are informed that the Turks applied to the Egyptian "king" to conclude an alliance against the crusaders and even pledged to embrace Shiism and to make many other concessions to them provided the Arabs wage the war on their side.[45] The crusaders agreed to give them back the cities captured by the Seljuks on condition that the "king of Babylon" would concede them Jerusalem. Finally the Egyptians sent legates to the Christians.

Some chronicles report that the "king-emir of Babyloniua" offered to make a treaty with Christians and to restore them the tower of David and the Mount Zion and even to have discussions about acknowledging the Christian faith.[46] Moreover, the "emir of Babylon" found it desirable that Christians should lay down their swords and continue their way to Jerusalem with the Egyptian escort of honour.[47] The response of the crusaders shocked the legates—they accused the Muslims of putting obstacles in the pilgrims' way and of capturing Jerusalem that by right belonged to Christians and will be recovered with arms "by God's countenance."[48] So we can conclude that the policy of the Fatimid Egypt is explained in detail by the chroniclers, whereas their notions with regard to the political hierarchy in the Arab world are far from distinct. By trying to characterize the status of the Egyptian rulers, the chroniclers hesitate between the Western title of 'king" and the Eastern title of "emir" and even invent a fantastic title "the king-emir," and in addition they do not tie a concrete person to these titles.

Among the Seljuk leaders the chroniclers feature Yagh-Syan, Kilij-Arslan and Karbuqa as epic Saracens. The Turkish "maiores" appear rather often in the chronicles. I would like to point to the story about the embassy of Shems-ad-Daul to the "king of Khorasan." This embassy was sent to Khorasan by the governor of Antioch Yagh-Syan (Cassianus) who is referred to sometimes as "emir," sometimes as "king" and also as "king and the ruler of the city."[49] It is noteworthy that the participants of the heated debates at the sultans' court virtually indicate the complex set of hierarchical relationships of the Seljuk Turks.

The system of the Seljuk political relationships is depicted in this episode (in accordance with reality) as a family clan in which all the great leaders appear to be brothers (*confratres*) related to each other by family bonds. In his message, Yagh-Syan warns his "brothers and rulers" about the Christian threat, subsequently the "Persian sultan" summons his subjects to take vengeance on Christians who have injured the "friends and relatives of the Turks."[50]

Turkish hierarchy seems to be closely interwoven with relations of consanguinity. It is not by chance that in the chronicles Turkish emirs call each other "brothers and friends."[51] In the fictitious speech of Kilij-Arslan at the headquarters of the sultan, he calls Yagh-Syan "our superior and kin." As stated by the Nicean sultan, Yaghi-Syan, the "friend and subject" of the Persian sultan "holds the city of Antioch and other lands by sultan's gift."[52] In my opinion the essence of the relationships is correctly reflected in this passage. Scholarly research has shown that the Seljuk governors were in fact a certain kind of vassals dependent upon the Persian sultan, who granted lands to them in exchange for their loyal service.[53]

As said by the chroniclers, the same type of relationships connected Yaghi Syan, "the king of Syria and the whole Armenia" with his tributaries, in particular, with the four "noblest and most powerful emirs quasi kings", each of whom possessed a hundred castles.[54] As stated by Albert of Aachen, the four most important towers guarding the central citadel in Antioch known to be the residence of Yagh-Syan gave names to these four emirs who were long-standing Yaghi Syan's protectors and defenders of the governor just like these towers.[55] Though the number of the vassals as well as their names are merely fictitious, the principle of the Seljuk hierarchy is properly outlined. Yaghi-Syan the eldest and the noblest among the emirs ("homo grandaevus") is one of the greatest "maiores" who are directly subject to the sultan.

No wonder Albert of Aachen awards Yagh-Syan with the Western *insignia* calling him the "ruler carrying the scepter."[56] Only Sultan Berqyārūq is invested with such signs of power. Though historically Yaghi-Syan was merely the governor of the sultan in Antioch, the chroniclers describe him as "the most powerful among the Oriental kings" who is second to the sultan.[57] It goes without saying that Yaghi-Syan is portrayed as an epic Saracenic ruler. Being passive and light-hearted, he was not able to protect his subjects and fled out of fear from the beleaguered city.[58] During his wanderings, he encountered his former subjects who recognized him immediately, took hold of his sword, cut his head off, and sent it to the crusader camp.[59]

Kilij-Arslan received no less attention of the chroniclers.[60] The Nicean sultan is depicted as one of the most powerful Turkish rulers. They know him to be the son of Suleiman ibn-Kutulmish (Solimanus Vetus) who "wrested the whole of Romania from the Emperor"[61] Albert of Aachen calls him "a powerful man, duke and prince of the Turks," "greatly renowned for his diligence and eloquence."[62] The power of Suleyman (Solimanus) is immense—he has subdued Nicea and Romania (Anatolia) and in a military campaign he summons to his assistance "emirs and dukes from all of the Oriental territories."[63] Because Suleyman holds Nicea and Romania (Anatolia) from the "Perisan king" in exchange for his loyal service, he is referred to as "the Turkish king" and even "the great king."[64]

As in other cases, chroniclers ascribe epic features to the sultan and create his image as a typical Saracen and villain. In the epic and historical tradition of the crusade, Christian knights always win, Saracens always lose. In the eyes of the chroniclers, Kilij-Arslan is one of the Muslim rulers who had his share of defeats at the hands of the Christians and therefore shows humility.[65] His fictitious speeches convey the chroniclers' idea of what a defeated Saracen should have said and of how he should have behaved. Thus after the defeat at Dorylaeum, Suleiman confesses how his army composed of cavalry archers was destroyed by the Frankish heavy cavalry. He praises the military valor (celestial or devilish) of the Christian knights enthusiastically, describing their armor and convincing the Turks not to join the battle with them.[66]

The story of valor of the Frankish knights as well of their armor "glittering more than the brilliance of the sun" is repeated in the sultans' headquarters where Kilij-Arslan arrives with the embassy of Shems-ad-Daul long after his defeat at Nicea.[67] This time Killij Arslan, being in an extremely desperate state (he plucks out his beard and hair), tells how his army was destroyed in Nicea and his family was taken prisoner and himself persecuted by Christians had to flee to Antioch in the hope of finding refuge. As Karbuqa starts mocking his speeches and boasting of his own victories over the Peter the Hermits' army and his alleged participation in the battle of Nicea, Kilij-Arslan attempts to crush his pride. He reproaches him for underscoring the strength of the Christian knights who vanquished the Turks by Nicea, he also lists the victories of the crusaders who conquered and subdued many towns and castles in Anatolia and Armenia.[68]

Whereas Kilij-Arslan is featured by the chroniclers as the typical Saracen leader who changed pride to humility after the defeat by Christians, Karbuqa, who has not yet experienced the courage of the Frankish warriors, is shown as an epic Saracen overwhelmed with pride and boasting of his eventual victories but also doomed to be defeated by Christian warriors.[69] Chroniclers put into his mouth most of the fictitious speeches that occur in their works.[70] At first glance their descriptions of the titles of Karbuqa are not very clear or distinct. They present him as "the Persian satrap" or "the principle of the army of Persian sultan" and even as "majordomo."[71] And it seems that he is never given the title "emir." On the contrary, as he tells his mother in one of the imaginary dialogues, there are "more powerful emirs at his disposal than in all the Christian army."[72] Karbuqa appears to be at the highest stage of the Muslim political hierarchy, he is the sovereign of Khorasan.[73] While his role in the real political life was rather insignificant, in the crusade historiography and *chansons de geste* of the crusade cycle he is depicted as the most powerful ruler, probably superior to the others. According to Albert of Aachen, Karbuqa is "the first in the court and second to the king of Khorasan."[74]

The residence of Karbuqa is placed by the chroniclers in Khorasan.[75] It is Karbuqa who, by the order of the sultan, sends dispatches throughout all the "kingdom of Khorasan" to summon warriors for the expedition to Antioch. As indicated by chroniclers, he is the most powerful military principal: greatest manpower resources are at his disposal, and all the other principals worship him "adorating him as God and heeding him as their leader."[76] These descriptions may sound exaggerated but they contain bits of true information. Karbuqa is known to be the atabeg of Mosul, this title (word derived from Turkic "ata" meaning ancestor and Iranic "beg" meaning lord) in the Seljuk state was usually conferred to a tutor and guardian of the minor heir, so to some extent Karbuqa was a "servant" (*familiaris*) in the sultan's family. Because the atabegs were usually appointed leaders of the army, the chroniclers always refer to Karbuqa as the "principal of the army of the sultan."[77]

In the chronicles, all the Seljuk emirs, *maiores* as well as *minores*, are subordinate to the Persian sultan. Being "the most powerful king" (*rex prepotentissimus*),[78] the sultan stands above "all the noblest majors" of the "kingdom of Khorasan."[79] It is "the king of Khorasan" who invites "noblemen and emirs" to a military council meeting notifying "our friends and brothers" about the threat of war against Christians; it is the sultan again who organizes the military campaign in order to rescue Turks besieged in Antioch.[80]

By referring to the sultan as "the mightiest knight," the chronicles lay stress on the military aspect of his power.[81] The military and secular power of the sultan is really great. This appreciation is rather close to reality; in fact, thanks to the Seljuks the idea of the secular power went on developing in the Islamic world. Though the sultan is invested with Western *insignia* and is described as "the holder of the scepter" (the same goes for the *chansons de geste*), his position in the political hierarchy of the Muslim world is denoted adequately.[82]

Khorasan, where the sultan receives the Seluk rulers, is also the residence of the caliph who is mentioned in the chronicles equally with sultan. Karbuqa addresses his bombastic letter to "our pope and our lord the king of Persians."[83] Guibert of Nogent is surprised to find that the Saracens have their pope "the same way as we do."[84] The chroniclers call the caliph "the blissful pope" as well as "apostolic Caliph," "Caliph our bishop," "pope our caliph,"[85] laying stress on his role as the religious head of the Muslim world. The crusaders surely differentiated between the Fatimid and Abbasid caliphs. It is evident that when they refer to the "Turkish pope,"[86] they are talking about the caliph of Baghdad, who was at that time Ahmad al-Mustazhif (1094–1118) but whose name they probably did not know.

The extract about the "Shems-ad-Dauls' embassy" can be paralleled in the "Song of Antioch." In this poem the emir sultan rules in his "kingdom of Persia," his residence being located in the town of Sarmazane where the embassy of Shems-ad-Daul arrives. The Turks from all over the Orient have assembled there to pray to the idol of Mohammed adorned with precious stones and held up in the air by magnet forces.[87] The sultan (Soudan) is a center stage in this passage. He is represented as a great sovereign who stands above all the pagans (*païens*). Nevertheless the caliph surpasses him in power being the mightiest ruler in the Muslims world—as stated by poets, his dominions "extend all the way to the setting sun."[88] The caliph personifies the supreme power; he is superior to all the representatives of the political hierarchy.[89]

Having heard the complaints of Yaghi-Syan and Soliman about their defeats and having made sure of the truthfulness of their accounts—it sufficed to show him a piece of the beard of Yagh-Syan given by him to the messengers as a token[90]—the sultan sends out letters to Baudas (may be Baghdad) to the apostolic caliph. Some 400 couriers carry these letters with the emir's seal to the supreme ruler spreading the news in fifty different languages.[91] Then the sultan summons the Muslim aristocrats to the council in the vicinity of Coronde. All the Oriental "kings" come to join the assembly (*parlement*) where the caliph announces a "rich pardon that Mahon will give us."[92]

The emir invites the three kings-brothers from Mecca to come with all their forces and bring the God Mohammad along with them. The kings-brothers arrive and bring their god Mohammad made entirely of gold and silver and seated on the elephant in a jeweled how-dah with a canopy over his head. Through enchantment, the devil (*aversier*) penetrates in the hollow statue of the idol and speaks to the infidels. The caliph interprets his words to the Saracens. The demon allows the Saracens to have twenty, thirty wives or as many as they fancy to increase the number of pagans able to fight against Christians. Everyone who seeks Mohammed's forgiveness and goes into battle will, should he die, have two bezants in one hand and a rock in the other; with the bezants they will buy their passage to the paradise, or if that fails, with the rock they can fight their way in, Mohammad will aid them and bring them to heaven at any rate.[93]

Just as the pope in the Catholic world is responsible for the salvation of the Christians' souls, the caliph, as the spiritual leader of the Muslim world, shows the way to the para-dise even if in this passage the Christian idea of the paradise is completely inverted.[94] The description is quite fantastic but the role of the caliph as the Muslim religious leader is comprehended properly. It is depicted symmetrical to the role of the pope.

We have a good reason for believing that the descriptions of the Muslim political reali-ties in the chronicles as well as in the crusade epic songs are a kind of mirror-image. The iconography seems to confirm this thesis. In the most lavishly decorated codex of the cru-sade chronicle (*Estoire d'Eracles*) a considerable part of the miniatures is devoted to the events of the First Crusade.[95] The Muslims who are often painted as old men are recogniz-able by their beards and turbans as, for instance, in the miniatures recounting the history of the siege of Nicea (Fig. 21.1). The representatives of the Muslim political hierarchy may be identified even easier. Some miniatures represent Karbuqa—one of the most important Muslim personages of the First Crusade chronicle and epic songs (Fig. 21.2).

We see Karbuqa at the moment of the siege of Antioch when he orders his archers to begin shooting. He differs greatly from his warriors who are depicted in short tunics and turbans on their heads. In contrast to them, Karbuqa is in a long mantel trimmed with squir-rel fur, he wears a crown on his head and looks very much like the European monarch.

Figure 21.1 An episode from the seige of Nicea (1097). Bibliothèque Nationale de France. Ms. Fr. 22495, f. 28.

Figure 21.2 A scene from the siege of Antioch by the army of Karbuqa (1098). Bibliothèque Nationale de France. Ms. Fr. 22495, f. 50v.

Figure 21.3   Generalized image of the siege warfare presented at the three-tiered miniature depicting the major events of the crusade. Bibliothèque Nationale de France. Ms. Fr. 22495, f. 9.

Figure 21.4   Two-tiered miniature: sultan sending a spy in the camp of the crusaders (on the right); Saracens set out to the military campaign against Christians (on the left). Bibliothèque Nationale de France. Ms. Fr. 22495, f. 280v.

The only features of his appearance that make him look different from Western kings are his beard and his dark face. The painter adjusts the size of the figure to the positions they hold so the figure of the Turkish ruler is remarkably larger than those of ordinary warriors. This social symbolism is of universal character, it is also applied to signify the Christian social hierarchy.[96] "Maiores" are usually painted in an identical manner in the miniatures of the illuminated chronicles.[97]

Here is one of the examples. At the very beginning of this illuminated manuscript codex, we see a three-tiered (two images in every tier) miniature dedicated to different themes of the crusade. This miniature introduces different subjects and personages of the history of the crusades including Saracens, so it plays a significant role in the iconographical program of the illuminated chronicle. It also familiarizes us with the generalized image of the Muslim ruler. This abstract Oriental personage (Fig. 21.3) is depicted according to the general principles of iconography: unlike the ordinary Saracens he wears a long mantel, his high rank being indicated by the crown which is the indispensable element to represent a Muslim ruler.

In the iconography as well as in the *chansons de geste* and the chronicles, the members of the political hierarchy are represented in the same way as the European kings. But like chroniclers, the medieval artists are aware of the differences between the hierarchies and attempt to get an insight of it. As a result, sometimes the painters ascribe to their personages two iconographic elements: the crown, which is a typical sign of power in Europe, and the turban, which is a constant iconographic attribute of the Saracens (Fig. 21.4).[98] The way the political otherness of the Muslim world is represented in the works of art is identical to that of the chronicles and the *chansons de geste*.

*****

So we see that in the chronicles and the *chansons de geste* of the First Crusade the political hierarchy of the Muslim world is symmetrical to the European. In fact, while the religious cult is usually depicted in the chronicles according to the inversion principles (in this case they serve as a sort of *camera obscura*) as paganism, which is believed to be an opposition to Christianity, the Muslims political institutions are mirror-images of the feudal hierarchy. As we have seen, the oral tradition is present in the chroniclers—medieval authors see the political hierarchy through the prism of this tradition and create epic portraits of the Saracen rulers. Nevertheless in their perception of the political otherness of the Muslim world, they go a step further than poets. They are knowledgeable about the lack of coincidence between the political hierarchies and try to make sense of it.

With this purpose, they antiquate the Muslim institutions, comparing them with the ancient ones and correlating the new experience with their general knowledge about political and administrative structure. In their attempt to approach the unfamiliar reality, they impose their conception of the feudal hierarchy on the Muslim world which results in the identification of the Muslim hierarchy with the European in the chronicles as well as in the iconography. The chroniclers cannot perceive the political structure of the Muslim world other than in terms of their proper culture.

Even if the chroniclers call the representatives of the Muslim political hierarchy kings and attribute to them other Western titles, they are very often close to understanding the specific character of political power in the Muslim East. Thus the title of emir is used by them equally alongside the ancient (prefect, procurator) and medieval (king, emperor) ranks. It serves to denote the Muslim ruler including different secular and military rank holders.

In order to emphasize the authority of the Muslim rulers, the medieval authors ascribe to them royal and noble ranks and *insignia*.

The essence of the relations within the Muslim hierarchy where the Seljuk emirs are represented as the tributaries of the Persian sultan is interpreted adequately. By analyzing the power relations between sultan and caliph, the medieval writers compare them with the pope and the emperor and as we have seen these parallels may be not unfounded.

Describing conflicts and alliances of the Seljuk and Egyptian leaders as well as negotiations between Christians and Muslims, chroniclers show sound knowledge of the *Realpolitik*. At the same time they attach less importance to the political relations per se, the focal point being their military victories and their political interests. If fictitious speeches of the Muslim rulers are cited in the chronicles, the Saracens usually dwell on their defeats suffered from the Christian army. If they boast of the eventual victories like Karbuqa, their speeches bring them to dishonor.

Nevertheless the Muslim political realities as mirrored in the First Crusade chronicles are depicted in a quite different manner in comparison to the Muslim religious rites which are normally represented as "heathen pollution."[99] The medieval authors are more tolerant in their descriptions of the Muslim political world. According to the chroniclers, *ritus gentilium* may agree with the respectful attitudes toward Christian shrines. The proof of it is the story about the visiting of the Church of the Holy Sepulchre by the vizier Al-Afdal. But after the defeat by Asclaon in August 1099, the Egyptian ruler, being an epic Saracen, swears to Mahomet and other gods to destroy the Holy Sepulchre and to raze to the ground the holy city of Jerusalem.[100]

NOTES

1 Peter Tudebode, *Historia de Hierosolymitano itinere*, ed. John H. Hill and Lauritia L. Hill, Paris, 1977, 91–92; *Gesta Francorum et aliorum Hierosolymitanorum*, ed. Lauritia Hill, London, 1962, 51–52; Guibert of Nogent, *Gesta Dei per Francos*, ed. R.B.C. Hyugens. Turnhout, 1996, 211; Baudri of Bourgueil, *Historia Hierosolymitana*, in RHC Oc IV, 59; Robert the Monk, *Historia Hierosolymitana*, in RHC Oc III, 811; Suzanne Duparc-Quioc, *Chanson d'Antioche. Étude critique*, 2 vols (Paris, 1977–1978), I, vv. 6786–6800.

2 These fictitious passages are based upon the historical events of the siege of Antioch (October 1097–June 1098). They recount the "embassy of Sensadolus," the son of the governor of Antioch Yaghi-Syan, to Khurāsān and his negotiations with the *Seljuk Sultan* Berqyārūq and Karbuqa. These passages are common to both the Old French crusade cycle, especially the "Song of Antioch," and the crusade chronicles, in particular that of Albert of Aachen. The issues about the links between epic and historiography of the First Crusade are discussed in many works. For example, *Chanson d'Antioche*; Jean Flori, Des chroniques à l'épopée ou bien l'inverse?, *Perspectives médiévales* 20 (1994), 36–43. See also the introduction to the translation of the "Chanson d'Antioche": *Chanson d'Antioche, the Old-French Account of the First Crusade*, ed. Suzan Edgington and Carol Sweetenham (Oxford, 2011), 3–85.

3 For the eschatological connotations that were associated with Khurāsān and might have been actualized during the crusades, see Alan V. Murray, "Coroscane: Homeland of the Saracensi n the Chansons de geste and the Historiography of the Crusades," in *Aspects de l'épopée romane. Mentalités. Idéologies. Intertextualités*, ed. Hans van Dijk and Willem Noomen (Groningen, 1995), 177–184.

4 Albert of Aachen, *Historia Ierosolimitana*, ed. Susan B. Edgington (Oxford, 2011), 612.

5 Albert, 248–250.

6 *Gesta*, 50–1, 67; Peter Tudebode, 90–91.

7 Albert, 594.

8 Fulcher, *Historia Hierosolymitana*, ed. H. Hagenmeyer (Heidelberg, 1913,), 247: "soltanus, rex scilicet Persarum"; 340.

9 Albert, 248, 613.

10 Hamilton A.R. Gibb, "The Caliphate and the Arab states," in *A History of the Crusades*, ed. K.M. Setton (London, 1969), 81–98.

11 Cahen Claude, "The Turkish Invasion: The Selchükids," in Setton, *A History of the Crusades*, 135–176; Barthold Vasilly, *Turkestan Down to the Mongol Invasion* (London, 1977).

12 The Seljuk sultan Tutush I was fighting against the Nicean sultan Suleiman ibn-Kutulmish who in his turn was seeking to seize the southern Syria. Ibn-Kutulmish was defeated by Tutush in 1086 but the latter himself was beaten and killed by his nephew Sultan Berqyārūq in February 1095. At the same time Berqyārūq was involved in the struggle in central Persia against his other brother Mohammad. See Joshua Prawer, *Histoire du royaume latin de Jérusalem*, 2 vols (Paris, 1975), I, 120.

13 Fulcher, 133; Radulf of Caen, *Gesta Tancredi in expeditione Hierosolymitana*, in RHC Oc III, 668–669.

14 For instance, Raymond of Aguilers notes that Egyptians are Shi'a and worship Ali' who was a relative of the prophet Muhammad: Raymond of Aguilers, *Le "Liber" Raimundi de Aguilers*, ed. J. Hugh and Lauritia L. Hill (Paris, 1969), 111 ("colerent Alim, ... qui est de genere Mahumet").

15 Raymond, 111.

16 Albert, 230: "grauissima ... erat discordia et odium."

17 Guibert, 100: "in re militari et equestri elegantia, animi etiam virtute prepollet."

18 Guibert, 189, 271.

19 For the most detailed story see: Albert of Aachen, 442–444.

20 Albert, 248–250.

21 Guibert, 208; Fulcher, 571.

22 *Chanson de Roland*, ed. Joseph Bédier (Paris, 1922), vv. 2649–2650.

23 See Matthew Bennett, "First Crusaders' Images of Muslims: The Influence of Vernacular Poetry?" in *Forum for English Language Studies*, 22 (1986), 105.

24 "dux de Caleph" (Raymond, 56); "Rodoam admiraldum Caleph" (*Gesta Francorum Iherusalem expugnantium*, in RHC Oc III, 497).

25 "Ducath, rex Damascenorum" (Fulcher, 373); "Decaccus admiraldum Damascenorum" (*Gesta Francorum Iherusalem expugnantium*, 340).

26 Jeanine Dominique Sourdel, *Dictionnaire historique de l'islam* (Paris, 2004), 78–79.

27 In the traditional *chansons de geste*, the title of emir is often identified with the title of king, but most frequently is left without translation. See Paul Bancourt, *Les musulmans dans les chansons de geste*, 2 vols (Aix-en-Provence, 1982), II, 839–844.

28 For instance, Karbuqa gives orders to his emir whom the chronicler calls "procurator." See Baudri of Bourgueil, 76: "procuratori suo quem admiralius vocant."

29 Guibert, 208: "Ierosolimorum praefectus, quos barbarica illi lingua admiravisos vocant."

30 Ibid., 192: "dudodecim de eorum primoribus viris, quos verbo Caldaico satrapas, secundum eorum barbariem, admiravisosiris vocant."

31 Baudri of Bourgueil, 51; *Gesta*, 41. Robert the Monk mentions twelve best Egyptians emirs: Robert the Monk, 788.

32 See *Chanson de Roland*, vv. 707–708.

33 Robert the Monk, 788: "Et quos admiraldos vocant, reges sunt, qui provinciis praesunt. Provincia quidem est, quae unum habet metropolitanum, XII consules et unum regem."

34 Ibid., 809.

35 Guibert, 211.

36 Albert, 504; Guibert, 298: "Babylonie princeps militiae, quem patrio lingua admiravisum vocant"; *Gesta Francorum et aliorum Hierosolymitanorum*, 91. Such were the real functions

of the emirs. See Dominique Sourdel, *Gouvernement et administration de l'Orient islamique jusqu'au milieu du XI siècle* (Leyden, 1988), *passim.*

37 For instance, Karbuqa entrusts the command of a citadel to an emir who takes an oath of fealty to his lord. See Peter Tudebode, 90.

38 Robert the Monk, 811: "maiores regni Persarum"; Albert, 646: "Babylonie potentes."

39 Peter Tudebode, 147; Raymond, 110; Guibert, 271.

40 Fulcher, 311.

41 For instance, Robert the Monk names the "Babylonian emir" Clemens which is not paralleled in other texts. As Carol Sweetenham has shown in her recent article, naming so the greatest enemy of the Christians was a way to comment on a contemporary political situation. The matter is that in the investiture conflict the antipope Wibert of Ravenna had taken the name of Clemens III. See Sweetenham Carol, "Crusaders in a Hall of Mirrors. The Portrayal of Saracens in the Robert the Monk's History," in *Languages of Love and Hate. Conflicts, Community and Identity in the Medieval Mediterranean*, ed. Sara Lambert and Helen Nicholson (Turnhout, 2011), 50–63, esp. 52–55.

42 Albert, 442.

43 Ibid., 444; Raymond, 110–111.

44 Raymond, 110 "Dubitaverat enim an faceret nobiscum amititiam, an cum Turcos." In this extract of the chronicle it is hard to tell "the king of Babylon" from the "emir." The guess is that the latter is al-Afdal.

45 Raymond, 111: "si venire cum ipsis contra nos in praelium, colerent Alim, quem ipse colit."

46 Albert, 230.

47 Robert the Monk, 791–792; Raymond, 110.

48 Robert the Monk, 793.

49 Albert, 248; Guibert, 249. Historically Yagh-Syan was a governor of Antioch nominated by Malik-shāh. Nominally Yagh-Syan was a vassal of Redwan of Aleppo and then of Dukak of Damascus.

50 Albert, 250, 260.

51 Ibid., 254.

52 Ibid., 252: "rex Darsianum … tibi subjectum et amicus tuoque munere urbes et terras tenentem."

53 Claude Cahen, "L'evolution sociale du monde musulman jusqu'au XII siècle face à celle du monde chrétien," *Cahiers de civilisation médiévale* 1 (1958), 451–463.

54 Albert, 194.

55 Ibid., 200: "quatuor insuperabiles turres … quoum praefati ammiraldi quatuor semper custodies et defensores regis Darsiani attitulati sunt."

56 Ibid., 248.

57 Radulf of Caen, 656: "regum orientalium potentissimus, uni Soldano qui regnum Persida regnaverat, secundus."

58 As said by Albert of Aachen, during the siege of the city, Yaghi-Syan, ignorant of the danger, sleeps soundly in his upper rooms through all the fighting. Albert, 248: "rex Darsianus … hactenus in omni conflict … in solio dormiens."

59 See Robert the Monk, 806; Albert, 286; Radulf of Caen, 655–656; *Chanson d'Antioche*, vv. 9365–9390.

60 Historically Kilij-Arslan is the ruler of the sultanate of Rum who destroyed the army of Peter the Hermit at Civitot in October 1096. In May 1097, the crusaders took his capital, the city of Nicea, and afterwards Kilij-Arslan was defeated by the Christians in the battle of Dorylaeum on July 1, 1097.

61 Robert the Monk, 764.

62 Albert, 32.

63 *Gesta Francorum Iherusalem expugnantium*, 495: "Solimanus admiraldus erat qui Nicaeam et totam fere Romaniam imperii suo subjugavit adhibitis sibi multis in auxilium orientalibus partibus admiraldos et ducibus."

64 Radulf of Caen, 620: "rex Turcius," 623, 625: "rex Solimannus"; Baudri of Bourgueil, 62: "Solimano regi magno."

65 Albert, 252: "nuper expertus est virtutem Christianorum."

66 See "Verba Solimanni": Robert the Monk, 764; *Gesta Francorum et aliorum Hierosolymitanorum*, 22.

67 Albert, 250. In the "Song of Antioch" (vv. 4995–5005) he arrives in Khurassan after Shems-ad-Daul. His host numbers only forty soldiers, all of them mutilated and wounded during the fights for Nicea.

68 See the accounts of Kilij-Arslan in the chronicles and the "Song of Antioch": Albert, p, 252–256; *Chanson d'Antioche*, vv. 5020–5045, 5070–5145.

69 Albert, 254: "vir contumax et plenus superbia feritate virtutes Christianorum parvipendens"; Robert the Monk, 811: "quae sibi conversa sunt in ignominia." Historically Karbuqa arrived at Antioch only on June 5, 1098 after having assembled the army of thirty thousand warriors. On June 28 he was defeated by the crusaders.

70 *Gesta Francorum et aliorum* Hierosolymitanorum, 50–53; Peter Tudebode, 89–90; Robert the Monk, 811, *Chanson d'Antioche*, vv. 4605–5150, 5376–5390, 6786–6840, 6838–6895.

71 Radulf of Caen, 664: "Persarum satrapa"; Baudri of Bourgueil, 50: " militiae soldanus Persiae magister"; Guibert, 165: "major domus vel potius militia princeps.

72 Robert the Monk, 813.

73 Albert, 312: "Corbahan princeps Corruzana."

74 Ibid., 254: "Corbahan vero familiaris et primus in aula regis et secundus a rege in regno Corruzana."

75 Guibert, 189.

76 Albert, 254.

77 Ibid., 264.

78 Ibid., 250.

79 Robert the Monk, 811: "regique Persarum soldano super omnes glorioso, majorisbusque regni Persarum proceribus."

80 Albert, 252, 254, 260.

81 *Gesta Francorum et aliorum Hierosolymitanorum*, 51: " nostri regi domino Soldani militi fortissimo."

82 In contrast to the chroniclers, the poets have no idea with regard to the character of the sultans' power and think of this title as a proper name. In the "Song of Roland" this rank is not even mentioned. See Bancourt, II, 846–849.

83 Guibert, 211.

84 Ibid., 208: "habent enim papam suum, ad instar nostri."

85 Ibid., 211: "papaeque beatissimo"; Peter Tudebode, 92: "Caliphas nostro episcopo"; Robert the Monk, 811: "religiosos papae nostro Caliphae, regique Persarum Soldano."

86 Raymond, 111.

87 *Chanson d'Antioche*, vv. 4877–4910.

88 Ibid., v. 5195: "Cil a le segnorage dusqu'a soleil couçant."

89 Ibid., v. 5194: "A Calife qui est sor les autres puissan."

90 Ibid., v. 4857.

91 Ibid., v. 5191.

92 Ibid., v. 5212.

93 Ibid., vv. 5323–5347.

94 The Muslim political world is very often an inversion of the Christian. See on this subject, Pascal Péron, *Les croisés en Orient: la représentation de l'espace dans le cycle de croisade* (Paris, 2008), 490–495. See also John Tolan, "Muslims as Pagan Idolators in the Chronicles of the First Crusade," in *Western Views of Islam in Medieval and Early Modern Europe. Perception of Other*, ed. David R. Blanks and Michael Frassetto (New York, 1999), 107–109.

95 The illuminators paint the scenes of the siege of Nicea, Antioch, and Jerusalem. See BNF. Ms. fr. 22495, f. 28, 32, 50v. See other illuminated codexes of the chronicle: fr. 9082, ff. 66v, 75v etc.
96 See the images of the Christian rulers in the same codex: 22495, f. 78.
97 See: BNF. Ms. fr. 9083, ff. 200v, 263v, 283v.
98 See other miniatures: BNF. Ms. fr. 2630, f. 129v etc.
99 See on this subject: Penny Cole, "O God, the Heathen Have Come into your Inheritance": The Theme of Religious Pollution in Crusader Documents, 1095–1188," in *Crusaders and Muslims in Twelfth Century Syria*, ed. Maya Shatzmiller (Leiden, 1993), 84–111.
100 Peter Tudebode, 147; Robert the Monk, 877–878.

CHAPTER TWENTY-TWO

CRUSADERS, MUSLIMS AND BIBLICAL STORIES: SALADIN AND JOSEPH

————— • ◆ • —————

Yehoshua Frenkel

INTRODUCTION

The Ayyubid sultan Saladin (Ṣalāḥ al-Dīn Yūsuf bn Ayyūb; 1137–93) is the undisputed hero of medieval Islam. His political and military career is well documented and has been extensively investigated. A considerable number of modern works, both in European and in Near Eastern languages, reflect upon his political career, the wars he fought and other achievements;[1] to these should be added the seemingly endless list of writings and other means of communication in the Arabic/Islamic worlds that center on him.

These literary products depend heavily upon the writings of Saladin's secretaries and court poets. They and their medieval successors aspired to present him as a great and valiant Muslim warrior and diplomat; to this end they were also ready to manipulate biblical stories that were familiar to medieval Muslim audiences. The presence of biblical heroes in the medieval Muslim imagination is illuminated by the drawing of an analogy between Saladin Joseph and the biblical Joseph (Yūsuf bn Yaʿqūb in Arabic). This comparison is a noticeable literary tool in the verbal arsenal that was available to the sultan's admirers and they employed it both in prose and in poetry.

Relying on detailed studies by competent scholars, the present work aims at looking into this apparent element in the construction of Saladin's image and the ensuing propaganda.[2] Yet, before turning to this principal goal, this chapter will dwell briefly on the career of Saladin and on the reception of the biblical story of Joseph by medieval Muslims. The succeeding section will deal with the representation of Saladin in passages written by Ayyubid contemporaries in which he is treated as a hero akin to the biblical Joseph.

SOURCES

The study of Saladin's image is based principally upon literary sources composed by his contemporaries or collected by their successors,[3] although inscriptions and material evidence provide useful information. The Ayyubid sultan paid great attention to recording his deeds and his political and military achievements and, undoubtedly, he was very successful in his efforts to project a fitting image and to boost his prestige as the ideal Muslim warrior.

His representation in Arabo-Muslim historiography attests to his success at achieving this goal. In these works he acquired the image of an outstanding Muslim political and military hero.[4] This role is visible in the texts used by me in this limited study.[5]

'Imād al-Dīn Muḥammad al-Shāfi'ī (519–97/1125–1201), who is known as the Secretary from Isfahan (*al-kātib al-isfahānī*), was a Persian émigré who came to Damascus in the summer of 1167 and joined the court of sultan Nūr al-Dīn Maḥmūd. After Saladin's capture of Damascus, the new sultan, who needed the services of skilled bilingual scribes, recruited 'Imād al-Dīn (in 1175). Being a close companion of Saladin, al-'Imād al-Isfahānī operated as a ghost-writer for the new commander of the armies of Jihad. 'Imād al-Dīn's major work, al-Barq al-Shāmī (*The Syrian Thunderbolt*), which tells the history of the reigns of Nūr al-Dīn and Ṣalāḥ al-Dīn, was completed after the latter's death.[6]

Bahā' al-Dīn Ibn Shaddād joined Saladin after the victory at Ḥaṭṭīn (in 1187) and was in his service during the Third Crusade and until the sultan's death in Damascus.[7] His training and professional career resembled that of many of his skilled contemporaries. These well-educated scholars, including those in the religious sciences (*'ālim*), served at the military command headquarters. A confidential servant of the victorious sultan (*al-Malik al-Nāṣir*), with whom he enjoyed long sessions, Ibn Shaddād claims to provide his audience with insightful information. Yet we should bear in mind that his primary aim was to portray his master as the archetypical holy warrior.[8]

Although Ibn al-Athīr's bias against Saladin is notorious,[9] his al-Kāmil (*The Complete Book in the Matters of History*)[10] and al-Bāhir (*The Dazzling Victory: On the History of the Zangids*) are major Arabic sources for the history of the crusaders. The *al-Kāmil fī al-ta'rīkh* was written over a considerable time and underwent various revisions.[11] In his narrative of the events, Ibn al-Athīr tried to place the story of the Franks in the Eastern Mediterranean within the framework of a global conflict between Islam and Christendom.

Abū Shāma the Damascene, an elder contemporary of Ibn al-Athīr, provides accounts from earlier sources that have not survived in his *al-Rawḍatayn* (*The Two Gardens*).[12] This book, appended with biographies of Muslim nobles, has the quality of an ego-document.[13] An admirer of the two sultans who are pivotal in his book, Nūr al-Dīn and Ṣalāḥ al-Dīn, Abū Shāma depicts their reigns as exemplary models for Muslim rulers and commanders.[14]

Ibn Wāṣil al-Ḥamawī was a scion of a Syrian elite family and served in the civilian administration of two dynasties. In late Ayyubid Cairo, he taught at the al-Aqmar mosque.[15] During the years of transition, from the Ayyubid dynasty to the Mamlūk sultanate, he composed a comprehensive history of the wars between Islam and the Franks.[16] In the chapters that he dedicates to reports on Saladin, Ibn Wāṣil based himself on earlier sources, while in the accounts of later decades he incorporates personal narratives. Such, for example, is the report on his diplomatic mission to Italy, which he visited as an ambassador of the Mamlūk sultan Baybars.[17]

THE POLITICAL CAREER OF SALADIN: PROPAGANDA AND IMAGE

The administrative, military and political career of Ṣalāḥ al-Dīn Yūsuf bn Ayyūb in Egypt, Syria and south-east Anatolia extended over nearly a half century (*c.* 1151–93). At approximately the age of fifteen, he joined the Asadiyya in Aleppo, which were the well-trained army battalion of his uncle, Asad al-Dīn Shīrkūh (both names mean lion). In 1164, he moved to Egypt for the first time. Five years later, after the death of his uncle, he became the commander of the Syrian contingent, which Nūr al-Dīn Maḥmūd had dispatched to the Nile Valley. Following the death of the last Fatimid caliph in Cairo (1171), he became the de facto ruler of Egypt and, for the next two decades, he was primarily engaged in efforts to strengthen his legitimacy as an heir of Nūr al-Dīn (d. 1174).

The victory at Ḥaṭṭīn (in 1187) established Saladin's image as a leading jihad commander, although even after this decisive triumph he was ready to negotiate truces with the Franks and even to recognize their rule over parts of the Latin Kingdom of Jerusalem. This willingness is apparent in the treaty he concluded with Richard Coeur de Lion in September 1192.[18] Following this event, Saladin's troops dispersed and he himself returned to Damascus, where he lived for a few months before succumbing to illness and death in March 1193.

As with other twelfth- and thirteenth-century warlords, Saladin was also deeply concerned with questions of legitimacy.[19] Hence he was very keen in constructing an image as a devoted Muslim, a close supporter of the Abbasid caliph, and a champion of combat against both internal and external threats.[20] To this end, he recruited soldiers, employed clerks, and paid poets. Thus, as already stated above, he was able to fashion a positive biography, which was composed by several of his companions. These texts contain glorifying poetry and official dispatches that portray the sultan as a devoted Muslim who cleaned up (*ṭahara*) the Abode of Islam from the contamination caused by internal heresies and external enemies.[21]

By steadily holding the reins of power, Saladin used the resources at his disposal to purchase public support.[22] Material evidence and inscriptions illuminate this sultanic policy.[23] This policy is highly visible in his socio-religious policy as the sultan endowed pious charities (*awqāf*).[24] The main beneficiaries of his "altruistic" investments were jurisconsults and sufi mendicants who were the backbone of his religious establishment. Another example of this point is an inscription from Damascus that reads:

> The construction of this school was completed during the days of al-Malik al-Nāṣir Ṣalāh al-Dunyā wal-Dīn the rescuer of Jerusalem from the hands of the polytheists.[25]

It should be emphasized here that scholars disagree in their evaluation of Saladin's jihad policy.[26] In the study of his anti-Frankish propaganda, which has deep roots in the historiography of the Latin Kingdom and of the contemporary Islamic dynasties, it is possible to detect two conflicting interpretations: either he was motivated by an anti-Christian jihad spirit[27] or he lacked a well-formulated ideology of holy war and opted for a policy of détente.[28] In this study of the sultanic eulogia, this question is of limited concern, although it is fitting to say that the image of Saladin as a reviver of religion is striking.[29]

JOSEPH (YŪSUF) IN THE QUR'AN AND IN ISLAMIC TRADITION

To facilitate a study of the analogy between the biblical Joseph and Saladin, which is plainly visible in Oriental and Occidental medieval sources, I will briefly turn to the story of biblical Joseph in the Islamic tradition.

Biblical "references" are detectable in various medieval Islamic historical-political narratives and reflect the familiarity of Muslim historians with the prophets and biblical tales.[30] Although exact literal biblical quotations are extremely rare in the various Islamic genres that narrated the history of the Children of Israel, biblical kings and prophets, and other related subjects, Islamic writings on these matters reflect deep familiarity with the Bible and the Midrash.[31] It is valid to claim that biblical legends were instrumental in Islamic historiography. Those chapters that represent Muhammad's mission as the final stage in the history of revelation serve as one example.[32]

Another case in the point is an account of the last chapter in the life of al-Amīn, the besieged Abbasid caliph (AH 198/AD 813).[33] This account is said to be based on testimony that was narrated by his nephew Ibrāhīm b. al-Mahdī. Its transmitters designed it as an ego-document and as such it is quoted by several later historians. It tells of a weary, depressed, and obviously frightened caliph who twice heard a voice coming from the Tigris River. The waters whispered, so we are told by his alleged companion: "The matter is decided whereon you enquire."[34] This phrase is taken directly from the Qur'anic verses that tell the story of Joseph in Pharaoh's prison.

The narrator of this presumed event certainly assumed that his audience was familiar with the "Stories of the Prophets." Although he transfers the event from the Nile Valley to the banks of the Tigris, he did not doubt that the audience would receive the story as reimagined by him. He further believed that the placing of the scene in Baghdad would not deter them from accepting the validity of his testimony.

Chapter 12 of the Qur'ān (*sūrat yūsuf*) is devoted to the story of Yūsuf bn Yaʿqūb (Joseph the son Jacob). The relating of his youth and the account of his career in Pharaoh's Egypt is the longest sustained narrative of any biblical character's life in the Qur'ān. The story of Joseph in this chapter reflects the basic paradigm of the Qur'ān: a young prophet is derided by his family and kin, is exiled to an alien territory, but is eventually vindicated and rises to prominence.[35]

In post-Qur'anic literature, and particularly in pietistic literature, Joseph serves as a model of virtue and wisdom.[36] His beauty and chastity are other salient topics in these texts.[37] Abū Jaʿfar Muḥammad b. Jarīr al-Ṭabarī (224–310/838–923), a highly esteemed historian and exegete, who is a crucial node in the transmission of Islamic juridical, historical and scriptural lore, brings in his bulky exegesis of the Qu'rān the following tradition:

> Some of the People of the Torah report that, according to the Torah, Joseph was sold by his brothers and brought to Egypt when he was seventeen years old. They say that he remained in the house of the ruler who bought him for thirteen years, and that when he reached the age of thirty the Pharaoh of Egypt al-Walīd b. al-Rayyān made him vizier.[38]

In his "Tales of the Prophets," al-Thaʿālibī transmits the following description of Joseph:

> The beauty of Joseph was like the light of day; his skin was fair, his face comely, his hair curly, eyes large, he stood upright, had strong legs, upper arms, and forearms, a flat belly with a small navel, he was hook-nosed, and had a dark mole on his right cheek which beautified his face; a white birth mark between his eyes resembling the Moon when it is full, and eye lashes like the fore-feathers of eagle wings. His teeth sparkled when he smiled, and light emanated from his mouth between his incisors when he spoke. No human would be able to describe Joseph, no one! It is said that he inherited his beauty from his grandfather Isaac, son of Abraham, who was the most beautiful man, Isaac means "the one who laughs" in Hebrew, and who, in turn, inherited his beauty from his mother Sarah.[39]

SALADIN YŪSUF AND THE BIBLICAL JOSEPH

Poets and other authors who were keen to promote Saladin's image exceedingly praised Yūsuf bn Ayyūb (Saladin).[40] A deviation from the main topic of their subject matter is a common literary device used in these writings. In order to eulogize the sultan Ṣalāḥ al-Dīn Yūsuf, these sources often take a digression before returning to the key subject of their account.[41] It is not rare, as was already suggested here, to stumble in these praising lines upon an analogy between Ṣalāḥ al-Dīn Yūsuf the son of Ayyūb (the Hebrew Job) and the biblical Joseph the son of Jacob (Yūsuf bn Yaʿqūb in Arabic).[42]

Shortly after his arrival at Damascus (in 562/August 1167), the secretary ʿImad al-Dīn al-Kātib al-Isfahānī, who would fill an important role at Saladin's court, visited Najam al-Dīn Ayyūb, Saladin's father. At that date the host's son and brother, Saladin and Asad al-Dīn Shīrkūha respectively, were heading toward completing their second Egyptian adventure.[43] At the reception, the secretary ʿImād al-Dīn recited a long poem, which contained prophetic verses:[44]

> The two will tomorrow kindle a corroding fire among the infidels / the tongue of fire will turn young to old // In the future Joseph will establish himself in Egypt / with it, after a long separation, Jacob will find security // There Joseph will meet his brothers / by God, with no reproach Allah will unite them at that day.[45]

On the arrival of Saladin to Egypt, the poet Ḥassan (known as ʿArqalah) said to him:

> the Turk [soldiers have] relinquished Egypt to be destroyed by the Bedouins / O Lord in the past you gave Egypt to Joseph the righteous (Yūsuf al-Ṣadīq), the son of Jacob / nowadays Egypt is governed by Yūsuf the faithful (al-Sādiq), the son of Ayyūb.[46]

Narrating the story of Saladin's rise to power, Ibn Wāṣil says that following the death of his young nephew, Asad al-Dīn, the former seized the command over the Syrian expedition forces that were stationed at Cairo. Then he goes on and tells about Ṣalāḥ al-Dīn's repentance:

> When the leadership was given to him he stopped from drinking alcohol and shunned from [non-Islamic] entertainments. From now on, till death, he acted sombrely and solemnity (al-jidd wal-ijtihād).[47]

In the plot woven by the narrator, the elevation of the young army commander was not a political turning point, but a deeply religious conversion. This literary technique is employed by some authors who glorify the achievements of Saladin by installing the sultan within the timeline of Islam's sacred history. They compared his successes with key events in a utopian past and compare his achievements with triumphs that occurred in the days of the founding fathers of Islam.[48]

Learning in Damascus of Ṣalāḥ al-Dīn's success in subduing a rebellion in Cairo (564/ August 1169), ʿImād al-Dīn dispatched a panegyrical poem to him:

> with Saladin gleamed the most respect praises in our days // I have to produce what is my duty of honour and to thanks him for his considerable efforts to present voluntary gifts

// He is Joseph of Egypt our hopes are directed toward him // You rendered the flooding two Nile Rivers: a river of dark blood and an attainment of grace [...] with your power you are confusing the Nile, well it is the time to conquest the Mediterranean's coasts // and to sanctify the Holy City, to clean her from the corrupted infidels, from the filth of the wicked barbarians.[49]

A second dispatch in response to a communication by Saladin, the secretary 'he s al-Dīn mentions his addressee's conflict with Shawār, a violent clash that ended with the execution of the Fatimid vizier.[50] This event was the subject of a panegyric poem that says:

Be delighted Egypt, Yūsuf [Joseph the son of Jacob] has seized control over you, God the All-merciful made him to accomplish something long awaited // Only David's killing of Goliath resembles the execution of Fatimid vizier Shāwar at the hands of Yūsuf [Joseph Saladin].[51]

The term "Pharaoh" (Fir'ūn) occurs in the Qu'rān seventy-four times. He is an evil king who, together with his household, did not believe in God. Later Islamic literature depicts Pharaoh as a symbol of evil and arrogance.[52] It is no wonder that in many legendary tales, Pharaoh is said to lead his followers to hellfire on the day of resurrection.[53] He is the symbol of absolute wickedness and biographers of Saladin were familiar with this tradition and manipulated it for their own purposes.[54] Often they used this motive to emphasize the anti-Fatimid policy of Saladin and to extol his measures to eliminate them from Egypt.[55]

Saladin, however, is portrayed as the redeemer of Egypt, who saved the Nile Valley from the heretics.[56] Verses by the Yemenite poet 'Umāra, who was in Cairo when Saladin abolished the Fatimid vizierate, can serve as an example to these dramatic formulas:

It is as if in those nights, I was a believer amongst the people of Pharaoh: I struggled to defend my religion, even though death was kept waiting.[57]

'Abd al-Mun'im al-Jilyānī (531–602/1136–1205), a second poet that witnessed this unification of father and son, wrote:

In the east the splendor of Najm al-Dīn has risen / his sons are unconsumed comets // They arrived like Jacob and the tribes, who have come / from Syria to the ruler of Egypt and joined him // Yet when the brothers arrived to this Joseph / they experienced no conflict or slander.[58]

To commemorate the death of al-'Āḍid and the end of the Fatimid regime in Egypt, 'Imād al-Dīn al-Isfahānī wrote a poem. Its verses contain a sharp political message:

al-'Āḍid the propagandist passed away never again an imposter will seized Egypt // with it the age of Pharaoh came to an end in Egypt / from tomorrow the reins of government will be in the hands of Yūsuf of Egypt.[59]

As a summary of this analogy between biblical Joseph and Saladin, we can use Ibn Wāṣil's narrative. This historian narrates an episode enriched with quotations from the Qur'ān:[60]

What happened to Ayyūb with his son Ṣalāḥ al-Dīn Yūsuf resembles to a considerable degree to what happened to Jacob with his son Joseph, when he arrived at Egypt and found that his son is the ruler of the Nile Valley. "So, when they entered unto Joseph, he took his father and mother into his arms saying, 'Enter you into Egypt, if God will, in security'."[61] It is narrated that when Ayyūb met with his son al-Malik al-Nāsir (the Victorious King) Ṣalāḥ al-Dīn, who was accompanied by the [Fatimid] caliph al-ʿĀḍid, a reciter chanted the adjacent verse: "And he lifted his father and mother upon the throne; and the others fell down prostrate before him. 'See, father,' he said, 'this is the interpretation of my vision of long ago; [my Lord has made it true]'."[62]

Moreover, in the texts studied by me, Saladin was compared not only to biblical Joseph. Thus, for example, it is reported that Saladin accepted, without complaint, the bad news about his army's defeat at Mongisard (Mount Gezer). His endurance was equal to the patience of Job, maintains the historian, and he is said to bewail the crushing defeat like King David.[63]

Subsequent to the victory at Jacob's Ford (*Vadum Jacob* or Chastellet; 575/August 1179)[64] the poet Ibn al-Sāʿātī composed the following verses:

You stopped at the Castle of the Ford // indeed it is a unique post that no other placement equals // you raised your yellow flag and shortly / afterwards your enemies shook // should a gang that lie while proclaiming their faith live in the land of the prophets // you advised them, and all know that warning is a religious duty / they scattered the house of Jacob and immediately Joseph came forward.[65]

The decisive victory of Saladin at Ḥattin is compared with the biblical story of Joseph in the land of Egypt, his arrest and release.[66] This image of Saladin was not limited solely to Muslim sources. The Christian historian Bar Hebraeus summarizes the transfer of power from the last Fatimid caliph to Saladin, the new lord of the Nile Valley and says: "And the poets also have composed a multitude of metrical harangues, saying 'The reign (*melkūtā*) of Pharaoh has come to an end, and that of Joseph (*yosefya*) has begun'."[67]

At the first sermon in the al-Aqṣā mosque, which was given after Saladin's victorious entry to Jerusalem, the preacher said, among other praises: "is not this house (i.e. al-Aqṣā) where God stopped the sun from descending over Joshua (Yūshaʿ [bn Nūn]) and slowed the coming of the night so that he will be able to conquest and to offer the sacrifice?"[68] "Is it not the shrine that Moses ordered his people to save and they all, except two men. He became angry and punished them by deporting them to the desert."[69] The preacher continued his words and said that after the Sons of Israel have averted from Him, God has chosen the Muslims in their place.[70]

The lengths that Saladin's entourage was ready to go in their efforts to praise him can be deduced from the description of his final hours:

I came across a letter by al-Qāḍī al-Fāḍil who wrote that a man saw a vision at the night of Saladin's death. A voice whispered "tonight Joseph was freed from his jail." These words are in line with the saying by the Prophet Muhammad: "The world is the prison of the believer and the paradise of the infidel." The transmitter added: "our Joseph was in this earthly world in prison, compared with his fate in the Paradise. God is pleased with his spirit and hence opened for him the gates of Heaven. This was the last opening (i.e. Conquest) that Saladin hopped to attain."[71]

The connection of biblical metaphors and the official language used by the courtiers of Saladin is plainly seen in the memorandum that was composed by ʿImad al-Dīn al-Isfahānī. In it, the chief secretary of Saladin reports to the caliph's court in Baghdad on the victories of 583/July 1187.[72] He opens his report with a carefully selected verse from the Qurʾān that reads: "For We have written in the Psalms (*zabūr*), after the Remembrance, 'The earth shall be the inheritance of My righteous servants'."[73]

As was demonstrated above, Saladin's admirers often saw him as equivalent to biblical Joseph.[74] This representation spread in the Near East already during Saladin's lifetime, as we can deduce from an anonymous Latin poem that says:

He was not a Joseph, should not have been a Joseph. In the king's bed by a crime against a woman, He corrupted his lady, adulterous man, a thief too bold … By general edict, Saladin became the first among princes, through such a crime becomes nearly the king's equal.[75]

SUMMARY

The sources analyzed here reflect the reception of the story of Joseph by many medieval Muslims, who assimilated and retold it. The identification with the biblical patriarchs was an integral component in their world vision and the use of biblical references in documents that portray Saladin illuminates it; his contemporaries drew analogies between him and Joseph the son of Jacob. It would not be difficult to append the handful of verses quoted above with numerous other stanzas and accounts that extol Saladin the sovereign of Egypt, who is said to resemble Joseph the vizier of Pharaoh.[76]

These passages also raise the question of the role of the Bible in their world vision.[77] That early generations of Muslims were familiar with biblical legends is agreed upon by students of Islam who have pondered upon the popularity of the *Isrāʾīliyyāt* genre during those centuries.[78] Yet, during the Mamlūk period a twist can be detected. Sources from that period make it clear that several well-respected Muslim scholars voiced their objection to the reception of this literary genre.[79]

However, from the texts studied here by me it is clear that the popularity of biblical narratives was unchallenged during the Ayyubid period. Moreover, the connection of Joseph with the ruler of Islamic Egypt did not end with the collapse of the Ayyubid house. Ibn al-Mughayzil (d. 1296), an early Mamlūk historian, transmits a tale that associates, perhaps for the first time, al-Ẓāhir Baybars (d. 1277), the new Mamlūk sultan of Egypt with the Biblical/ Qurʾānic tradition. One of the emirs of the Ayyubid ruler al-Ṣāliḥ Ayyūb (d. 1249) is quoted as saying to al-Ẓāhir Baybars: "God put you in the place of Joseph, and put in your hand the souls of his servants."[80] Facing a food crisis, the sultan nominated an inspector (*muḥtasib*) of the markets in Cairo (Misr), telling him: "you are a foreigner (*gharīb*), I am a foreigner and Joseph the righteous (*ṣadīq*) was an outsider."[81] A poet wrote that while on the road from Cairo to Mecca an emir was arrested (751/1351): "In the highest mountain peak in a fortress he was jailed. A lofty prison high as a shining star. / He will be welcomed by the mighty that provided hospitality to Jesus the son of Mary. As Joseph was delivered from the dungeon so will be you freed."[82]

NOTES

1 On his political and military career, see Hamilton A. R. Gibb, *The Life of Saladin: From the Works of Imad ad-Din and Baha ad-Din* (Oxford: Clarendon Press, 1973); *idem, Saladin: Studies in Islamic History*, ed. Y. Ibish (Beirut, 1974); Andrew S. Ehrenkreutz, *Saladin* (Albany: State University of New York Press, 1972); Malcolm Cameron Lyons and D. E. P. Jackson, *Saladin: The Politics of the Holy War* (Cambridge: Cambridge University Press, 1982); Yaacov Lev, *Saladin in Egypt* (Brill, 1999); *Anne-Marie Eddé, Saladin* trans. Jane Marie Todd (Cambridge, MA: Belknap Press of Harvard University Press, 2011).

2 Stanley Lane-Poole, *Saladin and the Fall of the Kingdom of Jerusalem* (New York, 1906), 377–401.

3 Fr. Gabrieli, "The Arabic Historiography of the Crusades," in B. Lewis and P. M. Holt (eds), *Historians of the Middle East* (London: Oxford University Press, 1962), 98–107; Claude Cahen, "Editing Arabic Chronicles: A Few Suggestions," *Islamic Studies* 15 (1976), 17–19; for a selected translation of these sources, see Fr. Gabrieli, *The Arab Historians of the Crusades* (London, 1969).

4 An early survey of this literary production was done by Hamilton A. R. Gibb, "The Arabic Sources for the Life of Saladin," *Speculum* 25 (1950): 58–72; Donald S. Richards, "A consideration of two sources for the life of Saladin," *JSS* 25 (1980): 46–65.

5 This facet is distinctly visible in Abū Shama's report on the relations between Nūr al-Dīn and Saladin and his evaluation of the sources that report on developments in Cairo and Damascus. Abū Shama ʿAbd al-Raḥman b. Ismaʿīl b. Ibrāhīm al-Shāfiʿī (599–665/1202–67), *Kitāb al-Rawḍatayn fī akhbār al-dawlatayn al-nūriyya wal-ṣalāḥiyya*, ed. Ibrahim Shams al-Dīn (Beirut: Dar al-Kutub al-ʿIlmiyya, 1422/2002), II: 77–79 (AH 564). I shall return to this issue further below.

6 Donald S. Richards, "Imad al-Din al-Isfahani: Administrator, Litterateur and Historian," in Maya Shatzmiller (ed.), *Crusaders and Muslims in Twelfth-Century Syria* (Leiden: E. J. Brill, 1993), 133–46; Nasser O. Rabbat, "My Life with Salah al-Din: The Memories of ʿImad al-Din al-Katib al-Isfahani," *Edebiyat* 7/2 (1996): 267–287.

7 Bahaʾ al-Din Abu al-Mahasin Yusuf b. Rafiʿ Ibn Shaddad (539–632/1145–1239), *al-Nawadir al-sultaniyya wal-mahasin al-yusufiyya* [*Sirat Salah al-Din*], ed. G. al-Shayyal (Cairo: Turathuna, 1964) (D. S. Richards (trans.), *The Rare and Excellent History of Saladin or al-Nawadir al-Sultaniyya waʾl-Mahasin al-Yusufiyya by Bahaʾ al-Din Ibn Shaddad* (Aldershot: Ashgate, 2001).)

8 Chase F. Robinson, *Islamic Historiography* (Cambridge: Cambridge University Press, 2003), 62–63.

9 See, however, the review by Françoise Micheau, "Le Kitāb al-kāmil fī l-tāʾrīkh dʾIbn al-Athīr: Entre chronique et histoire," *Studia Islamica* 104 (2007): 94–98.

10 ʿIzz al-Din ʿAli b. Abi al-Karm Muhammad Ibn al-Athir al-Jaziri (555–630/1160–1233), *al-Kamil fī al-taʾrikh*, ed. al-Daqqaq (Beirut: Dar al-Kutub al-Ilmiyya, 1424/2003) (Donald S. Richards (trans.) *The Chronicle of Ibn al-Athir for the Crusading Period from al-Kamil fiʾl-taʾrikh*, 3 vols (Aldershot: Ashgate, 2006–08).

11 S. Richards, "Some Consideration of Ibn al-Athīr's al-Tāʾrīkh al-Bāhir and its relationship to the Kāmil," in C. Vázquez de Benito and M. A. Manzano Rodríguez (eds), *Actas XVI Congreso UEAI* (Salamanca, 1995), 444.

12 Abū Shāma ʿAbd al-Raḥman b. Ismaʿīl b. Ibrāhīm al-Shāfiʿī (599–665/1202–67), *Kitāb al-Rawḍatayn fī akhbār al-dawlatayn al-nūriyya wal-ṣalāḥiyya*, ed. Ibrahim Shams al-Dīn (Beirut: Dar al-Kutub al-ʿIlmiyya, 1422/2002).

13 See the author's remarks on his birth and name: Abū Shāma, *Dhayl al-Rawḍatayn*, V: 50, 57–58.

14 On Abu Shāma's and Ibn Wāsil's life and production, see Konrad Hirschler, *Medieval Arabic Historiography: Authors as Actors* (London: Routledge 2006).

15 Ṣalāḥ aL-Buḥayrī, "Le décret de nomination de l'historien Ibn Wāṣil au poste de professeur de la mosquée al-Aqmar," *AnIsl* 12 (1975): 85–94.

16 Jamal al-Din Muhammad b. Salim Ibn Wāṣil (604–97/1207–98), *Mufarrij al-kurūb fī akhbar bani ayyub*, ed. al-Shayyal et al. vols 1–5 (Cairo, 1954).

17 Y. Frenkel, "Ayyubid and Mamluk Historiography: Eyewitness Accounts by Several Contemporaries," in K. D'Hulster and J. van Steenbergen (eds), *Continuity and Change in the Realms of Islam* (Leuven: Peeters, 2008), 245–260.

18 Y. Frenkel, "Muslim Responses to the Frankish Dominion in the Near East (1098–1291)," in Conor Kostick (ed.), *The Crusades and the Near East: Cultural Histories* (London: Routledge, 2011), 30–31.

19 R. Stephen Humphreys, "Legitimacy and Political Instability in Islam in the Age of the Crusades," in Hadia Dajani-Shakeel Ronald A. Messier (eds), *The Jihad and its Times dedicated to Andrew S. Ehrenkreutz* (Ann Arbor: MPublishing University of Michigan and Center for Near Eastern and North African Studies, 2011), 5, 7.

20 Peter Malcolm Holt, "Saladin and His Admirers: A Biographical Reassessment," *BSOAS* 46 (1983): 235–239.

21 Emmanuel Sivan, *L'Islam et la croisade: Idéologie et propagande sans réactions musulmanes aux croisades* (Paris: Librairie d'Amérique et d'Orient, 1968), 95–97.

22 Ibn Wāṣil, *Mufarrij al-kurūb*, I: 174.

23 Stephennie Mulder, "The Mausoleum of Imam al-Shāfiʿī," *Muqarnas* 23 (2006): 15–46.

24 Y. Frenkel, "Political and Social Aspects of Islamic Religious Endowments (*awqāf*): Saladin in Cairo (1169–73) and Jerusalem (1187–93)," *Bulletin of the School of Oriental and African Studies* 62 (1999): 1–20.

25 Gaston Wiet, "Les Inscriptions de Saladin," *Syria* (1922): 309, 312, 314 (note 4); A. S. Tritton, "Three Inscriptions from Jerusalem," *Bulletin of the School of Oriental and African Studies* 20 (1957): 537–539.

26 Hillenbrand, *The Crusades: Islamic Perspectives*, 248–250 (on the conflicting interpretations by Sivan and Köhler).

27 This thesis was advanced by Emmanuel Sivan in several works. See his *L'Islam et la croisade: Idéologie et propagande sans réactions musulmanes aux croisades* (Paris: Librairie d'Amérique et d'Orient, 1968).

28 Michael Köhler argues that the jihad propaganda of the Ayyubids should not to be taken at face value in every case. They, including Saladin himself, often opted for negotiations with the Franks and concluded treaties with them. Michael Köhler, *Alliances and Treaties between Frankish and Muslim Rulers in the Middle East: Cross-Cultural Diplomacy in the Period of the Crusades*, trans. Peter M. Holt, ed.and intro. Konrad Hirschler (Leiden: Brill, 2003), 213–267.

29 Andrew S. Ehrenkreutz, *Saladin* (Albany: State University of New York Press, 1972), 205–206. It is appropriate to translate his royal title "the reformer of religion and earthly things."

30 Uri Rubin, "Islamic Retellings of Biblical History," in Y. Tzvi Langermann and Josef Stern (eds), *Adaptations and Innovations Studies on the Interaction between Jewish and Islamic Thought and Literature from the Early Middle Ages to the Late Twentieth Century, Dedicated to Professor Joel L. Kraemer* (Louvain: Peeters, 2007), 299–313.

31 F. Rosenthal, "The Influence of the Biblical Tradition on Muslim Historiography, " in B. Lewis and P. M. Holt (eds), *Historians of the Middle East* (London, 1962): 41–44; Hava Lazarus-Yafeh, *Intertwined Worlds: Medieval Islam and Bible Criticism* (Princeton: Princeton University Press, 1992), 112.

32 Jalāl al-Dīn Abū al-Faraj ʿAbd al-Raḥman b. ʿAlī Ibn al-Jawzī al-Ḥanbalī (510–597/1117–1201), *al-Wafā bi-aḥwāl al-Muṣṭāfái*, ed. M. A. ʿAṭā (Beirut: Dār al-kutub al-ʿilmiyya, 1408/1988), 56–68; esp. 60 "in another Psalm hymn [David] said: 'God proclaimed him in Zion, a praiseworthy crown'. The crown indicates leadership and guidance, praiseworthy (*maḥmūd*) means Muhammad". Cf. Psalm 50: 2 "Out of Zion, the perfection of beauty, God shines forth."

33 Abū Jaʿfar Muḥammad b. Jarīr al-Ṭabarī (224–310/838–923), *Taʾrīkh al-rusul wal-mulūk*, ed. M. A. Ibrahīm (Cairo: Dār al-Maʿārif, 1386/1967), XIII: 476–477; Tayeb el-Hibri, "The Regicide of the Caliph al-Amin and the Challenge of Representation in Medieval Islamic Historiography," *Arabica* 42/3 (1995): 338–339.

34 Q. Sūrat Yūsuf, XII: 41 (trans. Arberry).

35 Sh. Goldman, "Joseph," in Jane Dammen McAuliffe (ed.), *Encyclopaedia of the Qur'ān* (Leiden: Brill, 2001), III: 55–57.

36 R. Firestone, "Yusuf," *The Encyclopaedia of Islam* (Leiden: Brill, 2002), XI: 352–354.

37 Abu al-Fida Isma'il Ibn Kathir (701–74/1301–73), *Qiṣaṣ al-anbiya*, ed. A. al-Farmawi (Cairo, 1417/1997), 304; For primary sources in English translation, see W. M. Brinner (trans.), *The History of al-Tabari. Vol. 2: Prophets and Patriarchs* (Albany 1987), 148–185; William M. Brinner (trans.), *Arā'is al-majālis fī qiṣaṣ al-anbiya*, or, *Lives of the Prophets as Recounted by Abū Ishāq Ahmad ibn Muhammad ibn Ibrāhīm al-Tha'labī* (Boston: Brill, 2002), 181–235; W. M. Thackston (trans.), *The Tales of the Prophets of al-Kisā'ī* (Boston 1978), 167–192; Abu al-Fida Isma'il Ibn Kathir (701–74/1301–73), *Stories of the Prophets: From Adam to Muhammad*, trans. Sayyid Jad et al. (Dar al-Manarah, 2001), 127–156; Brannon M. Wheeler (ed. and trans.), *Prophets in the Quran: An Introduction to the Quran and Muslim Exegesis* (London and New York: Continuum 2002), 127–145.

38 Brinner, *The History of al-Tabari*, 154–155.

39 Brinner, *Arā'is al-majālis fī qiṣaṣ al-anbiya*, 184.

40 Konrad Hirschler, *Medieval Arabic Historiography: Authors as Actors* (London: Routledge 2006), 81, 89–90.

41 Abu Shama, *Rawḍatayn*, II: 82, 83, 84, (AH 564; quotes *Dīwān 'Arqalah al-Kalbī*), 88, 89, 90.

42 Ibn Wāṣil, *Mufarrij al-kurūb*, II: 233, 235.

43 They were back in Damascus in September. Qiwām al-Dīn al-Fatḥ b. 'Alī al-Bundarī (586–643/1190–1245), *Sanā al-barq al-shāmī mukhtaṣar al-barq al-shāmī lil-'Imād al-isfahānī*, ed. R. Şeşen (Istanbul, 2004), 10–11.

44 Ibn Kathir, *Bidāyah*, XVI: 423 (AH 562/1167).

45 A reference to Q. 12: 92 "He said, 'No reproach this day shall be on you; God will forgive you; He is the most merciful of the merciful'" (trans.) Arberry.

46 Ibn Kathir, *Bidāyah*, 16: 421 (AH 562/1167; the first journey of Saladin to Egypt); Malcolm Cameron Lyons and D. E. P. Jackson, *Saladin: The Politics of the Holy War* (Cambridge: Cambridge University Press, 1982), 10–11.

47 Ibn Wāṣil, *Mufarrij al-kurūb*, I: 168 (quoting Bahā' al-Dīn).

48 Ibn Wāṣil, *Mufarrij al-kurūb*, II: 222; for the reception of pseudo-history as a source for events that presumably took place during the first generation, see Shams al-Dīn Muḥammad b. Ibrāhīm Ibn al-Jazarī (658–739/1259–1338), *Ta'rīkh Ḥawādithal-zamān wa-anbā'ih' wa-wafayāt al-akābir wal-a'yān min abnā'ih' al-ma'rūf bi-ta'rīkh Ibn al-Jazarī*, ed. A. A. al-Tadmurī (Beirut: al-Maktaba al-'Aṣriyya, 1419/1998), III: 667 (he quotes pseudo-Wāqidī, *Futūḥ al-shām* as an original work).

49 Ibn Wāṣil, *Mufarrij al-kurūb*, I: 177–78; Abu Shama, *Rawddatayn*, II: 88–89.

50 On Shawār, see F. Daftary, *The Isma'ilis: Their History and Doctrines* (Cambridge University PRess 1990), 271–272; 2nd edn (2007), 251–252.

51 Ibn Wāṣil, *Mufarrij al-kurūb*, I: 178; Abu Shama, *Rawḍatayn*, II: 90; Ibn Kathīr, *Bidāyah*, XVI: 433 (AH 564/1169); 'Izz al-Dīn Aḥmad ibn Ibrāhīm al-'Asqlānī al-Ḥanbalī (800–876/1398–1471), *Shifā' al-qulūb fī manāqib Banī Ayyūb* taḥqīq Madīḥah al-Sharqāwī (Cairo: Maktabat al-Thaqāfah al-Dīnīyah, 1415/1996), 98.

52 Also in present-day political writings. See, for example, Zainab al-Ghazali, *Return of the Pharaoh Memoir in Nasir's Prison*, trans. Mokrane Guezzou (The Islamic Foundation 1427/2006), esp. 171 (5 June 1967).

53 Reuven Firestone, "Pharaoh," in Jane Dammen McAuliffe (ed.), *Encyclopaedia of the Qur'ān* (Leiden: Brill, 2001), IV: 66–68.

54 Konrad Hirschler, "The 'Pharaoh' Anecdote in Pre-Modern Arabic Historiography," *Journal of Arabic and Islamic Studies* 10 (2010): 45–74, esp. 51.

55 For similar accusation voiced against an Ayyubid sultan, see Gary Leiser, "The Madrasa and the Islamization of the Middle East: The Case of Egypt," *Journal of the American Research Center in Egypt* 22 (1985): 44.

56 This is not the first time in Islamic history that poets manipulate this comparison to strengthen the image of their patron. Abū Shāma, *Rawḍatayn*, II: 131–132.

57 Pieter Smoor, "'Umāra's Poetical Views of Shāwar, Ḍirġām, Shīrkūh and Ṣalāḥ al-Dīn as Viziers of the Fatimids Caliphs," in Farhad Daftary and Josef W. Meri (eds), *Culture and Memory in Medieval Islam: Essays in Honour of Wilferd Madelung* (London: I. B. Tauris, 2003), 425; on 'Umāra, see Yaacov Lev, *Saladin in Egypt* (Brill, 1999), 90

58 Abū Shāma, *Rawḍatayn*, II: 100 (AH 565).

59 Ibn Kathir, *Bidāyāh*, XVI: 451–452 (AH 567/1171), and 453; and see resembling verses by 'Imad al-Din in Abū Shāma, *Rawḍatayn*, II: 128 (567/September 1171).

60 Ibn Wāṣil, *Mufarrij al-kurūb*, I: 186.

61 Q. 12: 99/100.

62 Q. 12 100/101.

63 Ibn Kathir, *Bidāyah*, XVI: 523 (573/November 1177); Ibn al-Athīr, *al-Kāmil fī al-taʾrīkh*, X: 85–86 (AH 573). On this event and report, see D. Richards "Ibn al-Athir and the later parts of al-Kamil," in D. O. Morgan (ed.), *Medieval Historical Writing in the Christian and Islamic Worlds* (London: SOAS, 1982), 89.

64 On the archaeological site, see Adrian J. Boas, "Archaeological Sources for the History of Palestine: The Frankish Period: A Unique Medieval Society Emerges," *Near Eastern Archaeology* 61/3 (1998): 157–158.

65 Ibn al-Sāʿātī (618/1221), *Dīwān* (Beirut, 1936), II: 409; 'Izz al-Dīn Aḥmad ibn Ibrāhīm al-'Asqlānī al-Ḥanbalī (800–876/1398–1471), *Shifāʾ al-qulūb fī manāqib Banī Ayyūb* ed. Madīḥah al-Sharqāwī (Cairo: Maktabat al-Thaqāfah al-Dīnīyah, 1415/1996), 117.

66 Ibn Kathīr, *Bidāyah*, XVI: 585; Qurʾān sūra 12.

67 Gregorii Barhebraei (AD 1226–86), *Chronicon Syriacum* (Paris, 1890), 344 (ll. 22–23) (E. A. Wallis Budge (trans.) *The Chronography of Gregory Abu'l-Faraj commonly known as Bar Hebraeus* (Oxford, 1932), 300.)

68 Ibn Wāṣil, *Mufarrij al-kurūb*, II: 223; cf. Joshua 10: 12 "Sun, stand still over Gibeon, and you, moon, over the Valley of Aijalon"; al-Ṭabarī, *Taʾrīkh*, ed. Ibrahim, 1: 440, 441.

69 Q. 5: 21–23.

70 Ibn Wāṣil, *Mufarrij al-kurūb*, II: 223–224.

71 Abū Shāma, *Rawḍatayn*, IV: 217.

72 Ibn Wāṣil, *Mufarrij al-kurūb*, II: 203.

73 Q. al-Anbiya, 105; cf. Psalms 37: 29: "The righteous shall possess the land and dwell upon it forever."

74 Anne-Marie Eddé, *Saladin*, trans. Jane Marie Todd (Cambridge, MA: Belknap Press of Harvard University Press, 2011), 156–160.

75 For this negative description that aimed at opposing the praised image of the sultan, see Eddé, *Saladin*, 470–471.

76 Ibn Wāṣil, *Mufarrij al-kurūb*, I: 183, 186; Abū Shāma, *Rawḍatayn*, II: 89, 95, 96 (by verses by 'Imad al-Dīn).

77 M. J. Kister, "Haddithu 'an Bani Isra'il wa-la harja. A Study of an Early Tradition," *Israel Oriental Studies* vol. 2 (1972), 215–239; reprinted in his *Studies in Jahiliyya and Early Islam* (London: Variorum 1980), art. 14.

78 Roberto Tottoli, "Origin and Use of the Term Isrāʾīliyyāt in Muslim Literature," *Arabica* 46/2 (1999): 193–210.

79 Yehoshua Fernkel, "Is there a Mamlūk culture?," *Ulrich Haarmann Memorial Lecture*, ed. Stephan Conermann (Berlin: EBVerlag, 2014), 20–21.

80 Ibn al-Mughayzil, *Dhayl Muffarij al-kurūb fī akhbār Banī Ayyūb*, ed. ʿUmar ʿAbd al-Salām Tadmurī (Beirut, 2004), 89–90. An amir who has beaten up Baybars in childhood told him after he seized the sultan's throne: "would not Joseph's brothers treating him badly he would not became the king of Egypt. The person who faces difficulties patiently will win at the end of the day. Suffering is the key for rewards." al-Nuwayrī al-Iskandrānī, *Kitāb al-ilmām*, VI: 5.

81 Mūsá ibn Muḥammad al-Yūsufī (676–759/1277–1358), *Nuzhat al-nāẓir fī sirat al-malik al-nāṣir*, ed. A. Ḥuṭayṭ (Beirut, 1986), 297 (l. 7; AH 736/1336); cf. Koby Yosef, "Mamluks and Their Relatives in the Period of the Mamluk Sultanate (1250–1517)," *Mamluk Studies Review* 16 (2012): 63–68.

82 Ṣalāḥ al-Dīn Khalīl. b. Aybak al-Safadī (696–764/1296–1363), *Ayām al-ʿaṣr wa-aʿwān al-naṣr* (Beirut, 1418/1998), II: 88 (ll. 5–6).

BIBLIOGRAPHY
Primary sources

Abū Shama, ʿAbd al-Raḥman b. Ismaʿīl b. Ibrāhīm al-Shāfiʿī (599–665/1202–67), *Kitāb al-Rawḍatayn fī akhbār al-dawlatayn al-nūriyya wal-ṣalāḥiyya*, ed. Ibrāhīm Shams al-Dīn (Beirut: Dār al-Kutub al-ʿIlmiyya, 1422/2002).

al-ʿAsqalānī, ʿIzz al-Dīn Aḥmad ibn Ibrāhīm al-Ḥanbalī (800–876/1398–1471), *Shifāʾ al-qulūb fī manāqib Banī Ayyūb*, ed. Madīḥah al-Sharqāwī (Cairo: Maktabat al-Thaqāfah al-Dīnīyah, 1415/1996).

Bar Hebraeus=Gregorii Barhebraei (AD 1226–86), *Chronicon Syriacum* (Paris, 1890). (Trans. E. A. Wallis Budge as *The Chronography of Gregory Abu'l-Faraj commonly known as Bar Hebraeus* (Oxford, 1932).

al-Bundarī, Qiwām al-Dīn al-Fatḥ b. ʿAlī (586–643/1190–1245), *Sanā al-barq al-shāmī (mukhtaṣar al-barq al-shāmī lil-ʿImād al-isfahānī*, ed. Ramazan Şeşen (Istanbul: Istanbul Üniversitesi Edebiyat Fakültesi Yayınları, 2004).

al-Ghazali, Zainab, *Return of the Pharaoh: Memoir in Nasir's Prison*, trans. Mokrane Guezzou (Leicester: The Islamic Foundation, 1427/2006).

Ibn al-Athīr, ʿIzz al-Dīn ʿAlī b. Abī al-Karm Muḥammad al-Jazirī (555–630/1160–1233), *al-Kāmil fī al-taʾrīkh*, ed. al-Daqqāq (Beirut: Dār al-kutub al-ʿilmiyya, 1424/2003). (Trans. Donald S. Richards as *The Chronicle of Ibn al-Athir for the Crusading Period from al-Kamil fi'l-taʾrikh*, 3 vols (Aldershot: Ashgate, 2006–08).)

Ibn al-Jawzī, Jalāl al-Dīn Abū al-Faraj ʿAbd al-Raḥman b. ʿAlī al-Ḥanbalī (510–97/1117–1201), *al-Wafā bi-aḥwāl al-Muṣṭafá*, ed. M. A. ʿAṭā (Beirut: Dār al-kutub al-ʿilmiyya, 1408/1988).

Ibn Kathīr, Abū al-Fidá Ismāʿīl (701–74/1301–73), *Qiṣaṣ al-anbiyā*, ed. ʿAbd al-Ḥayy al-Farmāwī (Cairo: Dār al-ṭibāʿa wal-nashr al-islāmiyya, 1417/1997). (Ibn Kathir, *Stories of the Prophets: From Adam to Muhammad* trans. Sayyid Jad et al. (Dar al-Manarah, 2001).)

Ibn Kathīr, Abū al-Fidá Ismāʿīl (701–74/1301–73), *Bidāyah wal-nihāya*, ed. ʿAbd Allah b. ʿAbd al-Muḥsin al-Turkī, 18 vols (Cairo: Hajar, 1998).

Ibn al-Mughayzil, *Dhayl Muffarij al-kurūb fī akhbār Banī Ayyūbi*, ed. ʿUmar ʿAbd al-Salām Tadmurī (Beirut: al-Maktaba al-ʿAṣriyya, 2004).

Ibn al-Sāʿātī, Riḍwān b. Muḥammad (618/1221), *Dīwān*, ed. Anīs al-Maqdisī (Beirut: AUB, 1936).

Ibn Shaddād, Bahāʾ al-Dīn Abū al-Maḥasin Yūsuf b. Rāfiʿ (539–632/1145–1239), *al-Nawādir al-sulṭāniyya wal-maḥāsin al-yūsufiyya* [*Sirat Ṣalāḥ al-Dīn*], ed. G. al-Shayyāl (Cairo: Turāthuna, 1964). (Trans. D. S. Richards as *The Rare and Excellent History of Saladin or al-Nawadir al-Sultaniyya wa'l-Mahasin al-Yusufiyya by Bahaʾ al-Din Ibn Shaddad* (Aldershot: Ashgate, 2001).)

Ibn Wāṣil, Jamāl al-Dīn Muḥammad b. Sālim (604–97/1207–98), *Mufarrij al-kurūb fī akhbār banī ayyūb*, ed. al-Shayyāl et al., 5 vols (Cairo: Dār al-kutub al-qawmiyya, 1953–77).

al-Jazarī, Shams al-Dīn Muḥammad b. Ibrāhīm (658–739/1259–1338), *Ta'rīkh Ḥawādithal-zamān wa-anbā'ih' wa-wafayāt al-akābir wal-a'yān min abnā'ih' al-ma'rūf bi-ta'rīkh Ibn al-Jazarī*, ed. A. A. al-Tadmurī, 3 vols (Beirut: al-Maktaba al-'Aṣriyya, 1419/1998).

al-Kisā'ī, Muḥammad b. 'Abd Allah (fl. eleventh century), *Qiṣaṣ al-abniyā'* [Vita prophetarum], ed. Isaac Eisenberg, 2 vols (Leiden, 1923). (Trans. W.M. Thackston as *The Tales of the Prophets of al-Kisā'ī* (Boston: Twayne Pub., 1978).)

al-Nuwayrī al-Iskandrānī, Muḥammad b. Al-Qāsim (775/1372), *Kitāb al-ilmām fīmā jarat fihi al-aḥkām wal-umūr al-muqḍiya fī waq'at al-iskandariyya*, ed. A. S. 'Aṭiya, 7 vols (Haydar-Abad: Da'irat al-ma'ārif, 1390/1970).

Qur'an = A. J. Arberry (trans.), *The Koran Interpreted* (New-York: Macmillan, 1955/1996).

al-Safadī, Ṣalāḥ al-Dīn Khalīl. b. Aybak (696–764/1296–1363), *Ayām al-'aṣr wa-a'wān al-naṣr* (Beirut: Dār al-fikr, 1418/1998).

al-Ṭabarī, Abū Ja'far Muḥammad b. Jarīr (224–310/838–923), *Ta'rīkh al-rusul wal-mulūk*, ed. M. A. Ibrahīm, 10 vols (Cairo: Dār al-Ma'ārif, 1386/1967). (Trans. Brinner W.M. as *The History of al-Tabari. Vol. 2: Prophets and Patriarchs* (Albany: SUNI, 1987).)

al-Tha'ālabī, Abū Isḥāq Aḥmad b. Muḥammad b. Ibrāhīm al-Nisābūrī (427/1035), *Arā'is al-majālis fī qiṣaṣ al-anbiyā*, trans. Brinner William M. as *Lives of the Prophets as Recounted by Abū Isḥāq Aḥmad ibn Muḥammad ibn Ibrāhīm al-Tha'ālabī* (Boston: Brill, 2002).

al-Yūsufī, Mūsá ibn Muḥammad (676–759/1277–1358), *Nuzhat al-nāẓir fi sirat al-malik al-nāṣir*, ed. A. Ḥuṭayṭ (Beirut, 1986).

Secondary sources

al-Buḥayrī, Ṣalāḥ. "Le décret de nomination de l'historien Ibn Wāṣil au poste de professeur de la mosquée al-Aqmar," *AnIsl* 12 (1975): 85–94.

Boas, Adrian J. "Archaeological Sources for the History of Palestine: The Frankish Period: A Unique Medieval Society Emerges," *Near Eastern Archaeology* 61/3 (1998): 138–173.

Cahen, Claude. "Editing Arabic Chronicles: A Few Suggestions," *Islamic Studies* 15 (1976), 9–32.

Daftary, F. *The Isma'ilis: Their History and Doctrines* (Cambridge: Cambridge University Press 1990; 2nd edn, 2007).

Eddé, Anne-Marie. *Saladin*, trans. Jane Marie Todd (Cambridge, MA: Belknap Press of Harvard University Press, 2011).

Ehrenkreutz, Andrew S. *Saladin* (Albany: State University of New York Press, 1972).

el-Hibri, Tayeb. "The Regicide of the Caliph al-Amin and the Challenge of Representation in Medieval Islamic Historiography," *Arabica* 42/3 (1995): 338–339.

Frenkel, Yehoshua. "Is there a Mamlūk culture?" *Ulrich Haarmann Memorial Lecturei*, ed. Stephan Conermann (Berlin: EBVerlag, 2014).

Firestone, Reuven. "Yusuf," *The Encyclopaedia of Islam* (Leiden: Brill, 2002), XI: 352–354.

———. "Pharaoh," in Jane Dammen McAuliffe (ed.), *Encyclopaedia of the Qur'ān* (Leiden: Brill, 2001), IV: 66–68.

Frenkel, Yehoshua. "Ayyubid and Mamluk Historiography: Eyewitness Accounts by Several Contemporaries," in K. D'Hulster and J. van Steenbergen (eds), *Continuity and Change in the Realms of Islam* (Leuven: Peeters, 2008), 245–260.

———. "Muslim Responses to the Frankish Dominion in the Near East (1098–1291)", in Conor Kostick (ed.), *The Crusades and the Near East: Cultural Histories* (London: Routledge, 2011), 27–54.

———. "Political and Social Aspects of Islamic Religious Endowments (*awqāf*): Saladin in Cairo (1169–73) and Jerusalem (1187–93)," *Bulletin of the School of Oriental and African Studies* 62 (1999): 1–20.

Gabrieli, Fr. "The Arabic Historiography of the Crusades," in B. Lewis and P. M. Holt (eds), *Historians of the Middle East* (London: Oxford University Press, 1962), 98–107.

————. *The Arab Historians of the Crusades* (London, 1969).

Gibb, Hamilton A. R. *Saladin: Studies in Islamic History*, ed. Y. Ibish (Beirut, 1974).

————. "The Arabic Sources for the Life of Saladin," *Speculum* 25 (1950): 58–72.

————. *The Life of Saladin: From the Works of Imad ad-Din and Baha ad-Din* (Oxford: Clarendon Press, 1973).

Goldman, Sh. "Joseph," in Jane Dammen McAuliffe (ed.), *Encyclopaedia of the Qurʾān* (Leiden: Brill, 2001), III: 55–57.

Hillenbrand, Carole. *The Crusades: Islamic Perspectives* (London: Routledge, 1999).

Hirschler, Konrad. *Medieval Arabic Historiography: Authors as Actors* (London: Routledge 2006).

————. "The 'Pharaoh' Anecdote in Pre-Modern Arabic Historiography," *Journal of Arabic and Islamic Studies* 10 (2010): 45–74.

Holt, Peter Malcolm. "Saladin and his Admirers: A Biographical Reassessment," *BSOAS* 46 (1983): 235–239.

Humphreys, Stephen R. "Legitimacy and Political Instability in Islam in the Age of the Crusades," in Hadia Dajani-Shakeel Ronald A. Messier (eds), *The Jihad and its Times Dedicated to Andrew S. Ehrenkreutz* (Ann Arbor: MPublishing University of Michigan and Center for Near Eastern and North African Studies, 2011), 5–13.

Kister, M. J. "Haddithu ʾan Bani Isra'il wa-la harja. A Study of an Early Tradition," *Israel Oriental Studies* 2 (1972): 215–239; reprinted in his *Studies in Jahiliyya and Early Islam* (London: Variorum 1980), art. 14.

Köhler, Michael. *Alliances and Treaties between Frankish and Muslim Rulers in the Middle East: Cross-Cultural Diplomacy in the Period of the Crusadesi*, trans. Peter M. Holt, ed. and intro. Konrad Hirschler (Leiden: Brill, 2003).

Lane-Poole, Stanley. *Saladin and the Fall of the Kingdom of Jerusalem* (New York, 1906).

Lazarus-Yafeh, Hava. *Intertwined Worlds: Medieval Islam and Bible Criticism* (Princeton: Princeton University Press, 1992)

Leiser, Gary. "The Madrasa and the Islamization of the Middle East: The Case of Egypt," *Journal of the American Research Center in Egypt* 22 (1985): 29–47.

Lev, Yaacov. *Saladin in Egypt* (Brill, 1999).

Lyons, Malcolm Cameron and Jackson, D. E. P. *Saladin: The Politics of the Holy War* (Cambridge: Cambridge University Press, 1982).

Micheau, Françoise. "Le Kitāb al-kāmil fī l-tāʾrīkh d'Ibn al-Athīr: Entre chronique et histoire," *Studia Islamica* 104 (2007): 81–101.

Mulder, Stephennie. "The Mausoleum of Imam al-Shāfiʿī," *Muqarnas* 23 (2006): 15–46.

Rabbat, Nasser O. "My Life with Salah al-Din: The Memories of ʿImad al-Din al-Katib al-Isfahani," *Edebiyat* 7/2 (1996): 267–287.

Richards, Donald S. "Ibn al-Athir and the later parts of al-Kamil," in D. O. Morgan (ed.), *Medieval Historical Writing in the Christian and Islamic Worlds* (London: SOAS, 1982), 76–108.

————. "A Consideration of Two Sources for the Life of Saladin," *JSS* 25 (1980): 46–65.

————. "Imad al-Din al-Isfahani: Administrator, Litterateur and Historian," in Maya Shatzmiller (ed.), *Crusaders and Muslims in Twelfth-Century Syria* (Leiden: E. J. Brill, 1993), 133–146.

————. "Some Consideration of Ibn al-Athīr's al-Tāʾrīkh al-Bāhir and its relationship to the Kāmil," in C. Vázquez de Benito and M.A. Manzano Rodríguez (eds), *Actas XVI Congreso UEAI* (Salamanca, 1995), 443–446.

Robinson, Chase F. *Islamic Historiography* (Cambridge: Cambridge University Press, 2003).

Rosenthal, F. "The Influence of the Biblical Tradition on Muslim Historiography," in B. Lewis and P. M. Holt (eds), *Historians of the Middle East* (London, 1962), 35–45.

Rubin, Uri. "Islamic Retellings of Biblical History," in Y. Tzvi Langermann and Josef Stern (eds), *Adaptations and Innovations Studies on the Interaction between Jewish and Islamic Thought and Literature from the Early Middle Ages to the Late Twentieth Century, Dedicated to Professor Joel L. Kraemer* (Louvain: Peeters, 2007), 299–313.

Sivan, Emmanuel. *L'Islam et la croisade: Idéologie et propagande sans réactions musulmanes aux croisades* (Paris: Librairie d'Amérique et d'Orient, 1968).
Smoor, Pieter. "'Umāra's Poetical Views of Shāwar, Ḍirġām, Shīrkūh and Ṣalāḥ al-Dīn as Viziers of the Fatimids Caliphs," in Farhad Daftary and Josef W. Meri (eds), *Culture and Memory in Medieval Islam: Essays in Honour of Wilferd Madelung* (London: I. B. Tauris, 2003), 410–432.
Tottoli, Roberto. "Origin and Use of the Term Isrāʾīliyyāt in Muslim Literature," *Arabica* 46/2 (1999): 193–210.
Tritton, A. S. "Three Inscriptions from Jerusalem," *Bulletin of the School of Oriental and African Studies* 20 (1957): 537–539.
Wheeler, Brannon M. (ed. and trans.), *Prophets in the Quran: An Introduction to the Quran and Muslim Exegesis* (London and New York: Continuum 2002).
Wiet, Gaston. "Les Inscriptions de Saladin," *Syria* (1922): 307–328.
Yosef, Koby. "Mamluks and Their Relatives in the Period of the Mamluk Sultanate (1250–1517)," *Mamluk Studies Review* 16 (2012): 55–69.

CHAPTER TWENTY-THREE

HISTORICAL MOTIFS IN THE WRITING OF MUSLIM AUTHORS OF THE CRUSADING ERA*

——·◆·——

Daniella Talmon-Heller

> The past was a very real presence in early medieval societies. It might provide a legitimiz-
> ing template for the current order of things, explaining how things were meant to be thus,
> or an image of an ideal order, a Golden Age against which the present could be judged.[1]

In his introduction to *Kitab al-Rawdatayn* (*The Book of the Two Gardens*, i.e. the reigns
of Nur al-Din and Saladin), the Damascene historian Abu Shama (d. 1268) writes about
the collection and the reading of his sources. He discloses how impressed he was with
the biographies of his protagonists, saying: "and I have found them, from among the later
generations, like the two ʿUmars of the early generations [ʿUmar ibn al-Khattab and ʿUmar
ibn ʿAbd al-ʿAziz],[2] as each one of them followed those predecessors regarding justice and
jihad and striving in every way for the glory of the religion of God." He adds, revealing
his motivation to record history: "it is our duty (*wajaba ʿalayna*) to commemorate their
merits." He also expresses his wish that such commemoration will inspire others to follow
their example.[3]

Several recent articles deal with Zangid and Ayyubid era Arab historiography, or more
generally, with the discourse of Arab writers of the crusading era. They address the way
Muslims had understood the crusaders' motives and goals, and their perception of the counter-crusade, or *jihad*, returning to questions raised by Emmanuel Sivan's seminal work of
1968.[4] Directing their attention to the literary sources and rhetorical devices used by these
Muslim writers of the twelfth to fourteenth centuries, most authors stress the religious characteristics of the discourse. Mourad, Lindsay, and Christie demonstrate, among others, the
quotation of *hadith*—especially *hadith* in praise of Syria, Palestine, and Jerusalem and their
religious merits (*fadaʾil*), or *hadith* in praise of *jihad*;[5] Lev, Leder, and Chevedden highlight
the construction of a firm link between personal piety and enlistment to the defense of Dar
al-Islam.[6] What I would like to add to these typologies are some comments on the use of
narratives about early Islamic history in Muslim crusading era discourse, an example of
which Abu Shama has provided for us in the excerpt quoted above.

The crucial role of narratives about the past in the constitution of group and individual identities, and in the interpretation of historical events experienced in the present,

has been established by scholars of various fields. In the sub-field of medieval Muslim historiography, this notion has been employed as a framework for enquiry in the work of Thomas Sizgorich, *Violence and Belief in Late Antiquity*.[7] Konrad Hirschler refers to this phenomenon, which he calls "historicizing," in his detailed study of the works of the above-mentioned Abu Shama and his colleague the chronicler Ibn Wasil (d. 1298). Hirschler deciphers the meaning of the chroniclers choice to place narratives about the past into specific continuities or discontinuities.[8]

A later strata of historical analogies, that making use of narratives of crusading-era history in Modern Arab historiography and political discourse, has been dealt with more widely. Emmanuel Sivan analyzes the creative ways in which twentieth-century Arab historians engage in comparisons between the twelfth- to thirteenth-century *jihad* against the crusaders and the nineteenth- to twentieth-century struggles with imperialism, colonialism, Zionism, and the West. One of the prominent lessons which were formulated by the Arab historians who made these analogies, claims Sivan, was an optimistic one: history is bound to repeat itself; the failure of the crusades and the victory of the Muslims predict the victory of the East in its present-day encounter with the West.[9] Another prominent Israeli historian, B.Z. Kedar, has dealt with allusions to the crusades in modern Hebrew historiography and publicist writing, and came up with some surprising analogies and several contradicting lessons.[10] Several works focus on Saladin's representations and the use of his figure in Ottoman and modern works of historians, publicists, and artists.[11]

I would like to begin my presentation of the historical motifs and analogies used by Muslim historians, preachers, poets, and men of religion of the crusading era, in their accounts of the events they were experiencing in their own times with a little known work of the Damascene historian and preacher Sibt ibn al-Jawzi (d. 1256). In the first decades of the thirteenth century, Sibt ibn al-Jawzi's fame was established on his weekly assemblies of exhortation, which drew huge enthusiastic crowds. To later generations he is best known as the author of the lively chronicle *Mir'at al-Zaman* (Mirror of the Time). The work I am referring to is his *al-Jalis al-Salih wa-l-Anis al-Nasih*, written in the genre of "mirrors for princes" and dedicated to his patron and friend, the Ayyubid ruler al-Malik al-Ashraf (r. 1229–37). The book includes a rather lengthy chapter on *jihad*, with a discussion of the lexical meanings of the term. Sibt ibn al-Jawzi explains that *jihad* may denote one of five: warfare on the battle field, combating one's passions, fighting with the devil, polemics against heretics and dissenters (combat by the tongue, known as *al-jihad bi-'l-lisan*), and the laborious struggle of the mystic to purify his heart and overcome all possible distractions that may lead him astray from total devotion to God. Sibt ibn al-Jawzi grades the virtue of the wars of the heart and soul above the virtue of combat on the battle field, in accordance with a well-known saying of the Prophet, who, coming home from the battlefield, confessed that he was returning from the 'lesser *jihad*' to the 'greater *jihad*'.[12]

Having concluded his discussion of the five meaning of the word *jihad* and of related terms, Sibt ibn al-Jawzi moves on to recall a series of stories (*hikayat*) about Muslim warriors of three historical periods: participants in the wars of the Prophet Muhammad against the people of the tribe of Quraysh; the warriors who went out to conquer Syria in the 630s during the caliphate of 'Umar ibn al-Khattab (634–44); the volunteers who enlisted for the war of attrition on the Arab-Byzantine frontier in the eighth to tenth centuries. I will follow his paradigm and divide my presentation into the same three parts.

At this point, it may not be superfluous to point out that the narratives and myths about the formative period of Islam had been constructed at least four centuries before the crusading era. The first four caliphs had been elevated to the rank of the 'Rightly Guided' Caliphs (*al-rashidun*), in what was to evolve into the Sunni camp,[13] already in the Umayyad period.[14] The extraordinary qualities and good virtues of the Companions of the Prophet (*al-sahaba*), and their great service for Islam, have become a favorite theme since the early second/ eighth century. Compilations of *hadith* of the third/ninth century devote special chapters to advertising their merits (*fada'il/manaqib*) and historians of that period contributed to the formation of the doctrine on their elevated status.[15] As eloquently argued by Thomas Sizgorich, the figure of the militant, pious ascetic warriors, "horsemen during the day and monks at night," was accorded a place of honor in the foundational narratives of the early Muslim community, interwoven into the master-narrative of "a grand drama" in which God had given the Muslim *umma* dominion over vast territories and immeasurable wealth.[16]

Sibt ibn al-Jawzi opens his chapter of stories about the warriors of old with anecdotes about the heroes of Badr, the first significant military confrontation between Muhammad's men (the coalition of his devotees from Mecca with their helpers at al-Medina) and their adversaries who had remained in Mecca. It had taken place in the second year of the *hijra* (624 CE) and ended in a great Muslim victory. Sibt ibn al-Jawzi emphasizes the role of the warriors who had expressed an explicit wish to die on the battlefield, and did indeed achieve martyrdom. Those include 'Umayr b. Abi Wiqqas, who insisted on joining the Muslim army despite his youth; the elderly lame 'Amr b. al-Jamuh, whose sons had tried in vein to convince him to stay at home, and Abu al-'Aqil, who lost an arm in Badr but nonetheless enlisted for the following campaign.[17]

Badr was a favorite theme. For example: the poet Ibn al-Qaysarani (d. 1153–54), a refugee from the coastal town of Qaysariyya who fled to Mosul, recalls the battle of Badr in his eulogy of Zangi's greatest victory—the conquest of Edessa in 1144. He enthusiastically describes angels who accompanied, as it were, Zangi's soldiers, alluding to the units of angels who had encouraged the men of the Prophet in 2/624.[18] The pinnacle of Saladin's career in the eyes of his contemporaries, the reconquest of Jerusalem in 1187, was also compared to Badr. This comparison was first suggested by the preacher Ibn al-Zaki, who had won the prestigious and much sought after appointment to the pulpit of the regained and hastily re-consecrated mosque of al-Aqsa, on the first Friday after the reconquest.[19]

A somewhat less dramatic victory of Saladin, achieved during the summer of 1179 in Marj 'Ayun (in southern Lebanon), was compared by the poet Abu 'Ali al-Hasan al-'Iarqi al-Juwayni (d. 1188–89), to Muhammad's victory at Hunayn, some 550 years earlier. In the valley (*marj*) of Hunayn, on the eighth year of the *hijra* (AD 630) shortly after the conquest of Mecca, the tribes of Hawazin had gathered their families and belongings. They prepared for an attack on the Muslim force, perhaps in anticipation of an attack on the temple of their goddess al-Lat. The "front force" of the Muslim army retreated disorderly and the Muslims were close to defeat, but they recuperated and returned to assault. Encouraged by the Prophet's war cry "One and One only,"[20] they finally won a great victory and plenty of booty. At Marj 'Ayun, as at Hunayn, a notable victory was attained by the Muslims even though the initiative was the enemy's. Surprised by a large Frankish force led by King Baldwin IV, and despite an initial reverse, Saladin managed to capture over 270 knights, including the heads of the Templars and Hospitallers and other prominent men. Those were later ransomed for huge sums of gold and the release of an impressive number of Muslim prisoners, including some important emirs.[21]

A rather unusual analogy, highlighting the similarities between the enemies of Islam "then"—in the days of the Prophet—and "now," was suggested in a poem propagated following the seizure of Damascus by Nur al-Din in 1154. Alluding to the deposed ruler of the city, Mujir al-Din, who preferred a treaty with the Franks to fighting against them, the poet recalls the Jews who betrayed Muhammad early on: "The governor of Damascus and its inhabitants are like the Jews of Khaybar who cooperated with the people of Quraysh [against the Prophet]." He concludes by saying: "Whoever defends the fortress of Islam is a believer, whoever does not, is an infidel."[22]

The most daring analogies between the crusading era and the times of the Prophet were suggested by 'Imad al-Din al-Isfahani (d. 1201), Saladin's personal secretary. First, he compared the significance of Saladin's reconquest of Jerusalem on the 27th of Rajab AH 583 (October 2, 1187) to that of the night journey of the Prophet to Jerusalem, known to have happened on the very same date. Second, in the opening paragraph of his *History of the Reconquest of Jerusalem*, he writes the following striking lines:

> I began this record at the beginning of the year 583 [1187] because histories usually begin either with the creation of mankind or with the succession of states ... I, on the other hand, chose to write my history from a second *hijra* ... this *hijra* being the *hijra* of Islam to Jerusalem, undertaken by the Sultan Salah al-Din ... History would do well to be dated from this year ... Indeed, this *hijra* is of more lasting significance than the first.[23]

A third dramatic comparison of the reconquest of Jerusalem is suggested in 'Imad al-Din's letter to the caliph in Baghdad. It is based on *sura* 20:37, "We had already showed you favor." Imad al-Din writes: "The first time was in the century of the Prophet and of his Companions. The second is the present time, which has seen Islam freed from the slavery of misfortune."[24]

One of the most surprising implicit positioning of Saladin on par with the Prophet may be found, according to Abu Shama, in the sultan's own words, allegedly uttered during his illness, away from home: "If I die, I have designated Abu Bakr, 'Umar, 'Uthman and 'Ali to succeed me." Alluding to his brother al-'Adil Abu Bakr, his nephew Taqi al-Din 'Umar, and his two sons al-'Aziz 'Uthman and al-Afdal 'Ali, the choice to designate them by that component of their names that recalls the first four caliphs in the order of their reign cannot be missed.[25] Perhaps one can read into this sequence also a proclamation of fidelity to Sunni Islam—which unlike Shi'i Islam endorses all four first caliphs—at a time in which the struggle against the crusaders was firmly linked to the attempt to revive absolute Sunni hegemony in Syria.[26] A reminiscent example is brought by 'Imad al-Din al-Isfahani, who upon the death of the emir Baha' al-Din 'Umar ibn Daya equates the friendship and fidelity of the five Banu Daya brothers toward Nur al-Din to the relationship between Abu Bakr, 'Umar, 'Uthman, 'Ali and Hasan, and the Prophet.[27]

The *futuh*, the great conquests of the Arabs that took place after the death of the Prophet, especially the speedy conquest of Syria in the 630s, are often alluded to in twelfth- to thirteenth-century sources. Ibn al-Zaki enumerates the decisive battles of the first Muslim conquest of Syria when he proclaims: "You [Saladin] have renewed for Islam the glorious days of al-Qadisiyya, the battle of Yarmuk, the siege of Khaybar, and the impetus attacks of [the celebrated general] Khalid ibn al-Walid."[28] The physician and poet Abu al-Fadl 'Abd al-Man'am b. 'Umar al-Jilyani (d. 1205–06), an Andalusi emigrant to Damascus, exclaims, in a *qasida* he composed in praise of Saladin, for the occasion of the reconquest of Jerusalem, "[it is as if] we are in the era of the Companions, and you [Saladin] are named al-Siddiq (the upright; Abu Bakr's epithet)."[29] 'Imad al-Din al-Isfahani claims a victory such as that achieved in Jerusalem was not seen since the days of the Companions.[30] Nur al-Din's council with a group of 'ulama' in Damascus (regarding the use of waqf money for fortifications) is compared by the protocol maker, as quoted by Abu Shama, to the custom of the Companions who got together in order to discuss the best interests of the Muslims.[31] From a slightly different perspective on this theme, Konrad Hirschler observes that the interest in governance and in the qualities of the ideal ruler is due to closer connection between historians and the ruling elites, typical of the later medieval period.[32]

The poet al-'Arqala (Husan b. Numayr al-Kalbi, d. c. 1171–72) compares Nur al-Din's gains to those of futuh al-Faruq (the conquests of 'Umar) "in the east and west, valley and mount."[33] Even earlier, following Zangi's successful campaign against the Frankish stronghold of Ba'rin (Montferrand), north of Hims, in 1137, Ibn al-Qaysarani expresses his wish that all the thughur (garrison towns of the Arab-Byzantine frontier) will return to the Muslims laughing, as if liberated by 'Umar, the second caliph.[34]

Being the caliph who received the surrender of the people of Jerusalem in 634 in person—according to Arab historians of the classical era—'Umar ibn al-Khattab is mentioned time and again in the poems composed on the occasion of the surrender of the people of Jerusalem to Saladin in 1187. The Egyptian poet Muhammad b. As'ad al- Juwayni (d. 1192) exclaims, turning to Saladin: "You are its Faruq (one of the laudatory names of the second caliph), 'Umar the most pure imam."[35] Ibn Shaddad praises Saladin's analysis of the condition of the forces in April 1190 (contrasting it with the faulty understanding suggested by his emirs and councilors), commenting, with hindsight: "It came about as the sultan said … befitting what the Prophet had meant when he said: 'In my community there are those with insight who speak up, and 'Umar is one of them.'"[36] Even Ibn al-Athir, known for his continuous loyalty toward the fallen house of the Zangids, and hence a rather reserved, if not biased attitude toward Saladin,[37] admits the semblance between the conquests of 634 (or 636) and 1187, saying: "This blessed deed, the conquering of Jerusalem, is something achieved by none but Saladin (God have mercy on him) since the time of 'Umar ibn al-Khattab (God be pleased with him). This is his sufficient glory and honor."[38]

The comparison to the two 'Umars (al-'Umarayn), as suggested by Ibn al-Athir (d. 1233) in his eulogy of Nur al-Din, both in his universal history (al-Kamil fi al-Ta'rikh) and in his chronicle of the Zangid dynasty (Ta'rikh al-Bahir fi al-Dawla al-Atabakiyya),[39] goes far beyond the military aspect. "Not since the rightly guided caliphs and 'Umar ibn 'Abd al-'Aziz," he writes, "have I seen a ruler whose conduct was neither better than that of al-Malik al-'Adil Nur al-Din, nor more just and fair. [He was] a man who has devoted his days and nights to the dissemination of justice, who has made it his jihad."[40] Nur al-Din's virtue of justice, which receives pride of place in his formal title "al-Malik-'Adil," is hailed also by other biographers, and inscribed in stone and wood on his endowed monuments.[41] This depiction of Nur al-Din, according to Yaacov Lev, is dominant in the twelfth- to thirteenth-century historiography of his reign, while his depiction primarily as a warrior of jihad is peculiar to Ibn al-Athir.[42] Donald Little notes that the first section of Ibn Shaddad's biography of Saladin, which is devoted to describing his virtues of justice, generosity, courage, zeal, steadfastness, humaneness, etc., is geared to demonstrate the correlation between his life and that of the Prophet.[43]

The humility and humane conduct of 'Umar ibn al-Khattab has been compared to the cruel savagery of the crusaders in Jerusalem in 1099.[44] 'Umar is said to have entered Jerusalem on foot, in shabby cloths, assuring the patriarch that the lives and property of its inhabitants will be protected. He refrained from prayer in the Holy Sepulcher, so as not to establish a precedent that may lead to the confiscation of the church, unrolled his prayer mat outside the church and knelt (or rather, prostrated) there. The doubts that some latter-day historians have raised regarding the historicity of Umar's conquest of Jerusalem in person,[45] are, of course, irrelevant. When Saladin entered Jerusalem after its surrender, according to the testimony of his secretary 'Imad al-Din al-Isfahani, some of the emirs that had taken part in the campaign called for the destruction of the Church of the Holy Sepulcher, so as to make sure that the Christians have no reason to ever return to it. Others argued that the Christian pilgrims are drawn to the place of crucifixion rather than to the edifice built upon it, and therefore the destruction of the church will bring no benefits. Some of them reminded the sultan that when 'Umar ibn al-Khattab, the commander of the believers conquered Jerusalem, he did not demolish the church, but rather confirmed the right of the Christians to the place.[46] This seems to have been a decisive argument.

Early traditions, repeated by Arab geographers of the fourth/tenth century and in eleventh-century compilations of the virtues of Jerusalem, mention 'Umar ibn al-Khattab's visit at the prayer niche of David (Mihrab Da'ud) upon his conquest of Jerusalem. Moreover, he is said to have appropriately recited Surat Sad (*sura* 38, of which verses 21–22 allude to the niche) on the spot, thus establishing the connection between the Qur'anic story of David and the place.[47] When Saladin recaptured the city, he renewed this connection. Ibn al-'Imad al-Isfahani, probably an eye-witness, writes that the sultan "provided for its restoration, and appointed an *imam*, two muezzins and servants."[48]

Comparisons to 'Umar b. 'Abd al-'Aziz, the exceptionally pious eighth Umayyad caliph, are likewise geared either to highlight commendable governance, or piety and praiseworthy personal virtue. Hence Nur al-Din is also depicted as indifferent to laudatory poems, "which was the way of 'Umar ibn al-'Aziz, the most frugal (*zahid*) caliph."[49]

Not only sultans and emirs, but also pious and devoted regular participants of the counter-crusade were likened to those companions of the Prophet who are said to have joined the great conquests, inspired by purely religious motives, rather than by the quest for glory or booty. The memory of the *sahaba* who fought in the great Islamic conquests was raised already in 1105, only six years after the arrival of the First Crusade, in a series of sermons delivered in Damascus by 'Ali b. Tahir al-Sulami (d. 1106).[50] Al-Sulami stressed the willingness of the Companions to give their lives for the conquest of Syria. Several decades later, the historian Ibn 'Asakir (d. 1176), author of a huge biographical dictionary entitled *The History of Damascus*, defines all the people of Syria as defenders "in the way of God" (*murabitun fi sabil Allah*) and as "God's army" (*jund Allah*) by their mere place of residence, citing a saying of the Prophet.[51] Usama ibn al-Munqidh praises his contemporaries, the shaykhs 'Abd al-Rahman al-Halhuli and al-Fandalawi by comparing them to the Companions. Those two elderly scholars who had left Damascus in 1148, in the midst of the siege imposed by the warriors of the armies of the Second Crusade, were happy to find martyrdom in their assault upon the enemy. Like al-Sulami, Ibn 'Asakir stresses the purity of the intents of the Companions, and their readiness to sacrifice their lives in the way of God.[52] Likewise, both 'Imad al-Din al-Isfahani and Ibn Wasil write about one of the fallen soldiers of a battle that took place in the vicinity of Acre in 1189, that he was a worthy descendent of his great forefather, Ibn Rawaha. The latter was a martyr of the first and unsuccessful (not to say catastrophic) loss of the Muslims to the Byzantines, at Mu'ta Transjordan, in 629. According to the Muslim version, only a handful of Muslims had confronted the 20,000 soldiers of Heraclius at Mu'ta.[53] "One died as a *shahid* at Mu'ta fighting the Byzantines, and the other died as a *shahid* at the plain [of Acre]," concluded Ibn Wasil.

The memory of those earlier exemplars of *talab al-shahada* (the active quest of martyrdom) was probably quite alive in the minds of the above-mentioned al-Halhuli and al-Fandalawi. A treatise on *jihad* compiled by one of those exemplars was read in public in Damascus during the Second Crusade: ʿAbd Allah ibn al-Mubarak's *Kitab al-Jihad*—a compilation of *hadith* on the merits of *jihad* and martyrdom (probably the oldest surviving work on this subject nowadays). Ibn al-Mubarak (d.797) was a model "embattled scholar" of the Arab–Byzantine frontier. He became famous for his asceticism, and for the courage he displayed both in his encounters with the Christian enemy and in his confrontations with Muslim political authorities. ʿAbd Allah ibn al-Mubarak and his comrades, who went out to fight the enemy in the war of attrition that was carried on from the later eighth century until the mid-tenth in the frontier zones (*al-thughur*)—especially those facing the Byzantine Empire, but also in the planes of central Asia, against the Turks—found their way into hagiographic tradition from early on. Their dedication to *jihad* and their uncompromising asceticism, as well as the tensions inherent in their very demanding way of life, is depicted in this literature in glaring colors.[54]

Kitab al-jihad by ʿAli ibn Tahir al-Sulami, read in the Mosque of Bayt Lahiya in the suburbs of Damascus in 1105, brought forth the example of Saʿid ibn al-Harith, who took part in a campaign against the Byzantines in 706–07. Saʿid fought zealously for three days—motivated by a dream in which he saw his future eternal wife and heard from her that she is promised to him upon his martyrdom, when he was mortally wounded and died. Lest taken to have fought only for heavenly joys, al-Sulami hastens to mention the importance of undertaking *jihad* out of piety, implying that this was indeed the case with Saʿid b. al-Harith's martyrdom on the Byzantine frontier.[55]

Sibt ibn al-Jawzi drew from a pool of reminiscent stories about the Arab–Byzantine frontier, both in his written and in his oral communications. One of them is about a devout Muslim who performed *hajj* and *jihad* in alternate years. In one of his *jihad*s he encountered a Greek face to face. When it was time to pray, the Muslim asked the Greek to allow him a pause, and then resume. The Greek agreed, and kept his promise. They continued fighting until the Greek's time to pray arrived. The Muslim gave his promise, but was tempted to break it. However, when he raised his sword, a heavenly voice stopped him, recalling a certain Qurʾanic verse. The Muslim's hand trembled and he dropped the sword. The Greek, truly impressed by God's care for the enemies of the Muslims, converted, proclaiming the *shahada* on the spot.[56] In another wonderous tale I had reiterated elsewhere, Sibt ibn al-Jawzi preaches *jihad* through the story of Ibn Qudama, a ninth-century veteran of the Byzantine frontier, who had witnessed an inspiring case of youthful martyrdom and maternal willing sacrifice.[57]

I had not found explicit analogies between the scholars and ascetics who volunteered to go out to the Arab–Byzantine frontier and those who joined the counter-crusades, if not for the actual fighting, at least as some kind of chaplains and propagandists. But it seems as if the twelfth- to fourteenth-century chroniclers and biographers who describe them make use of earlier models of embattled scholars. Depictions of shaykh Abu ʿUmar ibn Qudama (d. 1210) may serve as a good example. Abu ʿUmar, a native of the Palestinian village of Jammaʿil who became a charismatic preacher and communal leader in the Hanbali suburb of Jabal Qasyun by Damascus, is said to have "never heard of a jihad without joining in," volunteering for many expeditions against the Franks. He is also described as a rigorous ascetic, scrupulous in his care to avoid illicit food and luxuries, deeply devoted to prayer:

he always volunteered to stand on guard at nights, when the others slept, busying himself in prayer and recitation of the Qur'an. Despite the fact that prominent members of his clan usually enjoyed cordial relations with the rulers and governors of Damascus, Abu 'Umar is said to have refrained from any contact with ruling authorities, just like the eighth-century ascetic, warrior, and author 'Abd Allah ibn al-Mubarak. Even when al-Malik al-'Adil, Saladin's brother and heir came to visit him, Abu 'Umar, who was preoccupied with prayer in his tent, allegedly did not go out to greet him. Al-'Adil waited in the sun, until he despaired and went away.[58] Finally, *talab al-shahada*—the active quest for martyrdom on the battlefield, or at least the expression of the will to die "in the way of God"—was also attributed to Abu 'Umar, as to other scholars of the same circles.[59]

CONCLUSIONS

Arab Muslim historiography of the crusading era evokes the memory of earlier generations who struggled for the glory of Islam. It reproduces the myths of the campaigns of the Prophet, the great conquests, and the embattled scholars and martyrs of the Byzantine–Umayyad and early 'Abbasid frontier. By highlighting elements of moralistic continuity[60] with the Islamic golden age they obviously served well the cause of propaganda for the counter-crusade and the political legitimization of its leaders, contributing to the consolidation of the collective identity of the Muslims of Syria. Most Muslim historians of the twelfth to fourteenth centuries also partook in the discourse of piety, typical of that pious age. They employed not only the prowess, zeal to fight, and quest of martyrdom of the times of the Prophet, the first caliphs, and the early Islamic empire, but also their asceticism, humility, just conduct ('adl) and sincere personal religiosity. They especially stress their convergence of the two *jihad*s: holy war on behalf of the Muslims, and holy struggle with their lower soul.

As a literary device, early exemplars are often recalled for what Tarif Khalidi calls the "not since" motif ("not since the victories of Sa'd or Khalid have such victories been recorded").[61] Moreover, the images of earlier campaigns, especially those of the Prophet and his companions, and of the conquest of Syria in the 630s, seem to have influenced the ways in which Muslim authors of the Zangid, Ayyubid, and Mamluk periods constructed the events and protagonists of their own days. The representation of certain contemporary events as a sort of re-enactment of significant events that occurred in early Islamic history seems to be a means to make sense of current events and clarify their meaning,[62] if not to enhance their significance, and even to lift contemporaneous struggles to the heights of the divinely guided early heyday of the Muslim community. Of course the humbler intention of embellishing one's narration of contemporary history for "the literati who watch for brilliant purple passages," to quote 'Imad al-Din al-Isfahani's introduction to his major history *al-Barq al-Shami*, must not be overlooked.[63]

Returning to the purpose of historical writing in medieval Islamic civilization, on the basis of the examples brought above, history was obviously regarded as a mine of exempla, practical and moral lessons, which may help men, especially young princes—future rulers—in choosing their conduct.[64] In Ibn al-Athir's words: "The instructiveness of History has many aspects, and its usefulness, both in this world and in the other world, is very great ... Kings and persons in authority derive an additional advantage from the study of history."[65] This view cohabits, somewhat uneasily, with the notion that history is but the execution of the divine plan.[66] Such continuities and repetitions as the assistance of angels at Badr (624), at Edessa (1144), and in Jerusalem (1187) were depicted as part of this divine plan.

APPENDIX

"Yusuf b. Ayyub thus fights the powers of evil, just as did Yusuf b. Ya'qub"[67]—the re-enactment of Qur'anic episodes in the Ayyubid era, as depicted in Muslim historiography"

Analogies between Saladin and the prophet whose name he carried—Joseph/Yusuf—are replete in our sources. Several medieval authors make Saladin into a new Joseph, equating not only their names, but also their biographies: both left Syria (Palestine) for Egypt, rose to be the right hand of the Egyptian ruler, and acted on behalf of law and justice. Here are some examples, in the chronological order of the sultan's life story.

After Saladin's appointment as head of police (*shihna*) in Damascus by Nur al-Din in 1165, the witty poet al-'Arqala (d. *c*. 567/1171–72), playing on the Qur'anic story on the female guests of Potiphar's wife (known as Zulaykha) who, stupefied by Joseph's beauty, cut their fingers with their knives (Q. 12: 31), writes: "go softly, O thieves of Syria – this is my advice to you ... the hands of women were cut because of that Joseph, but this one cuts off the hands of men."[68] Two years later, upon the arrival of Saladin with his uncle Shirkuh to Egypt, he writes: "God, as you had it [Egypt] ruled by Yusuf al-Siddiq of the progeny of Jacob, may in our times rule over it Yusuf al-Sadiq of the progeny of Ayyub."[69]

Similar analogies are employed also after Saladin returned to Syria and engaged in warfare. Rejoicing at the fall of Tiberias to the Muslims in 575/1179–80, the poet 'Ali ibn Muhammad al-Sa'ati (d. 604/1207–08) addresses the defeated saying: "I give you good advice (and advice is a duty of religion): Leave the House of Jacob, for Joseph has come!"[70] Likewise, a long poem in praise of Saladin, presented to the sultan by al-Hakim Abu al-Fadl al-Jilani in 582/1187 and cited by Abu Shama, depicts the "tribes of Joseph" (*asbat Yusuf*) coming from the land of Egypt, in their zeal for Jerusalem.[71]

Finally, reporting about Saladin's deathbed illness, al-Qadi al-Fadil alludes to Joseph's ordeal in the Egyptian prison: "our Joseph – may God have mercy upon him – was in prison here below, compared to the place he occupies in the next world."[72]

NOTES

* I wish to thank the Israel Science Foundation, grant no. 1679/09 "The Formation of Muslim Society in Palestine (ca. CE 600–1500)," for supporting this study.

1 I. Hen and M. Innes, *The Uses of the Past in the Early Middle Ages*, Cambridge, 2000, 1.

2 'Umar ibn al-Khattab (r. 634–44), the second of the "righteous caliphs," and 'Umar b. 'Abd al-'Aziz (r. 717–20), the most righteous among the Umayyad caliphs.

3 Abu Shama, *Kitab al-Rawdatayn fi Akhbar al-Dawlatayn*, ed. M.H.M. Ahmad, 4 vols, Cairo, 1998–99, 1: 5–6. On Abu Shama's frequent references to the "Golden Age" of the Prophet and rightly guided caliphs, see K. Hirschler, *Medieval Arabic Historiography. Authors as Actors*, London, 2006, 79.

4 E. Sivan, *L'Islam et la croisade*, Paris, 1968. See also his later "Muslim Representations of the Crusades," in *Verso Gerusalemme*, Il convegno internazionale nel IX centenario della i crociata (1099–1999), ed. F. Cardini, M. Belloli and B. Vetere, Lecce, 1999, 131–132.

5   S. Mourad and J. Lindsay, "Rescuing Syria from the Infidels: The Contribution of Ibn 'Asakir of Damascus to the Jihad Campaign of Sultan Nur al-Din," *Crusades* 6 (2007): 37–55; S. Mourad, "Ibn 'Asakir of Damascus and the Radicalization of Sunni Jihad Ideology in Crusader-Era Syria," in *Just Wars, Holy Wars, and Jihads*, ed. S. Hashimi, New York, 2011, 116–119; Niall Christie, "Motivating Listeners in the *Kitab al-Jihad* of 'Ali ibn Tahir al-Sulami (d. 1106)," *Crusades* 6 (2007): 10. Christie also dealt with the use of curses against the Franks, in his "The Origins of Suffixed Invocation of God's Curse on the Franks in Muslim Sources for the Crusades," *Arabica* 48 (2001): 254–266.

6   Y. Lev, "The *jihād* of Sultan Nūr al-Dīn of Syria (1146–1174): History and Discourse," *Jerusalem Studies of Arabic and Islam* 35 (2008): 272; and S. Leder, "Sunni Resurgence, Jihad Discourse and the Frankish Presence in the Near East," in *Crossroads between Latin Europe and the Near East: Corollaries of the Frankish Presence in the Eastern Mediterranean (12th–14th centuries)*, ed. S. Leder, Wurzburg, 2011, 95; Christie, "Motivating Listeners," 1–14; P. E. Chevedden, "The View of the Crusades from Rome and Damascus: The Geo-Strategic and Historical Perspectives of Pope Urban II and 'Ali ibn Tahir al-Sulami," *Oriens* 39 (2011): 292–299 [257–329].

7   T. Sizgorich, *Violence and Belief in Late Antiquity*, Philadelphia, 2009. For a short presentation of the theoretical foundation, see ibid., 8–10.

8   Hirschler, *Medieval Arabic Historiography*.

9   E. Sivan, "Modern Arab Historiography of the Crusades," *Asian and African Studies* 8 (1972): 109–149; and "Modern Arab Historiography of the Crusades," in his *Interpretations of Islam, Past and Present*, Princeton, 1985, 3–44.

10 B.Z. Kedar, "Il Motivo della Crociata nel Pensiero Politico Israeliano," in *Verso Gerusalemme*, 135–150 and *idem*, "The Crusades' Motif in the Israeli Political Discourse," *Alpayyim* 26 (2004) [in Hebrew].

11 See D. Abouali, "Saladin's Legacy in the Middle East," *Crusades* 10 (2011): 175–185; J. Phillips, "Before the Kaiser: The Memory of Saladin and the Crusades in the Near East from the Fifteenth to the Nineteenth Centuries," in *Vor der Orientreise Wilhelms II. – Die Erinnerung an Saladin und die Kreuzzüge im Nahen Osten vom 15. bis zum 19. Jahrhundert*, ed. F. Hinz, Zurich and New York, 2014; S. Heidemann, "Memory and Ideology: Images of Saladin in Syria and in Iraq," in *Visual Culture in the Modern Middle East*, ed. C. Gruber and S. Haugbolle, Indiana, 2013, 57–81; E. Aubin-Boltanski, "Salāh al-Din, un héro à l'épreuve. Myth et pèlerinage en Palestine," *Annales HSS* 1 (2005): 91–107; A.M. Eddé, *Saladin*, trans. Jane M. Todd, Cambridge MA, 2011 (2008), 620–623.

12 Sibt ibn al-Jawzi, *al-Jalis al-Salih wa-l-Anis al-Nasih*, ed. F. S. Fawaz, London, 1989, 124–125.

13 On the gradual differentiation of Muslims to Shi'is and Sunnis, see J. Berkey, *The Formation of Islam*, Cambridge, 2003, 83–91.

14 P. Crone, "The Early Islamic World," in *War and Society in the Ancient and Medieval Worlds*, ed. K. Raaflaub and N. Rosenstein, Cambridge MA and London, 1999, 317 n. 38. For their representation in the *History* of Tabari (d. 923), see B. Shoshan, *Poetics of Islamic Historiography: Deconstructing Tabari*, Leiden, 2004, 94–97.

15 M. Muranyi, "Sahaba," in *Encyclopaedia of Islam*, 2nd edition, ed. C. Bosworth, *et al.* Leiden, 1995, 9: 828; A.I. Tayob, "Tabari on the Companions of the Prophet: Moral and Political Contours in Islamic Historical Writing," *Journal of the American Oriental Society* 119 (1999): 204–205.

16 Sizgorich, *Violence*, 190–191, 13. The thrust of Sizgorich's work—intercommunal relations in late antiquity—is beyond our point here.

17 Sibt ibn al-Jawzi, *al-Jalis*, 114–119.

18 H. Dajani Shakeel, "Jihad in 12th century Arabic Poetry," *Muslim World* 66 (1976): 107. The help of angels is also mentioned by 'Imad al-Din al-Isfahani in his poetic description of the liberation of Jerusalem by Saladin: "*wa-a'āna Allāhu bi-inzal al-mala'ika wa-l-ruh*" (Abu Shama, *al-Rawdatayn*, 2: 315).

19 See D. Talmon-Heller, *Islamic Piety in Medieval Syria*, Leiden, 2007, 101–102.

20 Shoshan, *Poetics*, 97.
21 A.S. Ehrenkreutrz, *Saladin*, Albany, 1972, 162; based on Ibn al-Athir, *al-Ta'rikh al-Bahir;* al-Bundari, *Sana al-Barq al-Shami*, ed. F. 'A. al-Nabrawi, Riyad, 1989, 166. See also Abu Shama, *al-Rawdatayn*, 2: 22–25; Ibn Wasil, *Mufarrij al-Kurub fi Akhbar bani Ayyub*, ed. G. al-Shayyal, S. 'Ashur and H. Rabhi, 5 vols, Cairo, 1953–77, 2: 75–77. For a detailed comparison between the works of Abu Shama and Ibn Wasil, see Hirschler, *Medieval Arabic Historiography.* For an evaluation of Ibn Wasil's coherence and evenhandedness, see R.S. Humphreys, *Islamic History. A Framework for Inquiry*, London, 1995, 395–396. The battle of Hunayn was recalled for the sake of comparison earlier: by Tabari, in his account of the rebellion of 144/760–761 (Shoshan, *Poetics*, 96–97).
22 Translation of Abu Shama, in D. Ephrat and M. Kabha, "Muslim Reactions to the Frankish Presence in Bilad al-Sham: Intensifying Religious Fidelity within the Masses," *al-Masaq* 15 (2003): 50–51.
23 T. Khalidi, *Arabic Historical Thought in the Classical Period*, New York, 1994, 182. Khalidi argues that Ayyubid and Mamluk historians present their own times as "a new era" (*idem*, 183–184). But this seems to be more relevant to their perception of the Mongol invasions as unprecedented, as he himself stresses, rather than to the wars against the Franks.
24 Eddé, *Saladin*, 177.
25 Al-Bundari, *Sana al-Barq al-Shami*, 269 trans. Eddé, *Saladin*, 177.
26 As noted in D.J. Stewart, "The Maqamat of Ahmad b. Abi Bakr b. Ahmad al-Razı al-Hanafı and the Ideology of the Counter-Crusade in Twelfth-century Syria," *Middle Eastern Literatures* 11 (2008): 228. On Sunni revivalism in the twelfth century, see for example N. Elisséeff, "The Reaction of the Syrian Muslims after the Foundation of the first Latin Kingdom of Jerusalem," in *Crusaders & Muslims in Twelfth-Century Syria*, ed. M. Shatzmiller, Leiden, 1993, 162–172; Y. Tabbaa, *The Transformation of Islamic Art during the Sunni Revival*, Seattle, 2001.
27 Abu Shama, *al-Rawdatayn*, 1: 388.
28 Trans. in C. Hillenbrand, *The Crusades: Islamic Perspectives*, Edinburgh, 1999, 191. The battle of Qadisiyya is also mentioned in a poem by al-Hakim Abu al-Fadl. He asks: "Have you seen the conquest of Qadisiyya in the surroundings of Lubya [where Saladin fought in preparation of the decisive battle at Hattin]?" (Abu Shama, *al-Rawdatayn*, 2: 369).
29 Abu Shama, *al-Rawdatayn*, 2: 331.
30 Abu Shama, *al-Rawdatayn*, 2: 318.
31 For a detailed description and analysis of this meeting, see S. Heidemann, "Charity and Piety for the Transformation of the Cities," in *Charity and Giving in Monotheistic Religions*, ed. M. Frenkel and Y. Lev, Berlin and New York, 2009, 169–172.
32 Khalidi, *Arab Historical Thought*, 184; see also D.P. Little, "Historiography of the Ayyūbid and Mamlūk epochs," *Cambridge History of Egypt*, ed. C.F. Petry, Cambridge, 1998, 413; Hirschler, *Historiography*, 14.
33 Abu Shama, *al-Rawdatayn*, 1: 347.
34 Abu Shama, *al-Rawdatayn*, 1: 89. On the attack, see Ibn al-Athir, *al-Kamil*, Beirut, 1966, 11: 51–52; trans. in F. Gabrieli, *Arab Historians of the Crusades*, London, 1969, 42–43.
35 Abu Shama, *al-Rawdatayn*, 2: 337.
36 D.S. Richards, *The Rare and Excellent History of Saladin or Nawadir al-Sultaniyya wa'l-Mahasin al-Yusufiyya by Baha' al-Din Ibn Shaddad*, Aldershot, 2001, 109.
37 D.S. Richards (trans.), *The Chronicle of Ibn al-Athir for the Crusading Period from al-Kamil fi'l-ta'rikh*, part 1, Aldershot, 2006, 2–3; part 2, Aldershot, 2007, 4; Lev, "The jihad," 238.
38 Richards, *Chronicle of Ibn al-Athir*, 2: 335. Ibn al-Athir relies mainly on Tabari for events prior to his lifetime (Little, "Historiography," 415).
39 For a comparison between the two works, see Ch. Robinson, *Islamic Historiography*, Cambridge, 2003, 99.

40 Ibn al-Athir, *al-Bahir*, 163; Richards, *The Chronicle of Ibn al-Athir*, 2: 222. Another ruler of the middle period who is honored with a comparison to ʿUmar ibn ʿAbd al-ʿAziz thanks to his just conduct is the hapless caliph al-Zahir b. al-Nasir, who got to the throne in 622/1225 at 52, for nine months only, yet found the time to abolish non-*sharʿi* taxes and to tend to many complaints on injustice (Ibn Kathir, *al-Bidaya wa-l-nihaya*, Beirut, 1993, 13: 126; Ibn al-Athir, *al-Kamil fi al-Taʾrikh*, Beirut, 2003, 10: 453). A comparison gone sour is mentioned in an anecdote about the caliph al-Mustansir, who in 633/1235–36 was angered by the apparent flattery of a scholar who told him: "were you present at the day of the *saqifa* (immediately after the Prophet's death), you would have been the first chosen." He was banished from Baghdad as punishment for insulting the first righteous caliphs (Ibn Wasil, *Mufarrij al-Kurub*, 5: 108).

41 Lev, "The jihad," 236–237, 270–272.

42 Lev, "The jihad," 277.

43 Little, "Historiography," 416.

44 A. Maalouf, *The Crusades through Arab Eyes*, New York, 1984, 51.

45 H. Busse, "ʿOmar's image as the conqueror of Jerusalem," *Jerusalem Studies in Arabic and Islam* 8 (1982), 149–169.

46 Al-Isfahani, *Hurub Salah al-Din wa-Fath Bayt al-Maqdis*, ed. I. Shams al-Din, Beirut, 2003, 95–96; or al-Isfahani, *Kitab al-Fath al-Qusi fi al-Fath al-Qudsi*, ed. C. de Landberg, Leiden, 1888, 69.

47 H. Busse, "The Tower of David - Mihrab Dawud: remarks on the history of a sanctuary in Christian and Islamic times," *Jerusalem Studies in Arabic and Islam* 17 (1994): 142–165."

48 Al-Isfahani, *al-Fath*, 68, trans. in Busse, "The Tower," 158. On Mihrab Daʾud, see A. Elad, *Medieval Jerusalem & Islamic Worship. Holy Places, Ceremonies,* Pilgrimage, Leiden, 1995, 131–134. An even more explicit connection between ʿUmar b. al-Khattab's building projects and those of Saladin is drawn by the Palestinian authors Fadi Salamiyya and Majdi al-Saʿdi, writing about the aftermath of the battle of the Horns of Hattin. They claim that Saladin renewed and enlarged a mosque that was established in the times of the second caliph in Hattin, adding to it a *khanqah* (named after him, al-Salahi) and a minaret (the first in the region, so they claim). They also attribute to Saladin the settlement of the depopulated village with refugees (F. Salamiyya and M. al-Saʿdi, *Qaryat Hittin*, Damascus, 2011, 42–43).

49 Abu Shama, *al-Rawdatayn*, 1: 584.

50 For the first study of his manuscript sermons, see. E. Sivan, "La Genèse de la contre-croisade: un traité damasquin de debut du XIIe siècle," *Journal Asiatique* (1966): 197–224; also in *Les relations des pays d'Islam avec le monde latin du milieu du Xe siècle au milieu du XIIIe siècle. Articles réunis par Françoise Micheau*, Paris, 2000, 26–51.

51 Ibn ʿAsakir, *Taʾrikh Madinat Dimashq*, ed. M.A. ʿU. al-ʿAmrawi, part 1, Beirut, 1995, 282.

52 J.-M. Mouton, "Yusuf al-Fandalawi: Cheikh des Malekites de Damas sous les Bourides," *Revue des études islamiques* 51 (1983): 63–75; D. Talmon-Heller, "Muslim Martyrdom and Quest for Martyrdom in the Crusading Period," *Al-Masaq, Journal for the Study of the Medieval Mediterranean* 14 (2002): 136. Lev estimates that not all of the defenders of the city were likewise motivated by the spirit of *jihad*, moreover, that the Second Crusade was exceptional to arouse such zeal at the time (Lev, "The Jihad," 275).

53 Ibn Wasil, *Mufarrij al-kurrub*, 2: 300–302. According to Hirschler, Ibn Wasil makes only occasional references to earlier periods, "since he considered the period treated in his text to be of equal importance with most of the preceding periods" (Hirschler, *Historiography*, 77).

54 M. Bonner, "The Naming of the Frontier," *Bulletin of the School of Oriental and African Studies* 57 (1994): 17–24; *idem*, "Jihad on the Arab-Byzantine Frontier," *Studia Islamica* 75 (1992): 26; *idem*, *Jihad in Islamic History*, Princeton, 2006, 98–101. For a detailed treatment of Ibn al-Mubarak's works on asceticism and *jihad*, see also Sizgorich, *Violence*, 180–189. For an amusing anecdote depicting (parodying?) the struggles of a certain ascetic of the ninth century, Ahmad ibn

Khazruya, see Farid al-Din Attar, *Muslim Saints and Mystics: Episodes from the Tadhkirat al-Auliya' (Memorial of the Saints)* trans. A.J. Arberry. London and Boston, 1966.

55 Christie, "Motivating Listeners," 12–13.

56 Sibt ibn al-Jawzi, *al-Jalis*, 107.

57 Sibt ibn al-Jawzi, *al-Jalis*, 106–107, and *idem, Mir'at al-Zaman*, Hyderebad, 1951–52, 8: 544–545, told in detail in D. Talmon-Heller, "Charity and Repentance in Medieval Islamic Thought and Practice," in Frenkel and Lev, *Charity*, 270–271.

58 Diya' al-Din al-Maqdisi, *Manaqib al-Shaykh Abu 'Umar al-Maqdisi*, ed. A.'A. al-Kundari, Beirut, 1997, 46.

59 See Talmon-Heller, "Muslim Martyrdom," *Al-Masāq: Islam and the Medieval Mediterranean* 14 (2002): 131–139.

60 I owe this phrase to Mourad and Lindsay, "Rescuing Syria," 45.

61 As formulated by Khalidi, *Arabic Historical Thought*, 186.

62 See also Robinson, *Islamic Historiography*, 122.

63 Translated in D.S. Richards, "'Imad al-Din al-Isfahani: Administrator, Litterateur and Historian," in Shatzmiller, *Crusaders and Muslims*, Leiden, 1993, 141.

64 E. Rosenthal, *A History of Muslim Historiography*, Leiden, 1968, 46–49.

65 D.S. Richards, "Ibn al-Athir and the Later Parts of the *al-Kamil*: A Study of Aims and Methods," in *Medieval Historical Writing in the Christian and Islamic Worlds*, ed. D.O. Morgan, London, 1982, 93–95; *Chronicle of Ibn al-Athir*, 1: 5; Rosenthal, *Historiography*, 298–300. For 'Imad al-Din's similar view, see D.S. Richards, "'Imad al-Din," 143.

66 On God and history in the writings of Muslim historians, see Robinson, *Islamic Historiography*, 129–134. Put shortly, despite the axiom that God was the engine of history, many historians presented their work as a record of human choices, from which their readers were to draw the appropriate lessons. On the prescriptive value of history, especially of the biographies of the Prophet and other exemplars, see ibid., 122.

67 See Ephrat and Kabha, "Muslim Reactions," 52.

68 Translated in Malcolm C. Lyons and D.E.P. Jackson, *Saladin. The Politics of Holy War*, Cambridge, 1982, 10.

69 Abu Shama, *al-Rawdatayn*, 2: 364, and similar allusion ibid., 449. For the comparison between the Mamluks and Joseph, and between Egyptian rulers (of various eras) and Joseph, both in Muslim and in late medieval European sources, see K. Yosef, "Mamluks and Their Relatives in the Period of the Mamluk Sultanate (1250–1517)," *Mamluk Studies Review* 12 (2011): 63–69.

70 *The Chronicle of Ibn al-Athir*, 2: 266.

71 Abu Shama, *al-Rawdatayn*, 2: 368.

72 Eddé, *Saladin*, 159, 507. Only extracts of the work of this senior official of Saladin have survived.

CHAPTER TWENTY-FOUR

LATIN CYPRUS AND ITS RELATIONS WITH THE MAMLUK SULTANATE, 1250–1517

——— •◆• ———

Nicholas Coureas

R elations between Latin Cyprus, a kingdom under the French Lusignan dynasty from 1192 to 1473 and a Venetian possession from 1473 until its conquest by the Ottomans in 1570, and the Mamluk Sultanate, which lasted from 1250 until 1517, the year in which the Ottoman sultan Selim II conquered it, were multifaceted. Furthermore, they spanned the entire period of the Mamluk sultanate from its inception to its abolition. This chapter shall cover relations between the two states in the following fields: war, diplomacy, cultural and religious exchanges and, finally, trade and settlement. Although these will be treated as distinct fields, it will be made clear that they were interrelated to a considerable extent, not separate from each other, with developments in one field affecting or affected by those in another.

WARFARE

War between the two states was intermittent from the mid-thirteenth century until 1426, when, following the defeat of the Cypriot king Janus at the battle of Khirokitia, the kingdom of Cyprus became a tributary of the Mamluk sultans, coming under their suzerainty. As early as 1252, King Henry I of Cyprus arrived in Latin Syria in person at the head of a large army in order to assist King Louis IX in strengthening the military capabilities of the Latin Christians there.[1] Such help did not halt the Mamluk re-conquest of the remaining Latin outposts in Syria and Palestine, beginning in 1263 under the Mamluk sultan Baybars, who attacked Acre in that year and in 1265 took Arsuf and Caesarea, as well as destroying Haifa. In 1266 several important Latin strongholds were captured, including the great fortress of Saphet in the interior. King Hugh III of Cyprus responded to the above developments by bringing forces from Cyprus over to Latin Syria. In 1265, 130 knights and mounted squires had been brought over, and a similar force was sent from Cyprus to Latin Syria in 1266. These forces, however, did not prevent the loss of the above localities to the Mamluks, and were probably utilised in reinforcing the Latin garrison at Acre.[2] King Hugh II's successor, Hugh III, continued the policy of despatching Cypriot forces to the defence of Latin Syria, but was unable to prevent Sultan Baybars from capturing Jaffa, Beaufort and Antioch in 1268.[3] In 1271 Baybars also took the great Hospitaller castle of Crac des Chevaliers, but desisted from attacking Tripoli because Hugh III despatched forces to the defence of Acre in conjunction with Prince Edward I of England, who arrived in the city at the head of 1,000 men. While journeying to the Holy Land, he had stopped off on Cyprus and had various supplies loaded onto his galleys transporting troops to Acre.[4] Cyprus's role in despatching both troops and supplies to the defence of Latin Syria brought the island to the attention of the Mamluk sultan Baybars. In an attempt to divert King Hugh III from the defence of Latin Syria, he conceived a naval attack on Limassol. The Mamluk galleys sailing there were painted black in the manner of Christian ships, and bore the sign of the cross on their sails so as to secure the element of surprise. The plan misfired, however, when the Mamluk fleet was driven aground on the shoals off the coastline of Limassol. The troops and sailors on board were all captured and transferred to Acre for the purposes of ransom, although a large number were able to make their escape from there. The fact that the fleet had been under the command of two admirals who did not get on with each other seems to have been the main reason why it ran aground, although some Mamluk authorities cite the attempts at deception, namely the painting of crosses on Mamluk ships, as having been impious, thereby provoking divine anger.[5]

This naval defeat off Limassol did not prevent the eventual success of the Mamluk land forces in Latin Syria. Sultan Kalavun, who obtained power in 1279 and was helped by the dispute between King Hugh III and Charles of Anjou the king of Naples from 1277 onwards for the kingdom of Jerusalem, stormed the coastal city of Tripoli in 1289, even though King Henry II of Cyprus had sent his brother Amaury to its defence at the head of a force of knights and soldiers. Cypriot assistance likewise failed to prevent the forces of Kalavun's successor, Al-Ashraf, from capturing Acre in 1291. King Henry II arrived in person to its aid with a force of 200 knights and 500 foot soldiers, or 100 knights and 200 foot soldiers according to a more conservative estimate. Following Acre's fall, Tyre, second in importance to the Latins after Acre, surrendered to the Mamluks without offering resistance, as did Sidon, which the Templars abandoned, fleeing to Cyprus.[6] Overall the experiences of the period from 1263 to 1291, in which the Latins of Cyprus attempted to aid their co-religionists in Latin Syria in confronting the final Mamluk onslaught, with virtually no assistance from Europe, clearly showed that the resources of Lusignan Cyprus could not prevent the final loss of Latin Syria to the Mamluks. If Cyprus were to contribute effectively to the crusading movement and to the defence of Latin Christendom against the Mamluks, this would have to be done in co-operation with other powers.

Steps in this direction were taken in the period from 1291 to 1307, when the forces of the Lusignan kingdom cooperated with those of the Catholic military orders, the Armenians and the Mongols against the Mamluks. In the decade following 1291, Cyprus served as a base for the organisation of naval raids against Mamluk Egypt and Syria. Some of the campaigns which the Latins of Cyprus participated in were not simply raids, but also had the recovery of the recently lost territories as their objective. In 1292 a Latin fleet of twenty galleys attacked Adalia, a port on the southern coast of Asia Minor, in conjunction with a Cypriot fleet of fifteen galleys. The combined fleet then proceeded to conduct a naval raid against Alexandria, the largest port of Mamluk Egypt.[7] In the decade following Acre's fall, both the Templars and the Hospitallers, who had transferred their respective military headquarters to Limassol on Cyprus, began to develop fleets with a view to implementing seaborne offensives against the Mamluks. In 1300 a combined Templar, Hospitaller and Lusignan fleet of sixteen galleys raided both Syria and Egypt, an expression of the new policy whereby Latin Cypriot forces were engaging the Mamluks in battle in alliance with those of the Catholic military orders.[8]

The Lusignan kings of Cyprus also attempted to engage the Mongols of Persia, the Mamluks' eastern foe, as allies in the warfare being waged against them. Such attempts foundered on the inability of both parties to coordinate their movements, but also because of fundamental differences in their respective aims. Whereas the Latins sought the re-conquest of territories lost to the Mamluks, the Mongols desired to raid Mamluk lands but not necessarily to conquer them. From 1299 to 1301, attempts by the Cypriot Latins to coordinate military operations with the Mongols met with failure. In 1299 the Mongols of Persia invaded Syria and invited the Templars, the Hospitallers and the Latin Cypriots to join them, but the Christian response was dilatory. Nonetheless, when the Mongol invasion took place late in 1299, King Henry's brother Amaury began operations against the Mamluks together with the Templars and the Hospitallers. In 1300 the island of Ruad off Tortosa was captured from them. The 300 Latin Cypriot knights who took part in the attack on Ruad represented the largest army ever mobilised by the Lusignan kings of Cyprus, and Amaury went on to capture Tortosa itself, where he waited for the Mongols' arrival. The Mongols, however, did not arrive until February 1300, and then departed after a brief sojourn, and so the Cypriot forces returned to Cyprus.[9] A second Mongol invasion of Syria resulted in a Mamluk defeat in 1301, but after advancing as far as Homs the Mongols withdrew again. The island of Ruad, taken in 1300, was retaken by a powerful Mamluk fleet late in 1302. The naval forces of the Latin Cypriots and of the military orders on Cyprus were unable to offer any assistance to the besieged Templars holding the island, and over 500 of them were either beheaded or led into captivity following their surrender to the Mamluks in 1302. Two Hospitaller military expeditions to the Christian kingdom of Cilician Armenia failed to result in effective action against the Mamluks.[10] When Amaury overthrew his brother King Henry II of Cyprus, in the coup of 1306 he invoked Henry's neglect of the defences of Cyprus, and he may have had in mind the failures to undertake concerted action against them mentioned above, as well as the limitations the king had imposed on the acquisition of incomes and properties on Cyprus by the military orders, whose power he was fearful of and anxious to circumscribe.[11]

Perhaps mindful of such criticisms, shortly after his restoration to the Cypriot throne in 1310 with Hospitaller assistance Henry submitted detailed proposals to the pope before the Council of Vienne, advocating Cyprus as a base not only for attacking the Mamluks but also for implementing a naval blockade designed to weaken them economically prior to the start of military operations. Being near both Egypt and Syria, Cyprus was proposed as the ideal base for offensive operations, because the Mamluks, unsure of which land would be attacked, would be forced to split their forces between them. But these proposals came to naught. With the dramatic rise of Turkish and especially Ottoman power in Asia Minor in the first half of the fourteenth century, crusading activity shifted from the Levant to the Aegean. In terms of political and strategic thinking, the Turks of Asia Minor were now perceived as the main threat, as opposed to the Mamluks of Syria and Egypt. As a result, offensive campaigns to recover of the Holy Places were superseded by the creation of defensive naval alliances aimed at combating Turkish piracy in the Aegean and the Mediterranean.[12]

Under King Peter I (1359–69), a reversion to the policy of war against the Mamluks occurred when he organised a crusade against Alexandria, the chief port of the Mamluk sultanate and Famagusta's main rival as a commercial entrepôt after the final loss of the Armenian port of Lajazzo to the Mamluks in 1335. Peter Edbury has argued that King Peter's crusade against Alexandria was actuated by commercial considerations, for following the lifting of the papal ban against direct trade with the Muslims in 1344 Famagusta had steadily been losing business to Alexandria.[13] Whether this or a determination to lead a crusade was the king's overriding motive, the long-term consequences of this venture, despite the immediate glory and renown it brought him in Western Europe, were disastrous. The Lusignan kingdom became embroiled in an expensive war with the Mamluks, the cost of which provoked internal unrest and was a factor leading to the murder of King Peter I in 1369 by disaffected nobles who resented the costs of his bellicose policies.[14] The sack of Alexandria was also resented in Venice and Genoa, as it had harmed their commercial interests. Genoese anger expressed itself in 1373 when it invaded Cyprus, seizing Famagusta, the main commercial port, and retaining it until 1464. In the peace treaty between Genoa and Cyprus of 1383, Cyprus was also forced to pay Genoa a heavy annual indemnity, further impoverishing the kingdom.[15]

This financial impoverishment impelled the Cypriots to wage a new type of warfare against the Mamluks: naval piracy. The first quarter of the fifteenth century was marked by systematic piracy against the Egyptian and Syrian coastlines by Catalan, Cypriot and Rhodian pirates operating from Cyprus, with the connivance and active encouragement of the island's nobles and the king himself, in straitened financial circumstances on account of the annual war reparations Cyprus had to pay Genoa after the disastrous Genoese invasion of 1373. The pirates seized Muslim ships and captured thousands of Muslims, who were sold as slaves in the markets of Rhodes and Cyprus, while those sold in Cyprus were often set to work in the highly profitable and labour-intensive sugar plantations at Kolossi and Episkopi in the district of Limassol and at Lemba near Paphos, belonging to the Hospitallers, the Venetian Corner family and the Crown.[16] The participation of Cypriots was certain, especially when King Janus of Cyprus took part in such raids. Furthermore, the Mamluks themselves conducted retaliatory raids against the Cypriot coasts and Genoese Famagusta in 1410–11, even though the Genoese had ransomed twenty-five Muslim captives in the previous year so as to send them to the sultan. Fearing more reprisals, the king of Cyprus concluded a peace treaty with the Mamluk sultan in 1410, promising not to allow pirates operating from Cyprus to raid Syria, not to offer victuals to pirates should they come to Cyprus and not to allow his subjects to purchase their ill-gotten goods.[17]

But subsequently the Cypriot nobles took a different line from both the king and the Western merchants based on Cyprus, who both desired peace in the interests of commerce and political stability. In 1413 the king's brother Prince Henry of Galilee together with some Catalans raided the Syrian coastline, capturing so many Muslims that the governor of Damascus sent an embassy with money to ransom them. A new peace treaty between the Cypriot Crown and the Mamluk sultan signed in 1414 was a dead letter precisely because it ran counter to the desire of the Cypriot nobles to enrich themselves through piracy and acquire workers for their estates. This need for workers also engineered an abrupt change in royal policy, for in 1415 King Janus, faced with declining royal revenues and an insufficient workforce for his sugar plantations, ordered the royal war galley to raid the Egyptian coasts, capturing 1,500 Muslims in the process. He refused to release them, despite the fury of the Mamluk Sultan al-Mu'ayad, replying to him that they were needed to work in the sugar plantations, although the Italian writer Emmanuel Piloti states that 535 persons captured in Cypriot piratical raids were ransomed in the same year.[18] Catalan pirates secured supplies from Cyprus and sold their plunder there, especially the captives, and some time after 1422 a Muslim captive escaping from Cyprus recounted to the sultan how high officers of the kingdom of Cyprus were supporting the pirates, singling out Philip de Picquigny, the royal *bailli* of Limassol. Salih ibn Yahya, a contemporary Muslim historian from Beirut, recounted how a ship loaded with soap and other goods belonging to the merchant Ahmad ibn al Hamim, a protégé of the sultan, was seized by Basque pirates as it left Tripoli for Damietta and was taken to Cyprus. Both these incidents steeled the sultan's resolve to attack Cyprus by way of punishment.[19]

Nemesis was not long in coming. In the summer of 1424 the Mamluk fleet defeated the Lusignan fleet off Limassol, the first Mamluk naval victory, pillaging the fortress of Limassol and villages on the Cypriot coastline. King Janus, overruled by his bellicose brother Henry and royal councillors whose interests in promoting piracy he had failed to check, had rejected the offer of a peace treaty made by the governor of Syria and various Mamluk emirs, even though personally disposed to accept it. A second punitive expedition followed, while the final expedition taking place in 1426 culminated in King Janus's defeat and capture in the battle of Khirokitia and in the Mamluk sacking and pillaging of Nicosia, the island's capital. The course of the military campaign is well known but it is worth emphasising that because of the parlous state of the Mamluk fleet, neglected since the beginning of the fifteenth century, the galleys constructed at the arsenal of Beirut proved defective, with the Venetian Emmanuel Piloti observing that there were not enough rudders for the galleys. Consequently the Mamluk war fleet transporting troops to Cyprus consisted of *djermas*, transport ships used on the Nile, and ships requisitioned from Western traders in Egypt.[20] This condition of the Mamluk fleet goes some way towards explaining why prior to 1424 Catalans, Rhodians and Cypriots were able to raid the Egyptian and Syrian coastlines with such impunity.

Some elements of Cypriot society opposed war with the Mamluks. The so-called 'White Venetians', Cypriots and Levantines resident in the East who were subjects of Venice and generally engaged in trade, not only opened the gates of Nicosia to the advancing Mamluks but even showed them where the revenues of the royal treasury were located.[21] It was the merchants in Cyprus who had opposed piratical operations against the Mamluks, favoured by the Cypriot nobility and eventually the Crown itself, and these actions of the 'White Venetians' smack of revenge. In addition, the Mamluk victory of 1426 over Cyprus did not stop completely pirates from raiding the coasts of Egypt and Syria and using Cyprus as a base. Genoese-occupied Famagusta lay territorially outside the kingdom and was used by Catalan and Biscayan pirates, acting in collusion with corrupt Genoese officials, for precisely this purpose well into the second half of the fifteenth century.[22] After 1426, however, the issues of war and piracy no longer dominated relations between Lusignan Cyprus and the Mamluk sultanate, given that the former was now a tributary of the latter.

DIPLOMACY

War and diplomacy are inextricably linked, and the history of diplomatic relations between Lusignan Cyprus and the Mamluk sultans must be examined. The records for the despatch of envoys and the diplomatic negotiations they engaged in derive mostly from Cypriot chronicles and Mamluk histories, for the state archives of both the Lusignan kingdom and the Mamluk sultanate are not extant. Furthermore, most evidence for diplomatic missions was shortly before, during or immediately after armed conflict between the states of Lusignan Cyprus and Mamluk Egypt, although missions concerning the payment of the tribute after 1426 are also attested, and here documentary evidence is extant. Most envoys were of high station, Cypriot nobles or Mamluk emirs, but some were merchants or clerks, and some were even religious converts, used on account of their understanding of the language and culture of their former faith. The treatment of the envoys could also vary, from honourable reception to imprisonment and even death. A truce of ten years, ten months and ten days, concluded after the customary Mamluk manner of making truces with Christians was made in 1289 between King Henry of Cyprus and the Mamluk sultan Al-Kalawun. An attack by crusaders from western Europe on Muslim peasants bringing produce to market in Acre that occurred in August 1290 gave the sultan, who was disinclined to observe the truce in any case, the pretext needed to begin the hostilities leading to the fall of Acre. An embassy of four men sent by the citizens of Acre to the new sultan Al-Ashraf shortly before the siege began in April 1291 were all imprisoned. Its leader, Sir Philip Mainboef, a native of the Holy Land fluent in Arabic, was not released from captivity until 1319, spending twenty-eight years in gaol, a dramatic example of the dangers attendant on diplomatic missions.[23]

The state of war between Cyprus and the Mamluk sultanate between the years 1366 and 1370 led to a flurry of diplomatic activity until the conclusion of a peace after the assassination of King Peter I. Envoys sent from Cyprus by the king but also from the Venetians and the Genoese, who desired peace in the interest of commerce, included nobles such as Sir James de Nores, Sir James le Petit and Sir Hugh de la Baume, as well as an erudite clerk named Anthony, an expert in law, the merchants Sir Cassan Cigala and Sir Nicholas Giustinani from Genoa and Venice respectively, and on one occasion two Muslim slaves. The latter, sent with letters from the king to the Mamluk sultan in the autumn of 1368, were sent following the mistreatment of Cigala and Giustiniani at Mamluk hands, causing the king to fear for the safety of Christian envoys. In the summer of 1366, one of the envoys sent from Cyprus to Egypt was the Catalan John d'Alfonso, a Jewish convert to Christianity.[24] Mamluk envoys sent to Cyprus included emirs, sometimes going there with a large retinue. Early in 1370 the sultan sent four Christian envoys, two Venetians and two Genoese merchants he had been keeping in custody, to conclude peace with Prince John of Antioch, the brother of King Peter I and regent of Cyprus following the king's assassination.[25] Shortly before invading Cyprus in 1426, the Mamluk envoy sent there to persuade King Janus to stop piratical activities was the son of an eminent Muslim sheikh named Muhammad ibn Khudaidar, sheikh of Damascus. This envoy was refused access to the king and returned empty handed. During the Mamluk invasion of June 1426, the Mamluks sent as an envoy following their capture of Limassol an old Mamluk who had long ago converted from Christianity to Islam, perhaps on account of his familiarity with the culture of the enemy, and he too was refused access to the king. The Mamluk envoy who did secure access to King Janus in July 1426, a peasant bearing a letter for the king, was tortured and maltreated so cruelly that he died, and on discovering his corpse the Mamluk troops vented their fury on the Cypriots, during the battle of Khirokitia.[26]

Diplomatic communication was generally conducted through letters borne by the envoys of the respective parties, but oral communication was also employed sometimes. With the reduction of the kingdom of Cyprus to a Mamluk tributary after 1426, diplomacy and the dispatch of envoys continued, often in connection with payments of the annual tribute. Mamluk delegations sent to Cyprus in the years after 1426 were numerous and costly to maintain for their Cypriot hosts.[27] Envoys from Cyprus also visited Mamluk Egypt, and were not always Cypriot nationals. Hence in 1437 the Castillian nobleman Pero Tafur journeyed to Egypt as King John II's envoy to Sultan Barsbay with three requests to the sultan, all of which were granted. One was for the sultan not to send numerous Mamluks to Cyprus to collect the tribute because much was spent on hospitality towards them, the second was for the camlets and other textiles sent as tribute in kind from Cyprus to be valued at Egyptian prices, which were higher than those paid in Cyprus, and the third was for Cypriot salt to be sold throughout the Mamluk lands duty free. Tafur was given a fine robe as a present during his embassy, and such robes were given as tokens of vassalage by the Mamluks to foreign ambassadors as early as the thirteenth century. He was chosen for his mission on account of his friendship with Carceran Suarez, a fellow Castillian who was the admiral of Cyprus, a post he had obtained after saving the life of King Janus during the battle of Khirokitia. Furthermore, he was assisted in his mission on arriving in Cairo by Taghribirdi, the chief interpreter at the Mamluk court, himself a converted Jew originally from Seville who was in receipt of an annual pension of 200 ducats from both King Janus and his son and heir King John II due to the assistance he had given King Janus whilst the latter was in captivity in Cairo.[28] Then as now, ethnic affinity and personal connections facilitated diplomacy.

Despite Tafur's reported success, at least one of the three requests he had been granted was subsequently disregarded, for in 1450 Barsbay's successor Sultan Jaqmaq ordered his Mamluk Faris-al-Turkmani to go to Cyprus, buy Mongol slaves there and have them sent to Cyprus. He gave him a sum of gold for this purpose and ordered him to use the tribute collected in Cyprus as well. The tribute due was not always paid promptly. In a letter Sultan Inal wrote just after his accession in March 1453 to King John II, he referred to a letter he had received from Peter Podocataro, a nobleman from a family of Greek extraction who was the king's ambassador to the Mamluk court. The letter informed the sultan of the festivities organised on Cyprus to celebrate Inal's accession, a practice also followed in the provinces of the Mamluk lands to celebrate victories, the accessions of sultans and governors and the building of new mosques. Pleased by this demonstration of loyalty, Sultan Inal commended King John to the Ottoman sultan Mehmet II, asking the latter to desist from piratical raids against Cyprus, and he also remitting arrears in the Cypriot tribute amounting to 16,250 ducats.[29] After King John's death in 1458 and the war of succession between his legitimate daughter Queen Charlotte, the rightful heir to the throne, and his natural son James, the issue of tribute actually determined Mamluk support for the latter's claim. The embassies sent by both Charlotte and James to Sultan Inal determinedly made bids for the sultan's support. Both were accompanied in their journey to Cairo in 1459 by the Mamluk ambassador Taghribardi-at-Tayyar, who had originally arrived in Cyprus in early 1459 to declare the sultan's support for James. In Cairo James's embassy, headed by the wily William Goneme, an Augustinian friar whom James later had appointed archbishop of Nicosia as a reward for his services, essentially outbid Charlotte's embassy, headed by Peter Podocataro, by offering double the annual tribute normally sent.[30]

During the civil war of the years 1460 to 1464 between the supporters of Charlotte and James, the latter, following his capture of Famagusta early in 1464, had to send another embassy to Cairo after massacring the Mamluk commander Janibeg and his troops following an armed clash when Janibeg refused to heed James's orders that the Mamluks in Cyprus were to stop kidnapping youths for forcible conversion to Islam and recruitment as Mamluks. The ambassador sent, referred to as 'James the Frank' by the contemporary Muslim historian ibn Taghribirdi, later returned to Cyprus with a Mamluk envoy named Sudun al-Mansuri. This envoy 'recounted many things' on his return from Cyprus. This suggests that he probably went there on a fact-finding mission after the massacre of Janibeg's Mamluks. James's embassy was ultimately successful, giving presents not only to the sultan but also to other important people in his entourage. In 1466 James also succeeded in obtaining papal recognition as King James II.[31] The Mamluk sultans were the suzerains of Cyprus and so their good will and recognition were sought whenever a change of government occurred there. On King James II's death in 1473, both his ousted sister Queen Charlotte and his Venetian widow Queen Catherine sent embassies to Sultan Qaytbay (1468–96). The latter embassy headed by Andrea Casoli, a burgess from Famagusta, and Anthony de l'Orsa was successful. The sultan refused to see Queen Charlotte's emissaries, but detained them and then handed them over to Queen Catherine's ambassadors for her to deal with at her pleasure, and they were sent back to Rhodes, where Queen Charlotte had been resident. The sultan also made known his good feelings towards Queen Catherine, adding apropos of the tribute that: 'he should be sent 24,000 ducats for three outstanding payments, and a good present because the queen has entered into her kingdom!'[32]

Venice effectively annexed Cyprus after the death of King James II and the flight from Cyprus of former supporters of his, predominantly Catalans and Sicilians, opposed to Venice. The diplomatic relations between Venetian Cyprus and the Mamluk passed through two phases. During the first phase, lasting until Queen Catherine's abdication in 1489, Venice was anxious to secure Mamluk recognition of Venetian control over Cyprus and to prevent the Mamluks from offering support and recognition to rivals of Venice wishing to control Cyprus. These rivals were Queen Charlotte and her daughter Carla, King Ferdinand of Naples and his natural son Don Alonso and the two natural sons of the late King James, Eugene and John. The second phase followed the abdication of Queen Catherine and the Mamluk recognition of Venetian direct rule over Cyprus in 1490, after which diplomatic relations largely centred on the prompt payment of the tribute from Cyprus and in ensuring that the camlets and other textiles sent were of acceptable quality, which was not always the case according to the Mamluks receiving them. A Venetian envoy sent from Cyprus in late 1474 or early in 1475 was ill treated at the Mamluk court, possibly because the Mamluk sultan thought that King Ferdinand of Naples might seize the island. By May 1476, however, the Mamluk sultan assured the queen's second envoy, the Cypriot Thomas Ficard, that the first envoy who had been detained would be sent back. He thanked her for the two years of delayed tribute sent to him and sent her valuable presents including a robe of gold brocade lined with ermine, the customary token of vassalage but also reconciliation. Indeed, the Venetians encouraged the queen to call herself 'Io tua schiava' in her correspondence with the sultan, who nonetheless appears to have kept his options open by welcoming Don Alonzo and Queen Charlotte on their arrival in Egypt in autumn 1478 and by sending an embassy in the years 1479–80. By this time, however, Venice had warned King Ferdinand to keep his fleet away from Cyprus, a warning that he heeded, and Venetian control was incontestable.[33]

Time, moreover, was working in Venice's favour. Carla's death in 1480, Queen Charlotte's sale of her rights over Cyprus to the dukes of Savoy in 1485, her own death in 1487, Don Alonzo's departure from Egypt in the same year and the arrest in 1488, followed by the incarceration and eventual execution of Rizzo di Marino, a former supporter of King James who had long plotted to overturn Venetian control over Cyprus, cut the ground from under the feet of Venice's enemies.[34] A second embassy of Thomas Ficard to the Mamluk sultan in 1483, just one year after Queen Charlotte's departure from Egypt, was crowned with success. Ficard, initially detained for non-payment of tribute, was released on assurances that the delayed tribute would be paid, given a robe of honour and expensive gifts for the queen and duly returned to Cyprus. In his written report he also pointed out that the sultan had refused an audience with the Neapolitan ambassador. The only hitch in the good relations between Venice and the Mamluks regarding Cyprus occurred in 1488 when the Mamluk sultan, angered by the above-stated arrest of Rizzo di Marino, who had led an embassy for the Mamluk sultan to Hospitaller Rhodes, had the Venetian consul in Damietta incarcerated. In addition, he refused to see Mark Malipiero, the Venetian ambassador sent to see him in April 1489 so as to justify Venice's decision to impose direct rule over Cyprus. Nothing daunted, Venice sent a second ambassador, Pietro Diedo, to Egypt in September 1489, securing Mamluk recognition of her imposition of direct rule over Cyprus by March 1490.[35] Furthermore, a Catalan envoy named Marchius who had also come to Cairo and expressed opposition to this takeover to Taghribirdi, the sultan's chief interpreter, was literally sent packing. This chief interpreter, a namesake of the one discussed above, was a Spanish or Sicilian Jew who had converted first to Christianity and then to Islam. He was in the pay of Venice, hence his denunciation of Marcius. Venice's diplomatic success over Cyprus is also to be placed in a wider context, this being the Mamluk sultan's desire to form a common front with Western rulers against the Ottomans, with whom he was at war. The sultan concluded treaties with Venice and Florence in March 1490 and sent his ambassador to the papal congress held in Rome with the aim of organising a crusade against the Ottomans, an aim that never materialised.[36]

CULTURAL AND RELIGIOUS EXCHANGES

The geographical proximity of Cyprus to Egypt and Syria resulted in a variety of cultural contacts. These took place notwithstanding the fact that Cyprus was a Latin kingdom with a Greek majority and large groups of Oriental Christians while the Mamluk sultanate was an officially Sunni Muslim state with groups of Orthodox and Oriental Christians. Indeed the Oriental Christians were an important though not exclusive factor in cultural interchanges. One of the earliest influences took place in the field of hunting, a sport highly popular in Cyprus among the Latin nobility as well as among other social classes and ethnic groups. King Hugh IV of Cyprus loved hunting and an anonymous English traveller visiting Cyprus in the years 1344–45 states that he used to employ leopards to hunt moufflons: Ludolf of Suchen, a German traveller who also visited Cyprus in the fourteenth century recounted how John of Ibelin, the count of Jaffa, also possessed leopards for hunting, which he was forced to sell in late 1342. One can surmise with a reasonable degree of certitude that they were imported to Cyprus from Egypt, the African country nearest to Cyprus and a country known to contain numerous species of wild animal, both endemic to the country and imported from Nubia and elsewhere further to the south. Indeed, these 'leopards' are almost certainly cheetahs. The fastest among all land animals, cheetahs were familiar in the medieval Islamic world and never confused with leopards. From Mamluk Egypt, where they were to be encountered in the Cairo menageries and were considered quite common, they could be easily imported from Alexandria to Cyprus. They were used for hunting in medieval Egypt and Syria. Such cheetahs were 'the companions of princes and sultans' who had them seated on the back of their horses for both hunting and parade ground purposes.[37]

Arabic was spoken on Cyprus before the Mamluk period, especially by the Maronites, Eastern Christians who though originally Monothelite had for the most part recognised papal primacy during the twelfth century. Following the Latin conquest and the establishment of the Lusignan dynasty, the number of Eastern Christians settling in Cyprus increased, with Arabic scribes mentioned among those encouraged by Guy, the founder of the Lusignan dynasty, to settle in Cyprus. Literary evidence exists proving that Arabic, besides being widely spoken in Cyprus, developed distinct characteristics in relation to other varieties of eastern Arabic. Izz ad-Din abu Ishaq Ibrahim bin Muhammad bin Tarxan as-Suwaydi's work titled 'Treatise on the Characteristics of Plant Names' (*Kitab al-simat fi asma al-nabat*) and written in the thirteenth century lists in separate sections the distinct usages of the Arabic names, given alongside their equivalents in other eastern and European languages, in Egypt, Palestine and Cyprus. This constitutes proof that by this time a distinct Cypriot Arabic idiom had come into existence.[38] It was further disseminated during the Mamluk era as the language of many Eastern Christians who migrated to Cyprus between 1260 and 1291, in the wake of the Muslim re-conquest of Latin Syria.

Arabic was also used by members of the Cypriot nobility. Among them were Isabella de Ibelin, who was married to King Hugh III of Cyprus in 1255 and transmitted her ability to swear and blaspheme in that language to her daughters Maria and Helvis. King Hugh IV of Cyprus and his second wife Alice de Ibelin knew Arabic and the Byzantine scholar and humanist Nicephorus Gregoras states that the Arabs of Egypt close to Cyprus often travelled across the sea to the king for the sake of stimulating conversation. King Janus de Lusignan likewise knew Arabic, a knowledge of which made his life easier during his detention in Cairo, following his capture by the Mamlūks in 1426 at the battle of Khirokitia. According to an admittedly partisan contemporary chronicler, Janus befriended the trainee Mamluk *julban* while in Cairo and visited prostitutes of both sexes. Likewise, when the Mamlūks reached Nicosia after the battle and hesitated on whether or not to enter, the knights Joseph, Bekhna and Raymond Audeth, Sir Khimi and his brothers and Sir Badin Goneme, who all knew Arabic and were all bar the last of Syrian origin, led them into the city and subsequently asked them to have various offices conferred upon them.[39]

The development of Famagusta into a major trading centre in the later thirteenth century, populated by varied groups of Arabic-speaking Eastern Christians who actively participated in this trade, often with their co-religionists remaining behind in the Mamluk sultanate, saw the emergence of the *drogumani* or *turcimanni*, persons able to translate commercial deeds and other commercial documents from and into Arabic, attested in fourteenth- and fifteenth-century Famagusta. Such persons included Latin, Melkite and Eastern Christian clergy, craftsmen and the anonymous writer of the third part of the early fourteenth-century manuscript known as the *Gestes de Chiprois*, a section now known as the 'Templar of Tyre', who was employed as a translator of Arabic in the Templar chancery. The Augustinian friar James of Verona and the Greek merchant Athanasios Lependrenos who visited Cyprus in the mid-fourteenth century commented on the Cypriots' ability to understand Arabic and Latin-based languages. Furthermore, the chronicle of George Boustronios suggests that there was a school of Arabic in fifteenth-century Nicosia, although this is not conclusive evidence. Arabic was also present in rural Cyprus. A donation of mulberry and olive trees to the church of St George in Kythraea dated 24 June 1499 was signed by one of the signatories witnessing it, a man named Isaac, in Arabic.[40]

Arabic medicine was highly appreciated in Cyprus. The Italian doctor Legno di Bologna journeyed to Syria in 1448 for treatment of problems with his eyesight, something he had been suffering from since 1446. This doctor, described as a *fisicus*, was a resident of Famagusta, then under Genoese occupation, and a member of the city's municipal council. On account of problems he was suffering with his eyesight, which could manifestly not be cured in Cyprus, he had taken four months' leave from work in order to journey to Damascus in Syria and undergo treatment there, after having secured assurances that his salary would continue to be paid to him while he was away. This doctor left Cyprus while Famagusta was under the administration of the Genoese captain Baliano de Porta.

He remained in Damascus, where his eyesight problems were indeed cured following treatment, for four months. Arabic medical works were translated for use on the island. Among those possessing such translations was Guy de Bagnolo, the physician of King Peter I of Cyprus, whose library was transported from Cyprus to Venice in 1368. Many of the medical treatises were translations from Arabic. Arabic medical works continued to be in demand on Cyprus during the following centuries. During the fifteenth century, the Cypriot nobleman James Singlitico purchased a medical manuscript that had been copied *c.* 1300 by the Greek Michael Loulloudes. The manuscript contains numerous marginal notes indicating that doctors familiar with Arabic were using it, for they simply transcribed into Greek Arabic medical terms that had no direct Greek equivalent. A better understanding of Arabic medicine also provided an incentive for the wider diffusion of the language throughout Cyprus. After the effective annexation of Cyprus by Venice in 1473, the Venetian Council of Ten in 1539 urged the local authorities in Cyprus to find a Copt fluent in Arabic so that they could pay him to teach the language to his fellow Copts resident in Cyprus and to others interested in learning it. In this fashion the books on medicine written in Arabic discovered in the Coptic monastery of St Macarius situated in the mountains to the north of Nicosia could be understood better and the knowledge therein disseminated more widely.[41]

King Hugh IV of Cyprus was himself a patron of Arabic art. A vessel from his court was a large and finely worked brass basin, formerly damascened with gold and silver, and measuring 57 centimetres across and 27.5 centimetres deep. The vessel is now in the Louvre Museum in Paris; similar types were made in the first half of the fourteenth century for King Hugh's contemporary, the Mamluk sultan a-Nasr Muhammad of Cairo. The stylistic similarities between this vessel and one in the St Louis Museum produced for an officer of Sultan al-Nasr Muhammad in the same monumental Thuluth script make it clear that the vessel with the French inscription was made at around the same time for King Hugh IV by craftsmen so familiar with the calligraphic techniques used for metal engraving in the Mamluk court that they must have been trained there. What makes the vessel commissioned for King Hugh IV stand out is the fact that it was commissioned for a Christian ruler. This vessel like others of similar dimensions and dating, commissioned for Christian patrons, were arguably not produced at the Mamluk sultan's court, but on Cyprus itself for the king. King Hugh consciously appropriated the courtly language of the damascened brass vessels made at the court of Sultan al-Nasir Muhammad and was almost alone among Western rulers in doing so. He may have wished to project the idea that he was the sultan's equal in importance and power.[42]

Contacts between Cyprus and the Mamluk lands spanned the domain of religion. The economic resources of the Latin Church of Cyprus, established in 1196, were used to support the embattled Latin sees in Latin Syria, suffering from Muslim raids and the re-conquest of Latin-controlled territories. In 1253 Pope Innocent IV granted Cypriot clerical tenths and the revenues of the archbishopric of Nicosia to help finance the fortification of the castle of Qusair, belonging to the Latin patriarch of Antioch and suffering from Muslim raids, and in 1256 this patriarch was granted the administration of the Cypriot see of Limassol to relieve his poverty. In 1291 Pope Nicholas IV granted the Dominican Patriarch Nicholas of Jerusalem exemption from paying tithes on two *casalia* his church owned in Cyprus to the Latin archbishop in Nicosia. This exemption was rescinded in 1291, by which time Latin Syria had been irretrievably lost in any case. In 1312, after the dissolution of the Order of the Templars, some of their villages in the diocese of Nicosia were granted to the titular patriarchs of Jerusalem, who were now resident on Cyprus. The loss of Latin Syria in 1291 also resulted in the relocation of the Latin bishopric of Tortosa to Famagusta, although the cathedral chapters of Famagusta and Tortosa remained separate. The Latin canons of the bishopric of Beirut found refuge in Nicosia. Papal hopes that the Mamluk sultan An-Nazir Muhammad might restore the Holy Land to Latins through peaceful negotiation led Pope John XXII to authorise the Dominican Peter de la Palude, titular patriarch of Jerusalem, and his household to visit and reside there, and to have the custody of the Latin churches there. He was also granted administration of the see of Limassol, exemption from paying tithes on the villages his patriarchate owned in Cyprus and the fines imposed on merchants excommunicated for transporting forbidden goods to finance his journey to the Holy Places. Reaching Cyprus in 1329, the patriarch went on to Egypt in 1330, but he failed to persuade the sultan to return the Holy Places and eventually returned to Avignon.[43]

Cyprus's proximity to the Holy Places made it an attractive point of departure for pilgrimages to the Holy Land. In 1326 Pope John XXII authorised King Hugh IV of Cyprus to send nuncios and 'explorers' of his own choosing to the Muslim lands around his kingdom in order to explore these lands. In another letter of around this time he also allowed him to send mendicants in his employ or in that of officials of his kingdom to these countries, and one wonders if this was a veiled reference to espionage carried out from Cyprus. From 1326 onwards, the popes began authorising Latin archbishops of Nicosia, members of the Latin clergy and Latin lay persons to perform pilgrimages to the Holy Places, so long as they did not transport prohibited strategic materials such as weaponry and timber there to finance their journeys, but only licit goods. In September 1333 the pope granted Helias de Nabineaux, the new Latin archbishop of Nicosia, permission to visit the Holy Places and also celebrate mass there in churches and oratories under Muslim occupation. Papal policy relaxed further in 1345 when Pope Clement VI authorised Archbishop Philip of Nicosia to grant absolution from excommunication, on payment of a monetary fine, to pilgrims who had visited the Holy Places without having first obtained papal permission, while also authorising him to visit the Holy Places successively with large numbers of companions, of between 100 and 300 on each occasion. By delegating the power of absolution to the archbishop, the pope was also saving petitioners on Cyprus from the time, expenses and dangers attendant on making a journey to Avignon for the purpose of obtaining absolution. From 1350 onwards visitors to the Holy Land travelling from Cyprus solicited and received papal licences as a routine procedure.[44]

The pilgrims' needs regarding accommodation, health care and even burial were also attended to. In 1328 the pope granted permission to the Genoese merchant Stephen Draperius to have a chapel to St Stephen founded within the confines of a hospital he had founded for the housing, care and burial of pilgrims in the cemetery attached to it. A hospital founded with papal permission on Mt Zion by the Florentine widow Sophia Philippi in 1353, run by women who had adopted the rule of the Franciscan Third Order and which had been damaged by Muslim raids carried out in retaliation for King Peter's attack on Alexandria in 1365, also received help from Cyprus. In 1370 Pope Urban V authorised Archbishop Raymond of Nicosia to receive donations for its restoration and for repayment of its debts. In 1372 he also authorised the bishop of Famagusta to allow Sophia to visit the Holy Places with 200 people, a way of raising funds for the hospital. Furthermore, in 1373 the pope granted indulgences to those assisting in its reconstruction, although now the foundation was also placed under direct papal supervision.[45]

The Spanish Dominican friar Alfonso Buenhombre, who knew Arabic, lived in Famagusta during the mid-fourteenth century. With a view to promoting missions to the East, he was engaged in translating works from Arabic into Latin, dedicating in February 1341 to Cardinal Pedro de Sotomayor a history of St Anthony he had discovered in a manuscript deposited in the library of the Coptic monastery of this saint in Famagusta. On Cyprus, Buenhombre continued a vocation of translator and commentator he had begun in Egypt with the aim of strengthening contacts between Eastern and Western Christians. Ascertaining that the mendicants established in Famagusta, arguably the most cosmopolitan of Cypriot cities, were ignorant of Arabic and lacked an interpreter, he lamented the divide separating the various Christian denominations. He observed that Arabic-speaking Christians had no linguistic access to the works of the great Latin Church fathers such as St Thomas Aquinas and Isidore of Seville while Western Christians were deprived of the teachings of the Egyptian anchorite fathers and Ephraim the Syrian. This Spanish Dominican promoting inter-denominational dialogue in Famagusta can be placed in a tradition of multilingual interpreters mentioned twenty years later by the Greek merchant Athanasios Lependrenos in his correspondence with the Byzantine scholar Nicephoros Gregoras.[46]

Interfaith contacts between Cyprus and the Mamluk lands involved religious polemic. The Syrian Melkites, who followed the Greek rite and were present on Cyprus, had co-religionists in the Mamluk lands and were directly involved in such polemic. It took the form of the so-called 'Letter from the People of Cyprus', an elegantly worded but highly contentious piece of Christian polemic initially written in the thirteenth century by the Melkite Bishop Paul of Sidon as a letter to a Muslim friend. In it Paul stated that he has travelled to the lands of the Christians at the request of his anonymous Muslim friend so as to discover Christian beliefs concerning Islam. He then proceeded, through a combination of citations of the Quran, sometimes altered to make them conform more closely to Christian belief, and logical reasoning to prove that the Quran supports and agrees with fundamental Christian beliefs, such as the Trinity, the duality of Christ and the Incarnation. His work maintained that the teachings of the prophet Muhammad were directed not to mankind as a whole but solely to the unlettered desert Arabs as a *preparatio evangelica*, a means whereby they might be made receptive to Christianity, the ultimate religious truth. This tract circulated widely in the thirteenth century and was known to Muslim scholars, one of whom, Shihab al Din al Qarafi, refuted it in his writings.[47]

During the early fourteenth century, this piece of Christian polemic was recast extensively by an anonymous author. His fluency in Arabic, thorough knowledge of the Quran and citations of the Bible in its Arabic translations suggest that he was either a Syrian Melkite or a convert from Islam to Melkite Christianity, who had perhaps fled to Cyprus after or even just prior to the Muslim re-conquest of Latin Syria to escape the Muslim punishment for apostasy. He deleted much of the original's logical reasoning, corrected the doctored citations of the Quran and added further such citations, as well as citations from the Bible, hoping thereby to make the text more acceptable, less easy to refute and ultimately more convincing for the Muslim audience it was aimed at. This sedulously revised 'Letter from the People of Cyprus' was then sent to two Muslim scholars in Damascus, Ibn Taymiyya in 1316 and al-Dimashqi in 1321. Al-Dimashqi wrote a comprehensive refutation of this piece of Christian polemic just four months after receiving it, arguing from a wholly Quranic perspective. It is not known whether this reply ever reached Cyprus and its survival in just one manuscript indicates a limited diffusion. The 'Letter from the People of Cyprus', composed either to boost Christian morale in the wake of the Muslim re-conquest of Latin Syria or to attempt conversion of Muslims by peaceful means, indicates that the Syrian Melkites living on Cyprus as well as the Latins were active in promoting the struggle against Islam, in the Melkites' case through the medium of religious polemic.[48]

Ibn Taymiyya likewise refuted this 'Letter from the People of Cyprus' in his famous work known as *The Right Answer* (Al-Jawab al-salih) some time after 1316, a landmark in the history of Christian–Muslim polemics. The main ideas developed in this work were anticipated in summary form, however, in an earlier work he had written in the years 1303–04, known as *Al-risala al-qubrussiya* or *The Cypriot Letter*. The letter's addressee has occasioned disagreement among scholars, who maintain him to have been either John II the lord of Jubail, a member of the Embriaci family living in exile on Cyprus at the time, or William de Villaret, the Hospitaller Grand Master between the years 1294 and 1305. In this letter, Ibn Taymiyya presents Islam as a golden mean, superior to Judaism in its severity towards unbelievers and superior to Christianity in its compassion towards believers. In the Cypriot letter, developing the Sufi tradition's three fundamental attributes concerning God of majesty, beauty and perfection, Ibn Taymiyya states that Moses had the attributes of majesty and severity, Jesus those of beauty and compassion, and Muhammad, 'the seal of the prophets', that of perfection. Christianity is accused of corrupt features, such as crosses allegedly suspended in mid-air, icons shedding tears and the 'Holy Fire' coming down in the Church of the Holy Sepulchre in Jerusalem during Easter, regarded as a fabrication. Christians are also accused of having renounced *jihad*, the duty to wage war on God's behalf. The letter states that the coming of the prophet Muhammad was revealed in the Old Testament book of Habakkuk 3:3–13. Ibn Taymiyya concluded *The Cypriot Letter* by maintaining that the Muslim captives on Cyprus had been seized wrongfully. This was because while Muslims were right to wage war against the Christians, who had corrupted God's religion, Christians could never be justified in waging war on Muslims because neither God, the Messiah or the apostles had ever sanctioned attacks on those following the religion of Abraham, by which he meant Islam. The letter's recipient is urged to treat Muslim captives on Cyprus humanely and to abstain from trying to change their faith.[49] This was an oblique acknowledgement that Muslim captives on Cyprus did sometimes convert to Christianity, as will be seen below.

TRADE AND SETTLEMENT

Trade between Lusignan Cyprus and Mamluk Egypt and Syria took place throughout the period under discussion, even when officially prohibited. As early as 1232, the Genoese, who had helped the Ibelin faction prevail in the civil war on Cyprus between the Ibelins and the Imperialists, secured shops in Famagusta, the Cypriot port opposite Syria, in the treaty they concluded with King Henry I. In his decrees of 1251 Archbishop Hugh of Fagiano, the Latin archbishop of Nicosia, condemned as excommunicated those 'false Christians' exporting timber, weapons and iron to the Mamluk lands, in line with successive papal prohibitions on the export of such goods to the infidels from the twelfth century onwards. His successor Archbishop Ranulf renewed this prohibition in 1280, and it is also found in the Greek translations of the *Assizes de la Cour des Bourgeois* executed in the fourteenth century, where in the second of the two extant codices it is a capital offence. That such goods were exported to Egypt and Syria from Cyprus at the time occasions no surprise, for Cilician Armenia also exported timber, iron and weapons to the Mamluk lands in the thirteenth and early fourteenth centuries.[50] The Mamluks were keen to acquire such goods, in short supply in their own territories, from any outside source. During and immediately after the Mamluk re-conquest of the coastal cities of Palestine and Syria under Latin rule between 1260 and 1291, completed by the capture of Acre and Tyre, numerous Latin and Syrian Christian refugees from those areas settled in Cyprus and especially in Famagusta. By the start of the fourteenth century, Famagusta had become the main port of the Lusignan kingdom, not least on account of its proximity to Egypt, Syria and above all to the port of Alexandria.[51]

The bull Pope Nicholas IV promulgated in August 1291 forbidding Christians to trade with the Mamluk lands for the next ten years, on pain of excommunication, followed by subsequent bulls forbidding the export of strategic materials to the Mamluks actually benefited trade between Cyprus and the Mamluk lands. As Anthony Luttrell has pointed out, 'a blockade which could only be enforced by those who stood to lose from it had little chance of success'. In practice the Cypriot authorities enforced the ban where possible on Western merchants travelling to Egypt or Syria while covertly allowing merchants based in Cyprus, Latins as well as Syrians or Greeks, to trade freely in those lands. Cyprus-based traders profited greatly as middlemen between the Western merchants coming to Cyprus to buy goods, including silks, spices and slaves, originating from the Mamluk lands, and the Muslim traders eager to buy Western textiles, timber, metals and weapons. And this despite repeated condemnation of their activities, in 1320, 1323 and 1324 by Pope John XXII. In actuality, the papacy developed a practice whereby merchants and others excommunicated for such illicit trade could obtain absolution, either on the payment of a monetary fine or by serving for a fixed period of time in campaigns organised against the Muslims. From around 1326 onwards, the papacy began granting permission for trade with the Muslims in licit non-strategic materials in return for a fee.[52] An anonymous trading manual compiled in around 1320 records the export of Cypriot camlets and the colours exported to various destinations. Emerald green, pistachio, light green, yellow, azure and white ones were sent to Alexandria, Cairo and Damietta, large quantities in all colours to Damascus and Beirut, emerald green, pistachio green and white were sent to Tripoli and green, white and a few pistachio green camlets were sent to Latakia. Cypriot camlets continued to be exported to the Mamluk sultanate and from 1426 onwards formed part of the tribute until the Ottoman conquest of Egypt and Syria in 1517.[53]

The papal embargo and its beneficial effects on Cyprus, however, were transitory. After 1335 the political instability affecting Iran and the Tatar kingdom of Southern Russia made it harder for goods to reach Western Europe via those lands, to the considerable detriment of Venetian and Genoese traders. Pressure was exerted on the papacy to lift the embargo, and in three letters of August 1343 Pope Clement VI granted Bishop Eudes of Paphos, the collector of papal taxes on Cyprus, permission to absolve from excommunication merchants and others in Cyprus found guilty of taking forbidden goods to Alexandria and other proscribed destinations on receipt of a suitable monetary payment, whereupon the sentence of excommunication would be commuted to a penance. The papal prohibition on trade between Western merchants and the Muslims was lifted under Pope Clement VI in 1344. From then onwards the Venetians and Catalans were permitted to send lines of galleys to the Mamluk lands regularly.[54]

With the resumption of direct trade between Western Europe and the Mamluk territories the role of Cypriot middlemen was undercut. While Venice continued to send six to eight state-sponsored trading galleys every year to the eastern Mediterranean, these galleys now had papal permits for trade with the Muslims and only around half came to Cyprus. During the years 1357 to 1359 inclusive, fourteen such galleys were equipped for trade with Alexandria and only nine for Famagusta. If this trend in Venetian trade is reflected in the other major trading nations involved in the transit trade between Western Europe and the East, it seems that fewer goods were available for sale on Cyprus. Fewer visits to the island on account of the merchants' legal as well as practical ability to sail directly to Egypt and Syria meant reduced customs dues for the Cypriot Crown. Hence in 1361 complaints were made of how people were falsely claiming Venetian nationality or importing as Venetian merchandise goods belonging to non-Venetians in order to claim exemption from customs payments. Disputes between Cyprus and Genoa in 1364 nearly erupted into war, and the agreement of April 1365 that averted this contained provisions humiliating to the kingdom of Cyprus. One long-running issue of contention was to what extent Eastern Christians under Venetian or Genoese protection, the so-called 'White Venetians' and 'White Genoese', could claim exemption from customs duties and other imposts, with the royal officials seeking to tax them and the Venetians and Genoese upholding their claims to exemption.[55]

The decline of Cypriot commerce caused by the resumption of normal trade between Western Europe and the Mamluk sultanate and the corresponding reduction in Cypriot royal revenues may well have been a key factor impelling King Peter I of Cyprus to attack Alexandria in 1365 with Hospitaller assistance, in the context of the crusade the pope had proclaimed. The ruinously expensive war this provoked with the Mamluks, discussed above, did nothing to benefit Cypriot trade, and the anger both Venice and Genoa felt towards King Peter, whose attack had harmed their own trading interests, only made things worse. Despite his desire to resume war with the Mamluks, the Venetians and Genoese secured papal backing for peace with them. In May 1368 the king authorised envoys from the mercantile republics of Venice and Genoa to negotiate a peace treaty on his behalf. Among the issues for the Cypriots in these negotiations was one important for Cypriot traders in Mamluk territory, namely the residence of the Cypriot commune in Alexandria, colloquially known as the *Han de la Moze*, the khan of Moses. This facility, like similar facilities existing in Egypt, Syria and other Muslim countries for merchants from Europe was a regulated commercial and residential facility for transitory and resident merchants as well as other travellers from Cyprus. Cypriots residing in Egypt came under the legal jurisdiction of the Cypriot consul there, at least in cases not involving bloodshed, and similar arrangements were in force for Venetians, Provençals, Catalans and other Westerners residing in Cyprus. The peace concluded between Lusignan Cyprus and the Mamluk sultanate and ratified in 1370, one year after King Peter's assassination, revived commercial contacts. These were boosted even more by the Genoese seizure of Famagusta in 1373, which toughened the competition Cypriot merchants faced and impelled them to make greater use of Egypt as an operational base.[56]

Early fifteenth-century Cypriot trading activity in Mamluk territories is recorded. A certain Maria of Cyprus, an innkeeper in Alexandria, lent four ducats to George Deliono, who possibly originated from the town of Nuoro in Sardinia and was resident in Famagusta. It is possible that Maria is identical to the 'Mariona de Zipro' mentioned in a notarial act of December 1421 regarding the purchase of eighty-one butts of wine by three Venetians resident in Candia, Crete. This wine, sent from Crete to Alexandria, was sold to three persons explicitly mentioned as tavern-keepers, one Greek, one Anconitan and one Coptic, as well as to Mariona, who although not mentioned as a tavern-keeper must have either been one or have been engaged in a similar occupation, for why else would she have purchased this wine? The participation of women in this trading activity is noteworthy and several Cypriot women maintained hostels in the city. Sometime before 1422 Peter Zexomeno, a Greek from Cyprus, became Cypriot consul there. A deed of July 1422 recounts how Peter's son James married Maria, an Abyssinian slave manumitted by her master Bartholomew Lomellini on the same day and given a dowry of 60 ducats by him, clearly so as to marry James. In Alexandria, notarial acts of the early fifteenth century record Cypriot ships visiting the harbour there.[57] One notes in this context that a community of Cypriot merchants similar to that at Alexandria also came to be established in Beirut during the mid-fourteenth century, when according to the Arab write Salih ibn Yahya Frankish ships began in this period to frequent this port tentatively so as to trade. Venetians were coming to Cyprus and the king of Cyprus used to despatch their goods to Beirut on board two ships that arrived there consecutively. He states that the Cypriots had a church in Beirut, although he does not state unfortunately which Christian denomination it belonged to, and a group among them took up residence there, maintaining their taverns and wine presses.[58]

The Mamluk invasion of Cyprus in 1426 and its reduction to tributary status actually boosted Cypriot exports to the Mamluk sultanate, since the tribute was payable in kind. Camlets have already been mentioned, and other products given by way of payment were silks, woollens and cloth, especially as sometimes the camlets were of poor quality. While Syrian cotton and bocasine were exported to Europe via Cyprus and to Cyprus itself in the fourteenth and fifteenth centuries, Cypriot cotton and bocasine were also exported to Europe. Genoese customs entries for the years 1376–77 record far more numerous such imports from Cyprus as opposed to Mamluk territory. Both Cyprus and the Mamluk lands produced sugar, but Cyprus appears to have produced it more cheaply. Cypriot sugar, including the cheaper molasses variety, was imported to Mamluk lands throughout the fifteenth century. In 1477 the Venetian government ruled that a Venetian galley from the regular Beirut convoy should stop at Famagusta and take Cypriot sugar on board before continuing to Beirut. Mario Sanudo the Younger recorded in his *Diarii* for the year 1504 the export of Cypriot sugar, molasses and honey to Syria. Sugar production in Egypt and Syria suffered on account of the technological stagnation there in comparison to Cyprus, the stifling of competition because privileges were granted to factories owed by the sultan and his emirs, and the management of the sultan's factories by corrupt officials. These phenomena, together with the inflation Egypt and Syria experienced on account of the export of silver to Europe and the import of copper, which in the early fifteenth century became the basis of Mamluk currency, all hampered Mamluk production and assisted rival Cypriot production of sugar, textiles and other goods.[59]

Wheat cultivation in Mamluk Syria and Egypt declined during the fifteenth century and was displaced by barley. Nonetheless, wheat and barley from these lands were imported to Cyprus throughout the fifteenth and early sixteenth centuries whenever the island suffered a bad harvest and Coptic merchants participated in such grain exports. Indeed, the depopulation of Egypt and Syria facilitated such exports to Cyprus down to the end of the period of Mamluk rule. Cyprus began to export wheat to Egypt regularly after the imposition of Mamluk suzerainty in 1426, and in 1436 Pero Tafur observed that the kingdom was bound by treaty to export wheat regularly to Egypt. Cypriot barley was also exported to Egypt and Syria throughout the fifteenth and early sixteenth centuries. Mastic from Chios was brought to Cyprus, with Jews from Chios active in selling it and Genoese Famagusta acting as a sale and distribution point throughout Cyprus but also to Syria and Egypt. Cypriot salt, first mentioned by Pero Tafur as an important Cypriot export article to the

Mamluk territories, was still being exported there according to Marino Sanudo in the early sixteenth century. Sanudo made the important observation in 1510 that many poor people in Cyprus made a living from the trading relations with Syria. Genoese merchants based in Famagusta and Nicosia imported pepper from Egypt to Cyprus. There were numerous soap factories in Egypt and Syria in the early fifteenth century. In 1427 Venetian merchants based in Alexandria sold some soap to King Janus and earlier a Copt based in Famagusta and working with a Genoese merchant in Nicosia also sold soap to a North African drago-man named Daut.[60]

Copts, mentioned above as merchants in connection with trade between Cyprus and the Mamluk lands, probably settled on Cyprus in the second half of the fourteenth century, although they may have arrived earlier. The punitive measures the Mamluks took against the Copts in retaliation for King Peter I's attack on Alexandria may have impelled some Copts to flee to Cyprus, but there is no conclusive evidence for this. The first Coptic bishop on Cyprus, Anba Michael, who subsequently became the metropolitan of Rhodes, is recorded as late as 1483, although this reference is important in showing that the Copts were numerous and organised enough by that time to have their own bishop. Coptic manuscripts were copied or edited on Cyprus and some time before 1535 the Copts had a church in Nicosia dedicated to St Benham. Two wills of 1451 and 1453 drawn up by members of the prominent Audeth family of Syrian origin record bequests to 'the four churches of the Copts'. Although their names and locations are unfortunately not men-tioned, they are probably the Coptic cathedral of St Anthony in Nicosia, the church of St Benham mentioned above, the Coptic church of St Anthony in Famagusta and the Coptic monastery of St Macarius of Klima founded near the village of Platani to the north of Nicosia. These four churches received 2,000 ducats in the will of the prominent Copt Sir Hanna Christodoulou, who died in 1518. The Coptic monastery of St Macarius was mentioned in a letter of the Venetian Council of Ten dated 24 May 1539. It commented favourably on the monks' abstemious lifestyle and regular worship and awarded them a grant from the public purse so that they could construct new buildings on account of an increase in the number of monks from four to sixteen. It was this monastery, moreover, that possessed the Arabic medical books that also attracted the Venetians' attention, as discussed above. Not everyone liked the Copts, and in 1580 the Dominican friar Stephen de Lusignan, writing at a time when Cyprus was under Ottoman rule, described them as obstinate and opinionated, although reluctantly acknowledging that they maintained a strict regimen.[61]

Muslims as well as Christians from the Mamluk sultanate also settled in Cyprus, albeit under very different circumstances. James the natural son of King John II of Cyprus pre-vailed over his legitimate sister Queen Charlotte in the civil war of the years 1460–64 with the help of an auxiliary force composed of Circassian Mamluks. Although some, for reasons explained above, were massacred following the capture of Famagusta, others, such as John the Circassian, the emir Curcuma and the Mamluk Taghribirdi, remained in the service of James, who granted fiefs to them by way of rewarding them. Although generally keeping their Muslim faith in some cases, they intermarried with Cypriot women and their chil-dren, Christians who nevertheless acknowledged their Circassian ancestry, as attested as fief holders in the Venetian period. Examples are Peter and Bernard Cercasso, sons of John the Circassian, while an unnamed son of his was killed in 1501 in the fighting that broke out when twelve Ottoman ships raided Lapithos on the northern coast of Cyprus. The persons Thomas, Jeronimo and Paris Cercasso recorded in sixteenth-century Venetian documents were probably also among John the Circassian's descendants. Jeronimo Cercasso, recorded in the list of feudatories owing military service dated 28 April 1560 drawn up by the Venetian proveditor general and syndic Andrea Dandolo, held the title of *magnifico*, an indubitable attestation of noble rank. He is indeed the only person of Circassian origin recorded as achieving noble status in Cyprus. The Cypriot interpreter Michel Membre who later worked in Venice claimed to be of Circassian origin while the *matthesep* (*muhtasib*) Battista Mamaluco who served in the Karpass peninsula sometime before 1559 was clearly descended from the Mamluks.[62]

Not all persons moving from the Mamluk territories to Cyprus or vice versa did so voluntarily. The movement of slaves, usually captured in warfare, is a case in point. Over 1,800 Muslims were taken captive near Limassol in 1271 when the fleet sent against Cyprus by Sultan Baybars ran aground. Many of them were sent to Acre to be ransomed and although a ransom price was not agreed, they escaped successfully from custody with the aid of saws and files which their warders, who had been bribed, smuggled in to them. As stated above, Ibn Taymiyya also referred to Muslim captives in Cyprus in his letter of 1303–04, probably addressed to John II the exiled lord of Jubail, and Ludolf of Suchen who visited Cyprus in the mid-fourteenth century referred to a vineyard called Engaddi in the Paphos district, where the Templars had employed over 100 Muslim captives to tend the vines daily, clearly before their dissolution in 1312. Christians were also taken captive in war, and when the besieged Templars on the island of Ruad surrendered to the Mamluk forces in 1302, those who escaped massacre were taken to Cairo as captives. According to the testimony of the Genoese witness Percival of Mar during the trial of the Templars taking place on Cyprus in the years 1310–11, they were kept in captivity for nearly ten years, deprived of food and water, yet they preferred dying in this state, or even decapitation, to renouncing Jesus Christ.[63]

The systematic raids conducted from Cyprus against the Mamluk coastlines of Egypt and Syria in the early fifteenth century brought numerous captives. King Janus of Cyprus acquired 1,500 Muslim captives in a raid of 1415, according to the Cretan Emmanuel Piloti, who were sent to work on the royal sugar plantations. An emissary from the Mamluk sultan sent to the king to request their return was told by him that they were far less than he needed. But sometimes captive Muslims were ransomed. In 1414, following a ceasefire between Cyprus and the Mamluk sultanate, a Muslim emir sent to Cyprus successfully negotiated the ransom of 535 Muslim captives, with the king paying in person for the ransom of 135 of them. In 1419 the Venetian government instructed its consuls in Damascus and on Cyprus to buy back numerous Muslim slaves purchased by Jean Corner, probably to work in his family's extensive sugar plantation in Episkopi near Limassol. The raids for Muslim slaves ceased following the Mamluk invasion of 1426. On account of the invasion, former Muslim captives who had become Christian fled from Nicosia and elsewhere to escape the wrath of their former co-religionists, who would have had them executed for apostasy had they discovered them. Between the years 1424 and 1425 the Mamluks seized over 1,000 Cypriots in retaliatory raids on the island's littoral, taking them into captivity. Some were killed for refusing to apostatise to Islam while others were sold as slaves. Following the Mamluk invasion of 1426 and their seizure of Nicosia, between 2,000 and 6,000 Cypriots were taken to Egypt in captivity, according to differing estimates. Some were ransomed, and the papacy ordered the churches of Spain, France, England and Italy to offer funds for their redemption. Others, however, were sold into slavery, with some converting to Islam and others executed for refusing to abjure Christianity.[64]

CONCLUDING REMARKS

Relations between Lusignan Cyprus and the Mamluk sultanate, which encompassed Egypt, the Holy Land and Syria, were multifaceted. They crossed religious, linguistic and ethnic boundaries but were continuous, involved fluctuating degrees of hostility and intervention by outside powers, notably the Mongols in the early fourteenth century and Venice from the late fifteenth century. This was not only because of the proximity of all these lands to each other but also because of the long period of time the relations covered, in the case of the Mamluk sultanate spanning the whole of its history. Initially beginning as relations between two sovereign states, from 1426 until the fall of the Mamluk sultanate in 1517 the relationship was between tributary and suzerain. Even after the Ottoman conquest of the Mamluk sultanate, Cyprus, under Venetian control since 1474, continued to be a tributary to the Ottomans. With the Ottoman conquest of 1570, however, Cyprus like the former lands of the Mamluk sultanate came under Ottoman rule. The political map of the eastern Mediterranean was radically and irrevocably altered.

NOTES

1 P. Edbury, *The Kingdom of Cyprus and the Crusades 1191–1374* (1991; 2nd edn, 1994), 83.

2 P.M. Holt, *The Age of the Crusades: The Near East from the Eleventh Century to 1517* (London and New York, 1986), 95–6; C. Marshall, *Warfare in the Latin East 1192–1291* (Cambridge, 1992; 2nd edn, 1994), 231–4, 238, 244; P. Thorau, *The Lion of Egypt: Sultan Baybars and the Near East in the Thirteenth Century* (London and New York, 1987), 158–62 and 166–71; Edbury, *Kingdom*, 89.

3 Holt, *Near East*, 96; Marshall, *Warfare*, 244 and 247–248; Thorau, *Lion*, 187–192; Edbury, *Kingdom*, 90, 92.

4 A. Forey, 'Cyprus as a Base for Crusading Expeditions from the West', in *Cyprus and the Crusades*, ed. N. Coureas and J. Riley-Smith (Nicosia, 1995), 76; Thorau, *Lion*, 206; Holt, *Near East*, 96; G. Hill, *A History of Cyprus*, 4 vols (Cambridge, 1940–52), 2:166–7; Edbury, *Kingdom*, 92.

5 Thorau, *Lion*, 206–7, 218 notes 110–12; Hill, *History*, 2:167; A. Fuess, 'Was Cyprus a Mamluk Protectorate? Mamluk Policies towards Cyprus between 1426 and 1517', *Journal of Cyprus Studies*, 11 (2005), 13.

6 *The 'Templar of Tyre' Part III of the 'Deeds of the Cypriots'*, ed. P. Crawford (Aldershot, 2003), 104–19; Holt, *Near East*, 102–4; Marino Sanudo Torsello, *The Book of the Secrets of the Faithful of the Cross: Liber Secretorum Fidelium Crucis*, trans. P. Lock (Farnham, 2011), 365–70; Marshall, *Warfare*, 244–5, 253–5; Edbury, *Kingdom*, 98–9; Hill, *History*, 2:188.

7 Sanudo, *Secrets*, 370; Edbury, *Kingdom*, 102.

8 A. Luttrell, 'The Hospitallers in Cyprus after 1291', in *Praktika tou Protou Diethnous Kyprologikou Synedriou*, 3 vols (Nicosia, 1972), 2:163 and esp. note 3.

9 J. Riley-Smith, *The Knights of St John in Jerusalem and Cyprus, 1050–1310* (London, 1967), 198–200; Luttrell, 'Hospitallers in Cyprus', 161–2.

10 Sanudo, *Secrets*, 385–6; Edbury, *Kingdom*, 105–6; 'Chronique d'Amadi' in *Chroniques d'Amadi et de Strambaldi*, ed. R. de Mas Latrie, 2 vols (Paris, 1891–3), 1:239; S. Schein, *Fideles Crucis, The Papacy, the West and the Recovery of the Holy Land, 1274–1314* (Oxford, 1991), 163–5; Luttrell, 'Hospitallers in Cyprus', 164 and note 4.

11 'Amadi', 241–5 note 8 and section I; N. Coureas, *The Latin Church of Cyprus, 1195–1312* (Aldershot, 1997), 136–8, 167–8; Schein, *Fideles*, 194–5.

12 L. de Mas Latrie, *Histoire de l'île de Chypre sous le règne des princes de la maison de Lusignan*, 3 vols (Paris, 1852–61), 2:118–25; Schein, *Fideles*, 212–13; Edbury, *Kingdom*, 156–7; N. Housley, *The Avignon Papacy and the Crusades 1305–1378* (Oxford, 1986), 23–5.

13 J. van Steenbergen, 'The Alexandrian Crusade (1365) and the Mamluk Sources: Reassessment of the *kitab al-ilmam* of an-Nuwayri al-Iskandarani', in *East and West in the Crusader States, Context-Contacts-Confrontations*, ed. K. Cigaar and H. Teule (Peeters, 2003), 123–37; P. Edbury, 'The Crusading Policy of King Peter I of Cyprus', in *idem, Kingdoms of the Crusaders from Jerusalem to Cyprus* (Aldershot, 1999), XII; *idem, Kingdom*, 171.

14 J. Richard, 'La révolution de 1369 dans le royaume de Chypre', in *idem, Orient et Occident au Moyen Age: contacts et relations (XIIe-XVe s.)*, 3rd edn, XVI (Aldershot, 1997), 110–15; P. Edbury, 'The Murder of King Peter I of Cyprus', in *idem, Kingdoms of the Crusaders from Jerusalem to Cyprus* (Aldershot, 1999), XIII; Fuess, 'Mamluk Protectorate', 14.

15 P. Edbury, 'Cyprus and Genoa: the Origins of the War of 1373–1374' and 'The Aftermath of Defeat: Lusignan Cyprus and the Genoese, 1374–1382', both in *idem., Kingdoms of the Crusaders from Jerusalem to Cyprus* (Aldershot, 1999), XIV and XV.

16 'Amadi', 498; *Excerpta Cypria Nova*, ed. G. Grivaud, vol. 1 (Nicosia, 1990), 61–2; E. Ashtor, *Levant Trade in the Later Middle Ages* (Princeton, 1983), 225; D. Jacoby, 'To emporio kai he oikonomia tes Kyprou', in *Historia tes Kyprou*, IV, *Mesaionikon Basileion, Henetokratia*, ed. Th. Papadopoullos (Nicosia, 1995), 444–5, 445 note 77.

17 M. Ouerfelli, 'Les relations entre le royaume de Chypre et le sultanat mamelouke au XVe siècle', *Le moyen Age*, Tome CX, 2 (2004), 330, 332–3.

18 'Amadi', 499–500; Ouerfelli, 'Relations', 333–4; Ashtor, *Levant Trade*, 225.

19 Ouerfelli, 'Relations', 335–36.

20 'Amadi', 500–9; Ouerfelli, 'Relations', 336; R. Irwin, 'Hoi eisboles ton Mameloukon sten Kypro', in *Historia tes Kyprou*, IV, *Mesaionikon Basileion, Henetokratia*, ed. Th. Papadopoullos (Nicosia, 1995), 159–76; A. Fuess, 'Rotting Ships and Razed Harbours: The Naval Policy of the Mamluks', *Mamluk Studies Review*, 5 (2001), 54–5; *idem*, 'Mamluk Protectorate', 15–16.

21 Leontios Makhairas, *Recital concerning the Sweet land of Cyprus, entitled 'Chronicle'*, ed. R. M. Dawkins, 2 vols (Oxford, 1932), 1:§693.

22 *Une enquête à Chypre au XVe siècle: Le Sindicamentum de Napoleone Lomellini, capitaine génois de Famagouste (1459)*, ed. C. Otten-Froux (Nicosia, 2000), 120–1, 141–6, 150–1, 153–8, 190–1, 218 note 31, 221 note 53, 247.

23 Crawford, *'Templar of Tyre'*, 101–4; Hill, *History*, 2:183–4; P.-V. Claverie, 'L' Ambassade au Caire de Philippe Mainebeuf (1291)', in *Egypt and Syria in the Fatimid, Ayyubid and Mamluk Eras*, vol. 7, ed. U. Vermeulen and J. van Steenbergen (Leuven, 2005), 383–93; *Early Mamluk Diplomacy (1260–1290) Treaties of Baybars and Qalawun with Christian Rulers*, ed. P. M. Holt (Leiden, 1995), 3–4, 9.

24 Makhairas, *Recital*, 1: §§181–2, 184–5, 189; Guillaume de Machaut, *The Capture of Alexandria*, trans. J. Shirley, introduction and notes by P. Edbury (Aldershot, 2001), 98–9.

25 Machaut, *Capture*, 96–8, 102–4; Makhairas, *Recital*, 1: §§297–300.

26 'Amadi', 502–5, 507; Makhairas, *Recital*, 1: §§661–7, 673, 676, 683; J. Pahlitzsch, 'The Mamluks and Cyprus: Transcultural Relations between Muslim and Christian Rulers in the Eastern Mediterranean in the Fifteenth Century', in *Acteurs des transferts culturels en Méditerranée médiévale. Ateliers des Deutschen Historischen Instituts Paris*, ed. R. Abdellatif, Y. Benhima, D. König and E. Ruchaud (Paris, 2010), 113.

27 Ouerfelli, 'Relations', 342 and note 84; M. Ziada, 'The Mamluk Conquest of Cyprus in the Fifteenth Century', *Bulletin of the Faculty of Arts*, 2 pt.1 (1934), 50–1, 50 note 1.

28 *Pero Tafur and Cyprus*, trans. C. I. Nepaulsingh (New York, 1997), 12–17; A. D. Stuart, *The Armenian Kingdom and the Mamluks: War and Diplomacy during the Reigns of Het'um II (1289–1307)* (Leiden, 2001), 72; Holt, *Near East*, 186, 188–9.

29 *Chypre dans les sources arabes médiévales*, ed. T. Mansouri (Nicosia, 2001), 95; B. Arbel, 'The Cypriot Nobility from the Fourteenth to the Sixteenth Century: A New Interpreatation', in *Latins and Greeks in the Eastern Mediterranean after 1204*, ed. B. Arbel, B. Hamilton and D. Jacoby (London, 1989), 189–90; Y. Frenkel, 'Public Projection of Power in Mamluk Bilad al-Sham',

Mamluk Studies Review, 11 (2007), 39–53; N. Iorga, *Notes et extraits pour servir à l'histoire des croisades au XVe siècle*, 3 vols (Paris, 1899–1902), 1:525–6.

30 *Chypre dans les sources arabes*, 89–91, 94–5; Ziada, 'Mamluk Conquest', 55–8; Hill, *History*, 3: 555–7; George Boustronios, *A Narrative of the Chronicle of Cyprus 1456–1489*, trans. N. Coureas (Nicosia, 2005), §§40–2; Fuess, 'Mamluk Protectorate', 18.

31 Boustronios, *Narrative*, §§88–90; *Chypre dans les sources arabes*, 94–5; P. Edbury, 'The Last Lusignans (1432–1489): A Political History', *Epeterida Kentrou Epistemonikon Ereunon* (henceforth EKEE), 36 (2011–12), 193 and notes 134–5, 204; Hill, *History*, 3:1159.

32 Boustronios, *Narrative*, §§111–12, 120, 132, 149; Otten, *Une enquête*, 141–2, 235 note 7; Mas Latrie, *Histoire*, 3:127 note 3.

33 Mas Latrie, *Histoire*, 405–6; Ashtor, *Levant Trade*, 458–9; B. Arbel, 'The Last Decades of Venice's Trade with the Mamluks: Importations into Egypt and Syria', *Mamluk Studies Review*, 8 (2004), 54; Hill, *History*, 3:606–6, 609, 725.

34 Hill, *History*, 3:609–12, 731 note 1, 741 and note 4; Boustronios, *Narrative*, §§278–9; Mas Latrie, *Histoire*, 3:431–5.

35 'Documents nouveaux servant de preuves à l'Histoire de l'île de Chypre sous le règne des princes de la maison de Lusignan', ed. L. de Mas Latrie, *Mélanges historiques*, 4 (1882), 518–21; *idem, Histoire*, 3:442 note 1, 444, 472–81; Hill, *History*, 3:739, 741, 821–4; A. Navagero, 'Historia Veneziana', in *Rerum Italicarum Scriptores*, ed. L.A. Muratori, 25 vols (Milan, 1723–51), 23: col. 1199; *Ambasciata straordinaria al sultanato d'Egitto*, ed. F. Rossi (Venice, 1988), 21–34, 254–5, 259–64.

36 Mas Latrie, *Histoire*, 3:443; Shai Har-El, *Struggle for Dominion in the Middle East: The Ottoman-Mamluk War 1485–1491* (Leiden, 1995), 197–200; N. Housley, *The Later Crusades from Lyon to Alcazar 1274–1580* (Oxford, 1992), 114.

37 Mas Latrie, *Histoire*, 2:201, 215; 'Anonymous Englishman', in *Supplementary Excerpts on Cyprus*, trans. Th. Mogabgab, 2 pts (Nicosia, 1941–43), pt 2:57; T. Buquet, 'Le guépard medieval, ou comment reconnaître un animal sans nom', *Reynardus, Yearbook of the International Reynard Society*, 23 (2010–11), 12–19; *idem*, 'Animalia extranea et stupenda ad videndium: Describing and Naming Exotic Beasts in the Cairo Sultan's Menagerie', in *Animals and Otherness in the Middle Ages: Perspectives Across Disciplines*, ed. F. de Ais Garcia Garcia, M. Ann Walker Vadillo and M. Victoria Chico Picazza, BAR International Series 2500 (Oxford, 2013), 31.

38 A. Borg, *Cypriot Arabic* (Stuttgart, 1985), 5–6, 150–1; *idem, Comparative Glossary of Cypriot Maronite Arabic (Arabic-English)* with an introductory essay by A. Borg (Leiden, Boston, 2004), xix–xxiii, 17–18; Edbury, *Kingdom*, 16–18.

39 W. Rudt de Collenberg, 'Les Ibelin aux XIIIe et XIVe siècles: Généalogie compilée principalement selon les registres du Vatican', *EKEE* IX (1977–79), 119, 157–8; *idem*, 'Les Lusignan de Chypre: Généalogie compilée principalement selon les registres de l'archivio segreto Vaticano et les manuscrits de la biblioteca Vaticana', *EKEE* X (1979–80), 288–9; *Syntagma Byzantinon Pegon Kypriakes Historias, 4os–15os aionas*, ed. V. Nerantzi-Varmazi (Nicosia, 1996), 159; for English translation see H. Pohlsander, 'An Anthology of Greek Texts of the Fourteenth and Fifteenth Centuries relating to Cyprus', in George Boustronios, *A Narrative of the Chronicle of Cyprus 1456–1489*, ed. N. Coureas (Nicosia, 2005), 233; Pahlitzsch, 'Mamluks and Cyprus', 116; Makhairas, *Recital*, I: §693.

40 *Notai Genovesi in Oltremare: Atti rogati a Cipro da Lamberto di Sambuceto (3 luglio–3 agosto 1301)*, ed. V. Polonio, Collana Storica di Fonti e Studi (henceforth CSFS) 31 (Genoa, 1982), nos 128 and 262; *Notai Genovesi in Oltremare: Atti rogati a Cipro da Lamberto di Sambuceto (6 luglio–27 Ottobre 1301)*, ed. R. Pavoni, CSFS 32 (Genoa, 1982), no. 13; *Notai Genovesi in Oltremare: Atti rogati a Cipro da Lameto di Sambuceto (11 Ottobre 1296–23 Giugno 1299)*, ed. M. Balard, CSFS 39 (Genoa, 1983), nos 27 and 121; *Chronaca del Templare del Tiro (1243–1314)*, ed. L. Minervini (Naples, 2000), 1–3 and §§74–5[310–11], 249[485] and 363[599]; Crawford, *'Templar of Tyre'*, 2–7 and §§310–11, 485, 599; *Nicola de Boateriis, notaio in Famagusta e Venezia (1355–1365)*, ed. A. Lombardo (Venice, 1973), no. 70; *Genova e Cipro: L'inchiesta su*

Pietro di Marco, capitano di Genova in Famagosta (1448–1449), ed. S. Fossati-Raiteri, CSFS 41 (Genoa, 1984), nos 32–3, 277 (9); G. Grivaud, *Entrelacs Chiprois: Essai sur les letters et la vie intellectuelle dans le royaume de Chypre 1191–1570* (Nicosia, 2009), 65, 104–13; Otten, *Une enquête*, 190–1, 207, 240; *The Synodicum Nicosiense and other Documents of the Latin Church of Cyprus 1196–1373*, ed. C. Schabel (Nicosia, 2001), 248–9; *Excerpta Cypria: Materials for a History of Cyprus*, trans. C. D. Cobham (Cambridge, 1908), 17; Nerantzi-Varmazi, *Syntagma*, 167; Boustronios, *Narrative*, §59; Pohlsander, 'Anthology', 239.

41 CSFS 41, nos. 13–14, 16; Grivaud, *Entrelacs*, 31, 81–2; *Anekdota engrapha tes kypriakes historias apo to kratiko arkheio tes Venetias*, ed. Aik. Aristeidou, 4 vols (Nicosia, 1990–2003), IV, no. 137.

42 H.-R. d'Allemagne, 'Note on a Brass Basin made for Hugh IV, King of Cyprus 1324–1361', in C. Enlart, *Gothic Art and the Renaissance in Cyprus*, trans. D. Hunt (London, 1987), 511–19; A. Weyl-Carr, 'Art in the Court of the Lusignan Kings', in *Cyprus and the Crusades*, ed. N. Coureas and J. Riley-Smith (Nicosia, 1985), 246–50; N. Coureas, 'Cultural Brokers at the Court of Lusignan Cyprus', in *Cultural Brokers at Mediterranean Courts in the Middle Ages*, ed. M. von der Höh, N. Jaspert and J. R. Oesterle (Paderborn, 2013), 237–8; U. Ritzerfeld, 'Made in Cyprus? Fourteenth Century Mamluk Metal Ware for the West – The Question of Provenance', in *The Harbour of All this Sea and Realm: Crusader to Venetian Famagusta*, ed. M. J. K. Walsh, T. Kiss and N. S. H. Coureas (Budapest, 2014), 107–33.

43 N. Coureas, 'The Role of Cyprus in Provisioning the Latin Churches of the Holy Land in the Thirteenth and Early Fourteenth Centuries', in *Egypt and Syria in the Fatimid, Ayyubid and Mamluk Eras*, vol. 5, ed. U. Vermeulen and K. D'Hulster (Leuven, 2007), 407–18; J. Dunbabin, *A Hound of God: Pierre de la Palud and the Fourteenth Century Church* (Oxford, 1991), 164–73.

44 N. Coureas, 'Controlled Contacts: The Papacy, the Latin Church of Cyprus and Mamluk Egypt, 1250–1350', in *Egypt and Syria in the Fatimid, Ayyubid and Mamluk Eras*, vol. 4, ed. U. Vermeulen and J. van Steenbergen (Leuven, 2005), 401–7; *idem, The Latin Church in Cyprus 1313–1378* (Nicosia, 2010), 175–6.

45 Coureas, 'Controlled Contacts', 402; *idem., Latin Church 1313–1378*, 170–1, 177–9.

46 Grivaud, *Entrelacs*, 65; Nerantzi-Varmazi, *Syntagma*, 167; Pohlsander 'Anthology', 239.

47 *Muslim-Christian Polemic during the Crusades: The Letter from the People of Cyprus and Ibn Abi Talib al-Dimashqi's Response*, ed. R. Ebied and D. Thomas (Leiden and Boston, 2005), 1–5.

48 Ebied and Thomas, *Muslim-Christian Polemic*, 5–35.

49 Ibn Taymiyya, *Lettre à un roi croisé (al-Risalat al-Qubrusiyya)*, ed. and trans. J. R. Michaud (Louvain-la-Neuve Tawhid, Lyon, 1995), 87–91, 125–202; D. S. Cucarella, 'Corresponding across Religious Borders: The Letter of Ibn Taymiyya to a Crusader in Cyprus', *Islamochristiana* 36 (2010), 187–212.

50 Schabel, *Synodicum*, 98–9, 136–7, 154–5; *The Assizes of the Lusignan Kingdom of Cyprus*, trans. N. Coureas (Nicosia, 2002), Codex One, §45, Codex Two, §46; D. Jacoby, 'The Economy of the Armenian Kingdom of Cilicia: Some Neglected and Overlooked Aspects', in *La Méditerranée des Armeniens*, ed. C. Mutafian (Paris, 2014), 267–71.

51 D. Jacoby, 'The Rise of a New Emporium in the Eastern Mediterranean: Famagusta in the Late Thirteenth Century', *idem, Studies on the Crusader States and Venetian Expansion* (Northampton, 1989), VIII.

52 J. Richard, 'Le royaume de Chypre et l'embargo sur le commerce avec l'Égypte (fin XIIIe-début XIVe siècle)', *idem, Croisades et Etats latins de l'Orient* (Aldershot, 1992), XVI; Housley, *Avignon Papacy*, 201, 212–13; Ashtor, *Levant Trade*, 39–44; Edbury, *Kingdom*, 133–4; Coureas, 'Controlled Contacts', 400.

53 D. Jacoby, 'Camlet Manufacture and Trade in Cyprus and the Economy of Famagusta from the Thirteenth to the Late Fifteenth Century', in *Medieval and Renaissance Famagusta: Studies in Architecture, Art and History*, ed. M. J. K. Walsh, P. W. Edbury and N. S. H. Coureas (Farnham, 2012), 15–42 and esp. 25–6; N. Coureas, 'The Tribute paid to the Mamluk Sultanate, 1424–1517:

The Perspective from Lusignan and Venetian Cyprus', in *Egypt and Syria in the Fatimid, Ayyubid and Mamluk Eras*, vol 7., ed. U. Vermeulen, K. D'Hulster and J. Van Steenbergen (Leuven, 2013), 364–7, 370.

54 Edbury, *Kingdom*, 151–2; Ashtor, *Levant Trade*, 64–70.

55 Edbury, *Kingdom*, 153–6, 166; D. Jacoby, 'Citoyens, sujets et protégés de Venise et de Gênes en Chypre du XIIIe au XVe siècle', *idem, Recherches sur la Méditerranée orientale du XIIe au XVe siècle* (London, 1979), VI, 161–4, 166–9, 178–83.

56 Mas Latrie, *Histoire*, 2:294 note 1, 306; Ashtor, *Levant Trade*, 99–103; O. R. Constable, *Housing the Stranger in the Mediterranean World: Lodging, Trade and Travel in Late Antiquity and the Middle Ages* (Cambridge, 2003), 252, 270; Jacoby, 'To emporio', 424–5, 430–1.

57 C. Verlinden, 'Marchands chrétiens et juifs dans l'Etat mamelouk au début du XVe siècle d'aprés un notaire vénitien', *Bulletin de l'Institut historique belge de Rome*, 2 (1981), 66, 69–70 and 81; Ashtor, *Levant Trade*, 410, 537 and 539; Jacoby, 'To emporio', 439–40.

58 Mansouri, *Chypre dans les sources arabes*, 101.

59 N. Coureas, 'Trade between Cyprus and the Mamluk Lands in the Fifteenth Century, with special reference to Nicosia and Famagusta', in *Egypt and Syria in the Fatimid, Ayyubid and Mamluk Eras*, vol. 5, ed. U. Vermeulen and K. D'Hulster (Leuven, 2007), 421–7; *idem*, 'Losing the War but Winning the Peace: Cyprus and Mamluk Egypt in the Fifteenth Century', in *Egypt and Syria in the Fatimid, Ayyubid and Mamluk Eras*, vol. 7, ed. U. Vermeulen, K. D'Hulster and J. van Steenbergen (Leuven, 2013), 354–5, 357–8.

60 Coureas, 'Losing the War', 356–9; *idem*, 'Trade', 420–3, 427–33, 438.

61 G. Grivaud, 'Les minorités orientales à Chypre (époques médiévale et moderne)', in *Chypre et la Méditerranée orientale*, ed. Y. Ioannou, F. Métral and M. Yon (Lyon, 2000), 49–50; N. Coureas, 'The Coptic Presence in Cyprus during the Fifteenth and Sixteenth Centuries', in *Egypt and Syria during the Fatimid, Ayyubid and Mamluk Eras*, vol. 5, ed. U. Vermeulen and K. D'Hulster (Leuven, 2007), 439–50.

62 B. Arbel, 'Venetian Cyprus and the Muslim Levant', in *Cyprus and the Crusades*, ed. N. Coureas and J. Riley-Smith (Nicosia, 1995), 174–7; N. Coureas, 'Mamluks in the Cypriot Chronicle of George Boustronios and their Place within a Wider Context', in *Continuity and Change in the Realms of Islam: Studies in Honour of Professor Urbain Vermeulen*, ed. K. D'Hulster and J. van Steenbergen (Leuven, 2008), 145–8.

63 Hill, *History*, 2:167; Mas Latrie, *Histoire*, 2:212; *The Trial of the Templars in Cyprus: A Complete English Edition*, ed. A Gilmour-Bryson (Leiden, 1998), 67–8.

64 'Amadi', 498–9, 512–14; Makhairas, *Recital*, 1:§677; Ziada, 'Mamluk Conquest', 91, 94, 98, 104; Hill, *History*, 2: 469–70, 470 note 1, 472 note 5, 474 and note 1; Ashtor, *Levant Trade*, 225; Ouerfelli, 'Relations', 333–4.

REFERENCES

Primary sources

Ambasciata straordinaria al sultanato d'Egitto, ed. F. Rossi, Venice, 1988

Anekdota engrapha tes kypriakes historias apo to kratiko arkheio tes Venetias, ed. Aik. Aristeidou, 4 vols, Nicosia, 1990–2003, 4

The Assizes of the Lusignan Kingdom of Cyprus, trans. N. Coureas, Nicosia, 2002

Chypre dans les sources arabes médiévales, ed. T. Mansouri, Nicosia, 2001

'Documents nouveaux servant de preuves à l'Histoire de l'île de Chypre sous le règne des princes de la maison de Lusignan', ed. L. de Mas Latrie, *Mélanges historiques*, 4 (1882)

Early Mamluk Diplomacy (1260–1290) Treaties of Baybars and Qalawun with Christian Rulers, ed. P. M. Holt, Leiden, 1995

Excerpta Cypria: Materials for a History of Cyprus, trans. C. D. Cobham, Cambridge, 1908

Excerpta Cypria Nova, ed. G. Grivaud, vol. 1, Nicosia, 1990

Genova e Cipro: L'inchiesta su Pietro di Marco, capitano di Genova in Famagosta (1448–1449), ed. S. Fossati-Raiteri, CSFS 41, Genoa, 1984

Muslim-Christian Polemic during the Crusades: The Letter from the People of Cyprus and Ibn Abi Talib al-Dimashqi's Response, ed. R. Ebied and D. Thomas, Leiden and Boston, 2005

Nicola de Boateriis, notaio in Famagusta e Venezia (1355–1365), ed. A. Lombardo, Venice, 1973

Notai Genovesi in Oltremare: Atti rogati a Cipro da Lamberto di Sambuceto (3 luglio–3 agosto 1301), ed. V. Polonio, Collana Storica di Fonti e Studi (henceforth CSFS) 31, Genoa, 1982

Notai Genovesi in Oltremare: Atti rogati a Cipro da Lamberto di Sambuceto (6 luglio–27 Ottobre 1301), ed. R. Pavoni, CSFS 32, Genoa, 1982

Notai Genovesi in Oltremare: Atti rogati a Cipro da Lambeto di Sambuceto (11 Ottobre 1296–23 Giugno 1299), ed. M. Balard, CSFS 39, Genoa, 1983

The Synodicum Nicosiense and other Documents of the Latin Church of Cyprus 1196–1373, ed. C. Schabel, Nicosia, 2001

Syntagma Byzantinon Pegon Kypriakes Historias, 4os–15os aionas, ed. V. Nerantzi-Varmazi, Nicosia, 1996

The Trial of the Templars in Cyprus: A Complete English Edition, ed. A Gilmour-Bryson, Leiden, 1998

Une enquête à Chypre au XVe siècle: Le Sindicamentum de Napoleone Lomellini, capitaine génois de Famagouste (1459), ed. C. Otten-Froux, Nicosia, 2000

Chronicles and narrative accounts

'Anonymous Englishman', in *Supplementary Excerpts on Cyprus*, trans. Th. Mogabgab, 2 pts, Nicosia, 1941–43, pt. 2

'An Anthology of Greek Texts of the Fourteenth and Fifteenth Centuries relating to Cyprus', ed. H. Pohlsander, in George Boustronios, *A Narrative of the Chronicle of Cyprus 1456–1489*, ed. N. Coureas, Nicosia, 2005

Chronaca del Templare del Tiro (1243–1314), ed. L. Minervini, Naples, 2000

'Chronique d'Amadi', in *Chroniques d' Amadi et de Strambaldi*, ed. R. de Mas Latrie, 2 vols, Paris, 1891–93

George Boustronios, *A Narrative of the Chronicle of Cyprus 1456–1489*, trans. N. Coureas, Nicosia, 2005

Guillaume de Machaut, *The Capture of Alexandria*, trans. J. Shirley, introduction and notes P. Edbury, Aldershot, 2001

Ibn Taymiyya, *Lettre à un roi croisé (al-Risalat al-Qubrusiyya)*, ed. and trans. J. R. Michaud, Louvain-la-Neuve, Tawhid, Lyon, 1995

Leontios Makhairas, *Recital Concerning the Sweet Land of Cyprus, Entitled 'Chronicle'*, ed. R. M. Dawkins, 2 vols, Oxford, 1932

Marino Sanudo Torsello, *The Book of the Secrets of the Faithful of the Cross: Liber Secretorum Fidelium Crucis*, trans. P. Lock, Farnham, 2011

Pero Tafur and Cyprus, trans. C. I. Nepaulsingh, New York, 1997

The 'Templar of Tyre' Part III of the 'Deeds of the Cypriots', ed. P. Crawford, Aldershot, 2003

Secondary works

Allemagne, H.-R. d', 'Note on a Brass Basin made for Hugh IV, King of Cyprus 1324–1361', in C. Enlart, *Gothic Art and the Renaissance in Cyprus*, trans. D. Hunt, London, 1987

Arbel, B., 'The Cypriot Nobility from the Fourteenth to the Sixteenth Century: A New Interpretation', in *Latins and Greeks in the Eastern Mediterranean after 1204*, ed. B. Arbel, B. Hamilton and D. Jacoby, London, 1989

———— 'Venetian Cyprus and the Muslim Levant', in *Cyprus and the Crusades*, ed. N. Coureas and J. Riley-Smith, Nicosia, 1995

———— 'The Last Decades of Venice's Trade with the Mamluks: Importations into Egypt and Syria', *Mamluk Studies Review*, 8 (2004)

Ashtor, E., *Levant Trade in the Later Middle Ages*, Princeton, 1983

Borg, A., *Cypriot Arabic*, Stuttgart, 1985

———— *Comparative Glossary of Cypriot Maronite Arabic (Arabic-English)* with an introductory essay by A. Borg, Leiden and Boston, 2004

Buquet, T., 'Le guépard medieval, ou comment reconnaître un animal sans nom', *Reynardus, Yearbook of the International Reynard Society*, 23 (2010–11)

———— '*Animalia extranea et stupenda ad videndum*: Describing and Naming Exotic Beasts in the Cairo Sultan's Menagerie', in *Animals and Otherness in the Middle Ages: Perspectives Across Disciplines*, ed. F. de Ais Garcia Garcia, M. Ann Walker Vadillo and M. Victoria Chico Picazza, BAR International Series 2500, Oxford, 2013

Claverie, P.-V., 'L' Ambassade au Caire de Philippe Mainebeuf (1291)', in *Egypt and Syria in the Fatimid, Ayyubid and Mamluk Eras*, vol. 7, ed. U. Vermeulen and J. van Steenbergen, Leuven, 2005

Constable, O. R., *Housing the Stranger in the Mediterranean World: Lodging, Trade and Travel in Late Antiquity and the Middle Ages*, Cambridge, 2003

Coureas, N., *The Latin Church of Cyprus, 1195–1312*, Aldershot, 1997

———— 'Controlled Contacts: The Papacy, the Latin Church of Cyprus and Mamluk Egypt, 1250–1350', in *Egypt and Syria in the Fatimid, Ayyubid and Mamluk Eras*, vol. 4, ed. U. Vermeulen and J. van Steenbergen, Leuven, 2005

———— 'The Coptic Presence in Cyprus during the Fifteenth and Sixteenth Centuries', in *Egypt and Syria during the Fatimid, Ayyubid and Mamluk Eras*, vol. 5, ed. U. Vermeulen and K. D'Hulster, Leuven, 2007

———— 'The Role of Cyprus in Provisioning the Latin Churches of the Holy Land in the Thirteenth and Early Fourteenth Centuries', in *Egypt and Syria in the Fatimid, Ayyubid and Mamluk Eras*, vol. 5, ed. U. Vermeulen and K. D'Hulster, Leuven, 2007

———— 'Trade between Cyprus and the Mamluk Lands in the Fifteenth Century, with Special Reference to Nicosia and Famagusta', in *Egypt and Syria in the Fatimid, Ayyubid and Mamluk Eras*, vol. 5, ed. U. Vermeulen and K. D'Hulster, Leuven, 2007

———— 'Mamluks in the Cypriot Chronicle of George Boustronios and their Place within a Wider Context', in *Continuity and Change in the Realms of Islam: Studies in Honour of Professor Urbain Vermeulen*, ed. K. D'Hulster and J. van Steenbergen, Leuven, 2008

———— *The Latin Church in Cyprus 1313–1378*, Nicosia, 2010

———— 'Cultural Brokers at the Court of Lusignan Cyprus', in *Cultural Brokers at Mediterranean Courts in the Middle Ages*, ed. M. von der Höh, N. Jaspert and J. R. Oesterle, Paderborn, 2013

———— 'Losing the War but Winning the Peace: Cyprus and Mamluk Egypt in the Fifteenth Century', in *Egypt and Syria in the Fatimid, Ayyubid and Mamluk Eras*, vol. 7, ed. U. Vermeulen, K. D'Hulster and J. van Steenbergen, Leuven, 2013

———— 'The Tribute Paid to the Mamluk Sultanate, 1424–1517: The Perspective from Lusignan and Venetian Cyprus', in *Egypt and Syria in the Fatimid, Ayyubid and Mamluk Eras*, vol. 7, ed. U. Vermeulen, K. D'Hulster and J. Van Steenbergen, Leuven, 2013

Cucarella, D. S., 'Corresponding across Religious Borders: The Letter of Ibn Taymiyya to a Crusader in Cyprus', *Islamochristiana* 36 (2010)

Dunbabin, J., *A Hound of God: Pierre de la Palud and the Fourteenth Century Church*, Oxford, 1991

Edbury, P. W., *The Kingdom of Cyprus and the Crusades 1191–1374*, 1991; 2nd edn, 1994

———— 'The Crusading Policy of King Peter I of Cyprus', in *idem*, *Kingdoms of the Crusaders from Jerusalem to Cyprus*, Aldershot, 1999, XII

———— 'The Murder of King Peter I of Cyprus', in *idem, Kingdoms of the Crusaders from Jerusalem to Cyprus*, Aldershot, 1999, XIII

———— 'Cyprus and Genoa: the Origins of the War of 1373–1374', in *idem, Kingdoms of the Crusaders from Jerusalem to Cyprus*, Aldershot, 1999, XIV

———— 'The Aftermath of Defeat: Lusignan Cyprus and the Genoese, 1374–1382', in *idem, Kingdoms of the Crusaders from Jerusalem to Cyprus*, Aldershot, 1999, XV.

————'The Last Lusignans (1432–1489): A Political History', *Epeterida Kentrou Epistemonikon Ereunon* (henceforth EKEE), 36 (2011–12)

Forey, A., 'Cyprus as a Base for Crusading Expeditions from the West', in *Cyprus and the Crusades*, ed. N. Coureas and J. Riley-Smith, Nicosia, 1995

Frenkel, Y., 'Public Projection of Power in Mamluk Bilad al-Sham', *Mamluk Studies Review*, 11 (2007)

Fuess, A., 'Rotting Ships and Razed Harbours: The Naval Policy of the Mamluks', *Mamluk Studies Review*, 5 (2001)

———— 'Was Cyprus a Mamluk Protectorate? Mamluk Policies towards Cyprus between 1426 and 1517', *Journal of Cyprus Studies*, 11 (2005)

Grivaud, G., 'Les minorités orientales à Chypre (époques médiévale et moderne)', in *Chypre et la Méditerranée orientale*, ed. Y. Ioannou, F. Métral and M. Yon, Lyon, 2000

———— *Entrelacs Chiprois: Essai sur les letters et la vie intellectuelle dans le royaume de Chypre 1191–1570*, Nicosia, 2009

Hill, G., *A History of Cyprus*, 4 vols, Cambridge, 1940–1952, 2 and 3

Holt, P. M., *The Age of the Crusades: The Near East from the Eleventh Century to 1517*, London and New York, 1986

Housley, N., *The Avignon Papacy and the Crusades 1305–1378*, Oxford, 1986

———— *The Later Crusades from Lyon to Alcazar 1274–1580*, Oxford, 1992

Iorga, N., *Notes et extraits pour servir à l'histoire des croisades au XVe siècle*, 3 vols, Paris, 1899–1902

Irwin, R., 'Hoi eisboles ton Mameloukon sten Kypro', in *Historia tes Kyprou*, IV, *Mesaionikon Basileion, Henetokratia*, ed. Th. Papadopoullos, Nicosia, 1995

Jacoby, D., 'Citoyens, sujets et protégés de Venise et de Gênes en Chypre du XIIIe au XVe siècle', in *idem, Recherches sur la Méditerranée orientale du XIIe au XVe siècle*, London, 1979, VI

———— 'The Rise of a New Emporium in the Eastern Mediterranean: Famagusta in the Late Thirteenth Century', *idem, Studies on the Crusader States and Venetian Expansion*, Northampton, 1989, VIII

———— 'To emporio kai he oikonomia tes Kyprou', in *Historia tes Kyprou*, IV, *Mesaionikon Basileion, Henetokratia*, ed. Th. Papadopoullos, Nicosia, 1995

———— 'Camlet Manufacture and Trade in Cyprus and the Economy of Famagusta from the Thirteenth to the Late Fifteenth Century', in *Medieval and Renaissance Famagusta: Studies in Architecture, Art and History*, ed. M. J. K. Walsh, P. W. Edbury and N. S. H. Coureas, Farnham, 2012

———— 'The Economy of the Armenian Kingdom of Cilicia: Some Neglected And overlooked Aspects', in *La Méditerranée des Armeniens*, ed. C. Mutafian, Paris, 2014

Luttrell, A., 'The Hospitallers in Cyprus after 1291', in *Praktika tou Protou Diethnous Kyprologikou Synedriou*, 3 vols, Nicosia, 1972

Marshall, C., *Warfare in the Latin East 1192–1291*, Cambridge, 1992; 2nd edn, 1994

Mas Latrie, L. de, *Histoire de l'île de Chypre sous le règne des princes de la maison de Lusignan*, 3 vols, Paris, 1852–61, 2 and 3

Navagero, A., 'Historia Veneziana', in *Rerum Italicarum Scriptores*, ed. L. A. Muratori, 25 vols, Milan, 1723–51

Ouerfelli, M., 'Les relations entre le royaume de Chypre et le sultanat mamelouke au XVe siècle', *Le moyen Age*, Tome CX, 2 (2004)

Pahlitzsch, J., 'The Mamluks and Cyprus: Transcultural Relations between Muslim and Christian Rulers in the Eastern Mediterranean in the Fifteenth Century', in *Acteurs des transferts culturels en Méditerranée médiévale. Ateliers des Deutschen Historischen Instituts Paris*, ed. R. Abdellatif, Y. Benhima, D. König and E. Ruchaud, Paris, 2010

Richard, J., 'Le royaume de Chypre et l'embargo sur le commerce avec l'Égypte (fin XIIIe-début XIVe siècle)', *idem, Croisades et Etats latins de l'Orient*, Aldershot, 1992, XVI

——— 'La révolution de 1369 dans le royaume de Chypre', in *idem, Orient et Occident au Moyen Age: contacts et relations (XIIe-XVe s.)*, 3rd edn, Aldershot, 1997, XVI

Riley-Smith, J., *The Knights of St John in Jerusalem and Cyprus, 1050–1310*, London, 1967

Ritzerfeld, U., 'Made in Cyprus? Fourteenth Century Mamluk Metal Ware for the West – The Question of Provenance', in *The Harbour of All this Sea and Realm: Crusader to Venetian Famagusta*, ed. M. J. K. Walsh, T. Kiss and N. S. H. Coureas, Budapest, 2014

Rudt de Collenberg, W., 'Les Ibelin aux XIIIe et XIVe siècles: Généalogie compilée principalement selon les registres du Vatican', *EKEE* 9 (1977–79)

——— 'Les Lusignan de Chypre: Généalogie compilée principalement selon les registres de l'archivio segreto Vaticano et les manuscrits de la biblioteca Vaticana', *EKEE* X (1979–80)

Schein, S., *Fideles Crucis, The Papacy, the West and the Recovery of the Holy Land, 1274–1314*, Oxford, 1991

Shai Har-El, *Struggle for Dominion in the Middle East: The Ottoman-Mamluk War 1485–1491*, Leiden, 1995

Stuart, A. D., *The Armenian Kingdom and the Mamluks: War and Diplomacy during the Reigns of Het'um II (1289–1307)*, Leiden, 2001

Thorau, P., *The Lion of Egypt: Sultan Baybars and the Near East in the Thirteenth Century*, London and New York, 1987

van Steenbergen, J., 'The Alexandrian Crusade (1365) and the Mamluk Sources: Reassessment of the *kitab al-ilmam* of an-Nuwayri al-Iskandarani', in *East and West in the Crusader States, Context-Contacts-Confrontations*, ed. K. Cigaar and H. Teule, Peeters, 2003

Verlinden, C., 'Marchands chrétiens et juifs dans l'Etat mamelouk au début du XVe siècle d'aprés un notaire vénitien', *Bulletin de l'Institut historique belge de Rome*, 2 (1981)

Weyl-Carr, A., 'Art in the Court of the Lusignan Kings', in *Cyprus and the Crusades*, ed. N. Coureas and J. Riley-Smith, Nicosia, 1985

Ziada, M., 'The Mamluk Conquest of Cyprus in the Fifteenth Century', *Bulletin of the Faculty of Arts*, 2 pt.1 (1934)

CHAPTER TWENTY-FIVE

CHRISTIAN MERCENARIES IN MUSLIM LANDS: THEIR STATUS IN MEDIEVAL ISLAMIC AND CANON LAW

———•◆•———

Michael Lower

Many Latin Christian mercenaries fought for Muslim regimes during the classic era of crusading. Some were prominent exiles, waiting for the political winds to shift back in their favor at home. Others were true soldiers of fortune, who sought riches beyond the borders of Christendom. Most were fighters with expertise in particular forms of warfare—heavy cavalry combat, naval operations, artillery (especially the crossbow), and demolition—that made them attractive to Muslim rulers looking to diversify their armed forces. They were popular for other reasons as well. Their status as Christians made them useful for carrying out politically sensitive tasks, such as collecting taxes, and for providing disinterested protection to the ruler, whom they often served as personal bodyguards. These mercenaries usually fought in internecine struggles between Islamic states, especially in Anatolia, North Africa, and al-Andalus (Richard, 1952: 174). Sometimes, though, they found themselves opposing crusader armies. This was the case in 1270, when Abu ʿAbd-Allah Muhammad al-Mustansir, emir of Tunis, deployed his elite Catalan guard against King Louis IX of France's forces during the future saint's ill-fated final campaign (Lower, 2006: 508).

It is easy to see the Christian mercenary in Islamic lands as a transgressive figure, whose search for fame, fortune, or just a decent livelihood drove him to violate widely held ideals on both sides of the religious divide. In some normative Christian literature, he appeared as a traitor. The *Siete partidas* (1972: III, 139; Burns, 2001: IV, 997), the thirteenth-century Castilian law code, condemned him for twofold treason—to the realm and to Christianity. Muslim rulers who hired Christian mercenaries could encounter disapproval as well. An early fourteenth-century emir of Tunis, Ibn al-Lihyani, was walking down the street one day, surrounded as usual by his Christian bodyguard, when he was spotted by the pious ascetic al-Qarawi, who ran up to him and shouted, "O faqih Abu Yahya, that is not permitted!" Because they had once studied together, al-Lihyani stopped and asked him what he meant. Al-Qarawi reminded the emir of an ancient Maliki prescription: "God has forbidden seeking the aid of a polytheist" (Brunschvig, 1940–47: I, 447). In Christian and Islamic legal traditions that offered crusade and jihad as the default stance of each faith toward the other, there would seem to be little room for accommodating the mercenary who took up service for a religious rival.

Given how entrenched interreligious mercenary warfare was in medieval Mediterranean culture, it is important to take a closer look at the legal theory that developed around it. Once we move beyond the stern admonition of the *Siete partidas* and al-Lihyani's awkward encounter in the streets of Tunis, we find a surprising diversity of opinion among the Christian canonists and Muslim jurists who analyzed interfaith military collaboration. Far from condemning the Christian mercenary as a kind of anti-crusader and his Muslim employer as a betrayer of the jihad, the traditions afforded both parties considerable flexibility in their dealings with each other. This generally accommodating stance provided the context in which the thriving Mediterranean mercenary market of the Central and Later Middle Ages developed. It also raises a larger question about the relationship between norms and practice in that world. Thanks to the work of David Nirenberg (1996) and others, it is widely recognized that religious boundaries were far from impermeable in the rough and tumble ports of the medieval Mediterranean. Medieval Mediterranean merchants, craftspeople, mariners, and even soldiers enthusiastically crossed religious borders in the name of profit or a living wage. It is often assumed that these crossings took place against a backdrop of official condemnation, or at least disapproval. Even as interreligious contact flourished, religious authorities are thought to have maintained formal ideologies of separation, division, and conflict. The mercenary case, however, raises an intriguing possibility: could these authorities have actually encouraged rather than inhibited the cross-cultural contact that allowed Christian mercenaries to spread far and wide in Islamic lands?

ISLAMIC JURISPRUDENCE ON MILITARY ASSISTANCE FROM NON-MUSLIMS

The questions of how, to what extent, and for what reward non-Muslim troops might collaborate with Muslim armies went back to the earliest days of Islam. As Islamic tradition stressed, Muhammad's first efforts to build up a religious movement in Medina involved a complex series of accommodations and confrontations with the major Jewish tribes of the city and the pagan Quraysh of Mecca (Donner, 2010: 43–50). The result was a corpus of traditions that described the Prophet as rejecting military assistance from non-believers on some occasions and accepting it on others. This diversity among the Prophetic *hadith*s supported contrasting stances among the early Muslim jurists on the legitimacy of seeking military aid from non-believers.

Wadad al-Qadi (2004) lists five Prophetic *hadith*s that show Muhammad refusing help from non-Muslims for his military campaigns. Three of these were thematically linked and, as Luke Yarbrough (2015) has argued, shared a common origin in eighth-century Medina. The most widely circulated of these Medinese *hadith*s was traced back to 'A'isha, the Prophet's wife, and told of a polytheist (*mushrik*) who approached Muhammad as he was on his way out to Badr, where he and his followers would attack a caravan organized by the Quraysh of Mecca in 624. When the polytheist asked if he could join the raiding party, Muhammad replied with a question of his own: did he believe in God and his Prophet? The man said no, so the Prophet told him to go back from where he came, declaring: "I will not seek the assistance of a polytheist." Sometime later, the same man again approached Muhammad, who was taking shade under a tree. They repeated the conversation they had on the way to Badr. Finally, they met for a third time in the desert, and the man proclaimed his belief in God and his Messenger, to which Muhammad replied, "Come along then" (Sahnun, 1994: I, 525). A year later, the Meccans launched an attack on Medina that resulted in defeat for Muhammad and his followers at the battle of Uhud (625). In a *hadith* from Sa'd b. al-Mundhir, it was reported that on his way out to the battle, the Prophet saw a fine squadron and asked who they were. When told they were 'Abd-Allah b. Ubayy b. Salul and his clients among the Banu Qaynuqa', a Jewish tribe, the Prophet urged them to convert to Islam. After they refused, he turned them away, saying: "We will not seek the assistance of polytheists against polytheists" (al-Tahawi, 1996: VI, 417). The Prophet delivered the same message to the grandfather of Khubayb b. 'Abd al-Rahman b. Khubayb, who approached Muhammad with another man from his tribe before a raid and expressed shame that their tribe would fight without them because they had yet to embrace Islam. In this *hadith*, once the Prophet had told them that he would not "seek the assistance of polytheists against polytheists," Khubayb converted and went on to fight in the battle, thus reconciling his martial and spiritual values (al-Tahawi, 1994: VI, 407–419). The two final *hadith*s in which Muhammad spurns assistance from non-believers used different language to express this rejection. In a *hadith* from al-Zuhri, the Prophet said, "We do not need them," when his Medinese supporters asked if they should call on their Jewish allies to fight with them at the battle of Uhud (Sahnun, 1994: I, 525); and he declared that "booty was not licit for anyone before us" in a tradition related by Abu Hurayra—a statement that some later jurists would interpret as prohibiting non-Muslims from sharing in the spoils of battle (Ibn Hazm, 1964: VII, 391).

On the basis of these *hadith*s, the Maliki school of jurisprudence that flourished in medieval North Africa came to oppose military collaboration with non-believers. Because Malik b. Anas, the school's eponymous founder, did not comment on the issue in his *Muwatta*, it was left to the other formative figure of Maliki *fiqh*, Sahnun b. Sa'id, to stake out the *madhhab*'s position. Citing 'A'isha's *hadith* about the polytheist of Badr and al-Zuhri's about the Prophet rejecting Jewish help before Uhud, Sahnun stated that Muslims may not call upon the aid of polytheists, but added two qualifications: "unless they are sailors (*nawatiyya*) or servants (*khadam*), for I see no objection to that" (Sahnun, 1994: I, 524). As Wadad al-Qadi (2004: 137–144) has shown, early Muslim fleets employed Egyptian Copts as sailors, who manned the ships and left the actual fighting to the Muslims. Sahnun may have carved out an exception for sailors to his general ban on interreligious military alliances with this practice in mind. Prestige may have been a factor as well. By lumping the sailors together with the servants, Sahnun suggested that while non-believers could perform low-status tasks for the armed forces, the glories of combat should be reserved for the Muslims.

Later Maliki jurists adhered to Sahnun's strictures, loosening them only a little over the course of centuries. Ibn Abi Zayd al-Qayrawani (922–96) added to Sahnun's list of acceptable ways for non-Muslims to assist Muslim armies. In his *Kitab al-Nawadir*, a major compendium of Maliki *fiqh*, Ibn Abi Zayd proposed that non-Muslims could also demolish strongholds, shoot siege artillery, and make useful things. In addition, if the Imam made peace with some residents of the house of war (*dar al-harb*), these *harbi*s could supply him with weapons that he could use to fight other *harbi*s with whom he was at war (Von Bredow, 1994: 29).

This idea of auxiliary support on the fringes of the Muslim war effort found its fullest expression in the legal writing of Ibn Rushd al-Jadd (1058–1126), the Andalusian Maliki *faqih* and grandfather of the famous philosopher. He posited the case of a group of Christian residents of the house of Islam (*dar al-Islam*) who live near the frontier of the *dar al-harb*. Acting on their own initiative, these *dhimmi*s decide to launch a raid against their *harbi* co-religionists across the border. If the *dhimmi* raiders take plunder during the expedition, should it be subject to the *khums*, the fifth part of the spoils traditionally reserved for the Imam? Ibn Rushd al-Jadd concluded that they might keep all the booty they have taken, provided that they were really raiding on their own, separately from the Muslims. He also envisioned a scenario whereby *dhimmis* could supply weapons to the Imam and even follow along on his campaigns to "urge on" the army, provided that they remained outside the Muslim camp (Ibn Rushd al-Jadd, 1988: III, 5–10).

By maintaining the ban on direct military collaboration between Muslims and non-Muslims while exploring a wide range of secondary support roles for the latter to play, Ibn Rushd al-Jadd pushed against but did not break through the parameters of the Maliki position. The restrictions the school placed on interreligious military alliances remained in place through the Later Middle Ages. In his popular epitome of Maliki law, Khalil b. Ishaq (d. 1365) simply paraphrased Sahnun when summarizing the rules of jihad: "It is forbidden to ask for the aid of polytheists other than for auxiliary services" (Fagnan, 1908: 5).

Another Sunni *madhhab* that came to prominence in the western Mediterranean echoed this view. Ibn Hazm al-Qurtubi (d. 1064), the Andalusian polymath who was central to the juridical and theological innovations of the Zahiri school, argued that Muslim armies could use non-believers only as guides. Like the Maliki jurists, he quoted ʿAʾisha's *hadith* about the polytheist of Badr in support of this restriction. Unlike other jurists who shared his opposition to interreligious military collaboration, however, he also explored a broader corpus of Prophetic traditions relating to non-Muslim participation in Muhammad's campaigns (Ibn Hazm, 1964: VII, 391–392). Although Ibn Hazm would ultimately reject the implications of these *hadith*s on technical grounds, other jurists would use them to argue for the legality of using non-Muslims in direct military roles.

Several of these pro-alliance *hadith*s described Muhammad allowing Jews to fight in his wars. Al-Zuhri reported that when the Prophet used to go raiding with the Jews, he would give to them the same shares of the spoils as the Muslims received (Ibn Hazm, 1964: VII, 391). A *hadith* from al-Waqidi stated that Muhammad also gave ten Medinese Jews an equal share of the plunder after they fought with him at the battle of Khaybar (629) (al-Qadi, 2004: 112). In another unidentified battle, Ibn ʿAbbas related that the (Jewish) Banu Qaynuqaʿ joined the Prophet's forces but received only a little of the booty, not the full shares given to the Muslims (Abu Yusuf, 1938: 40). Some *hadith*s showed polytheists as well as Jews participating in the early Islamic conquests. It was reported on the authority of Abu Hurayra that the Prophet and Abu Bakr hired a polytheist from the tribe of al-Diʾl as a guide to show them along the coastal road (Ibn Hazm, 1964: VII, 392). Safwan b. Umayya was said to have fought at the battle of Hunayn (630) alongside Muslim forces before he embraced Islam himself (al-Shafiʿi, 1961: IV, 261). Finally, a *hadith* that circulated in Hanafi legal scholarship had the Prophet say: "In truth God will aid this [Islamic] religion by means of men who do not have a place in the hereafter" (al-Sarakhsi, 1971: IV, 1422–1423; 1989: III, 56).

For a majority of the key figures in the formative and classical era of Islamic jurisprudence, these texts offered persuasive evidence that the Prophet's habitual practice was to call upon the aid of non-believers in his military campaigns. Among this majority we can include al-Shaʿbi (d. 722–23), Qatada (d. 725), Abu Hanifa (d. 767), al-Awzaʿi (d. 774), Sufyan al-Thawri (d. 778), Abu Yusuf (d. 798), al-Shaybani (d. 805), al-Shafiʿi (d. 820), Abu ʿUbayd al-Qasim b. Sallam (d. 838), al-Tabari (d. 923), al-Tahawi (d. 933), al-Mawardi (d. 1058), al-Sarakhsi (d. 1090), and, according to one report, Ahmad b. Hanbal (d. 855) (Ibn Hazm, 1964: VII, 391–392; Friedmann, 2003: 36; al-Qadi, 2004: 113). These jurists came to approve of military cooperation with non-Muslims, but not without reservations.

They qualified their support for the practice, just as the Maliki and Zahiri legal scholars qualified their opposition.

One of the most important conditions that pro-alliance jurists envisioned for licit military collaboration across religious lines was that Muslims retain overall command of the combined forces. In his *Kitab al-siyar*, the Hanafi jurist Muhammad b. al-Hasan al-Shaybani (1966: 258; 1975: 249) gave his opinion in the form of a dialogue with his master, Abu Hanifa:

> I asked whether there is any harm for the Muslims in seeking the assistance of unbelievers against the inhabitants of the territory of war …

> He replied: There is no harm in seeking their assistance, provided the command is in the hands of the Muslims, but if the command were in the hands of the unbelievers, the Muslims should not participate in the fighting along with unbelievers, unless they were fearful for their safety—[in such cases it would be alright to fight with them] in self-defense.

In his commentary on this passage, Shams al-A'imma al-Sarakhsi, another leading Hanafi jurist, emphasized the subordinate status of the Christian auxiliaries: "We thus understand that there is no harm in asking aid [of non-Muslims]. It resembles the aid that one expects from dogs to fight the unbelievers" (al-Sarakhsi, 1971: IV, 1422–1423; 1989: 56–57). Just as animals could be useful to the war effort, even though they were not Muslims, so too could human non-believers, provided they were tightly controlled.

Another requirement for licitly drawing on non-Muslim military assistance was need. Following al-Shaybani's analysis, fear of the enemy could even justify fighting under non-Muslim command. There is also a discussion of need in this context from Ibn Rushd al-Jadd, the anti-alliance Maliki jurist discussed above. He cited a certain Abu al-Faraj, who in turn quoted Malik b. Anas as saying "that he did not object to the Imam calling on the assistance of polytheists if he had need of it, taking as evidence [the Prophet's] statement to the *ansar* (his Medinese helpers), 'We do not need them'" (Ibn Rushd al-Jadd, 1988: III, 6). This was a reference to al-Zuhri's *hadith*, in which Muhammad gave this answer to his supporters who wondered whether they should ask the Jews for help before Uhud. While usually cited as grounds for opposing interreligious military cooperation, here it served to raise the possibility that on other occasions the Prophet might have required non-Muslim aid.

A seeming corollary to the condition of need was that non-believers bring some benefit to the Muslims when they fought together. Muhammad b. Idris al-Shafi'i (1961: IV, 269–270) was particularly insistent on this. The imam should not allow non-believers who might harm the Muslim cause to participate in his campaigns. He should be especially watchful for hypocrites who might lie to the Muslims, dampen their spirits, and help their enemies instead of them.

If the non-believers had to bring a benefit to the Muslim war effort, what should they receive in return? The relevant Prophetic *hadith*s offered a variety of answers, from no reward at all, to some compensation from the booty, to the full share claimed by the Muslim soldiers. While two Umayyad-era jurists, 'Abd al-Rahman al-Awza'i and Sufyan al-Thawri, argued for full shares, most of the later jurists settled on giving non-Muslims a little reward from the plunder (al-Tabari, 1933: 21; 2007: 89–90; al-Qadi, 2004: 115). This policy was not wholly satisfactory to al-Shafi'i, however, who worried about non-Muslims gaining even a little booty when many Muslims who might become involved in military campaigns, such as women and minors, received none. His solution was to call for non-Muslims to be hired, so that they would serve on predetermined terms (al-Shafiʻi, 1961: IV, 261).

Even as al-Shafiʻi permitted the employment of non-Muslim troops, he was aware of the traditions in which the Prophet was said to have rejected the practice. He was perhaps the first jurist to attempt to reconcile the two conflicting sets of proof texts. To do so, he invoked the juridical concept of abrogation (*naskh*), arguing that earlier reports of the Prophet rejecting non-Muslim help at the battles of Badr (624) and Uhud (625) had been superseded by later ones of him accepting it at the battles of Khaybar (629) and Hunayn (630) (al-Shafiʻi, 1961: IV, 261). One difficulty with this chronological approach was that several pro- and anti-alliance *hadith*s were not linked to a particular episode in the Prophet's biography. The a-temporal quality of some of the *hadith*s (e.g. "God will aid this religion by means of sinners") encouraged later jurists to harmonize the conflicting traditions on less technical grounds. Luke Yarbrough (2015) discusses two important attempts along these lines. Al-Tahawi (1994: VI, 417–419) distinguished between "seeking assistance" and "fighting with": Muhammad would not ask non-believers to join his forces, but he would fight alongside them if they wound up on the battlefield with him. The fourteenth-century Shiʻa jurist al-ʻAllama al-Hilli maintained that the Prophet's seemingly straightforward statement, "I will not seek the assistance of a polytheist," actually contained two implicit conditions. Muhammad would not seek assistance unless (1) he needed it and (2) he could trust the non-Muslims who offered it. If one of these conditions were lacking, he would turn them away. That was why he rejected Khubayb, for example, in the oft-cited anti-alliance *hadith*. These conditions, presented here as implicit in the Prophet's declaration, featured explicitly in the Hanafi analyses of interreligious military alliances that we reviewed above. The Hanafi stalwart al-Sarakhsi (1971: IV, 1422–1423; 1989: 56–57) explained away the contradictions in the *hadith* corpus by turning to still another qualification: Muslim operational control. Muhammad refused assistance from Jewish fighters on the way to Uhud because they were autonomous and did not want to fight under his banner, but he accepted help from the Banu Qaynuqaʻ (against the Banu Qurayza) and from Safwan b. Umayya (at Hunayn) because they acknowledged his command.

Despite these efforts at reconciliation, classical Islamic jurisprudence remained divided on the question of accepting military aid from non-believers. By the Central Middle Ages, two schools had emerged, with a majority approving of interfaith collaboration under certain conditions and a strong minority, led by the Malikis, opposing direct military aid but allowing auxiliary services. There was a spectrum of opinion within the two schools and at times the outer reaches of each position came close to overlapping. Al-Sarakhsi's restrictive approval of interfaith alliances was not far removed from Ibn Rushd al-Jadd's measured, exception-laden disapproval. There was sufficient diversity within and across the two main positions to afford Muslim rulers ample leeway in their military arrangements, even in areas where Maliki *fiqh* predominated, such as North Africa and al-Andalus. Maliki strictures certainly did not deter Ibn al-Lihyani, the fourteenth-century emir of Tunis who walked the streets with his Christian bodyguards in tow. When al-Qawari upbraided him about seeking the assistance of non-believers, he responded, "Why, yes" and kept right on going. As Robert Brunschvig noted (1940–47: I, 447) long ago, the moral of the story is clear enough: even in Maliki North Africa, only "the excessive zeal of a rigorist" could disapprove of the employment of Christian guards. If the development of the Islamic legal tradition on interfaith military collaboration explains why this might be so, we are still left with a further question: how did religious authorities in Latin Christendom regard the Christian mercenary who took up service with a Muslim prince? Al-Lihyani's bodyguards may not have feared official Muslim disapproval, but were they risking their immortal souls along with their lives in offering him protection?

CANON LAW ON CHRISTIAN MERCENARIES

On the face of it, these mercenaries would seem to have serious cause for concern. The papacy had long taken a dim view of mercenary warfare within Europe, never mind beyond its borders and on behalf of avowed religious rivals. The most important early ecclesiastical attempts to deal with mercenaries had their roots in the Peace and Truce of God, a movement to limit and channel the violence that had been an endemic feature of European life since the tenth century. First at assemblies of local people, later at church councils presided over by high churchmen and sometimes even the popes in person, a formal ban would be placed on waging war against vulnerable members of society and at certain times of year.

Although mercenaries had fought in medieval armies since Carolingian times, they first became the focus of Peace legislation in the mid-twelfth century, when they emerged as a social problem for ecclesiastical authorities (Géraud, 1841–42). In regions where claims to power were many, groups of fighters banded together to offer their services to the highest bidder. Though known under many names, the men who belonged to these companies were most commonly called *routiers*, from the Latin *ruta* or *rupta*. The usage derived from a term for clearing brush—an earthy evocation of the destructive path these bands carved through war-infested areas of Europe (France, 2008: 6–8).

The region the *routiers* hit hardest was southern France; and it is no surprise to find a cleric of the Midi issuing the first Peace of God decree against them. In 1139 Archbishop Guillaume of Auch (Sainte-Marthe and Hauréau, 1715–1865: I, 162; Housley, 2002: 86) called on secular authorities to suppress the "pestilential bands of mercenaries" by force. To those who took up the challenge he offered a partial indulgence: forgiveness of two years of enjoined penance. Those who died in the campaign would receive the full crusade indulgence. Calling on local nobles to take military action against violators of the Peace was standard procedure by this time. Granting them crusade indulgences was not.

Hard line or not, the archbishop's decree did little to stanch the flow of *routiers* into southern France. It did, however, provide a model for Pope Alexander III when churchmen from the region pressed him to take action against mercenaries at the Third Lateran Council in 1179. He issued a decree censuring the "Brabanters, Aragonese, Navarrese, Basques, *Coterelli*, and *Triaverdini*, who practice such cruelty upon Christians that they respect neither churches nor monasteries, and spare neither widows, orphans, old or young nor any age or sex, but like pagans destroy and lay everything waste" (Tanner, 1990: I, 224–225). Some of these terms for the mercenaries were regional designations, while others were generic. *Coterelli* and *Triaverdini*, for example, can be roughly defined as "men of the companies" (France, 2008: 6–8). However named, the canon condemned them all, in effect, for violating the Peace of God. Their crime lay in attacking the vulnerable groups protected by peace legislation: the clergy, the old and the young, and women lacking male defenders.

These attacks removed the mercenaries from the community of the faithful. The decree likened them to pagans and linked them to another threat to Christian social order: heretics. The first part of the canon noted the spread of heresy in southern France and placed heretics, their supporters, and defenders under anathema. In similar fashion, those who "hire, keep, and support" the mercenaries were to be denounced publicly and refused communion unless they abjured "their pernicious society and heresy." This program of de-Christianization climaxed with a call to oppose mercenaries and heretics with crusading force. The canon granted the full Holy Land crusade indulgence to those who died in the course of combating these twinned evils and remission of two years' penance to survivors of the proposed campaign. Those who fought the mercenaries and heretics would receive the papal protection of persons and property extended to Holy Land crusaders by Pope Eugenius III in his crusade bull of 1145, *Quantum praedecessores*.

Alexander III's decree was carefully targeted. Fighting for pay was common in the late twelfth century and enforcing an outright ban on it would have been impractical. Instead, the pope focused on particular groups (the named mercenary bands) and particular actions (attacking vulnerable members of society). In doing so, he implicitly recognized a kind of soldier who could legitimately receive wages. Distinguishing this soldier from the mercenary, however, was no easy task. The names used to identify the *routier* companies in the canon only helped so much—presumably, for all the mercenaries recruited from these areas, there still could be found soldiers of Brabant, Aragon, and Navarre serving blamelessly for pay. The distinction would have to be grounded in an analysis of what mercenaries did, not who they were.

Despite the interpretive challenges it posed, Alexander III's mercenary decree would receive little attention from canon lawyers. This was because it did not find its way into the *Liber extra*, the authoritative collection of church law promulgated by Pope Gregory IX in 1234. The mercenaries, however, did attract the attention of a prominent group of pastoral theologians, including Peter the Chanter, Robert of Courson, and Thomas of Chobham. Against the backdrop of widespread mobilization of paid troops in the early thirteenth-century conflicts between England and France, they would attempt to apply Alexander III's teachings to the realities of contemporary warfare.

Robert of Courson explicitly differentiated between illicit mercenaries, whom he called *Coterelli*, and licit fighting men, whom he called *milites stipendarii*, or "salaried knights" (Baldwin, 1970: I, 221). To make clear what separated the two categories of paid soldiers, he turned first to just war theory, stating plainly that knights may receive wages if they fight in a righteous campaign (Baldwin, 1970: I,: 222). Defined initially in the Christian tradition by Augustine, the just war had received its most influential legal formulation in the mid-twelfth century, courtesy of *causa* 23 of Gratian's *Decretum*. There Robert and his colleagues could read that "a just war is waged by an authoritative edict to avenge injuries" (Friedberg, 2000: I, col. 895). The definition gave equal weight to two factors: the justice of the cause for which the war was fought and the legitimacy of the authority waging it. In differentiating mercenary combat from other forms of salaried warfare, however, the pastoral theologians tended to stress just cause as the crucial factor over legitimate authority. Thus Peter the Chanter offered the case of a city under papal interdict: could a knight draw wages to fight in its defense without incurring excommunication? The answer was yes, so long as the knight could not make a living any other way and, crucially, the city was being unjustly attacked. Even when the legitimacy of the war-waging authority was in doubt, a knight could still serve it in return for wages if the cause were just (Baldwin, 1970: I, 222; Russell, 1975: 241).

If fighting in a just war was one hallmark of the salaried knight, the other was that he did not earn more than he was due. The salaried knight had to fight not only in a just war but also for a just price. In the eyes of Robert of Courson (Baldwin, 1970: I, 222), it was robbery for a fighting man to receive anything beyond his contracted wages. Looting, plundering, and pillaging were sinful appropriations of unearned wealth. Thomas of Chobham (Russell,

1975: 241) argued that mercenaries were particularly liable to receive more than the just price for their work, since they not only devoted themselves to plunder but also neglected their other duties in the process.

Once set apart from the legitimate wage-earning soldier, the mercenary could be condemned unambiguously. Thomas of Chobham declared the mercenary enterprise dangerous to the soul. Robert of Courson said that those who pursued it were evil and guilty of sacrilege, while Peter the Chanter called for them to be refused the Eucharist because they made their living by killing innocent people. He advised mercenaries to find another line of work, but not before undergoing penance (Russell, 1975: 241). These views helped to solidify an anti-mercenary norm in Latin Christendom in the early thirteenth century. The question was whether this norm applied to Christian soldiers who fought in Muslim lands. If military service represented an acceptable form of wage labor under certain conditions, could these conditions be met outside of Christendom?

LATIN CHRISTIAN RELIGIOUS AUTHORITIES ON MILITARY AID TO MUSLIMS

Initially, at least, the answer was no. Writing at the end of the twelfth century, the canonist Huguccio argued that Christian soldiers sinned when they freely offered their services to Muslim regimes (Russell, 1975: 121). The popes of that era shared his view and expressed particular concern about the Iberian Peninsula, where Christians had long fought for Muslim regimes. The Umayyad caliphate that ruled Muslim Spain in the ninth and tenth centuries was probably the first Islamic power in the region to employ Christian troops (Clément, 1997: 120). It was the collapse of the dynasty in the eleventh century, though, that ushered in the heyday of the Christian mercenary in al-Andalus. The breakdown in central authority during the ascendancy of the *ta'ifa* kings created a market for Christian warriors, the most famous of whom was Rodrigo Diaz, el Cid. His death in 1095 ushered in an era of sharper religious division on the peninsula. From the north, crusading ideology crossed the Pyrenees and imbued the Christian reconquest of Spain with the aura of holy war. From the south, two reformist Islamic regimes from North Africa—the Almoravids and the Almohads—crossed the Straits of Gibraltar in succession and forged al-Andalus into a more unified and aggressive neighbor to the Christian kingdoms of the north. Religious scruples, however, did not prevent either dynasty from having frequent recourse to the services of Christian mercenaries. Nor did it stop them from entering into alliances with Christian powers when expedient (Burns, 1972).

These practices continued even after a grand alliance of Christian Iberian powers defeated the Almohads at Las Navas de Tolosa in 1212. Although Christian Spain seemed unified like never before, ecclesiastical authorities were soon complaining that Christian knights were flocking to the banners of Muslim princes once again. Writing around 1218 to "all the knights of the whole of the kingdom of the king of Castile," Archbishop Rodrigo of Toledo noted with dismay "how some of you by yourselves and some with your lords and friends, deserting your people and your land, are trying to enter into an alliance with the Saracens so that, if you are able, you can fight and oppress the Christian people with them" (Pick, 2004: 211–212). These worries found an echo in the decrees of secular rulers. In the *Siete partidas*, the mid-thirteenth-century Castilian law code promulgated under King Alfonso X, those who left the realm to take up arms with Iberian Muslims were declared traitors to God and country alike:

When a nobleman leaves his country of his own accord, and the king does not banish him, and he goes to the land of the Moors, his vassals should not follow him. This is the rule because he commits treason in two ways: first, he commits it against God, because he goes to the assistance of the enemies of the faith; second, he commits it against his natural lord, by making war against him and ravaging his country, and his vassals are guilty of the same treason if they accompany him in order to assist him.

(Siete partidas, 1972: III, 139; Burns, 2001: IV, 997)

The decree resonated with the language of betrayal. Nonetheless, the policy it enacted was less restrictive than such terminology might imply (Garcia Sanjuan, 2006: 446). It excluded from the ban those whom the king had expelled and it seemed most concerned with subjects who fought directly against the king alongside his Muslim enemies in Iberia. It did not address the possibility of fighting in North Africa.

The papacy shared the concerns of ecclesiastical and secular authorities about Christian military support for Muslims in Spain, and on similar grounds. Popes objected to the practice for two main reasons: it could harm Iberian Christians and it could hamper the crusading plans of Iberian monarchs. These objections emerge with particular clarity from the correspondence of Pope Celestine III (1191–98), a fervent advocate of crusading against Muslim Spain who struggled to unite the Christian rulers of the Peninsula behind his plans (Smith, 2008). In 1195, at the battle of Alarcos, the Almohads defeated a crusade Celestine had preached. In the wake of this victory, Caliph Abu Yusuf Ya'qub al-Mansur recruited two Christian rulers to his side: Duke Sancho of Navarre and King Alfonso IX of León. Writing to Sancho in 1196, Celestine (Kehr, 1970: II, 574–576, no. 220) wondered whether he had reflected carefully enough on the fact that Muslims "thirst after the blood of all Christians" before forging his agreement with the Almohads. Allying with these pagans was an offense toward God because they were "enemies of the church, persecutors of the faithful, and agents of evil." Warning Sancho to abjure their company, the pope urged him to take up arms against them on crusade instead. While hoping to lure Sancho back to the Christian side, Celestine judged King Alfonso of León to be incorrigible. In 1197 he excommunicated Alfonso, absolved the people of León from their oaths of fidelity to him, and declared his lands open for occupation by Catholic princes (Colomé, 1895: 423–424, no. 3). At the same time, the pope granted crusader privileges to the king of Portugal to invade León (Erdmann 1970: 376, no. 154).

Later popes would not go so far as to preach crusades against those who provided military support to Iberian Muslims, but they were more than willing to deploy their most powerful spiritual sanctions against them. In 1214, as the euphoria generated by the Christian triumph at Las Navas two years earlier began to fade, Innocent III ordered clergy throughout Spain to excommunicate any Christian who supported Muslims in combat against other Christians (Barton, 2002: 24–25). Once again, the harm such support did to Iberian Christians supplied the rationale for the papal intervention. In 1250, King Jaime I of Aragon asked for papal help against the Christians and Muslims who were working together to de-stabilize his rule over Valencia. Pope Innocent IV threatened excommunication against any Christian who "presume[d] to give advice and help to the Saracens against [Jaime], to the danger of their souls" (Quintana Prieto, 1987: II, 563, no. 620). Whether kings played the role of perpetrator or victim, the issue for the papacy was the same: it would not tolerate military aid to Muslims that harmed Spanish Christians or their crusading ventures.

In addition to forbidding Christian military support to Muslims, the papacy also prohibited interreligious trade in war materials. Perhaps because they addressed an important economic issue—cross-cultural commerce in the Mediterranean—these papal measures were incorporated into the *Liber extra* as decretals. Unlike papal pronouncements on mercenaries in Europe, therefore, they generated considerable decretalist commentary.

In the decretal *Ita quorundam*, Pope Alexander III lamented that:

> Cruel avarice has so seized the hearts of some that though they glory in the name of Christian they provide the Saracens with arms and wood for galleys and become their equals or even their superiors in wickedness and supply them with arms and other necessaries to attack Christians. There are even some who for gain act as captains or pilots in galleys or Saracen pirate vessels.
>
> (Tanner, 1990: I, 223; Friedberg, 2000: II, col. 773)

The pope went on to declare that such persons should be excommunicated and deprived of their possessions, and could legally be enslaved by those who captured them.

Ita quorundam seemed to envisage a broad embargo, prohibiting the supply of military materials and naval expertise to Muslims for any reason at any time. In the decretal *Significavit* (Friedberg, 2000: II, col. 775), Pope Clement III (1187–91) considered two possible exceptions to this general ban. The first exception related to trading war materials for pious purposes. Could merchants active in the markets of Alexandria sell prohibited items in order to redeem Christian captives? Clement answered that they could, provided that they offered nothing in aid or subsidy beyond the redemption fee. The second exception Clement considered raised the issue of timing. Could merchants trade prohibited items in Alexandria during a truce between Muslim and Christian powers? Here the answer was no: the embargo remained in force at times of peace, war, and truce. While re-affirming the broad temporal scope of the Alexandrian embargo, Clement also expanded the list of prohibited trade items. In the decretal *Quod olim* (Friedberg, 2000: II, col. 775), he ruled that during periods of war between Christians and Muslims there could be no Christian commerce at all with the Islamic world. In addition to a total wartime embargo, *Quod olim* added new categories of prohibited Christian military activity on behalf of Muslims. Whereas at Third Lateran Alexander had excommunicated only those who served as captains or pilots on Muslim warships, Clement leveled this spiritual sanction against those who "by some other means" provided "any kind of aid or advice to them, while war was underway between us and them." Although Clement allowed a significant exception in the case of redeeming captives, the overall effect of his rulings was to increase the number of papal prohibitions on Christian military aid to Muslims.

Under Pope Innocent III (1198–1215), the papal embargo achieved its classic form. His version of the ban appeared in the crusade decree *Ad liberandam* issued during the Fourth Lateran Council of 1215 (Tanner, 1990: I, 270; Friedberg, 2000: II, col. 777–778). In *Ad liberandam*, Innocent re-asserted the total ban on trade in arms and timber with Muslims. He also made three changes to the embargo. First, he added iron, galleys, and ships to the list of goods that Christians could never sell to Muslims. Second, he repeated Clement's ban on military aid or advice to Muslims, but did not limit the prohibition to periods of war. In effect, Innocent barred Christians from providing military support to Muslims at all times, making this ban consistent with the trade embargo. Third, he justified the prohibitions in terms of Christian safety and the security needs of the Crusader States of Syria and Palestine. Those who engaged in such illicit practices did so "in opposition to Christ and the Christian people" and "to the detriment of the Holy Land."

With Innocent III's embargo, church teachings on interreligious military aid and trade reached a crossroads. One path led toward a complete prohibition of all forms of Christian military support to Muslims at all times: there was certainly language in the decree to justify this restrictive turn. Another path, however, led toward a more flexible policy. Because Innocent had given the embargo a specific purpose—to prevent injury to Christians and Christian settlements in the Holy Land—it became possible to envision military assistance to Muslims that did not violate the embargo's intent. In their analyses of *Ad liberandam*, canonists stressed the harm that could come to Christians and the Holy Land by providing military aid to Islamic powers. According to Bernardus Papiensis "We are prohibited from giving or sending arms to Saracens ... because they are accustomed to fighting us with our own arms; we know, from the desolation of the kingdom of Jerusalem, that this is something that has happened in our own day" (Papiensis, 1956: 210). Pope Innocent IV, in his commentary on the decretals, confirmed that selling galleys to Muslims was prohibited because "with these they could cause great injury to Christians" (Innocent IV, 1570, fol. 507). Christian pirates who colluded with their Muslim counterparts were also subject to ecclesiastical censure "because of the following words, in aid of the Holy Land" (Innocent IV, 1570, fol. 507). Ramón of Peñafort (1744, fol. 26) held that "we may not send arms to Saracens, with which they could fight us."

Ramón's expertise in this matter was well known. In 1234, the heads of the Dominican and Franciscan communities of Tunis sent him a long list of questions about their ministry there, many of which related to the trade embargo. Their concerns were to provide pastoral guidance to the Christian residents of the city and to impose ecclesiastical discipline correctly. They wrote to Ramón because he was a papal penitentiary for Pope Gregory IX and as such dealt with matters relating to the forum of conscience across the church. His expertise in canon law and enthusiasm for missionary work in the Islamic world made him particularly well attuned to their concerns. When Ramón replied, he did so in the name of the pope. He explained at the beginning of his letter that his answers were authoritative statements of the church's penitential discipline:

> You asked to be instructed by the Apostolic See about what you ought to hold regarding the following articles; therefore, once the pope had personally subscribed to these articles I had the answers that he promulgated after due deliberation noted so faithfully by this special order that you may judge according to their tenor in the penitential forum.
> (Balme and Paban, 1898, no. 18)

Ramón's responses reveal how difficult it was to apply the papal embargo to real-life situations and how creative some merchants could be in trying to skirt its penalties. What goods were included under the ban? Should horseshoes, bridles, and saddles be considered arms? What about victuals, such as wheat and beans? Were these to be defined as war materials, and thus banned at all times, or should they be considered licit commercial goods and thus prohibited only in times of war? Did a merchant's original intentions for a prohibited item matter in determining whether a violation had occurred? For example, what if a merchant brought a large supply of swords, lances, and daggers into Muslim lands, not to sell, of course, but for self-defense, then ran out of money and had to sell the weapons in order to survive? Did that merchant face excommunication? (The short answer: yes.)

Amid this proliferation of cases, the mendicants of Tunis needed a uniform standard of judgment. To provide it, Ramón turned to the criteria that had emerged out of

Ad liberandam, decretalist commentary on it, and the long-standing papal disapproval of Christian military support for Muslims in Iberia: furnishing military goods or aid to Muslims merited excommunication only if it harmed Christians or the Christian cause in the Holy Land. Over and over again, Ramón used these criteria to distinguish licit from illicit Christian interaction with Muslims. When asked, therefore, whether those who provided support to Muslims by their arms should be excommunicated, he replied "no, unless it was done to the detriment of the Holy Land or other Christians" (Balme and Paban, 1898, no. 18). With that statement, Ramón and Gregory IX set forth the church's teaching on the Christian mercenary who served a Muslim regime. Even though his occupation frequently led to sin, and in other contexts could expose him to charges of heresy and paganism, he was not necessarily to be cast out of the community of the faithful. Even though he carried out his duties beyond the bounds of Christendom, in the service of a rival faith, he could remain a Christian in good standing.

CONCLUSION

Christian mercenaries who fought for Muslim states were valuable commodities in the medieval Mediterranean. For Muslims rulers, they offered military force that was not enmeshed in local networks of power. However powerful and thus potentially useful a Christian mercenary captain might be, the religious difference ensured that he could never seriously threaten his Muslim employer's supremacy within the state. Retention of their natal faith also allowed the mercenaries to maintain ties with their home countries, which enabled them to act as intermediaries in cross-Mediterranean diplomacy and trade. These arrangements benefited the mercenaries and their home countries, too. For the mercenary, service abroad was a potential path to riches, or at least an escape from poverty or troubles at home. For the Christian kingdoms of Iberia especially, the availability of military employment outside the realm provided a safety valve when political tensions between the monarchy and the nobility became unbearable. Many a thirteenth-century Iberian Christian noble was able to resume his accustomed position in the political order after a cooling off period in al-Andalus or the Maghreb (Barton, 2005: 125–127).

The fighting men who took up this option were so useful to their home and host societies that they may have been able to thrive even in the face of official disapproval. In reality, though, they rarely had to transgress religious norms to do their work. Most Muslim and Christian medieval religious authorities permitted interfaith mercenary warfare, with only Maliki jurists placing significant restrictions on the practice. Across many cultures and historical eras, the figure of the mercenary has often been associated with outlawry and sin. Strangely enough, the medieval Christian mercenary who fought for Muslims usually avoided this negative portrayal.

REFERENCES

Abu Yusuf, Ya'qub b. Ibrahim, 1938, *al-Radd 'ala siyar al-Awza'i*, ed., Abu al-Wafa al-Afghani. Beruit: Dar al-Kutub al-'Ilmiyya.

Baldwin, J., 1970, *Masters, Princes, and Merchants: The Social Views of Peter the Chanter and His Circle*, 2 vols. Princeton: Princeton University Press.

Balme, F. and Paban, C. (eds), 1898, *Raymundiana: Seu documenta quae pertinent S. Raymundi de Pennaforti vitam et scripta*. Rome: In domo Generalitia and Stuttgart: Apud Jos. Roth, bibliopolam.

Barton, S., 2002, "Traitors to the Faith? Christian Mercenaries in al-Andalus and the Maghreb, c. 1100–1300," in Collins, R. (ed.) *Medieval Spain: Culture, Conflict and Coexistence; Studies in Honour of Angus MacKay*. Houndmills, Basingstoke, Hampshire: Palgrave Macmillan, 23–45.

―――― 2005, "From Mercenary to Crusader: The Career of Álvar Pérez de Castro (d. 1239) re-examined," in Martin, T. and Harris, J. (eds), *Church, State, Vellum, and Stone: Essays on Medieval Spain in Honor of John Williams*. Leiden: Brill, 111–129.

Bredow, M. von (ed.), 1994, *Der Heilige Krieg (Gihad) aus der Sicht der Malikitischen Rechtsschule*. Beruit: Franz Steiner Verlag.

Brunschvig, R., 1940–47, *La Berbérie orientale sous les Hafsides, des origines à la fin du XVe siècle*, 2 vols. Paris: Librairie d'Amérique et d'Orient.

Burns, R., 1972, "Renegades, Adventurers and Sharp Businessmen: The Thirteenth-Century Spaniard in the Cause of Islam," *Catholic Historical Review* 58, 341–366.

―――― (ed.), 2001, *Las Siete partidas*, trans. Parsons Scott, S. 5 vols. Philadelphia: University of Pennsylvania Press.

Clément, F., 1997, *Pouvoir et légitimité en Espagne musulmane à l'époque des* taifas *(Ve/XIe siècle): L'imam fictif*. Paris: L'Harmattan.

Colomé, F., 1895, "Bulas históricas del reino de Navarra en los postreros años del siglo XII," *Boletín de la Real Academia de la Historia* 26, 417–460.

Donner, F, 2010, *Muhammad and the Believers: At the Origins of Islam*. Cambridge, MA: Harvard University Press.

Erdmann, C. (ed.), 1970, *Papsturkunden in Portugal*. Berlin: Abhandlungen der Gesellschaft der Wissenschaften zu Göttingen, 1927. Repr. Göttingen: Vandenhoeck and Ruprecht.

Fagnan, E., 1908, *Le djihâd ou guerre sainte selon l'école malékite*. Alger: Typographie Adolphe Jourdan.

France, J., 2008, "Introduction," in France, J. (ed.) *Mercenaries and Paid Men: The Mercenary Identity in the Middle Ages: Proceedings of a Conference held at University of Wales, Swansea, 7‑9 July 2005*. Leiden: Brill, 1–13.

Friedberg, E. (ed.), 2000, *Corpus iuris canonici*, 2 vols. Leipzig: Tauchnitz, 1879–81. Repr. Union, NJ: Lawbook Exchange.

Friedmann, Y., 2003, *Tolerance and Coercion in Islam: Interfaith Relations in the Muslim Tradition*. Cambridge: Cambridge University Press.

Garcia Sanjuan, A., 2006, "Mercenarios cristianos al servicio de los musulmanes en el norte de Africa durante el siglo XIII," in *La Peninsula Iberica entre el Mediterraneo y el Atlantico; siglos XIII-XV*. Cadiz: Diputación de Cádiz, 435–447.

Géraud, H., 1841–42, "Les routiers du douzième siècle," *Bibliothèque de l'École des Chartes* 4, 125–147.

Housley, N., 2002, "Crusades Against Christians: Their Origins and Early Development, c.1000–1216," in Madden, T. (ed.) *The Crusades: Essential Readings*. Oxford: Blackwell, 71–97.

Ibn Hazm, Abu Muhammad ʾAli, 1964, *al-Muhalla*, ed. Haras, M., 11 vols. Cairo: Maktabat al-imam.

Ibn Rushd al-Jadd, Muhammad b. Ahmad, 1988, *al-Bayan wa-l-tahsil wa-l-sharh wa-l-tawjih wa-l-taʾlil fi masaʾil al-Mustakhraja*, ed. Hijji, M. 22 vols. Beruit: Dar al-Gharb al-Islami.

Innocent IV, 1570, *Commentaria super libros quinque decretalium*. Frankfurt.

Kehr, P. (ed.), 1970, *Papsturkunden in Spanien*, 2 vols. Berlin: Weidmann, 1926–28. Repr. Göttingen: Vandenhoeck & Ruprecht.

Las siete partidas del Rey Don Alfonso el Sabio, 1972, ed. Real Academia de la Historia, 3 vols. Madrid: Imprenta Real.

Lower, M., 2006, "Tunis in 1270: A Case Study in Interfaith Relations," *International History Review* 28, 504–514.

Nirenberg, D., 1996, *Communities of Violence: Persecution of Minorities in the Middle Ages*. Princeton: Princeton University Press.

Papiensis, B., 1956, *Summa decretalium*, ed. Laspeyres, T. Graz: Akademische Druck- u. Verlagsanstalt.

Pick, L., 2004, *Conflict and Coexistence: Archbishop Rodrigo and the Muslims and Jews of Medieval Spain*, Ann Arbor: University of Michigan Press.

al-Qadi, W., 2004, "Non-Muslims in the Muslim Army in Early Islam: A Case Study in the Dialogue of the Sources," in Khasawnih, S. (ed.) *Conference on Orientalism: Dialogue of Cultures*. Amman 22–24 October 2002. Amman: University of Jordan, 109–159.

Quintana Prieto, A. (ed.), 1987, *La documentación pontificia de Inocencio IV (1243–1254)*, 2 vols. Rome: Instituto español de historia eclesiastica.

Ramón of Peñafort, 1744, *Summa*, Verona: Ex Typographia Seminarii, Apud Augustinum Carattonium.

Richard, J., 1952, "An Account of the Battle of Hattin Referring to the Frankish Mercenaries in Oriental Muslim States," *Speculum* 27, 168–177.

Russell, F., 1975, *The Just War in the Middle Ages*, Cambridge: Cambridge University Press.

al-Sahnun, 'Abd al-Salam b. Sa'id, 1994, *al-Mudawwana al-kubra*, 5 vols. Beruit: Dar al-Kutub al-'Ilmiyya.

Sainte-Marthe, D. de and Hauréau, B. (eds), 1715–1865, *Gallia Christiana*, 14 vols. Paris: Lutetiae Parisiorum.

al-Sarakhsi, Abu Bakr Muhammad b. Ahmad b. Abi Sahl Shams al-A'imma, 1971, *Sharh kitab al-siyar al-kabir li-Muhammad b. al-Hasan al-Shaybani*, ed. al-Munajjid, S. 5 vols. Cairo: Ma'had al-Makhtutat bi-Jami'at al-Duwal al-'Arabiya.

——— 1989, *Le grand livre de la conduit de l'état, commenté par Abu Bakr Muhammad ibn Abu Sahl Ahmad Chams al-A'immah as-Sarakhsi (400–483 H./1009–1090)*, trans. Hamidullah, M. 4 vols. Ankara: Editions Türkiye Diyanet Vakfi.

al-Shafi'i, Muhammad b. Idris, 1961, *Kitab al-umm*, ed. Zahri al-Najjar, M. 8 vols. Cairo: Maktabat al-Kuliyat Al-Azhariyya.

al-Shaybani, Muhammad b. al-Hasan, 1966, *The Islamic Law of Nations: Shaybani's siyar*, trans. Khadduri, M. Baltimore: Johns Hopkins Press.

——— 1975, *al-Qanun al-dawli al-Islami: Kitab al-siyar li-l-Shaybani*, ed. Khadduri, M. Beruit: Al-Dar al-Muttahida li-l-Nashr.

Smith, D., 2008, "The Iberian Legations of Cardinal Hyacinth Bobone," in Smith, D. and Doran, J. (eds) *Pope Celestine III (1191–1198): Diplomat and Pastor*. Farnham, Surrey: Ashgate, 81–113.

al-Tabari, Abu Ja'far Muhammad b. Jarir, 1933, *Das Konstantinopler Fragment des Kitab ihtilaf al-fuqaha'*, ed. Schacht, J. Leiden: Brill.

——— 2007, *Al-Tabari's Book of Jihad: A Translation from the Original Arabic*, trans. Ibrahim, Y. Lewiston: Edwin Mellen Press.

al-Tahawi, Ahmad b. Muhammad, 1994, *Sharh mushkil al-athar*, ed. al-Arna'ut, S. 16 vols. Beirut: Mu'assasat al-Risala.

Tanner, N. (ed.), 1990, *Decrees of the Ecumenical Councils*, 2 vols. Washington, DC: Georgetown University Press.

Yarbrough, L., 2015, "I'll not Accept Aid from a Mushrik," in Delattre, A., Legendre, M. and Sijpesteijn: (eds) *Authority and Control in the Countryside, Late Antiquity and Early Islam: Continuity and Change in the Mediterranean 6th-10th Century*. Princeton: Darwin Press.

PART VI

ARCHAEOLOGY OF THE CRUSADES

———•◆•———

CHAPTER TWENTY-SIX

CRUSADER FORTIFICATIONS: BETWEEN TRADITION AND INNOVATION

———•◆•———

Mathias Piana

The most impressive remnants left by the crusaders from their two hundred years' rule in the Levant are certainly the castles and urban fortifications they erected. Substantially preserved examples such as Krak des Chevaliers/Qalʻat al-Ḥiṣn, Margat/al-Marqab and Saône/Ṣahyūn in Syria, Giblet/Ǧubayl and Sidon/Ṣayda in Lebanon, Kerak/al-Karak and Montréal/aš-Šawbak in Jordan, as well as Belvoir/Kawkab al-Hawā and Chastel Pèlerin/ʻAṯlīt in Palestine still bear witness to the fortified landscape the crusaders had established in the East. Although many of these sites were studied and excavated during the past decades, there are still a lot of questions raised by them, and the debate on some key issues is still going on. They range from formation conditions, sociocultural influences, the distinction between castles and fortified settlements/towns, encastellation processes and settlement patterns, the representative and residential requirements of builders, to military and strategic functions and the significance of these fortifications for the exertion of governance. One major issue raised by scholars from the beginning of scientific research was the influences that shaped their layout and architecture (Lawrence 1988: xxi–xl; Piana 2011). Their physical appearance, often determined by a dominating monumentality, and their novel design, implementing cutting-edge defensive elements and principles, going far beyond the achievements of contemporary European military architecture, always puzzled travellers and scholars having dedicated themselves to their study (Fig. 26.1).

HISTORY OF RESEARCH

While the remnants of these fortifications were well noticed by the many travellers to the Eastern Mediterranean during the past centuries, it was not until 1871, when the French historian Emmanuel Guillaume Rey published the first systematic study dedicated to them (Rey 1871). Rey's book, based on the results of three scientific journeys to the respective areas, also addresses urban fortifications, although being less well preserved, recognising their importance for the development of military architecture. With his work, Rey lay the foundation of the scholarly investigation of these objects, providing many useful observations of details since lost, the more so as he was accompanied by one of the early photographers,

Figure 26.1   Krak des Chevaliers (Syria), the best-preserved crusader castle and a paramount example to illustrate the defensive qualities of the castles of that period. Photograph: Author.

Louis de Clercq, who left a series of 222 photographs in six volumes, entitled *Voyage en Orient*, of which one (vol. II) was especially dedicated to the *Châteaux du Temps des Croisades en Syrie* (de Clercq 1881). Rey's approach to embed the fortifications in their historical setting was advanced by Max van Berchem who brought to mind the complexity of the building history of many of these sites by analysing – in most cases for the first time – their Arabic building inscriptions (van Berchem 1888, 1897).

A remarkable study, originally an undergraduate thesis, was published in 1936 by the young Thomas Edward Lawrence, the later Lawrence of Arabia, who presented the results of his tour of 1909 through Syria (Lawrence 1988). His most important contribution to the study of crusader fortification was the recognition that the early castles of the keep-and-bailey type reflect a strong Western influence. Both Rey and Lawrence, however, were mistaken about their view that Templar and Hospitaller castles could be distinguished by the shape of their towers, an opinion completely discarded by later research. However, their assumption of a decisive Byzantine influence has found a wider acceptance today – backed by a better knowledge of Byzantine fortifications – than in earlier decades.

The year 1926 marks the starting point for the archaeological investigation of crusader fortifications, when a team from the Metropolitan Museum in New York excavated the castle of Montfort in Galilee (Dean 1927). The main objective of this campaign, however, was to obtain medieval artefacts from a promising site. In the following year the French historian Paul Deschamps set out for Syria, where he conducted three large campaigns studying the crusader fortifications there and in the neighbouring countries. Deschamps's masterpiece was the exploration of the Krak des Chevaliers, of which he published the results in 1934 (Deschamps 1934). This work was the first to assess a major Levantine fortification with a high degree of accuracy, a comprehensive documentation and an exhaustive exploration of the historical sources. It is the result of an intense preoccupation with the building history of the site, unique for the time in his methodological approach. Deschamps's oeuvre concerning the architecture and topography of the Latin states in the Levant certainly laid the foundation of any modern research on crusader fortification in all its aspects (Deschamps 1939, 1973; Richard 1991).

A principal criticism against the 'French school' of historians, of which Deschamps was a major exponent, was their nationalistic approach, undoubtedly rooted in the spirit of the time (Ellenblum 2007a). This era ended when British researchers entered the scene in the 1930s, supported by the British Mandate Department of Antiquities of Palestine. One major figure was Cedric N. Johns from the British School of Archaeology in Jerusalem. After having participated in the clearing and conservation works at the castle of 'Aǧlūn/Qal'at ar-Rabaḍ in Jordan 1927–29 (Johns 1997: viii), he directed the excavations at 'Athlīt from 1930 to 1934, which comprised not only the castle but also the adjacent town (Johns 1997: ii–vi). This was the first excavation of a crusader fortification where modern principles of archaeology such as stratigraphy and the analysis and documentation of artefacts were employed. Thereafter, from 1934 to 1939, Johns led a major excavation campaign at the Citadel of Jerusalem (Johns 1997: vii). Another important exponent was T.S.R. Boase whose most important contribution – still of relevance, though with some modifications – was the theory of an autonomous crusader art and architecture, influenced by European, Byzantine, Armenian and Arabic cultures (Boase 1967, 1971). The scientific research on the Frankish topography in Israel was established by Joshua Prawer, who promoted several projects in this field. During his time and with his support, several excavations were conducted: Caesarea (1960–64, 1972, 1975–76, 1979), Belvoir (1963–67) and Acre/Hospitaller quarter (1955–64).

Although since then many further studies were conducted, the medieval fortifications of the Eastern Mediterranean, including those erected by Armenian, Byzantine and Muslim rulers, which are to be considered in any study in that field, are far from being sufficiently researched. Only very few of the sites under review have experienced a comprehensive study, taking into account not only the architecture but also the many other functions fortified sites are seen to be related to within the framework of modern-day research. Issues discussed in current European castellology such as encastellation processes (Creighton 2012: 140–45), the symbolic and iconological values of fortifications (Zeune 1996; Perbellini 2000; Creighton and Higham 2005: 166–173; Kühtreiber 2009; Piana 2015) and the environmental context (Liddiard 2005; Hansson 2006; Creighton 2012: 125–46) were hitherto only marginally addressed. Therefore, there is still a wide range of open questions and topics for further studies.

The picture is somewhat complicated by the fact that – more than in medieval Europe – the distinction between the 'classical' castle and other walled precincts such as citadels, fortified manors (*maisons fortes*), fortified monasteries, walled villages or small towns with a castle-like appearance, of which many existed especially in Syria and Mesopotamia, is not clear. The more so, as the contemporary chroniclers were equally ambiguous about that matter (Ellenblum 2007a: 84–102; Kedar 2009; Pringle 2010). Here, one has to keep in mind that the majority of the several hundred fortifications which were owned by the crusaders throughout the period of their rule, did either exist before that period or was erected on pre-existing sites (Ellenblum 2007a: 167, Table 11.1). Newly built ones at a place which has never been fortified before are primarily found in rural areas and in Palestine, where less pre-crusader fortifications existed.

FORTIFICATION AND THE DEVELOPMENT
OF THE CRUSADER STATES

When the first crusaders arrived in the East, they encountered an already well-developed fortified landscape, due to the Arab–Byzantine wars from the seventh to the eleventh centuries and the Fatimid–Seljuq rivalries during the latter. Especially the fierce and long struggle along the Arab–Byzantine border zone in Northern Syria and Mesopotamia, the *ṯuġūr*, left its imprint in form of a network of fortified settlements (Hellenkemper 1976; Bianquis 1992; Eger 2008). One can even go so far as to say that at the arrival of the crusaders in the end of the eleventh century every larger settlement in Northern Syria, the area of the Levant entered by them first, was either walled or protected by another kind of fortification. This is easily comprehensible from the sources related to the First Crusade and the subsequent period which leave no doubt that almost any place conquered by the crusaders was fortified. The rapid advancement of the crusading forces resulted in the occupation of a significant number of these sites. According to contemporary sources between 165 and 200 *civitates et castra* in Syria were conquered prior to the taking of Antioch in June 1098 (Hagenmeyer 1901: 145, 147, 151). Although the figures may be exaggerated, they nonetheless reflect the density of fortifications in that area.

These facts shed light on an important prerequisite for the study of crusader fortification, hitherto not adequately taken into account. Before beginning to construct their own fortifications in the years after 1100, the crusaders already possessed around sixty fortifications of Byzantine origin (Fig. 26.2) and about forty Islamic ones, to which some Armenian may be added (Piana 2014b), which had undoubtedly served as models (Bianquis 1992: 136–7). In view of an enemy skilled in all current siege and mining techniques, it was of utmost importance to adopt approved local fortification principles. Therefore, in order to prevail against an opponent abreast with its latest developments, the study of the local fortification and its characteristics was a vital need for this new player in the field. As we can derive from their early fortifications, which boast many elements unknown to the West at that time, the crusaders undoubtedly benefited from the possession of well-fortified places such as Antioch, the second-best fortified city of the time after Constantinople, Tarsus, Adana, Mamistra, Anavarza, Edessa, Lattakia, Raphania, Tortosa, Caesarea maritima, Jaffa and, finally, Jerusalem. Additionally, the crusaders had co-religionist Byzantine and Armenian workers and masons at their disposal who counted among the best of their time, acquainted with all aspects of Eastern defence technology (Prouteau 2008).

The development of crusader fortified architecture is closely intertwined with the history of the crusader states (Ellenblum 1996; Ehrlich 2003). It may thus be divided into distinct phases:

I.a (1097–*c.* 1110): conquest and acculturation – occupation of pre-existing fortified sites

I.b (first quarter of twelfth century): formation of the crusader states – conquest of the remaining coastal cities, first crusader fortifications

II (second quarter of twelfth century): settlement and colonisation – construction of castles and refortification of cities/towns

III (*c.* 1150–87): maximal expansion of crusader states – advancement of fortification employing novel developments

IV.a (1187–91): consolidation after heavy losses by Saladin's campaigns

Figure 26.2   Saône (Syria), east section showing walls of tenth-century Byzantine castle (left) and crusader front tower. Photograph: Author.

IV.b (1191–1229): reconquest of the coast and restitution of territories – refortification of recovered coastal towns (Gaza, Ascalon, Jaffa, Caesarea, Acre, Sidon, Beirut)

V (1220–63): consolidation – foundation/reinforcement of fortresses (Margat, Tortosa, Krak des Chevaliers, Sidon, Beaufort, Montfort, Chastel Pèlerin/'Aṭlīt, Saphet) by the Military Orders and reconstruction of town walls by King Louis IX of France (Arsur, Jaffa, Caesarea, Haifa, Acre, Sidon)

VI (1263–1302): decline of the crusader states on the mainland – coastal towns as last bulwarks (Acre until 1291, Giblet/Ǧubayl until 1298, Tortosa and Arwād until 1291/1302)

Five phases are of special interest. Phase I is marked by the first wave of fortifications erected by the crusaders, most of them built by the king and his magnates. These early strongholds are all situated at places of a strategic interest. They played a role in the protection of the newly conquered areas, the control of important routes, and in the conquest of cities such as Antioch, Tripoli and Tyre. Three siege castles placed around the walls of Antioch in November 1097 and March 1098 (Malregard, La Mahomeria, Castrum S. Aegidii) were the first fortifications in stone built by the crusaders. Further such castles were Montpèlerin (Ar. Qal'at Sanǧīl), founded in 1102 by Raymond IV of Saint-Gilles opposite of Tripoli (Piana 2010: 309–10), and Scandalion (Ar. al-Iskandarūna), erected in 1117 by King Baldwin I to blockade and attack Tyre from the south. In 1105 Baldwin constructed Qaṣr Bardawīl, bearing the king's name, and in the following year Chastel Arnaud

(Ar. Yālū) (Pringle 1997: 106–07, 117). Qaṣr Bardawīl was located on the Golan Heights to control the Hauran and Chastel Arnaud on the road from Jaffa to Jerusalem 'to ensure the safety of pilgrims passing along that route' (Babcock and Krey 1943: II, 58). During the same time Hugh of Falkenberg, lord of Tiberias, founded the castles of Toron (Ar. Qal'at Tibnīn) and Chastel Neuf (Ar. Hūnīn) on the road from Damascus to Tyre, to serve as bases for raids against the latter (Piana 2008c: 396–7).

This phase, a period of fierce struggles and temporary losses of previously conquered places, is equally marked by a fortification or better refortification of towns, for which reasons it may be considered as a phase of entrenchment and consolidation. Although castles at that time played a stronger military role, previous paradigms of castles and other fortified places as predominantly military entities necessary to enforce power and sway within a colonial settlement and to defend the frontiers of the new crusader states (Prawer 1951; Smail 1956) is now abandoned in favour of a more differentiated view, supported by the results of surveys and archaeological interventions from the past decades (Ellenblum 1995).

Phase II is marked by an upsurge in the construction of Frankish castles, now to a lesser extant for military reasons but rather according to the need of the new sovereigns to establish themselves as feudal rulers. The castles, and similarly the fortified small towns in this period, were necessary to secure and to administer the appropriated land and to serve as residences. This phase is therefore marked by private fortifications of a new elite devoted to establish a seigneurial landscape according to the model of their homelands. Defensive capabilities seem to have played a minor role in the castle building of that period. This is also due to the fact that all major towns in Northern Syria and along the Levantine coast were in Frankish hands and all of them were fortified. Urban fortifications thus formed the defensive backbone of the crusader states in that period. That the castles erected at that time predominantly served as seigneurial centres, being constituents within a feudal settlement landscape, may be derived from their spatial distribution (Ellenblum 2007a: 165–86). They were situated in safer inland areas, though often at strategic points, rather than in border zones.

Most of these seigneurial castles, especially in rural areas, were of the keep-and-bailey type, consisting of a central tower surrounded by an enceinte (Fig. 26.3). More than hundred such castles are reported (Pringle 1994; Major 2003). The central tower or keep was identified as an import from the West. There, the keep not only served as the residence of a lord but also equally figured as the symbol of seigneurial power and status. The usually quadrangular enceinte, however, clearly refers to a model prevailing in the East, the *castrum*. It is derived from the Roman legionary camp and consists of a quadrilateral enclosure usually furnished with corner towers and a gate in the centre of one of the curtain walls. The combination of both has therefore been labelled as 'marriage of *turris* and *castrum*' (Smail 1956: 228) but may as well be viewed as the transfer of the motte-and-bailey castle, a common European prototype, to the Eastern sphere, where the Romano-Byzantine *castrum* scheme was a widespread pattern of fortified architecture. A common advancement of this scheme was the attachment of collateral barrel-vaulted halls at the interior of the curtain walls. This feature is prefigured in the array of chambers along the walls of Romano-Byzantine *castella* from the third to the sixth centuries (Qaṣr Busīr in Jordan, Androna/al-Andarīn in Syria) or the Byzantine examples from the tenth and eleventh centuries such as Maṣyāf and Ṣahyūn (upper wards). One of the first crusader castles implementing this scheme was Montpèlerin near Tripoli (Piana 2008d: 426–31; 2010: 332–4). There, the inner ward representing the

Figure 26.3   Giblet (Lebanon), an example of a keep-and-bailey castle marking the seigneurial phase of crusader castle building. Photograph: Author.

first building phase from the time of Raymond of Saint-Gilles features a modified *castrum* scheme with continuous vaulted halls along the enceinte, most probably combined with a central tower. The nearby Byzantine castle of Maṣyāf with a similar arrangement may have served as a model. However, Montpèlerin was reportedly erected with Byzantine support or by Byzantine masons.

Montpèlerin, as well as the contemporary castle of Saône, shows a further characteristic of these fortifications. They were usually associated with a settlement, which could be accommodated in an outer bailey or a *faubourg*. More often, this was an open village (*casale*) or an agricultural estate. Sometimes, fortifications acted as a starting point for a new settlement, as at Montpèlerin, where a suburb developed at the foot of the castle hill during the Frankish period (Piana 2010: 315–18). These settlements were often secondarily fortified, thus initiating an urbanisation process, in which the former castle turned into the citadel of the new urban entity. This development, which in cases such as Arsur (Roll 2011: 11–12) or Caesarea (Mesqui 2014: 77–99) already took place in the pre-crusader period, becomes obvious regarding the examples of Tortosa (Piana 2014a: 136) and Kerak (Meulemeester and Pringle 2008). In both cases the castles turned into citadels of the emerging towns during the Frankish period (Fig. 26.4).

AN APOGEE IN THE ART OF FORTIFICATION

The following phase from the middle of the twelfth century to the break caused by Saladin's campaigns against the crusader states in 1187–90 is characterised by a step change in the development of fortification. The promoters of this development were the Military Orders, or more specifically the Hospitaller and Templar Orders. Their growing financial resources and their increasing relevance for the defence of the crusader states led them to play a major role as builders of fortifications. Another factor contributing to the upsurge in the building of fortifications in this period was the growing threat from Muslim attacks led by Nūr ad-Dīn and Saladin. After a period of quiet, the crusader states had to face a long series of attacks starting from the late 1140s, when Nūr ad-Dīn began to seize one after another Frankish strongpoint in Syria, and later, in the 1160s, in Palestine, continued by Saladin in the 1170s (Ellenblum 1996: 523–29).

The principles and elements now employed were the concentric design, large projecting towers to enable flanking fire, casemated arrow-slits, barbicans and other arrangements to protect the gates, measures against undermining such as basing walls on bedrock and upon a talus or a glacis (stone revetment of slopes beneath fortification walls), and moats with stone-lined scarps. All these elements are already known from earlier Byzantine and Islamic fortifications but were now systematically employed and even advanced.

The concentric design is an advancement of the double wall scheme, consisting of a main wall and a lower forewall at a short distance. This arrangement, which offered several advantages such as a staggered defence from different firing levels and the prevention of a direct access to the main wall, is already known from the Late Chalcolithic in Egypt and was in use in the lands of the Fertile Crescent more or less incessantly until the Middle Ages. The most important pre-medieval promoter of this scheme and therefore the mediator of its use in later periods was the Byzantine emperor Justinian I (r. 527–65) who renewed the fortifications of major cities in the East. During the subsequent centuries,

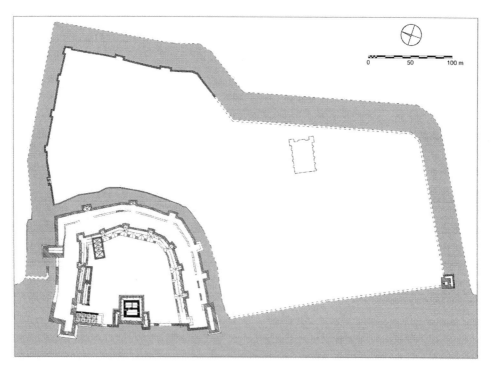

Figure 26.4 Tortosa (Syria), layout of medieval town and citadel in the thirteenth century.
Source: Author.

this principle was also employed at smaller fortifications. At the time when the crusaders arrived in the East, all larger coastal towns as well as major inland towns such as Kayseri, Tarsus, Antioch, Anavarza, Artasia/Artāḥ, Birtha/Birecik, Edessa/Urfa, Marasion/Maraş, Melitene/Malatya, Kaisum/Kaysun, Resafa, Manbīğ, Raqqa, Marra/Ma'arrat an-Nu'mān and Jerusalem, as well as the citadels of Adiyaman, Aleppo, Cyrrhus, Arka and Apamea were protected by double walls, be it Byzantine or Islamic fortifications (Piana 2007). For the advancement of this arrangement to the concentric scheme consisting of two independent lines of defence no clear transition can be determined. However, it is already realised at the pre-crusader Byzantine castles in Syria, as examples such as al-Manīqa, al-Ḥawābī and Maṣyāf indicate.

One of the first crusader castles featuring this design was Montpèlerin near Tripoli. The advancement of the second line of defence there is attributed to the time span between 1112 and 1137 (Piana 2010: 334). The first castles where this design was implemented from scratch were Beth Gibelin (Ar. Bait Ğibrīn) and Belmont (Ar. Ṣūbā). Beth Gibelin was built by King Fulk of Anjou in 1134 as a siege castle against Ascalon and entrusted to the Hospitallers upon completion two years later, as related by William of Tyre. They were, however, certainly involved in the planning and construction. The castle, consisting of a classical *castrum* with corner towers surrounded by an outer enceinte with adjacent halls (Fig. 26.5), was set in the north-west corner of the Byzantine city walls of Eleutheropolis, making use of some of its towers (Kloner and Cohen 2008). Belmont marks a step forward in the development. It was erected by the Hospitallers most probably in the mid-1150s on a hill west of Jerusalem (Harper and Pringle 2000). The rock surface on top of that hill was shaped to form a steep polygonal glacis surrounding its base,

Figure 26.5 Beth Gibelin (Israel), outer wall with gate (foreground) and *castrum*-type main ward (background). Photograph: Author.

partly rock-cut and partly built, with a regular ashlar facing enclosing a rubble core. This arrangement may be regarded as an advancement of the stone-lining of the slopes of castle hills, a phenomenon known from Islamic fortifications such as the citadels of Aleppo, Ḥārim, Šayzar, Hama, etc., lending not only an armour-like appearance to the walls but also impeding their undermining and the use of siege towers. The main ward consists of a walled quadrangle with hall ranges on three sides, no doubt adopting the traditional *castrum* scheme. Structures of the *castrum* type in hilltop position were not uncommon in the preceding Byzantine period, as examples from the upper wards of Maṣyāf and Ṣahyūn demonstrate. Remains of a hall range to the south-west at intermediate level indicate that the castle did have a concentric layout.

A contemporary example employing the same principles, though on flat ground, is the citadel of Tortosa (Ar. Ṭarṭūs) on the Syrian coast. A devastating raid of Nūr ad-Dīn in spring 1152, followed by the conflagration of the former town, led the local bishop to entrust the ruins to the Templars with the obligation to rebuild the fortifications. They constructed a new citadel on the lines of the former town walls, most probably not long after 1155, when a truce was agreed with Nūr ad-Dīn. Here, too, the walls and towers were based on bedrock where possible, which in most cases was hewn to form a sloping talus (Fig. 26.6). The layout of the citadel is marked by a concentric design, consisting of a main ward developed from the *castrum* scheme with continuous hall ranges along the enceinte, and – separated by a ditch – a lower outer enceinte of the same build (see Fig. 26.4). The ensemble was completed by an outer moat, once filled with sea water, with scarps partly rock-cut partly stone-lined. A further novel feature are open-backed towers, equally prefigured in Montpèlerin and earlier sites (Piana 2014a). These principles were applied to

Figure 26.6 Tortosa (Syria), north-east corner of the citadel displaying rock-based walls of outer enceinte. Photograph: Author.

another Templar stronghold in the hinterland of Ṭarṭūs, Chastel Blanc (Ar. Ṣāfītā), which was completely rebuilt after the earthquake of 1170 and a temporary occupation by Nūr ad-Dīn in the following year. There, a concentric castle was erected on top of a hill, similar to Belmont with a steep glacis all around the outer enceinte, which was, however, furnished with open-backed towers and a central keep accommodating a church at ground floor level and a hall above (Piana 2008a).

This period saw the equivalent advancement of private castles. At Saône the most vulnerable east side of the castle was furnished with massive rectangular towers around the mid-twelfth century. The largest of which, 24.5 m square, located at the centre of this section and overlooking the deep rock-cut ditch, acted as a front tower commanding the entire eastern part of the castle and the area beyond the ditch (see Fig. 26.2), where a settlement had emerged (Michaudel 2011). Beaufort (Ar. Qalʿat aš-Šaqīf) was conquered in 1139 and refortified in the following decades, as well as Kerak, where a new castle was erected by Pagan the Butler who transferred his residence from Montréal/Šawbak to this place. According to William of Tyre, his successors strengthened it by adding towers and a moat. The castle was located at a strategic position, on the narrow ridge connecting the plateau on which the town lies with the main Moab plateau. On both ends of the castle deep rock-cut ditches were dug, adding much to the impregnability of the place (Fig. 26.7). An outer wall to the west delimited a lower bailey, which might correspond to the *barbacana* ceded to

Figure 26.7   Kerak (Jordan), south front of the castle with lower bailey (left) overlooking a deep rock-cut chasm. Photograph: Author.

the Hospitallers in 1152, and halls alongside the curtain walls, but was not concentric in the narrow sense of the term (Meulemeester and Pringle 2008).

A number of analogies to the citadel of Tortosa leads to the assumption that the same workforce was in charge, when the Krak des Chevaliers was newly built after the severe earthquake of 1170, which had completely ruined the castle. The Hospitallers had received the place in 1142 from Count Pons of Tripoli who had temporarily lost it to the Muslims two years before and could not afford its defence any more. It consisted of a trapezoidal enceinte with adjacent halls delimiting a courtyard, revealing borrowings from the *castrum* scheme, indicated by the corner towers and the central tower at the south side. In this first phase the Hospitaller castle was not fully concentric but had a forewall at three and a half sides. A barbican in front of the gate and a bailey on the south side completed the ensemble (Zimmer et al. 2011).

At about the same time the Hospitallers commenced another, even more ambitious forti-fication project, in which the concentric principle found its culmination. In 1168 they took over the castle of Belvoir (Ar. Kawkab al-Hawā) in Palestine, a border stronghold overlook-ing the Jordan valley, and reconstructed it in the subsequent period (Biller 1989). There, a classical quadrangular *castrum* with four hall ranges, four corner towers and a gate tower at the central west side was surrounded by another, though pentagonal, *castrum* of the same build – here with an intricate entranceway at the east side through a large projecting tower-like structure, an arrangement similar to that at the citadel of Tortosa. The towers of the outer enceinte all rest on high taluses rising from the bottom of the surrounding moat, with the intermediate slopes of the scarp equally revetted with regularly coursed ashlars (Fig. 26.8). With this programmatic concept, often referred to as a 'castle within a castle', Belvoir marks an apogee in the art of fortification. Additionally, all novel elements of fortification were employed: hall ranges with flat roofs for the mounting of artillery, postern gates leading to the bottom of the moat to enable the active defence of the same, casemated arrow-slits, flank-ing towers rising from taluses, stone-lined hill slopes, and multiple-bended entranceways exposing an enemy to direct fire. Hence it forced Saladin to a siege of one and a half years and despite all these measures the Hospitallers finally surrendered in 1189 after the collapse of the large structure at the central east side, which might have been a tower or a barbican.

REVIVAL AFTER SALADIN'S CAMPAIGNS

The heavy losses inflicted on the crusader states by Saladin evoked several new crusades, in the aftermath of which many of the lost towns and castles were either recaptured or restored. Phase IV is thus marked by the refortification of the regained places, which almost all had been destroyed and their walls and towers dismantled, due to fear of Saladin and his succes-sors that the crusaders could re-establish themselves in the respective areas. Gaza, Ascalon, Jaffa, Caesarea and Acre were retaken by King Richard I of England in 1191 who imme-diately began to reconstruct their fortifications. In the following year, however, Gaza and Ascalon were again lost to the Ayyubids, Jaffa only in 1197, followed by the dismantling of all its walls, while Caesarea was left in ruins. Its citadel was rebuilt in 1218 but again destroyed in the following year. Its walls were, however, rebuilt prior to the arrival of the German crusade of 1228–29 and again slighted in 1244. While Gaza was never again forti-fied by the crusaders and Ascalon not until 1239, Jaffa's citadel was reconstructed from its foundations by Emperor Frederick II 1228–29, whereby the surrounding ditch was cleared from debris and lined with stones, commemorated by two preserved inscriptions (Sharon

Figure 26.8 Belvoir (Israel), south-west corner tower of outer ward surmounted by remains of inner ward, constituting a concentric *castrum* concept. Photograph: Author.

and Shrager 2012). Beirut and Sidon, where Saladin had razed the town walls in 1190, were both re-conquered in 1197, but while the walls of Beirut were subsequently reconstructed, those of Sidon were subject to further destruction after the crusader had army left the town. On a small island immediately north of Sidon, however, two towers were erected by English and French crusaders in 1227–28, constituting the nucleus of the later Sea Castle (Piana 2008b: 374–83). Beirut was given to John of Ibelin between 1200 and 1205 whereupon he rebuilt the town walls and the keep inside the citadel. The magnificent furnishing of which is admired by Wilbrand of Oldenburg in 1212 (Pringle 2012: 118–19). Wilbrand also describes the fortifications of the citadel, which might have been rebuilt by the king already before the capture of the town by Saladin in 1187. They consisted of a double wall with strong towers and a deep, stone-lined ditch. In 1995 the ground walls of the south-eastern corner tower on the landward side of the citadel were excavated (Antaki 2002). The tower was 19 m square with walls between 4.2 and 4.8 m thick, featuring a masonry of large rusticated ashlars with ancient columns employed as headers. The double wall, described by Wilbrand, is attested at the adjoining south wall, where the tower had a postern gate that led to the bottom of the ditch, which at this point was 14 m wide. In 2005 a section of the west wall of the citadel was exposed, displaying the same characteristic masonry (Fig. 26.9). In front of this wall a 9 m wide free space is delimited by a parallel wall, probably representing the moat and a section of the city wall. To the north the 5 m thick wall bends back at a right angle to abut the rock of the ancient tell. This corner was once taken up by a tower which at its base measured 18 by 16 m. To the south of the tower, a secondarily walled-up postern gate is located. The parts of the citadel once located on the peninsula, which jutted out to the sea between these two sites, do not exist any more as the peninsula was ablated when the new harbour was built in the 1890s.

Figure 26.9 Beirut (Lebanon), outer west wall of the citadel showing crusader masonry with columns used as headers (foreground) and main ward of citadel (background). Photograph: Author.

At Tyre, which was not conquered by Saladin, the Genoese built a castle near the town wall in 1192. The heavy earthquakes of 1202/03 almost completely ruined the fortifications, which were reconstructed in the course of the thirteenth century. At Jerusalem, where the walls had been razed by al-Malik al-Muʻaẓẓam in 1219, construction works are recorded at the citadel during the Frankish period of 1229–39 (Johns 1997: vii; Ellenblum 2007b; Leistikow 2008). Besides Ascalon, where some stretches of the walls attributed to Richard I have survived (Pringle 1984), in neither of these towns substantial remains of the walls are preserved.

In this phase some new castles were erected and existing ones strengthened. Both at Margat and at the Krak des Chevaliers, the decades after 1200 were characterised by large-scale construction programmes. The latter was extended by adding an outer enceinte and a new polygonal gate tower. Additionally, the three towers at the south section of the main ward were enlarged and furnished with rounded front sides, their curtain walls strengthened by a high glacis with arrow-slits and a casemate inside to operate them (Zimmer et al. 2011: 263–77) (see Fig. 26.1). D-shaped towers, most probably a Western import (Piana 2013: 236–7), were now favoured, as the castle of Silifke (Cr. Seleph) from the same period indicates. There, the Hospitallers refortified a former Byzantine stronghold overlooking the town of the same name, after they had it taken over in 1210. They strengthened the Byzantine main wall and forewall, added a series of D-shaped towers on three sides, and a glacis in front of the forewall. This was surrounded by a moat, the counterscarp of which lined with masonry and a third wall erected on top of the rampart having accumulated by digging out the moat (Fig. 26.10). On the north side a gate tower with a bended passage-way was erected, which could only be accessed via an outer gate followed by a barbican.

Figure 26.10   Silifke (Turkey), south section of the castle illustrating Hospitaller reinforcements such as rounded towers, a stronger forewall, a stone-lined moat and a counterscarp wall.
Photograph: Author.

The castle, centre of a newly founded Hospitaller march in Cilicia, had to be surrendered to the Armenians in 1226 (Piana 2013).

THE ERA OF THE GREAT FORTRESSES

The fortifications of the thirteenth century are different from those of the twelfth. Baronial and royal castles, having shaped the fortified landscape of the latter, became less important. The brunt of defence and fortification of the remaining Frankish territories was born by the Military Orders who built new fortifications and refortified older ones on a larger scale. This period (phase V) is further marked by the refortification programme King Louis IX of France executed at a number of the major coastal towns of the Levant. The achievements in fortification from the preceding century are now systematically implemented, but only very new elements employed. One of these may have been the machicolations which are now found more often, another the establishment of a third line of defence beyond the moat. However, the fortification of the thirteenth century is marked by a stronger Western influence. At all sites with buildings from that period can be found not only Gothic vaulting and sculpture but also construction principles developed in the West at that time. These were a more deliberate planning, the employment of geometric design patterns, and the use of smaller, regularly cut stones (*petit appareil*).

From 1217 to 1222 the Templars erected a new fortress on the peninsula of 'Aṯlīt (Cr. Chastel Pèlerin) and a large *faubourg* on the adjacent mainland. The place was intended to become the main Templar stronghold in the Kingdom of Jerusalem and so were its defensive works. To the landward side a main wall, 12 m thick and over 30 m

451

high, flanked by two huge rectangular towers more than 34 m high, overlooked a forewall, 6.5 m thick and 16 m high, furnished with three smaller towers in a staggered arrangement protecting the curtains of the main wall. The forewall contained a vaulted passage at the towers' first floor level providing access to the casemated arrow-slits of the curtain walls and the tower chambers at that level. The wall was once crowned by a battlemented parapet, most probably furnished with merlons pierced by arrow-slits, as at the other Templar fortifications. These towers, which acted as gate towers having lateral entrances protected by machicolations, overlooked a 25 m wide moat delimited by a walled counterscarp forming a third line of defence. The forewall and its towers, as well as the counterscarp, had all sloping sills. The interior of the castle follows a concentric plan with a rectangular inner ward and a polygonal outer enceinte, both accompanied by sequenced hall ranges (Johns 1997: ii–vi). Although Chastel Pèlerin ranked among the strongest fortified sites of the crusaders, additionally favoured by natural advantage, it had to be abandoned after the fall of Acre in 1291.

Montfort, the main castle of the Teutonic Knights in the East, was founded in the mountains of Galilee in 1226. Its main ward, erected on a slightly sloping spur, was protected at the east side by two rock-cut ditches and a huge D-shaped front tower resting on a plinth, which contained a cistern and a chapel and had an outer facing of large ashlars with plain bosses. The outer dimensions of the latter are some 24 by 21 m, its wall thickness amounting to more than 7 m, and its height to about 25 m. The narrow main ward consisted of an elongated hall building with a massive, trapezoidal structure of tower-like dimensions added at its western end. It certainly was of a residential character and contained a noble hall with vaults resting on a central octagonal pier (Boas 2012). An outer enceinte at a lower level completed the ensemble, which fell to Sultan Baybars in 1271, who had it subsequently dismantled.

At the citadel of Tortosa the walls of the main ward were heightened during the thirteenth century, adding two further firing galleries with arrow-slits alternating with square openings, probably for the use of siege-crossbows. Additionally, a new castle chapel was built and a great hall added at the inner north section of the main wall (Piana 2014a). The castle of Saphet (Ar. Ṣafad), once erected to guard the route from Damascus to Acre and labelled as the 'key (fortress) of all Galilee', had been dismantled during the 1220s by al-Malik al-Muʿaẓẓam. After it had been restored to the Templar Order in 1240, it was refortified on a massive scale and at a vast expense. Its construction is reported in a treatise from 1264, entitled *De constructione castri Saphet*, which represents the most detailed contemporary account we have of the building of a medieval castle, even providing dimensions of its major elements (Huygens 1981). The castle was oval in shape, covering a hilltop (300 by 130 m) overlooking the town of the same name. It was built on a concentric plan, with ditches between the inner ward and forewall and in front of the latter. Although the earthquakes of 1837 and 1927 had left a heap of ruins, recent excavations at the south-west section of the inner ward revealed some evidence (Barbé and Damati 2004). According to this and the specifications given in *De constructione*, the main ward was enclosed by a wall, some 3 m thick on top and about 40 m high, furnished with seven rectangular towers, 20 m square with walls 4 m thick, surmounting the curtain walls by 4 m. The outer wall had a height of about 20 m and was equally furnished with towers. They were round, as one example having survived under its Ottoman superstructure at the north-west side of the castle indicates. This wall seems to have been built on top of a glacis containing casemates which were connected with the inner ward by underground tunnels and from which crossbowmen could operate great ballistas. The fortifications were completed by an outer ditch enclosed by a rampart. During the same time, Ascalon was refortified after it had been occupied by Count Theobald IV of Champagne in 1239. This rebuilding, however, concerned merely the citadel at the north-west corner of the former town. It was furnished with a double wall and a high glacis covering the slopes of the Bronze Age ramparts, sections of which are still visible. Additionally, the principle layout of the intricate entrance passage at the north gate could be reconstructed (Boas and Piana 2008). One of the few baronial castles refortified during that period was the citadel of Arsur (Ar. Arsūf), completely rebuilt by John of Ibelin in 1241. The castle, or better the citadel, is situated on the cliff edge in the north-western part of the town overlooking a small harbour. During the past decades, the remains of the castle were completely exposed. A small ward around the central octagonal keep is delimited by halls and a pentagonal enceinte with rounded towers at the corners. The gate at its east side is flanked by two U-shaped towers, undoubtedly an adoption from Western models of the time. This enceinte is enclosed by a forewall forming semi-circular bastions around the towers and the gate, resting on a glacis. Of this forewall, which overlooks a deep moat between 21 and 30 m wide, only scant remains have survived. On the opposite side a polygonal wall on top of a rampart defines a third line of defence, turning this small but compact castle to a heavily fortified structure. Architectural analysis reveals a strong Western influence, tangible not only from the tower shapes but also from the repertoire of Gothic forms and building principles employed (Roll 2011).

In 1250 King Louis IX of France arrived at Acre after his unsuccessful campaign against Egypt and he subsequently ordered the walls of the new suburb of Montmusard to be refortified. As at the city wall proper, this new enclosure had a main wall and a forewall, both furnished with towers at regular intervals. After donations of the necessary land in 1192 and 1194, the Hospitallers established their main quarter in the city. It was located at the northern city wall and incorporated a tower and one of its gates. Its layout is based on the *castrum* scheme. The excavations during the past decades revealed considerable remains allowing for the reconstruction of the medieval buildings, which comprised a church dedicated to St John and several large halls and magazines. The main quarter of the Templar Order was once located on a promontory jutting out into the sea at the south-west corner of the city. Today almost nothing has survived but, to conclude from the sources, it must have been strongly fortified in the thirteenth century (Kedar 2006; Jacoby 2008).

The ruined fortifications of Caesarea were rebuilt by King Louis IX in 1251–52 on a massive scale (Fig. 26.11). The walls enclose a rectangle, covering an area of about 450 by 240 m, on three sides with the fourth side to the west encompassing a small harbour. They still followed the lines of the Islamic city wall but were now furnished with a high talus and sixteen open-backed towers, with three of them acting as gate towers, one in each wall, of which the north and east gates had bended passageways. The uprising walls surmounting the talus were lavishly furnished with casemated arrow-slits connected by covered wall-walks. Postern gates leading into the moat allowed for sallies. The south wall ends at the sea side at a neck ditch which separates a peninsula south of the harbour. There, a rectangular keep, now heavily mutilated, was located, defended to the landward side by two massive rectangular towers with ancient columns used as headers within a masonry of huge bossed ashlars. The latter are now contributed to the refortification campaign of 1228, while the keep may have been the work of the king of Jerusalem, John of Brienne, executed in 1217–18 (Mesqui 2014).

Figure 26.11   Caesarea (Israel), east wall of the fortification erected by King Louis IX of France (1251–52). Photograph: Author.

Figure 26.12   Sea Castle at Sidon (Lebanon), reflecting the last crusader phase in its layout when it served as a base for the Knights Templar (1260–91). Photograph: Author.

Other towns refortified by King Louis IX were Haifa (where the walls of the citadel, having been razed by Saladin, were repaired), Jaffa and Sidon. Jaffa, where Louis IX had stayed a full year (1252–53), was subjected to a major refortification programme. The citadel had already been rebuilt by Emperor Frederick II in 1228–29, and subsequently fortified by Patriarch Gerald of Lausanne by two towers constituting his own residence. Louis IX had then refortified the town walls, 'from sea to sea', with twenty-four towers, three gates and a ditch. This work seems to have been unfinished by March 1267, which may have facilitated the conquest by Sultan Baybars one year later (Peilstöcker 2006; Kedar 2006). Excavations in 2007–08 have brought to light the glacis of a huge round tower (diameter *c.* 35 m) in the area of the Franciscan Hospital, attributed to the works of King Louis IX. The appurtenant tower seems to have been a corner tower, accommodating a gate, as indicated by remains suggesting this, which were excavated on top of the structure (Re'em 2010). At Sidon, the king's activities (1253–54) are related to the second building stage at the Sea Castle. It is represented by the extension of the existing fortification, consisting mainly of two towers, to a construction of the *castrum* type with corner towers, of which only the south-eastern one has survived within later additions. This tower protected a postern gate immediately west of it and the castle's main gate adjoining to the north, defended by a portcullis and a murder hole. This ensemble was refortified at a massive scale most probably after 1260, when the castle was destroyed by the Mongols and subsequently ceded to the Templars (Fig. 26.12). A further work of King Louis IX may be seen in the glacis around the land castle of Sidon, which until today is named after the king. Nothing, however, has survived from the town walls, which he had 'fortified with great walls, mighty towers, deep and cleaned ditches inside and outside' (Piana 2008b). Tyre, which was so badly damaged by the earthquake of 1202 that 'all the towers but three, and the walls except for the outer barbican' had collapsed. These were the famous triple walls on the landward and the double walls on the sea side, which had already existed when the crusaders conquered the town in 1124. The refortification must have been accomplished by 1283, when Tyre was described by Burchard of Mount Sion who wrote that 'on the east side ... it was surrounded by triple wall, strong and high, and 25 feet thick, ... fortified with twelve very strong towers, ... linked to the citadel or castle, which is very strongly defended and situated on a rock in the midst of the sea, ... likewise fortified with towers and solidly-built residences'. The castle may be identified with the one already mentioned in 1190 and of which King John of Brienne disclosed in 1212 that he had begun to (re)build it. A contemporary source reported that it was situated near the harbour and had four high towers (Pringle 1995: 85–87; Antaki 2011).

CONCLUSION

Regarding the fortifications erected by the crusaders in the light of research conducted so far, it becomes clear that certain traits of its development may well be assessed. However, many questions remain open to debate. What is ascertained is that we cannot speak of the crusader castle as a typological entity, due to the wide range of forms and types found. Many of the building principles, architectural forms and defensive elements that often occur are equally found in Byzantine, Armenian and Islamic fortification. Even if the ancient *castrum* scheme, which is, however, varied and advanced, is so often found that we may speak of it as a hallmark of crusader fortification, there are many fortifications utilising the advantages of the terrain for the positioning of walls and towers. An indispensable feature of any ambitious fortification from the very beginning was the main wall–forewall–moat scheme, often combined with a ditch between the walls or a rampart beyond the moat with or without a (third) wall on top. The advancement of the forewall to a more independent structure with adjacent halls constituting the full concentric fortification, although already pre-figured in Byzantine castles of the region, is a true achievement of the crusader period. The main promoters of this concept were the Military Orders who developed this principle to a hallmark of their fortifications, which in turn had repercussions on European castle building (Piana 2014b).

A further frequently found principle is the setting of walls on bedrock, a measure against undermining, usually combined with a sloping of its base in form of a talus or with a glacis. Stone lining is also applied to the opposite flank of the moat or ditch, the counterscarp, and even to the bottom of which. During the thirteenth century, casemates were built into the glacis, thus enhancing the defensive capabilities of such a structure. Fortification walls became thicker over time, from about 2 m to 4 m and more during the thirteenth century, reflecting the developments in siege artillery. Towers are almost always rectangular during the twelfth century, while during the thirteenth rounded fronts became popular, most probably a Western import due to the specific forms. Other than at the very beginning, when buttresses and smaller towers prevailed, towers usually projected from the adjoining curtain walls, in order to provide flanking fire and a better overview of the ground zone in front of them. A further development, equally adopted from earlier (Byzantine) fortifications, were open-backed towers. Arrow-slits were rapidly introduced but also advanced during the twelfth century, with casemates and longer openings with sloping sills, and their bases widened for a more effective operation. A further characteristic element were arrow-slits in the centre of merlons.

Although during the thirteenth century European influences grew much stronger, even then we notice a peculiar mixture of archaic forms such as bulky rectangular towers and splendid Gothic halls. One example is the Sea Castle of Sidon, where a massive rectangular tower with a masonry of rusticated ashlars and columns used as headers at the east tower contrasts with its much more elegant counterpart at the west side with a polygonal layout and a rounded front (see Fig. 26.12). Another example is Arsur, where Western forms such as the gate with its twin U-shaped towers are combined with a forewall, a glacis and a counterscarp wall as a third line of defence, an old fortification pattern from the East, to be found for example at the pre-crusader fortifications of Constantinople and Tripoli. The development of the concentric fortification scheme, however, shows that elements were not only adopted and maintained but also advanced. Thus the fortification of the crusaders may not be regarded simply as a syncretic phenomenon but rather as an eclectic one, born out of Eastern fortification traditions and combining the best-proven elements and principles according to the military, economic, sociocultural, administrative and representative needs of their builders and of the era they lived in.

REFERENCES

Antaki, P. (2002) 'Le château croisé de Beyrouth. Étude préliminaire', in *Beirut – History and Archaeology & Water in the Pre-Modern Near East. ARAM. 12th International Conference, Beirut, 13–15 April 1999* (ARAM periodacals, 13/14), Oxford, 323–53.

——— (2011) 'Les fortifications de Tyr à la lumiére des sources médiévales', in P.-L. Gatier, J. Aliquot and L. Nordiguian (eds), *Sources de l'histoire de Tyr. Textes de l'Antiquité et du Moyen Âge*, Beyrouth, 179–200.

Babcock. E.A. and Krey A.C. (1943) *William of Tyre: A History of Deeds Done Beyond the Sea by William Archbishop of Tyre*, 2 vols (Columbia University Records of Civilization, 35), New York.

Barbé, H. and Damati, E. (2004) 'Le château de Safed; sources historiques, problématique et premiers résultats de recherches archéologiques', in N. Faucherre, J. Mesqui and N. Prouteau (eds), *La fortification au temps des Croisades*, Rennes, 77–93.

Berchem, M. van (1888) 'Le château de Bâniâs et ses inscriptions', *Journal Asiatique*, 12, 440–71.

―――― (1897) *Inscriptions arabes de Syrie*, Le Caire.

Bianquis, T. (1992) 'Les frontières de la Syrie au milieu du Ve/XIe siècle', in J.-M. Poisson (ed.), *Frontière et peuplement dans le monde méditerranéen au moyen âge: actes du colloque d'Erice – Trapani (Italie) tenu du 18 au 25 septembre 1988*, Madrid, 135–50.

Biller, T. (1989) 'Die Johanniterburg Belvoir am Jordan: zum frühen Burgenbau der Ritterorden im Heiligen Land', *Architectura*, 19, 105–36.

Boas, A. (2012) *Montfort Castle. The Western Wing and the Great Hall*, Haifa.

Boas, A. and Piana, M. (2008) 'Die Kreuzfahrerstadt Ascalon', in Piana, 2008, 263–73.

Boase, T.S.R. (1967) *Castles and Churches of the Crusading Kingdom*, London.

―――― (1971) *Kingdoms and Strongholds of the Crusaders*, London.

Clercq, L. de (1881) 'Inventaire d'une collection de photographies executées dans le cours d'un voyage en Orient', *Archives de l'Orient latin*, 1, 365–71.

Creighton, O. (2012) *Early European Castles. Aristocracy and Authority, AD 800–1200*, London.

Creighton, O. and Higham, R.A. (2005) *Medieval Town Walls. An Archaeological and Social History of Urban Defence*, Stroud.

Dean, B. (1927) 'A Crusaders' Fortress in Palestine. A Report of Explorations made by the Museum 1926', *Bulletin of the Metropolitan Museum of Art*, 22, Part II, 1–46.

Deschamps, P. (1934) *Les Châteaux des Croisés en Terre Sainte*, vol. I: *Le Crac des Chevaliers. Étude historique et archéologique*, text and album (Bibliothèque archéologique et historique, 19), Paris.

―――― (1939) *Les Châteaux des Croisés en Terre Sainte*, vol. II: *La Défense du Royaume de Jérusalem. Étude historique, géographique et monumentale*, text and album (Bibliothèque archéologique et historique, 34), Paris.

―――― (1973) *Les Châteaux des Croisés en Terre Sainte*, vol. III: *La Défense du Comté de Tripoli et de la Principauté d'Antioche. Étude historique, géographique, toponymique et monumentale*, text and album (Bibliothèque archéologique et historique, 90), Paris.

Eger, A. (2008) 'The Spaces Between the Teeth: Environment, Settlement, and Interaction on the Islamic-Byzantine Frontier', PhD diss., University of Chicago.

Ehrlich, M. (2003) 'Crusaders' castles – the fourth generation: reflections on Frankish castle-building policy in the 13th century', *Journal of Medieval History*, 29, 85–94.

Ellenblum, R. (1995) 'Settlement and society formation in crusader Palestine', in T. Levy (ed.), *The Archaeology of Society in the Holy Land*, London, 501–11.

―――― (1996) 'Three generations of Frankish castle building in the Latin Kingdom of Jerusalem', in M. Balard (ed.), *Autour de la Première Croisade* (Analecta Sorbonensia, 14), Paris, 517–51.

―――― (2007a) *Crusader Castles and Modern Histories*, Cambridge.

―――― (2007b) 'Frankish castles, Muslim castles, and the medieval citadel of Jerusalem', in I. Shagrir, R. Ellenblum, and J. Riley-Smith (eds), *In Laudem Hierosolymitani. Studies in Crusades and Medieval Culture in Honour of Benjamin Z. Kedar* (Crusades – Subsidia, 1), Aldershot, 93–110.

Hagenmeyer, H. (1901) *Epistulæ et chartæ ad historiam primi belli sacri spectantes, quæ supersunt, ævo æquales et genuinæ. Die Kreuzzugsbriefe aus den Jahren 1088–1100. Eine Quellensammlung zur Geschichte des ersten Kreuzzugs*, Innsbruck.

Hansson, M. (2006) *Aristocratic Landscape. The Spatial Ideology of the Medieval Aristocracy*, (Lund Studies in Historical Archaeology, 2). Stockholm: Almqvist & Wiksell.

Harper, R.P. and Pringle, D. (2000) *Belmont Castle. The Excavation of a Crusader Stronghold in the Kingdom of Jerusalem* (British Academy Monographs in Archaeology, 10), Oxford.

457

Hellenkemper, H. (1976) *Burgen der Kreuzritterzeit in der Grafschaft Edessa und im Königreich Kleinarmenien. Studien zur historischen Siedlungsgeographie Südost-Kleinasiens* (Geographica Historica, 1), Bonn.

Huygens, R.B.C. (1981) *De constructione castri Saphet. Construction et fonctions d'un château fort franc en Terre Sainte*, Amsterdam.

Jacoby, D. (2008) 'Die Kreuzfahrerstadt Akko', in Piana, 2008, 242–51.

Johns, C.N. (1997) *Pilgrim's Castle ('Atlit), David's Tower (Jerusalem) and Qal'at ar-Rabad ('Ajlun). Three Middle Eastern Castles from the Time of the Crusades*, ed. D. Pringle (Variorum Collected Studies Series, 579), Aldershot.

Kedar. B.Z. (2006) 'Les murailles d'Acre franque', *Bulletin Monumental*, 164, 45–52.

———— (2009) '*Civitas* and *Castellum* in the Latin Kingdom of Jerusalem: Contemporary Frankish Perceptions', *Burgen und Schlösser*, 50–4, 199–210.

Kloner, A. and Cohen, M. (2008) 'Die Kreuzfahrerburg Beth Guvrīn', in Piana, 2008, 285–92.

Kühtreiber, T. (2009) 'Die Ikonologie der Burgenarchitektur', in O. Wagener, H. Laß, T. Kühtreiber and P. Dinzelbacher (eds), *Die imaginäre Burg* (Beihefte zu Mediävistik, 11), Frankfurt/M, 53–92.

Lawrence, T.E., ed. (1988) *Crusader Castles by T.E. Lawrence*. A new edition with introduction and notes by D. Pringle, Oxford.

Leistikow, D. (2008) 'Der "Davidsturm" in der Zitadelle von Jerusalem', in Piana, 2008, 326–35.

Liddiard, R. (2005) *Castles in Context. Power, Symbolism and Landscape, 1066 to 1500*. Macclesfield: Windgather.

Major, B. (2003) 'Castles, towers and vaults. Second report on the field surveys in the Syrian Littoral', in A. Pellitteri (ed.), *Maġāz. Culture e contatti nell'area del Mediterraneo. Il ruolo dell'Islam* (La Memoria, 15), Palermo, 73–94.

Mesqui, J. (2014) *Césarée maritime. Ville fortifiée du Proche-Orient*, Paris.

Meulemeester, J. and Pringle, D. (2008) 'Die Burg Kerak (al-Karak) in Jordanien', in Piana, 2008, 336–42.

Michaudel, B. (2011) 'Le château de Saône/Sahyûn en Syrie, creuset de l'architecture médiévale en Orient', *Chronos*, 23, 67–104.

Peilstöcker, M. (2006) 'La ville franque de Jaffa à la lumière des fouilles récentes', *Bulletin Monumental*, 164, 99–104.

Perbellini, G. (2000) 'City walls and their symbolic significance', in G. Perbellini (ed.), *The Town Walls in the Middle Ages. Les Enceintes Urbaines Au Moyen Âge* (Europa Nostra IBI Bulletin, 53), The Hague, 7–18.

Piana, M. (2007) 'Frühe Zwinger- und Vorbefestigungen an Burgen der Kreuzfahrerzeit', in H. Müller and R. Schmitt (eds), *Zwinger und Vorbefestigungen. Tagung vom 10. bis 12. November 2006 auf Schloss Neuenburg bei Freyburg (Unstrut)*, Langenweißbach, 53–62.

———— (2008), ed. *Burgen und Städte der Kreuzzugszeit* (Studien zur internationalen Architektur- und Kunstgeschichte, 65), Petersberg.

———— (2008a) 'Die Templerburg Chastel Blanc (Burğ aṣ-Ṣāfītā)', in Piana, 2008, 293–301.

———— (2008b) 'Die Kreuzfahrerstadt Sidon (Sagette, Ṣaidā)', in Piana, 2008, 367–83.

———— (2008c) 'Die Kreuzfahrerburg Toron (Qal'at Tibnīn)', in Piana, 2008, 396–407.

———— (2008d) 'Die Kreuzfahrerstadt Tripoli (Triple, Ṭarābulus)', in Piana, 2008, 422–37.

———— (2010) 'From Montpèlerin to Ṭarābulus al-Mustajadda: The Frankish-Mamluk succession in Old Tripoli', in U. Vermeulen and K. D'hulster (eds), *Egypt and Syria in the Fatimid, Ayyubid and Mamluk Eras VI* (Orientalia Lovaniensia Analecta, 183), Leuven, 307–54.

———— (2011) 'Die Wehrarchitektur der Kreuzfahrer zwischen Tradition und Innovation: die Frage nach den Einflüssen', *Burgen und Schlösser*, 52, 240–55.

———— (2013) 'The Castle of Silifke, a neglected Hospitaller fortification in Cilicia', in I.C. Ferreira Fernandes (ed.), *Castelos das Ordens Militares. Atas do Encontro Internacional, 10–13 de outubro de 2012 – Tomar, Convento de Cristo – Portugal*, Lisboa, II, 227–51.

———— (2014a) 'A bulwark never conquered: the fortifications of the Templar Citadel of Tortosa on the Syrian coast', in M. Piana and C. Carlsson (eds), *Archaeology and Architecture of the Military Orders: New Studies*, Farnham, 133–71.

———— (2014b) 'Wehrelemente an Befestigungen der Kreuzzugszeit und ihr potentieller Einfluss auf den europäischen Wehrbau', in *"Dem Feind zum Trutz" – Wehrelemente an mittelalterlichen Burgen. Tagung des Wissenschaftlichen Beirats der Deutschen Burgenvereinigung e.V., Goslar, 15.-17. März 2013*, Braubach.

———— (2015) 'Monumentality and the medieval fortification architecture of the Levant: origins and meanings', in K. D'hulster and J. van Steenbergen (eds), *Egypt and Syria in the Fatimid, Ayyubid and Mamluk Eras VIII* (Orientalia Lovaniensia Analecta), Leuven (forthcoming).

Prawer, J. (1951) 'Colonization activities in the Latin Kingdom of Jerusalem', *Revue belge de philologie et d'histoire*, 29, 1063–118.

Pringle, D. (1984) 'King Richard I and the Walls of Ascalon', *Palestine Exploration Quarterly*, 116, 133–47.

———— (1994) 'Towers in Crusader Palestine', *Château Gaillard. Etudes de Castellologie médiéval*, vol. XVI: *Actes du colloque international tenu à Luxembourg (Luxembourg) 23–29 août 1992*, Caen, 335–50.

———— (1995) 'Town defences in the Crusader Kingdom of Jerusalem', in I.A. Corfis and M. Wolfe (eds), *The Medieval City under Siege*, Woodbridge, 69–121.

———— (1997) *Secular Buildings in the Crusader Kingdom of Jerusalem. An Archaeological Gazetteer*, Cambridge.

———— (2010) 'Perceptions of the castle in the Latin East', in P. Ettel, A.-M. Flambard-Héricher and T. McNeill (eds), *Études de castellologie médiévale. Château et représentations. Actes du colloque international de Stirling (Écosse) 30 août–5 septembre 2008* (Château Gaillard, 24), Caen, 223–29.

———— (2012) 'Wilbrand of Oldenburg's journey to Syria, Lesser Armenia, Cyprus, and the Holy Land (1211–1212): a new edition', *Crusades*, 11, 109–37.

Prouteau, N. (2008) '"Beneath the battle?" Miners and engineers as 'mercenaries' in the Holy Land (XII–XIII Siècles)', in J. France (ed.), *Mercenaries and Paid Men. The Mercenary Identity in the Middle Ages. Proceedings of a Conference held at University of Wales, Swansea, 7th–9th July 2005*, Leiden and Boston, 105–17.

Re'em, A. (2010) 'Yafo, the French Hospital, 2007–2008. Preliminary Report', *Hadashot Arkheologiyot – Excavations and Surveys in Israel*, 122, 24 November 2010 (online publication).

Rey, E.G. (1871) *Étude sur les Monuments de l'Architecture Militaire des Croisés en Syrie et dans l'Ile de Chypre* (Collection des documents inédits sur l'histoire de France. Première Série. Histoire politique), Paris.

Richard, J. (1991) 'Notice sur la vie et les travaux de Paul Deschamps, membre de l'Académie', *Comptes-rendus des séances de l'Académie des Inscriptions et Belles-Lettres*, 135, 336–46.

Roll, I. (2011) 'The site, the settlement and the Crusader Castle at Arsur' in O. Tal (ed.), *The Last Supper at Apollonia. The Final Days of the Crusader Castle in Herzliya*, Tel Aviv, 8–51.

Sharon, M. and Shrager, A. (2012) 'Frederick II's Arabic Inscription from Jaffa (1229)', *Crusades*, 11, 139–58.

Smail, R.C. (1956) *Crusading Warfare, 1097–1193*, Cambridge.

Zeune, J. (1996) *Burgen – Symbole der Macht. Ein neues Bild der mittelalterlichen Burg*, Regensburg.

Zimmer, J., Meyer, W. and Boscardin, L. (2011) *Krak des Chevaliers in Syrien. Archäologie und Bauforschung 2003 bis 2007* (Veröffentlichungen der Deutschen Burgenvereinigung, Reihe A: Forschungen, 14), Braubach.

CHAPTER TWENTY-SEVEN

CRUSADER BATTLEFIELDS: ENVIRONMENTAL AND ARCHAEOLOGICAL PERSPECTIVES

———•◆•———

Raphael Y. Lewis

The following description by Ibn al-Athir of the fields of Hattin, given two years after the decisive Ayyubid triumph in Hattin, is well known:

> About two years later I passed by the site of the battle and saw the ground covered with their bones, visible from afar, some of them heaped up and others scattered about and this was apart from those that torrents had swept away or wild beasts in those thickets and hollows had taken.

(Ibn al-Athir, 2007: 324)

These words inspired travelers and scholars who visited, studied, and described the decisive historical event occurring on the on 4 July 1187 on the fields to the west of the volcanic hill "the Horns of Hattin" (Wilson, 1880: 63–66; Rae Wilson, 1824: 220–221; Conder, 1897: 147–160; Prawer, 1964: 117–124; Guérin, 1985: 125–133; Kedar, 1992: 190–207; Herde, 2002: 97–153; Ehrlich, 2007: 16–32; Lewis, 2013). But Saladin's biographer is doing more than just providing a strict and neutral observation of the battlefield. In fact, he is giving us a preliminary (and almost scientific) geomorphologic observation of the fields of Hattin associating a cause—torrents and wild beasts—with an effect—bones taken and swept away. Today, we can corroborate al-Athir's observation knowing the tendency of the clay-ish Basalt soil, covering a major part of the Hattin plain, to be swept easily by rain water (Avisar, 1973: 132–136; Liphschitz and Biger, 2004: 242–246).

Hundreds of years of change and development span between the present and historical events such as the Battle of Hattin, Arsuf and other battlefields. The people opposing each other were under the influence of manmade and natural forces before and during the fighting itself and the material signature left by them was exposed to environmental and manmade forces operating from the time of the event itself to present days. Environmental conditions such as soil, heat, humidity, radiation, sunlight, and moonlight have direct influence on both military campaigns in all periods and on the preservation of finds. In order to be able to reconstruct historical events, we must consider the environmental conditions mentioned above (and others).

Sir Basil H. Liddel Hart understood that no natural hazard could measure to the obstacles people could impose on each other (Liddell Hart, 1989: 92). It is obvious that some landscapes can be traveled faster, easier, and safer than others. Manmade features such as roads, walls, earthworks, ditches, trenches, and plowed fields can influence the movement of men in a given landscape. Therefore, in order to understand the historical event, a map representing the landscape in which the event took place should be presented. Archaeological features should be taken into account and be considered together with the environmental and historical data in order to get a picture as close as possible of the studied arena. The dynamic nature of the landscape usually presents a fundamental problem in studies which are based only on written accounts and on preliminary observations of the battlefield's topography. The researcher should cross the boundaries of his discipline and examine the subject from the widest angle possible (Arnold, 1986: 32; Bloch, 2002: 66, 99–104). Therefore, the data presented in studies of historical events should consist of three main categories of evidence: (1) environmental considerations; (2) material cultural remains; (3) written sources.

This chapter will demonstrate the significant contribution which environmental and archaeological perspectives can have on the understanding of events such as battles. The two case studies are based on the two decisive events from the days of the Latin Kingdom of Jerusalem which have recently been studied archaeologically by the writer of this chapter (Lewis, 2013; Lewis, forthcoming): the Battle of Hattin[1] (3–4 July 1187) and the Battle of Arsuf[2] (7 September 1191).

Just a little more than four years separate the two events, and some of the chief participants were present at both. But still the two open field battles were fought in very different landscapes: the Battle of Hattin was waged in the middle and eastern Lower Galilee and the Battle of Arsuf took place along the coastal plain of the Mediterranean. This makes the two events interesting case studies to follow. It should also be noted that the archaeological characteristics of the two battles (presented below), as with other open battlefields, are very different from the ones previously studied archaeologically in the Levant. First, the Battle of Hattin and the Battle of Arsuf took place over a vast landscape when the Muslim (Ayyubid) and Frankish (crusader) armies were almost constantly on the move, marching through different terrains, and the campaign lasting no more than a few days. Second, although there were many casualties, the dead bodies and other remains related to the fighting were not buried within a destruction layer but were left lying in the field in a way that was more vulnerable to post-residual processes caused by nature and man. In order to overcome these fundamental methodological challenges, it was required to look beyond the boundaries of conventional archaeological field-survey and site-detection methods, and develop a new perspective that would help to define the work within dynamic and ever-changing landscapes.[3]

A SHORT SUMMARY OF THE EVENTS OF THE BATTLE OF HATTIN[4]

The Hattin campaign was part of the jihad war declared on the Latin Kingdom of Jerusalem years before. The Muslims, led by Saladin, started to gather at the eastern part of the Jordan River in April 1187 (Lane-Poole, 1964: 201–203; Ehrlich, 2007: 24; Ibn al-Athir, 2007: 319; Asbridge, 2010: 344). On 1 May 1187, the Battle of Cresson occurred as a result of a large group of Muslim cavalry crossing into the Galilee (for a disputed reason) and meeting with a Frankish party led by the grand masters of the Templar (Gerard de Ridefort) and Hospitaller (Roger de Moulins). The collision between the two forces by the springs of Cresson (Fontaine de Cresson/Croisson) was catastrophic to the Franks, with only the grandmaster of Templar surviving the engagement and a few of the parties' follow- ers (Lane-Poole, 1964: 201–203; Baldwin, 1978: 87–92; Prawer, 1984: 529–530; Edbury, 1996: 156–157).[5] The Battle of Cresson is important not only because it led to the Battle of Hattin, but also because it made a good deal of the Muslim senior officers familiar with the same landscape as the Battle of Hattin (Lewis, 2013: 337) (Fig. 27.1).

The Muslims reinvaded the Galilee in late June 1187. They crossed the Jordan River (27 June) took the village of Kafr Sabt (30 June) and positioned themselves in other vantage points (such as Mount Tabor) in the eastern Lower Galilee and along the Safori-Tiberias road (Kedar, 1992: 193–194; Lewis, 2013: 336–337). On 2 July, one of the Muslim forces conquered Tiberias and placed its castle under siege (Kedar, 1992: 194–195; Nicolle, 1993: 61). Eventually, after a quarrel between the grandmaster of the Templar knights and Count Raymond of Tripoli, the Muslim provocation caused the Franks, led by King Guy of Lusignan, to evacuate their camps at the springs of Safori and to march on Tiberias (Kedar, 1992: 194–195; Nicolle, 1993: 62; Ehrlich, 2007: 30).

The Frankish forces started moving on 3 July. When they reached the valley of Turan, the Muslims began harassing them with endless attacks from their mounted archers (Prawer, 1964: 122; Ehrlich, 2007: 30). The march was slow and made at the pace of the infantry, which most probably circled the three main bodies of mounted knights in rings of defense (Smail, 1956: 156–157, 198; Prawer, 1980: 491; Ehrlich, 2007: 30). According to a letter written by Saladin, the Franks managed to take over one of the water sources which was on their way (most likely the spring of Turan) but later abandoned it (Lyons and Jackson,

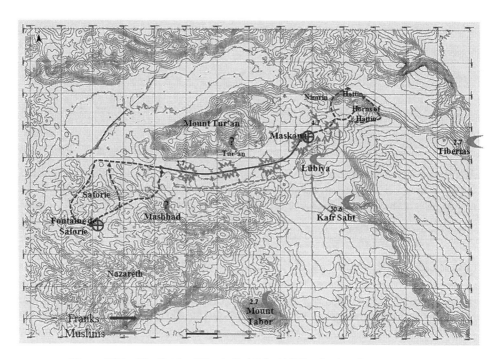

Figure 27.1   The Battle of Hattin 3–4 July 1187 battle plan. Source: Author.

1982: 259–260; Melville and Lyons, 1992: 209; Kedar 1992: 196). When they reached Maskana, known for a big seasonal pool to its south, the Franks were heavily attacked, and the rearguard led by Balowin de Iblin retreated (Smail, 1956: 196; Nicolle, 1993: 75; Ehrlich, 2007: 31).[6]

At sunset of 3 July 1187, the fighting did not stop. The Franks camped around Maskana, while the Muslims brought convoys of provision to the front line, and at the same time kept harassing the Frankish camp (Prawer, 1980: 493; Kedar, 1992: 199–200; Herde, 2002: 121). At sunrise the Franks were on the move again. The men and their horses were in total exhaustion. It was argued by some scholars that Count Raymond of Tripoli took a northern route leading to the Springs of Hattin in order to quench their thirst (Prawer, 1980: 493). Other researchers argue that on 4 July the Franks were still heading toward Tiberias as planned (Kedar, 1992: 202–203). Reading through the different sources and studies, it is hard to follow the exact order of the events, but we know that at a certain point the Muslims burned the fields around the Franks. At another point, the vanguard led by Raymond of Tripoli got the command (and honor) to charge against the Muslim troops that blocked their way. But instead of the two forces colliding, the Muslims opened their ranks and Raymond's troops went right through them, never returning to the battle-field. It is also unclear at which point the infantry fled to the Horns of Hattin, leaving the main body unprotected behind, and at which point cavalry charges made in the direction of Saladin himself were initiated by the Franks and restrained by the Muslims (Prawer, 1980: 496–499; Lyons and Jackson, 1982: 262–264; Kedar, 1992: 204; Herde, 2002: 139–140). The Muslims' victory is marked by the capture of the relic of the "True Cross," the fall of the Frankish king's red tent, his imprisonment, the massacre of the Templar and Hospital knights as well as the beheading of Count Reynald de Chatillion (Prawer, 1980: 500; Kedar, 1992: 204; Nicolle, 1993: 76–79). The total defeat of the Franks led to the fall of the holy city and the Latin Kingdom of Jerusalem. The detailed landscape archaeology study done during the Battle of Hattin Archaeological Project and the reconstruction of the Hattin landscape, allowed us, for the first time, to place the events just mentioned chrono-logically and also to point to the space where they could have occurred in the landscape (for more details see Lewis, 2013: 335–373).

A SHORT SUMMARY OF THE EVENTS OF
THE BATTLE OF ARSUF

The decisive Frankish defeat at the Battle of Hattin (3–4 July 1187 CE), the capture of the "True Cross" and the fall of Jerusalem, all led to the Third Crusade (Prawer, 1964: 117–124; Kedar, 1992: 190–207; Herde, 2002: 97–153; Ehrlich, 2007: 16–32; Lewis, 2013: 335–373; Lewis, forthcoming). The ultimate goal of the campaign was to reclaim Jerusalem, an objective that was not in fact achieved. The Battle of Arsuf was the central violent engagement of the Third Crusade which took place in an open field (Roll, 2007: 36). After Acre's surrender to the Crusaders on 12 July 1191 and the departure of Philip II Augustus to France, Richard I decided to besiege Jerusalem. Therefore, he marched on Jaffa and captured its important port in order to secure his men with constant provisions and potential reinforcements. The Arsuf battlefield was only a continuation of the monumental siege warfare taking place (from August 1191 to November 1192) on the plain of Acre and on its walls (Prawer, 1984: 63–64, 70–71). Due to the three years of siege, both the Muslims and the crusaders were looking for a decisive move before the crusaders planned to finish crossing the coastline and particularly the Sharon plain (Ehrlich, 2014: 109). The crusader forces started marching along the coastline on 22 August 1191 close to the seashore with their right flank protected by the sea (Gillingham, 1999: 174). The force was divided into several sections, each protected by infantry. The infantry suffered from the Muslim skirmishers, therefore they were split—one marched closer to the enemy while the other to the west recuperated (Nicolle, 2005: 67).

On 1 September 1191 the crusaders left Caesarea and marched for 5 km to Flum Mort (the "Dead River", modern Hadera River). On 3 September 1191 they suffered many losses because of the Muslim fire and the heat.[7] Then they camped and stayed for two days at Flum Sale (the "Salty River", modern Alexander River). On 5 September 1191 they marched into the Arsuf forest to Flum de Rochetaillée (Nahar al-Falik, modern Poleg River) with almost no casualties. On Saturday 7 September 1191, the crusaders made their way to Arsur (Arsuf/Apollonia, on modern Herzliya north-western town limits) positioned 8 km to the south (Oman, 1924: 304–309; Lyons and Jackson, 1982: 334–336; Prawer, 1984: 72–74; Gillingham, 1999: 174–178; Ibn Shaddād, 2002: 170–174; Nicolle, 2005: 55–66; Roll, 2007: 36–37; Ibn al-Athīr, 2007: 390–391).

According to Ibn Shaddād: "He [Saladin] rode out and drew up his divisions for battle, with every intention of bringing the enemy to a pitched battle, that day" (2002: 174). Richard I was probably aware of this situation and therefore moved up and down the line of men on the march (Ambroise, 1976: 252, 6207–6210; Gillingham, 1999: 176; Nicolle, 2005: 67).

Saladin's skirmishers attacked the crusaders from the early morning (Fig. 27.2), and close to Arsuf (in mid-morning, or "at the third hour" according to the *Intinerarium*, i.e. 09:00) the Muslims intensified their attack, killing many of the crusaders' horses. The Hospitallers in the rear were the target of many constant attacks (Stubbs, 1864: 262; Ambroise, 1976: 252–253, 6212–6300; Ibn Shaddād, 2002: 174; Nicolle, 2005: 74). Richard I endured, while Saladin kept raising the pressure on the crusaders' rearguard, sending his personal guard as reinforcement (Ibn Shaddād, 2002: 175; Nicolle, 2005: 75). Finally, the grand master of the order, Garnier de Naples, and one of the knights (who had come with Richard I), Baldwin Carew, could restrain themselves no more and charged from the rear, crying: "Saint Jorge [George]!" (Ambroise, 1976: 258–259, 6420–6433). They were soon followed by the rest of the host. Though a premature charge had been made, Richard I seized the moment and supported the Hospitallers' attack. Soon thereafter almost all of the knights[8] broke through the infantry line and swept the field from west to east. But the first premature cavalry charge did not throw the Muslims off balance, and it took at least two more attacks to achieve this. The series of charges made by the crusaders pressed Saladin to withdraw, leaving the field with many of his men dead and others wounded and scared. He found no consolation even from his admirer, Bahā al-Dīn Ibn Shaddād. Saladin's son (al-Afḍal) was among those who stood firm but "was shaken by this day" (Ibn Shaddād, 2002: 175–176).

The Battle of Arsuf is considered to be one of the key events of the Third Crusade, and consequently, it has been the focus of a good deal of historical research (Oman, 1924: 305–319; Smail, 1956: 156–165; Gillingham, 1999: 188–191; Lyons and Jackson, 1982: 337–339; Prawer, 1984: 74–77; Nicolle, 2005: 55–89; Roll, 2007: 35–38; Asbridge, 2010: 466–476; Ehrlich, 2014: 109–118). Some of the studies adopted a more multidisciplinary approach, considering mainly aspects of geography and topography. But like many other battlefields in the Levant, the Hattin and Arsuf battlefields were excluded from archaeological

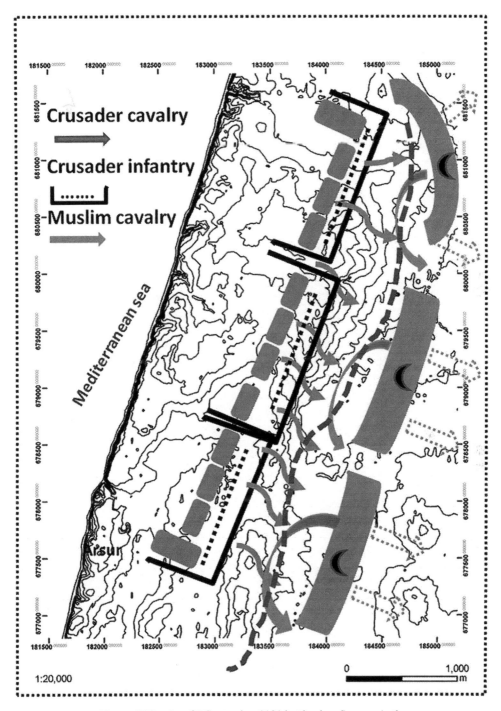

Figure 27.2 Arsuf 7 September 1191 battle plan. Source: Author.

study (Lewis, 2013: 1–3; Ehrlich, 2014: 110–111).[9] Written sources are probably the most important evidence we have for an historical account, but they are always written after the fact from a certain subjective perspective. I believe that considering related environmental and archaeological perspectives can supplement significantly our understanding of historical events because it conserves part of the traces of the original event.

ENVIRONMENTAL ASPECTS

As mentioned above, environmental conditions such as natural water sources, soil, heat, humidity, radiation, sunlight, and moonlight have direct influence on military campaigns and on the preservation of finds. Therefore in order to reconstruct historical events and especially military campaigns, environmental conditions must be considered, as will be shown below (Lewis, 2013: 141).

Geographic overview of the two battlefields

The Battle of Hattin

The Battle of Hattin took place in the central and eastern parts of the Lower Galilee (Fig. 27.3), a region which characterized by mountain ridges with wide valleys between them, laying on a west to east axis. The Nazareth Mountains are of soft limestone, which allows the growth of vegetation and in the past was cultivated intensely. The Turan Mountain, however, is characterized by hard dolomite stone, creating a landscape with

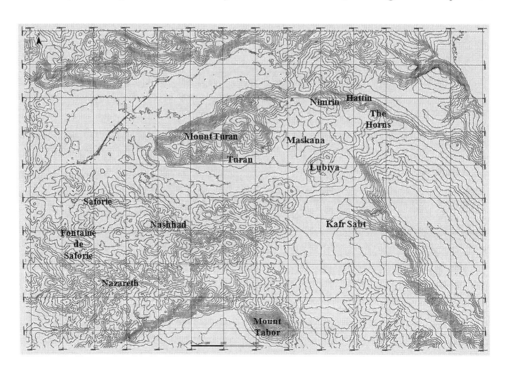

Figure 27.3 Main settlements on topographic map of the central and eastern Lower Galilee.
Source: Author.

almost no vegetation. The valley of Turan, located between these two mountains, is rich with a thick layer of alluvial soil which tends to be flooded during the rainy season. So is the valley of Beit Netofa/ al-Batuf to the north of Mount Turan.

The eastern Lower Galilee is characterized by a series of tilted blocks covered with basalt stones. The western edge of the tilted block of Arbel and the north-western border of the tilted block of Poria is characterized by soft limestone which creates a hilly landscape lying south-north and separates the Maskana plateau from the plain of Hattin. This area is the highest in the eastern Lower Galilee: the Nimra mount (by the abandoned village of Nimrin) is 392 m above sea level, Kibbutz Lavi stands at the height of 313 m above sea level, and the hill of Lubia is 326 m above sea level (Bitan, 1982: 7).

The volcanic hill known as the Horns of Hattin was formed 4–4.3 million years ego. The hill has two volcanic craters, main and a secondary, both are open to the south-west creating the two mountain peaks— giving it its name. While the hill gradually climbs from west to east, on its eastern side the slope drops rapidly (Mazor, 1980: 116–117).

The battlefield of Hattin stretches over an area of 26 km, and a good deal of that area went through significant development during the twentieth century. Therefore it was decided to concentrate in the event taken place in the area between Maskana and the Arbel Valley, a timeframe confined to the eve of 3 July and to midday of 4 July 1187. This area is also less developed from the one to its east. Kibutz Lavi and Hodayot are the main settlement in that area but there is also highways, an industrial area, a museum (in Golani Junction) and the sanctuary of Nabi Shu'ayb.

The Battle of Arsuf

The Battle of Arsuf took place in the southern part of the Sharon plain (central coastal plain of Israel). This region extends between the Yarqon River in the south and the Taninim River in the north (5 km to the north of Caesarea). The Sharon plain is about 15 km in width and extends from east to west, from the foothills of the Samaria hills to the Mediterranean (Fig. 27.4). Early coastlines had created three Kurkar ridges of hills (Kurkar is fossilized dune sandstones) parallel to the Mediterranean coastline and to each other, subdividing the Sharon plain into three valleys. The streams running from the foothills of Samaria to the sea penetrated the kurkar ridges and enabled sand from the sea to create dunes; when the streams were blocked, the kurkar ridges swamps were thus created. The first kurkar ridge is the closest to the coast and occasionally it is characterized by a steep cliff. Some of the larger ancient settlements in the Sharon plain including Caesarea and Apollonia-Arsuf were built on it (Gophna and Ayalon, 1998: 8). On its eastern side the ridge gradually slopes to the "Sharon Swale", an elongated valley that extends between the first and second kurkar ridges. The traditional and the present coastal trunk road runs along its eastern border. The second ridge is constructed from a stronger type of kurkar rock, serving as an adequate platform for the emergence of settlements throughout the ages. Since it provided a useful foundation for building purposes, it was also used for quarrying building-stones and for hewn burial caves and agricultural installations (Gophna and Ayalon, 1998: 8; Gibson, 2003: 8). The valley to the east of the second ridge is blanketed with alluvial soil. The third kurkar ridge is almost completely covered today with a red sandy soil and appears to merges with the red sand hills (*hamra*) located to its east (Gophna and Ayalon, 1998: 8). The Sharon region, and especially the eastern valley, is poorly drained and occasionally in the rainy season water accumulates creating waterholes. Throughout the nineteenth and twentieth

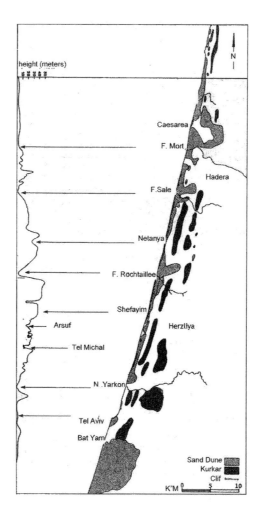

Figure 27.4   Map of the Sharon Plain. Location of kurkar ridges and sand
dunes (after Gavish and Bakler, 1990: map 2). Source: Author.

centuries the area was well known for its swamps (Gophna and Ayalon, 1998: 8). Due to
the bad drainage of the Sharon plain, it was sparsely populated throughout most eras. Only
when a centralized power invested in draining the swamps did it became more hospitable,
and permanent settlements were founded. Drainage systems had to be maintained and once
neglected the swamps reappeared. The Sharon was unattractive for agriculture and settlement in many periods, therefore throughout most of the human history the Sharon plain
served mainly as a route through which people traveled (Safrai et al., 1990: 249; Ehrlich,
2014: 113–114). Today the Sharon region is one of the most densely populated and cultivated areas in Israel.

The battlefield supposedly lies under the modern towns of Herzliya and Kibbutz
Shefayim, and the villages of Rishpon, Kfar Shmaryahu, Arsuf and Arsuf-Kedem and an
abandoned military factory.

Sunlight and moonlight

Sunlight and moonlight can have a great effect on organisms (humans are not excluded), but surprisingly there are hardly any references to such elements in the literature with regards historical events. Time calendars of sunlight and moonlight are of enormous use in modeling military campaigns, and in many cases can help us learn more about the actual events or even to put them into a more limited timeframe.

According to the cosmological data,[10] on 3 September 1187 the Frankish forces had more than fourteen hours of daylight to reach Tiberias from Saforie. This means they had to cover a distance of about 30 km at a pace of a little more than 2 km per hour. This does not look like an impossible challenge for a healthy group of people, but in war conditions this is becoming almost impossible. We should also take into account that the Franks were marching on both 3 and 4 July, facing the sun, which was probably another factor contributing to their exhaustion. According to the cosmological data, on 3 July the sun rose at 04:37 and set at 18:50. At sunset on 3 July 1187 the fighting did not stop. It is interesting that in those light conditions the Muslims were still able to bring from the east convoys of provision and at the same time keep harassing the Frankish encampment at Maskana. The moon, however, rose only fourteen minutes after midnight, hence five hours and twenty-four minutes after sunset. And when it rose, it was shining only in 28.2% moonlight capacity: five hours of complete darkness on that dark night. These are definitely not ideal conditions for horse riding, but one could easily find cover in the dark.

The sun rose (on both armies) the next morning again at 04:37, so we should consider the possibility that the order to continue the march eastwards was given only after the sun was high in the sky and out of the eyes of the Frankish archers facing east. In Arsuf the lunar conditions were almost exactly the opposite. The sun rose at 05:22 on 6 September 1191 and set at 17:50.[11] This gave the two forces at least twelve hours of sunlight. If the battle had not taken place in the fields of Arsuf, the crusader forces would have had to march to Jaffa, a distance of close to 20 km. This would not have been an easy challenge and an almost impossible task to accomplish under fighting conditions.[12] The moon during that night rose 1.27 hours after sunset. Since the night of 5 September 1191 had a full moon, it was most likely a very clear night. In these lunar conditions the two rivals could theoretically be at each other's throats continually through the night. Such a clear night could have made night-time horse-riding possible, but there would have been hardly any cover from arrows with such moonlight.

Next morning the moon set only at 06:35, which was 1.12 hours after sunrise. Another point that should be taken into account regarding the battle of Arsuf is that the crusader force was marching to the south, but during their march the Muslim archers were standing to the east of the crusaders, which gave the former a clear advantage during early morning over the Latin forces facing not just the Muslims but also the sun. So we should consider the possibility that the order to continue the march southwards was given to the crusader forces, just as with Hattin, each day of their march only after the sun was high in the sky.

Water sources

The decisive defeat of the Frankish forces at Hattin is explained by the written sources and researchers in different ways. But there is no dispute over one thing: the Muslims' total control of the main water sources along the Safori-Tiberias road and the slow movement of the Frankish forces—carrying their own provisions, heavily armed in the extreme heat of July—had led to the complete exhaustion of the Frankish army. There are few more important points that should be taken into account regarding the water sources which were in Frankish reach. The springs along the Safori-Tiberias road were discussed in past research, special attention was given to the spring of Turan in relation to the mention of a water source taken by the Franks and then abandoned (Prawer, 1980: 493; Lyons and Jakson, 1982: 259–260; Kedar, 1992: 196–97; Melville and Lyons, 1992: 208, 209, 211). Prawer noted that the spring of Turan was unreachable for the Franks due to the presence of Muslim bowmen in their flanks (Prawer, 1980: 493). Kedar showed that the water discharge of the spring of Turan was significantly lower than other springs in the region, and therefore would not be able to provide enough water for the thousands of men and animals in the Frankish force (Kedar 1992: 196–197). The spring of Turan is located at the end of a narrow gorge/wadi 1.5 m in length and no more than 60 m in width. The spring flowing out of a plastered cave has almost no open space around, so it will not be possible for more than a few men and horses to group at its entrance (Lewis, 2013: 350). The two spurs running along the two sides of the wadi are controlling it from a height of sometimes tens of meters. In fact, due to the extreme topography, the spring of Turan would be unreachable if one does not control the two spurs running above it. It would make more sense that the water source mentioned in Saladin's letter (Melville and Lyons, 1992: 209, 211) was actually water flowing down the wadi from the spring gathered at the entrance of Wadi Turan or where the modern Turan village is located. But if Kedar's observation is right, the spring's low water discharge would not make it all the way to the bottom of the wadi without trickling into the ground (Lewis, 2013: 350).

Another possibility is that Saladin in his letter was actually referring to the seasonal pool located to the south of the ruins of Maskana, Talmudic Mashkena[13] (Marecalcia/Mareschaucie), which was considered in the past also by several sources as possible water source available to the Franks (Prawer, 1980: 489–490; Kedar, 1992: 198–199; Lewis, 2013: 350). Maskana pool is a small seasonal pool, and though it is based on what looks like a volcanic crater, it was modified and maintained by people in the past (Fig. 27.5). We can learn this from several features located at the north-eastern and south-eastern points of the pool. The first north-eastern feature is a channel that was cut and then built with basalt stones.

The channel runs north from the north-eastern corner of the pool, and along the basalt plateau to its east and the western edge of the settlement. It was probably built by the inhabitants in order to enlarge the catchment basin of the pool from the west and served to maximize the collecting basin of the Maskana pool. Another feature which meets the north-eastern part of the pool is a small road leading from the settlement of Maskana which overlooks it. Today, due to modern development, only the beginning of the road can be seen, but it is evident in aerial photos taken in 1945. The feature located at the south-eastern part of the pool is an access ramp connecting the pool to the empyreal roman Sefori-Tiberias road. This road was dated in the past, and again during the Battle of Hattin archaeological project to the first half of the second century CE was in constant use to the beginning of the twentieth century. The village of Maskana was inhabited during the Late Roman, and the Byzantine periods and it is mentioned in the Ottoman cadastral register of 1555–1556. It was mentioned in Frankish sources regarding the Battle of Hattin as a casale (a village) (*L'estoire de Eracles*: 63; *Libellus*: 223; Kedar, 1992: 198–199) and therefore Kedar concludes that it is very likely that it was also inhabited during the twelfth century. Twelfth-century pottery was found during three different archaeological surveys done at the site of Maskana support

Figure 27.5 Milestone positioned at the center of the Maskana pool probably for estimating water level, and the same milestone by the Roman Road (Lewis, 2013: 293, fig. 83). Source: Author.

Kedar's assumption (Leibner, 2004: 336–337; Lewis, 2013: 351). Maskana pool is an open reservoir, and it is possible that the quality of water was not high. According to British Intelligence in 1918, the water in the pool were considered to be good for animals but not for men (Kedar, 1992: 200–201, n. 36). Today, though declared as a small national park, the water in the pool is polluted by cattle and most likely also by the road traveling north, a gas station, and an army camp located nearby.

Additional information regarding the pool of Maskana was gathered during the Battle of Hattin Archaeological Project. It seems that the seasonal pool of Maskana is not as seasonal as was expected in the past. Apparently, once in every few years, the pool remains with substantial amount of water throughout the whole summer. After the channel leading water into the pool from the north was reopened accidently, due to earthworks, during the winter of 2008 the pool stayed with water until summer 2014. On 3 July 2009 the pool was measured and had approximately 1.2 million liters of water in it (Fig. 27.6) (Lewis, 2013: 295). According to the Canadian Agri-Food Research Council an average-size horse (545 kg) when not working hard drinks about 27 liters of water a day. Therefore during 3 July 2009 there was enough water in the pool to sustain 44,444 (not very thirsty) horses (Lewis, 2013: 351, n. 386). It should also be noted that apart from the Maskana pool there are four other seasonal pools along the Roman road and in the Lubia/Hattin plain, although less impressive than the one just discussed, and it is very likely that they were already dry in late spring, just as today.[14]

As Herde suggested, because of the subtropical climate conditions in this region, water cisterns were always the most common and repayable water source in the Levant

471

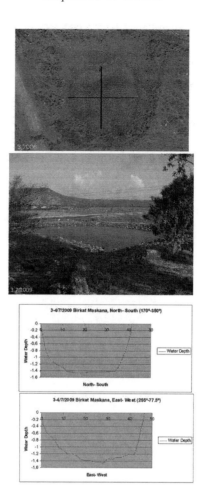

Figure 27.6   Maskana pool (from top to bottom): aerial photo from March 2006 with two sections, pool with water 4 July 2009, two sections taken for estimation of amount of water (Lewis, 2013: 294, fig. 84). Source: Author.

(2002: 111–112). There are hundreds of such installations between Safori and Hattin, and though water cisterns are hard to date by archaeological excavations, it is very likely that because of their relations to other features in the landscape and the dating of the main settlement in the region, most of the water cisterns were built in the Early Roman to Byzantine periods and sustained by the villagers and farmers until 1948; in other words, they could have been operating at the time of the battle of Hattin. Only in the village of Lubia, which had continuous occupation from the Early Roman period to the mid-twentieth century, are there over 200 water cisterns (Khalidi, 1992: 527; Alexandre, 2003: 27–9; Leibner, 2004: 341–343; Lewis, 2013: 246–250, 296, fig. 86, 297–298). Apart from a few rare cases of water cisterns which were built from basalt stones and plastered, most of the water cisterns are cut into limestone, and therefore can be found mainly were this rock formation exists (Lewis, 2013: 297–298). The survey done during the Battle of Hattin Archaeological Project enabled us to follow, for the first time, the exact route traveled by the Frankish forces through most of the area between Maskana and the Horns of Hattin (Lewis, 2013: 354–360). The Franks walked through most of 3 and 4 July 1187 in the valley of Turan and the plain of Hattin, which are covered with a thick layer of alluvial soil with no water cisterns on their way, while the Muslims were controlling the hills around them, which are dotted with plenty of water cisterns. This could give the Muslims another considerable advantage over the Franks. Seven water cisterns (only one is functional today) were located during the survey on Maskana (Lewis, 2013: 296). The artifacts destitution analysis shows that the Franks crossed the watershed not far from two big water cisterns,[15] but even if those water cisterns were not contaminated by the Muslims and available to the Franks, still the Muslims total control of the water cisterns should be considered as a major factor in their decisive victory.

The march to Jaffa during the Third Crusade shows that the Latin forces preferred to locate their encampments near running-water streams. Hence it was interesting to learn how much daytime the crusaders would have had in order to get from one encampment to the next during each single day. As mentioned earlier, by camping by the Wadi al-Falik the night before the battle, the crusaders were provided with a good source of water, and this also allowed them to camp on a well-protected position overlooking the land to the north, east, and south. This would have been very important on the very clear night of 6 September 1191.

Albedo

Apart from sunlight and the availability of water sources, there is another environmental factor that can effect human exhaustion. Albedo is the amount of electromagnetic radiation, reflected from the sun, which is bounced back to the atmosphere after hitting and heating different surfaces. The closer a man or animal is to the surface, the more they are affected by the heat and radiation. The brighter a surface is, more electromagnetic radiation will be returned from it to the atmosphere: snow, for instance, returns the highest amount of radiation, but darker surfaces will absorb more of the radiation which could turn to heat (Hall et al., 2005: 801–802, 810). During the Battle of Hattin, the Franks could have used the volcanic crater and the basalt plateau overlooking the Maskana pool as an encampment for the night of 3 July, but in the morning, walking from that point eastwards on the dark soil of the basalt plateau, the heat generated from it would have been a major factor adding to the heat and thirst from which they were already suffering (Lewis, 2013: 153–156, 365–367).

During the Battle of Arsuf, the sun could be reflected into the eyes of the crusaders and Muslims. Theoretically, the albedo could have heated the sand dunes close to the shore, but it is more likely that the crusader forces were marching between the first and second kurkar ridges (Lewis, forthcoming), an area with more chance of coverage by coastline vegetation, which will reduce the albedo effect to a minimum.

Wind direction and velocity

It is clear that wind direction and velocity could have a significant influence on humans, especially on their capabilities of maneuvering and on their sight. It will also have great effect on the accuracy and range of ballistic weapons. Those could be very important to the outcome of historical events and understanding them. [16]

The wind on the Hattin plain during summertime tends to blow from west or south-west. The wind is strongest at about 11:00, at about 17:00 it will slow down, and then it starts blowing stronger again at about 02:00. Table 27.1 gives data from the agro-metallurgical station at Kibbutz Lavi (positioned on the Hattin plain) for the last five years.

The wind direction at Hattin blows from west to south-west and has two implications for the battle. First, it will give considerable advantage to those shooting ballistic weapons from the west—with the wind direction. An experimental archaeology test made during the Battle of Hattin reenactment in 2011 showed that the range of an arrow shot from a 60 lb composite bow, at a 45 degree angle, can reach a distance of over 60 m when shot with the wind direction and not against it.[17] Second, and just as important, the western winds blowing on the Hattin plain meant that the Muslims could only light a fire after the Franks had crossed the Muslims line and the Franks were positioned to the east of them. Any fire lit when the Franks were situated to the west of the Muslims troops would play into Frankish hands, creating a screen of smoke between the two forces, cutting communication between the Muslim units or even burning the Muslims themselves (Lewis, 2013: 154–155, 365–367).

The wind in Arsuf, as in the coastal region of the eastern Mediterranean, usually starts blowing in the morning, first from the south-west, and then during the day it moves clockwise and reaches the north-west in the afternoon. Usually the wind stops in the evening, and starts up again during the second half of the night. It grows stronger, with the wind coming from the highland region. According to Jaffe and Fledel (1990: 100), this is the general characteristic of the wind throughout the year, but especially in summer. Changes from the characteristics mentioned above usually happened between seasons (such as in September). At that time (and in winter), hot, dry, and turbulent eastern winds descend from Mount Carmel and Samaria to the Sharon. These can reach the speed of 20 knots (37.04 km per hour) and more (Jaffe and Fledel, 1990: 100).

When the crusaders entered the forest of Arsuf, they were worried that the Muslims would set it on fire (Ambroise, 1976: 248, 6095–6100). Through most of their march to the south, the wind was blowing at the back of the marching crusaders, giving them an advantage in ballistic range, the carrying of dust, and the direction that a forest fire would spread. The wind direction can also provide another explanation as to why Saladin preferred attacking the rearguard (at the north) throughout most of the march. Positioning his troops to the east or to the south-east of the marching crusaders not only would have put his archers in an inferior position but also would have unnecessarily risked the lives of his people owing to the danger of forest fires extending from the north-west. By contrast, if we consider the account by the Regis Ricardi, of clouds of dust covering both the crusaders and Muslims

Table 27.1 Wind speed (agro-metallurgical station Kibbutz Lavi)

Date	Highest wind speed (meters per second)	Date	Highest wind speed (meters per second)	Date	Highest wind speed (meters per second)
2.7.2009	9.9	3.7.2009	9.7	4.7.2009	8
2.7.2010	8.7	3.7.2010	9	4.7.2010	9.4
2.7.2011	9.1	3.7.2011	9.3	4.7.2011	10.1
2.7.2012	9.4	3.7.2012	7.9	4.7.2012	8.5
2.7.2013	7.6	3.7.2013	8.2	4.7.2013	9

(Stubbs, 1864: 271), this must be seen to be more than just a metaphor which was meant to dramatize the event. It is likely therefore that in the early hours of 7 September, the wind was not blowing hard or in a clear direction, and that as a result it did not provide an advantage to either of the two rivals.

Temperature and humidity

Different levels of temperature and humidity can create a false reading of their effect on the human body. Only by putting the temperature and humidity one against the other can we really get an idea of the extent of the heat burden (Lewis, 2013: 152).

The temperature at the eastern Lower Galilee and Hattin is the same as for the rest of the Levant, the highest during the month of August. The maximum temperature ever measured in this region, 49°C, was at the Sea of Galilee. During summer at daytime, temperatures will be between 20° and 23°C at 6:00 and will reach its maximum of 30° to 36°C at about 14:00. In Nazareth the average temperature during summer is 30°C (Table 27.2).

Table 27.3 gives data from the agro-metallurgical station at kibbutz Lavi concerning relative humidity measured from the last five years.

The climate in the Sharon plain, and Arsuf, is of Mediterranean temperatures. August is the hottest month in the year, but the highest temperatures in the Sharon were actually measured during the fall and spring. The temperature between the two main seasons can rise up to 40°C (in the shade). The number of days in which the temperature is higher than 30°C near the coastline is relatively low. The radiation in the Sharon is relatively lower than in other regions in Israel because it is covered with clouds for many days throughout the year (165 calories per square cm). However, fog during daytime is a rare phenomenon in the Sharon, and if it happens, it disappears soon after sunrise (Jaffe and Fiedel, 1990: 99–100). Though humidity is at its highest during the winter months, it is also high in summer and the relative humidity is between 70% and 85% during the day, and at night can rise up to 95%. In addition, there are 200–240 nights of dew in a year, and a good number of these are during the summer (Jaffe and Fiedel, 1990: 100).

One of the differences between the Battle of Hattin and the Battle of Arsuf is that on 6 September on the Sharon plain the two rivals stopped their quarrel for the night. At Hattin, the fighting did not stop on the night of 3 July, and the Muslims archers continued to harass the Franks at their encampment throughout the night, after a long day of fighting in the blazing Levantine summer. In Arsuf, however, at least some of the warriors could get some rest and even some sleep. But just as importantly, the Franks were sweating under intense physical and mental difficulty. When one is wearing several layers of clothing, the sweat can hardly evaporate. This helps with cooling the body during daytime, but at night, when the relative humidity percentage can easily go over 90%, not taking off the armor and drying the moisture under it would contribute significantly to the body's dehydration and exhaustion, even when at rest.[18]

ARCHAEOLOGICAL ASPECTS

Archaeology deals with a wide range of material culture. However, at this point I would like to present only two case studies where archaeology can contribute significantly to the understanding of a historical event that took place in the landscape; in other words, locating time in space.

Table 27.2 Temperature (agro-metallurgical station Kibbutz Lavi)

Date	Temperature in Celsius	Ground temperature 5 cm at 08:00	Date	Temperature in Celsius	Ground temperature 5 cm at 08:00	Date	Temperature in Celsius	Ground temperature 5 cm at 08:00
2.7.2009	23–36	28.6	3.7.2009	25.9–32.6	27.8	4.7.2009	25.8–31.5	27.6
2.7.2010	18.3–32.4	26.6	3.7.2010	20–33.1	27.1	4.7.2010	19.2–36.3	27.4
2.7.2011	19.6–34.1	24.9	3.7.2011	20.3–36.1	25.5	4.7.2011	21–35	26.1
2.7.2012	18.3–34.3	27.2	3.7.2012	23.6–33.4	28.5	4.7.2012	21.8–32.9	27.6
2.7.2013	18.6–31.7	26.7	3.7.2013	20.4–33.1	27.1	4.7.2013	18.6–33.8	26.9

Table 27.3 Relative humidity (agro-metallurgical station Kibbutz Lavi)

Date	Relative humidity %	Date	Relative humidity %	Date	Relative humidity %
2.7.2009	17.4–81.2	3.7.2009	29.4–90.7	4.7.2009	36–90.2
2.7.2010	38–86.3	3.7.2010	42.7–87.4	4.7.2010	34.3–91.8
2.7.2011	32–84.2	3.7.2011	32.8–86.2	4.7.2011	24.5–88
2.7.2012	27.9–88.6	3.7.2012	21.4–79.4	4.7.2012	28.5–78.9
2.7.2013	34–87.1	3.7.2013	39.4–88.5	4.7.2013	29.8–93

Communications: road systems

Topography usually determines the way in which a network of roads is laid out in the landscape. Generally, there is a strong link between land structure and the location of roads in antiquity (Safrai et al., 1990: 253; Gibson, 1995: 237–258; Lewis, 2013: 269). In addition, continuity is one of the most important aspects in landscape archaeology. In relation to roads, we find that people used the same tracks or lines in the landscape for thousands of years. Because of these two factors (topography and continuity), roads should be classified and understood as part of the structural features of the long durée.

Archaeologists have suggested different ways in which to classify roads (Gibson, 1995: 237; Roll, 1996: 153–154; Wilkinson, 2003: 60, 62, 113, 116). Due to the landscape archaeology approach of those two case studies, I adopted Gibson's model for the categorization of roads: international roads (highways); regional roads; local roads.

The main difference between Gibson's approach to that of other researchers is that his classification is free from directly referencing a specific construction technique, period, or culture.[19] Gibson regards roads as communication systems linking different types or levels of settlements and trade centers with other landscape components such as agricultural fields, industrial and agricultural installations, or burial complexes (Gibson, 1995: 237; Lewis, 2013: 269).

During the Battle of Hattin Archaeological Project, eighteen pre-modern roads (of all the three different levels mentioned above) and nineteen road junctions were found, surveyed, and in some cases excavated. Many of those roads were already present during the Battle of Hattin and served travelers in this region for hundreds of years before and after the Hattin campaign (Lewis, 2013: 269–291). One of the main questions that came up in studies concerning the battle was whether on the morning of 4 July 1187 the Franks were marching to the springs of Hattin or were still following their initial plan, getting to Tiberias (Prawer, 1980: 493; Kedar, 1992: 202–203; Lewis, 2013: 373). The artifact distribution analysis done during the Battle of Hattin Project points out that the Franks crossed the watershed (the hills of Lavi) at exactly the location where they left the international road to Tiberias and climbed north to the Hattin plain. Initially, it would seem that the climbing by the Franks north toward the Hattin plain while leaving the Saforie-Tiberias road supports Prawer's theory that at that point they were aiming toward the Springs of Hattin. But a more detailed look at the road system map drawn during the Battle of Hattin Project will suggest otherwise, as it reveals that even from the Hattin plain the Franks could continue advancing toward Tiberias on a regional road, bypassing the Horns of Hattin from the south (Fig. 27.7). This road that runs along the southern border of the Hattin plain and an extensive co-axial field system could eventually lead them back to the Saforie-Tiberias road they had left earlier (Lewis, 2013: 277 fig. 74, 278, 283–284 table 19, 285–289, 373). Once it was understood where the watershed was crossed, we could reconstruct it chronologically and suggest a point where other events, mentioned by the sources, occurred. Those series of events (which will not be discussed here), accompanied by the fire ignited by the Muslims after they crossed them to the east, drove the Franks to make a last stand on the volcanic hill on the eastern border of the plain and on the fields just to its west (Prawer, 1980: 497–500; Kedar, 1992: 204; Nicolle, 1993: 65–79; Herde, 2002: 139–140; Lewis, 2013: 3360–3373).

Due to their terrible state of preservation, it is hard to reconstruct the ancient road systems in the western part of the Sharon plain based on the existing archaeological record.

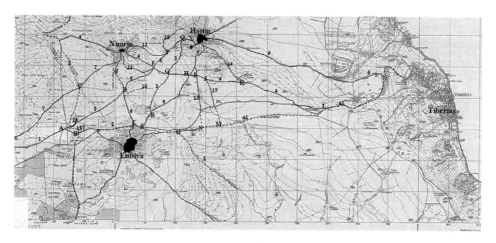

Figure 27.7 Map of roads and junctions between Maskana and Tiberias studied during the Battle of Hattin Project. Source: Author.

Learning about the road system can be done mainly by relying on sources such as the position of one or two ancient urban centers, mid-nineteenth- to mid-twentieth-century cartography, and aerial photographs taken before the intensive modern development (Roll and Ayalon, 1989: 222–223; Safrai et al., 1990: 249, 256–258; Roll, 1994: 38–40; Wilkinson, 2003: 33–37; Lewis, 2013: 120–123, 133–188; Lewis, forthcoming).

Smail argued that the Franks were not dependent on roads when applying the fighting technique known as the "fighting-march" (1956: 304–305). Smail's analysis infers that the study of road systems is neither relevant for the Arsuf and Hattin campaigns nor for any other Frankish military affair that involved this tactic. I tend to disagree with this, since even if physically Frankish men and their horses did not have to walk on the paved roads, they were still bound to travel on the same network of roads which was based on the region's infrastructure.

It is evident from the road-system map that there were at least four land roads (Roll and Ayalon, 1989: 229, fig. 140) in the sub-region, among them one international and three regional roads, leading to and from Apollonia-Arsuf (Fig. 27.8). Crossroads are points for decision-making; if one wants to influence the decision of an opponent then a road junction will be just the right place to do this. The road junction near Arsuf must be regarded as a regional focal point. Connecting different levels of roads, it was the most important junction between Caesarea and Jaffa. It is evident that this focal point attracted a lot of human activity, including that of military conflicts (Gichon, 1990: 289–317).[20] In fact, the Arsuf road junction could be the key for understanding why the event took place in this specific location between Caesarea and Jaffa. The Arsuf junction presents a dilemma: either going south along the coast to Jaffa or proceeding to the east toward Jerusalem.

Arsuf was the first place to be encountered in the march down the coast from where the crusaders could actually leave the coastal road and then go east to Jerusalem. Marching to Jerusalem through the broad Lydda (Lod) plain could suit their battle tactics in the best way.[21] Saladin undoubtedly took a greater risk by attacking the crusaders at Arsuf: a decisive loss on his side might have sent the crusader army straight on to Jerusalem. I would like

Figure 27.8   Road and junctions at the vicinity of Apollonia/Arsuf. Aerial photograph
(dev-12 60196021. 28.1.1946). Source: Author.

to suggest that Saladin was not fully aware that their target at that point was in fact Jaffa and
not Jerusalem. As mentioned earlier, the Muslim defeat at Arsuf was no more than a moral
blow, but the capture of Acre was much more significant.

Saladin took the risk and attacked with all his might. He lost the battle, but the assault
at Arsuf contributed significantly to the fact that the crusader forces decided not to march
straight on to Jerusalem (Lewis, forthcoming).

The Walls of Hattin

During the archaeological Project of Hattin many areas and features, which went through tremendous changes over the years, were studied archaeologically. One evident change that was made relates to the ancient fortification walls surrounding the Horns dated to the Late Bronze Age and to the Iron Age IIa–b. The excavation of several archaeological features on the Horns of Hattin itself exposed a complicated complex. Late Bronze and Iron Age IIa-b settlements existed on the mountain. It seems that the basalt soil eroded into the main crater, together with the laying of the co-axial field system in the second century CE on a good deal of the eastern Lower Galilee, covered a series of buildings and structures dated to those periods and maybe others (Gal, 1992: 213–214; Lewis, 2013: 260–268) (Fig. 27.9).

This is the testimony of one of the villagers of Hattin who during the 1948 Arab–Israeli war defended their village from the top of the Horns just as strategic reasoning would recommend:

> We joined our lookouts on the Horns of Hi[a]ttin. Numerically, we were fewer; however, our position overlooked theirs … we saw every move they made. As they advanced towards us … we fought them fiercely for more than four hours and forced them to halt. A few of us went down the mountain and dug in behind the rocks; when they opened fire, the Jews thought that they were trapped and decided to retreat.

(Khalidi, 1992: 522–523)

Figure 27.9 Main features on the Horns of Hattin. Source: Author.

After the Israeli Independence War and taking over the Horns of Hattin (in the second attempt) during Operation Dekel, the Israeli Defense Forces and the city officer of Tiberias fortified the mountain. Comparing the photos taken before and after 1948 demonstrates that new roads were cut into and around the Horns and that trenches were dug into the ancient walls themselves. This information has tremendous implications for our understanding of the final stages of the battle. Back in 1823 Rae Willson still had to get off his mule in order to climb to the Horns and so did other pilgrims and travelers (Rae Wilson, 1824: 221; Hodder, 1878: 273). It is evident, however, that when the Frankish army reached the Horns of Hattin, probably toward midday of 4 July, the walls circling them would have been much closer in character to those visible on the images taken before 1948.

The secondary crater is also open to the south-west, but unlike the main crater, there is no natural or manmade feature which can prevent horses from getting to its peak through the field that climbs gradually to it. Though the crater is accessible from the west, its peak can still be well protected. This is due to the fact that the Iron Age IIa–b wall runs along its southern border and a natural wall of basalt boulders is running along its northern edge. The field between those two walls measures 120 by 80 m. Approaching the northern Horn, would mean crossing through a blind spot. It would seem that due to this special layout of archaeological and natural features, the northern Horn could be approached by horses and could also be easily defended. At the peak of the Horn there is an open area (about 8.5 m in diameter). This feature, which is probably the top of the volcanic chimney of the secondary crater, is almost clear of stones. Despite the different obstacles mentioned, the battlefield south-west and south of the peak can be viewed easily from the height of a man standing at this point on the peak of the northern Horn (Fig. 27.11). The fact that the peak of the Horns can be approached by cavalry, it can be protected and that the battlefield can be viewed

Figure 27.10 Looking west to the battlefield from the peak of the northern horn.
Photograph: Author.

Figure 27.11 Eye sight from the height of 1.7 m. The area covered is marked in white (Socet GXP, courtesy of BAE Systems; Lewis, 2013: 369, fig. 126). Source: Author.

from it would make it the most appropriate place for King Guy's position during the final stages of the battle. However, only a handful of people and horses could stand together on the northern Horn's peak.

It seems that, unlike suggestions in the past (Prawer, 1980: 499), there is evidence that horses (at least in large numbers) could not climb into the main crater of the volcano and definitely could not be grouped and charge toward Saladin's position.[22] It seems that only infantry could climb into the main crater and up to the southern Horn. But a small group of horses and riders could climb up to the peak of the northern Horn and use it as a last stand, or could serve the Frankish king and his company as a stronghold where he was finally captured. Moreover, as just mentioned above, since only a small group of horses could group on the northern peak, it would seem that most of the knights were cornered against the volcanic hill without being able to use it as refuge. If the typical western winds were also blowing on the plain on that day, carrying the fire and their arrows eastward, the Muslims would have had another considerable advantage on the encircled knights.

THE LOCATION OF THE BATTLE OF ARSUF AND THE LOCATION OF THE ARSUF (SHARON) FOREST

The forest of Arsuf/Arsur was once part of a very large area of woodland stretching over most of the Sharon plain of modern Israel (Waisel and Agami, 1990: 118–120; Ehrlich, 2014: 113).

One of the great enigmas concerning the reconstruction of the landscape of the southern Sharon plain on the eve of the battle pertains to the location of the Arsuf forest. According to Conder and Kitchener: "The country south-west of Mukhalid is an open woodland of oak, the trees attaining a fair size" (1881: 136). The two explorers identify the wood as the crusader's forest of Arsur, located between the Salt River (Nahr Iskanderuneh/modern Alexander) and Rochetaillie (al-Falik/Poleg) (Conder and Kitchener, 1881: 136). The forest may also be seen delineated on the Survey of Western Palestine map from 1880 together with the legendary "Oak Forest" (Conder and Kitchener, 1881, Sheet X, scale one inch to the mile). The forest is marked on the map approximately at the village of Mukhalid and extends southwards from the al-Falik stream, south-east to Kefar Saba, and almost as far as al-Haram (Sayiduna [Sidna] ʿAli) on the south-west.

According to Ambroise, on the day before the battle the crusader forces came out of the forest and camped on open land near Rochetaillie. It could be understood from Ambroise that the Arsuf forest's southern border was on the banks of Rochetaillie/al-Falik (Prawer, 1984: 74), but it is clear from the eye-witness cited in Ibn Shaddād's description of the battle that the three charges made against the Muslims took place near the woods and in that direction (Ibn Shaddād, 2002: 175).

It seems that the literary sources on the Battle of Arsuf actually give us the approximate western boundary of that famous and long-gone forest. According to Ibn Shaddād, the crusader forces charged three times against their enemy. Those cavalry charges were directed (mainly) toward the east, because of the danger of being drawn into an ambush (in the forest), and thus the charges were stopped at its edge (Ibn Shaddād, 2002: 175). Ibn al-Athīr tells us: "close to the Muslims there was a grove of dense trees which the Muslims entered and the Franks suspected that it was a trick, so they withdrew and took the pressure off them" (2007: 391). Ambroise claims that the Muslims fled into the woods, climbed up trees and hid behind the bushes (1976: 261, 6519–6520).

The detailed archaeological field study, done at the valley located between the first and second kurkar ridges and just north-east of Arsuf, leads us to believe that this is where the Battle of Arsuf took place. Though the fields of Arsuf went through great changes due to modern development, a decision was made after the reconstruction of the landscape to try to look for the material signature of the Battle of Arsuf. Fortunately, a handful of finds[23] that could be related to the battle were located in close proximity to each other by a metal detector (Lewis, forthcoming).

Though we might have some sources that may suggest that the crusaders chased the Muslim for a distance of up to two leagues or in the direction of the sea (Ambroise, 1976: 261, 6523–6529; Edbury, 1996: 180), I think there is good reason to believe that the three charges described were made toward the east and were stopped at the forest's edge. If the charge was made by the crusader forces toward the east, and taking into account the artifacts found during the survey together with the range of an arrow and the distance of an affective cavalry charge, it is reasonable to point to the approximate distance from the battlefield to the western border of the Arsuf forest.

It has been shown how crucial and vital archaeological and environmental aspects can be for the understanding of historical events. But it seems that the case of the Battle of Arsuf shows that this works in both directions, when the written and archaeological evidence can help us point to the approximate location of the lost forest of Arsuf.

CONCLUSION

There are many other matters which were studied during the Battle of Hattin and the Battle of Arsuf Projects, which were not brought up here. The main objective of this chapter was to show the importance of widening our point of view, on what was once considered as strictly historical objective. Hattin and Arsuf were the first time that a research framework for the discipline of Battlefield Archaeology[24] was presented and applied successfully in the Levant. The fact that the two case studies chosen were of crusader battlefields is not coincidental and relates to the great number of sources and the eminence of the historical studies on them. Those works were fundamental for this archaeological field study which attempted to find and understand the material imprint of the short durée. Those studies were also important because some of them already initiated a multidisciplinary approach. But it was mainly demonstrated here that written, environmental, and archaeological perspectives should always be considered at an almost equal level when looking into a historical event such as a field battle and warfare including our subject matter—the Latin East.

NOTES

I am indebted to Prof. Tal and the Israel Antiquities Authority (IAA) for supporting this study during the academic year 2013–14. I would also like to thank Dr. Huake Kenzler for his remarks on the script and the rest of the Apollonia excavation team from the Tel Aviv University and the University of Tübingen, for their support during the project.

1 The Battle of Hattin Project was carried out by the author of this chapter during his doctoral study. The PhD thesis titled *Archaeology of Conflict: The Decisive Stage of the Battle of Hattin as a Case Study*, supervised by Prof. A. Boas, was granted by the University of Haifa.

2 The Battle of Arsuf Project was carried out as a post-doctoral research project by the author at Tel Aviv University, Department of Archaeology and Ancient Near Eastern Cultures, under the supervision of Prof. O. Tal.

3 In my dissertation I argued that historical events such as battles, political assassinations, and even natural disasters, which are of short duration, have to be examined in the light of the structural (i.e. long durée) and the circumstantial-cyclical (i.e. medium durée) categories as well. Events cannot really be fully understood without the researcher initiating the broader perspective, moving from the macro (as represented by the landscape) to the micro (as represented by the specific artifact). In fact, the approach taken by the Annales School has been adopted here, and seems to contribute to the broadening of our knowledge more than the Historical-Positivist School (Lewis, 2013: 80–4).

4 The summary of events on the two battles discussed is presented at this point for the general orientation of the reader. The main preliminary sources for the battle where presented, debated and assessed mainly by Prawer and Kedar (Prawer, 1980: 484–486; Kedar, 1992: 192). The main preliminary sources for the battle are: Theodericus, *Libellus de Locis Sanctis*, eds. M.L. and W. Bulst, (1976), Heidelberg; *L'estoire de Eracles empereur la conqueste de la Terre d'Outremer*, (1844–1859), RHCr.Occ., II, Paris: 52; L. de Mas Latrie, (ed.), (1871), *Chronique d'Ernoul et de Bernard le Trésorier*, Paris: 155–166; Röhricht, R. (1893–1904), *Regesta regni hierosoly-mitani* and *Additamentum*, Innsbruck No. 664a, No. 658, Nos. 661 and 661 Additamentum, No. 660; Principes transmarinae Ecclesiae ad Fridericum I, M. G. H. SS., XXI, 475; Ibn al-Athir,

The Chronicle of Ibn al-Athir for the Crusading Period from Al- Kāmil fi'l-ta'rikh, trans. D.S. Richards (2007), Ashgate: Aldershot: 322–324; Kraemer, J. (1952), *Der Struz des Königreichs Jerusalem (583/1187) in der Darstellung des 'Imad ad-Din al- Katib al- Isfahani*. Wiesbaden; Abū Shāma (1898), *Le livre des deux jardins*, in RHC. Or. vol. 4, Paris: 286–287ss.; MS REG. LAT. 598.; Al-Safadi, *al-Wāfi bi-l Wafāyāt*, ed. A. al-Arnā'ūt and T. Mustafā, (2000), vol 6 of 29, Beirut p.117; MS 6024; Bahā'al-Din Ibn Shaddād (1884), *Anecdotes et beaux Traits de la Vie du Sultan Youssof* in RHC. Or. vol. 3, Paris.

5   The location of this battle is still uncertain; a few possible locations were suggested in the past by travelers and scholars (Palmer, 1881: 122; Conder and Kitchener, 1881: 413; Abel, 1938; 422; Prawer, 1984: 529–530; Guerin, 1985: 111–112; Pringle, 2001: 239; Ibn al-Athir, 2007: 319; Lewis, 2013: 10–11). A recent archaeological study undertaken by the author of this chapter shows that a violent event occurred at the springs of Saforie during the late twelfth to early thirteenth centuries. This could strengthen Ibn al-Athir's account about the location of the battle by those springs (Ibn al-Athir, 2007: 319; Lewis, 2013: 345–346).

6   It is unclear if Balowin de Iblin himself retreated already at this point or later in the battle.

7   Richard I himself was also injured by an arrow.

8   The Normans and English (Anglo-Normans) were held in reserve (Gillingham, 1999: 178; Nicolle, 2005: 78).

9   The main preliminary sources for the battle are: Ltin peregr. Gest. Regis Ricardi, c. XVII–XX (ed. W. Stubbs: 260–77); Ambroise, L'Estorie, v. 6125–6730 (ed. G. Paris, cols. 163–180); cf. Hubert and La Monte 1941: 249–68; Bahā al-Dīn Ibn- Shaddād (trans. D. S. Richards) (2002), The Rare and Excellent History of Saladin. Aldershot; Imad ad-Din al-Katib al-Isfahani (tr. H. Massè), Conuête de la Syrie et de la Palestine par Saladin, 383–388 (340–4), Paris; Abu Shamah, Kitab al-Rawdatayn' in Recueil Historens des Croidades: Historiens Orientaux, IV&. V, Paris (1898).

10   According to the Wise Observatory Center in Ramon (http://wise-obs.tau.ac.il/~eran/Wise/wise_calen.html).

11   According to the Wise Observatory Center in Ramon (http://wise-obs.tau.ac.il/~eran/Wise/wise_calen.html).

12   During the march to Tiberias from Saforie on the 3 July 1187 the Franks covered a distance of about 17 km.

13   "Mashkena"–Mishkenot–Mishkan in Hebrew means 'dwellings'.

14   One east of Maskane Poll (188600/242986), another on the plain of Hattin (192730/244950) both unnamed, a third pool located south of the Horns of Hattin (194000/244590), which is called on the Survey of Western Palestine map Birket el- Kurum (The vineyards' pool) and a fourth pool located today at the eastern edge of Kibutz Lavi (191990/244000) which was given on the map of Tiberias 1:20.000 from 1942 a very unpromising name – Birkat er-Riqq (the empty pool).

15   One which still functions today was dated during the survey to the Early Roman period.

16   It should be taken in to account that the data available on the two battlefields are different due to the fact that there is an agro-metallurgical station of the Hattin battlefield. This is not the case in Arsuf.

17   Wind speed on this specific day was as high as 10.1 m. per second, the highest speed recorded and presented in Table 27.1.

18   During the Battle of Hattin reenactment of 3 July 2010, four of the reenactors where monitored physically by the author of this chapter. Data were collected on: height, weight, percentage of water (and alcohol), body temperature, and blood pressure. Though there were only four subjects measured, it was interesting to see that while three of the subjects maintained their body temperature around 37°C through the walk (of 17 km), the fourth subject's body temperature dropped to 34.5°C (hypothermia) at 15 km and because of this he could not continue to the next day.

19   Roll classified roads into four categories: countryside roads; local roads; main roads; and Roman roads (Roll, 1996: 153–154). Wilkinson's classification is: formal and paved roads; paved roads in highlands; cutting (mountain crossings); linear hollows; rural tracks with boundary walls; stepped tracks; wheel ruts; desert tracks (Wilkinson, 2003: 60, 62, 113, 116).

20 Because of structural reasons, Arsuf remained an important junction even after it was taken by the Mamluk army in late April 1265 (Tal and Roll, 2011), and the settlement itself had no apparent significance.

21 Saladin probably remembered very clearly the event occurring on that same plain on 25 November 1177, later known as the Battle of Montgisard, during which his army suffered a major loss at the hands of the Franks led by Baldwin IV and he was almost killed there (Ehrlich, 2013).

22 On the possible location of Saladin during the final stages of the battle in relation to what can be viewed from dominating point over the battlefield and a study of eyesight in relation to different features, see Lewis, 2013: 368–70.

23 Two arrowheads, a horse harness fittings (part of curb bit?), a horseshoe nail (violin key type) and a punctured metal plate (part of a Great Helm?) (Lewis, forthcoming).

24 It was agreed in 2008, during the 5th Biennial Fields of Conflict Conference in the city of Ghent, that Battlefield Archaeology is a sub-discipline of Archaeology of Conflicts (Bradley, 2008: 30; Lewis, 2003: 3).

BIBLIOGRAPHY

Printed and translated sources

Abū Shāma (1898), *Kitab al-Rawdatayn' in Recueil Historens des Croidades*, Historiens Orientaux, IV & V, Paris.

Bahā'al-Din Ibn Shaddād (1884), *Anecdotes et beaux Traits de la Vie du Sultan Youssof* in RHC. Or vol. 3, Paris.

Historia de expeditione Friderici imperatoris, ed. A. Chroust (1928), in *Quellen zur Geschichte des Kreuzzuges Kaiser Friedrichs I*, Monumenta Germaniae Historica, SS n.s. 5, Berlin.

Hugonis et Honorii chronicorum continuationes weingartenses, ed. L. Weiland (1869), Monumenta Germaniae Historica SS 21, Hannover.

R. B. C. Huygens (ed.), (1994), *Peregrinationes tres: Saewulf, Johannes Wirziburgensis, Theodericus, Corpus Christianorum, Continuatio medievalis*, vol. 139, Turnhout.

Imad ed-din el-Katib el Isfahani, *Conquete de la Syrie et de la Palestine par Salah ed-Din*, ed. C. de Landberg (1888), Leiden.

Kraemer, J. (1952), *Der Struz des Königreichs Jerusalem (583/1187) in der Darstellung des 'Imad ad-Din al- Katib al- Isfahani*, Wiesbaden.

L'estoire de Eracles empereur la conqueste de la Terre d'Outremer, (1844–59), RHCr.Occ., II, Paris.

L. de Mas Latrie (ed.), (1871), *Chronique d'Ernoul et de Bernard le Trésorier*, Paris.

Ltin peregr. Gest. Regis Ricardi, c. XVII–XX (ed. W. Stubbs, 260–277).

Röhricht, R. (1893–1904), *Regesta regni hierosolymitani* and *Additamentum*, Innsbruck.

Al-Safadi, *al-Wāfi bi-l Wafāyāt*, ed. A. al-Arnā'ūt and T. Mustafā, (2000), vol. 6 of 29, Beirut.

Stubbs, W. (1864), *Chronicales and Memorials of the Reign of Richard* I. Vol. 1. *Chronicles and Memorials of Great Britain and Ireland during the Middle Ages*, London.

Theodericus (1976), *Libellus de Locis Sanctis*, ed. M.L. and W. Bulst, Heidelberg.

Secondary sources

Abel, F. M. (1933, 1938), *Géographie de la Palestine*. Tome I, II. Librairie Lecoffre: Paris.

Alexandre, Y. (2003), Lubya (West). *Hadashot Arkheologiyot, Excavations and Surveys in Israel.* Electronic volume 115: 27 (Hebrew).

Ambroise (2005), *The History of the Holy War, History in Verse of the Third Crusade*, trans. I. Kahaneman. Yad Ben-Zvi Press: Jerusalem (Hebrew).

——— (1976), *The Crusade of Richard Lion-Heart*, trans. M. J. Hubert and J. L. La Monte. Octagon Books: New York.

——— (1941), *The Crusade of Richard Lion-Heart*, trans. M. J. Hubert and J. L. La Monte. Columbia University Press: New York.

Arnold, C. J. (1986), Archaeology and History: The Shades of Confrontation and Cooperation. In J. L. Bintliff, and C. F. Gaffney (eds.), *Archaeology at the Interface: Studies in Archaeology's Relationships with History, Geography, Biology and Physical Science*, 32–39. BAR International Series 300: Oxford.

Asbridge, T. (2010), *The Crusades: The War for the Holy Land*. Simon & Schuster: London, New York, Sydney, Toronto.

Avisar, O. (1973), *Book of Tiberias*. Keter-Books: Jerusalem.

Baha' al-Din Ibn Shaddād (2002), *The Rare and Excellent History of Saladin* or *al- Nawadir al-Sultaniyya wa'l- Mahasin al- Yusufiyya*, trans. D.S. Richards. Ashgate: Aldershot.

Baldwin, M. W. (1978), *Raymond III of Tripolis and the Fall of Jerusalem (1140–1187)*. Princeton University Press: Princeton.

Bitan, A. (1982), *Changes of Settlement in the Eastern Lower Galilee (1800–1978)*. Yad Izhak Ben Zvi Publications: Jerusalem (Hebrew).

Bloch, M. (2002), *Apologie Pour L'Historie ou Métier d'historien*, trans. Z. Zamiri. Bialik Institute: Jerusalem (Hebrew).

Bradley, R. (2008), Report from the Frontline: A Review of the Fifth Biennial Fields of Conflict Conference. Ghent, Belgium, 17–19 October 2008. *Rosetta* 5: 30–33.

Conder, C. R. (1897), *The Latin Kingdom of Jerusalem 1099 to 1291 A.D.* P.E.F: London.

Conder, C. R. and Kitchener, H. H. (1881), *The Survey of Western Palestine, Memoirs of the Topography, Orography, Hydrography, and Archaeology*. Vol. I: *Galilee*. P.E.F: London.

Edbury: W. (1996), *The Conquest of Jerusalem and the Third Crusade, Sources in Translation*. Ashgate: Aldershot.

Ehrlich, M. (2007), The Battle of Hattin: A Chronicle of a Defeat Foretold? *The Journal of Medieval Military History* 5: 16–32.

——— (2013), Saint Caterine's Day Miracle – The Battle of Montgisard. *Journal of Medieval Military History* 11: 95–106.

——— (2014), The Battle of Arsur: A Short-Lived Victory. *Journal of Medieval Military History* 12: 109–118.

Gal, Z. (1992), Saladin's Dome of Victory at the Horns of Hattin. In B. Z. Kedar, (ed.), *The Horns of Hattin*, 213–215. Yad Izhak Ben-Zvi, Israel Exploration Society: Jerusalem.

Gavish, E. and Bakler, N. (1990), The Sharon Costal Strip – Geomorphlogical and Sedimentological Factors and Processes. In D. Grossman, A. Degani, and A. Shmueli (eds.), *Hasharon Between Yarkon and Karmel* 61–82. Tel Aviv (Hebrew).

Gibson, S. (1995), *Landscape Archaeology and Ancient Agricultural Field Systems in Palestine*. PhD thesis, University College, London.

——— (2003), From Wildscape to Landscape: Landscape Archaeology in the Southern Levant-Methods and Practice. In A. M. Maeir, S. Dar, and Z. Safrai, (eds.), *The Rural Landscape of Ancient Israel*, 1–25. BAR International Series 1121: Oxford.

Gichon, M. (1990), The Sharon from a Military-Geographic Perspective. In D. Grossman, A. Degani, and A. Shmueli, (eds.), *Hasharon between Yarkon and Karmel*, 289–315. Ministry of Defense Publishing House: Tel Aviv (Hebrew).

Gillingham, J. (1999), *Richard I*. Yale University Press: New Haven and London.

Gophna, R. and Ayalon, E. (1998), *Archaeological Survey of Israel: Map of Herzliyya (69)*. Israel Antiquities Authority: Jerusalem.

Guérin, V. (1985), *Description Géographique, Historique et Archéologique De La Palestine Vol. VI. Galilee (a)*. Yad Izhak Ben Zvi Publications: Jerusalem (Hebrew).

Hall, K. Staffan Lindgren, B. and Jackson: (2005), Rock Albedo and Monitoring of Thermal Conditions in Respect of Weathering: Some Expected and Some Unexpected Results. *Earth Surface Processes and Landforms* 30: 801–811.

Herde (2002), Die Kämpfe bei den Hörnern von Ḥiṭṭīn und der Untergang des Kreuzritterheeres (3. und 4. Juli 1187). Eine Historisch-Topographische Untersuchung. In E. Halbband (ed.), *Peter Herde, Studien zur Papst- und Reichsgeschichte, zur Geschichte des Mittelmeerraumes und zum kanonischen Recht im Mittelater,* 97–153. Anton Hiersemann: Stuttgart.

Hodder, E. (1878), *On Holy Ground or, Scenes and Incidents in the Land of Promise.* Nimmo, Hay & Mitchell: Edinburgh.

Ibn al-Athir (2007), *The Chronicle of Ibn al-Athir for the Crusading Period from Al- Kāmil fi'l-ta'rikh,* trans. D.S. Richards. Ashgate: Aldershot.

Jaffe, S. and Fledel, H. (1990), The Climate of the Sharon. In D. Grossman, A. Degani, and A. Shmueli (eds.), *Hasharon Between Yarkon and Karmel,* 99–102. Ministry of Defense Publishing House: Tel Aviv (Hebrew).

Kedar, B. Z. (1992), The Battle of Hattin Revisited. In B. Z. Kedar (ed.), *The Horns of Hattin,* 190–207. Yad Izhak Ben- Zvi, Israel Exploration Society: Jerusalem.

Khalidi, W. (1992), *All that Remains, The Palestinian Villages Occupied and Depopulated by Israel in 1948.* Institute for Palestinian Studies: Washington.

Kitchener, H. H. (1877), Notes and News. Camp Tiberias, 30 March, *PEFQST* July 1877: 116–120.

Lane-Poole, S. (1964), *Saladin and the Fall of the Kingdom of Jerusalem.* Khayats: Beirut.

Lewis, R. Y. (2013), *Archaeology of Conflicts: The Decisive Stage of the Battle of Hattin as a Case Study.* PhD dissertation, University of Haifa.

———— (Forthcoming), Carpe Momento: The Battle of Arsuf (7 September 1191): Environmental and Archaeological Perspectives.

Liddell Hart, B. H. (1989), *Thoughts of War.* Maarachot, Tel-Aviv (Hebrew).

Leibner, U. (2004), *History of Settlement in the Eastern Galilee During the Hellenistic, Roman and Byzantine Periods in Light of an Archaeological Survey.* PhD dissertation, Bar-Ilan University: Ramat-Gan (Hebrew).

Liphschitz, N. and Biger, G. (2004), *Green Dress for a Country: Afforestation in Eretz Israel, The First Hundred Years 1850–1950.* Ariel: Jerusalem.

Lyons, M. C. and Jackson, D. E. P. (1982), *Saladin, The Politics of the Holy War.* Cambridge University Press: Cambridge.

Mazor, I. (1980), *Geology with an Israeli Hammer.* Open University. Tel-Aviv.

Melville, C. P. and Lyons, M. C. (1992), Saladin's Hattin Letter. In B. Z. Kedar (ed.), *The Horns of Hattin,* 208–212. Yad Izhak Ben-Zvi, Israel Exploration Society: Jerusalem.

Nicolle, D. C. (1993), *Hattin 1187, Saladin's Greatest Victory.* Osprey Military: London.

———— (2005), *The Third Crusade 1191: Richard the Lionheart, Saladin and the Struggle for Jerusalem.* Osprey: Oxford.

Oman, C. (1924), *A History of the Art of War in the Middle Ages.* Methuen & Co: London.

Palmer, E. H. (1881), *The Survey of Western Palestine, Arabic and English Name Lists, Collected During the Survey by Lieutenants Conder and Kitchener.* P. E. F.: London.

Prawer, J. (1964), The Battle of Hattin. *Israel Exploration Journal* 14: 160–179.

———— (1980), *Crusader Institutions.* Clarendon Press: Oxford.

———— (1984), *A History of the Latin Kingdom of Jerusalem, Vol. 2: The Crusades and the Second Kingdom.* Bialik Institute: Jerusalem (Hebrew).

Rae Wilson, W. (1824), *Travels in Egypt and the Holy Land.* Londman, Hurst, Rees, Brown and Green: London.

Pringle, D. (2001), The Spring of the Cresson in Crusading History. In M. Balard, B. Z. Kedar, and J. Riley-Smith, (eds.), *Dei Gesta per Francos, Crusader Studies in Honour of Jean Richard,* 231–240. Ashgate: Aldershot.

Roll, I. (1994), Survey of Roman Roads in Lower Galilee. *Excavetions and Survets in Israel* 14: 38–40.

———— (1996), The Types of Roads in the Land of Israel During the Roman and Byzantine Periods. *Ariel* 119–120: 151–156.

———— (2007), The Encounter of Crusaders and Muslims at Apollonia-Arsuf as Reflected in the Archaeological Finds and Historical Sources. In I. Roll, O. Tal, and M. Winter (eds.), *The Encounter of Crusaders and Muslims in Palestine,* 9–104. Hakibbutz Hameuchad: Tel Aviv (Hebrew with English abstract).

Roll, I. and Ayalon, E. (1989), *Apollonia and Southern Sharon, Model of Coastal City and Its Hinterland.* Tel Aviv (Hebrew with English abstract).

Safrai, Z., Grossman, D., Frenkel, J. and Rainey, A. F. (1990), The Roads of the Sharon. In D. Grossman, A. Degani, and A. Shmueli (eds.), *Hasharon Between Yarkon and Karmel,* 249–262. Ministry of Defense Publishing House: Tel Aviv (Hebrew).

Smail, R. C. (1956), *Crusading Warfare (1097–1193).* Cambridge University Press: Cambridge.

Tal, O. and Roll, I. (2011), Arsur: The Site, Settlement and Crusader Castle, and the Material Manifestation of Their Destruction. In O. Tal (ed.), *The Last Supper at Apollonia: The Final Days of the Crusader Castle in Herzliya,* 8-51. Eretz Israel Museum: Tel Aviv.

Waisel, Y. and Agami, M. (1990), The Vegetation of the Sharon plain. In D. Grossman, A. Degani., and A. Shmueli (eds.), *Hasharon between Yarkon and Karmel,* 109–122. Ministry of Defense Publishing House: Tel Aviv (Hebrew).

Wilkinson, T. J. (2003), *Archaeological Landscapes of the Near East.* The University of Arizona Press: Tucson.

Wilson, C. W. (1880), *Picturesque Palestine Sinai and Egypt,* Vol II. Virtue and Co: London.

Maps

Conder, C. R. and Kitchener. H. H. (1880), *Map of Western Palestine in 26 sheets,* sheet number 10. London

Palestine Survey Department (revised July 1942), *Tiberias* Series 1:20,000 Sheet 19/24

Internet

Wise Observatory Center in Ramon: http://wise-obs.tau.ac.il/~eran/Wise/wise_calen.html

The agro-metallurgical station at Kibbutz Lavi: www.mop-zafon.org.il/csv/index.html

CHAPTER TWENTY-EIGHT

THE HOSPITALLER CASTLE OF BELVOIR: SETTING THE SCENE FOR A DISCUSSION OF THE TOPOGRAPHY, GEOLOGY AND ARCHITECTURE

——•◆•——

Vardit Shotten-Hallel, Eytan Sass and Lydia Perelis Grossowicz

INTRODUCTION

A detailed archaeological and historical study of Belvoir Castle is currently underway as part of a long-term research project.[1] The aim of this chapter is to provide an introductory platform for engaging some questions regarding the architecture of Belvoir. While these questions are not new and were indeed addressed in the past, this chapter attempts to look closely at the core features of Belvoir and infer only those relevant to the timeframe and the unique social fabric in which it was shaped. The study of these features requires a multidisciplinary approach. Hence, the methodology applied here is based on an examination of the castle's various components, the analyses of the building materials and the integration of the data with the historical documents and the archaeological finds.

Whether we perceive Belvoir as a 'concentric castle',[2] 'enclosure castle' or 'double *castrum*',[3] we must first examine the core features in order to decipher their meaning. They relate to the construction and the architecture of Belvoir and particularly to one of its most important components: the chapel. The church or chapel of any castle or monastic establishment is a key element for the understanding of its plan and the interrelations between its various, religious and lay, modules. The first part of this chapter examines the architectural layout of the castle. By analysing several building elements and distinguishing between different construction phases, we are able to propose a location for a chapel.[4] The second part of this study deals with the topographical and geological settings, including a discussion of the main building materials used in the castle and the recently surveyed quarries located in its vicinity. This analysis, in our view, is a key element in understanding the architecture of Belvoir. In the synthesis we will focus on the building materials used to engage the question of the *identity* of Belvoir chapel, and specify attributes typical to Hospitaller church or chapel buildings. We suggest, although there is no certainty as to the original

490

location of the 'castle chapel', that from the surviving elements it is possible to draw several preliminary conclusions about its plan. As work, both archaeological and historical, is still in progress, we will focus on the following questions and suggest a point of departure for future discussion.

OUTSTANDING QUESTIONS

The general plan of Belvoir consists of a deep moat, open on the east, and outer defences built from the bedrock as a glacis. Posterns leading to the moat were located in the outer defence line which in the level of the castle formed vaulted halls and galleries. An open area separated the outer line of defence and the inner castle, which was built around a central courtyard. Four towers were located at each of the inner castle corners. A staircase from the south side of the courtyard ascends to the upper level where dormitories and a chapel were probably located during the second and probably also during the first phase of Hospitaller presence at Belvoir (Fig. 28.1).

The first issue addressed here relates to the *dating* of the castle chapel. The architectural analyses and the historical documentation will be used to aid this, yet some gaps cannot be bridged at present. Although it is accepted that the castle was built anew in one campaign, we will try to break down the chronology of the construction by looking at the different occupation phases. This model will provide explanations to construction phases and to issues relating to heterogeneous architectural style of the elements found in the site. The initial construction of Belvoir Castle commenced in the third quarter of the twelfth century when the Hospitaller Order was led by Gilbert d'Assailly (1163–70). Under his mastership,

Figure 28.1   Aerial photograph of Belvoir. Photograph: Dubi Tal, 2004.

the order was deeply involved in large-scale military and financial projects: in the Egyptian campaigns of King Amalric, in purchasing large tracts of lands, farms and building and in the defence of several castles.[5] The second issue to consider relates to *identity*. Belvoir is classified as a well-designed military castle, built by the Hospitaller Order of St John. Its location on the eastern frontier of the Latin Kingdom, the topographical setting, its plan and architectural features qualify to the highest standards of military construction. The dual character of the Hospitaller Order, as a military and a religious institution, imposed creating a unique fabric of establishment that had to accommodate military and monastic functions at the same time. Therefore, design scheme principles and architectural components corresponding to its military function and its religious identity had to be implemented and could, at times, come into conflict. The estimated location and the plan of the castle chapel in particular embodied the complexity of a castle built by a military religious order in the Latin East. The third issue relates to *materiality*. The materials employed in the castle, especially stone, are the key to understanding and reconstructing the architectural plan of the castle chapel. Although the location of the chapel has not yet been confirmed, we are able to distinguish now the architectural elements, the sculptures and the masonry of the chapel from those of the castle.

Dating

The first Frankish settlement in the area was during the reign of Fulk of Anjou (1131–43).[6] The two periods of Hospitaller presence at Belvoir discussed here begun during the mastership of two grand masters. The first period, from *c.* 1168, begun in the years of Gilbert d'Assailly (1163–70). With his controversial resignation only a couple of years after the acquisition of Belvoir, a period of growth in power, possessions and acquisitions of the Hospitaller Order was ending.[7] The second Hospitaller occupation of the site began, most probably, during in the years of Peter of Vieille Bride (1240–42) and lasted until the rise of Baybars and his raid of the Galilee between 1263 and 1266 when the Templar Castle of Safed fell.[8]

The question of *dating* is relevant for the identification of the architecture of Belvoir chapel and to several other elements including the west tower of the inner castle, the adjacent rooms and the staircase in the central courtyard.[9] These architectural elements are essential for analysing the arrangements of functions within the castle. At present it is hard to establish whether these elements were built at the first phase of Hospitaller occupancy of the site, altered by the Ayyubid, renewed during the second Hospitaller phase or during the Mamluk period. The assumed second Hospitaller occupancy of the site (1241–66) was a little longer than the first (1168–89), if we take 1266 as a last possible date.[10] By the middle of the thirteenth century there was no doubt about the need to refortify and garrison the castle to face the new threats from Egypt and the Khwarizmians who occupied Jerusalem (1244). This must have been a challenging task after the devastating result and the great casualties of the battle of La Forbie later that year, which also caused financial deficiency in the order.[11] There is no explicit evidence regarding settlement at Belvoir after 1266.[12]

Identity

In the research of Frankish architecture, Belvoir is regarded as 'one of the finest castle designs produced by the Franks in the East',[13] 'the first of the concentric castles',[14]

492

and 'a milestone in castle design',[15] to mention just a few. The meaning ascribed to this well-designed structure was habitually military and the monastic or cloistral character of Belvoir has only scarcely been discussed.[16] This aspect was overlooked by contemporary Latin and Muslim sources who also associated Belvoir with a military stronghold, in the same way that the Order of the Hospital was perceived.[17] Theodoric, writing in 1172, a few years after the construction of Belvoir reported: 'In cuius vicino monte praecelso hospitarii fortissimum et amplissimum castrum constituerunt, ut adversus Noradini, halapiensis tyranni, insidias terram citra Jordanem sitam possint tueri.'[18] William of Tyre also refers to it as a castle. 'castrum novum cui nomen est hodie Belveir'.[19] In the Muslim sources, Belvoir appears as a military stronghold. In a letter al-Fadl addressed to Saif al-Din, Belvoir is described as the Hospitaller base where their leader, weapons and munitions are concentrated:[20]

وهى كرسى الاسبتارية ودار كفرهم, ومستقر صاحب امرهم وموقع سلاحهم وذخرهم.

Even if Belvoir was not regarded as a monastic institution by its contemporary viewers, there is no doubt that its proprietors strove to integrate the order's military requirements with those of its monastic way of life. Master Gilbert d'Assailly himself stressed this particular exceptional characteristic, amongst others, of his order: 'Nos itaque et fratres nostri, religioni miliciam commiscentes, in ejus defensione continue labore.'[21] This dual insight is manifested in the building: from the layout, design and architecture, through the various functions and even more so, in the visual appearance of several components. The Augustinian Rule, from which the Hospitaller Rule drew inspiration, discloses no building requirements or standards. It is intriguing then to examine how Belvoir, no doubt a military structure, functioned at the same time as a monastic establishment, although by the time the castle was built the character of the order was yet to be developed, as reflected in the statutes of 1182 where the first mention of *fratribus armorum* appears.[22] To do so we can compare the distinctive architectural components of each type. Table 28.1 illustrates how these components are manifested at Belvoir.

Presenting a compacted plan we can assume the external castle was inhabited by the lay community and served for storage and defence, the ground floor of the inner castle was used for the domestic activities (kitchen, refectory) and the upper level was for the use of the brethren (dormitories, chapel, possibly a chapter house, private chambers for officials). The architectural differentiation between secular and religious buildings was also articulated in the materiality of the castle's construction and the castle chapel was recognisable not only by form but also by material as the external fortifications were built using different material from the inner castle.

Materiality

Topographical and geological setting

Belvoir Castle is situated 298 m above sea level, in the north-west Jordan Valley of Israel. Located on the east slope of the Kokhav Plateau, convenient access to the site is from the west, a significant factor in terms of roads for transporting large quantities of building materials.[23] The Kokhav Plateau, formed by a series of faults, is located at the western margin of the African-Syrian Rift. The area is built mainly of Neogene (23–2.6MA) and

Table 28.1   Features of concentric castle and cloistral monastic establishment at Belvoir

Features	*Concentric castle*	*Cloistral monastic establishment*
Location	Evidently located in a frontier area, Belvoir was located S of Tiberias, an area administered by the Hospitallers during the last quarter of the twelfth century.	Ideally isolated from urban centres.
Topography	Manmade cut in the escarpment of Kokhav plateau, vacating the site for the castle and a surrounding moat.	No Holy Sites are associated with the purchase of Belvoir.
Water supply	Two water reservoirs: small cistern in the inner court and a larger one in the outer bailey (providing, according to Ben-Dov, more than 500 cubic m).	Source of water: cistern, spring or manmade basin used for the sacraments.
Burial grounds	NE	NE
Architectural components		
Moat	Surrounded by a dry moat (bridge on the W face?). Access was via the main gate in the SE corner of the castle.	NA
Barbican	E face of the castle, protruding the outer line of defence.	NA
External fortifications	Outer line of walls.	NA
Glacis	The surrounding glacis is alternating with the natural rock, inconsecutive along all faces.	NA
Inner castle	Inner castle well defended and self-contained with water and storage spaces for food, weapons and munitions.	Serve as a cloister for the brother knights, separating them from the lay community.
Fortifications/ towers	Corner towers projected from a glacis pierced only with posterns in both outer and inner fortifications.	NA
Church/Chapel	Castle chapel	Church/Chapel located at the N of the convent. In Belvoir the chapel/s was probably located in the W inner tower.
Bell tower	NA	Required in Hospitaller houses.[a]
Chapterhouse	NE	NE – presumably on the upper level.
Kitchens	Located in the SE area of the courtyard. Cooking vessels and other kitchen utensils were found during the excavations.	
Refectory	According to M. Ben-Dov, the refectory was located adjacent to the kitchen.[b]	The community ate twice a day in common, the meals divided to two shifts.[c]
Dormitories	Halls for the castellan (*castellanus*), chaplain and other high-rank officers or visitors, these were likely to be separated. Halls for knights and for brother sergeants that might have been joined.	Separated halls for chaplain, knights, brother sergeants and lay personnel.

Latrines	NE		NE	
Cellars	Inner vaults for shelter, safe movement and storage of wine and foodstuff.		Storage of wine and foodstuff.	
Treasury	NE		NE	
Drapery	NE		NE[d]	
Infirmaries	NE		NE	
Walls	Thick walls arranged in number of lines		NA	
Windows	In the inner castle only.		Required for lighting and ventilation. There is no evidence of windows in the remains of the ground floor.	
Sorties (and staircases)	Inner courtyard, inner wall staircase (SE). Posterns to the moat.		Day stairs	Staircase in the inner courtyard served to approach the upper level.
			Night stairs	NE
Galleries	Galleries for additional firing positions.		Providing separated area for the knights.	
Staircases	Wide enough to accommodate fully equipped knights' movement.		Staircase in the inner courtyard served to approach the chapel.	
Firing and viewing apertures	Firing and viewing apertures in inner towers.		NA	
Scriptoria	NA		NE	

Notes: *NA* – not applicable; *NE* – no evidence.

a The Statutes of Hugh Revel as decreed in the Chapter General of 19 September 1262 *Cart* III, 43–54, no. 3039: 31: the bell for dinner was sounded on a fixed time, daily and on the occasion of Fridays and Festivals. In clause 27, the requirement to come to the Sunday Procession: 'Statutum est quod omnes diebus dominicis fratres veniant ad processionem, illis exceptis qui erunt aliquo domus negocio occupati.'

b Ben-Dov, M. (1969) Excavations in the Crusader Fortress of Kokhav Hayarden. *Qadmoniot* (in Hebrew), 2 (1): 22–7, at 26.

c *Cart* I, 62–8 no. 70 (Rule) 11; Cart. II, 536–47, no. 2213 (*esgarts*) 26–7; Cart II, 547–61, no. 2213 (*usances*) 105, 124.

d *Cart* II, no. 2213, *esgart* 39, *usance* 109.

Quaternary (2.6MA till present) volcanics and sediments.[24] The stratigraphic sequence consists of over 600 m that include: 1) the Lower Basalt (part of the Hordos Formation, Tiberias Group, lower to middle Miocene, base not exposed in the area); 2) the Dead Sea Group (late Miocene – Pliocene) sediments and volcanics that include a) the Umm Sabune conglomerate (0–200 m consisting mainly of basaltic pebbles and granules eroded from the Lower Basalt), b) the marine Bira Formation (marls, dark clays, sandstone, chalks and limestone mostly composed of thinly laminar calcareous shales, that pass gradually upwards into evaporitic gypsum and anhydrite), c) the Gesher Formation (marls, chalks, gypsum and limestone which were deposited in lagoons or shallow lakes), and d) the Cover Basalt, whose rocks are exposed in the area of the castle, at the top of the escarpment.

Building materials

Two main rock types were used for the construction of Belvoir: the Cover Basalt and limestones of the Gesher Formation. Some similarly decorated architectural elements, including elbow columns and thick leaf capitals, were produced in both types. The Cover Basalt, extracted on the site to form a dry moat, was the main building material for the defence elements: the glacis, external towers, external walls and posterns. Vertical columnar joints and horizontal fractures in the basalt, the latter measuring between 0.3 and over 1 m, caused during the cooling process, created 'natural' segmentation of the rock, which no doubt eased the stone cutters' work. This phenomenon is clearly seen along the outer face of the moat cut, on the south side and also on the north inner face of the glacis (Fig. 28.2).

In the inner castle, large and small building blocks of basalt were used in the lower courses of the ground floor and incorporated in the defence structures: in the towers and in the construction of walls, foundations, openings and vaults. The basalt building blocks were both hewn stones (range: 0.3–0.9 x 0.4–0.7 m) and rough, unfinished stones including some trapezoids (boulders, 0.3–0.7 x 0.3–0.5 m). Smaller stones (0.2 x 0.5 m) were incorporated between the large rough stones and in the vaults and the higher parts of the walls (Fig. 28.3). Maintaining high standards of construction, hewn stones were commonly used in door and window frames, while the rough stones were used in the lower courses and for the curtain walls between the constructive elements (i.e. doors, windows, embrasures). The appearance of these walls suggests that they were plastered.[25] Basalt was used in the lower part of the openings, particularly embrasures, and the western gate of the castle as well as gates to the rectangular towers. In addition, thin basalt chips (3–10 mm) were inserted in the joints between the limestone blocks. This method was retained as standard all over the castle, regardless of joint widths. Occasionally joints were of less than 5 mm wide. It was implemented only on walls built in nodular limestone. No such method was detected on walls constructed in basalt.[26]

Figure 28.2 South face of the moat: columnar jointing and boulders retrieved from the castle during excavations 1963–66. Photograph: Vardit Shotten-Hallel.

The Cover Basalt exposed in the area of the castle is characterised by: a) columnar structure in the upper part of the flow, some of which are curved and tapering towards the top of the flow and are fractured horizontally; b) concentric lava flows around basalt pebbles (Fig. 28.4 showing the outburst of lava upwards splitting on both sides of the centre, r20 cm, r5 cm respectively); c) ferric oxides imprints on the face of the rocks (Fig. 28.4); d) thin stripes of small vesicles (Fig. 28.4) differ to the round/longitudinal/pipe vesicles shown on some of the rough building stones showing three vesicular stones positioned on different directions to the flow); e) zeolites.

All the above features are seen on construction blocks throughout the castle. In addition, basalt granules were added to the mortar mixture used in the basalt construction levels.

Limestone for the construction and decoration of the castle and of the chapel was extracted from different quarries. Those quarries represent two members of the Gesher Formation, showing different characteristics in hand specimens and in petrographic sections. Throughout the castle, the builders used limestone from the upper layer of Gesher Formation (the varied layers, henceforth nodular limestone).[27] Major characteristics include: a) laminated structure, b) thin layers of darker mineral, possibly bentonite, and c) nodules. The nodular limestone was incorporated in the construction of the inner castle and was used for walls, arches and openings and staircases. The relatively large blocks were not carved perfectly to rectangular shapes. The stone cutters rather followed the natural structure of the rock with its nodular structure (Fig. 28.5). The blocks perimeter therefore is only coarsely

Figure 28.3 SE wall of the inner court. Basalt and limestone construction. Thin basalt chips inserted between coarsely hewn limestone blocks. Photograph: Vardit Shotten-Hallel. Scale in photo is of 15cm.

Figure 28.4 Characteristics of the cover basalt exposed in the moat of the castle: oval iron imprint, lava flows, stripes of vesicles in the lower part of the moat. Photograph: Vardit Shotten-Hallel.

cut. To fill the irregular joints between the layers of stones, the builders inserted thin basalt chips (see Fig. 28.3 above).

The architectural fragments, retrieved from the houses of the village of Kawkab al-Hawa, and now piled north of the moat, were used for the reconstruction of the architectural elements of the castle chapel (Fig. 28.6). Amongst these are: a) three-sided pillar base; b) portal fragments (Fig. 28.7a); c) window fragments (Fig. 28.7b); d) rib vaulting vertebrae (Fig. 28.7c); e) surrounding cornice nave and apse; f) elbow columns; g) arches; h) round and semi-round columns in various sections; and i) thick leaf capital. All these details were extracted from the mid member of Gesher Formation and they differ in texture and colour from the nodular limestone described above. These features, prominent in the final appearance of the blocks, include: a) white colour; b) thin grain size; and c) homogenous compact structure. They regulate high standards of the construction method enabling subtle architectural detailing and precise courses.

Additional types of rocks were employed for specific structural and decorative elements such as portals and sculptures. The bossed blocks in the jambs of the south-east entrance to the castle, secondary use, were carved in fine quality limestone, yellow-red in colour

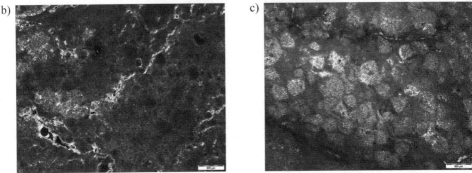

Figure 28.5 Characteristics of the Gesher Formation nodular limestone (the varied layers) of building block from the castle: a) W jamb of opening to the NE hall in the inner castle; b) peloidal mudstone containing mottled structure areas – no clear boundaries between patches and abundant cross-cutting calcite veins; c) compact crystalline patches within mottled structure, developed in peloidal mudstone. Fine calcite veins. Photographs: Vardit Shotten-Hallel.

Figure 28.6 Lapidary, the concentration of elements retrieved by Meir Ben-Dov, north of the moat. Photograph: Vardit Shotten-Hallel.

a)

b)

c)

Figure 28.7   Architectural elements retrieved from the village Kaukab al-Hawa: a) portal fragments; b) window fragments; c) rib vaulting vertebrae. Photographs: Vardit Shotten-Hallel.

(whose source is currently unidentified) and show well-preserved bivalves. Two marble sculpted pieces, currently on display in the Israel Museum in Jerusalem, were retrieved from the cistern in the courtyard.[28] Originally coming from at least two different elements, these include the bearded head and the head of a youth (see below: sculptural elements).

The quest for quarries

While exploiting the immediate source for basalt in the site itself, it appears that the Hospitallers spared no effort to secure distant sources for other building materials, especially limestone for the construction and decoration of their chapel. Two limestone quarries were surveyed in the vicinity of the castle, both located less than 2 km from the castle (c. 300m above sea level). North east of the castle (249841/723371, and 290 m below), a quarry site occupies some 90 sq m of slopes in the Kokhav Stream. The remaining exposed limestone bed suggests a good source for quarrying. On the site remains an exceptionally large quantity of stone wedges and man-made trenches for extracting blocks, horizontal surfaces indicating the place where blocks were removed (Fig. 28.8a). A second quarry was identified some 1500 m (point to point) north-west of the castle (248378/724342, 8 m below sea level) on the south slope of Tabor stream. In the site that was surveyed in the past, three surfaces of quarry along c. 15 m, 90 cm high each and clefts for extraction of blocks are still visible.[29] Thin sections of samples from both quarries were examined under polarising microscope. The thin sections show peloidal wackestone, poor sorting of round to oval micritic ooids, unidentified ostracods valves, some conserving their original shape (Fig. 28.9a and Fig. 28.9b). Both samples contain gastropod shell or moulds. As none of the examined building stones from the castle contained any, these quarries apparently did not serve for the construction of Belvoir.

During survey of the area, we identified a quarry site in Hagal Wadi, located some 6,000 m (point to point) north of Belvoir, south of the Hagal spring (250716/727858). The exposed rocks in the quarry belong to the Gesher Formation, which consist of limestone beds with thin dark layers of bentonite. The appearance of rock on the north and east faces is similar to that of the building blocks in the castle. The quarry site stretches from both side of the road and is mostly covered with fresh soil. This is evidently the result of the topographical conditions. The quarry is a plane located below the slopes where soil is constantly sliding. In the winter of 1188–89 in a letter addressed to Saif al-Din, al-Fadhel describes the weather conditions in the vicinity of the castle. The description depicts heavy rains, floods and mud, literally causing a shallow landslide. The current situation in the quarry site, where most of it is covered by soil that has washed down from higher areas, echoes this description while describing the area in the vicinity of Belvoir when he describes the streams full of water, the mountains covered with snow and walking the narrow roads resembles a prisoner in chains:

وكان نزولنا علي كوكب والشتاء في كوكبه، وقد طلع من الانواء في موكبه، والثلوج تنشر علي الجبال طي ملائها، والاودية قد عجت بمائها ... ومشيت المطلق فيها مشية الاسير في الحلقات[30]

Samples from the quarry and from building blocks in the castle were analysed in petrographic thin sections. Samples show textural differences in some areas but similar content and similar character: mottled texture of micritic grain, heterogeneous texture, limonite patches and veins of sparry calcite. Since the Gesher Formation is characterised by great variability, these minor differences are anticipated. At this stage we assume the quarry could have served the castle's builders as a source of stone for construction of the inner castle buildings. A quarry located elsewhere, unidentified to this date, served for the construction and decoration of the chapel.

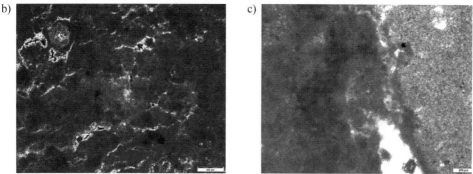

Figure 28.8 Quarry in Hagal Wadi, Gesher Formation. Petrographic sections of a sample from the quarry: a) limestone quarry, Gesher Formation, clefts shown where blocks were extracted; b) peloidal mudstone displaying a mottled structure – no clear boundaries between patches; c) contact area between mottled texture and compact calcite crystals (130μm) patches, veins separating between the two structures. Photographs: Vardit Shotten-Hallel.

THE CASTLE CHAPEL

The constant struggle to maintain their rule over the Holy Land required that both the Franks and their Muslim rivals demonstrate their hold over urban centres and especially over religious sites. Hence the urge to accentuate the symbols of their faiths.[31] The chapel or church in a castle became an important visual element just as military components; for example, fortified towers and thicker walls, were emphasised.[32]

The existence of a chapel at Belvoir is beyond doubt.[33] However, important data are missing: there is no direct archaeological evidence of the chapel's original location.

At present we do not know its plan or whether it was rebuilt at different times in the castle's history. The documentation provides only a general time framework within which various phases can be proposed. We suggest that there may have been a sequence of chapels on site. Prior to the Hospitallers, the first settlement in the area of the castle was probably built in the 1140s while Fulk of Anjou was king of Jerusalem, although no direct documentation or archaeological trace were found to support this.[34] The site was in the hands of Ivo Velos who sold it to the order for the sum of 1,400 bezants.[35] As a settlement of a Christian nobleman, one would assume a chapel dedicated already in this early stage.[36] The site came into Hospitaller hands in 1168 at the latest, and was held by them until 1189. A chapel must have been built at the very first stage. We refer to this chapel as *Castle Chapel I*. Saladin, who conquered the castle after a long siege, would probably have destroyed this chapel, at least partially, to demonstrate his conquest. From 1241, during the second Frankish occupation of the site, a second chapel was probably constructed, which is referred to as *Castle Chapel II*. The hypothetical reconstruction of chapel history is listed in Table 28.2.

We were able to distinguish the elements of the chapel from those of the inner castle by their distinct petrographical features. All the elements were carved of oolitic limestone from Gesher Formation. This type of rock is of higher quality and its appearance is considerably superior to those of stones cut of the varied layers member (nodular limestone). The oolitic limestone was used when precision in details and superior workmanship were of first priority.[37]

Table 28.2 Hypothetical summary of chapel generations at Belvoir

Generation	Date	Fate	Elements	Estimated location
Private chapel(?)	*c.* 1140	Unknown. Demolished by the Hospitallers with the rest of the buildings?	No identified remains.	Unknown.
Castle Chapel I	*c.* 1168–89	Demolished or partly demolished, possibly by collapse of the roof by Saladin.	Most of the remains were possibly reused for chapel II.	Unknown. Possibly on the second level of the inner castle.
Castle Chapel II	*c.* 1241–66	Last occupation by the Hospitallers, complete demolition probably by Baybars.	Materials remained in the site and were reused in the houses of the village Kaukab al-Hawa and in Muslim tombs in cemetery located near H. Gebul, SW of the castle (719085/248126).	1 In the same place as the first chapel, i.e. on the second level of the inner castle. 2 A new location on the second level. 3 Unknown. A new location on ground level.

a) 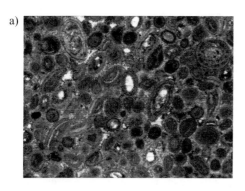 b)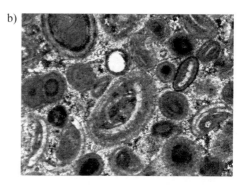

Figure 28.9   Rib vault fragment (see Fig. 28.7c) petrographic sections, under plane-polarised light.

a) Oolitic limestone. Oval ooids, cemented by sparry calcite, occurring in two size modes: larger ooids (750–850μm) and small ones (~250μm). The nuclei of the ooids commonly consist of either fragmental or whole ostracod valves, and occasionally of ostracod containing intraclasts.

b) Mostly oval ooids formed around ostracod valves. Oval ooid formed around a number of valves, thick brown coating. A single ostracod valve, micritic filling. A single valve with dark rim around it. Over layered valves with micritic filling and thin brown rim surrounding each. Photographs: Vardit Shotten-Hallel.

The samples described in Figure 28.9 were extracted from the same layer of Gesher Formation. The stone is probably extracted from the same quarry and the minor variations in the analysed samples are typical to this formation.

Proposed architectural plan

As no trace of the original building survived, we can only assume its location and the methods of construction. However, the remaining architectural elements allow for a partial reconstruction and estimation of the size of the building and its appearance. The 'third generation' chapel, the *Castle Chapel II*, we assume, as suggested by M. Ben-Dov, was located in the second level of the west tower.[38] Changes in the original plan of this area enabled the construction of a chapel here. The principal entrance was therefore probably located on the south façade, to enable for a convenient access from the broad staircase leading from the courtyard. Another entrance was probably located on the north side of the chapel to allow direct access to the dormitories and more importantly for rituals and processions.

According to the architectural fragments, currently under study, the plan of the chapel consisted of an independent structure of two bays measuring approximately 18 by 8 m internally: a single nave covered with cross vaults and a sanctuary.[39] A triple clustered column was the division element between the nave and the apse and the springing point for the transverse rib and the diagonal ribs of both spaces.[40] The nave measured approximately 14 m in length and was accessed via at least one opening. So far, the single window of the sanctuary was reconstructed from the remaining fragments, yet it is possible that more windows were located along the nave. These dimensions were concluded from cornice fragments of the apse. The dimensions of the main portal were derived from the reconstruction of the tympanum where a stone slab presenting an angle was probably located. This slab is one of three sculptures found *ex situ* during the excavation of the castle.

Sculptural elements: interpretation of architectural context

Three sculptural elements found during the excavation of the site pose questions of identity, dating and original position. They certainly do not attest to the complete original sculptural programme of Belvoir chapel. In fact, it would have been a very difficult task to identify the three elements with one programme, had we not known they all actually came from the same source. However, the only plausible building to which these highly adorned elements belonged was the chapel. The elements are: a) a stone slab, part of a tympanum, presenting a hovering angel and an unidentified (damaged) object or creature above it (Fig. 28.10); b) a bearded head, decorated with foliage in the rear (Fig. 28.11), c) a head of a youth, decorated with foliage (Fig. 28.12).[41] Two of these elements were studied and published by M. Barasch after the excavation.[42] Barasch detailed the artistic features of both elements at length and suggested that their stylistic origin was in the 'southern regions of twelfth century Europe'.

Customary scenes depicted in portals of the twelfth or thirteenth century include the Ascension, the Last Judgement, the Last Supper, Annunciation and Adoration of the Magi. But subjects and representations were endlessly diverse. The interpretation of the elements retrieved from Belvoir points to a different, perhaps unique, scene that was depicted on the main portal and façades of its chapel. The iconographical oddities evident in these three elements allow no traditional or familiar Western interpretation.

Reconstruction of the chapel's plan and that of the sculptural programme demands reconsideration of these three elements and analysing their original function. To do so, and to aid decipher their identity, we summarised their properties in Table 28.3.[43]

Hovering angel

The architectural form of the 'Hovering Angel' slab suggests it was the left part of a tympanum of the main portal. The main portal in the principal entrance was not necessarily located on the west façade.[44] The left side of the slab was where the arch of the portal rested: a chamfer on the upper part of the slab was conformed with the curve of the arch so the slab tapered. The remaining gap was filled, on the left side and above, with stones adjusted to the arch.

With one angel on the left side of the tympanum, the more obvious scenes would be *Majestas Domini* (Christ in Majesty), where Christ is depicted flanked with the four evangelists who were often represented by their symbols or the Ascension in which Christ is seen with angels on both his sides (usually holding the mandorla). In the first scene the angel would have represented St Matthew, winged and holding a square shape object that appears to be a book. Above the angel is an unidentified remains of a creature/object that was severely damaged, probably for the same reason that caused the angel's wings to be impaired. The remains of scrolls on the left side of this figure suggest this was the depiction

505

Figure 28.10   Stone slab presenting a hovering angel and an unidentified (damaged) object or creature above it. Courtesy of Israel Museum, Jerusalem. Photograph: Vardit Shotten-Hallel.

of St Mark as a Lion. To complete the scene a similar relief slab on the other side would present the symbols of the evangelists St Luke as an ox and St John as an eagle. The middle block in this type of scene would be the relief of Christ himself enthroned.

This reconstruction is problematic for a number of reasons. First and foremost we have only the relief of the angel and above it some obscure figure; the other parts have not been discovered yet. Second, the position of the angel contradicts the common iconography as he is depicted turning outside of the scene focal point which is Christ; even his face is not looking back but rather further left, a very unusual gesture. In addition, in most representations of this scene the angel appears at the upper part and the lion/St Mark below.[45] Notable examples include Chartres' West façade, central portal tympanum showing the angel on top left and the eagle on top right. The lion and the ox are on the lower parts, their bodies turn outward but their heads turned inward. In the portal of St Trophime in Arles, the evangelists are represented holding a book each, except for St John who rests as an eagle upon a scroll. All figures are presented when they are turning in the direction of Christ and so are their faces.[46]

Table 28.3   Summary of properties for three sculptural elements

Element/ Additions	Material/ Dimensions	Oddities/ Interpretation	Function/ Construction details	Original position
Hovering angel/ square object, possibly a book	Oolitic limestone (Gesher Fm.)[a] 117 x 58 x 31 cm	The angel is turning away from the scene in an unusual gesture. Unidentified damaged element above it.	Slab, part (1/3) of a tympanum. Reverse left unworked hence the slab was inserted to the construction, mortar remains on the right side of the slab.	Out. Portal, principal entrance. Left part of the tympanum.
Bearded head/nil	Proconnesian marble 41 x 37.5 cm		Trumeau (?)/double-sided capital: figured on the obverse, foliage on the reverse. The capital is worked of all sides: front – bearded head; back – foliage; sides – flattened to receive slabs. The lower part is delineated by an astragal.[b]	In and out. Portal, principal entrance. The sides of the capital show the mould of narrow slabs attached on both its sides. The base of the capital is rounded to fit a 150cm column.
Head of youth/nil	Thasos marble 33 x 32 x 32 cm	Furrows and mouth suggesting a grimacing expression.[c]	Cornice (?) Right side unworked, left side flattened, possibly to fit continuation of the cornice.	Out. Surrounding external cornice, attached to the construction on one face.

Notes:

a   For a detailed study of this type of limestone, see 'Building stone' section in this chapter.

b   Jacoby, Z. (1982) The Workshop of the Temple Area in Jerusalem in the Twelfth Century: its Origin, Evolution and Impact. Zeitschrift fur Kunstgeschichte, 45/4: 325–94, at 376.

c   Barasch interprets the expression to be a smile comparing the 'formula' to two more heads from Acre. M. Barasch (1971) Crusader Figural Sculpture in the Holy Land: Twelfth Century Examples from Acre, Nazareth and Belvoir Castle. Ramat Gan, 192–3.

Bearded head

According to the architectural finds studied so far, the portal was framed by a double colonnette, of which components of the left jamb survived (see Fig. 28.7 components of the left jamb), and was possibly divided to two by a trumeau formed by the bearded head and a round column. The trumeau was seen from both its sides: the front sculpted with

b)

a)

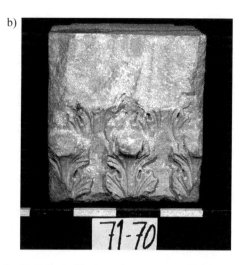

Figure 28.11   Trumeau. Bearded head, decorated with foliage. Photographs: courtesy of IAA, Mariana Salzberger.

the face and the back with foliage. The trumeau was probably situated between two thin lintels above which was the tympanum framed by the archivolts, making the portal height significantly larger. It rested upon a column shaped to fit its base. A base for the trumeau column has not yet been identified. Although associated with the angel detail of the portal, the foliage in the rear of the trumeau conform to the foliage details carved in the *head of youth* element. The acanthus leaves in the reverse seem to be carved in the same way as those in the front left part of the *head of youth.* This could imply the same artist working on the different elements.

Head of youth

The original function of this element was probably in a surrounding cornice, located in an opening of a door or a large window. Its right side was hidden inside a wall and its left side was worked to receive the neighbouring fragment of the cornice. Barasch and Folda seem to agree that the expression on the youth's face represents a smile by observing the mouth and furrows. Barasch dated this piece to the middle and second half of the twelfth century.[47] Grimaces of laughter and mockery appeared frequently as demonstrated by N. Kenaan-Kedar.[48] Alternatively, we propose to identify the youth as *grimacing* rather than smiling. Looking for parallel examples of this expression and main features, such as the dominant hair, yields no prominent example. In the tympanum of the main portal of Sainte-Foy, Conques, a few demonic figures illustrate comparable features (Fig. 28.13). The demons are carved with furrows, prominent chin, swollen lips and an open mouth. Additional features include the carving of the hair (spirals) and the holes drilled in the eyes. Moreover, to the right of Christ are four angels depicted, each turns in a different direction.[49]

The following discussion deals first with the hovering angel as representing one scene depicted on the portal, which belong to the celestial hierarchy of saints and angels, and then

Figure 28.12   Head of a youth, decorated with foliage. Photograph: courtesy of
Israel Museum, Jerusalem, photographer: unknown.

Figure 28.13   Detail of portal, west façade, Saint Foy, Conques. Note features of the bottom-left
demon. Photograph: courtesy of R. Kool.

with the two elements representing visual physiognomic features (open mouth, wide-open eyes) connected to the representation of sinners, dammed, demonic or fantastic creatures (Fig. 28.14). The heads are isolated, with no human and animal body attached, and carry no objects acting as symbols. Both elements were most probably displayed on the outer side of the chapel. The rear of the bearded head as a trumeau displayed foliage which was facing the interior of the chapel.

Whether we adopt the moralising or apotropaic approach, our interpretation of the sculpture from Belvoir is based on the meaning ascribed to them and by our reading of the dual character of the Hospitaller Order. The heads of Belvoir represent fantastic and demonic creatures alongside celestial creatures.[50] Regardless of how complete the sculptural programme was, with only three elements surviving there is still enough to draw the difference between the elements and to emphasise some principles regarding the visual vocabulary used in a Hospitaller chapel.[51]

Figure 28.14 The bearded head and the head of youth. Courtesy of Israel Museum, Jerusalem. Photograph: Vardit Shotten-Hallel.

SYNTHESIS: DATING, IDENTITY
AND MATERIALITY

In this work we have attempted to analyse the architecture of Belvoir through different prisms: historical, archaeological, architectural and geological. By enquiring into issues of dating, identity and materiality of Belvoir Castle, we can now suggest a new point of departure for a detailed study of the castle and in particular of the castle chapel. It is possible to identify a number of attributes of chapel construction directly associated with the Order of the Hospital. These attributes are based on new reading of the finds from Belvoir and parallels with a limited number of other Latin–East Hospitaller churches.[52] Each of these churches provides us only with a fractional image of its original sculptural programme and plan. En masse they allow the visualisation a more complete image of each chapel. Three attributes relate to the materiality, and additional four relate to architecture and art. Both types of attributes reflect an image different from the one common so far regarding the architecture of Hospitaller churches in the Latin East.

1   Variety of materials
     Many of the Frankish churches in the Latin Kingdom were built using different materials for construction and for decoration. At Belvoir, marble elements were incorporated in the sculptural programme.[53]
2   Spolia
     The use of spolia in churches is evident throughout the kingdom. In the second generation chapel (*Castle Chapel II*) of the thirteenth century, many elements of spolia could have come from the first chapel (*Castle Chapel I*) built by the Hospitallers on site in the twelfth century. While all the construction and decoration were exectured in limestone of the same type, the two marble sculptures form an exception. Thus they cannot be 'dated' or attributed to either of the stages (twelfth or thirteenth century). Their identification will have to be based on grounds of style and contemporary parallels, as the Franks, as argued by Nurith Kenaan-Kedar, used models of symbolic themes in the architectural components of their churches.[54]
3   Limestone
     As a general rule, the majority of Frankish churches incorporated limestone in construction details. At Belvoir, ex situ elements of oolitic limestone can accordingly be attributed to the chapel/s.
4   Location
     In Hospitaller compounds of the Latin East, the church/chapel is not always located in the traditional customary place, that is in the northern area of the cloister.[55] In the Hospitaller convent in Acre, the church was located south of the main compound.[56] The same applies to the church at Bethgibelin which was located south of the refectory and courtyard. At Belvoir we suggest that the chapel (*Castle Chapel II*) was located in the west tower of the inner castle.
5   Visibility
     The visibility of the church was significant as much as any other military component, hence the tendency to locate the church in the upper levels, not only for reasons of segregation of the religious from the lay community, but also to visibly demonstrate

511

Christian rule. At Belvoir it is at the western tower upper level, at Athlit at the highest point in the castle, and at Arsur, we also suggest its location at the western tower's upper level.

6   Single apse plan

The choice of plan evidently derived from a wide range of considerations. Size and scale of the convent were relatively of minor significance. The chapels in Belmont (near Tripoli), Crac des Chevaliers, Margat (Marqab) and most likely that of Arsur, show all plans based on a single nave and apse.

7   Monsters and demonic creatures

The most intriguing attribute relates to the introduction of monstrous creatures. The representation of these creatures is abundant in Western churches of the twelfth and thirteenth century. Demons and other monsters and hybrid creatures representing evil (manticores, centaurs) were extensively used in churches throughout Europe.[57] In the Latin Kingdom demonic creatures appear in the Church of the Annunciation, Nazareth (twelfth century)[58] and in the cathedral church of St John the Baptist, Sebastia (twelfth century).[59] It is important to note that the two remaining sculptures from Belvoir are both heads carved into most significant building details. They convey a message not only as an image but as a vital building component. A recent discovery at Arsur, retrieved from the fills of the castle's western façade in 2010, further emphasises the introduction of monsters into church buildings.[60] At Arsur, as at Belvoir, this element was a significant component of the castle chapel as designed by the Hospitallers.

CONCLUSIONS

In this chapter we propose an interpretation to the chronology of Hospitaller presence in Belvoir, while trying to decipher some of the castle's architectural components. We focused on the numerous fragments of architectural elements, ex situ, which in our view represent two different generations of chapels in the castle: *Castle Chapel I* (*c.* 1168–89) and *Castle Chapel II* (*c.* 1241–66).[61] A two-chapels chronology as proposed here may provide a partial explanation for the eclectic nature of the detailed assemblage and for the multi-type construction details relative to the estimated size of the chapel.[62] The Hospitaller church in Abu-Ghosh, contemporary to Belvoir, followed a basilica-type plan, which allowed flexibility and 'room' for several technological solutions to be applied throughout.[63] At Belvoir the chapel was an independent structure, consisting of two bays: a single nave and a sanctuary, measuring approximately 18 by 8 m internally. Despite its relatively small scale, the structure was complex since the builders used several supportive elements to construct the vaults. Clustered column served as the division element between the nave and the apse. An impost below the vaulting marked the springing point for the transverse arch and the diagonal ribs of the vaulting. The impost followed the nave and the curve of the apse where a single window was set. The chapel was built exclusively of oolitic limestone, while marble elements were incorporated only in the sculptural programme.

The rather 'eclectic' nature of the architectural components, suggesting two generations of chapels, does not allow us to rely on any of the features to provide a distinct consecration date. Yet, in light of parallel features abundant in some twelfth-century Jerusalem area churches (e.g. elbow columns), it would be reasonable enough to assume a twelfth-century origin for most of the details studied so far. The proposed hypothetical history of chapels built in Belvoir as a result of different occupation phases also resolves the conflict regarding the construction of the western tower. According to the pieces so far retrieved from Belvoir, *spolia* elements were used for both construction and for the decoration of the chapel.[64] As suggested already by M. Ben-Dov and by T. Biller, the tower is yet to be studied in order to trace the different phases. However, if we take into account that it was either refortified by the Mamluk or/and by the Hospitallers themselves in the thirteenth century, it could have provided the foundation for the upper-level chapel.

The discussion of the sculptural programme of the chapel is for the moment reduced to three elements, all currently on display in the Israel Museum in Jerusalem. At least two of these were probably used in the portal of the principal entrance to the chapel. Their theme remains enigmatic at this stage.

Engaging questions that concern the dating and the identity of the chapel in Belvoir through examination of the materiality allowed new interpretation to come forward. This reading of the architectural plan of the castle allows ascribing a chapel to the second Hospitaller phase in the thirteenth-century castle.[65] The proposed location of the chapel, the heart of religious life, on the upper level of the inner fortified tower echoes the words of the Hospitaller master who built Belvoir, reflecting the duality of the Hospitaller Order as it appears at Belvoir:

Nos itaque et fratres nostri, religioni miliciam commiscentes.

NOTES

Special thanks are due to the directors of *Mission archéologique de Belvoir*, Professor Jonathan Riley-Smith, Meir Ben-Dov, Na'ama Brosh, Dr Moshe Shirav, Dr Shimon Ilani and Alexis Rosenbaum, Professor David Jacoby, Professor Amnon Linder, Florian Renucci, Simon Dorso, Dr Sebastián Ernesto Salvadó, Dr Robert Kool and to Dr Gil Fishof. All the sculptural and architectural elements mentioned in this chapter are at present in the site itself and in the Israel Museum in Jerusalem.

1 *Mission archéologique de Belvoir* (IAA licence No. G 51 / 2013, G 47 / 2014) is led by Professor Bruno Phalip, Université Blaise Pascal Clermont-Ferrand and Dr Anne Baud-Chemain, Université Lyon II in cooperation with Dr Hervé Barbe of the Israel Antiquities Authority. The first author is part of the mission and a PhD candidate at the Hebrew University of Jerusalem, supervised by Professor Benjamin Z. Kedar with the guidance of Professor Eytan Sass.

2 Ellenblum, R. (2008) *Crusader Castles and Modern Histories*. Cambridge University Press, 283–4.

3 Boas A. J. (2006) *Archaeology of the Military Orders: A Survey of the Urban Centres, Rural Settlements and Castles of the Military orders in the Latin East (c. 1120–1291)*. Routledge, 13, 122–3; (2009) *Crusader Archaeology: The Material Culture of the Latin East*. Routledge, 103–6.

4 At this stage the exact location and layout of the castle chapel has not yet been identified. The structure seen today above the west tower was built by the restoration team of the castle, following the excavations of 1966. Meir Ben Dov excavated the site on behalf of the Department of Antiquities and the National Parks Authority. He identified and isolated the stones originally belonging to the chapel and which we are now studying. Other stones used in this reconstruction were retrieved from the dismantling of the village Kawkab al-Hawa.

5 Riley-Smith, J. (2012) *The Knights Hospitaller in the Levant*. Palgrave, 33. See also: Burgtorf, J. (2008) *The Central Convent of Hospitallers and Templars: History, Organization, and Personnel (1099/1120–1310)*. Brill, 65–6; Hamilton, B. (2014) The Crusades and North East Africa. In: John, S. Morton, N. (eds) *Crusading and Warfare in the Middle Ages: Realities and Representations*. Ashgate, 169–70.

6 J. Prawer noted the problematic documentation of the first settlement in Belvoir. Victor Guerin, based on a text by Jacques de Vitry, was contemplating the construction of the castle under the leadership of King Fulk of Anjou, between 1138 and 1140: *Cum igitur ciuitates memoratas pluresque alias, maximè mediterraneas, nostri subiugare non possent, in extremitatibus ter-rae suae, vt fines suos defenderent, castra munitissima & inexpugnabilia inter ipsos & hostes extruxerunt, scilicet Montem Regalem, & Petram Deserti, cuius nomen modernum est Crac, vltrà Iordanem, Sapheth & Belvoir, cum multis aliis munitionibus, citra Iordanem. Est autem Sapheth castrum munitissimum inter Accon & mare Galileæ, non longè à montibus Gelboë situm. Belvoir vero, non longè à monte Thabor iuxta civitatem quondam egregiam & populosam Iezraël, inter Citopolim & Tyberiadem, situm est in loco sublimi* (Jacques de Vitry, chap. 49, éd. Moschus: 83–4; éd. Bongars: 1074). Marino Sanudo, who copied de Vitry almost verba-tim, included this passage in his chronology dating the construction to the end of King Fulk's reign, or to 1143, at the latest. Contradicting the opinion of Guerin and his immediate suc-cessors, Van Berchem, M. (1902) *Notes sur les croisades*, 413–14, https://archive.org/stream/notessurlescroi00bercgoog#page/n43/mode/2up (accessed online 22 February 2015). Van Berchem already noted that Jacques de Vitry did not mention any date for construction of vari-ous castles mentioned in this passage. Prawer, J. (1967) *The History of the Fortress of Kaukab el-Hawa Belvoir.* Yedi 'ot ha-Hevrah la-hakirat Erets-Yisra'el ve-'atikoteha Vol. 31. Jewish Palestine Exploration Society, 236–49 at 237–8.

7 Alongside his ambitious moves, d'Assailly will be most remembered for the crises caused in his time: the Order's involvement in the Egyptian campaigns initiated by King Amalric and for his resignation. Nevertheless his time as master for nearly a decade was characterised by great sta-bility in personal terms: King Amalric was crowned in 1163 and was king of Jerusalem until his death in 1174, he was accompanied by one preceptor – Guy of Mahón (1163–70). In the *Chronicle of the Deceased Masters*, d'Assailly was commemorated as 'Hic fuit antiquus valdè, et brevi tempore que vixit multa bona religioni procuravit, et dominis infirmis servivit multum benignè.' Dugdale, W. (ed. 1817–30) *Monasticon Anglicanum*, Cronica magistrorum defunctorum, 8 vols, London, VI, 796–8, at 797.

8 Blochet, E. (trans. 1908) *Histoire d'Égypte de Makrizi traduite de l'arabe et accompagnée de notes historiques et géographiques*, Earnest Leroux, 471, n. 2. Kaūkab is mentioned amongst other sites returned to the Franks ('Les villes dont les Francs se rendirent maîtres de nouveau furent: Jérusalem, Béthléem, Ascalon et la province qui en dépend, Baīt-Djibrīl et sa province, Medjdel Yabā la province qui en dépendent: Safad, Kaūkab, Toūr, Tibnīn, la province de Ghaza sauf la ville de Ghaza elle m la province de Ghaza sauf la ville de Ghaza elle même, Tibériade et ses dépendances, les deux Shakīf, et en somme tout le Sāhel'). For the fall of Safed, see Barbé H. (2010) Le château de Safed et son territoire a l'époque des croisades. PhD diss., Hebrew University of Jerusalem (French; Hebrew summary), 31–5.

9 For a proposed reconstruction of the W gate see: *Biller, T.* (1989) Die Johanniterburg *Belvoir* am Jordan: zum frühen Burgbau der Ritterorden im Heiligen Land. *Architectura* 19: 105–36, at 119.

10 It should be clearly noted that we have no historical document confirming Hospitaller reoccupa-tion and rebuilding of Belvoir castle.

11 For the financial instability, see Bronstein, J. (2008) The Decree of 1262: A Glimpse into the Economic Decision-Making of the Hospitallers. In: Mallia-Milanes, V. (ed.) *The Military Orders: History and Heritage.* Ashgate, 197–8. It seems that the order was able to restore man power, however, their income suffered from significant loss of agricultural territories. In October 1259 the order was relieved from the payment of full tithes and pay only the twentieth part of some of its crops ('pour le dixmes de Belveer et ses dépandance ... l'ordre ne payera dorénvant que la vingtièm partie du bled d'orge, féve, pois chiches, lentilles, vins et huiles, et qu'il sera exempt de toute autre sorte de dixme pour les dites terres'); *Cart* II, no. 2937, p. 883. The original document was lost (Marseille, Arch. Des B. du-Rh., ordre de Malte, H. invent. Des chartes de Syrie, no. 318 (XVIII s)).

12 Prawer noted the treaty of Qalāwūn where Kaukab al-Hawa is listed amongst other cities under his rule. See Prawer, J. *The History*, 237. For the treaty of 682/1283 and translation of the text and list of the cities and sites, see Holt, P. M. (1995) *Early Mamluk Diplomacy, 1260–1290: Treaties of Baybars and Qalāwūn with Christian Rulers*. Brill, 69–88.

13 Boas, *Archaeology of the Military Orders*, 229.

14 Ellenblum, *Crusader Castles*, 249.

15 Piana, M. and Carlsson, C. (2014) *Archaeology and Architecture of the Military Orders: New Studies*. Ashgate, 179.

16 Comments in Boas, *Archaeology of the Military Orders*, 202: the dormitories of Belvoir were probably 'located in the vaults north or south to the cloister/courtyard'; Kennedy, H. (1994) *Crusader Castles*. Cambridge University Press, 61: 'In Belvoir we can see clearly how the inner court functioned as a monastic cloister for the knights'; Riley-Smith, J. (2012) *The Knights Hospitaller in the Levant, c.1070–1309*. Palgrave, 112: 'the construction of the castles had also to take account of religious life. Enclosure … was an important issue.'

17 See a discussion in Riley-Smith, *The Knights Hospitaller*, 32–4.

18 *Theodorici Libellus de Locis Sanctis*, XLIV (1172). Tobler, T. (ed.) Paris, 1865, 97–8.

19 Prawer already noted that the castle is called 'new' although it was probably built three years before. Prawer, *The History*, 237.

20 Letter of al-Fadhel, *Recueil des Historiens des Croisades, Historiens Orientaux*. IV, 387, 388–9, at 389. http://gallica.bnf.fr/ark:/12148/bpt6k51581f (accessed 10 January 2015).

21 Delaville le Roulx, J. (1894) *Cartulaire général de l'ordre des Hospitaliers (1100–1310)*, 4 vols. Ernest Leroux, IV, 247–8, no. 310.

22 *Cart.* I, 425–9, no. 627

23 For the geology of the site consult also the *Geological Map* of Belvoir Area: Sneh, A., Bartov, Y. and Rosensaft, M. State of Israel, Ministry of National Infrastructures, Geological Survey of Israel, Jerusalem 1998. Geological Map of Israel 1:200,000 Sheet 1.

24 Schulman, N. (1962) The Geology of the Central Jordan Valley. PhD thesis, Hebrew University, Jerusalem (in Hebrew); Shaliv, G. (1991) *Stages in the Tectonic and Volcanic History of the Neogene Basin in the Lower Galilee and the Valleys*. Report GSI/11/91 (in Hebrew).

25 Plaster remains on the inner walls of the castle as shown on the S wall of the courtyard. The dating of this wall is still questionable.

26 Compare this standard persistently kept in Belvoir with the construction of walls in Vadum Jacob, the Templar stronghold built N to the Sea of Galilee, where in the limestone construction (e.g. of the north wall) the builders randomly used chips of both basalt and limestone.

27 Typical section in the lower Tabor Stream consist of three members. The base: thin grain laminated limestone, max. 22 m, hardly exposed in the area. The middle layer is the 'Oolitic limestone' and on top the 'varied layers' (Schulman, The Geology of the Central Jordan Valley; Shaliv, *Neogene Basin in the Lower Galilee*).

28 M. Ben-Dov, 2014 personal communication.

29 Zvi Gal, Israel Antiquities Authority Survey Map 'Gazith – 46, 1991.

30 Letter of al-Fadhel, *Recueil des Historiens des Croisades, Historiens Orientaux*. IV, 389. http://gallica.bnf.fr/ark:/12148/bpt6k51581f (accessed 10 January 2015)

31 Replacing the crescent with a cross and vice versa as a visual symbol of replacing the authority and the dominant faith. See, for example, Goldhill, S. (2008) *Jerusalem*. Harvard College, 55. Another aspect is the integration of architectural elements originated from churches in the construction of Muslim buildings. See, for example, Guidetti, M. (2009) The Byzantine Heritage in the dār al-Islām: Churches and Mosques in al-Ruha between the Sixth and Twelfth Centuries. *Muqarnas*, 26: 1–36. https://univie.academia.edu/MattiaGuidetti (accessed 8 February 2015).

32 The exceptionally large number of religious institutions formed in the Latin Kingdom during less than two centuries goes beyond the mere religious needs of the Frankish society. See Pringle, D. (1993) *Churches of the Latin Kingdom of Jerusalem*. Cambridge University Press, I, 1.

33 Finds directly associated with a chapel were discovered during the excavations led by Meir Ben-Dov. See Ben-Dov, M., (1969) Excavations in the Crusader Castle at Kochav Hayarden, *Qadmoniot* Israel Exploration Society, Jerusalem II, 1, 5: 22–7, at 26–7. Two column fragments, from the chapel, were found on the ground floor north and south to the west tower. Meir Ben-Dov, personal communications, 2015. We thank Meir Ben-Dov for his contribution.

34 Prawer, *The History*, I. 241. *Mission archéologique de Belvoir* Excavations of 2014 revealed architectural elements which were not identified with any of the Hospitaller phase. Most probably they belong to the earlier phase of construction on site.

35 *Cart.* I, 271–2 no. 398: 'damus et concedimus in elemosinam castrum de Coquet, quod vulgariter Belvear nuncupatur cum suis divisis et pertinentiis quod Ivo Velos Suique heredes pretio mille et quadringentorum bisantiorum Hospitali … vendiderunt.' Cf. Röhricht, R. (ed.) (1960) *Regesta Regni Hierosolymitany (MXCVII–MCCXCI)*. No. 448, p. 117. Libraria Academica Wageriana. www.archive.org/details/regestaregnihie00rhgoog (accessed 8 February 2015).

36 There is no indication of nobility regarding Ivo Velos's origins. His signature only appears in the document. For private chapels, see Kieckhefer, R. (2010) The Impact of Architecture. In: Bornstein, D. E. (ed.) *Medieval Christianity*. Augsburg Fortress, 109–46, at 133.

37 Regardless of these differences, in terms of preservation both types of rocks proved to be durable. Hardly any changes are seen on both types as a result of natural weathering processes or physical deterioration.

38 During the survey of the castle walls, we identified limestone chips between basalt boulders in the inner walls of the outer castle. The chips, cutting waste, were found only in the NW side. This might indicate the stone masons' workshop area that was situated close to the site of the chapel.

39 Calculations are based on two elements of a rounded impost that was placed in the apse. The radius of the elements is 3.73 m which indicate the dimension of the apse 7.46 m and interior of the nave of no more than 8 m. Reconstruction plan of the chapel is currently under preparation.

40 A similar element was recorded by C. N. Johns in the parish church of 'Atlit. Johns, C.N. (1997) *Pilgrims' Castle ('Atlit), David's Tower (Jerusalem) and Qal'at ar-Rabad ('Ajlun): Three Middle Eastern Castles from the Time of the Crusades*, ed. D. Pringle. Ashgate, 124, fig. 2, plate LXXIV 5.

41 Photos of the three sculptural elements exhibited at the Israel Museum, Jerusalem. Courtesy of the Israel Antiquity Authority.

42 Barasch, M. (1971) *Crusader Figural Sculpture in the Holy Land: Twelfth Century Examples from Acre, Nazareth and Belvoir Castle*. Ramat Gan, 189–207, fig. 46; Folda, J. (1995) *The Art of the Crusaders in the Holy Land, 1098–1187*. Cambridge University Press, 395, pl. 9.36d.

43 The reconstruction is based on analysis of the sculptural elements. Further elements, should they be found, will shed more light and might suggest a different reconstruction. The analysis is mostly based on the architectural function of these three elements rather than on their style.

44 Barasch suggested it decorated the porch of the chapel. Barasch, *Crusader Figural Sculptures*, 203.

45 For the traditional location of the Evangelists, see Fishof, G. (2012) The Master of the Tympanum of Saint-Hilaire in Semur-en-Brionnais: Rethinking the Meaning of Style and Concepts of Decline in Burgundian Romanesque Sculpture. *Annales des Bourgogne* 84–3: 245–80, at 255.

46 For a detailed discussion of the iconography of Majestas Domini scenes, see Vergnolle, É. (2008) Maiestas Domini Portals of the Twelfth Century. In: Hourihane, C. (ed.) *Romanesue Art and Thought in the Twelfth Century. Essays in Honour of Walter Cahn*. Princeton Index of Christian Art and Penn State University, 179–80; Skubiszewski, P. (2006) 'Maiestas Domini' et liturgie. In: Arrignon, C., Debies, M.-H., Galderisi, C. and Palazzo, E. (eds) *Cinquante années d'études médiévales, Actes du colloque organise à l'occasion du cinquanteniaure de CESCM les 1er 4 septembre 2003*. Brepols, 309–408.

47 Barasch, *Crusader Figural Sculptures*, 196–7.

48 Kenaan-Kedar, N. (1995) *Marginal Sculpture in Medieval France: Towards the Deciphering of an Enigmatic Pictorial Language*. Aldershot, 14.

49 This is not to suggest any further connection between the portal at Conques to the elements found in Belvoir. For the dating of the portal, see Kendall, C. B. (1989) The Voice in the Stone: the Verse Inscription of Ste.-Foy of Conques and the date of the Tympanum. In: Gallacher, P. J. and Damico, H. (eds) *Hermeneutics and Medieval Culture.* State University of New York Press, 163–82. For the origin of Gilbert, see Poplimont, Ch. (1870) *La France Héraldique*, vol. 1. Bruges, 83. The origin of the master of the Hospital, Gilbert of Assailly, has not been established as coming from Assailly, which is in the Aveyron department, Midi-Pyrénées region. Assailly is only some 300 km from Conques and by the time Gilbert left for the East, the church and the tympanum were long built.

50 Recent scholarship differs in this field of research: Dale, T. E. A. (2011) The Monstrous. In: Rudolph, C. (ed.) *Blackwell Companion to Art History, A Companion to Medieval Art: Romanesque and Gothic in Northern Europe.* Blackwell; Steel, K. (2012) Centaurs, Satyrs, and Cynocephali: Medieval Scholarly Teratology and the Question of the Human. In: Mittman, A. S. and Dendle P. J. (eds) *The Ashgate Research Companion to Monsters and the Monstrous.* Ashgate, 257–74.

51 Criticising the use of monstrous creatures in cloisters, Bernard of Clairvaux also stressed the use of marble: 'Tam multa denique, tamque mira diversarum formarum apparet ubique varietas, ut magis legere libeat in *marmoribus*, quam in codicibus, totumque diem occupare singula ista mirando, quam in lege Dei meditando'. *Apologia ad Guillelmum abbatem*, 29.

52 These chapels include: the chapel of Belmont near Tripoli, chapel of Crac des Chevaliers, chapel of Margat (Marqab) and a proposed location and plan for a Hospitaller Chapel in Arsur.

53 According to the recent analysis, Belvoir seem to be an exception in that respect as no other materials were identified, excluding the marble elements. The possibility of integrating basalt and limestone details, such as the elbow columns, has yet to be proved.

54 Kenaan, N. (1973) Local Christian Art in Twelfth Century Jerusalem. *Israel Exploration Journal*, 23, 4: 221–229, at 222 in relation to the Holy Sepulchre. For the use of spolia in the Frankish East see, for example, Boas, A. J. (2006) *Archaeology of the Military Orders.* Routledge, 108. 183, 186 (Belvoir), 190, 217.

55 Lawrence, C. H. (2014) *Medieval Monasticism: Forms of Religious Life in Western Europe in the Middle Ages*, 3rd edn. Taylor & Francis, 158, 306.

56 Shotten-Hallel, V. (2015, forthcoming) Ritual and Conflict in the Hospitaller Church of St John in Acre: The Architectural Evidence. In: Schenck, J. and Carr, M. (eds) *Military Orders 6, Culture and Conflict.* Ashgate.

57 Ambrose, K. (2013) *Marvellous and the Monstrous in the Sculpture of 12th-century Europe.* Boydell, 95–9.

58 Jacoby, Z. (1981) Le portail de l'eglise de l'Annonciation de Nazareth au XIIe siécle: Un essai de reconstitution. *Monuments et memoirs Academie des inscriptions et belles letters Fondation Eugene Piot*, 64: 141–94, at 21–2. These include fragment of a capital, devil's head, great arch stone from the external archivolt decorated with manticore and from the western portal of the church, demons with bow and arrow and demon with shield.

59 A corbel with a monster's head.

60 *The Last Supper at Apollonia* (2011) Exhibition Catalogue, 41, Fig. 17 (in Hebrew).

61 The assemblage of architectural details are currently studied by the mission members Florian Renucci, Anne Flammin and the first author.

62 Elbow columns were found in the Church of our Lord's Resurrection in Abu-Ghosh and also in the church of St Mary of the Germans in Jerusalem. Both churches share similarity in details in addition to the similarity between their plans. See Grabiner, E. (2001) From Raw Materials to a Compound and Back Again: A Look at One Element of Crusader Architecture. *Assaph – Studies in Art History*, 6. http://arts-old.tau.ac.il/departments/images/stories/journals/arthistory/Assaph6/05grabiner.pdf (accessed 9 February 2015).

63 The plan of the Church in Abu-Ghosh is based on three aisles separated by rectangular piers, the aisles are flanked with pilasters, and are covered with pointed groin vaults with transverse arches. The nave arches rest upon elbow columns. Two sets of double elbow columns are positioned

on the west façade to receive the transverse arches of the side aisles. Two surrounding cornices separate the clerestory from the lower part of the walls, continuing around the three apses.

64 Few elements of spolia were used in the castle, in the SE inner tower, in the SE external gate and in the south jamb of the western inner gate. See Ben-Dov, *Excavations*, 27.

65 Forthcoming excavations will no doubt add to our knowledge of Belvoir Castle and its architecture. This chapter aimed at sharing the work currently underway and at providing a preliminary platform for future discussion.

CHAPTER TWENTY-NINE

MARITIME COMMERCE IN THE LATIN EAST AS REFLECTED IN THE IMPORT OF CERAMICS

———•◆•———

Edna J. Stern

INTRODUCTION

Coinciding with the establishment of the crusader states in the East during the twelfth century and following in the thirteenth century, maritime travel and commerce in the Mediterranean was at its peak. The new maritime trade network that developed between the western Mediterranean ports and the Frankish ports in the eastern Mediterranean was led mainly by the Italian maritime commercial cities. Ports throughout the Mediterranean developed and flourished as the maritime technology of the period necessitated stopping at various ports along the way. The many ships that anchored at these ports brought various goods, among them ceramics, from one region of the Mediterranean to another. These imported glazed tableware, containers for foodstuff and other kitchen ware, brought by the medieval shipmen, travellers and merchants, were exposed in numerous archaeological excavations in various urban and rural sites within the Latin Kingdom of Jerusalem (modern-day Israel). Discarded ceramic vessels broke into many fragments and as they are not perishable, hundreds of years later sherds can be collected in archaeological excavations. When studied and categorized, their provenience can be traced using typology and analytical studies. Although pottery was not the most important product traded, it can represent a wide range of medium-priced bulk products such as cloth, glass or metals and staple foods as grain, oil and wine that either did not survive, or whose provenience is harder to trace. The study of the ceramics traded throughout the Mediterranean may contribute in filling gaps left by written sources on trade as these bulk products and foodstuffs are the basic elements of any economic system. Tracing their movement can give us a new perspective on patterns of maritime commerce and the economic systems of the Latin East. We would like to suggest here to consider the use of ceramic evidence as yet another source for assessing and reconstructing the patterns of maritime trade of the Latin East; or in other words, to convert ceramic evidence into an acceptable source relevant to other scholars studying the Crusader World, not only those interested in archaeology or ceramic studies.

Denys Pringle was the first to look into the connection between ceramics and trade among the crusader states (Pringle, 1986). Following a discussion on the types of pottery found in the East, Pringle pointed to three main features. The first was the homogeneity of thirteenth-century ceramic assemblages in Frankish Cyprus, Syria, and the Latin Kingdom of Jerusalem, indicating the existence of an intensive system of coastal distribution of ceramics produced in the crusader states and southern Italy, Byzantine Greece and Muslim Syria. The second was the observation that fine wares were not the only items of trade. Coarse wares were distributed by sea, containers and cooking wares. The third feature was the existence of documentary evidence from the crusader states that points to coastal trade in coarse wares. Nevertheless, Pringle stated that the archaeological study of medieval pottery in the Levant is still in its infancy, and suggested to further research the topic by sampling and analyzing distributed pottery with the purpose of identifying the sources of production, by applying quantitative and qualitative analyses to these ceramic wares, in order to measure the volume of the various traded wares as well as to conduct additional research on the unglazed coarse wares.

The study of crusader ceramics has advanced considerably since and some of Pringle's suggestions for further research have been adopted. These will be shortly reviewed below as they are essential for the discussion of our topic. Ceramics from the eastern and western Mediterranean as well as from the Latin Kingdom of Jerusalem have been scientifically sampled with the purpose of identifying the sources of production. The results of these enable identifying some of the production sites. Quantitative and qualitative analyses of Crusader period ceramics and additional research on the unglazed coarse wares have also been carried out in various excavated sites. For instance, Acre and Jaffa, two main ports of the Latin Kingdom of Jerusalem, in which large-scale excavations were conducted in the past years and the crusader-period ceramic assemblages, were extensively studied. This chapter will use the results of these studies to present the ceramic evidence relevant for the study of the Latin East maritime trade.

BACKGROUND

This section provides some background material for the topic under discussion here, the trade and distribution of pottery throughout the Mediterranean during the crusader period. These include general historical sources pertaining to Mediterranean maritime trade, nautical data concerning ships, ballast, sailing routes and navigation techniques that prevailed during this period. Finally, we will shortly review the excavations of Acre and Jaffa whose ceramic assemblages are used here to study maritime trade.

Historical background

The opening of the trade routes between Western Europe and the Levant following the establishment of the Latin kingdoms and principalities in the eastern Mediterranean had great consequences for the Western economy. This period has been described by some scholars as an age of "commercial revolution." During this time the Italian maritime cites dominated the Mediterranean maritime transportation as they were developing more sophisticated business techniques and becoming more daring in their commercial activities. With the First Crusade, the Genoese, Pisan, and later the Venetians assisted the crusading armies, mainly with ships for naval battles and to bring supplies to the East. This resulted in economic privileges and quarters that these Italian maritime cites received in the main coastal towns and were the core for the establishment of trade colonies on the Levantine coast.

Their possessions in the coastal towns and cities included hostels, warehouses, markets and churches. Citizens from the mother-cites resided in these quarters, where they had their consuls and their own legislation. The skill and initiative in commerce of the Italian maritime cities was on a par with none. They also had the biggest fleets, making the European trade with the Levant dependent mainly on them in the twelfth century. Along with the gradual growth in the power of the Italian cities in the Levantine trade, during the end of the twelfth century and the beginning of thirteenth, merchants from Catalonia and Provence also began to be active in trade (Abulafia, 1995: 1, 17–18; 2000; Day, 2002: 800; Richard, 1987: 172–3, 179–82).

The Levant maritime trade was very active in long-distance, mid-distance and local trade. Long-distance maritime trade between the Levant and Europe had existed before the crusades, but became larger in volume thereafter. Mid-distance maritime trade connected the Levant, Egypt and the Byzantine Empire. Local maritime trade, also known as tramping, was characterized by ships plying the length of the Levantine coast from Asia Minor to Egypt, buying and selling merchandise and picking up and unloading passengers in the various ports along the way. The ships used for this traditional activity along the Mediterranean coast were either small or medium-sized and belonged to local traders, or larger ships of European traders and seamen (Abulafia, 2000: 336; Jacoby, 1998).

The geographical locations of Acre and Jaffa on the coast resulted their being two of the main ports in the Latin Kingdom of Jerusalem, trading with Europe, the Muslim states and the Byzantine Empire as well as serving as a gateway for pilgrims (Fig. 29.1). Jaffa served as the main port of Jerusalem, the twelfth-century capital, and Acre was in fact the capital in the thirteenth century, in addition to serving as a thriving commercial center, both for over land and maritime trade. The Pisans were granted a quarter in Jaffa, and controlled the trade through its port, while at Acre the Genoese, Venetians and Pisans were granted quarters and commercial privileges from the twelfth century in the town, contributing greatly to the city's growing commercial importance (Boas, 1999: 32–41, 49–50).

Nautical background

In light of the fact that pottery arrived at Acre primarily by sea, it is imperative to consider issues related to maritime transportation. The nature of the ships, the issue of ballast, the sailing routes, and technological advances in navigation are all intrinsically related to the movement of pottery (and other goods) around the Mediterranean.

A change in ship-building in the western Mediterranean took place shortly before the First Crusade. Ship-builders of the Italian maritime cities began to build larger vessels that were technologically superior to the existing ships (Pryor, 1988: 29–31, figs. 5–8). Known as the round ship or *navis*, this type represented the most advanced of the sailing ships plying the Mediterranean at the time. Such ships usually carried cargo, but could take up to a thousand passengers and up to a hundred horses (Pryor, 1994: 64). As they grew larger, their capacity increased and they also became faster due to technological innovations, as detailed below. The galley ship, also known as the long ship or *galea*, increased in size during the crusader period as well. These ships were not usually used for cargo and occasionally were used only for short-distance trading. In the thirteenth century, as the ships grew and improved, they could carry more cargo and they sailed more frequently between the Mediterranean ports (Byrne, 1930: 5–6; Pryor, 1988: 26–32, 1994; Balard, 1994: 131–135).

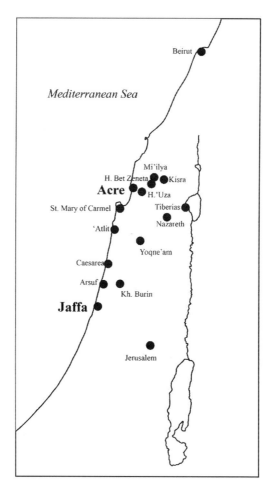

Figure 29.1 Map with the major sites mentioned in the text.

Ballast is a heavy object that provided ships with greater stability and better maneuverability. The antiquity of this practice is attested to by ancient Mediterranean shipwrecks from the Late Bronze period onwards (McGrail, 1989: 357). Ballast, which usually consisted of rubble, stone, gravel or sand, took up valuable space in the ship. Eventually, it was realized that a ship could take on heavy, salable goods, such as metal ingots, marble or millstones. Two goals could then be achieved: a well-ballasted ship and a profit from selling those goods. This type of cargo has been defined by archaeologists studying shipwrecks as "saleable ballast" (McGrail, 1989: 354–357; Parker, 1992: 91–92). Support for this can also be found in medieval written sources. Venetian lists of maritime freight charges and Genoese marine contracts classified cargo into light and heavy goods. The latter were called *merces de savurra*, which literally means ballast (Dotson, 1982: 56–59). The idea of medieval pottery serving as ballast has previously been suggested by Abulafia (1985: 294). He pointed out the presence of Tunisian medieval pottery at Pisa, and suggested that it can indicate that large cargo ships that transported grain to Tunisia brought back only low-weight products and thus the pottery served as both a space filler and as saleable ballast.

The sailing routes in the Mediterranean in the twelfth and thirteenth centuries more or less hugged the coast (Pryor, 1988: 14, fig. 2; Stern, 2012a: 155, fig. 8.2). Although there were ships that could cross the sea at that time, merchant and passenger ships preferred the littoral route in order to trade at the different ports, to restock food and water, and to break the monotony of the long, slow voyages. The main commercial trunk routes developed along the chain of islands in the northern part of the Mediterranean for this reason, as well as to overcome the prevailing winds in the east–west voyage, which made the crossing of the open sea from east to west more challenging, although not impossible. They could be avoided by hugging the coast and taking advantage of the currents and daily cycle of the land and sea breezes close to the shore. For the west–east journey, the prevailing winds were more favorable, this was important at the time since ships were generally powered by wind (Pryor, 1989: 70–73; 1994: 74).

Finally, the technological leaps in navigation of the period included the invention of the mariner's compass and more sophisticated nautical charts, tables, and maps. These, in addition to the bigger and better ships in use during this period and the improved Mediterranean sailing routes, resulted in reduce of shipping costs and led to an increase in the number of ships sailing from Europe to the eastern Mediterranean (Lane, 1966: 332–337, 341; Balard, 1994, 131, 134).

Archaeological background

Archaeological excavations have been conducted by the Israel Antiquities Authority since the 1990s both at Acre and at Jaffa due to the growth and development, and at Acre also for the promotion of tourism sites. These archaeological excavations have revealed different parts of the crusader-period towns. The two main excavations conducted at Acre (Stern and Syon, in preparation), are the compound of a Military Orders: the Hospitallers (Fig. 29.2; Stern, 2002, 2006) and a residential and commercial quarter at the Knights Hotel (Syon and Tatcher, 1998), yielded almost 10,500 ceramic fragments and vessels that were comprehensively studied (Stern, 2012a). At Jaffa, a large number of medium to small salvage excavation have been conducted (Fig. 29.3; Peilstöcker, 2006, 2011; Arbel, 2009; Re'em, 2010), exposing various parts of the town. Over 1,000 ceramic shreds and vessels from the Kishle site (Burke and Stern, forthcoming) and the French Hospital (Stern, in preparation) have been studied. The wide variety of ceramic wares imported from many regions throughout the Mediterranean stood outstanding in the ceramic assemblages from both Acre and Jaffa. These include pottery types from the western Mediterranean that were not previously identified in crusader-period contexts in Israel or at other sites in the Levant, and consist mainly of glazed table wares, but also included some unglazed plain wares, cooking vessels and transport amphorae.

THE CERAMIC EVIDENCE

As shown above, glazed tableware coming from many different regions in the Mediterranean were found in the two ports of the Latin Kingdom, serving the kingdom's capitals (Fig. 29.4). In order to use pottery as evidence to reconstruct patterns of the marine commerce in the Latin East, it is required to shortly present the ceramic wares imported to the Latin Kingdom

Figure 29.2   The Hospitaller Compound, Acre, 1992 excavation season. General view of the central courtyard, looking east. Photograph: Howard Smithline, courtesy Israel Antiquities Authority.

Figure 29.3   The Kishle site, Jaffa, 2007 excavation season. Courtyard with cistern and remains of domestic buildings, looking south. Photograph: Yoav Arbel, courtesy Israel Antiquities Authority.

Figure 29.4 Glazed bowls imported to Acre from a wide range of regions throughout the Mediterranean. Photograph: Howard Smithline, courtesy Israel Antiquities Authority.

of Jerusalem, to determine the production areas, the distribution and consumption areas, and which ceramic forms were the most commonly traded by sea, and why. Then ceramic assemblages from other consumption areas in the Mediterranean will be observed and compared to Acre.

Imported ceramics

As noted, the ceramics found in the large-scale excavations at Acre and Jaffa are used here to represent the ceramics imported to the Latin Kingdom of Jerusalem. The Acre ceramics were grouped according to production regions as determined by fabric and form and as based on the existing crusader-period pottery typologies as well as on the results of provenance studies and archaeological remains of pottery production (see below and Stern, 2012a: 33–101). The pottery from Jaffa was studied in a similar way, allowing it to be easily compared to Acre's pottery (Burke and Stern, forthcoming; Stern, in preparation). The twelfth- and thirteenth-century pottery groups are listed here together; however, while studying the assemblages each type was dated, and it was found that there was an increase in the provenances of imports in the thirteenth century (Stern, 2012a: 27, table 3.3).

The pottery that was imported by sea to Acre and Jaffa came from various regions, including wares produced on the Lebanese coast within the borders of the Latin Kingdom (Fig. 29.5). The Lebanese coastal ware include amphorae, jugs, and oil lamps (LE.PL: Stern, 2012a: 38–40), some other unglazed cups, jugs and oil lamps (BE.PL: Stern, 2012a: 40, 41), glazed cooking ware (BE.CW; Stern, 2012a: 41–44) and glazed table wares, jugs and oil lamps (BE.GL; Stern, 2012a: 44–47). From the Muslim territories of central

Syria, soft-paste ware (SY.GL: Stern, 2012a: 52–54), with typical oriental floral and geometric designs painted in black and blue, and covered with a transparent alkaline-based glaze, was imported to the ports and also the rural sites of the Latin Kingdom. The forms include jugs, jars, *albarelli*, and bowls. It is interesting to see that despite the antagonistic nature of Muslim–Christian relations, commerce, at least in such goods, continued. The vividly decorated glazed Port St. Symeon Wares were imported from the Principality of Antioch (al-Mina) and possibly similar vessels were also manufactured in the neighboring Armenian Kingdom (in Kinet and Misis). The finds from Acre included four decoration schemes and mainly bowls and other open forms. Some jugs, *albarelli*, flasks, oil lamps, and even a figurine and tiles were also identified (NSY.GL; Stern, 2012a: 55–58). The ceramic industry flourished in thirteenth-century Frankish Cyprus, as vast amounts of ceramics were traded from there to the urban and rural sites within the Latin Kingdom of Jerusalem (Stern, 2008, 2014). These mainly include glazed tablewares and oil lamps, decorated either with monochrome green or yellow glaze, slip painted, or incised decoration, with or without enhancement of green or/and yellow glaze (CY.GL: Stern, 2012a: 60–65) that arrived in larger numbers, with smaller numbers of handmade cooking pots (CY.CW: Stern, 2012a: 59, 60) and jugs (CY.PL: Stern, 2012a: 58, 59). Pottery was also imported from other parts of the eastern Mediterranean. From mainland Greece and the Aegean Sea, glazed tablewares with a variety of decorative styles (GR.GL: Stern, 2012a: 65–69) were shipped to the Latin Kingdom. Some of these vessels are coarsely potted and the wall thickness is uneven, as well the incised decoration being quickly executed. All this seems to

Figure 29.5   Cooking wares and glazed table ware found in Acre and produced in Beirut and its vicinity. Photograph: Howard Smithline, courtesy Israel Antiquities Authority.

indicate mass production of this ware that apparently was destined for maritime distribution. This is also evident by underwater excavations of shipwrecks where these types of glazed wares were found in the cargo in commercial quantities (see Armstrong, 1991, 1997; Stern, 2012a: 149–153). From Asia Minor and the Black Sea region amphorae were shaped for maritime transport (TUR/GR.PL: Stern, 2012a: 70–72), and were commonly found in shipwrecks (Stern, 2012a: 149–153) and glazed tablewares of the Zeuxippus-Ware group (TUR/GR.GL: Stern, 2012a: 72–76) were imported. The forms of these include cups, plates and bowls with very thin walls and incised decorations. Pottery was also imported from southern Italy and Sicily and from northern Italy. The large quantities of various types of Proto-maiolica wares (Fig. 29.6; SIT.GL.2-6: Stern, 2012a: 77–80) that have been found in Acre emphasize the impact of the central geographical location of southern Italy and Sicily on trade (Stern, 2012a: 154). This ware is characterized by its pale yellow or buff fabric, decorated with tin glaze painted designs in brown, blue, and yellow, occasionally green or only brown. Common forms are bowls and plates, less common are jugs. Spiral Ware (SIT. GL.1: Stern, 2012a: 76, 77) was less common than the former, although it was imported from those regions as well. The decoration on these glazed bowls is uniform and consists of four spirals, painted alternately in green and brown. The glazed wares from northern Italy

98-3118

Figure 29.6   A Proto-maiolica glazed bowl with a depiction of a woman holding a lily.
Photograph: Clara Amit, courtesy Israel Antiquities Authority.

(NIT.GL: Stern, 2012a: 80–82), most likely imported from Venice, seem to have been produced there from the late thirteenth century and inspired by some Late Byzantine ceramic types, mainly the Zeuxippus ware mentioned above. The forms imported include mainly bowls but also some jugs and *albarelli*. Identified thus far mostly at Acre, with a few examples at Jaffa, ceramics were transported also from the western Mediterranean. Cooking ware made of a characteristic orange-red coarse fabric was imported from areas along the Ligurian coast to Catalonia (NIT/SFR/CA.CW: Stern, 2012a: 87, 88), and with a gray fine fabric from the coast of Provence and Languedoc in southern France (SFR.CW: Stern, 2012a: 83, 84). A glazed jug (SFR.GL: Stern, 2012a: 84) and some unglazed crucibles, small pinched bowls and thick walled basins also came from southern France (SFR.PL: Stern, 2012a: 82, 83), perhaps for the use of a chemist, metal producer, or for any other craftsman. Various types of glazed wares were imported from Catalonia at the end of the thirteenth century (CA.GL: Stern, 2012a: 85–87), among them a simple, utilitarian, coarsely made basin, and table ware including jugs and bowls, the latter are decorated with green and brown painted designs. Tunisia on the northern African coast was a natural port of call for trading ships and therefore it is not surprising that bowls, basins, and jugs of the locally produced Blue and Brown painted ware (TU.GL: Stern, 2012a: 88, 89) were shipped to Acre and Jaffa, as well as to Paphos, Alexandria and the western Mediterranean. Large jars with impressed decoration either unglazed or glazed were also found in small quantities in Acre and in Jaffa (SP/NA.PL,GL; Stern, 2012a: 89–91). These jars, used as containers for liquid or grain, were produced in Spain and/or North Africa and were also found in two shipwrecks in Corsica and Catalonia, suggesting they were used on the ships as water receptacles. Finally, green-glazed, fine stoneware vessels were imported from China to Acre (CH.GL: Stern, 2012a: 91, 92). The celadon ware may have arrived at Acre with Venetian merchants who traded with China, by land routes through central Asia and the Black Sea, or by a maritime route to the Red Sea, and from there to Alexandria for further distribution. The Celadon vessels found at Acre were not only in transit, but were also used by the local population, as attested by the finds there.

Production areas

As stated above, pottery was imported to the Acre and Jaffa from a range of regions throughout the Mediterranean, including the area of present-day Syria, Turkey, Cyprus, Greece, Italy, Sicily, France, Spain, Tunisia, and China. The provenance of the imported ceramics was determined primarily by traditional archaeological methods, such as typological and stylistic consideration, or by identifying archaeological remains of production sites, that is, workshops or kilns (e.g. a cluster of workshops excavated at Paphos and Lemba in Cyprus that produced similar pottery vessels [CY.GL] see Papanikola-Bakirtzi, 1996: 215–216; von Wartburg, 1997: 336; Cook, 2014).

In order to obtain more precise and scientifically grounded results to define production areas, two main methods of provenance analysis were applied to the study of medieval Mediterranean ceramics, beginning in the 1980s. These are petrographic analysis, which identifies the geology of the region from which the clay and/or the added temper was obtained, and chemical analysis (also known as elemental analysis), which provides a compositional "fingerprint" of each pot (see Stern, 2012a: 14–17). These methods of analysis were also employed to crusader-period pottery found within the borders of the Latin Kingdom of Jerusalem (Boas, 1994; Acre: Goren, 1997; Waksman et al., 2008; Shapiro,

2012; Waksman, 2012; Beirut: Waksman, 2002; François et al., 2003) and at other regions in the Latin East (Kinet: Blackman and Redford, 2005; Cyprus: Megaw and Jones, 1983; Armstong and Hatcher, 1997; Megaw, Armstong and Hatcher, 2003; Waksman and von Wartburg, 2006; Waksman, 2014). The results of these studies have been incorporated in the description of the ceramic groups above.

After establishing the locations of the production sites from which pottery was exported to the Latin East, it was obvious that most of these pottery workshops were situated in coastal areas, in some cases very close to the coast: Beirut (BE.PL, CW.GL) and the Lebanese coast (LE.PL), al Mina and Kinet (NSY.GL), Paphos (CY.GL), Apulia and Gela (SIT.GL.2–6), Venice (NIT.GL), the Ligurian coast to Catalonia (NIT/SFR/CA.CW), Provence and Languedoc (SFR.PL,CW), Catalonia (Barcelona?, CA.GL) and Tunisia (TU.GL). Exceptions are the soft-paste wares from central Syria (SY.GL) and the celadon wares from China (CH.GL), which were apparently brought overland to the ports and were then redistributed by sea.

Clustering these workshops into regions and determining the percentages of ceramics coming from each region can reveal some interesting data. But first, it is necessary to explain sherd quantification, before the results of the counts of ceramics found in the excavations at Acre and Jaffa (Stern, 2012a: 24–31; Burke and Stern, forthcoming; Stern, in preparation) will be discussed. In order to assess a ceramic assemblage and compare either various factors within the assemblage, or compare it with another, we need to know how much of any given item is there. This is done by identifying and quantifying all the sherds of the rims found in the excavation by form and function.

Tabulating the sherd counts according to production regions shows that the glazed tablewares imported to Acre and Jaffa (as represented by the Kishle and French Hospital sites) are predominantly from the Eastern Mediterranean, with 44.2% at Acre and 43.37% at Jaffa (Fig. 29.7; Table 29.1; Stern 2012a: 31, table 3.7; Burke and Stern, forthcoming; Stern, in preparation). The second largest group comes from northern and central Syria and Lebanon (the Levant; in Acre – 29.3%; Jaffa –30.92%), and then Italy (Acre, 23.1%; Jaffa, 22.49%). In both sites the smallest proportions come from the western Mediterranean (Acre, 3.3%, Jaffa, 3.21%) and China (Acre, 0.2%, Jaffa, none). Therefore Acre's and Jaffa's ceramic imports reflect an orientation toward the Byzantine world, the trade of which was dominated by the Italian mercantile cities of Genoa, Pisa and Venice.

Distribution and consumption areas

The pottery groups that were shortly described above, were, as noted, all found in Acre and most of the groups were also found at Jaffa. The crusader-period pottery from Acre and Jaffa was divided to two phases according to stratigraphy and according to the presence or absence of certain securely dated pottery types, to an early assemblage dating roughly to the twelfth and early thirteenth centuries, and a late assemblage, dated to the thirteenth century. While assessing and comparing the early assemblages from Acre and Jaffa, the ratio between the local and the imported wares is almost the same, with a slight inclination toward 10% more imported ceramics at Jaffa than at Acre. Comparing the late assemblages shows that the ratio between the local and the imported wares is almost the same, but there is slight inclination toward imported ceramics at Acre (Stern, in preparation). Although this may be coincidental, the fact that Jaffa served as the main port for Jerusalem, the capital of the Latin Kingdom in the twelfth century, and Acre was the capital of the Latin Kingdom

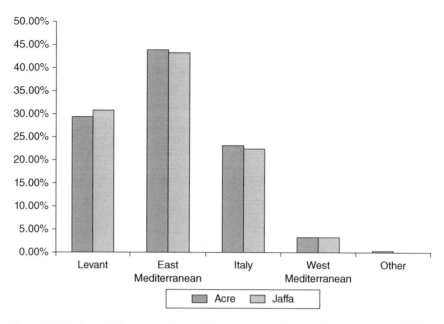

Figure 29.7   Quantitative comparison of imported ceramic types between Acre and Jaffa.
Drawing: Nimrod Getzov.

of Jerusalem in the thirteenth century, in addition to being one of the busiest ports in the Levant, may explain this.

The same imported pottery groups were distributed to and consumed at other Frankish sites along the Levantine coast (Fig. 29.1) including 'Athlit (Johns, 1934, 1936; Pringle, 1982), Caesarea (Pringle, 1985; Brosh, 1986; Boas, 1992; Arnon, 2008) and Apollonia, Arsuf (Roll, 2007; Tal and Roll, 2011; Ayalon et al., 2013). At sites further inland most of the ceramic groups listed above were also consumed (BE.GL, NSY.GL, SY.GL, CY.CL, GR.GL, TUR/GR.GL, and SIT.GL). Interestingly, these are also the groups found in larger quantities at Acre (Stern, 2012a: 31, table 3.7) and Jaffa (Burke and Stern, forthcoming). The inland Frankish sites in which these groups have also been found include Horbat 'Uza (Fig. 29.8; Stern and Tatcher, 2009), Mi'ilya (Stern, 2012b), the Monastery of St. Mary of Carmel (Pringle, 1984; Gabrieli and Stern, in preparation), Tiberias (Amir, 2004; Stern, 2013), Nazareth (Alexandre, 2012) and Yoqne'am (Avissar, 1996, 2005), as well as at non-Frankish sites inhabited by indigenous population; for example, Horbat Bet Zeneta (Getzov, 2000), Kisra (Abu 'Uqsa, 2006) and Horbat Burin (Kletter and Stern, 2006). (For a comprehensive list of sites in the Latin East with imported pottery see Avissar and Stern, 2005, 40–80, 105, 106 and Stern, 2012a, 38–47, 52–99.)

Quantification of the ceramic assemblages unearthed at urban and rural Frankish sites and at non-Frankish rural sites has shown that the differences between these sites lay in the relative quantities of imported pottery types consumed at each site (Fig. 29.9; Table 29.2). This has been seen in a comparative study of the ceramic assemblages from Acre (Stern, 1997), an urban Frankish site and rural sites in which either Franks (Horbat 'Uza; Stern and Tatcher, 2009) or indigenous population resided (Horbat Bet Zeneta; Getzov, 2000; Stern, forthcoming). While the rural indigenous population consumed more handmade

Table 29.1   Quantitative comparison of imported ceramic types between Acre and Jaffa
(numbers=vessel rims)

Region and Ware Group	Jaffa	Acre
Levant		
BE.GL	56	292
SY.GL	1	29
NSY.GL	10	216
Sub-totals	*67*	*537*
East Mediterranean		
CY.GL	31	410
GR.GL	33	47
TUR/GR.GL	3	349
Sub-totals	67	806
Italy		
NIT.GL	–	81
SIT.GL	46	342
Sub-totals	46	423
West Mediterranean		
SFR.GL	–	1
CA.GL	–	52
TU.GL	6	8
Sub-totals	6	61
Other		
CH.GL	–	4
TOTALS	186	1831

wares (43.3%), and less local glazed bowls (23.3%), and even less imported glazed bowls (0.4%), the rural Frankish population consumed relatively less handmade vessels (10.9%), and more imported glazed bowls (15.6%). The urban Frankish population consumed considerably more imported glazed wares (44%), but nearly no handmade wares (0.7%). These interesting results suggest that the choice of vessels was not related to a preference for a certain type, and was most likely not consciously used as a display of ethnic identity. Rather, choices seemed to have stemmed initially from dining and food preparation habits, as well as other practical factors such as at which market they shopped and which vessels were available on the market.

The same pottery groups found in the Latin Kingdom were also found at excavated ports throughout the Mediterranean that were active in the international maritime trade during the twelfth and thirteenth centuries including: Beirut (el-Masri, 1997–98; Waksman, 2002; François et al., 2003), Tripoli (Salamé-Sarkis, 1980), al-Mina (Lane, 1937; Vorderstrasse, 2005: 118–127), Kinet (Redford et al., 2001; Blackman and Redford, 2005), Paphos (Megaw, 1971, 1972, 1975; von Wartburg, 2003), Istanbul (Hayes, 1992; Megaw, 1968), Corinth (Morgan, 1942; MacKay, 1967; Williams and Zevros, 1993, 1994; Sanders, 1987), Split (Buerger, 1979), Venice (Saccardo, 1998; Saccardo et al., 2003), Genoa (Cabona et al., 1986; Capelli et al., 2005; Benete, 2010), Marseilles (Marchesi and Vallauri, 1997;

Figure 29.8   Imported glazed bowls found at Horbat 'Uza. 1, 2: Cypriot thirteenth-century glazed ware, 3: Port St. Symeon Ware, 4: North African Blue and Brown Wares. Photograph: Tsila Sagiv, courtesy Israel Antiquities Authority.

Vallauri and Démians d'Archimbaud, 2003), and Alexandria (François, 1999). All these sites yielded substantial and amply published ceramic finds that could be compared to the ceramic assemblages of Acre and Jaffa (see below).

What was the most common ceramic form traded by sea, and why?

For reconstructing marine commerce patterns in the Latin East, a comparison of relative quantities imported types by function can reveal what was the most common ceramic form traded by sea. Once the count results are organized by functional type (glazed bowls, cooking ware and jars and amphorae), it is clearly demonstrated that the ratios between functional groups of pottery vary. The most frequent import by far are the glazed bowls, of which 875 were found, 11.1% were imported cooking ware, and only 4.2% were imported jars or amphorae (Stern, 2012a, fig. 3.2). Hence it is clear that the great numbers of glazed vessels for individual dining were imported to Acre in what could be defined commercial quantities.

Glazed bowls shipped in commercial quantities were also recorded in ten Mediterranean and Black Sea shipwrecks dated to the twelfth and thirteenth centuries. These were found in large enough quantities to suggest that they were part of the cargo and not items for

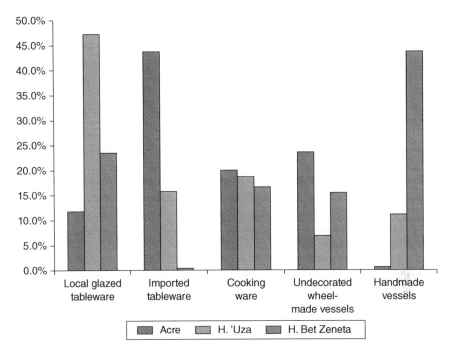

Figure 29.9   Quantitative comparison of general ceramic types between Acre, Horbat 'Uza and
Horbat Bet Zeneta. Drawing: Nimrod Getzov.

the personal use of the passengers (Stern, 2012a: 149–151, table 8.1: nos. 1, 3, 4, 5, 7–9,
16, 18, 19, fig. 8.1). These shipwrecks reveal interesting evidence regarding the maritime trade and ceramic distribution. Occasionally glazed bowls were found together with
amphorae and other goods, like at the Novy Svet shipwreck (Zelenko, 1999; Waksman
et al., 2009), indicating that they were part of a compound cargo. Fulford (1987: 60–1) and
Parker (1986: 36), archeologists who studied ancient shipwrecks, suggested that pottery
was probably always part of a compound cargo, mainly because of the lack of cargoes with

Table 29.2   **Quantitative comparison of general ceramic types between Acre, Horbat 'Uza
and Horbat Bet Zeneta (numbers=vessel rims)**

Pottery Group	*Acre-Courthouse site*	*H. 'Uza*	*H. Bet Zeneta*
Local glazed tableware	36	348	106
Imported tableware	133	117	2
Cooking ware	61	138	75
Undecorated wheel-made vessels	72	51	70
Handmade vessels	2	82	197
Total	304	736	450

only pottery in shipwrecks from various ancient periods. Multiple manufacturing sources of the cargo demonstrate that merchants were engaged in tramping, sailing along the coastline from one port to another, buying and selling goods along the way (see above section 'Nautical background'). This suggests that medieval pottery could have a double capacity as both a sale item and a space filler or salable ballast (see above, and Stern, 2012a, 153–154).

But why fill a ship with merchandise that according to contemporary written sources was apparently relatively inexpensive and available almost everywhere (Stern, 2012a: 146)? It is possible that ships unloading merchandise in ports wanted to fill the space that was created, or more importantly, that they needed the extra weight on the ship for its stability on the sea. The ship master or sailors could buy some ceramics to later sell along the sailing route, or/and in the meantime it could be used as a secondary, heavy cargo, like ballast. The advantage of using ceramics as ballast, as opposed to lead or brass mentioned in medieval sources, was that it could be sold once the space was needed for more valuable goods, and even if it could not be sold, as its value was not very high, it could be dumped into the sea, as were stones that were used as ballast. Bowls were very convenient for this purpose, since they could be packed easily, one inside the other, to avoid breakage. In addition, standardized glazed dinning vessels were also the most common form, in use everywhere.

"Mediterranean Mix"

The diverse pottery groups imported to Acre and Jaffa during the crusader period, locally produced and transported by sea from relatively nearby sites on the Lebanese coast, as well as vessels coming from more distant venues, enable us to examine the extent of Mediterranean trade, as well as its distribution patterns. It has been shown above that similar pottery was found at contemporaneous port cities throughout the Mediterranean. This comprised a unique assemblage termed a "Mediterranean mix" (Stern, 2012a: 133–135, table 7.1). Sixteen of the main subgroups of imported pottery found at Acre were also found at these excavated sites, including glazed table and cooking ware from Beirut (BE. GL and BE.CW); soft-paste wares from central Syria (SY.GL); Port St. Symeon Ware from the north Syrian coast (NSY.GL); Cypriot thirteenth-century glazed ware (CY.GL); glazed ware from Greece (GR.GL); Zeuxippus Wares, (TUR/GR.GL), and amphorae (TUR/GR.PL) from the eastern Mediterranean; Protomaiolica Ware (SIT .GL) from southern Italy and Sicily; glazed ware from Venice (NIT .GL); cooking ware and glazed ware from southern France (SFR.CW and SFR.GL); glazed ware from Catalonia (CA .GL); cooking ware from the western Mediterranean coast (NIT /SFR/CA .CW); North African Blue and Brown Wares from Tunisia (TU.GL); and celadon ware from China (CH.GL). These groups were compared, and it has been found that the sites yielding the highest similarity to the sixteen imported ceramic subgroups from Acre are Marseilles, Paphos, Venice, Genoa, Alexandria, and al-Mina. These sites are major cities, some of them serving as ports of call of the main ruling powers of the time. Marseilles was an important port in the western Mediterranean and also the home port of Provençal merchants who traded with the Levant from the end of the twelfth to the thirteenth centuries (Abulafia, 1980: 20–21, 29; Lopez, 1987: 342). Venice and Genoa were two of the major Italian maritime powers (Pryor, 1999). Alexandria was one of the three main Egyptian ports through which much of the international trade and merchandise coming from the Red Sea passed (Abulafia, 1987). Al-Mina, situated on the northern part of the Levantine coast, was also a significant port (Heyd, 1959: 133–134, 168–169). Sites that yielded fewer comparisons to the Acre "Mediterranean mix" assemblage, yet were also engaged in international maritime trade, are Kinet, Tripoli, Corinth, and Split. Notably, Beirut and Istanbul yielded small quantities of the imported ceramic subgroups found at Acre, although both are known to have been active international ports. This could simply be due to the lack of excavations or publication of pottery assemblages from these sites.

The two ceramic groups that were found at most Mediterranean ports during the twelfth and thirteenth century are the glazed pottery produced at various locations in Greece (GR.GL) and the Syrian soft- paste wares (SY.GL). It is not surprising that the glazed wares from Greece were frequently circulated since these wares were also the most common in the shipwrecks of this period (Stern, 2012a: 152). This abundance is most likely related to the extensive influence of the Byzantine Empire at that time and its diverse maritime connections. The subgroup of Syrian soft-paste wares (SY.GL), however, seems to have reached Acre and other sites by overland routes from their origin in central Syria; their presence at other Mediterranean coastal sites was most likely the result of redistribution from Acre, Beirut, and various Syrian ports. Closely following are Proto-Maiolica Ware (SIT .GL), found at ten sites, Port St. Symeon Ware (NSY.GL) and Zeuxippus Wares (TUR/GR.GL), both found at nine sites. It seems that the high frequency of the Proto-maiolica Ware from southern Italy and Sicily is due to both the significant involvement of Italian merchants in the long-distance maritime trade during the twelfth and thirteenth centuries and the location of these regions on the main sea routes from the western to the eastern Mediterranean that made them a natural stopping point on the way. Some of the ports of southern Italy and Sicily were en route for ships sailing from Genoa, Pisa, and Venice to other destinations, and goods were apparently loaded and unloaded there. The distribution of the Port St. Symeon Ware from ports along the Syrian coast (just as the Syrian soft-paste ware described above) is an indication of the great volume of Levantine trade and the large number of ships that called frequently at these ports. Although the exact provenance of Zeuxippus Ware is presently unknown, it is assumed that there was more than one production region, presumably situated within the area of the Byzantine Empire (Waksman and François 2005). As with the most frequent subgroup, GR.GL, discussed above, the abundance of this ware can be explained by the continuation of trade with the areas that were previously under control of the Byzantine Empire. The Cypriot thirteenth-century glazed ware (CY.GL) was found at eight of the sites. Cyprus is situated on the crossroads of the eastern Mediterranean and most ships sailing toward the Levantine coast passed by the island. It seems that during the thirteenth century, the Paphos Region workshops were producing pottery targeted mainly to the Levantine market. Further to the north at Kinet, Istanbul, and Corinth, Cypriot wares were not recorded, however, some small fragments of glazed bowls of the Paphos region workshops were found at ten sites on the southern coast of Asia Minor, but definitely not in the quantities as in the Latin Kingdom (Böhlendorf-Arslan, 2014: 80–85, figs. 2–4). It thus seems that Cypriot wares were distributed mainly to markets southeast of Cyprus and not to its north or west, although they have been found in very small quantities in major trading centers in the western Mediterranean (Venice and Marseilles), where they were probably brought by merchants from those cities who visited Cyprus (Stern, 2008, 2014).

Acre, Alexandria and Venice

What additional information can be gleaned from comparing selected imported ceramic groups at medieval Mediterranean ports? For this, we must take a look at quantitative data from Acre, Alexandria, and Venice. Imported glazed wares from excavations at Alexandria (François, 1999: 155–162) and Venice (Saccardo, 1998: 66–70) were quantified in a similar way to Acre (Stern, 2012a: 135–137), making them the only two port sites that could be compared to Acre (Fig. 29.10; Table 29.3). The data indicates a great increase in glazed imports to Alexandria during the thirteenth century, tripling from the twelfth to the thirteenth centuries (François, 1999: 157, figs. 37, 38), similar to the accordance in Acre (Stern, 2012a: 25, tables 3.1, 3.2). However, Venice experienced an increase in imported glazed ceramics at the end of the twelfth century and the beginning of the thirteenth century, followed by a decrease in the second half of the thirteenth century, then the number of local glazed wares increased and they appeared ten times more frequently than the imported wares (Saccardo, 1998: 68–70, tables 5–9). It seems, therefore, that the local glazed wares were the main types of pottery in use during the late twelfth and thirteenth centuries at Venice. Thus, the pattern of imported and local glazed wares observed at Acre and Alexandria differs from that noted at Venice. As Fig. 29.10 clearly indicates, the imported glazed wares outnumber the local ones in Acre (84.7%) and Alexandria (93%), while in Venice, the opposite was the case: the local glazed (81.7%) wares outnumber the imported ones (18.3%).

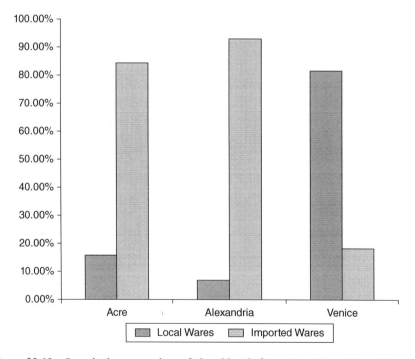

Figure 29.10 Quantitative comparison of glazed bowls from Acre, Alexandria and Venice. Drawing: Nimrod Getzov.

Table 29.3 **Quantitative comparison of glazed wares from Acre, Alexandria and Venice (numbers=vessel rims)**

	Acre	*Alexandria*	*Venice*
Local wares	294	24	1123
Imported wares	2063	320	252

One would expect that in the main harbor and capital of a rich and prosperous maritime power such as Venice, many types of foreign and exotic ceramic wares would have been imported for the use of the inhabitants, especially the families of the merchants involved in the long-distance trade. However, it has been demonstrated that Acre and Alexandria, which served as transit ports through which a large volume of trade passed, had more imported than local glazed ceramics. This may suggest that the presence of imported wares is connected to the volume and the nature of trade going through the port, rather than to the socioeconomic status or functional and commercial requirements of the inhabitants. At transit ports such as Acre or Alexandria, the ships could have unloaded pottery in order to load local products and goods in transit from distant locales, all destined for the western Mediterranean. Consequently, it seems that ship owners rarely returned to their homeports with ceramics as cargo, but with more expensive, lucrative goods.

CONCLUSIONS

Pottery was just one of the many products that circulated within the framework of the Mediterranean maritime trade network, and certainly not a main one. However, its durability in the archaeological record as opposed to other perishable goods makes it into a worthy representative of these. The reasons for maritime pottery trade seem to have been quite practical and closely linked to the opening of the Mediterranean to maritime traffic between East and West that could happen in the period following the First Crusade due to the sophisticated maritime trade system that developed with the innovative navigation methods, the establishment of sailing routes and the progress in ship construction. The main agents responsible for distributing the pottery and the many other products were the maritime merchants and seafarers involved in the bustling thirteenth-century maritime traffic, mostly the Genoese, Pisans, and Venetians, as well as merchants from southern France, Catalonia, Tunisia, and various other sites.

In summary, the ceramic evidence of maritime trade discussed above reveals the following points:

- Production sites: for the most these were situated on the coast, and in many cases nearby or in important economic ports that were very active in the international maritime commerce.
- Consumption sites: these were also situated on the coast, and most of them were also the ports engaged in the maritime trade. In addition, some also had pottery workshops. Consumption sites also include inland sites, however, there the quantities of the imports are notably lower than at the coastal sites.
- Correlation between production and consumption sites: there is a clear correlation between the contemporary Mediterranean sailing routes that started from or passed

through major maritime centers and the origin of the majority of the ceramics that were consumed at Acre, Jaffa, and other Mediterranean ports.

- Correlation between pottery type and consumption: it seems that whether the pottery was Cypriot, Levantine, Aegean, or Sicilian was of little concern to the traders and consumers alike. They probably bought a glazed bowl for its function mainly.
- Pottery as ballast: the ceramic wares in the ships were mostly secondary cargo or "saleable ballast," although it should be kept in mind that smaller quantities of pottery may also have traveled as personal property of merchants, sailors, or other individuals, such as pilgrims who arrived at Acre.

With the suggestion to use ceramic evidence as yet another source for assessing and reconstructing the patterns of maritime trade of the Latin East, I would like to direct attention to the following information that emerged from the study of the imported ceramics:

- Most of the pottery types imported to Acre and Jaffa originate from the Eastern Mediterranean, from regions that were parts of the Byzantine sphere. This can indicate the volume of trade from those areas.
- Ports with the most similar "Mediterranean mix" types of pottery as Acre, namely al-Mina, Paphos, Alexandria, Venice, Genoa, and Marseilles, may indicate a similar volume of trade.
- The slight differences in the relative frequencies of imports at Jaffa and Acre, namely slightly more imported glazed bowls at twelfth century Jaffa in contrast to slightly more at thirteenth-century Acre, seem to indicate that more ships were attracted to Jaffa's harbor in the twelfth century and to Acre's harbor during the thirteenth century.

As this information is coming from one study, these suggestions above should be taken with caution and carefully further examined as quantitative data from other sites becomes available. Clearly, more data relevant for the study of maritime trade can be gleaned from the study of the pottery assemblages. Hopefully, future studies will both develop the study of traded ceramics and utilize the information available from the archaeological ceramic data to study medieval maritime trade.

REFERENCES

Abu 'Uqsa H. 2006. Kisra. *'Atiqot* 53:9*–19* (Hebrew; English summary, 196–197).
Abulafia D. 1980. Marseilles, Acre and the Mediterranean. In P. W. Edbury and M. Metcalf eds *Coinage in the Latin West*. Oxford. 19–40.
——— 1985. The Pisan Bacini and the Medieval Mediterranean Economy: A Historian's Viewpoint. In C. Malone and S. Stoddart eds *Papers in Italian Archaeology IV; The Cambridge Conference, voll. IV, Classical and Medieval Archaeology* (BAR International Series 246). Cambridge. 287–302.
——— 1987. Asia, Africa and the Trade of Medieval Europe. In M.M. Postan, E. Miller and C. Postan eds *Cambridge Economic History of Europe*, II *Trade and Industry in the Middle Ages* (2nd edn). Cambridge. 402–473.
——— 1995. Trade and Crusade, 1050–1250. In M. Goodich, S. Menache and S. Schein eds *Cross Cultural Convergences in the Crusader Period*. New York. 1–20.
——— 2000. Industrial Products: The Middle Ages. *Mediterranean Encounters, Economic, Religious, Political, 1100–1550* (Variorum Collected Studies Series). Aldershot. 333–358.

Alexandre Y. 2012. The Pottery. In Y. Alexandre. *Mary's Well, Nazareth. The Late Hellenistic to the Ottoman Periods* (IAA Reports 49). Jerusalem. 57–88.

Amir R. 2004. Pottery. In Y. Hirschfeld. *Excavations at Tiberias, 1989–1994* (IAA Reports 22). Jerusalem. 153–167.

Arbel Y. 2009. Yafo, the Qishle. *HA – ESI* 121. www.hadashot-esi.org.il/Report_Detail_Eng. aspx?id=1051&mag_id=115 (accessed 23 December 2014).

Armstrong P. 1991. A Group of Byzantine Bowls from Skopelos. *Oxford Journal of Archaeology*. Oxford. 10:335–346.

———— 1997. Byzantine Glazed Ceramic Tableware in the Collection of the Detroit Institute of Arts. *Bulletin of the Detroit Institute of Arts* 71: 4–15.

Armstrong P. and Hatcher H. 1997. Byzantine and Allied Pottery, Phase II: Past Work on Materials Analysis and Future Prospects. In H. Maguire ed. *Material Analysis of Byzantine Pottery*. Washington, DC. 1–8.

Arnon Y.D. 2008. *Caesarea Maritima, the Late Periods 700-1291* (BAR International Series S1171). Oxford.

Avissar M. 1996. The Medieval Pottery. In A. Ben-Tor, M. Avissar and Y. Portugali eds *Yoqne'am I: The Late Periods* (Qedem Reports 3). Jerusalem. 75–172.

———— 2005. *Tel Yoqne'am: Excavations on the Acropolis* (IAA Reports 25). Jerusalem.

Avissar M. and Stern E. J. 2005. *Pottery of the Crusader and Mamluk Periods in Israel* (IAA Reports 26). Jerusalem.

Ayalon E., Tal O. and Yehuda E. 2013. A Twelfth-Century Oil Press Complex at the Crusader Town of Arsur (Apollonia-Arsuf) and the Olive Oil Industry in the Latin Kingdom of Jerusalem. *Journal of Eastern Mediterranean Archaeology and Heritage Studies* 1, 4: 259–291.

Balard M. 1994. Coastal Shipping and Navigation in the Mediterranean. In R.W. Unger ed. *Cogs, Caravels and Galleons*. London. 131–138.

Benente F. 2010. La ceramica d'importazione dal Mediterraneo tra X e XIV secolo. Aggiornamenti e dati di sintesi per la Liguria. In S. Gelichi and M. Baldassarri eds *Pensare/Classificare. Studi e ricerche sulla ceramica medievale per Graziella Berti* (Ricerche di Archeologia Altomedievale e Medievale, 37). Florence. 53–70.

Blackman J. and Redford S. 2005. Neutron Activation Analysis of Medieval Ceramics from Kinet, Turkey, especially Port Saint Symeon Ware. *Ancient Near Eastern Studies* 42: 83–186.

Boas A.J. 1992. Islamic and Crusader Pottery (c. 640–1265) from the Crusader City (Area TP/4). K. G. Holum, A. Raban, and J. Patrich eds *Caesarea Papers* 2 (*JRA* Suppl. S. 35). Portsmouth, R.I. 154–166.

———— 1994. Import of Western Ceramics to the Latin Kingdom of Jerusalem. *IEJ* 44: 102–122.

———— 1999. *Crusader Archaeology. The Material Culture of the Latin East*. London.

Böhlendorf-Arslan B. 2014. Medieval Pottery In Turkey and Germany: An Overview of Distribution in Archaeological Sites and Collections. In Papanikola-Bakirtzi D. and Coureas N. eds *Cypriot Medieval Ceramics. Reconsiderations and New Perspectives*. Nicosia. 77–103.

Brosh N. 1986. Pottery of the 8th–13th Centuries C.E. (Strata 1–3). In L.I. Levine and E. Netzer eds *Excavations at Caesarea Maritima, 1975, 1976, 1979, Final Report* (Qedem 21). 66–89.

Buerger J. 1979. The Medieval Glazed Pottery. In S. MacNally, J. Marasovic and T. Marasovic eds *Diocletian's Palace* III. Split. 11–50.

Burke K. S. and Stern E. J. Forthcoming. Crusader Pottery from the Kishle Excavations. In Y. Arbel, ed. *Excavations at the Ottoman Police Compound (Kishle), in Jaffa* (The History and Archaeology of Jaffa). Los Angeles.

Byrne E.H. 1930. *Genoese Shipping in the Twelfth and Thirteenth Centuries*. Cambridge, MA.

Cabona D., Gardini, A., Pizzolo, O. 1986. Nuovi dati sulla circolazione delle ceramiche mediterraneedallo scavo di palazzo Ducale a Genova (secc.XII–XIV). In *La ceramica medievale nel Mediterraneo occidentale, Siena-Firenze, 1984*. Firenze. 453–482.

Capelli C., Cabella R., Riccardi M.P. and Waksman Y. 2005. Caratterizzazione archeometrica di ceramiche graffite medievali (*Port Saint Symeon Ware*) rinvenute a Beirut, Genova e Marsiglia.

In C. D'Amico ed. *Atti del III Congresso Nazionale di archeometria, Bressanone, febbraio 2004.* Bologna. 193–202.

Cook H. 2014. From Boom to Bust: The Impact of the Crusades upon the Glazed Pottery Paphos, Cyprus, during the Thirteenth and Fourteenth Centuries A.D. from the Theater Workshop Perspective. In Papanikola-Bakirtzi D. and Coureas N. eds *Cypriot Medieval Ceramics. Reconsiderations and New Perspectives.* Nicosia. 29–43.

Day J. 2002. The Levant Trade in the Middle Ages. In A.E. Laiou ed. *The Economic History of Byzantium.* Washington D.C. 179–806.

Dotson J.E. 1982. A Problem of Cotton and Lead in Medieval Italian Shipping. *Speculum* 57: 52–62.

François V. 1999. *Céramiques médiévales à Alexandrie.* (Études alexandrines 2). Cairo.

François V., Nicolaïdes A., Vallauri L. and Waksman Y. 2003. Premiers éléments pour une caractérisation des productions de céramique de Beyrouth entre domination Franque et Mamelouke. In Ch. Bakirtzis ed. *VIIe Congrès International sur la Céramique Médiévale en Méditerranée. Thessaloniki 11–16 Octobre 1999.* Athens. 325–340.

Fulford M. 1987. Economic Interdependence among Urban Communities of the Roman Mediterranean. *World Archaeology* 19: 58–75.

Gabrieli R.S. and Stern E.J. In preparation. The Pottery. In E.J. Stern, C. Qualls, J. Stones, and M.J. Nestler eds *The Monastery of St Mary of Mount Carmel: Site Report for the 1988–1992 Excavation Seasons* (IAA Reports). Jerusalem.

Getzov N. 2000. An Excavation at Horbat Bet Zeneta. *'Atiqot* 39: 75*–106* (Hebrew; English summary, 202–204).

Goren Y. 1997. Excavation of the Courthouse Site at 'Akko: Preliminary Petrographic Analysis of the Ceramic Assemblage. *'Atiqot* 31: 71–74.

Hayes J.W. 1992. *Excavations at Saraçhane in Istanbul.* II: *The Pottery.* Princeton.

Heyd W. 1959. *Histoire du Commerce du Levant au Moyen-Age.* Amsterdam.

Jacoby, D. 1998. The Trade of Crusader Acre in the Levantine context: an Overview. *Archivio Storico del Sannio* 1–2: 103–120.

Johns C.N. 1934. Medieval Slip Ware from Pilgrims' Castle, 'Atlit. *QDAP* 3: 137–44.

——— 1936. Excavations at Pilgrims' Castle, 'Atlit (1932–3). Stables at the South-West of the Suburb). *QDAP* 5: 31–74.

Kletter R. and Stern E. J. 2006. A Mamluk-Period Site at Khirbat Burin in the Eastern Sharon. *'Atiqot* 51: 173–214.

Lane A. 1937. Medieval finds in Al-Mina in North Syria. *Archaeologia* 87: 19–78.

Lane F. C. 1966. The Economic Meaning of the Invention of the Compass. *Venice and History. The Collected Papers of Frederic C. Lane.* Baltimore. 331–344.

Lopez R. S. 1987. The Trade of Medieval Europe: The South. In M. M. Postan, E. Miller and C. Postan. eds *Cambridge Economic History of Europe,* II: *Trade and Industry in the Middle Ages* (2nd edn). Cambridge. 306–400.

Mackay T.S. 1967. More Byzantine and Frankish Pottery from Corinth. *Hesperia* 36: 249–320.

Marchesi H. and Vallauri L. 1997. Structuration et évolution du quartier. In H. Marchesi, J. Thiriot and L. Vallauri eds *Marseille, les ateliers de potiers du XIIIe s. et le quartier Sainte-Barbe (Ve–XVIIe s.)* (Documents d'Archéologie Française 65). Paris. 19–108.

el-Masri S. 1997–98. Medieval Pottery from Beirut's Downtown Excavations. The First Results. *ARAM* 9–10 (1997–98): 103–119.

McGrail S. 1989. The Shipment of Traded Goods and Ballast in Antiquity. *Oxford Journal of Archaeology* 8(3): 353–358.

Megaw A.H.S. 1968. Zeuxippus Ware. *ABSA* 63: 68–88.

——— 1971. Excavations at "Saranda Kolones", Paphos: Preliminary Report on the 1966–67 and 1970–71 Seasons. *RDAC* 1971: 117–146.

——— 1972. Supplementary Excavations on a Castle Site at Paphos, Cyprus, 1970–71. *DOP* 26: 322–343.

——— 1975. An Early Thirteenth Century Aegean Glazed Ware. In G. Robertson and G. Henderson eds *Studies in Memory of David Talbot Rice*. Edinburgh. 34–45.

Megaw A.H.S. and Jones R.E. 1983. Byzantine and Allied Pottery: A Contribution by Chemical Analysis to Problems of Origin and Distribution. *ABSA* 78: 235–263.

Megaw A., Armstrong P. and Hatcher H. 2003. Zeuxippus Ware: An Analytical Approach to the Question of Provenance. In Ch. Bakirtzis ed. *VIIe Congrés International sur la Céramique Médiévale en Méditerranée, Thessaloniki 11–16 Octobre 1999*. Athens. 91–100.

Morgan C.H. 1942. *The Byzantine Pottery. Corinth* XI. Cambridge, MA.

Papanikola Bakirtzis D. 1996. *Medieval Glazed Pottery of Cyprus: Paphos and Lapithos Ware*. Thessaloniki (Greek; English summary, 213–220).

Parker A.J. 1986. The Evidence Provided by Shipwrecks for Ancient Economy. *Les Thraces et les Colonies Grecques. Sozopol 6–10 Octobre 1985* (Thracia Pontica III). Sofia. 30–45.

——— 1992. Cargoes, Containers and Stowage: the Ancient Mediterranean. *The International Journal of Nautical Archaeology* 21(1): 89–100.

Peilstöker M. 2006. La Ville Franque de Jaffa à la Lumière des Fouilles Récentes. *Bulletin Monumental* 164–1: 99–104.

——— 2011. The History of Archaeological Research in Jaffa, 1948–2009. In M. Peilstöcker and A.A. Burke eds *The Jaffa Cultural Heritage Project 1*. (The History and Archaeology of Jaffa). Los Angeles. 17–32.

Pringle D. 1982. Some More Proto-Maiolica from 'Athlit (Pilgrims' Castle) and a Discussion of its Distribution in the Levant. *Levant* 14: 104–117.

——— 1984. Thirteenth-Century Pottery from the Monastery of St. Mary of Carmel. *Levant* 16: 91–111.

——— 1985. Medieval Pottery from Caesarea: the Crusader Period. *Levant* 17171–202.

——— 1986. Pottery as Evidence of Trade in the Crusader States. In G.Airaldi and B. Z. Kedar eds *I Comuni Italiani nel Regno Crociato di Gerusalemme*. Genoa. 451–475.

Pryor J.H. 1988. *Geography, Technology, and War. Studies in the Maritime History of the Mediterranean, 649–1571*. Cambridge.

——— 1989. Wind, Waves, and Rocks: The Routes and the Perils Along Them. In K. Friedland ed. *Maritime Aspects of Migration*. Wein. 71–85.

——— 1994. The Mediterranean Round Ship. In R.W. Unger ed. *Cogs, Caravels and Galleons*. London. 59–76.

——— 1999. The Maritime Republics. In D. Abulafia ed. *The New Cambridge Medieval History* V: *c. 1198–1300*. Cambridge. 419–446.

Redford S., Ikram, S., Parr E.M. and Beach T. 2001. Excavations at Medieval Kinet, Turkey: A Preliminary Report. *Ancient Near Eastern Studies* 38: 58–138.

Re'em A. 2010. Yafo, the French Hospital, 2007–2008. *HA – ESI* 122. www.hadashot-esi.org.il/report_detail_eng.aspx?id=1566&mag_id=117 (accessed 23 December 2014).

Richard J. 1987. Frankish Power in the Eastern Mediterranean. *Mediterranean Historical Review* 22: 168–187.

Roll I. 2007. The Encounter of Crusaders and Muslims at Apollonia-Arsuf as Reflected in the Archaeological Finds and Historical Sources. In I. Roll, O. Tal and M. Winter eds *The Encounter of Crusaders and Muslims in Palestine as Reflected in Arsuf, Sayyiduna 'Ali and Other Coastal Sites*. Tel Aviv. 9–103 (Hebrew; English summary).

Saccardo F. 1998. Venezia. Le Importazioni Ceramiche tra XII e XIII secolo. In S. Gelichi ed. *Ceramiche città e commerci nell-Italia Tardo-Medievale. Ravello, 3–4 Maggio 1993*. Mantova. 49–73.

Saccardo F., Lazzarini L. and Munarini M. 2003. Ceramiche Importate a Venezia e nel Veneto tra XI e XIV secolo. In Ch. Bakirtzis ed. *VIIe Congrès International sur la Céramique Médiévale en Méditerranée. Thessaloniki, 11–16 Octobre 1999*. Athens. 395–420.

Salamé-Sarkis H. 1980. *Contribution à l'histoire de Tripoli et sa région à l'époque des Croisades*. Paris. 156–237.

Sanders G.D.R. 1987. An Assemblage of Frankish Pottery at Corinth. *Hesperia* 56: 161–195.

Shapiro A. 2012. Petrographic Analysis of Crusader-Period Pottery from the Old City of Acre. In E. J. Stern, *'Akko I. The 1991–1998 Excavations. The Crusader Period Pottery* (IAA Reports 51). 2 vols. Jerusalem. 103–126.

Stern E. 2002. Excavations in Crusader Acre (1990-1999). In Calò Mariani M.C. ed. *Il cammino di Gerusalemme. Atti del II Convegno Internazionale di Studio. Bari-Brindisi-Trani 18-22 maggio 1999.* Bari. 163–168.

———— 2006. La Commanderie de l'Ordre des Hospitaliers à Acre. *Bulletin Monumental* 164(1): 53–60.

Stern E. and Syon D. In preparation. *'Akko, the Excavations of 1991–1998 II: The Late Periods* (IAA Reports). Jerusalem.

Stern E.J. 1997. Excavations of the Courthouse Site at 'Akko: The Pottery of the Crusader and Ottoman Periods. *'Atiqot* 31: 35–70.

———— 2008. Production and Export of 13th-century CE Cypriot Pottery: the Evidence from the Crusader Kingdom of Jerusalem. *Report of the Department of Antiquities, Cyprus* 2008: 455–465.

———— 2012a. *'Akko I. The 1991–1998 Excavations. The Crusader-Period Pottery* (IAA Reports 51). 2 vols. Jerusalem.

———— 2012b. Mi'ilya: Evidence of an Early Crusader Settlement. *'Atiqot* 70: 63*–76*.

———— 2013. Crusader, Ayyubid and Mamluk-Period remains from Tiberias *'Atiqot* 76: 183–208.

———— 2014. The Paphos Glazed Wares: Distribution and Consumption in the Latin Kingdom of Jerusaelm. In Papanikola-Bakirtzi D. and Coureas N. eds *Cypriot Medieval Ceramics. Reconsiderations and New Perspectives*. Nicosia. 61–76.

———— Forthcoming. Pottery and Identity in the Latin Kingdom of Jerusalem. A Case Study of Acre and Western Galilee. In J. Vroom. *Medieval and Post-Medieval Ceramics in the Eastern Mediterranean*. Turnhout.

———— In preparation. The Crusader-Period Pottery. In A. Re'em ed. *Yafo, The French Hospital* (IAA Reports). Jerusalem.

Stern E.J. and Tatcher A. 2009. The Early Islamic, Crusader and Mamluk Pottery from Horbat 'Uza. In N. Getzov, D. Avshalom-Gorni, Y. Gorin–Rosen, E.J. Stern, D. Syon and A. Tatcher eds *Horbat 'Uza. The 1991 Excavations. Volume II: The Late Periods* (IAA Reports 42). Jerusalem. 118–175.

Syon D. and Tatcher A. 1998. 'Akko, Hanyon Ha-Abirim. *HA* 108: 17–24 (Hebrew).

Tal O. and Roll I. 2011. Arsur: The Site, Settlement and Crusader Castle, and the Material manifestation of their destruction. In *The Last Supper at Apollonia: The Final Days of the Crusader Castle at Herzliya*. Tel Aviv. 10–79 (Hebrew).

Vallauri and Démians d'Archimbaud 2003. La Circulation des céramiques Byzantines, Chypriotes et du Levant Chrétien en Provance, Languedoc et Corse du Xe au XIVe siècle. In Ch. Bakirtzis ed. *VIIe Congrès International sur la Céramique Médiévale en Méditerranée. Thessaloniki 11–16 Octobre 1999.* Athens. 137–152.

Vorderstrasse T. 2005. *Al-Mina. A Port of Antioch from Late Antiquity to the End of the Ottomans.* Leiden.

Waksman S.Y. 2002. Céramiques levantines de l'époque des Croisades: Le cas des productions à pâte rouge des ateliers de Beyrouth. *Revue d'Archéométrie* 26: 67–77.

———— 2012. Chemical Analysis of Western Mediterranean Ceramic Imports. In E. J. Stern ed. *'Akko I. The 1991–1998 Excavations. The Crusader Period Pottery* (IAA Reports 51). 2 vols. Jerusalem. 127–132.

———— 2014. Archaeometric Approaches to Ceramic Production and Imports in Medieval Cyprus. In Papanikola-Bakirtzi D. and Coureas N. eds *Cypriot Medieval Ceramics. Reconsiderations and New Perspectives*. Nicosia. 257–297.

Waksman S.Y. and François V. 2004–2005. Vers une redéfinition typologique et analytique des céramiques byzantines du type *Zeuxippus Ware. BCH* 128–129: 629–724.

Waksman S.Y. and von Wartburg, M-L. 2006 "Fine-Sgraffito Ware", "Aegean Ware", and other wares: new evidence for a major production of Byzantine ceramics. *Report of the Department of Antiquities of Cyprus*. Nicosia. 396–388.

Waksman S.Y., Stern E.J., Segal, I., Porat N. and Yellin J. 2008. Some Local and Imported Ceramics from Crusader Acre Investigated by Elemental and Petrographical Analysis. *'Atiqot* 59: 157–190.

Waksman S. Y., Teslenko, I. and Zelenko S. 2009. Glazed Wares as Main Cargoes and Personal Belongings in the Novy Svet Shipwreck (13th c. AD, Crimea): a Diversity of Origins Investigated by Chemical Analysis. In: *Actas del VIII Congreso Internacional de Cerámica Medieval*. Ciudad Real. 851–856.

von Wartburg M.-L. 1997. Lemba Ware Reconsidered. *Report of the Department of Antiquities of Cyprus* 1997: 323–340.

——— 2003. Cypriot Connections with East and West as Reflected in Medieval Glazed Pottery from the Paphos Region. In Ch. Bakirtzis ed. *VIIe Congrès International sur la Céramique Médiévale en Méditerranée. Thessaloniki 11–16 Octobre 1999*. Athens. 153–166.

Williams C.K. and Zevros O.H. 1993. Frankish Corinth:1992. *Hesperia* 62: 1–52.

——— 1994. Frankish Corinth:1993. *Hesperia* 63: 1–56.

Zelenko S. 1999. The Results of the Underwater Archaeological Research at the Black Sea by Taras Shevchenko Kiev University (1997–1999). *VITA ANTIQUE* 2: 223–234 (Russian).

CHAPTER THIRTY

DOMESTIC LIFE IN THE LATIN EAST

————•◆•————

Adrian J. Boas

How well we have become acquainted with the military and religious activities of the crusaders and Frankish settlers in the East. In a society in which so much activity centred around battlefields, fortifications and churches, and with the perception, not infrequently encountered even today that matters of day-to-day life are predictable, tedious and of little significance, it is hardly remarkable that scholars of the crusader period often entirely circumvent the examination of domestic life. However, this trend is slowly changing, and following a very brief discussion of daily life in the Kingdom of Jerusalem published over four decades ago by Meron Benvenisti (Benvenisti 1970: 371–81) and a more expansive one by Urban Tignor Holmes which relied principally on evidence in contemporary literature (Tignor Holmes, 1977), a growing number of examinations of life under crusader rule, combining the written sources with archaeological evidence have begun to appear. In recent volumes of what might be regarded as the most prestigious journal of the crusader studies today – *Crusades* – we find a handful of papers on a range of domestic topics such as daily life in Acre (Jacoby, 2005), urban development in Acre (Arad, 2006), the use of money (Kool, 2003), food (Bronstein, 2013), gambling and gaming (Lampina, 2013), disease (Wagner and Mitchell, 2011) and death and burial (Riley-Smith, 2008). In 2010 I published a book dealing with domestic architecture and day-to-day activities in the crusader states (Boas 2010a). An increasing volume of publications dealing with all aspects of material culture are appearing and a growing number of scholars working in the field of archaeological research are involved in expanding such topics.

This slow but positive trend, might have been expected to come much earlier, as did numerous European studies in the wake of Marc Bloch, Fernand Braudel and the Annales School, but the Latin East had until recently remained something of a backwater in this regard. It is chiefly the outcome of increasingly extensive archaeological work on crusader sites and examinations of Frankish material culture carried out over the past three decades that has brought about the realisation that such topics can contribute much to our understanding of historical events.

URBAN LIFE

A number of descriptions of Frankish Jerusalem have been published examining different aspects of life in the Holy City (Prawer, 1985, 1991; Pringle, 1990–91; Bahat, 1991; Boas, 2001). In his paper on everyday life in Frankish Acre, David Jacoby discussed various urban activities and painted a multi-faceted picture of this cosmopolitan port city (Jacoby, 2006: 73–105; see also Boas, 2010b). However, daily life in other crusader cities has hardly been touched upon, mainly because whereas both Jerusalem and Acre were described in detail in various contemporary sources, among these some quite detailed accounts by visiting pilgrims, this was not the case for most other cities. In addition, although recent archaeological work has added to our knowledge of certain aspects of daily life in some of the lesser towns, notably, Jaffa (Peilstökker, 2011), Yoqne'am (Ben-Tor et al., 1996; Avissar, 2005) and Arsur-Apollonia (Roll and Tal, 1999; Tal and Roll, 2011), the volume of material evidence from both Jerusalem and Acre far outweighs that of all the other towns together. The outcome of this is that our acquaintance with day-to-day life in crusader cities is almost entirely based on the two principal cities of the Kingdom of Jerusalem. Indeed, each of these cities provides information on aspects of daily life that the other is less informative on, and the combined information from the two cities paints us a picture which covers a great many aspects of urban life. Acre, for example, is a copious source of both written and archaeological evidence on all types of domestic buildings: palaces, merchant houses, private and communal houses (Figure 30.1), while information on domestic architecture in Jerusalem is comparatively slender and is almost limited to written sources (though of these there are some of considerable interest). However, with regard to public commercial structures, in particular market buildings, Jerusalem has the fore, with five twelfth-century covered bazaars, standing and still in use (see below). Acre has only one, well-preserved but largely hidden within modern structures (Kedar and Stern, 1995). A possible second bazaar can be observed on early twentieth-century aerial photographs (Boas, 1997).

Living conditions

Living conditions in a city were influenced by its size and importance, by location, particularly with regard to its position on commercial or pilgrimage routes, by the wealth or poverty of its inhabitants, by crowding and pollution, and by many other factors that are often observable both in written sources and in archaeological remains. Acre, being the chief port of the Kingdom of Jerusalem, its most cosmopolitan city and one which was seasonally inundated with traders, pilgrims and soldiers, was, not surprising, severely affected by overcrowding and pollution. Ibn (c. 1185) described Acre's roads and streets as: 'choked by the press of men, so that it is hard to put foot to ground' (Ibn Jubayr, 1952: 318). Archaeological evidence shows a steady process of expansion of domestic construction into open areas, private or public, as space dwindled. Houses were raised to three or four storeys, courtyards were built into (Boas, 2010a: 216) and in the outer parts of the city new houses were constructed in formerly open gardens and fields, sometimes even protruding over the city moat (Arad, 2006: 193–4). In the second half of the twelfth century, a Greek pilgrim described appalling conditions in the city, placing the blame for this on the 'enormous influx of strangers' who corrupted the air, causing the outbreak of various diseases and frequent deaths (John Phocas, 1892: 11). Refuse from the markets and waste from the city's

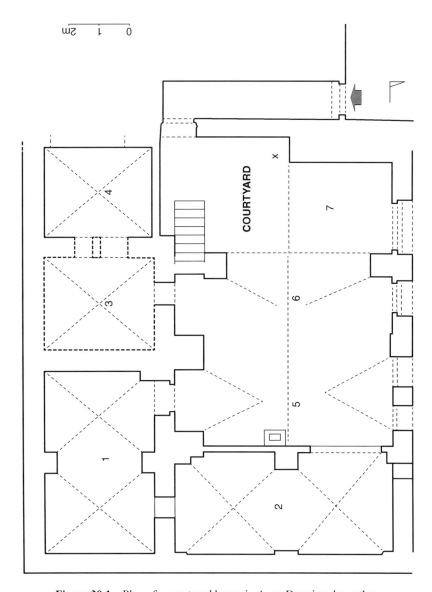

Figure 30.1   Plan of a courtyard house in Acre. Drawing: by author.

sewers and drains, including a large sewage system excavated under the Hospitaller compound (Avissar and Stern, 1995), appears to have turned the enclosed port into a large open sewer and explain why it became known in contemporary sources as 'the Filthy Sea' (*lordemer* in French, *a mari quod dicitur immundum* in Latin) (Jacoby 1993: 88–91). Although Jerusalem also experienced a degree of crowding in the festive seasons, it was less prone to such problems and in the twelfth century was probably much as it is described two centuries later when Ludolf of Suchem described its 'wholesome air' (Ludolf of Suchem, 1895: 97). The same was probably true of other towns such as Sebaste (Samaria) and Nicosia in Cyprus (Aerts, 2000: 209; Ludolf of Suchem, 1895: 42).

546

Urban layout

None of the crusader cities had much to show in the way of urban planning. Instead, like medieval cities elsewhere in both the West and the East, they were full of narrow streets, warrens and cul-de-sacs. With the exception of the small town that grew up outside the Templar castle of Chateau Pelerin, all crusader towns had long histories, and those which in classical times had shared the benefits of Hellenistic or Roman/Byzantine town planning had lost most traces of this long before the arrival of the Franks. None-the-less, a limited degree of planned layout did exist, either where traces of the principal Roman/Byzantine roads survived (albeit built over and subdivided as was the case in Jerusalem) or in the Italian communal quarters in Acre and Tyre where a sort of standard plan was used, based on certain urban components outlined in the terms of treaties – such as the famous *pactum Warmundi* between the Venetians and the Patriarch of Jerusalem which promised the Venetian commune that in every city it would have an ecclesia (church), a *ruga* (street), *platea* (square), balnea (bathhouse), and a *furna* (bakery). In the case of Acre a mill (molendina), scales and other installations are also mentioned (William of Tyre, 1986: 12:25, I, 578; in English trans., I, 553). This model served as a prototype for the other communes and this type of layout can still, to a certain degree, be observed in the former Genoese quarter in Acre. Here the location of the quarter's principal church, San Lorenzo, has been identified with the present Greek orthodox church of St George; the square, possibly with the open area that surrounds the church even today but covering a larger area to the west and south; and the *ruga* with the vaulted street (apparently the Genoese *Via Cooperta*) which extends from adjacent to the church in a roughly easterly direction right across the quarter to what may have been the main north–south street of the city, *Via Publica* (now Market Street) (Kedar and Stern 1995; Kool 1997). Along the length of the vaulted street were some of the quarter's principal *palazi* (large residential buildings for merchants of the commune).

Planning, however, was difficult to maintain, particularly in a crowded port city like Acre which experienced large influxes of population during and following the brief shipping seasons known as the *passagia*, when the fleets arrived from the West twice a year. At these times armies might arrive, and always merchants, mainly from Italy, as well as vast numbers of Christian pilgrims. The German pilgrim Theoderich recalls seeing over eighty pilgrim ships in the harbour of Acre when he visited the city in Easter week of 1169 (Theoderich, 1896: 60). Such seasonal crowding would have made municipal management difficult and can be seen as the cause for much of the obstructive building and the pollution which is recalled in written accounts of the period and later (John Phocas, 1892: 11; Ibn Jubayr, 1952: 318).

In Jerusalem where so much public construction changed the face of the city, some important projects were aimed at improving the city's infrastructure for the benefit of the general population. Examples of public works include the establishment of new and better commercial centres in the city including covered market street constructed by Queen Melisende in 1152 (*Regesta*, no. 278) (Fig. 30.2), the improvement of sewage and drainage works such as that constructed outside the city walls in the east to carry winter rain water in the Valley of Jehoshaphat out of the path of the Church of the Tomb of the Virgin Mary (Seligman, 2012), major development of the city's water supply and new burial grounds. In 1152 Melisende enforced the clearance of the area before the principal gate into the city, Porta David, and the removal of a mill constructed by the lepers of St Lazarus, which was

Figure 30.2 Twelfth-century market street in Jerusalem. Photograph: Author.

partly obstructing passage into the city (*Regesta*, no. 269). Even in the brief period in the thirteenth century when the Franks regained the city following the Treaty of Jaffa (1229) and until its final loss in 1244, some important public structures seem to have been established, possibly including new market buildings that were even larger and more impressive than those built by Melisende (Fig. 30.3).

Commercial activity

Forms of commerce varied, depending on the nature of the town. A vast range of goods would have been available in coastal towns, specfically those that served international commerce, in particular Acre and Tyre. These ports had autonomous Italian communities and separate quarters of other nationals, and the commodities passing through their markets would have included products brought from the West, from Far Eastern and Middle Eastern lands, alongside locally produced and manufactured goods. Such merchandise was intended

Figure 30.3   Possible thirteenth-century market street in Jerusalem. Photograph: Author.

not only for international trade but also for use by the city's Italian merchants, crusaders, local Franks, Eastern and Western Christian pilgrims, Moslems and Jews. In Jerusalem, a city which, other than being an administrative centre, was largely involved in its role as the centre of Christian pilgrimage, commercial activities focused on pilgrims' needs for food, clothing, keepsakes and devotional objects such as holy relics. Thus, if Acre's markets sold a variety of local and imported ceramics (Fig. 30.4), as archaeology has indeed shown (Stern, 2012), glass vessels (Gorin-Rosen, 1997, 2013), metal objects, textiles, spices, raw materials and so on, several of Jerusalem's markets specialised in local produce, cooked food, textiles and clothing, palm branches for processions, candles, holy objects and keepsakes (as, indeed, its markets largely do today).

Urban industrial activity

The peripheral areas of towns, both within and outside the walls, were the location of certain urban industries. Such industries are recorded in written sources, identifiable on occasion in site names that have occasionally been preserved, and are observable in archaeological finds. In Jerusalem the name Tanners' Gate, at the eastern part of the southern city wall, identifies the location of this industry. Within the gate which was exposed in excavations in the 1970s, a series of channels and plastered tanks of medieval date, possible remnants of the tannery, were uncovered. Similarly, plastered channels and basins found in a structure excavated south of the citadel and adjacent to the royal palace may be

Figure 30.4   Imported ceramics from Acre. Collection of Israel Antiquities Authority.
Photograph © The Israel Museum, Jerusalem, by Avraham Hay.

remains of the dye works which were located in that area (Reem, 2002: 8). Indeed, a medieval Jewish traveller, Rabbi Benjamin of Tudela, records Jewish dyers under the citadel
(Benjamin of Tudela, nd: 23). In Acre, a sugar mill was located outside the eastern city
wall (Imad ad-Din: 296) and near the old north wall a manufacturer of pilgrim keepsakes
(Syon, 1999). Other industries, mainly those that did not create foul smells and smoke,
were more centrally located, such as the gold and silversmiths who occupied workshops
in the heart of Jerusalem.

RURAL LIFE

We are now much better informed than in the past as to the extent, organisation and nature
of Frankish rural life in the East. Recent historical and archaeological studies (Ellenblum,
1998; Pringle 2000; Boas, 2003) have not changed our understanding that most of the
Frankish population in the crusader states lived, worked and died in the cities. However,
we are now more aware of the nature of their rural activities which, other than defence,
fall largely under three categories – administration, agriculture and industry. Each of these
activities left their different and distinctive marks on the landscape.

Rural estate centres

Being a minority consisting, as we have noted, of a largely urban population, the Franks
were dependent for their food and for many of their manufactured goods on a non-Frankish peasant class, a substantial part of which was potentially hostile. Consequently, the
nature of rural administration in the crusader states had to be well organised and efficient.
A system of overseers in charge of running the rural economy, in particular in the collecting of taxes and dues, was established early on, adopting some local customs but to a
large degree based on Western feudal customs. The backbone of this system was a large

number of rural administrative centres and depots. These centres appear to have altered somewhat in size and form as conditions in the Latin East changed. This development can best be observed in the twelfth century when the extent and effectiveness of settlement activities and rural administration fluctuated according to political stability, external threats and internal security (Boas, 2007). The earliest phase was that which developed together with the occupation of the Holy Land after the initial conquest in 1099. The Franks set up a network of fortified towers and small castles, the primary purpose of which was defensive, but in many cases the structures were also intended to serve the equally important task of enabling the Franks to achieve and retain a degree of control over the local peasant population and to regulate agricultural activities and the collection of taxes. By the 1140s security conditions in parts of the kingdom had begun to improve, to a large degree a result of the presence of these buildings together with a growing number of larger fortresses. The most important of the latter were castles built in problematic areas near major roads, frontier areas and particularly around the coastal town of Ascalon which had remained a Muslim enclave in the Frankish territory and a base for raids into the kingdom. The neutralising of this problem, especially with the occupation of Ascalon in 1153 seems to have led to the first attempts at Frankish rural settlement. It also meant that administrative buildings no longer needed to be fortified, at least not to the same degree as in the past. The result of this was that from the middle of the twelfth century a series of larger buildings, usually of a courtyard plan and often with little or no defences, were constructed in important areas of agricultural activity. Examples of these are found in densely populated regions around the larger cities but also, on occasion, further afield. Perhaps the best-known and best-preserved example is the Hospitaller building of Aqua Bella located on the road between Jerusalem and Jaffa, 7 km south-west of modern Jerusalem (Fig. 30.5). These buildings served a double purpose. They were houses for the *locators* (rural overseers, representatives of the landowners) and they were storage facilities for the goods and livestock collected as taxes from the peasants. They also, on occasion, contained certain installations, feudal monopolies of the lords such as mills which the farmers were required to use, and pay for their use. When conditions within the kingdom's borders deteriorated, notably at the time of the rise to power of Salah ad-Din and his invasions into the kingdom from 1170 onwards, many of these buildings were strengthened with fortifications. Quite possibly similar developments in rural areas occurred in the thirteenth century relating to the various ups and downs in the security conditions, which became even more insecure after 1187, but of these we are less informed from archaeological evidence.

Frankish villages

A large number of villages, often referred to as *casals*, appear in documents but of most of these we know little or nothing at all. Quite frequently we are not even certain of their location and whether or not they were settled by Christians, let alone Franks. Of these settlements perhaps the most interesting are a small group of villages consisting of single lines of narrow elongated houses set adjacent to one another along either side of a single street (Figs 30.6, 30.7). This type of 'street village' or 'string village' was entirely new to the region and at present, with only a handful of such sites, we are not at all certain that this was a widespread phenomenon. Rather, at the present state of research it seems that it may be a quite exceptional one and possibly geographically limited to the region

Figure 30.5   Aqua Bella. A rural administrative building. Photograph: Author.

between Jerusalem and Nablus. Various attempts at identifying similar layout at Akhziv (*Casal Imbert*) (Benvenisti, 1970: 223) on the northern coast and near Belvoir Castle above the Jordan Valley have come to nothing.

Frankish farms

A few isolated rural buildings appear to have been farms rather than administrative centres, although in some cases they possibly served both functions. Together with domestic apartments and some storage vaults, these buildings might have stables, cattle sheds, pig pens, chicken coops and water reservoirs, and were surrounded by orchards and fields. A farm at Khirbet Lowza, a few kilometres south-west of Jerusalem, which has been partly excavated (Ellenblum et al., 1996) was constructed around a courtyard, with nearby fields and a reservoir (Fig. 30.8). A farm at Har Hozevim to the west of Jerusalem consisted of a large hall-house but also had two enclosed courtyards containing a small stable, animal pens and a chicken coop.

Agricultural activities

One of the earliest examinations of rural settlement and agricultural activities in the Latin East was a short dissertation written at the University of Pennsylvania at the turn of the twentieth century (Preston, 1903). This was followed by a number of studies over the following years (Benvenisti, 1970: 213–67; Prawer, 1972: 355–81; 1980, 143–200; Smail, 1973: 80–88; Richard, 1985; Ellenblum, 1998; Boas, 1999: 60–90; 2003; Pringle, 2000). Under the Franks numerous traditional crops were grown, viticulture underwent a revival

Figure 30.6 Al-Kurum. A Frankish street village near Jerusalem. Photograph: Author.

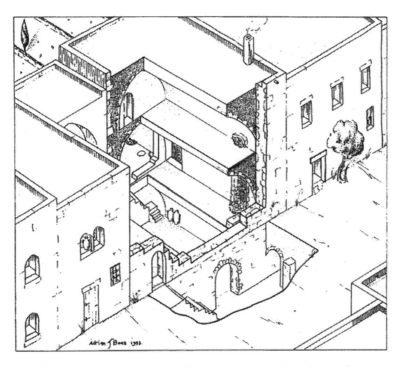

Figure 30.7 Reconstruction of street in al-Kurum. Drawing: Author.

Figure 30.8 Khirbat al-Lowza. A Frankish farm near Jerusalem. Drawing: by David Hully, courtesy of Ronnie Ellenblum.

after centuries during which Islamic rule was not favourable towards the manufacture of wine. Similarly there was no doubt an increase in the raising of pigs. With the development of sugar refining and its expansion into a major industry, the growing of sugar cane probably greatly increased.

LIFE IN A CASTLE

Archaeology is a particularly useful source of information on aspects of life in a crusader castle. Excavations and publication of finds from several major and minor castles has enabled us to gain an insight into how life was lived by castle garrisons (Johns, 1997; Pringle, 1986; Harper and Pringle, 2000; Biller et al., 2006). The layout of domestic apartments in castles is not difficult to follow, in particular in Hospitaller, Templar and Teutonic castles where regular garrison life was modified by the monastic framework that the military orders adopted.

Many finds from excavations of castles relate to daily life. Items relating to food preparation include mortars and pestles (Montfort, Belvoir), knives and spoons (wooden spoons from Montfort), mixing bowls, cooking vessels and ceramic and glass tablewares are frequent finds. Objects of dress are occasionally recovered, mainly buckles but occasionally fragments of textiles and in one case footware (a child's shoe and a sandal from Montfort, now lost). Saddlery includes buckles, horseshoes, spurs and other items. Work tools include hammers (Montfort), spades (Vadum Iacov, Chateau Pelerin, Montfort) axes, (Chateau Pelerin, Montfort), sickles, picks, hoes and pruning knives (Vadum Iacov) pliers (Belvoir), chisels and nails (Fig. 30.9).[1]

0   10   20cm

Figure 30.9   Spade recovered in excavations at Montfort Castle. Photograph: Author.

LIFE IN MONASTERIES AND IN THE MILITARY ORDERS

Numerous monastic foundations were active in the Latin East, mainly Augustinian, Benedictine, as well as a few Cistercian, Premonstratensian and other establishments. Most of these retained for their houses, with few changes, the cloistral layout that had evolved and been adopted by most of the monastic orders in Europe. Daily life of the monks and nuns in the East would in most aspects have differed little from that of their brother and sister foundations in the West (see Boas, forthcoming).

A typical cloistral monastic house in the Latin East was the Cistercian abbey of Belmont, established on a hilltop south-east of Tripoli in 1157 (Fig. 30.10). Although it later passed into Orthodox hands and has been largely rebuilt in modern times, its original layout can still be observed, and a plan of it was published by Camile Enlart in 1923 (Enlart, 1923: plate 1 between pages 2 and 3). It followed the characteristic layout of Cistercian monasteries in the West, with the church in the north of the cloister, the refectory and kitchen to the south, the dormitory and chapterhouse to the east and the cellars to the west (Enlart, 1923: 4). Monastic life within this physical framework was probably little different from that of monasteries in the West with the daily round of prayer (prime, terce, sext, none, vespers and compline) in the church, lessons and meetings in the chapterhouse, meals in the refectory, and a variety of labours in the kitchen, bakery, cellars, garden, and scriptorium.

A new introduction in the East was the adaptation by military communities of monastic rule and the cloistral setting. The establishment of the military orders was an original and highly successful innovation of Frankish society in the East, one that Joshua Prawer referred to as an exception to the rule that crusader society lacked innovation and originality (Prawer, 1972: 252). Retaining very closely the monastic routine and the six prayer sessions as the framework of daily life, the knight brothers of these orders introduced into it military activities; combat training and taking care of their equipment and horses.

COMMERCIAL ACTIVITIES

Commerce in the Latin East thrived as a result of the activities of Italian merchant fleets and the communes that they established in the towns of Acre and Tyre. The presence of the communes gave the principal towns a distinctive cosmopolitan character which can be observed in physical remains and written descriptions. The quarters in these towns were inhabited by different ethnic communities, much more varied than in the internal towns, and they seasonally hosted waves of soldiers, merchants and pilgrims, and consequently were crowded, noisy and dirty. They contained numerous churches, hospices and hospitals, money exchanges, manufacturing quarters and specialised markets.

INDUSTRY

A number of industries supplied goods for the Frankish population as well as items for export by the Italian merchant fleets to the West. Some of these were traditional industries of the region, including manufacture of glass, pottery and textiles, dyeing, wine and oil manufacture. Others were entirely new developments of the twelfth and thirteenth centuries, such as the refining of sugar which became one of the most profitable industries of the crusader states. Prior to the twelfth century, the preparation of a primitive sweet from sugar cane was a household activity. Under the Franks the refining of sugar was organised into

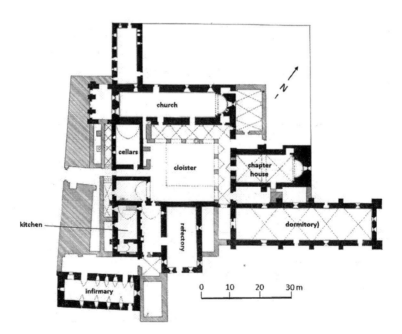

Figure 30.10   Plan of the Cistercian abbey of Belmont near Tripoli (after C. Enlart, 'L'Abbayecistercienne de Belmont en Syrie', Syria 4, 1923).

a large-scale, technically highly developed industry. The Franks built a large number of refineries in the cane-growing regions along the coast and in the Jordan Valley (Stern, 1999) and these were introduced in to Cyprus after the island came under their control in 1191 (Fig. 30.11). The process, from harvesting to grinding, cooking and the final manufacture of liquid sugar (molasses) and crystalised sugar of varying qualities in ceramic moulds, has been outlined in a number of recent studies (Stern, 1999; Peled, 2009). The products of this industry were not only intended for export. Archaeological finds and written sources have provided evidence for the extensive involvement of the Hospital of St John and, to a lesser extent, the Teutonic Order in the refining of sugar which was not only a lucrative activity but also had a practical use in preparation of medicines for use in their hospitals.

Glass manufacture was a traditional industry in the Syro-Palestine littoral and with the increased trade from the Latin East to the West in this period it underwent an expansion and development. Kilns for glass manufacture and workshops for decorating vessels with enamel were established. For export and local consumption these produced drinking vessels (Fig. 30.12), glass lamps and window glass, including stained glass. Analysis of stained glass finds from Montfort Castle in the Western Galilee show them to have been locally produced (Whitehouse et al., forthcoming).

Figure 30.11   The Hospitaller sugar refinery at Kolossi, southern Cyprus. Photograph: Author.

Figure 30.12 Glass (prunted beaker) from Beit She'an, manufactured in the Holy Land. Courtesy of the Eretz Israel Museum, Tel Aviv Collection.

Another industry that took off in the crusader period was the manufacture of religious items intended for pilgrims or for clergy looking for holy objects to take back to their monasteries and churches. Not only the discovery or invention of holy relics, but the manufacture of vessels (reliquaries) to contain them, developed into an important source of revenue. Pilgrim keepsakes were manufactured in towns (above, Syon, 1999) and villages (a mould for pilgrims' cross pendants was found in the excavation of a village and pilgrim site near Jerusalem – see Boas, 1999: 162) and sold to or acquired by visiting pilgrims (Fig. 30.13).

HOUSEHOLD WORK AND LEISURE

Although no cookbooks from the Latin East are known to have survived, references to cooking occasionally appear in written sources. As in other activities, in preparing and serving food the Franks sometimes adopted local customs and habits. One interesting example

a) b)

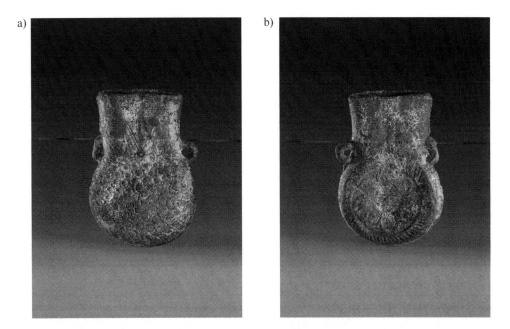

Figure 30.13   Lead ampulae. Courtesy of the Eretz Israel Museum, Tel Aviv Collection.

is given by the Syrian writer Usāmah Ibn-Munqidh, who describes his visit to a retired Frankish knight who, on observing the former's hesitation to partake of a meal he had prepared, informed him that he employed Egyptian cooks and served no pig flesh (Usāmah Ibn-Munqidh, 1964: 169–70). Regarding food, cooking and meal-taking we can learn a great deal from the statutes and rules of monastic institutions and the military orders. These are a wealthy source of information on what foods were eaten by the brothers, when, where and in what conditions (Bronstein, 2013).

No less informative is a wealth of archaeological evidence in the form of kitchens, hearths, cooking and baking ovens, installations used in preparation of foodstuffs, olive mills, grape presses, vessels of metal, stone, ceramic and glass used for storage or prepara-tion of foods, tableware, cutlery (Fig. 30.14), and actual remains of foods (animal bones, seeds, etc.). Meat consumption has been examined at a few sites including the Red Tower (Burj al-Akhmar – Cartledge, 1986), Yoqne'am (Kolska Horowitz and Dahan, 1996) and Margat (Kováts, 2012) and plant remains have been examined at the Red Tower (Hubbard and McKay, 1986).

The local Frankish population living in the towns and villages in the Latin East enjoyed pastimes and leisure activities that were traditional in the West but also adopted some local ones. Hunting was a pastime or sport as much as a necessity for the Frankish population. There are references to hunting and falconry in historical sources (John of Joinville, 1963: 292; Usāmah Ibn-Munqidh, 1964: 226, 239; Burchard of Mount Sion, 1896: 24, 43; on Cyprus, see Edbury, 2005: 83–4). Fulk of Chartres refers to hunting with falcons and dogs (Fulcher of Chartres, 1969: 298). Fulk of Anjou is recorded as having died falling from his horse while chasing a hare near Acre (William of Tyre, 15:27, II, 134). John of Joinville recorded lion hunting near Caesarea (John of Joinville, 1963: 289). Restrictions were occa-sionally placed on hunting for members of the military orders (Upton-Ward, 1992: 32–3).

A few archaeological finds can be connected to hunting. An example is small balls of fired-clay, about 2.5 cm in diameter, found in excavations in Acre, which may possibly have been shots for slingshots used to wing birds (Boas and Melloni, forthcoming).

One partial influence of the East on the Frankish lifestyle was frequent visits to the bath-house. This appears to have become a fairly widespread activity in both urban and rural settlements. Whereas in Islam ritual bathing was an important part of religious life, with the Franks, the bathhouse was for comfort and pleasure. In the Latin East public bathing would seem to have been regarded with less ambivalence than in the West where the Church sometimes remained hostile for fear of debauchery. The influence of Eastern culture on the Franks of the Latin East may have played a role in changing Western attitudes in regard to the importance of hygiene.

Even in the East, bathing could occasionally ignite the contempt of Church leaders, but these were particularly outsiders, the best-known example being Jacques de Vitry who in a general condemnation of the *pullani* (colts – a term which was used to designate native-born Franks, and occasionally a derogatory term for children of Frankish father and Muslim mother) referred to them as being: 'more used to baths than battles' (Jacques de Vitry, 1896: 64). John of Joinville, who accompanied Louis IX on the Seventh Crusade to the Holy Land (1248–54), mentions taking a room near the bathes in Acre (John of Joinville, 1963: 266). Some rather colourful and often quoted passages of Usāmah Ibn-Munqidh describe certain Frankish practices in bathhouses (Hillenbrand, 1999: 276–82). There appear to have been some rather inappropriate practices carried out by the brothers when accompanying donats on their way from the bathhouse in Acre that necessitated a warning in the Hospitaller Rule (Statute of Rr. Hugh Revel, no.19, King, 1934: 77–8). The custom of eating and sleeping at the bathhouse was also looked askance upon as a statute of the Hospitaller Order suggests, albeit of later date but possibly reflecting earlier attitudes (King, 1934: 107).

In Acre a Frankish bathhouse was excavated in the suburb of Montmusard (Smithline et al., 2013). Heating was provided by a large furnace that distributed hot air through channels to each room with a hypocaust system of rectangular limestone pillars supporting a marble floor. Other bathhouses of Frankish date have been found at Chateau Pelerin – 'Atlit (Johns, 1997 (II): 124–9), Mount Tabor (Battista and Bagatti, 1976: 65) and Jerusalem (Boas, 2001: 161–3).

Figure 30.14 Wooden spoon from Montfort. Photograph: Mariana Salzberger. Courtesy of IAA, Rockefeller Museum, Jerusalem.

Pursuits of leisure could take other forms. Franks frequented taverns and brothels (Joinville, 1963: 292). Nobility were involved daily in jousting, games and tournaments (Ludolf of Suchem, 1895: 52; Philip de Novare, 1936, vi (112), vii (113): 65–66). Games and gambling were commonplace in taverns and private houses, castles and monastic houses. John of Joinville mentions King Louis's brothers playing dice in Acre (John of Joinville, 1963: 278). Six bone dice were found at Chateau Pelerin (Fig. 30.15), and there are occasional references to board games such as morelles, backgammon and chess. Games were popular in all levels of society, no less among religious orders as among the general Frankish population. Indeed, most examples of board games, dice, tokens and counters found in excavations have come from monasteries and houses and castles of the military orders (Boas, 1999: 168–70; 2006: 203–4; Sebbane, 1999; Lampina, 2013).

MUSIC

No serious study has been carried out regarding music in private and liturgical practices in the Latin East and information on this aspect of daily life in the crusader states is not extensive. No doubt there were local musicians, and certainly with the arrival of pilgrims and in festive seasons the presence of foreign musician and minstrels would have become noticeable. John of Joinville refers to minstrels from Greater Armenia, performing musicians who performed acrobatic tricks (John of Joinville, 1963: 297). On the whole archaeology provides us only with minor evidence, although the major discovery of two musical instruments in the grounds of the Church of Nativity in Bethlehem are important – an organ and a carillon throw light on the use of music in sacred contexts. The organ consisted of 221 copper fistulae and the carillon had twelve different-sized bronze bells. These latter were removed from the bell tower of the church in 1452 or perhaps earlier on the order of Mohammed II and were buried nearby where three of them were discovered in 1863 and

Figure 30.15 Bone dice from Chateau Pelerin. Courtesy of IAA.

fourteen more in 1906. The largest bell had a dragon-shaped mount and the smallest was inscribed with the words '*Vox Domini*' (Voice of the Lord). The organ pipes apparently came from a water-powered organ.

ILLNESS AND DEATH

Disease and injury, medical treatments and hospital care is an area of study which was largely neglected until recent years but has now become the topic of some interesting and useful publications. The evidence for various illness and injuries suffered by people in the Latin East is obtained from human remains recovered from a number of crusader period sites; for example, at Vadum Iacob and Jezreel (Tel Yizra'el). Examining human bone finds from these sites (Mitchell, 1998; Mitchell et al, 2006) has indicated the types of injuries suffered, often as the result of participation in battle, and, on occasion, something of the manner in which they were treated. Microbiological material that has been recovered in excavations of latrines and cesspools in Acre has enabled the identification of the various intestinal parasites that plagued the inhabitants of the Hospitaller compound in Acre and has suggested something about the nature of the food that the inhabitants of the city consumed and how it was prepared (Mitchell, 1998, 2008; Mitchell et al., 2008). These add to a number of informative studies based on con-temporary sources and archaeological studies describing the Jerusalem hospital, an important institution run by the Knights of the Hospital of St John which occupied a large area to the south of the Church of the Holy Sepulchre (Kedar, 1998; Edgington, 1998, 2005). These stud-ies not only enlighten us on the building itself but also on the activities carried out within it and the conditions of care and treatment which the inmates of the hospital experienced.

Only a few investigations on the subject of death and burial customs in the Latin East have been carried out. There are some important studies of the epigraphy of numerous

Figure 30.16   Grave marker in the Mamilla cemetery, Jerusalem. Photograph: Author.

tombstones found in the Kingdoms of Jerusalem and Cyprus (Chamberlayne, 1894; Claverie, 2013; Clermont-Ganneau, 1899: 106–11, 276–9, 279–90; Pringle, 2004, 2007; de Sandoli, 1974). Burial grounds and tombs have been uncovered in Acre, Caesarea, Jerusalem (Fig. 30.16) (Boas, 2001: 180–8; Reem, 1999) and Nazareth as well as in rural sites including Tel Jezreel, al-Qubaiba (Baggati, 1993: 77–9), Bethany and Casale Santa Maria (Abud). Burials have also been examined at Caesarea (Yule and Rowsome, 1994), Tel Jezreel (Bradley, 2006: 33; 1994: 63; Ussishkin and Woodhead, 1997: 56; al-Qubaiba (Bagatti 1993: 77–8) and in the Kingdom of Cyprus (Enlart, 1899/1987; du Plat Taylor, 1938; Imhaus, 2004). A few graves in the cemetery outside the faubourg of the Templar castle, Chateau Pelerin ('Atlit), were excavated by British archaeologist C.N. Johns in 1934 (Johns, 1997, I, 92–4). A recent PhD dissertation examined the layout of the cemetery (Thompson, 2013) and plans are underway for a more expansive study of this large burial ground which contains over 900 tombs.

NOTE

1 Many of the small finds from Montfort Castle will be published in a monograph due for publication in 2016. See Boas and Khamisy, forthcoming.

REFERENCES

Primary sources

Benjamin of Tudela, *The Itinerary of Benjamin of Tudela*, trans. and commentary M.N. Adler, London, nd.

Burchard of Mount Sion, *A Description of the Holy Land*, English trans., A. Stewart, Palestine Pilgrims' Text Society, vol. 12, London, 1896.

Fulcher of Chartres, *A History of the Expedition to Jerusalem 1095–1127*, trans. F.R. Ryan, ed. H.S. Fink, New York, Knoxville, 1969.

Ibn Jubayr, *The Travels of Ibn Jubayr*, trans. R.J.C. Broadhurst, London, 1952.

Imad ad-Din in Abu Shama, 1898, 'Livre des Deux Jardins', *Recueil des Historiens des Croisades, Historiens orientaux*, vol. 4, Paris, 296.

Ludolf of Suchem, *De Itinere Terrae Sanctae*, English trans., A. Stewart, *Palestine Pilgrims' Text Society*, vol. 12, London, 1895.

Jacques de Vitry, *A History of Jerusalem, A.D. 1180* (erroneous date), trans. A. Stewart, *Palestine Pilgrims Text Society*, vol. 11, London, 1896.

Joannes Phocas, *Descriptio Terrae Sanctae*, English trans. A. Stewart, *Palestine Pilgrims' Text Society*, vol. 5, London, 1892.

John of Joinville, *The Life of Saint Louis*, in *Joinville and Villehardouin*, trans. R.B. Shaw, New York, 1963.

Philip de Novare, 1936, *The Wars of Frederick II Against the Ibelins in Syria and Cyprus*, trans. J.L. La Monte, New York.

Regesta Regni Hierosolymitani, ed. R. Röhricht, Innsbruck, 1893.

Theoderich, 1896, 'Theoderich's Description of the Holy Places', trans. A. Stewart, *Palestine Pilgrims Text Society*, vol. 5, London.

Usāmah Ibn Munqidh, *Memoirs of an Arab Syrian Gentleman* (*Kitāb al I'tibār*), trans. P.K. Hitti, Beirut, 1964.

William of Tyre, 1986, *Guillaume de Tyr, Chronique*, ed. R.B.C. Huygens, Corpus Christianorum, Continuatio Mediaevalis LXIII, Turnhout; English trans., E.A. Babcock and A.C. Krey, *A History of Deeds Done Beyond the Sea*, New York, 1943.

Secondary sources

Aerts, W.J., 2003, 'A Byzantine Traveller to One of the Crusader States', in K. Ciggaar and H. Teule (eds), *East and West in the Crusader States. Context-Contacts-Confrontations. Vol. 3: Acta of the Congress held at Hernen Castle in September 2000*, Leuven, Dudley, MA, 165–221.

Arad, P., 2006, 'Thanks to a Bad Neighbour's Reputation: Reconstructing an Area of Thirteenth Century Acre', *Crusades* 5: 193–7.

Avissar, M, 2005, *Tel Yoqne'am. Excavations on the Acropolis, IAI Reports* 25, Jerusalem.

Avissar, M. and E. Stern, 1995, 'Akko, the Old City', *Excavations and Surveys in Israel* 14: 24–5.

Bagatti, B., 1993, *Emmaus-Qubeibeh. The Results of Excavations at Emmaus-Qubeibeh and Nearby Sites (1873, 1887–1890, 1900–1902, 1940–1944)*, English trans. R. Bonanno, Jerusalem.

Bahat, D., 1991, 'Topography and Archaeology' in J. Prawer and H. Ben-Shammai (eds), *The History of Jerusalem* (Hebrew), Jerusalem, 68–120.

Battista, A. and B. Bagatti, 1976, *La fortezza saracena del monte Tabor (SBF.CMi 18)*, Jerusalem.

Ben-Tor, A., M. Avissar and Y. Portugali, 1996, *Yoqne'am I: The Late Periods, Qedem Reports* 3, Jerusalem.

Benvenisti, M., 1970, *The Crusaders in the Holy Land*, Jerusalem.

Biller, T., D. Burger, G. Ulrich Grossmann, H.-H. Häffner, W. Meyer, M.-L. Boscardin, T. Radt and R. Scmitt, 2006, *Der Crac des Chevaliers. Die Baugeschichte einer Ordensburg der Kreuzfahrerzeit*, Regensburg, Berlin, Stuttgart.

Boas, A.J., 1997, 'A Rediscovered Market Street in Frankish Acre', *Atiqot* XXXI: 181–6.

———— 1999, *Crusader Archaeology: The Material Culture of the Latin East*, London, New York.

———— 2001, *Jerusalem in the Time of the Crusades*, London and New York.

———— 2003, 'Street Villages and Rural Estate Centres: The Organization of Rural Settlement in the Latin Kingdom of Jerusalem', in A.M. Maeir, S. Dar and Z. Safrai (eds), *The Rural Landscape of Ancient Israel*, BAR International Series 1121, Oxford, 137–48.

———— 2006, *Archaeology of the Military Orders, A Survey of the Urban Centres, Rural Settlements and Castles of the Military Orders in the Latin East (c.1120 1291)*, London and New York.

———— 2007, 'Three Stages in the Evolution of Rural Settlement in the Kingdom of Jerusalem during the Twelfth Century', *In Laudem Hierosolymitani – Crusades subsidia* 1: 77–92.

———— 2010a, *Domestic Settings. Sources on Domestic Architecture and Day-to-Day Activities in the Crusader States*, Leiden and Boston.

———— 2010b, 'Daily Life in Frankish Acre', in A. Killebrew and V. Raz-Romeo (eds.), *One Thousand Nights and Days: Akko through the Ages*, Haifa, 49–54.

———— forthcoming, 'Archaeological Evidence for Monastic Layout in the Latin East', in E.J. Stern, C. Qualls, J. Stones, and M.J. Nestler (eds), *The Monastery of St Mary of Mount Carmel: Site Report for the 1988–1992 Excavation Seasons* (IAA Reports), Jerusalem.

Boas, A.J. and R.G. Khamisy (eds) forthcoming, *Montfort. History, Early Research and Recent Studies of the Principal Teutonic Fortress in the Latin East*, Leiden and Boston.

Boas, A.J. and G.P. Melloni, forthcoming, *Acre-East: 1999, 2000: Two Seasons of Excavations in the Possible Quarter of the Teutonic Knights in Akko*.

Bradley, M., 1994, 'Preliminary Assessment of Medieval Christian Burials from Tel Jezreel', *Levant* 26: 63–5.

———— 2006, 'The Medieval Christian Cemetery at Tel Jezreel', *Levant* 38: 33–5.

Bronstein, J., 2013, 'Food and the Military Orders: Attitudes of the Hospital and the Temple between the Twelfth and Fourteenth Centuries', *Crusades* 12: 133–52.

Cartledge, J., 1986, 'Faunal Remains', in D. Pringle (ed.), *The Red Tower* (al-Burj al-Ahmar), London: 176–86.

Chamberlayne, T.J., 1894, *Lacrimae nicossienses: recueil d'inscriptions funéraires, la plupart fran-çaises, existant encore dans l'île de Chypre: suivi d'un armorial chypriote et d'une description topographique et archéologique de la ville de Nicosie*, vol. 1, Paris.

Claverie-V., 2013, 'Les difficultés de l'épigraphie franque de Terre sainte aux XIIe et XIIIe siècles', *Crusades*, 12: 67–89.

Clermont-Ganneau, C., 1899, *Archaeological Researches in Palestine*, vol. 1, trans. A. Stewart, London.

Edbury, P.W., 2005, 'Franks', in A. Nicolaou-Konnari and C. Schabel (eds), *Cyprus, Society and Culture, 1191–1374*, Leiden, 63–101.

Edgington, S., 1998, 'Medical Care in the Hospital of St John in Jerusalem', in *The Military Orders*, vol. 2, ed. H. Nicholson, Aldershot and Burlington, 27–34.

———— 2005, 'Administrative Regulations for the Hospital of St John in Jerusalem dating to the 1180s', *Crusades* 4. 21–37.

Ellenblum, R., 1998, *Frankish Rural Settlement in the Latin Kingdom of Jerusalem*, Cambridge.

Ellenblum, R., R. Rubin and G. Solar, 1996, 'Khirbet al-Lawza, a Frankish Farm House in the Judaean Hills in Central Palestine', *Levant* 28: 189–98.

Enlart, C., 1987, *Gothic Art and the Renaissance in Cyprus* (trans. of 1899 edition, D. Hunt), London.

———— 1923, 'L'Abbaye cistercienne de Belmont en Syrie', *Syria* 4: 1–22.

Gorin-Rosen, Y., 1997, 'Excavation of the Courthouse Site at Akko. Medieval Glass Vessels (Area TA), *Atiqot* 31: 75–85.

———— 2013, 'Glass Finds from the Crusader-Period Bathhouse in 'Akko (Acre)', *Atiqot* 73: 109–16.

Harper, R. and D. Pringle, 2000, *Belmont Castle: The Excavation of a Crusader Stronghold in the Kingdom of Jerusalem*, London.

Hillenbrand, C. 1999, *The Crusades. Islamic Perspectives*, Edinburgh.

Hubbard, R.N.L.B. and McKay, J. 1986, 'Medieval Plant Remains', in D. Pringle (ed.), *The Red Tower (al-Burj al-Ahmar): Settlement in the Plain of Sharon at the Time of the Crusaders and Mamluks (AD 1099-1516)*, London, 187–91.

Imhaus, B. (ed.), 2004, *Lacrimae Cypriae: Les larmes de Chypre ou Recueil des inscriptions lapidaires pour la plupart funéraires de la période franque et vénitienne de l'Île de Chypre*, Nicosia, 2 vols.

Jacoby, D., 1993, 'Three Notes on Crusader Acre (Lordemer and Ecology)', *Zeitschrift des Deutschen Palästina-Veriens* 109: 83–96.

———— 2005, 'Aspects of Everyday Life in Frankish Acre', *Crusades* 4: 73–105.

Johns, C.N., 1997, *Pilgrims' Castle ('Atlit) David's Tower (Jerusalem) and Qal'at Rabad (Ajlun): Three Middle Eastern Castles from the Time of the Crusades*, Aldershot.

Kedar, B.Z., 1998, 'A Twelfth Century Description of the Jerusalem Hospital', in *The Military Orders*, vol. 2, ed. H. Nicholson, Aldershot and Burlington, 3–26.

Kedar, B.Z and E. Stern, 1995, 'A Vaulted East-West Street in Acre's Genoese Quarter?', *Atiqot* 26: 105–11.

King, E.J., 1934, *The Rule, Statutes and Customs of the Hospitallers*, London.

Kolska Horowitz, L. and E. Dahan, 1996, 'Animal Husbandry Practices During the Historic Periods', *Yoqne'am I, The Late Periods, Qedem Reports* 3, Jerusalem, 246–55.

Kool, R., 1997, 'The Genoese Quarter in Thirteenth-Century Acre: A Reinterpretation of its Layout', *Atiqot* 31: 187–200.

———— 2003, 'Coins at Vadum Jacob: New Evidence on the Circulation of Money in the Latin Kingdom of Jerusalem during the Second Half of the Twelfth Century', *Crusades* 1: 73–88.

Kováts, I., 2012, 'Meat Consumption and Animal Keeping in the Citadel of Marqab', in *The Military Orders*, vol. 5, ed. P.W. Edbury, Farnham and Burlington, 43–50.

Lampina, E., 2013, 'Gambling and Gaming in the Holy Land: Chess, Dice and other Games', *Crusades* 12: 121–32.

Mitchell, P., 1998, 'The Archaeological Approach to the Study of Disease in the Crusader States, as employed at Le Petit Gerin', in *The Military Orders*, vol. 2, ed. H. Nicholson, Aldershot and Burlington, 43–50.

———— 2008, 'A Comparison of Health at a Village and Castle in the Kingdom of Jerusalem during the Twelfth Century', in *The Military Orders*, vol. 4, ed. J. Upton-Ward, Aldershot and Burlington, 23–8.

Mitchell, D., Y. Nagar and R. Ellenblum, 2006, 'Weapon Injuries in the 12th Century Crusader Garrison of Vadum Iacob Castle, Galilee', *International Journal of Osteoarchaeology* 16: 145–55.

Mitchell, D., J.P. Huntley and E. Stern, 2008, 'Biological Analysis of the Latrine Soil from the Thirteenth-Century Hospital of St John at Acre, Israel', in *The Military Orders*, vol. 3, ed. V. Mallia-Milanes, Aldershot and Burlington, 213–23.

Peilstöcker, M. and A.A. Burke (eds), 2011, *The History and Archaeology of Jaffa 1*, The Jaffa Cultural Heritage Project 1, *Monumenta Archaeologica* 26, Los Angeles.

Peled, A., 2009, *Sugar in the Kingdom of Jerusalem. A Crusader Technology between East and West*, Jerusalem (Hebrew).

du Plat Taylor, J., 1938, 'Medieval Graves in Cyprus', *Ars Islamica* 5: 55–86.

Prawer, J., 1972, *The Latin Kingdom of Jerusalem. European Colonialism in the Middle Ages*, London.

——— 1980, *Crusader Institutions*, Oxford.

——— 1985, 'The Jerusalem the Crusaders Captured: A Contribution to the Medieval Topography of the City', *Crusade and Settlement: Papers Read at the First Conference of the Society for the Study of the Crusades and the Latin East and Presented to R.C. Smail*, ed. P.W. Edbury, Cardiff, 1–14.

——— 1991, 'Political History of Crusader and Ayyubid Jerusalem', in J. Prawer and H. Ben-Shammai (eds), *The History of Jerusalem* (Hebrew), Jerusalem, 1–67.

Preston, H.G., 1903, *Rural Conditions in the Latin Kingdom of Jerusalem*, PhD thesis, University of Pennsylvania, Philadelphia.

Pringle, R.D., 1986, *The Red Tower (al-Burj al-Ahmar): Settlement in the Plain of Sharon at the Time of the Crusaders and Mamluks (AD 1099–1516)*, London.

——— 1990–91, 'Crusader Jerusalem', *Bulletin of the Anglo-Israel Archaeological Society* 10: 105–13.

——— 2000, 'Crusader Settlement and the Landscape: Some Reflections on Method in the Light of Recent Archaeological Work', in D. Pringle, *Fortification and Settlement in Crusader Palestine*, Aldershot (UK) and Burlington (US), chapter IV: 1–11.

——— 2004 'Crusader Inscriptions from Southern Lebanon', *Crusades* 3: 131–51.

——— 2007, 'Notes on Some Inscriptions from Crusader Acre', in I. Shagrir, R. Ellenblum and J. Riley-Smith (eds), *In Laudem Hierosolymitani: Studies in Crusades and Medieval Culture in Honour of Benjamin Z. Kedar*, Crusades – Subsidia, vol. 1, Aldershot, 191–209.

Reem, A., 1999, 'Burial Customs in the Crusader Kingdom of Jerusalem', in S. Rozenberg (ed.), *The Knights of the Holy Land*, Jerusalem, 256–61.

——— 2002, 'The Kishle Excavations', in B. Zissu (ed.), *New Discoveries in the Citadel of Jerusalem and its Surroundings*, Jerusalem, 7–15 (in Hebrew).

Richard, J. 1985, Agricultural Conditions in the Crusader States, in K.M. Setton (ed.), *A History of the Crusades*, vol. 5, Madison, 251–94.

Riley-Smith, J., 2008, 'The Death and Burial of Latin Pilgrims to Jerusalem and Acre, 1099–1291', *Crusades* 7: 165–79.

Roll, I. and O. Tal, 1999, *Apollonia-Arsuf. Final Report of the Excavations*, Tel Aviv.

de Sandoli, S., 1974, *Corpus Crucesignatorum Inscriptionum Terrae Sanctae (1099–1291)*, Jerusalem.

Sebbane, M., 1999, 'Board Games: A Crusader Pastime', in S. Rosenberg (ed.), *Knights of the Holy Land*, Jerusalem, 286–91.

Seligman, J., 2012, 'A Wall Painting, a Crusader Flood Diversion Facility and Other Archaeological Gleanings from the Abbey of the Virgin Mary in the Valley of Jehoshaphat, Jerusalem', in L.D. Chupcała (ed.), *Christ is Here: Studies in Biblical and Christian Archaeology in Memory of Michele Piccirillo*, Milano.

Smail, R.C., 1976, *The Crusaders in Syria and the Holy Land*, London.

Smithline, H., E.J. Stern and E. Stern, 2013, 'A Crusader-Period Bathhouse in 'Akko (Acre)', *Atiqot* 73: 71–108.

Stern, E.J., 1999, The Sugar Industry in Palestine during the Crusader, Ayyubid and Mamluk Periods in Light of the Archaeological Finds (2 vols., Hebrew with English abstract), unpublished MA thesis, Hebrew University of Jerusalem.

———— 2012, '*Akko I. The 1991–1998 Excavations The Crusader Period Pottery*, *IAA Reports*, 2 vols, Jerusalem.

Syon, D., 1999, 'Souvenirs from the Holy Land: A Crusader Workshop of Lead Ampullae from Acre', in S. Rozenberg (ed.), *Knights of the Holy Land*, Jerusalem.

Tal, O. and I. Roll, 2011, 'Arsur: The Site, Settlement and Crusader Castle, and the Material Manifestation of their Destruction,' in O. Tal (ed.), *The Last Supper at Apollonia: The Final Days of the Crusader Castle in Herzliya*, Tel Aviv.

Thompson, J.A., 2013, Death and Burial in the Latin East. A Study of the Crusader Cemetery at 'Atlit, Israel. ProQuest Dissertation Publishing (UMI U584117), Ann Arbor, MI, 2013.

Tignor Holmes, U., 1977, 'Life Among the Europeans in Palestine and Syria in the Twelfth and Thirteenth Centuries' in H.W. Hazard (ed.), K.M. Setton (gen.ed.), *The Crusades*, vol. 4, Wisconsin 1977, 9–13.

Upton-Ward, J.M., 1992, *The Rule of the Templars*, Woodbridge.

Ussishkin, D. and J. Woodhead, 1997, *Excavations at Tel Jezreel 1994–1996: Third Preliminary Report*, Tel Aviv 24, 6–72.

Wagner, T.G. and Mitchell, P., 2011, 'The Illnesses of King Richard and King Philippe on the Third Crusade: An Understanding of *arnaldia* and *leonardie*', *Crusades* 10: 23–44.

Whitehouse, D., T.B. Husband, L. Pilosi, M.B. Shepard and M.T. Wypyski, forthcoming, 'Glass Finds in the Metropolitan Museum of Art from the 1926 Expedition', in Boas, A.J. and R.G. Khamisy (eds), *Montfort. History, Early Research and Recent Studies of the Principal Teutonic Fortress in the Latin East*, Leiden and Boston.

Yule, B. and P. Rowsome, 1994, *Caesarea Maritima. Area 114, Excavations – the 1993 Season. Interim report on the excavation of a sondage through sediments filling the Herodian Inner Harbour and an overlaying Arab and Crusader sequence.* Caesarea Inner Harbour Evaluations (CIHE), Caesarea. Rural Settlement.

CHAPTER THIRTY-ONE

CONQUEST AND EUROPEANISATION: THE ARCHAEOLOGY OF THE CRUSADES IN LIVONIA, PRUSSIA AND LITHUANIA

———•◆•———

Aleksander Pluskowski and Heiki Valk

INTRODUCTION

In the early 1170s, a letter from Pope Alexander III addressed to Scandinavian magnates offered indulgences to those who would fight against the pagans in Estonia (Fonnesberg-Schmidt 2007: 59–61). This heralded the start of the crusades in the eastern Baltic, a series of penitential wars sanctioned by the papacy with the aim of protecting Christian converts and converting the indigenous population. Crusading here would begin in 1198 and then in 1200 under the leadership of bishop Albert of Buxhövden and authorised by Innocent III. By 1230 much of the lands corresponding to the modern territories of Latvia and Estonia had been militarily subjugated and parallel crusades had begun against the southern Baltic tribes – the Prussians (see Christiansen 1997; Urban 1997). Fighting continued for many decades, and whilst Prussia was officially subdued by 1283, resistance in Livonia continued until 1290. The mechanism of crusading provided a regular supply of Christian armies to the eastern Baltic, whilst conquered territories were secured by castles largely built by the Teutonic Order. Between 1202 and 1236, the Sword Brothers – a military order formed by Albert in Riga – had spearheaded the crusades into Latvia and Estonia, after which they suffered a crippling defeat by a Samogitian army at Saule (Schaulen) and the remnants were quickly incorporated into the Teutonic Order as its Livonian branch (or Livonian Order). Northern Estonia was conquered by a Danish army in 1219 and remained under royal control until it was sold to the Order in 1346, following an unsuccessful indigenous rebellion in 1343. The rest of the annexed territories were sub-divided between the Teutonic Order, bishops and their cathedral chapters (Fig. 31.1). Throughout the fourteenth century, the Teutonic Order waged a relentless war against the Grand Duchy of Lithuania and Samogitia, which had remained independent and resisted Christianisation until it was accepted by the Grand Duke in 1387. After the final collapse of the crusader states in the Latin East in 1291, the eastern Baltic became the main theatre of crusading for the European knightly class.

Traditionally, our understanding of the Baltic crusades has been dominated by historians. The events of the crusades were documented in a series of narratives written by German clerics; Henry's *Chronicle of Livonia* (Brundage 2004) and the anonymous *Livonian Rhymed*

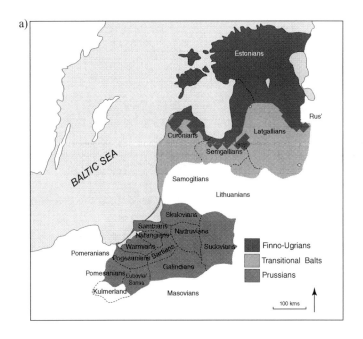

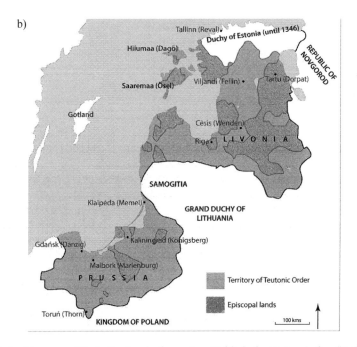

Figure 31.1 The geopolitical situation in the eastern Baltic before (a) and after (b) the crusades.
Map: by Maria Smirnova.

Chronicle (Smith and Urban 2006), written during the period of active crusading, whilst Peter of Dusburg's *Chronicle of Prussia* (Wyszomirski and Wenta 2011), later rendered into German by Nicholas of Jeroschin (Fischer 2010), drew on earlier sources but was written several decades after the official end of the Prussian Crusade. There is also a substantial body of papal correspondence which sheds important light on the eastern Baltic within the broader context of the crusading movement (Arbusow 1928; Fonnesberg-Schmidt 2007). However, since the late nineteenth century, and particularly from the 1950s, archaeological data have provided information on various aspects of the cultural transformations that accompanied the crusades – the final phase of indigenous Baltic societies and the formation of Christian polities governed by a militarised Catholic theocracy, dominated by the Teutonic Order. Investigations have been largely concerned with the fortifications built or procured by crusaders, as well as the newly established towns supporting both military campaigns and Christianisation. Crusading and commerce went hand in hand, and the events of the thirteenth century sustained a war economy in the Baltic Sea region, contributing to the development of the Hanse. However, the crusades, also laid the foundations for a type of apartheid distinguishing much of the surviving indigenous populations from the colonists, one that would become more pronounced in the later fourteenth and fifteenth centuries.

THE ARCHAEOLOGY OF THE CRUSADES IN LIVONIA AND ESTONIA

The German conquest of the Eastern Baltic was initially driven by the interests of merchants seeking to access the markets of the Rus' principalities, alongside an emerging agenda of Christianisation. It began in the territory of the Livs – a small Finnic ethnic group inhabiting the lower course of the expansive Daugava River, the main inland waterway to the east. From the Livs, whom the colonists met first, also originates the name of Livonia which became a common nomination for the German-ruled area east of the Baltic Sea following the crusades. The name *Estonia* was used for present-day northern Estonia; the Danish province in the post-conquest period.

The attempts of Meynard, the first bishop of the Livs (1186–96), to Christianise the indigenous population were of a peaceful character, but unsuccessful. Crusading activities were launched in 1198 by his follower, Bishop Berthold, who organised the first crusading army and was killed that same year in a battle. The third bishop, Albert (1199–1229), launched a full-scale crusade which ended with the conquest of those areas which largely correspond to the present-day territory of Estonia and Latvia, that is, with the making of medieval Livonia.

The geography and chronology of the Livonian crusades reflects the aim of taking control over the main communication and trading routes. First, control was established over the Daugava waterway. The wars against the Livs ended in 1206/1210 and the Latgallians, settled in the mid-course of the Daugava en route to the Rus' Principality of Polotsk, had accepted Catholic Christianity and German overlordship by 1208. Crusades against the Estonians were launched in the same year, motivated by the need to take control over the territory leading to Pskov, and ended in 1227 with the subordination of the Osilians (Saaremaa island), a dangerous maritime group in the eastern Baltic. Fighting against the Curonians of western Latvia lasted from 1210 to 1267, and the wars against the Semigallians from 1220 to 1272/1290.

The archaeological record of medieval Livonia provides evidence of a clear watershed between the colonists and the conquered natives of Livonia and Estonia (Mugurēvičs 1973;

ARE 2006: 159–92; 205–21; Šnē 2009b). The stone castles, towns and monasteries established during and after the crusades follow a Latin European cultural pattern, while rural settlements, local village cemeteries and sacred natural sites are indicative of the persistence of indigenous traditions.

The settlement pattern and native inhabitants

Although villages were severely plundered during the crusades, as described in Henry's *Chronicle*, the conquest did not result in discontinuity in the settlement pattern in the territory of Estonia. Here, the occupation layers of villages provide evidence of continuity from the Final Iron Age to the medieval period. There are no signs of abandonment and no distinct hiatus between the pre- and post-conquest period can be observed. Even if villages ceased to exist for a short time, they were soon re-established. A valuable source concerning the settlement pattern during the period of the crusades in northern Estonia is the Danish Census Book *Liber Census Daniae* (Johansen 1933), originating from about 1240 and documenting the numbers of plough-lands associated with villages. The villages mentioned in *the Liber* have survived until the present day and their location can be identified archaeologically in the landscape. The emergence of several village cemeteries, in areas where graves are not known from the Final Iron Age, provides evidence of settlement expansion after the crusades. This process is also indicated by pollen data from southern Estonia (Niinemets 2008; Valk et al. 2009: 138), which shows the occupation of formerly uninhabited areas from the mid-thirteenth century onwards. In western Latvia, however, the population was greatly reduced, partly due to population losses, partly due to emigration to Lithuanian areas.

The situation of the native population after the conquest is relatively poorly reflected in the written record (Ligi 1968: 153–13; Šterns 2002: 577–624; Šnē 2009a: 65–6; Selart and Valk 2012: 63–73). The crusades resulted in substantial changes in land ownership, and villages were offered to new owners, partly of German, partly of native origin. Having its roots in the Iron Age, a network of manors developed after the conquest of Livonia, first in core areas. In Estonia, it developed most rapidly in Harrien, north Estonia, the area under Danish rule. The subordinated natives, although personally free, preserving their own laws and the right to bear arms, to have movable and immovable property and to inherit it, had accepted, together with Christianity and the crusaders' overlordship, a suite of new duties. These included paying tithes and taxes, participating in the wars against pagans and Russians, and assisting in the building of castles, churches and roads. Furthermore, the labour duty for the agricultural requirements of manors and castles, although initially limited to only a few days each year, also appeared in the mid-thirteenth century.

In contrast to Prussian territories occupied by the Teutonic Order, no rural colonisation by German settlers took place in Livonia. The number of Germans remained small in the countryside, being limited to the inhabitants of castles, manors and the newly established semi-urban settlements which emerged alongside the castles.

The archaeology of conquest

Although the direct evidence of the crusades is hard to observe in the archaeological record, the siege of Estonian Final Iron Age strongholds by crusading armies can be identified by finds of specific of crossbow bolts, typical for the 1210s–1220s, maybe also in the 1230s–1240s, but not subsequently used (Mäesalu 1991: 170–4; bolt types AI: 1–2). Such projectiles have been found at fourteen strongholds in Estonia (Fig. 31.2); also from sites not mentioned in Henry's *Chronicle* (Lang and Valk 2011: 293–6). The hill fort of Lõhavere (Tõnisson 2008: 271–5), two-thirds of which has been excavated, was destroyed by fire in the early thirteenth century crusades (Fig. 31.3); judging by Henry's *Chronicle*, either in 1215 or 1223. A craft and jewellery box was recovered from the context of the last destruction phase (Laul and Tamla 2014). In Viljandi/Fellin the final siege of the hill fort by the crusaders in 1223, described in Henry's *Chronicle* (CHL XXVII: 2) is reflected in the archaeological record (Valk 2001a; Lang and Valk 2011: 296–301; Valk 2015: 18–25). Henry's note, that the work of the besiegers' trebuchets was strongly hindered by Estonian crossbowmen, corresponds well to the fact that on the hills within 110–140 m of the stronghold the remains of trebuchet platforms have been discovered (Fig. 31.4). On one of the hills (*c.* 100 m²), forty-one crossbow bolts, shot to hinder the builders of the platform, alongside an iron spade, were found. In south-eastern Estonia the unfinished condition of some hill forts enables us to connect the last stage of their fortification with the uprising of 1223–24 (Lang and Valk 2011: 306–13) when Otepää, the central stronghold, together with its hinterlands surrendered without a struggle. Furthermore, traces of digging out the ramparts – a siege tactic mentioned by Henry – can be observed at some Estonian strongholds (Keava and Lohu). Henry's note that in 1220 the Danes gave holy water to the peasants in north Estonia, asking them to baptise themselves (CHL XXIV: 2) – given it was important to precede the German priests with baptism for political reasons – may also be

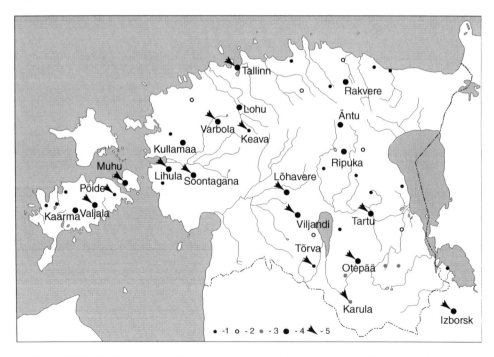

Figure 31.2 Native strongholds in Estonia in the thirteenth century. 1, 3–5 – crusade period strongholds, 2 – supposed crusade period stronghold, 3 – unfinished stronghold, constructed or re-constructed probably for the uprising of 1223, 4 – Estonian strongholds mentioned in the thirteenth-century written data, 5 – finds of crusaders' crossbow bolts. Map: by Maria Smirnova.

Figure 31.3   Fortifications on the hill fort of Lõhavere, Estonia, burnt by the crusaders in 1215 or 1223: the reconstruction and archaeological reality (after Tõnisson 2008, figs. 67 and 131).

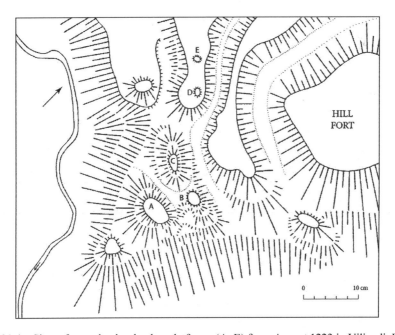

Figure 31.4   Sites of crusaders' trebuchet platforms (A–E) from August 1223 in Viljandi, Estonia. The system of moats was probably different at that time, but the origins of the east–west directional moats/valleys are glacial. Map: by Maria Smirnova.

573

reflected in the archaeology. Numerous finds of "Hanseatic bowls" from the Danish area in north Estonia, sometimes in sets of several items, may be evidence of this rushed baptism (Tamla 1999).

The introduction of stone castles

Control over the conquered territories was established through a network of castles (Tuulse 1942; Caune and Ose 2004). A significant innovation introduced during the crusades was stone buildings constructed using lime mortar. The first stone castles of Livonia, in Ikšķile and Martinsāla (Holm) on the Daugava River, were already built before the crusades, *c.* 1185 and 1186 (CHL I: 6–8). Excavations on Ikšķile, Holm (Caune and Ose 2004: 209–15, 442–6), as well as on Riekstu kalns in Cēsis (Wenden) (Apala and Apals 2014), show that the earliest German castles were surrounded by a stone wall, and this was also likely in Estonia. From Viljandi there is archaeological evidence for the use of bricks already between 1215 and 1223 (Valk 2001a: 70). Beside castles, fortified monasteries (Daugavgrīva and Kärkna) played an important role in the forging of a new European society in Livonia.

As the resources of the crusaders were limited, the first stone castles were constructed at the most strategic sites in terms of power and communications. They were often built on the sites of local hill forts (e.g. Tartu, Otepää, Viljandi, Lihula, Tallinn in Estonia; Turaida, Koknese, Tērvete, Embūte in Latvia), where the earlier timber fortifications were replaced with stone walls, or in their immediate vicinity (Cēsis, Tērvete, Sigulda, Aizkraukle). In Viljandi a set of mid-thirteenth-century capitals provides evidence of the magnificent interior of the first Livonian Order castle, replaced by the convent house *c.* 1300 (Alttoa 2015). When the natives had accepted baptism, the most important strongholds were initially manned jointly by them and German garrisons. This practice was ended in Estonia following the major uprising in 1223 when German colonists were killed or captured in a perfidious way (CHL XXVI: 5–7).

The network of castles gradually expanded in Livonia during the thirteenth century. By the end of the century their number was at least seventeen in Estonia, and in Latvia around fifty have been mentioned, including timber castles and hill forts used in the post-conquest period. Then, in addition to those mentioned above, in eastern Latvia (Mugurēvičs 1973: 34, table 1); for example, the castles of Riga, Adaži, Jelgava, Lielvārde, Sigulda, Valmiera, Gaujiena and Daugavpils (Caune and Ose 2004), in western Latvia those of Ventspils, Kuldīga, Grobiņa, Aizbute and Embute, and in Estonia those of Kuressaare, Pärnu, Karksi, Helme, Põltsamaa, Haapsalu, Paide, Rakvere, Narva and Kirumpää were founded. Trial excavations of the earliest occupation layers of Karksi castle, dated to the last two decades of the thirteenth century, provide evidence of the colonising, German lifestyle of its first inhabitants, marked for example by the lack of local wheel-thrown pottery and the use of stave bowls (Valk et al. 2013a : 74–8). Although in Latvia there were several crusaders' timber castles from the thirteenth century, in Estonia strongholds with timber fortifications and of pre-conquest origin belonged mainly to the native nobility.

The fate of strongholds and the native elite

The fate of prehistoric strongholds was different following the Christianisation of different regions of Livonia, depending on local circumstances, the manner and conditions of surrender and the role of the native elite in the new power structures. In western and northern Estonia where part of the local nobility obtained the status of vassals in the new feudal society (Valk 2009), some of the strongholds remained continuously in use. The lack of traces of "European" cultural innovations in the archaeological record indicates these sites continued to be used in a traditional, native way. Presently there exists archaeological data indicating the post-conquest use in the thirteenth century of twelve strongholds in Estonia – seven certain and at least five probable cases (Fig. 31.5). The use of some strongholds in the 1230s and in the context of Estonian uprisings of 1260

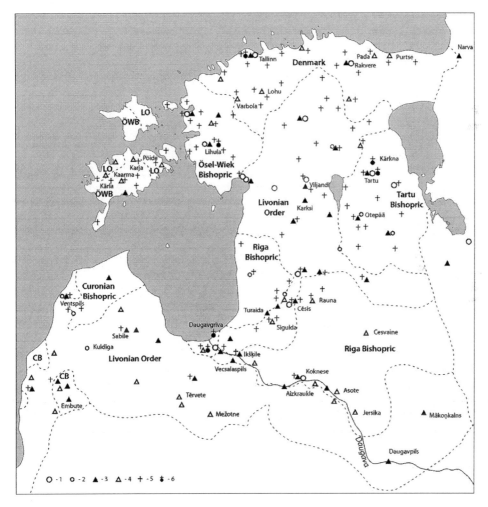

Figure 31.5   Livonia after the end of the crusades: castles and churches around AD 1300 and strongholds of post-conquest use (after EAA 2006; Latvian castles after Caune and Ose 2004; Estonian post-conquest strongholds after Valk 2014; Latvian post-conquest strongholds after Šnē 2009a and b and Mugurēvičs 1973). 1 – town, 2 – large urban settlement without town rights, 3 – castle, 4 – timber castle or hill fort, 5 – church, 6 – monastery. Map: by Maria Smirnova.

575

(Kaarma) and 1345 (the sites were not named, but probably were Karja Purtsa, Varbola and Lohu) is also reflected in the written record (Valk 2014). In Varbola, the strongest and largest of the Estonian Final Iron Age strongholds, the reconstruction of the gates can be dated by coins from 1210/20 to 1288/90 (Valk 2014: 447). In Virumaa, Purtse hill fort was in use in the late thirteenth or even early fourteenth century and a post-conquest occupation seems also highly likely for the large hill fort at Pada. However, having lost their former hinterlands, now split between various smaller vassals, the economic basis of the large strongholds effectively collapsed. As timber fortifications required permanent care, those sites which were not strategically important for the authorities of medieval Livonia probably gradually lost their military significance. In Latvia, the share of vassals of native origin was larger than in Estonia, where they even dominated in the thirteenth century (Šterns 2002, 614–19; Šnē 2009a: 65). There also exist archaeological traces or written data of the post-conquest use of prehistoric strongholds in Latvia alongside the new German castles; for example, Asote, Cesvaine, Jersika, Rauna (Tanīsa kalns), Sēlpils, Mežotne, Tērvete, Sabile and Sigulda/Satesele (Mugurēvičs 1973: 32; Šnē 2009a: 67; 2009b: 131–2; Zemītis 2014).

The continuity of power in the thirteenth century was, probably, the most pronounced in Saaremaa (Mägi 2002: 148–50) which accepted Christianity without a final battle. There the local elite preserved their place within the new power structures, and may also have participated in the foundation of the first stone churches (Mägi 2004: 31–3; Markus et al. 2003: 11–12). The spatial connections between Late Iron Age stone graves and hoards, and medieval manors, in Saaremaa are suggestive of the prehistoric origins of the latter (Mägi 2001). The situation was also similar in western and northern Estonia, Curonia and most of eastern Latvia where stone castles were rare in the thirteenth century. The rights of the natives remained particularly extensive in the peripheral border areas, as shown by finds from the cemetery of Siksälä in south-eastern Estonia (Laul and Valk 2007; Valk and Laul 2014; Valk, Ratas and Laul 2014). There, grave goods – axes, spears and spurs – point to the warrior status of the local men up to the fifteenth century.

The crusades and the genesis of towns

There were no towns within the territories of Estonia and Latvia before the crusades. Riga, the first town in Livonia, founded in 1201, became the main centre for the crusaders. During the thirteenth century, towns emerged only in the immediate vicinity of stone castles in Livonia, in places suitable for long-term communication and trading (Fig. 31.5). From the perspective of the natives, however, the town was a fortified site and this is reflected in the name of the new phenomenon in both the Estonian and the Latvian language (Valk 2014: 101, 104). In addition to towns, some large urban settlements without town rights also developed alongside castles.

Archaeological information concerning the earliest phase of Livonian towns has accumulated unevenly. From Latvia there is a vast quantity of archaeological data relating to the earliest history of Riga (Caune 1984, 2007). In Estonia the process of early urbanisation (Pärn 2004a) has been studied on the basis of the archaeological record in Viljandi (Valk 2005; Haak and Russow 2013) and Haapsalu (Pärn 2004b, 2009), but archaeological data from the thirteenth century is also rich from Tartu. In the material culture of the thirteenth-century towns, the parallel existence of building traditions of German and indigenous origin (houses of brick and timber-frame construction *versus* cross-log houses) can be observed. The meeting of different cultures is also reflected in the types of recovered artefacts (Mugurēvičs 1990). While German culture is characterised by the use of stoneware and stave bowls, native traditions are represented by ordinary wheel-thrown pottery. Human osteological data refers to the multi-ethnic composition of the early urban population (Kalling 1997: 55–7). In the early urban churchyards the presence of the native population can also be observed on the basis of jewellery and textile remains.

The crusades and the religion of the natives

The Livonian crusades resulted in the official baptism of the indigenous peoples and the establishment of a network of churches (Fig. 31.5). Their number was quite large in Estonia (*c.* 70 rural churches by around AD 1300) (EAA 2006), but little is known about the formation of the network of parish churches within Latvian territory. Churches were numerous in its core areas, but there were almost no stone churches in Curonia, Semigallia and large eastern areas of Latvia during the Middle Ages (Caune and Ose 2010). Although the land was formally Christianised, the process of religious transformation remained unfinished and was limited by dual faith and syncretism (Valk 2003). Sacred natural sites remained in use in Estonia and Latvia (Urtāns 2008), despite the crusades and Christianisation. Sacred groves, trees, hills, stones and springs are remembered until the present day, on the basis of continued use (e.g. Vaitkevičius 2004; Urtāns 2008), and their network existed in parallel to and independently of the network of churches and chapels (Valk 2004). In addition, crusading and Christianisation laid the foundation for a network of rural chapels, which was densest in Livonia in the late medieval period. Votive coins from St Nicholas' hill, southern Estonia, situated at the historical military and trade route from Cēsis to Otepää and Tartu, point to an already existing chapel in the second quarter of the thirteenth century (Valk et al. 2013b, 121–2, 125–7). Located close to the crusaders' assembly and camp site, mentioned by Henry, the chapel was evidently built on the place where common sermons for the Christian army took place before the raids to Ugaunia.

Despite the official baptism, the system of local village cemeteries remained in use in Livonia, in parallel to the newly founded churchyards, also following the conquest. The background for this concession was the papal letters from 1214/1215 forcing the bishop of Riga and the Sword Brothers to give the neophytes the right to choose burial according to their will (Arbusow 1928: 296–7, 323). Although large grave goods mostly disappeared during the thirteenth century and Christian grave orientations became predominant in Livonia, local village cemeteries with burials furnished with small grave goods (knives, jewellery, coins, etc.) remained in use everywhere (e.g. Valk 2001b; Muižnieks 2011). In Latvia no clear boundary between prehistoric and early medieval burial rites can be observed during the thirteenth century, and in areas further from the centres even later (Mugurēvičs 1973). In Estonia, where the rate of cremation and inhumation graves was more or less balanced in late pre-Christian times (with certain regional differences), the crusades and Christianisation prompted a rapid decrease in cremation practices: these ceased completely in northern and western Estonia and were greatly reduced in the south. In Curonia, however, cremation was widely practised up to the fifteenth century, and cremations occurred sporadically up to that time in eastern Latvia and southern Estonia as well, in the latter even up to the 1530s.

The archaeological record of the cemeteries has regional differences. In the Latgallian areas of eastern Latvia and south-eastern Estonia (Muižnieks 2011, 54; Valk 2001a, 70–2) a gender-based opposite orientation of male and female graves, having its roots in prehistoric times, can be observed. In western and northern Estonia the continuity of Iron Age jewellery and fashion traditions can be observed both in village cemeteries and in rural churchyards until the second half of the thirteenth century, but then it rapidly disappears (Valk 2009: 4–279). Most likely, the principal change in costume and jewellery traditions was caused by the transition to new, "European" fashions. The reason for this change might be that the local native elite, involved in new power structures, was numerous enough to mediate cultural innovations to the indigenous society. A similar situation can be suggested also for most of Latvia where the rich sets of jewellery characteristic of the Iron Age disappeared from the graves by the late thirteenth century. In southern Estonia where the local nobility, evidently mistrusted by the Germans after the rebellion of 1223, was not involved in the vassal system, such profound changes cannot be observed. Southern Estonia and eastern Latvia remained conservative, retaining jewellery traditions of Iron Age origin. The cultural situation remained especially conservative in the eastern peripheries of Livonia where the only innovation in burial rites linked to Christianisation was the decrease of cremation practises: gender-based opposite orientation and burial with a rich set of jewellery continued, whilst men were buried with weapons until the fifteenth century (Laul and Valk 2007). Grave finds indicate a similar situation also existed in the eastern periphery of Latvia (Berga 2007). In the Middle Ages, graves furnished with jewellery also exist in the rural churchyards of Livonia.

Thus despite officially accepting Christianity and being governed by a militarised theocracy, the transformation of the indigenous population into the type of culture characteristic of medieval Europe – of Christendom – remained incomplete up until post-medieval times in Livonia. The old society adapted to the new situation and continued its existence in parallel to the newly introduced centres and networks of "European" society – those of a colonising origin. An important reason for this lack of assimilation was the segregation of society into German and non-German (Estonians, Latvians, Livs) groups – the *Undeutsch*. The roots of this differentiation stretch back to the crusades which laid the foundation for the watershed between the German-speaking victors and the natives, subordinated by force.

THE ARCHAEOLOGY OF THE CRUSADE IN PRUSSIA

The Prussian Crusade was technically a series of crusades sustained over five decades. The mid-point of these crusades was the Treaty of Christburg in 1249, which consolidated the Teutonic Order's hold over western Prussia. Conflict with western Natangia lasted until 1253 and the following year Barta and Galindia had been officially included within the conquered territories. In 1255 Sambia was initially occupied with the aid of Ottokar II of Bohemia, although it was not pacified until nearly a decade later, whilst eastern Natangia was overwhelmed by the Order's armies in 1256. The Great Prussian Uprising saw an unlikely alliance with neighbouring Christian Pomerelia (eastern Pomerania) and endured until 1274, after which Nadruvia and Scalovia were occupied and the Order's armies pushed further east again. Sudovia was finally occupied by 1283, when Peter of Dusburg (PD III: 221) notes the end of the wars with the Prussians. Archaeologically, a cultural transformation is evident over the course of the thirteenth century, albeit at a relatively low resolution (for a detailed regional survey see Pluskowski 2012).

The destruction, re-use and construction of strongholds

The impact of the crusades can be linked with a chronological hiatus representing the final occupation phases of many Prussian strongholds. A number of these sites appear to have been abandoned before the crusades, perhaps as the result of Polish or Rus' military activity. For example, the limited human activity in parts of Galindia after the eleventh century, resulting from some internal demographic or economic crisis, has been connected with Polish and later Danish incursions (Wróblewski et al. 2003: 168), although some areas continued to be occupied as suggested by settlements such as Święta Góra near Staświny, as well as palynological evidence for continued human impact on the landscape from the eleventh century (Białuński 1996: 20; Wacnik et. al 2014). Further north, the distribution of strongholds within the vicinity of Klaipėda that were destroyed or abandoned in the thirteenth century provides dramatic evidence of the creation of a precarious frontier with Samogitia (Fig. 31.6); the lack of indigenous sacred place names in this region

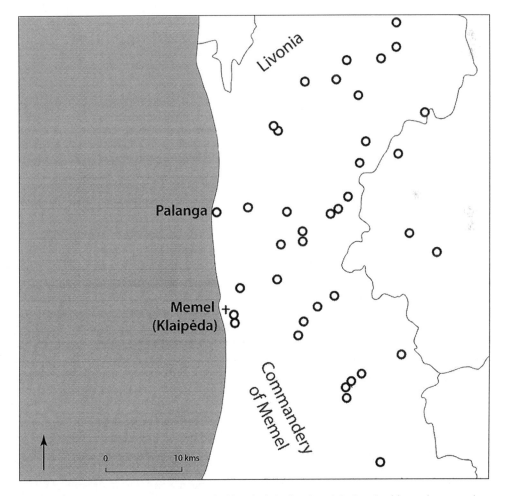

Figure 31.6   The distribution of strongholds (circles) abandoned during the thirteenth century in western Lithuania (after Zabiela; www.piliakalniai.lt/index_en.php). Map: by Maria Smirnova.

may reflect the long-term impact of the crusades in southern Curonia (Vaitkevičius 2004). Palynological studies at the stronghold and settlement of Impiltis have indicated the regeneration of woodland following the crusades, a general trend in this borderland giving rise to a significant belt of wilderness referred to as *Die Große Wildnis* (Stančikaitė et al. 2009), although ceramics recovered from sites such as Posejnele and Półkoty (Prussian Sudovia) hint at the survival of sporadic communities in some parts of this largely depopulated zone (Engel et al. 2006: 202).

The earliest *castra* constructed by the Teutonic Order were offensive structures, built quickly with the aim of securing territorial gains and facilitating Christianisation (Arszyński 2000). The re-use of existing structures is described in Peter's account for a number of the Order's *castra* (Poliński 2007b: 42, note 2), and archaeologically has been attested at a range of sites (Kochański 2001: 468). The entry point of the crusades – the Kulmerland – had only recently seen Prussian occupation, and here the Order established its bases within former Slavic strongholds. This was repeated further down the eastern side of the Vistula valley which had seen extensive Pomeranian colonisation in previous centuries. Excavations at the Order's castles in Toruń (Thorn), Pokrzywno (Engelsburg), Grudziądz (Graudenz) and Rogózno (Rogasen) also revealed earlier, Slavic timber-earth structures dating to the late twelfth/early thirteenth century (Poliński 2007b: 45). At the stronghold of Zamkowa Góra in Stary Dzierzgoń (Alt Christburg), excavations in 2009 uncovered both Prussian and Teutonic Order material culture, and German archaeologists working at the site in the 1930s had speculated it was re-fortified in 1230 in response to the threat from the crusading host, but the Order successfully attacked and occupied the stronghold (Szczepański 2010; Gazda and Jezierska 2014). At Königsberg, the Order's castle is assumed to have been constructed on the site of the stronghold of Tuwangste, and this has been partially verified archaeologically by excavations in Kaliningrad (Kulakov 1990), whilst other Sambian strongholds have yielded both Prussian and Teutonic Order material culture (Wendt 2011).

Whilst there are certainly instances of re-used sites, there are also examples of newly constructed buildings on fresh, unoccupied sites. The timber stronghold uncovered under the outer bailey courtyard of the Order's castle at Elbląg (Elbing) in 2012–13, incorporated 200-year-old oaks within its superstructure and several phases of construction were identified before the island fortification was replaced by the stone and brick convent (Fig. 31.7).

The thirteenth-century *castrum* was sited on a riverine island, exemplifying an acute awareness of the broader landscape consistently demonstrated in the strategic location of castles; overlooking rivers, close to or on major routes and making use of the natural topography in much the same way as earlier communities had done. There is even some evidence the Order utilised old trees as watchtowers and fortified points (Poliński 2007b: 43). The variety of forms during the crusading period indicates the construction of fortifications was tailored to the specific needs of the Order's garrisons and associated settlements. These included relatively simple, moated and embanked ring-works enclosing a courtyard with a timber-framed building constructed on stone foundations. Some had fortified outer baileys; others contained *mottes* of various sizes. Occasionally gate house or perimeter towers were located at the edges of embankments (Kochański 2001). From the onset, these strongholds functioned as key centres of administration, managing the Order's newly acquired territory which was sub-divided into *Komturei* or commanderies, each overseen by a convent headed by a commander. Once a level of political and economic stability had been established in Prussia, castles began to be built and re-built from more durable materials, although even before 1280 there is evidence of field stones being combined with

Figure 31.7 Remains of the thirteenth-century timber castle excavated in Elbląg (Elbing) in 2012.

brick, whilst timber and earth structures continued to be built by the Order into the fifteenth century (Poliński 2007a: 241). At Papowo Biskupie (Bischöflich Papau), the oldest known regular quadrangular castle in Prussia was constructed between 1287 and 1292 largely from field stones (Fig. 31.8).

Very little is known about the organisation of space in these early castles from the fragmentary archaeological record. It is reasonable to speculate the internal organisation of these sites would have been tailored to the specific needs of the garrisons. Peter of Dusburg's descriptions of the Order's thirteenth-century fortifications suggests the brothers did practice a communal lifestyle, but until the development of the conventual castle it is difficult to describe them as fortified monasteries. Archaeologically, it is possible to distinguish three diachronic phases in castle design: the use of earlier structures; the introduction of transitional fortifications combining the elements of early medieval strongholds with those of later castles (such as residential towers); and the conventual castle built from more durable materials (Poliński 2005). However, castles built during the crusading period

Figure 31.8 The castle at Papowo Biskupie. Photograph: Magnus Elander.

certainly played a role in the perceived spiritual war waged against the pagans: named after Christ, the Virgin, angels and saints, with their chapels as repositories of relics, they vividly mapped a Christian landscape onto the conquered tribal territories (Rozynkowski 2006: 229–40). When a standardised rectilinear plan was eventually adopted for castle building, it was used in the majority of the Order's Prussian convents, clearly promoting a corporate identity revolving around a monastic lifestyle and the ideology of holy war (Herrmann 2007: 81–3).

The most dramatic outcome of the crusades was the realignment of core and peripheral territories, which influenced the late medieval settlement pattern. The great castle of Marienburg (Malbork) began to be constructed from brick from the 1270s, and would undergo a significant programme of expansion after it was designated as the Order's headquarters in 1309, following the annexation of Gdańsk and Pomerelia (Fig. 31.9). Located in the thirteenth-century Pomeranian/Prussian borderlands, its commandery would become the heartland of the theocratic polity and a major stimulus for colonisation of the Vistula fens. In contrast, where the north-eastern extent of the Order's territory stretched up the Curonian spit, the convent of Memmel (Klaipėda), founded in 1252, would become a base for attacks into Samogitia, coinciding with a collapse of the indigenous settlement pattern in this region (Zabiela 1995), including the abandonment of the major trading hub at Palanga (Žulkus 2007).

Colonising Prussia

A defining feature of the Prussian Crusade was a deliberate, sustained process of colonisation linked to the gradual development of an administrative structure to manage the conquered territories. The western and southern borderlands with Prussia had seen earlier

a)

b)

Figure 31.9 View of Malbork castle (Marienburg) from the south-west (a) with examples of the earliest brick courses in the Wendish bond from the lower north wall of the high castle (b). Photographs: Author.

phases of Slavic colonisation, particularly associated with the expansion of the Polish state, and this process was revived and intensified during the crusading period. Flourishing, well-connected settlements contained a pool of skilled labour essential for constructing and maintaining fortifications, generated wealth for the Order and provided military and logistical support, particularly in terms of provisioning. Whilst the organisation of the crusades in Prussia quickly became the responsibility of the Teutonic Order, these campaigns – and the foundations of associated settlements – were very much a collaborative effort. For example, Polish princes and the Burgrave of Magdeburg, together with the Order, founded Thorn, Kulm and Marienwerder (Dygo 2009: 75), the crusading contingent of Henry III, the Burgrave of Meissen, founded Elbing, whilst the Bohemian king Przemysl Ottokar II contributed to the foundation of Königsberg, although the majority of investment here would come from the Order (Czaja 2009).

The number of colonists coming into Prussia during the period of active crusading was relatively small, and the majority established themselves within the protected confines of settlements and towns attached to the Teutonic Order's castles. The locations of colonies established during the crusading era are described in written sources, however, only a few are well known archaeologically. An exceptional rural site with a transitional occupation has been located at Biała Góra just south of Malbork, and although no internal settlement plan has yet been identified, the range of material culture indicated both a military and a mercantile presence, with evidence for the exploitation of a diverse spectrum of environmental resources (Pluskowski et al. 2014). The Order encouraged individual knights to promote the process of colonisation in the Kulmerland and Pomesania following military conquest. In 1233, the Order built a watch tower 4 kilometres north of Marienwerder which three years later was given to the German knight Dietrich of Tiefenau, along with 300 *hufen* (one *hufe* or hide is around 40 acres) – a sizeable amount of land for a colonising settlement. By the end of the decade this was augmented with additional territory between Marienwerder and Christburg (Dygo 2009: 77). Excavations at the settlement revealed that the main tower of Dietrich's stronghold, framed by posts with walls of tightly packed oak beams, appears to have combined the functions of a residence, defensive keep and observation post. The site was destroyed during the First Prussian Uprising (1242–49), although occupation may have continued for a few more decades (Haftka 2007). The volatility of the crusading period is clearly archaeologically evident in massive fires that destroyed parts of Thorn in the 1260s (Czacharowski 1983: 45) and Elbing in 1288 (Nawrolska 2001).

The next phase of colonisation only began after the suppression of the Second Prussian Uprising, with the first peasant settlements documented from the 1280s (Czaja 2009). Few colonists took their own initiative; all settlements were planned and financed by new landlords, whilst their appointed locators travelled to recruit settlers, and to ensure that key occupations were represented in each colony. Incentives included a large farm free from taxes for several years followed by lower permanent taxes, as well as aid with constructing dwellings and tilling land. Buschinger and Olivier (2007: 131) estimate that between 10,000 and 15,000 colonists came to the lands occupied by the Order and Prussian bishops at the turn of the fourteenth century, primarily focused on the Kulmerland, the lower Vistula and the coastal zone leading up to the Sambian Peninsula. They were largely Silesians and Germans from Brandenburg and Lübeck, with some individuals coming from Scandinavia and Holland. The southern regions were colonised by many Poles, especially in the Kulmerland where settlement was very intensive. Here, until *c.* 1343, some 328 rural settlements are documented (Poliński 2003: 10). In contrast, comparatively few colonists settled in Sambia where indigenous communities survived the longest. Archaeologically, the increasing use of brick in buildings within the urban colonies can be dated to this phase of colonisation, and Prussian town communities would develop their own distinct form of material culture (Gaimster 2005).

Indeed, at the level of individual sites the process of colonisation following the crusades is associated with distinctive types of material culture. The most striking is the appearance of a new type of kiln firing technology, producing wheel-thrown, slender and diverse forms of 'grey ware', fired in a reductive atmosphere at a temperature of 900°C, and contrasting with both Slavic and Baltic ceramic traditions. This technology does appear earlier on the fringes of Prussian lands, particularly in the Kulmerland from the first half of the twelfth century; however, it is far more typical of the period of colonisation (Poliński 1996). The largest and most studied assemblages of grey ware from a single site within Prussia have been recovered from excavations in Elbląg, where their dating has been supported by dendrochronology (Marcinkowski 2003). Here, one of the earliest structures associated with ceramic production was a pottery kiln uncovered in the north-eastern part of the town near the defensive earthen embankment. Nearby were the remains of a timber house, which dated this complex to the turn of the 1280s until 1288, when it was destroyed by fire. Some 82,451 ceramic fragments of wheel-thrown, mostly flat-bottomed 'grey ware' were recovered from the site, including pots, jugs, bowls, plates, covers, lamps, spindle whorls and fishing net weights. The general absence of spherical bottoms, a form associated with Westphalia and the Rhineland, was interpreted as reflecting the potter's origins from Thuringia through Silesia or from Upper Saxony. The appearance of greyware within Prussia is the most commonly used archaeological proxy of the crusading period and an indicator of the presence of colonists, and/or the Teutonic Order. Other forms of material culture associated with the earliest phases of colonisation include coins minted by the Order (e.g. dating the final phase of the settlement complex at Kałdus; Chudziak 2003), the introduction of timber-framed and brick housing, churches, heating systems and new forms of weaponry, especially crossbows (for an overview see Pluskowski 2012).

Individual settlements were organised (and re-organised) under a series of laws, two drawn from the Holy Roman Empire – the Madgeburg and Lübeck laws – and two particular to Prussia – the Kulm law and the Prussian law (*Iura Prutenorum*). The latter governed settlements of indigenous Prussians, who were treated differently to incoming Christian colonists. There is in fact relatively little written data on the ethnic diversity within medieval Prussian settlements and disagreement between scholars on the levels of segregation. In the commandery of Balga and in Sambia it appears that Prussians also lived in settlements under the Kulm Law, and in the latter region they even functioned as colony locators (Długokęcki 2009: 205). This is perhaps one important area where future archaeological research has the potential to further our understanding of the impact of the crusade on the indigenous population. At present the persistence of indigenous communities is almost entirely known from five cemeteries where burials with weapons and equestrian equipment continue, despite the earlier prohibitions in the Treaty of Christburg (Shiroukhov 2012: 250).

THE ARCHAEOLOGY OF THE LITHUANIAN *REISEN*

The crusades in Prussia and Livonia resulted in the depopulation of the borderlands with Samogitia and the Grand Duchy of Lithuania. Despite sustained attempts at unifying both regions of the Baltic *Ordensland*, the Teutonic Order was only able to consolidate its hold with the convent and town of Memel, situated at the northern end of the Curonian lagoon at Klaipėda in modern western Lithuania. This frontier remained militarised and volatile into the fifteenth century and the convent at Memel was unable to sustain itself from its commandery due to persistent Lithuanian raids, requiring regular imports of food produce (Žulkus 2002). Attacks across the border into eastern Prussia and southern Livonia also had a significant impact on settlement; in the former region the process of colonisation was only stabilised from the second half of the fourteenth century, whilst settlements in southern Sudovia and Semigallia abandoned at the end of the thirteenth century would not be reoccupied until the fifteenth century (Jarockis 2003).

At the same time, the Teutonic Order fostered a culture of crusading targeting Samogitia and Lithuania which attracted the knightly class of Christendom, and resulted in the eastern Baltic becoming the destination par excellence for crusaders in the fourteenth century. According to Peter of Dusburg, the war with Lithuania began immediately after the official end of the Prussian Crusade in 1283. However, seasonal campaigns across the borderlands which came to be known as *Reisen* and saw regular participation from European aristocrats and their retinues, began in the early fourteenth century. The details of these, including the participants, are known entirely from written sources (Paravicini 1989). The campaigns were clearly framed in religious ceremonial, particularly related to the cult of the Virgin (Dygo 1989), alongside spectacular chivalric trappings: banquets, hunts and pageantry. This interwoven relationship between the secular and religious aspects of aristocratic culture defined the crusading movement in the fourteenth century.

From an archaeological perspective, the *Reisen* themselves remain largely intangible. Settlement archaeology and palynology consistently indicate limited human activity in the borderlands throughout the fourteenth century. The earliest phase of the easternmost Prussian castle at Lyck (Ełk), a fortified timer structure dating to the early fifteenth century and built on an island in one of the largest lakes in Masuria, is indicative of pressing security concerns (Herman forthcoming). Alongside a series of border castles, the most important base for launching these expeditions was Königsberg (Kaliningrad) (Paravicini 1989: 281). However, the archaeology of its convent and associated three towns remains extremely limited to date. Wall paintings in the cathedral which no longer survive attested the presence of visiting knights, some of whom were buried there and memorialised. Part of a wall painting in the cathedral from 1360 (heavily modified during nineteenth-century restorations) represented pilgrims arriving in Prussia as crusaders (Nowakowski 1994: 34). In other cases, the casualties of the Lithuanian frontier were shipped back to their homelands, as suggested for the 'St Bees Man', identified as Sir Anthony de Lucy who died whilst fighting alongside the Teutonic Order in Lithuania in 1386. He was buried wrapped in lead and beeswax-coated shrouds in St Bees Priory in Cumbria, north England (Knusel et al. 2010). The regular presence of European military retinues had a significant economic impact on the urban complex of Königsberg, although participants would also visit other convents, towns and smaller castles en route to and from the frontier. Occasional finds, such as a fourteenth-century sword pommel recovered during excavations in Frombork and decorated with a heraldic eagle of Thuringian or Hessian origin (Chodyński 2003: 29) provide glimpses of European knights moving through the *Ordensland*.

The official conversion of the Grand Duchy of Lithuania to Catholicism prompted an ideological crisis within the Teutonic Order, which saw the *Reisen* intensify. Samogitia was finally incorporated into the *Ordensland* in 1398, although this was followed by two major uprisings and the borders in this region would not become fixed until the Treaty of Melno in 1422. By this point the Teutonic Order was in terminal decline, severely weakened after its defeat by the Polish-Lithuanian army at Grunwald (Tannenberg, 1410). The loss of its *raison d'être* and the gradual reduction of its lands over the course of the fifteenth century heralded the eventual secularisation of the Order: in Prussia in 1525 and in Livonia in 1561.

CONCLUSION

The crusades in the eastern Baltic were a brutal and formative episode in the history of north-eastern Europe, resulting in the transformation of indigenous tribal societies into Christian polities governed by German theocratic elites, and in north Estonia by the Danish crown until 1346. The archaeology of the thirteenth century across the eastern Baltic region varies, with striking differences between Prussia and Livonia.

In Prussia and southern Curonia, indigenous power structures were completely destroyed, reflected in the abandonment of strongholds and the re-alignment of political, religious and economic authority to the Teutonic Order's convents and episcopal centres with their associated colonies. The indigenous population was not entirely eradicated and remained particularly visible in eastern Prussia, although now re-organised, disenfranchised and subject to taxation and tithes. The Prussian language was slowly replaced by German (and in the southern regions also by Polish), and would become extinct by the seventeenth century. From an archaeological perspective the indigenous population becomes largely invisible after the thirteenth century. The exceptions, to date, are five east Prussian cemeteries where earlier depositional practices continued into the fifteenth century, although the tradition of ritual animal killing and deposition at such sites of public cult activity was suppressed. Later written sources indicate that attempts at Christianising the indigenous population here generally failed, and the proliferation of the new religion was largely driven by incoming colonists who sponsored churches to meet their own spiritual needs. Excavations over the last century have almost entirely focused on the colonising culture established during and after the Prussian Crusade – castles and towns, which have yielded a completely new range of material culture, including new kiln technologies, metalworking, coinage, architectural traditions and imported tableware, more aligned with Catholic, Western European and particularly German-speaking Hanseatic, rather than local Baltic, societies. Future archaeological research may yield new information on the surviving indigenous population in the eastern regions of the Prussian *Ordensland*, or at least problematise our understanding of the encounters between the colonists and the colonised.

In Livonia, as a result of the crusades, some of the Late Iron Age central places were developed into stone castles for the new German (in north Estonia, Danish) authorities, some were destroyed or abandoned, but some continued to operate almost into the mid-fourteenth century, reflecting a different relationship between the incomers and the indigenous population. The regional differences depended on the manner and circumstances of subordination and this also influenced the roles of the native social elite within the new power structures. Evidently, the native elite mediated cultural innovations of European character among the indigenous people. Although the crusades resulted in significant population losses, especially in southern Estonia and Semigallia, the rural population soon recovered at the local level. In contrast to Prussia, the German colonisation of Livonia remained primarily limited to towns, manors, castles and monasteries, with no associated peasant immigration.

In Livonia, the native population preserved much of its social customs, religious and material practices, clearly evident in the archaeology of rural settlements and cemeteries. Religious practices, as represented in both the archaeological and the written record, provide evidence of vernacular religion where rites of pre-Christian origin survived, in parallel to Christian introductions, in a way that cannot be seen in the core areas of medieval Europe. This is clearly visible in the use of local village cemeteries alongside churchyards, and by the use – and large number – of sacred natural sites. The planned urban colonies were inhabited both by colonists and by the indigenous population, and here native forms of architecture and material culture could also be found. However, urban dwellers of indigenous origin appear to have accepted Christianity more readily than people in the countryside. Future archaeology will contribute further to our understanding of these cultural encounters and dynamics, both in towns and in rural areas.

REFERENCES
Primary

CHL = Brundage, J. A. (trans.) (2004) *The Chronicle of Henry of Livonia*. New York: Columbia University Press.

CP = Fischer, M. (trans.) (2010) *The Chronicle of Prussia: A History of the Teutonic Knights in Prussia, 1190–1331*. Farnham: Ashgate.

LRC = Smith, J. C. and Urban, W. L. (trans.) (2006) *The Livonian Rhymed Chronicle*. London: Routledge Curzon.

PD = Wyszomirski, S. and Wenta, J. (trans.) (2011) *Piotr z Dusburga. Kronika Ziemi Pruskiej*. Toruń: UMK.

Secondary

Alttoa, K. (2015) 'Viljandi ordulinnuse arhitektuur/On the Architecture of Viljandi Castle', in *Viljandi ordulinnus ja Lossimäed läbi aja/The Teutonic Order's Castle and Castle Hills in Viljandi through time*. Viljandi Muuseumi Toimetised, V. Viljandi: Viljandi Museum, 87–110.

Apala Z. and Apals, J. (2014) 'The Vendic hill fort on Riekstu kalns in Cēsis', in H. Valk (ed.), *Strongholds and Power Centres East of the Baltic Sea in the 11th–13th centuries*. Tartu: Institute of History and Archaeology, 115–38.

ARE 2006 = Archaeological research in Estonia 1865–2005. *Estonian Archaeology*, 1. Tartu.

Arbusow, L. (1928) *Römischer Arbeitsbericht, I. Acta Universitatis Latviensis XVII*. Riga: Latvijas Universitāte.

Arszyński, M. (2000) 'Zamki i umocnienia krzyżackie', in Z. H. Nowak (ed.), *Państwo zakonu krzyżackiego w Prusach: podziały administracyjne i kościelne w XIII–XVI wieku*. Toruń: UMK, 29–43.

Berga T. (2007) *Augšdaugavas 14.–17. gadsimta senvietas: no Krāslavas līdz Slutišķiem*. Riga: Latvijas Vēstures Institūts.

Białuński, G. (1996) *Osadnictwo regionu Wielkich Jezior Mazurskich od XIV do początku XVIII wieku – starostwo leckie (giżyckie) i ryńskie*. Olsztyn: Ośrodek Badań Nauk. im. Wojchiecha Kętrzyńskiego.

Buschinger, D. and Olivier, M. (2007) *Les chevaliers teutoniques*. Paris: Ellipses.

Caune A. (1984) *Zhilischcha Rigi XII–XIV vv. po dannym arheologiocheskih raskopok*. Rīga: Zinātne.

––––––– (2007). *Pētījumi Rīgas arheologijā : rakstu izlase*. Riga: Latvijas Vēstures Institūts.

Caune, A. and Ose, I. (2004) *Latvijas 12. gadsimta beigu – 17. gadsimta vacu pilu leksikons*. Riga: Latvijas Vēstures Institūts.

CHAPTER 31: *The archaeology of the crusades*

——— (2010) *Latvijas viduslaiku mūra baznīcas. 12. gadsimta beigas – 16. gs. sākums.* Riga: Latvijas Vēstures Institūts.

Chodyński, A. R. (2003) *Broń i barwa w czasach krzyżackich od XIII do połowy XVI wieku.* Malbork: Muzeum Zamkowe w Malborku.

Christiansen, E. (1997) *The Northern Crusades*, 2nd edn. London: Penguin.

Chudziak, W. (2003) *Wczesnośredniowieczna przestrzeń sakralna in Culmine na Pomorzu Nadwiślańskim.* Toruń: UMK.

Czacharowski, A. (1983) 'Toruń średniowieczny (do roku 1454)', in M. Biskup (ed.), *Toruń dawny i dzisiejszy: Zarys dziejów.* Warsaw: Państwowe Wydawnictwo Naukowe, 31–131.

Czaja, R. (2009) 'Urbanizacja kraju', in M. Biskup, R. Czaja, W. Długokęcki, M. Dygo, S. Jóźwiak, A. Radzimiński and J. Tandecki (eds), *Państwo zakonu krzyżackiego w Prusach. Władza i społeczeństwo.* Warsaw: Wydawictwo Naukowe PWN, 177–99.

Długokęcki, W. (2009) 'Prusy w starożytności i we wczesnym średniowieczu', in M. Biskup, R. Czaja, W. Długokęcki, M. Dygo, S. Jóźwiak, A. Radzimiński and J. Tandecki (eds), *Państwo zakonu krzyżackiego w Prusach. Władza i społeczeństwo.* Warsaw: Wydawnictwo Naukowe PWN, 25–50.

Dygo, M. (1989) 'The political role of the cult of the Virgin Mary in Teutonic Prussia in the fourteenth and fifteenth centuries', *Journal of Medieval History*, 15/1: 63–81.

——— (2009) 'Poczatki i budowa władztwa zakonu krzyżackiego (1226–1309)', in M. Biskup, R. Czaja, W. Długokęcki, M. Dygo, S. Jóźwiak, A. Radzimiński and J. Tandecki, *Państwo zakonu krzyżackiego w Prusach. Władza i społeczeństwo.* Warsaw: Wydawnictwo Naukowe PWN, 53–78.

EAA 2006 = Kriiska, A., Tvauri, A., Selart, A., Kibal, B., Andresen, A., Pajur, A. *Eesti ajaloo atlas.* Tallinn: Avita.

Engel, M., Iwanicki, P. and Rzeszotarska-Nowakiewicz, A. (2006) '"Sudovia in qua Sudovitae". The new hypothesis about the origin of Sudovian Culture', *Archeologia Lituana*, 7: 184–211.

Fonnesberg-Schmidt (2007) *The Popes and the Baltic Crusades 1147–1254.* Leiden: Brill.

Gaimster, D. (2005) 'A parallel history: the archaeology of Hanseatic urban culture in the Baltic c. 1200–1600', *World Archaeology*, 37/3: 408–23.

Gazda, D. and Jezierska, J. (2014) 'Badania archeologiczne obiektu warownego w Starym Dzierzgoniu w latach 2010 – 2011', in E. Fudzińska (ed.), *XVIII Sesja Pomorzoznawcza I.* Malbork: Muzeum Zamkowe w Malborku, 365–83.

Haak, A. and Russow, E. (2013). 'On the development of the town of Viljandi in the light of earliest archaeological find complexes', *Estonian Journal of Archaeology*, 17/1: 57–86.

Haftka, M. (2007) 'Wieża mieszkalno-obronna XIII-wiecznej siedziby rycerskiej w miejscowości Podzamcze w Pomezanii', *Archaeologia Historica Polona*, 17: 307–17.

Herman, R. (forthcoming) 'Badania archeologiczne i architektoniczne zamku w Ełku w latach 2011–2012', in Hoffmann M., Karczewski M. and Wadyl S. (eds), *Warmińsko-Mazurska Sesja Sprawozdawcza.*

Herrmann, C. (2007) *Mittelalterliche Architektur in Preussenland: Untersuchungen zur Frage der Kunstlandschaft und -geographie.* Petersberg: Michael Imhof Verlag.

Jarockis, R. (2003) 'Lietuviškosios Žiemgalos dalies apgyvendinimo raida XIII–XVI amžiuje', *Lietuvos archeologija*, 24: 9–16.

Johansen, P. (1933) *Die Estlandliste des Liber Census Daniae.* Copenhagen: Hagerup.

Kalling, K. (1997) 'Uusi paleoantropoloogilisi andmeid Tartu Jaani kirikumatuste kohta. – Arheoloogilisi uurimusi', *Tartu Ülikooli Arheoloogia Kabineti Toimetised*, 9: 54–70.

Knusel, C. J., Batt, C. M., Cook, G., Montgomery, J., Müldner, G., Ogden, A. R., Palmer, C., Stern, B., Todd, J. and Wilson, A.S. (2010) 'The identity of the St Bees lady, Cumbria: An osteobiographical approach', *Medieval Archaeology*, 54/1: 271–311.

Kochański, R. (2001) 'Fosy i mosty jako element obronności zamków krzyżackich w Prusach', *Materiały Zachodniopomorskie*, 46: 457–81.

Kulakov, V. I. (1990) *Drevnosti prussov VI–XIII vv.* Moscow: Nauka.

Lang, V. and Valk, H. (2011) 'An archaeological reading of the Chronicle of Henry of Livonia: Events, traces, contexts and interpretations', in M. Tamm, L. Kaljundi and C. S. Jensen (eds), *Crusading and Chronicle Writing on the Medieval Baltic Frontier*. Aldershot: Ashgate, 291–316.

Laul, S. and Tamla, Ü. (2014) *Peitleid Lõhavere linnamäelt*. Tartu-Tallinn: Tartu Ülikooli arheoloogia osakond, Tallinna Ülikooli Ajaloo Instituut, Õpetatud Eesti Selts.

Laul, S. and Valk, H. (2007) *Siksälä: A Community at the Frontiers. Iron Age and Medieval*. Tartu-Visby: University of Tartu, Institute of History and Archaeology.

Ligi, H. (1968) *Talupoegade koormised Eestis 13. sajandist 19. sajandi alguseni*. Tallinn: Eesti Raamat.

Mäesalu, A. (1991) 'Otepää linnuse ammunooleotsad', in L. Jaanits and V. Lang (eds), *Muinasaja teadus, 1. Arheoloogiline kogumik*. Tallinn: Eesti Arheoloogiaselts, Eesti Teaduste Akadeemia Ajaloo Instituut, 163–81.

Mägi, M. (2001) 'Landed estates on Saaremaa 1100–1400 as recorded in a study of the parish of Pöide', in M. Auns (ed.), *Lübeck Style? Novgorod Style? Baltic Rim Central Places as Arenas for Cultural Encounters and Urbanisation 1100–1400 AD*. Riga: Nordik, 315–28.

——— (2002) *At the Crossroads of Space and Time. Graves, Changing Society and Ideology on Saaremaa (Ösel), 9th–13th centuries AD*. Tallinn: Insitute of History.

——— (2004) 'From paganism to Christianity. Political changes and their reflection in the burial customs of 12th–13th century Saaremaa', in D. Kattinger, J. E. Olesen and H. Wernicke (eds), *Der Ostseeraum und Kontinentaleuropa 1100–1600. Einflussnahme – Rezeption – Wandel*. Schwerin: Thomas Helms Verlag, 27–34.

Marcinkowski, M. (2003) 'Średniowieczny warsztat garncarski ze Starego Miasta w Elblągu', *Pomorania Antiqua*, 19: 194–250.

Markus, K., Kreem, T.-M. and Mänd, A. (2003) 'Sissejuhatus', in *Kaarma kirik*. Tallinn: Muinsuskaitseamet, 11–16.

Mugurēvičs, E. (1973) 'Vidus- un Austrumlatvija 13.-14. gs', *Arheoloģija un etnogrāfija*, 10: 27–39.

——— (1990) 'Interactions between indigenous and western cultures in Livonia in the 13th to 16th centuries', in D. Austin and L. Alcock (eds), *From the Baltic to the Black Sea. Studies in Medieval Archaeology*. London: Routledge, 168–78.

Muižnieks V. (2011) *Arheoloģiskās liecības par 14.-18. gs. apbedīšanas tradīcijām Latvija teritorijā*. Rīga: Promocijas darba kopsavilkums.

Nawrolska, G. (2001) 'Domestic architecture in Elbląg', in B. Dahmen, M. Gläser, U. Oltmanns and S. Schindel (eds), *Lübecker Kolloquium zur Stadtarchäologie im Hanseraum III: der Hausbau*. Lübeck: Schmidt-Römhild, 473–90.

Niinemets, E. (2008) *Vegetation and Land-use History of the Haanja Heights (SE-Estonia) during the Holocene*. Dissertationes geologicae Universitatis Tartuensis, 22. Tartu: Tartu University Press.

Nowakowski, A. (1994) *Arms and Armour in the Medieval Teutonic Order's State in Prussia*. Łódź: Oficyna Naukowa MS.

Paravicini, W. (1989) *Die Preußenreisen des europäischen Adels* (2 volumes). Sigmaringen: Thorbecke.

Pärn, A. (2004a) 'Die Städtegründung en in Estland – Einfluss faktoren auf die Siedlugsentwicklungen', in J. Staecker (ed.), *The European Frontier. Clashes and Compromises in the Middle Ages*. Lund: Almqvist & Wiksell International, 259–82.

——— (2004b) 'Külaehitiste jäljed Haapsalu varases linnaehituses', in *Linnusest ja linnast. Uurimusi Vilma Trummali auks. Muinasaja Teadus*, 14. Tartu-Tallinn: Ajaloo Instituudi arheoloogiaoskond, Tartu Ülikooli arheoloogia õppetool, 269–90.

——— (2009) 'Die Rolle der Esten bei den Städtegründungen Westestlands', in J. Staecker (ed.), *The Reception of Medieval Europe in the Baltic Sea Region*. Visby: Gotland University Press, 109–25.

Pluskowski, A. G. (2012) *The Archaeology of the Prussian Crusade: Holy War and Colonisation*. London: Routledge.

Pluskowski, A. G., Sawicki, Z., Shillito, L.-M., Badura, M., Makowiecki, D., Zabilska-Kunek, M., Seetah, K. and Brown, A. (2014) 'Biała Góra: The forgotten colony in the medieval Pomeranian-Prussian borderlands', *Antiquity* 88/341: 863–82.

Poliński, D. (1996) *Przemiany w wytwórczości garncarskiej na ziemi chełmińskiej u schyłku wczesnego i na początku późnego średniowiecza*. Toruń: UMK.

—— (2003) *Późnośredniowieczne osadnictwo wiejskie w ziemi chełmińskiej*. Toruń: UMK.

—— (2005) 'Gród czy zamek? Z badań nad najwcześniejszymi krzyżackimi obiektami obronnymi w ziemi chełmińskiej', *Archaeologia Historica Polona*, 15/1: 181–96.

—— (2007a) 'Krzyżackie warownie drewniano-ziemne w świetle badań archeologicznych', *Archaeologia Historica Polona*, 17: 241–57.

—— (2007b) 'Wczesne warownie krzyżackie w Prusach w kontekście miejscowych obiektów obronnych w umocnieniach drewniano-ziemnych'. *Archaeologia Historica Polona*, 16: 41–61.

Rozynkowski, W. (2006) *Omnes Sancti et Sanctae Dei: Studium nad kultem świętych w diecezjach pruskich państwa zakonu krzyżackiego*. Malbork: Wydawnictwo Muzeum Zamkowe w Malborku.

Selart, A. and Valk, H. (2012) 'Muutused ja järjepidevus 13. sajandi Liivimaal', in Selart, A. (ed.), *Eesti ajalugu II. Eesti keskaeg*. Tartu: Tartu Ülikooli ajaloo ja arheoloogia instituut, 63–80.

Shiroukhov, R. (2012) 'Prussian graves in the Sambian Peninsula, with imports, weapons and horse harnesses from the tenth to the 13th century: The question of the warrior elite', *Archaeologia Baltica* 18: 224–55.

Stančikaitė, M., Šinkūnas, P., Risberg, J., Šeirienė, V., Blažauskas, N., Jarockis, R., Karlsson, S. and Miller, U. (2009) 'Human activity and the environment during the Late Iron Age and Middle Ages at the Impiltis archaeological site, NW Lithuania', *Quaternary International*, 20: 74–90.

Szczepański, S. (2010) '"Góra zamkowa" w Starym Dzierzgoniu w świetle średniowiecznych dokumentów, tradycji i badań archeologicznych', *Komunikaty Mazursko-Warmińskie*, 2/268: 191–7.

Šnē, A. (2009a) 'The emergence of Livonia: The transformations of social and political structures in the territory of Latvia during the twelfth and thirteenth centuries', in Murray, A. (ed.), *The Clash of Cultures on the Medieval Baltic Frontier*. Aldershot: Ashgate, 53–72.

—— (2009b) 'The early town in Late Prehistoric Latvia', in Staecker, J. (ed.), *The Reception of Medieval Europe in the Baltic Sea Region*. Visby: Gotland University Press, 127–36.

Šterns I. (2002) *Latvijas vēsture 1180–1290. Krustakari*. Rīga: Latvijas Vēstures Institūts.

Tamla, T. (1999) 'Bronzeschalen. Zeugnis der Christianisierung Estlands im 13. Jahrhundert?', in M. Müller Wille (ed.), *Rom und Byzanz im Norden. Mission und Glaubenswechsel im Ostseeraum während des 8.–14. Jahrhunderts*. Mainz: Akademie der Wissenschaften und der Literatur, 9–36.

Tõnisson, E. (2008) 'Eesti muinaslinnad./Prehistoric strongholds of Estonia', in Ain Mäesalu and Heiki Valk (eds), *Muinasaja teadus*, 20. Tartu – Tallinn: Tartu Ülikooli Ajaloo ja Arheoloogia Instituut.

Tuulse, A. (1942) *Die Burgen in Estland und Lettland*. Verhandlungen der Gelehrten Estnischen Gesellschaft. Dorpat: Dorpater Estnishcer Verlag.

Urban, W. (1997) *The Baltic Crusade*, 2nd edn. Chicago: Lithuanian Research and Studies Center.

Urtāns, J. (2008) *Ancient Cult Sites of Semigallia. Zemgales senās kulta vietas*. Riga: Nordik.

Vaitkevičius, V. (2004) *Studies into the Balts' Sacred Places*, BAR International Series 1228. Oxford: Archaeopress.

Valk, H. (2001a) 'Besieging constructions from 1223 in Viljandi', *Arheoloogilised välitööd Eestis/ Archaeological Field Work in Estonia*, 2000: 65–79.

—— (2001b) *Rural Cemeteries of Southern Estonia 1225–1800 AD*. Visby: Gotland University College, Centre for Baltic Studies; Tartu: University of Tartu, Archaeology Centre.

—— (2003) 'Christianisation in Estonia: A process of dual-faith and syncretism', in M. Carver (ed.), *The Cross goes North. Processes of Conversion in Northern Europe, AD 300–1300*. Woodbridge: Boydell, 571–9.

—— (2004) 'Christian and non-Christian holy sites in medieval Estonia: A reflection of ecclesiastical attitudes towards popular religion', in J. Staecker (ed.), *The European Frontier. Clashes and Compromises in the Middle Ages*. Lund: Almqvist & Wiksell International, 299–310.

591

———— (2005) 'The genesis of Viljandi (Fellin): archaeological data', in I. Misāns and H. Wernicke (eds), *Riga und der Ostseeraum. Von der Gründung 1201 bis in die Frühe Neuzeit*. Marburg: Verlag Herder-Institut, 95–107.

———— (2009) 'From the Iron Age to the Middle Ages. Local nobility and cultural changes in Estonia in the 13th century', in J. Staecker (ed.), *The Reception of Medieval Europe in the Baltic Sea Region*. Visby: Gotland University Press, 273–92.

———— (2014) 'The fate of Final Iron Age strongholds of Estonia at transition to the Middle Ages', in H. Valk (ed.), *Strongholds and Power Centres East of the Baltic Sea in the 11th–13th Centuries*. Tartu: Institute of History and Archaeology, 333–384.

———— (2015) 'Viljandi muinasaeg/The prehistory of Viljandi', in *Viljandi ordulinnus ja Lossimäed läbi aja/The Teutonic Order's Castle and Castle Hills in Viljandi through Time*. Viljandi Muuseumi Toimetised, V. Viljandi: Viljandi Muuseum, 5–23.

Valk, H., Pluskowski, A., Thornley, D., Brown, A. and Summerfield, C. (2009) 'Fluxgate gradiometry survey in the ruins of Karksi castle and palaeoenvironmental analysis in its hinterlands', *Archaeological Fieldwork in Estonia* 2007: 134–40.

Valk, H., Rannamäe, E., Brown, A.D., Pluskowski, A., Badura, M. and Lõugas, L. (2013a) 'Thirteenth century cultural deposits at the castle of the Teutonic Order in Karksi', *Archaeological Fieldwork in Estonia* 2012: 73–92.

Valk, H., Kama, P., Rammo, R., Malve, M. and Kiudsoo, M. (2013b) 'The Iron Age and 13th – 18th century cemetery and chapel site of Niklusmägi: grave looting and archaeology' *Archaeological Fieldwork in Estonia* 2012: 109–32.

Valk, H. and Laul, S. (2014) *Siksälä kalme. I: muistis ja ajalugu*. Tartu: Tartu Ülikooli Ajaloo ja arheoloogia instituut.

Valk, H., Ratas, J. and Laul, S. (2014) *Siksälä kalme II: matuste ja leidude kataloog*. Tartu: Tartu Ülikooli Ajaloo ja arheoloogia instituut.

Wacnik, A., Kupryjanowicz, M., Mueller-Bieniek, A., Karczewski, M.and Cywa, K. (2014) 'The environmental and cultural contexts of the late Iron Age and medieval settlement in the Mazurian Lake District, NE Poland: Combined palaeobotanical and archaeological data', *Veget Hist Archaeobot*. DOI 10.1007/s00334–014–0458-y.

Wendt, A. (2011) *Samländische Burgwälle*. Bonn: Habelt-Verlag.

Wróblewski, W., Nowakiewicz, T. and Bogucki, M. (2003) 'Terra desolata. Wczesnośredniowieczna Galindia w świetle badań mikroregionu Jeziora Sałęt', in W. Wróblewski (ed.) *Studia Galindzike* 1. Warsaw: Instytut Archeologii Uniwersytetu Warszawskiego, 157–180.

Zabiela, G. (1995) *Lietuvos medinės pilys*. Vilnius: Diemedis.

Zemītis, G. (2014) 'The hill fort of Satesele – a power centre in the territory of the Livs in the 10th–13th century', in H. Valk (ed.), *Strongholds and Power Centres East of the Baltic Sea in the 11th–13th centuries*. Tartu: Institute of History and Archaeology, 445–461.

Žulkus, V. (2002) *Medieval Klaipeda: Town and Castle. Archaeology and History*. Vilnius: Žara.

———— (2007) *Palanga in the Middle Ages. Ancient Settlements*. Vilnius: Versus aureus.

CHAPTER THIRTY-TWO

INTESTINAL PARASITES IN THE CRUSADES: EVIDENCE FOR DISEASE, DIET AND MIGRATION

————•◆•————

Piers D. Mitchell

INTRODUCTION

In recent years a number of archaeological excavations have identified latrines and cess-pools at Frankish sites in the Latin East. These have been analysed in order to gain further information about the contents when they were in use. This may include the intestinal para-sites present in those using the latrine, the diet of these users, the rubbish that may be thrown in, whether plant materials were used for personal hygiene, the types of fly that bred there, the rodents that scavenged there, and the pollen present indicating the type of vegetation in the region of the town (Mitchell et al., 2008a).

This chapter focuses on evidence for intestinal disease in crusaders and Frankish settlers who used these latrines in the Latin East. First we will explain how we can detect ancient parasites eggs, then summarise the positive results for parasites at crusader sites. With this knowledge we can gain insights into levels of sanitation, diet and cooking efficacy, detec-tion of migration from Europe, and the health consequences of parasitism upon those cru-saders, pilgrims, merchants and settlers who suffered from them.

HOW TO DETECT ANCIENT PARASITES

Parasitic worms (helminths) that infect humans die and decompose soon after they are out-side their host. However, the eggs of many species of parasites are extremely tough and can survive in a recognisable form for long periods in archaeological contexts. They cease to be infective after a few months, but can be identified from their preserved outer wall for hundreds, and sometimes thousands, of years. Parasites that infect the soft tissues of the body are usually only preserved in mummies, and these have not been found from crusader contexts. However, the eggs of intestinal parasites can be found in latrines and cesspools, in coprolites (preserved human stool), and in the pelvic soil of burials, where the intestines of that individual were located during life. These sources of ancient faeces have the potential to be recovered from crusader contexts.

— Piers D. Mitchell —

In order to see if the remains of medieval faeces contain the eggs of intestnal parasites, the material has to be suspended in a solution, known as disaggregation (Anastasiou and Mitchell, 2013a). A number of different methods are available to then separate out the eggs from the soil, including flotation, sedimentation and microsieves. My preferred technique is that of microsieves, as it minimises the need for the use of chemicals that may cause environmental polution after the analysis. The solution of ancient faecal soil is passed through sieves of 300, 160, and 20μm diameter mesh size. As the eggs of instestinal worms are generally 25–150μm in size, they will be trapped on the 20μm mesh. This material is then mixed with glycerol, a drop placed on a microscope slide, and viewed with digital light microscopy at x400–x600 magnification.

Eggs can be identified by their size, shape, colour and special characteristics and standard parasite identification texts can be consulted (Garcia, 2009; Gunn and Pitt, 2012). They may be round, oval, lemon-shaped, have a lid at one end, have a protruding spine, or a special texture to their surface coat. Eggs from intesinal worms are often stained brown by the bile produced by the liver that is secreted into the intestines to aid digestion. Most human intestinal parasites can be identified to species level from their appearance, but some cannot. For example, oocysts of the pork tapeworm (*Taenia solium*), which is contracted by eating undercooked pork, and the beef tapeworm (*Taenia saginata*), contracted by eating undercooked beef, appear identical at this stage of their life cycle so cannot be differentiated with light microscopy alone.

Single-celled parasites can be hard to detect using microscopy in archaeological sediments, as they are much more fragile than the eggs of intestinal worms. This means they are easily damaged or deformed, and so hard to identify from their physical appearance. In consequence, enzyme-linked immunosorbent assay (ELISA) can be used to detect the proteins unique to each species. This technique has been used with success to detect the protozoal organisms that cause dysentery, such as *Entamoeba histolytica* and *Giardia duodenalis* (Goncalves et al., 2002, 2004).

If we want to understand the importance of any parasites at crusader sites, we first need to know what parasite species were present in the Middle East before the time of the crusades, and also what parasites were present in Europe and so would have infected the first crusaders as they headed to the eastern Mediterranean. Once the range of species of parasite is determined, we can use our knowledge of the parasite life cycle and their known distribution in the past to improve our knowledge of what it was like to live in the Frankish states of the Latin East.

PARASITES IN THE MIDDLE EAST PRIOR TO THE CRUSADES

Prior to the arrival of the crusaders, a number of species of parasites are known to have been present in the Middle East. The earliest case of abdominal parasitism so far published from the region is an individual with schistosomiasis dating from 4,500–4,000 BC (Anastasiou et al., 2014). This was located at the site of Tell Zeidan in Syria, on the confluence of the Euphrates and Balikh rivers. The flatworm *Schistosoma haematobium* lives in the bladder and kidneys of people who wade in warm fresh water such as ponds and farming irrigation chanels. It causes anaemia from blood loss in the urine. The parasite has also been found in Egyptian mummies at sites along the River Nile (Deelder et al., 1990). While this parasite does not seem to have ever been endemic along the coastal strip of the Levant, this

594

means that crusaders and pilgrims travelling to Egypt or Syria would have been at risk of contracting the parasite there.

A number of archaeological sites in the southern Levant have been analysed for intestinal parasites. These include Iron Age Jerusalem 700–500 BC (Cahill et al., 1991), the site of the Essenes sect 100 BC–AD 100 at Qumran (Harter et al., 2004; Zias et al., 2006), and Nahal-Mishmar cave AD 160 (Witenberg, 1961). The species identified include roundworm, whipworm, lancet liver fluke, hydatid worm, pinworm, and the beef/pork tapeworm. Ectoparasites in the form of head lice and body lice have been recovered from the fortress of Masada 100 BC–AD 800 (Mumcuoglu and Zias, 1988; Mumcuoglu et al., 2003) and Nahal-Hemar cave 6900–6300 BC (Mumcuoglu and Zias, 1991).

In Egypt a range of mummies and jars of eviscerated organs have been analysed for ancient parasites. Sites studied include Antinoe, Dakhleh Oasis, El-Deir, Hawara, Karnack, Saqqara, Thebes West and the Valley of the Nobles, which date from 3000 BC to AD 500. Species of helminths identified include roundworm, whipworm, Guinea worm, hydatid worm, pinworm, threadworm, liver fluke, fish tapeworm, filarial worm, beef/pork tapeworm, trichinosis and schistosomiasis. The single-celled parasites toxoplasmosis, visceral leishmaniasis and falciparum malaria were also identified, as were head lice (Mitchell, 2013; Anastasiou and Mitchell, 2015).

In Cyprus the only sites where parasites have been studied date from prehistory, so the species present at the time of the crusades may well have been rather different. However, at Shilliourokambos (8300–7000 BC) and at Khirokitia (7000–6000 BC) the parasites found included the roundworm, whipworm, beef/pork tapeworm, fish tapeworm and liver fluke (Guilaine et al., 2005).

PARASITES IN EUROPE PRIOR TO THE CRUSADES

A large range of archaeological sites across many European countries have been studied for ancient parasites. Certain species are found right across the continent, while others seem to be restricted to certain areas. This was often due to the contraints of the parasite life cycle or to the dietary and culinary habits of different cultural groups. The earliest parasite egg identified so far is roundworm, which was found in France and dates from 28,000 to 22,000 BC (Bouchet et al., 1996). Species of parasite infecting humans in Europe prior to the time of the crusades include roundworm, whipworm, beef/pork tapeworm, hookworm, fish tapeworm, liver fluke, bile duct flukes, dicrocoelium, capillaria, giant kidney worm, entamoeba dysentery and giardia dysentery (Anastasiou, 2015).

We can see there is quite a difference in species between Europe and the Middle East/Egypt, and this is in part due to the life cycle of many parasites. The Middle East and Egypt are warm and support a range of insects that can transmit the single-celled parasites such as leishmaniasis. A number of parasites from the Middle East cannot survive the cold winters of Europe, such as schistosomiasis and the guinea worm. In Europe we see changes in species over time, as the species we inadvertently contract from eating wild animals (such as capillaria, giant kidney worm and dicrocoelium) become very rare by the medieval period. However, other species spread by the fecal contamination of food (by fertilising crops with human faeces and not washing hands before cooking food for others) become quite common in Europe by the medieval period. Key examples of such species are the roundworm and whipworm.

Some species were common in certain parts of Europe but absent in other regions. One good example is the fish tapeworm, which was common in northern Europe but rare south of the Alps. Fish tapeworm is acquired by eating raw, pickled, or smoked freshwater fish. In the colder parts of northern Europe it was common to preserve fish by smoking, pickling or drying it while this did not work so well in the warmer climate of the south (Yeh et al., 2014). So far, all examples of entamoeba dysentery found in the world at sites that date to before the medieval period were in Europe. This has led to the suggestion that *Entamoeba histolytica* may have evolved as a species in Europe, before being spread around the world by trade, migratons and wars (Le Bailly and Bouchet, 2015).

This overview helps us to appreciate which kinds of parasites crusaders and pilgrims may have been infected with when they travelled to the eastern Mediterranean, and also which species of parasite were already present in the East. It is clear that some parasites were present in both regions, such as roundworm and whipworm. However, other parasites were only found in one region or the other. This means that some Europeans may have brought species with them that were not present in the Middle East at that time, while others may have arrived and been exposed to new parasites they had never experienced before.

EXCAVATIONS AT CRUSADER SITES

Sarandra Kolones Castle

The Frankish castle of Sarandra Kolones (Forty Columns) was built to defend the port of Paphos in Cyprus (Megaw, 1971; Rosser, 1985). The island was taken from Isaac Comnenus by King Richard I of England in AD 1191, during the Third Crusade. Richard sold the island in 1192 to Guy de Lusignan, the former king of Jerusalem, and the Lusignans ruled the island until 1489. The exact date of the castle's construction is unknown, but must have been built between 1191 and 1222 when it was destroyed in an earthquake. After the earthquake, the ground level shifted so that the medieval port at Paphos dried up. In consequence, the castle was never rebuilt as it was no longer needed to defend the harbour (Boas, 1999: 93–104; Nicole, 2007: 27). This means any parasites found here must date from this narrow thirty-year period. It is the only example of a concentric castle on the island, and its design included four large piers. In one pier there was a well for drinkng water, but in each of the other three piers latrines were built (Figure 32.1). These were located on upper and lower floors, with the faecal waste falling into a cesspool below (Megaw, 1971; Rosser, 1985). Sediment from one of these cesspools was sampled and analysed for the eggs of intestinal parasites.

The eggs of roundworm and whipworm were found in the cesspool soil, but no other species of parasite were observed (Anastasiou and Mitchell, 2013b). Roundworm and whipworm are faecal oral parasites, as they are spread by the contamination of food by faeces. These species of helminth were found across Europe and the Middle East by the medieval period. The results indicate that at least some members of the garison of the castle were infected with these worms, but as the faeces were mixed in a cesspool we cannot tell what proportion of people were infected. The presence of these parasites would be compatible with poor hand washing among cooks in the castle, or the consumption of food that had been grown in fields fertilised using human faeces as manure.

While these two parasite species had been found in Cyprus in prehistory (Guilaine et al., 2005), the other species from prehistory (beef/pork tapeworm, fish tapeworm and live fluke)

Figure 32.1   Latrine from Sarandra Kolones castle in Cyprus (Image Evilena Anastasiou).

were not. This may be a result of the random nature of the samples taken for analysis, and more species may have been detected if the other two cesspools had survived in better condition to permit their analysis. Alternatively, it may reflect changing lifestyle and diet from prehistory to the medieval period, so that the species of parasites that commonly infected people on the island may have changed over that 8,000-year period.

The complex of St John in Acre

The Order of St John built a large complex in the coastal city of Acre, in the Frankish Kingdom of Jerusalem. This has been excavated in recent decades and the internal layout is gradually becoming clear (Goldmann, 1994). Ongoing excavations have identified a latrine block built on several floors. Thirty-five toilet seats (Figure 32.2) were arranged on two floors, with a large cesspool beneath. An irrigation system collected rainwater from the roof and washed throught the drainage shutes with water. The cystern was connected via a drain to larger drains under the city. Samples of sediment were collected from the cystern and drain at the time of its excavation, and underwent analysis for parasites, pollen, seeds and other environmental indicators. Radiocarbon dating has shown that material from the base of the cesspool dated from 1260 to 1310 AD. Since Acre was attacked and destroyed in 1291 AD, the faecal material analysed from this cesspool probably dates from about 1260–91 (Mitchell et al., 2008b).

Figure 32.2   Toilet seats from the latrines of the Order of St John in Acre (Image Piers Mitchell).

Large numbers of fly pupae were recovered, highlighting how flies must have bred in the cesspool. A bone from a small rodent was also recovered, showing how rats or mice must have inhabited the drains and sewers (Mitchell et al., 2008a). Parasite analysis identified the eggs of whipworm, fish tapeworm (Figs 32.3 and 32.4) and roundworm (Mitchell and Stern, 2001). The protozoan parasites *Entamoeba histolytica* and *Giardia duodenalis* were also identified using ELISA analysis, and these organisms can cause dysentery (Mitchell et al., 2008b).

Private houses in Acre

Excavations at Acre have also identified cesspools in private houses dating from the time of the crusader period. In contrast to the large multiseat, mutlifloor latrines of the military orders, private houses generally had more modest cesspools with a single seat. Fewer people would have been using these toilets (perhaps the members of just one family), so we might expect the range of parasites to have been more limited.

A site at the corner of Ha-Amal and Ha-Gedod Ha-'Ivri roads in Akko was excavated in 2003, and this exposed a crusader period cesspool. It is thought to have been located within a private house rather than within a military order or religious order complex. Fragments of ceramics and five crusader coins indicate it was in use during the thirteenth century. The pear-shaped chamber of the cesspool measured 1.77 m in height and 1.4 m in diameter. Parasite analysis detected the eggs of whipworm and the oocysts of beef/pork tapeworm (Figure 32.5) (Mitchell and Tepper, 2007). The samples were also tested with ELISA for the organisms that cause dysentery, but the results were negative (Mitchell et al., 2008b).

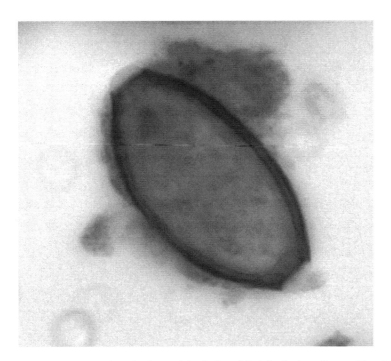

Figure 32.3   Whipworm egg from latrines of the Order of St John in Acre (Image Piers Mitchell).
Egg dimensions 52x21µm.

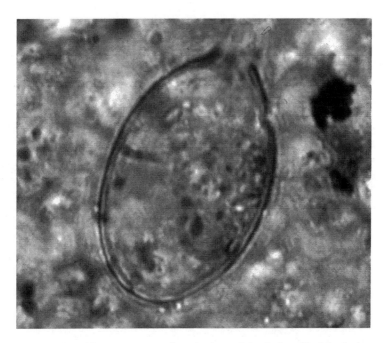

Figure 32.4   Fish tapeworm egg from latrines of the Order of St John in Acre
(Image Piers Mitchell). Egg dimensions 60x45µm.

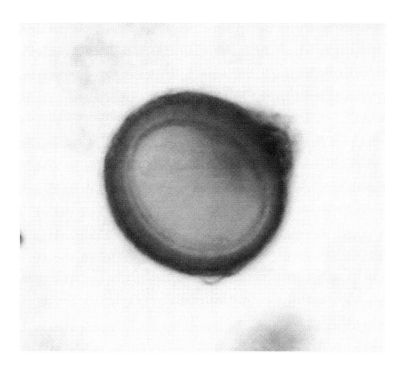

Figure 32.5   Beef/pork tapeworm egg from private house excavated near Ha-Amal and Ha-Gedod Ha-'Ivri roads in Acre (Image Piers Mitchell). Oocyst dimensions 33x34μm.

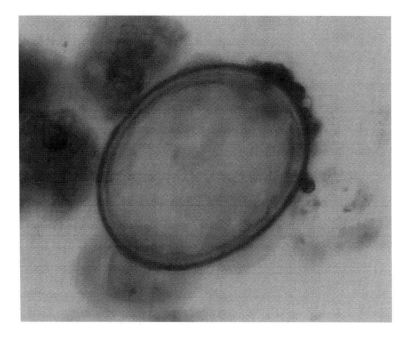

Figure 32.6   Roundworm egg from cesspool in private house excavated near Weizman Street in Acre (Image Piers Mitchell). Egg dimensions 48x37μm.

Table 32.1   Species of Parasite Found in Crusader Period Cesspools

Parasite	Location
Roundworm (*Ascaris lumbricoides*)	Sarandra Kolones Castle Acre, St John Acre, house
Whipworm (*Trichuris trichiura*)	Sarandra Kolones Castle Acre, St John Acre, house
Beef/pork tapeworm (*Taenia saginata/solium*)	Acre, house
Fish tapeworm (*Diphyllobothrium latum*)	Acre, St John Acre, house
Entamoeba dysentery (*Entamoeba histolytica*)	Acre, St John
Giardia dysentery (*Giardia duodenalis*)	Acre, St John

In 2007 a complex of crusader buildings were excavated adjacent to Weizman Street in Akko. Again, these were thought to be in a residential quarter of the old city. Several cesspools were identified, and one was sampled for parasite analysis. This cesspool measured 2.9 m long, 1.7 m wide and about 2 m deep. It was connected to the toilet seat above via a vertical shute. Radiocarbon dating of a fragment of animal rib from the cesspool indicated a likely date for the contents of between 1265 and 1303 AD to 84% probabilty. Since the city was destroyed in 1291, it is likely the contents date from before then. Parasite analysis showed the present of the eggs of roundworm (Figure 32.6) and the fish tapeworm (Table 32.1) (Mitchell et al., 2011).

WHAT THESE DISCOVERIES TELL US

While a range of parasite species have been detected from different crusader sites, we can see quite a variety at each location. No species of parasite has been found at every site. This suggests that people living there were not all infected with the same range of species, and we cannot assume that all people had intestinal parasites. However, our knowledge of the life cycle of those parasites that have been found can help us to understand better the areas of sanitation, diet, migration and health of those living in the Latin East at the time of the crusades.

Sanitation

Some of the species of parasite identified from these latrines indicate the level of effective sanitation for the population. Whipworm and roundworm are parasitic worms that are spread by the accidental consumption of human faeces that contain the eggs (Garcia, 2009; Gunn and Pitt, 2012). This may occur if food plants are eaten that were fertilised with human faeces and not then cooked thoroughly afterwards. Transmission may also take place if a cook prepares and served food without washing their hands thoroughly after going to the toilet themselves. There is some evidence for the efficacy of sanitation in the Frankish States of the Latin East. As we can see from the cases discussed above, the construction of cesspools and latrines was fairly standard in the towns. We also know that some towns such as Acre had a basic system of drains and sewers build under the city (Pringle, 1997; Syon et al., in press). However, when the Muslim traveller Ibn Jubayr passed through Acre during the twelfth century, he noted that the city was 'full of refuse and excrement' (Ibn Jubayr, 1952). It is not easy for us to know whether this indicates Acre was a particularly unsanitary medieval city, or just that Ibn Jubayr wanted to make a point that he felt Muslim cities were cleaner than those of the uncultured European invaders. Either way, it would at least suggest that he was not struck by its cleanliness. Whipworm, roundworm or both were found in each of the cesspools so far analysed at crusader period sites. This would indicate that levels of sanitation allowed the spread of these helminths. However, comparison with medieval towns across Europe shows a similar picture (Anastasiou, 2015), so there is no reason to think that sanitation in Acre was any worse than was the case in Europe at that time.

Diet and cooking

Certain parasites can only be contracted by eating particular foods. For example, fish tapeworm, beef tapeworm and pork tapeworm can only be acquired by eating fish, beef and pork as their names imply. This means that when we find the eggs of these intestinal worms in archaeological samples, we know that these foods were being eaten by the infected individuals. These parasites live for a number of years in the intestines so finding the eggs in a crusader period latrine does not necessarily mean the parasites were contracted in the same town. It is theoretically possible that the meat containing the eggs came from Europe but was consumed in the East (Pryor, 1988), or that the person contracted the parasites in Europe before traveling to the East. However, the recovery of butchered animal bones at a number of crusader period sites in the East such as Belmont Castle, Sumaqa and Caymont shows that a wide range of animals were being farmed or caught from the wild and eaten, such as sheep, goat, cattle, pig, donkey, camel, deer, chicken, pigeon, goose and fish (Croft, 2000; Horwitz and Dahan 1990, 1996). Those species of parasite that are known to have been present in the Middle East prior to the arrival of the crusaders could clearly have been contracted from eating those local foods such as beef and pork.

The eggs of parasitic worms transmitted in food are killed by the heat of cooking. This means that no one would have any fish, beef or pork tapeworms if they cooked these meats thoroughly. People eating pickled, smoked or dried fish or meat consume parasite eggs that are just as viable as the day the animals was killed and butchered. Similarly, no one would suffer with dysentery from giardia or entamoeba if they boiled their drinking water thoroughly. While people in the medieval period did not realise the health benefits of cooking parasite eggs before they ate and drank, we can use this information to help us understand how food was being prepared, stored and cooked. Written texts from the medieval Middle East show that indigenous people there did not eat pickled, salt or dried fish or meat in that state. It was always cooked before consumption (Lewicka, 2011; Rodinson, 2001; Zaouali, 2007). In contrast, northern Europeans often ate smoked, pickled, dried or salted meat and fish (Yeh et al., 2014). This would have put them at increased risk of contracting parasites contained within these foods.

Migration

The crusades were a series of events when large numbers of people travelled from Europe to the East in sequential waves of migrations (Mitchell and Millard, 2009, 2013). Many crusaders and pilgrims suffered with infectious diseases at some stage on their journey (Wagner and Mitchell, 2011). It is not surprising that some spread these diseases from Europe to the East, while others brought them back to Europe (Mitchell, 2011). When we find the eggs of parasites in a new region for the first time, this often indicates that people have migrated from an endemic area taking their parasites with them. Two groups of parasites seem to have been brought to the eastern Mediterranean by crusaders. Fish tapeworm was common in northern Europe during the medieval period, but absent in southern Europe and the Mediterranean region. The finding of fish tapeworm eggs in crusader period latrines suggests that crusaders or pilgrims from northern Europe had travelled to the east with fish tapeworms in their intestines (Mitchell et al., 2011). However, the fact that this parasite is not indigenous to the region today suggests that its life cycle was probably not compatible with the environment of the Middle East, and that it never became endemic there.

Similarly, the single-celled parasite *Entamoeba histolytica* that causes dysentery in humans is thought to have originated in Europe (Le Bailly and Bouchet, 2015). It has never been found in the Middle East prior to the crusades, but has been detected in the latrines of the Order of St John dating from the thirteenth century (Mitchell et al., 2008b). Historical accounts of the Seventh Crusade to Egypt record how in AD 1249 large numbers of the army suffered with dysentery. Indeed, King Louis IX of France suffered so badly that he had the lower part of his breeches cut away so he did not need to pull them down each time he had diarrhoea (John of Joinville, 1955). It may well be that Europeans travelled to the East with dysentery leading to such outbreaks, and so spreading it to the region.

Health

Infection with low to moderate numbers of some intestinal parasites seems to cause no ill effects upon health. In a well-fed person, having a few roundworms, whipworms or a beef tapeworm may well go unnoticed. However, heavier worm loads are known to cause energy malnutrition and anaemia, especially in children who can then experience stunted growth and reduced IQ (Goto et al., 2009; Stephenson et al., 2000). Not everyone with the protozoal parasites entamoeba or giardia develop symptoms of dysentery. However, a proportion of people infected will suffer with severe diarrhoea, and a proportion may die from it (Garcia, 2009, 274).

There were frequent descriptions of famine events during the crusades, sometimes due to sieges, sometimes from natural disasters such as crop failures. Study of named individuals in a number of different two- to three-year-long crusade expeditions suggest that about 15–20% of nobles and clergy died from either malnutrition or infectious disease (Mitchell, 2004). We might expect even higher numbers of poor footsoldiers to have starved, since they had less money and smaller reserves of food. In such circumstances, we would expect that crusaders with intestinal parasites might be at higher risk of starvation if they had to share what little food they had with their worms.

CONCLUSION

It has been shown that study of the contents of latrines and cesspools dating from the crusader period can enlighten us regarding many aspects of life in the medieval period. While information can be acquired from surviving fragments of food, pollen, fly pupae and rodent remains, this chapter focuses on the eggs of intestinal parasites. We have shown evidence for six species of parasites in crusader contexts, namely roundworm, whipworm, fish tapeworm, beef/pork tapeworm, *Entamoeba hystolytica* and *Giardia duodenalis* that cause dysentery. The implications of each parasite for our understanding of diet, health, sanitation and migration have been discussed in order to demonstrate the fascinating new information that can be acquired from human waste.

REFERENCES

Anastasiou, E., Parasites in European populations from prehistory to the industrial revolution. In: Mitchell, P.D. (ed.) *Sanitation, Latrines and Intestinal Parasites in Past Populations* (Farnham: Ashgate, 2015, 203–17).

Anastasiou, E. and Mitchell, P.D., Simplifying the process for extracting parasitic worm eggs from cesspool and latrine sediments: a trial comparing the efficacy of widely used techniques for disaggregation. *International Journal of Paleopathology* 3 (2013a): 204–7.

––––––– Human intestinal parasites from a latrine in the 12th century Frankish castle of Saranda Kolones in Cyprus. *International Journal of Paleopathology* 3 (2013b): 218–23.

––––––– Human intestinal parasites and dysentery in Africa and the Middle East prior to 1500. In: Mitchell, P.D. (ed.) *Sanitation, Latrines and Intestinal Parasites in Past Populations* (Farnham: Ashgate, 2015, 121–47).

Anastasiou, E., Lorentz, K.O., Stein, G.J. and Mitchell, P.D., Prehistoric schistosomiasis parasite found in the Middle East. *Lancet Infectious Diseases* 14 (2014): 553–4.

Boas, A.J., *Crusader Archaeology: the Material Culture of the Latin East* (New York: Routledge, 1999).

Bouchet, F., Baffier, D., Girard, M., Morel, P., Paicheler, J.C. and David, F., Paléoparasitologie en contexte pléistocène: premières observations à la Grande Grotte d'Arcy-sur-Cure (Yonne), France. *Comptes Rendus de l Academie des Sciences (Paris)* 319 (1996): 147–51.

Cahill, J., Reinhard, K., Tarler, D. and Warnock, P., It had to happen: scientists examine remains of ancient bathroom. *Biblical Archaeological Review* 17 (1991): 64–9.

Croft, P., The Faunal Remains. In: R.P. Harper and D. Pringle (eds) *Belmont Castle: The Excavation of a Crusader Stronghold in the Kingdom of Jerusalem* (Oxford: Oxford University Press, 2000), 173–94.

Deelder, A.M., Miller, R.L., de Jonge, N. and Krijger, F.W., Detection of schistosome antigen in mummies. *The Lancet* 335 (1990): 724–5.

Garcia, L.S., *Practical Guide to Diagnostic Parasitology*, 2nd edn (Washington DC: ASM Press, 2009).

Goldmann, Z., *Akko in the Time of the Crusaders: The Convent of the Order of Saint John* (Akko: Government Tourist Office, 1994).

Gonçalves, M.L.C., Araújo, A., Duarte, R., da Silva, J.P., Reinhard, K., Bouchet, F. and Ferreira, L.F., Detection of Giardia duodenalis antigen in coprolites using a commercially available enzyme-linked immunosorbant assay. *Transactions of the Royal Society of Tropical Medicine and Hygiene* 96 (2002): 640–3.

Goncalves, C.L.M., Da Silva, V.L., De Andrade, C.M., Reinhard, K., Da Rocha, G.C., Le Bailly, M., Bouchet, F., Ferreira, L.F. and Araújo, A., Amoebiasis distribution in the past: first steps using an immunoassay technique. *Transactions of the Royal Society of Tropical Medicine and Hygiene* 98 (2004): 88–91.

Goto, R., Mascie-Taylor, C.G.N. and Lunn, P.G., Impact of intestinal permeability, inflammation status and parasitic infections on infant growth faltering in rural Bangladesh. *British Journal of Nutrition* 101 (2009): 1509–16.

Guilaine, J., Le Brun, A., Mort, F.L., Vigne, J.D., Bouchet, F. and Harter, S., Premières données parasitologiques sur les populations humaines précéramiques Chypriotes (VIIIe et VIIe millénaires av. J.-C.). *Paleorient* 31 (2005): 43–54.

Gunn, A. and Pitt, S.J., *Parasitology: An Integrated Approach* (Chichester: Wiley-Blackwell, 2012).

Harter, S., Bouchet, F., Mumcuoglu, K.Y. and Zias, J.E., Toilet practices among members of the Dead Sea scrolls sect at Qumran (100 BCE–68 CE). *Revue de Qumran* 21 (2004): 579–84.

Horwitz, L.H. and Dahan, E., Subsistence and environment on Mount Carmel in the Roman-Byzantine and mediaeval periods: the Evidence from Kh. Sumaqa. *Israel Exploration Journal* 40 (1990): 287–304.

———— Animal husbandry practices during the historic periods. In: A. Ben-Tor, M. Avissar and Y. Portugali (eds) *Yoqne'am I. The Late Periods* (Jerusalem: Israel Exploration Society, 1996), 246–55.

Ibn Jubayr, *The Travels of Ibn Jubayr*, trans. R.J.C. Broadhurst (London: Jonathan Cape, 1952), 318.

John of Joinville, *The Life of Saint Louis*, ed. R. Hague (London: Sheed and Ward, 1955), 24.

Le Bailly, M. and Bouchet, F., A first attempt to retrace the history of dysentery caused by *Entamoeba histolytica*. In: Mitchell, P.D. (ed.) *Sanitation, Latrines and Intestinal Parasites in Past Populations* (Farnham: Ashgate, 2015, 219–28).

Lewicka, P.B., *Food and Foodways of Medieval Cairenes* (Leiden: Brill, 2011).

Megaw, A.H.S., Excavations at 'Saranda Kolones', Paphos. Preliminary Report on the 1966–67 and 1970–71 Seasons (Nicosia: Report for the Department of Antiquities, 1971), 117–46.

Mitchell, P.D., *Medicine in the Crusades: Warfare, Wounds and the Medieval Surgeon* (Cambridge: Cambridge University Press, 2004), 143.

———— The spread of disease with the crusades. In: B. Nance and E.F. Glaze (eds) *Between Text and Patient: The Medical Enterprise in Medieval and Early Modern Europe* (Florence: Sismel, 2011), 309–30.

———— The origins of human parasites: exploring the evidence for endoparasitism throughout human evolution. *International Journal of Paleopathology* 3 (2013): 191–8.

Mitchell, P.D., Anastasiou, E. and Syon, D., Human intestinal parasites in crusader Acre: evidence for migration with disease in the Medieval Period. *International Journal of Paleopathology* 1 (2011): 132–7.

Mitchell, P.D., Huntley, J. and Sterns, E., Bioarchaeological analysis of the 13th century latrines of the crusader hospital of St. John at Acre, Israel. In: Mallia-Milanes, V. (ed.) *The Military Orders: volume 3. Their History and Heritage* (Aldershot: Ashgate 2008a), 213–23.

Mitchell, P.D. and Millard, A.R., Migration to the medieval Middle East with the Crusades. *American Journal of Physical Anthropology* 140 (2009): 518–25.

———— Approaches to the study of migration during the crusades. *Crusades* 12 (2013): 1–12.

Mitchell, P.D. and Stern, E., Parasitic intestinal helminth ova from the latrines of the 13th century crusader hospital of St. John in Acre, Israel. In: M. La Verghetta and L. Capasso (eds) *Proceedings of the XIIIth European Meeting of the Paleopathology Association, Chieti Italy* (Teramo: Edigrafital S.p.A. 2001), 207–13.

Mitchell, P.D., Stern, E. and Tepper, Y., Dysentery in the crusader kingdom of Jerusalem: an ELISA analysis of two medieval latrines in the city of Acre (Israel). *Journal of Archaeological Science* 35 (2008b): 1849–53.

Mitchell, P.D. and Tepper, Y., Intestinal parasitic worm eggs from a crusader period cesspool in the city of Acre (Israel). *Levant* 39 (2007): 91–5.

Mumcuoglu, K.Y. and Zias, J., Head lice, Pediculus humanus capitis (Anoplura:Pediculidae) from hair combs excavated in Israel and dated from the first centrury BC to the eight century AD. *Journal of Medical Entomology* 25 (1988): 545–7.

———— Pre-Pottery Neolithic B head lice found in Nahal Hemar Cave and dated 6900–6300 BCE (uncalibrated). *Atikot* 20 (1991): 167–8.

Mumcuoglu, K.Y., Zias, J., Tarshis, M., Lavi, M. and Stiebe, G.D., Body louse remains in textiles excavated at Masada, Israel. *Journal of Medical Entomology* 40 (2003): 585–7.

Nicolle, D., *Crusader Castles in Cyprus, Greece and the Aegean 1191–1571* (Oxford: Osprey Publishing Limited, 2007).

Pringle, D., *Secular Buildings in the Crusader Kingdom of Jerusalem: An Archaeological Gazetteer* (Cambridge: Cambridge University Press, 1997), 17.

Pryor, J.H., *In subsidium terrae sanctae*: export of foodstuffs and raw materials from the Kingdom of Sicily to the Kingdom of Jerusalem, 1265–1284. *Asian and African Studie,* 22 (1988): 127–46.

Rodinson, M., Studies in Arabic manuscripts relating to cookery. In: Rodinson, M. (ed.) *Medieval Arab Cookery: Essays and Translations* (Totnes: Prospect Books, 2001), 91–164.

Rosser, J., Excavations at Saranda Kolones, Paphos, Cyprus, 1981–1983. *Dumbarton Oaks Papers* 39 (1985): 81–97.

Stephenson, L.S., Latham, M.C. and Ottesen, E.A., Malnutrition and parasitic helminth infections. *Parasitology* 121 (2000): S23–38.

Syon, D, Stern, E. and Mitchell, P.D., Water installations at Crusader 'Akko. *'Atiqot* (in press).

Wagner, T.G. and Mitchell, P.D., The illnesses of King Richard and King Philippe on the Third Crusade: an understanding of arnaldia and leonardie. *Crusades* 10 (2011): 23–44.

Witenburg, G., Human parasites in archaeological findings. *Bulletin of the Israel Exploration Society* 25 (1961): 86.

Yeh, H.-Y., Pluskowski, A., Kalējs, U. and Mitchell, P.D., Intestinal parasites in a mid-14th century latrine from Riga, Latvia: fish tapeworm and the consumption of uncooked fish in the medieval eastern Baltic region. *Journal of Archaeological Science* 49 (2014): 83–9.

Zaouali, L., *Medieval Cuisine of the Islamic World*, trans. M.B. De Bevoise (Berkeley: University of California Press, 2007).

Zias, J.E., Tabor, J.D. and Harter, S., Toilets at Qumran, the Essenes, and the scrolls: new anthropological data and old theories. *Revue de Qumran* 22 (2006): 631–9.

PART VII

ART AND LITERATURE

———•◆•———

CHAPTER THIRTY-THREE

DECORATIVE ARCHITECTURAL SCULPTURE IN CRUSADER JERUSALEM: THE EASTERN, WESTERN, AND ARMENIAN SOURCES OF A LOCAL VISUAL CULTURE

————•◆•————

Nurith Kenaan-Kedar

Since its beginnings, the study of architectural and monumental stone sculpture of the Latin Kingdom of Jerusalem focused mainly on issues of style. It has tried to demonstrate that crusader art depended mainly on French Romanesque and early Gothic art and consequently considered it as an extension or a provincial version of artistic centers in France. Such an approach was expressed by Camille Enlart in the 1920s, whose work on crusader architecture and monumental stone sculpture remains indispensable (Enlart, 1928). Enlart based his study on historical documents and immaculate pictorial comparative style-analysis with Romanesque and Gothic art in various regions of France. In the 1930s Paul Deschamps continued Enlart's work and developed additional methods for stylistic study (Deschamps, 1931). Both Enlart and Deschamps systematically defined any crusader form alien to French and Western medieval sculpture as "Byzantine."

Successive generations of scholars of crusader art have continued to investigate its development in comparison with contemporaneous Western art. The study of monumental sculpture in Jerusalem concentrated on the Church of the Holy Sepulchre, while the other monuments were not always studied in detail. Consequently, whenever similar forms were observed in the Holy Land, Apulia, France, or Sicily, links between specific Western and Eastern objects were proposed. In 1973 I argued that local masons preserved local traditions in the crusader southern façade of the Church of the Holy Sepulchre (Kenaan, 1973). Valentino Pace, however, introduced the concept of Frankish artists who, though born in the Holy Land, remained connected to the traditions of the West (Pace, 1982). This chapter focuses on one major issue: the role and meanings of the goudron frieze in the Crusader churches of Jerusalem.

A NEW URBAN PANORAMA

I believe that in crusader Jerusalem, and mainly during the reign of Melisende as queen or regent for her son (1131–61), one can differentiate between the monuments of the historical city the crusaders found when they arrived, reconstruction of old buildings such as the Church of the Holy Sepulchre, and the construction of new projects.

609

The historical buildings, primarily the Templum Domini and the Templum Salomonis in the Temple area, actually dictated the traditional panorama of the city and thus also served as the model for the new construction undertaken in the Church of the Holy Sepulchre.

The crusaders, accustomed to regard Solomon's temple as an ideal, literary prototype of a church, were confronted in Jerusalem with an earthly Templum Domini built upon the site of Solomon's temple, as well as with Solomon's palace, which was sometimes called Templum Salomonis. At the same time they encountered the church of the Holy Sepulchre, an age-old model for many churches in the West. The crusaders established manifold ties between the temple and the sepulchre and their kings were prominently linked, as well as to the palace of Solomon.

It is plausible to assume that this complex situation led to the choice of a dome for the definite vaulting of the new crusader church of the Holy Sepulchre and to the construction of the double portals, both charged with symbolic meaning (Kenaan-Kedar, 1986).

MELISENDE AS PATRON

Five of the newly constructed projects under the patronage of Queen Melisende created a new urban landscape. The new buildings were constructed in various locations throughout the city, thus bestowing the holy places with an additional layer that reflected the new power and function of the kingdom and the attitudes and intentions of the royal patronage in creating a new urban panorama.

The five building projects and their pictorial language

These are the five main projects which were reconstructed, at least in great part, under the patronage of Melisende and with her great support:

- The Church of the Holy Sepulchre in the center of the city.
- The Abbey Church of Saint Anne in the north-eastern corner of the city, near the eastern city wall. According to William of Tyre, in 1140 she rebuilt the convent of Saint Anne and later the convent of Bethany and endowed it with vast property. Her sister Yveta was installed at Saint Anne as abbess until the convent in Bethany above the tomb of Lazarus could be completed (Folda, 1995: 131–3, 246–9).
- The Armenian Cathedral of Saint James in the south-western sector of the city. It was probably built during her time, since John of Würzburg describes it in 1162 as completed.
- The Armenian Church of the Archangels, not far from the Cathedral of Saint James.
- The royal tombs of Morphia and Queen Melisende in the ancient Church of Saint Mary in the Valley of Jehoshaphat outside the walls facing the eastern city wall which was reconstructed in several parts in the twelfth century (Folda 1995).

I argue that the usage of the goudron frieze on four of these new projects, two Latin (the Church of the Holy Sepulcre, and the Church of Saint Anne) and two Armenian, (the Saint James Cathedral, the Church of the Archangels, and the Tomb of Queen Melisende in the Church of the Assumption of the Virgin) is meaningful and reflects the queen's involvement in the patronage of these projects. It is a declaration of the attitudes and stances of Queen Melisende as the common patron of both the Latin and the Armenian projects and communities of Jerusalem.

The repertory of forms of these churches, their architecture and ground-plans as well as the system of supports such as domes, varied sorts of pillars, and capitals, in addition to their decorative architectural sculpture reveal a wide range of pictorial sources and a distinct relationship of the creators of each of the churches to a pictorial language and its sources. However, even if the vocabulary of forms did vary, four of these projects, with the exception of the Church of Saint Mary in the Valley of Jehoshaphat, share the prominent appearance of the goudron frieze on their façades.

THE GOUDRON FRIEZE: MEANING AND ICONOGRAPHY

As the goudron frieze constitutes a prominent element in the decoration of the portals of the southern façade of the Church of the Holy Sepulchre, it was numerous times an issue of discussion concerning its origins and character. While several scholars ignored it, most scholars relating to it have considered the goudron frieze an "alien" and "foreign" form, and are in agreement that it was a "Muslim" motif (Kenaan-Kedar, 1998: 83–5). It is believed to have first appeared on the Bab-el-Futuh, the wall gate to the city of Cairo built in the eleventh century, a fact brought to support the argument for its Muslim origin. This long-held view was repeated in a new context as late as 1998 (Folda, 1998: 248). However, the same author changed his view in 2012 (Folda, 2012: 470).

I would like to contend that the goudron frieze is a meaningful form that poses its own iconographical significance. Furthermore, I believe it to be an Armenian—or at least a north-Syrian—form, and that its usage constitutes a deliberate declaration. By shedding some light on Armenian art in the Holy Land of the twelfth century, I hope to demonstrate that these Armenian forms were also present elsewhere in the East, but have not been systematically studied. In the following I shall attempt to show that "Armenian" forms belonged to the pictorial tradition of what constituted the Eastern Roman Empire and cannot be defined as simply "local" or "crusader."

However, I was not able to find the goudron frieze in Armenian monasteries, but only similar forms. It was adopted in Syria, Egypt, and in the Holy Land (Utudjian, 1968), as well as in a very few places in the West, as a meaningful symbol by patrons conscious of its significance.

What are the origins of the goudron frieze? Its predecessors had appeared in endless formal variations in Greater Armenia on church portals since at least the sixth century. One prominent example is that from the gate tower of the monastery of Tatevi Egemidzin Gayiane dated to 885 CE (Thierry, 1989). It also appears in northern Syria, and indeed some scholars regard this frieze as being typically north Syrian (Creswell, 1952: 210–11). Its representation on the Bab-el-Futuh in Cairo in the eleventh century in the same form as in Jerusalem is of the utmost significance. The goudron frieze was used here as an isolated element, as it would appear in the future Armenian projects in Jerusalem. The Bab-el-Futuh, like the other gates of the eleventh-century Cairo city walls, was built by Badr el-Djamali, the Fatimid commander-in-chief and vizier (Tyerman, 2006: 128). Of Armenian ethnic origin and a former slave of the Syrian amir, Djamal al-Dawla died in 1094 at over eighty years of age and we know very little about his activities as governor. He provided Cairo with its second wall and its three strong city gates, including the Bab-el-Futuh (Becker, 1960: 869–70; Pringle, 2014: 351). The use of the goudron frieze here was no coincidence. By employing it as a major element in this triumphal gate the governor of Egypt was firmly declaring his origins and ethnic inclinations.

THE GOUDRON FRIEZE IN TWELFTH-CENTURY JERUSALEM

The goudron frieze has a different form and is placed in a different context in the Latin and the Armenian projects. When it becomes part of the decorative architectural sculpture of the two Latin churches, the Church of the Holy Sepulchre and Saint Anne, both of them symbolizing royal power, the goudron frieze is enframed by additional friezes with motifs of classical origin and becomes thereby a local element, part of the routine traditional vocabulary. The goudron frieze stands out on the southern façade of the Church of the Holy Sepulchre, the main project of the Latin Kingdom, as a prominent architectural decoration. It surrounds the double portal in the first floor and the double windows in the second floor, accompanied by additional friezes: a rosette frieze on the double portal and a leaf frieze on the double upper windows. Enframed by a palmette frieze, the goudron frieze appears on the upper window of the abbey church of the Saint Anne Latin convent that was headed by Yvetta, the queen's sister, and supported by Melisende.

The Armenian projects the Cathedral of Saint James—in effect, the largest project constructed in Jerusalem after the Church of the Holy Sepulchre—and the Church of the Archangels. In the Cathedral of Saint James, the goudron frieze surrounds the monumental portal leading from the narthex to the cathedral. It surmounts a smaller frieze in the shape of a rope, installed in the inner portal's tympanum. The form of each unit of the goudron frieze is flatter than the voluminous units in the Latin projects, and may be compared to the Armenian decorative systems in the monastery of Tatev (Thierry, 1989). The goudron frieze in the Church of the Archangels surrounds its portal leading from the narthex to the church, while its units are put very compactly together.

THE WORKSHOPS

Queen Melisende has been presented as the most prominent patron of the arts in Jerusalem between 1131 and 1161, as well as being instrumental, *inter alia*, in getting the masons from the Church of the Holy Sepulchre to work also for the Armenians. Thus the Cathedral of Saint James has remained subject to the traditional belief that as the Church of the Holy Sepulchre was the most prominent architectural project in twelfth-century Jerusalem, the masons employed by the Armenians could have come only from this major project, and the cathedral is of secondary importance (Folda, 1995: 249).

However, I believe that since Melisende was the patron of several building projects in Jerusalem, there were several workshops operating in Jerusalem. These workshops had their pictorial traditions, so that their repertory of forms presents their own significant forms, but feature the goudron frieze at the same time as a prominent element of their façades.

The workshop of the Church of the Holy Sepulchre was responsible for the southern façade, whose two floors are unique in Jerusalem (Fig. 33.1). Even if they may be perceived as Western, their pictorial language is totally different from the Romanesque pilgrim churches with two-floor façades. In the west façade of Saint Sernin in Toulouse, the surrounding window archivolts are built toward the window (Hearn, 1981: 139–41), while in the Puerta de las Platerias in Santiago de Compostela the decorative archivolts have been constructed toward the inner parts of the window enframed by a multilobed arch, a typical Spanish form (Hearn, 1981: 142–6). In addition, a sculptural program is presented between the two floors.

Figure 33.1   Southern façade of the Church of the Holy Sepulchre, Jerusalem.
Photograph: Sarit Uzieli, courtesy of Nurith Kenaan-Kedar.

In the Church of the Holy Sepulchre, however, the friezes accompany the goudron frieze while being installed on the edifice's wall. Moreover, the workshop here is aware of the classical heritage, deliberately employing not Romanesque elements but rather antique forms at large. Outstanding are the cornices in a late antique style and installation: the lower one above the double portal has the form of a meander, maintaining its secondary decorative elements, while the upper one is above the second-floor windows. It is difficult to know whether the installation of the lower cornice is a secondary usage or an imitation of an antique cornice. The capitals recall Justinianic capitals and the rosette friezes relate to antique traditions of the Holy Land. Above all, the double portal is carrying on a dialogue with the double portals of the Golden Gate in the eastern city wall through which Christ was believed to have made his triumphal entry (Kenaan, 1973).

Thus the façade demonstrates extensive use of antique elements. And then, in the middle of this program appears the goudron frieze (Kenaan, 1973). It is difficult to know who initiated this pictorial program, but the work demonstrates great awareness of the classical world at large. The appearance of the goudron frieze thus gains momentum in this façade with decorative elements of antique sources.

The second workshop seems to have been employed on the church of Saint Anne. The façade of the church of Saint Anne is medieval in character, and can be compared to diverse churches in various regions in France, featuring a limited decorative repertoire with antique elements. However, the goudron frieze appears on the single window in the upper part of the façade accompanied by a palmette frieze (Fig. 33.2). The nave capitals of Saint Anne bear no resemblance to the Church of the Holy Sepulchre; they are not chiseled but engraved,

Figure 33.2 West façade of the Church of Saint Anne, Jerusalem.
Photograph: Sarit Uzieli, courtesy of Nurith Kenaan-Kedar.

and display great similarities to sixth-century Syrian capitals, and to capitals on the city wall of Ani in Armenia (Cowe, 2001). Thus the mason workshop of the inner church of Saint Anne presents an independent vocabulary of form, deviating from the façade and capitals of the Church of the Holy Sepulchre.

The third and fourth workshops introduced to the Armenian projects a rich and complex pictorial language of Armenian forms deviating completely from the Latin pictorial tradition. It seems plausible that the third workshop worked on the Cathedral of Saint James, with its own repertory of forms for the inner dome, goudron frieze pillars and the capitals. The fourth workshop worked on the goudron frieze of the portal of the church of the Archangels, and on the capitals in its nave. Furthermore I believe that it worked on the decoration of the outer dome of the Cathedral of Saint James with a series of blind arches carried on twin columns. These Armenian projects represent an autonomous visual culture.

THE ARMENIANS IN JERUSALEM: ASPECTS OF HISTORY AND VISUAL CULTURE

A brief overview of the Armenian community in Jerusalem is called for in order to present the specific visual culture of their monuments (Pringle, 2014). The history of the Armenian community in the Holy Land and Jerusalem goes back to early Christianity. Armenian traditions relate the existence of the community to the third century, while early Armenian monasticism in the Holy Land has been documented at least from the fourth century.

Armenian tradition maintains that the head of St. James the Great was kept in the cathedral, which subsequently became a most holy place of veneration. In addition, several sixth-century mosaic pavements with Armenian inscriptions from sepulchral monuments testify to Armenian awareness of their ethnicity and to artistic activity and active patronage. One example is the mosaic pavement still in situ near Nablus Road, with the Armenian inscription "For the memory and salvation of all the Armenians, whose name the Lord knows." This mosaic pavement depicts vine scrolls stemming from an amphora, spread out symmetrically, each one enframing a bird. Birds were often interpreted as images of the believers' souls. Other inscriptions refer to the monastery of the Armenians.

The relationship between the Armenian principalities and communities in the East, although beyond the scope of this chapter, is a major component for understanding Armenian culture and art in Jerusalem. Constant ties between diverse Armenian communities and the migration of their various populations from one center to another were a factor throughout the Middle Ages. From the end of the eleventh and during the twelfth centuries, the Armenians maintained extensive relations with the arriving crusaders. As was demonstrated (Prawer, 1976), the Armenians enjoyed a privileged position among the other local Christian communities. This was due to two reasons: the vast Armenian population in the crusader principalities, mainly in Edessa and Antioch, and intermarriage between the Frankish and Armenian royal houses and nobility. Baldwin I, first count of Edessa and then king of Jerusalem, married Arda, the daughter of Prince Toros of Edessa, whom he later settled in the Jerusalem convent of Saint Anne. The most influential marriage, however, was that of Baldwin II, king of Jerusalem, to Morphia, the daughter of Gabriel, governor of Melitene. Morphia gave birth to four daughters: Melisende, who was to become the most prominent queen of Jerusalem; Hodierna, princess of Tripoli; Alice, princess of Antioch; and Yveta, who had been a hostage in her childhood and therefore could not marry, but became the Abbess of Saint Anne and later of the convent of St. Lazarus in Bethany through the very strong support and lavish donations of Queen Melisende, her elder sister (Prawer, 1976; Kenaan-Kedar, 1998).

THE TWELFTH-CENTURY ARMENIAN BUILDING PROJECTS

The Church of the Archangels

This church is a three-aisled basilica, preceded by a narthex. There is one portal leading from the narthex to the church. The portal's arch is enframed by the goudron frieze only, with the units put together very compactly (Fig. 33.3). The nave of the church is supported by piers which carry cross-ribbed vaults emerging from stepped machicouli (Fig. 33.4). The capitals are very similar to the capitals bearing the blind arched decoration on the outer face of Saint James dome. These machicouli can also be compared to several capitals from the ninth-century monastery of Tatev.

The Cathedral of Saint James and the third workshop

The Armenian cathedral was the center of the Armenian community of Jerusalem. In a Jerusalem which was not densely built, the cathedral presented a visual world and culture completely different from that of the Church of the Holy Sepulchre. It was not connected to

Figure 33.3   Goudron frieze framing the portal from the narthex to the church, Armenian Church of the Archangels. Photograph: Garo Nalbandian, courtesy of Nurith Kenaan-Kedar.

the classical or Byzantine world, even if certain elements of its architecture were based on them. Armenian pilgrims and travelers frequented the cathedral, in addition to the Church of the Holy Sepulchre.

The twelfth-century Armenian Cathedral of Saint James has been surveyed and described. However, interpretations of the meaning and function of the edifice, in the context of life in the twelfth-century Armenian community in Jerusalem, have not been presented. The cathedral was, however, described in detail and defined as having "an Armenian, that is oriental design" (Folda, 1995: 247). It was also described as a middle Byzantine creation (Kühnel, 1994).

The ground plan of the cathedral as well as its architectural elements demonstrate some affinity with Byzantine and Armenian architectural traditions of the eleventh and twelfth centuries, thus differing consciously from the crusader plan of the Church of the Holy Sepulchre. Its narthex can be only partly evaluated, as the original façade was destroyed in the seventeenth century. While it is Byzantine in origin, the pictorial language of its portal, however, consists of the goudron frieze as its main decoration accompanied by a small frieze in the portal's tympanum. The particular flat form of the goudron frieze differs

Figure 33.4   Main nave, Armenian Church of the Archangels. Photograph: Garo Nalbandian, courtesy of Nurith Kenaan-Kedar.

significantly from the one on the façade of the Holy Sepulchre church and can be compared with Armenian decorative systems (Fig. 33.5).

The frieze accompanies the arches and is cut in the wall surfaces. On the walls beside it are elbow capitals receiving the ceilings ribs and "elbow colonnettes."

The most prominent element of the cathedral is its dome which presents completely different forms in its inner and outer forms (Figure 33.6). The inner dome is decorated with six intersecting ribs which form a star on a square base with a decorative schematic garland frieze, thus deviating from the Byzantine hemisphere dome. The supporting piers are square, with four capitals on each side, suggesting the original existence of half columns decorated with large smooth leaves. These capitals with animals carved on their leaves do not show any similarity with the capitals of the other projects mentioned above. However, the outer dome is decorated in a completely different pictorial language than the inner one. The outer form of the dome and its decoration has not yet been considered by scholarly literature. This decoration consists of a series of blind arches carried alternatively by small twin and single columns with uncarved capitals running all around the dome. Their form is very similar to the blind arches decoration of the dome of the Redeemer Church at Ani, from the eleventh century, which possesses the same form of capitals and columns; it resembles also the capitals in the form of stepped machicouli of the central nave of the Church of the Archangels. Evidently, this outer form of the dome, which is Armenian and might even be considered archaic, was created by one of the Armenian workshops (Figs 33.7 and 33.8). This decoration has no relationship to Latin architecture and presents a completely different perception compared to the dome of the Church of the Holy

617

Figure 33.5 Goudron frieze framing the portal from the narthex (the Etchimiadzin chapel) to the Cathedral of Saint James. Photograph: Garo Nalbandian, courtesy of Nurith Kenaan-Kedar.

Sepulchre, which is a hemisphere and is decorated on its outer face with ninety-six corbels (Kenaan-Kedar, 1992).

I believe that this form of dome is distinctly Armenian. Thus, the choice of two sets of Armenian formal systems, one for the inner dome and one for the outer dome of the Armenian cathedral, was no coincidence but must have been intentional and symbolical for the Armenian community and Queen Melisende.

The Tomb of Melisende in the Church of Saint Mary in the Valley of Jehoshaphat

Melisende was buried in the church of the Tomb of the Virgin Mary in the Valley of Jehoshaphat, much patronized by the royal house (Kenaan-Kedar, 1998: 86–90; Folda, 1995: 324–6; Bagatti et al., 1975: 83–93). The queen supported the church with many gifts during her reign, making the convent one of the richest in the kingdom.

618

Figure 33.6   The inner dome, Cathedral of Saint James. Photograph: Sarit Uzieli, courtesy of Nurith Kenaan-Kedar.

The Church of the Tomb of the Virgin Mary was probably founded in the fourth century. However, it was rebuilt and enlarged in the twelfth century under the crusaders (Bagatti et al., 1975: 84). It is known that the queen's mother, the Armenian Queen Morphia, was already buried there probably on the left side of the stairs. William of Tyre describes the location of Melisende's sepulchral chamber precisely: "The first chamber on the right when descending the stairs" (William of Tyre, 1986: 18.32, 858).

The royal sepulchral chamber is entered through a large arch decorated with floral *cassettoni* recalling an antique arcosolium. The inner space of the chamber has been planned with meaningful architectural elements. Two niches are situated in the southern and northern walls of the chamber, for the placement of two sarcophagi. The niches are enframed with quasi pediments cut with inner profiles, as is routine in Armenian architecture. The chamber's most outstanding element, however, is the domed lantern crowning its center.

The dome is built on a square ground plan with an octagonal base on squinches and a round form in its upper part. It is thus a characteristic Armenian dome, like those in

Figure 33.7 Outer panorama of the dome of the Cathedral of Saint James. Photograph: Sarit Uzieli, courtesy of Nurith Kenaan-Kedar.

Figure 33.8 Outer panorama of the dome of the Cathedral of Saint James: detail. Photograph: Sarit Uzieli, courtesy of Nurith Kenaan-Kedar.

the monastery churches of *Haphpat* from the end of the eleventh century (Thierry, 1989: 534–5, fig. 734). The use of a dome for a sepulchral chamber is unique in itself. None of the crusader kings were buried under a dome, nor any contemporaneous Western king, as far as I am aware. Thus, the dome symbolizing eternity appears here again to be reflecting a deliberate choice (Fig. 33.9).

It has been suggested that the sepulchral dome was derived from the dome of St. Helen Chapel in the Church of the Holy Sepulchre (Bagatti et al., 1975: 131; Folda, 1995): The dome of St. Helen, however, is a regular Byzantine hemispheric one and has no relation to Melisende's tomb. Thus, in the choice of an Armenian dome—recalling the dome crowning the Armenian cathedral—for her own royal tomb, Melisende deliberately associated herself with the Armenian cathedral.

THE GOUDRON FRIEZES: THEIR ROLE AND MEANING IN THE NEW BUILDING PROJECTS

The goudron frieze reflects the work of different workshops and traditions. It stands out most clearly on the façade of the Church of the Holy Sepulchre. It is larger and more voluminous while the accompanying friezes remain two-dimensional. In a similar form it appears around the upper window on the west façade of Saint Anne. The flat and compact goudron frieze in its particular Armenian form appears as the major decoration around the central entrance portal from the southern narthex to the Cathedral of Saint James and the Church of the Archangels introduces to Jerusalem Armenian architectural decoration, creating a local and unique visual panorama.

Figure 33.9 Dome of the Tomb of Melisende. Photograph: Garo Nalbandian, courtesy of Nurith Kenaan-Kedar.

THE GOUDRON FRIEZE IN THE WEST

In the twelfth century, the goudron frieze made its first appearance in the West, in the Church of Santa Maria del'Admiralio, the Martorana, in Palermo and in a little church in Marignac (Saintonge). I believe that in these two places, too, the frieze was selected for its significance, in this case via appropriation of meaning for a different place and purpose.

In the Martorana, the frieze appears only on the entrance bell tower. The church, as is well known from surviving documents as well as from the imagery of its mosaic decoration, was built by George of Antioch, admiral to King Roger II, as a sepulchral monument to his mother, his wife, and himself. In his architectural analysis of the church, Slobodan Čurčič suggested that a workshop from the Holy Land came to Palermo to work on the bell tower and introduced the goudron frieze (Čurčič, 1990). I suggest that in the traditions of the eastern Mediterranean, George of Antioch, a Greek Orthodox, wished to display the goudron frieze, a traditional symbol of eternal victory, on the church bell tower in order to inform posterity of his Syrian origins.

An additional appearance of the goudron frieze is in the Church of Marignac, where it decorates the inner arches of a triconch apse recalling the rotunda of the Church of the Holy Sepulchre (Semur, 1984: 176). Consequently, this frieze may be regarded as proclaiming the church patron's association with the Church of the Holy Sepulchre as a pilgrim or a crusader.

CONCLUSION

In this chapter, I have attempted to show that both Melisende as patron, and the workshops she employed, were familiar with Armenian and Western pictorial traditions and their respective roles and meanings. The exclusive usage of prominent Armenian forms in the Armenian projects in such a small distance from the Latin churches demonstrate the awareness of the builders and the patron of the power and meanings of architectural images and their decorations. This plural perception of the unique visual traditions of each of the communities contributed to the new urban scenic view and panorama of Jerusalem.

REFERENCES

Bagatti, B., Piccirillo, M., and Prodomo, A. (1975) *New Discoveries at the Tomb of Virgin Mary in Gethsemane*, Jerusalem: Franciscan Printing Press.

Becker, C.H. (1960) "Badr al-Djamali," in *the Encyclopaedia of Islam*, vol. 1, Leiden and London: Brill, 869–70.

Creswell, K.A.C. (1952) *The Muslim Architecture of Egypt*, 2 vols, Oxford: Clarendon Press.

Cowe, S.P. (2001) *Ani: World Architectural Heritage of a Medieval Armenian Capital*, Sterling, VA: Peeters

Čurčič, S. (1990) "The architecture," in E. Kitzinger (ed.), *The Mosaics of St. Mary's of the Admiral in Palermo*, Washington, DC: Dumbarton Oaks.

Deschamps, P. (1931) *La sculpture française en Palestine et en Syrie a l'époque des Croisades*, Paris: Ernest Leroux.

Enlart, C. (1928) *Les monuments des croisés: le royaume de Jérusalem: architecture religieuse et civile*, Paris: P. Geuthner.

Folda, J. (1995) *The Art of the Crusaders in the Holy Land, 1098–1187*, Cambridge: Cambridge University Press.

——— (1998) "The south transept façade of the Church of the Holy Sepulchre in Jerusalem: an aspect of 'rebuilding Zion'," in J. France and W.G. Zajac (eds), *The Crusades and Their Sources: Essays Presented to Bernard Hamilton*, Aldershot: Ashgate, 239–57.

——— (2012) "Melisende of Jerusalem: queen and patron of art and architecture in the Crusader kingdom," in T. Martin (ed.), *Reassessing the Roles of Women as "Makers" of Medieval Art and Architecture*, 2 vols, Leiden: Brill, 429–77.

Hearn, M.F. (1981) *Romanesque Sculpture: The Revival of Monumental Stone Sculpture in the Eleventh and Twelfth Centuries*, Oxford: Phaidon.

Kenaan, N. (1973) "Local Christian art in 12th century Jerusalem," *Israel Exploration Journal*, 23: 165–75, 221–9.

Kenaan-Kedar, N. (1986) "Symbolic meaning in Crusader Architecture," *Cahiers archéologiques*, 34: 109–15.

——— (1998) "Armenian architecture in twelfth century crusader Jerusalem," in *Assaph, Studies in Art History*, Section b, 3: 77–91.

——— (1992) "The ninety-six corbels of the Church of the Holy Sepulchre," *Israel Exploration Journal*, 42, 1–2:103–13, figs. 1–13.

Kühnel, B. (1994) *Crusader Art of the Twelfth Century: A Geographical, an Historical, or an Art Historical Notion?* Berlin: Gebr. Mann.

Pace, V. (1982) "Italy and the Holy Land: import and 2: the case of Apulia," in J. Folda (ed.), *Crusader Art in the Twelfth Century*, Oxford: B.A.R., 245–69.

Prawer, J. (1976) "The Armenians in Jerusalem under the Crusaders," in M.E. Stone (ed.), *Armenian and Biblical Studies*, Jerusalem: St. James Press, 222–35.

Pringle, D. (2014) "Crusader Castles and Fortifications: The Armenian Connection," in G. Dédéyan and C. Mutafian (eds.), *La Méditerranée des Arméniens, XIIe–XVe siècle*, Paris: Geuthner, 353–72.

Semur, F. (1984) *Abbayes, prieurés et commanderies de l'ancienne France: Poitou-Charentes, Vendeé*, Bannalec: F. Semur.

Thierry, J.-M. (1989) *Armenian Art*, New York: Abrams.

Tyerman, C. (2006) *God's War: A New History of the Crusades*, Cambridge: Belknap Press.

Utudjian, E. (1968) *Armenian Architecture*, Paris: Editions A. Morancé.

William of Tyre (1986) *Guillaume de Tyr, Chronique*, ed. R.B.C. Huygens, Corpus Christianorum, Continuatio Mediaevalis LXIII, Turnhout.

CHAPTER THIRTY-FOUR

CRUSADER ART AND THE WEST: THOUGHTS ON ASSESSING THE IMPACT OF ART FROM THE CRUSADER EAST ON MEDIEVAL ART IN WESTERN EUROPE, ESPECIALLY IN CENTRAL ITALY

——•◆•——

Jaroslav Folda

INTRODUCTION

In attempting to address the complex issue of the impact of crusader art on the art of western Europe in the twelfth and thirteenth centuries, it is worth noting that this is a topic very little discussed to date.[1] Furthermore there are certain important problems that are directly relevant to such a discussion which must be taken into account as research goes forward. Looking at the second point first, it is clear that although the idea and existence of what is perhaps most accurately called the art of the crusaders in the Holy Land, and also known as crusader art for short, is now widely accepted, there are still dissenting views about it. On the one hand, whereas the art of the crusaders in the Holy Land has been argued to be a major chapter in the history of medieval art in the Mediterranean world between 1098 and 1291, the older more doubtful view, first voiced before 1957, is still occasionally found.[2] And even though a wide consensus about the existence of crusader art and crusader artists continues to grow and develop, the fact is that our understanding of what constitutes a work of crusader art is also changing. Indeed as we learn more about the characteristics of certain kinds of crusader art, most recently in particular, about icons and panel paintings, icons once considered Byzantine have been reinterpreted to be crusader. Certain characteristics pertaining to the overwhelming majority of works identified as crusader icon painting continue to be recognized, namely the fundamental Byzantinizing tradition that the crusader artist creates in his own idiom. But the subtlety and sophistication of the ways a crusader painter could appropriate, emulate, and also reinterpret the artistic characteristics of Byzantine originals in certain innovative ways are increasingly coming to light. One of the most notable examples of an icon formerly held to be Byzantine, but recently argued quite persuasively to be crusader, is the well-known mosaic icon of the Virgin and Child *Hodegetria* (bust-length) now in the Monastery of St. Catherine on Mount Sinai, probably done in Constantinople

624

sometime shortly after 1204, that is, shortly after the crusader conquest of the city (Fig. 34.1).[3] Given our new understanding of this icon, we must first signal that there are other Byzantine-looking icons like this one which are currently in the process of being reconsidered and reinterpreted from differing points of view. And we must keep these dynamics in mind as we attempt to consider the impact of crusader art on the West. The fact is that in this chapter we can only offer some preliminary discussion about this issue and raise some important questions, while the basic identification of works of art as "crusader" goes on, and some new examples of ways crusader art appears to have had an impact on the art of western Europe are proposed. Our focus here will therefore be on sharpening our understanding of what characterizes certain crusader icons, and starting to assess the impact of crusader icon painting on the medieval art of western Europe, especially central Italy.

At the outset we can recall that the attention of modern scholars to the existence of the art of the crusaders in the Holy Land began in the 1950s. Between 1957 and 1976 new discoveries in the field of crusader painting identified over twenty manuscripts for which arguments were presented locating their place of production in Jerusalem, Acre, and Antioch during the time of the crusader states in Syria/Palestine during the twelfth and thirteenth centuries.[4] Meanwhile approximately some 120 "western influenced icons" were identified in the collection of the Holy Monastery of St. Catherine on Mount Sinai of which somewhat less than half were published in a series of articles by Kurt Weitzmann between 1963 and 1982.[5] These icons were argued to have been done by crusader artists and/or for crusader

Figure 34.1   Crusader icon of the Virgin and Child *Hodegetria Dexiokratousa*, bust-length, in Mosaic, Constantinople or Sinai, Monastery of St. Catherine, Sinai, *c.* 1250s. (47.3 x 33.7 cm).
Photograph: Elizabeth Bolman and Jaroslav Folda, by permission.

patrons mainly at St. Catherine's or in Acre. This newly identified material created a core of work focused on painting, whereas the crusader presence in the Holy Land had previously been largely identified through works of architecture and architectural sculpture, starting in the second half of the nineteenth century. These discoveries also generated interest in the art of the crusaders not only in the Holy Land, but also elsewhere, such as the existence of art done for crusaders in the Latin Empire of Constantinople[6] and on Cyprus.[7] It also stimulated study of other media, such as metalwork, coinage, fresco painting, mosaics, and glass, as well as renewed interest in figural and decorative sculpture and architecture commissioned by and/or for the crusaders. The result has been a series of broad-based studies which have attempted to assess what is known about and document the art of the crusaders in the Holy Land, and articulate the state of the question. Notable among these studies have been a four volume study of the churches of the crusaders and two volumes on the art of the crusaders in the Holy Land between 1098 and 1291.[8]

It was during this same period, when art commissioned by or produced by the crusaders was coming into focus, between the 1950s and the early 1980s, that study of the art of Byzantium had developed to a point where art historical scholarship also generated renewed attention on the dynamics of East–West interchange and, in particular, the impact of Byzantine art in the West. In 1970 Otto Demus published a volume entitled *Byzantine Art and the West*, which was based on the Wrightsman Lectures given by him in 1966. The purpose of that book was, "to show the role played by the art of Byzantium in the development of Western art."[9] But it was a limited role, "not all the Byzantine elements," but "only those which have something to do with art in the proper sense of the term and especially with the creation and the evolution of the artistic language in the figurative arts."[10] Demus was, of course, not the first scholar to plunge into to this topic; Wilhelm Köhler had given a famous paper with a slightly different title, "Byzantine Art in the West," at the inaugural symposium held at Dumbarton Oaks in 1940.[11] But the six lectures published by Demus represented a considerable expansion of scholarly inquiry into this field, not only by him, but also by others.

These lectures by Demus were stimulated by or formed part of an ongoing then current international discourse in examining the role of Byzantine art as having had an important impact on the art of western Europe from the Carolingian period to the high Middle Ages. Three other important and contemporary art historical events generated particular attention to the understanding of the Byzantine artistic tradition and how it was manifested and participated in the development of medieval art in the West. First, there was the Council of Europe exhibition in Athens in 1964, "Byzantine Art, a European Art," with a Symposium in Athens, from which seven papers were published in 1966.[12] Second, there was the symposium at Dumbarton Oaks in 1965 dealing with "The Byzantine Contribution to Western Art of the Twelfth and Thirteenth Centuries." Selected papers of this conference were published in the *Dumbarton Oaks Papers*, vol. 20, for 1966.[13] Third, there was an exhibition entitled "The Year 1200" held at the Metropolitan Museum of Art from February to May, 1970, with a symposium held in March 1970. The papers given at that 1970 symposium were overwhelmingly focused on art in the West—only one paper dealt at length with Byzantine art as compared to twenty-four on works of art in western Europe—but these papers could be said to have complemented and expanded the scholarship presented at the earlier symposia in certain ways.[14]

The result was that by the 1970s a framework of understanding about the dynamics and timing of the impact of the Byzantine artistic tradition on the Latin West had been formulated with regard to the twelfth and thirteenth centuries. Within this framework, we can recognize the following overall assessment: "Byzantine art exerted its strongest, deepest, and most diverse influences upon the Latin West in the twelfth and thirteenth centuries."[15] Kurt Weitzmann then distinguishes certain levels of impact, two of which we can restate for purposes of introduction:

1   "The first level, that of the most direct impact of Middle Byzantine art, is found in those centers where Byzantine artists were commissioned to execute large projects in their own style and to emulate the high artistic standards of Constantinople."[16] Venice and Sicily provide the key examples.
2   "The second level of penetration of Byzantine art can best be studied in Italian panel painting of the Duecento."[17] Weitzmann goes on to say, "the sudden outburst and mass production of panel painting in the thirteenth century in the Latin West and especially in Italy ... was obviously due to a strong stimulus from the Greek East."[18] "In this outburst of artistic activities ... Byzantine icons played a major role."[19]

Otto Demus agreed with Weitzmann, and he commented on it this way: "had it not been for ... Byzantine icon painting and the transfer of this art form to the West, the chief vehicle of Western pictorial development [by which he meant Italian panel painting] would not have existed or would have come into existence a good deal later."[20]

But if both Weitzmann and Demus agreed that Byzantine icons were of major importance, the two of them, and Ernst Kitzinger as well,[21] had major reservations and questions about how the Italians could have known about the Byzantine icons. Indeed, specifically what Byzantine icons could the Italians have known? How could the Italian painters have learned about them and from them? What other ways might the Italian artists have learned about the Byzantine tradition?

One issue they sought to assess therefore was what original Byzantine icons on wood panels the Italian painters could have seen in Italy during the thirteenth century, that is, icons surviving today that were known to be there before 1300. Kurt Weitzmann set out to do this with the result that among the best known there were three of note. First, there is the Virgin of Spoleto from the twelfth century, an icon which had formerly belonged to Petrus of Alipha, a crusader of the entourage of Robert Guiscard.[22] Second, there is the Virgin *Hagiosoritissa* in Freising from the mid-thirteenth century.[23] And third, there is the Virgin *Hagiosoritissa* in the Cathedral of Fermo, from the second half of the thirteenth century. To this number may be added a fourth, quite modest Byzantine icon, an image of the Virgin and Child *Hodegetria* (bust-length) from the church of the Carmine in Siena, now in the Pinacoteca Nazionale on deposit. It clearly appears to have been done in the early thirteenth century and was apparently brought to Siena by the Carmelites shortly after it was done.[24] This fourth example is important because, unlike the first three, it is an icon type widely venerated in the East and West,[25] and it was located in a center, Siena, known to be important for the development of Tuscan painting in the thirteenth century.

Weitzmann's assessment is, in any case, completely valid that the original Byzantine icons known to be in Italy in the thirteenth century are "surprisingly limited in number" and that "such imports were obviously too few in number to be held responsible for the start of a mass movement of creating panel paintings in the style of the *maniera greca*."[26] With this in mind, Weitzmann, Demus and Kitzinger considered—directly or indirectly—the idea that crusader icons might have also played a role in this process, given their strongly

Byzantinizing character, despite the fact that at that time, in 1965, even fewer crusader icons could be documented as being located in Italy in the thirteenth century.[27] Ernst Kitzinger proposed to identify the Virgin and Child *Hodegetria Dexiokratousa* now in Grottaferrata as one such example, but of course we do not know exactly when it reached Italy.[28] Otto Demus himself, writing in 1970, was thinking along similar lines when he said: "recent research in the art of the Crusader States, Jerusalem, Acre and Cyprus, by Professor Buchthal and Professor Weitzmann suggests that the hybrid art which grew up in these regions from the symbiosis of Byzantine, Armenian and Western artists may have had much more important repercussions on Western art, and especially on Italian art, than we were led to believe until now."[29] Weitzmann's idea was that in effect since not many Greek icons appear to have reached Italy at this critical time, the tradition of Byzantine style and imagery became known mostly through what he called "intermediary copies."[30] Of the intermediary copies that might be possible, one can mention portable objects such as sketches in model books and miniature paintings in manuscripts, intermediaries also discussed by Kitzinger and Demus.[31] But the most interesting intermediaries that Weitzmann proposed had to do with crusader icons, and in his 1984 article he discusses a small number of specific examples.[32]

By briefly having retraced selected outlines of the arguments offered by these three scholars, we arrive at the point where we can now entertain more fully the important idea that to some extent crusader icons, and crusader painters, were responsible for transmitting what I am calling the "Byzantinizing tradition" from the Byzantine and crusader East to western Europe, and specifically to central Italy. And let me be clear: by "Byzantinizing tradition" I refer to the Byzantine-inspired artistic ideas which the crusader painters appropriated and reinterpreted to produce icon painting for their patrons which, while often strongly Byzantine in character, combined innovative versions of the artistic form, the imagery, the techniques and the content of their icons derived from their own ancestry, training and experience to produce what we call crusader icon painting. "Byzantinizing" refers to the hybrid combination of Byzantine, crusader and Western characteristics, which differentiated a crusader icon from a pure Byzantine icon. The Byzantinizing tradition also refers to the style, imagery and content of these icons as distinct from what came to be called by Vasari and others much later as the *maniera graeca* in Italy. Whereas from an Italian Renaissance point of view the *maniera graeca* was largely seen as a negative development in earlier Italian painting, the "Byzantinizing tradition" of crusader icons and icon painters and its impact on Italian panel painters was a positive development in medieval art that generated important stimulus and innovative ideas for the Italian artists, especially the central Italian panel painters whose work we study in the period from *c.* 1225 to 1311, and some of whose names we know, artists such as Coppo di Marcovaldo, Guido da Siena, Cimabue, and Duccio.[33] In sum, from the point of view of this discussion, it is important to understand that whereas the influence of Byzantine art on the art of the medieval West has been an issue of scholarly concern for some time, the realization that crusader art could be and often was the vehicle for the transmission of Byzantine artistic ideas via the Byzantinizing tradition is rather a more recent development. As we continue to understand more clearly the nature and characteristics of the art of the crusaders in the period from 1099 to 1291, it is gradually becoming possible to identify the various ways crusader art could and did have an impact on medieval art in the West.

In order to demonstrate the characteristics of a newly identified crusader icon and its Byzantinizing tradition as an innovative work in crusader terms and as a possible "intermediary copy" in Weitzmann's terms, consider the well-known mosaic icon from Sinai referred to above (Fig. 34.1).[34] Initially this relatively small icon (34 x 23 cm, without the frame) was attributed to Constantinople as the work of a Byzantine artist reflecting the monumental style of the early thirteenth century. The artist worked in the most refined technique, with minute tesserae which, in the areas of flesh on the faces, hands, and feet of the two figures are almost undiscernible by the naked eye. The individual tesserae, while tiny, are however visible on the Virgin's purple maphorion with chrysography, and in the decorative background of stylized rosettes, which imitate cloisonné enamel. The imagery represents the Virgin and Child *Hodegetria Dexiokratousa*, a variation on the original type said to have been painted by St. Luke, on which the Child appears on the Virgin's left arm. One also notes the inclination of the Virgin's head toward the child is slightly more pronounced than usual, suggesting a closer relation of Mary to Jesus, without impairing "the aloofness and emotional restraint" of the Virgin. Also somewhat unusual is the way the Child braces the scroll he holds against his knee with a closed fist. These points observed by Weitzmann served to situate this icon in the scholarly discussion until a new interpretation was recently proposed by Bissera Pentcheva.[35]

With regard to special characteristics in the imagery of this icon, Pentcheva goes beyond Weitzmann's observations to note three additional items which she links to distinctive imagery that "proleptically evoke Christ's crucifixion." First, we see the bare feet of the Child with the sole of one exposed to the viewer. Second, there is the special Greek blessing gesture of Christ, and third, the fact that he turns his blessing hand toward his Mother. These features appear to have been inspired by earlier images, exemplified by the fresco of the Virgin and Child at Lagoudera, c. 1192, images not necessarily depicting the Virgin and Child *Hodegetria*.[36] The result here, as argued by Pentcheva, is that the fragility, the vulnerability, the psychological complexity found in the Lagoudera image has appealed to the patron and been introduced in the mosaic icon, possibly for a crusader patron, where these qualities are combined skilfully with the stately and emotionally restrained aspects of this Virgin type in the Byzantine tradition. What we have is a representation of the Virgin and Child *Hodegetria* with a certain suggested emotional tenderness where the two figures exist in a pictorial space for the viewer's prayer and devotion. It is notable that neither figure engages the worshipper or looks at each other, but rather they engage each other in discreet prayerful dialogue by gesture. It is also notable that they appear before an elegant decorative background, with equal-armed red crosses, and stylized rosettes in medallions set against a gold ground, everything—the rectangular icon, the *siglae* medallions, the two haloes—framed with red, white and black crenellations, a decorative repertoire linked to that of Byzantine cloisonné enamels and imperial Byzantine art. The argument that these special hybrid characteristics may indicate a crusader patron and possibly a crusader artist who has worked hard to create an icon that reflects what I am calling the Byzantinizing tradition seems valid and defensible. But there are additional aspects of this icon which clearly indicate its crusader characteristics.

Pentcheva goes on to observe that on this icon the standard *siglae* found on an icon of the Virgin and Child *Hodegetria* have been reduced to the abbreviated red medallions with "Mater Theou" alone, without the abbreviated initials of Jesus Christ. These *siglae* clearly place great emphasis on the Virgin as the Mother of God, an emphasis found in Byzantine icons to be sure,[37] but it is an emphasis which is given powerful visual expression here with the introduction of chrysography over the maphorion of the Virgin, a feature which is not found in Byzantine icons. Both figures are of course given a nimbus to indicate their sanctity in the venerated Byzantine image type of the Virgin and Child *Hodegetria*, and also here in this variation of the *Dexiokratousa*. But here, with regard to the use of chrysography, there is a significant departure from the normal Byzantine practice. Jesus is given chrysography on his tunic, which is the standard Byzantine imagery, but also Mary is given chrysography on her maphorion, which is not. By giving Mary this chrysography she is raised to the same status as that of her Child, Jesus, both of them radiant with divine light of holiness. Indeed chrysography is virtually never seen on the Virgin of Byzantine icons of the Virgin and Child *Hodegetria*. But significantly it is frequently found on crusader icons of this classic type, but only rarely on the Dexiokratousa variation. A crusader icon of the classic *Hodegetria* portrait now in the Monastery of St. Catherine on Mount Sinai provides us with an excellent comparative example (Fig. 34.2).[38]

The Sinai crusader icon of the Virgin *Hodegetria* mentioned above (Fig. 34.2) is, of course, normally dated into the third quarter of the thirteenth century, usually about 1260 and therefore much later, whereas the crusader mosaic icon (Fig. 34.1) has consistently been attributed to Constantinople in the early thirteenth century. How can we understand this new attribution and what is its significance? I see no reason to doubt the possibility that this icon was produced in Constantinople by a first-rate artist; indeed, the artist may have been "crusader," but could well have been Byzantine. But given the choices made, which include the unByzantine use of chrysography on the Virgin's maphorion and other

Figure 34.2 Crusader icon of the Virgin and Child *Hodegetria*, bust-length, Sinai or Acre (?), Monastery of St. Catherine, Sinai, *c.* 1260s. (37.3 x 27.9 cm). Photograph: Elizabeth Bolman and Jaroslav Folda, by permission.

variations drawn from what appear to be a number of various possible sources, in order to satisfy a non-Byzantine patron, it seems clear the patron was certainly very likely a crusader. Finding a crusader patron in Constantinople in the early thirteenth century, of course, also clearly suggests the possibility that this work was ordered and carried out shortly after the Fourth Crusade took the city in 1204. And an important aspect of the significance of this icon for our understanding of the development of crusader art is that it is the earliest extant example of a crusader icon of the Virgin and Child *Hodegetria* on which we see the innovative use of chrysography found on the Virgin's maphorion to indicate her radiant holiness as the human mother of Jesus, who was represented as both divine and human.

In light of our proposal to see this icon as the result of a commission by a crusader patron in Constantinople, between 1204 and *c.* 1210, what evidence can we see that this icon, or a crusader image like this, could have served as an "intermediary copy" in relation to central Italian panel painting in the thirteenth century? To start with, Kurt Weitzmann provided a striking thirteenth-century Byzantine example of the Virgin and Child *Hodegetria Dexiokratousa*, the sort the crusader artist of the mosaic icon could have modeled his example on.[39] It is a large Byzantine icon, 117.3 x 79.5 cm, which is painted in tempera and gold, not done in mosaic, but its imagery is similar to the crusader mosaic icon: in particular the elements of Jesus blessing in the Greek manner, his bare feet and the sole of his left foot exposed, and the fact that he holds a scroll resting on his leg—all are specifically comparable. The Byzantine artist of course does not use chrysography on the figure of the Virgin, and the angels in the paired medallions on the Byzantine icon are transformed into the *siglae* of the *Mater Theou* on the crusader mosaic icon.

By comparison in the West, there are very few examples of the Virgin and Child *Hodegetria Dexiokratousa* (bust-length) found in Tuscany and Umbria in the thirteenth century. The one prominent example that does exist as a bust-length icon is in Pisa, the so-called "Madonna di sotto gli Organi" (93 x 55 cm), currently on view on an altar in the left transept of the Duomo (Fig. 34.3).[40] It is also probably done in the first quarter of the thirteenth century; it is also painted in tempera, not done in mosaic, it is roughly twice as big as the Sinai mosaic icon, and, perhaps most significantly, the Virgin has no chrysography on her garments. There are other differences as well: no *siglae* at all, the Child remarkably holds an open book rather than a scroll,[41] and his costume differs; the Virgin's pose is more upright and she has the equal-armed star crosses on her maphorion and tunic, whereas the Virgin of the Sinai mosaic icon has none. Nonetheless there are certain details that the two icons do hold in common which should be noticed: the depiction of the Virgin's right hand under the Child is the same, but not the same as the Virgin's hand on the Byzantine model mentioned above (note 39). Jesus and Mary look past each other, not at each other, and the smallish round-headed pug-nose face of Jesus is quite similar. It is also notable that the equal-armed cross star on the cuff of the Virgin's tunic on the Pisan painting is a detail found often on crusader images of the Virgin, not so often on Byzantine icons of the Virgin *Hodegetria* during the thirteenth century.[42] And the fact is that crusader artists did numerous examples of the Virgin and Child *Hodegetria Dexiokratousa* (bust-length) in the thirteenth century.[43] Despite the fact that none of them includes chrysography on the maphorion of the Virgin, except the crusader mosaic icon, the mixture of certain specific details such as those mentioned above, seems to suggest there were many examples of this icon type in circulation in the crusader East, one or more of which the artist of the Madonna in the Pisa Duomo may have had access to and was inspired by.

Figure 34.3   Italian panel painting: Virgin and Child *Hodegetria Dexiokratousa*, bust-length, known as the "Madonna di sotto gli Organi," now in the cathedral in Pisa, first quarter of the thirteenth century. Photograph: Genevra Kornbluth.

There were of course examples of the traditional Virgin and Child *Hodegetria* (bust-length) images for which crusader examples again could have served as "intermediary copies." There is in Siena a small (28 x 21.9 cm) and quite modest (no gold ground, yellow painted nimbi, but nonetheless Jesus is given the standard chrysography) Byzantine icon formerly in the church of the Carmine, and now on deposit in the Pinacoteca Nazionale, as mentioned above. It probably was done in the first half of the thirteenth century and brought to the West sometime by the mid-century.[44] It reflects the basic image type which a crusader artist would have known in Sinai or Acre who painted his own version,[45] but for which his patron commissioned him to give the Virgin copious chrysography, unlike whatever Byzantine model(s) he might have been using. Examples of these kinds of icons, both from the Byzantine tradition of the former type and from the Byzantinizing tradition of the latter Crusader type—the "intermediary models"—must have been available to the Tuscan artists who painted, for example, the devotional icon panels now in Pisa, inv. 1575 in the Museo Nazionale di San Matteo (86 x 57 cm) (Fig. 34.4)[46] and the celebrated image of the Madonna del Voto in the Duomo in Siena (112 x 82 cm) (Fig. 34.5).[47] Both were done *c*. 1265–70 in Pisa and Siena respectively. Both are hauntingly beautiful images which have appropriated the use of chrysography on the figure of the Virgin from crusader painting of the Byzantinizing tradition like the Sinai icon mentioned above (Fig. 34.2). In the case of the Pisan panel, inv. 1575, there are aspects of the chrysography and the imagery that suggest the artist could have known not only a Byzantine icon (e.g. the child blessing in the Greek manner), but also a Crusader icon (the copious chrysography on the Virgin), and

Figure 34.4   Italian panel painting: icon of the Virgin and Child *Hodegetria*, bust-length, with angels, now in the Museo Nazionale, Pisa (inv. 1575), from the church of San Giovannino dei Cavalieri, *c.* 1265–70 (?) (86 x 57 cm). Photograph: Genevra Kornbluth, by courtesy of the MiBAC/Soprintendenza Pisa.

Pisan painting like the Pushkin Madonna (the chrysography is boldly designed and given a number of Italian decorative forms including the numerous rhomboidal connectors on the maphorion) (Fig. 34.6). With the Madonna del Voto in Siena (Fig. 34.5), this artist obviously may have seen the Byzantine icon in the church of the Carmine, mentioned above, and the more restrained interpretation of the *Virgin Hodegetria* type is reflected in this artist's work. The presence of the chrysography on the figure of the Virgin also reflects influence from a crusader work of the Byzantinizing tradition, although the Madonna del Voto artist may also have seen Pisan work like the Pushkin Madonna. What is evident, however, is that the Madonna del Voto master has refined the chrysography in terms of elegant and decorative linear designs, including the copious miniaturized rhomboidal connectors found now all over the Virgin, and indeed now the Virgin even has chrysography on her red coif, something found often on Tuscan panel painting and also seen infrequently on crusader images of the Virgin Hodegetria.[48]

It is striking however, that whereas there were relatively few examples of this specific type of Virgin *Hodegetria* (bust-length), or the Virgin *Hodegetria Dexiokratousa* (bust-length) icon that have survived in the West, there is another version of this greatly revered type, the Virgin and Child *Hodegetria* enthroned full-length and flanked by angels, which was widely produced by central Italian painters in the later thirteenth century. And for this type we not only have many well-known Italian altarpieces extant, but also there are a number of crusader examples which we may evaluate as "intermediary copies."

Figure 34.5 Italian panel painting: Virgin and Child *Hodegetria* (Madonna del Voto) by the Madonna del Voto Master, *c.* 1265–70(?) (112 x 82 cm). Photograph: Foto LENSINI Siena, by permission.

Figure 34.6 Italian panel painting: Virgin and Child *Hodegetria* enthroned, with angels, the Pushkin Madonna, from Pisa, now in the Pushkin Museum, Moscow, *c.* 1260. Photograph: Linda Docherty, by permission.

The first of these examples is another example of an icon which was originally thought to be Byzantine, which on the basis of further consideration can clearly be seen to be crusader. I am referring to the medium-sized icon (34.5 x 26 cm) in the collection of the Monastery of St. Catherine on Mount Sinai which Weitzmann attributed to "Constantinople, 1200–1250" (Fig. 34.7), and where he drew attention to the fact that "the gold striation is an even more conspicuous feature [than what is seen on the Sinai mosaic icon discussed above], which has an abstracting as well as luminous effect. This technique was particularly popular in the thirteenth century, when relations with the West and especially Italy were very close."[49] This icon later appeared in the great exhibition *Byzantium: Faith and Power (1261 – 1557)* in 2004 where Elka Bakalova concluded her discussion in the catalogue by saying, "this small icon of great artistic merit was probably painted in the ateliers of the Monastery of Saint Catherine by a master painter working for the Crusaders."[50]

Several additional specific features of this icon fully support this attribution to a possible crusader artist. In the first place the two figures of the Virgin and Child *Hodegetria* appear enthroned on a lyre-backed throne, about which Anthony Cutler commented that it is found

Figure 34.7   Crusader icon of the Virgin and Child *Hodegetria* enthroned on a lyre-backed throne, with angels, Sinai or Acre (?), Monastery of St. Catherine, Sinai, *c*. mid-thirteenth century (35 x 26 cm). Photograph: Elizabeth Bolman and Jaroslav Folda, by permission.

on crusader icons with the Virgin *Hodegetria*, but the Virgin *Hodegetria* is "never associated with the lyre-backed throne in medieval Greek art."[51] A second point is that the clarity of organization and composition found on most middle Byzantine icons is here somewhat blurred. For example, the gesture of the enthroned Virgin toward Christ "misses" him, in effect, by pointing above his head, because here the Child is so tiny and seated down below in her lap. Also the red inscriptions which provide the *nomina sacrae* are curiously all lined up along the top of the panel, mixing the holy name of the *Mater Theou* with those of the two archangels, Michael and Gabriel. The abbreviated letters of *Mater Theou* are only differentiated at all by being very slightly enlarged in size. And conspicuously, the inscription identifying Jesus Christ is again omitted, as it was on the earlier crusader mosaic icon. The most remarkable feature, however, is certainly the copious chrysography, which covers not only the Virgin and Child and the archangels, but also the lower part of the throne, its cushion and its footstool. It is particularly notable on the figure of the Virgin, however, because it covers her maphorion and her tunic, as well as the coif she wears under the veil of her maphorion, a most unusual detail. These particular characteristics provide what I take to be clear evidence that this icon was very likely done by a crusader artist for a crusader patron, who may have been a pilgrim to the Holy Monastery of St. Catherine. With this possibility in mind, it is important to recall that the monastery had originally been dedicated to Mary, the *Theotokos*, "God-Bearer," and continued to be known this way even after the relics of St. Catherine were brought to the monastery in the middle Byzantine period.[52]

Given the wide variations of the dating of this icon found in the literature, and the difficulty of being very precise without further documentation, an attribution to mid-century seems to be reasonable. And associated with this innovative example of a crusader artist producing an icon of the Virgin and Child *Hodegetria* enthroned full-length and flanked by angels we can recognize three additional more or less contemporary examples of crusader work. The first is found on the central panel of what is known as the "Acre Triptych" (68.5 x 49.7 cm) probably dating from the late 1250s in Acre;[53] the second is known as the Kahn Madonna, a large icon (123 x 72 cm) probably produced in Constantinople *c*. 1260 now in the National Gallery in Washington, DC,[54] and the third is known as the Mellon Madonna, a somewhat smaller icon (84 x 53 cm) also probably produced in Constantinople possibly in the same workshop as the Kahn Madonna at about the same time, also in the National Gallery in Washington.[55] These four icons all also share the characteristic of Virgin figures seated frontally on monumental thrones, albeit thrones of various interesting types. These four icons done in the crusader East can all be considered as "intermediary copies" and considered as exemplifying crusader paintings that central Italian artists appear to have used as models for important new commissions done from 1261 to 1311.[56]

Although these four icons I am proposing to be crusader examples from the years around 1260 can be thought of as "intermediary copies," they take on special importance because there are so few contemporary Byzantine examples the crusaders—or the Italian painters—could have seen. The fact is that the Byzantine examples from which they might have been inspired are varied and widely spread out. Basically those Byzantine examples which show full-length images of the Virgin and Child enthroned—for example, either cult images such as the apse mosaic of Hagia Sophia in Constantinople, dated 867, or devotional images such as the thirteenth-century illustration in a Greek Psalter, MS Gr. 61 in the library of the Monastery of St. Catherine, dating *c*. 1274[57]—have the Virgin seated frontally with the Child also on her central axis, and in any case they are mostly not images of the *Hodegetria* type. Although there were icons of the full-length seated

Virgin *Hodegetria* in the pre-Iconoclastic period, in the post-Iconoclastic period the Virgin and Child *Hodegetria* enthroned "was never generally accepted in Byzantium," at least not up until about 1300.[58] This seems to indicate therefore that the crusader appropriation of the Byzantine icon of the Virgin and Child *Hodegetria* in the thirteenth century to produce these examples of the Virgin and Child *Hodegetria* enthroned full-length with angels involved a creative and innovative merger. The Virgin and Child enthroned had, of course, been a major feature of Western imagery in the twelfth and early thirteenth century, in Romanesque and Gothic sculpture especially, particularly in France. But it was the crusaders who explored this imagery in painting in works found in the Latin Kingdom of Jerusalem, such as the icon on the Bethlehem nave column dated 1130, on the headpiece in the Psalter of queen Melisende from Jerusalem, done c. 1135, and from the headpiece in the Riccardiana Psalter, probably done in Acre *c.* 1225.[59] And it was apparently the crusader painters who produced the newly minted result of the traditional *Hodegetria* type integrated with the imagery of the Virgin enthroned in the mid-thirteenth century, of which the four examples cited above are extant, namely the Sinai icon, the Acre Triptych central panel, the Kahn Madonna, and the Mellon Madonna. The possible reasons for this creative work have not been examined as yet, but no doubt the transition from the smaller Byzantine icon of the bust-length Virgin and Child *Hodegetria*, which functioned as a devotional image, to the different needs of larger crusader panels, some of which must have been used as altarpieces for the Latin liturgy (e.g., the Kahn Madonna and the Mellon Madonna) is an important consideration.

These crusader panels with the Virgin and Child *Hodegetria* enthroned full-length with angels therefore provide our most important evidence for sources that the central Italian painters could have known about in the period around the years 1260 ff. for their new altarpieces commissioned in Tuscany. The two earliest of these Tuscan panels appear to be the Pushkin Madonna, done by a Pisan artist *c.* 1260, presumably in Pisa (Fig. 34.6), and the Madonna del Bordone, painted by Coppo di Marcovaldo in Siena, commissioned by the Servite Order for the church of Santa Maria dei Servi in 1261 (Fig. 34.8). These two works seem to be effectively contemporary, but it is particularly important to note that the work by Coppo is firmly dated 1261, and is therefore the earliest of these Tuscan panels given this kind of documentation. If we ask the question whether either of these two early Tuscan paintings appear to reflect the impact of crusader icons as exemplified by the four examples cited above, the answer is that both of them do, but the specifics differ greatly in each case. Bearing in mind the fact that the four crusader works all appear to be icons of various sizes and different functions, and the Tuscan works both appear to be altarpieces, and thereby placed in a distinctive Western liturgical context,[60] we can consider just how these two Tuscan panels seem to reflect the possible influence of crusader models as "intermediary copies" in the Byzantinizing tradition.

With the Pushkin Madonna (173 x 84 cm)[61] (Fig. 34.6) there are four aspects that seem to be important reflections of the artist's inspiration from a crusader model or models, quite apart from the characteristic Pisan Byzantinizing style of the artist and some features of the imagery, such as the bust-length flanking angels above. First the composition features a Virgin seated in essentially a frontal position as characteristic of the four Crusader Virgin *Hodegetria* icons mentioned above. Second, there is also the variation in her specific pose, with her head slightly inclined toward her upright son, who is depicted as a diminutive ruler blessing and holding a scroll upright on his leg. These aspects appear to draw on imagery also found in the mosaic icon of the Virgin and Child *Hodegetria Dexiokratousa* from

Figure 34.8   Italian panel painting: altarpiece for the Church of the Servites in Siena: Madonna del Bordone, by Coppo di Marcovaldo, 1261 (220 x 125 cm). Photograph: Genevra Kornbluth, by permission of the Arcidiocesi di Siena.

Constantinople discussed above (Fig. 34.1), an iconographical type also noted as exceedingly popular among crusader artists. Third, the Virgin's throne is clearly given a lyre-back as seen in a slightly more simplified version on the smaller Sinai icon from the mid-century also discussed above. And fourth, the Pisan master has bathed the Virgin of the Virgin and Child *Hodegetria Dexiokratousa* in chrysography as found uniquely on crusader icons from the East. The presence of the chrysography can, I submit, be understood as having been drawn from a crusader source, without being able to identify any one specific model, but the formal characteristics of this chrysography also shows features already distinctively Italian; for example, the remarkable number of rhomboidal connectors on the maphorion which neither Byzantine nor Crusader chrysography employs.

With the much larger Madonna del Bordone (220 x 125 cm) done in 1261 (Fig. 34.8),[62] the situation is somewhat different with regard to the impact of crusader icon painting. Coppo's commission from the Servite Order was apparently to create an image of the Virgin as Queen of Heaven for a major liturgical altarpiece in their church. Coppo's relationship to the Byzantinizing tradition of crusader art or the slightly earlier works in Pisa as discussed above, while clearly indebted to the crusader tradition with the use of the lyre-backed throne and the boldly designed chrysography, is quite distinctive and has its own innovative characteristics. Furthermore, Coppo's Madonna was significantly altered in the early Trecento, presumably shortly after 1311, with the repainting of the face and hands in a Ducciesque style and the addition of the Duccio-type inner veil (replacing the original coif).

Among the new features introduced by Coppo in 1261 at the behest of his patrons, the Servite Order in Siena, we notice the enormous size of this panel, responding to the new function which this cult image was to serve. At 220 x 115 cm this altarpiece was over four times bigger than the Sinai Crusader icon of the Virgin and Child *Hodegetria* enthroned from *c*. 1260 (Fig. 34.7).

For the image of the Virgin and Child, Coppo appears to have combined the idea of a crusader image of the Virgin and Child *Hodegetria* enthroned on a flat-topped lyre-back throne, as seen in the Sinai panel, together with the distinctively Byzantine imagery of the bare-legged and bare-footed child seated upright on his mother's arm, wearing a blue harness over his tunic, blessing (in the Latin manner) and holding a red scroll, as seen on several thirteenth-century Byzantine icons linked to Cyprus in origin.[63] Despite the impact of these crusader and Byzantine sources, however, Coppo chose to depict the Virgin in a costume that while it maintains the dignity and stature of the Byzantinizing tradition, it nonetheless departs significantly from the standard garments that he would have known from any crusader or Byzantine icon. Instead of the Virgin wearing the normal tunic Coppo introduces here, for the first time in Tuscan painting, a Western-style maroon tunic/dress with a tightly fitted bodice and torso with horizontal folds across her ribs, secured with a silver belt tied in a bow at the center with tassels hanging down (Fig. 34.8). She has long fitted sleeves, a full tunic-skirt below, and above, a high round and jeweled neckline no longer visible under the white veil added in the early fourteenth century. Instead of a maphorion, this Virgin wears a long regal blue cloak tied with white silk strands, also known from Gothic sources. On her head this Virgin wears a splendid yellow silk veil perhaps represented as "cloth of gold." Furthermore it is lined in red silk, decorated with çintamani and given a hem of rich red maroon with tiny pearls. On this scarf we also see medallions decorated with frontal eagles featuring displayed wings, a remarkable, indeed unique, iconography first applied to the person of the Virgin here, by Coppo. Under this scarf, originally Coppo included a coif over her hair as seen in the Byzantinizing tradition, a coif now covered with a white inner veil added later.

As argued by Lila Yawn-Bonghi, Rebecca Corrie, and Gianna Mina, this costume is inspired by Gothic examples of the Virgin as Queen of Heaven found in contemporary Gothic manuscript illustration and even early Gothic church sculpture.[64] Mary here wears a tailored *bliaut* or tunic/dress, red shoes, a regal cloak and a headscarf like the Queen of Heaven, but without the crown so widely seen in Gothic France. This scarf represented in yellow-gold silk is of course a Western Gothic idea, but the form the scarf takes on her head, that is, the shapes of its folds formed in deep dark blues creates a remarkable maphorion-like covering. In this way Coppo synthesizes East and West in this unique image, which sets an important standard for Sienese images of the Virgin in the later Dugento, from Coppo to his more famous colleagues slightly later, Guido da Siena and Duccio.

Coppo crystallizes his vision of the Virgin *Hodegetria* as Queen of Heaven by giving her a radiance of the most remarkable chrysography. Far from emulating the configurations of the Pushkin Madonna (Fig. 34.6), which seems not to have been very influential here, or the crusader icons he might have been inspired by, such as the small Sinai panel with its copious linear coverage, splashes and spikey rays (Fig. 34.7), he again takes the ideas of his sources and reinvents them to produce a Virgin of impressive monumentality and distinctive radiant character. As she holds her beloved Child, who is intensely radiant with his red and blue garments covered with gold, and his blue harness belt, her chrysography complements his by representing her as Queen and mother, who is both regally divine and human. And the theme of their joint humanity is unified not only by the tender touch she gives his foot, but also by his vulnerability expressed by his bare legs and feet, his chubby baby-like body, the design of his striped belt harness with a flourished "proleptic knot," which leads our thoughts to the loin cloth he would eventually wear at his crucifixion, and the abundant folds of the cloth he sits on, which foreshadows his shroud in the tomb.

In sum, we find realized on the Madonna del Bordone (Fig. 34.8) the remarkable achievement of Coppo di Marcovaldo who carried out the special commission he received from the Servite Order, perhaps from the first Sienese director general himself, Fra Jacopo da Siena, in 1261. Coppo was able to draw on the resources of several traditions, Eastern and Western—that means, crusader, Byzantine and Gothic, as well as his own Tuscan tradition—to produce a magnificent altarpiece that was truly original in the way that he synthesized and harmonized these diverse traditions. But for our purposes here I particularly want to make the special point that, among other things, Coppo was brilliantly innovative in the way that he conceived, designed and executed the chrysography on the figure of the Virgin. In doing this he was apparently the first artist in Siena to produce a major altarpiece in the Dugento with a full program of radiance and reflection in which the Virgin was depicted as the human Mother of God, *Theotokos*, as the Hodegetria enthroned with Christ, and as the glorious Queen of Heaven. Valentino Pace has argued that the imagery of Mary as the Queen of Heaven wearing a crown was well known in Italy, especially in Rome, and south Italy, from very early on in the Middle Ages. But it is also true that as he says, "in the territories of the Orthodox Church, this message of royalty was never accepted,"[65] at least not in the same terms. But Coppo di Marcovaldo here in Siena in 1261 brilliantly succeeded in creating a new image of the *Regina Coeli*, without a crown, but rather transformed and developed out of the Byzantine and crusader imagery of the *Theotokos* and rooted fundamentally in the traditional iconography of the *Hodegetria*.

These two Tuscan altarpieces stand at the beginning of a remarkable development of liturgical images of the Virgin and Child *Hodegetria* enthroned full-length with angels, or some few bust-length, seen especially in Siena and elsewhere in Tuscany and Umbria between 1261 and 1311, all of which to some extent reflect the Byzantinizing tradition from the crusader East. In each case careful analysis can reveal the extent to which the painting from the crusaders in the Holy Land contributed to these works, but in every case the Byzantine icon type of the Virgin and Child *Hodegetria* and the crusader innovation of using chrysography as part of the essential imagery of the Virgin as Queen of Heaven is found. We cannot explore these further examples here, because of limitations for the size of contributions in this volume, but we can conclude with some important conclusions about the impact of the art of the crusaders in the Holy Land on the art of western Europe.

First, we have seen that with regard to icons and panel paintings, work identified as crusader in the thirteenth century is closely associated with Byzantine examples. It is important therefore to reexamine carefully the Byzantine icons we have in order to clearly identify and understand their Byzantine characteristics as distinct from those works by crusader artists who were inspired by and emulated Byzantine originals.

Second, the work done by crusader artists is characterized by the synthesis of their appropriation from the Byzantine tradition, the contribution made from their own training, experience and development as artists in the West and/or as residents in the crusader East, and their creative originality and innovation in formulating works for their patrons in what we are calling the Byzantinizing tradition.

Third, even though we cannot as yet document crusader work and/or crusader artists in central Italy independently by the existence of crusader icons in situ or specific evidence about individuals found in written historical sources from the period, we can see the impact of the Byzantinizing tradition on Tuscan panel painters in the years around 1260 as discussed above.

Finally, it is clear that systematic analysis of the contributions made by crusader painters and artists working in other media, as well as architects, is yet to be carried out with regard to medieval art and architecture in the European West in the twelfth and the thirteenth century. This is a large task for future scholarship. But my hope is that the discussion in this chapter will provide a sample of how scholars could proceed and offer some useful considerations methodologically along with examples of the kind of results we can expect to find.

NOTES

1 See, for example, Kurt Weitzmann, "Crusader Icons and Maniera Greca," in *Byzanz und der Westen*, ed. Irmgard Hutter (Vienna: Österreichischen Akademie der Wissenschaften, 1984), 143–170; Jaroslav Folda, "Crusader Art and its Impact on the West," Epilogue for *Crusader Art: The Art of the Crusaders in the Holy Land, 1099–1291* (Aldershot and Burlington: Lund Humphries, 2008), 164–169; Rebecca Corrie, "Sinai, Acre, Tripoli, and the Backwash from the Levant," in *Approaching the Holy Mountain: Art and Liturgy at St Catherine's Monastery in the Sinai*, eds. Sharon Gerstel and Robert Nelson (Turnhout: Brepols, 2010), 415–448.

2 Steven Runciman, *A History of the Crusades*, vol. III (Cambridge: Cambridge University Press, 1954), 367–386; see more recently, David Winfield, "Crusader Art: Sir Steven was right," in *Byzantine Style, Religion and Civilization*, Essays in honour of Sir Steven Runciman, ed. Elizabeth Jeffreys (Cambridge: Cambridge University Press, 2006), 159–173.

3 Bissera Pentcheva, "8. Mosaic Icon of the Virgin Hodegetria," in *Holy Image, Hallowed Ground: Icons from Sinai*, eds. Robert Nelson and Kristen Collins (Los Angeles: The J. Paul Getty Museum, 2006), 140–143.

4 Hugo Buchthal, *Miniature Painting in the Latin Kingdom of Jerusalem* (Oxford: Clarendon Press, 1957); Jaroslav Folda, "A Crusader Manuscript from Antioch," *Atti della Pontificia Accademia Romana di Archeologia: Rendiconti*, XLII (1969–70), 283–298; Jaroslav Folda, *Crusader Manuscript Illumination at Saint-Jean d'Acre, 1275–1291* (Princeton: Princeton University Press, 1976).

5 Kurt Weitzmann, "Thirteenth Century Crusader Icons on Mount Sinai," *Art Bulletin*, 45 (1963), 179–203; *idem*, "Icon Painting in the Crusader Kingdom," *Dumbarton Oaks Papers*, 20 (1966), 51–83; *idem*, "An Encaustic Icon with the Prophet Elijah at Mount Sinai," *Mélanges offerts à Kazimierz Michalowski* (Warsaw, 1966), 713–723; *idem*, "Four Icons on Mount Sinai: New Aspects in Crusader Art," *Jahrbuch der Österreichischen Byzantinistik*, 21 (1972), 279–293; *idem*, "Three Painted Crosses at Sinai," *Kunsthistorische Forschungen: Otto Pächt zu seinem 70. Geburtstag* (Salzburg: Residenz Verlag, 1972), 23–35.

6 Cecil L. Striker, "Fresco Cycle of the Life of St. Francis of Assisi," in *Kalenderhane in Istanbul, the Buildings, Their History, Architecture and Decoration*, Final Reports: 1966–78, eds. C.L. Striker and D.G. Kuban (Mainz: Verlag Philipp von Zabern, 1997), 128–142.

7 T.S.R. Boase, "Ecclesiastical Art, The Arts in Cyprus," in *The Art and Architecture of the Crusader States*, ed. Harry W. Hazard, vol. IV of *A History of the Crusades*, ed. Kenneth Setton (Madison and London: University of Wisconsin Press, 1977), 165–195, 343–348; Jaroslav Folda, "Crusader Art in the Kingdom of Cyprus, 1275–1291: Reflections on the State of the Question," 209–237, and Annemarie Weyl Carr, "Art in the Court of the Lusignan Kings," 239–274, in *Cyprus and the Crusades*, eds. N. Coureas and Jonathan Riley-Smith (Nicosia: Cyprus Research Center, 1995).

8   Denys Pringle, *The Churches of the Crusader Kingdom of Jerusalem: A Corpus*, 4 volumes (Cambridge: Cambridge University Press, 1993, 1998, 2007, 2009); Jaroslav Folda, *The Art of the Crusaders in the Holy Land, 1098–1187* (Cambridge: Cambridge University Press, 1995), and *idem, Crusader Art in the Holy Land, from the Third Crusade to the Fall of Acre, 1187–1291* (Cambridge: Cambridge University Press, 2005).

9   Otto Demus, *Byzantine Art and the West* (New York: New York University Press, 1970), vii.

10 Ibid., 2.

11 This lecture was published a year later: Wilhelm Köhler, "Byzantine Art in the West," *Dumbarton Oaks Papers*, I (1941), 61ff.

12 *Byzantine Art, An European Art*, 9th Exhibition held under the auspices of the Council of Europe (Athens: Department of Antiquities and Archaeological Restoration, 1964); and *Byzantine Art, An European Art, Lectures* (Athens: Department of Antiquities and Archaeological Restoration, 1966), with papers by Steven Runciman, D. Talbot Rice, Hugo Buchthal, Anastasios Orlandou, H.F. Volbach, Ernst Kitzinger, and Kurt Weitzmann.

13 Papers by Hugo Buchthal, Ernst Kitzinger, James Stubblebine, and Kurt Weitzmann were included. The paper by Otto Demus given at the symposium was not published here, presumably because his views were spelled out in some detail in his 1966 Wrightsman Lectures, mentioned above.

14 *The Year 1200*: A Centennial Exhibition at the Metropolitan Museum of Art, vol. 1, catalogue, ed. and written by Konrad Hoffman (New York: Metropolitan Museum of Art, 1970); *The Year 1200: A Background Survey*, vol. 2, ed. Florens Deuchler (New York: Metropolitan Museum of Art, 1970), with an essay by Margaret Frazer, "Byzantine Art and the West," 185–230; *The Year 1200: A Symposium*, ed. Jeffrey Hoffeld (New York: Metropolitan Museum of Art, 1975), with an essay by Kurt Weitzmann, "Byzantium and the West around the Year 1200," 53–93.

15 Kurt Weitzmann, "Various Aspects of Byzantine Influence on the Latin Countries from the Sixth to the Twelfth Century, *Dumbarton Oaks Papers*, 20 (1966), 3.

16 Ibid., 20.

17 Ibid.

18 Kurt Weitzmann, "Crusader Icons and Maniera Greca," in *Byzanz und der Westen*, ed. Irmgard Hutter (Vienna: Österreichischen Akademie der Wissenschaften, 1984), 143.

19 Kurt Weitzmann, "Various Aspects of Byzantine Influence," 20.

20 Demus, *Byzantine Art and the West*, 205.

21 Ernst Kitzinger, "The Byzantine Contribution to Western Art of the Twelfth and Thirteenth Centuries," *Dumbarton Oaks Papers*, 20 (1966), 34–37.

22 Weitzmann, "Crusader Icons and Maniera Greca," 144 and n. 7.

23 Ibid. 145 and n. 8. This type, as Weitzmann points out, is quite unusual and was rarely copied. For an explanation of the type, see: Nancy Sevcenko, "Virgin Hagiosoritissa", *Oxford Dictionary of Byzantium*, vol. III (New York and Oxford: Oxford University Press, 1991), 2171.

24 Hans Belting, *Likeness and Presence: A History of the Image before the Era of Art*, trans. E. Jephcott (Chicago and London: University of Chicago Press, 1994), 364, color pl. VI.

25 Ibid., 75–76.

26 Weitzmann,"Crusader Icons and Maniera Greca," 3.

27 The issue of how the Italian artists may have known about crusader icons is a separate issue that we are dealing with in a separate study. The fact is, however, that this remains as a significant problem to be explained.

28 Kitzinger, "The Byzantine Contribution to Western Art," 35, and Weitzmann agreed with this identification, see *idem*, "Various Aspects of Byzantine Influence," 75, and fig. 52.

29 Demus, *Byzantine Art and the West*, 30.

30 Kurt Weitzmann, "Various Aspects of Byzantine Influence," 20.

31 Weitzmann, "Icon Painting in the Crusader Kingdom," 74 ff., where he takes up the issue of "transmission." See also, Kitzinger, "The Byzantine Contribution to Western Art," 34 ff; Demus, *Byzantine Art and the West*, 29 ff.

32 Weitzmann, "Crusader Icons and Maniera Greca," 143–170.

33 I examine this Byzantinizing tradition more fully in a book entitled *Byzantine Art and Italian Panel Painting: The Virgin and Child* Hodegetria *and the Art of Chrysography* (New York: Cambridge University Press, 2015).

34 Cf. above, n. 3.

35 Kurt Weitzmann, *The Icon: Holy Images—Sixth to Fourteenth Century* (New York: Braziller, 1978), 36, 102, pl. 32, and *idem*, "Crusader Icons and Maniera Greca," 147–148; and Bissera Pentcheva, "8. Mosaic Icon of the Virgin Hodegetria," in *Holy Image, Hallowed Ground: Icons from Sinai*, ed. Robert Nelson and Kristen Collins (Los Angeles: J. Paul Getty Museum, 2006), 140–143.

36 Illustrated in the Pentcheva entry cited above, ibid., 141.

37 See, for example, the twelfth-century Icon of the Virgin *Brephokratousa* with Old and New Testament figures now at Sinai: Titos Papamastorakis, "Icon of the Virgin *Brephokratousa* … ," in *Mother of God*, ed. Maria Vassilakis (Athens: Benaki Museum, 2000), 315, and a detailed discussion by Father Justin Sinaites, "Sinai, MS GR. 2: Exploring the Significance of a Sinai Manuscript," in *Approaching the Holy Mountain*, 278–281.

38 Folda, *Crusader Art in the Holy Land*, 455, fig. 289, 534–535, no. 22.

39 Weitzmann, "Icon Painting in the Crusader Kingdom," 81, fig. 66.

40 Lorenzo Carletti, "16. Icona," in *Cimabue a Pisa: La pittura pisana del Duecento da Giunta a Giotto*, eds. Mariagiulia Burresi e Antonino Caleca (Pisa: Pacini editore, 2005), 130–131. Scholars have debated whether this icon in Pisa was done by a Tuscan painter or a Byzantine painter. See, Valentino Pace, "Between East and West," in *Mother of God*, ed. Maria Vassilaki (Athens: Benaki Museum, 2000), 424–427. One might wonder if it was possible the artist had visited the Crusader East in any case?

41 There is another Crusader icon in which the rare imagery of the Child holding an open book appears, so it is a motif available from Crusader sources. See, Folda, *Crusader Art in the Holy Land*, 140, fig. 76 (679).

42 See, for example, the Virgin on the Crusader diptych with St. Procopios and the Virgin and Child Kykkotissa from the late thirteenth century (Folda, *Crusader Art in the Holy Land*, 445, fig. 272, 549ff., no. 110) and the Virgin on the Crusader Virgin and Child *Hodegetria Dexiokratousa* from the early thirteenth century (Folda, *Crusader Art in the Holy Land*, 140, fig. 76, 540, no. 57). In the case of the latter example, we see the only other example known to me where the Child holds an open book in his hand, instead of the customary scroll.

43 I count six extant examples in my annotated handlist. See, Folda, *Crusader Art in the Holy Land*: 140, fig. 76 (679), 328, fig. 181 (55), 445, fig. 272 (1783), 535, fig. 360 (180), 542, fig. 375 (588), 558, fig. 414 (131).

44 Hans Belting, *Image and Likeness*, trans. Edmund Jephcott (Chicago and London: University of Chicago Press, 1994), 341, 591 n. 32, colorplate VI.

45 Weitzmann, "Icon Painting in the Crusader Kingdom," 81, pl. 67, and Folda, *Crusader Art in the Holy Land*, 454–455, 534–535, colorplate 11.

46 Pisan panel inv. 1575: Lorenzo Carletti, "54.Icona: Madonna col Bambino e due angeli," in *Cimabue a Pisa*, 197; and E.B. Garrison, *Italian Romanesque Panel Painting: An Illustrated Index* (Florence: Leo S. Olschki, 1949), no. 339, 128.

47 Madonna del Voto: Silvia Georgi, *Duccio: Alle Origini della Pittura Senese*, 54–55. I am as yet unable to accept the attribution to Dietisalvi di Speme however, and prefer for the time being to retain the name of this painter as the anonymous "Master of the Madonna del Voto". See also, Helmut Hager, *Die Anfänge des italienischen Altarbildes* (Munich: Anton Schroll & Co., 1962), 134–137, 152–153, figs. 187–189; and E.B. Garrison, *Italian Romanesque Panel Painting: An Illustrated Index* (Florence: Leo S. Olschki, 1949), no. 650, 233.

48 See below, for example, the medium-sized Sinai icon of the Virgin and Child *Hodegetria* enthroned full-length, flanked by angels, here interpreted to be a work of crusader art.

49 Kurt Weitzmann, "The Icons of Constantinople," in *The Icon*, eds. Kurt Weitzmann, Manolis Chatzidakis, et al. (New York: Alfred A. Knopf, 1982), 20, 66.

50 Elka Bakalova, "208.Icon with the Enthroned Virgin and Child," in *Byzantium: Faith and Power (1261–1557)*, ed. Helen C. Evans (New York: Metropolitan Museum of Art, 2004), 348.

51 Anthony Cutler, "The Lyre-Backed Throne," in *Transfigurations* (University Park and London: Penn State Press, 1975), 34.

52 The dedications of the monastery that is known today as the Monastery of God-trodden Mount Sinai, and popularly called the Monastery of St. Catherine, is discussed by many. Here I can cite Father Justin Sinaites, "Sinai, MS GR. 2: Exploring the Significance of a Sinai Manuscript," in *Approaching the Holy Mountain*, 278, "described by Procopios in the sixth century as the Monastery of the Holy Virgin." In the thirteenth century we note that the German pilgrim, Thietmar, on pilgrimage in 1216–17, made the clear distinction between the "beautiful church in honour of Our Lady the Blessed Virgin," and the tomb of St. Catherine "in the same church next to the choir." See, "Thietmar Pilgrimage (1216–1217)," in *Pilgrimage to Jerusalem and the Holy Land, 1187–1291*, trans. Denys Pringle (Farnham and Burlington: Ashgate, 2012), 124–125.

53 The Acre Triptych: Folda, *Crusader Art in the Holy Land*, 310–318, figs. 155–163; Jaroslav Folda, "216. Triptych with the Virgin and Child Enthroned, Scenes from the Life of the Virgin, and Saints Nicholas and John the Baptist," in *Byzantium: Faith and Power (1261–1557)*, 357.

54 The Kahn Madonna: Rebecca Corrie, "The Kahn and Mellon Madonnas and their place in the history of the Virgin and Child Enthroned in Italy and the East," in *Images of the Mother of God: Perceptions of the Theotokos in Byzantium*, ed. Maria Vassilaki (Aldershot and Burlington: Ashgate, 2005), 293–303; Jaroslav Folda, "Icon to Altarpiece in the Frankish East: Images of the Virgin and Child Enthroned," in *Italian Panel Painting of the Duecento and Trecento*, ed. Victor M. Schmidt, *Studies in the History of Art*, vol. 61 (Washington, DC: National Gallery of Art, 2002), 127–132; Jaroslav Folda, "The Kahn and Mellon Madonnas: Icon or Altarpiece," in *Byzantine East, Latin West: Art-Historical Studies in Honor of Kurt Weitzmann*, eds. C. Moss and K. Kiefer (Princeton: Department of Art and Archaeology, Princeton University, 1995), 501–510

55 The Mellon Madonna: Rebecca Corrie, "The Kahn and Mellon Madonnas and their place in the history of the Virgin and Child Enthroned in Italy and the East," in *Images of the Mother of God: Perceptions of the Theotokos in Byzantium*, ed. Maria Vassilaki (Aldershot and Burlington: Ashgate, 2005), 293–303; Folda, "Icon to Altarpiece in the Frankish East," 127–132; Joseph Polzer, "The 'Byzantine' Kahn and Mellon Madonnas ... " *Arte Cristiana*, XC (2002), 410. Most recently he has declined to attribute both works to the same artist: *idem*, "Concerning Chrysography ... ," *Arte Medievale*, IV serie, anno II (2012), 180; Jaroslav Folda, "The Kahn and Mellon Madonnas: Icon or Altarpiece," in *Byzantine East, Latin West: Art-Historical Studies in Honor of Kurt Weitzmann*, eds. C. Moss and K. Kiefer (Princeton: Department of Art and Archaeology, Princeton University, 1995), 501–510.

56 These four works by crusader painters all possibly done in the years around 1260 in the crusader states or in Constantinople, and all four with distinctive chrysography, are discussed at length in chapters 3 and 4 of my book, *Byzantine Art and Italian Panel Painting*. Due to appear from Cambridge University Press in 2015. Due to limitations of space it is not possible to consider them further here.

57 Jennifer Ball, "202.Greek Psalter," in *Byzantium: Faith and Power (1261–1557)*, 343–344, and Nancy Sevcenko, "The Mother of God in Illuminated Manuscripts," in *Mother of God*, ed. Maria Vassilakis (Athens: Benaki Museum, 2000), 161.

58 Victor Lasareff, "Studies in the Iconography of the Virgin," *Art Bulletin*, 20 (1938), 54. Lazarev discusses this imagery at length noting that although it is "in no sense characteristic of the art of Constantinople," it does appear on seals and on ivory carvings and relief sculpture in other media. He goes on to say that "in the thirteenth and fourteenth centuries, the seated Hodegetria appears less frequently in the art of Byzantium than in the previous epoch."

59 For all three of these images, see, Folda, "Icon to Altarpiece in the Frankish East," 123–127.

60 Victor M. Schmidt, "Die Funktionen der Tafelbilder mit der thronenden Madonna in der Malerei des Duecento," *Papers of the Netherlands Institute in Rome*, 55 (1996), 44–72.

61 Victor Lasareff, "New Light on the Problem of the Pisan School," *Burlington Magazine*, no. 395, LXVIII (1936), 61–62, and see now the bibliographic outline of the citations and attributions by Victoria Markova, in the catalogue entry (in Russian) of *the State Pushkin Museum of Fine Arts: Italy: VIII-XVI Centuries, Collection of Paintings* (Moscow: Galart, 2002), 53, with further discussion on 51ff.

62 Gianna Mina has published an excellent article on the Madonna del Bordone based on her unpublished 1992 PhD dissertation: eadem, "Coppo di Marcovaldo's Madonna del Bordone: political statement or profession of faith?," in *Art, Politics, and Civic Religion in Central Italy: 1261–1352*, eds. Joanna Cannon and Beth Williamson (Aldershot and Brookfield: Ashgate, 2000), 237–293; Rebecca Corrie, "The Political Meaning of Coppo di Marcovaldo's Madonna and Child in Siena," *GESTA*, XXIX (1990), 61–75, and eadem, "Coppo di Marcovaldo's Madonna del bordone and the Meaning of the Bare-Legged Christ Child in Siena and the East," *GESTA*, XXXV (1996), 43–65. See also, Miklos Boskovits, "The Art of Coppo di Marcovaldo," in *The Origins of Florentine Painting: 1100—1270* (Florence: Giunti Gruppo Editoriale, 1993), 116–130, and his entry on the Madonna del Bordone, 510–523, with exhaustive bibliography. Most recently see Joseph Polzer, "Concerning Chrysography in Dugento Tuscan Painting and the Origin of the Two Washington Madonnas," *Arte Medievale*, IV serie, anno II (2012), 172ff., and Joanna Cannon, *Religious Poverty, Visual Riches* (New Haven and London: Yale University Press, 2013), 76–79. See also the excellent study by Lila Yawn-Bonghi, "A Case of Careful Tailoring: Costume and Meaning in Coppo di Marcovaldo's Madonna del Bordone" (1990), MA thesis for the Department of Art, University of North Carolina at Chapel Hill.

63 Corrie, "Coppo di Marcovaldo's Madonna del Bordone," 50–51, and the publications of Doula Mouriki which first focused attention on this special imagery. See, Doula Mouriki, "Thirteenth-Century Icon Painting in Cyprus," *The Griffon*, n.s. 1–2 (1985–86), figs. 2, 6, 26, 27, and eadem, "A Thirteenth-Century Icon with a Variant on the Hodegetria in the Byzantine Museum in Athens," *Dumbarton Oaks Papers*, XLI (1987), 403–414, and fig. 1 (117.5 x 75 cm).

64 Lila Yawn-Bonghi, "A Case of Careful Tailoring: Costume and Meaning in Coppo di Marcovaldo's Madonna del Bordone" (1990), MA thesis for the Department of Art, University of North Carolina at Chapel Hill, 37–39, figs. 21–23; See also, Corrie, "Coppo di Marcovaldo's Madonna del Bordone," 70, n. 10, who interprets this costume as "a celestial version of the costume of a contemporary European queen," and Mina, "Coppo di Marcovaldo's Madonna del Bordone," 238–239.

65 Valentino Pace, "Between East and West," in *Mother of God*, 425–532.

CHAPTER THIRTY-FIVE

NARRATOLOGICAL READINGS OF CRUSADE TEXTS

———•◆•———

Marcus Bull

NARRATIVE UNDERSTANDING AS A TECHNICAL DISCIPLINE

Medieval history is, methodologically speaking, a house of many mansions. In large measure because of the relative scarcity of primary evidence from the Middle Ages, many of the types of sources that do survive are the subject of dedicated fields of study. Examples include numismatics, sigillography, epigraphy, palaeography, codicology and diplomatic. The need for in-depth technical training, a specialist vocabulary and the ability to read significance into what to a non-specialist might seem very slight differentiations within the source corpus, all these characterize such fields. A challenge that faces specialists in these areas is to maintain, and deepen, the technical rigour of their respective disciplines while navigating between two sets of scholarly demands and expectations. Are such areas of study to be understood as 'auxiliary sciences', their primary function being to offer up data for other scholars, perhaps themselves less technically accomplished in the fields concerned, to work into syntheses that draw on multiple source types? Or are they self-standing academic projects? In recent decades, the field of archaeology has perhaps done most to confront this choice, resisting the once prevalent expectation that it was in the business of feeding raw material into discussions of historical change and of material culture that were predominantly framed in non-archaeological terms. Instead, archaeology is able to deliver its own answers to its own questions, within discursive and methodological parameters that certainly have affinities to other disciplines, such as anthropology, but have been developed to be specific to it and are markers of a distinctive disciplinary identity. On a smaller scale, prosopography has confronted a similar challenge: is it a facilitator of the study of social, cultural and political history, or does it isolate a facet of human experience that is sufficiently discrete, significant, and well served by the sources to merit its own self-standing academic domain?

The aim of these opening remarks is to point up a contrast with another field of study, narratology, that has never been part of the canon of historical auxiliary sciences, at least *eo nomine*. By extension it has never needed to situate its identity in relation to historical study in the round. There have in recent decades been some notable and productive conjunctions:

the study of ancient Greek and Roman history-writing has been particularly enriched by narratologically informed readings (see Dewald 2005; Feldherr 2009; de Jong 2014). But narratology's disciplinary reach largely continues to reflect its origins in literary scholarship, where indeed it has faced challenges of means-end definition closely analogous to those we have just noted within the historical context. Is narratology a thing one 'does' in itself, as one might 'do' New Historicism, queer theory, or postcolonialism? Or is it a set of tools that facilitates something else? (See Fludernik 2005; Herman 2005.)

Narratology's absence from most medieval historians' methodogical toolkits or conceptual apparatus is noteworthy, given the important place of texts characterizable as narrative, as well as of types of evidence that contain narrative elements, within the global corpus of extant primary sources. Any in-depth study of the Middle Ages must engage with narrative material in a number of genres. This is so much an obvious fact of life that it can stifle further reflection on its implications. A defensive position on the part of a practising medieval historian, wary perhaps of cluttering up the subject with 'ologies' and technical jargon, might be that the close study of narrative sources has developed and grown successfully over the past several centuries of historical inquiry. It can draw upon a suite of technical (sub-)disciplines such as codicology, etymology and the study of rhetoric. It may not always engage expressly with the concept of intertextuality, but it appreciates the value of identifying a work's regime of borrowing, adaptation, allusion and quotation for understanding the textual culture of which the work is part. Moreover, this historian might argue, historical training *inter alia* involves a progressive honing of reading skills that need not come freighted with jargon or informed by hard theory but are nonetheless effective in pragmatic terms, flexible and adaptive. Such a training serves to refine an intuitive facility in a kind of polymorphous inductive reasoning suitable for a wide variety of texts. The proof of this, our putative historian might further argue, is the sheer volume and range of excellent scholarly work either directly about narrative sources or based on them.

This line of argument is very compelling. Its grounding in experience and what seems like professional common sense ultimately derives from the ubiquity of narrative in all cultures. Young children mature and learn to function as social beings in large part by developing skills in understanding narratives and making narratives of their own. Narrative is central to language acquisition and is deeply implicated in the development of memory. Indeed, for many scholars narrative is not merely a necessary complement of selfhood but also a major part of its constituent matter (e.g. Bruner 1986; Maynes et al. 2008; Randall 1995). Witness Oliver Sacks's moving accounts of patients who, either because of pathology or trauma, suffered damage to the brain that severely impaired their ability to remember and tell stories; troubling reflections emerge from these cases about the vulnerability of personal identity and self-possession when an individual's narrative facility is lost (Sacks 1986). And what seems to be true of individuals has been scaled up to collective experience. Societies remember with narratives; and narratives of many sorts, from myths of origin to cultural scripts big and small, not only frame social experience but also in some measure constitute it (Connerton 1989; Cubitt 2007; Fentress and Wickham 1992).

In such circumstances, narrative might appear to be too diffuse and multiform to be reducible to a technical field. Even within the limited range of textual genres left to us by medieval culture, it could be argued, narrative is self-evidently a much larger and looser category than those types of objects, such as coins, seals and charters, that benefit from the specialized approaches we noted above. The aim of this chapter is not to disprove this line of argument, which appears wholly reasonable, but to turn it around: the ubiquity of narrative in life 'out there' and its prominent place in our primary source repertoires are not reasons to avoid technical or theoretical engagements. On the contrary, they are challenges to see how much a field such as narratology can add to an already rich and deep reserve of scholarly insight and experience. In specific terms, this chapter will explore these issues by drawing upon three well-known crusade narratives chosen as a representative sample: the anonymous *Gesta Francorum* from the First Crusade, the *De expugnatione Lyxbonensi*, which recounts the conquest of Lisbon in 1147 and is now ascribed to an Anglo-Norman cleric named Raol, and Robert of Clari's narrative of the Fourth Crusade, *La conquête de Constantinople*.

WHAT IS A NARRATIVE AND WHAT IS NARRATOLOGY?

But before we consider these texts, some general remarks are necessary. First of all, what is narrative? There are as many definitions as there are theorists who have pronounced upon it. But a workable formulation that captures the essentials would be the representation of human action by means of signs. At the risk of straying into tautology, narratives may also be defined as any communicative act that displays the quality of narrativity. In its simplest terms, that is to say with regard to the briefest possible narrative utterances, there is some debate among theorists as to what is necessary and sufficient for narrativity to be present. Does one action suffice, for example, or must there be at least two? If the latter, how close must the causal, temporal or other connection between the actions be? Does narrative require some form of awareness, however low-level and left to inference, on the part of human or human-like agents, or does an account of a herd of animals stampeding or a meteor hitting a forest possess narrativity? Such seemingly abstruse questions about the minimum requirements of narrativity actually have a practical bearing upon the medieval source base to a greater degree than might be supposed, because a number of source types are on or near the margins of narrativity: many administrative, financial and legal records, for example, offer up brief flashes of narrated human action, sometimes in nothing more than a clause or participle. At a somewhat higher level of narrative complexity one encounters many sources in which a short but recognizable, and more or less coherent, narrative is present, even though the primary function of the source, its reason for being, is not to tell a story as such. Dominique Barthélemy borrowed the term *narrativité* to capture a recurrent feature of the eleventh- and twelfth-century charters from his chosen area of central-western France, namely the documents' narrative adumbration of background circumstances, such as the twists and turns of a property dispute, or changes in a pious donor's familial circumstances and religious aspirations (Barthélemy 1993). Similarly Joel Rosenthal has emphasized the narrative dimension within late medieval English legal records (Rosenthal 2003).

Most narratological study, however, concerns itself with higher-order texts, complexes of multiple units of minumum narrativity that may themselves be designated as a narrative in the singular. Within the medieval source corpus, such texts would include saints' lives, *miracula*, *translationes* and other hagiographical genres, as well as historiographical writings of all types. (The limit case here would be sets of annals comprising series of individually laconic utterances that appear, at least on first reading, thematically unconnected to one another but in fact possess underlying narrativity: cf. Foot 2005). And just as texts characterizable as narrative in their generic make-up may contain passages of non-narrative such as description and argument, so also complex, sometimes even lengthy, sequences of narrative are to be found nested in texts such as doctrinal treatises, sermons and letters that are not themselves principally narrative in their content, form and horizon of reader expectations.

The study of the crusades is well served by narrative source survivals. As is well known, the First Crusade was the stimulus for a rich florescence of narrative histories dedicated in whole or in substantial part to the events of 1095/6–99 (and sometimes beyond). Although good news for the historian of the First Crusade, the sheer richness of this body of material has had the effect of making the narrative corpora relating to all later crusades seem impoverished by comparison, even in those instances such as the Third Crusade and the Albigensian Crusade where significant clusters of narrative sources survive. It is important to stress how very unusual the First Crusade was as an historiographical phenomenon, for reasons that have only recently begun to be explored systematically, and which have something to do with, but certainly do not boil down to, the novelty value of the First Crusade as idea and experience. The First Crusade also lent itself to multiple retellings because it fulfilled its principal objectives whereas other crusades, those to the East at any rate, never attained the same level of satisfying narrative closure. On one level, then, the First Crusade narrative corpus sets up expectations that subsequent bodies of crusade texts are bound to disappoint, but subsequent crusade historiography is for all that a rich and variegated resource: witness, for example, the manner in which Robert of Clari's and Geoffrey of Villehardouin's narratives of the Fourth Crusade were at the forefront of the innovative extension of Old French prose to the writing of contemporary history. Put another way, the whole crusade corpus, not just that concerning the First Crusade, participated fully in central and late medieval historiographical culture, and consequently the insights into it that narratology may afford are potentially of similarly wide application.

But what, specifically, is narratology? (See Abbott 2010; Keen 2003; Rimmon-Kenan 2002.) The word's etymology would suggest that it is the study of narrative and narration in the round, but in practice its operational boundaries have been more tightly drawn. Nor is it simply a synonym for 'narrative theory'. Narratology is essentially a subset, or a survival, of Structuralism, and as such amounts to a collection of approaches to the study of narratives in which the main categories of analysis reflect their structuralist inspiration in their dyadic (or sometimes triadic) configurations. Narrative appears in all types of communicative media (hence the inclusion in the above definition of the phrase 'by means of signs'), but in practice most narratologists most of the time have worked on written texts. (But see e.g. Lewis 1999 for the application of narratological approaches to visual material.) Although theorists offer up an all-embracing vision of narratology's applicability to any and all species of narrative, in practice the discipline has concentrated on literary texts, more specifically novels written between the eighteenth and twentieth centuries as well as modernist and postmodernist texts that subvert the story-telling norms of the 'classic' novel in ways that neatly comport with narratological categories of analysis. Narratology's literary grounding is one reason for many historians' wariness of it – as one very distinguished historian of medieval Europe exclaimed in a seminar a few years ago, there was a grave danger of simply 'treating sources just like novels'. More specifically, it raises questions about the fit between historical and literary catagories of textual analysis. And it thereby shades into debates about what, if anything, differentiates fictional from non-fictional discourse. By extension, narratology gestures in the direction of postmodernist critiques of historical writing's claims to truth and extratextual referentiality; that is to say, attacks on mainstream history's central premises most associated, of course, with the work of Hayden White (see esp. White 1978, 1989, 1999). Limitations of space mean that it is not possible to go into a detailed discussion of these wider debates. But one particular set of remarks is in order.

Narratology's roots in Structuralism mean that it can be isolated in large measure from the implications of the later intellectual movements that to a large extent reacted against structuralist paradigms. In other words, to apply narratological approaches to a given historical text is not tantamount to smuggling in radical claims about the fictive basis of all historiographical utterance and the historian's thoroughgoing imposition of narrative order upon the chaos of the world. This is not to say that narratology is 'safe' or 'easy', nor is it necessarily ideologically neutral, but it does not carry the anti-historical (and, frankly, anti-historian) baggage that characterizes a good deal of poststructuralist theory. In the last two decades or so narratology has significantly expanded its range of critical and theoretical engagements, informing, for example, feminist, postcolonial and queer-theory readings of texts. This ability to go with the intellectual flow is doubtless a positive sign. But it is also noteworthy how much textbook-type treatments of narratology, from the perspective of this non-specialist at least (and this is anecdotally supported by several students' remarks), lose much of their expositional clarity and systemic sharpness when they shift from what is sometimes termed 'classical' narratology to various of its recent theoretical applications (see e.g. Bal 2009). The practising historian confronted with a narrative text, and seeking some analytical purchase on it, is almost certainly not intending to become a fully fledged narratologist. Nor, for that matter, is she or he aiming to enshrine the text in question in narratology's canon (though this might prove a salutary indirect consequence down the line). She or he is simply looking for tools; and classical narratology is the best place to find the initial toolkit. In due course, the toolkit may, if research directions so suggest, be expanded to embrace post-classical narratology's broader suite of concerns, the thematic overlaps with cultural historical inquiry suggesting many possible synergies.

Narratology's own narrative of origins tends to begin with the linguistics of Ferdinand de Saussure (1857–1913), and then works up through various schools and movements, such as the Russian Formalists of the 1920s and 1930s and the Prague School of the 1930s, building towards its defining intellectual moment: French Structuralism of the 1960s and 1970s as represented by such scholars as Roland Barthes, Algirdas Greimas, Claude Bremond, Gérard Genette and Julia Kristeva. It was another of these theorists, Tzvetan Todorov, who coined the term *narratologie* in his 1969 study of Boccaccio's *Decameron*. Their insights were extended and systematized between the 1970s and 1990s, in particular by theorists in the United States and Israel, and it is largely from this body of work that classical narratology has emerged within anglophone scholarship. (Other academic traditions, notably that in the German-speaking world, have followed somewhat different trajectories.)

NARRATOLOGICAL SUBJECTS: TIME

What are classical narratology's signature concerns? One is to ask what is fundamental, and what simply incidental, to the workings of narrative. Action is central to all definitions of narrative, so it is unsurprising that this has attracted a great deal of attention, in particular insofar as action, even interior mental process, necessarily involves movement through time. There is a pointed contrast to be made here with the typical narrative treatment of space. Some narratives devote a good deal of attention to filling out the details of the settings in and through which their characters move, what is sometimes termed the 'diegesis' (a helpful but not altogether unambiguous term) or 'storyworld'. But most narratives most of the time prove on close inspection to function with very little or even no diegetic detail. It is true that reader inference goes to work even on – or especially on – diegetically bald texts. To say that a crusader rode into battle, for instance, is to trigger the reader's mental conjuring up of a horse even if it is not explicitly mentioned. Most of the implications that a narrative suggests are only trivially true, though much of the historian's task when engaged in close reading is constantly to be scanning for that subset of all possible inferences that might prove meaningful: 'If X is the case, what does this imply that the source is not mentioning?' That said, the amplitude of the storyworld, that expressly supplied and that left to inference, is very much at the mercy of the individual text, a point well illustrated by crusade narratives.

For example, the account of the First Crusade in the *Gesta Francorum* (and the text known as the *Peregrinatio Antiochie* which may have been its progenitor) focuses much of its attention on the deeds not of the Franks collectively but on one of the crusade's leaders, Bohemond of Taranto. Indeed, the work may have originated in a material assembled for a planned *Gesta Boamundi*, before the author's expanding conception of the crusade led him to enlarge his substantive and ideological frames of reference. Given Bohemond's importance within the plot of the *Gesta Francorum*, it is noteworthy how little we are told about Bohemond himself, his appearance and physical presence. The nearest we come is the fleeting mention of a no less fleeting wry smile that plays across Bohemond's lips after he is thwarted when the other crusade leaders spot his (rather telegraphed) attempt to deceive them (*Gesta Francorum* 1962: 45). The *Gesta Francorum* is not unusual among crusade narratives in its parsimonious realization of its storyworld. Other texts may include passages of dense description, but these tend to announce themselves as interludes precisely because they are exceptional. This general tendency has important implications, incidentally, for historians' habitual inclination to privilege so-called eyewitness sources, of which, of course, crusade historiography supplies many examples. But the diegeses that these eyewitnesses construct are usually skeletal. And even when the eyewitness author's own perceptions are at play, this is often expressed obliquely. Robert of Clari, for example, does not tell the reader that Venice and Constantinople are marvellous cities to behold on the basis of his having seen them for himself; he says what it was like for the fourth crusaders (of whom he was one) when they saw these places (Robert of Clari 1936: 39, 67; 2005: 10, 50).

If the world of visual (and other sensory) perception is only fitfully realized in narratives such as crusade histories, the situation is altogether different with respect to the handling of time. Time is embedded in all action itself as well as in the durative or punctual verbs that express action; and the manner in which a narrative handles time is perhaps the single most important guide to understanding that it offers the reader. Especially since Genette's groundbreaking work on Proust's manipulation of time in *A la recherche du temps perdu*, time has been a central focus of narratological study (see Genette 1980; also Chatman 1978: 62–84). Genette showed how 'text time' – a metaphor for the amount of space on the page occupied by a given sequence – constantly dances around the notionally measurable passage of clock- or calendar-time that can be extrapolated from, or projected onto, the events in the storyworld. Narratives can slow down time, speed it up, skip over it, describe once a type of event that happened several times, or return several times to an event that happened once. Genette's predeliction for technical neologisms with Greek roots has left us with perhaps his two most useful concepts: prolepsis, which is when a narrative flashes forward to anticipate the future before returning to the moment in the main narrative arc that it had reached, the 'now' of its storyworld; and analepsis, or flashback, often directed towards the filling in of explanatory background. The latter device in particular, in the hands of a skilful author, can send out powerful signals about the regime of causation, human motivation, and interconnectedness between events that is brought to the fashioning of the text's storyworld. For example, Robert of Clari's history of the Fourth Crusade includes substantial and well-signposted analepses, reaching back more than twenty years and embracing the Latin East as well as Byzantium, in order to explain the dysfunctional state of Byzantine imperial dynastic succession in the period after the death of Manuel Komnenos, and the vengeful animus felt by Boniface of Monterrat towards the Greeks (Robert of Clari 1936: 46–57, 59–66; 2005: 20–36, 40–8).

TIME, COORDINATION AND REFERENCE

Robert's thoughtful handling of time helps to give the lie to the still persistent stereotype of crusade narratives, in particular those written by participants, as unsophisticated accumulations of loosely coordinated statements with little underlying sense of interconnection and pattern. The textual feature most often adduced in support of this stereotype is parataxis, the use of generally snappy main clauses featuring one or few subjects performing one or few actions and linked by coordination rather than subordination. What parataxis ostensibly loses is the scope for nuance, amplification and qualification that subordination offers. And even within the system of coordination itself, extreme parataxis favours the more punctual and neutral forms ('and', 'then', 'next') over those that imply, however dimly, the presence of some connection or rationale ('for', 'so', 'therefore'). Paratactical text would seem to communicate a one-dimensional view of time in which one thing happens, then another, then another, and in which the human scale of the action remains more or less constant: such passages tend not to jump back and forth between small and large events, nor between instantive occurrences and circumstantial background. As will be readily apparent, paratactical delivery carries powerful associations with infantile speech patterns, and by extension it can easily be read as evidence of unsophisticated literary craft. The presence of paratactical sequences in the *Gesta Francorum*, for example, has contributed to the persistent belief that it is the work of a 'simple' crusader (whatever that means), probably a knight. Such a characterization is demonstrably incorrect: the stylistic craft on show in the text and its rich interlay of biblical quotation and allusion point to a quite well-educated author, almost certainly a cleric. Moreover, the passages of sustained parataxis that have been taken to be the text's signature style in fact occupy only a fairly small proportion of the work as a whole. In other words, parataxis represents a choice, an expression of literary creativity (however modest), rather than the best rendering of action in time that an unsophisticated author could manage.

Robert of Clari is another supposedly 'simple' author – he *was* a knight, after all – who draws on parataxis. Again, however, authorial artifice is evident. For example, in narrating, within an extended analepsis, the swift rise to power of the emperor Alexios III Angelos (1195–1203), Robert states:

> Afterwards it happened one day that the emperor [Isaac II Angelos] went hunting in the forest, and what does Alexius his brother do but go into the forest where the emperor was and take him by treason and put out his eyes. Then when he was done with this, he had

him put in prison in such a way that no one knew anything about it. And when he had done this, he came back to Constantinople and made them believe that the emperor his brother was dead, and he had himself crowned emperor by force.

(Robert of Clari 1936: 57; 2005: 36)

Within the bald sequence of events that can be reassembled from this passage, time is layered in interesting ways. Beyond the framing event of the imperial hunt (the work of one day, or several days spent away from Constantinople?), time in the longer term stretches back to the putative origin of Alexios's ambitions for power at his brother's expense (which the text has not mentioned up to this point). It could be argued that the passage permits a reading of Alexios's action as the result of a spur-of-the-moment, opportunistic impulse, but this is not very plausible: Alexios's pre-formed purpose is implied by our being told of his going into the forest; and although this is the first point at which the reader is made aware of Alexios's apparently 'true' character, his behaviour is consistent with the negative view of the instability of Byzantine political culture and public life that subtends the narrative as a whole. Further questions are posed by the rendering of Alexios's actions back in Constantinople. What sort of act or acts of persuasion and deception are subsumed within 'made them believe' (*fist acroire*), and over how long a period? One speech or a sustained campaign of misinformation? How long was the interval between Alexios's return and his coronation? How far ahead has Robert jumped by means of the construction 'and he had himself crowned' (*se fist couronner*)?

These are questions that, in principle and to some extent in fact thanks to the availability of other sources, could be answered with reference to modern historians' reconstructions of what happened in 'real' time in and around Constantinople in 1195. But it is important to remember that the storyworld that Robert's narrative calls forth is not that of modern historical reconstruction, even if there happen to be numerous homologies between the two, and even though Robert's stated aim was to write the truth (see Robert of Clari 1936: 128; 2005: 132–4). Robert was not doing a bad job of being a modern-day historian: his manipulations of time point to his crafting of a storyworld that faces inwards into the workings of the text at least as much as, and probably more than, it attempts a correlation with the chronological ordering of historical actuality as we would understand it. The jump in time expressed by 'and he had himself crowned' is part of the meaning-making operations of the text (whatever meanings we choose to read off it), rather than a case of Robert, so to speak, looking at a calendar for 1195 and deciding to skip the space between two points on it as a matter of convenience.

The important distinction at stake in this example is often missed in modern historians' readings of medieval historical narratives, which tend to cut straight through the storyworlds of the texts to the extratextual reference, to the extent at least that this can be retrieved from the available evidence. Questions of a text's historical 'reliability' and 'value' are then posed and answered with reference to an external master-narrative. Illustrative in this regard are the notes to the editions and translations of historical narratives that do such helpful work as supplying dates (note that Robert does not specify when Alexios's coup took place), offering potted biographies, transposing the location of events onto modern geography, and generally filling out the contextual background. It is salutary to remember that, useful as such notes can be, their cumulative effect is to stage a confrontation between the text in question and the modern historian's master-narrative that envelops it, an unequal contest that will always turn out in favour of the latter. Of the various approaches that fall

653

under the umbrella of narratology, it is perhaps our ability to dissect a text's handling of time, deploying categories of analysis supplied by Genette and other scholars, that is most useful in this regard. For this creates a constant *Verfremdungseffekt* reminding us that a medieval historical narrative should be understood with respect to its own world-making operations, not just the empirical world of the contextualizing footnote.

THE COMMUNICATIVE MODEL: IMPLIED AUTHORS AND NARRATORS

This Janus-like quality of medieval historiography, looking both inwards into its own textual operations and outwards to the actuality of the past (or at least a decent approximation to it), also bears upon another of narratology's major concerns, namely how to understand a text as a communicative act. How does a written text effect some illocutionary connection between the author who writes it and the reader who reads it? The reader will probably not have personal knowledge of the author. She or he may have some paratextual information to bring to a reading of the text, such as generic markers in the title (if there is one) or familiarity with other works by the same author. But by and large the text itself must shoulder the communicative burden, which is where the narratological focus on a work's poetics, its meaning-making operations, comes into play. Narratology's approach has been to model the communicative process as a series of moves, or textual levels, interposed between the author and the reader and linked by directional markers representing the communication flow. Different models have been proposed, but the neatest and best known is that developed by Seymour Chatman, in which everything between the real author and the real reader is to be found within the pages of the text (Chatman 1978: 147–51):

real author > implied author > narrator > narratee > implied reader > real reader

Classical narratology has by and large devoted most attention to the entities on the left-hand side of this diagram, although the recent growth of narratological interest in cognitive poetics and forms of reception theory has shifted the centre of gravity somewhat further to the right. Valuable, however, as are the levels on the right-hand side of the diagram in the context of medieval historiography – for example, when thinking about a work's intended readership or the extent to which its manuscript transmission provides evidence for its cultural impact – it is probably the left-hand side that has the potential to contribute more to an understanding of medieval narrative sources.

Before we turn to the narrator, the single most important level, it is useful to consider the implied author. There is lively scholarly debate over whether the implied author is something (or some*one*) planted within a text by the real author as a kind of persona or 'front'. Is it simply a secondary effect or incidental by-product of a narrative's communicative functions? Or is it a mental projection generated by the real reader's cognitive processing of what she or he is reading (in which case *inferred* author would be the more accurate term)? (See Kindt and Müller 2006.) Viewed pragmatically as the solution to a kind of biographical mystery, the implied author represents an anthropomorphized synthesis of all the various answers that a text can be made to deliver to the question 'What does this say about the person who wrote it?' Some of the answers to this question will relate to the author's external circumstances, such as where and when she or he lived, or to matters of cultural background, such as linguistic competence and knowledge of other texts. According, however,

654

to Wayne Booth, who first devised the concept of the implied author in his 1961 work *The Rhetoric of Fiction* and whose formulation perhaps remains the most elegant and convincing, the implied author also has an ethical function as the perceived source of the values and sensibilities that inform the text. Some theorists, such as Genette, would dispense with the implied author altogether, arguing that it contributes nothing to an understanding of a text's communicative dynamic; but most scholars accept that, however difficult to pin down in practice, it is a valuable addition to the communication model.

From the perspective of the practising medieval historian, the concept of the implied author is especially useful as a warning-shot across the methodological bows, a reminder to avoid the kind of conceptual short-cut that is nicely illustrated by two recurrent turns of phrase. The first of these typically appears in 'The Author' sections of the introductions to the editions or translations of historical texts, and is some variant on the form 'Everything that/most of what we know about the author has to be derived from the text itself.' With respect to the more or less objective biographical information that can be derived in this way, the what and where of the author's life, this is a perfectly sound move, though even here we know so little about almost every medieval author that it is deceptively easy to slip into 'must have' (stereo-)typing in an attempt to flesh things out. Booth's notion of the implied author as ethical source provides a valuable added dimension. For although modern-day scholars are generally less confident than were their nineteenth- and early twentieth-century predecessors about calling forth the character and personal qualities of an author from the depths of the text, one regularly encounters the sort of conflation of work and author in the second symptomatic formulation, which goes along the lines of 'Orderic Vitalis is our best source for late eleventh- and early twelfth-century Normandy.' The fact that this form of shorthand is so common, and feels so natural, illustrates the biographism that still dominates much discussion of medieval historiography. The implied author is not a stand-in or double for the real author, in such a way that to characterize the one is always to get an accurate fix on the other. The implied author is a distillation or refinement of the personal experience and ethical positioning of the real author. Biographist readings can lose sight of this important distinction.

Modern-day scholarship has been very good at digging into medieval historical texts themselves, in the process often arriving via more intuitive and less theoretically freighted routes at the same sorts of insights that narratology and other branches of literary study afford. But when one moves from the text itself to the nexus between text and the author, approaches tend to remain more old-fashioned. This explains, for example, the persistence of the thesis that the author of the *Gesta Francorum* was a knight, a position based on an invalid syllogism rooted in the old-fashioned assumptions of the nineteenth-century historians Heinrich von Sybel and Heinrich Hagenmeyer, who came up with it: simple texts are the work of simple authors (highly debatable); the *Gesta Francorum* is a simple text (demonstrably incorrect); therefore the author of the *Gesta Francorum* was a simple crusader, whose biographical circumstances as inferred from the text demonstrate that he was a knight (almost certainly incorrect). The concept of the implied author is a good protection against slipping into this sort of deterministic biographism. Texts do not write themselves, of course, and real authors are, and were, real people moving in real historical time. But placing some distance between the implied and real author is a good protection against the tendency to short-circuit debates about a text's significance by over-emphasizing the real author as against the other levels in the communicative process.

If the implied author is a debated concept, the figure of the narrator is even more so (see Currie 2010). Simply put, the figure of the narrator responds to the feeling on the part of an attentive reader that she or he is being told the story by a human or human-like interlocutor. It is noteworthy how much the metaphorical language used to describe this effect and the manner of readers' awareness of it presupposes a close analogy between the reading of a written narrative and oral communication: the reader 'hears' the 'voice' that is 'speaking' or 'telling' the story. These metaphors also illustrate how easy it is, using face-to-face conversation as the guide model, to project anthropomorphic qualities, even a full persona, onto what is a textual effect. It must be emphasized that the narrator is not a homunculus (or female equivalent) mysteriously at large within the pages of a book. Some more rigorous-minded theorists attempt to get round the trap of easy anthropomorphism by means of circumlocutions such as 'narrating instance' and the use of the pronoun 'it' rather than 'she' or 'he', though the results of such scrupulousness are seldom elegant or indeed clearer than the traditional terminology. The persistence of the term 'narrator' in scholarly discourse is reinforced, moreover, by the fact that almost all narratives almost all of the time – including every medieval historiographical text above the level of the most skeletal of annals – work to construct a sense of a consciousness controlling the content and form of the narrative. But, it might be asked, is this consciousness not simply that of the (real) author? Why is the figure of the narrator necessary? Indeed, a sceptic might be forgiven for wondering whether the narrator functions as a kind of free pass or alibi, permitting scholars to argue in anthropomorphic terms when confronted with the traces of human creativity and craft that narratives present on every page, while deferring to critical strictures about the death of the author. But that certainly would be too jaundiced a view, for narratologists make a strong case for the independent value of the concept of the narrator.

Narrators come in a multitude of guises and equipped with a wide range of competences. Is the narrator able to jump instantaneously across time and space, or does it appear to be constrained by the same physical limitations that act on a real-world individual? Does the narrator bring a God-like omniscience to its knowledge of its storyworld, or are there blind spots and grey areas? *Pari passu*, is the narrator able to drill into characters' brains to extract what they are thinking and feeling, even the 'mind stuff' which is beyond their own conscious awareness? Or is the construction of characters' rational and emotive states limited by the same constraints that govern real-world social interactions? Is the narrator 'reliable' (another anthropomorphism), or has it either got its facts wrong or misunderstood the correct facts at its disposal? Is the narrator internally consistent, or does it flick between easy omniscience and disavowals of knowledge? Most importantly of all, perhaps, where does the narrator stand in relation to the storyworld that its own narrative is fashioning? Here, once again, Genette's Greek-based neologisms have become useful scholarly jargon. Thus, for example, a homodiegetic narrator functions as a character within the storyworld, while a heterodiegetic narrator speaks from outside it. A reading of crusade narratives reveals all these sorts of distinctions at play.

In our three sample texts, as in crusade histories in general, the narratorial situatedness is broadly characterizable as heterodiegetic; the crusaders are spoken of in the third person plural by a narrator to whom knowledge is mostly, as it were, spontaneously and fully available, and who does not routinely disclose the sources of that knowledge, though exceptions to this are made in mentions of specific interlocutors or documents, or in references to disembodied rumour and common report. But there is also movement in and out of homodiegetic narration, typically signposted by a switching to the first person plural. To give just one small example, the *De expugnatione* remarks that 'we saw' (*vidimus*) an unusual fish, a species of ray, on an Iberian beach (*De expugnatione* 2001: 64–5). Presumably the reader is meant to picture the author himself among those on the shore that day, but the experience is generalized and abstracted by the use of the plural. First person singular narration is quite rare, much of what there is being concerned with brief, nested autobiographical segments or disavowals of knowledge. Other than such disavowals, the scopes of the texts' knowledge and understanding push outwards in the direction of omniscience: the narrator of the *Gesta Francorum*, for instance, famously knows details of the conversation between the Turkish generalissimo Kerbogha and his mother on the eve of the battle of Antioch (*Gesta Francorum* 1962: 53–6); while Robert of Clari's narrator knows how the inhabitants of cities on the Adriatic coast reacted to the sight of the crusade fleet, and what high-status Byzantine women felt and said to one another when they witnessed the crusaders' chivalric prowess in action from the windows and walls of Constantinople (Robert of Clari 1936: 43, 75; 2005: 16, 60).

Narrators can also imply that they have access to greater stores of knowledge than appear on the page: the narrator of the *De expugnatione* reassures the reader that he has edited out the more bumptious contributions to a debate among the crusaders, while 'reality effect' moments of seemingly unmotivated precision, such as, in the same text, details of the exact depth of the water over which the crusaders are sailing off Britanny and the dimensions of a siege tower, evoke a narrator that is observant, precise, and authoritative (*De expugnatione* 2001: 58–9, 100–1, 142–3). In places the absence of narratorial guidance to the reader can be as significant as its presence. For example, Robert of Clari's narrator withholds explanation or comment when reporting that the people of Constantinople did not recognize the imperial pretender Alexios when he was paraded before them by the Venetians. The narrator usually supplies some rationale or motivation for the pay-off in such narrative sequences, so why not here? Are Alexios's credentials (he will fall out with the Franks later in the narrative) being undermined in this passage? Other effects that are present in these texts, as in many others, include the quickening of time across 'slack' periods, and at the other end of the scale the slowing down of narrative time by means of compacted detail: one plot situation in which such temporal retardation seems to have become conventional is the climactic moment in a siege in which the attackers break through or surmount the defences, or a similar moment of touch-and-go tension. Narrators also signpost transitions in subject and theme, select examples to illustrate recurrent events, and frame particular episodes as synecdoches of larger patterns of mood and behaviour: the narrator of the *De expugnatione*, for example, makes such contextualizing remarks about the predispositions of the crusaders from Cologne and Flanders (*De expugnatione* 2001: 170–1).

CONCLUSION

It should be emphasized that the foregoing discussion has covered only some of the principal concerns of narratological study. Particular mention should also be made of the question of focalization: this identifies the manner in which the narration of action may be filtered through the consciousness of one or more observers present within the diegesis or positioned outside it. In the *Gesta Francorum*, for example, the initial awareness of changes in situation is regularly routed through Bohemond's eyes, as if his perceptual acuity reflects a particularly shrewd appreciation of the crusaders' circumstances (e.g. *Gesta Francorum* 1962: 7, 18, 36). It should be emphasized that crusade texts are not, in narratological terms, a class apart from other types of medieval historiography, nor do they constitute a discrete genre that is characterizable by certain narrative conventions. The fact that crusade histories almost always narrate movement over long distances (as well as periods of stasis) means that their handling of the dynamic between space and time, or 'chronotope' – present in, for example, choices about what to linger over in descriptive detail and what to skip over, when to fast-forward and when to pause – can be more overtly 'exoskeletal' than in some other types of historical writing. But this is not an invariable. The fact that several crusade texts were written by those who had participated in the events, at least to some extent, can problematize the construction of the narrator, who, often within the space of a single text, can retreat into use of the third person and hetero-diegetic non-visibility; adopt an intermediate series of positions expressed through the first person plural, where the exact extent of the 'we' in any instance is usually unstated and is at best left to inference from the story logic; or insert itself into the diegesis by means of the first person singular. Even in this last case there are variables, however, for the first person singular narrator can be fully involved in autobiographical mode as an actor within the storyworld or strive for semi-detachment by appearing as an observer or checker of detail after the fact. Again, these features can be interestingly foregrounded in crusade texts but are not specific to them. All the above remarks would fully apply, for example, to Galbert of Bruges's eyewitness account of the events surrounding the murder of Count Charles the Good of Flanders.

The figure of the narrator is especially interesting because it has become a focal point of debates about the relationship between fictional and non-fictional writing. Scholars such as Dorrit Cohn who have defended the separation of these two discourses against the critiques of speech-act theorists and philosophers of history, foremost among them of course Hayden White, have argued that the figures of the (real) author and narrator are co-extensive in works of non-fiction such as history, but not in fiction (Cohn 1999; Doležel 2010). This is a strong argument, but its drawback from a medievalist's perspective is that it works best with regard to historical writing in the academic idiom that has emerged since the nineteenth century. It does not follow that because medieval historical writings stake out some reference to events that existed beyond the text, and may even be accurate in many of their truth claims, they must fall on the non-fictional side of a binary that is grounded in post-medieval taxonomies. For their part, modern-day historians can be as invested as literary scholars in the preservation of this binary, which is why the claim that, say, there is a narrator or narrators in texts such as the *Gesta Francorum* or the *De expugnatione* can seem unsettling. But it is not a case of the authors of such works lying or of their pretending to be someone or something else. And it is not about treating these texts as if they were novels (cf. Otter 2005; Stein 2005). Narratology is not a theoretical creed or an end in itself, simply a suite of analytical tools to be used in whatever permutations a given text warrants. These tools are flexible: despite attempts to differentiate between stylistics and narratology, for example, these clearly overlap, as they both do with rhetoric. But narratology is not a magic key. It simply complements and extends the close reading of texts in ways that can invite new insights, and it brings a technical vocabulary and conceptual precision to bear on that reading. For these reasons it has the potential to enrich our understanding of crusading's extensive narrative source base.

REFERENCES

Abbott, HP 2008, *The Cambridge Introduction to Narrative*, 2nd edn, Cambridge University Press, Cambridge.

Bal, M 2009, *Narratology: Introduction to the Theory of Narrative*, 3rd edn, University of Toronto Press, Toronto.

Barthélemy, D 1993, *La société dans le comté de Vendôme de l'an mil au xivᵉ siècle*, Fayard, Paris.

Booth, W 1961, *The Rhetoric of Fiction*, University of Chicago Press, Chicago.

Bruner, J 1986, *Actual Minds, Possible Worlds*, Harvard University Press, Cambridge, MA.

Chatman, S 1978, *Story and Discourse: Narrative Structure in Fiction and Film*, Cornell University Press, Ithaca.

Cohn, D 1999, *The Distinction of Fiction*, Johns Hopkins University Press, Baltimore.

Connerton, P 1989, *How Societies Remember*, Cambridge University Press, Cambridge.

Cubitt, G 2007, *History and Memory*, Manchester University Press, Manchester.

Currie, G 2010, *Narratives and Narrators: A Philosophy of Stories*, Oxford University Press, Oxford.

De expugnatione Lyxbonsensi: The Conquest of Lisbon 2001, ed. and trans. CW David, rev. JP Phillips, Columbia University Press, New York.

Dewald, C 2005, *Thucydides' War Narrative: A Structural Study*, University of California Press, Berkeley.

Doležel, L 2010, *Possible Worlds of Fiction and History: The Postmodern Stage*, Johns Hopkins University Press, Baltimore.

Feldherr, A (ed.) 2009, *The Cambridge Companion to the Roman Historians*, Cambridge University Press, Cambridge.

Fentress, J and Wickham, C 1992, *Social Memory*, Blackwell, Oxford.

Fludernik, M 2005, 'Histories of narrative theory (II): from structuralism to the present' in *A Companion to Narrative Theory*, eds J Phelan and PJ Rabinowitz, Blackwell, Oxford, 36–59.

Foot, S 2005, 'Finding the meaning of form: narrative in annals and chronicles' in *Writing Medieval History*, ed. N Partner, Hodder Arnold, London, 88–108.

Genette, G 1980, *Narrative Disscourse: An Essay in Method*, trans. JE Lewin, Cornell University Press, Ithaca.

Gesta Francorum et aliorum Hierosolimitanorum 1962, ed. and trans. RMT Hill, Thomas Nelson & Sons, Edinburgh.

Herman, D 2005, 'Histories of narrative theory (I): a genealogy of early developments' in *A Companion to Narrative Theory*, eds J Phelan and PJ Rabinowitz, Blackwell, Oxford, 19–35.

de Jong, IJF 2014, *Narratology and Classics: A Practical Guide*, Oxford University Press, Oxford.

Keen, S 2003, *Narrative Form*, Palgrave Macmillan, Basingstoke.

Kindt, T and Müller H-H 2006, *The Implied Author: Concept and Controversy*, Walter de Gruyter, Berlin.

Lewis, S 1999, *The Rhetoric of Power in the Bayeux Tapestry*, Cambridge University Press, Cambridge.

Maynes, MJ, Pierce, JL and Laslett B 2008, *Telling Stories: The Use of Personal Narratives in the Social Sciences and History*, Cornell University Press, Ithaca.

Otter, M 2005, 'Functions of fiction in historical writing' in *Writing Medieval History*, ed. N Partner, Hodder Arnold, London, 109–30.

Randall, WL 1995, *The Stories We Are: An Essay in Self-Creation*, University of Toronto Press, Toronto.

Rimmon-Kenan, S 2002, *Narrative Fiction: Contemporary Poetics*, 2nd edn, Routledge, London.

Robert of Clari 1936, *The Conquest of Constantinople*, trans. EH McNeal, Columbia University Press, New York.

———— 2005, *La Conquête de Constantinople*, ed. P Noble, Société Rencesvals British Branch, Edinburgh.

Rosenthal, JT 2003, *Telling Tales: Sources and Narration in Late Medieval England*, Pennsylvania University Press, University Park, PA.

Sachs, O 1986, *The Man Who Mistook His Wife for a Hat*, Picador, London.

Stein, RM 2005, 'Literary criticism and the evidence for history' in *Writing Medieval History*, ed. N Partner, Hodder Arnold, London, 67–87.

Todorov, T 1969, *Grammaire du Décaméron*, Mouton, Paris.

White, H 1978, *Tropics of Discourse: Essays in Cultural Criticism*, Johns Hopkins University Press, Baltimore.

——— 1989, *The Content of the Form: Narrative Discourse and Historical Representation*, Johns Hopkins University Press, Baltimore.

——— 1999, *Figural Realism: Studies in the Mimesis Effect*, Johns Hopkins University Press, Baltimore.

PART VIII

STUDYING THE CRUSADES

———•◆•———

CHAPTER THIRTY-SIX

FROM SEPPHORIS TO NAZARETH: ASPECTS OF CRUSADER HISTORIOGRAPHY AND A NEW READING OF THE NAZARETH SCULPTURE

------- • ◆ • -------

Gil Fishhof

INTRODUCTION

From its beginning in the second half of the nineteenth century and through much of the twentieth century, the study of crusader art concentrated on several major questions (Folda, 1995: 5–17). One such question related to identifying the origin of those artists working at major crusader sites. For such French scholars as Camile Enlart or Paul Deschamps, these origins were absolutely clear. For them, crusader art was above all an extension, beyond the sea, of French art and architecture and constituted a sort of regional school, equivalent to the great schools of French Romanesque art such as those of Burgundy or Languedoc (Enlart, 1925–28; Deschamps, 1931). In a celebrated quotation, Enlart claimed that if a church from the Latin Kingdom of Jerusalem would have been transported to the valleys of the Rhône, the Allier or the Garonne rivers, it would have been hard to distinguish it from the indigenous churches (Enlart, 1925–28: I, 32).

From these early formulations of the origins of crusader art, several directions evolved. Attempts were made to identify ever more accurately the origins and itineraries of specific Western masters arriving in the Holy Land, the most notable of whom was a master working in Nazareth, whose style was identified on a capital in the church of Saint-Martin in Plaimpied (Berry) and whose itinerary through the Rhone valley and from there to the Holy Land was elaborately traced by Alan Borg (Borg, 1982).

At the same time, the understanding of the nature of crusader art became greatly enriched. As early as the work of Thomas Boase in 1939, the impact of Byzantine art on the art of the Latin Kingdom was recognized (Boase, 1939), especially in mural and mosaic cycles such as those of Bethlehem. Examination of the complex connections between Byzantine and crusader arts was later elaborated by Gustav Kühnel (Kühnel, G. 1988) and Annemarie Weyl Carr (Weyl Carr, 1982), while the artistic links between the Latin Kingdom and southern Italy were studied by Helmut Buschhausen (Buschhausen, 1978) and Valentino Pace (Pace, 1982). Additionally, more nuanced and detailed studies of workshops active in the Latin Kingdom were conducted by Zehava Jacoby, who developed the concept of the 'Workshop of the Temple Area' (Jacoby, 1979, 1982, 1985). This concept was later criticized by Lucy-Anne Hunt, who in place of an organized workshop proposed, rather, the model of individual sculptors entering into partnerships for particular projects (Hunt, 2000).

A major development took place in 1973, when Nurith Kenaan-Kedar began considering the local character and components in crusader sculpture (Kenaan, 1973), identifying not only continuous local traditions but also specific local (Jerusalemite) models such as, for example, the Golden Gate for the double portal of the southern façade of the Holy-Sepulchre, or the two domes of the Temple Mountain for the two domes of the rebuilt crusader church of the Holy-Sepulchre (Kenaan-Kedar, 1986).

In the 1990s, after more than a century of scholarship had greatly expanded our knowledge of crusader sites, the time was ripe for new considerations of the general notion and development of crusader art. Jaroslav Folda placed major emphasis on the evolution and chronological development of crusader art and, therefore, arranged the chapters of his 1995 volume according to the reigns of the kings of the Latin Kingdom of Jerusalem (Folda, 1995: 15). Bianca Kühnel re-examined the very notion of crusader art, wondering if it should be understood as a geographical, historical, or art historical notion (Kühnel, B., 1994). In the very same years Denys Pringle began his monumental four-volume corpus of crusader churches, providing extensive archeological analysis of all known crusader ecclesiastical edifices (Pringle, 1993–2009). The hundreds of entries in Pringle's indispensable corpus include a wealth of textual sources, from charters to pilgrims' accounts, as well as new plans and sections of numerous churches. The time was also ripe for wide-scope studies on both the urban and the institutional levels, and so Adrian Boas published comprehensive studies of Jerusalem in the time of the crusades (Boas, 2001) and of the archaeology of the military orders (Boas, 2006). In the first of these studies, Boas offers a wide-ranging panorama of the physical setting of the crusader holy city, including its fortifications, quarters, palaces, streets and squares, as well as churches, thus enabling a re-evaluation of the visual culture of the city as a complex entity. The second of these studies is devoted to the extensive building activity of the military orders, including the administrative centers in Jerusalem and Acre, rural possessions, castle typology and design as well as specific elements of fortification.

Alongside these major contributions to the study of crusader monumental art and architecture, important contributions were also made to the study of the minor arts—especially ivories and book illuminations. Cases in point are the famous ivory book covers of Queen Melisende's psalter, which contain a cycle of six scenes from the Life of David. These have been interpreted as relating to Fulk V of Anjou—Melisende's husband and king of the Latin Kingdom of Jerusalem—constituting a Kingly Statement (Norman, 1980; Kühnel, 1991). Since the fundamental study of miniature painting in the Latin Kingdom of Jerusalem by Hugo Buchtal (Buchtal, 1957), studies have been dedicated to specific manuscripts (Mahoney, 2010), or to specific periods and places of production as well as specific scriptoria (Folda, 1976). An additional important strand of scholarship focuses on crusader imagery as it appears in monumental cycles in the West, in places such as Vézelay (Katzenellenbogen, 1944), Auxerre (Denny, 1986), Poncé-sur-le-Loir (Lapina, 2009), Le-Puy (Derbes, 1991), Saint-Gilles-du-Gard (O'Meara, 1977) and elsewhere.

One of the major developments in the study of crusader art, and one which was to have a fundamental influence on the state of research in the late twentieth and early twenty-first century, has been an increasing awareness of the role and involvement of patrons—both ecclesiastical and secular—in the development of crusader art. Indeed, the historiography of crusader art reveals a growing acknowledgment of the importance of tracing the attitudes and intentions of the patrons for the understanding of the multilayered functions and meanings of crusader art. Central in this regard have been the studies by Nurith Kenaan-Kedar on the Holy Sepulchre in Jerusalem (Kenaan-Kedar, 1986), interpreting the symbolic meaning of its architecture in regard to the multiple functions of the church, including its use for the coronation and burial of the Kings of Jerusalem, as well as her studies on the Armenian architecture of Jerusalem (Kenaan-Kedar, 1998) and on the Western donors and models of the cathedral of Sebaste (Kenaan-Kedar, 1992).

ASPECTS OF CRUSADER HISTORIOGRAPHY IN THE LATE TWENTIETH AND EARLY TWENTY-FIRST CENTURIES: PATRONS, VIEWERS AND IDENTITIES

One important aspect of the studies examining the role of the patron is that the particular choice of specific forms or styles began to be studied not only in terms of abstract "influences," or resulting only from practical considerations, but was perceived as an intentional choice, interpreted as manifesting notions of cultural and historical identity or political stance. This shift in focus, which places so much more emphasis on meaning than on archaeological problems or on the origins of the artists, has opened the way in the late twentieth and early twenty-first centuries to new questions, such as how specific forms or styles were perceived by their spectators, and what sort of notions were they able to manifest. The studies by Robert Ousterhout and Lucy-Anne Hunt demonstrate how different answers to these questions have led to completely different views about the purpose and meaning of architectural and sculptural forms.

Ousterhout begins his interpretation with the observation that the crusader church of the Holy Sepulchre contains visible architectural disjunctions, and that although each of the major building phases stands in stark opposition to the principal architectural concepts of the earlier phases, each building phase nonetheless preserved large parts of its predecessors. Rather than seeing this incorporation of earlier building parts as merely the result of constructional needs or lack of resources, Ousterhout sees this as a meaningful choice by the designers. In his explanation of this choice, Ousterhout places great emphasis on the efficacy of a holy site, which results from its ability to provide a direct and tangible link between ritual, place of veneration, and the sacred event it commemorates. According to him, the preservation of the earlier building phases provided such a link to the historical event, resulting in the fact that the structure of the Holy Sepulchre has become sacred, a relic in itself, and so the stones of the Holy Sepulchre have been reused whenever possible (Ousterhout, 2003).

With this notion in mind, Ousterhout turns to the sculpted friezes and capitals of the southern façade of the Holy Sepulchre, focusing on use of the Late Antique style and on the reuse of antique pieces incorporated into the fabric of the façade as spolia or (as has been suggested) carved by the crusaders as a sort of "pseudo-spolia." Following Kenaan-Kedar (Kenaan, 1973), Ousterhout notes that many of the capitals and sculpted friezes of the façade follow local models, among them fifth- or sixth-century Syro-Palestinian models, while yet other sculpted elements are based on western European models. What, however, is the meaning of this mixture of Late Antique styles? For Ousterhout it is again the desire to preserve the old stones, considered as relics, that stands behind this choice. For him the use of the ancient stones or of sculptures carved in Late Antique style functioned to visually connect and unite the sacred event and the architectural setting in which it was commemorated. In Ousterhout's interpretation, it was the very "antiqueness" and locality of the style which were important and which were perceived and recognized as such by the designers as well as the spectators.

A new direction was chosen by Lucy-Anne Hunt. Hunt similarly notes the diversity of stylistic vocabulary on the southern façade, but while Ousterhout focuses mainly on the way these forms were perceived as "ancient" and therefore created a connection to the sacred past, Hunt interprets them in light of the relationship between the different Christian communities in the Latin Kingdom and their position within the Holy Sepulchre, especially the relations of the Eastern Christians with the Western settlers, stating that the Church of the Holy Sepulchre was one of the prominent shrines in the Latin Kingdom in which the liturgy was performed according to both the Orthodox and the Latin rites, and that the Armenians and the Syrian-Jacobites possessed chapels in the church (Hunt, 1995a).

It is this coexistence of the different Christian communities that Hunt sees as the cause of the different stylistic languages of the southern façade. For her, the decision to use these diverse sculptural styles was the consequence of a necessity to coexist, which led to the toleration or even acknowledgment of these artistic languages within the artistic program sponsored by the Latins. Thus, if at the heart of Ousterhout's interpretation lie the forms of the southern façade being perceived by patrons and viewers as manifesting antiqueness, according to Hunt they each had a special resonance for the community of Eastern Christians who worshiped at the Holy Sepulchre. They were understood not as antique but as bearers of notions of communal and religious identity.

THE SCULPTURAL PROGRAMS OF THE CHURCH OF THE ANNUNCIATION IN NAZARETH: ASPECTS OF HISTORIOGRAPHY

The sculptural programs of the Church of the Annunciation in Nazareth, which include the celebrated five capitals discovered in 1908 by Father Prosper Viaud (Viaud, 1910: 55–56), as well as numerous additional fragments excavated by Bellarmino Bagatti in the 1950s–1960s (Bagatti, 1969: 31–70, 89–129), constitute a good example demonstrating the significant shifts and changes of interests marking the historiography of crusader art.

Four of the Nazareth capitals are polygonal and one is rectangular. As is well known, the four polygonal capitals present scenes from the lives of the Apostles Matthew, Thomas, Peter, and James the Great, some of which display extremely rare iconography dedicated to the mission of the Apostles to the East and to the far corners of the earth, such as the depiction of the mission of Matthew to Ethiopia, and his struggle with sorcerers (Folda, 1986: 31–43). On the rectangular capital is depicted a crowned female figure leading a nimbed male figure by the hand, in the midst of terrible demons holding bows and other weapons (Figure 36.1). Often identified as an image of *Ecclesia* or Faith leading an apostle or a believer, Jaroslav Folda has, however, identified the female figure as Mary, in connection to the Greek tradition of the descent of the Virgin into Hell and her pleading on behalf of the tormented souls (Folda, 1986: 43–51; Barasch, 1971: 146–153).

Figure 36.1   Church of the Annunciation, Nazareth, Rectangular capital, depicting Ecclesia/Mary leading a sainted male, middle – second half of twelfth century, courtesy of the Studium Biblicum Franciscanum.

Among the many archeological, stylistic, and iconographical questions which have attracted scholarly attention, one of the most challenging was the explanation of the choice of subjects on the capitals, especially the decision to depict a cycle of the Apostles on the four polygonal capitals. An analysis of the different answers given to this question has much to reveal in regard to the changing focus of the historiography of crusader art.

Interpreting the mission of the Apostles as a revered biblical model for the crusaders, Moshe Barasch has seen the depiction of the Apostles in the East on the Nazareth capitals as giving legitimation to the crusader settlement in the Holy Land; while the depiction of the female figure leading the male figure out of harm's way on the rectangular capital emphasizes the redeeming power of faith and offered reassurance to the frightened Christian inhabitants of Nazareth during the final years of the Latin Kingdom (Barasch, 1971: 150–154). The notion of using the mission of the Apostles as a revered biblical model for the crusaders is well known (Katzenellenbogen, 1944); and recently William J. Purkis has shown that the ideal of the imitation of the Apostles held a very important place in crusader spirituality, including the notion of living in unanimity of spirit (Purkis, 2008). The suggestion by Barasch that the mission of the Apostles depicted on the capitals legitimized the crusaders is thus very valuable. However, we should note that his interpretation has remained general and does not relate to the specific concerns of the patrons. Similarly, Lucy-Anne Hunt has suggested that the cycle as a whole should be interpreted in the context of a mission to convert the Muslims—again a plausible but general interpretation (Hunt, 1995b). Zahava Jacoby, investigating the apostolic iconography in light of the more extensive iconographical program of the west portal, sees the capitals as expressing the authority of the Church, within a program culminating in Christ's triumphant Second Coming and the Last Judgment (Jacoby, 1981, 1986). Thus, similarly to Barasch, Jacoby does not attempt a more specific interpretation that takes into account also the political and ecclesiastical circumstances in Nazareth.

The studies by Jaroslav Folda on the Nazareth sculpture, and especially his extensive monograph published in 1986, mark a significant development in the historiography of the capitals. Folda has suggested that the decision to embellish the Church of the Annunciation was intended to increase its fame in comparison to the other major sacred sites of the Holy Land, and that it was initiated by the Archbishop of Nazareth, Lethard II (Folda, 1986: 20–21). Folda contended that the choice of scenes from the lives of the Apostles for the capitals was motivated by Archbishop Lethard and that it was a part of a claim to an apostolic foundation raised by Nazareth in order to acquire additional fame and prestige, since of the three greatest holy sites, Nazareth was the least important for pilgrims during the twelfth century, perhaps because it was difficult to access from Jerusalem (Folda, 1986: 35–36).

Folda's interpretation differs from previous suggestions in that it is anchored in the specific circumstances of Nazareth, and not in general formulations of crusader ideology. However, additional motivations can also be discerned, rooted in the political struggles of the Archbishop of Nazareth and in the specific ecclesiastical circumstances of his archbishopric.

THE ARCHBISHOP OF NAZARETH AND THE SCULPTURAL PROGRAMS OF HIS CHURCH: A NEW INTERPRETATION

My own interpretation of the Nazareth sculpture[1] contends that it was part of an attempt by the Archbishop of Nazareth to manifest and consolidate the legitimacy of his ecclesiastical status in the face of internal diocesan challenges.

The images of St. Peter included within the cycle serve as a focal point of my interpretation, especially his depiction on a monumental jamb statue (Figure 36.2) discovered during the excavation of 1966 (Bagatti, 1969: 102–105). St. Peter is depicted frontally, holding in his right hand the Keys of Heaven and in his left a detailed model of a church. A prominent feature of this church is its three rounded apses, resembling those of the crusader church in Nazareth. Although the three apses of the actual crusader church were set into a rectangular configuration at the eastern end, and so the round outline of the apses was not visible from the outside—unlike the case of the model in St. Peter's hand—depictions of church models from early Christian art onwards indicate that there should be little doubt that St. Peter is holding a model of the Church of the Annunciation itself.[2]

The tradition of portraying patrons and donors as holding a model of the church they had built goes back to early Christian times. However, this iconography was usually reserved for non-canonized donors and patrons, be they secular or ecclesiastical, who were depicted presenting the model of the church to a saintly recipient (Lipsmeyer, 1981: 34–89). In Nazareth the situation is different. Rather than an ordinary patron it is the saint himself who holds the model of the church. In Nazareth, therefore, an important shift in meaning has occurred. Instead of the Archbishop of Nazareth presenting the church to

Figure 36.2   Church of the Annunciation, Nazareth, trumeau statue of St. Peter holding the keys and the model of the church, middle – second half of twelfth century, courtesy of the Studium Biblicum Franciscanum.

St. Peter, it is the saint himself who is portrayed as protector and as the source of authority and prestige for the Nazareth church, and from whom the archbishop receives legitimacy and authority.

This visual statement had a special and specific importance for Nazareth and for its archbishop. Traditionally, Nazareth had been the seat of an Orthodox bishop (Hamilton, 1980: 60). However, in the first years after the Latin conquest no attempt was made to reconstitute a diocesan organization in the Galilee, and Pope Paschal II granted the Abbot of Tabor archiepiscopal authority throughout the region (Hamilton, 1980: 60; Pringle, 1993–2009: II, 64).

It was only gradually that the See of Nazareth rose back to prominence. At the instigation of Gibelin of Arles, papal legate and newly elected Patriarch of Jerusalem, the See of

Nazareth was newly established and the newly appointed bishop, first appearing in the documents in 1109, enjoyed jurisdiction throughout the Galilee (Hamilton 1980: 60). Another development took place in 1129, when William, the second Latin bishop of Nazareth, was promoted to the rank of archbishop and Nazareth became the metropolitan see for Galilee instead of Scythopolis (Bethsan), which was the metropolitan see in Orthodox times but had become almost deserted by the twelfth century.[3]

I believe that the placement of St. Peter at the focal point of the west portal was meant to manifest and consolidate the legitimacy of both the transfer of the bishopric from Mount Tabor to Nazareth,and Nazareth's new status as an archbishopric, both of which were instigated or recognized by the papacy. Indeed, until a relatively late period, the crusaders were well aware that the elevation of Nazareth to an archbishopric constituted a break from tradition, and William of Tyre noted that "Scythopolis is the capital of Palestina Tertia ... It is also called Bethsan. Nowadays Nazareth, which is situated at the same diocese, enjoys its prerogative" (William of Tyre, 1986: 1030). It thus seems that throughout the twelfth century the status of the archbishop of Nazareth appeared to require explanation; and, perhaps also from his own point of view, consolidation. The image of St. Peter and his unique appearance holding the model of the Church of the Annunciation provided both.

Similarly to the image of St. Peter, the unique depiction of the crowned female figure leading to safety the male figure attacked by demons, can also be interpreted in regard to the concerns of Nazareth and of its archbishop.

As I have already mentioned, Jaroslav Folda identified the female figure as Mary, in connection to the tradition of the descent of the Virgin into Hell and her intercession on behalf of the anguished souls. According to Folda's explanation, Nazareth suffered from a liturgical problem resulting from the fact that the Feast of the Annunciation, celebrated on March 25, usually fell in the Lenten season. Therefore, in Nazareth, there was a need to find a way to harmonize the cult of the Virgin with the focus of Christianity on the Resurrection of Christ in the period of Lent and Holy Week. The choice of the rare iconography of the capital, based visually on the image of the Anastasias, responded to this need (Folda, 1986: 47).

SEPPHORIS AND ITS STRUGGLE FOR PILGRIMS

I wish to suggest an additional explanation for the choice of this unusual iconography, and to contend that it served also to increase the prestige and importance of Nazareth, in the face of growing competition by the developing site of Sepphoris.[4]

From early times Sepphoris had been associated with the Virgin and with her parents. In the sixth century the Pilgrim from Piacenza refers to relics of the Virgin found at Sepphoris, which included a basket, a flagon, and the chair on which she was sitting at the time of the Annunciation (Pilgrim of Piacenza, 1965: 130). Twelft-century sources, including Theodoric and Fretellus, mention that St. Anne was born at Sepphoris (Folda, 1991: 88; Pringle, 1993–2009: II, 211; Grabiner, 2006: 116–117), while John of Würzburg recounts that it is said that the Virgin Mary herself was born in Sepphoris (John of Würzburg, 1994: 80–81).

Sometime in the middle or second half of the twelfth century, a crusader church was built in Sepphoris. Both Jaroslav Folda and Esther Grabiner claim that several characteristics of the building suggest that it was more than just an ordinary parish church, and that it might have been intended to mark the holy site of St. Anne's house (Folda, 1991: 90–94; Grabiner, 2006: 114–115). Among these they mention the large size of the church and the unusual richness of the architectural articulation and decoration. An important feature of the church in this regard is the visible presence of the living rock, rising into the central apse. Crusader architecture at important holy sites often reveals an attempt to incorporate parts of the natural landscape (caves, rocks), and in so doing create a visible link between the geography of the holy site and the edifice built on that site (examples of rocks and caves visible in crusader churches include the hill of Calvary; the grotto of the Nativity, and many others). It is important to note, however, that Pringle has claimed that when taking into account the floor level in the twelfth century, the rock would seem to have registered only minimally at the time, if at all (Pringle, 1993–2009: II, 213).

Considering all this, a picture emerges according to which a holy site was established at Sepphoris and traditions were cultivated that were directly in competition with those of Nazareth—especially in the claim that the Virgin was born in Sepphoris. Indeed, contrary to the claim raised at Sepphoris, Theodoric describes how in the grotto of Nazareth "there is an arched structure having only a single cross engraved beneath it, in which the blessed mother of God when she was born came out of her mother's womb" (Wilkinson, 1988: 312). It is important to note that the clash between the claims of both sites to being the birthplace of the Virgin was noted by John of Würzburg, who, when mentioning that it is said that the Virgin Mary was born in Sepphoris, also adds, however, that he knows from Jerome that the Virgin was born in Nazareth (John of Würzburg, 1994: 80–81).

Returning to Archbishop Lethard II and his ambitious rebuilding and decoration of the Church of the Annunciation, we can now ask whether the iconography of the rectangular capital responds to the challenges of Sepphoris. I believe that the attempts of Sepphoris to proclaim itself as an important Marian center (and as the birthplace of the Virgin) may have played a part in the choice of this iconography, which places such emphasis on the redemptive power of the triumphant Virgin. After all, as this capital was installed in the Church of the Annunciation, the protective role of Mary which is referred to by this image can be understood as directed toward the pilgrims arriving at this holy sanctuary, thus making a strong visual claim regarding the benefits to be gained by those who visit the Virgin's sanctuary in Nazareth.

CONCLUSION

As I have sought to show, the historiography of crusader art in the last decades of the twentieth century and the beginning of the twenty-first century reveals a growing interest in the intensions of the patrons, as expressed via the iconographical and stylistic choices in the monuments related to them. As the examples of Nazareth and Sepphoris reveal, the specific political, economic, and regional interests of these patrons, and their struggles to achieve influence and prestige, should also be considered as important factors in the development of crusader art.

NOTES

1 My interpretation of the Nazareth sculpture is fully elaborated in (Fishhof, forthcoming, a).
2 As studied by Elizabeth Lipsmeyer, such models are often an abbreviation of the structure represented, and include a reduced number of repeated elements. They are often a combination of the symbolic with the actual or realistic features of the represented building (Lipsmeyer, 1981).

3 In a document from early 1129 William is named bishop, while in a document dated to March 1129 he is already named archbishop (Rozière, 1849: 138–139, note 67, and 81–83, note 44).

4 I examine the influence of the competition for pilgrims on the sculpture of Nazareth also in (Fishhof, forthcoming, b).

REFERENCES

Bagatti, B. (1969) *Excavations in Nazareth*, 2 vols., Jerusalem: Franciscan Printing Press.

Barasch, M. (1971) *Crusader Figural Sculpture in the Holy Land: Twelfth Century Examples from Acre, Nazareth and Belvoir Castle*, Ramat-Gan: Massada Press.

Boas, A. (2001) *Jerusalem in the Time of the Crusades: Society, Landscape and Art in the Holy City under Frankish Rule*, London: Routledge.

———— (2006) *Archaeology of the Military Orders: A Survey of the Urban Centers, Rural Settlement and Castles of the Military Orders in the Latin East (c.1120–1291)*, London: Routledge.

Boase, T.S.R. (1939) "The arts in the Latin Kingdom of Jerusalem," *Journal of the Warburg and Courtauld Institutes*, 2: 1–21.

Borg, A. (1982) "Romanesque sculpture from the Rhone valley to the Jordan valley," in J. Folda (ed.), *Crusader Art in the Twelfth Century*, Oxford: BAR, 97–121.

Buchthal, H. (1957) *Miniature Painting in the Latin Kingdom of Jerusalem*, Oxford: Clarendon.

Buschhausen, H. (1978) *Die süditalienische Bauplastik im Königreich Jerusalem von König Wilhelm II. bis Kaiser Friedrich II*, Vienna: Österreichische Akademie der Wissenschaften.

Denny, D. (1986) "A Romanesque fresco in Auxerre cathedral," *Gesta*, 25: 197–202.

Derbes, A. (1991) "A crusading fresco cycle in the cathedral of Le Puy," *Art Bulletin*, 73: 561–76.

Deschamps, P. (1931) *La sculpture française en Palestine et en Syrie a l'"époque des Croisades*, Paris: Ernest Leroux.

Enlart, C. (1925–28) *Les monuments des croisés: le royaume de Jérusalem: architecture religieuse et civile*, 2 vols., Paris: P. Geuthner.

Fishhof, G. (forthcoming, a) "The role and meanings of the image of Saint Peter in the crusader sculpture of Nazareth: A new reading," in E. Lapina and A. Morris (eds), *The Crusades and Visual Culture*, Farnham, UK and Burlington, VT: Ashgate.

———— (forthcoming, b) "The sculpted images of St. Peter and the Virgin in the crusader Church of the Annunciation—rival traditions, competition for pilgrims and regional context," in M. Rojas (ed.), *Warfare and Peace at the Time of the Crusades*.

Folda, J. (1976) *Crusader Manuscript Illumination at Saint-Jean d'Acre, 1275–1291*, Princeton, NJ: Princeton University Press.

———— (1986) *The Nazareth Capitals and the Crusader Shrine of the Annunciation*, Philadelphia: Pennsylvania State University Press.

———— (1991) "The Church of Saint Anne," *The Biblical Archaeologist*, 54/2: 88–96.

———— (1995) *The Art of the Crusaders in the Holy Land, 1098–1187*, Cambridge: Cambridge University Press.

Grabiner, E. (2006) "Les vestiges de l'église Franque de Séphorie," *Bulletin monumental*, 164/1: 113–20.

Hamilton, B. (1980) *The Latin Church in the Crusader States—the Secular Church*, London: Variorum Publications.

Hunt, L.-A. (1995a) "Artistic and cultural inter-relations between the Christian communities at the Holy Sepulchre in the 12th Century," in A. O'Mahony and G. Gunner (eds.), *The Christian Heritage in the Holy Land*, London: Scorpion Cavendish, 57–96.

———— (1995b) "Excommunicata generatione: Christian imagery of mission and conversion of the Muslim other between the first crusade and the early fourteenth century," *Al-Masaq* 8: 79–153.

———— (2000) "Crusader sculpture and the so-called 'templar workshop': A reassessment of two carved panels from the dome of the rock in the Haram Al-Sharif museum in Jerusalem," *Palestine Exploration Quarterly*, 132: 131–56.

Jacoby, Z. (1979) "The tomb of Baldwin V, King of Jerusalem (1185–1186) and the Workshop of the temple Area," *Gesta*, 18/2: 3–14.

———— (1981) "Le portail de l'église de l'annonciation de Nazareth au XIIe siècle—un essai de reconstitution," *Monuments et mémoires de la Fondation Eugène Piot*, 64: 141–94.

———— (1982) "The workshop of the temple area in Jerusalem in the twelfth century: its origin, evolution and impact," *Zeitschrift fur Kunstgeschichte*, 45/4: 325–94.

———— (1985) "The Provencal impact on crusader sculpture in Jerusalem: more evidence on the temple area atelier," Zeitschrift für Kunstgeschichte, 48/4: 442–50.

———— (1986) "The composition of the Nazareth workshop and the recruitment of sculptors for the Holy Land in the twelfth Century," in V.P. Goss (ed.), *The Meeting of Two Worlds—Cultural Exchange Between East and West During the Period of the Crusades*, Kalamazoo: Western Michigan University, Medieval Institute Publications, 145–59.

John of Würzburg (1994) *Descriptio Locorum Terrae Sanctae*, R.B.C. Huygens (ed.), in *Corpus Christianorum. Continuatio Mediaevalis*, 139, Turnhout: Brepols.

Katzenellenbogen, A. (1944) "The central tympanum at Vézelay. Its encyclopedic meaning and its relation to the first crusade," *The Art Bulletin*, 36: 141–51.

Kenaan, N. (1973) "Local Christian art in 12th century Jerusalem," *Israel Exploration Journal*, 23: 165–75, 221–9.

Kenaan-Kedar, N. (1986) "Symbolic meaning in crusader architecture," *Cahiers archéologique*, 34: 109–15.

———— (1992) "The cathedral of Sebaste: its western donors and models," in B.Z. Kedar (ed.), *The Horns of Hattin*, Jerusalem and London: Yad Izhak Ben Zvi and Variorum, 99–121.

———— (1998) "Armenian architecture in twelfth-century Jerusalem," *Assaph—Studies in Art History*, 3: 77–92.

Kühnel, B. (1991) "The kingly statement of the book covers of Queen Melisande's psalter," *Jahrbuch für Antike und Christentum Ergänzungsband (Tesserae–Festschrift für Josef Engemann)*, 18: 340–57.

———— (1994) *Crusader Art of the Twelfth Century: a Geographical, an Historical, of an Art Historical Notion?* Berlin: Gebr. Mann.

Kühnel, G. (1988) *Wall Painting in the Latin Kingdom of Jerusalem*, Berlin: Gebr. Mann.

Lapina, E. (2009) "La représentation de la bataille d'Antioche (1098) sur les peintures murales de Ponce-sur-le-Loir," *Cahiers de civilisation médiévale*, 52: 137–57.

Lipsmeyer, E. (1981) "The donor and his church model in Medieval art, from early Christian times to the Late Romanesque Period," unpublished dissertation, Rutgers University.

Mahoney, L. (2010) "The 'Histoire ancienne' and dialectical identity in the Latin Kingdom of Jerusalem", *Gesta*, 49: 31–51.

Norman, S. (1980) "The life of King David as a psychomachia allegory—A study of the Melisende psalter book covers," *Revue de l'université d'Ottawa*, 50/2: 192–201.

O'Meara, C.F. (1977) *The Iconography of the Facade of Saint-Gilles-du-Gard*, New York and London: Garland.

Ousterhout, R. (2003) "Architecture as relic and the construction of sanctity: The stones of the Holy Sepulchre," *Journal of the Society of Architectural Historians*, 62: 4–23.

Pace, V. (1982) "Italy and the Holy Land: import and export 2: the case of Apulia," in J. Folda (ed.), *Crusader Art in the Twelfth Century*, Oxford: BAR, 245–69.

Pilgrim of Piacenza (1965) *Itinerarium*, P. Geyer (ed.) in *Corpus Christianorum. Series Latina*, 175, Turnhout: Brepols.

Pringle, D. (1993–2009) *The Churches of the Crusader Kingdom of Jerusalem: A Corpus*, 4 vols, Cambridge: Cambridge University Press.

Purkis, W.J. (2008) *Crusading Spirituality in the Holy Land and Iberia c. 1095–c. 1187*, Woodbridge, UK and Rochester, NY: Boydell Press.

Rozière E. de (1849) *Cartulaire de l'église du Saint Sepulchre de Jerusalem*, Paris: L'Imprimerie Nationale.

Viaud, P. (1910) *Nazareth et ses deux églises: de l'Annonciation et de Saint-Joseph*, Paris: Picard.

Weyl Carr, A. (1982) "The mural paintings of Abu Ghosh and the patronage of Manuel Comnenus in the Holy Land," in J. Folda (ed.), *Crusader Art in the Twelfth Century*, Oxford: BAR, 215–44.

Wilkinson, J. (1988) *Jerusalem Pilgrimage 1099–1185*, London: Hakluyt Society.

William of Tyre (1986) *Historia rerum gestarum in partibus transmarinis*, R.B.C. Huygens (ed.), in *Corpus Christianorum, Continuatio Mediaevalis*, 63A, Turnhout, Belgium: Brepols.

CHAPTER THIRTY-SEVEN

AFTER TWENTY-FIVE YEARS: JOSHUA PRAWER'S CONTRIBUTION TO THE STUDY OF THE CRUSADES AND THE LATIN KINGDOM OF JERUSALEM RECONSIDERED

———•◆•———

Sophia Menache

The crusader epos in the Holy Land, with all its images and metaphors, is part and parcel of Israeli culture. Fructiferous scholarly investigation and popular publications, along with an ever-increasing number of lectures and tours, are clear manifestations of the wide interest displayed by Israeli society in the crusades. Such attention could easily be explained by the visual impact of crusader remains throughout the country, with castles, strongholds, cities, and villages being a ubiquitous component of daily life.[1] The geographical landscape, notwithstanding its weight, cannot shadow the leading influence of Joshua Prawer (1917–90), one of the most influential figures in the Israeli academia from the 1950s on, in turning the crusades into a mainstream of Israeli culture. Though Prawer's historiographical contribution to our understanding of the crusades and the Latin East had enjoyed satisfactory attention in recent decades,[2] his influence from an Israeli perspective is less known. This chapter is devoted, therefore, to an analysis of the fertile interchange between Prawer and Israeli society as a whole, with special emphasis on his impact on the research of the crusades and the Latin Kingdom of Jerusalem.

Joshua Prawer was born to a prosperous Jewish merchant family in Bedzin, Polish Silesia. From his youth, he excelled in his studies, especially mathematics and foreign languages, acquiring a wide knowledge of Polish, German, Hebrew, French, Latin, Yiddish, and English. In a successful attempt to leave Poland prior to the Second World War (1936), he registered at the Hebrew University of Jerusalem—a prerequisite to circumventing the immigration limitations imposed by the British Mandate on Palestine. During Israel's War of Independence, he served as liaison officer with the Christian institutions in Jerusalem; soon afterwards, began a successful career at the Hebrew University. There, under the supervision of Richard Koebner—to whom he often referred as "my teacher and rabbi"— Prawer began his research on crusader settlements and the colonization process in the Holy Land, a subject matter that attracted his lifelong interest. He gradually acquired prestige as an outstanding scholar and an inspiring, charismatic teacher. In parallel, he played an active role in academic administration at the Hebrew University, officiating, *inter alia*, as dean of the Faculty of Humanities (1961–65) and prorector; as such, he promoted the founding of additional centers of higher studies in both the north of the country, the University of Haifa (1963), and the south, Ben-Gurion University of the Negev (1969). Prawer was also active beyond the "ivory tower," fostering important reforms for Israeli secondary education, the emergence of pre-academic units, and cultural agreements with institutions all over the world. His creative academic career advanced his election to the Israeli Academy of Sciences, and to the chairmanship of its Humanities section, and culminated in his being honored as an Israeli Prize Laureate for the Humanities in 1969.

The many fields in which Prawer was active did not eclipse his most cherished goal, of incorporating the crusades into mainstream Israeli culture. The physical environment undoubtedly influenced and stimulated his work; as remarked by his colleagues: "Living, as he did, on the scene of the events he described, he could fully exploit the advantage which he held over his illustrious predecessors in this particular field. It sharpened his understanding of the geopolitical context of the world in which the crusaders lived and of their, as well as their opponents', strategic concepts."[3] Prawer's immediate knowledge of Israel's physical environment had distinct advantages, as was clearly reflected in both the map of the crusading kingdom, which he produced with Meron Benvenisti,[4] and his analysis of the geographical factors and their weight in the crucial Battle of Hattin (1187).[5] Moreover, as chairman of the Jerusalem Institute for Israel Studies and a member of the board of both the Israel Archaeological Society and the Yad ben Zvi Institute, Prawer fostered a wider awareness of the influence of the crusader period on the history of the Holy Land. He also encouraged the creation of a new field of area studies that focused on the Land of Israel throughout the ages, a subject that enjoys much popularity in Israel and worldwide to the present time.[6] His great prestige and influence in political circles facilitated the allocation of extensive government funding for the restoration of crusader sites, such as St. Louis's walls and the mural towers at Caesarea and the Hospitaller castle at Belvoir, allowing their accessibility to the wide public.[7] Aware of the importance of archeological research, Prawer strongly supported the excavations in the City of David against the limitations advocated by extreme religious groups. Benjamin Z. Kedar could therefore rightly claim, "It is difficult to think of another historian who played so important a role in uncovering the physical remains of the period with which he dealt."[8]

As "a citizen of earthly Jerusalem," in Sylvia Schein's portrayal of the man,[9] Prawer devoted much attention to the historical development of the city before, during, and after the crusader conquest, as well as to its unique status in all monotheistic religions.[10] When honored as a "Distinguished Citizen of Jerusalem" (1989), Prawer declared his personal conviction that "Jerusalem of today is a universal city, belonging to all cultures."[11] Though a fervent partisan of the Jewish State, Prawer was from a cultural perspective a true cosmopolitan, who easily adapted to foreign environments. His main merit in this regard was to make Jerusalem a main center of crusader studies on the same level of well-known, older institutions in France, England, and Germany. He succeeded in fostering interest among young Israelis in the history of the crusades and the crusader states as a bridge between European history and the Land of Israel. It would be no exaggeration to assert that most medieval historians teaching at Israeli universities at the end of the previous and the beginning of the present centuries have been among Prawer's students at some stage of their careers.[12] These scholars eventually advanced the study of the crusades worldwide, notwithstanding the lack of archives and primary sources in Israel. Such a chronic disadvantage dictated close links with the continent, where Prawer encouraged many of his students to pursue their PhD studies. The close links he forged abroad gained Prawer recognition of his work worldwide. He received an honorary doctorate from the University of Montpellier (1969), and his two-volume *Histoire du royaume latin de Jérusalem* (1969–70) earned him the *Prix Gustave Schlumberger* of France's *Académie des inscriptions et belles lettres*. Prawer was appointed a Corresponding Fellow of the Medieval Academy of America (1967) and a Visiting Fellow at All Souls College, Oxford (1974). No wonder, therefore, that his death (Jerusalem, April 30, 1990) was widely regretted abroad, as well as in Israel.[13] The question still arises: What was the secret of Prawer's personal magnetism? At the academic level, Prawer appears as the rare mixture of an illuminating scholar, a brilliant teacher, and a most convincing writer, whose language was accessible to a broad public.[14] As his former student during the early 1970s, I clearly remember Prawer's charming rhetoric, enhanced with a sophisticated sense of humor, and his listening carefully to his students at all levels. Yet, he did not welcome criticism, especially when coming from his students (*non jurat ad verba magistri!*); eventually, he was ready to accept some remarks, when satisfactorily proved, in a humoristic tone (*touché*).[15] Perhaps it was this peculiar combination that ensured Prawer's extraordinary influence on the study of the crusades.

When Prawer began his research on the crusades and the Kingdom of Jerusalem at the mid-twentieth century, the subject had already become a traditional component of Western culture. The massive publication of original sources throughout previous centuries created, indeed, a solid base for research and findings that were better documented.[16] It did not, however, radically change the thirteenth-century baronial jurists' perspective with regard to an ideal feudal state, in which the monarch wielded a purely nominal authority as *primus inter pares*. This approach was first undermined by M. Grandelaude's research in the 1920s. It was Prawer's main merit—in parallel with the studies of leading French medievalists of the time, first and foremost Claude Cahen and Jean Richard—to reveal the changing interaction between the monarchy and the privileged groups in the kingdom, the nobility at their head, but also the Military Orders, the Italian merchants, and the Frankish burgesses.[17] Prawer argued that in the first decades of the crusader kingdom the kings of Jerusalem were able to maintain a rather strong, stable position. The continuous state of war, however, brought about some deterioration in the status of monarchy, which was forced to make many compromises with its tenants-in-chief. Most of the early kings' concessions—the *regalia* mentioned in the *Livre au roi*—eventually eroded the status of the monarchy, with the balance of power tilting in favor of the aristocracy, as clearly manifested in the *Assise sur la ligece* of King Amaury. Frederick II's problematic crusade reflects a turning point, the nobility then being able not only to ignore royal rights but also to express far-reaching claims on behalf of the High Court, composed by their vassals. Prawer thus concluded that the thirteenth century provided one of the earliest examples of the development of a *Ständenstaat*, with the different sociopolitical groups developing a sense of community, strengthened by oath. In his book, *Crusader Institutions* (Oxford, 1980),[18] Prawer further developed former studies, clarifying the legal structure of the realm. He emphasized the presence of marked non-feudal elements in the kingdom's organization, and devoted much attention to the development of the *Cour des Bourgeois* and the role played by the burgesses in royal and seigniorial administration.

From a sociological perspective, Prawer expanded the conceptual framework of an immigrant society at work, focusing on the importance of immigration, on the one hand, and the peril of manpower shortage, on the other. Throughout a long series of articles and four monographs,[19] he examined almost every aspect of crusader history, providing a more complex, yet still vivid reflection of crusader life. He devoted much attention to land projects and agriculture and urban settlements, and the role of the Italian communes.[20] He did not confine his research to the Latin Kingdom of Jerusalem, but also brought a refreshing view of the agrarian/social history of the lordship of Tyre, based on the report of the Venetian agent in Syria (1243).[21] One of the most important assertions advanced by Prawer related to the very essence of crusader society, which he encapsulated in the name of his monograph on the subject, *The Latin Kingdom of Jerusalem: European Colonialism in the Middle Ages*. Research on crusader society, especially its way of life, economy, and institutions, led Prawer to posit the existence of a colonial society, whose lack of knowledge of or interest in its neighbors eventually brought about its collapse. Crusader society was not, in this view, characterized by acculturation performs, but by the forced importation of Western European practices to the Holy Land. A continuous lack of security and, most especially, the crusaders' situation as a minority surrounded by a powerful enemy, further justified in Prawer's eyes their concentration in fortified cities and fortifications; thus, only the indigenous inhabitants lived in rural areas and engaged in agriculture.[22] Prawer concluded that the crusader kingdom was the first European colony established overseas, characterized as it was by a strict, continuous apartheid between exploiting conquerors and exploited natives. The sense of insecurity characteristic of crusader society as a whole, moreover, did not arise solely from the external danger; it was generated from the potential collaboration of the indigenous Christian and Muslim populations with external enemies, as well. Prawer thus presented a Frankish society of immigrants, who lived in strict political, social, and cultural segregation from the Syro-Christians and Muslims, a state of affairs that he described as "apartheid."

Toward the end of his life, Prawer published *The History of the Jews in the Latin Kingdom of Jerusalem,*[23] a subject to which he had devoted much attention throughout his life.[24] Basing his analysis on the rich documentation of the Cairo Geniza and the Hebrew itineraries to the Holy Land, Prawer was able to reconstruct the major trends of community life, first and foremost in Acre; later on in other major cities—Tiberias, Jaffa, Ashkelon, and Gaza; and eventually in Jerusalem. He reached the unforeseen conclusion that a decade or so after the slaughter that characterized the crusader conquest in 1099, the Jewish communities enjoyed relative security and comfort under the rule of the king and the Latin overlords, to whom they paid taxes and whose laws they strictly obeyed. Like other subject peoples, the Jews, as a corporation among many others of this kind, enjoyed religious freedom and conducted their lives according to their own ritual laws. Fortified by a continuous current of pilgrims, the Jews of the Crusader Kingdom were united by their age-old belief in the forthcoming redemption of the Promised Land, a belief that revealed the crusaders to be a punishment for the Jews' sins (*peccatis nostris exigentibus*), but still a transitory phenomenon as had been the Greeks, the Romans, the Byzantines, and the Muslims before them.

Although Prawer's conclusions were essentially based on his wide knowledge of medieval sources and years of investigation spent at leading academic centers worldwide, they provided food for controversy and sometimes also biased criticism. Thus, referring to Prawer's approach to the Crusader Kingdom as a colonial society, Josep Torró concludes, rather deterministically: "De toute evidence, l'historien israélien parlait d'une situation qui, à titre personnel, ne lui était pas étrangère." Considering the policy of apartheid to be a common denominator defining the crusaders then and the Israelis today, Torró did not refrain from oversimplifications, further claiming in a footnote, "L'intérêt des médiévistes israéliens pour le royaume de Jérusalem ne peut pas s'expliquer en fonction de la seule coïncidence géographique."[25] The biased approach that characterized the Catalan historian aside, the debate over Prawer's main conclusions in fact embraces all fields of crusader history. Although Prawer's pioneering research left a mark on crusader historiography, some of his premises were later questioned and eventually invalidated by younger Israeli researchers, first and foremost by those who had previously been numbered among his students. For the purposes of this study, we will focus on the main revisions of Prawer's thesis in four complementary fields: material conditions (especially fortresses and castles), art, economy, and military organization.

New archeological evidence and documentary testimonies uncovered over the past thirty years have revealed cross-cultural influences between the Latins and the different inhabitants in the area, not only Muslims, but also East Christians, Druzes, and Jews,[26] thus undermining one of the main pillars of Prawer's apartheid thesis. Showing the shortcomings of the colonialist–segregationist premise, Ronnie Ellenblum convincingly connects Frankish military architecture to its local environment and to the medieval framework as a whole.[27] In his extensive survey and study of Frankish rural settlements, castles, and construction techniques, Ellenblum reconstructs a considerable number of crusader agricultural settlements, some of them close to those inhabited by Oriental Christians. In addition to disclosing greater numbers of Latin settlers than those estimated by Prawer, he also found strong evidence of the existence of Latin settlers living together with Syrians. According to Ellenblum, moreover, crusader castles, too, should be regarded as the "most evident visual expression of the cultural dialogue between East and West. Not because one of the sides 'borrowed' an architectural expression from the other, but because they were the outcome of a lengthy, ongoing dialogue between two schools of military tactics and approaches."[28] The reconstruction suggested by Prawer with regard to the crucial Battle of Hattin, as well, received new light from one of his most prominent students, Benjamin Z. Kedar.[29] Discussing the road system and water resources at that site, Kedar contributed additional information on the material-physical factors that influenced the battle and, in so doing, basically revised his former teacher's thesis.[30] Moreover, when investigating the meeting points between opposing religions/cultures/societies, Kedar further weakened the foundations of Prawer's segregation thesis.[31] Kedar's book, *Crusade and Mission: European Approaches toward the Muslims* (Princeton, 1984), faithfully reproduces the two main options facing medieval Christendom: either mission by peaceful means as advocated by the Franciscans, with Francesco d'Assisi and Ramon Lull at their head, or a continuation of the *bellum sacrum* in its most extreme manner in an attempt to purify the Holy Land of the Muslim presence. Kedar convincingly proves that mission and crusade were not mutually exclusive options, and there were many combinations of the two alternatives.

Yvonne Friedmann, too, analyzed additional aspects of the encounter between crusaders and Muslims. Her illuminating monograph, *Encounter between Enemies: Captivity and Ransom in the Latin Kingdom of Jerusalem* (Leiden, 2002), examines the customs, legal codes, and socioeconomic mechanisms that evolved from the encounter between Christians and Muslims. The book clarifies the main changes in Western mentality and acculturation processes, from which the imperative to redeem captives eventually emerged and which made payment of ransom to the heretic not only conceivable but also acceptable. It is rather symbolic that Friedman's book opens with the tragic story of the Israeli navigator Ron Arad, who fell captive in Lebanon (October 1986) and for whom all ransom efforts unfortunately failed (p. xi). The very mention of Arad hints at the link, which Friedman acknowledges outright, between Israeli research of the crusades and current political reality.[32] Such a link, however, did not influence genuine research characteristic of historical investigation, rather the contrary. Friedman also wrote a considerable number of articles on the various concepts of ransoming captives from among the different social and religious groups that fought one another in the Levant for the two hundred years marking the overall crusader period.[33] Taking a more optimistic viewpoint, she is now advancing investigation of conciliation and peace-making processes in the Crusader Levant, a subject that has not lost its validity in this troubled region to this very day.[34]

The dialogue between the crusaders and the native population indeed impregnated every facet of daily life; that it was reflected in crusader art comes as no real surprise and further weakens Prawer's apartheid concept. Faithful to his basic premise of the colonialist nature of the Crusader Kingdom, Prawer regarded crusader art as lacking original or authentic elements of its own.[35] With the improved access to crusader structures and fragments after the Six Day War (1967), especially in Jerusalem, the "colonialist view" began to be challenged by various Israeli art historians, led by Nurith Kenaan-Kedar.[36] Her pioneering contribution focuses on the discovery of a local crusader school in Jerusalem, which she saw as a faithful reflection of its ethnic environment.[37] The immediate contact with crusader sites and remnants, no longer limited to Prawer, now began to play a key role in stimulating new, challenging art perspectives on the meeting points between local innovation and foreign influences.[38]

Important archeological developments in the past two decades, which were due in part to extensive government funding through the Israeli Archeological Society, have revealed additional facets of crusader history while further undermining Prawer's segregation model. The studies by Adrian Boas clarify various aspects of daily life in both urban and rural Latin settlements, including domestic architecture and ceramics, as well as in fortifications.[39] In addition, new findings of ceramics and glass objects[40] and about the sugar industry have brought to light commercial ties in the geopolitical space and the development of technology in crusader times.[41] Robert Kool produced a series of articles on the coins of the Crusader Kingdom, their relation to Islamic jewelry, and their contribution to the development of trade and its scope in the Levant.[42]

Prawer's approach to the economy of the Latin Kingdom from a Eurocentric and colonial perspective, and as such as having been underdeveloped and exploited by Western traders, too, encountered severe criticism. It was the merit of another of Prawer's former students, David Jacoby, to prove the vitality and market-orientation of agriculture and industry, the crucial role of local traders, and the importance of the service sector to the kingdom's economy.[43] His focus on Mediterranean commerce and trade brought Jacoby closer to the history of the Italian communes and the Frankish principalities in the Levant,[44] which are now viewed as having constituted a major factor in the development of medieval trade. His new reading of published and unpublished primary sources, which he analyzed within their contemporary context and in a comparative framework, provided a new perspective of Mediterranean trade, with Venice in the lead, and the economy of the Frankish States.[45]

In his book on *The Latin Kingdom of Jerusalem: European Colonialism in the Middle Ages*, Prawer devoted a most illuminating chapter to pilgrims and pilgrimage in the crusader period, while putting emphasis on the emergence of a "sacred geography."[46] It was a new reading of the geographical "reality" of the Holy Land, with its emphasis on the holy places, real or imaginary. Another of Prawer's disciples, the late Aryeh Grabois, presented still newer perspectives in his book, *Le pèlerin occidental en Terre Sainte au Moyen Âge*

(Paris-Bruxelles, 1998). Dealing with challenging questions regarding both spiritual and material factors that encouraged medieval people to leave their familiar homeland, Grabois reveals in some depth the pilgrims' encounter with the Holy Land, its fauna and flora, vis-à-vis the biblical heritage, thus further clarifying additional facets of what Prawer had called "sacred geography." Indeed, throughout the two hundred years of the Crusader Kingdom of Jerusalem, the never-ending search for the holy places where Jesus and the apostles lived and preached, and where some of them also died, encouraged pilgrims to report their experiences. The result was the development of a unique literary genre that became very popular in the crusader period, the itineraries.[47] Yvonne Friedman, as well, analyzed the spiritual and ideological factors behind pilgrimages,[48] while clarifying some practical matters, such as the available road systems in the Holy Land.[49]

From a chronological perspective, Prawer focused on the "classical" period of the crusades; namely, from Pope Urban II's call in Clermont in 1095 until the fall of Crusader Acre in 1291. He further restricted the definition of crusade to those expeditions led by the papacy whose ultimate goal was to conquer or to secure Christian rule in the Holy Land and, by extension, all places holy to Christianity in the Levant. Sylvia Schein, one of Joshua Prawer's closest students, extended research about the crusades up to 1314, thus expanding by more than twenty years the chronological framework established by her teacher.[50]

Although Prawer was well aware of the importance of the Military Orders, to which he devoted one chapter in his study *The Latin Kingdom of Jerusalem: Colonialism in the Middle Ages*, he wrote but a single article on the subject.[51] The Orders, however, received much more attention in the work of some of Prawer's former students, notably the author of this chapter, who extensively wrote about the Templars, in both the Holy Land and Europe,[52] and the Military Order of Calatrava in Castile.[53]

Another subject that was considerably amplified by Prawer's students was the Muslim perspective of the crusades. Emmanuel Sivan, who investigated in depth the Muslims' reactions to the crusades, placed special emphasis on Islamic religious culture and values.[54] He provided a fresh view of the particular condition of Muslim and Oriental Christian communities under foreign rule and the place of Jerusalem in Islamic ideology during the crusader period.[55] Daniella Talmon-Heller, Reuven Amitai, Yaacov Lev, and Yehoshua Frenkel, to name just a few among the Israeli scholars dealing with the subject, widened our understanding of the Muslim world in the crusader period by bringing new insights from the perspectives of socioeconomic, political, and intellectual history. Several examples may illustrate this point: Talmon-Heller focuses on Islamic piety and religion and the very concept of public space in the crusader period.[56] Yaacov Lev's research on Fatimid Egypt, Saladin, and Nur-al-Din has become an integral component of crusader bibliography.[57] Of great relevance to attaining a more comprehensive understanding of the political and military world of the crusades are Reuven Amitai's studies on the Mongols, their tactics, and their varying relations with Christendom and the leading powers in the Levant.[58]

About twenty-five years after the death of Joshua Prawer, it is rather clear that Israeli historians have reevaluated many of his premises and conclusions, altering some of them and completely reversing others. This scholarly mechanism reveals the complete autonomy of crusader research in Israel, free of ideological and political considerations. Despite superfluous arguments that Israeli research of the crusades is actually subject to extra-scholarly considerations of the different contesting ideological wings that delineate the contemporary Israeli public sphere,[59] one can argue that such generalizations are detached from the actual work of Israeli historians. Simply put, such claims do not justice to the work of these scholars. The historiographical transformations in Israelis' research of the crusades, their causes and outcomes, do not reflect changing ideological or political fashions. Quite the reverse. The continuous development of research on the crusades and the Latin Kingdom of Jerusalem, in all its many and rich facets, is clearly rooted in the process of the accumulation of and continuous improvement in historical knowledge gained from both written documentation and archeological finds. When Prawer began his research, the native aspects of the crusades were almost *terra incognita*. It was Prawer's zeal that made this field a legitimate and developing area of research. The limited scope of historical and archeological finds in Prawer's time—and not any ideological bias—dictated the segregation model. Later generations of Israeli historians and archeologists entered this newly formed field and added their insights. Gradually, quantity became quality, and the scholarly perspective completely changed. In the same vein, one may expect that future findings and interpretative paradigms will again sustain new schools, and these in turn will argue with their predecessors as, at the same time, they continue them.

NOTES

1 Ronnie Ellenblum, *Crusader Castles and Modern Histories* (Cambridge, 2007), 61. See, also, Yael Katzir's documentary films, such as *A Walk in Crusader Jerusalem* (1980), *Christianity and Christians in Jerusalem,* (1981), *In Quest of the True Cross,* (1985), and *In the Footsteps of the Crusaders in Caesarea and St Jean d'Acre* (1996).

2 Any attempt to offer a bibliographical summary of Prawer's contribution to the history of the crusades would prove exhausting. See, for instance, Jonathan Riley Smith, "History, the Crusades and the Latin East, 1095–1204: A Personal View," in *Crusaders and Muslims in Twelfth-Century Syria,* ed. Maya Shatzmiller (Leiden, New York, 1993), 2.

3 Giles Constable, Kenneth M. Setton, and Hans Eberhard Mayer, "Memoirs of Fellows and Corresponding Fellows of the Medieval Academy of America: Joshua Prawer," *Speculum* 66, 3 (1991), 727–729. A similar view was expressed by Christopher Tyerman, *The Invention of the Crusades* (Houndmills, 1998), 123.

4 "Crusader Palestine: Map and Index," in *Atlas of Israel* (Jerusalem, 1960).

5 Joshua Prawer, "La bataille de Hattin," *Israel Exploration Journal* 14 (1964), 160–179.

6 He strongly opposed, however, any analogy between the Crusader Kingdom and the State of Israel, emphasizing the fact that modern Zionists settled and worked the land, whereas the crusaders ruled over a conquered land worked by natives and that was too limited to ensure permanency. Although he refrained from any scholarly writing on the subject, Prawer often expressed his view in a series of interviews to the media in Israel and abroad. See, also, Jonathan Riley Smith, *The Crusades: A History* (London, 2005), 304; and Ellenblum, *Crusader Castles and Modern Histories,* 57.

7 Joshua Prawer, "The Archaeological Research of the Crusader Period," in *Thirty Years of Archaeology in Israel. 1948–1978* (Jerusalem, 1981), 117–128.

8 Benjamin Z. Kedar, "Joshua Prawer (1917–1990): Historian of the Crusading Kingdom of Jerusalem," *Mediterranean Historical Review* 5 (1990), 113.

9 Sylvia Schein, *Gateway to the Heavenly City: Crusader Jerusalem and the Catholic West (1099–1187)* (Aldershot, 2005), dedicatory page.

10 See, Joshua Prawer, "Jerusalem, Capital of the Crusader Kingdom," in *Judah and Jerusalem* (Jerusalem, 1957), 90–104 [Hebrew]; *idem, Jerusalem – Living City* (Jerusalem, 1968, translated into English, French, German, and Spanish); *idem,* "Jérusalem terrestre, Jérusalem celeste. Jérusalem dans la perspective chrétienne et juive au haut moyen âge et à la veille de la première

croisade," in *Jérusalem: l'unique et l'universel* (Vandôme, 1979), 17–27; *idem*, "Jerusalem in the Christian and Jewish Perspectives of the Early Middle Ages," in *Settimane di studi sull'alto medio evo* (Spoleto, 1980), 1–57.

11 Liat Collins, "Expert on 'Knights' Honored," *The Jerusalem Post* (17 November, 1989).

12 Among Prawer's students who reached international recognition in the field, one should mention David Jacoby, Aryeh Grabois, Benjamin Kedar, Emanuel Sivan, Yvonne Friedman, Sylvia Schein, Sophia Menache, and Ronnie Ellenblum. On their research and critical revision of Prawer's main thesis, see below.

13 "Joshua Prawer, Renowned Scholar Dies at 73," *The Jerusalem Post* (2 May, 1990); Hyam Maccoby, "Obituary: Joshua Prawer," *The Independent* (4 May 1990); David Abulafia, "A Crusading Revisionist: Obituary of Joshua Prawer," *The Guardian* (4 May 1990).

14 On the innovative character of Prawer's use of the Hebrew language and its attraction, see, Kedar, "Joshua Prawer (1917–1990)," 108–109.

15 Ibid., 110.

16 One should mention, *inter alia*, the pioneer studies of R. Röhricht, René Gousset, and Sir Steven Runciman, as well as the work of Arthur Beugnot, Emmanuel G. Rey, Hans Prutz, Gaston Dodu, and John La Monte. See, Christopher Tyerman, "Modern Historiography," in *The Crusades: An Encyclopedia*, ed. Alan V. Murray, 4 vols. (Sta. Barbara, 2006), II, 582–588.

17 Jonathan Riley-Smith asserted, along with Jean Richard, that Prawer "wrote institutional studies of lasting value and ... rewrote the constitutional history of the Kingdom of Jerusalem." *The Crusades: A History*, 2.

18 The book includes eleven revised articles, five of them previously appearing in French and one in Italian. Reviewed by Robert B. Patterson, *The American Historical Review* 86 (1981), 822.

19 *A History of the Latin Kingdom of Jerusalem*, 2 vols. (Jerusalem, 1963, 1971); *The Latin Kingdom of Jerusalem: Colonialism in the Middle Ages* (London, 1972); *Crusader Institutions* (Oxford, 1980); *A History of the Jews in the Latin Kingdom of Jerusalem* (Oxford, 1988). For a complete list of Prawer's publications, see *Outremer: Studies in the History of the Crusading Kingdom of Jerusalem presented to Joshua Prawer* (Jerusalem, 1982), 7–13.

20 See Prawer's early studies in this regard, such as, "The Settlement of the Latins in Jerusalem," *Speculum* 27 (1952), 490–503; "Colonization Activities in the Latin Kingdom of Jerusalem," *Revue belge de philologie et d'histoire* 29 (1951), 1063–1118; "The *Assise de Teneure* and the *Assise de Vente*: A Study of Landed Property in the Latin Kingdom," *Economic History Review* 41 (1951–52), 77–87; "Les premiers temps de la féodalité dans le royaume latin de Jérusalem," *Revue d'histoire du droit* 22 (1954), 401–424; "La noblesse et le régime féodal du royaume latin de Jérusalem," *Moyen âge* 65 (1959), 41–74.

21 Joshua Prawer, "Etude de quelques problèmes agraires et socialux d'une seigneurie croisée au XIIIe siècle," *Byzantion* 22 (1952), 5–6, 23; (1953), 143–169.

22 Prawer, *The Latin Kingdom of Jerusalem*, 524. Reviewed by James A. Brundage in *Speculum* 50–1 (1975), 145–147.

23 Reviewed by D. Richards, *British Journal of Middle Eastern Studies* 18 (1), 109–110.

24 Joshua Prawer, "The Jews in the Latin Kingdom of Jerusalem," *Zion* 11 (1946), 38–82; "The Jewish Population in Palestine: Arab Rule; the Crusaders; the Mameluk Period (640–1516)," *Three Historical Memoranda Submitted by the General Council of the Jewish Community of Palestine* (Jerusalem, 1947), 27–51; "The Friars of Mount Zion and the Jews of Jerusalem in the Fifteenth Century," *Bulletin of the Jewish Palestine Exploration Society* 14 (1948–49), 15–24; "Jewish Resettlement in Crusader Jerusalem," *Ariel* 19 (1967), 60–66; "Notes on the History of the Jews in the Latin Kingdom of Jerusalem," *Immanuel* 9 (1979), 81–87.

25 Josep Torró, "Contre les stéréotypes: Etudes sur la colonization et l'ésclavage – Jérusalem ou Valence: La première colonie d'Occident," *Annales* 55 (2000), 985.

26 See a critical review of Prawer's premises and conclusions, along with important new data, by Benjamin Z. Kedar and Muhammad al-Hajjuj, "Muslim Villagers of the Frankish Kingdom of

Jerusalem: Some Demographic and Onomastic Data," in *Itinéraires d'Orient: Hommages à Claude Cahen*, ed. Raoul Curiel and Rika Gyselen (Bures-sur-Yvette, 1994), 145–156.

27 Ronnie Ellenblum, *Frankish Rural Settlement in the Latin Kingdom of Jerusalem* (Cambridge, 1998), 3–38; *idem, Crusader Castles and Modern Histories*, 55 ff.

28 Ibid., 304.

29 See a brief biographical note and a list of publications in *In Laudem Hierosolymitani: Studies in Crusades and Medieval Culture in Honour of Benjamin Z. Kedar*, ed. Iris Shagrir, Ronnie Ellenblum, and Jonathan Riley-Smith (Aldershot, 2007), IX–XXIII.

30 Benjamin Z. Kedar, "The Battle of Hattin Revisited," in *Horns of Hattin*, ed. Benjamin Z. Kedar (Jerusalem and London, 1992), 190–207.

31 Benjamin Z. Kedar, *Franks, Muslims, and Oriental Christians in the Latin Levant: Studies in Frontier Acculturation* (Aldershot, 2006). See, also, *idem*, "The Subjected Muslims of the Frankish Levant," in *Muslims under Latin Rule, 1100–1300*, ed. James M. Powell (Princeton, 1990), 135–174; *idem*, "Some New Sources on Palestinian Muslims before and during the Crusades," in *Die Kreuzfahrerstaaten als multikulturelle Gesellschaft*, ed. H. E. Mayer (Munich, 1997), 129–140; *idem*, "Multidirectional Conversion in the Frankish Levant," in *Varieties of Religious Conversion in the Middle Ages*, ed. J. Muldoon (Gainesville, 1997), 190–199.

32 Yvonne Friedman, "Crusades and Settlement – Crossroads and Paths in Research," *Cathedra* 100 (2000), 264–268 [Hebrew].

33 *Eadem*, "Women in Captivity and Their Ransom in the Crusader Period," in *Cross-Cultural Convergences in the Crusader Period*, ed. M. Goodich, S. Menache, and S. Schein (New York, 1996), 75–87; *eadem*, "The Ransom of Captives in the Latin Kingdom of Jerusalem," in *Autour de la Première Croisade*, ed. M. Balard (Paris, 1996), 177–189; *eadem*, "The 'Great Precept' of Ransom: The Jewish Perspective," in *La Liberazione dei 'captivi' tra Christianità e Islam*, ed. G. Cipollone, Collectanea Archivi Vaticani 46 (Citta del Vaticano, 2000), 161–172; *eadem*, "Captivity and Ransom: The Experience of Women," in *Gendering the Crusades*, ed. S. Lambert and S. Edgington (Cardiff, 2001), 121–139.

34 *Eadem*, "Gestures of Conciliation? Peacemaking Endeavors and Cultural Consequences," in *In Laudem Hierosolymitani*, 31–48; *eadem*, "Christian-Muslim Peacemaking in the Medieval Latin East," in *Peace, War, and Violence*, ed. Jost Duellfer and Robert Frank (Essen, 2009), 45–63.

35 Prawer, *The Latin Kingdom of Jerusalem*, 416–468.

36 On her important contribution to the history of crusader art, see Gil Fishhof, "Reading Pictorial Languages: Art as Text," in *Pictorial Languages and Their Meanings: Liber Amicorum in Honor of Nurith Kenaan-Kedar*, ed. Christine B. Verzar and Gil Fishhof (Tel Aviv, 2006), xxix–xxxi. Her list of publications appears on xxxiii–xxxviii.

37 Nurith Kenaan-Kedar, "Local Christian Art in Twelfth-Century Jerusalem," *Israel Exploration Journal* 23 (1973), 167–175, 221–229; *eadem*, "Symbolic Meaning in Crusader Architecture: The Twelfth-Century Dome of the Holy Sepulcher Church in Jerusalem," *Cahiers archéologiques* 34 (1986), 109–117; *eadem*, "A Neglected Series of Crusader Sculpture: The Ninety-Six Corbels of the Church of the Holy Sepulchre," *Israel Exploration Journal* 42 (1992), 103–114; *eadem*, "The Role and Meaning of Crusader Architectural Decoration: From Local Romanesque Tradition to Gothic Hegemony," *Schriften des historischen Kollegs* 37 (1997), 165–178; see, also, *eadem*, "The Cathedral of Sebaste: Its Western Donors and Models," in *The Horns of Hattin*, 99–120.

38 Esther Garbiner, "Israeli Research of Crusader Art and Its Local Character," *Mutar* 7 (1999), 33–38 [Hebrew].

39 Adrian J. Boas, *Crusader Archeology: The Material Culture of the Latin East* (London, 1999); *idem, Jerusalem at the Time of the Crusades* (London, 2001); *idem, Domestic Settings* (Leiden, 2010).

40 Y. Rosen, "Excavation of the Courthouse Site at 'Akko: Medieval Glass Vessels (Area TA)," *Atiqot* 31 (1997), 75–85 [Hebrew]; Y. Gorin-Rosen, "The Glass Vessels," in *Tel Yoqne'am Excavations on the Acropolis*, ed. M. Avissar, *IAA Reports* 25 (2005), 103–109 [Hebrew]; Edna Stern, *Trade*

and Distribution of Ceramics in the Mediterranean during the Twelfth and Thirteenth Centuries as Reflected in the Excavations of Crusader Acre (PhD dissertation, University of Haifa, 2007) [Hebrew].

41 Edna Stern, "The Excavations at Lower Horvat Manot: A Medieval Sugar Production Site," *Atiqot* 42 (2001), 277–308 [Hebrew]; *eadem, The Sugar Industry in Palestine during the Crusader, Ayubid, and Mamluk Periods in Light of Archeological Finds* (MA thesis, Hebrew University of Jerusalem, 1999).

42 Robert Kool, "The Khirbet Shatta Hoard: European and Latin Coins and Islamic Jewellery from the Late Thirteenth Century," in *The Gros Tournois: Proceedings of the Fourteenth Oxford Symposium on Coinage and Monetary History*, ed. N. Mayhew (Oxford 1997), 257–278; *idem*, "A Fatimid Amulet-Box with European Coins from the Eleventh Century," *American Journal of Numismatics* 11 (1999), 47–68; Robert Kool and Haim Gitler, "Coins in the Frankish East (1099–1291)," in *Terra Santa: Dalla Crociata alla Custodia dei Luoghi Santi Catalogo e mostra*, ed. M. Picherillo, S. Folda, and M. Arslan (Milan, 2000), 231–235, 241–243.

43 David Jacoby, "Mercanti genovesi e veneziani e le loro merci nel Levante crociato," in *Genova, Venezia, il Levante nei secoli XII-XIV*, ed. Gherardo Ortalli and Dino Puncuh, *Atti della Società Ligure di Storia Patria*, n. s. 41 (115)/1 (2001), 213–256; *idem*, "The Economic Function of the Crusader States of the Levant: A New Approach," in *Europe's Economic Relations with the Islamic World – 13th–18th Centuries*, ed. Simonetta Cavaciocchi (Firenze, 2007), 159–191; *idem*, "The Supply of War Materials to Egypt in the Crusader Period," *Jerusalem Studies in Arabic and Islam* 25 (2001), 102–132.

44 *Idem, Société et démographie à Byzance et en Romanie Latine*, (London, 1975); *idem, Studies on the Crusader States and on Venetian Expansion* (Northampton, 1989); *idem, Trade, Commodities, and Shipping in the Medieval Mediterranean* (Aldershot, 1997); *idem, Byzantium, Latin Romania, and the Mediterranean* (Aldershot, 2001); *idem, Commercial Exchange Across the Mediterranean* (Aldershot, 2005).

45 *Idem*, "A Venetian Manual of Commercial Practice from Crusader Acre," in *I comuni italiani nel regno crociato di Gerusalemme*, ed. Benjamin Z. Kedar and G. Airaldi (Genoa, 1986), 403–428; *idem*, "Venetian Anchors for Crusader Acre," *The Mariner's Mirror* 71 (1985), 5–12; *idem*, "The Venetian Presence in the Latin Empire of Constantinople (1204–1261): The Challenge of Feudalism and the Byzantine Inheritance," *Jahrbuch der Osterreichischen Byzantinistik* 43 (1993), 141–201; *idem*, "Venetian Settlers in Latin Constantinople (1204–1261): Rich or Poor?" *Biblioteca dell'Istituto Ellenico di Studi bizantini e postbizantini di Venezia* 19 (Venice, 1998), 181–204; *idem*, "Pèlerinage médiéval et sanctuaries de Terre Sainte: La perspective vénitienne," *Ateneo Veneto* 24 (1986), 27–58.

46 J. Prawer, *The Latin Kingdom of Jerusalem*, 200–227.

47 A. Grabois, "Les pèlerins occidentaux en Terre Sainte et Acre: d'Accon des croisés à Saint-Jean d'Acre," *Studi Medievali* 3, 24 (1983), 247–264; *idem*, "De la "géographie sacrée à la 'Palestinographie': Changements dans la description de la Palestine par les pèlerins chrétiens au XIIIe siècle," *Cathedra* 31 (1984), 43–54; *idem*, "Les pèlerins occidentaux en Terre Sainte au Moyen Age: Une minorité étrangère à sa patrie spirituelle," *Studi Medievali* 3, 30 (1989), 15–48.

48 Yvonne Friedman, "Pilgrimage to the Holy Land as an Act of Devotion in Jewish and Christian Outlook," in *Rashi et la culture juive en France du Nord au moyen âge*, ed. G. Dahan and G. Nahon (Paris, 1997), 278–301; *eadem*, "Pilgrims in the Shadow of the Crusader Kingdom," in *Knights of the Holy Land*, ed. Silvia Rosenberg (Jerusalem, 1999), 100–110; *eadem*, "'In the Name of God and Profit'—Holy Land *Itineraria* in the Mamluk Period," in *Eretz Israel and Jerusalem* 4–5 (2007), 199–217.

49 Yvonne Friedman and Anat Peled, "Did the Crusaders Construct Roads?" *Qadmoniot* 20 (1988), 119–123 [Hebrew]; *eadem*, "The Map of Roads in Galilee in the Middle Ages," in *Hikrei Eretz: Studies in the History of the Land of Israel*, ed. Y. Friedman, Y. Schwartz, and Z. Safrai (Ramat Gan, 1997), 323–341 [Hebrew].

50 Sylvia Schein, *Fideles Crucis: The Papacy, the West, and the Recovery of the Holy Land (1274–1314)* (Oxford, 1991), *passim*.

51 Joshua Prawer, "Military Orders and Crusader Politics in the Second Half of the Thirteenth Century," in *Die geistlichen Ritterorden Europas*, ed. J. Fleckenstein and M. Hellmann (Sigmaringen, 1980), 217–229.

52 Sophia Menache, "Contemporary Attitudes Concerning the Templars' Affair: Propaganda Fiasco?" *Journal of Medieval History* 8 (1982), 135–147; *eadem*, "The Templar Order: A Failed Ideal?" *The Catholic Historical Review* 79 (1993), 1–2; *eadem*, "A Clash of Expectations: Self-Image Versus the Image of the Knights Templar in Medieval Narrative Sources," *Analecta Turonensia* 13 (2005), 47–58; *eadem*, "Elections in the Military Orders in the Late Middle Ages: An Achilles' Heel?" *Analecta Turonensia* 14 (2007), 1–15; *eadem*, "Rewriting the History of the Templars According to Matthew Paris," in *Cross-Cultural Convergences in the Crusader Period: Essays Presented to Aryeh Grabois* (New York, 1996), 183–213; *eadem*, "Jacques de Molay, the Last Master of the Temple," in *Knighthood of Christ: Essays on the History of the Crusades and the Knights Templar presented to Malcolm Barber on his 65th Birthday* (Ashgate, 2007), 229–240.

53 *Eadem*, "La Orden de Calatrava y el Clero Andaluz (siglos XIII–XV)," in *En la España medieval: Estudios en memoria del Profesor D. Claudio Sánchez Albornoz*, 5, 1 (1986), 633–653; *eadem*, "A Juridical Chapter in the History of the Order of Calatrava: The Mastership of Don Alonso de Aragón (1443–1444)," *The Legal History Review* 55 (1987), 321–334; *eadem*, "Una personificación del ideal caballerezco en el medioevo tardío: Don Alonso de Aragón," *Revista de la Universidad de Alicante* 6 (1987), 9–29; *eadem*, "Medieval States and Military Orders: The Order of Calatrava in the Late Middle Ages," in *In Laudem Hierosolymitani*, 457–468.

54 Emmanuel Sivan, *L'Islam et la croisade: Idéologie et propaganda dans les reactions musulmanes aux croisades* (Paris, 1968); *idem*, *Modern Arab Historiography of the Crusades* (Tel Aviv, 1973); *idem*, "La genèse de la contre-croisade: Un traité damasquin du début du XIIe siècle," in *Les relations des pays d'Islam avec le monde latin du milieu du Xe siècle au milieu du XIIIe siècle*, ed. Françoise Micheau (Paris, 1966, 2000), 26–51; *idem*, "Muslim Representations of the Crusades," in *Verso Gerusalemme*, 125–133; *idem*, "Islam and the Crusades: Antagonism, Polemics, Dialogue," in *Religionsgespräche im Mittelalter*, ed. Bernard Lewis and Friedrich Niewohner (Wiesbaden, 1992), 207–215.

55 *Idem*, "Notes sur la situation des chrétiens à l'epoque ayyubide," *Revue de l'histoire des religions* 172, 2 (1967), 117–130; *idem*, "Le caractère sacré de Jérusalem dans l'Islam aux XIIe-XIIIe siècles," *Studia Islamica* 27 (1967), 149–182; *idem*, "Réfugiés syro-palestiniens au temps des croisades," *Revue des études islamiques* 35 (1967), 135–148.

56 Daniella Talmon-Heller, *Islamic Piety in Medieval Syria: Mosques, Cemeteries, and Sermons under the Zangids and Ayyūbids* (Leiden, 2007); *eadem*, "Hanbalite Islam in 12th–13th Century Jabal Nablus and Jabal Qasyun," *Studia Islamica* 79 (1994), 103–120; *eadem*, "Religion in the Public Sphere: Rulers, Scholars, and Commoners in Zangid and Ayyubid Syria (1150–1260)," in *The Public Sphere in Muslim Societies*, ed. M. Hoexter, S. N Eisenstadt, and N. Levtzion (Albany, 2002), 49–64.

57 Yaacov Lev, *State and Society in Fatimid Egypt* (Leiden, 1991); *idem*, *Saladin in Egypt* (Boston, 1999); *idem*, *Charity, Endowments, and Charitable Institutions in Medieval Islam* (Gainesville, 2005); *idem*, "The Social and Economic Policies of Nur al-Din (1146–1174): The Sultan of Syria," *Der Islam* 81 (2004), 218–242; *idem*, "Aspects of the Egyptian Society in the Fatimid Period," in *Egypt and Syria in the Fatimid, Ayyubid, and Mamluk Eras*, ed. U. Vermeulen and J. Van Steenbergen (Leuven, 2001), 1–33; *idem*, "The Fatimids and Byzantium," *Graeco-Arabica* (2000), 156–169.

58 Reuven Amitai, "Mongol Raids into Palestine (A.D. 1260 and 1300)," *Journal of the Royal Asiatic Society* (1987), 236–255; *idem*, "Mamluk Espionage among Mongols and Franks," *Asian and African Studies* 22 (1988), 173–181; *idem*, "Mamluk Perceptions of the Mongol-Frankish Rapprochement," *Mediterranean Historical Review* 7 (1992), 50–65; *idem*, "The Mongols and

Karak in Trans-Jordan," *Archivum Eurasiae Medii Aevi* 9 (1995–1997), 5–16; *idem*, "Foot Soldiers, Militiamen, and Volunteers in the Early Mamluk Army," in *Texts, Documents, and Artifacts: Islamic Studies in Honour of D. S. Richards*, ed. Chase F. Robinson (Leiden, 2003), 232–249; *idem*, "A Mongol Governor of al-Karak in Jordan? A Re-examination of an Old Document in Mongolian and Arabic," *Zentralasiatische Studien* 36 (2007), 263–275; *idem*, "Mongol Provincial Administration: Syria in 1260 as a Case-Study," in *In Laudem Hierosolymitani*, 117–143.

59 David Ohana, *Neither Canaanites nor Crusaders* (Jerusalem, 2008), 307–319 [Hebrew].

CHAPTER THIRTY-EIGHT

WHAT *ARE* THE CRUSADES?

——•◆•——

Gary Dickson

A cynic might give an immediate answer—an academic industry, although there is more than a grain of truth in such a response. The first, pamphlet-sized *Bulletin* of the newly founded Society for the Study of the Crusades and the Latin East appeared in 1981. Listed were 103 members. The 2012 issue of number 32 of the *Bulletin* listed 531 members, according to my unscientific count. That represents a considerable jump in the membership. What is even more impressive is how cosmopolitan the membership has become. Not only do members come from all over Europe, North America, and the Middle East, but also from Australia, Malta, Cyprus, Turkey, Russia, China, Japan, Iran, and Brazil. Truly it can be said that the crusades now have a global audience.

When one supposes that very many of these members, probably the overwhelming majority, are engaged in university teaching, that means a good number of undergraduate and postgraduate students are studying the crusades, which also means that they need books on the crusades. Some will be purchasing books on the crusades; some will be checking out library books. Consequently, libraries, especially university libraries, will definitely be purchasing books on the crusades. So are publishers interested in the subject? So will lecturers be writing articles and books on the crusades? The total of recent publications completed by members of the Society for 2012 climbs to approximately 313 essays and books, including encyclopedia entries. Proof, were it needed, that the crusades have entered the academic mainstream. Moreover, there is an obvious subsequent question. How many of the postgraduates now studying and doing doctoral research on the crusades hope to go on to teach their subject?

To those who know its history, the crusade trajectory is familiar, although dating the steps in the process is likely to be contested. By the time the First Crusade became the Second Crusade, a variety of other crusades were soon added, not only to the Holy Land, but also beyond the frontiers of Christian Europe, and summoned for causes other than combatting the Muslims. Thus, along with the idea of the crusade, still much debated by scholars, came the crusading movement, a perception that the crusades would continue regardless of how dispiriting the results were following any individual enterprise.

When the crusades began is nearly always (but not always) dated 1095. When it came to an end is more controversial. Jonathan Riley-Smith affirmed in 1987 that "the crusading movement ended with the fall of Malta on 13 June 1798," not to a Muslim prince, but to Napoleon Bonaparte (Riley-Smith, 2002: 89). That ringing declaration was modified somewhat in 2009, when our pre-eminent crusade historian volunteers: "I am much less ready nowadays to provide a terminal date." There are, he states, sixteenth- and seventeenth-century possibilities, but even in the nineteenth century the crusades cast "a long shadow," a shadow which extends, as Riley-Smith is all too aware, into the twenty-first century (Riley-Smith, 2009: 90–92). The nature of that "long shadow" provides one answer to the question of what the crusades *are*.

Well before the crusading movement ceased, however—and while the idea of the crusade was still very much alive—the crusades had become a plan, a program for future success. At the time plans for the recovery of lost territory in the Holy Land were being composed, Acre had not yet fallen (1291). Humbert of Romans (d. 1277), a preacher of Louis IX's ill-fated crusade to Damietta and former master general of the Dominican Order, wrote his *Opus tripartitum* for the Second Council of Lyons (1274). In it, he attempted to deal with public opinion adverse to the crusade, urged closer rapport or reunion with the Greeks, and suggested ways of raising much-needed funds (Bird, 2006: II, 612–613). Humbert cited an unforgotten example of an inspirational crusade preacher. "O shame on our times! … a poor hermit, Peter, moved all of Christendom." Another great one would incite others to such fervor (Humbert of Romans, 1690: II, 200). Past triumphs led to messianic hopes.

Fidenzio of Padua (d. *c.* 1291) was an Italian Franciscan missionary to the Holy Land, who knew the Muslim enemy well, having tended the Christian prisoners after Safed fell (1266) and also at Antioch (1268). Fidenzio probably attended the Second Council of Lyons where Pope Gregory X asked him to submit a written plan for the reconquest and retention of the Holy Land which became his *Liber recuperationis Terre sanctae*, which he completed in 1291 a few months before the fall of Acre.

Fidenzio's treatise is remarkable for its comprehensiveness, encompassing past and future, military strategy and Christian morality. Sufficient, well-armed Christian forces need to be virtuous and well commanded. An excellent captain must be found (*dux populi Xpistiani*), an overall leader, not a luxury-lover, a man of regal qualities. Here again there is crusade messianism, the search for a savior. Realism and utopian hope commingle in Fidenzio's recipe for crusade success (Grabois, 2006: II, 426–427; Fr. Fidenzio de Padua, 1913: II, 1–61).

Pierre Dubois (d. after 1321) probably wrote his *De recuperatione Terre Sancte* (*The Recovery of the Holy Land*) around 1306. He was ill informed about European history and his knowledge of the Holy Land was based on what he read. What is interesting in his proposal was its sweeping scope. For the Holy Land to be recovered and retained, the Church had to be morally reformed; attractive, educated Christian women had to be persuaded to marry Saracens and convert them; those Christians who made war in Europe would be exiled to the Holy Land; the military orders would be combined; the political rivalries in the empire and the Italian cities would be resolved. Finally, France would emerge with a kingdom in the East and with increased sway in the West. In Dubois's vision a successful crusade would be a stepping stone to a utopian reordering of Christian Europe (Pierre Dubois, 1956; Jacques Paviot, "Dubois, Pierre," 2006: II, 366). Similarly, in some of today's "crusades" there is more than a hint of utopianism.

After Constantinople became Istanbul, the geo-political sphere of crusading continued to expand. One modern scholar alleges that "the principal motivating factor responsible for the discovery of the New World" was "the medieval crusading spirit." He is discussing

"[Christopher] Columbus the crusader." Bartolomé de Las Casas, who claims to have recorded and paraphrased Columbus's journal, quotes him directly in this passage "for so I declared to Your Highnesses that all the gain of this my Enterprise should be spent in the conquest of Jerusalem." This was prior to 1492. Later, in 1503, he wrote a letter to the Spanish Sovereigns, saying the Abbot Joachim prophesied that the rebuilder of Jerusalem would be a Spaniard (Hamdani, 1979: 39–40, 44). Utopian hopes are grounded in a prophetic future. That, too, has present-day resonances.

Fifteenth- and sixteenth-century *exhortatoria* urged renewed crusading warfare against the Turks (Housley, 1992: 384–387). Then, when Jacques Bongars published his mighty collection of chroniclers of the crusades in 1611, he chose the same ringing title for it that Guibert of Nogent had given his chronicle of the first crusade in the early twelfth century—the *Gesta Dei per Francos*. As exemplified by the canonized crusader-king Saint Louis, French participation in the crusading movement defined a sense of French identity—an elect people in the service of God and Christendom. Medievalists helped to perpetuate the memory of that tradition. During the reign of Louis XIV, the great medieval Latinist Charles Du Fresne Du Cange published his edition of Joinville's *Histoire de S. Louis de France*, dedicating it to the saint's modern royal namesake (Du Cange, 1668), while the dedicatory epistle which the Gallican, Jesuit historian Louis Maimbourg attached to his *Histoire des croisades* (1675–76) likens Louis XIV to the heroic crusaders of France's medieval past (Maimbourg, 1682). Efforts to promote a new crusade in the seventeenth century were also endorsed by Leibniz, the papacy, and French royal counselors (Dickson, 2010: 168). Thus the crusade remained a living enterprise in the post-medieval world. Moreover, the possibility of its re-appearance kept the memory of the crusades alive. That memory the twenty-first century retains.

The eighteenth-century *philosophes*, however, generally saw the crusades as wholly consigned to a medieval past, a past that, thankfully, was over and done with. In his *History of England*, the Scottish philosopher David Hume summed up "the Crusades ... which have ever since engaged the curiosity of mankind, as the most signal and most durable monument of human folly that has yet appeared in any age or nation. ... [T]his universal frenzy ... spread itself by contagion throughout Europe" (Hume, 1786: 292). Here Hume directly borrows from Voltaire's *maladie épidémique* in his *Histoire des croisades* (Voltaire, 1752: 103). Another Scottish historian, William Robertson, names the crusades as the most "singular event" in "the history of mankind", characterizing it as "an extraordinary frenzy of the human mind" (Robertson, 1824: IV, 214). Then came Edward Gibbon, laying down his final verdict: "the principle of the crusades was a savage fanaticism" (Gibbon, 1946: III, 2160). Irrational to its the core, the crusades were the absolute antithesis of what Enlightenment intellectuals advocated. Certainly, a negative picture of the crusades persists in the present, especially among those who deplore warfare, religious zeal, and collective enthusiasm. Therefore, for some people, the legacy of the *philosophes* defines the crusades today. Yet that is not the whole eighteenth-century story.

Upon Voltaire's historical foundations, Condorcet constructed his rationalist–progressivist interpretation of the crusades. In his *Sketch for a Historical Picture of the Progress of the Human Mind* (1795), Condorcet prepared the way for a rehabilitation of the crusades according to Enlightenment principles by celebrating their inadvertently happy consequences.

"These wars, undertaken in the cause of superstition, served in destroying it." To Condorcet, the crusades were not so much an essential feature of the Middle Ages—the general perspective of medievalists today—as a determining factor in the dissolution of the medieval world (Condorcet, 1955: 92). Medievalists usually encounter this relentlessly modernist perspective only in connection with the Renaissance and the Reformation. Nevertheless, Condorcet's progressivist view of the crusades deserves credit for opening up a host of interpretive strategies which would be exploited later on.

Bonaparte's Egyptian campaign of 1798–99 did not lead to the recapture of Jerusalem. Still, its galvanizing impact upon French orientalism (and with it the historiography of the crusades) is not in doubt. Napoleon's expedition to Egypt, rekindling, as it did, memories of St. Louis' Egyptian crusade, not only revivified interest in the crusading movement; it also meant that a fresh look at crusade history was needed; for in the Napoleonic age, the Enlightenment interpretation of the crusades began to look increasingly old-fashioned, obstructing its proper integration into the history of France.

Challenging the assumptions of the Enlightenment was romantic medievalism, and particularly the idealizing Catholic imagination of François René de Chateaubriand, who published his *Génie du Christianisme* in 1802. In it he put forward as the only "two noble subjects for epic poetry in modern times," namely, "the crusades and the discovery of the new world" (Chateaubriand, 1871: I, pt 2, 173–174). In the English-speaking world, Chateaubriand's contemporary, Sir Walter Scott, was romantic medievalism's most illustrious spokesman. His best-known novel, *Ivanhoe*, was published in 1819. The two heroic protagonists of the novel were King Richard I of England and Ivanhoe, both returning from the Third Crusade, both exemplars of chivalry. Ivanhoe fought at Acre and acquited himself well. Yet Cedric, Ivanhoe's father, thinks that returning crusaders are "dissolute." The villains of the story are Templars (Scott, 1988).

Scott's later reflections on the crusades and chivalry are similarly ambiguous. "[Chivalry] ... blazed forth with high vigour during the Crusades, which indeed may be considered as exploits of national knight-errantry." Nevertheless, "the genius alike of the age and of the order tended to render the zeal of the professors of Chivalry fierce, burning, and intolerant." A Christian knight faced with an infidel who denied the doctrines of the faith should thrust his sword "six inches into the accursed bowels' of that infidel" (Scott, 1892: 14–15, 107). Scott's romantic medievalism, so warmly embraced by American southerners of the civil war era, was tinctured with Scottish Enlightenment reservations. Nonetheless, romantic medievalism still figures, unambiguously, in cinematic depictions of the Middle Ages, and, in some instances, of the crusades as well.

In 1806 the History and Literature section of the Institut de France announced a new prize competition. Its subject would be the crusades. Candidates were called upon "to examine ... the influence of the crusades on the civil liberty of the peoples of Europe, on their civilization, on the progress of enlightenment, on commerce and industry" (Franquet de Franqueville, 1895–96: II, 402). As one would have expected, the phrasing of the question is sober and judicious. There is no hint of Chateaubriand-style romantic idealization. Nor, when it alludes to the *progrès des lumières*, does the Institut de France disavow the legacy of the Enlightenment. Rather, historiographical continuity and change are nicely balanced. Stripped of its Voltaire-inspired negations, Condorcet's rationalist-progressivist interpretation opens the door to an ideologically uncontentious way of reconciling the French past with the French present. The question-setters seem to be saying that another old-fashioned assault upon the Middle Ages was no longer what was needed. What was desired instead was a scholarly affirmation of the benefits brought by the crusades (sub-text: as dominated by the French) to "the peoples of Europe," their liberty, civilization and economic development (sub-text: Europeans could expect analogous benefits to flow from an expanded French role in the contemporary world).

Of the two essayists who split the prize, one was a Frenchman, Maxime de Choiseul-Daillecourt, the other a German, A. H. L. Heeren. Neither essay merits attention. Nevertheless, it is clear that the Institut de France, in reaffirming the significance of the crusades for European history, were very much aware that the historical interpretation of the crusades was moving in a new direction.

After the prize competition, the European significance of the crusading movement begins to emerge as an important intellectual and historiographical problem. Indeed, the crusades in some sense become one of the earliest bridges upon which the perceived chasm between the Middle Ages and the modern world was to be crossed. So, perhaps, what is most interesting about the phrasing of the question of our 1806 prize competition is what was omitted. The role of papacy and Church was passed over in silence, effectively dechristianizing the crusades. Thus the crusading movement was implicitly secularized. A secular modern world was happy to cross a bridge to the Middle Ages, but only on its own terms. Religious enthusiasm, the Christian fanaticism detested by the *philosophes*, no longer overshadowed the crusades. But, paradoxically, the Middle Ages which proved accessible to modernity had first to be modernized.

When a field of learning acquires its own history, it has come of age. For the study of the crusades, that moment came in 1841, when Von Ranke's student Heinrich von Sybel initiated the historiography of the crusades with the publication of his *Geschichte des ersten Kreuzzuges*. Von Sybel refers to the 1806 essay competition and its prize winners (Von Sybel, 1861). So, too, do several influential nineteenth-century histories of Latin Christianity. Throughout the nineteenth century and well into the twentieth, writers on the crusades were expected to include a chapter on the significance and meaning of the crusading movement, invariably translated into the terms of the 1806 prize competition as influence, consequence, or significance.

Historical interpretations, as we would expect, vary, as do moral judgments. What is interesting to observe is that, for many historians, the crusades represent more than a narrative of events. In the late nineteenth century Thomas Archer and Charles Kingsford applaud the crusading movement so enthusiastically that twenty-first century historians might find their views problematic. "The Middle Ages were ... as important and fruitful for mankind as any other epoch of the world's history. The Crusades were their crowning glory of political achievement" (Archer and Kingsford, 1894: 451). "Political achievement" sounds strange if it refers to the Latin states of *outremer*. Could it mean the transitory co-operation of European Christians of diverse regions in the crusading enterprise? Louis Bréhier in 1907 was also laudatory, but more balanced. "It would be unjust to condemn out of hand these five centuries of heroism ... which left behind in the consciences of modern peoples a certain ideal of generosity and a taste for sacrifice ... which the harshest lessons of reality will never erase completely" (Bréhier, 1964: 87).

In the reprint of his *Encylopaedia Britannica* article of 1923, Ernest Barker begins with the "significance of the crusades" and displays his moderate judgment with the comment that Europe's cultural debt to the crusades "has perhaps been unduly emphasized" (Barker, 1936: 6). Arnold Toynbee goes further. In accounting for "the Crusaders' eventual failure" he states that "the Medieval Western Christian competitors for dominion over the Mediterranean Basin were neither strong enough to subdue their neighbours nor cultivated enough to captivate them" (Toynbee, 1964: 74). Hence the Western crusaders were defeated both militarily and culturally.

Worse still, Sir Steven Runciman feels that the crusades were, morally and religiously, "a tragic and destructive episode." At the end of three volumes, he pronounces his last judgment: "the Holy War itself was nothing more than a long act of intolerance in the name of God, which is a sin against the Holy Ghost" (Runciman, 1955: III, 480). Runciman was a philhellene in the nineteenth-century British mode. For Runciman, the crusaders' sack of Constantinople amounted to desecration.

Astonishingly, in our own time Runciman's concluding condemnation has been echoed by no less a personage than Joseph Ratzinger, Pope Benedict XVI. Without mentioning the crusades, he unmistakably speaks of them. "The cruel consequences of religiously motivated violence are only too evident to us all. Violence does not build up the kingdom of God, the kingdom of Humanity. On the contrary, it is a favorite instrument of the Antichrist, however idealistic its religious motivation may be. It serves, not humanity, but inhumanity"[1] (Joseph Ratzinger/Pope Benedict XVI, 1211: pt 2, 15).[2] The pope who is speaking is not, of course, Urban II. Still, it must be said that the legacy of the crusades, however interpreted, continues to be ambiguous as well as morally resonant.

In absolute contrast, for one extremely well-known Protestant preacher, the crusades carried an entirely positive moral resonance. The celebrated American Christian evangelist Billy Graham conducted over 400 US and world missions beginning in 1947 and only coming to a triumphant halt in 2013. These evangelical preaching tours were witnessed by thousands, while Graham vigorously urged members of his audience, potential converts among them, to step forward. His well-publicized, well-attended services were widely broadcast to millions on radio and television. His global missions were called Crusades (Strober and Strober, 2006: xiv–xv, 39).

Consequently, what the crusades *are* is not necessarily what the crusades *were* historically or historiographically. The point is what the crusades now *signify*. Crusade scholars continue to wrestle with this question, for what the crusades now mean to them is what the crusades now *are*, at least to them. What crusading means to the general public is a different matter. Yet how scholars think of crusading governs how the crusades are now taught. Obviously, the awareness of scholars-teachers of the historiography of the crusades allows for an overview of previous interpretations, which can be passed on to students. Giles Constable offers the best précis of crusade historiography, from its first days to the brink of the present, as well as an excellent typology of academic approaches to the crusades. Crusade history has been and continues to be reinterpreted; for, as Constable affirms, "both the learned world and the general public show a voracious appetite for works on the crusades" (Constable, 2008: 3–43, 31).

In surveying the aftermath of the crusading movement, Hans Eberhard Mayer, another outstanding contemporary crusade scholar, comes to this conclusion: "the consequences of the crusades for both Western Christendom and Islam must be judged to be either insignificant or possibly harmful." Concerning Eastern Christendom, he believes, it was definitely the latter. All in all, what "the [crusades] cost in … human life was out of all proportion to the goal that was sought." That goal, Mayer insists, comes down to one thing: the recapture of the Holy Sepulchre (Mayer, 1972: 280–283).[3]

As for the significance of the crusades, Norman Housley strongly disagrees with Mayer. Housley argues that probably nobody would dispute (except for Mayer?) that "the crusades played a central rather than a peripheral role in the development of medieval Europe." Futhermore, Housley examines the varied impact of the crusades on trade, papal and royal power, papal taxation, the association of the Church with violence, the negative effect of the crusades on "interfaith relations," pogroms against the Jews, and holy wars against heretics (Housley, 2006: 144–166).

To a greater or lesser degree, the crusades were involved in all these spheres. Both Mayer and Housley touch upon the moral issues raised by crusading, but neither places them as uppermost. At present, however, moral issues do come to the fore with the vexed question over imperialism and colonialism between the West and the Islamic world. Nineteenth-century European imperialism was perceived by Arab nationalists as the modern continuation of the crusading movement (Hillenbrand, 1999). As Riley-Smith puts it, this perception still casts "a long shadow" (Riley-Smith, 2009: 91–92). Added to that is the early-twenty-first-century American "crusade against terror" which many Muslims perceive as directed against them. In an editorial, the British newspaper *The Independent on Sunday* comments that the "ideology" of "the so-called Islamic State ... sees Western foreign policy as a crusade against Muslims" (5 October 2014).

Certainly aggravating that issue is the acrimonious dispute between the Israelis and the Palestinians over a territory, *terra sancta*, and especially a city, Jerusalem, which Jews, Christians, and Muslims claim as historically, religiously and hence rightfully theirs.

Naturally, we would expect that for the scholars of Israel the history of the crusader state would be central. Yet, just as in Jewish history the polarities of *Galut* (or Diaspora) and *Eretz Yisrael* (the Holy Land) begins early (certainly from Philo's Alexandria), so, too, do the histories of the crusader state and that of medieval European Jewry intertwine. While since 1948 the people of Israel have become the territorial legatees, touristic custodians, historians and archaeologists of what once was the kingdom of the crusaders, no Israeli crusade scholar can ignore the fact that the worst European persecutions the Jews suffered up to that time, the Rhineland massacres of 1096, were inflicted upon them by crusaders en route to conquer Jerusalem; and that virtually every popular crusading movement thereafter (apart from the children's crusade of 1212) slaughtered Jews, while official crusaders frequently had to be prevented from doing so. Hence the lines of connection which normally function in crusade scholarship between medieval Western Europe and *Outremer* carry a particular meaning for the crusade historians of Israel.

The founding father, the Abraham, of Israel's crusade historiography, was Joshua Prawer (1917–90). Arriving as a young immigrant to Palestine in 1936, he went on to receive his PhD at the Hebrew University. His teacher was the scholar of Roman, British, and French imperialism, Richard Koebner (Koebner, 1961). Koebner's intellectual influence would be apparent in Prawer's later interpretation of the crusader state. Decades afterwards, Prawer "proudly accepted" the title of "Koebner's pupil", referring to Koebner as "my revered teacher" (Prawer, 1992: 360–361).

Of his many books, perhaps the best known is *The Latin Kingdom of Jerusalem: European Colonialism in the Middle Ages* (1972). Prawer's international reputation (founding President of SSCLE) and eminence in academic and civic society considerably raised the profile of crusade studies in Israel. Benjamin Kedar has discussed very perceptively how Prawer's keen appreciation of the problems faced by the crusaders in their new homeland impacted upon (and indeed was enriched by) his concerns for the security and stability of Israel. In Kedar's words, Prawer "loves his crusaders, identifies with their worry about the future of their kingdom, and sounds genuinely angry with those who did not offer [them] sufficient assistence" (Kedar, 1990: 109). Territorial security; frontiers; worrying patterns of demography; settlements—all had special resonances for an Israeli scholar.

In addition, what Sophia Menache writes is worth bearing in mind. "As the … father of crusader studies in Israel, Prawer saw the crusader period as an integral part of the country's history. This was a bold act, for which he was repeatedly attacked."[4] Indeed, whether we realize it or not, the crusades have a "Prawer thesis." A stimulating symposium was devoted to it ("The Crusading Kingdom of Jerusalem–the First European Colonial Society?"), chaired by Giles Constable, and subsequently published in *The Horns of Hattin* (Kedar, 1992: 341–366).

Particularly valuable about Prawer's reply to his critics was his broadening of political and economic definitions of "colonialism" to include a "colonial mentality" and a "colonial culture." "For two hundred years," Prawer insists, "they [the Frankish settlers] lived among Muslims and Greeks, who had something to teach Europe—but the Crusader Kingdom … never [became] a bridge, neither of Greek nor of Arab culture, to Europe. The bridges are in Sicily, in Spain—never in the Holy Land" (Prawer, 'The Crusading Kingdom of Jerusalem': 365). This was Prawer the European medievalist, Prawer the cosmopolitan. Could he perhaps have been also addressing his fellow countrymen, advising them to be guided by history—and to choose another path? Thus does historiographical memory impinge upon the present.

When historical memory is transmuted into metaphor its diffusion over space and time is guaranteed, although not without cost. The idea of a crusade as a heroic, high-minded struggle between good and evil—the crusade as a controlling metaphor—is alive today. American crusades were always metaphorical holy wars, stretching back to the days of Thomas Jefferson's "crusade against ignorance" through the nineteenth-century's "holy crusade for the abolition of slavery" to the Temperance movement's "crusade against alcohol" ("the demon rum") to Dwight D. Eisenhower's Second World War memoirs, *Crusade in Europe* (1948), right on to contemporary "crusades" against poverty and drugs and terrorism (Dickson, 2003: XIV, 838; 2010: 8). Metaphorical crusading will insure that the crusades have a present as well as a future. Once they become timeless, however, history, oversimplified and distorted, will bear the cost.

NOTES

1 I owe this reference to my University of Edinburgh colleague, Owen Dudley Edwards.

2 For what follows I am much indebted to B.Z. Kedar's, 'Joshua Prawer (1917–1990), Historian of the Crusading Kingdom of Jerusalem', *Mediterranean Historical Review*, 5 (1990): 107–116. See also B.Z. Kedar, H.E. Mayer, R.C. Smail (eds.), 'Joshua Prawer--an Appreciation', *Outremer: Studies in the History of the Crusading Kingdom of Jerusalem* (Jerusalem, 1982), 1–4. Although I am deeply grateful to Benjamin Kedar for his kind help, I alone am responsible for the views expressed here.

3 The 2nd edition, 1998, lacks chapter 15, "The Aftermath" of the first edition.

4 Sophia Menache, 'Israeli Historians of the Crusades and their Main Areas of Research, 1946–2008', *Storia della Storiografia*, 53 (2008), 3–24. Sophia Menache thoughtfully forwarded me an off-print of her article, for which I thank her.

REFERENCES

Archer, Thomas A. and Charles L. Kingsford. *The Crusades* (G.P. Putnam's Sons, New York, 1894). In: *The Crusades: Motives and Achievements*, J.A. Brundage (ed.), (D.C. Heath & Co., Boston, 1964) 66–68.

Barker, Ernest. *The Crusades* (Barker, Ernest. 'The Crusades', *Encyclopaedia Britannica*, 11th edition Cambridge, 1910), VII, 524–52; *The Crusades*, revised & reprinted (Oxford University Press, Oxford, 1936).

Bird, Jessalynn. "Humbert of Romans," *The Crusades: an Encyclopedia* (Santa Barbara, CA, Denver, CO, Oxford, England, 2006).

Bréhier, Louis. *L'Église et L'Orient au moyen âge: les Croisades*, 2nd edition (Librairie Victor Lecoffre, Paris, 1907), 50–54. Trans. by J. A. Brundage in his *The Crusades: Motives and Achievements* (D.C. Heath & Co., Boston, 1964), 85–87.

Brundage, James A. (ed.) *The Crusades: Motives and Achievements* (D.C. Heath & Co., Boston, 1964).

Chateaubriand, François René de. *Génie du Christianisme*, new edition (Garnier, Paris, 1871).

Condorcet, Antoine-Nicolas de. *Sketch for a Historical Picture of the Progress of the Human Mind.* J. Barraclough (trans.) (London, 1955).

Constable, Giles. "The Historiography of the Crusades" in his *Crusaders and Crusading in the Twelfth Century* (Ashgate Publishing, Farnham, Surrey & Burlington, VT, 2008), 3–43.

Dickson, Gary. "Crusade as Metaphor" in "Crusades," *Encyclopedia Britannica*, 15th edition, 26th printing (Chicago, 2003), Vol. 16.

Dickson, Gary. *The Children's Crusade: Medieval History, Modern Mythistory*, (Palgrave Macmillan, Basingstoke, 2010).

Dubois, Pierre. *The Recovery of the Holy Land*, translated by W. I. Brandt (Columbia University Press, New York, 1956).

Du Cange, Charles Du Fresne. *Histoire de S. Louis de France* (Mabre Cramoisy, Paris, 1668).

Fidenzio de Padua. "Liber recuperationis Terre sanctae," in *Biblioteca Bio-Bibliografica della Terra Santa e dell'Oriente Francescano*, 1st ser., II, 1–60, Girolamo Golubovich (ed.), (Collegio di S. Bonaventura, Quarracchi, 1913).

Franquet de Franqueville, A.C.E. *Le premier siècle de l'Institut de France*, II (J. Rothschild, Paris, 1895–96).

Gibbon, Edward. *The Decline and Fall of the Roman Empire*. J.B. Bury (ed.) (The Heritage Press, New York, 1946).

Grabois, Aryeh. "Fidenzio of Padua," *The Crusades: an Encyclopedia* (Santa Barbara, CA, Denver, CO, Oxford, 2006).

Hamdani, Abbas. "Columbus and the Recovery of Jerusalem," *Journal of the American Oriental Society*, 99 (1979), 39–48.

Hillenbrand, Carole. *The Crusades: Islamic Perspectives* (Edinburgh University Press, 1999).

Housley, Norman. *The Later Crusades from Lyons to Alcazar, 1274–1580* (Oxford University Press, Oxford, 1992).

Housley, Norman. *Contesting the Crusades* (Malden, MA & Oxford University Press, Oxford, 2006).

Humbert of Romans, *Rerum* II in Edward Brown, *Appendix ad Fasiculum Rerum* (Richard Chiswell, London, 1690).

Hume, David. *The History of England*, new edition (Printed for T. Cadell, London, 1786).

Kedar, Benjamin. "Joshua Prawer (1917–1990)", *Mediterranean Historical Review*, 5 (1990), 107–16.

Kedar, B.Z. (ed.) *The Horns of Hattin* (Variorum, Jerusalem and London, 1992), 341–66.

Koebner, Richard. *Empire* (Cambridge University Press, Cambridge, England, 1961).

Maimbourg, Louis. *Histoire des Croisades*, 4 Vols. 2nd edition (Mabre Cramoisy, Paris, 1682).

Mayer, Hans Eberhard. *The Crusades*. 1st edition. John Gillingham (trans.) (Oxford University Press, Oxford, 1972).

Mayer, Hans Eberhard. *The Crusades*. John Gillingham (trans.) 2nd edition (Oxford University Press, Oxford, 1998).

Prawer, Joshua. *The Latin Kingdom of Jerusalem: European Colonialism in the Middle Ages* (Weidenfeld & Nicolson, London, 1972).

Prawer, Joshua. "The Crusading Kingdom of Jerusalem–the First European Colonial Society?" in B.Z. Kedar (ed.), *The Horns of Hattin* (Variorum, Jerusalem and London, 1992), 341–66.

Ratzinger, Joseph/Pope Benedict XVI. *Jesus of Nazareth*. Philip J. Whitmore (trans.) (Doubleday, London and San Francisco, 2011).

Riley-Smith, Jonathan. *The Crusades: a Short History* (Yale University Press, New Haven, CT, 1987).

Riley-Smith, Jonathan. *What were the Crusades?* 3rd edition (Palgrave Macmillan, Basinstoke, England and New York, 2002)

Riley-Smith, Jonathan. *What were the Crusades?* 4th edition (Palgrave Macmillan, Basingstoke, England and New York, 2009).

Robertson, William. *History of the Reign of the Emperor Charles V with a View of the Progress of Society in Europe.* In Robertson, *The Works*, IV (printed for W. Sharpe & Son, London, 1824).

Runciman, Sir Steven. *History of the Crusades* (Cambridge University Press, Cambridge, 1955).

Scott, Sir Walter. "Essays on Chivalry." In his *Essays on Chivalry and Romance* (Frederick Warne, London, 1892).

Scott, Sir Walter. *Ivanhoe*, Graham Tulloch (ed.) (Edinburgh University Press, Edinburgh, 1998).

Strober, Deborah H. and Strober, Gerald S. *Billy Graham, an Oral and Narrative Biography* (Jossey-Bass, San Francisco, CA, 2006).

Toynbee, Arnold J. *A Study of History* (Oxford University Press, Oxford, 1954). VII, 363 reprinted in J.A. Brundage (ed.) in *The Crusades: Motives and Achievements* (D.C. Heath & Co., 1964), 69–74.

Voltaire. *Le Micromégas avec une histoire des croisades.* Printed for J. Robinson (London, 1752).

Von Sybel, Heinrich. *The History and Literature of the Crusades*, Lady Duff Gordon (transl. & ed.) (Chapman & Hall, London, 1861).

INDEX

———•◆•———

margrave of Meissen 62
Marguerite, wife of King Louis IX 87
Maria Comnena 226, 230
Marienberg/Malbork Castle 119, 582
Marienwerder 584
Marignac, the little church 622
Marīnids 176
Marino Sanudo 270, 407–408, 513
Mariona de Zipro 406
Marj 'Ayun 74–75, 380
markets 521, 545, 548
Marra (Ma'arrat an-Nu'mān) 445
Marseilles 11, 531, 534, 538
Marsilio Zorzi 181–188, 194, ns. 1, 4, 5, 6, 7, 236, 238
Martinsāla 574
martyrs 62, 105, 289; martyrdom 64, 262, 289, 384
Mary of Champagne 205
Mas-Deu 115, 123
Maskana 77, 463, 467, 469–471, 473, 485, n. 14
Masuria 586
massacre 71
Maṣyāf 442–443, 445–446
Material Culture 55, 475, 544, 576, 580, 584,- 585, 587–588, 646
Matilda, queen of England 115
Matilda, countess of Tuscany 54
Matthew Blastares 261
Matthew Paris 88
Maurienne (St Jean-de-Maurienne) 11
Mayer, Hans Eberhard 693
Mecca 75, 353, 369, 380, 420
Meccans 315
medicine 401
Medina 420
Mediterranean Sea/region 11–14, 20, 31, 34, 43, n. 57, 62, 68, 90–91, 112–114, 121, 168, 198, 212, 219, 271, 316, 318–319, 324, 367, 405, 420, 422, 429, 439, 461, 467, 474, 520–523, 528, 531, 535–537, 594, 603, 692; commerce 680; policy 177
Mehmet II, sultan 397
Meinhard, bishop of Üxküll 150
Melisende (Milesende), queen of Jerusalem 4, 54, 59, 216, 225–226, 229, 239, n. 3, 547–548, 609, 612, 618, 622; psalter of 637, 664; tomb of 610
Melisende of Lusignan 208, 226
Mellon Madonna 637
Memel 85, 586

Memmel River 582
Men-at-arms *(armigeri)* 85
merceneries 419–431
merces de savurra 522
merchants 519, 534–535, 549, 570
Mergentheim 121
Mérida 169
merlons 452
Mesagne 120
Mesarites 295
Mesopotamia 329, 439–440
Messina 113, 121
metals 405, 559
metalwork 626
metaphors 656
Metz, bishop of 130
Meynard, bishop of Livs 570
Mežotne 576
mice 597
Michael IV Autoreianos 261
Michael Palaiologos 270
Michael VIII Palaiologos 301
Michael VIII 268, 270–272
Michael of Cesena 248–249
Michael Loulloudes 401
Middle Ages 1, 32–33, 70, 82, 84, 146, 164–167, 173–174, 176, 196, 252, 277, 286, 420, 422, 424, 444, 577, 615, 640, 646–647, 678, 680–681, 691–692
Middle East 31, 69–72, 320, 325, 596, 602, 688
Mieszko III, duke of Poland 148
migration 3, 597, 602–604
mihrab 320
Mi'ilyā 214, 530
Milan 116, 121, 123
military orders 2, 73–74, 84, 87–88, 90, 93, 104, 443, 456, 523, 559
milites Christi 136
milk 187
mill (*molendina*) 122–123, 187, 216, 547
millstones 522
Mīmās 217
minting 283
Miriam the Sash-Maker 317
missionaries 49, 152–153
Moab 447
Moclín 91
Modon 120
Mogunz 151
Mohammed/Muhammad 353, 358, n. 12, 403, 420–421